PRINCIPLES
and PATTERNS
of PUBLIC SPEAKING

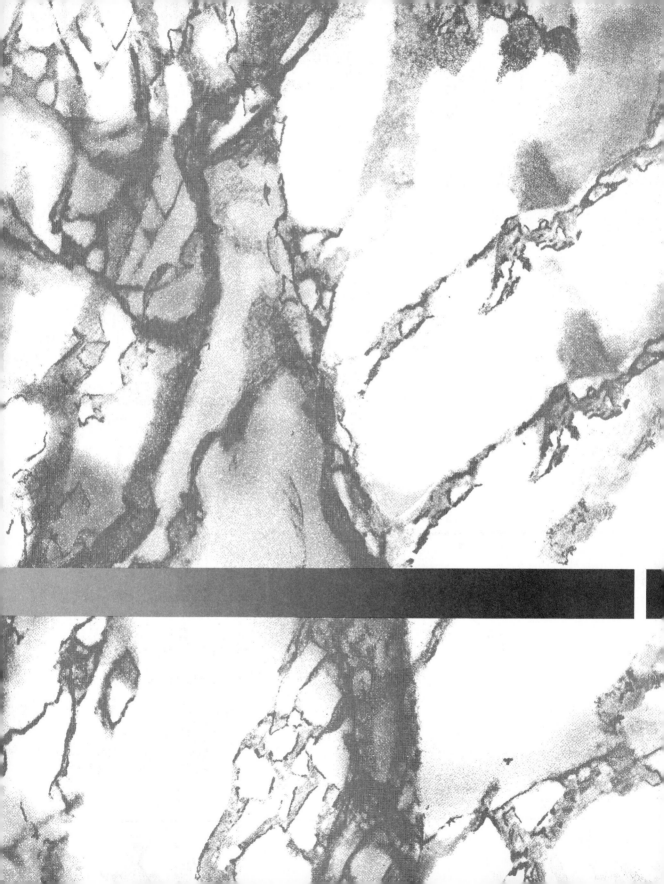

PRINCIPLES
and PATTERNS
of PUBLIC SPEAKING

Richard A. Katula

University of Rhode Island

Wadsworth Publishing Company
Belmont, California
A Division of Wadsworth, Inc.

Communications Editor: Kristine M. Clerkin

Special Projects Editor: Judith McKibben

Editorial Assistant: Sharon McNally

Production Editor: Andrea Cava

Managing Designer: Lisa Mirski

Print Buyer: Barbara Britton

Designer: Donna Davis

Copy Editor: Gregory Gullickson

Photo Researcher: Stuart Kenter

Compositor: Graphic Typesetting Service

Cover: Mark McGeoch

Signing Representative: Ira Zuckerman

Printed in the United States of America   49

1 2 3 4 5 6 7 8 9 10---91 90 89 88 87

Library of Congress Cataloging-in-Publication Data

Katula, Richard A.
    Principles and patterns of public speaking.

    Includes bibliographies and index.
    1. Public speaking. I. Title.
PN4121.K335   1987   808.5′1   86-24594
ISBN 0-534-07656-4

To
Bill Buys at Western Michigan
Carl Dallinger at Northern Illinois
Marie Hochmuth Nichols at University of Illinois, C-U

Three cherished advisors

BRIEF CONTENTS

Part I
PRINCIPLES / 1

Part II
PATTERNS / 231

DETAILED CONTENTS

Part I
PRINCIPLES / 1

MODEL SPEECHES

PHOTO ESSAYS

PREFACE

PRINCIPLES AND PATTERNS OF PUBLIC SPEAKING is intended for an introductory course in public speaking. The course serves those students who are taking the introductory course as preparation for other communication courses and those for whom this will be the only speech course taken during college.

The ability to compose and present a speech, a report, a lecture, or some other formal communication is essential to the educated person. Surveys in such diverse fields as politics, business, teaching, law, and government reveal that the ability to shape an idea into a formal speech and to present that idea enthusiastically and intelligently is a prerequisite for success. Students at the college entry level consistently cite the need to develop their analytical powers and communication skills. The purpose of this text is to provide students with analytical principles related to formal communication and with the skills and opportunity to practice public speaking.

About the Book's Approach

For many years, one popular format for an introductory course in speech communication has been to divide the text into *principles* of speech communication, which the students learn, and *types* of speech communication, which they practice. The types of speech are usually labeled "persuasive," "informative," "special occasion," or described in similar terms. This text follows the familiar division into principles and types but makes some essential changes in the method and content of these two parts.

Terms such as persuasive and informative indicate the purpose of a speech. In their original formulation, such purposes were designed to motivate speakers to think about their role in a given speech situation and the goal toward which they and the audience were moving as a result of the situation. In recent years, purpose has become the controlling principle in speech composition.

Principles and Patterns of Public Speaking shifts the focus of speech communication instruction away from speeches named after general purposes and toward a recognition of patterns of thinking and reasoning that can be used to analyze topics and organize them into speeches. The text does emphasize the concept of purpose but in its appropriate place as a preparatory phase of the speech composing process during which speakers analyze their situation, their role in the situation, the audience, and the way the topic must be developed for that audience. Thus, the book offers a balanced treatment of speech communication, based on sound principles of reasoning and analysis and sound practices in speech composing and presentation.

Part I of the text focuses on establishing a relationship between the canons of invention and organization. This goal is accomplished by introducing students to conceptual patterns of critical thinking as a way to probe their topic—that is, to see it from its various perspectives, and then to choose one perspective as a way of organizing the speech. Part I also covers traditional areas such as listening, language, delivery, outlining, and composing speech parts such as the introduction, conclusion, and thesis statement. In addition, students will find new and essential information on such topics as the question-answer session, recording ideas and experiences, drafting a critical-thinking statement, the psychology of composing a speech, computer graphics, sexism in language, communication apprehension, and rescripting the speech or "ad-libbing."

Part II develops the six most commonly used conceptual patterns as full patterns of reasoning that students can use to compose their own speeches. Narrative is treated as a pattern of reasoning through which we share and discover meaning in our experiences. The process pattern is introduced as a practical method through which we gain insight and information into how things work. Cause-effect is developed as a pattern through which knowledge is acquired by adherence to logical criteria. The analysis pattern is developed as a means for breaking down problems, issues, policies, and objects for purposes of information and advocacy. The definition pattern is introduced as a means for analyzing and discussing essential meanings. Finally, the classification pattern is introduced as a pattern of reasoning through which we establish classes into which things fit.

Each pattern is introduced as a way to think about the world around us. The pattern is then placed into real situations so that students will have an idea when the pattern will best work for them.

Students are then shown how to use the pattern to compose their own speeches.

The conceptual patterns approach offers several advantages for instruction in speech communication, three of which are worth immediate mention. First, the speech communication course should be a place where thinking about ideas is a central concern of instruction. Critical thinking requires one to be aware of innate or learned patterns in the mind that are used in the natural process of developing ideas and experiences. Students are introduced to six often-used thought patterns and taught to use them in both the invention and organization of a speech. Thus, an instructor using this text would probably wish to stress the relationship between thought and communication, a relationship that makes communication a substantive and natural process.

Second, the public speaking course should focus on the process by which an idea grows from its incipient stages in the mind into a completed speech. Using the patterns approach upon which this text is based allows one to follow the path of an idea in all its twists and turns from its beginnings to delivery of the speech.

Finally, using the patterns approach gives the public speaking instructor a broad spectrum of assignments. If each pattern is used just once, at least six and up to nine very different speech assignments result, usually more than enough to provide students with adequate practice. Thus, the patterns approach, while it does not neglect the role of purpose, offers a great deal of variety.

Teaching and Learning Features

Model speeches are valuable teaching aids; *Principles and Patterns of Public Speaking* has an abundance of these models throughout Part II. Students will find that the models serve both to stimulate their thinking about speech topics and to aid them in the development of their own speeches. A list of the model speech topics with the pattern they have followed and the speech purpose follows the table of contents.

A notable addition to the text is the *boxed material.* Designed to show that speech has a central place in the student's liberal arts training, the facts and opinions presented about human communication show its practical uses and its intrinsic fascination as an art form.

The *photo essays* in each of the final six pattern chapters have been carefully chosen and developed to demonstrate visually the patterns and to stimulate student speech topics. In each essay, a topic or issue is explored using the pattern of the chapter and corresponding photographs. These should be additional help to students in understanding the patterns and in developing their own speech topics.

In addition to these specific features, readers will find a thorough discussion of the art of asking and answering questions, a section on sexism in language, a discussion of computer graphics, and a thorough, up-to-date review of speech anxiety. The text offers a comprehensive guide to researching information, as well as practical advice on interviewing, listening to the speeches of others, and developing a composing and delivery style. Also included is a section on the art of ad-libbing for the student who shows a readiness for this technique.

Acknowledgments

Preparing a textbook is a team effort involving the commitment and talents of many individuals. I have been most fortunate during the development of this text to have been guided and encouraged by a host of dedicated professionals. I wish to thank them publicly at this time.

I extend my deepest gratitude to Kris Clerkin, Judith McKibben, Naomi Brown, and Ira Zuckerman from Wadsworth Publishing. Through their encouragement and skill, these four committed professionals kept this text on course when the wind in my sails was errant. I am truly fortunate to have them with me on this venture. In addition, many other fine people at Wadsworth played key roles in the development of this text: Andrea Cava, Patricia Brewer, Bob Kauser, Kevin Howat, Lisa Mirski, and Barbara Britton.

Other individuals in the publishing profession who helped me along the way are Paul O'Connell, Pat Parrott, and Else Kramer. For technical advice I want to thank Gerry Phillips, my cherished colleague, and Blaine Goss, whose advice was most helpful in Chapter 2 on listening.

I extend great thanks to Professor Agnes Doody from the Speech Communication Department at the University of Rhode Island. Agnes's wisdom graces every page of this manuscript—from the photos to the inserts to the text itself. She has been both taskmaster and friend. Others in my department who have helped me throughout this process are Winifred Brownell, L. Patrick Devlin, Ethel Thompson, and George Dillavou. From the English Department, Celest Martin contributed notably to Chapter 7 on language. Without such gifted scholars and colleagues to push and prod and advise, this project would not have succeeded.

Reviewers play a critical role in the development of a text. This project was guided by the following scholars: John Bee, University of Akron; Willard Booth, Delta State University; John Campbell, University of Washington; Robert Chamberlain, Seattle Pacific University; Marlene Cohen, Prince Georges Community College; Sonja Foss, University of Denver; Richard W. Halley, Weber State College; Carl Kell, Western Kentucky University; Gerald M. Phillips, Pennsylvania State University; Dan Rothwell, Cabrillo College; and Kathy Wahlers, Valdosta State College.

On a personal level, I want to thank my wife, Patricia, and my son, Michael, for their faith in me and for their encouragement on those late Saturday and Sunday nights when cleaning fish seemed preferable to drafting text at my CoCo. To all these people and to others whose names I do not know, you have made the journey easier and the result more satisfying.

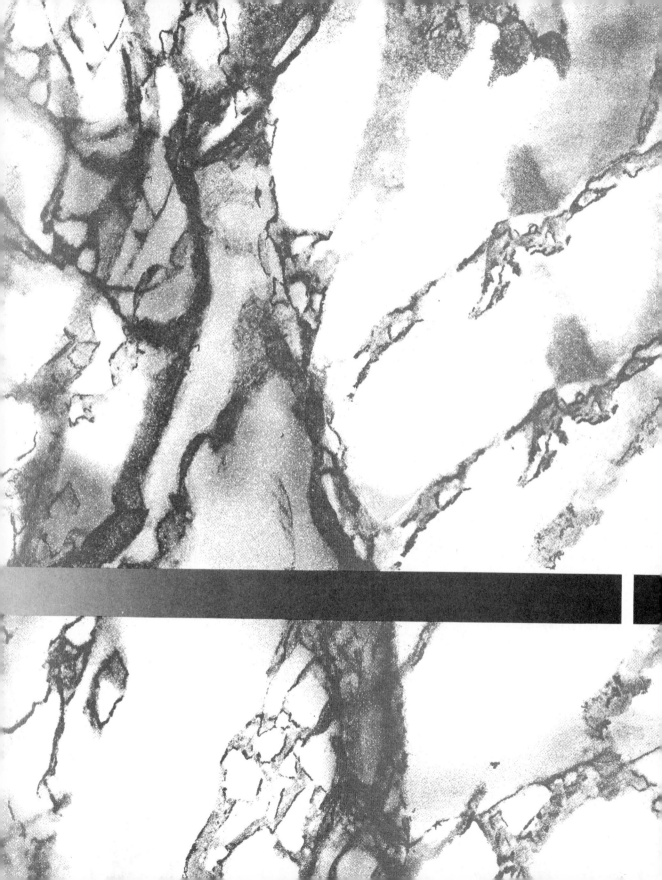

PART I - PRINCIPLES

A course in the fundamentals of public speaking begins with a study of the principles that govern public speaking. The main purpose of the first eight chapters of this text is to introduce you to a body of knowledge about public speaking, principles and guidelines that will make you aware of the broader public-speaking context and help you craft a speech when you play the role of speaker. The principles presented in Part I will provide you with a framework for practicing public speaking throughout the course. Part I has other purposes, however, two of which we want to specify at the outset.

First, although we use the public-speaking context as our vehicle, we intend this course of study to be about fundamentals that apply to all human communication. Much of the information you gather in the next eight chapters will be applicable to any communication situation. All communication requires articulate speakers and attentive listeners; all communication should be an expression of a person's ideas—a piece of a person's mind; all communication involves purpose—a goal toward which the talking is directed; and finally, all communication is couched in words and nonverbal cues, the delivery system. Thus, the principles you learn here infuse all communication events, and you can apply them as such.

Second, a course of study focusing on public speaking specifically and human communication in general should be an integral part of your general education. Public speech is a vital force in the life of our culture. The public lecturer, the pulpit orator, the politician, and citizens addressing their peers are continually reconstituting—defining and changing—our society. Because public speaking is, in many ways, the shaper of democratic action, we should learn about it as a phenomenon in our daily lives. Part I of this text will introduce you to facts about public speech. You will learn names, dates, places, events, and ideas that are particular to public speech as a mode of expression and a social artifact.

So, this course involves more than developing skills in public speaking. Developing skills is important, but as a singular goal it is too narrow to hold your attention or to justify a course of study. Although we want you to become familiar with principles and guidelines that govern public speaking, we also intend that you understand more about yourself as a communicator, more about human communication in general, and more about the role of public speech in a democratic society.

Chapter 1 · Basic Principles of Public Communication

She moved with nervous but resolute steps toward the front of the room: Virginia was a woman in her early thirties, quite heavy, clothed in a draping black dress. Upon reaching the speaker's stand, she turned to her classmates, took a deep breath, and announced: "During this semester I have listened carefully to each one of you present your speeches; you have also listened courteously to me. As this last round of speeches begins I want to share with you my feelings about this course." Everyone in the room perked to attention as Virginia continued.

> *For most of my adult life I have been obese, "fat" it's called behind my back. I have never been what you would call attractive, overly successful, or much involved in the life of my community, state, or nation. A sociologist would probably label me "the average housewife." I am seldom the center of attention, only occasionally when, for instance, I cook a gourmet meal. As a result, my ideas have not quite seemed to matter to me or to others. I have never really felt that my life has made a difference.*

> *During this speech course, however, I have felt the wonder of communication. You have made me think and express my ideas. You have made me feel that my opinion counts, and you have helped me understand that each one of us does make a difference—excuse me—must make a difference.*

> *You know, I may never present another speech, but that's okay because I've learned so much about myself and about you, and that is reward enough for me. And now, here's my final speech.*

Before Virginia could start her speech, the class interrupted her with applause—the kind that is spontaneous and meaningful, not simply polite. After a moment or two of silence, Virginia gave her final speech and returned to her seat.

About two years had passed when I had a chance meeting with this memorable student. She told me that, contrary to what she had expected then, she had given two speeches since our class: the first at her Overeaters Anonymous meeting, the second at a public hearing concerning the building of a racetrack in her community. Her speech training had worked for her in two valuable ways: once to help her discover more about herself and once again to help her shape the future of her own community.

Public speaking is a time-honored activity in Western civilization. Its function has been to bring together the social, cultural, and political values of the people. From Patrick Henry's "Give me liberty or give me death," to Reverend Jessie Jackson's "Let us put hope in our brains, not dope in our veins," the utterances of the public speaker have served to inform and inspire us. The public speaker and the public speech serve as a rallying point for our hopes, dreams, frustrations, and ambitions.

Experience in public speaking has a place in your education whether or not you ever find yourself in front of a large audience. For some of you this will be your only course in communication. As such, it is an integral part of your general education, introducing you to facts and ideas about human communication that will broaden your understanding of human behavior. Those of you who take further communication coursework can use this course as a foundation for future studies and speaking experiences. Most importantly, a course in public speaking provides you with those theories, principles, and skills that will help you to become a more articulate, forceful speaker and an effective, thoughtful listener. Regardless of your situation, the study of public communication has other rewards.

One reward of a speech-communication class is that it can broaden your perspective on the ideas and issues confronting us as a society. The public speeches you will listen to in the classroom will add to your knowledge, and you will learn that for any topic there are numerous perspectives. You will question your stance on the controversies of the day, and you will discover truth in the adage "There are at least two sides to every issue." From the trivial to the profound, information will become the focus of attention in the classroom, and it will stay with you long after the class has ended.

Presenting speeches in the classroom is also an excellent forum for crafting your critical-thinking skills, testing your ideas, and discovering how to defend them. A well-prepared speech involves ana-

Developing Speech-Making Skills

"In 1642, when Harvard University, America's first college, set up its curriculum, it required students to study public speaking on an almost daily basis. Since then, training in public speaking has been a central part of liberal education in the United States."

Karl Wallace
A History of Speech Education in America

lyzing your ideas and attitudes, developing a speech topic with supporting details, and organizing the speech in a logical pattern so that you clearly communicate your ideas to your audience.

But perhaps the greatest reward of a course in speech will be a new level of competence, confidence, and enjoyment you feel when communicating with others. Indeed, the experience of the woman in black is often repeated in the speech-communication classroom. Like Virginia, we are all learning more about ourselves and the world around us. Most of us have felt that basic urge to speak out on an issue, hoping to make a difference in its outcome. Training in public speaking can be the key that unlocks those doors to understanding ourselves and the world. For those of you who make the commitment, this course will be, as it was for Virginia, both educational and enjoyable.

Features of Public Communication

All forms of human communication share several features. Communication is a basic social activity through which we make contact with our fellow human beings. It involves the use of symbols—words and nonverbal messages that we exchange with others as we search for understanding between and among ourselves. It is also a purposeful activity, leading us to new information and to changes in our beliefs, attitudes, and values. Finally, communication is a powerful activity because our success or failure in life is often determined by our ability to communicate properly.

While certain features of communication are present whether the situation is a friendly conversation at a local restaurant or a public speech in a crowded auditorium, public speaking differs

Real people do give public speeches. In a survey of speaking habits of 478 adults in the New York area of Albany-Troy-Schenectady, between 55 and 63 percent of them had presented at least one speech in the past two years. In addition, people with more education and income had given speeches most frequently.

Kathleen Kendall
"Do Real People Ever Give Speeches?"
ERIC document 255 974, 1985

from other forms of communication because it is a highly defined situation that involves much prior planning and attention to the dynamics of the situation. Let's explore the features that distinguish the public-communication situation from others.

The Public Speech Situation

Communication occurs in a variety of situations, sometimes called *contexts*. The situations in which we find ourselves as communicators range from informal, casual conversations to highly formalized public debates. While situations do change, the qualities necessary for effective communication do not. Since many people begin a course in public speaking with the assumption that they know little about it, let's look at the similarities and differences between conversational speech and public speaking.

Conversational speech involves all those features so far discussed. A conversation is a social activity involving both nonverbal and verbal cues conveyed or interpreted with word symbols. It may seem to move randomly about, but in reality the participants attempt to organize their thoughts and to move the conversation toward some aim or purpose. Conversational speech is powerful: it can enhance understanding and conviction, and it can reach the sphere of art when engaged in conscientiously. The words of philosopher Joost Meerloo sum up the qualities of a conversation:

> *All conversations exert a formal influence. Consider whom you choose for company; unwittingly you take over their language, their gestures and their habits of thought. People need to receive and differentiate all varieties and amounts of words, to form new adjustments and modifications—and this is only possible in direct contact with diverse companions.*[1]

There are, however, significant differences between conversational situations and the setting for a public speech. Because each distinction requires adjustment on the part of the communicator, it is important to understand the differences clearly.

First, a conversation is usually spontaneous. It involves from two to perhaps eight or ten people who gather and begin talking, and it occurs in dialogue form: first one person talks, then another, and so forth. Thus, no speaker is required or expected to speak for long periods of time, and each subsequent speaker is expected to respond to something a previous speaker has said.

A public speech is a planned event involving a large group of people. One person is required to speak for an extended period of time while others listen. Adjustments do and should occur in the public-speaking situation, but the stream of speech is one-way, from speaker to listeners in a form of monologue.

Second, because a conversation is spontaneous, the participants have usually not prepared their remarks in advance. Some ideas may have been thought through and some participants may even have a strategy or a goal they are pursuing, but it is unlikely that those gathered have conscientiously prepared their messages in advance. In fact, too much preplanning violates the spirit of a conversation.

As opposed to a conversation, a public speech involves an extended stream of speech requiring the speaker to prepare his or her remarks in advance. Thus, a public speech is prepared according to principles and guidelines designed to help the speaker compose the speech in advance and deliver it effectively to a live audience. Finally, the speaker has a strategy in mind: she or he has analyzed a topic and the audience, practiced delivering the message, and tried to control the outcome of the communication.

Certain recurring situations in our society require formal communication: speeches at public hearings or at meetings of an organization; oral reports in the classroom or the conference room; and occasional fragmentary presentations, perhaps as part of a larger debate on an issue under discussion at church, school, or on the job. These situations have built into them certain expectations and principles that other, less formal, communication situations generally do not have. Let's look carefully at the individual components of the situation and the expectations that go with them.

The Speaker

In a public-speaking situation, the speaker is responsible for initiating the communication. Since the speaker will present the entire message without interruption, he or she controls much of what happens during the speech. If you have ever sat in a large auditorium listening to a lecture, you are aware that the communication climate in that room is to a great extent the creation of the speaker. The speaker controls the public-speaking situation.

A speaker can do much to enhance his or her chances of success with the speech. First, the speaker must be enthusiastic about the topic, since the audience will often adopt the same attitude toward the topic that the speaker exhibits. The speaker must also have something important to contribute to the topic, so that the audience will feel the speech bears listening to. Finally, the speaker must compose the speech carefully, so that it is accurate and can be delivered fluently. One of the great orators of the nineteenth century, Ralph Waldo Emerson, observed that a great speaker was someone who said what everyone else would have said had they been able to express their thoughts clearly.[2] That is the speaker's role: to say what needs to be said about the topic.

The Topic

The topic is the heart of the message the speaker sends to the audience. The speaker is responsible for choosing a topic that is relevant to the audience and the occasion, for analyzing the topic carefully, and for delivering the topic to the audience. Speakers must take great care to choose the right topic for the speech situation.

Some speech topics will require limiting or expanding to meet the needs of the situation. Every speech topic will require supporting detail to give credibility to the idea and will need to be organized carefully. Throughout this text we will be suggesting topics for you to consider speaking on yourself, or to use as a basis for comparison as you select a topic of your own.

The Audience

The audience is the group of people to whom the message is addressed. In one sense, each member of the audience is an individual, while in another sense the audience is a group that responds in a composite way to the speech. An effective public speech is one that is adapted to the needs of an audience both as individuals and as a group.

The use of the word *adapted* in the previous sentence is not meant to imply that the speaker should say whatever he or she believes the audience wants to hear. To do so would be both unethical and self-defeating. The people in the audience are listening to a speech in order to learn more about the topic or to adjust their attitudes on it. The speaker must therefore focus on the information the audience *needs to hear* in order to learn the most or to make the most reasoned decision.

Adapting a speech to an audience means something other than pandering to the audience's predispositions. Adapting means showing the audience that the topic is relevant to them; it means using language that they can understand. Adapting also means using lively examples and other forms of support to illuminate the topic. We can never change the facts to suit our desires or our audience's biases, but we can and should make every effort to maximize our audience's understanding of a topic.

Later in this text, in Chapter 3, we will discuss audience analysis completely. If you will remember for now that your success as a speaker is a decision the audience makes, this will be an important step toward competence in public speaking.

Feedback

Feedback is the response you get from the listeners. In a public speech, you will usually get verbal feedback only when you have finished (unless you say something exceptionally pointed and the audience replies, "Bravo," "Right on," or "Amen"). But feedback also occurs in nonverbal forms, and effective speakers monitor the nonverbal cues they receive from the audience as the speech progresses. Based upon this feedback, the speaker adjusts to the audience.

Think of a public speech as a form of energy passing between two objects. You, the speaker, are one object, and the audience is the other. The energy passing from you to the audience is both verbal (words) and nonverbal (your vocal and bodily behavior). The energy passing from the audience to you is usually only nonverbal, but it is nonetheless as important as yours. This audience energy is feedback, and it warrants spontaneous attention as you speak so that you use your energy wisely.

Feedback also occurs after a speech in the form of questions, comments, applause, and so on. Effective public speakers must know how to handle feedback following the speech, or risk losing whatever success occurred during the speech. A complete section of Chapter 2 will address this important type of feedback—the questions and comments that follow a speech.

The Speech Channel

One final feature of the public-communication situation is the channel, the medium through which the speech is delivered. In the speech-communication classroom the channel is normally direct, live interaction between the speaker and the audience. On occasion, however, you may find yourself speaking to an audience over the radio or on a television screen. Public speeches occur in a variety of contexts, each of which requires adjustment.

The model of the public-communication situation in Figure 1.1 shows the variables just discussed as they occur in the speech process. Notice that the model shows the variables of speaker, topic, audience, feedback, and channel in a balanced way. It does so to stress that each variable is equally important in effective speech making, and that each must be considered when planning a public speech. Notice also that while a model must, by nature, show the features separately, in the actual speech these features interact simultaneously; that is, speaking and listening, with all the attendant activities, occur all at once during the speech.

In addition to the variables that make up the public-speech situation, it will be helpful for you to know the principles governing the study of this form of communication. Let's turn our attention to these principles.

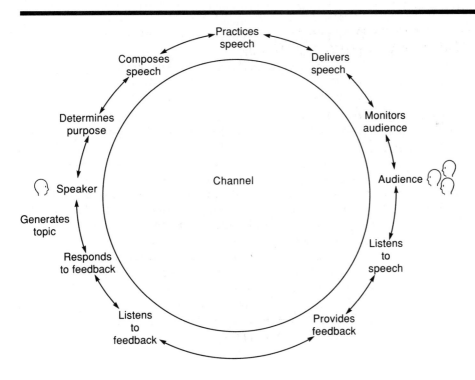

Figure 1.1
The features of public communication

The Principles of Public Communication

The first handbooks on public speaking were written approximately 2,500 years ago during the age of the flourishing Greek democracy in Athens. The study of public speaking was known then as "rhetoric," a term still used today. (Today, however, the term is sometimes used to denote empty or bombastic language.) The principles of public speaking, which were developed during this period and later during the early years of the Roman Empire, are referred to as the "canons" of rhetoric.[3] Traditionally, the study of rhetoric is divided into five parts or canons: invention, organization, style, delivery, and memory. It is important to understand these principles, since they are a reference point, a basic vocabulary, for talking about public speaking.

Invention

Invention involves the study of ideas, including how we get them, what we do with them, how we feel about them, and how we make them purposeful for others. The classical definition of *invention*, coined by Charles Sears Baldwin, is "the investigation, analysis, and grasp of the subject matter."[4]

This text will introduce you to a systematic method for analyzing your experiences and your ideas and for developing speech topics. The critical-thinking system introduced in Chapter 3 will show you how to ask questions about your topic that will help you see the many ways the topic can be developed. We call this process "probing." You will also be shown how to determine the appropriate role and purpose for your speech, and how to adapt your speech to the audience. You will be shown how to put these critical decisions about your topic into a "critical-thinking statement," a paragraph that capsulizes your plan for the public speech you are to give.

Once you have reflected on your topic and grasped it fully, you will need to develop it. Chapter 4 will show you how to support and expand your speech topic with a variety of materials from facts to opinions. Thus, invention involves both sound reasoning and hard work as you flesh out your speech topic.

Organization

Organization is related to invention, since critical thinking is itself a structured process.[5] Organization focuses on patterns used to arrange thoughts for purposes of communicating them to others. A

> Tradition has it that the first persons to systematically study the art of rhetoric were Corax and Tisias, two teachers in the city of Syracuse in Sicily. The first handbook of rhetorical principles was written by Corax and Tisias during the second quarter of the fifth century B.C. (450–475).
>
> *George Kennedy*
> The Art of Persuasion in Greece

carefully analyzed topic, clearly structured for the audience, moves the speech in an orderly way toward the purpose. In this text, you will discover that the same critical-thinking system you used to probe your topic will help you organize your speech clearly. Taken together, the principles of invention and organization represent a way to reason through a speech topic. In fact, using the same critical-thinking system for invention and organization of a speech makes the art of public speaking a much more organic and natural process.

Style

Style is related to both invention and organization, but it mainly involves the language that is appropriate for the speaker in a particular situation. *Style* can be defined as "diction," or "the choice of words and their combination in phrases, clauses, and sentences."[6] Chapter 7 of this text focuses on qualities of style such as clarity, appropriateness, and vividness, offering advice on wording the speech to give it a professional sound.

Delivery

Delivery concerns those vocal and physical attributes that help get a message across to an audience in a pleasing, convincing manner. Public-speaking delivery style is an extension of interpersonal delivery style, with added emphasis and projection and with fewer of the random gestures, movements, and vocal nonfluencies. In Chapters 6 and 8 of this text we will examine the qualities of personal style that you will need to develop as you master delivering a public speech.

Memory

The canon of memory is often dismissed as the lost or artificial practice of memorizing a speech. Actually, *memory* is best defined as "the firm retention in the mind of the matter, words, and arrangement."[7] A public speaker should not memorize a speech, because doing so would preclude adaptation to the live speech event, thus eliminating one of those important and distinctive features of the public-speaking situation discussed earlier. But having in mind one's pattern of organization, a key phrase, or a revealing story, and always keeping in mind the goal or purpose toward which a speech is headed, are marks of the professional public speaker. In Chapter 6 you will learn how to develop a notation system to help you remember your speech, and you will learn about a rehearsal system that will help you remember your speech without memorizing it.

The Process of Public Communication

You can apply the above principles of public speaking to the development of a speech in a step-by-step process. Generally, one principle or another dominates each phase of the development of a public speech. Let's turn our attention to that process so that you can preview the steps you will be taking in this course to develop a public speech.

Step 1: Understanding the Speech Event

In some situations you will not be assigned a public speech; rather, you will receive a phone call or a letter asking you to speak on a particular topic. Similarly, you might personally decide to speak on some matter that interests you, perhaps an issue in your community or on your campus. In the speech-communication classroom, instructions are generally given for each speech assignment. But regardless of the circumstances leading to the speech, some general guidelines will help you off to a good start. First, take notes about the speech event, including time, place, audience size, and peculiar circumstances that might prevail. In some situations you will need to consider the speech channel—the medium through which the speech is to be delivered, such as a microphone, radio, television, or videotape recorder. A microphone, for instance, can put constraints on your movement, so you want to be certain you have prepared in advance for such an exigency. Then, ask any questions about the speech that come to mind. And finally, ask or think about the size of the audience that will be present for the speech.

Step 2: Thinking About the Speech Situation

Once you understand the speech assignment, you must choose— or refine—the topic by analyzing your interests and experiences. In addition, you will have to settle on your role as a speaker and on a purpose for your speech, variables that will guide you in the beginning phases of the composing process. Having thought about topic, purpose, role, and situation, you should draft a statement that accurately reflects your understanding of the situation.

Step 2 requires that you thoroughly analyze your audience. The Roman statesman Gracian is quoted as saying, "A speech is like a feast, at which the dishes are made to please the guests, and not the cooks."[8] As you think about your speech you may want to keep these words in mind. For every speech you give you need to ask yourself: "What does this audience need to know about my topic to understand it?" "What questions are they likely to ask?" "What is my reputation with them?" As noted earlier, Chapter 3 will provide a complete guide to audience analysis.

Step 3: Composing the Speech

Having planned your speech carefully, begin researching your topic, gathering materials, outlining, wording, and generally getting involved in composing your speech. You may well find information about your topic throughout the speech-composing process, but during this third stage you will focus on fleshing out the idea.

One critical choice you must make at this stage is to choose a pattern with which to organize your speech. The pattern you choose will become the starting point of a speech outline and will guide you to the proper location of facts, stories, arguments, and other supporting materials within the speech. Later in this text you will be given a variety of patterns for organizing a speech, and in Part II you will see each pattern fully developed and at work in the public-speaking situation.

Step 3 may also involve preparing visual aids, or at least thinking about visual aids that might make your ideas clearer to the audience. Preparation of visual aids is discussed in Chapter 6.

Step 4: Preparing the Final Draft of the Speech

Earlier, in step 2, you wrote a planning statement *to guide you* in your thinking about the speech. In step 4, you will need to write a *thesis statement*, a single sentence that you will state in your speech *to guide the audience* through the topic. Preparing the final draft of a speech also involves drafting an introduction and a conclusion, and composing the details of the body of the speech. You will discover the frustration and exhilaration of drafting your thoughts into some final form as you discover your own composing style.

Before you actually deliver the speech you will prepare the final format, the notes or outline from which you will actually deliver the speech. A variety of formats appear in Chapter 6. Whether you choose to draft a few words or a complete speech will depend on the advice of your instructor, the speech situation, and your own composing preference. But whichever method you choose for the final form of your speech will determine what you bring with you to the lectern as you prepare to deliver the speech.

Step 5: Practicing and Rehearsing the Speech

During this step you will put the final touches on the speech by practicing it. Some speakers practice with friends, in front of a mirror, or into a tape recorder. Whichever method you develop, keep in mind that "spontaneity" in public speaking is crucial. Thus, you will want to know the speech well enough to feel comfortable about presenting it but not so comfortable that the speech sounds memorized when you actually present it. Chapters 6 and 7 are devoted to helping you develop a spontaneous communication style.

Step 6: Delivering the Speech

Delivering a speech successfully requires that you cope with your nervousness, respond to and monitor the audience, adjust to the speech event as it occurs, and get your message across with clarity and enthusiasm. To accomplish this you will need to have a final format with which you feel comfortable and a delivery style that is lively and dynamic. Your presentational style will develop naturally as you deliver speeches during the course. As noted earlier, much of the focus in a public speaking course is on helping you through the actual speech presentation and on coping with nervousness in public speaking.

Step 7: The Question-Answer Session

After you have completed your speech you will often be given a chance to address questions from members of the audience. In a question-answer session you will need to think on your feet, and at times you will need to defend your position on an issue without losing control of the situation. The question-answer session is a time to clarify points you made during the speech, fill in gaps in information, and, in some situations, win the audience to your point of view. Chapter 2 covers guidelines for handling the question-answer session.

Step 8: Analyzing the Speech Experience

During this final step you will receive an evaluation from your instructor and perhaps from others in the class. This evaluation, whether in written or oral form, usually comments on the ideas you presented in the speech and on your level of success in applying the principles of public speaking. If the speech has been recorded on audio or videotape, you may be asked to analyze it. Analyzing the speech experience, perhaps with an instructor or with colleagues or peers, is an important final step that leads to improvement in future speech experiences.

As you can see, the variables of the public-speaking situation (speaker, topic, audience, feedback, and channel) combine with the principles of public speaking (invention, organization, style, delivery, and memory) to make up the process of public communication. Although this process might seem quite complex at first, you will find that through classroom instruction, exercises, speaking experiences, and reading this text, the process is comprehensible. In fact, a major objective of this text is to increase your enjoyment of public communication, a topic toward which we now turn our attention.

Enjoying Public Communication

Communication is one of our most natural activities. As small children, we gained enormous pleasure from chatting with parents or with those close to us. In our early teenage years, most of us spent endless hours on the telephone with friends, often talking aimlessly simply because we enjoyed the human contact that speech provided. Even today, most of us find gratification in communication with others.

In fact, it may be harder to remain silent than to talk. The most difficult experience for many people is simply to be cut off from communication with others. Ask soldiers stationed far from home or a prisoner in solitary confinement: they will tell you how joyous, even redemptive, a communication from a friend, a loved one, or even a stranger is. In this course, we want to transfer the basic pleasure derived from casual communication to the public-speaking situation. We want you to enjoy the course so that you, and your listeners, will enjoy the art of public speaking.

Increasing Self-Esteem

If communication can be such a joyous activity, then why is it that many people fear giving a public speech? Two reasons appear over and over again: lack of personal confidence and apprehension about some aspect of the speech experience itself. Training in public speaking is designed specifically to help you deal with these two common problems, and it can do much to improve your self-esteem.

Virginia's story, which opened this chapter, is typical of many students' experiences. You will find, for instance, that audience members are learning from your speeches. You will notice that your speaking can move them and affect their thoughts and actions. Each speaking experience will buoy your self-esteem because you will come to see yourself as a person with ideas and attitudes that have value for others. Many students have said after completing their speech course, "I enjoyed giving the speeches. Sure the anxiety was

At least two presidents have been involved in the study of speech communication. John Quincy Adams, sixth U.S. president, was inducted as first Boylston Professor of Rhetoric and Oratory at Harvard University in 1806; Lyndon B. Johnson, thirty-fourth U.S. president, was a speech teacher and debate coach at Sam Houston High School in 1930.

Karl Wallace
A History of Speech Education in America; *and*
Robert Caro
The Years of Lyndon Johnson: The Path to Power

difficult to handle at first, but I learned that there is a little ham in me and I love to make the audience react."

"Sure the anxiety was difficult to handle at first" is a common remark students make about their first attempts at public speaking. In fact, communication apprehension (sometimes referred to as speech fright or speech anxiety) is probably the single most common reason given for avoiding formal presentations.[9] The objective of training in public speaking is to help you come to grips with communication apprehension by learning what causes it and how to cope with it. If you will make an effort to understand and cope with anxiety, this course will be a pleasurable experience. A large section of Chapter 8 is devoted to helping you do just this.

Ethics of Public Speaking

Appreciating public speaking also means recognizing that when we communicate we share our values and shape the values of others. Many successful people from presidents to business executives to activists have used speech to change public opinion. Lawyers, politicians, advertisers, and evangelists spend a disproportionate amount of their time engaged in what has been called "the engineering of consent," a phrase coined by Edward Bernays, the founder of public relations, to describe the vast array of strategies and techniques professional communicators employ to lure us with words.[10] In a society founded on the principles of free speech, communication is often a vehicle to power and profit.

Because communication is so powerful an instrument, we must consider the ethical implications of our communication with others. Ethics in communication involves the conscious choices we make about our tactics and about our intentions toward our audience.[11] Coercion and deceit have no place in communication. In the long run, strategies that reduce the options an audience has or that provide an audience with inaccurate or misleading information hurt all concerned. We have the right to take whatever position we favor on an issue, but we must intend to address our audience with accurate, original communication. To do otherwise is to break the bond of communication that holds society together.

Ethical communicators recognize that all communication is about values. Audiences should be urged toward what P. Albert Duhamel has called "the discovery of and persuasion to right action."[12] In other words, if we choose to speak about an issue, we should investigate all sides of that issue and our research should be thorough

Credo for Free and Responsible Communication in a Democratic Society

Recognizing the essential place of free and responsible communication in a democratic society, and recognizing the distinction between the freedoms our legal system should respect and the responsibilities our education system should cultivate, we members of the Speech Communication Association endorse the following statement of principles:

WE BELIEVE that freedom of speech and assembly must hold a central position among American constitutional principles, and we express our determined support for the right of peaceful expression by any communicative means available to humans.

WE SUPPORT the proposition that a free society can absorb with equanimity speech which exceeds the boundaries of generally accepted beliefs and mores; that much good and little harm can ensue if we err on the side of freedom, whereas much harm and little good may follow if we err on the side of suppression.

WE CRITICIZE as misguided those who believe that the justice of their cause confers license to interfere physically and coercively with the speech of others, and we condemn intimidation, whether by powerful majorities or strident minorities, which attempts to restrict free expression.

WE ACCEPT the responsibility of cultivating by precept and example, in our classrooms and in our communities, enlightened uses of communication; of developing in our students a respect for precision and accuracy in communication, and for reasoning based upon evidence and a judicious discrimination among values.

WE ENCOURAGE our students to accept the role of well-informed and articulate citizens, to defend the communication rights of those with whom they may disagree, and to expose abuses of the communication process.

WE DEDICATE ourselves fully to these principles, confident in the belief that reason will ultimately prevail in a free marketplace of ideas.

Endorsed by the Speech Communication Association, December, 1972,[13]
Reprinted by permission of the Speech Communication Association.

and up-to-date.[14] If we seek to make others laugh, we should do so at no one's expense. Communication is a powerful instrument that can be enjoyed only if we recognize its potential for good *and* harm.

In order to encourage ethical speech, the Speech Communication Association has endorsed a Credo for Free and Responsible Communication in a Democratic Society. Published in 1972, the Credo states the principles of ethical communication to which professional speech communication instructors have subscribed. It is reprinted on the opposite page so you may be aware of and understand the commitment professional speech teachers have made.

These, then, are the ethical principles underlying instruction in public speaking. But what principles should you adopt as your commitment to ethical communication? Although each one of us chooses his or her path to morality, the following list of ethical principles should serve as a guide in this course.

Principles of Ethical Communication
for the Practitioner of Speech Communication

THE ETHICAL SPEAKER has a well developed sense of social responsibility. This person recognizes that when she or he speaks, others will be influenced. The ethical speaker, then, is partly responsible for the actions of others and speaks accordingly.

THE ETHICAL SPEAKER recognizes that there are at least two sides to every issue, and that it is the responsibility of the public speaker to represent the spectrum of viewpoints for any topic.

THE ETHICAL SPEAKER presents only those ideas that are a product of his or her critical thinking. A public speech that is poorly prepared or plagiarized does not further the purposes of a free society. In this same regard, ethical speakers use and cite only accurate, up-to-date sources.

THE ETHICAL SPEAKER cares about the feelings of others, even those who might hold opposing views. The ethical speaker achieves her or his purpose without personal attack (argument ad hominem) or sarcasm by focusing on ideas and issues.

THE ETHICAL SPEAKER is sincere and speaks only on issues in which he or she is interested and truly believes.

Use these principles as a guide to your conduct as a public speaker. Remember that you alone make the ultimate decision about your ethical behavior, but remember also that ethical communicators ultimately enjoy public speaking much more than those who are not.

Summary

A fundamentals course in the art of public speaking should be both an educational and an enjoyable experience. As a part of a general education, the study of public speaking leads to an understanding of human interaction and the role of communication in society. As the study of a specific art, coursework in public speaking leads to the development of principles and skills that can be applied throughout one's lifetime.

Certain features reappear in human communication regardless of the context. Communication is a social activity; it appears in both verbal and nonverbal forms; it is a symbolic activity using words as the principal mechanism for understanding. Communication is a practical, purposeful activity that has lasting import for members of a society.

The contexts in which communication takes place range from informal to formal. Conversational speech is casual and informal and is distinguished by the number of participants and the dialogue format. A public speech takes place in a one-to-many situation, is planned in advance, and is delivered as a monologue. The public-speech situation includes the speaker, the topic, the audience, the channel, and feedback.

The principles governing the art of public speaking are sometimes known as "the canons of rhetoric," and they serve as the formative principles of this text. There are five canons: invention, organization, style, delivery, and memory. Each is covered in detail in the various chapters of this text.

Public communication is a process. The process is discussed in this text in eight steps, ranging from gathering the basic information concerning the speech assignment to the analysis following the delivery of the speech. The public-speaking process combines the variables or features of public communication with the principles of public speaking.

There is an old saying, "A lie can be around the world before the truth has time to put its pants on." Training in ethical communication is the best chance truth has to catch up to deceit, the best chance we have for a world founded on hope rather than hype.

Craig Randall
"Hype Springs Eternal," *United,* November 1985

Finally, public communication—and especially coursework in public speaking—should be an enjoyable experience. Many people shy away from presenting a public speech because they do not have the confidence to present a speech or they are overwhelmed by their apprehension of the speech situation. Communication is most enjoyable when it is based upon a clear set of ethical guidelines. In this course we want to stimulate enjoyment of public speaking by helping increase your self-confidence and by providing you with a clear set of principles to insure ethical communication.

Exercises

1. Try an in-class experiment with words. Without looking back to the text, try to write a definition of style in public speaking in approximately twenty words or less. Having done so, compare your definition with the one in the text on p. 13. Is it the same? Close? Did anyone in the class write the same definition? See whether you can discover why people responded as they did. Use this experiment to initiate a discussion with others in the class about the elusive nature of speech.

2. On a blank sheet of paper draw a picture representing the following scene. Imagine that you are outside your speech-communication classroom looking in and you see yourself giving your first speech. What do you see? Allow yourself about ten minutes for your sketch and then compare your picture with others. What did you emphasize? Did you draw yourself first? Did you include all five variables of the speech-communication process? A picture such as this is a rough characterization of the picture you have in your mind concerning the art of public communication. Now

is the time to discuss your understanding of the speech process, your concerns about this course, and so on. The picture will help stimulate the discussion. Save it until the end of this course to see how you have changed.

References

1. Joost A. Meerloo, "Conversation and Communication," in *The Human Dialogue*, ed. Ashley Montagu (NY: The Free Press, 1967), p. 144.

2. Frederick J. Antczak, *Thought and Character: The Rhetoric of Democratic Action* (Ames, IA: Iowa State University Press, 1985), p. 111.

3. George Kennedy, *The Art of Persuasion in Greece* (Princeton: Princeton University Press, 1963), pp. 10–11.

4. Charles Sears Baldwin, *Ancient Rhetoric and Poetic* (Gloucester, MA: Peter Smith, 1959), p. 43.

5. Frank D'Angelo, *A Conceptual Theory of Rhetoric* (Cambridge: Winthrop Publishers, 1975), p. 14.

6. Baldwin, p. 22.

7. Cicero, *Ad Herennium*, trans. Harry Caplan, Loeb Classical Library (Cambridge: Harvard University Press, 1968), p. 7.

8. Chaim Perelman and L. Olbrechts-Tyteca, *The New Rhetoric: A Treatise on Argumentation* (Notre Dame: University of Notre Dame Press, 1969), p. 24.

9. James C. McCroskey and Virginia Richmond, *The Quiet Ones: Communication Apprehension and Shyness* (Dubuque: Gorsuch Scarisbrick Publishers, 1980), p. 26.

10. Craig Randall, "Hype Springs Eternal," *United*, November 1985, p. 130.

11. B. J. Diggs, "Persuasion and Ethics," *Quarterly Journal of Speech* 50 (1974), pp. 359–373.

12. Ralph T. Eubanks and Virgil Baker, "Toward an Axiology of Rhetoric," in *Contemporary Theories of Rhetoric: Selected Readings*, ed. Richard L. Johannesen (NY: Harper and Row, 1971), pp. 340–356.

13. The Speech Communication Association of America. Used by permission.

14. Eubanks and Baker, pp. 353–354.

Chapter 2 · Listening
to a Public Speech

What image enters your mind when you think of the principle of freedom of speech? Perhaps you visualize an average person standing before a public assembly expressing an opinion. This is one common way to capture the idea of freedom of speech. Freedom to express one's ideas and opinions is a basic commitment of any democracy. But freedom to speak would be a hollow principle, indeed, if it were not accompanied by the responsibility to listen. That image of freedom of speech is incomplete without an audience.

The study of public speaking, as was stressed in Chapter 1, is more than the study of a skill. Public speaking is designed to engage a speaker and a group of listeners in the free exchange of ideas, the result of which is the full flowering of one's thoughts in words. Ideas grow and develop not simply in the act of speech making but also and as much in the act of speech receiving.

Noted journalist-philosopher Walter Lippmann goes so far as to call the listener the "indispensable opposition," without whom an idea might languish on the rocks of self-approval and flattery. Says Lippmann: "Opposition is indispensable. A good statesman, like any other sensible human being, always learns more from his opponents than from his fervent supporters. For his supporters will push him to disaster unless his opponents show him where the dangers are."[1] While those close to us may mean well and encourage us out of a sense of love and loyalty, the critic gives us a more objective response, one that leads to a truer evaluation of our thoughts.

Of course, we listen not simply to evaluate the ideas of others but to learn new information, to appreciate the words of others, and to be inspired. Listening purposes range from the critical to the purely therapeutic. Just as a speaker must have some goal in mind, listeners will also be more successful if they know why they are listening. As Andrew Wolvin and Carolyn Coakley, authors of *Listening*, note, "Recognizing that there are many purposes for listening and that a listener cannot hold all listening purposes at once, we recommend that the listener consciously determine the purpose most suitable for the listening occasion during the early stages of each communicative act."[2]

It goes without saying that most of us will be part of an audience more frequently than we will be the speaker. Thus, one objective of this course in public speaking is to help you improve listening ability. This entire course involves listening, but the present chapter in particular focuses on this most neglected art, beginning with a definition of listening and a model of the listening process. We then present and discuss guidelines that, if followed conscientiously, will lead to more active listening. The chapter concludes by examining the question-answer session that follows a speech, since during this phase of the public-speaking experience critical listening most plays a part.

The Listening Process

The act of listening is often confused with the act of hearing, but they are actually quite different. Hearing is a physiological process in which sound waves are transformed into auditory nerve impulses. For example, a horn sounds while you are talking to someone. You hear the sound even though you had not intended to hear it. More to the point, you can also hear someone talk without consciously attending to his or her words. The fact that you hear the horn or the person speaking does not mean that you are listening. As Lyman K. Stiel, president of the International Listening Association, says, "Listening is more than simply hearing what someone else is saying."[3] What, then is listening?

Most definitions of listening identify it as a conscious process beginning with the recognition of a verbal stimulus that is translated into a meaningful unit of language and then reflected upon.[4] Of course, in the context of public speaking, listening is incomplete without a response, or a critical comment. For our purposes, then,

We listen faster than we speak. The normal speaking rate is approximately 125–150 words per minute. However, studies have shown that listeners can cope successfully with single-sentence commands compressed to 400 words per minute. Our thinking rate has actually been suggested to be about 400 words per minute. But in terms of general listening comprehension, David Orr concluded that 275–300 wpm was the optimum rate for maximum comprehension. Using the maximum-comprehension-rate figure as the appropriate one for public-speaking situations, it is clear that we can listen comprehensively twice as fast as the speaker is speaking. This is one good reason for focusing attention on the speaker: to avoid daydreaming or attention lag.

Carl Weaver
Listening

listening is the conscious process of receiving symbols—primarily through the sense of hearing reinforced by the other senses—assigning meaning to those symbols, reflecting critically on the message, and responding to it.

In order to more fully understand how the listening process works and where it often fails, let's look at a practical model of listening, one developed by Blaine Goss[5] (see Figure 2.1). The Goss model divides the listening process into three phases: signal processing, literal processing, and reflective processing. Each phase, represented by a circle in Figure 2.1, has a distinctive component and an overlapping component.

Signal Processing

We are continuously bombarded with the sounds of speech. Think about a time when you were in a crowded room with dozens of conversations taking place simultaneously, or a time when you attended a sports contest or a concert where a din of voices formed the background for the event. In such situations, speech sounds impinge more or less involuntarily on your sense of hearing. Any of these sounds that has the potential to be consciously recognized by you is called a *signal*.

Listening begins by consciously attending to one or more of the signals one hears. A parent listening from inside the house to a group of children chattering in the backyard may not consciously attend to the sounds until one, perhaps a word of anger, catches the parent's attention and he or she decides to attend to the chil-

Figure 2.1
The Goss Model of Listening
(Reprinted by permission of *Communication Quarterly.*)

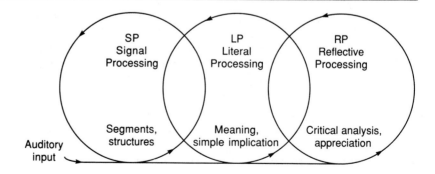
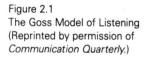

dren's talking. Signal processing requires that the listener recognize the voice of another as a distinct signal.

But consciously focusing on one set of sounds such as a person's voice is only the beginning of signal processing, the recognition phase. In addition, the listener must segment the spoken sounds into words, phrases, and sentences. Look at the following string of letters: iamtakinganicecoldshower. If you were to hear these sounds you would need to make a decision. Has the person said, "I am taking a nice, cold shower" or "I am taking an ice-cold shower"? Your decision, made instantaneously as you attended to the stream of speech, gives the statement its initial meaning: its structure and sequence as a unit of language.

In order to accomplish signal processing, the listener must understand the language and also apply basic rules of language, grammatical and structural rules both learned and acquired through experience with the language. The listener puts the letters together into meaningful word units and recognizes the basic sentence pattern used to make the statement. Having gathered the stream of speech into a meaningful unit of language, the listener has moved from the phase of signal processing into the overlapping phase of literal processing.

Literal Processing

Literal processing involves organizing the spoken words into meaningful statements the listener believes the speaker is producing. The distinctive phase of literal processing is analogous to a computer sorting out commands received from a program. Like a computer, the mind applies its logic to the message in an effort to understand the message, almost as if to say, "Here is what I am assuming you mean by what you are saying." Notice that understanding the message does not imply judgment of it. That comes later.

Literal processing requires the listener to use his or her store of knowledge to decipher the message. Consider the following statement: "The cognitive continuum is concerned with objectives related to knowledge and to the intellectual abilities and skills rising from comprehension to evaluation." If one were a scholar in a field such as psychology, this statement might stand on its own and be translated immediately into a meaningful unit of speech. If one were not trained in the area discussed in the statement, however, more information might be required, perhaps an example or a restatement in simpler terms, for the statement to take on meaning. Thus, in the literal-processing phase knowledge is required for understanding the message.

It is important to note that the meaning assigned to a message is always determined by the listener and is based upon what the listener already knows about the topic being discussed, or about the language being used to discuss the topic. Some basic implications of the message occur as a result of the listener's ability to comprehend, implications such as "This is confusing" or "This is out of my league." As these implications begin to surface, the listener moves into the final phase of listening, reflective processing.

Reflective Processing

Reflective processing of a message involves critical analysis. During this stage the message is assigned a degree of importance, compared to other messages, and interpreted in light of the comparison. One listener might say that a speech was "interesting and informative," meaning that to the listener the message was comparatively new and insightful. Another listener might disagree based upon his or her own experience. Each listener brings to a message a set of experiences, motives, and attitudes that become part of the message itself.

Some writers on the art of listening refer to reflective processing with such terms as *registering, interpreting,* or *assimilating,* to indicate that reflective processing involves making inferences and assessments about the overall impact of the message. Summing up and appreciating the message as a whole completes the listening cycle, since the listener now becomes an active part of the communication event, a contributor to the meaning and interpretation of the message originated by the speaker.

Understanding the listening process is an important first step to increasing communication effectiveness. For the speaker, this understanding provides a full measure of caution. Speakers should be aware that they must gain the attention of their audience and, having done so, should speak clearly and plainly. Failure to do so may result in a communication breakdown at the most basic level: signal processing.

The speaker should also recognize that while he or she intends a meaning, the listener assigns a meaning. Speakers must therefore monitor the audience with the eyes, looking for signs of confusion, perplexity, and misunderstanding. Furthermore, speakers must adapt their messages to the listeners, being careful to speak neither beneath them nor above their comprehension level.

Finally, speakers should recognize that, in addition to knowledge, the audience begins with a set of motives and attitudes that will interact with the message, changing it dramatically at times. Speakers should anticipate responses from the audience by asking what interpretations and reactions are most likely for a given message. By anticipating audience response, the speaker can fine-tune the message during the composing process and can be more responsive during the question-answer session following the speech.

In subsequent chapters of this text we will attend to the listening variables speakers must understand. You will learn, for instance, how to analyze the audience and how to secure their attention, as well as how to deliver your message clearly and articulately. Later in this chapter, you will learn how to handle questions from the audience. But this chapter is devoted to the listener's role in the listening process, and we want to look carefully at ways to improve listening to a message. In order to focus our discussion, we will use the popular expression *active listening*, because it captures the notion that listeners are as much a part of communication as speakers.

Guidelines for Active Listening

Noted psychologist Carl Rogers is responsible for coining the term *active listening*.[6] Although Rogers was concerned with communication between analysts and patients and between managers and workers, *active listening* is a helpful term for critical listening in a public-speaking situation because it suggests that listening is an active processing of information by a receiver, a processing designed to help the speaker understand how accurately he or she has communicated. Far from being the passive recipients of a communication, receptacles into which a message is placed, active listeners reflect on the message as it is delivered, responding with gestures, facial expressions, and other nonverbal cues in an effort to help the speaker understand the impact of the message. By following the guidelines presented here, you can become an integral part of the communication event, reacting and responding to the communication.

Put Yourself in the Speaker's Position

Active listening begins when the listener puts himself or herself in the place of the speaker. Carl Rogers notes that active listening "requires that we get inside the speaker, that we grasp from the speaker's point of view just what it is he or she is communicating to us. More than that, we must convey to the speaker that we are seeing things from his or her point of view."[7] This fundamental act of role reversal is important because it helps us process the message literally before we make judgments about it. Unfortunately, placing ourselves in the other person's position is not easy to accomplish.

When the speaker is taking a position that we find offensive, it is difficult to recognize why the person has taken that point of view and, further, to show through our listening posture that we respect the person's right to take the position. It is much easier to turn someone off or show them nonverbally that we disagree.

When the speaker is someone we dislike or someone we find offensive, it is difficult to put ourselves in that person's shoes. It is tempting to send the speaker the message that we dislike him or her rather than to offer our attention and respond to the person's message.

Finally, situations occur when the person speaking is a subordinate. Once again, it is tempting to show our superiority rather than listen. We have all encountered those who are struggling with language or who are new at the art of public speaking. On such occasions it is easy to feel superior. Should this occur, our weighting of the person's message (our reflective processing) may be influenced more by the person's status than by the message. Communication breaks down in such situations. As Charles Kelly writes, "If you are reacting to another as being dishonest, unethical, stupid, tedious—or as a college professor, or Republican, or student rioter, or disgruntled parent—it will be difficult for you to accurately perceive what that person is trying to say."[8]

Direct Your Listening

Have you ever known a person who had an "ear" for music? Most likely that person knew what to listen for. When people with a trained ear for music listen to a song, they hear it both in parts and as a whole; that is, they hear chords, beat, lyrics, and make judgments about the sophistication of the music on each separate component. This analysis is added to their overall reaction, giving them a total judgment of the song. Active listening requires that we listen to a speech the way trained critics listen to music.

One way to direct your listening is to become acquainted with the criteria many instructors use for evaluating speeches. While certain variables and the emphasis placed on them vary from instructor to instructor and listener to listener, the following list shows the key elements to listen for in a successful speech.

I. Content
   A. Topic
      1. Suited to speaker and audience
      2. Worthwhile, creative, interesting
      3. Limited to time and situation
   B. Purpose and thesis
      1. Clearly stated
      2. Consistently maintained throughout speech
   C. Introduction
      1. Gains attention
      2. Relates to topic
      3. Establishes credibility and good will toward audience
   D. Conclusion
      1. Summarized clearly
      2. Memorable
   E. Body of speech
      1. Clearly organized
      2. Ideas amply supported
      3. Supporting material authoritative, up-to-date, relevant
      4. Transitions varied and informative

II. Delivery
   A. Vocal quality
      1. Pitch
      2. Rate
      3. Quality
      4. Volume
   B. Physical quality
      1. Eye contact
      2. Posture
      3. Gestures
      4. Facial expressions
   C. Style
      1. Natural
      2. Dynamic
      3. Articulate
   D. Language
      1. Hesitations, pauses, hedges
      2. Pronunciation
      3. Grammar
      4. Word choice

We spend a great deal of our time listening. In the course of our everyday affairs, the average person spends approximately 55% of his or her verbal communication time listening, as opposed to 24% speaking, 13% reading, and 8% writing. In the speech-communication classroom, a student may spend up to 80% of the classroom time in the listener's role. Listening, then, is an art in which one engages a large majority of the time.

Andrew Wolvin and Carolyn Coakley
Listening

Some instructors make comments orally and/or on a prepared form. Regardless of the method of criticism, the basic criteria of speech effectiveness are generally agreed upon. When using these criteria as your guide to listening, make each entry a question: "Did the introduction move me to listen?" "Was that statistic up-to-date?" and so on. Add your assessment of each criterion to an overall evaluation of the speech. By putting together your individual reactions with your overall reaction, you will have a more thorough understanding of the message.

Take Notes

When taken properly, notes help listeners focus on key ideas and information. In a study conducted by Francis DiVesta and G. Susan Grey, subjects who took notes during a 3–5 minute speech were able to recall more ideas from the message than subjects who did not take notes.[9]

Note taking begins with having a pen or pencil and a note pad ready. Write down key words and thesis statements, but also note your reactions in shorthand form. Look at the following statement taken from a speech and the notes one might take based upon it.

TRANSCRIPT   *Many New Yorkers are angry because they believe justice is rarely achieved in the courts. The word* vigilante *strikes them as the justice of the streets, the kind that is swift and based upon a sort of eye-for-an-eye philosophy. George Will called vigilantism "private enterprise in the justice business." But vigilantism can quickly become anarchy, and that means a return to a "wild*

*West" mentality that puts all of us in jeopardy. What is clearly
needed is reform in the court system so that justice is speedy
but civilized. Only then will the vigilantes disappear.*

NOTES

*People become vigilantes because it provides swift justice, while
courts are slow.
But vig. = anarchy.   (ask for repeat of Will quote)
Thus, need swifter court system.*

Of course, everyone's notes will look somewhat different and may
appear in a variety of ways on a note pad. If you focus on key words
and phrases and on developing a system you feel comfortable with,
you will soon find yourself taking rapid, informative notes.

But when should one take notes? Goss reports a study by Aron-
son, who noted that "people use the pauses found in a speaker's
natural speaking pattern to process what is being said."[10] In other
words, think about the message as the speaker talks, and take notes
during the speaker's natural pauses.

Listen for Ideas, Not Just Words

A speaker will often use words that grab attention or that cause
confusion. Jot such words down, but try not to let one word cause
you to miss the rest of the speech. During the question-answer
session you may want to ask the speaker why he or she used the
word, but during the speech you should concentrate on ideas. Here
are two ways to do this.

First, listen carefully for the pattern of organization, for the direction in which the speech is moving. Note the point at which the
speaker moves from the introduction to the body to the conclusion.
Within the body of the speech, listen for the main points. If the
speaker says three main points will be covered in the speech, listen
for them and write them down. Structure is a key to the reasoning
the speaker is using in the speech (a point that will become apparent
by the end of this course). For now, listen for the statements that
move the speech from one point to the next.

Second, rather than jotting down the exact words a speaker used
(which often becomes a chore in itself), try to restate the speaker's
point in your own words on your note pad. This skill is called
paraphrasing, and it is used extensively by those who listen as a
part of their professional work. Thus, if the speaker says, "But vigilantism can quickly become anarchy, and that means a return to a

'wild West' mentality that puts all of us in jeopardy," you might note that "vigilantism is like the wild West" to capture the idea the speaker intends.

React to the Speaker During the Speech

Use nonverbal cues such as eye contact and head nods to provide feedback. A quizzical look will let the speaker know that you are confused; a friendly smile says that you agree. Keep that nonverbal dialogue going throughout the speech. By so doing, you help the speaker adjust to you and you keep yourself actively involved in the speech.

Suspend Judgments

It is not a good practice to decide early in a speech whether you agree or disagree with the speaker. Doing so can cause you to become defensive. "Defensive behavior," according to Jack Gibb, "engenders defensive listening, and this in turn produces postural, facial, and verbal cues which raise the defensive level of the original communicator."[11] In addition, evaluating the message too early causes the listener to be on the lookout for "what is wrong with the speech" rather than simply what the message is. By suspending judgment about a speech until you have listened to it entirely, you pass through the literal-processing phase of listening before reflective processing, thus increasing the accuracy of your judgments.

Listen with Your Eyes as Well as with Your Ears

Listening, as our definition notes, is a multisensory activity. Take note of the speaker's appearance and delivery style. Listen for tones as well as words. Note any contradictions between the speaker's content and delivery. If the speaker concludes by saying, "We should all give blood because people who need blood are people who need people," but says it while walking away from the lectern or while shuffling note cards, you might well want to mention that you liked the words in the conclusion but not the physical activity that accompanied them.

Listening is an essential component of a general education. We are taught to read, write, speak, and compute—these are considered basic elements of literacy. Recently, however, educators have begun to recognize that training in listening is vital especially in an age dominated by mass oral media. In 1978, the Primary and Secondary Education Act added listening to the basic skills noted above, and it is now considered a mark of literacy.

Andrew Wolvin and Carolyn Coakley
Listening

One of the most opportune times to practice active listening is during the question-answer session following a speech. The question-answer session can be one of the most enjoyable parts of a speech situation, especially when speaker and listeners engage in a critical evaluation of the ideas presented. The next section offers suggestions on how listeners can ask the right questions and how speakers can best respond to them.

Listening and the Question-Answer Session

Actively listening to a thought-provoking speech often leads to a lively exchange after the presentation. The speaker's role shifts back and forth from speaker to listener, and audience members have an opportunity to express their opinions. Because the discussion period following a speech is so perfect a time to practice active listening, let's take a look at the art of asking and answering questions.

Asking Questions Following a Public Speech

Questions may be about any aspect of a speech. Sometimes, in the speech-communication classroom, questions may be asked or comments made about the learning process of speech making. It is not unusual, for instance, to hear a comment such as "You seemed much more natural this time—how do you account for your improvement?" While such questions are important, in this section we want to concentrate on questions and comments about the ideas expressed during a speech.

QUESTIONS SEEKING INFORMATION. Questions addressed to the speaker often focus on more information. Here are examples of typical information-seeking questions:

I am not sure I understand your point. You gave us a great deal of information about AIDS but didn't tell us what to do with it. Maybe we're not supposed to do anything—I don't know—your speech was interesting, but I need to know what to do at this point. (question related to thesis)

You were going too quickly for me. Could you go over those steps again, briefly? (question related to organization and delivery of speech)

I've heard that word microchip *before, but to be honest I really don't know what a microchip is. Could you explain how you were using that term in your speech? (question related to content)*

QUESTIONS CONCERNING DISAGREEMENTS. You may disagree with the speaker and want to ask a question challenging an assertion in the speech. All too often, audience members hesitate to ask argumentative questions because they prefer to avoid confrontations. But confronting ideas is the way to make them sharper, and it is in the area of disagreement that you will come closest to Walter Lippmann's ideal of the indispensable opposition.

There is, of course, an appropriate tone and style for disagreement: unemotional, straightforward, and inquisitive, rather than accusatory. Although it is not possible to capture the tone of an argumentative question here, it is possible to show the right and the wrong way to phrase a question of disagreement.

Example 1: question following a speech entitled "English: The Unofficial Language of America."

A. Wrong: "You mean to tell me that English is not the official language of this country? I can't believe that!"

B. Right: "You said in your speech that America has no official language. What do you mean by official? Don't we all just assume that English is the official language, since it is the one taught in the schools and used in all official documents and transactions? I would be interested to know how you arrived at that conclusion and where you got that piece of information?"

Example 2: question following a speech advocating passage of the Equal Rights Amendment.

A. Wrong: "Every time I hear women complaining about discrimination, it makes me laugh. Women run this country and everyone knows it." (Notice that this is not actually a question but a comment that elicits an answer as though it were a question.)

B. Right: "After listening to you, I would agree that women have suffered discrimination—at least your research demonstrates that—but does that mean we should pass ERA? Aren't there other ways to address the problem? What is the reasoning of those who oppose ERA?"

MAKING COMMENTS THAT ARE NOT QUESTIONS. It is often appropriate to make a comment that does not require a response from the speaker. Such comments may be either positive or negative. The only requirements are that the comment be directly related to the speech and that it not be too long—listeners should not give their own speeches. Here are two examples of appropriate comments following a speech, one positive and one negative.

Positive: "I want to tell you, I really enjoyed your speech. I had no idea what had happened to the Vietnamese people after the American pullout, although I had often wondered. Your speech was thorough and the visual aids really helped me to see Vietnam today. I still believe that we had to get out of there, so I disagree with your thesis, but at least your opinion was well supported and reasonable. Good job."

Negative: "I guess I want to disagree with your speech. There is no reason that American auto makers cannot compete without import quotas. In fact, *Newsweek* recently ran a story about how auto makers have made huge profits and given large bonuses to executives, while at the same time increasing auto prices and freezing workers' salaries. If fair market competition had been allowed, the Big Three could still have made a profit and our system of free enterprise would not have been undermined by import quotas."

Questions and comments come in all shapes and sizes, of course, and the above are only representative samples. The important point is to join the discussion. We turn now to the parallel art of answering questions from the audience: the speaker as listener.

Answering Questions Following a Public Speech

In the previous discussion on asking questions, you probably noticed that some questions were good and some pretty bad. Regardless of the quality of the question, however, the speaker must handle the question clearly and diplomatically, listening intently and then responding positively.

The most common speaker error is defensiveness. You will often find that the value of your response lies in your tone and your attitude toward your listeners. Questions and comments from the audience should be seen as creative opportunities. The following are strategies for succeeding in the question-answer session.

BE RESPONSIVE TO EVERY QUESTION OR COMMENT. Responsiveness is the opposite of defensiveness. Being responsive means focusing on the person asking the question and, regardless of the question, giving a reasoned response. In the following example, notice how even a negative comment can be turned around by making a positive response.

Question: "Look, the whole problem with automation is that it takes jobs away from people like you and me. You won't be so fired up about the machine that takes your job."

Answer: "I appreciate what you're saying—nobody wants to be replaced by a machine. But, if you'll remember, during my speech I pointed out that more jobs, and actually more skilled jobs, result from technological innovation, since it takes more total people to design and maintain the innovation than it does to provide the work that the machine now performs. So, more people are added to the work force than are replaced by the machine. Of course, that doesn't make it any easier for the person who loses a job; we need to help that person retrain so that she or he can work in the new areas created by the technology."

In this example, the speaker has shown a willingness to listen and an appreciation for the remark. Further, the speaker has turned the question into a positive response, citing facts given in the speech. Whenever possible, turn emotion into reason, and avoid needless confrontations.

RESPOND TO THE ENTIRE AUDIENCE. All too often a speaker becomes involved with one person in the audience only to find later that he or she has won that person over but lost the audience. Address all answers to the entire audience, focusing on the person who asked but drawing all listeners into the response.

> Listeners often get the urge to interrupt, especially when emotions are running high or when the question is not being adequately phrased. On such occasions, another technique seems to work well: silence. Silence allows someone else to finish a comment, and it often leads to greater understanding between communicators.
>
> *Dorothy Molyneaux and Vera W. Lane*
> Effective Interviewing

REPEAT THE QUESTION, AND REPHRASE IF NECESSARY. Often a question will be asked too softly or be poorly phrased. If that happens, repeat and rephrase the question before responding. The following is an example of how to do this.

Question: "You said something about child abuse and I guess something like this law favors parents. I can't believe that. Are you sure about this law?"

Answer: "Your question, I assume, refers to the laws regarding child abuse and parental custody. I am glad that you asked about this. I meant to point out in my speech that while agencies want very much to remove children from situations in which they are abused by parents, quite often the courts are reluctant to issue such orders because presumption has traditionally been with the parents; that is, the parent-child relationship had been held sacred by the courts and there must be compelling evidence before the courts will intervene and break up this fundamental relationship. I should add that many judges are now rethinking the strictness of this rule, especially given the many examples of child abuse I cited in my speech."

KEEP ANSWERS BRIEF. Answers to questions should be concise and to the point. Brevity is the mark of a skillful answer. Remember, a question-answer session often lasts only a few minutes, and your goal is to answer as many questions as possible during that time. Therefore, do not wander to provide irrelevant detail. Stick to the heart of the matter.

There will be times when an appropriate response to a question will require a long answer. In such cases, ask the questioner if he or she would be interested in speaking with you later, when time would permit a full response.

LEARN TO SAY, "I DON'T KNOW." If you do not know the answer to a question, say so. Do not fudge an answer, since it will generally come back to haunt you at a later time. It is a sign of maturity to say, "That's a good question; I'm not sure I know the answer to it, but I'll check it out and have something for you at the next meeting." You may also want to ask other members of the audience whether they have an appropriate answer to the question. Audiences appreciate candor more than deception.

ANSWER ONLY QUESTIONS RELATED TO YOUR TOPIC. Quite often, someone will ask you to speculate, or to answer a question related to a different topic. Similarly, on occasion a question or comment will be addressed to you regarding your character. Such questions are irrelevant, and the best response is a polite "No response." It is enough to say that you are not the appropriate person to ask, or that the question is a good one but not related to your topic. By doing so you will avoid the all-too-common situation of drifting away from your planned topic into areas that you are not prepared to speak about. Such discussions usually bear little fruit and often lead to audience boredom.

Summary

A society founded on the concept of democracy must include freedom of speech, which includes not only the freedom to speak but the responsibility to listen. Listening is the indispensable counterpart to speaking. Most of us will be listeners more than we will be speakers, so learning to listen actively is a fundamental part of our education.

Listening is defined as "the conscious process of receiving symbols, primarily through the sense of hearing reinforced by the other senses, assigning meaning to them, reflecting critically on the message, and responding to it." The listening process involves three stages: signal processing, literal processing, and reflective processing. Each stage has a distinctive phase and an overlapping phase. Each time we listen we make a conscious effort to attend to a stimulus. We then translate the stimulus or signal into meaningful language units, search for the meaning in the message, and then reflect on the message by comparing it to other messages we have heard. The result of listening is an overall judgment about a message. In the public-speaking situation it is important that our assessment of the message be communicated to the speaker. Listening to a public speech requires a response.

Understanding the listening process prevents numerous break-downs caused by skipping phases or by improperly processing the information at each stage. When we consciously focus on the message to understand it and help the speaker adjust to us, we are said to be engaged in active listening. Active listening helps complete the process of communication. In this chapter we suggested guidelines for active listening: (1) put yourself in the speaker's position; (2) direct your listening to the criteria for successful communication; (3) take notes; (4) listen for ideas, not just words; (5) react to the speaker during the speech; (6) suspend judgments; and (7) listen with your eyes as well as your ears.

Active listening is often practiced during the question-answer session that follows a speech. The following guidelines will aid the listener when asking a question: (1) ask questions to gain more information about the topic; (2) challenge assertions made in the speech if you disagree with them; (3) make comments that are not questions if you feel they are appropriate; (4) join in the discussion.

Answering questions following a speech is an important way to win adherents to your position on the topic. It is important not to become defensive, and to follow these guidelines: (1) be responsive to every question or comment; (2) respond to the entire audience; (3) repeat the question, and rephrase it if necessary; (4) keep your answers brief; (5) learn to say, "I don't know"; and (6) answer only questions related to your topic.

Exercises

1. Listening involves interpreting messages. Very often, words set off an emotional reaction in a person that prevents the person from hearing the entire message. What words do that to you? Try to list five words that break your attention and cause you to miss whatever comes after the word. After all members of the class have listed words, separate into groups of five or six and share your lists, commenting as you go around the group on why each word affects you the way it does.

2. A visually impaired student in a speech-communication class developed the following exercise. Prepare a 2–3 minute presentation on some topic of interest to you. Then, four volunteers should be asked to present their speeches to the class. The first two speakers should speak blindfolded. The second two speakers should present their speeches to a blindfolded audience. After this procedure, address the following questions, either in small groups or as a whole class.

a. How does the blindfold affect you as a speaker?

b. How does the blindfold affect you as a listener?

c. Do other senses compensate for the one that is masked?

3. This exercise requires an active class. One person volunteers to prepare a 5-minute speech on an issue of his or her choice. As the person presents the speech, audience members should interrupt whenever a comment or a question occurs. Interruptions should be polite but firm, and the speaker must listen to each interruption but cannot respond. In this exercise comments or questions may refer to either the ideas or the delivery of the speech. Afterward, the speaker should report on his or her reaction to the experience. Discuss the value, or lack thereof, of interruptions—or as they are sometimes called, "immediate feedback."

References

1. Walter Lippmann, "The Indispensable Opposition," *Atlantic Monthly*, August 1939, p. 189.

2. Andrew Wolvin and Carolyn Gwynn Coakley, *Listening* (Dubuque: William C. Brown, 1982), p. 50.

3. Lyman K. Stiel, "Secrets of Being a Better Listener," interview in *U.S. News and World Report*, May 16, 1980, p. 65.

4. Wolvin and Coakley, pp. 30–31.

5. Blaine Goss, "Listening As Information Processing," *Communication Quarterly* 30 (Fall 1982), p. 305.

6. Carl Rogers and Richard Farson, "Active Listening," in Richard Huseman, Cal Logue, and Dwight Freshley, *Readings in Interpersonal and Organizational Communication*, 2d ed. (Boston: Holbrook Press, 1974), pp. 541–557.

7. Rogers and Farson, p. 546.

8. Charles M. Kelly, "Empathic Listening," in John Stewart, ed., *Bridges Not Walls* (Reading, MA: Addison-Wesley, 1973), p. 73.

9. Francis J. DiVesta and G. Susan Grey, "Listening and Note-Taking," in Richard Huseman, Cal Logue, and Dwight Freshley, *Readings in Interpersonal and Organizational Communication*, 2d ed. (Boston: Holbrook Press, 1974), pp. 558–570.

10. Goss, p. 306.

11. Jack Gibb, "Defensive Communication," in John Stewart, ed., *Bridges Not Walls* (Reading, MA: Addison-Wesley, 1973), p. 73.

Chapter 3 · Thinking About Public Communication

What is so hard as getting started? Watching a young child struggle for that first step, stumbling our way through that first day on the job—we have all sympathized with the beginner or laughed at ourselves over those tortuous moments of starting up. Who cannot relate to distinguished novelist Joseph Conrad when he writes: "I have written one page. Just one page. I went about thinking and forgetting—sitting down before the blank page to find that I could not put one sentence together. . . . I am frightened when I remember that I have to drag it all out of myself."

But start we must, and we begin the process of speech making with one advantage: the knowledge that contained within each one of us are all the capacities needed to give a successful speech—we simply need to put them to use. This chapter examines the initial steps a speaker must take to think of a speech topic and compose a speech. You will learn how to develop speech topics, record your topics for future reference, analyze the speech situation, develop a sense of purpose for the speech, and draft a critical-thinking statement that will act as a guide throughout the speech-composing process. In short, this chapter is intended to help you take that first step toward a successful speech.

Exploring Experiences and Ideas

Very early in most speech-communication courses, one question races through the minds of the students: "What am I going to talk about?" Here are the comments of three students who were asked to think about and then respond to the question "How do you find a topic for your speech?"

STUDENT ONE

It is difficult to discern the steps I take immediately after a speech assignment is given. Normally, I do not have an idea for a speech right away; most of the time my ideas seem to pop into my head when I least expect it. For example, I was totally at a loss as to what I was going to do for my last speech. Then, one morning, I woke up at 4:00 A.M., and all of a sudden I knew exactly what my speech would be on, as well as where I would obtain my information and visual aids. This may seem a little strange, but I have my best ideas for speeches from spur-of-the-moment ideas that seem to spring up out of nowhere. Another time I was typing away at work when suddenly an idea for a speech came to mind. Usually, when this happens, I try to jot it down and jot down other ideas that will be vital to the speech.

I get all my ideas by meditating. I go to the Catholic Center on campus and into an old-fashioned confessional in the back of the church where it is dark and quiet. I let my mind roam freely over the events of the day. I find that everything that has happened to me personally is somehow related to an issue. All I have to do is connect things up. If I slip on the ice and feel embarrassed I think to myself, "Slipping on snow and ice—sue the university—no! Learn to be more relaxed; laugh things off instead of getting angry—don't be so self-conscious. What about handicapped people? Think how hard it must be for them on the snow and ice. What is being done to make this campus more accessible to the handicapped? Now there's a good topic—saw a piece on that in the newspaper yesterday." Anyway, that is sort of how it goes with me.

I have kept a diary all of my life. Each day I write down all the things that have happened to me: thoughts and feelings; especially if I hear a good joke I write it down because I can never remember them. I get most of my ideas for speeches from my diary. The rest I get by browsing through USA Today, which is always in the lounge in my dorm.

How would you respond to such a question? Where will you get topics for your speeches? In informal communication we rarely run out of things to talk about; we want now to make that the case for formal communication situations. The best speech topics come from a search through our bank of personal experiences or from an inventory of ideas in which we are interested. Let's pursue these two sources for speech topics in greater detail.

Experiences

There are basically two kinds of experiences: personal and vicarious.[1] Personal experiences are those that happen directly to us. A personal experience can be anything from a fleeting instant, perhaps a look someone gives us that sets off a chain reaction of emotions; to a lifelong event such as a relationship with a parent, sibling, or friend; to major events such as a new job, a trip abroad, or marriage.

Vicarious experiences are those that actually occur to others, but that we participate in either mentally or emotionally. Watching a movie that makes you cry is a vicarious experience, as is your reacting to a tragic news story. When we are relating to an experience that someone else is having or has had, we are experiencing it vicariously.

Experiences, both personal and vicarious, often lead to speech topics. It has been said that experience is the child of invention. Our experiences are our most tangible contact with reality. Much of what we believe is predicated on our collective experience, so powerful is its force. Reflecting on the experiences that have shaped us is a vital step toward becoming effective communicators simply because we will be talking about what we know, our own experience.

When reflecting on your experiences in order to find a speech topic, consider those that have made a difference in the way you think or the way you live. Start with a heading on a sheet of paper and then fill the page as in the following example:

Experiences that have changed my thinking:

My trip to an art gallery and a symphony concert in the evening

My parents' divorce

Working in an internship program in the inner city

Having a child

Experiences that have changed my life-style:

Living for one semester with a neat-freak

Paying the bills for the first time

Watching my friend's father die from lung cancer

Hearing the parents screaming at us on the Little League field

Look for the subtle as well as the grand experiences in your life. Let your mind drift through and around an experience, searching for the meaning in it.

Ideas

As an active mind makes contact with the external world, the inevitable result is an idea. Ideas are formulated thoughts or opinions that develop through conscious attention to or interest in something.[2] It is natural to have ideas, and they come in all shapes, sizes, and levels of intensity. There are a number of ways to get an idea for a speech topic.

Listening to the speeches of others is one common way to formulate an idea of your own. You might, for instance, hear a speech recommending that the Olympics be located in one place permanently. If you are listening actively, that speech might lead you to think about a number of ideas for your speech: great Olympians, the sports-politics connection, amateurism versus professionalism in sports, and so on. Each one of these ideas can be turned into a speech topic.

Ideas for speech topics often come from reading. Just as Student Three (mentioned earlier) noted that her speech topics came from browsing through a newspaper, so your reading can lead to ideas. Make a point of looking at one newspaper each day, and read magazines, novels, poems, and essays with a view toward developing your own ideas. As you reflect on the ideas of others you will begin to get your own.

One further way to get ideas for speech topics is to become a list-maker. A list is simply a column of words or phrases that reflect your current interests. A list might represent some free associating you do with one idea, turning it into a variety of new ideas, as shown in this example:

Idea: Senior citizens desire to remain active in community life but often lack the opportunity to do so. Seniors could be asked to write narratives of the great moments in their lives, which could be published in the local paper. Seniors might enjoy working on community-action boards such as the conservation commission or the recreation board.

Listing can also be done by categories. Start with a broad group such as sports, hobbies, medicine, food, travel, or music. Now, begin to list under each heading some formulated thought or opinion you have for the category, as we have done for music in this example:

Music:

My first piano lesson

Starting up a band

A rating system for rock music as a form of censorship

The difference between jazz and blues

Each speech you present should be a public statement of some inner view you hold about the world. We speak in order to share our experiences and ideas with others, hoping that this sharing might make a difference for us and the audience.

Each one of us has an idea of what is good, what makes life meaningful, and how the world works. We all have attitudes on questions of current concern: apartheid, abortion, capital punishment, health costs, and so on. The fact is that each one of us is actively and creatively thinking. The point, then, is to develop a system for recording our experiences and ideas and a systematic method for analyzing them.

Recording Experiences and Ideas

Think back to the comments of Student Three noted earlier in this chapter (p. 47). She said, "I have kept a diary all of my life. Each day I write down all the things that have happened to me...." It is a common practice of many people to record their thoughts, perhaps in a diary but also in a number of other ways. Few things are more frustrating than losing a good topic because you forgot to write it down—something equivalent to forgetting the camera after leaving on a vacation.

Since so many good topics for speeches often occur fleetingly, it is helpful to store them in some external source. Professional speakers and writers use a variety of recording techniques ranging from scraps of paper stored under a book to full-scale diaries. This sec-

The brain is divided into two hemispheres that are joined by the corpus collosum. Each hemisphere is highly specialized. The left hemisphere processes information analytically, sequentially, rationally. The right hemisphere processes information differently, and is responsible for creativity, imaginative thinking, intuition, and so on. Sometimes the two hemispheres function simultaneously and sometimes independently, but both operate in the production of ideas.

Frank D'Angelo
A Conceptual Theory of Rhetoric

tion covers three commonly used techniques for storing your experiences and ideas for later use in a public speech.

Tape Recorders

Consider the following comment from a student in a speech-communication class:

> A friend of mine bought one of those new, little miniature tape recorders, about the size of a pocket camera. He keeps it in his car on the dash or between the seats. While he's driving and thinking about things, sort of like we all do, he thinks out loud into the tape recorder. Most of the time it just comes out garbage and he tapes over it, but every once in a while a great idea pops into his head—you know, the kind you can never remember when you go back to it. He's got the idea on tape.

Not only does the person mentioned above have his good ideas on tape; he also has potential speech topics. While we may feel somewhat silly at first, recording our thoughts on a tape recorder or even on a note pad is a highly useful activity. Even if the end result is not a speech topic, the recorded thoughts could help fill in some part of the speech at a later stage of development.

Journals

Another way to capture experiences and ideas is to keep a journal. A journal is similar to a diary except that it does not have to be systematic or arranged by dates. The point of keeping a journal is to write freely about anything that comes to mind. If you hear an interesting anecdote, put it in the journal. If you encounter a topic that you would like to know more about, record your initial impressions in your journal. If you are working on a research project for a speech course, keep random thoughts about it in the journal. Ever catch yourself coining a clever phrase? Record it in the journal before you forget it.

A journal can be a small but sturdy note pad or a full-sized, 8½-by-11-inch, personally engraved booklet. Some journals are easily carried in a back pocket or a handbag, while others need to be stored in a briefcase. It is not the size or the shape of the journal that matters as much as the ease with which one can use it.

The following anecdote from a speech-communication professor reveals the value of recording experiences and ideas: "I was driving one day to a convention to present a speech on a research project. On the radio I heard an announcer talking about Murphy's Law—you know, if anything can go wrong, it will. A caller phoned in to the show and said, 'Have you heard of Lieberman's Law? It goes like this: Everybody's lying these days, but it doesn't matter because nobody's listening.' Well, my speech was on deception in political communication, and there it was—my introduction. I pulled over at the next rest stop, jotted it down, and then used it later that day at the convention with much success."

Commonplace Books

A commonplace, in classical rhetoric, was originally an oration on an acknowledged truth.[3] Students much like yourselves in ancient Athens or Victorian England would be asked to speak on topics such as the following:

"If the more difficult of two things is possible, then the easier is possible also."—a common principle

"A fool and his money are soon parted."—a proverb

Commonplaces were used as exercises to sharpen the mind and to test one's skill at arguing. Today the notion of commonplaces has changed somewhat. We now think of a commonplace as an idea one encounters that might later be worthy of reflection and development, perhaps in a speech or an essay. In fact, some of the boxed selections in this text are commonplaces. A commonplace book is a notebook that is systematically arranged according to specific headings and corresponding commonplaces. It can be extremely helpful for inspiring speech ideas.

If you wish to develop a commonplace book, you can arrange the headings in any convenient, logical system. One system is to have a section for each department at your school, so that when you encounter an idea from a course you are taking, you can record it. Following is a sample page from a commonplace notebook to give you an idea of how one could look:

Philosophy

1. "A philosopher is someone who, when you point your finger at reality, wants to study your finger."—Professor Smith

2. "One no longer loves one's insight enough once one communicates it."—Friedrich Nietzsche

3. "No thinker shall suffer for his thoughts is equivalent to the rule: nothing important shall ever happen."—William Ernest Hocking

4. "The public is the fairy story of an age of understanding, which in imagination makes the individual into something even greater than a king above his people."—Sören Kierkegaard

5. "I *am* only in communication with another."—Karl Jaspers

It is possible to have a page for any number of areas: sports, medicine, drugs, dance, and so on. Each time you write down a thought or a direct quotation, you should consider whether it might make an interesting speech topic or perhaps fit into a topic you are considering. Once you have begun recording experiences and ideas, you have taken a major step toward developing speech topics.

Thinking Critically About the Speech Topic

Once we have decided on a topic for a speech, we need to begin thinking about it in a systematic, or critical way. Critical thinking is a matter of discovering meaningful patterns or relationships in a subject, and of seeing the subject from a variety of perspectives. For example, when journalists conduct interviews they follow a standard set of questions designed to draw out all relevant information needed for their stories. As public speakers we also need a list of questions to help us grasp our topics fully. The activity of thinking critically about a speech topic through questioning is called "probing," because it suggests a sort of "poking at" or "digging into" the subject matter at hand.

But where shall we get a list of questions appropriate to probing a speech topic? Consider where the journalists obtain theirs. They have to cover a story so that readers get all the facts in a brief amount of space or time. As the various types of journalism have evolved (newspapers, radio, TV), and based upon an analysis of reader response, professional reporters have fine-tuned their standard questions so that the questions accomplish two things: give the readers all the angles and facts on a story, and provide the reporter with a basic structure for writing up the story. Public speakers follow the same sort of logic in the development of a list of questions for probing a subject.

The Topics of Aristotle

The philosopher Aristotle was the first person to be concerned with a list of questions one could apply to discover appropriate arguments for a speech. Aristotle called his questions the *topoi* or "common topics," and he listed twenty-eight of them.[4] Some of Aristotle's topics were definition (determining the meaning of something), division (breaking the topic into parts), and time (looking at events in a sequence to see how each led to the next). Each time one asks a different question about the speech topic (For example: What is it? What are its parts? How did it happen?), a different perspective emerges, different facts are revealed, and the topic is seen more fully. For Aristotle, a speech concerning public affairs or anything else was not complete until all the common topics had been used to reveal the subject matter fully.[5]

The Categories of Invention

Contemporary scholars of communication and composition have refined and expanded Aristotle's system of common topics. Today, the common topics are referred to as "categories of invention," because by analyzing an experience or idea according to one of these categories, we "invent" something about it. While Aristotle's common topics were derived from his understanding of the qualities existing in the universe, the categories of invention are based upon research by psychologists and communication scholars into how the mind naturally sorts out and processes information.[6] Let's look into this notion more deeply.

Although each one of us is a creative thinker and although our thoughts may seem to be jumbled together at times, the products of our thinking—our speaking and writing—reveal consistent categories. We all classify, for instance, and we all generally tell stories in chronological order. It is reasonable to infer from the categories we see in speaking and writing, then, that our thinking is structured and governed by the same categories.

The categories of invention used in this text are based upon two logical concepts: time and space. It is easy to see that people think in time by simply observing the number of stories people tell as a way of explaining or reasoning in communication with others. A story is a sequence of events, one event following the other, in a time-governed order. Time is a common concept used in thinking and communication, and it is relatively easy to observe people using time as the controlling concept while they think.

Similarly, space is a controlling concept for thinking. When we divide apples up, for instance, and say, "There are three colors of apples: red, green, and yellow," our dividing is based not on time but on some spatial relationship we see among the various colors of apples. When we classify one type of music and then another, our classification system is based upon the differences we observe between the two styles; the concept of time plays no part in our analysis. So the concepts of space and time are separate as well as exhaustive, because they cover the range of possibilities for thinking about a subject.

When the two basic concepts, time and space, are divided into categories of invention, we see the following breakdown. Time can be used in three different ways to process information: narration, process, and cause-effect. Space can also be used in three ways to process information: definition, analysis, and classification. When each category of invention is further developed into a standard question format we get the following list:

Narration—a recounting of a sequence of events focusing on the question "What?"

What happened?

When and where did it happen and to whom?

Process—a recounting of a sequence of events focusing on the question "How?"

How does it work?

What are its stages or steps?

How would someone do it?

Cause-Effect—a recounting of a series of events focusing on the question "Why?"

Why did it happen?

What are the reasons behind it?

How does it relate to something else?

What effects has it produced, or will it produce?

Definition—*thinking about the boundaries or limits of a thing in terms of its differences*

What is it?

What is its history?

What is it composed of?

Analysis—*dividing anything complex into simple units or components*

How can it be divided?

What are its key components?

What is its logical form?

Classification—*thinking about the boundaries or limits of a thing in terms of its similarities*

How can it be categorized?

What common attributes make up the whole?

Of course, the categories of invention overlap because of their inherent grounding in the concepts of time and space. Aristotle recognized overlap in his common topics also. But in the same way that many sports are alike in that they involve putting a ball into a goal but are nevertheless distinct in the way the players go about doing this, so categories of invention overlap and yet are distinctive in the speaking or writing that develops from them. Each time we ask a different question we get somewhat different information, thus adding both breadth and depth to our understanding of the topic.

Because these categories of invention are so important and because they make up the critical-thinking system upon which this entire text is based, let's look at a sample speech topic to show how it can be thought about systematically by applying each category of invention and the attendant probes, or questions, to it.

We will assume that you have returned recently from a trip to Washington, D.C. One memorable experience for you was a visit to the Vietnam Veterans Memorial. The experience moved you so much that it struck you immediately as a possible speech topic, and you jotted the topic down on a piece of paper (in your journal, perhaps). You now want to think systematically about it to discover all the possible ways you might talk about it. Your probing might yield something like the following:

You could talk about walking around the memorial, capturing the scene: the people, the events, people's feelings and reactions to the monument. A thorough recounting of events might convince others to visit the memorial, or simply move them to relate vicariously to your experience.

NARRATION

You could talk about how the memorial was built. From the time it was proposed to the opening ceremonies, how did the project take shape? You might remember news stories that focused on the controversy surrounding such steps as the choice of black marble stone, or the site upon which the memorial was constructed. You could expand on the news story with your experience and some research of your own into the process of constructing the memorial.

PROCESS

You could talk about the controversy surrounding the memorial. Why was it built? What effect has the monument had on perceptions of the Vietnam War? On those who served in it?

CAUSE-EFFECT

You could talk about the meaning of this memorial. Is this a memorial in the classic sense of the term? Many have argued, you recall, that a monument should be uplifting and glorious, while the Vietnam memorial strikes you as sad and funereal. Does this memorial meet the criteria?

DEFINITION

You could talk about the arguments made for and against the memorial. By looking at the pros and cons you might convince others that the memorial was a good idea or a bad idea. You might also divide your talk into the characteristics of the memorial that give it distinctness: shape, color, size, and so on.

ANALYSIS

There are many kinds of monuments such as statues, obelisks, and entire buildings. How would you classify the various monuments you have observed around Washington or elsewhere? Where would the Vietnam memorial fit into this scheme?

CLASSIFICATION

You can probe any topic in a similar manner. Notice that some questions yield or lead us to "invent" more or better information than others. You might do some initial thinking at this point about which approach will be most interesting to an audience or which represents the way you see the subject. At any rate, you have thought critically about your topic and reflected on it with a variety of categories.

Learning the categories of invention and the questions/probes that are peculiar to each category is important beyond their use as an analytical tool. Later in this text you will see that these same categories of invention can be used to organize the body of your speech. That is, you can use the narrative category to think about and invent a topic, and you can also use the narrative category as a pattern for developing your entire speech. Using the same principles to organize your speech that you used to analyze your topic makes the art of developing a speech much more natural and developmental, since this approach involves a natural progression from thinking to speaking.

Critical thinking about the speech subject is essential to success in speaking. The more we know about the topic—the more ways we can see it as a living entity, as a piece of our mind—the more successful we will be. A speech, however, involves more than analysis of the topic. It is a live event and must be carefully adapted to the situation in which it will be presented. Considering in an integrated way the variables of speaker, topic, audience, and situation aids our understanding of the art of public speech-making. Let us therefore turn our attention to this important consideration: the speech event.

Considering the Speech Situation

Considering the speech situation requires that we examine the variables of the speech-communication process as they interact with one another. Each time a speaker delivers a message to an audience in a particular place, it is an original event. A successful speech is one that you have some interest in presenting and that you can make interesting to an audience in the time you have and the room you are in. Let's look at these variables in some depth.

Audience Analysis

Audience analysis begins with careful attention to general characteristics of those attending the speech. In a speech-communication class you may need to do this only once, perhaps at the beginning of the semester. The following questions will help you develop a composite picture of the audience.

1. What are the physical, social, and economic conditions of the audience?

2. What about factors such as age, home environment, ethnic background, income level, and health or handicaps?

3. What is the general educational level of the audience?

4. What values and ethical standards do audience members hold?

A topic should be relevant for the audience addressed in that the audience should have a general interest in the topic or be able to develop one. Recently, for instance, a student gave a speech to a group of eighteen-year-old college students on the problems involved with raising preadolescent children. There was little natural interest in the topic, since no students in the audience were parents; and, try as she did, the speaker could generate little enthusiasm for the topic during the speech.

Choose topics that have a chance to succeed. Older audiences have different tastes than younger audiences. Predominantly male audiences have different interests than predominantly female audiences. In fact, each time a dimension is added to the audience—sex, race, age, education—it must be considered in audience analysis.

Audience and Topic

Once you have determined that audience members have or could be led to have an interest in the topic, you need to determine their specific relationship to the topic. In order to do so consider the following questions:

1. How much does the audience already know about the topic?

2. What would motivate this audience to accept my ideas?

3. Will the audience consider the topic too trivial or too technical?

4. What is the audience's opinion on the topic, as far as can be determined?

Obviously, you would not want to talk about a topic that the average person already knew about. A speech on how to preregister for classes, most of which comes from a recent article in the school newspaper, is probably of little value to the audience. Similarly, a speech on fifteenth-century tapestry techniques is probably remote enough for the average audience to confound them in a short speech.

The best topics are those about which the audience knows something, but about which it could learn more in the time allotted.

A trivial topic is one that is too simple, is overdone, or is a bit too obvious. Whether your topic is trivial or not is, of course, a decision you must make in your situation. In order to help you, however, here are some topics that have been looked upon as trivial in speech-communication classes:

Too Simple	*Overdone*
My first time drunk	Joining a fraternity/sorority
How to make brownies	Legalizing marijuana
Potting a plant	Going away to school
"Feel good" topics:	What's wrong with X
Being against war/for peace	How to meet men/women
Treating everyone politely	
Studying hard and getting ahead	

Add your own topics to this list as your situation dictates, and subtract from this list topics that you feel would be right for your audience. A helpful rule of thumb is this: if your topic is trivial or overdone, you will either run out of material in a minute or two or you will find so much material that you will soon think that everyone must have given a speech on this topic at one time or another.

A topic that is too complex will be difficult for the audience to follow. Scientific or technical processes, deeply philosophical topics, or topics involving excessive numbers such as computer programming or accounting fit into this category. Once again, this is not to say that any topic should be ruled out for every audience, but simply to suggest that highly complex topics require a special effort to be made clear for the specific audience. Following is a list of topics that have failed in speech communication classrooms because they were too difficult for the audience:

Existentialism (or any philosophy) as a way of life

Writing your own computer programs/novels/poems/ and so on

DNA, or any physiological or anatomical process or system that requires a large amount of technical vocabulary

The rise and fall of the Roman Empire

Finally, think about why the audience would like your topic. To what natural interest does it appeal? What gratification does it offer the audience? Approach the speech situation realistically: people listen to you because they are getting something from your speech. You need to decide what others might gain from listening to you.

Audience and Speaker

An effective speech topic is one that the audience finds believable coming from you. Judgments that audience members make about you, the speaker, will affect their judgments about your speech. It is important, therefore, that you consider the following questions as you think about the speech situation.

Do I have any credibility for this topic with the audience?

What is the overall opinion audience members have of me?

Am I interested enough in this topic to do the work involved?

Am I interested enough in this topic to speak enthusiastically about it?

So critical is speaker credibility to successful communication, that enough research is available on the subject to fill this entire text.[7] We know, for instance, that the speaker's credibility is affected across three time periods: before, during, and after the speech. In other words, speakers must be concerned about credibility from the time they choose a topic until the time the speech has been

Recent studies in social communication (conversation) reveal that the social use of language depends as much on the knowledge of the audience as on the knowledge of language itself. In conversational speech, speakers adjust their language naturally to the responses of the audience. In public speaking, audience adjustment is not natural and must be consciously attended to.

Robert Krauss and Sam Glucksberg
"Social and Nonsocial Speech"
Scientific American, Feb. 1977

evaluated in the minds of the audience. In the chapter on delivery (Chapter 8) we will be concerned with enhancing credibility during and after the speech. At this point we need to be most concerned with establishing credibility through topic selection.

What are the dimensions of speaker credibility? Credibility is the result of the impression we make on our audience—specifically, the character, intelligence, and good will we demonstrate.

Speaker credibility based on character is related to perceived moral and ethical qualities. An audience can get the wrong impression of us if it perceives anything deceptive or exploitative about our speech. Using too much material from one source can cause such a perception. Similarly, a student once gave a speech on the thrill of stealing a flag from the local fast-food restaurant. He thought the audience would be amused and impressed: it was not. Speeches that proselytize (that is, preach dogmatically for the acceptance of some doctrine) may also be viewed negatively by the audience.

We also establish credibility by respecting our audience's intelligence and time. When it is your turn to speak, you want the audience to look forward to listening to you. This will happen if you choose topics that are challenging, interesting, and enjoyable. Too many students have failed in a speech assignment by attempting to recycle a high-school topic or an essay from their composition class. Others have failed by choosing a topic far below their own intelligence level as well as that of the audience. On the other hand, students who take the challenge, who choose topics that stimulate, are often rewarded for their efforts by the audience's attention and gratitude.

Good will refers to the enthusiasm and care we show for the speech. Enthusiasm begins early, and, as the questions on the previous page indicate, you should decide immediately whether you can sustain the excitement for your topic that you will need to get through the planning and composing stages of the speech. Many speeches have failed because speakers could not maintain enthusiasm throughout their speeches. Later, we will emphasize the need to show enthusiasm during your speech; choosing the right topic now can make that a much easier task.

Time and Place: The Speech Situation

It is easy to overlook the location of the speech or the time allotted for the speech. To do so, however, can cause an otherwise carefully planned speech to fail. Consider the following questions when thinking about the environment in which you will present the speech.

Can I say something meaningful about this topic in the time allotted?

Will this topic require props or demonstrations that are possible in the situation?

Will there be a lectern, a podium, sufficient lighting, portable chairs, desks, or any other furniture or physical problems?

Many excellent speech topics suffer simply because they are too long for the time allotted. You would not be able, for instance, to develop the topic "Creationism versus Evolutionism" very effectively in a 3–5 minute speech (although it has been tried). Reduce the scope of your topic to meet the constraints of the situation.

A topic like "Apartheid in South Africa" is much too large, but as you begin to probe the topic you will see facets of it emerging. A speech on the topic "Apartheid: What Does It Mean?" limited to the category of definition would be much more manageable. You can limit the scope of your topic most easily by applying the questions listed on pp. 55–56.

The speech-communication classroom can be a quite lively place. Speech instructors have seen goats, sail boats, parents, and all manner of objects brought into the classroom to add color and visual support to a speech. But there are limits! As you think about speech topics, consider whether you will be able to use the props and perform the demonstrations that such topics might require. Chapter 6 contains a thorough discussion of the preparation and use of visual aids.

Finally, take some time early in the semester to look around the room you are in. Think about each feature of the room and decide how it will affect you. You may, for instance, have a lectern or a

---

The term *credibility gap* is often used to refer to problems between a person's words and his or her actions. This term was coined by journalist David Wise on May 23, 1965, in reference to the notorious credibility gap in the presidential administration of Lyndon B. Johnson.

Warren Rogers
"The Truth About LBJ's Credibility"
Look, May 2, 1967

---

speaker's stand that you know will be a hindrance to you but also a temptation. Think about how you will handle the speaker's stand during the semester. Will there be a microphone? Think also about how to manage visual aids in the room, and whether the room has electrical outlets should you need them. Each variable in the speech environment adds a shade of meaning to your topic selection and to your general thinking about the public-speech situation.

Developing a Clear Sense of Role and Purpose

In many speech situations you will begin with a clear sense of your role and purpose; that is, who you are and what your goal is in the speech situation. Members of the city council, for instance, might ask a local historian to explain for them the history of zoning ordinances in the city so that the council might adopt a new zoning plan. The historian's role and purpose are clear: he is an expert on the matter and is to bring the council information they need to make decisions in the future. On another occasion, a representative from the local Chamber of Commerce might ask to speak at the city council meeting in favor of a particular plan to increase commercial zoning. Once again, the Chamber of Commerce official knows his or her role and purpose: to speak as an advocate for one zoning plan in an attempt to convince the council to pass it into law. Although there are many similarities in the two situations, each situation carves out a clear path down which each speaker and each audience will travel.

It is also possible to be in a situation where purpose is unclear. A speech in the classroom may require you to cast yourself in a role and to develop for yourself a clear sense of the outcome you intend for the audience. A speech on the nutritional value of fast food, for instance, could take many directions. The speaker might act as a source of information, as an advocate against fast food, or even as a humorist/satirist on the topic. The decision the speaker makes is important because the audience will be naturally curious to know where he or she is leading them.

Knowing one's role and purpose in a speech situation is important for another reason: should you make a mistake and confuse your role and purpose, your speech, well-intentioned and insightful as it may be, will quite likely fail. Recently, a female professor with thirty years of teaching experience at a large university was asked by the local women's caucus to address the topic "Life Before Affirmative Action." The professor decided to approach the subject light-heartedly, relating her experience as one of only five females on a faculty of over three hundred. While her intent was to amuse the audience with her experiences and still make a serious point, the audience had expected her to present a serious analysis of discriminatory practices that warranted affirmative-action legislation. The result was a communication breakdown between the speaker and the audience.

From examples such as those just given it is clear that one's role and purpose are essential concerns in developing a speech. In this text we think of purpose as a two-fold concept: as the response intended by the speaker, and as the response sought from the audience, since if either the speaker or the listeners are confused about the purpose of the speech, communication will break down.[8] In light of its importance to the public speaker, let's take a close look at the concept of purpose in the making of a public speech.

Classifying Speech Purposes

There are numerous methods for classifying the various purposes of a public speech. Public-speaking teachers in ancient Athens and Rome believed that all speeches were intended to persuade the audience to the speaker's point of view. This belief arose because speeches were presented in three situations: the courtroom (forensic speeches), the legislative chamber (deliberative speeches), and public ceremonies (epideictic speeches). Each of these situations required that the speaker gain the assent of the audience, whether that assent was a verdict, a vote, or applause.[9]

The notion that a public speech is an instrument of persuasion remains strong today. Some scholars, such as David Berlo, assert that language itself is inherently persuasive, since the words we choose to represent an idea signal a bias on our part and therefore an attempt to move the audience in our direction.[10] Other scholars, such as Edward P. J. Corbett, continue to argue that even situations that appear purely informative still rely on convincing the audience to accept the information.[11] The predominant view today, however, is that not all purposes for a speech are persuasive in nature.[12] Let's look briefly at the development of this notion.

In the eighteenth century, an influential scholar named George Campbell argued that persuasion was not the only purpose for a speech. Based upon his belief that the mind was composed of various "faculties" such as reason, emotion, and will, Campbell asserted that a public speech ought to be addressed predominantly to one faculty or another. The art of public speaking was, for Campbell, "the art or talent by which discourse is adapted to its end." For Campbell, there were four ends corresponding to faculties in the mind: "All the ends of speech are reducible to four: every speech being intended to enlighten the understanding, to please the imagination, to move the passions, or to influence the will."[13]

During the early decades of the twentieth century, the concept of purpose Campbell spelled out came to dominate public-speaking instruction. Authors of texts on public speaking began to list purposes, some noting as many as seven, with the average being around five. The most influential public-speaking text of this period, *Public Speaking*, by James Winans, listed four purposes: to interest, to make clear, to induce belief, and to influence conduct, with the caution that "no classification of topics in this discussion seems entirely satisfactory."[14]

In 1935, a book published by Alan H. Monroe, *Principles and Types of Speech*, transformed some of the frequently used purposes into types of speeches.[15] That is, while purpose had traditionally been considered as one critical component in planning a speech, Monroe made purpose the central or controlling element in the entire development of the speech. Thus, speeches came to be labeled by the purpose toward which they were directed. Monroe listed four types of speeches: speeches to inform, speeches to entertain, speeches to stimulate through emotion, and speeches to convince through reasoning.[16]

Through Monroe's transformation, purpose became the controlling principle in the teaching of public speaking. A speech to inform, for instance, would be taught differently from a speech to persuade. The idea that purpose is the critical distinction among various types of speeches has some following today, but classifying speeches by purpose also causes problems for public speakers when they actually compose speeches.

One problem is that purposes greatly overlap. Every speech should be informative, persuasive, or entertaining, a fact that leads some to suggest that speeches are classified by purpose simply for instructional reasons.[17]

A more serious problem with the classification of speeches by purpose is that knowing whether one's purpose is, for instance, informative or persuasive does little to help one analyze and organize the topic. Whether one is presenting a speech to inform, to entertain, or to persuade, one still needs to analyze, support, and organize the topic and deliver the speech enthusiastically. As an analytical tool, then, knowing one's purpose is only one means to an end, not an end in itself.

Topic Analysis, Role, and Purpose

Why, then, is purpose important in thinking critically about a public speech? Think back a few pages to our discussion of the categories of invention (pp. 54–58). Six categories were presented, each of which, when applied to a speech topic, yielded different information about the topic or, at the very least, a different angle from which to view the topic. In addition, you looked at an example (the Vietnam-memorial visit on pp. 56–57) of the categories at work and saw for yourself the vast amount of information that a simple experience can generate. In fact, you probably noted that in one speech you could not possibly cover all the information or all the angles generated by your probing of the topic. You probably also discovered that some of the categories yielded information or perspectives that were not relevant or useful in a practical way for a public speech. Your observations were correct.

The question a public speaker must ask is, "Which information generated from which categories would be most appropriate for the speech I have to present?" In other words, if you were to use all the categories to probe your topic, which one or ones would give you the primary direction for your speech? The answer to this question lies in your analysis of your role and in the purpose of your speech. This will be clearer with an example.

Let us assume that you and several other students are going to speak at a meeting of the student senate at your school. The subject of the speeches is the campus-wide parking problem. Because of time constraints, it has been predetermined that each speaker will be given five minutes to present his or her opinion on the matter (this is often the case in such situations). You decide that you are an advocate for a plan that would change one underused staff parking lot to a lot for use by commuter students. The response you want from the student senators is passage of a resolution supporting your proposal. So your role and purpose are clear, but how do you carry out your role and achieve your purpose?

Of course, your delivery will be a factor in your success, as will an infinite number of variables over which you have little or no control, such as the mood of the audience, other speakers on the topic, the audience's knowledge, and so on. In addition to delivery, you can control your material, and if you analyze it carefully your chances for success improve dramatically. So you probe the speech with the categories of invention, selecting those categories that yield information relevant to the situation. Your probing might go something like this:

NARRATION	*I could talk about the hassles of parking on campus, and then ask the senate to support our resolution. That might work.*
PROCESS	*I could review the process by which parking lots are designated staff, faculty, commuter, and so on, and then argue that this process has caused the problem. Not too relevant.*
CAUSE-EFFECT	*I could show why this problem has surfaced, tracing it from the change in the number of commuters on campus, to the lack of spaces, to the need for reallocation. This way, my proposal seems like a readjustment to the situation rather than a pleading for my special interest. I'll keep this one in mind.*
DEFINITION	*What is the parking problem? Everyone agrees about this already. Not a good approach.*
ANALYSIS	*I could approach this simply from a problem-solution point of view. Here's the problem, and here's the solution. If they see the data they'll sign the resolution. Highly possible.*
CLASSIFICATION	*Does the problem come from the classification system used here? Could lots simply be open on a first-come, first-served basis? This approach takes me far afield from the immediate problem. I think I'll pass on this one.*

Through probing, the speaker now has a number of angles from which to approach the topic. Eventually, the speaker will choose those categories that yield relevant information and one category that will be used to organize the speech (organization is covered in Chapter 5). The speaker now sees, in other words, a relationship between the purpose and the approach most suitable to that purpose. Having analyzed role, purpose, and pattern, the speaker is now ready to draft a statement that will serve as a guide throughout the process of developing the speech.

You will notice as you become familiar with the categories of invention that, while each category can serve an entire range of purposes one might have for a speech, some categories are generally used more for one purpose than another. In Chapter 5 of this text, where you will learn how to use the categories of invention as patterns for organizing a speech, we will describe the purposes for which each category is normally used. Also, in Part II of this text, when each category is developed in detail as a formal pattern of public speaking, we will indicate through discussion and speech models the purposes for which the patterns are commonly used. Having analyzed role, purpose, and the categories of invention, the speaker is now ready to draft a purpose statement that reflects all the critical thinking that has gone into planning the speech.

The Critical-Thinking Statement

The speaker writes a critical-thinking statement for use as a guide as the speech develops. In Chapter 5 we will discuss the thesis statement, an actual statement that is given during the speech. For now, however, we are talking about a critical-thinking statement as something written to help guide the speaker during the composing process of a speech. To work well as a guide or focus of a speech, a critical-thinking statement should include something about the speech situation itself, about the speaker's role, and about the purpose of the event, and some suggestion of the probe or category most appropriate for the event.

Start drafting the critical-thinking statement by reducing the situation to a brief profile—for example, "I am signed up to speak in favor of a resolution to change Parking Lot F from staff to commuter." Be certain that you have assessed the situation properly before going on.

Next, think about your role in the situation. At this point, it helps to use the infinitive forms of verbs to characterize your role. Following are some verbs that are commonly used to describe the speaker's role:

To inform	To move to action
To enlighten	To entertain
To convince	To stimulate
To impress	To expose
To refute	To praise

Add to this general notion of your role a statement describing who you are in the situation: "I am an advocate trying to convince..." or "I am a consultant trying to enlighten...."

Add to the general notion of your role in this situation a statement concerning what you seek from the audience. Here is a sample of some common responses sought from audiences:

To sign a petition

To enjoy an experience or relate to it

To vote in favor of an ordinance, law, and so on

To accept a point of view as valid

To adopt a new attitude toward something

To understand something more clearly

To pass an appropriation for X amount

Finally, indicate the method of analysis or category of invention you feel will most effectively work in the situation as you have described it. Will narration be best? Will this situation require a demonstration of a process? Is it best to define terms here? Part II of this text will make many suggestions about when each approach might work best. For now, finish up your critical-thinking statement by merging all your considerations into one.

The speaker who has signed up to address the student senate on the parking problem might draft a critical-thinking statement something like the following:

I am signed up to speak in favor of the resolution to change Parking Lot F from staff to commuter [the situation]. My role is to be an advocate and convince the senate to pass the resolution to change the lot [role and purpose]. A problem-solution analysis would most directly support my request [the category].

The critical-thinking statement, when written clearly during the planning phase of speech composing, will serve as a guide during the rest of the process. It will assure that speaker and audience are moving toward compatible ends. In Part II of this text you will see critical-thinking statements written for each speech pattern. These model statements will guide you as you develop your own. Take the time to draft a critical-thinking statement that accurately reflects the situation, your role in it, the end or purpose toward which the speech is moving, and the method most appropriate for achieving it.

Summary

The preparatory phases of a public speech are critical to success on the day of presentation. In this chapter we have discussed essential considerations that precede the speech-making process.

The first step in critical thinking about a speech involves exploring experiences and ideas. There are two kinds of experiences: personal and vicarious. Each kind can lead to a topic for a public speech. Experiences lead to ideas, which are the fruit of carefully nurtured experiences and inspirations. Ideas also lead to speech topics. The best speeches come from within the self rather than from some external source such as a friend who says, "I gave a speech on such-and-such and it went pretty well—want to borrow it?"

The best way to keep track of experiences and ideas is to record them. In this chapter we covered three methods for recording experiences: talking to a tape recorder, writing in a journal, and starting a book of commonplaces. You may have another system that works best for you. The point is to keep track of experiences and ideas so that you can use them for speech topics and in the speech itself.

Critical thinking about ideas and experiences, which is essential to a thorough understanding of a speech topic, involves probing a topic by asking questions about it. In this chapter we introduced six categories of invention, categories based upon the concepts of time and space, and we developed questions appropriate to each category. By applying the probes to a speech topic, the speaker can be sure that he or she has seen the topic in all its facets and developed a clear sense of how the material might be communicated to an audience.

Turning from content to the speech situation, we looked at the interacting variables of the actual speech event: speech, audience, speaker, and environment. Anticipating the speech situation requires that we conduct a basic analysis of the audience, followed by an analysis of the relationship between the audience and the speech topic, between the speaker and the audience, and between the topic and the environment.

In the last section of this chapter we discussed the essential components of role and purpose in a speech. We noted that purpose, the end toward which one is moving, involves the speaker's role, the goal toward which one is moving, and the categories of invention that are most appropriate to achieving purpose. We considered each of these variables and showed how an analysis of each leads one to a precise critical-thinking statement, a short paragraph that serves as a personal guide throughout the speech-making process.

Having considered the preparatory variables in speech making, we can turn our attention to supporting a speech topic.

Exercises

1. A FIRST SPEECH. Here is a speech assignment you can try while reading the chapters in Part I. The assignment gives you an opportunity to try speaking and stating your opinions in front of the class, but it is easy enough to minimize your anxieties. The assignment is also a good first speech because it will introduce you to a number of topics of current concern, some of which you may want to pursue later in other speeches.

   a. Look in reputable newspapers and magazines for an editorial, a letter to the editor, or a syndicated column on a current-events topic. Choose one to which you have a strong reaction.
   b. Type out the article triple-spaced. Mark it with notes to yourself.
   c. Prepare the speech in three parts:
      (i) Prepare a short background to give the audience basic information about the article: author, topic, the nature of the issue being discussed, key names, dates, places, and so on.
      (ii) Now read the article to the class as you imagine the author would. Try to emphasize key ideas with your voice, and put the appropriate tone into the speech. Most importantly, as you read the article try to maintain some eye contact with the audience.
      (iii) Having read the article, comment on it. Tell the audience whether you agree or disagree with the author and tell them why. Be as reasonable as you can. Answer any questions audience members may have.

2. In an in-class discussion, try a free-association exercise to generate speech topics. One person begins by throwing out a word that is important to her or him. Another person says the first word that comes to mind, followed by another person, and so on. Each time a word suggests a speech topic, stop the associating and write the word down or discuss it with the group.

3. Bring a copy of a newspaper to class. In a group discussion, list stories from the paper that strike you or the group as potential speech topics. Each person should say why a story interests her

or him. When the group has finished, each person should have one firm speech topic. Now, as an out-of-class assignment, probe the speech topic using each category of invention. Follow the Vietnam memorial model on pp. 56–57 as your guide, writing one paragraph for each category of invention.

4. Fill in the following inventory so that you have a thorough analysis of the speech situation as the semester begins. Place this completed exercise in your speech-communication notebook and use it as a guide to topic selection and audience analysis throughout the semester.

EXPERIENCES:
● List the five most important/interesting people you have met.
● List the three most interesting/humorous/tragic events in your life.
● List the three most interesting places you have been.
● List five movies/books/stories that have moved you.
● What is the craziest thing you did as a child?
● List the five things you enjoy doing most and least?

EXPERIENCE/SELF/AUDIENCE: For each list above, which item could you most meaningfully speak about to this audience?
● Person
● Event
● Place
● Book/movie/story
● Craziest thing
● Most enjoyable thing
● Least enjoyable thing

AUDIENCE: Looking back at our audience-analysis discussion, which specific aspect of the audience affected your choice of items most? Based on this consideration, which two topics from your list above would be most appropriate for this audience?

IDEAS:
● List the five most serious problems/issues you see in the world today.

- List five values or attitudes you consider important to you.
- List the three most interesting ideas you have ever heard from someone else.
- List your three favorite proverbs or famous quotations.
- List two crazy ideas that have popped into your head.
- List five fads or trends you see around you.

IDEAS/SELF/AUDIENCE: For each list above, choose one item that you would feel comfortable talking about and that you think the audience might be interested in or benefit from.

- Problem/issue _____

- Value/attitude _____

- Idea heard from someone else _____

- Favorite saying _____

- Crazy idea _____

- Fad/trend _____

AUDIENCE: Looking back at our discussion of audiences, what specific aspect of audience affected your choice of the item? Choose two items from the list above that you think the audience would most appreciate hearing about.

5. In a 250-word essay, answer the following question: How do you want others to remember you after this course? Your instructor might decide to ask class members to share their essays with one another in a warm-up group discussion, so be prepared to talk about what you have written. This exercise can lead to an awareness of how your experience and ideas compare with those of others in the class, and can thus be used as a guide in topic selection for a speech.

6. If you have given a public speech prior to this class, you might find this exercise interesting. Draft a critical-thinking statement for the speech you gave, explaining the situation, your role in it, the goal you had for the audience, and the approach or probes you used to reach your goal.

References

1. Frank D'Angelo, *Process and Thought in Composition*, 2d ed. (Cambridge: Winthrop Publishers, 1980), pp. 7–10.

2. Lewis Mumford, *The Pentagon of Power* (NY: Harcourt, Brace, Jovanovich, 1969), p. 422.

3. Gail Price, "A Case for a Modern Commonplace Book," *College Composition and Communication* 31 (May 1980), pp. 175–182.

4. Lane Cooper, trans. *The Rhetoric of Aristotle* (NY: Appleton, Century, Crofts, 1932), p. 159.

5. Cooper, p. 157.

6. Frank D'Angelo, *A Conceptual Theory of Rhetoric* (Cambridge: Winthrop Publishers, 1975), p. 26.

7. See, for instance, Kenneth Anderson and Theodore Clevenger, Jr., "A Summary of Experimental Research in Ethos," *Speech Monographs* 30 (1963), pp. 59–78.

8. David Berlo, *The Process of Communication* (NY: Holt, Rinehart, and Winston, 1960), p. 17.

9. Cooper, p. 17.

10. Berlo, p. 12.

11. Edward P. J. Corbett, *Classical Rhetoric for the Modern Student*, 2d ed. (NY: Oxford University Press, 1971), pp. 3–4.

12. See, for instance, Donald Bryant, "Rhetoric: Its Function and Scope," in Douglas Ehninger, ed., *Contemporary Rhetoric* (Glenview, IL: Scott, Foresman, 1972), pp. 15–38.

13. James J. Golden and Edward P. J. Corbett, eds., *The Rhetoric of Blair, Campbell, and Whately,* (NY: Holt, Rinehart, and Winston, 1968), p. 145.

14. James Winans, *Public Speaking* (NY: The Century Co., 1920), p. 109.

15. Alan H. Monroe, *Principles and Types of Speech* (NY: Scott, Foresman, and Co., 1935), p. 183.

16. Monroe, Part II.

17. See, for instance, Joseph A. DeVito, *The Elements of Public Speaking* (NY: Harper and Row, 1984), p. 17.

Chapter 4 · Supporting a Speech with Evidence and Research

In Chapter 3 we examined the initial steps in the speech-making process: exploring and recording experiences and ideas, analyzing the speech situation, thinking critically about speech topics, and developing a clear purpose. As we saw, these aren't discrete steps; often we cover several simultaneously. In fact, a dynamic speech topic is one that inspires us to think critically about our speech from the moment of recognition through the question-and-answer session with our audience.

In preparing a speech, however, we often need to rely on more than our own ideas and experiences. We need to cite concrete evidence and research to support our topic. Indeed, our audience does—and should—expect us to back up ideas with proof and evidence. For example, a speaker's personal experience may lead to a speech showing that offshore oil exploration is a menace to marine life, but a simple statement of personal opinion would lack credibility with the audience, and perhaps integrity as well. But if the speaker presented reliable and varied evidence supporting his or her view, the audience would be more likely to accept that view. This chapter, then, examines the different kinds of supporting evidence and research that can be used in a speech, and offers guidelines on conducting research and gathering supporting material.

Forms of Support for a Speech

There are many ways to develop a speech topic with supporting material—to put flesh on the bones of your ideas, so to speak. A highly personal narrative speech may require a careful search of one's self and of the meaning of events in one's life, while an analysis of a controversial topic will mandate a large amount of information from objective, authoritative sources. In this section we will discuss five major forms of support: opinions, facts, examples, comparisons, and numerical data. We will also provide guidelines for using the supporting material correctly.

Opinions

An opinion is a statement that has merit in relation to its source, the person or persons who are responsible for it. An opinion can add a personal touch to a speech, or, if scientifically generated, can become a way of proving one's point. There are three kinds of opinion: personal, public, and expert. Each differs from the others and can support a speech topic.

PERSONAL OPINION. If you have had firsthand experience with the topic on which you are speaking, that experience may lead you to express an opinion in the course of your speech. The audience will accept your opinion to the degree that they accept you as a legitimate source of information. In the following speech segments, the first student's opinion is not acceptable, while the second student's is:

> *My second reason for favoring capital punishment is that life imprisonment is more cruel and unusual than death. I know that if I had to live the rest of my life in an eight-foot-by-ten-foot cell I'd just as soon die, and I am willing to bet that most "lifers" feel the same way.*

> *The second rule in choosing an investment broker is not to mix business and social relationships. I can tell you that my first experience with an investment broker was a disaster because I chose him on the basis of a friend's advice, and I decided on him without visiting any other firms. As it turned out, this broker did not spend much time with my portfolio, and I finally had to drop him, a painful experience since a friend was involved. Now I invest with a broker whose only ties to me are through my wallet. It works out much better.*

Notice that both examples given may be accurate, or both may be inaccurate: Choosing an investment broker who is also your best friend might work out perfectly. The point is that the second opinion is based upon an actual experience the speaker had, and this gives the opinion just enough veracity with the audience to make it a useful form of support for the speech topic.

Avoid using too many personal opinions in the body of your speech; of course, the more expert you are perceived to be on the topic, the more weight your opinion will carry with the audience. Quite often, personal opinions are used in the conclusion of a speech, since the conclusion sums up the data presented in the body of the speech.

PUBLIC OPINION. Most of us have seen a public-opinion poll. It is usually composed of responses to a question put before a randomly selected, nonexpert audience. Television reporters often stand on the street asking people for their opinion on a political candidate, a new building, or a recent news event. The information generated represents a nonscientific sampling of the public. Public-opinion polls are also conducted by professional polling agencies in such a highly scientific and reliable way that the results often reflect quite accurately the entire population. Public opinion can add valuable support and color to a speech when used appropriately. Look at the following segment from a speech on the phenomenon known as the "Christmas Blues."

> *After reading the psychologist's analysis of the "Christmas Blues" I decided to ask people at work if they ever suffered any of the symptoms reported by Dr. Stone. My manager told me he hated Christmas because he didn't like to be happy on command, especially when the weather was so poor and he had to travel three hundred miles home each year. The owner of the restaurant said he liked Christmas because business was so good, but that Christmas also reminded him of many bad childhood experiences, and that gave him the blues. Finally, I asked one of our regular customers, and she told me that Christmas made her feel sad because all of her children were now grown and moved away and she missed them during the holidays most of all. I guess Dr. Stone was right: Christmas is a bad time for quite a few people.*

In this example the opinion of ordinary people was appropriate because it supported an expert's opinion and also because the opinions added color to the speech and represented a variety of views on the topic, views to which audience members could relate.

Public opinion can be found in most newspapers and magazines, and scientific public-opinion polls such as the Gallup Poll are published in yearly volumes under the title *The Gallup Reports.* You can also seek out your own public opinion in a journalistic way and use it in your speech when appropriate.

When using public opinion, select statements from the entire body of opinions collected so that the opinions expressed in your speech represent a fair sample. If you have gathered ten opinions, nine in favor of an idea and one against, represent that balance in the three or four comments you actually use in the speech. Reporting only one favorable and one unfavorable opinion without presenting the percentage of responses is unethical.

EXPERT OPINION. For almost any speech topic there are experts to testify on one side or the other. Expert opinion is often used as a form of support in speeches that use cause-effect, analysis, and process patterns. In the following sample from a speech, expert opinion is used effectively:

> Mortimer Adler, a twentieth-century pioneer and champion of liberal education, writes in his book The Paidaeia Proposal: "As compared with narrow, specialized training for a particular job, general schooling is of the greatest practical value. It is good not only because it is calculated to achieve two of the three main objectives at which basic schooling should aim— preparation for citizenship and for personal development and growth. It is also good practically, because it will provide preparation for earning a living."

Notice that the person and the source of the quotation were stated in the speech. The audience can now judge whether the quotation is biased or unbiased, whether it comes from a legitimate source, and whether the information is firsthand or secondhand. Notice also that the quotation is an opinion, much like what you might get from any person if you questioned him or her on the value of a general education: the difference is that Adler is a noted expert and the presumption is that his opinion counts for more than that of someone who is not a recognized expert. Finally, remember that some experts are not always known to the audience. If you quoted from Jimmy Carter you would not necessarily have to note that he was president of the United States from 1976 to 1980, but if you were quoting from an expert like Adler, for instance, you would need to tell why he was an expert.

A clever turn of phrase, an interesting comparison, or a revealing quotation can work at any point in your speech. When you use expert opinion, tell the audience where the statement originated, and give credit to the person from whose work you took it.

Examples

An example is a particular instance of an idea or experience. Effective examples, which provide a context for ideas and help an audience to grasp and apply ideas, are used as a form of support in all varieties of speeches. This section examines three types of examples: specific instances, illustrations, and hypothetical examples.

SPECIFIC INSTANCES. A specific instance is a brief example or a series of brief examples that support an assertion. We have all used specific instances as a way of helping our listeners visualize a point we are trying to make. In the following model, we can see specific instances used to support a point:

> *The most widely talked about aggravation of the health center is the lengthy waiting period each visit entails. There is almost always at least a twenty-minute wait before a student receives any kind of medical attention. The main room is always filled with unhappy, often irritated faces; all eyes glance suddenly toward any little noise, grasping for some indication that their turn for treatment will be next. One student with an asthmatic condition who was having considerable difficulty with his breathing didn't get to see a physician for two hours. Another student had to wait for over an hour to get a prescription filled when the pharmacist informed him, "I'm not here now, I'm on lunch." Another student, told to return to the center to review test results with the doctor, sat for thirty minutes before the nurse informed him that the doctor would not be in for another hour.*

Specific instances are often strung tightly together:

> *Professional writers are usually people whose personal lives are awash in booze. Of the nine American Nobel Prize-winners in literature, three were alcoholics. William Faulkner, Sinclair Lewis, and Eugene O'Neill were lushes. So were Fitzgerald, Hemingway, and Steinbeck.*

> *Truman Capote's speech at Towson State University was so incoherent that he had to be carried off the stage. Jack London committed suicide while drunk at age forty. And Tennessee Williams was involuntarily committed to a mental institution in 1969.*

Whether the instances are simply listed or given brief explanations, they add color and specificity to an assertion.

ILLUSTRATIONS. An illustration is a fully developed example. It can be a personal narration or it can be about others. Notice the difference between the following illustration and a specific instance:

Simplicity is by no means the only attraction to recycling. Many groups and individuals have put forth successful efforts to reap economic gain from recycling.

Two twenty-eight-year-old Chicago men took a creative approach to turn the country on to the economics of ecology through paper recycling. First, they bought the rights to catchy illustrations for one hundred dollars each and went into the greeting card business. Starting with only Christmas cards, they landed a $12,000 card order from Chicago's Marshall Field and Co. department store. From that initial success, they have now expanded to birthday cards, Easter cards, and occasional card lines. Orders have virtually doubled every year since. In a 1977 news release, Recycled Paper Products was projecting a volume of 160 million cards and a gross of ten million dollars. This is a prime example of the money that can be generated from recycled paper.

The value of such an extended example is that it adds concreteness to an assertion by demonstrating the assertion in full detail. In order to add credibility to your speech, use examples that are representative and typical rather than extreme or sensational.

HYPOTHETICAL EXAMPLES. A hypothetical example (or scenario) is an extended example that characterizes an imaginary situation, a situation that has not happened but could, or a situation that represents a composite picture of a number of real examples. Hypothetical examples can be used when a real example is unavailable or when you are attempting to visualize what might occur if certain conditions came to pass. The following hypothetical example, taken from a student speech, shows how this form of support can be used to good effect:

Sensory aphasia is different from motor aphasia. When one has motor aphasia it is difficult if not impossible to speak the words one has in mind. Sensory aphasia involves a loss of meaning for words and numbers. Imagine yourself being transported to a street in downtown Moscow. People are talking everywhere. You hear the words spacibo *and* do svidanya, *and they make absolutely no sense to you. After a period of time you would become frustrated, even fearful. That is how sensory aphasics hear their own native tongue: like a jumble of sounds and syllables from a foreign language. Unlike the American in downtown Moscow, however, no matter how hard the person tries, for the aphasic the language will never make sense.*

Of course, examples must adhere to certain guidelines. First, they should be typical—they should represent the average type or average occurrence. If the examples are extreme or unrepresentative, the speaker should so indicate. Second, there should be enough examples to justify the conclusion reached. Common sense will usually dictate the number needed for a given situation. Third, there should not be examples that would show the exact opposite of the one used. To use an example that is easily negated by another takes away the credibility of the example.

Facts

A fact is an object of agreement, something no rational person would argue about. Psychologist Abraham Maslow noted that facts are things that are clear enough, certain enough, real enough, beyond the point of doubt enough, that they call for action or belief on the part of others.[1] Whereas opinions are credible only in relation to a source, a fact stands on its own unless obscured by source or context.

Facts surround us. Cincinnati won the World Series in 1975; interest rates soared to 18 percent in 1979; the sky is blue, salt dissolves in water. . . . Each year, the *World Almanac* publishes approximately one thousand pages of facts on every conceivable topic, so vast are the facts we accept. Because facts, by their very nature, are beyond doubt, they serve as an excellent form of support in a speech.

Facts make up a large body of supporting data in a speech, and they can come from two sources. Some facts are observed: oranges are round, human beings are different from fish, and so on. And some facts come from others: the solar system has nine planets, rubber is a poor conductor of electricity. Regardless of the source of the fact, the speaker must follow concrete guidelines so that the facts he or she presents others will stand on their own.

First, use credible sources of facts. One of the most common problems concerning the use of facts arises when the source of the facts reduces the information from fact to opinion. Many sources obscure facts, present them out of context, or simply misstate them. Notice in the following hypothetical example how this is done:

Half-truth: *According to the* National Exposer, *one out of every ten persons has psychic power.*

Fact: *According to psychologist E. B. Rhone, and based upon a ten-year research study, only one out of ten subjects showed extrasensory capacity, a statistically insignificant number, according to Rhone.*

In this case, the same fact is changed by the way it is presented. Notice also that in the second statement the speaker is citing a study rather than a secondary source that quoted from the study. First-hand, primary information is much better than secondhand; whenever possible, go directly to the original source rather than to an intermediate one, even if it is credible.

Second, use facts in their proper context. Facts are sometimes used out of the context in which they occurred. Consider the following example of facts that are true, but when taken out of context mean something altogether different:

At a public hearing at a state legislature concerning passage of a container-deposit law, opponents of the so-called "bottle bill" testified that "according to federal studies, beer sales in Maine declined 4.4 percent between 1977 and 1978, the first year of Maine's bottle bill." The effect cited was a significant decrease in sales-tax revenues, thus the opposition to the bottle bill. Supporters of the bottle bill decided to look at the federal study quoted from to see if the opposition's facts were accurate, and sure enough, the passage in the actual study went like this: "Beer sales declined 4.4 percent between 1977 and 1978, but grew again in 1979. One distributor stated that only part of the decline was attributable to the deposit law, adding that sales recovered and grew steadily. Maine changed its legal drinking age from eighteen to twenty in 1977 also, which may have reduced beer consumption."

In this example the facts were correct, but the way they were used in the context of the speech slanted them in a particular direction. Be sure to question not only the source of facts but also the context in which the facts were originally used.

We are a nation of facts, a society bent on the production of information. However, as John Naisbitt says so concisely in his book *Megatrends*, "We are drowning in information, but starved for knowledge."[2] Use facts as the backbone of assertions you make, but use them to reveal, not to conceal.

Comparisons

Comparisons are involved in such stylistic devices as analogy, metaphor, and simile (see pp. 193–196, 189–191). In addition, comparisons are used as a form of support for an idea. Let's take a look at two kinds of comparisons that are often used in public speeches.

LITERAL COMPARISONS. A literal comparison establishes a relationship between two closely related phenomena. Literal comparisons are often used to show that if something worked in one place it would work in another place, since both places were similar. In the following example a student uses her experience at her previous university to argue for a proposal at her new one:

> *The mealbook plan at Western allowed us to choose weekend meals or not. By doing so, many of us who commuted on weekends to work did not have to pay for meals we could not eat. Now this school is really a lot like Western. Many students commute and don't eat meals here on campus. Because of the system here, though, we have to buy a mealbook plan that covers weekends, and so we end up having to pay for meals we can't eat because we aren't here. I believe that what worked at Western would work here and would be fairer to commuter students.*

Literal comparisons reassure audience members by showing that your idea has worked somewhere else. When making such comparisons, however, be certain that the phenomena you are comparing are alike enough to justify one being used to talk about the others. The appropriate guideline is whether the similarities outweigh the differences between the things being compared. If they do, conclusions you might draw from the comparison are more justified.

HYPOTHETICAL COMPARISONS. Unlike a literal comparison, which involves two related phenomena, a hypothetical comparison makes one unrelated phenomenon clear by comparing it to something the audience already understands. Even though the things compared are not the same, as they were in a literal comparison, the audience sees a resemblance between the two, thus making the comparison work. The following example will make this clear.

> *You might think that paying basketball star Ralph Sampson $2 million each year is extravagant, but look at it this way. What if you and four friends went out shovelling snow to make a little extra money. You ended up doing most of the work while your friends fooled around more than helped. By the end of the day you had made a total of $100. After some argument everyone finally agreed that you should get $50, since you did most of the work; so the other four split the remaining $50, which amounts to $12.50 each—still not bad for fooling around. Well, that is the way it is with Ralph Sampson and the Houston Rockets. He gets about 50 percent of the money allocated by the franchise for players' salaries. The other guys get the rest, which still averages out to $166,000 per player. Not bad for just fooling around.*

Philosopher Chaim Perelman describes a comparison as a "resemblance of relationships."[3] By this definition Perelman means that, in a strictly logical sense, a comparison is never valid, since no two things are literally alike; however, a comparison is reasonable because the audience accepts the relationship involved in the comparison. If the comparison makes common sense, if it is reasonable, it can support an idea as validly as a fact, statistic, or example.

Statistical Support

Statistics are one of the most frequently used forms of support for a speech topic. This is so because numbers imply a certain exactness and correctness not found in other forms of support. When using numbers, however, remember the old saying that "figures lie and liars figure." In order to use numerical support ethically and productively, we need to follow certain guidelines.

First, by themselves statistics do not often mean much to an audience. How would you react if a speaker said, "Every twenty-three minutes someone dies from an auto accident caused by a drunk driver." You might be shocked, but you might also be puzzled. The number itself is accurate, but it would be much more revealing if it were related to other numbers, perhaps in this way: "Every twenty-three minutes someone dies from an auto accident caused by a drunk driver. That makes drunk driving the single leading cause of death in America—greater than cancer, heart disease, or homicide." Now that the number has been related to something, its significance to the audience is clearer.

Second, avoid using too many numbers at one time. An audience can drown in a sea of numbers. Because a speech is presented in the oral medium and heard only once, too many numbers at one time are difficult to comprehend. In the following excerpt, the speaker has valuable statistical data but a bit too much of a good thing:

Crime rates are dropping across the nation. An FBI report covering the period from 1976 to 1985 shows that homicides

When using supporting materials, remember:

Use material from a variety of legitimate sources.

Cite primary rather than secondary sources.

Use different forms of supporting material.

Consider the source of the data and announce it in your speech.

Support ideas with current information and give dates in your speech.

Use material within the context in which it was produced.

Be certain your material actually supports your thesis.

Connect supporting material with ample commentary.

Place complex data on visual aids.

per 1,000 persons have gone from 4.8 to 3.6; rape is also down from 13.1 to 10.6, aggravated assault from 62.4 to 56.4, and burglary from 135.8 to 121.7. These statistics are for the violent crimes only, but even domestic crimes such as gambling and forgery are down 10% and 8% respectively.

The statement is well intended and informative, but the speaker would have been more successful if he had given one or two examples and put the overall figures on a visual aid. Sometimes a summary quotation by an official who gathered the data plus one or two illustrations will suffice for a large body of numbers.

Third, qualify numerical support. Often we can achieve better results with fewer numbers and more qualifying phrases, or at least with a balance of both. The following statements illustrate how to qualify numbers:

Satisfactory	*Better*
70 percent of those sampled said they would vote for a qualified woman for president of the United States.	70 percent of those sampled said they would vote for a qualified woman for president of the United States. This is compared to 37 percent who held this view in 1937, which is about half the percentage. Of course, the word *qualified* meant many things to those sampled. Even if we take that into account, the percentages are still open to question.

Finally, put numerical detail in visual form. An audience often finds statistics and numerical data easier to comprehend if they are presented visually in graphs, charts, or tables. Chapter 6 addresses preparing and using visual aids.

There are, of course, countless ways to use and abuse numbers. When presenting statistical support, always give the source and the date of your information, and add whatever qualifications you think are necessary for the audience to understand the number correctly.

Supporting a speech topic requires creative use of a variety of supporting materials. There are many other ways to support an idea besides those major ways presented here. Humorous anecdotes, myths, fairy tales, proverbs, truisms, and jokes have worked in many speeches to support an idea convincingly. Use your own common sense when deciding what will work to get your idea across to the audience.

Where and How to Gather Supporting Material

Where do we find public-opinion polls, facts, and statistics that we need to support our ideas? This section examines a number of sources of supporting material available to the speech-communication student. We will cover nonlibrary sources first, then turn our attention to using the library and taking notes. Keep in mind, however, that gathering supporting material takes time; allow yourself enough time to get the material you need.

The Government

Local, state, and federal agencies are a vast source of information. The federal government, in particular, has information on every conceivable topic. Of course, many libraries have a government-documents section, and you may choose to start there. However, should you want or need to go directly to the federal government for information, the following advice should help a great deal.

ELECTED OFFICIALS. Some elected officials have people on their staffs who respond to inquiries from constituents. Consequently, you may want to use the resources of your elected officials to help you to gather data for speeches. Most elected officials have a local office listed in your phone directory; also, your library should have the *Congressional Directory,* a document that lists congressional representatives' phone numbers and addresses.

Your elected officials can help you in three specific ways: by contacting the right federal agency for the topic you are exploring, by helping you find material from the Government Printing Office, and by sending you material on pending legislation.

GOVERNMENT AGENCIES. Executive agencies of the government are a useful source of information, producing a pamphlet or a story on just about any topic imaginable. Your congressperson can access these agencies much more quickly than you, but should you want to go directly to an agency your library should have a copy of the *U.S. Government Organization Manual*, which describes the origin and purpose of each agency and tells how to contact the agency. You might also wish to send for a free copy of the *Consumer Information Catalog* by writing to New Catalog, Pueblo, Colorado, 81009. This document lists thousands of pamphlets published by the government and tells how to acquire them. Here, for instance, is a partial listing of health topics on which research pamphlets were available for just one season, Winter 1983–84:

Aspirin: possible risks and proper use

Baldness: products and treatments

Contact Lenses: health, care, and safety factors for all types

Contraception: nine common methods of birth control

Food and Drug Interactions: drugs and nutrition

Generic Drugs: compares generic drugs with name brand drugs

Hearing Aids: how and where to find help

Interferon: is it a miracle drug?

Prescription Drugs: dangers involved

Biofeedback: the most commonly asked questions

Laser Surgery: the pros and cons

Tamper Resistant Packaging: requirements and precautions

Tranquilizers: use and abuse

Valium: use and abuse

What's in Your Medicine Chest: tips for safe and proper storage

THE GOVERNMENT PRINTING OFFICE. The GPO has more than twenty-four thousand documents on those aspects of our lives about which some federal agency has an interest. Once again, check with your elected officials first for easy access to GPO documents. Many libraries also carry *The Monthly Catalog of U.S. Government Publications*, which lists titles of new studies. To order a study directly from the GPO write to Superintendent of Documents, U.S. Government Printing Office, Washington, D.C. 20402. You must include the reference number for the study and a check for the document. Congresspersons get two copies of each study free of charge, however, which is another good reason to start with their offices.

Groups and Organizations

There are often specific local, national, and worldwide organizations that are concerned with your topic. Most of them are listed in the *Encyclopedia of Associations* (located in the library), but many local-interest groups can also be found in the pages of your phone book. One student who was doing a speech on gun control wrote to the National Rifle Association in Washington for data opposing gun control and called a statewide organization, Handgun Alert, for material supporting gun control. Once she combined this material with her other research, she had ample information for an incisive pro-con analysis of gun control.

Sometimes a group or organization is right under your nose, on campus perhaps. Check with your student senate or student association for a list of all campus-affiliated interest groups. The campus phone directory can lead you to professional, faculty, and student groups. For example, a student who was interested in the integration of sororities in America discovered through the campus directory that the national headquarters of a large sorority was located on her campus. She visited the headquarters and found a complete file on the topic of racial integration of fraternities and sororities.

Campus or Local Experts

You probably walk by three experts each day on campus or in the local area and are not aware of it. How do you find these people, experts who can either tell you all you need to know or who can lead you to information for your speech?

Sometimes you can think of the department of your campus that is most likely to be pursuing the topic; for instance, if you were doing your speech on robots, the engineering department would be a good first stop. Ask the secretary or someone in the office if anyone in the department might be involved in your topic. Quite often you will get a name. Call that person and ask for an appointment.

Another way to find people with information is simply to ask around. A student once asked an instructor whether he knew someone who might know about preservation of historic buildings. As luck would have it, the instructor had just recently attended a talk on the Historic Preservation Act given by a local businesswoman who was involved in the issue of zoning for historic buildings. The student contacted the businesswoman and conducted a successful interview. If this student had not asked, he might have missed the key resource for his speech, even though it was only one mile down the road.

Actively seeking information outside the library can make the process of researching a speech topic both enjoyable and educational. Make use of the resources available and you will find your speeches increasing in sophistication and complexity.

Conducting an Interview

Many students hesitate to seek firsthand sources of information because they are unsure about conducting an interview. An interview can be an enjoyable and profitable experience for both parties if the interviewer has prepared carefully.

First, contact the person you want to interview well in advance. People with information are usually busy people who need advance notice of your visit. It is good to call one week or so before you want to conduct the interview. Of course, if the person lists certain times when she or he will be in, go to the person's office at that time and ask for a few minutes to talk.

Write out your questions in advance of the interview. The probes given in Chapter 3 (pp. 55–56) are often helpful in an interview. In addition, it is important to ask questions that elicit a response other than "Yes" or "No." You should ask, for instance, "What artifacts did you find and how were they identified?" rather than "Did you find any artifacts?". Make certain your questions keep the conversation going.

The questions you ask should serve as an outline, but the interview should flow like a conversation. React spontaneously to the person you are interviewing. Stick to the point and follow your outline, but do not simply ask questions mechanically and then write down the responses. Doing so makes an interviewee uncomfortable. Also, if you want to tape record the interview, ask permission to do so.

Be on time for the interview and stay only as long as the person requests. It is a good idea to settle the matter of time at the outset of the interview or when you make the appointment. When the interview has concluded, thank the person, clarify any points you don't understand, and leave. When you have returned home, go over your notes and sift out the important points.

The Library

Looking for material in a library can try the patience of even experienced professionals. Books are often checked out, microfilm machines break down, lines are long. And yet, for those who are patient, the library will usually yield all that is needed for a successful speech. The following list of tips should help make that trip to the library more enjoyable and productive.

1. START EARLY AND GO EARLY.   Waiting until the night before your speech is due is a sure road to failure. Go to the library as soon as you can after the assignment has been given. Additionally, try to go in the morning or early-afternoon hours, since, according to reports, the library is least busy during these times.

2. ASK FOR HELP.   If you need assistance, ask for it at the reference desk or ask the head librarian. You will find that librarians pride themselves on being able to help people, and if you ask for help courteously and precisely, you will usually get what you need. Many libraries stock handouts and pamphlets that also help in using the library's resources.

3. HAVE THE NECESSARY MATERIALS WITH YOU.   Bring a pen, a pencil, a pad of paper, and some note-taking material such as note cards. Also, bring along any material you may need to find your source or to study while at the library.

4. TAKE CAREFUL NOTES.   When you look up a book or article, take down all the information on your pad or note card. Keep the first note card for each source separate and use it as your bibliography card. Also, when you take notes from the article or book, be sure you use quotation marks if you quote directly; if you are paraphrasing from the material (using your own words to sum up the ideas contained in the article), do not use quotation marks. Keep accurate note cards now, so that when you compose your speech later you will know whether you said something or the author said it. Figures 4.1 and 4.2 show two typical note cards.

While you are taking notes, add notes to yourself as they come to you. Look at the bottom of the first sample note card in Figure 4.1: the student has made a note about where the quotation might be used in the speech. By making notes to yourself you are thinking about the speech as you research. When you reach the final-draft stages, the research and the notes to yourself will be invaluable.

Many speech-communication instructors schedule a trip to the library early in the semester or invite a librarian to class to speak

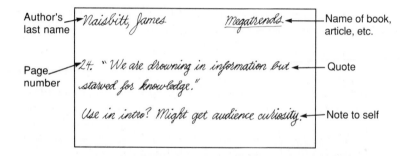

Figure 4.1
Sample of a note card using a
direct quotation

Author's last name → Naisbitt, James   Megatrends ← Name of book, article, etc.

Page number → 24. "We are drowning in information but ← Quote
starved for knowledge."

Use in intro? Might get audience curiosity. ← Note to self

on using the library. Also, most libraries offer tours and pamphlets to help users: take advantage of the library's help. Often the reference librarian or assistant can guide you to useful sources. The five most important sources of library material for the speech-communication student are books, magazines and periodicals, newspapers, government documents, and computer printouts.

FINDING A BOOK.   Although in the near future many libraries will use computers to catalog their books, the card catalog is still the source for finding a book at most libraries. Books are filed by subject, author, and title. The following guidelines should help you find the book quickly.

1. Cards are filed word-by-word and then letter-by-letter within the word:
    New York
    Newark

Figure 4.2
Sample of a note card using
paraphrased material

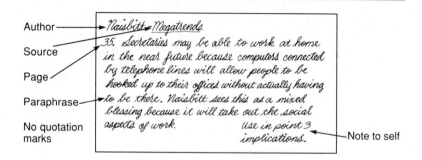

Author → Naisbitt → Megatrends
Source →
Page → 35. Secretaries may be able to work at home in the near future because computers connected by telephone lines will allow people to be hooked up to their offices without actually having
Paraphrase → to be there. Naisbitt sees this as a mixed blessing because it will take out the social
No quotation marks → aspects of work.   Use in point 3
implications. ← Note to self

2. Articles (*a, an, the*) at the beginning of titles in all languages are not used. Titles are filed by the next word.

3. *Mc* and *Mac* are interfiled as if spelled "Mac."

4. Acronyms are filed as a word if they are pronounced as a word, (NATO, FORTRAN); otherwise, they are filed at the beginning of the letter (AAA, VFW).

5. Universities and colleges are filed under their names in spoken order: Brigham Young University, University of Virginia.

6. If last names, place names, and titles all start with the same word, they are filed by person, then place, then thing:
   Boston, Orland William
   Boston, Children's Museum
   Boston, Musical Reviews

Once you have found the book you need, write down the call number located in the left-hand corner. Then look for the library directory that will tell you where the call number is located. If you can't find a book, ask for it at the checkout counter, and the attendant will put a trace on the book and locate it for you. Figure 4.3 shows a sample catalog card with notes to help you read it.

MAGAZINES AND PERIODICALS. Libraries subscribe to popular magazines, which are published either weekly or monthly, and scholarly journals, which often are published every four months. All articles that are published in magazines or periodicals can be found by using an index, a book or booklet that lists all the publications for magazines or periodicals that it covers.

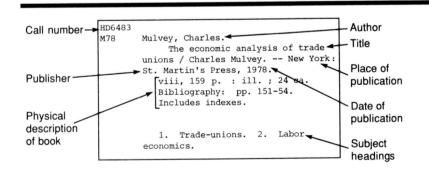

Figure 4.3
The catalog card

The most popular index for magazines and a few periodicals is the *Reader's Guide to Periodical Literature*. This index lists all articles published in over 180 technical and nontechnical publications, including the popular weekly magazines such as *Time, Newsweek,* and *U.S. News and World Report.* You can look for an article by either author or subject. Each entry provides all the necessary information for locating the article. Figure 4.4 shows two sample entries from the *Reader's Guide* with marginal notes.

Very often, you will need to find more specialized information. If so, one or more of the following indexes might be of help:

Applied Science and Technology Index

Art Index

Biological and Agricultural Index

Education Index

Humanities Index

Index to Legal Periodicals

Social Sciences Index

Figure 4.4
Sample entries from the
*Reader's Guide to Periodical
Literature*

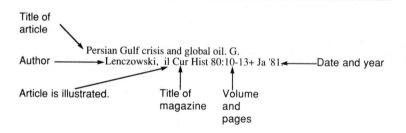

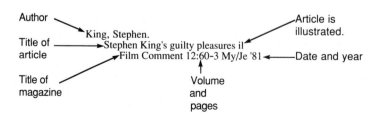

Once you have found the articles you need for your topic, consult your library's list, which indicates where all magazines and periodicals can be found. Magazines and periodicals can usually be taken out from the library for only short periods of time, if at all; consequently, when using such sources plan to stay in the library to do your work.

NEWSPAPERS. Many libraries subscribe to various newspapers. Although newspaper articles are difficult to find, two indexes might help: the *New York Times Index* and the *Wall Street Journal Index*. Figure 4.5 is a sample entry from the *New York Times Index* with marginal notes to help you read the entry.

When you have determined which articles you want to see, you will most likely need to ask a librarian where the newspapers are filed and how to use them. Some libraries put all newspapers on microfilm, while some keep them stored in a temperature-controlled room.

GOVERNMENT PUBLICATIONS.   As mentioned earlier, many libraries subscribe to government publications. You can find government documents by following these steps:

1. Begin with the subject, author, or title index of the *Monthly Catalog of the United States Government Publications*, located in the government publications area or at the reference desk.

2. The entry number from the index will refer you to the main entry in the *Monthly Catalog*, where you will find the government publications call number.

3. The call number will refer you to the government publications shelflist (card catalog), which is arranged alphanumerically by

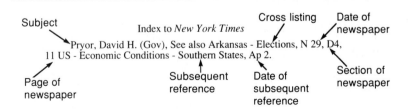

Figure 4.5
Sample entry from the *New York Times Index*

call number. If the library has the item, you will find a card for it that will indicate whether the item is held in paper copy or microform.

The very best way to locate a government document is to ask a librarian for help. Many libraries insist that you do so, since the process can be frustrating.

COMPUTER SEARCHING. An increasingly important source of information in many libraries, especially the larger ones, is computer searching. A computer search can yield a list of selected writing available on a topic. For instance, if you were interested in the topic "Acid Rain," a computer search could provide you with a bibliography for that topic, thus saving you the time of pouring through all the various indexes noted above. Following are some steps for initiating a computer search, should your library have such a system.

1. Make an appointment. Most searching is done by a specialist in the library. You may need to fill out a form indicating what you are interested in finding, and the librarian will tell you what indexes the library can search in that field.

2. Complete the search. In most cases, you will help the librarian type onto the computer all the information needed. As references begin to appear, you can change or alter your strategy until you start to get references that are relevant to your topic.

3. Pay the fee for the search. Most computer-search services charge for their work. Though charges vary greatly, most searches can be accomplished for between two and fifty dollars, a reasonable sum considering the hours of time such a procedure can save.

Summary

This chapter has been devoted to the art of expanding on ideas and experiences, filling them out for the purpose of developing a speech. Expanding an experience or an idea into a speech requires understanding the various forms of supporting material and gathering supporting material from a variety of sources.

There are many ways to expand upon a speech topic. In this chapter we have focused on five common ways to support an idea: facts, opinions, examples, comparisons, and numerical data. When used appropriately, each form of support adds validity, color, and concreteness to the idea. In order to help you use supporting material successfully, a set of guidelines was provided for each form of support.

Supporting material comes from a variety of places. In this chapter we have discussed nonlibrary and library resources, and we have given advice for conducting an interview, contacting elected officials, and ordering material from the government. We have also provided information on the five major sources of support in the library: books, magazines and periodicals, government documents, newspapers, and computer-based data.

This chapter concludes the planning and preparation stages of speech composition. We have learned what experiences and ideas are, how to explore them, and how to give them purpose. We have also learned how to expand on our ideas and experiences, and where to get supporting material. We turn now to the process of composing the final draft of the speech, a process each one of us will find challenging and educational.

Exercises

1. Read the model speech "Controlling the American Pet Population," on pp. 329–337. List the different types of supporting material used in the speech and give an example of each type from the speech. Then answer the following questions:
   a. What support does the speaker have for her assertions?
   b. How much variety does the speaker have in her supporting material?
   c. How else could the speaker have supported her topic to make it more convincing?
   d. Does the speaker's use of statistics conform to the guidelines given in this chapter? Explain.

2. Complete the following questionnaire as a way of familiarizing yourself with the resources available to you.
   a. Who are are your elected officials?

   U.S. senator   1. _____ local office phone no.
                  2. _____ local office phone no.

U.S. representative 1._____ local office phone no.
State senator
State representative

b. Where are resources in your locality?
Local repository of government documents
Indexes available in your library

Five organizations in the community that provide information to the public

Five campus organizations that provide information to the public

Two faculty members and their areas of expertise

3. In an in-class group discussion react to the following statistically based statements using the guidelines suggested in this chapter. Indicate whether the statements are acceptable as they are and why, or how each might be restated.
   a. The average salary of a worker in New York is $27,500, while the average salary of a worker in Wyoming is $20,250. Obviously, workers in Wyoming are poorly paid.
   b. Americans consume huge quantities of salt, especially in processed food. For instance, cornflakes contain 4,559 mg. of salt per pound, processed cheese spread 1,371 mg. per pound, peanut butter 2,740 mg. per pound, and white bread 2,300 mg. per pound.
   c. The average normal temperature in Arizona is 39°F in December, 55°F in April, 78°F in July, and 69°F in September.
   d. Every five minutes someone dies from cancer.
   e. In last week's ratings, NBC finished with a share of 18.9, while CBS finished second at 17.8 and ABC third at 16.6.

References

1. Abraham Maslow, *The Farthest Reaches of Human Nature* (NY: Viking Press, 1983), p. 76.

2. James Naisbitt, *Megatrends: Ten New Directions Transforming our Lives* (NY: Warner Books, 1983), p. 24.

3. Chaim Perelman, *The New Rhetoric* (Notre Dame: University of Notre Dame Press, 1969), p. 372.

Chapter 5 · Composing a Public Speech

On November 19, 1863, President Abraham Lincoln delivered a speech most people consider a masterpiece of oratory, perhaps the greatest speech ever given by a notable American. The speech, given as part of a ceremony to consecrate the new burial ground at Gettysburg, Pennsylvania, four months earlier the site of the bloodiest battle of the Civil War, was 269 words long and took approximately five minutes to deliver. Some fifteen thousand people heard the address without the aid of a public-address system. Lincoln's timeless oration has become known as the Gettysburg Address, and is reprinted here.

LINCOLN'S GETTYSBURG ADDRESS

Four score and seven years ago our fathers brought forth on this continent a new nation conceived in liberty and dedicated to the proposition that all men are created equal.

Now we are engaged in a great civil war, testing whether that nation or any nation so conceived and so dedicated, can long endure. We are met on a great battlefield of that war. We have come to dedicate a portion of that field as a final resting place for those who here gave their lives that that nation might live. It is altogether fitting and proper that we should do this.

But in a larger sense, we cannot dedicate, we cannot consecrate—we cannot hallow—this ground. The brave men, living and dead, who struggled here, have consecrated it far beyond our poor power to add or detract. The world will little note nor long remember what we say here, but it can never forget what they did here. It is for us the living, rather, to be dedicated here to the unfinished work which they who fought here have thus far so nobly advanced. It is rather for us to be here dedicated to the great task remaining before us—that from these honored dead we take increased devotion to that cause for which they gave their last full measure of devotion—that we here highly resolve that these dead shall not have died in vain—that this nation, under God, shall have a new birth of freedom—and that government of the people, by the people, and for the people, shall not perish from the earth.

Short and simple as the Gettysburg Address is, it belies the effort Lincoln put into it. Historians know, for instance, that Lincoln worked carefully on the address for several days before he delivered it, actually writing it out at least twice.[1] Later, when preparing the address for publication and posterity, Lincoln wrote the speech at least three more times. Thus, there were five drafts for one 269-word speech, not to mention the hours of thought and practice Lincoln put into the text and into the delivery of the speech.

Lincoln's Gettysburg Address is but one instance of a meaningful speech that succeeds not through the strokes of a genius but through the perseverance of a craftsman. Composing a speech involves creativity and imagination, but even more, it requires an understanding of the speech-composing process and a commitment to following that process.

Many professional speakers and writers agree that the hardest part of composing a speech is sitting down in a chair and staying there until they have accomplished the goal they have set for themselves. With the many distractions facing us, it is quite difficult to close off the rest of the world, plunk ourselves down at a desk, and start to work on a speech.

Discovering Your Composing Style

Planning a Timetable and Setting Goals

A common reason for failure in a speech is lack of time spent in the composing process, especially if the speech is composed the night before it is due. It is a good idea, then, to plan a timetable when a speech assignment is first given. Start early enough to complete the assignment at your normal working pace, remembering always that you may need two or three drafts until you get the one with which you feel satisfied.

In addition to planning time, set a small goal for each day. Rather than saying, "Tonight, I'm going to concentrate on my speech," it is better to say, "Tonight, I'm going to arrange my evidence for the body of the speech." By dividing the total process into a series of manageable steps, you may feel more successful at the end of the composing session. Here is a sample timetable with a set of goals based upon one composer's schedule:

Day One: Start at 2:00 P.M.—get notes together. Stop at library for book.

Day Two: Start at 9:00 A.M.—work on outline. See Dr. Wilson for interview at 10:00. Finish critical-thinking statement.

Day Three: Morning—fill in outline. Draft thesis. After dinner—draft up introduction and conclusion.

Day Four: 2:00 P.M.—work up note cards. Get visuals prepared.

Day Five: Practice, practice, practice.

Your timetable might look quite different; the point is to have a plan, a game plan, that gets you to the lectern fully prepared.

Helpful Hints for Composing

When you actually sit down to compose a speech, what can you expect? As any professional speech writer will tell you, the hardest part will be simply shutting off everything around you and focusing your attention on the task at hand. Having settled in to a period of concentration, you can increase your chances of a productive work session by applying the following guidelines.[2]

First, pick a place to work where you feel comfortable, but not so comfortable that you will become drowsy shortly after you begin. Avoid places that are filled with distractions. Finally, go to the same location and make working in one location a habit.

Second, most of us have favorite writing tools. Find a pen and paper with which you feel comfortable. Have your tools set out before you. It can be quite distracting to have a steady flow of ideas coming and then have to interrupt that flow to sharpen a pencil or search for a note card. Just as a carpenter arrives at a job with a complete set of tools, so you should arrive at your composing place fully equipped to write.

Third, have a manageable goal for each work session and start writing. One excellent idea to start you toward your goal is to make a list of what you are thinking, actually numbering your thoughts as they occur. Scribble thoughts, write them out, make pictures of them—in short, do what *you* need to do to get your creative juices flowing.

A useful technique for a composing session is to talk your speech out. Write as though you were conversing with friends. Give yourself a voice and give potential audience members a voice. One scholar whose research focuses on the behaviors and habits we are now addressing says that it is a good idea to "speak onto your paper."[3] Remember, however, that you are not writing an essay; you must compose your speech with that composite view of your audience always in mind.

Fourth, walk away from your task if you reach a prolonged "dead spot." All composers experience the need to allow an idea to digest or to allow thoughts to unscramble. There will be times when the tension of composing requires us to stop for a while. Having done so, you may discover that your thoughts are flowing smoothly again once you return.

Finally, when the words and thoughts start to flow, work until you are exhausted. It is not a good idea to put a time limit on your composing—to say, "Tonight I will work from seven to eight and then watch my show on TV"—since, if your most creative and productive moments happen to begin around seven thirty, you will be quitting just at the key moment. Allow yourself an open end so that you can continue to work at peak moments.

The composing process is original to each person in the sense that each person has a favorite writing instrument, location, time of day, and so on. The moments one experiences during composing, however, are fairly common and the steps for successful composing are generally understood. Recognize in advance, then, what you and others can expect as you set out to compose a speech, and you will find the experience much more enjoyable and productive.

Now we want to look at the specific tasks you need to perform in order to compose a speech. We begin by showing you how to organize and outline your speech, then how to write a thesis statement, and finally how to compose a preview of the speech, an introduction, and a conclusion. You may at times compose your speech in another order, perhaps writing your introduction before the body if you are inspired to do so. The goal here is to provide you with principles and guidelines for each specific task in the speech-composing process.

Peter Elbow captures the relationship between composing a speech and speaking in this statement: "I see the writer at her desk conjuring up her audience before her in her mind's eye as she writes. She is looking *at* them—more aware of the sounds of her spoken words in her ear than the sight of her written words on paper. She is the writer as raconteur. The writer with the gift of gab."

Peter Elbow
"Shifting Relationships Between Speech and Writing"
College Composition and Communication 36(1985).

Organizing the Body of a Speech

In Chapter 3 of this text we noted that the categories of invention used to probe a topic would be used again to organize the body of the speech. Using the same techniques to generate information about the topic and to organize the speech itself turns the art of composing a speech into a more natural, reasoned process.

A well-organized speech is one that moves thoroughly, comprehensibly, and convincingly through a topic, allowing listeners to share in and absorb the main point(s) of a message with maximum ease. Furthermore, a consciously designed organizational plan helps the speaker put his or her data in the right place—it helps to prevent those numerous stressful moments caused by not knowing where something fits or where the speech itself is headed.

To say that a speech is organized means that it proceeds in one consistent direction from beginning to end. In order to accomplish this, the speaker needs a pattern to follow, much as a designer needs a pattern in order to cut cloth into a particular shape. We call the pattern a public speaker uses to organize a speech a *pattern of discourse.*

Understanding the Patterns of Discourse

The patterns of discourse are simply the categories of invention you learned about in Chapter 3, turned into basic outline patterns for use when composing a speech. In Part II of this text each pattern will be developed in great detail. For present purposes, here is a list of the patterns of discourse with a brief description of each, including purposes for which the patterns are often used.

NARRATIVE

A pattern of discourse that helps us arrange events in a consistent chronological order. Often used in storytelling and television documentaries, and in recounting personal experiences, narratives are used to satisfy the complete range of purposes and have, in particular, a subtle, persuasive aim. The narrative pattern focuses on the question "What happened?" Begin to use the narrative pattern by listing the key moments in the total event:
Event 1
Event 2
Event 3 . . .

PROCESS

A pattern of discourse used to explain the steps or stages in the development of something in a consistent manner. Process speeches are practical in nature and are most often used to con-

CHAPTER 5

vey information in how-to-do-it and do-it-yourself situations such as orientation lectures and cooking demonstrations. The process pattern helps us organize the results of our investigation into how to do something or how something works. The process outline begins with a listing of the essential steps or stages:

Step 1   Phase 1
Step 2   Phase 2
Step 3...   Phase 3 ...

A pattern of discourse that guides an investigation into the reasons for something or the results of something. Cause-effect speeches are often used to organize arguments on controversial issues and explain how some condition has come to be. Thus, cause-effect speeches satisfy both informative and persuasive purposes and can, in fact, be used for the entire range of communicative situations. The cause-effect pattern helps us organize in a sequential, chronological order so that we can answer the question "Why did something come to be?" or "What are the effects of some condition?" Begin to organize the cause-effect speech by noting the critical moments in the development of something, or the main effects of something:

CAUSE-EFFECT

Cause 1   Cause
Cause 2   Effect 1
Cause 3 ... Effect 2
Effect   Effect 3 ...

A pattern of discourse that helps us divide some whole into its component parts. Analysis speeches serve all purposes and are frequently given by consultants or lobbyists to explain complex topics, by advocates such as lawyers to argue for or against something, and by lecturers to break down a complex idea into reasonable parts. The analysis pattern takes many forms, all of which are guided by the essential question "How can the topic be logically divided?" Here are some ways to begin outlining an analysis:

ANALYSIS

Problem   Issue   Policy
Solution 1   Proponents   Implication 1
Solution 2   Opponents   Implication 2
Solution 3 ... Interpretation ... Implication 3 ...

A pattern of discourse through which the essential nature of something is determined. Definition speeches are used in per-

DEFINITION

suasive situations when the meaning of something is at issue and in informative situations to clear up confusion about terms. The definition pattern is also often used in speeches designed to entertain. It helps us organize our search for an answer to the question "What is it?" Basic outlines for the definition speech look like this:

Term	*Term*
Meaning 1	*Standard meaning 1*
Meaning 2	*New meaning 1*
Meaning 3 . . .	*New meaning 2 . . .*

CLASSIFICATION

A pattern of discourse that leads to a logical grouping of things into classes or categories. Often used to arrange lectures, to explain complex ideas, and to see matters in a different, sometimes humorous light, classification speeches fit a wide range of speech purposes. Use the classification pattern to organize your response to the question "What are its common attributes or its basic categories?" Begin organizing the classification speech by looking for the following essential elements:

Type 1	*Class 1*
Type 2	*Class 2*
Type 3	*Class 3 . . .*

Using the Patterns of Discourse

Each pattern, you may have noticed, responds to a question. You begin to organize a speech by focusing on the question you want to answer. The question you ask about your topic will determine

---

Kenneth Burke, one of the great figures in rhetoric in the twentieth century, said that "form [organization] is a way of experiencing," and that "there are no forms which are not forms of experience outside of art," and that "a work has form insofar as one part of it leads a reader to anticipate another part, to be gratified by the sequence." In these words we see the basis of organization and its importance to a speaker.

Kenneth Burke
Counterstatement

---

the total direction of the speech. In other words, if you decide to focus on the question "Why did something happen?" your speech will move according to the principles of cause-effect. If you decide to focus on the "What is it?" aspect of your topic, the speech will move according to the definitional pattern, and so on for each question.

Each time you ask a different question you begin to get a much different speech. Thus, it is critical that you write out the question you want to answer in your speech, looking carefully at the key words to be sure they represent the approach you want to take. In order to show you more clearly how to organize a speech using the patterns of discourse, let's look at an example.

Assume that a speaker has chosen to speak on the topic of television viewing. Quite obviously, this is a huge topic and the speaker needs to focus on one aspect. Thinking critically, the speaker begins to ask questions about the topic, to probe the topic with the categories of invention. Let's hypothesize some possible approaches to the topic resulting from just three categories of invention.

CAUSE-EFFECT. The speaker, during the course of reading about the topic, might come across the statement that excessive television watching causes people to listen passively, to blur the distinction between fantasy and reality, and to model negative behavior seen on television. Thinking the audience might profit from development of this idea into a full speech, the speaker might focus on the question "What effects does excessive television viewing have on people?"

CLASSIFICATION. The speaker might discover that a citizens' group is classifying television programs according to levels of violence, a classification scheme that has caused the group to propose banning programs that fall into the high-violence categories. The speaker might decide that a good argument could be made for or against such a classification system, focusing on the question "What are the classes or categories in the system, and what criteria were used to establish the system?"

ANALYSIS. The speaker might be aware of or read about problems facing the television industry, such as cable piracy and radar-dish licensing. Thinking that such problems deserve audience attention, the speaker might decide to explore them in detail and/or offer a solution.

Notice that each time the speaker looked at the problem with a different category of invention, he or she generated a new perspective and a new way to focus on the topic. Now the speaker must choose one category, turn it into a pattern for organizing the speech, and then stick to that pattern throughout the composing process. The other categories of invention may still be helpful as supporting material in the speech, but only as support. Once the pattern is chosen, the speaker is committed to it. Let's see how this works by continuing our example of the speech on excessive television viewing.

Assume that the speaker decides that, for this speech situation, the most interesting way to approach the topic is the one generated by the cause-effect category of invention. The cause-effect category now becomes a pattern of discourse used to organize the entire body of the speech. Thus, the speaker has the main components for an outline: three effects of excessive television viewing.

EFFECT 1   *Excessive television viewing causes people to become passive listeners.*

EFFECT 2   *Excessive television viewing causes people to blur the distinction between fantasy and reality.*

EFFECT 3   *Excessive television viewing causes people to model negative behaviors seen on television.*

At this point, the speaker is prepared to fill in the outline, arranging supporting material under the headings generated. You will see how this is done in the next section.

There is nothing essentially mysterious or difficult about organization, although students often cite it as their greatest weakness. Most failures in organization result from not having one consistent pattern that serves as a guide throughout the composing process, or from not having a pattern at all. Having too many points of view leads to a speech that moves randomly around a topic, never developing depth of detail or making a point. Having no point of view leads to a laundry list of assertions and comments about the topic—leading, once again, nowhere. Thus, the beginning step toward an organized speech is clear: choose a pattern of discourse and stick with it.

An outline is a carefully crafted plan that shows the essential ingredients of the entire speech: the chosen pattern of discourse and the main supporting material. Outlining is essential to clear thinking because it allows you to focus on one aspect of the speech while having a sketch of the whole speech in front of you as a reference point. Speech outlines, in their skeleton form, look like this:

Outlining the Speech

Introduction

Thesis
(Preview)

Body

  I. Main point 1
    A. Subpoint 1
    B. Subpoint 2 ...

 II. Main point 2
    A. Subpoint 1
    B. Subpoint 2 ...

III. Main point 3
    A. Subpoint 1
    B. Subpoint 2 ...
Conclusion

In some situations, such as a long speech, the introduction and conclusion may also be outlined. We will look at the thesis, introduction, and conclusion shortly. For now, let's focus on outlining the body of the speech. As you go about the task of outlining your speech, keep in mind the following guidelines, since they will make the task easier and more effective.

Each main point in the outline corresponds to a main idea in the speech. For instance, if the speech is based on a process, each main point is an essential step in the process; if the speech is organized with the classification pattern, each main point is a separate class. Start an outline, then, by listing each main point separately.

Make sure that each main point has only one idea in it. Look at the following statement of a main point:

  I. Immigration policy in the United States is based upon political and moral considerations.

Notice that the speaker has collapsed two ideas into one main point. The first idea is that immigration policy is based upon political considerations, while the second idea is that immigration policy is based upon moral considerations. It would have been better to break this statement into two statements:

I. Immigration policy in the United States is based upon political considerations.
   A. Published surveys show that policy changes are consistent with the philosophy of the political party in power. (expert opinion)
   B. Elected officials have admitted to basing their policy on constituent pressure. (expert testimony)

II. Immigration policy in the U.S. is based upon moral considerations.
   A. Old Testament doctrines about immigrants, including the parables of the stranger at the gate and the good Samaritan, have influenced policy debates. (fact)
   B. Immigration officials themselves cite moral principles such as the tenant-versus-owner concept to shape policy. (quotations from experts)

In this corrected version of the outline, each idea is allotted a main point, making it easier for the speaker to develop each point and easier for the audience to follow the discussion.

Keep the language of main points consistent. Write main points and subpoints in sentence form, using the same sentence structure for each. In the above example on immigration policy, notice that each main point begins with the same words: "Immigration policy in the United States is based upon. . . ." The speaker on television viewing might similarly list the three effects uncovered in his or her research in the following way:

I. *Excessive television viewing causes* people to become passive listeners.

II. *Excessive television viewing causes* people to blur the distinction between fantasy and reality.

III. *Excessive television viewing causes* people to model negative behaviors seen on television.

Wording the main ideas consistently gives the speech a literary quality and makes it easier for the speaker to follow.

Main points must have parallel weight and balance. You should subordinate to subpoint status items that do not characterize the essential pattern being used to organize the speech. Notice how the person speaking on the effects of television viewing placed each effect in the outline as a main point because each was distinctive. Had the speaker uncovered a court trial concerning the commission of a crime closely resembling a crime committed on a recent television movie, this piece of supporting material would most appropriately have fit as a subpoint of main point II, since it would have supported the idea that television viewing caused people to imitate what they saw on TV, rather than itself being a separate effect. The speaker would have added a new main point only if he or she had uncovered a new effect, one completely different from those already listed.

Each subpoint supports a main point. Subpoints can clarify, qualify, illustrate, or prove the main point. They can be facts, opinions, statistics, illustrations, comparisons, definitions, or simply good reasons that elaborate on the main idea.

At least two subpoints should support each main point. Look for a variety of ways to support a main idea. One statistic, one opinion, one illustration, is seldom enough to elaborate adequately on the main point. In the speech on the effects of television viewing, for instance, we noted that the speaker listed as a subpoint a crime in which violent behavior portrayed on television was imitated in the commission of a crime. That crime is a specific instance of the main point, so it was placed as subpoint A under main point III:

III. Excessive television viewing causes people to model negative behaviors seen on television.
    A. A gang of youths in Boston poured gasoline on a man and ignited it the day after they had seen this done on TV in the movie *Fuzz*.

But while one instance is revealing, the audience quite likely will want more to convince them of this effect. So, the speaker will have to add another subpoint, preferably a different kind of supporting material. In the course of researching the topic, the speaker may have discovered an experiment to test the effects of television viewing. This experiment can be used to support the main point as subpoint B. Main point III would now be developed like this:

III. Excessive television viewing causes people to model negative behaviors seen on television.
   A. A gang of youths in Boston poured gasoline on a man and ignited it the day after they had seen this done on TV in the movie *Fuzz*. (specific instance)
   B. A study by Bandura and Walters shows that by observing aggressive behaviors on television programs, and under certain conditions, people will model their behavior after that of aggressive television characters. (statistical data)

Now the main point has more credibility. Also, the subpoints are more clearly distinguished from the main points because there are two of them.

If possible, avoid dividing the subpoints in a speech. In some situations a subpoint will need clarification, qualification, or illustration. But since the very role of subpoints is to support by illuminating the main point, material should be chosen and developed so that it need not be divided itself.

The outline may now be completed by adding details to each main point as the speaker discovers material during the research process. Having stated the main points clearly, according to the pattern chosen for developing the speech, the speaker now simply needs to place the material where it is most appropriate, and the speech begins to unfold neatly. Look at the completed outline for the speech on television viewing:

Title: Television Viewing May Be Bad for Your Health

Introduction

Thesis:
(Preview)

Body

I. Excessive television viewing causes people to become passive listeners.
   A. Media literacy studies show that people accept what they hear on TV without questioning it. (fact)
   B. Authorities such as Kenneth Boulding believe that because

television is a one-way system of communication, listeners, having no chance to respond, fall into a passive state. (expert opinion)

II. Excessive television viewing causes people to blur the distinction between fantasy and reality.
   A. Gerbner and Gross showed that heavy television watchers think of the world as a more dangerous place than those who do not watch television heavily. (expert opinion)
   B. During the Vietnam War, many studies showed that people watching the evening news coverage of the war did not perceive the war as real but only as another program. (statistical survey)

III. Excessive television viewing causes people to model negative behaviors seen on television.
   A. A gang of youths in Boston poured gasoline on a man and ignited it the day after they had seen this done on TV in the movie *Fuzz*. (example)
   B. A study by Bandura and Walters shows that by observing aggressive behaviors on television programs, and under certain conditions, people will model their behavior after that of aggressive television characters. (statistical data)

Of course, the speaker will need to expand on each point during the speech, "talking out" each form of support. While composing the speech, however, the speaker need only place all the material where it fits most appropriately. The steps in the outlining process apply to any speech. Outlining becomes a natural, habitual activity flowing out of critical thinking and choosing a pattern of discourse for the entire speech. Following an outline is one way to ensure that your speech is organized and thorough.

The Thesis Statement

You will remember from the discussion of purpose (pp. 69–70) that a critical-thinking statement guides the speaker throughout the development of a speech, giving him or her a composite picture of the entire speech situation. You were also told that when choosing an organizational pattern, you should ask a question that would lead you to the most appropriate pattern of discourse for your speech. When composing the speech itself, however, the speaker needs one sentence that will normally be stated in the speech and will act as the controlling idea behind it. That statement is called the thesis statement.[4]

The word *thesis* derives from an ancient Greek term meaning "to set" or "to place." That original meaning has evolved so that today we think of a thesis as the place where the central idea of a speech is located, a statement that each audience member can keep in mind throughout the speech as a way of connecting individual parts to the whole. An exact thesis statement may come to mind early in the speech-composing process, or it may not evolve into final form until well into the final draft of the speech. Write the thesis statement as soon as you think of it, but be prepared to revise it should your central idea change as you compose.

Whether you discover your ultimate thesis—the controlling idea of your speech—before, during, or at the end of the composing process, you should follow certain principles and guidelines in formulating the thesis statement.

Principles of the Thesis Statement

The first principle of a good thesis statement is that it be a single, declarative sentence. Thesis statements that ask a question are unsuccessful because they are too tentative. Thesis statements that command or request the audience to do something capture only a part of the message. Look at the following three statements:

Today, I would like to ask, "Are America's blacks accurately portrayed in the media?" (a question)

Today, we must fight for the real picture of blacks in the media! (a command)

Three key features make up the distorted image of blacks as portrayed in the media. (a declarative sentence)

Notice that the first statement, a question, is tentative. The audience cannot be certain whether the question will be answered or in what way the speaker will proceed to answer it. The second sentence tells the audience what it must do, but suggests no reasons, no basis for their action. The third sentence states quite clearly that the speech will be devoted to analyzing the image of blacks in an effort to convince the audience that the image is a distorted one. Thus, a single declarative sentence cues the audience to the main idea under consideration.

The thesis statement should suggest how the speech will be organized. Use a key word whenever possible to cue the audience to the pattern of discourse you will be using. Look at the following two thesis statements to see the value of cueing the audience to the organization of the speech:

In my speech today, I would like to talk about seat-belt laws and review my research on this matter.

As you will see, seat-belt laws are a controversial but effective solution to the problem of highway deaths.

The first statement is not effective because it fails to cue the audience to the direction the speech will take. Audience members are left to guess at the controlling idea, which seems to focus as much on the "talking" as on the topic. The second sentence makes an assertion—that seat-belt laws are good—and indicates that the speech will follow a problem-solution (analysis pattern of discourse) organizational plan. The audience is now clear about the idea controlling the speech and the direction in which the speech is headed. Part II of this text will show you effective thesis statements for each pattern.

The thesis statement should be worded clearly and concretely. In addition to suggesting the pattern a speech will follow, the thesis statement should avoid figurative language or indirect wording of the controlling idea. Read the following thesis statements:

There's an old saying, "A new broom sweeps clean," and that's what this speech is all about.

Marshall McLuhan stated that a thesis was originally a topic that was both paradoxical and abstract. That is, a thesis would contain an apparent contradiction such as, "All people are really one," and would be about something removed from a particular time and place. A thesis, then, became the focal point for classroom arguments, disputations used to train public speakers.

Marshall McLuhan
The Gutenberg Galaxy

Hundreds of bankrupt corporations have failed because they refused to innovate and change with changing conditions.

The first sentence might well work in the conclusion of the speech as a memorable, catchy way to sum up the point of the speech. As a thesis statement, however, it is ambiguous—the language is too figurative to indicate the central idea of the speech. The second sentence is much better as a thesis statement because the words indicate clearly the central idea of the speech. Furthermore, the key word *because* suggests the pattern of discourse the speech will follow: cause-effect.

The thesis statement may suggest the purpose of the speech. This principle is sometimes referred to as adjusting the thesis to the audience and situation, since purpose is a concept related to the speaker-audience interaction.[5] (See Chapter 3, pp. 61–62.) Following are two thesis statements for the speech previously outlined on excessive television viewing (pp. 113–119).

Today, my speech is about television viewing, and how too much of it is no good.

Excessive television viewing has lasting consequences, the three most detrimental of which I would like to explain.

The first sentence is declarative, but it does not work as well as the second because the second statement is less awkwardly written and suggests the purpose: to explain.

Not all thesis statements use purpose words like *persuade, inform, inspire,* or *entertain.* Sometimes the purpose of a speech is simply suggested, most notably in narrative speeches. Also, a speaker may have a variety of purposes for speaking, based, perhaps on the variety of people in the audience and the speaker's role in the speech situation. On such occasions, the purpose may not need to be reduced to one word such as *persuade* or *inform.*

Guidelines for Using the Thesis Statement

A thesis statement is said to control the speech because once the speaker states it, he or she must then move directly to support the idea and to follow the pattern of discourse chosen. Therefore, a thesis statement is often written for the final time at or near the end of the composing process, when the speaker is most clear about the controlling idea and the ultimate direction of the speech. Guideline number 1, then, is to have a tentative thesis statement in mind as you compose, but to write your final thesis statement only when you are certain about the central idea, your pattern, and possibly your purpose.

Since the thesis statement also becomes the audience's focal point for listening to the speech, as a practical matter it should normally be presented early in the speech. But this is only a guideline, not a rule. In some situations a thesis might be stated later in a speech, for instance, when summing up the results of an experience. Consider where your thesis statement would most help the audience. On most occasions, you will find that it works best just before you move to the body of the speech.

Having a clear thesis statement is essential in a public speech. The audience hears you only once—they cannot go back through your speech as if it were an essay. If you are to be understood and convincing, you will need a thesis statement that cues the audience to the controlling idea of your speech. Writing thesis statements may seem artificial at times. We often feel that our central idea will simply jump out at the audience—be ridiculously obvious. Experience shows, however, that in an oral-communication situation, the speaker must take nothing for granted in the development of the speech. Especially when learning the art of public speaking, it is better to be obvious than obscure.

Previewing the Speech

A thesis statement is often followed by a transitional section that previews the speech. The preview can serve three purposes: to provide background, to give definitions, and/or to state the key points that the speech will cover. Let's look at each purpose separately.

Previewing Through Background

Often the audience needs times, dates, and places to qualify the thesis and to orient themselves to the topic under discussion. For example, a speech focusing on the process of taking the federal census would profit from a preview explaining the origin of the census:

> *Before I proceed to the process of taking a federal census, I thought it would be helpful for you to know that the census is*

mandated by Article I, Section 3, of the U.S. Constitution. Its original intent was to determine the number of representatives each state would be allowed in the House of Representatives. The census is to be taken every ten years and is still the basis for reapportionment of the House of Representatives, although today the census is used for every imaginable objective from discovering who can read to how many of us have indoor plumbing.

In this example, the speaker provides the audience with a basic understanding of the history of the census and might go on to add more historical detail based upon his or her analysis of the audience.

Previewing Terms

If the speech will involve using new, unfamiliar, or commonly misunderstood terms, these terms can be previewed after the thesis and prior to launching into the body of the speech. Recently, during a speech on the problem of improving conditions for the handicapped at a school, the speaker stated her thesis and then added:

Let me take a minute before I get to the heart of this matter to clear up the term handicapped. *According to Titles 6 and 7 of the Civil Rights Act of 1964, a handicapped person is anyone with a "physical or mental disability that substantially impairs or restricts one or more such major life activities as walking, seeing, hearing, speaking, working, or learning." Actually, today we prefer the term* physically challenged *to refer to those who have physical disabilities. You can see, now, that the problem I will be addressing here has broad implications on our campus.*

By clarifying the key term in the speech, the speaker prevented possible misunderstanding during her speech. Whenever key terms in the speech will not be carefully defined in the body, a definition preview will aid the audience.

Previewing Key Points

It is often necessary to cue the audience to the key points that will be covered to support the thesis. An issue analysis, for instance, often benefits from a preview of the arguments made for or against the issue. In the following example, the speaker previews his argument in favor of bilingual education:

As support for my thesis, I intend to offer the following two reasons: that bilingual education is in keeping with the American tradition of education for all people, and that bilingual education costs are less than the costs associated with dropping out.

The speaker then proceeded to develop each point in the body of the speech. By previewing the two key points, he had cued the audience to what was to follow.

Previewing the speech is an effective way to expand on or clarify the thesis, and it serves as an aid to the audience, facilitating comprehension. Although it is a short part of the speech, the preview should be given careful thought and attention during the composing process.

Composing an Introduction

Professionals in various fields such as feature writing, advertising, and public relations agree on one principle of successful communication: you have just a few seconds to get the audience involved. If you fail to create that strong first impression, if you fail to excite others instantly, you have lost them. According to a well-established axiom, originally coined by noted psychologist William James, "What holds attention determines action."[6] What is true in the professional world and accepted in the theories of psychologists such as James is no less valid for the public speaker.

James Winans, a most influential public-speaking teacher and a pioneer in the field of speech communication, wrote in his classic 1915 text *Public Speaking:* "At any moment there are innumerable ideas and sensations struggling to get into the focus of your attention. The strongest—that is, the strongest at the moment—wins."[7]

For the student of public speaking, the message is that, regardless of the quality of the ideas in the body of the speech, success in public speaking requires that the audience first be made interested in the entire speech event. Audience interest in a speech begins with the introduction.

The introduction to a speech should gain audience attention, develop within the audience an awareness of and interest in the topic, and establish in the audience a sense of good will toward the speaker. Let's look at some of the methods most frequently used to fulfill the purposes of an introduction and at some examples of successful introductions from both student and professional speeches.

Humor

Most people like a good joke or a humorous story. Although there is only slight evidence that humor has much persuasive value, as a factor in getting the audience involved in the speech, humor is clearly a primary technique of experienced public speakers.[8] In the following introduction, notice how the speaker, a noted expert in education, uses humor to gain attention, develop an interest in the topic, and show his good will toward the audience.

> *There's a story about a chicken and a pig who were passing a church, when they noticed the signboard and the weekly message: WHAT HAVE YOU GIVEN TO GOD TODAY? The chicken looked at the pig, the pig looked at the chicken, and each allowed as how it had been a long time since either one of them had given God anything.*
>
> *"Pig," said the chicken, "I think we ought to mend our ways."*
> *"I agree," said the pig. "What exactly do you have in mind?"*
>
> *The chicken thought for a minute, then said, "Pig, you and I ought to give God a plate of ham and eggs." "You can't be serious," replied the pig.*
>
> *"Why not?" said the chicken, offended that his suggestion had been rebuffed. "Don't you think God would be pleased by our token offering?"*
>
> *"That's just the point," the pig retorted. "What for you may be a token offering, for me is total commitment."*
>
> *There seems to be a lot of poultry and pork in our society, even among educators. Some of us are ready to admit that we haven't necessarily been paragons in the profession; we've barely paid our dues, let's say. Call it a guilt trip, if you will, brought by reading too many letters to the editor in News-week; or call it an instance of consciousness raising, if you prefer that jargon. In any case, let's grant that there are many teachers and administrators—most of them at least as sincere as we are—who sense the need for a fresh start. Call it rejuvenation or being born-again, these educators (perhaps*

you are one of them) are just a little cautious, just a little gun
shy, of speakers like me and topics like mine. You've grown
weary of pep talks and wary of platitudes. Like the pig in the
story, you understand fully the difference between a token
offering and total commitment. You know that the cost of
total commitment to becoming and being a teacher means
nothing less than life itself. And you wonder if it's worth the
cost. (reprinted by permission of Vital Speeches)

Of course, humor can backfire. If the humor is directed at some group or a member of the audience, if it makes fun of someone or something, or if it is sarcastic, it can backfire even while gaining attention.

Humor that does not get a response—is for some reason not funny—can also backfire. A speaker recently gave the following introduction to a speech on the topic "What Makes Someone a Good Sport?": "There are two kinds of people in this world; those who divide the world into twos, and the rest of us. The same is true in sports: there are good sports and bad sports." Not only didn't audience members get the humor of the remark; they missed the connection between the introduction and the topic.

One final caution about using humor. Many amateurish speeches begin with a joke, taken from a joke book, that has nothing to do with the topic. It is difficult to transplant humor in this way. A humorous introduction must be an integral part of the speech and fit both the speaker and the occasion.

Startling Statements

Some topics, such as controversial ones, often begin with a startling statement. In the following introduction to a speech concerning crimes committed by blacks against other blacks, the speaker uses statistics to shock her audience into attention:

Did you know that more blacks were killed by other blacks in
the year 1977 than were killed in the entire Vietnam War?
Most of the 5,734 blacks killed on the battlefield of black
America could have survived the Vietnam War, since the
blacks who died there added up to 634 per year. This astound-
ing figure only begins to underscore the seriousness of black-
on-black crime. Nearly 87 percent of the robberies, rapes,
assaults and murders committed on blacks are committed by

other blacks. The result is that mistrust, fear, and anxiety are a permanent part of the black community. (reprinted by permission of the author)

Notice in this example that the speaker gains audience attention but also focuses on the topic. If startling statements are to be used in the introduction, they must relate to the topic and not be simply a gimmick. One speaker recently walked to the lectern, drew a starter's pistol, and fired it into the air to startle his audience into thinking about his speech on gun control. The audience was not impressed.

Questions

A question or a list of questions is often used to arouse audience curiosity. In the following example, a familiar question is used with an unfamiliar answer to pique audience interest in the topic:

Who's the leader of the club that's made for you and me? Mickey Mouse—No. It's Leonard S. Crutcher. What's the club? You've probably heard about it, but as college students you haven't found time to join. Well, it's Book-of-the-Month Club and you are about to hear three good reasons for belonging.

Sometimes a question can be planted in the minds of audience members to get them involved. The question-implantation method was recently used to introduce a speech called "How to Tell If Someone is Lying":

Have you ever looked directly into a person's eyes and asked, "Are you telling me the truth?" Have you ever wondered, "Am I being taken for a ride?" Well, if you have you are about to find out how to tell when someone is lying and when they are telling the truth.

When used to generate curiosity for the topic, questions are a useful technique for an introduction.

References to the Occasion

In some situations, an introduction provides an orientation to the occasion. The speaker captures the mood and the purpose of the event as a way of getting the audience involved. In the example shown here, from his eulogy on Sir Winston Churchill, Adlai Stevenson characterizes the occasion:

> Today we meet in sadness to mourn one of the world's greatest citizens. Sir Winston Churchill is dead. The voice that led nations, raised armies, inspired victories and blew fresh courage into the hearts of men is silenced. We shall hear no longer the remembered eloquence and wit, the old courage and defiance, the robust serenity of indomitable faith. Our world is thus poorer, our political dialogue is diminished and the sources of public inspiration run more thinly for all of us. There is a lonesome place against the sky.

Stories, Anecdotes, Personal Experiences

Speakers often use brief narratives to show their interest in and experience with the topic. Sometimes a humorous account of something works well, but, as in this example, a serious personal experience can also capture the audience's attention:

> There I was, nineteen years old, staring down the barrel of an M-16 rifle, sweating like an ice cube in hell, bleeding from a shrapnel wound in my thigh, and wondering why I was going to die before I hit twenty. But I made it out of Da Nang thanks to a medic with the face of a dirty angel and a chopper pilot who could land on a raindrop. I think back on it now and ask, "Why was I blamed for Vietnam? I was just trying to do my job."

Sometimes, historical anecdotes can be used to get an audience involved:

> John Paul Getty, the richest man in the world, was once asked the secret to attaining wealth. He replied, "Getting rich requires you to do three things: rise early, work late ... strike oil."

Narratives that do not work are those that threaten, preach, condescend, or are self-congratulatory. Here is an example of how not to establish good will with an audience:

Actor and anti-nuclear activist Paul Newman has said about the issue of nuclear arms that "there is no other issue." He is right! You may be concerned about the environment, about the economy, or about drug abuse, but those issues aren't really important compared to the nuclear arms issue. What good is a clean environment if we're on the brink of nuclear war?

I have spent the last two years of my life marching and pro-testing against nuclear arms. I wish more people would get off their duffs and do this. Too many of us let the other guy solve our problems. Today, I am going to convince you to do something about, as Newman put it, "the only issue there is," nuclear arms proliferation.

This might be a good speech topic, but the introduction puts the audience on the defensive. From this point on, the speaker will need to work extremely hard, not to convince the audience of his point but simply to get them to listen.

There are, of course, as many good introductions as there are good speech topics. Look to your topic for something that will get the motors running in your audience. Avoid trite introductions such as, "Today my speech is on so and so." Similarly, do not give the title of your speech in the introduction. Worst of all, do not announce the process by which you arrived at the topic: "I was puzzled about what to speak on so I finally decided to talk about. . . ."

Compose your introduction when you feel you have found the story, question, statistic, or whatever that will grab the audience. You may need to scrap your first introduction or rewrite it at some point in the process. It is important that you think about the introduction throughout the composing process and draft it out when the inspiration comes.

Composing a Conclusion

Equally as important as the introduction is the conclusion of a speech. Too many otherwise excellent speeches have failed because they arrived at a "Well, that's about it . . ." ending. The purposes of a conclusion are to provide a sense of completeness to the speech, to repeat and summarize in some manner the key ideas in the speech, and, in some speeches, to appeal to the audience to adopt an appropriate belief or behavior pattern.

Providing a Sense of Completeness

When a speech has ended, the audience must sense that the topic has been fully covered. The conclusion signals the audience that the message is complete. For example, one speaker concluded a speech in the following way:

> *Christians believe in Jesus Christ and have pledged their love and lives to Him. Naturally, Christians are curious and interested to know what Jesus Christ looked like. The Shroud of Turin holds that promise, and the possibility of having an exact picture of Christ is exciting. So far, however, and at least until the Vatican allows Carbon-14 testing to determine the Shroud's authentic age, Christians must live with the fact that the Shroud is only a possibility. There are still many unanswered questions concerning the Shroud of Turin, that, as of now, only God knows the answers to. (reprinted by permission of* Vital Speeches*)*

One test of a conclusion is that if the audience heard only the conclusion, it would know what the speech was about. This is the case for the conclusion given above. You can tell how the speech began and how the issue stands as the speech ends. By closing with a statement that grasps the general idea of the whole speech, the conclusion has worked.

Summarizing Key Ideas in a Speech

Closely related to the first goal—providing completeness—is the second goal of a conclusion: to repeat and summarize key ideas. This technique is sometimes known as *reiteration,* meaning repetition of something. Key ideas may be summarized in a variety of ways: through a personal experience, an interesting anecdote, a quotation, or a wise saying. In the following example, the speaker summarizes the key points she has made about the importance of fashion in contemporary society by simply rewording and restating the main points made in the body.

> *Fashion is, in my opinion, generally misunderstood by the public. As a fashion design major I have tried to dispel some of the myths that many hold about fashion, and to convince all of you that fashion should be recognized as a central mechanism in shaping the social order of our modern world. Fash-*

ion design is not an irrational process; it follows a predictable pattern of growth. True fashions are not intended as crazes or fads, but as permanent and enduring symbols of a society's values. Finally, fashion is not anarchic. Instead, fashion introduces order and uniformity into the social order. Fashion listens and then leads.

If the conclusion has summarized well, it has captured—although sometimes in slightly different wording—the thesis and the way in which the thesis was developed in the body of the speech. Notice how the conclusion to the speech on fashion does this in a creative way. Poor conclusions often summarize key ideas mechanically. Consider how the conclusion above might have been given:

So, in conclusion, my thesis is that fashion is a central mechanism in maintaining social order. I developed three main points in my speech to prove my thesis. First, fashion is a rational process. Secondly, real fashions are not crazes or fads. Thirdly, fashion introduces uniformity into a chaotic world. So, that's my speech. Thank you and please ask questions if you have them.

Appealing to the Audience

Some speeches attempt to move the audience to accept an appropriate attitude, value, or belief, or produce an appropriate behavior. Many great speeches of our time provide excellent models of conclusions that appeal to the audience's attitudes or values. Here is the well-known conclusion of John F. Kennedy's inaugural address of January 20, 1961:

And so, my fellow Americans, ask not what your country can do for you—ask what you can do for your country. My fellow citizens of the world: ask not what America will do for you, but what together we can do for the freedom of man.

Finally, whether you are citizens of America or citizens of the world, ask of us here the same high standards of strength and sacrifice which we ask of you. With a good conscience our only sure reward, with history the final judge of our deeds, let us go forth to lead the land we love, asking His blessing and His help, but knowing that here on Earth God's work must truly be our own.

Conclusions focusing on a specific action are not often found in the lofty, inspirational settings of the pulpit or the political soapbox. More commonly, appeals for audience action are presented in speeches on local or controversial issues. Appeals for action are quite often appropriate for speeches in the communication classroom. In the following example, a student appeals to members of the audience to get involved in student government.

We are students today, but tomorrow we are our nation's leaders. In the words of the immortal poet Longfellow:

> *In the world's broad field of battle,*
> *In the bivouac of life,*
> *Be not like dumb and driven cattle,*
> *Be a hero in the strife!*

Longfellow's words can be our inspiration. Be a leader, not one of the led; do something that will improve your own condition.

Next month, student elections will be held. As I have said in my speech, we need effective student government to protect our interests at the university. Part of that voice could be you. Nominations are this week. I have brought with me the nomination papers you need to fill out to have your name placed on the ballot. I am going to run—I'd like you to also.

The conclusion is a good place for a memorable quotation, such as the one from Longfellow in the above conclusion. Parallel sentences such as those at the beginning of the Kennedy example, and vivid language such as that used in humor, also work well in a conclusion. Sometimes a familiar proverb or maxim can capture the message of an entire speech. A touch of the literary leaves the audience with a positive feeling about the speech, and since vivid language is most memorable, a literary conclusion gives the audience something by which to remember your speech.

The conclusion to a speech should be positive. Speeches that end by scolding or appealing to negative emotions such as fear or anger will seldom win over an audience. Look at the above conclusion of the speech on becoming involved in student government. What if that conclusion had sounded like this:

So look, student government elections are next month. I am going to run. If more of you would shake yourselves out of that student lethargy, we could have some power around here. Remember, if you get dumped on by this administration, it's your own fault. If you don't run for office, you've got no one to blame for the problems on this campus but yourselves.

A conclusion like this is not going to work. It appeals to fear and apathy, and is accusatory in tone. Being positive, even when you feel like being negative, is a much better approach to the audience.

Spend time developing your introduction and your conclusion. Use the rhetorical techniques suggested and shown here, and have a clear function in mind as you compose. You will find that your speech is most successful if it has a creative beginning and a literary ending.

As with an introduction, compose your conclusion when the right idea comes to you. If you hear a quotable quote on your topic, jot it down and see how it looks as a conclusion to your speech. You may have to rewrite or revise your conclusion once or twice during the composing process, so having it always on your mental agenda keeps you alert to possibilities as they occur.

Summary

Composing a public speech requires effort, determination, skill, and a commitment to process. It takes time and attention; in fact, the hardest part may be focusing on the task at hand. In this chapter we have reviewed the principles and guidelines that aid in the speech-composition process.

As with any complex activity, composing a speech involves having a timetable and setting goals. Many speeches fail simply because the speaker composed the speech at the last minute and followed no plan. In addition, many speakers fail while composing because they are not familiar with the experience of writing. In this chapter we have looked at some common stages through which composing moves. Our goal has been to help speakers anticipate the composing experience so that they can more readily adjust to the moments of frustration and take advantage of the productive periods.

Organization is a key element in public speaking, and one that students and professionals often find baffling. Organization involves moving a speech in one consistent direction from beginning to end. In this chapter we introduced six "patterns of discourse" that can be used to organize the body of a speech. By focusing on one question, the speaker can choose one pattern of discourse for organizing the speech. Since the patterns of discourse are based upon the categories of invention used for thinking critically about a topic (see

Chapter 3), the processes of developing an idea and organizing it for purposes of communication with others are related in a natural, systematic way.

Choosing a pattern of discourse with which to organize a speech is the first step in outlining. Outlining a speech involves listing the main points and the subpoints, the latter arising from the supporting materials. In this chapter we provided a set of principles and guidelines for creating an outline.

A speech must include a thesis statement, which is a single, declarative sentence that indicates the central idea of the speech. The thesis statement cues the audience to the main idea of the speech and sometimes to the goal toward which the speech is moving. It is often stated after the introduction.

Once the body of the speech is outlined, the speaker needs to concentrate on three elements of a public speech that give it finish and completeness. First, many speeches need a preview—a short statement following the thesis that cues the audience to what is to follow. There are three common previewing techniques: previewing through background, previewing through definition of key terms, and previewing key points. The speaker must determine the type of preview best for each speech during the composing process.

The second element giving finish to a speech is the introduction. An introduction must gain attention, suggest the topic, and establish good will with the audience. We suggested a number of techniques for composing an introduction, including humor, startling statements, questions, stories, anecdotes, and personal experiences.

The final element of a speech is the conclusion. The purposes of a conclusion are to provide a sense of completeness, to summarize or reiterate main points, and/or to appeal to the audience for belief or action.

Introductions and conclusions can be composed at any point in the speech-composition process. They must both avoid gimmickry and be integral to the idea under discussion.

1. Famous author William Styron (*The Confessions of Nat Turner, Sophie's Choice*) said the following when asked about his composing style:

Exercises

I've always tried to work every day when I'm in the course of a specific work. I try to write four hours each day but often it's three hours or two. I start in the midafternoon and try to work through six or seven. . . . When it's going well I can write a page in 15 minutes. When it's going hard I can take two hours.

How would you respond to the question "How do you compose a speech?" What steps or stages do you follow? What bad habits do you need to work on? Is your experience similar to or different from the stages discussed on pp. 108–109? When do you compose your introduction and conclusion? You may discuss these questions in class or respond to them in a short essay.

2. Indicate whether each of the following statements is an appropriate thesis statement and why or why not.
   a. Is aid to South Africa morally responsible?
   b. Origami, the Japanese art of paper folding, is a five-step process that is easy to learn.
   c. The term *avant-garde* is steeped in both paradox and contradiction, and has meaning far beyond its popular sense.
   d. Join me in protesting any system for classifying rock-and-roll music.
   e. Who of us can ever forget that first date with a special someone?

3. Read the following statements and indicate, either in a homework assignment or in an in-class discussion, the pattern of discourse each suggests. Underline the key word or phrase that cues you to the pattern.
   a. Anyone who has taken a test knows that there are four easy steps to flunking.
   b. The life of Jane Fonda reminds us most emphatically that talented people can ply their skills in a variety of arenas.
   c. Achievement tests are not a very good indicator of success in higher learning and should be abolished as an entrance requirement.
   d. We are reminded by the new moral censors that the American character is generally dark with suspicion.
   e. Three important arguments characterize the debate over nuclear power.
   f. Photosynthesis is a process that even biologists do not fully understand.
   g. You can always tell a lot about people by the way they wear their hair.
   h. The feeling of loneliness is both deeply felt and deeply misunderstood.

i. Riding in a Hobie Cat is the thrill of a lifetime.

j. Rock musicians fall into three distinct groups.

4. Read the following introductions to three well-known speeches, and discuss why each succeeds or fails. Be sure to indicate the technique each speaker uses.

a. Elizabeth Cady Stanton, "The Case for Universal Suffrage" (1867):

In considering the question of suffrage, there are two starting points: one, that this right is a gift of society, in which certain men, having inherited this privilege from some abstract body and abstract place, have now the right to secure it for themselves and their privileged order to the end of time. This principle leads logically to governing races, classes, families; and, in direct antagonism to our idea of self-government, takes us back to monarchies and despotisms, to an experiment that has been tried over and over again, 6,000 years, and uniformly failed.

b. Spiro Agnew, "Television News Coverage" (1969):

Tonight I want to discuss the importance of the television news medium to the American people. No nation depends more on the intelligent judgment of its citizens. No medium has a more profound influence over public opinion. Nowhere in our system are there fewer checks on vast power. So, nowhere should there be more conscientious responsibility exercised than by the news media. The question is, Are we demanding enough of our television news presentations and are the men of this medium demanding enough of themselves?

c. Patricia Roberts Harris, "Religion and Politics: A Commitment to a Pluralistic Society" (1980):

In recent weeks newspaper columns and the television airwaves have been filled with the allegedly new phenomenon of the entry of American Evangelicals into the elective political process. The news-cum-entertainment program (or is it the other way around) "Sixty Minutes" this week gave us the unedifying spectacle of overt threats to targeted political figures because they failed to agree with the political position of putative religious leaders on several issues.

That "Sixty Minutes" has reported the phenomenon confirms its reality and, indeed, its pervasiveness. What we need to remember is that this invasion of the political process by those purporting to act in the name of religion is neither new nor a matter for entertainment.

References

1. Louis A. Warren, *Abraham Lincoln's Gettysburg Address* (Columbus, OH: Charles E. Merrill Publishing Co., 1968), pp. 4–7.

2. See, for example, Herdi Swarts, Linda S. Flower, and John R. Hayes, "Designing Protocol Studies of the Writing Process: An Introduction," in *New Directions in Composition Research,* ed. Richard Beach and Lillian S. Bridwell (NY: The Guilford Press, 1984), pp. 53–71.

3. Peter Elbow, "The Shifting Relationships Between Speech and Writing," *College Composition and Communication* 36(1985), pp. 283–303.

4. The term *thesis* is relatively new in speech texts. In the past, the term *proposition* was used to identify the thesis as an assertion on one or another side of an issue. The term *thesis* is more appropriate today when we think of public-speaking topics that are not the focus of debate but simply "themes to be developed." See, for example, Jo Sprague and Douglas Stuart, *The Speaker's Handbook* (NY: Harcourt, Brace, Jovanovich, 1984), pp. 18–21.

5. Frank D'Angelo, *Process and Thought in Composition,* 3d ed. (Boston: Little-Brown, 1985), p. 35.

6. William James, *Psychology: The Briefer Course* (NY: Harper and Row, 1961), p. 315.

7. James Winans, *Public Speaking* (NY: Century, 1920), p. 51.

8. Raymond Ross, *Persuasion: Communication and Interpersonal Relations* (NY: Prentice-Hall, 1974), pp. 163–164.

Chapter 6 · Preparing and Practicing the Final Speech

Franklin Delano Roosevelt was president of the United States from 1932 until his death in 1945. He led our nation through a lingering economic depression and a prolonged world war. Among the many qualities on which Roosevelt prided himself was his ability as a communicator, and he is today remembered as the first great radio orator. In David Halberstam's book *The Powers That Be*, the author provides insight into Roosevelt's success as a speaker:

> *He spoke in an informal manner. His speeches were scripted not to be read in newspapers, but to be heard aloud. He worked carefully on them in advance, often spending several days on a speech, reading the words aloud, working on the rhythm and the cadence, getting the feeling of them down right. When aides questioned the immense amount of time he devoted to just one speech, Roosevelt said that it was probably the most important thing he would do all week. He had an intuitive sense of radio cadence. Unlike most people who speeded up their normal speech pattern on radio, Roosevelt deliberately slowed his down. He was never in a rush. He had often memorized a speech before he began, and so he seemed infinitely confident, never seemed to stumble.*[1]

Halberstam's commentary on Roosevelt is instructive for many reasons. First, Roosevelt was not a gifted speaker. Beneath most "gifts" lie techniques and practice, and Roosevelt practiced endlessly—listening to himself, thinking about just the right way to accent a word or to get the most out of a pause.

Second, Roosevelt studied the situation. He thought consciously about being on the radio, about talking so that average Americans could understand, and about the gravity of his message. Having analyzed his audience, Roosevelt adjusted his vocabulary, tone, and rate of speech to meet the needs of the situation.

Most importantly, however, Roosevelt demonstrated in his speaking the art of sounding spontaneous, even though, as Halberstam notes, he had practiced so much that he knew his material extremely well, often to the point of memory. As the audience listened to FDR, it appeared to them that the words were coming in to his mind as Roosevelt spoke them. Achieving that spontaneous sound is a goal all public speakers seek.

In this chapter you will learn three ways to enhance spontaneity in communication. First, we will show you how to turn your outline into a final format, one that you can bring with you to the speaker's stand and that will aid, not hinder, you as you speak. Second, we will show you how to prepare visual aids and use them during the speech. And finally, you will learn how to practice your speech so that you are fully prepared and comfortable on the day of presentation.

The Final Format of a Speech

A common impediment to spontaneous communication in public speaking is the form of the final draft. The final format, prepared from your outline, is the notation system you take with you to the speaker's stand. You need a format that helps you get the information across accurately, as well as one that allows you to focus your attention on the audience. To put it another way, you need to create the impression Roosevelt created: that you are talking with the audience as though all that you are saying is coming to you as you speak, even though you have thoroughly prepared your speech in advance.

Chapter 6 examines three final formats for a speech: manuscript form, word-outline form, and sentence-outline form. Your choice of a final format will depend on your familiarity with the topic, the pattern of discourse you are using, the format you feel most comfortable with, the amount of temptation you feel to read the speech, and instructions from your speech teacher.

You will find that different speeches require different formats. Personal speeches, speeches that you have given time and again, or speeches that you have practiced to the point of memory will each succeed with a different format. In fact, the same speech, if given a few times, may require progressively fewer notes in the final format. Consider variables such as topic complexity, length of speech, familiarity with and type of topic, and your sense of ease about the speech situation. Having done so, choose the format that allows you to be the most natural and spontaneous.

Manuscript Form

A manuscript form, a final format in which the speech is written out entirely, is useful when you need to give a very long speech, a highly technical speech, or a speech with which you are quite unfamiliar. For normal-length classroom speeches the manuscript format is not recommended. Remember, the manuscript must not become a crutch, a place to hide your eyes and face, or an excuse for avoiding interaction with the audience. Even if you are using a manuscript, you must deliver the speech as if it were largely spontaneous. If you become aware of the pitfalls to which manuscripts are prone, and you practice enough to avoid them, a manuscript final format may be the right choice for you. Success in public speaking is not so much a variable of final format as of how one works with the final format and the audience.

In the following model speech, a problem-solution analysis intended to move the audience, the speaker produced a complete manuscript from her outline but then moved away from it during the speech as the situation demanded. Thus, she was sure to have all her words down as she wanted them, but was also aware enough of the audience to react and adjust to them as the situation progressed.

DRINKING AND DRIVING:
THE NATIONAL NIGHTMARE CONTINUES

Introduction: Gets audience interested.

I would like you to clear your mind of other thoughts for a minute and picture, if you will, the entire freshman and sophomore class here at the university—all six thousand of us—assembled on the lawn outside the student union. Imagine that someone snaps a finger and all of us disappear, never to be seen again—this quickly [snaps finger].

Gesture gains attention.

Speaker uses startling statistic to preview topic through background.

Each year approximately six thousand teenagers like you and me die—not from disease, not from suicide, not from crime. No! The teens about whom I speak die for another reason: we'll call it "personal irresponsibility." They die in automobile accidents caused by drunk driving.

Speaker establishes credibility with audience.

I have to be honest with you at the outset. I have driven while under the influence of alcohol, and I look back and thank God that I am still alive. Like many of you listening to me now, I know the problem firsthand. As we all know, the drinking age has been a center of controversy for quite some time. Raising the drinking age seems to be the typical knee-jerk reaction that politicians make to any problem. But simply raising the drinking age is not enough.

Thesis statement: Suggests pattern of discourse, problem analysis, and purpose of speech—to move the audience to act.

The problem of drinking and driving is a complex one to analyze, and it requires a variety of solutions, some of which I want to urge you to support.

Body: Speaker establishes dimensions of problem with statistics and comparisons.

The dimensions of this problem are staggering. According to the U.S. Department of Transportation, although teenagers number only 8 percent of the total driving population, they number over 15 percent of the casualties in alcohol-related accidents. A recent issue of *Ladies Home*

Journal notes that one in three high school students rides in a car driven by a heavy drinker at least once a month, and that 23 percent of all high school students drink in their cars. More teenagers die each year in drinking-related automobile accidents than die of health and medical problems.

Style: Speaker states sources of data.

Speaker supports existence of problem by example.

Statistics such as these are starkly revealing, but listening only to numbers can actually numb us to the real pain of losing a brother, sister, or loved one. The numbers I offer you, no matter how many times I repeat them, cannot convey the reality of broken bodies, burned flesh, grief-stricken families, or the pain and guilt of survivors. Statistics cannot change the fact that death by alcohol is an unnecessary waste of human potential.

Consider the following example of five teenage girls from the Boston area whose tragic end is outlined in the *Ladies Home Journal* in this way:

"It began innocently enough. They had told their parents they were going to a movie. As their Volkswagen rounded a curve on the highway, rock music blasting from the tape deck, it suddenly swerved across the double line and plowed into an Oldsmobile. When rescuers were finally able to pry the wreckage apart, only one of the girls could be saved.

Style: Speaker quotes directly from article, but reads with eyes focused on the audience as much as on the manuscript.

"Soon afterward, investigators revealed what they had found: bottles of vodka, brandy, and beer amid shards of glass and twisted steel at the accident site; the driver's license of one girl's twenty-one-year-old sister, which had been used as identification to buy liquor; and enough alcohol in the blood of the dead girls to classify them all as legally drunk. Indeed, the blood alcohol level of the girl who was driving was a staggering 47 percent, a level medical examiners likened to surgical anesthesia."

Style: Notice how the speaker translates statistics for the audience. This aids comprehension.

Can you imagine the sorrow these families must live with for the rest of their lives? According to an article in 1984 in *Seventeen* magazine, statistics show that on a typical Friday or Saturday night, when alcohol consumption is at its peak, fully 10 percent of all the drivers out there are legally intoxicated. That means that one out of every ten cars becomes a weapon to the other nine. With statistics and personal tragedies such as those I have outlined here, it is no wonder that *Time* magazine in a recent essay called drunk driving a "national epidemic."

By the way, I am focusing on teens and drunk driving, but we are not the only ones to blame. Alcohol abuse at the wheel covers every age group. The reason I am specifically pointing out teens and alcohol is that

Style: Speaker makes a digression from development of the problem to build relevance into the speech for this audience.

most of us are in the category, and also because teenagers are more likely to be maimed or killed when mixing drinking and driving. The main reason for this is what anthropologists call "youthful risk-taking behavior." This effect is seen mostly in teenage boys, and it refers to their trying to test their limits and prove they are "cool." They take out dad's car, have a few beers, and show everyone that they can handle it—that they are cool. Well, youthful risk-taking behavior has become a national risk to all of us.

Style: Speaker makes a transition from problem *to* solution.

You can see by now that alcohol abuse and driving is a crisis—what we need are solutions to combat this problem, and I would like to discuss solutions that I think are most effective.

Body: A Solution 1—raise the drinking age.

As I mentioned before, raising the drinking age is not the only solution, and for many of us who are still teens it seems like a punishment instead of a solution to a problem. But, I must reluctantly support legislation to raise the drinking age to twenty-one as one part of the solution, since studies have shown that it works. At the present time, Senator Claiborne Pell has sponsored a bill in the United States Senate to require a national drinking age of twenty-one. The bill would require states to raise their drinking age to twenty-one or lose 10 percent of their federal highway-construction funds. Pell said that the Presidential Commission on Drunk Driving found that 739 fewer deaths per year would result from passage of such a law. To quote Pell, "The American people are sick to death with the drunk driver and want to see the slaughter on our highways ended once and for all." I think we should all support this bill.

Style: Direct quotations add credibility and literacy to a speech.

Body: B Solution 2— education programs and stiffer penalties.

Recently, parents have formed groups to combat the drunk-driving problem. MADD, Mothers Against Drunk Driving, was started in 1980 when Cari Lightner, a fourteen-year-old girl, was struck and killed by a drunk driver. Mrs. Candy Lightner was shocked to see the leniency of vehicular homicide laws and the lack of public knowledge about how such cases are prosecuted. She then formed MADD to pursue stiffer criminal-sentencing statutes, and to help educate the public about this problem. Since then, other groups such as SADD, Students Against Drunk Driving, and RID, Remove Intoxicated Drivers, have launched public-awareness programs of their own. SADD has brought parents and their children together to talk openly about their problem and to sign agreements that the parents will pick up their child if he or she calls home while intoxicated, with no questions asked. The National Traffic Safety Administration in Washington is happy to provide education and advice to any group interested in this problem. I will give you their address following this speech.

Style: Facts are plentiful and accurate, thus adding to quality of speech.

This combination of raising the drinking age, public awareness, and stiffer penalties for drunk driving will do much to solve this problem, but the ultimate solution is for each one of us to accept the personal responsibility not to drink and drive and to stop others from so doing. Car pool if you have to, but make sure there is always a sober driver. If the driver is drunk, call a taxi or walk, but do not get into the car. If you are able, take the keys away from a drunk driver. Any one of us might save a life tonight if we will stop someone from driving while he or she is drunk.

Body: C Solution 3—personal responsibility.

I have detailed the problem for you and presented a number of solutions. I am hoping that with your help we can lessen the number of deaths from six thousand per year to four thousand or maybe even two thousand. To further motivate you to get involved in this problem, let me close by reading to you from a speech by Kevin Tunnel, who was involved in an alcohol-related accident in 1981. He was driving home drunk and came around a sharp curve at 50 MPH, hitting a car head-on. The girl he killed in that accident went to a school nearby; she and Kevin had never met before that night. Kevin's license was revoked and he was placed on probation until he was twenty-one. His sentence was one that many people felt was not severe enough. It wasn't a jail sentence but one that would last him the rest of his life. He was sentenced to one year of giving speeches about his accident. Many people felt he didn't get what he deserved, but maybe Kevin can relate to more teens out there and stop more of them from drinking and driving. Here is an excerpt from his speech:

Conclusion: Returns to the introduction to add completeness.

"There's a national emergency in the United States today and not many of you are willing to admit it. The problem is drunk driving. And I challenge the youth of America to do something about it. Twenty-six thousand people die each year because of drunk driving. That's two hundred people each day, one every twenty-two minutes. It scares me to think that one out of every two of you will be involved in an alcohol-related accident sometime in your life. You don't think it will happen to you—I didn't think it would happen to me. I was a drunk driver; I caused one of those twenty-six thousand deaths. You see, on the night of December 31, 1981, I thought I could handle it. If I could see Susan now there is so much I would say to her. In essence, it would all come down to, 'I'm so sorry—I really didn't go out looking for you that night.' "

Style: Speaker uses a quotation to capture the essence of the speech and leave audience with a memorable idea.

When speaking from a manuscript, you must follow certain guidelines. Look carefully at the following suggestions to help you avoid the pitfall of manuscript speaking: getting buried in the text.

1. *Cue the manuscript.* Go over the manuscript with a colored marker in hand. Underline words you want to emphasize, make notes to yourself to use a particular gesture or to refer to a visual aid. Let's look at how our speaker on drinking and driving might have marked one paragraph of her speech:

> *The dimensions of this problem are staggering [shaded yellow]. According to the U.S. Department of Transportation [refer to visual], although teenagers number only 8 percent of the total driving population, they number over 15 percent of the casualties in alcohol-related accidents. A recent issue of* Ladies Home Journal *[hold up] notes that [emphasize] one in three high school students rides in a car driven by a heavy drinker at least once a month, and that 23 percent [emphasize] of all high school students drink in their cars. More teenagers die each year in drinking-related automobile accidents than die of health and medical problems [pause].*

2. *Triple-space the manuscript.* Type the manuscript on hard bond paper in triple space to allow room for cues and for ease of reading. Do not write or print the manuscript in your own hand, and do not cue the manuscript with the same script or font used to produce it. You do not want to lose your place or read your cues; following the triple-space guideline will help you move smoothly through your manuscript.

3. *Use your index finger as a guide to reading.* Place your index finger under the words as you read them to help you keep your place. As you gain experience you will be able to read a line or so ahead of your actual place in the manuscript, in which case you can place your index finger ahead, at the beginning of the next statement.

4. *Keep your focus on the audience.* Even though you are reading, you must make eye contact with the audience and gesture with your free hand. Also, you must use vocal pauses and emphases that suggest oral communication. Chapter 8 will be of particular value to you in following this guideline. As long as you remember that you are presenting a *speech*, not an *essay*, you will be on the right track.

5. *Be prepared to move away from your manuscript.* If the audience reacts to something you say, react to them rather than simply continuing to read. If a good example or a personal experience comes into mind as you read, add it to the speech spontaneously. Though you must avoid overdoing the digressions, you need to adjust to the speech event as it occurs. You may want to read the section on ad-libbing, pp. 166–169, now.

Professional speakers sometimes use a manuscript that is printed by means of a keyboard onto a teleprompter, a glass screen that is positioned in front of the speaker so that he or she can read the speech as it scrolls. Television news-reporters most often are reading from such a prompter. You will probably not have access to a teleprompter for speeches in the classroom setting, but you should be aware that they exist should you find yourself in a situation where a long speech, a highly technical speech, or a carefully time-controlled speech such as a television editorial comment mandates a special aid such as a teleprompter.

Word-Outline Form

The second final format for a speech is a word outline. In a word outline key terms are recorded on note cards that trigger your memory. Use as many words as you need, but not so many that your note cards are cluttered. Word outlines are excellent for allowing you to focus on the audience and, if you have practiced giving the speech enough times, to sound truly spontaneous. But word outlines require as much practice as manuscript outlines, especially for topics that are complex. Most professional speakers prefer a word outline, especially if they have given the speech several times or if they have adequate visual aids to help them move through their material.

Put your word outline on a sheet of heavy stock paper or on three-by-five or five-by-seven-inch cards, so that your notes will not crumple as you refer to them. The model note cards on the following pages show how the speech on drinking and driving might have appeared in a word-outline format.

To use word outlines successfully, the speaker must follow certain guidelines. Let's review those guidelines here.

1. *Use visual aids.* The most common problem with a word outline is forgetting material. Visual aids are also memory aids because they contain information the speaker wants to communicate. Use visual aids to help you present all the information you have.

2. *Keep the note cards inconspicuous.* It is distracting to an audience to hear note cards being shuffled or to see them being turned. Some awareness of a speaker's cards is acceptable—for instance, if a speaker takes a card or two with him or her to the visual aid being used—but too much reference to the cards can reduce the speaker's effectiveness.

3. *Don't use the outline as note cards.* There is a temptation, usually precipitated by time considerations, to simply cut up an outline

Divide the note cards according to some logical system, such as the main points of the speech.

1

INTRODUCTION

--6,000--entire fresh. and soph. class gone

--"Personal Irresponsibility"

--I have driven while drunk

--Not speech on raising DA

Place thesis statement on separate card so it cannot be missed. See card 2.

Use abbreviations for familiar terms. See card 2, for instance.

2

THESIS

D and D a complex problem to analyze with a variety of solutions.

Use only necessary words to cue you to key point.

3

THE PROBLEM--STATS.   *emphasize*

1. Teens 8% of drivers/15% of casualties

2. 1 of 3 teens drives with heavy drinkers

3. 23% drink in cars

4. More teens die in cars than from health/medical problems

4

THE PROBLEM--EXAMPLE

--Stats. are not enough

--Broken bodies, grief-stricken families,
  guilt of survivors

(read example from LHJ)

hold up copy for audience

5

"It began innocently enough. They told
their parents they were going to a movie.
As their Volkswagen rounded a curve on the
highway, rock music blasting from the tape
deck, it suddenly swerved across the
double line and plowed into an Oldsmobile.
When rescuers were finally able to pry the
wreckage apart, only one of the girls
could be saved.
    Soon afterward, investigators
revealed what they had found: bottles of
vodka, brandy, and beer amid shards of
glass and twisted steel at the accident
site; the driver's license of one girl's

6

twenty-one year old sister, which had
been used as identification to buy
liquor; and enough alcohol in the blood of
the dead girls to classify them all as
legally drunk. Indeed, the blood alcohol
level of the girl who was driving was a
staggering 47%, a level medical examiners
likened to surgical anesthesia."

Add cues to yourself in colored ink, as shown in cards 3, 4, 11, and 13.

Number the cards in case they get dropped or shuffled.

Talk spontaneously about the data; add information such as source and date. Add interesting anecdotes as they occur to you.

Direct quotations should be typed on note cards and read word for word in the interest of accuracy. See cards 5 and 6.

7

THE PROBLEM--MAGNITUDE

1. Friday and Sat. night, 10% intoxicated

2. Time Mag. quote--"National epidemic"

Read the direct quotations with enthusiasm and with maximum eye contact with audience.

8

THE PROBLEM--NOT JUST TEENS

1. Focus on teens--most likely to die

2. "Youthful Risk Taking"

3. Being cool--national problem

Turn the cards over or place them on the bottom of the stack as you finish.

9

THE SOLUTION

1. Raise the drinking age

2. Pell bill--21 or lose 10%

(read Pell quote)

```
                    10

PELL QUOTE
"The American people are sick to death
with the drunk driver and want to see the
slaughter on our highways ended once and
for all."
```

Some speakers use a blue card for direct quotations and white cards for other information.

```
                    11

SOLUTION--EDUCATION AND AWARENESS   state
                                    full name
1.   MADD--Lightner, 1980           of each
                                    group
2.   SADD

3.   RID

4.   Nat. Traffic Safety Admin.
     (put address on board)
```

Do not tap the cards on speaker's stand or in any other way allow them to become a distraction.

Notice that the speaker has made a last-minute note on card 11 in pencil. Do this when necessary.

```
                    12

SOLUTION--PERSONAL RESPONSIBILITY

1.   Don't do it!

2.   Stop others

3.   Call a friend or a taxi

4.   Take keys away

5.   Walk
```

Do not be afraid of the pause required to look at each card. It seems longer to you than to the audience.

13

CONCLUSION

1. Lower from 6,000 to 2,000
2. Kevin Tunnel story *slow down, emphasize*
(read Tunnel quote)

14

TUNNEL QUOTE

"There's a national emergency in the United States today and not many of you are willing to admit it. The problem is drunk driving. And I challenge the youth of America to do something about it. 26,000 people die each year because of drunk driving. That's 200 people each day, one every twenty-two minutes. It scares me to think that one out of every two of you will be involved in an alcohol related accident sometime in your life.

Vivid or emotional quotations such as the one used in this conclusion require extra practice to capture the feelings behind them.

15

You don't think it will happen to you-- I didn't think it would happen to me. I was a drunk driver; I caused one of the 26,000 deaths. You see, on the night of December 31, 1981, I thought I could handle it. If I could see Susan now there is so much I would say to her. In essence, it would all come down to, 'I'm so sorry--I really didn't go out looking for you that night.'"

into note-card size. Doing so is not a substitute for making up a word outline on standard note cards.

Sentence-Outline Form

Many speakers feel most comfortable with a sentence outline. A sentence outline is often organized in the classical deductive style already shown in Chapter 5, pp. 115–119. The main points in sentence outlines begin with Roman numerals; the various levels of subpoints begin with capital letters, arabic numbers, small letters, and so on. Each new level used is indented in relation to the previous level. Sentence outlines have almost as much information as a manuscript and much more than a word outline. Thus, they can be used for speeches of any type or level of complexity.

As with any final format, the sentence outline can become a crutch for the speaker if he or she simply reads from it. So long as the speaker is focused on the audience, a sentence outline is a valuable aid. Let us look at the speech on drinking and driving as it might have appeared in sentence-outline form.

Topic: Drinking and Driving: The National Nightmare Continues

Introduction

I. Clear your mind and picture the entire freshman and sophomore class—six thousand people—assembled on the lawn in front of the union. Someone snaps a finger [snap finger] and we are all gone.

II. Each year approximately six thousand teens die almost as suddenly.
   A. They do not die from disease, suicide, or crime.
   B. They die from "personal irresponsibility"—from auto accidents caused by drunk driving.

III. I have driven while drunk and thank God I am alive.

IV. I am not here just to make a pitch for raising the drinking age, but to look at the entire problem.

Thesis

I. The problem of drinking and driving is a complex one to analyze, and it requires a variety of solutions, some of which I want to urge you to support today.

Body: The Problem

I. The dimensions of the problem are staggering [statistics].
   A. Only 8 percent of drivers are teens, but 15 percent of the casualties are teens.
   B. The *Ladies Home Journal* states that one in three high school students rides in a car driven by a heavy drinker.
   C. Twenty-three percent of all high school students drink in their cars.
   D. More teens die each year from auto accidents than from health and medical problems.

II. Statistics do not tell the real story of suffering, pain, and guilt suffered by family members and survivors.
   A. Statistics cannot change the fact that death from an alcohol-related auto accident is an unnecessary and tragic waste of human potential.
   B. Consider the following example from *LHJ* about five teenage Boston girls:

   [read quote from *LHJ*]
   C. Imagine the suffering these families must live with.
   D. According to *Seventeen* magazine, on a Friday or Saturday night fully 10 percent of all the drivers out there are legally intoxicated.
   E. *Time* magazine has called drunk driving a "national epidemic."

III. This is not only a teenage problem.
   A. But most of us in the audience are in that category.
   B. Teenagers are the most likely ones to be maimed or killed.
   C. The main reason for this is what anthropologists call "youthful risk taking."
      1. Teen boys try to drink and then test their limits.
      2. Teen boys try to prove they are cool.
   D. Youthful risk taking has become a national risk to all of us.

Body: Solutions

I. Raise the national drinking age to twenty-one.
   A. Senator Claiborne Pell has sponsored a bill to raise the drinking age to twenty-one.
   B. States not passing the bill would lose 10 percent of their federal highway-construction funds.
   C. Read Pell quotation.

II. Form or join a group concerned with education, awareness, and fair punishment.

   A. MADD was organized by Mrs. Candy Lightner after her daughter Cari was killed by a drunk driver who was then given a light sentence. Mrs. Lightner tries to change vehicular homicide laws and educate the public about drunk driving and the law.

   B. SADD is a student group concerned with getting other teens to vow not to drink and drive. SADD gets students together with parents to talk about problem and to sign an agreement that if the student has been drinking, he or she can call the parent for a ride home with no punishment the following day.

   C. RID has about the same goals as SADD, except that RID works to keep drunk drivers off the road.

   D. The National Traffic Safety Commission can provide education and advice to any group. I will put their address on board.

III. Each of us has a personal responsibility.

   A. Car pool when going out, and be sure there is a sober driver.

   B. Stop others from driving while drunk—take their keys if necessary.

   C. Call a taxi or walk if you are drunk.

   D. Do not get into a car with a drunk driver.

Conclusion

  I. I want to get that death rate down from six thousand to two thousand.

  II. To motivate you, I want to tell you the story of Kevin Tunnel and then read from a speech he delivered to a group of teens.

Speech instructors often require the sentence outline, and many will ask that speakers turn in a version of the sentence outline on the day the speech is to be given. For this reason alone, the sentence-outline format shown here should be studied carefully. Following certain guidelines for speaking with a sentence outline will assure greater success. Let's look at these guidelines.

   1. *Cue the outline.* Just as with the manuscript and word outlines, a sentence outline can be marked with notes to the speaker.

Simply use a colored-ink pen to note directions on the outline, as in the following excerpt:

Solutions [emphasize]

Look at audience

  I. Raise the national drinking age to *twenty-one.*
     A. Sen. Claiborne Pell has sponsored a bill to raise the drinking age to *twenty-one* [emphasize].
     B. States not passing the bill would lose 10 percent of their federal highway-construction funds.
     C. [Read Pell quote.]

Outline cues can pertain to gestures, tones, visual aids, or anything the speaker needs to be more fluent.

2. Use the outline to speak, not to read. A full-sentence outline can become a temptation. Resist the impulse to read from the outline by preparing visual aids, cueing yourself with notes to "look at audience," and practicing.

Part II of this text will present many speech models, all of them in sentence-outline format. The sentence-outline format is used because it is the best format for demonstrating all the principles and techniques of each pattern of discourse. You should, however, use the final format that meets your needs or the particular objectives your instructor has in mind for the assignment.

Visual Aids: Preparation and Presentation

Visual aids are an effective way to display information. When used properly, visual material aids audience comprehension, adds color to the speech, serves the speaker as a sort of enlarged note card, and, in some cases, helps reduce speech anxiety. Since the advantages of using visual material far outweigh the disadvantages, it's a good idea to consider using aids each time you compose a speech.

Like anything that seems so good, however, visual aids can detract from an otherwise effective speech if not prepared and presented properly. In this section we will look at a variety of visual materials most often used in the speech-communication classroom, give some examples of successful visuals, and discuss the advantages and disadvantages of each.

Charts

Unless a computer can be used to render the visual, a chart is usually presented on a poster board large enough to be seen by all those in the audience. Charts are used for three purposes: to simplify complex data, to list the steps in a process, and to present key words that you want the audience to remember. Figure 6.1 shows a chart listing the key ethnic groups of Yugoslavia. The chart was used in a speech on the 1984 Olympics. Because the speaker listed each ethnic group on the chart, the audience was able to keep unfamiliar names in mind as the speech progressed. Figure 6.2 shows a chart used to enhance comprehension of the steps in a process.

Charts are relatively easy to prepare if you use poster board and take pains to be neat. They are also easy to transport to the classroom and easy to use in the speech itself. Be sure to have necessary display materials with you, such as tape and tacks, since charts can slip and fall unless properly displayed. All things considered, charts are many speakers' first choice for visual aids.

Graphs

Although computer-assisted graphs are used quite often today, graphs, like charts, can be effectively prepared on poster board. A graph is

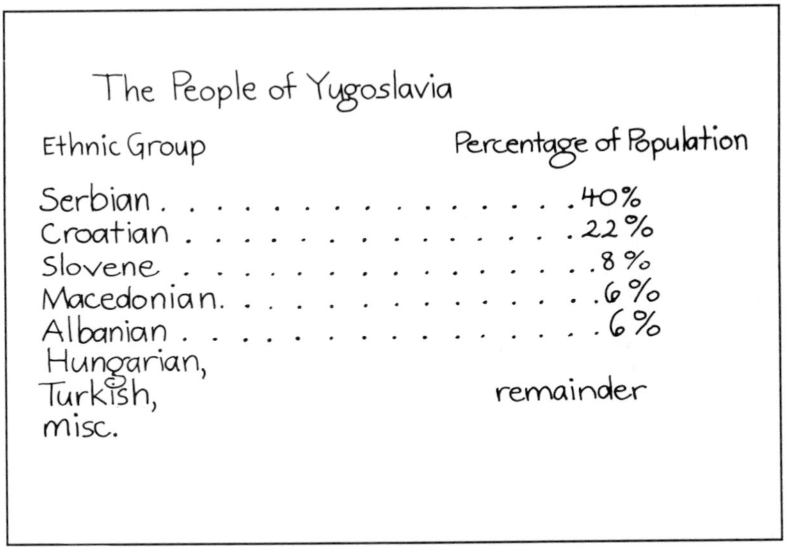

The People of Yugoslavia

Ethnic Group	Percentage of Population
Serbian	40%
Croatian	22%
Slovene	8%
Macedonian	6%
Albanian	6%
Hungarian, Turkish, misc.	remainder

Figure 6.1.
Key ethnic groups in Yugoslavia.

Running for Elected Office

1. Contact party officials.
2. Call potential volunteers.
3. Find a campaign manager.
4. Develop economic and political strategies.
5. Check laws governing filing and running.
6. File nomination papers.
7. Declare candidacy to public.

Figure 6.2
Steps in the process of running for office.

often used to display numerical supporting material. If the data reveal distribution, or percentages of some whole, a pie graph is an effective way to display the information. Figure 6.3 shows a pie graph of truancy in the New York schools. Notice how it aids comprehension by showing relationships among the percentages.

If you are preparing a pie graph to show a breakdown of percentages, start by tracing a circle and then dividing it into one hundred equal segments. Then, simply count the number of segments needed to show the percentages. Pie graphs can be shaded and color-coded to highlight features or provide secondary data.

Bar graphs or line graphs are usually used to show interrelationships among data. Figure 6.4, which shows starting salaries for college graduates over a period of eight years, was used in a speech on the decline of teaching as a career. Notice how clearly this decline is indicated by comparing salaries in teaching to those in other careers such as engineering.

When preparing and using graphs, consider the advantages and disadvantages of doing so. Graph preparation requires a bit of skill in the mechanical arts. On the other hand, graphs provide the audience with a comprehensive way to absorb a great amount of detail, and they provide the speaker with a handy source of information.

Maps

Maps are used to show geographical relationships. The maps that appear in *National Geographic* magazine are useful for many speeches.

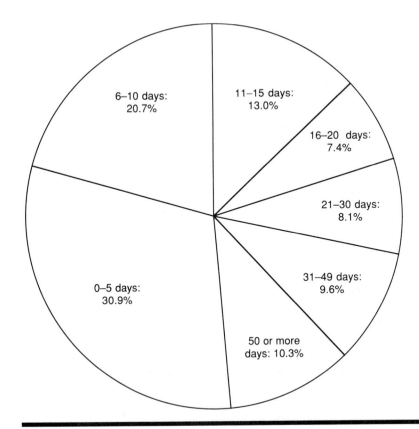

Figure 6.3
Truancy in New York High Schools during a Ninety-Day Semester, 1982. (From *The Wilson Quarterly,* New Year's 1984. Copyright 1984 by The Woodrow Wilson International Center for Scholars. Used by permission.)

Quite often, however, it is necessary to trace the map and then provide the supporting material on the traced version. Simply displaying a map is often not sufficient, since the detail will not be clear.

When using maps, be sure that the lettering is large enough for the audience to read. A map can be distracting if audience members have to strain to read or see it. Also, when showing a map, consider using a pointer of some kind so that the geographical relationships are visible while you are working with the aid.

Models and Exhibits

Models often make excellent visual aids. They can be used to demonstrate a process, exemplify a hobby or a collection, show a fin-

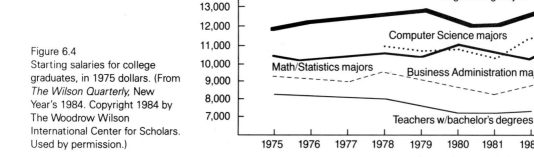

Figure 6.4
Starting salaries for college graduates, in 1975 dollars. (From *The Wilson Quarterly*, New Year's 1984. Copyright 1984 by The Woodrow Wilson International Center for Scholars. Used by permission.)

ished product, and so on. Models and exhibits can add a dimension of realism to a speech. Obviously, a real fan is more revealing than a drawing of one. Be careful, however, when using models or exhibits. First, if the model is to be borrowed, be certain that it will be available when you need it. Second, be sure that your model or exhibit can be brought to and presented in the room where you are speaking. Third, take special precautions with live exhibits such as animals: count on the unexpected happening and have a good line ready for when it does. Finally, be sure that the exhibit will not produce loud noises or in any other way distract other classes. Careful rehearsal with a model or an exhibit is a must, but once you feel comfortable and competent, models and exhibits can add color and variety to your speech.

The Chalkboard

Teachers and lecturers use a chalkboard to highlight key words and phrases. This is the only use of a chalkboard that we recommend for a speech. Writing on a chalkboard is not easy, and some who do it regularly never quite get the hang of it. If you should choose or need to do it, follow these guidelines. First, be sure that you have a piece of chalk. Second, if possible, put your material on the board before the speech and cover the board if desired. Third, work from left to right, as you would when writing on paper. And finally, write legibly and large enough for easy comprehension by the audience. Your instructor may want you to avoid chalkboard visuals, so check with him or her beforehand.

Handouts

Handouts are used in a speech to reinforce information, and may include photographs, pamphlets, and samples, among other things. In one speech, for instance, the speaker handed out a three-by-eight-inch card with the credo of Alcoholics Anonymous printed on it, plus information about joining the organization. Handouts are best given out after the speech, so they do not distract the audience during the speech. Occasionally, if a demonstration is involved, such as in a speech on paper folding, handouts must be given out during the speech. Caution must be exercised in such situations, however, so that the focus of the speech remains the speaker-message-audience interaction.

Audiovisual Aids

Audiovisual aids include such items as slides, overhead projections, and recordings. Such visuals are best avoided if possible, since they often require lighting or nonlighting that is not possible in the room, they often break down, and they require much rehearsal. If you decide to use them, be sure that there is an electrical outlet and that you have brought along an extension cord should you need one.

Using Yourself as a Visual Aid

A speech situation may arise in which you want or need to use yourself as a demonstrator. One speaker, for instance, recently spoke about fundamental differences among various martial arts, using himself to show certain positions and movements characteristic of each form. Using yourself as a visual aid is not recommended, since it is difficult to be both speaker and demonstrator at the same time. Should you decide to use yourself, however, follow these guidelines. First, be sure you can do what you intend. One student recently used himself to show juggling techniques, but because he was nervous he could not do the juggling he had planned and his speech lost much of its impact. Second, practice the demonstration as you practice your speech. Be sure you have timed the demonstration to synchronize with the text of the speech.

Computer Graphics

In recent years, computers have been developed for transforming lengthy texts and vast amounts of numerical data into easily digestible visual aids.[2] Pictorial as well as graphic material can be produced quickly and cheaply in a matter of minutes, for about one-tenth the cost of artist-produced visuals. Most commonly used today by businesses and government agencies, computer graphics are likely to be a common tool for students in the near future. Because computers can render many of the visual aids shown in this section, and because so many students in a speech-communication course may own or have access to computerized graphic hardware, it will be helpful to look at the equipment and the capabilities of computer-rendered graphics technology.

Computer-graphic hardware is being developed so rapidly that no text can keep up with it. The equipment ranges from the personal, typewriter-sized pen writer that produces bar, line, and pie graphs, to the huge, corporate-sized systems like the AVL Starburst computer package capable of the complete range of visuals. A typical system would include a sixteen-bit microprocessor, disk drives, a color monitor, a keyboard, a film recorder, a digitizing board for drawing, and software programs. Among the programs commonly used today are the Lotus 1-2-3 and the IBM Storyboard.

Computer-graphic equipment can produce pie, bar, and line graphs, logos, symbols, and maps. In addition, graphic computers can produce black-and-white slides, 35-mm color slides, and color prints. Some systems offer up to sixteen million colors and high-resolution film recorders. Other programs allow for free-form art, text formatting, and three-dimensional video presentations. With the press of a key, a bar graph may be transformed into a line graph or a pie graph. In short, computer-graphics equipment is available to produce virtually any type of aid one might need for a public speech.

In addition to producing graphics, hardware is available to project graphics from the computer monitor onto a large screen for viewing by others. With projection equipment, the speaker can simply locate the visual where it is stored on the disk, at which point the visual appears on the monitor while being simultaneously projected onto the large screen for the audience. Today, such equipment is usually found in the most sophisticated boardrooms, but in the near future we can expect visual-projection equipment to be available to students.

Most computer-graphic equipment is easy to use. A software program is loaded into the computer and may be accessed with a keyboard, a pointer, or a "mouse" (a small, rectangular box). The user may give commands to the computer or respond to choices, called "prompts," that appear on the screen in either visual or symbol form. For instance, a prompt may appear on the screen offering the user a choice of six pictures; the user simply chooses the picture most appropriate to his or her visual and the computer presents it on the screen, ready to be printed out or added onto.

There is no limit to future developments in the area of computer graphics. As of this writing, computer graphics are a new phenomenon, but we can expect them to dominate in the professional world of tomorrow. Though learning to use computer-graphic equipment is helpful in the speech-communication classroom today, it may be even more helpful in preparing one for the world of tomorrow.

Guidelines for Using Visual Aids

Regardless of the kind of visual aids you use, observe the following guidelines. Doing so will greatly enhance your use of visual aids in the speech-communication classroom and in later situations.

1. *Do not let the visual aid overwhelm you and your message.* A visual aid is just that: an aid. Shocking, illegal, or otherwise distracting aids will often produce an effect opposite to the one you intended and will shift attention away from you, the speaker. Similarly, visuals that are not synchronized carefully into the flow of the speech are a distraction. An important component of speech rehearsal should be practicing with the visual aids that you will use in the speech.

2. *Keep your focus on the audience.* When using your visuals, make as much audience contact as possible. Turning your back on the audience for too long a period of time can be distracting. The best way to use a visual that is behind you is to stand at an angle between the aid and the audience and to address the audience as you use the aid.

3. *Display visuals so that all can see them.* If some members of the audience have to crane to see your visuals, this will distract them from the speech. If you are using such visuals as models on a table, you may need to arrange the speaker's area of the room so that all can see.

When used properly, visual aids add color and meaning to a speech. With every speech, you should consider whether a visual will serve your purpose. Ask your instructor about special provisions he or she might have for the use of visual aids in your speech-communication classroom.

There are many ways to expand upon a speech topic. In this chapter we have focused on five common ways to support an idea: facts, opinions, examples, comparisons, and numerical data. When used appropriately, each form of support adds validity, color, and concreteness to the idea.

As any successful coach will tell you, practice is what shows up in the performance. This maxim is no less true in public speaking: practice is what shows up at the speaker's stand. Let's look at a system for practicing a speech.

Practicing the Speech

There are many ways to practice a speech. How one goes about it is more a matter of individual style than of a set of rules. Here, for instance, is what one exceptional student wrote about practice in her self-evaluation for a course in speech communication:

> When I practice speeches, usually about three days before they are due, I begin by reading my manuscript aloud. Next, I try to deliver the speech without the manuscript or my note cards. At this point, I have researched the speech twice. I now prepare my final outline and note cards.
>
> Once my note cards are set up, I set everything aside until the day of the speech. On the assignment date, in order to refresh my memory, I re-read the manuscript. Then I place the note cards on a table, look at the clock, and begin to practice.
>
> While practicing, I have found it helpful to stand in front of a mirror or to move around the room, or to do busywork like making my bed.
>
> My last rehearsal is always on my way to class. As I drive to class I practice the speech aloud. By now, I have begun to feel quite comfortable.

Practicing a speech may not follow a pattern such as the one this student has developed, but you should adopt a routine of your own. Following are practice techniques that have worked for student and professional speakers.

Reciting the Speech Aloud

Recitation is probably the most common practice technique. Take your note cards, outline, or manuscript and recite from them aloud as you walk around your room, an empty classroom, or any place where you feel comfortable. Speakers have been known to practice in front of mirrors, in front of friends who volunteered, in shower rooms, on park benches, and in closets. You will feel awkward listening to yourself, but each time you go through the material you will feel more comfortable with it.

Each time you read or recite the speech, use your notes less. See how many words, key ideas, and supporting materials you can recall each time you go over the material. Make notes on your manuscript, outline, or note cards as you practice.

Practicing with a Tape Recorder

This routine is the same as the previous technique, except that once you have taped the speech, you can listen to it and evaluate it on your own. After you have made notes about the taped speech, tape it again and listen to the first and second versions. Each time you tape, polish the speech, time it, and deliver it with fewer notes. You will notice yourself becoming a bit more fluent each time you go through the routine of taping and listening.

Practicing by Yourself

Many speakers practice a speech throughout the day as they go about their normal routines. You may be grocery shopping, working at a job, or walking from one place to another and at the same time practicing your speech. You'll be surprised at the results.

How do you know when you have rehearsed enough? Many speakers believe they have practiced enough when they can deliver the entire speech while focusing on the audience. That is, when they feel they can react to the audience's reactions to what they are saying, the speech is ready. Try your speech out on a friend, and ask that friend to give you a number of unusual nonverbal cues. When you can react to these cues and not lose your place, the speech is ready.

We have placed a great deal of emphasis on practice because classroom speakers often neglect it. In order to reach the point of spontaneity, you often need to go through stages during which you and your speech are like strangers getting to know one another: awkward moments, stumbling speech, and clumsy gestures. Once you have worked through these initial fumbling moments, you are ready to move to an advanced technique of effective public speaking that we shall call *ad-libbing*.

Rescripting the Speech: The Art of Ad-Libbing

We mentioned earlier that an essay is completely written out (scripted), so that it is in final form when it is read. A speech may be written out or not, depending upon conditions noted earlier in this chapter. Regardless of the final format chosen, however, the key to successful speaking is to appear spontaneous. A speech that sounds memorized or canned will surely draw mixed to poor reactions. Practicing a speech until you feel comfortable enough with it to react to the audience is the first step. The question is, how do you react? Effective speakers know how to ad-lib their way through a speech. Let's discuss this a bit more fully.

A speech-communication professor, William S. Howell, conducted a survey of people who did a great deal of public speaking.[3] He asked these speakers if they ever found themselves saying things they did not plan to say. All answered that they did. He then asked the speakers if they found themselves doing more or less of this as the years went by; all replied, "More." Finally, Howell asked the speakers how they felt about these unplanned comments. All responded that they were the best part of the speech.

Student speakers say the same thing in their self-evaluation papers. Here is a sampling:

In the actual presentation of a speech I do not always follow my notes. I may have written out note cards to follow, but if I feel that the audience is slipping away from me, I will try some clever example or story to win back their attention.

Ad-libbed statements have always worked for me. An unexpected comment gives a speech a less formal and more relaxed sound.

I found that once I had my manuscript and notes in front of me I wouldn't follow them but would just talk my way through.

*If I saw that the audience was getting restless, I would try to
throw in an interesting bit of information that I didn't plan on
until that moment.*

Almost all good speakers learn to work away from their notes and
manuscripts when the situation requires. Sometimes a humorous
aside shows spontaneity, as in the following:

*The science of raising laboratory animals has reached
advanced stages. Two scientists in England recently developed
a machine that milks mice and collects the milk in a sterile
environment for research purposes. [laughter from the audience, followed by this unprepared remark] The worst part, the
scientist said, was getting up so early in the morning.*

React to the audience. If the audience looks puzzled or startled
by a statement or a piece of data, react to their nonverbal signals by
going back over the information or stating it in another way. They
will appreciate your concern, and you will appear less "canned."

React to your speech. If you are speaking and something comes
to mind—a story, perhaps—break away from your notes and use it.
Once again, you will add an element of spontaneity to your speech.

Of course, like anything good, too much ad-libbing can become
a problem. Most commonly, drifting too often and too far away from
prepared remarks causes a time problem and can also cause needless digressions from the main body of the speech.

As you practice your material, try to ad-lib once or twice during
the speech. Time the speech so that you can tell whether your ad-
libs are causing trouble for you in terms of your timing.

Another common problem with ad-libbing is failure. A joke that
sounded funny the first time you heard it can bomb in its new
context. Also, you can find yourself stuck for words if the ad-lib is
really spontaneous. To return for a moment to the notion of cueing
yourself, whether on a manuscript or note cards, you may want to
have a few "prepared" ad-libs to meet special circumstance. For
example, you might write "Add own experience with X if time permits," or "Tell John Tyler story." You won't write these ad-libs out,
of course, but you should know them well enough to present them
without stumbling, so include them in your rehearsal time.

Ad-libbing is an advanced technique of public speaking. With
practice and with close attention to the guidelines presented here,
you will find that this creative form of rescripting is the best way to
achieve that naturalness essential to success in public speaking.

Summary

The goal of every public speaker is to sound spontaneous. To achieve this goal, one must have an effective final format and rehearse adequately. This chapter has examined three final formats: the manuscript, the word outline, and the sentence outline. In addition, we discussed the preparation and use of visual aids in the presentation of the speech, and presented systematic advice on practicing the speech.

Speaking from a manuscript is appropriate in special situations, such as in very long or highly technical speeches. But for normal-length classroom speeches the manuscript format is not recommended, since it is often a temptation to avoid audience contact. If you find the manuscript format appropriate for your situation, you should prepare a triple-spaced, cued text that you can read as though you were talking the speech. Also, be prepared to adjust spontaneously as the situation requires.

A word outline includes key terms or phrases that trigger the speech. Word outlines are usually placed on three-by-five or five-by-seven-inch cards for delivery to an audience. When using a word outline, consider using visual aids, keep the note cards inconspicuous, and avoid reading from them.

Many speakers feel comfortable with the sentence-outline format, which uses numerals and letters to code key statements to be made in the speech. The sentence outline works well if the speaker cues the outline with notes about delivery and avoids reading from it.

Visual aids are a valuable addition to a public speech, and the speaker should consider them on every occasion. Visuals add color to a speech and can lead to increased audience comprehension. Most importantly, however, they help the speaker achieve spontaneity.

Visual aids come in many forms. In this chapter we reviewed the advantages and disadvantages of using the following visuals: charts, graphs, maps, models and exhibits, chalkboards, handouts, and electronic aids. In addition, we considered recent developments in computer-assisted graphics, discussing their present capabilities and their promise for the future. Finally, we presented guidelines for using visuals during the speech.

Practice is critical to success in public speaking. Although no hard-and-fast rules govern the process, one can follow certain guidelines in rehearsing a speech. In this chapter we covered three rehearsal techniques: reciting the speech, practicing with a tape recorder, and practicing silently by yourself. We also learned about the art of ad-libbing—of adjusting spontaneously to the speech as it occurs.

If you follow the principles and guidelines suggested here, you will learn techniques and information that will serve you well throughout your life. We turn our attention now to language, looking for knowledge and techniques with which to put the finishing touches on our speech.

1. The following exercise works well as a warm-up in a speech-communication classroom. Look for a letter to the editor or an editorial that you find moving, humorous, shocking, or thought-provoking. Practice reading the letter or editorial while following the guidelines given in this chapter. You should even mark up the letter or editorial with cues to yourself, or type the letter/editorial onto a triple-spaced manuscript. Bring your selection to class and read it as though you were the author. Try to concentrate on the audience, make gestures, and read as though you were speaking. This can be done in small groups or in front of the class.

2. You can use part of exercise 1 for the following exercise. Practice reciting your letter and then tape-record it. Bring your tape to class and play it to a group of classmates. The group should comment on the spontaneity and naturalness of your sound. Follow up on this classroom session by recording the selection again on the same tape and evaluating, either in writing or in a class discussion, the differences you notice between the two tape recordings.

3. Look at Figure 6.1, a chart showing the various ethnic groups in Yugoslavia. Convert that chart to a bar graph and then to a pie graph. Discuss with others in the class any differences you see in the three formats. Does any one format have advantages over any other? State which type of visual you prefer and the reasons for your preference.

1. David Halberstam, *The Powers That Be* (NY: Alfred Knopf, 1979), p. 16.

2. Peggy Salfon, "Doing Business Graphically," *American Way,* October 29, 1985, p. 61.

3. William S. Howell, *The Empathic Communicator* (Belmont, CA: Wadsworth Publishing Co., 1982), p. 220.

Chapter 7 · Using Language
in Public Communication

The story of words is the story of human civilization itself. In fact, according to Thomas Pyles, author of *The Origin and Development of the English Language*, "We may be fairly sure that our ancestors were making use of the complicated and highly systemized set of vocal sounds that go to make up language when the wooly-haired rhinoceros and the mammoth roamed the earth."[1] As you have probably learned in history class, oral language predated written language by centuries. The human manipulation of sounds into words continues to be a subject of fascination and speculation, and one of the oldest debates about language has centered on the question of whether language shapes reality or whether reality shapes language.[2]

Whatever the answer to this question, the words we choose and the way we arrange those words mark not only our uniqueness as a species but also our individuality within that species. We form our first impressions of others when we take in their physical appearance, but our second, and sometimes more lasting, impression of others occurs when they begin to speak—to put together words intended to convey meaning, to put together "language."

A language may be defined as an organized set of symbols with both stated and unstated rules governing their use. A symbol is defined as something that stands for something else. In this chapter we are particularly concerned with speech symbols—words—since they are the stock-in-trade of the public speaker.

One note of caution as you begin this chapter: public speakers have a special problem when it comes to using words. Since a public speech is a formal situation, the public speaker is expected to use speech that is clear and correct, with even a touch of the literary. The public speaker must develop a style that keeps the audience involved and adds force to the idea. At the same time, however, she or he must appear natural and spontaneous rather than pretentious and rehearsed. Thus, wording a public speech is largely a matter of individual taste, of each person finding that line between the too formal and the too casual, between stuffy and sloppy.

We develop effective speech over the course of a lifetime. Understanding words and using them correctly requires continual attention. The educated person searches for new words, seeks new shades of meaning in familiar words, and checks that his or her speech is correct and appropriate. Improving our facility with words is a full-time concern, one to which each of us must commit ourselves.

In each chapter in Part II of this text you will find a discussion of style and language problems related to the pattern examined in that particular chapter. The present chapter is intended to infuse you with a bit of "logomania," a healthy preoccupation with words and how they are used. The chapter is organized according to three qualities of effective speech: clarity, accuracy and appropriateness, and vividness. As you read each section, ask yourself how you can use language to present your ideas as eloquently and thoughtfully as possible.

Clarity

Above all else, a speaker must be clear. You may be thinking, "Well, of course a speaker should be clear." Clarity may seem too obvious a quality of effective speaking to mention; however, clarity is not always easy to achieve. Sometimes, without realizing it, you may choose words that have one meaning for you and another for your audience. Or, you may slip in a cliché so overused it has no meaning. At other times, you might even misuse a word or expression. All of these common errors interfere with the clarity of your speech and impede understanding between you and your audience. The audience ends up with only a fuzzy notion of what you had in mind when you composed the speech, or worse yet, a total misunderstanding of your message.

How can you maximize the clarity of your speech and minimize misunderstanding? None of us can be positive we are clear all the time, but there are some impediments to clarity we can try to avoid and some positive measures we can take. The following sections will help you in your efforts to be as clear as possible when you speak publicly.

The Denotation-Connotation Distinction

One impediment to clarity is inherent in the nature of language: with the exception of articles, prepositions, and conjunctions, a language contains very few neutral words. "Neutral words" are words on whose definition everyone agrees, words like *tree* or *table* or *animal*—most concrete nouns. Neutral words, as a rule, do not cause your listener to respond emotionally to what you are saying.

In public speaking, however, many of your topics will center around words or phrases that do provoke emotional responses in your audience, words like *arms race* or *alcoholism* or *environmental protection*. There is nothing wrong with provoking emotional responses in your audience—that's part of what public speaking is about—

---

but you want to be sure it's the response you intended. When dealing with emotionally charged topics, then, it is especially important to be aware of the difference between the denotative and connotative meanings of a word.

The denotative meaning of a word is its dictionary definition, its actual meaning content. But the connotative meaning of a word involves the associations we bring to a word as a result of personal experience. With some words, the connotative meanings cling to the word so strongly that they may override the original, denotative meaning. Take the word *discrimination*, for example. For most people, this word connotes injustice. A person who discriminates is a bigot. Yet the original, innocent meaning of *discrimination* is "the quality or power of making fine distinctions." Since the 1950s, however, Americans have viewed *discrimination* in only the negative sense of making distinctions against something—a race, a nationality, a religious group. It has lost its original, more neutral meaning.

You want to ensure that your audience will not lose the meaning you intend because of their own associations or connotations of the term. You can't guarantee complete agreement, but you can minimize misunderstandings by defining potentially unclear terms throughout your speech. By doing so you won't run as great a risk of misinterpretation. Suppose, for example, you were talking about child abuse. It would be embarrassing to finish a speech and have someone say something like this: "I thought your topic was 'abuse.' I didn't hear you say anything about beating children or locking them in closets for hours or days. Your emphasis is on things parents *don't* do. To me, abuse means physical assault—that's what I see as the problem of child abuse."

At that point, you as the speaker would need to explain that you were concerned only with emotional abuse in your speech, with the issue of parents withholding affection from children as a means of punishment. Your reaction would be that the audience member who asked the question wasn't very smart if he or she couldn't figure out what you were talking about. But both you and your audience member must share equally the blame for the misunderstanding. You failed because you neglected to define, or "denote," the way in which you intended to use the word *abuse*, and the audience member blocked your intended meaning of the word because his or her own connotations of the word were stronger.

A classic illustration of a denotation-connotation problem concerns the Department of Defense, which until the end of World War II was called the War Department. The name "War Department" was intended to denote that this agency of the government was the military agency, the one that went to war when war arose. But the suggested, or connotative, meanings attached to the word *war*, such as "imperialist," "aggressor," and "conqueror" led political leaders to change the name to Department of Defense, a name with fewer negative connotations, and one that suggested responding to war rather than making it. Today, this agency has the same mission as before World War II, but the way this mission is captured in the name "Defense Department" has changed (and has been the subject of criticism by those who feel the name is misleading).

The following list of words shows even more clearly how connotations change the intended meaning of a word.

Denotation	*Connotations*
Slim: of small diameter in proportion to height	Scanty, small, adroit, crafty
Slender: spare in frame or flesh	Gracefully slight
Skinny: lacking sufficient flesh	Emaciated

In this example, the words *slim, slender,* and *skinny* have approximately the same denotation; their connotations, however, are quite different, ranging from the positive "graceful" to the negative "emaciated." Other examples abound: a leader of a political party is referred to as a "statesperson" by supporters and a "boss" by opponents; loyalty to one's country can be called "patriotism" or "chauvinism,"

Although *Webster's Third English Dictionary* lists about 450,000 words, the complete English vocabulary consists of close to one million words according to Mario Pei. The average person's vocabulary contains between 35,000 and 70,000 words, not bad given estimates that Shakespeare himself used only between 16,000 and 25,000 words in all of his literary works. Most of us, however, get along quite well with about 1,000 workable words. In fact, the telephone company estimates that the average telephone conversation rarely exceeds a vocabulary of 750 words.

Mario Pei
The Story of Language

---

depending upon one's intent. Clarity in the use of words requires us to understand not only the dictionary meanings of words, but the effects our words have on others.

Abstract Versus Concrete Language

We can use language abstractly or concretely. One student began his narrative this way: "Traffic was terrible this morning. It ruined my day." Later, the same student explained the situation to his instructor like this:

> *What a day I had! There was an overturned tractor trailer spread across three lanes of traffic on the interstate. There I was, sailing along, singing with the radio and wondering what this line of stopped cars in front of me meant. The worst part is that I had a calculus exam scheduled for eight this morning. And . . . my professor feels that we should always factor emergency time into commuting, so she wasn't too sympathetic about my making up the exam.*

This second description would have been a more effective way to begin the speech because it provides a concrete mental picture for the audience. When your purpose as a speaker is to create understanding and possibly empathy in your audience, use language that is concrete, words that will help your audience form a mental picture like the one of the traffic tie-up. Sometimes beginning speakers confuse concreteness with descriptiveness, and unfortunately, many people equate being descriptive with using a long string of adjectives. Instead, make your nouns and verbs do the work. If you choose precise nouns and verbs, you needn't dress them up with excessive adjectives and adverbs. In fact, language scholar S. I. Hayakawa developed the "abstraction ladder" as a series of nouns, each more specific than the next.[3] As you can see in Figure 7.1, the words become more and more abstract as you go up the ladder.

In the following examples, notice that while some concreteness develops from the addition of qualifying words, most of it derives from a more precise choice of nouns, noun phrases, and verbs.

Abstract	*Concrete*
They could really put *a stop to* serious crimes by *coming*	Criminal-court judges could reduce violent crimes such as

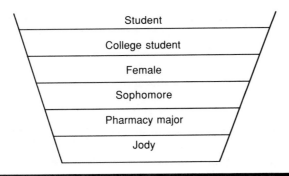

Figure 7.1
The abstraction ladder.

down hard on offenders the first time. It'd be a *lesson* to anyone else and would keep crime out of the minds of other *punks.*

murder, rape, and armed assault by applying their legislated right to deny bail and impose mandatory sentences on first offenders. Denying bail would put more criminals behind bars, while stiff mandatory sentences would serve as a warning from the bench to potential offenders.

Officials have been unable to account for the sudden surge in the *market.*

Eliot Janeway, noted economist and stock-market analyst, could not account for the surge in the Dow-Jones stock averages from 1210 to 1265 during the previous thirty-day period.

The narrower the reference you give, the more specific the meaning. Also, the more concrete the words you choose, the less chance that your audience's connotation of a word will overpower what you mean. Thus, concreteness helps solve the denotation-connotation problem discussed earlier. In some situations general terms serve a purpose—for instance, when they are used to introduce a topic and are later qualified. Also, we often need more words to be concrete; this does not create wordiness, however, if clarity is enhanced.

The Active Voice

Most statements follow an active form:

subject———verb———object

or

Agent————Action————Goal

Clear speaking involves using this active form most of the time.[4] We can modify the (subject-verb-object) form with adjectives, adverbs, qualifying phrases, and clauses, but the core of our statement should most often follow the S-V-O form, since it is the one audiences most easily comprehend.

Statements based upon the S-V-O form are said to be in the active voice. That is, the agent does something—the action. The goal of the statement is the object of attention: that which the agent changes, attends to, or influences through the action:

Agent	Action	Goal
Congress	passed	bill

This statement can be developed more fully:

> *A reluctant Congress, wary of public opinion, passed a tax-cut bill providing those who face reelection with a popular campaign issue.*

In this example, the statement is developed not by altering its basic structure but by modifying the structure with other parts of speech. The statement remains "active" because the agent still performs the basic action leading to the goal.

Too often, the basic structure of a statement is altered to make it seem more sophisticated, most often by reversing the goal and the agent:

Goal	Action	Agent
Bill	was passed	Congress

When a speaker makes this common alteration the statement is said to be in the passive voice. The passive voice is sometimes acceptable. It can be used to emphasize the object or goal rather than the subject or agent, or to lend variety to statements. Generally speaking, however, the active voice is clearer and more economical. The passive voice, when used improperly or too often, can cause confusion. Look at the following example:

Inflation has been blamed by voters on excessive union wage demands.

Who is doing what to whom is unclear in this passage. The subject of the statement, voters, is lost in the first prepositional phrase. Moreover, the goal of the statement is unclear. In the active voice the speaker would have said this:

Voters blame inflation on unions' excessive wage demands.

In the active voice the statement is shorter and clearer. Often we use the passive voice to evade stating the agent, either because we don't know who the agent is or because we want to avoid assigning responsibility for the action. For example,

A final report was never issued, causing the action to be tabled for lack of information.

Who failed to issue the final report? In cases where your audience needs to know who is responsible for an action, use the active voice.

Nominalizations

One of the most common undesirable qualities in a speech, especially a technical or bureaucratic speech, is stuffiness.[5] More often than not, a speech becomes stuffy through nominalizing. A nominalization is a noun made out of a verb or an adjective. Here are some common examples:

Word	*Nominalization*
use (v)	implementation
react (v)	reaction
determine (v)	determination
careless (adj)	carelessness
equitable (adj)	equitability

Nominalizations muddy up a statement by inverting the basic S-V-O form:

A presidential announcement was made to the American people indicating that carelessness in congressional spending would lead to even greater deficits.

In this statement, the president is actually announcing—he is the agent performing the action. But by inverting the natural order of spoken English, the speaker confuses the matter to the point where the audience cannot be certain who actually made the announcement or who was careless about spending. Here is the statement worded more clearly:

The president announced to the American people that careless spending by the Congress would lead to even greater deficits.

Nominalizations are usually wordy and cause confusion. Whenever possible, use verbs and adjectives rather than noun forms.

Pompous Diction

We have all heard the police officer who, when interviewed on the news, speaks of "perpetrators" and "correctional facilities," rather than simply "criminals" and "prisons." Recently, the Internal Revenue Service announced that Yuppies are a group of people who have "a relatively high values-based predisposition to noncompliant

---

The Story of Language tells us that English is a borrowed language, taking words from neighbors and conquerors, friends and foes alike. The original basis of English is Anglo-Saxon, a language of the Germanic or Teutonic branch of Indo-European. Yet, only 40 percent of the English spoken today is of Anglo-Saxon origin. The rest of the words are borrowed.

Mario Pei
The Story of Language

---

behavior." Of course, the IRS meant that yuppies like to cheat on their taxes—the language used is simply a pompous way to say it.

We tend to choose the "big" word over the familiar one, and in formal speaking situations that tendency often overrules our common sense. But pompous diction, the use of words strictly for impression, usually leads to confusion rather than clarity. Following is a list of favorite pompous words. See whether you can find a better term for each:

perpetrator	contingent upon	actuate
interface	subsequent to	determinative of
facilitate	ubiquitous	contemporaneous

Of course, this kind of language has a proper place, and you do want to expand your vocabulary. The point is, you should speak within your own style, using a vocabulary that you feel comfortable with and that your audience can easily understand. You don't need a thesaurus to do so.

Accuracy

Accuracy is another major quality of effective speech. Closely related to clarity, accuracy in speech leads the audience most directly to your meaning. Accuracy may hinge on the simple act of looking up a word in a dictionary or on an ethical decision by a speaker. In this section, we will look at three common problems speakers face in the search for accuracy.

Word Choice

The most common cause of inaccuracy is choosing the wrong word. Most words have shades of meaning, and while we might intend one meaning, another can result. To give you an example of how carefully we must choose our words, let's look at a list of terms that are related and yet distinct, terms speakers often misuse:

empathy———pity———sympathy

prototype———archetype———stereotype

prejudice———discrimination———bias

cooperate———collaborate———conspire

law———ordinance———statute

Distinguish the meanings among the words in each set. If you look up the words in a dictionary, you will find that each term is related to yet distinct from the other. It is a good idea to know the finer meanings of words we use regularly.

Inaccuracy is also caused by using words incorrectly. Here is a short list of words that speakers frequently misuse:

Very unique, most unique, absolutely unique	*Unique* means "one of a kind." It cannot be qualified by terms such as *very*.
Irregardless	There is no such word. The proper word is *regardless*.
Imply/infer	*Imply* is what the speaker does; *infer* is what the listener does.
Revert/revert back	*Revert* means literally "to turn back." Therefore, to say "revert back" is redundant. Choose either *go back* or *revert*, but not both.
The suffix *-wise*	Speechwise, the suffix *-wise* is meaningless. Don't use it.
The suffix *-ize*	Instead of saying "finalize," say "finish." Instead of "prioritize," say "rank."
120 percent	Sometimes a speaker will go as high as 1000 percent to characterize the amount of drive and hustle someone has given, but anything over 100 percent is usually overkill.
Oriented	Often confused with *orientated* (which actually means facing to the East), *oriented* means intellectually acquainted with something.

Loaded Words

A special category of the connotation problem discussed earlier is the use of loaded words, words that trigger an emotional reaction or otherwise bias the statement. Some words are obviously loaded, as in the following statement:

> Betty Friedan, noted radical feminist of the turbulent sixties, has now entered a matriarchal phase in her thinking about male-female relationships.

In addition, many words are only subtly loaded, as in the following:

> Larry Sigler, a former Nixon lieutenant, is now once again working his way through the Republican machine to a position of prominence.

Notice in the last example that the appositive, "a former Nixon lieutenant," loads the reputation of Mr. Sigler with numerous negative attributes. The use of *machine* rather than *party* also adds a touch of aggression to the phrase. Such language is loaded, even if not obviously so.

In the following list, notice how a neutral, objective term can be loaded to elicit a favorable or unfavorable reaction.

Favorable	Neutral	Unfavorable
spokesperson	party leader	political boss
patriot	citizen	chauvinist
reserved	quiet	boring
reason	persuade	manipulate
up-to-date	contemporary	faddish

Loaded words are a form of inaccuracy, and it is important to be as objectively accurate as possible. A word is loaded only when it purposely misleads the audience about a topic; when a word accurately captures a quality (there *are* fads, bosses, and manipulators in the world) the use is not loaded, and your intent is honest. Remember, though, whenever you choose to use loaded words, you risk a greater chance of a connotation problem than usual.

Slang and Colloquial Speech

The term *vernacular*, in its broadest sense, refers to the everyday language use of a particular culture or region, a use that differs in vocabulary and syntax from the accepted literary or "prestige" form of the language. For example, British people refer to the prestige dialect of their language as "the King's English." Americans call theirs "network standard." If you have studied foreign languages, you have probably heard of "Castilian Spanish" or "Parisian French."

Sometimes people who grow up speaking a nonstandard form or dialect of their language work hard at losing all traces of their vernacular; in their quest for economic success and social respectability, they perceive the prestige dialect as a more powerful tool. But while it is true that the standard form of a language is required much of the time in formal speaking, ability to use the vernacular of a region is also an accomplishment.

The best speakers gauge their audience and try to use an appropriate mix of both prestige and vernacular forms. Most occasions require that the speaker sound neither stuffy nor uneducated. Overuse of the literary form often produces stuffiness; total reliance on the vernacular may connote sloppiness and cause the audience to question the speaker's qualifications. Developing sensitivity to the language of those you are addressing and broadening your own linguistic range are important aspects of being a successful public speaker.

Language does change. Over a long period of time and usage, the once unacceptable becomes acceptable. There was a time, for example, when teachers pointed out to their students that "*ain't* ain't in the dictionary." But when *Webster's International Dictionary* appeared in 1961, teachers lost their base of support for correcting this particular error. Formal speech begins with vernacular speech, and today's household words were yesterday's jargon. Slang goes and comes, but it is useful to recognize what it is and how it differs from colloquial speech.

SLANG.   Slang is often defined as substandard speech: the speech of subgroups or of the street. In fact, the word *slang* comes from the phrase *thieves language,* later shortened to *slang.* Carl Sandburg, the poet and biographer, said, "Slang is language which takes off its coat, spits on its hands, and goes to work."[6] Slang can be words or phrases coined to express new meanings or to show membership in a group. Slang expressions abound when a movement or a fad becomes popular or controversial. Thus, the women's movement has given us terms such as *male chauvinist pig,* the anti-nuclear power movement terms such as *nuclear holocaust,* and the civil rights movement terms such as *oreo.* The following are recent slang expressions.

Safety net	What catches people who lose financial aid because of federal cutbacks
Yuppies	Young urban professionals
Stagflation	Inflation caused by a stagnating economy
Whacked	An organized-crime word for *assassinated*

Use slang terms carefully. Since they are often new, and often peculiar to one group, they can be confusing and inaccurate. Like loaded words, slang increases the number of connotations your audience may assign to your words, thereby increasing the risk of misinterpretations. On the other hand, when used consciously and cautiously, slang can add color to a speech.

COLLOQUIAL SPEECH. Related to slang, colloquial speech employs expressions that are acceptable in ordinary conversation but that may strike the public-speech audience as too "chatty" or casual. Colloquial terms or expressions are often synonyms, such as *dad* for *father,* *guy* for *man,* or *lousy* for *inferior.* Here is an example of colloquial speech:

> *Some of* Reagan's buddies *urged him to choose cabinet members who were not just political* hacks *but who had* busted their humps *to become qualified for these top posts.*

Colloquial expressions are not always in poor taste, and like slang, they can add color to a speech. To say that someone "got her act together" may be colloquial, but it can also add the right emphasis to a speech when used strategically. In fact, while we have cautioned

Some notes from *The Joy of Lex*: The word *no* is the first word spoken by over 50 percent of the population in the English-speaking world. In conversation, the word *I* is the most frequently used word. The longest English word in the *Oxford English Dictionary* has twenty-nine letters, *floccinaucinihilipilification.*

Giles Bandreth
The Joy of Lex

that slang expressions may be inaccurate, there are times when either slang expressions or colloquialisms may convey your meaning more precisely than their counterparts in standard language.

Sexist Language

Language is sexist when it arbitrarily assigns roles or characteristics to people on the basis of sex.[7] The words we choose when we speak, often on the basis of habit or tradition, may suggest a bias toward the male sex or a stereotype of either sex that limits the horizons of members of that sex. For example, words such as *fireman* and *man-made* suggest that only males appropriately fit the role or the behavior the term indicates. It is more appropriate to use neutral terms such as *firefighter* or *synthetic* whenever possible. We need to be aware of sexism in language and adopt speech conventions that help to overcome it. In order to become sensitive to sexism in language, let us look at some common errors.

OMISSIONS OF WOMEN. The most common category of sexist language, omission of women, concerns words such as those listed above: *policeman, mankind, best man for the job,* and so on. Avoid these masculine markers by using alternatives such as *police officer, humanity,* and *best worker.* For every sexist term there is usually a sensible alternative, one that avoids absurd expressions like *person-hole cover* and *personhood.*

PARALLEL TERMS. Instead of referring to occupations with male and female markers, use alternatives. For instance, rather than referring to stewards and stewardesses, use *flight attendant;* or instead of *salesman* use *sales representative.* Once again, you need not choose absurd alternatives: reasonable alternatives can always be found.

USING THE GENERIC HE. Because English has no common sex pronoun, it has been traditional to use *he* to refer to neutral nouns. Thus, "Each student should bring *his* paper to class." Using the term *he* in all cases is subtly exclusionary to women and should be avoided. (Say "*Students* should bring *their* papers to class.") In written language, it has become customary to use *his or her* or some such convention to resolve the problem. In oral speech, it is correct to use the *his or her* alternative or the plural pronouns *they* and *their* to deal with the problem.

DEMEANING WOMEN.   Men and women should be treated equally and consistently when they are described, whether the description involves appearance, marital status, or titles. For example, it is incorrect to refer to men as "lawyers" and women as "lady lawyers," or to use descriptive terms such as the ones in this sentence: "Two representatives were chosen to represent the State of Montana: Bill Lindgren, a savvy political veteran; and Mary Walsh, an alluring blonde housewife."

PATRONIZING OR TRIVIALIZING WOMEN.   In a similar manner to terms demeaning women, some terms and phrases patronize or trivialize women. Examples would be *the girls in the office* rather than *the secretaries,* or *an old wives' tale* to refer to a superstitious belief. Avoid stereotypical expressions such as *libber* or *coed* when referring to women. Use nonsexist terms such as *feminist* or *female student* as substitutes.

EXAMPLES.   Use women as well as men as examples in speeches. If you need an historical example to show the bravery of early Americans, mention a woman as well as a man. Men and women are equally capable of experiencing the complete range of emotions and they are capable of the same sorts of actions: show your awareness of this in your use of instances and examples.

Since we are all becoming more aware of language in this course, we should become aware of the fact that while language describes reality, it can also shape that reality. We can elevate or demoralize with our speech, and our purpose should be to improve the condition of everyone through our use of symbols.

There was a time, not long ago, when a great distance separated speaker and audience. It was considered proper for the speaker's language level to be well above that of the audience. The prestige

Vividness

form of the language was more than acceptable; it was expected. Speakers were, after all, "educated people," and most of the "common folk" were not. This was the Age of Oratory in America, a period that reached its zenith in the second half of the nineteenth century, when public speaking was a high and celebrated art form.[8]

The orator and oratory were once the central attraction of holiday gatherings and other festive occasions. When a famous orator, a Daniel Webster or an Edward Everett or a Carrie Nation, was in town, local citizens would often parade to the speaker's hotel balcony demanding "a few words of wisdom." As torches blazed deep into the night the crowd would listen, often for hours, to the speaker's spellbinding words.

Like television today, public speaking was at one time a dominant form of entertainment. But more than television is today, oratory was once the premier vehicle for the expression of shared cultural values.[9] Through oratory the public speaker reinforced the moral and spiritual principles of the time and transformed individual listeners into a group with shared sentiments. The old oratory spread itself out, was spacious enough to appeal to all members of the audience. Look at this excerpt from a speech by Daniel Webster (1782–1852), the person many consider the greatest orator in American history. In the speech, given in 1802 but only discovered in manuscript form in 1882, Webster is addressing a Fourth of July audience of local townspeople in Fryeburg, Maine. In this excerpt Webster focuses on the meaning of the U.S. Constitution. The terms in the margin refer to specific techniques Webster uses, elements of style that will be explained in this section.

Metaphor

Rhythm: short/long sentences

Parallelism built on the word what

Rhetorical question

Parallel phrase built on the words "for the"

The American Constitution is the purchase of American valor. It is the rich prize that rewards the toil of eight years of war and of blood: and what is all the pomp and military glory, what are the victories, what are the Armies subdued, fleets captured, colors taken, unless they end in the establishment of wise laws—and national happiness? Our revolution is not more renowned for the brilliancy of its scenes than for the benefit of its consequences.

Metaphor

Allusion to Greek Temple

Repetition

Repetition

The Constitution is the great memorial of the deeds of our ancestors. On the pillars and on the arches of that dome their names are written and their achievements recorded. While that lasts, while a single page or a single article can be found, it will carry down the record to future ages. It will teach mankind that glory, empty, tinkling glory, was not the object for which America fought. Great Britain had carried the fame of her arms far and wide. She had humbled France and Spain. She had reached her arms across the continent and given laws on the banks of the Ganges. A few scattered colonists did not rise up to contend with such a nation for mere renown. They had a nobler object, and in pursuit of that object, they manifested a courage, constancy, and union that deserve to be celebrated by poets and historians as long as language lasts.[10]

Metaphor

Alliteration

This passage may seem overdone—even archaic—yet if you take the time to read it aloud, you will probably find yourself admiring its sound and rhythm. But why dwell on this notion of oratory, an admittedly old-fashioned form of speaking?

Rhetoric is the study of the way ideas are brought to life and communicated to others. You might have a superb idea, but if you communicate the idea to others with enthusiastic tones and lively words, the idea itself has a better chance to succeed. This age-old truth is regaining favor, perhaps because the pendulum has swung away from the casual oratory of the 1970s, or perhaps because of the enthusiastic response given to firebrands of our day such as Jesse Jackson. Whatever the reason, "a ringing rhetoric," as columnist William Safire calls it, is back, not in its old-fashioned garb but in the cloak of contemporary times.[11]

In the old oratory we see most clearly the concept of vividness. As you can see from the Webster excerpt, the old oratory is filled with rhetorical techniques and figures of speech that give life to an idea. This section introduces and illustrates some of the more vivid rhetorical techniques so that you can learn to recognize and use them in your speaking.

Analogy

An analogy is a comparison of two things that, on the surface, may seem dissimilar. People skilled in expressing ideas extract common qualities from seemingly dissimilar entities and help their audience gain new perspectives. In fact, sometimes the more unlikely the two objects compared, the more vivid and memorable the analogy. Consider the following example:

I see nothing wrong with divorce. Married life, like a second glass of a rare wine, is not to be properly judged until one experiences it at least twice.

In outline form, the analogy shown above looks like this:

Married Life	is to	Divorce
	as	
Wine	is to	Second Glass

Of course, married life and good wine are not similar commodities to most people; a comparison, however, implies a common quality—in this case, improvement the second time.

If the belief expressed in an analogy captures the experience of the body of people addressed, if it creates in the audience a sensation of "Ah-ha, that's right," then the analogy is successful. Constructing analogies requires reasoning skill, since the most successful analogies require a near match of inherent qualities rather than of physical features. The outcome, however, is well worth the attempt.

Many speakers have used analogies to convey their point convincingly and colorfully. Here is just one example, from a speech by actor Alan Alda to the students of Drew University:

I think it is safe to say that a lot of you, maybe most of you, are going to experience this, the sentence "What's the purpose of all this?" is written in large letters over the mid-life crisis butcher shop. You can't miss it as you lug the carcass of your worldly success through the door to have it dressed and

It has been estimated that there are 2,796 different languages spoken in the world. Of these, only thirteen languages are spoken by fifty million people or more: Chinese, English, Hindustan, Russian, Spanish, German, Japanese, Arabic, Bengali, Portuguese, Malay (Indonesian), French, and Italian. As a native tongue, English is used in over one-fifth of the world. Chinese is the language most used by human beings, having approximately 800,000,000 speakers, compared to 450,000,000 speakers of English.

Mario Pei
The Story of Language

trimmed and placed in little plastic packages for people to admire. "What's the purpose of all this," you may ask yourself that next year or twenty years, but when you do, when you do think of that, at that moment you are going to remember what I am going to tell you now. This is getting good, isn't it? You thought I was just going to tell a bunch of jokes. Okay, it is this. It seems to me that your life will have meaning when you can give meaning to it, and only then, because no one else is going to give meaning to your life.[12]

Allusion

An allusion is an implied or indirect reference to something with which the audience is familiar; that is, an allusion is made without actually stating the reference. Some allusions are more obvious than others. If, for instance, a speaker were to say, "There should be no more Vietnams, no more Afghanistans, no more Cambodias; each of us must despise imperialism of any type," the speaker would be making an obvious reference to unpopular conflicts of recent times. An allusion can tantalize an audience into thinking about the original reference without actually stating it. John F. Kennedy once said, "If we cannot end now our differences, at least we can help make the world safe for diversity." In this allusion to a famous line from President Woodrow Wilson's declaration-of-war address to Congress in 1917, "The world must be made safe for democracy," Kennedy suggests America's willingness and resolve to fight not for one governmental philosophy but for the right of each country to determine its own form of government.

Closely related to the allusion is the representative example. This rhetorical technique takes a specific object with which audience members are familiar and makes it stand for a general condition. "Joe Six-Pack" is a common representative example often used to stand for all those supposedly average Americans who work hard for a living all day and then in the evening curl up to a good TV sitcom and a can of beer. In the following example, you can see how the representative example, presented as a simile, adds a stylish touch to a speech:

Before: Taking the family out to a fast-food restaurant for a hamburger and a soft drink has pretty much replaced the traditional Sunday dinner of roast beef and mashed potatoes.

After: Packing the family into the Chevy van and racing off for a Big Mac and a Coke may be as American today as Sunday roast beef and mashed potatoes was a generation ago.

The reference works if the audience is familiar with it.

Alliteration

Alliteration, a rhetorical technique involving the repetition of a sound, has probably been the most popular device of orators throughout history. During the 1984 Democratic Convention, candidate Jesse Jackson remarked, "My constituency is the damned, the disinherited, the disrespected, the despised." At that same convention, Governor Mario Cuomo spoke of "the lucky and the left out, the royalty and the rabble." If you listen carefully you will notice that alliteration adds rhythm and tone to a speech. It is not a difficult technique to use, and with a little practice you will be able to use it in your own speeches.

Parallelism

After alliteration, parallelism is probably the most common rhetorical technique speakers use. One form of parallelism involves the repetition of a key word or phrase to emphasize a point. It is frequently used in the conclusion of a speech, as in the following excerpt:

He found acting in the theater more inspiring than acting in the movies, and acting in the movies more inspiring than acting in television. What he never found inspiring, however, was acting for free.

Antithesis is another form of parallel structure, in which two thoughts are contrasted through a key word or phrase that serves as the connector. In a recent speech-communication class, a student summarized her speech on the need for a national health-care program in this way: "A person's health is not a privilege, it is a fundamental right." In this example the words *right* and *privilege* are contrasted to create the antithesis.

Creating parallel phrasing is relatively easy. Find a term or phrase in the idea you want to convey and repeat it in the same grammatical pattern. The parallel term can be the subject, the verb, or the object of the sentence. The statement is parallel if the key term or phrase is used in the same way throughout the statement. Like the successful analogy, the effective parallel phrase remains in the memories of the audience members for two reasons: first, the phrase itself is memorable because of its balance and its distinctiveness from ordinary sentence patterns; second, your use of rhetorical patterns marks you as a sophisticated user of language and therefore a more credible speaker. Use parallel phrases whenever you want to emphasize the essence of an idea or to illustrate how ideas work together.

Metaphor

The word *metaphor* comes from a Greek word meaning "to transfer." While analogies play upon the common quality in two dissimilar objects, a metaphor is a word or phrase that applies literally to one object but is used figuratively to give meaning to another. Like analogies, metaphors invite us to see an old or a too-familiar idea in a new way. By transferring meaning from one thing to another, we bring originality and vividness to our ideas. Metaphors are often convincing to an audience in the same way that analogies are—they help the audience "see" something that was perhaps too abstract for them to see clearly in a literal sense. Look at the following two ways to say the same thing:

Literal: A friend is someone you can demand be on your side, someone whose praise you can expect.

So creative is the English language that it is improbable that any twenty-word spoken sentence was ever uttered before, says Peter Farb. One linguist calculated that it would take 10,000,000,000,000 years (two thousand times the estimated age of the earth) to speak all the possible English sentences that use exactly twenty words.

Peter Farb
Word Play

Metaphorical: Always demand praise from friends. Seas of it. Crush honesty, prod gush. Always be a parasite on your friend's fund of adjectives.

The second version captures figuratively the acceptable demands placed on friends, adding a colorful, literary quality to the idea but also showing a playful, tongue-in-cheek tone suggesting that the author may be exaggerating just a trifle.

Semanticist I. A. Richards has given us two terms for understanding metaphor: *tenor* and *vehicle.*[13] The tenor is the thing being compared, and the vehicle is the term that does the comparing. In a metaphorical expression, the tenor is seen through the vehicle, as in this excerpt from a student speech:

There are two ways to slice the pie of human interaction. You can cut it into even pieces and try to please everyone by giving each an equal slice, or, you can cut each piece according to the appetite or wishes of the person being served. I prefer not to treat everyone the same way, but to adjust to each person as I encounter them.

In this metaphor, the image of a piece of pie helps the audience visualize the speaker's personal philosophy concerning interactions with others. Slicing a pie is the *vehicle* for communicating the more abstract concept of human interaction, which, in this metaphor, is the tenor or subject being spoken about.

Good metaphors are difficult to create. The philosopher Aristotle says in *The Rhetoric:* "By far the greatest thing is to be a master of metaphor. It is the one thing that cannot be learned from others. It is a sign of genius, for a good metaphor implies an intuitive perception of similarity among dissimilars."[14]

Because metaphors are hard to create, speakers often resort to using *dead* metaphors. A dead metaphor is one that has lost its vividness and the value of the meaning transfer, and has become a denotation for the object being symbolized; it has assumed a literal meaning. Metaphors such as *the bed of a river* or *bird's-eye view* now have exact, literal meanings, and as such have little value as metaphor.

Besides dead metaphors there are cliché metaphors, those that have been used too often to have much vividness left. How many times has a speaker discussed government as "the ship of state" and the president as "the captain"? Similarly, using the vocabulary of sports to talk about politics or personal affairs is also a bit trite:

We may be behind in the polls, but we still have a turn at bat and we plan to rally in the late innings and pull this election out.

I have made my final appeal to the board. As far as I am concerned, the ball is in their court.

As ineffective as dead metaphors and cliché metaphors are *mixed* metaphors. A mixed metaphor is one that uses two vehicles to give one tenor:

About all we can do is run the idea up the flagpole *and see* if it floats.

During his entire life Picasso struggled against the currents, *finally proving to the world that a man can withstand the* blows of society *and still* answer the final bell.

Besides being trite, both examples show confused language, and therefore, in the audience's mind, a confused speaker. In the second statement, for instance, the image of Picasso struggling upstream is a good one, but then the speaker switches to a new image, a boxer struggling to make the final round. As a result, the image is mixed and the result is confusion rather than colorfulness. Sometimes mixed metaphors are funny, but when humor is not the intended effect, the speaker only appears careless.

Simile

Similes, which are closely related to metaphors, create an immediate comparison between two objects, both of which are named. In a speech given at the Grand Ole Opry, commemorating the eighty-first birthday of singer Roy Acuff, Ronald Reagan noted, "My opponent's promises are like Minnie Pearl's hat: they both have a big price tag hanging from them."

Notice the use of the word *like* to connect the two objects. Similes usually use the words *like* or *as* to signify the comparison, and so are quickly recognizable by the audience. They require less time for an audience to process than do metaphors or analogies, but they are also less subtle. Similes are fairly easy to construct and can be very effective. However, we are sometimes tempted to overuse them because of the very ease of construction. Avoid relying on similes as your sole experiments with figurative language; try creating the more difficult metaphors and analogies as well.

The old oratory fell into disrepute because it overused figurative language at the expense of substance. What began as eloquence became mere ornamentation. Ideas were left behind in the rush for the quotable quote, the passionate phrase. The new oratory seeks a balance between ideas and the words used to communicate them. There is no reason that an idea cannot be communicated with style through rhetorical techniques such as those detailed in this section. But it is important to realize that figures of speech such as those we have just discussed cannot substitute for the substance of an idea.

Summary

Words form the history of human beings. Students of formal discourse must make a continuous effort to improve their understanding of words. Public speakers must know how to word a speech so that it appears both spontaneous and natural, and each one of us must find our own rhetorical style so that we can best express our ideas.

This chapter examined three qualities of effective speech. Clarity, the first quality, involves choosing words selectively and precisely. We discussed clarity in relation to denotation and connotation, abstract versus concrete language, active versus passive voice, nominalizations, and pompous diction.

A second quality of effective speech is accuracy, which involves leading the audience most correctly to the meaning intended. In the section devoted to accuracy we examined word choice, loaded language, and slang and colloquial speech.

A third quality of effective speech is vividness, which is best achieved through the use of rhetorical figures of speech and colorful, imaginative language to convey an idea. In our discussion of vividness we introduced some of the more commonly used stylistic techniques: analogy, allusion, alliteration, parallelism, metaphor, and simile.

Through careful attention to style, you can elevate a public speech to the status of an art form. The great orators, some of whom have shaped our nation, know the value of style. After reading this chapter you should know the difference between a plain speech and an oration.

A speech must flow out of your personality. Speech that strikes an audience as insincere, unrealistic, or pompous will surely cause problems for the speaker. Use this chapter as a reference point in composing your speech. Check to see whether your speech is clear, accurate, and vivid, as these qualities are defined and exemplified here.

1. Following is a list of neutral words. For each word list a synonym that gives the word a positive connotation and one that gives it a negative connotation. The first word is provided to give you an idea of how to do this exercise. Share your responses with others in a class discussion.

Positive	Neutral	Negative
individual rights	freedom	
	poor	
	homemade	
	rain	
	test	
	inebriated	
	anxious	
	attractive	
	different	
	house	

2. Rewrite the following statements so that the abstract words are more concrete.
   a. Campus security should be *more responsive* to student complaints.
   b. Recreation is *really* fun.
   c. Traveling in the South can be a *great way* to get away from the snows of winter.
   d. I think politicians should be more *up-front* with the public.
   e. When played correctly, rugby can be a *truly awesome* sport.

f. *Clothing* makes the person.

g. Things looked *pretty bad* for me as I faced the bull.

h. The stadium was *packed.*

3. Following is a list of prefixes and suffixes with their meanings. Try to list five words using each prefix and suffix.

Prefix	*Meaning*
retro-	back, backward
para-	near, resembling
micro-	small
macro-	large
contra-	against
Suffix	*Meaning*
-mania	exaggerated desire
-logy	science or study of
-phobia	fear of
-ous	possessing
-ize	to cause or to become

4. Read any of the speech models presented in Part II of this text, making a note of rhetorical figures the speaker uses. In a short essay, critique the speaker's use of language. Conclude the essay with your opinion concerning whether the speech meets acceptable standards for oratory.

References

1. Thomas Pyles, *The Origin and Development of the English Language,* 2d ed. (NY: Harcourt, Brace, Jovanovich, 1971), p. 1.

2. John B. Carroll, ed., *Language, Thought, and Reality: Related Writings of Benjamin Lee Whorf* (Cambridge, MA: MIT Press, 1956).

3. S. I. Hayakawa, *Language in Thought and Action,* 2d ed. (NY: Harcourt, Brace, and World, 1964).

4. Hans P. Guth, *New English Handbook*, 2d ed. (Belmont, CA: Wadsworth Publishing Co., 1985), pp. 165–166.

5. Joseph Williams, *Style: Ten Lessons in Clarity and Grace* (Glenview, IL: Scott, Foresman and Co., 1981), p. 12.

6. Richard Wolkomir, "Slipping the Mitten to a Catawamptious Wally: The Slang Gap Revisited," *Smithsonian*, March 1983, p. 96.

7. See, for example, Alleen Pace Nilsen, et al., *Sexism and Language* (Urbana, IL: National Council of Teachers of English, 1977).

8. See, for example, Frederick J. Antczak, *Thought and Character: The Rhetoric of Democratic Education* (Ames, IA: Iowa State University Press, 1986).

9. Richard Weaver, "The Spaciousness of Old Rhetoric," in *The Ethics of Rhetoric* (Chicago: Henry Regnery Co., 1953), pp. 164–186.

10. Daniel Webster, "American Government Unique," in *Modern Eloquence*, ed. Thomas B. Reed (Philadelphia: John D. Morris and Co., 1900), p. 1156.

11. William Safire, "Ringing Rhetoric: The Return of Political Oratory," *The New York Times Magazine*, August 19, 1984, p. 22.

12. Alan Alda, "Commencement Address at Drew University," in *Contemporary American Speeches*, ed. Will A. Linkugel, R. R. Allen, and Richard L. Johannsen (Dubuque: Kendall, Hunt Publishers, 1982), p. 146.

13. I. A. Richards, *The Philosophy of Rhetoric* (London: Oxford University Press, 1936), p. 99.

14. Aristotle, quoted in Williams, p. 156.

Chapter 8 · Delivering a Public Speech

Have you ever noticed how flawlessly newscasters, preachers, and politicians deliver their messages on television? Wouldn't we all like to sound like Dan Rather, Jesse Jackson, or Geraldine Ferraro? Of course, such professionals have practiced their craft for years, and that practice has borne fruit. Beyond practice, however, successful speakers have come to realize the qualities that go into a successful presentational style.

Chapter 6 emphasized that, regardless of the final format used, the speaker's goal was to look and sound spontaneous. We suggested that if the speaker didn't seem spontaneous, the message, no matter how ingeniously conceived, would suffer in the actual communication situation. In this chapter we want to focus on speech presentation, looking for ways to achieve spontaneity. We begin by looking at style—the way in which we present ourselves to our audience—and then examine the qualities and techniques that lead to effective speech delivery.

Presentational Style

Each one of us has his or her own style. It shows up in the way we carry ourselves, in the way we dress, and in our attitude toward ourselves and others. As intangible as it may sometimes seem, our style is something peculiarly our own.

One distinctive element of personal style is the way each one of us communicates with others. No one gestures exactly the way you do, has the same vocal qualities, or has your peculiar communication habits. Linguists have even determined that within each personal style there are numerous substyles that characterize communication in various situations.[1] Think, for instance, how you look and sound when engaged in a conversation, reading aloud, talking on the telephone, or reciting a favorite poem from memory. In each situation you communicate with a slightly different style.

Each one of us also has a distinctive public-speaking style. There are principles, guidelines, and qualities for effective delivery of a public speech, and yet each one of us will appear as a distinctive person while at the speaker's stand. Effective speech delivery requires that we find our own style and develop it.

As public speakers we need to get as clear an idea as possible about the way we look and sound to others. Then we should emphasize those aspects of our personal style that help us succeed in a speech and eliminate those aspects that hinder us. When you have finished this course, you should have a clear understanding of how you come across to others when you give a speech, and of what qualities, uniquely yours, you need to emphasize. In short, you will have developed your own presentational style.

Scholars who study public speaking notice that all great speakers share certain characteristics. Even though each speaker has a distinctive style, that style shows three common qualities: naturalness, dynamism, and articulateness. In fact, even speakers who are poles apart in their views—speakers such as Jesse Jackson and Ronald Reagan—share these same speaking qualities.

Qualities of Effective Delivery

Naturalness

A twentieth-century scholar in the field of rhetoric, Chaim Perelman, notes that one of the first judgments an audience makes about a speaker is whether the person is sincere and trustworthy.[2] An audience wants to feel that you are personally involved in your speech, that you care about your topic, and that you care about their interest in it. You create these feelings in the speaking situation by looking and sounding natural. Let's look at some of the common reasons for failure to achieve naturalness and then at how naturalness can be developed.

The most common reason for failure to achieve naturalness is that the speaker is reading too much. No one wants to listen to someone read a speech. What could be less spontaneous? A member of an audience once told a speaker, "Look, if you're going to read to me, why not just make a copy of the speech and I'll read it when I get a chance." Few listeners will be that outspoken, but many will feel that way if the speaker reads the entire speech—and they should.

You may, of course, have to read direct quotations or critical information during a speech, and as you know from Chapter 6, sometimes you may need to present the speech from a prepared manuscript. When you are required to read or to speak from a manuscript, follow the guidelines given on p. 146, and remember to try to sound as though you were speaking rather than reading: vary your voice, pause for emphasis, and look at your audience. In short, give the material life. A wise person once said, "Writers turn blood into ink; speakers turn ink into blood." If you must read, turn that ink into blood.

The second reason for failing to achieve naturalness is reciting a speech completely from memory. If you recite a memorized speech, you simply won't sound like yourself—you won't sound natural. When a speaker recites from memory, unless he or she is quite skilled, the speech tends to sound a little like a recorded message. Do not memorize the speech; let your words flow naturally.

The third reason speakers fail to achieve naturalness is that too frequently they call attention to themselves. An audience does not want the speaker to distract them from the message with outrageous emotional displays or obviously rehearsed theatrics. Do not make demonstrative gestures or pace the floor randomly simply because you have seen someone do it. If an audience member comes up to you after your speech and says, "Wow, what a show you put on today," it may be an unwanted compliment because it can mean you were not yourself. Natural delivery style is achieved by using realistic vocal tones, normal physical mannerisms, and behavior patterns that are particular to the speaker.

But how does one achieve naturalness? One way is to adjust to the situation as it occurs, perhaps by ad-libbing but certainly by moving away from prepared remarks if necessary. Handling unexpected situations is a sign of naturalness because it gives the audience the feeling that you are involved with them in a live event. Thus, if someone comes in late and disrupts the audience, and you, the speaker, adjust to it, perhaps by reacting with a look or a word to the person, you will put the audience at ease by your naturalness.

Another way to achieve naturalness is to build into your speech personal experiences and examples that you can talk about without notes. It is always helpful to reach a point in a prepared speech where you can look at the audience and say, "One example of this stands out in my mind ..." and then launch into an account of something you know well enough simply to talk about.

A third way to achieve naturalness is through practice. Experienced speakers know that the more times they rehearse a speech (or actually present it) the more relaxed and natural they feel. You will notice also that each time you present your speech it will come more "trippingly off the tongue," to paraphrase a famous line from Shakespeare's *Hamlet*.

Remember, finally, that naturalness does not mean sounding just the way we do in conversation. In formal public speaking we want to diminish as much as possible those errors in fluency that often accompany our casual speech. For instance, too much filler speech ("you know," "like," "um"), some of which might be acceptable in a conversation, can detract from an otherwise effective speech. We will discuss many of these errors in the section on articulateness. For now, remember that naturalness means sounding and looking like yourself when you are in your formal voice.

Dynamism

In ancient Athens, where the court system as we know it today had its start, litigants (those brought to trial), having no lawyer to represent them, soon learned to be as demonstrative as possible when pleading their case. Plaintiffs and defendants would wail loudly, beat their breasts, and, in both voice and body, show as much anger, disgust, fear, and revulsion as they could toward their opponents. Speech making in the Athenian court was as much devoted to entertainment as to securing justice. In fact, the two goals were clearly related.

Today, professional speakers realize that displaying emotion is no less important than it was two thousand years ago. Lawyers, politicians, and evangelists, among others, understand that an audience is moved in the heart as well as the head. Most importantly, effective speakers realize that the enthusiasm they show for their topic is often transferred to their audience. You have probably caught yourself at one time or another smiling because the speaker smiled, or

---

The most elaborate account of delivery surviving from ancient times was written by the noted Roman orator and teacher Quintilian. Here is a vivid historical description of how an orator conducted himself in the Roman forum. "When called, he rises and secures a few moments for reflection while he arranges his toga. He then turns to the judge, but still does not launch into his speech. A dramatic tension is built up as he strokes his head, or looks at his hands, or even sighs. Then, his feet slightly apart, standing straight but not stiffly, his face serious but not sad, his arms slightly out from the body, his right hand extending from the folds of his toga before his breast, he begins to speak calmly, with dignity, seeking the sympathy and the good will of the jury."

George Kennedy
Quintilian, p. 100

---

frowning the same frown you saw etched on the speaker's face. Emotional display is one sure way to get the audience involved.

Dynamic delivery means that the speaker shows energy and enthusiasm. You do not need to beat your breast or wail loudly, but you must demonstrate to the audience that you feel strongly about your topic. Your dynamism reveals your conviction, and, as with anything, your listeners will be about as convinced as you appear to be.

Dynamism is also important for keeping the audience's attention. In a public speech, you are asking others to listen for an unnatural period of time. Think of it: if someone at your lunch table talked for six to eight minutes without stopping you would quite rightly be upset. Thus, in a public speech you must keep the audience involved with you and your ideas by showing your enthusiasm.

You may object to this appeal for dynamism, arguing that a speech should be judged successful because of its merits, not because it has been hyped up through delivery. But, as F. G. Bailey says, human beings are "romantics who long for contact with 'real' persons. Displays of emotion can be reassuring, having a power that reason lacks."[3] The audience judges a public speech on both its content and the presentation—this is simply a fact of life all speakers must understand.

Delivery dynamics should not cloud judgment or appear as insincere demonstrations. The point is to get involved with your speech and let your message come through to the audience not by words alone but with the full power of your voice and body.

Articulateness

Articulateness is the third quality that effective speakers demonstrate. In the strict sense of the term, to articulate means to make all the sounds in the word correctly, as they appear in the dictionary. In a more general sense, however, as a quality of effective delivery style, to be articulate means to be capable of clear and even pleasing expression. Articulateness involves producing a steady, fluent stream of speech that is free of distracting physical and vocal habits. Let's look at the most common problem leading to speaker inarticulateness.

Failure to achieve articulateness is frequently the result of excessive nonfluencies, sometimes called "filler speech." Filler speech includes such words and phrases as *you know, like, right,* and *um,* which are used to fill in the pauses that occur between words in a

CHAPTER 8

stream of speech. The following transcription from a speech will give you some idea of this problem:

> *I, myself, have chosen to, um, not use marijuana. I'll tell ya, though, you know, I'm not, you know, sure that I have the right to decide for others, you know what I mean? I think like this, um, it's like we have a conscience of our own, right? You know, each one of us should have the right to decide, right?*

Most of this nonfluent speech creeps into our style during our adolescent years, and unless we become conscious of it, it stays in our speech indefinitely.

In casual conversation, a certain amount of filler speech is natural; even network news anchors say "um" now and then. But even in informal speech, too much nonfluency is distracting. In formal discourse, especially public speaking, it can be a singular cause for rejection of one's ideas, since, according to published research, filler speech suggests a lack of intelligence.[4] Here are three suggestions for coping with filler speech:

1. Be conscious of your filler words in conversational speech. Cutting down on fillers is a full-time job; make a commitment to working on it all day long, not just when presenting a speech.

2. Imitate the speech of people who are quite fluent. Picking a role model and keeping this person in mind when you speak is an idea that has worked for many others.

3. Ask a friend, a classmate, or your instructor to write down your filler words during your next speech. Keep an accurate count of nonfluencies and work during the course to cut the number down significantly.

Articulateness is further achieved through the use of correct oral grammar and diction. Oral grammar is word use, while diction is choice of words. It is not possible, of course, to review all the errors in grammar and diction that speakers have been heard to utter throughout the years. Whenever you are uncertain about your diction, consult a handbook of English grammar and usage. Following are simply a few of the most common errors in oral grammar and diction. Consult this list and add your own entries to it.

1. Misuse of *good* and *well.* Probably the most common error in oral grammar, and understandably so. *Good* is an adjective that mod-

ifies nouns, as in "It was a good movie, and I enjoyed the acting." *Well* is nearly always an adverb, usually modifying a verb: "He swam well." One way to avoid this common mistake in grammar is to avoid the overuse of the word *good* altogether.

2. Misuse of *get* and *got*. Rather than saying, "It's got to get better," say, "It must improve." Rather than saying, "I've got to agree with this opinion," say, "I must . . ." or "I have to agree with this opinion."

3. *A lot*. Although it is acceptable, the phrase *a lot* is commonly overused. Rather than using *a lot* all the time, substitute the word *many*, as in "He has struck out many times."

4. Dropping the *-ly* from adverbs. The *-ly* is often and incorrectly dropped from adverbs. Rather than saying, "The party was run real nice," say, "The party was managed nicely."

5. Word repetition. It is easy to seize upon a word or phrase and use it habitually. Avoid overuse of words and phrases such as *significantly, outstanding,* and *more or less,* or whatever phrase happens to be in vogue as you read this text.

6. Obscenity and profanity. There are few, if any, occasions when obscene or profane language adds to a public speech. Usually such language reveals a lack of vocabulary and self-control. This is not prudishness, simply good advice.

Articulateness is as much a matter of motivation as of knowledge. Most of us know the correct way to say all that we are thinking, and actually doing so will lead to positive results.

The three qualities we have discussed—naturalness, dynamism, and articulateness—are the marks of professional-level public speaking. For the student of formal communication, they are goals to be sought. Although each one of us will develop these three general qualities within the confines of our own personal style, certain specific behaviors will help us achieve them. In other words, we can improve the quality of our delivery by attending to some specific communicative behaviors, or elements of effective delivery.

Elements of Effective Delivery

The behaviors involved in presenting a public speech can be divided initially into physical attributes and vocal attributes. A speaker must use the body to gesture, move, and show feelings, and the voice to emphasize ideas and express emotions. Let's look at the aspects of the body and the voice to see what each adds to the presentation of a public speech.

Physical Aspects of Delivery

GESTURES.   Gesturing in informal communication situations is quite natural for most of us. If we were to pay close attention we would notice that our hands, arms, legs, and other mobile parts of our body move more or less automatically with our words, as if following an unconscious rhythm between voice and body. The objective in formal speaking is to use the same natural gestures we use in casual conversation, but to be a good deal more conscious and purposeful about it. In formal communication, gestures must be visible to the entire audience, made a little "larger than life," but not faked. Most of us will learn to gesture naturally as we practice speeches, by simply allowing our bodies to move with the meaning we intend.

Most importantly, we must become conscious of habits that irritate or distract an audience, such as locking our hands in our pockets, toying with jewelry or clothing, using only one gesture throughout the speech, clicking pens, tapping feet, shuffling note cards, or pulling on sleeves. If you have an opportunity to see yourself on videotape, look for these habits in your gestures and try to get rid of them.

POSTURE.   In informal communication our posture reflects how interested we are in the communication, how wide awake we are, how disciplined, and so on. Posture conveys much about our personal style. When delivering a speech, display the posture you assume when you are enthused about the person you are speaking with. Common posture problems to be aware of include leaning on the lectern or against the chalkboard, shifting weight from one foot to the other, hanging onto the back of a chair, slouching forward or backward, and crossing the feet or arms throughout the speech.

You can improve your posture through conscious attention. As you situate yourself at the speaker's stand or at the front of the room, run through a mental checklist to be sure your weight is resting equally on both legs, your arms and hands are not clutching an object, and you have an erect bearing. This little list, if run through during the course of the semester, will lead to better posture.

MOVEMENT. In many instances, you will speak from a lectern or a speaker's stand where little movement is possible. Unless circumstances require it, however, it is better to move away from possible "crutches" such as the speaker's stand. Doing so allows you to put your entire body into the speech, thus increasing your dynamism and your audience's interest.

Movement is effective when it reinforces some point in the message. Moving purposefully toward an audience member whose attention may have wandered will often draw the person back into the speech. A student was recently presenting a speech on the art of paper folding when she spotted one seemingly disinterested listener. Reacting appropriately, the speaker caught the person's attention by walking to his seat and asking him to serve as a demonstrator for the next fold. By so doing, the speaker recaptured her listener's attention. Similarly, even if you are confined to a lectern, a movement to one side or the other can break down the barrier between you and your audience. But learn to avoid the common mistakes of randomly pacing across the front of the room or around audience members, standing rigidly in one spot with feet planted too firmly, turning away from the audience to use visuals, and rushing away from the lectern after finishing the speech.

FACIAL EXPRESSION. The face is our most expressive feature. Effective delivery requires us to scan the audience with our eyes, moving evenly from side to side, focusing on one person for an instant, then moving to another, and so on. The face must express our feelings about our topic. Most of us have caught ourselves mimicking an actor's emotion while watching television; an audience reacts much the same way: their faces unconsciously reflect the speaker's own facial expression. Thus, thoughtful speakers learn to read their audience's expressions. Be aware of this the next time you are in a public-speaking situation.

Most problems with facial expression result from inexperience or nervousness. The speaker's jaws seem to lock, leaving a blank expression on the face. If the speech has been poorly prepared or memorized, the speaker often loses contact with the audience as he or she frantically searches for words. Try to avoid these common facial habits: looking too long at one member of the audience; gazing outside the room, perhaps through the window; looking above the eyes of the audience; looking downward; and facing only part of the audience.

Vocal Aspects of Delivery

A speaker's vocal attributes, such as pitch and volume, are just as important as her or his physical attributes, such as movement and facial expression. Most speakers naturally combine vocal and physical elements; for example, when they raise their vocal pitch their facial expression changes naturally with it.

PITCH.   Pitch is the highness or lowness of the voice. It is an axiom in the theater that bad actors show emotion in only one way: they raise their voice, increasing their pitch. The next time you watch television, notice how many characters tend to "yell" at one another in a normal conversation. How much better it is to use variety in vocal range. Most of us have at least one octave of sound under our control, and, interestingly enough, most emotions can be expressed as well by lowering the voice as by raising it. Let us take an emotion, anger, to see if it can be expressed in two ways. Speak the following sentence from a student speech on the drinking age in both a high and a low pitch, showing anger each time:

> *I am disgusted with the attitude of our own legislators toward young adults, and I am sick and tired of being treated like an adult when it comes to war and like a child when it comes to having a drink.*

Which is most effective, a high or a low pitch? What pitch would you use if you were trying to convince the audience of your point of view? With a little practice you will learn to vary your pitch so that you keep the audience involved with your speech.

VOLUME.   Closely related to pitch is volume, the loudness or softness of the voice. On a fundamental level, no speaker can be effective if he or she cannot be heard. We need to adjust our volume so that everyone in the room can hear us, but we do not want to drive anyone out of the room with our stentorian tones.

   Beyond this basic necessity of being heard, we can use volume just as we did pitch: to express emotion. If, for instance, a speaker has a characteristically soft voice, he or she can raise it to express an emotion. Try raising and lowering your volume while reading aloud the following paragraph, just to prove to yourself that you can use volume to express yourself.

It is an unattractive human truth, but a truth nonetheless, that most of us are not particularly talented, beautiful, or charismatic. Set free to discover "our true selves," we often find that there is nothing there at all. Set free to "do our own thing," we often learn that we have little of note to do.

The most common problem with volume in the speech-communication classroom is speaking too softly. Our normal conversational volume will usually not suffice in a public speech. Therefore, we must all project our voices by raising the volume enough so that those in the back of the room can hear. A useful tip to help you adjust your volume correctly is to practice your speech in the room in which you will give it, or at least in a similar room. Ask a friend or classmate to listen to you from several locations in the room. Sometimes you can open a window or create some noise that will force you to adjust your volume as you speak.

RATE. The average person speaks about 150 words per minute and can listen at a rate of 500 words per minute. There is a wide latitude, therefore, in the rate of speech that is appropriate for a given person. The most important point to remember about rate is that, as we monitor the audience with our eyes, we should adjust our rate if the audience does not appear to be following. Also, our rate of speech is too fast if it is affecting our ability to pronounce words correctly.

Speaker anxiety causes many problems with rate, the speaker's rate going up as the anxiety level rises. This is natural, and if we anticipate it happening we can cope with it in advance of the speech by consciously reminding ourselves to slow down.

PAUSE AND EMPHASIS. Pausing for key words and emphasizing key terms are two effective ways to keep a speech dynamic. For those

---

Demosthenes (384–322 BC), considered the greatest orator of his time, practiced speaking while facing the roaring waves of the sea off the coast of Greece in order to improve his ability to project his voice.

William Jennings Bryan
The World's Famous Orations

---

of us afflicted with a monotone voice, pausing and emphasizing help keep audience interest, as well as affecting the meaning and importance an audience attributes to a particular statement. Repeat the following statement, changing your emphasis each time to the underlined words:

A woman of charm, a woman of wit, and clever enough to sneak the dawn past a rooster.

A woman of charm, a woman of wit, and clever enough to sneak the dawn past a rooster.

A woman of charm, a woman of wit, and clever enough to sneak the dawn past a rooster.

You should be able to detect a subtle shift in meaning as you shift your emphasis. One time you focused on the metaphorical expression, another time on the woman's cleverness, and still another time on the two other qualities she possesses. Pause and emphasis help the audience follow your meaning, and you will notice your ability increasing each time you employ them.

FLUENCY. We have considered fluency already in our discussion of articulateness. Effective speakers keep up a steady stream of speech that is as free as possible from nonfluencies. Common fluency problems in public speaking include filler speech; in-sentence switches such as "I, um, arrived at the infirmary, but, well, first I had to get my car started, but, anyway . . . ; repetitions of a word or phrase; and incoherencies such as "I would like to quote from Grebelkop [Gorbachev] or whatever his name is. . . ." By paying attention to these common fluency problems, and by speaking in complete sentences, you will soon find yourself increasing in fluency.

PRONUNCIATION. Just about everyone stumbles over pronunciation every now and then, especially when presenting a public speech. Interestingly, we often read so quickly that we are not aware that we mispronounce words—it is in speaking that we hear ourselves stumbling. The best way to enhance pronunciation is to practice reading aloud, preferably in front of others. Any number of speakers may compose thoughtful speeches on paper, but unless they practice them out loud, they risk making embarrassing errors in pronunciation that will ultimately detract from their speeches.

Another way to strengthen pronunciation is to listen to others, noting how they pronounce difficult words. National newscasters, in particular, work diligently on their pronunciation. In 1983, many Americans had no idea how to pronounce *Grenada*, until that isolated island figured prominently in the news. Newscasters taught most Americans the correct pronunciation (although it took some of them a few days to figure it out!).

Here are some common errors many of us make. Note your own difficulties and add them to this list.

1. Clipping off the ends of words. In formal discourse, we are expected to make all of the sounds in the words. Many of us need to practice this until it becomes habit. Learn to say "going," not "goin," and to make all of the "ed" sounds at the ends of the words. These sounds can be made without exaggerating them or calling attention to the fact that they are being made.

2. Using too many contractions. In oral communication, of course, speech contractions are acceptable, but using too many can lower the quality of one's speech. The most commonly misused contractions are *don't*, in expressions such as "He don't like to use the library," rather than "He does not like to use the library" or "He doesn't like to use the library; and *ain't*, as in "This ain't the best speech I have in me."

3. Hyper-correcting words. Sometimes, in an effort to sound too formal, we overcorrect or unnaturally inflate our pronunciation. The best example is pronouncing the *t* in the word *often*, but there are many more. Regional pronunciations are not examples of hyper-correcting; in fact, to pronounce a word one way in a region where it is usually pronounced in another way is not appropriate if you normally use the dialect of the region. The following list presents words that are pronounced differently in various regions of the country and that are also mispronounced.

route	vegetables	athlete	important
tomato	relevant	nuclear	catsup
February	library	picture	unusual
hundred	environment	walked	aunt

Check your pronunciation of these words by recording yourself pronouncing them. Then look in a dictionary to see whether you pronounce them according to a standard dictionary pronunciation. You may legitimately pronounce the words according to a regional dialect, but you should also be aware of the pronunciation favored by a reputable dictionary such as *Webster's Ninth New Collegiate Dictionary.*

We have now discussed the qualities that make up the personal style of a successful public speaker, and we have discussed common elements of delivery that all of us will encounter and try to develop. One component of effective delivery remains, however, a component that for most of us is the most serious problem we will encounter as public speakers: speech anxiety.

Understanding and Coping with Speech Anxiety

One particular concern in a speech-communication course is "communication apprehension," an anxiety or fear syndrome associated with real or anticipated communication with others. In one study, James McCroskey reported that 15 to 20 percent of the college-student population suffered from severe communication apprehension.[5] Of the many communication situations in which a person might find him or herself, the public-speaking situation is generally regarded as producing the greatest amount of communication apprehension. In fact, many individuals avoid taking a course in public speaking because of their level of apprehension.

The communication apprehension associated specifically with presenting a public speech is called "public-speaking anxiety." While it is common to experience a moderate degree of apprehension for any communication situation, it is also common to experience a high degree of anxiety about giving a public speech. As McCroskey and Richmond note in their booklet *The Quiet Ones: Communication Apprehension and Shyness:* "In a national survey of adults in the United States, it was found that their number one fear was of speaking in public. This fear was felt by more people than any other, outranking such common fears as fear of death, fear of heights, and fear of water."[6]

In 1970, a team of scholars led by McCroskey developed an inventory to measure public-speaking anxiety. The instrument, called the Personal Report of Public Speaking Apprehension (PRPSA), is often used today to provide a general awareness of anxiety.[7] The PRPSA is reproduced at the end of this chapter in exercise 3 should you want to fill it out.

The sources of public-speaking anxiety are not completely clear. Besides relating to the general anxiety many feel because of their personality type, public-speaking anxiety seems to be related to low self-esteem, fear of failure and of evaluations that might follow the speech, and inexperience with the public-speaking situation. In general, the public-speaking anxiety one feels on a given occasion is the result of the interaction of the speech, the situation, and the speaker.

There are three treatment methods for public-speaking anxiety: systematic desensitization, cognitive modification, and skills training. Because we are interested in helping you cope with public-speaking anxiety, let's take a careful look at each treatment procedure.

Systematic Desensitization

Systematic desensitization is a procedure for treating public-speaking anxiety originally developed by Gordon Paul.[8] Since it requires assistance from a person trained in the method, its use should be restricted to institutions where trained professionals are available to help, perhaps in a laboratory setting.

The systematic desensitization process involves three basic steps. First, the subject completes a PRPSA so that progress can be measured after treatment. Then a hierarchy of anxiety-producing situations is established by the student with the help of the counsellor.

Daniel Webster, considered by many to be the greatest orator of the nineteenth century, wrote of himself that he was terrified to give a speech before his classmates. Webster wrote, "Many a piece did I commit to memory and rehearse in my room, over and over, yet when the day came to hear declamations, when my name was called, and I saw all eyes turned to me, I could not raise myself from my seat." But through sheer determination and practice, Webster overcame his fears and became the prized speaker at his college, Dartmouth.

David J. Brewer
A Library of the World's Great Orations

For a public-speaking situation, the hierarchy might include the following list:

1. You've just been told that you are expected to present a speech.

2. You're sitting at your desk trying to decide on a good topic for your speech, which is to be given two weeks from now.

3. You've determined a topic for your speech, which is due to be presented in one week. You're organizing your speech and deciding about main ideas.

4. You're in class listening to a fellow student present a speech.

5. You're in class. A classmate is presenting a speech and is nervous while doing so, so nervous you take notice.

6. It's two days before you give your speech; you are alone in your room practicing the speech out loud.

7. Now it's the day before your presentation. You're practicing the speech in front of a friend.

8. Your preparation and practice are virtually completed now. You'll present your speech tomorrow. You're thinking about how you'll do.

9. The day of your presentation is here. You're in the classroom waiting for the instructor to arrive.

10. You are the third speaker of the day. The first speaker has just finished a presentation. You take a moment to glance at your notes.

11. The second speaker has finished. It is now your turn. You get out of your chair and move to the front of the room. As you turn to the audience you see their faces. Look at them for a moment.

12. You begin your speech. You're trying to remember what you intended to say while keeping your eyes on the audience.

13. You're still speaking. Your speech is almost over and you're about to move to the conclusion. You pause momentarily to check your notes.

14. You've finished the speech. An audience member raises a question. You respond.

15. You've returned to your seat. You're listening to the instructor and a few of your classmates about your speech.[9]

Once this hierarchy is established, the instructor and student focus on the steps or stages that produce the most anxiety and discuss the matter.

The second step in systematic desensitization is relaxation training, which involves the tensing and relaxing of particular muscles. There are many variations of this procedure, but generally it involves playing a deep muscular relaxation tape, followed by specific relaxation instructions from the instructor.[10]

Once the tape has been played and relaxation instructions have been given, the anxiety-producing hierarchy is paired with the relaxation technique. That is, the subject is asked to picture himself or herself engaging in a particular activity. If the subject begins to experience anxiety while thinking about or visualizing the activity, he or she raises a finger and the instructor asks the subject to stop visualizing and to relax. After a period of relaxation time, perhaps thirty seconds, the subject is asked to visualize the situation again until he or she reports no anxiety. Treatment is completed when the subject is able to visualize each item on the hierarchy without becoming tense.

Systematic desensitization has been cited as being particularly effective for public-speaking anxiety.[11] The Deep Muscle Relaxation tape is reasonably priced (six dollars as of this writing) and is available through the Speech Communication Association. A copy of the essay explaining the entire procedure accompanies the tape. If your school has a systematic desensitization program, you might want to take advantage of it. If your school does not have such a program, you might want to suggest that one be developed or explored.

Cognitive Modification

The second treatment method for speech anxiety is cognitive modification. Actually, cognitive modification is not one specific technique but a label used to cover all speech-anxiety treatments designed to help individuals think and talk more positively about the public-speaking situation. In other words, individuals learn that their negative feelings about giving a speech are self-defeating; thus, if they can learn to think and talk positively about the situation, their anxiety will decrease.

Cognitive modification does not require personnel trained specifically in the method; in fact, it is the basis for many classroom treatments of public-speaking anxiety and has been shown to be effective.[12] In order to give you some idea of how cognitive modification works, let's look at one variation of it for coping with public-speaking anxiety, a treatment that focuses on two of the most common self-defeating tendencies.

THE SPEECH ANXIETY PEAK EXPERIENCE. Most of us think of speech anxiety as something we have throughout the speech experience. But if we think carefully about this, we realize that we actually have different levels of speech anxiety at various moments during the total speech experience.[13] For instance, most people feel the greatest anxiety just before the speech. If the speech gets off to a successful start, anxiety will normally taper off and actually disappear toward the end of the speech. Figure 8.1 shows the range of anxiety levels for various moments in the speech experience.

The realization that speech anxiety is not a constant part of the speech event is valuable for two reasons. Most importantly, simply knowing that anxiety is not going to haunt one through the entire speech can make the speaker feel more positive about the experience. The speaker now has a clearer understanding that "giving a speech" is not an event to be dreaded. Except for those initial moments, the anxiety is not a significant hindrance, and the experience, overall, can be enjoyable and anxiety-free.

Second, discovering those moments when one will feel anxiety helps the speaker zero in on specific ways to cope with that anxiety. For instance, if, as with most speakers, our anxiety level is greatest during the introduction of the speech, then we can focus on strategies to get us through those moments, recognizing that if we are successful our anxiety level will go down appreciably, if not disappear altogether. Understanding that you will feel some anxiety, but that it will not be a constant part of the speech, usually lessens tension.

THE TENDENCY TO EXAGGERATE AUDIENCE EXPECTATIONS.
Many of us have an unrealistic picture of the audience. We imagine a group of people who are listening critically to our every word, waiting to pounce on us at the slightest falter in our voice. Most other thoughts we have about the audience are equally negative. By creating this mental picture of the audience we put ourselves in a "me-against-them" frame of mind, a state that will surely cause our anxiety level to rise.

The cognitive modification procedure tries to get us to look at the facts about audiences. Most students come to realize that the

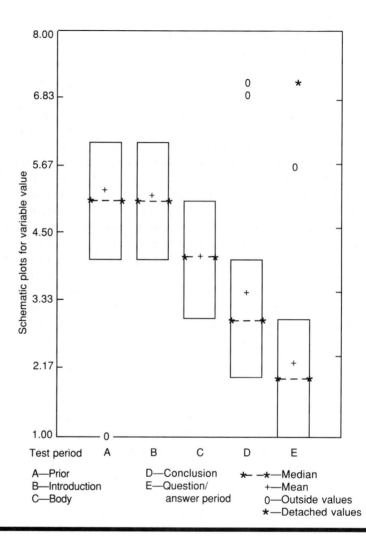

Figure 8.1
Plot of communication-anxiety
ratings by test period for the
entire sample. (Reprinted by
permission of *Communication
Quarterly.*)

audience is almost never as frightening as it appears to be. Here are
some commonly accepted opinions about audiences that should
give you a more realistic picture.

1. *Most audiences want the speaker to succeed.* This is especially
true of student audiences, since everyone is in the same situation.
But even in other situations, you will find that most audiences want
you to succeed in presenting the speech. Even if they disagree with
your point of view, the audience wants you to deliver the speech
successfully.

CHAPTER 8

2. *Most audiences are not experts on the topic.* You are the expert for your speech. You have thought about your topic, done the research, prepared the notes, and practiced. Even if the members of the audience are familiar with your topic, they want to learn more about it just as much as they want to pick apart statements you might make.

3. *You control the speech situation.* The speaker initiates the communication. You shape the environment with your words and your delivery style. Speakers act—audiences react.

4. *Audiences do not focus on your speech anxiety.* Audiences generally focus on your speech topic. They have come to hear you speak, not to assess how well you handle your anxiety. If you ask audience members after a speech whether the speaker was nervous or not, some may have noticed, but most will say they are unsure because they were not looking for signs of nervousness.

Most negative talking goes on in the mind of the speaker. The reality of the speech situation is quite different. Sometimes a teacher can counsel a student individually to get the student thinking more positively about the experience. Most of us, however, can modify our own understanding of the speech situation and thereby relieve some of the anxiety ourselves.

Skills Training

The third method for treating speech anxiety is designed to help students develop behaviors, coping strategies, that help in the actual presentation of the speech. Once again, there are many variations on this method, ranging from personal counseling to laboratory exercises. Following are steps that speech teachers often recommend for reducing anxiety.

1. *Draft a clear critical-thinking statement.* Research studies show clearly that confidence in public speaking is related to careful planning.[14] If you understand *why* you are giving the speech and keep that purpose in mind throughout the speech, your anxiety will be reduced. Draft a critical-thinking statement following the guidelines suggested in Chapter 3 of this text. Learning the preparatory skills associated with public speaking is the first step toward anxiety reduction within the skills-training approach.

2. *Use visual aids.* Visual aids work as a handy source of notes. As you work with your visuals you will feel more relaxed about keeping your place in the speech and getting all of your data before the audience. Furthermore, visual aids tend to shift the audience's

focus away from you to the aids, thus relieving you of the feeling that the audience is staring at you.

3. *Make continuous audience contact.* You might think that you will get more nervous if you look at the audience, but in fact the opposite is true: if you look away from the audience or over their heads, you will feel a sense of uneasiness about their reactions to your speech. Scan the audience as we suggested earlier and you will notice that the audience is not as intimidating as you might have thought.

4. *Avoid memorizing your speech.* Memorizing your speech will usually cause you to be more nervous than otherwise. It is much better to have a final format that you feel comfortable with, and some ad-libs to get you through a rough spot should one occur. At the very most, memorize your introduction if you find that this helps you get through the speech-anxiety peak.

5. *Take your time getting started.* Don't rush to the lectern and burst into your speech. Rather, take a few deep breaths, organize your formatted speech carefully, look at it, look at the audience, and when you feel ready, begin. What might feel like an eternity to you is only an instant to the audience.

6. *Let your natural abilities take over.* Each one of us has many years of experience communicating. Over this period of time we have all developed natural abilities to get our messages across to others. If you start thinking about yourself—about how you look or how you sound—you can become self-conscious and start feeling more anxiety. Let your natural ability, your natural skills, get you through the public-speaking situation.

Finally, do not give up if you get overly nervous the first time. All of us have experienced the sweaty palms, the shortness of breath, dryness in the mouth, and fidgeting associated with public-speaking anxiety. If you will recognize this anxiety as a natural phenomenon and try one of the treatment methods suggested here for coping with it, you might find yourself agreeing with the two students quoted below:

> *During my first speech I was so nervous my thoughts all seemed to run together. As soon as I saw all those faces looking at me, I forgot almost all of what I had prepared. Later, I became more familiar with the situation, I began to understand my nervousness, and my anxiety level went down appreciably.*

After I gave my speech and went back to my seat, I realized that I couldn't remember a word I had said, but those sitting near me were saying, "Nice job, Phyllis, that was really interesting." That made me feel a little better. As I gained experience in front of the group I learned that most of the people were hoping I would succeed, maybe because they had to speak that night also, but maybe more so because people are generally pretty polite in the class, and they seem to want to help us communicate our ideas.

Summary

The key to effective delivery is to become aware of and develop one's own personal style. Delivery style in a formal public speech is simply a projection of the personal style one exhibits in a conversation to the needs of a larger audience. The objective is to accentuate the positive components of one's style and eliminate negative behaviors.

Three qualities account for success in delivery: naturalness, dynamism, and articulateness. Each quality is achieved by avoiding some behaviors and emphasizing others.

Naturalness is achieved by adjusting to the situation as it occurs. Overreliance upon the manuscript, as though one were reading a prepared script, hinders naturalness, as does reciting a speech completely from memory. Speakers who call attention to themselves with gestures that are overly demonstrative or vocal expressions intended simply to incite the audience lack naturalness.

Dynamism involves displays of emotion or energy, and is captured in the enthusiasm the speaker shows for the topic through movement, tone, and gesture. Displays of dynamism reassure an audience that the speaker is involved in the speech.

The third quality, articulateness, involves clear and pleasing expression. An articulate person maintains a steady, fluent stream of speech and, most importantly, eliminates excessive nonfluent speech, vocal pauses, and incorrect oral grammar and diction.

The three qualities of effective delivery are developed by attending to specific communication behaviors, usually divided into physical and vocal attributes of delivery. The physical attributes of effective delivery are meaningful gestures, natural but erect posture, purposeful movement, and dynamic facial expressions. Vocal attributes of effective delivery include variety in pitch, volume appropriate to the surroundings, a comprehensible rate of speech, pause and emphasis, fluency, and accurate pronunciation.

One common problem associated with delivering a speech is speech anxiety. Many people suffer from public-speaking anxiety, and many avoid presenting a public speech because of their fear. While the sources of speech anxiety are varied and related to the situation, it is possible to measure one's general anxiety with an inventory called the Personal Report of Public Speaking Apprehension (PRPSA). Knowing one's anxiety level is helpful because it allows one to measure improvement generated through treatment and practice.

There are three treatment procedures for helping individuals cope with their speech anxiety. The first, systematic desensitization, requires professional assistance and involves deep muscle relaxation techniques. The second, referred to as cognitive modification, involves numerous classroom techniques for overcoming negative feelings about the public-speaking situation. The third treatment for speech anxiety is called skills training, and it involves practicing speech making and developing strategies for coping with anxiety during preparation and delivery.

Exercises

1. Many speakers find it difficult to reveal their enthusiasm for their topic through facial expressions, perhaps for fear of seeming too dramatic or affected. And yet, the audience wants expressiveness in the speaker. One good way to practice facial expressiveness is to attend a play, perhaps on campus or in the local community. Choose one of the better actors and, during the play, try to imitate that actor's facial expressions. Notice how wide the mouth opens to make all of the sounds, and notice how the actor exaggerates normal expressions such as eye movements ever so slightly to project to the audience. Finally, notice how the actor tilts the head to show concern, anger, or some other emotion. The more you imitate the expressions of other skillful persons, the more expressive you are likely to become yourself.

2. Conduct an interview with a person who does a good deal of public speaking. The person might be an elected official, a member of the local clergy, or a chief administrator at your school. Ask that person about any delivery techniques she or he has found effective over the years, and share the results of your interview

with class members in a group discussion. Compile a list of useful techniques or anecdotes that might help the entire class and report on these.

3. Following is the most popular instrument for measuring public-speaking anxiety, the Personal Report of Public Speaking Apprehension (PRPSA). Fill out the questionnaire and then determine your score by following the scoring instructions included after the questionnaire.

DIRECTIONS: This instrument is composed of thirty-four statements concerning feelings about communicating with other people. Indicate the degree to which the statements apply to you by marking whether you (1) strongly agree, (2) agree, (3) are undecided, (4) disagree, or (5) strongly disagree with each statement. Work quickly, recording your first impression.

PRPSA

1. While preparing for giving a speech I feel tense and nervous.

2. I feel tense when I see the words SPEECH and PUBLIC SPEECH on a course outline when studying.

3. My thoughts become confused and jumbled when I am giving a speech.

4. Just after giving a speech I feel that I have had a pleasant experience.

5. I get anxious when I think about a speech coming up.

6. I have no fear of giving a speech.

7. Although I am nervous just before starting a speech, I soon settle down after getting started and feel calm and comfortable.

8. I look forward to giving a speech.

9. When the instructor announces a speaking assignment in class, I can feel myself getting tense.

10. My hands tremble when I am giving a speech.

11. I feel relaxed while giving a speech.

12. I enjoy preparing for a speech.

13. I am in constant fear of forgetting what I prepared to say.

14. I get anxious if someone asks me something about my topic that I do not know.

15. I face the prospect of giving a speech with confidence.

16. I feel that I am in complete possession of myself while speaking.

17. My mind is clear when giving a speech.

18. I do not dread giving a speech.

19. I perspire just before starting a speech.

20. My heart beats very fast just as I start a speech.

21. I experience considerable anxiety while sitting in the room just before my speech starts.

22. Certain parts of my body feel tense and rigid while I am giving a speech.

23. Realizing that only a little time remains in a speech makes me very tense and anxious.

24. While giving a speech I can control my feelings of tension and stress.

25. I breathe faster just before starting a speech.

26. I feel comfortable and relaxed the hour or so before giving a speech.

27. I do poorly on speeches because I am anxious.

28. I feel anxious when the teacher announces the date of a speaking assignment.

29. When I make a mistake while giving a speech, I find it hard to concentrate on the parts that follow.

30. During an important speech I experience a feeling of helplessness building up inside me.

31. I have trouble falling asleep the night before a speech.

32. My heart beats very fast while I present a speech.

33. I feel anxious while waiting to give my speech.

34. While giving a speech I get so nervous I forget facts I really know.

SCORING: After you have filled out the PRPSA, *add* the scores for the following items: 1, 2, 3, 5, 9, 10, 13, 14, 19, 20, 21, 22, 23, 25, 27, 28, 29,

30, 31, 32, 33, and 34. Next, *add* the scores for items 4, 6, 7, 8, 11, 12, 15, 16, 17, 18, 24, and 26. Now, to get your PRPSA, simply do the following. Begin with the number 132. From that number subtract the total from the first set of numbers; then add to this figure the total from the second set of numbers. Your score is your PRPSA.

ANALYSIS: Your score should range between 34 and 170, or you have made a mistake in computation. Following is a list of ranges to compare your score to:

34–84 = very low anxiety
85–92 = moderately low level of anxiety
93–110 = moderate anxiety
111–119 = moderately high level of anxiety
120–170 = very high level of anxiety

Used by permission of the Speech Communication Association and the author.

References

1. Elinor O. Keenan and Tina L. Bennett, eds., *Discourse Across Time and Space* (Los Angeles: University of Southern California Press, 1977), p. 56.

2. Chaim Perelman, *The New Rhetoric* (Notre Dame: University of Notre Dame Press, 1969), pp. 320–321.

3. F. G. Bailey, *The Tactical Uses of Passion* (Ithaca: Cornell University Press, 1984), p. 11.

4. Mark Knapp, *Nonverbal Communication in Human Interaction* (NY: Holt, Rinehart, and Winston, 1978), p. 356.

5. James C. McCroskey, "Classroom Consequences of Communication Apprehension," *Communication Education* 26 (1977), pp. 27–33.

6. James C. McCroskey and Virginia Richmond, *The Quiet Ones: Communication Apprehension and Shyness* (Dubuque: Gorsuch Scarisbrick Publishers, 1980), p. 15.

7. James C. McCroskey, "Measures of Communication Bound Anxiety," *Speech Monographs* 37 (1970), pp. 269–277.

8. Gordon L. Paul, *Insight Versus Desensitization in Psychotherapy: An Experiment in Anxiety Reduction* (Stanford: Stanford University Press, 1960).

9. Douglas J. Pederson, "Systematic Desensitization as a Model for Dealing with the Reticent Student," *Communication Education* 29 (1980), p. 230.

10. James C. McCroskey, "The Implementation of a Large Scale Program of Systematic Desensitization for Communication Apprehension," *Speech Teacher* 21 (1972), p. 263.

11. Susan R. Glaser, "Oral Communication Apprehension and Avoidance: The Current Status of Treatment Research," *Communication Education* 30 (1981), p. 337.

12. Glaser, p. 331.

13. Winifred Brownell and Richard A. Katula, "The Communication Anxiety Graph: A Classroom Tool for Managing Speech Anxiety," *Communication Quarterly* 32 (1984), pp. 243–249.

14. Gerald M. Phillips, "Rhetoritherapy Versus the Medical Model Dealing with Reticence," *Communication Education* 26 (1977), p. 43.

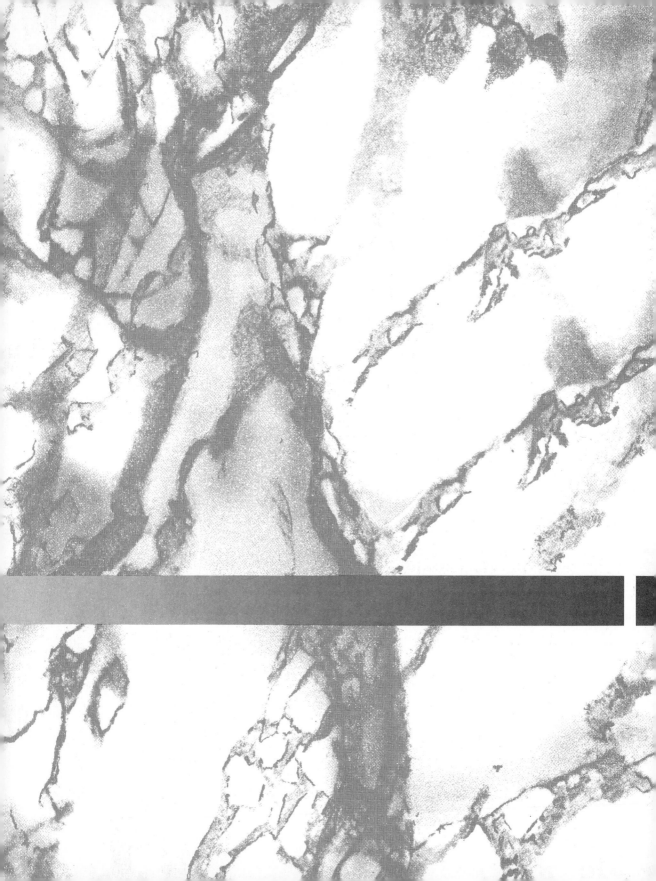

PART II - PATTERNS

Part II of this text develops in complete detail the patterns introduced in Part I. You have already seen the patterns functioning as a tool for analyzing a topic and for organizing that topic into a speech. Our goal now is to see each pattern as a pattern of reasoning and as a practical phenomenon in human communication.

The patterns we encounter in Part II of this text are patterns of reasoning. That simply means that each pattern is based upon a fundamental mode of human thought, either time or space, and that each pattern is governed by certain rules that, when followed, help us to draw inferences and make judgments about things. By following the rules for definition, for instance, we learn how to discover the essential meaning of things; by adhering to the rules for causality, we learn how to infer relationships among events; by knowing how to classify, we learn to recognize the systems according to which our world is organized. So, while you practice the patterns through the vehicle of public speech, you will also be developing your ability to think critically, an ability you will be able to apply to many situations.

Furthermore, each pattern you will study in Part II of this text is one that is commonly used when people communicate, whether it be in a public speech or another mode of formal human communication such as an essay, an oral report, or a classroom lecture. Narration, for instance, the first pattern you will learn about, is encountered almost daily in the form of stories or documentary accounts of social or political movements. Analysis, the pattern covered in Chapter 12, is another pattern we see in common use: when we witness a debate, see a group struggling to understand a problem or an object, or attempt to tease out the ramifications of a proposed policy. Because we encounter these patterns on an almost daily basis, we should understand them fully and know how and when to use them ourselves.

Around the patterns discussed in Part II speech assignments will be structured for this course. You can use the material in each chapter as a guide to the development of your topic. We will show you how to use the pattern as a way to think about ideas and experiences, then as a way to analyze and structure a speech on your chosen topic. Included in each chapter are the rules that govern the pattern, as well as helpful hints on using the pattern and at least one model speech that exemplifies the pattern. The model speeches are annotated to add to your understanding of the pattern.

Chapter 9 · Narrative

In the year 1873, at Chautauqua Lake, New York, a popular educational and cultural movement known as the chautauqua originated. Its original purpose was to organize large campground meetings at which lectures were given on religious matters, public affairs, science, literature, and the dramatic arts.[1] The chautauqua idea spread rapidly throughout rural America, and by World War I chautauquas had become highly successful commercial enterprises, involving three- to seven-day tent shows featuring popular American figures addressing a complete range of topics from science to poetry. For many Americans, the chautauqua meetings were the principal form of education and entertainment.

One popular feature of the chautauqua was storytelling.[2] Chatauqua companies would send out highly trained storytellers who held their audiences spellbound for hours with tales of courage and cowardice, loyalty and treason, adventure and romance. Noted political figures such as William Jennings Bryan and William McKinley, reformers such as Jane Addams and Susan B. Anthony, and literary figures such as Mark Twain and James Whitcomb Riley spoke rapturously about the America they knew. Through their lively and dramatic tales, millions of Americans—many immigrants and most living in tiny rural outposts—came to know "the American experience" and to know themselves as Americans. As Frederick Antczak writes, "Chautauqua probably did more than any other factor to make the expanding America of the late nineteenth and early twentieth centuries one nation culturally. . . ."[3]

Although the heyday of the chautauqua camp meeting has long since passed, we live today in a world equally vibrant with storytellers and their stories. Although the camp meeting has been replaced by the theater, radio, and television, rarely a day passes without our hearing a story: Charles Kuralt goes "on the road" to tell us about a woman who operates an opera house on the Nevada desert; public television sponsors a series on the Vietnam experience; Garrison Keillor takes to the radio microphone with humorous yarns from the fictional Lake Wobegon, Minnesota. Indeed, the oral tradition of storytelling still thrives as a vital component in the sharing of our collective experience as human beings.

Storytelling is one familiar instance of the pattern of discourse known as narrative. In a broader sense, narrative is used in documentaries that trace the history of something, perhaps a social movement; in fictional and nonfictional literature such as Charles Dickens's *Oliver Twist* or Joseph McGinniss's *Fatal Vision;* in the humorous monologues of the comedian; and in the religious parables so central to the pulpit oratory of preachers like Billy Graham. Whenever a person feels compelled to understand or share an experience or idea by recounting a sequence of events, that person has begun to use the narrative pattern.

Discovering meaning in events through narrative satisfies a basic human urge to understand life through the sharing of experience. As Walter Fisher writes, "The meaning and significance of life in all its social dimensions require the recognition of its narrative structure."[4] Thinking in terms of stories, then, is an essential way to relate to others, and is one reason that human beings have been referred to as "the story-telling animal."[5]

What is it about the narrative pattern of discourse that so attracts us? Certainly the pattern is simple; in fact, it is usually the first pattern we learn to recognize. Based on the concept of time, narratives occur in chronological order—one event after another—and although some narratives become complex tapestries of human drama, most follow essentially the same order in which we live out our lives.

Narrative further attracts us as a pattern of discourse because it involves characters engaged in the drama that is life. Whether our particular attraction is to a character on a soap opera or to the life of an American hero, in their collective sense narratives show us what is good and what is bad, what is acceptable behavior and what is not. Narrative discourse creates, to a great extent, the social norms by which we live.[6]

But beyond creating a shared social consensus, narratives help us understand ourselves as individuals. Recall a time when you were told a parable such as the one about the good Samaritan, or a fairy tale like "Cinderella." Stories such as these evoke in us the need to reflect on our own successes and shortcomings as human beings. Narratives are like mirrors we look into privately for the answer to that most perplexing question: Who am I?[7]

So far we have established that narratives are simple, colorful, educational, and at times cathartic. The full power of a narrative, however, is often realized in yet another function it assumes—moral persuasion.

The Narrative Intention: Roles, Situations, and Purposes

Many narratives contain subtle lessons in morality. The familiar line "And so the moral of the story is ..." serves as a caution to behave one way and not another, to believe X and not Y. Read the following story from the oral tradition of the Hausa tribe of Nigeria:

This is about the Chief of Lies and the Chief of Truth who started off on a journey together. They came to a large town, and lo, the mother of the King of this town had just died, and the whole town was mourning. Then the Chief of Lies said, "What is making you cry?" And they replied, "The King's mother is dead." Then he said, "You go and tell the King that his mother shall arise." In the evening the Chief of Lies went and caught a wasp, the kind of insect that makes a noise like Kurururu, and he put it in a small tin. No sooner had the people departed from the grave, the Chief of Lies opened the mouth of the grave slightly and brought the wasp and put it in, and then closed the mouth as before. Then he sent for the King, and said that he was to come and put his ear to the grave—meanwhile this insect was buzzing—and when the King had come, the Chief of Lies said, "Do you hear your mother talking?" Then the King arose, he chose a horse and gave it to the Chief of Lies, he brought gold and gave it to him, and the whole town began to rejoice because the King's mother was going to rise again. Then the Chief of Lies said, "Well, your father is holding your mother down in the grave and they are quarrelling." And he continued, "Your father, if he comes out, will take away the kingdom from you," and he said that his father would also kill him. When the King told the people this, they piled stones on the grave, and the King said, "Here Chief of Lies, go away. I give you these three horses." Certainly falsehood is more profitable than truth in this world.[8]

Notice the moral of this story; that lying is more profitable than telling the truth. Whether one accepts this as true or not is, of course, an individual choice. More important for us is the fact that a narrative is often the best way to demonstrate what might normally be considered an irrational idea. One unique feature of narratives is that they help us explain those phenomena of the world that are not always given to logical analysis.[9] Let's look further at this important feature.

We often assume that if something is valid it can be proven so through logic. We are taught that, as Fisher so rightly observes, "the world is a set of logical puzzles which can be resolved through appropriate analysis and application of reason conceived as an argumentative construct."[10] That is, there are rules for reasoning one's way through an idea (as you will see in patterns that follow logical formulas such as cause-effect), and if the idea meets the tests for validity and rationality, it deserves our acceptance.

But it is not always possible to account for the logic of events with traditional rational models. When logic fails us, when it fails to account for the world as experienced, we turn to narrative as our path to understanding. Because it answers the question "What happened?" and allows the "why" to surface through the events themselves, a narrative, to prove its point, need only be true to the audience's sense of how experience works. Narratives rest for their truth value on what the philosopher Aristotle called the natural tendency for people to know the truth when they hear it.[11]

Narrative is frequently the pattern of discourse used in a public speech. Short narratives can be used throughout a speech structured according to another pattern, but narratives can also serve as the analytical probe and organizational structure of an entire speech. Two of the most notable addresses of recent times, Richard Nixon's 1952 "Checkers' Address," in which he defended himself against charges of having a political slush fund; and Edward M. Kennedy's 1969 "Chappaquiddick Address," in which he explained the events surrounding the death of one of his aides, Mary Jo Kopechne, are just two examples of significant public speeches that followed primarily a narrative pattern.[12]

In the speech-communication classroom a narrative is a practical and interesting speech. Besides providing the opportunity to analyze and organize a topic with the narrative pattern, narratives help class members come to know one another, and they frequently generate interesting classroom discussions. Thus, whether you are assigned to present a narrative in the class or choose to present a narrative in another communication situation, you are engaging in a pattern of discourse that is central to human interaction.

So far in this chapter we have established that human beings are by nature storytellers. The narrative situation arises whenever we feel compelled to communicate a human experience that leads to a lesson or moral that is most easily explained through experience. The narrator is a storyteller cast in many specific roles; documentarist, political apologist, entertainer, teacher, and advisor. Narratives function to delight, instruct, and even persuade others. At some time or another, most of us will find ourselves needing and using the narrative pattern of discourse.

Choosing a Topic For a Narrative

A narrative is concerned with the question "What happened?" and it focuses on people and events in motion—that is, heading toward some point. When the communication situation (the event, your role, and your intent) suggests narrative, begin by asking, "What has happened to me or to someone else that is worth sharing with this audience?"

Almost any narrative can result in an interesting speech if you have thought about it deeply, sorted the events out in your mind, and come to understand your reaction. A narrative can recount an experience with another person or with an object or event. It can cover a long period of time, two or more seemingly unconnected units of time, or a brief but lucid moment. Here is a list of topics that students in a speech-communication course recently developed into narratives.

Learning not to chew gum in school

Living through my parents' divorce

Traveling behind the Iron Curtain

Escape from Vietnam

The only female on a male soccer team

Sometimes a winning narrative can result from an examination of the subtler experiences of life. On the other hand, choosing the first idea that comes to mind, or the most obvious, can lead to a trivial speech. Here is a list of overused or trivial topics gleaned from a number of speech instructors:

The first time I got drunk

My summer job

The first day away at college

Meeting a new roommate

My favorite pet

Of course, our presenting these lists does not mean that a similar topic would or would not work for you. Most importantly, think about experiences from which you have learned, experiences that have affected you deeply or made you the person you are today.

A narrative topic may or may not require outside reading and research, since a successful narrative is often the result of turning inward and thinking about your life. At other times—when discussing a social movement, perhaps—you might need outside documentation, including dates, times, places, and character data. Your topic will dictate the amount and type of information you need.

Developing a Narrative

Begin developing a narrative by drafting a critical-thinking statement, following the guidelines given in Chapter 3 of this text. Be certain the statement gives some indication of your role, the situation, and the outcome you intend. In the following sample critical-thinking statement, the speaker provides herself with a clear understanding of the communication situation in which she will present her narrative:

> *Running for senior-class president was the most memorable experience in my life. I want the audience to understand the emotional roller coaster that a political campaign is, and to learn that taking a challenge has its own rewards, win or lose. My point is the familiar one: it's not how you finish the race but how you get there that counts.*

Having determined your role and intent, the next step in the development of the narrative is to analyze the story itself. A complete narrative has three main ingredients: a theme, a story line, and character development.

The Theme

The theme of a narrative is the underlying "why" of the story, the lesson or moral you want to communicate by telling the story. Notice how the speaker quoted above finished her critical-thinking statement: "My point is the familiar one. . . ." By capturing her theme the speaker has a sense of the whole narrative.

A theme is stated in the form of a belief, an attitude, or a "truth" one has gleaned from an experience. Sometimes you will find a familiar expression that captures your theme, while at other times you will have to find the exact words yourself. Whichever is the case, word the theme as concisely as possible, even adding a touch of vividness to the statement (see Chapter 7).

The theme may or may not be stated in your analysis exactly as it will appear in the speech, but the point should be the same. Notice in the model speech on pages 245–248 that the speaker's theme is "Love is a fire that extinguishes as quickly as it ignites." In the story itself, however, the speaker says, "Both my loves ended as suddenly as they had begun." The words are different but the theme is consistent.

The Story Line

The story line is made up of the events necessary to accomplishing the goal. Start to develop the story line by listing the events that comprise your experience. Recognize that any story has an infinite number of events and that any single moment can be discussed endlessly. Thus, the narrator must mark off the boundaries of any particular experience, making decisions about the beginning, middle, and end of the experience, and about which events are absolutely essential to the audience's understanding of the theme.

The beginning of an experience is the moment we realize that something has happened to us, that some condition is changed or changing. The body of a narrative captures the sequence of events that explains how the condition came about, and the conclusion explains how the condition was resolved, what changes occurred, or what we have learned or deeply felt.

Events should be chosen with the audience in mind. What does the audience need to know in order to understand the theme? Once the audience has heard the story, they should feel that there are no loose ends, that the theme is completely understandable through what has gone before. Events that do not aim the audience toward the theme are called digressions. If there are too many digressions in a speech, audience members may lose track of the narrative.

The Characters

Narratives require attention to character development. Characters must be described concretely, their physical and mental qualities plainly communicated. It is not enough, for instance, to say, "Agnes was the most magnetic person I had ever met." The audience is left to wonder what the word *magnetic* might possibly mean. Qualities such as "magnetism" are the result of real things: physical features and traits of personality. Look at the way a speaker in a narrative might describe "magnetism" more concretely:

Agnes was the most magnetic woman I had ever met. She possessed compelling physical features: white hair piled in layers on top of her head, hair that some rumored touched her waist; strong hands that dominated any handshake; and steely blue eyes that, once fixed, remained on their target relentlessly searching for the person behind the face-mask. When she spoke, Agnes' voice exuded confidence and candor, and yet there was a softness about it that said, "Want to talk?" Agnes used that voice to draw others irresistibly into her favorite sport, debating. You never knew when you might be the next fly caught in that perfectly spun web.

Notice that the "magnetism" now becomes something tangible, a quality the audience can see in the person being described.

Describing characters serves an important purpose. Listeners must be able to understand through character description why the person would behave as she or he does. People act as they do because their physical and mental makeup interacts with events in a unique way. A person who is fearful will react differently than one who is confident in the same situation. A person who feels subordinate will behave differently than someone who feels superior, even in equal circumstances. When listeners understand the characters through concrete description, the characters' behavior is no longer a mystery.

Organizing and Outlining a Narrative

Experiences generally occur in strict chronological order: event 1 leads to event 2, which leads to event 3, and so on. In our minds, however, an experience often occurs in some other order—in reverse order, for instance, if we do not bother to sort out the events of the experience until it has had some impact on us. Organizing a narrative, however, is different from thinking about it and analyzing it.

Begin by writing out the critical thinking statement at the top of the outline; then proceed to list the characters and the events that will form the outline of the story. In the model speech "Two Love

Affairs" (pp. 245–248), the speaker begins with a critical-thinking statement and then a skeleton outline of characters and events:

Critical-Thinking Statement: I want to share with the audience my first two experiences with falling in love, each of which has had a lasting emotional impact on me. But more importantly, each taught me one lesson: that love is a fire that extinguishes as quickly as it ignites.

I. Characters
  A. I
  B. Demerara (the horse)
  C. Suzanne

II. Events
  A. I meet the horse.
  B. I fall in love.
  C. Demerara becomes a champion.
  D. Demerara falls and must be destroyed.
  E. My heart is broken.
  F. I meet Suzanne.
  G. We fall in love.
  H. She goes away to school.
  I. I become injured.
  J. The relationship disintegrates.
  K. My heart is broken.

Having listed the essential characters and events in the narrative, the speaker begins to fill in details. Look, for instance, at how the speaker describes the moment when the horse is put away:

I was also there the afternoon when, as she raced for the lead on the first turn at Suffolk Downs, she shattered her left front foreleg. I ran toward Demerara in a full panic. Tears filled my eyes, but I did not care if anyone saw. I will never forget that look on her face when they had to put her away. It was a sad look that said both thanks and goodbye, a look that said, "Take care of yourself, Steve."

Note that the words shown in the transcript presented in this text are the words the speaker chose when he gave the speech. Each telling of a narrative requires spontaneity and adjustment to the audience. When filling in a narrative outline, then, do not become enamored of one particular description to the point that you have it memorized. Work out your details so that you can outline your speech, but speak spontaneously during the speech itself, according to the guidelines suggested in Chapter 6. The final outline for a narrative might look like this:

A. Event 1
   1. Description and character sketches
   2. Details of the event

B. Event 2
   1. Descriptions
   2. Details

C. Event 3
   1. Descriptions
   2. Details

There are variations on this outline form, and your choice of sentences or words will depend upon the experience itself. The only variations not appropriate in a narrative are long digressions from the events or a sequence that has no sensible order.

Wording and Delivery

Narratives can be boring if the speaker uses the same words and phrases over and over to keep the story moving, such as "So then . . ." and "Next, we. . . ." Use a variety of transitions to move from event to event, such as "After our arrival . . ." or "Following this occurrence . . ." or "Once the music began. . . ." Most of the cues in a narrative pertain to time, and time can be conveyed by a word such as *then* or *next*, so it is important to think consciously about alternatives.

Narratives also require variety in the use of action verbs to create drama or movement in the story. Overusing the same verbs makes a narrative dull. Instead of saying, "So he says to me . . ." say, "He shrieked . . ."; instead of saying, "Next, she turned the car over . . ." say, "Suddenly she flipped the car. . . ." The model speeches in this chapter will show you other verbs that speakers have used to give color and drama to the events in their narratives.

As mentioned briefly earlier, narratives are more interesting and meaningful if concrete, specific language is used to describe the characters and events. To say, "She was the most awesome coach I ever had" is vague, since the jargon term *awesome* can mean any number of things. The following list of phrases shows you more clearly how to make your language specific, and at the same time emotive and expressive:

AMBIGUOUS: The rain was unbelievable.

CLEAR: The rain beat hard against my window like the drum roll in a circus act.

AMBIGUOUS: He was a vicious brute.

CLEAR: He created a fearful impression with his nostrils flared, brow knitted, and teeth bared.

AMBIGUOUS: I was, like, so cold.

CLEAR: I was so cold my teeth rattled like a ticker-tape machine.

Narratives frequently include dialogue. Using the exact words a character used and speaking in that character's voice add color to the narrative by capturing the exact shades and tones of the character's personality. Dialogue takes practice, and you should rehearse it carefully, trying to say the words exactly as the person spoke them originally. Though it is acceptable to paraphrase the person's words, actual dialogue is better. Try some in your speech.

Narratives are best delivered without notes, or with a simple notation system such as a word outline. Few notes should be necessary for a narrative about a personal experience; and for narratives that focus on the experiences of others, notes pertaining to key names, dates, places, and events should be all you need.

Focus your delivery on the audience. Use vocal emphasis and variety to capture the mood and tone of the experience, and try to imitate facial expressions you remember as being particularly vivid during the experience. In general, the goal in delivering a narrative is to capture as accurately and vividly as possible the experience as it occurred.

Summary

Storytelling, one of our most familiar and cherished traditions, is a common manifestation of a pattern of communication known as narrative. Narrative is also found in documentaries, literature, and

CHAPTER 9

oratory, and public speakers frequently use it to analyze and organize their speeches. Discovering meaning through narrative satisfies a basic human urge to share the experience that is life.

Narratives serve a variety of functions. They can be entertaining, educational, and subtly persuasive, and they help us understand those common experiences in life that are so unyielding to logical analysis. Narratives work because they make "common sense" out of events and reinforce the truisms by which we act out our lives.

Narratives can recount long periods of time or brief moments. Although they can range from the most personal experiences to stories about others, the best ones are always those for which there is some lasting effect on the narrator.

Planning a narrative begins with a critical-thinking statement suggesting your role and your intention for the narrative. From this statement, planning proceeds according to three main ingredients of a narrative: theme, story line, and character development.

The theme of a narrative is the lesson or moral embodied in the events, while the story line is the series of events that forms the beginning, the development, and the conclusion of the narrative. Finally, characters must be described concretely and vividly for the audience to make sense of their actions.

Organizing a narrative involves listing the characters and outlining the events in the order in which you want them to appear. Filling in the outline with details—descriptions and examples—adds color and clarity to the story.

Narratives can be boring if the speaker uses repetitive transitional phrases or if there is little variety in the use of action verbs. Use specific details, concrete descriptions, and dialogue to add color to the narrative. Deliver a narrative with as few notes as possible, focusing on the audience and creating, as much as possible, the tone and drama of the original events.

Two Love Affairs

The model speech presented below recounts two series of events in order to make one point. The narrative worked well in getting the audience to empathize with the speaker on a topic familiar to all of us: love.

Topic: Two Love Affairs

Critical-Thinking Statement: I want to share with the audience my first two experiences with falling in love, each of which has had a lasting emotional impact on me. But more importantly, each taught me one lesson: that love is a fire that extinguishes as quickly as it ignites.

I. Characters
  A. I
  B. Demerara (the horse)
  C. Suzanne

II. Events
  A. I meet the horse.
  B. I fall in love.
  C. Demerara becomes a champion.
  D. Demerara falls and must be destroyed.
  E. My heart is broken.
  F. I meet Suzanne.
  G. We fall in love.
  H. She goes away to school.
  I. I become injured.
  J. The relationship disintegrates.
  K. My heart is broken.

Introduction: Speaker piques audience curiosity, lets audience know that these are personal experiences, signals the sequence of events with the words first time.

Two experiences in my life have happened to me quite suddenly, both almost without warning. In both cases I was at one moment just a naive young boy and in the next moment I was in love. Let me tell you about the first time.

Language: Notice the detail in description of characters. Vividness in description helps the audience participate in the experience.

Demerara was an absolutely beautiful young creature. It was her eyes that captured me on that first, fateful meeting. They were the eyes of an angel: deeply set, dark, luminous, and filled with a sort of gentleness that made her seem wise far beyond her young years. Her hair was the color of polished mahogany and it shone in the sun's rays as she stepped toward me. I will never forget those eyes sparkling with energy and spirit as she gazed at me for the first time. For me it was love at first sight. She was a horse, a filly, who had a heart as big as a mountain. We were together for three years.

Language: Notice the use of figurative comparisons: heart as big as a mountain, eyes of an angel. Narrators can use figurative language to rouse the emotions of the audience.

Demerara loved to be petted and whispered to, especially in the early morning hours before her workouts. She was seldom moody, and most often would prance gaily about the stable yard. We would take frequent long walks together, neither one of us feeling the need to communicate with words. A light touch, a nuzzle, would always say more.

Demerara would always call out to me in the morning as I arrived for work, and she would often sense my presence long before I actually arrived at the barn. Some of the other workers called it "horse sense," but I called it intuition.

Demerara could always sense my mood, and if I was depressed or grumpy she would know just what to do to lighten my mood. She could sense sadness in me and could heal my hurt with one look. She helped me on many occasions to heal the normal hurts of adolescence. We were comfortable together.

Other people noticed our love growing and would warn me to go slowly. "Hearts are meant to be broken," they would whisper. But you know that love is blind and I never listened.

"Dem," as I called her, won over thirty thousand dollars during her thoroughbred racing career. She won fourteen out of her twenty-three races. I was there for all her victories and my heart leaped every time she crossed the finish line in first place.

I was also there the afternoon when, as she raced for the lead on the first turn at Suffolk Downs, she shattered her left front foreleg. I ran toward Demerara in a full panic. Tears filled my eyes, but I did not care if anyone saw. I will never forget that look on her face when they had to put her away. It was a sad look that said both thanks and goodbye, a look that said, "Take care of yourself, Steve." Demerara knew she was going to die that day. She knew it as surely as she knew when she had won her first race. She was an incredible lady; she was also gone.

I promised myself that night that I would never fall in love again. I was sixteen years old then, but like most of us at that age, I felt I had experienced it all.

My second experience with love happened quite as suddenly as the first. I was walking to the locker room after football practice. As I turned the corner she was there. It was her eyes that first caught my attention: they were big, deep, and they shone as they caught the sun. She looked wise much beyond her years. Suzanne looked back at me smiling faintly,

Note the speaker's use of the term three years *(second paragraph), which helps the audience follow the time order of the narrative. Placing characters in time is important for an audience to follow a narrative.*

Language: The use of actual dialogue does much to capture the moment and the mood of a narrative.

Transition: Notice how the speaker ends the first experience by explaining its effect on him. This helps set the tone for the second experience and cues the audience that the two experiences are to be connected.

Compare the description of the second love with the one of the horse in the second paragraph. The speaker is cueing the audience to the parallels between his two loves.

and she kept walking. Her hair was the color of polished gold. She was beautiful and I was in love.

We would walk and talk for hours at a time, once we got to know one another. We bared our souls to each other, but then at times we would not talk for hours. The silence we shared was relaxing.

Notice once again how the speaker uses repetition to compare the two relationships.

Suzanne cried when I told her about Demerara. Her sorrow over the horse only made me love her more. People, especially my friends, noticed our love growing and they warned me to be careful, but I did not listen—I did not want to listen. I was hopelessly in love.

Language: Speaker makes a larger point out of the experience. Doing so makes the audience realize that all events have meaning.

It would be nice to say that we lived happily ever after, but we did not. Like most things in life, I have learned, love is not simple.

Suzanne went away to college and I stayed home to save the money I needed to go to college also. During that time I was smashed up in a serious motorcycle accident. Suzanne could not get away from school to be there when I needed her. I tried to understand this but I also knew that if our situations had been reversed I would have been there for her.

When she finally arrived to see me weeks later during her Christmas break, her eyes read the story in mine. Our relationship had died a geographical death. I was nineteen at the time and I swore I would never fall in love again.

Conclusion: Speaker begins to connect the events in order to resolve them.

My love affair with Suzanne was over. It was over as definitely as Demerara was dead. Dead things do not come back to life.

My two experiences with love were alike in many ways. Both loves were alike in many ways. Their eyes shared a loveliness that drew me toward them. They both loved to be whispered to and both loved to take long walks—quiet and peaceful walks in the woods. Both of my loves ended as suddenly as they had begun. My friends were right.

I will never forget these experiences. They seem like one experience, actually, the feeling of love. I remember that I had no control over the events or my feelings. My young life was deeply affected by love and continues to be so today.

In the following model speech the narrator talks about a hunting trip with his father during which he learned a valuable lesson. The speech is moving, and it reinforces for the audience a value central in the minds of most of us.

Hunting in the Maine Woods

Topic: Hunting in the Maine Woods

Critical-Thinking Statement: I want to share with the audience a moment of personal pride and growth stemming from an experience in the Maine woods with my father. The point of my story is that, win or lose, you always play fair.

I. Characters
   A. I
   B. My father
   C. The hunter by the truck

II. Events
   A. We embark on our last hunting trip.
   B. We stop at the donut shop.
   C. We start to hunt.
   D. We stop for lunch.
   E. We try "still" hunting in the afternoon.
   F. The hunting day ends.
   G. We return to the truck.
   H. I stop the other hunter from shooting the buck.
   I. My dad responds.
   J. Reflections on the experience.

I grew up in a little town called Brunswick in Maine. Up in Maine, hunting is a popular sport, and so it was sort of natural that my father and I were avid hunters. We used to go out every other day during the season.

Introduction: Speaker provides background essential to the point of the story. He sets the scene for us.

The last year I lived in Maine was my sophomore year in high school. My parents had divorced and my father was living in New Jersey. The only chance we had to go hunting was the last day of the season. We knew this might be our last hunting trip together in the woods.

Thesis: Although not stated directly, the speaker clearly implies that his pattern is narrative and that he wants to share with the audience a new understanding.

What we did not know was that this trip would bring us closer together than we had ever been before, and it would teach me a lesson I would never forget.

We had a ritual: up at 3:00 A.M., off to Dunkin Donuts, then out to the woods. We'd spend the morning hunting, get lunch, and then go back to the woods until 4:15, the official end of the hunting day. On this last trip, we got dressed up in our boots, long underwear, and heavy pants. Then quietly, so as not to wake my mother and sister, we loaded up the truck and headed off to the place my father humorously called "Drunken Donuts," because of some of the people we would meet at that time of the morning.

Arriving at the donut shop, we slogged down a couple of cups of coffee, three donuts each, and listened to the stories of other hunters, most of which were about the big eight-pointer that had eluded their sights, or the friend who was nearly laced with buckshot by an overanxious weekend Daniel Boone. When we left the shop it was about 5:00 A.M. and just a five-minute ride to the preserve.

Actual hunting starts at 6:00 A.M., so we couldn't load up our guns till then. My dad was a stickler for the rules of hunting, always telling me, "If the deer can't cheat, neither can we." When we finally walked into the woods we immediately came upon a scrape that had been made by the deer. It was about one foot square.

For those of you who don't know what a scrape is, I'd better tell you. The deer scrapes off the topsoil—I should say the buck—and then urinates in the middle. This marks off the buck's territory. My father decided to hunt about fifty yards away from the scrape in hopes of getting a shot at a doe or another buck coming to investigate the scrape. I walked about two hundred yards up the trail that led to the scrape, hoping to get a shot at a deer from that vantage point. Well, I sat there for about three hours, listening to the squirrels above me making all sorts of noise, as if to warn the deer that I was there. It reached 11:00 A.M., so I decided to go see what dad had accomplished, and, as expected, he had seen nothing. We left for lunch.

Lunch was nothing more than a cup of soup and a donut at the same shop we had visited in the morning. The same men were there, telling the same stories about tracks and scrapes and rustling in the bushes— but not one deer had been shot. Dad said, "If this was baseball, Bruce, the deer would have a shutout right now."

Returning to the woods about 12:30 that afternoon we walked back to the scrapes. They had been freshened even more. Another layer of topsoil had been scraped off and there was fresh urine in the center. We decided to try our luck at "still" hunting.

Still hunting is a process of taking three to five steps, stopping, looking around, taking another three to five steps and looking around some more. Dad and I split up for this part of the day and we didn't meet up again for a good two hours. We talked softly as we walked about this being our last time hunting. Dad said, "Bruce, this is more about you and me than it is about us and the deer. I'll miss these trips."

Language: The speaker defines another term, thus showing his concern for the audience.

The time finally came. It was 4:15. The day was over; the deer had won and would live another year. We did not feel mocked, just defeated. We returned to the truck, opened it, and started to load our gear into the back. We put in our guns, hunting vests, jackets, sweaters, and shirts that we had layered ourselves with that morning.

Language: Notice the words the time finally came. *Such cue words help the audience follow events.*

While we were packing up, the hunter who had parked his truck next to ours came by. He leaned his gun against the front of his car and started unloading his gear into the truck. When I had finished I climbed into the front of our truck and looked up the ridge. Behind the scrapes, standing on the ridge and looking down at us was that buck. While I was admiring him, the hunter next to me walked over, picked up his gun, shouldered it and took aim at the buck on the ridge. When I heard the safety go off I knew what he intended to do. By now it was 5:00 P.M. and the hunting season was over. So at the exact time my dad leaned over and hit the horn I opened the truck door and slammed it into the hunter. His gun went flying and he fell crumpled to the ground. After about a minute, the hunter stood up, picked up his gun and gave me an angry, evil look. There was a long standstill in our staring match, but I did not give in. Finally, the hunter picked up his weapon, loaded it into his truck, and drove off.

The speaker uses simple but effective verbs to show action in the sequence of events.

I thought at first I had done wrong. My heart raced as I looked toward my father. But he leaned over to me, grabbed my hand and said, "Bruce, you did good work. That was the right thing to do."

Language: The speaker attempts a sample of dialogue. Dialogue helps a narrative by giving the audience a better feel for the characters and by adding an element of real life to the story.

I learned at that moment that hunting wasn't just a way of killing for food. Hunting was a sport and at 4:15 that afternoon the buck had won, won the right to live another year. When that hunter picked up his gun and aimed it at the deer it was like taking a punch at your opponent after the bell has rung.

Language: The speaker makes a good attempt at metaphor, comparing the illegal shot attempted by the hunter to punching someone after the bell.

Conclusion: The speaker reflects upon the point of the experience, actually stating his thesis, not exactly as he had worded it in his critical-thinking statement but as it came to him during the speech itself.

As I look back on the situation now, I know that there were better ways to handle it. I hope the other hunter learned the same lesson I learned: when you play a sport you play by the rules. Hunting is a game, and when it's over, it's over. Sometimes you win and sometimes you lose, but you never cheat. All you can do is hope for better luck next time.

What I remember most, though, is my father's words, "You did good work." That was our last hunting trip, and I see Dad only once or twice a year now, but we have a bond between us that spans the miles, a bond we forged in the woods of Maine.

Exercises

1. The following exercise is useful for drawing the meaning out of an experience. In a group discussion, describe an experience you have had today (a meal, waking up and preparing to leave for work or school) to others in the group. Having done so, see whether you can describe the experience again, this time trying to add detail to each moment and trying to make some point out of the experience. If you are listening, try to ask one question that might draw the speaker into revealing more detail.

2. Find a short fable or parable that has a clear moral stated in it (one good source is James Thurber's *Fables for Our Time* [Harper and Brothers Publishers, 1940]). Bring the fable to class, and either read it to the whole class or share it with a small group. Try to explain why the moral makes sense to you. If you are listening to the story, try to think of a counterpoint to the moral, a good reason that it does not work. See whether you can think of an experience that reinforces the counterpoint.

3. Prepare and present a narrative speech to your class. Your instructor will provide details for the assignment.

References

1. Frederick J. Antczak, *Thought and Character: The Rhetoric of Democratic Action,* (Ames, IA: Iowa State University Press, 1985), pp. 74–75.

2. Fred S. Sorrenson, *Speech for the Teacher* (NY: Ronald Press, 1952), p. 348.

3. Antczak, p. 80.

4. Walter Fisher, "Narration as a Human Communication Paradigm: The Case of Public Moral Argument," *Communication Monographs* 51 (1984), p. 3.

5. Fisher, p. 8.

6. William G. Kirkwood, "Storytelling and Self-Confrontation: Parables as Communication Strategies," *Quarterly Journal of Speech* 69 (1983), p. 73.

7. Kirkwood, p. 73.

8. Peter Farb, *Word Play* (NY: Bantam Books, 1975), p. 34.

9. Fisher, pp. 6–10.

10. Fisher, p. 4.

11. Fisher, p. 9.

12. For a critical analysis of Kennedy's speech see David Ling, "A Pentadic Analysis of Senator Edward M. Kennedy's Address to the People of Massachusetts, July 25, 1969," *Central States Speech Journal* 21 (1970), pp. 81–86. For an interesting analysis of Nixon's address, see Irving J. Rein, *The Relevant Rhetoric* (NY: The Free Press, 1969), pp. 203–209.

Model Speeches:
1. Steven Studley, "Two Love Affairs." Used by permission.
2. Bruce Kidman, "Hunting in the Maine Woods." Used by permission.

Whenever a person feels compelled to understand or share an experience by recounting a sequence of events, that person has begun to use the narrative pattern. Narratives often tell a story, and they function to instruct, entertain, and even persuade others of truths gained from experience.

A narrative speech can grow from any meaningful experience. For example, perhaps you once were hiking through the countryside and came upon a littered clearing like the scene in the above photograph. Maybe you were so disgusted with the sight that you became involved in a community clean-up and recycling project. Your experience could form the basis for a narrative speech.

Your narrative could recall the moment you felt the urge to get involved in the recycling project. You could focus on the significant events of the project—those humorous or dramatic moments when the experience came alive: a grueling yet inspiring week spent cleaning up the remote wilderness, long afternoons surrounded by mountains of garbage, the sudden realization that litterbugs tend to use a particular brand of drink. You could end the narrative with a statement about the meaning of the experience—for you and perhaps for the audience.

A narrative like this not only informs your audience about recycling and tells them about you, but also subtly persuades them to care for their environment.

Chapter 10 · Process

One of the most endearing faces on the television screen belongs to Julia Child, the world-renowned culinary expert who, on her television show "The French Chef," prepares some of the world's most tempting dishes. Each show follows the same formula. Through an introductory narrative Child creates a setting, perhaps a festive occasion such as Thanksgiving. She then provides a background preview, giving the audience facts about the origin of the occasion, or key names, dates, and places. An essential ingredient of the background is a list and/or a description of the food that traditionally is prepared and eaten on the occasion. This list serves as a transition to the focus of each show, preparation of the food itself.

Once into the body of the show, Child shows each step in the preparation of the food, commenting colorfully about her personal experiences, presenting little-known facts about the food, or telling humorous anecdotes pertaining to cooking. The show ends when Child places the food in a setting resembling that for the occasion and proceeds to sample it.

The Process Intention: Roles, Situations, and Purposes

Even those not familiar with "The French Chef" will recognize the pattern just described. Shop teachers in high school often follow the same pattern to show how an engine or a power tool operates. Counselors guide clients in the same way through a "stop smoking" program or a clinic in "dressing for success." At public hearings on controversial issues, speakers frequently talk about the development of a budget or the steps required to get a bill passed. These examples strike us as similar because they are all based on the same concept: the concept of process.

Curiosity about how to perform an action or about how things work is natural.[1] Consider for a moment the number of times you have asked a question beginning with the word *how*. How does an airplane fly? How do I prepare my income-tax forms? How should I study for tomorrow's test? Whenever we think about the steps, stages, or phases that characterize some activity or object, we are thinking with the process pattern.

The process pattern usually follows a chronological order to explain a series of steps, stages, changes, or operations that lead to a specific conclusion. A process becomes difficult when it has numerous steps or alternatives, or when it involves technical expertise. Indeed, we have all felt frustrated when trying to follow instructions that are billed as "a few easy steps" but then tell us, "Attach lift tube to leg lift pivot with the pivot pin, flat washers, and pushnut. Make sure cupped end of lift tube is facing down." Thus, while the process pattern is often used, it requires adherence to guidelines to be effective.

The process pattern is intended to serve the practical needs of many situations. There are times, for instance, when we want to understand the stages, steps, or operations involved in the development of something. At other times we may be curious about how something works in order that we might use it ourselves. The process pattern allows us to focus on development without having to worry as much about the people involved.

The process pattern serves a functional purpose.[2] It is not concerned with appeals to the imagination or with the interactions between characters and events as much as with facts and information that explain something concretely. Thus, while narrative is concerned with "what happened" as a way of understanding why it happened, process focuses on clarity and understanding for their own sake.

The process pattern is usually used in a public speech to satisfy practical, functional ends. For example, speeches orienting new employees to a corporation are often structured around the notion of "how things work around here—Standard Operating Procedures." Analyzing your topic and structuring your speech for the speech-communication classroom are appropriate whenever your main concern is to answer questions such as "How does it work?" "How would it work?" or "What are its stages or steps?"

When you choose this pattern for a speech, your role is to describe a process or change to your audience so that they can either perform the process themselves or understand how something works or has evolved. For example, a student who worked part-time in her college's registration office presented a speech on the computerized registration system to a group of new students. She emphasized the sequence of steps the students would have to follow and also let them know how these steps would simplify a process most students had come to detest: registration.

A speaker's concern with informing an audience about why certain key steps are important makes the difference between an interesting, vibrant speech and a boring, mechanical one. Effective speakers think through a process carefully, figuring out the most appropriate sequence of steps and determining how to subordinate less important to more important steps in order to facilitate audience comprehension. So, while a process speech does involve intensive analysis of the topic, the speaker always keeps in the forefront of his or her thinking the audience that will need to understand the process.

Choosing a Topic for a Process Speech

As we mentioned previously, the process pattern is appropriate whenever your role as a speaker is to teach your audience how to do something or how something works. In a speech in the preceding chapter on narrative, the speaker used a narrative pattern in order to lead his audience to understanding a lesson he learned on a hunting trip with his father (pp. 249–252). His purpose was to relate to the audience a new understanding about life he had gained through his experience, and the best pattern for carrying out that intent was narrative.

What might have happened had the speaker decided that his intent was to use that experience and others he might have had to address the topic "Steps to Take in Tracking a Deer"? The narrative pattern would not have promoted this purpose. Indeed, much of what the speaker said about the experience would have been meaningless with the process focus. What would the moment when he confronted the hunter have mattered? What would it have mattered that he and his father always stopped at the donut shop? For a topic focusing on steps, the right pattern would have been process.

With the process pattern, the speaker's focus would have been on steps involved in deer hunting, steps such as obtaining a license, preparing for the hunt, and reporting in at the ranger station. Comments about the father-son relationship or about significant moral lessons learned on one particular day would have been secondary or irrelevant. The process pattern is used, then, to convey how something works or how to do something.

A process speech can concern either a physical or a mental process. The best topics are those that lend themselves to linear, sequential steps rather than those involving several simultaneous actions or numerous minute actions. Consider whether you can speak creatively about your topic. Here is a list of topics that have worked well:

How the federal budget is drafted

A preventive dental hygiene program

How to make a gravestone rubbing

Preparing for a job interview

The metamorphosis from preppie to yuppie

Some topics are too simple for a process speech, either because the steps are completely familiar to the average person or because the process involves only a few easy steps. The following are some topics not sufficiently challenging for a speech using the process pattern:

How to pot a plant

Changing a flat tire

How to brush your teeth

Other processes may be too complex for a speech because they are too technical. The following topics have failed for this reason:

How to play a musical instrument

Programming a computer

How a star becomes a black hole in the universe

You too can become a professional photographer

Of course, you might be able to adapt one of the above topics to your situation. The point is to consider the situation and especially the audience in your topic selection, so that your topic is neither too simple nor too complex for the time allotted or the level of understanding you seek with your listeners.

Once you have chosen your topic, begin to develop it. Planning should begin with a critical-thinking statement that indicates your role in the situation and the outcome you seek for the audience. In the sample critical thinking statement that follows, the speaker demonstrates a detailed understanding of the speech situation:

Developing a Process Speech

Many of us could decorate our rooms or apartments with secondhand furniture that looks like new, but most of us approach the task of refinishing the wrong way. There is no reason that furniture refinishing should be a smelly, time-consuming, and even dangerous chore. In my speech I intend to pass along my years of experience and my knowledge of furniture refinishing so that the audience will know how to do it, and perhaps even learn that it can be an enjoyable and practical hobby.

Once you have written the critical-thinking statement in its final form so that you have a clear sense of the entire situation, the next step in the development of a process speech is to analyze the topic itself. It is important to note at the outset that an analyzed process is not a speech. A speech based on the process pattern includes not only the steps in the process, but two other ingredients as well: the background or setting, and commentary on the process, including applications. We need to look at each of these ingredients carefully.

Background for a Process Topic

Every process has a history. Look for key dates, times, places, people, and events that help the audience see the process in its historical setting. In the model speech on pages 268–271, the speaker notes that spaghetti does not come from Italy but was brought there from China by Marco Polo. Such information helps the audience understand the topic and also enjoy it more.

A process occurs in a typical setting. Food is prepared and served in a certain type of room; furniture is refinished in a work area of some kind. It is always helpful to create a sense of setting for the audience so that they can mentally place the event as you speak about it. Many process speeches use visual aids that help simulate the setting for the audience, and this might be possible for your topic. The object is to create for the audience a feeling for the process itself through background narratives, facts, and settings.

As you are reading about your process, then, it is critical to look for elements that surround the process and provide the touches you need to create a process speech. Watch for humorous anecdotes about the process. Look for interesting or unusual facts about it; jot down personal experiences that might add to the speech itself. All such supporting material will aid you in the speech, whether in the background or preview step, or in the commentary that runs throughout the speech. In fact, one common problem in a process speech is not having enough things to say while performing or showing a step; anticipate this problem when planning the speech by locating adequate background material or historical information.

Steps in the Process

The steps in the process are the framework for your speech, so as you analyze the process, make a list of the steps or stages involved. As you develop the list, keep two guidelines in mind.

First, list the key steps or stages and then fill in subordinate steps as appropriate. For instance, in the process of studying for a test, a key step might be "Arrange a time and place for the group to meet." Under that main step might be subordinate steps such as "Make certain the location is not going to distract the group," or "Be sure the place is available." Later, these steps will appear in the outline as key points and subpoints; for now, list them with the idea that some are distinct steps while others are part of another step.

Second, as you think and read about the topic, take nothing for granted. Sometimes a step you perform routinely will be completely new to your audience. "Take a three-point stance," or "Fold the mixture into the egg whites" may seem perfectly obvious to you but may be completely baffling to inexperienced audience members. It is better to err on the side of too much information than to leave audience members hung up on a term or step so that they miss the rest of the process.

A process speech often requires dress rehearsal, especially if you are using visuals or if the speech requires a demonstration. If you plan such a process speech, be certain that you have prepared and practiced each step in advance. One student demonstrated the art of making ceramic pottery by showing the clay, then the clay-formed pot, then the same type of pot after glaze had been applied, and finally another pot representing the finished product after baking (firing). Preparing each step in advance is essential to keeping the speech moving along.

As you rehearse the process, think about commentary that might accompany the steps. Add fascinating anecdotes, tips for completing a step that perhaps do not appear in the directions, and personal experiences that add realism to the process. Look at the following commentary for a speech on making a gravestone rubbing. It added nicely to audience enjoyment of the speech.

You can see that the rubbing I am holding up here is only half finished. I am holding it up to remind you of an important step in gravestone rubbing. I was in a beautiful old graveyard in a little town in Vermont one afternoon near dusk. As I was busily rubbing I heard the footsteps and pawsteps of a woman and her German shepherd swiftly approaching me from the rear. They thought I was a vandal who had been defacing stones in the yard recently. I did not have time to explain as I moved far faster than I thought was possible to my car. The step is simply this: get permission to do the rubbing before you settle into your work.

Having analyzed the steps and having thought about the essential details necessary for understanding each step, proceed to planning the final ingredient of the process speech: the application of the process.

Commentary on the Process

We have mentioned the need to have a running commentary on the process as you present the steps. It is also essential to have some commentary on the finished process. Commentary on the process can include such information as what the final product might look, taste, or smell like. A speech on how to make a food, for instance, might include some tasting, smelling, or looking at pictures of variations on the recipe.

Similarly, commentary might include a personal experience that places the process into a lifelike framework. In the following excerpt from a speech on preparing a living will, the speaker added the following personal commentary:

As we sat around the table talking about what we might do if one of us were to die we realized that death is an experience that is very much a part of life and that we were simply discussing an event that each one of us would face; we had sort of demystified the whole experience and learned that a living will is just as important in the process of dying as making out the inheritance.

The most important purpose of the commentary is to show the process as it might appear in the real environment. This might require visual aids or narrative. When planning the process speech, include commentary that makes the process come alive for the audience.

Organizing and Outlining a Process Speech

Since the process pattern is based on time, the steps in the process should be listed as they occur: step 1, step 2, step 3, and so on. For instance, the speaker organizing the speech on the electronic synthesizer (see the model speech on pages 271–274) began by listing the three basic steps in the process:

Step 1: Generating electrical current

Step 2: Generating sound

Step 3: Modifying the sound to make the music

The next step is to begin filling in details for each step. Here is how the speaker filled in her outline for the process of making synthesized music:

Step 1: Generating electrical current
    A. Modules create current.
    B. Matrixes connect electrical signals between modules.

Step 2: Generating sound
    A. Oscillators provide five basic wave forms.
    B. Dual-noise generators provide white or pink sound.

Step 3: Modifying the sound to make the music
    A. Sound can be modified with a filter.
    B. Sound can be modified with an envelope generator.

You must flesh out the essential outline for a process speech. Begin adding background, history, terms that may need to be defined, and commentary concerning setting and application for the audience. The final outline for a process speech might look like this:

  I. Introduction

 II. Thesis

Wording and Delivery

Speeches that emphasize process contain words that cue the audience as the speech moves forward. Since a process speech details the growth and evolution of something, the language you use in the speech should suggest this evolution to the audience. Words such as *change, step, phase, condition, function*, and *transformation* indicate growth and evolution, and thus are the kinds of words that work well in a process speech.

Words such as *next* and *then* also signal movement through a process but are often overused. A speech that continuously uses *next* as a transition from one step to the next will soon begin to sound mechanical. When practicing the process speech, try to use some of the synonyms for *next* suggested above, and look for words of your own that signal the movement of the process.

A process speech can be quite technical; at the very least, it concerns something with which the audience is not familiar. As a result, process speeches often require technical terms to explain aspects of the process. Look, for example, at the model speech on the music synthesizer (pp. 271–274). The speaker needs to use a few technical terms because of the nature of the topic, so she defines the ones she thinks the audience will be unfamiliar with.

When the process speech involves technical terms, certain guidelines will help you communicate your ideas without being simplistic. First, eliminate terms that are not essential—jargon terms, overly technical formulas or equations, and confusing terms. Define the terms you must use, either on a visual aid or on a handout. Define the terms in the speech also, and check the audience with eye contact to be certain they have followed your definitions.

Second, use metaphors, similes, synonyms, and other rhetorical techniques you learned in Chapter 7, to achieve vividness. In the following example, for instance, notice how use of rhetorical techniques makes the revised version clearer than the first version:

FIRST VERSION: *The socio-normative process is one of diffuse osmosis, as variegated as is each interaction and as enigmatic as is the inevitable conflict resulting from the ricochet effect caused by the cultural dialectic.*

REVISED: *New values take hold in a society through a complex process. First, the millions of conversations going on each day among the people of the culture produce values by a sort of "sinking in," something like a sponge absorbing water. This phase is usually followed by a period of conflict as the new values clash with the old, a sort of "wringing out" effect in which some values wash down the drain while others remain in the sponge that is society.*

A speech based on the process pattern is a perfect opportunity to practice using visual aids. Along with the entire variety of visual aids discussed in Chapter 6, one that accompanies a process speech quite effectively is a visual with terms defined on it. As we mentioned above, display such a visual during the speech, or include a handout that audience members may refer to during the speech.

Process speeches sometimes require a demonstration, and this can be troublesome in certain situations. For instance, if a speaker were to show the audience how to remove old paint from furniture, he or she would need to perform some of the steps during the speech. In such situations, it is important to follow certain precautions. First, check the room in advance to be sure that the demonstration can be performed. Check for tables, electrical outlets, lighting, and so on—in short, for anything that will be necessary to the demonstration. Second, practice the steps to be demonstrated so that you will be able to perform them fluently and in view of all audience members. You should also consider simulating steps (showing the audience how to sand something without actually touching the wood, for instance), if that will accomplish your objective.

In general, delivering a speech organized around a process requires the same attention to naturalness, dynamism, and articulateness that all other speeches require. Be sure to review principles of effective delivery as you prepare the speech, and apply those principles as you deliver it.

Summary

Curiosity about how things work and about how to do things is natural. When we feel the need to explore the steps, stages, phases, or development of something, we turn to the concept of process. The process pattern is a chronological way to structure a speech and is often used in public speaking. It is usually used in situations where the audience needs explanations and information. The role of the speaker in such situations is to teach or guide the audience in an effort to clarify a process.

Choose the process pattern whenever your particular interest in a topic has to do with answering the question "How does it work?" or "How do you do it?" Topics come from all areas of life: science, hobbies, business, sports, the arts, and everyday activities. When selecting a topic, be careful to avoid overly technical or simplistic ones, and consider whether the topic might be clearly explained to the audience in the time allotted.

A process speech has three parts: the background or setting, which includes historical facts and descriptions that create interest in the topic; the process itself, including an analysis of both main and subordinate parts; and the commentary on the completed process, especially on the applications of the process.

A process speech is organized around the steps themselves, which are listed as they occur. They are also placed in key or subordinate positions. The outline is then filled in with details that flesh out the process and, of course, with an introduction, thesis, and conclusion.

A process speech should be worded to cue the audience to the movement of the speech. Use a number of synonyms to avoid repetition of words like *next* and *then.* Process speeches often involve technical terms, which should be carefully defined or explained by means of rhetorical techniques such as metaphor.

Visual aids can be very important in a process speech. You must plan them carefully and rehearse with them if they are to be effective.

Making an Authentic Italian Spaghetti Dinner

The following model speech on the art of making an authentic Italian spaghetti dinner was presented by a foreign exchange student. While presenting the speech, the student demonstrated many of the steps he spoke about.

Topic: Making an Authentic Italian Spaghetti Dinner

Critical-Thinking Statement: To many Americans, a spaghetti dinner is fast food. Since spaghetti is the native dish of my homeland, Italy,

I want to show the members of the audience that making a real spaghetti dinner is an art that takes a little time but that leads to a delicious, nutritious meal at a reasonable price, and that fits into almost any mealtime setting.

I. Step 1: Making the spaghetti
   A. Obtain three ingredients: flour, water, and salt.
   B. Mix the ingredients into heavy, uniform dough.
   C. Press the dough against disc to get spaghetti strands.

II. Step 2: Cooking the spaghetti
   A. Bring pot of water to boil—add two pinches of salt.
   B. Add strands of spaghetti, being sure not to crack them.
   C. Check for perfect cooking.
   D. Add olive oil.

III. Step 3: Making the sauce
   A. Make the meatballs.
   B. Add them to hot olive oil and other ingredients.
   C. Add skinned tomatoes.
   D. Drain off other ingredients, mash tomatoes and meat.
   E. Cook for one to one and a half hours.

IV. Step 4: Adding sauce to spaghetti
   A. Warm the spaghetti and put it on plate.
   B. Add sauce, layer of cheese, and more sauce.

Buon Giorno or good morning! What do you think of when you think of Italy? Maybe its fashion, or its bureaucracy, or its leg shape. Or maybe you think of delicious food. I am from Italy, and I am now visiting the United States for the first time. I want to tell you that the food is, as you might have guessed, very delicious in Italy.

Introduction: The speaker establishes his credibility for the topic.

Especially delicious is the spaghetti, the pasta, which I am going to show you how to make the real Italian way today.

Thesis: Notice the use of cue words how to make.

I hope I do not disappoint you, but spaghetti does not come from Italy. Marco Polo was a Venetian explorer in the 1600s, and on his way back from China, Cathay as it was called then, he brought back some strange noodles. Well, those are what became spaghetti, from the Italian word *spago,* which means "string."

Background: Such information adds much to the essential process. The speaker began to display his ingredients as he spoke.

I spoke with Ms. Nancy Garnett, who is the head dietician on campus, and to my surprise she told me that spaghetti is not very high in calories. An average portion without sauce contains approximately 190 calories, but when the sauce is added, the calories jump to about 300 to 350 per serving. Ms. Garnett's main concern was that spaghetti lacked fiber, even though it is rich in vitamins, especially Vitamin B.

Spaghetti is very easy to make, and has three basic ingredients: flour, water, and salt. Depending on taste, some people add egg. All these ingredients are mixed together until a heavy dough, uniform in quality, is produced. *After this,* the dough is put in a special machine like the one in this picture, which has a disc on the end of it with many holes. The dough is pressed against the disc and out comes the spaghetti, looking like this spaghetti I have here in my hand.

But now we must cook the spaghetti. *First* of all, you need a big pot of boiling water, to which you will add two pinches of salt. *As* the water boils, you *add* the spaghetti, *making sure* not to crack the strings in half, by pushing them into the pot as the tips soften. The spaghetti must cook approximately six to fifteen minutes, depending on the quality and thickness of the strings. I personally find that Italian spaghetti cooks much faster than American spaghetti, although I cannot explain why.

About a minute before the spaghetti should be ready, take a string out and taste it. Be careful not to burn your tongue; blow first on the strand. The spaghetti must be what we call *al dente* or "to the tooth," meaning each string must be bitable and not rubbery. *Once* the spaghetti is ready for eating, pour the contents of the pot into a colander and then return the spaghetti to the pot, perhaps sprinkling a little olive oil on the strings to prevent them from sticking.

The next step is the important one: making the sauce. Personally, I prefer a very basic meat sauce. To hot olive oil you add little meatballs that you have rolled in the palm of your hand, chopped onion, parsley, chopped mushrooms, and a clove of garlic, which you will later remove so it will not leave an aftertaste. *Sauté* the sauce for about fifteen minutes. Now *add* some cut-up and skinned tomatoes, making sure they are well drained. *Add* oregano, salt and pepper to taste, and a bay leaf. You must now mash these ingredients to incorporate the meat into the tomatoes. *Cook* the sauce until the desired thickness is reached, usually about one to one and a half hours.

During this time the spaghetti has cooled and has taken on all of its flavor. When the sauce is ready, warm the spaghetti, but not too much. *Put* the spaghetti on a plate and pour the sauce on it; then add a layer of Parmesan cheese, then the rest of the sauce. This is done so that the cheese melts and ties all the sauce's ingredients together, and therefore it holds onto the spaghetti.

As you can see, spaghetti is a relatively easy meal to make, but most people just throw it into a pot, boil it, and douse it with some canned sauce from the A and P. Make a gourmet meal out of it. Spaghetti, when made the proper way, is both delicious and nutritious. So, I leave you with those familiar words, "Mangia, mangia."

The speaker tells the audience why a step is important, a good way to emphasize and subordinate.

Conclusion: The speaker might use more summary to make his key points memorable, but his friendly gesture works to leave the audience with a positive attitude toward the speech.

The final model speech in this chapter was referred to earlier in the section on organizing and outlining a process speech. The speaker for this speech was a music student who wanted to study composing on the synthesizer. She felt that although the subject was a bit complex, she could explain it to the audience. She used an audio tape to play the sounds made by the synthesizer and displayed pictures of various synthesizers around the room.

The Synthesizer and the Creation of Music

Topic: The Synthesizer and the Creation of Music

Critical-Thinking Statement: As a music student at the university, I have been introduced to the workings of the synthesizer, an instrument most people know only from hearing it at rock concerts. The synthesizer has changed the face of music so much that I wanted the audience to know the basic process by which the synthesizer produces sound and music.

  I. Step 1: Generating electrical current
   A. Modules create current.
   B. Matrixes connect electrical signals between modules.

 II. Step 2: Generating sound
   A. Oscillators provide five basic wave forms.
   B. Dual-noise generators provide white or pink sound.

III. Step 3: Modifying the sound to make the music
   A. Sound can be modified with a filter.
   B. Sound can be modified with an envelope generator.

Introduction: The speaker shows that the topic is relevant today.

It is often said that the arts reflect cultural progress and the stature of an era. If this is so, then it is little wonder that electronics have become such an important part of twentieth-century music. The electronic synthesizer, which is the most notable example in twentieth-century music, arrived at precisely the right time to link culture and the arts in the Western world.

Background: The speaker takes time to show the origins of the instrument and to give the audience enough background to understand the importance of the synthesizer.

The synthesizer was invented in 1955 by RCA, interestingly enough not for music but for processing voice patterns. Once it was discovered that this machine could be used for music, composers flocked from all over the world to learn how to use it. The RCA synthesizer at its best was precise and accurate, but at its worst was cumbersome and difficult to use. But it did give electronic music a start.

The popularity of the synthesizer soon spread, and smaller versions were invented in the 1960s. The most popular of the new synthesizers were the Buchler of San Francisco and the Moog of New York. The Moog is the one most of you have probably heard of. These synthesizers transformed the large RCA synthesizers to a much smaller, easier-to-use instrument. By the 1970s, many other versions were invented—the ARP, the Putney, and the Nirona being the most famous.

Thesis: Notice the cue word process and the creative way the thesis is worded.

Although the synthesizer is a highly complex instrument, there are three phases that are relatively easy to explain and that are responsible for the endless variety of sounds possible. I think that because we hear so much synthesized music today, you will all find interesting the process by which this lush array of sounds is produced through the magic of electronics.

Body: The speaker has a complex topic here, and so she repeats an idea at times during the speech if she feels the audience needs this to comprehend the material.

The first phase in the production of synthesized music is the generation of electrical current. Synthesizers do not make sound; synthesizers make electrical currents. Stereo amplifiers that receive these currents make the actual sound. Modules, which are small boxes about the size of a shoe box and are housed in the synthesizer body, are used to create the electrical currents. The modules, however, are not hooked up to one another and may be easily removed or changed around at the composer's will to make different electrical currents.

In addition to the modules, matrixes, which are a system of pegs running along the top and bottom, over and under the modules, are used to hook up electrical signals between the modules. One simply lines up the matrix on one horizontal line and electrical signals are connected to the modules.

The second step in understanding the synthesizer's ability to make music is understanding how sound is generated; that is, how synthesizers make sound. There are two ways to make sound on a synthesizer. The first way is with oscillators. An oscillator is an electrical device capable of producing a flow of electricity that changes from maximum flow to minimum flow as the operator wishes.

Most synthesizers are equipped with five to seven oscillators, which provide the composer with the five basic wave forms needed to make sound. The electronic wave forms are simply disturbances created in the air by the speaker cone of the amplifier.

The simplest wave is the "sin" wave, which is shown on this chart. Another type of wave is called the triangle wave because, as you can see, it is shaped like a triangle. As you can hear from this audio tape, the triangle wave sounds much like the sin wave.

The third wave, shaped like a square, is called the square wave, appropriately enough. The fourth wave, and the most complex wave, is the sawtooth wave. The final type, and probably the one most often used by composers, is the pulse wave.

With these five basic wave forms the composer is able to imitate any orchestral instrument. Five simple waves and the symphony spreads out before you. It is truly remarkable.

In addition to oscillation, the synthesizer uses something called the dual-noise generator to produce sound. The dual-noise generator produces two sounds: white sound, which sounds like hissing steam, and pink sound, which sounds like a waterfall.

The third and final step in understanding how synthesizers make music is understanding sound modification. Although the composer is equipped with the seven sounds I have played for you, it becomes boring and monotonous after a while just to hear these seven sounds. Modification allows the composer to vary these seven sounds.

Body: The speaker used visuals and the audio tape to advantage so that the audience could see what each wave looked and sounded like.

Notice that the speaker defines the unclear term oscillator.

Body: After covering the five waves, the speaker showed how each could be used to imitate the sound of an instrument such as the organ.

Body: The speaker played a tape of the hissing steam and the waterfall sound to help us understand.

Body: Notice that the speaker uses words like first *and* last *to help us follow the process.*

Notice that the speaker puts synthesized music into a setting to show one of its practical applications.

Conclusion: With the process explained, the speaker begins to show the relevance of the topic for audience members and begins to make her point: that synthesizers are more than a rock-and-roll curiosity piece, but are instead part of a new generation of sounds that composers will use to make the music of our culture.

The first type of sound-modification device is a filter, which allows part of the wave to pass and part to be filtered out, thus changing the sound of the wave. Envelope generators are the other type of wave-modification device, and they work with the filters to change sounds. The remaining parts of the synthesizers do not generate or modify sound; they simply store effects into a memory bank to be used later.

Most synthesized music is not played live, because it is so difficult to operate the modules and matrixes at the same time. Because of this, smaller versions of the synthesizer have been invented such as the mini-Moog, and it is this version that you see at most rock concerts. Listen, now, to a tape of a concert using synthesized music. It is really beautiful.

The synthesizer has freed composers. They are now their own performers, limited only by dexterity, not musical ability. Composing is still as challenging today as it was when Beethoven was working on the piano, and the synthesizer has added an exciting new dimension to music by bringing it into the cultural mainstream of the electronics revolution, a perfect blending of high technology and the arts.

Exercises

1. This exercise is designed to help you distinguish the process pattern. Think about a time, while growing up, when you made something with a parent: cookies, a gym set, or a sand castle, for example. Either in a classroom discussion or in a short essay, describe the experience two times. The first time, focus on the interaction between you and your parent. Try to capture the feelings as events progressed. Wrap up the description by making some point out of it, some lesson learned or some new awareness gained. In the second episode, focus on the object you are making, from start to finish. Try to remember little things you learned or little things that went wrong. Comment on the finished product and make a point out of its quality.

   Notice that each pattern forced you into a different perspective on the same event. In the narrative pattern you focused on which events? What different moments of the experience surfaced in the second telling? How did the different moments of the experience lead you to a different end? You should now begin to see clearly the difference between process and narrative, and, indeed, the distinctive pattern that is process.

2. This exercise is designed to help you think about the three parts of a process speech. Take a recipe from a recipe book, one that is at least somewhat complex or exotic. Now, do some research. Find out where the recipe was first tried, or take one ingredient (a spice works very well) and discover something distinctive about it. You might even try the recipe and make a note of things that happen to you that are not in the book. Having completed this exercise, ask yourself what you learned about the ingredient that might be of interest to others. Would the background make the recipe itself more inviting? Would knowing something about the origins of the recipe make others more interested in trying it? You should discover that a process is a simple series of steps or stages, while a process speech is brought to life by filling in the basic steps with a variety of interesting commentary.

3. Prepare and present a public speech using the process pattern. Your instructor will provide you with the relevant details.

References

1. Frank D'Angelo, *A Conceptual Theory of Rhetoric* (Cambridge: Winthrop Publishers, 1975), p. 15.

2. Cleanth Brooks and Robert Penn Warren, *Modern Rhetoric*, 3d ed. (NY: Harcourt, Brace, and World, 1970), p. 142.

Model Speeches:
1. David Fischer, "Making an Authentic Italian Spaghetti Dinner." Used by permission.
2. Donna Hopkins, "The Synthesizer and the Creation of Music." Used by permission.

A View of the Process Pattern: Fashion Design

The process pattern is a practical pattern used primarily by speakers seeking to inform others. It is concerned with how events are linked together and with how things work. A process may be as simple as booting up a computer or as momentous as the series of events that led to the meltdown of the Chernobyl nuclear reactor in the Soviet Union in 1986. The process pattern may be used in a variety of situations—for purposes that are purely entertaining to those of a serious and debatable nature.

Processes surround us and we don't often notice them. For example, although we all wear clothes, most of us don't consider them as the product of a particular process.

Yet clothes do indicate a process—from the designer's original idea for a garment and the first rough design renderings, to the weaving of the fabric (above), to form-fitting the fabric (following page, top) to the pattern cutting (following page, bottom) and garment sewing, and finally to the finished product—although most of us find ourselves less elaborately suited-up than the model on the previous page!

While we may not give much thought to the events that led to the clothes on our backs, to those in the fashion industry it's an important and finely tuned process.

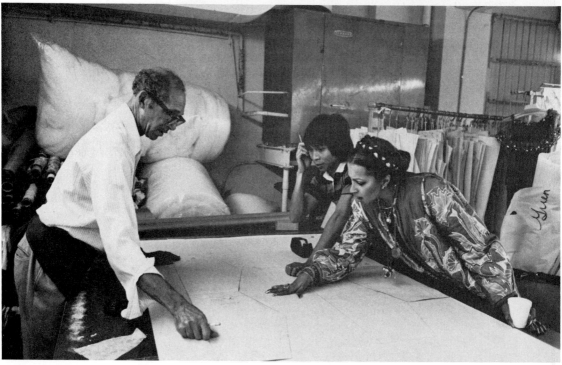

Chapter 11 · Cause-Effect

In 1859, Charles Darwin published his controversial work *On the Origin of Species*, a book that sparked a debate still raging today over whether life on Earth is the result of evolution or divine creation. Darwin believed that all living things were connected through an evolution in which one life form grew out of another, and in which each evolving life form continually adapted to its environment or perished. Darwin's research led him to conclude that an organism's form was an effect of its ability to adjust to its situation.[1]

Darwin's theory was subjected to intensive scholarly debate, as well as satire and ridicule. For instance, one unknown writer, in a humorous broadside lampooning Darwin's seeming overreliance on the theory of evolution, concocted the following scenario to account for the rise and fall of the British Empire:[2]

> *Old people keep ———cats which eat———mice, which otherwise might destroy ———bumble bees, which are needed for ———clover pollination, required for——— clover hay, necessary for———cavalry horses, essential to———the defense of the British Empire———thus, it follows that old people are essential to the maintenance of the British Empire.*

Although intentionally absurd, this example demonstrates the use of a powerful pattern of human thought, one used frequently for the most serious decision making—cause and effect. This pattern is used to investigate the workings of the natural universe and to determine guilt and innocence in our courts of law; it is used by essayists, novelists, and public speakers to support their proposals. In countless ways we use this pattern to help us reason through the problems and puzzles of our lives.

Reasoning from cause to effect, or from effect to cause, is natural, because as we observe our world we observe dependent relationships all around us. A stone skips along the surface of a pond, its ripples extending to every shore, and we see a relationship between the throwing of the stone and the turbulence of the water. So compelling is our understanding of the cause-effect sequence in nature that philosopher Chaim Perelman, among others, refers to the pattern as a basic structure of reality.[3]

The cause-effect pattern has a different focus from the other patterns based on the concept of time—narrative and process. It helps us answer that most provocative question, "Why?" Narratives are concerned with the question "What happened?" and only indirectly concerned with why those events occurred. A narrative focuses on descriptions of the common experiences of life and the lessons to be drawn from them. Process is concerned with how events are linked together, and has the practical goal of explaining the workings of things in the world. Cause-effect goes beyond description or explanation and probes into that most difficult domain, the search for why things happen as they do. Although this may appear to be a simple shift in focus, the emphatic concern with the question "Why?" distinguishes the cause-effect pattern most dramatically.

One of the most difficult questions human beings must answer is why things are as they appear. Our collective responses to the question "Why?" account for much of what we consider knowledge of the world around us. That is, if someone demonstrates to others that smoking causes cancer, that demonstration stands as proof until another person comes along to disprove it. Thus, the cause-effect pattern of thought involves us in description and explanation; even more importantly, it involves us in evaluation and judgment.

Because the cause-effect pattern of thinking is so critical to our understanding of the world, we have developed an intricate set of rules to govern our investigations, a logical method to follow in our search for proof of the assertions we make.

To prove something means to demonstrate it to others. Proof might mean that others who investigate the problem independently, and who follow the same rules for investigation, will arrive at the same conclusions. In other cases, proof might mean surpassing the "reasonable doubt" standard of a critical audience such as a jury by providing them with good reasons for an assertion. Whatever the criteria for judgment, causes and effects are real in the universe, but human beings must discover and prove that the relationships exist.[4]

Cause-effect thinking involves hypothesizing or asserting that the events in a sequence are dependent on one another. A cause is a force or influence that produces an effect; it is a person or operation that is responsible for some result. An effect is the result of the person's actions or of the operation. A person who makes the assertion must present a plausible case for the relationship asserted. Thus, while the events themselves are simply a sequence, a person identifies the connections between them.

The cause-effect pattern is used in every walk of life. Federal investigators probe the wreckage of a plane crash looking for the cause; medical experts search for the cause of AIDS, cancer, and multiple sclerosis; environmentalists search for the causes and effects of acid rain. In these and many other endeavors, we see the cause-effect pattern structuring our knowledge of the world around us.

The Intention of Cause-Effect: Roles, Situations, and Purposes

Regardless of one's profession, cause-effect reasoning ability is a prerequisite for success. Businesspersons must assess the results of public-relations campaigns; lawyers must analyze the events in a criminal investigation; scientists need to demonstrate the effects of nuclear power, genetic engineering, and new vaccines. Anyone actively engaged in the life of his or her community will find use for the cause-effect pattern.

Public speakers often use the cause-effect pattern to analyze and structure discourse. In a recent speech to a joint session of Congress, President Ronald Reagan reported on the effects of a summit meeting he had just attended with Soviet Premier Mikhail Gorbachev. As Alan Monroe and Douglas Ehninger point out in regard to cause-effect reasoning, "There is, perhaps, no other form of reasoning so often used by speakers," and they caution, "nor is there any form of reasoning which may contain so many flaws."[5]

The cause-effect pattern can be used to explain events. Recently, author William Broyles, Jr., traced the causes of war in an essay entitled "Why Men Love War."[6] Cause-effect essays and speeches are often lighthearted and humorous, as when science-fiction writer Isaac Asimov probed the effects of digital timekeeping on future generations in his essay "Dial Versus Digital."[7] Similarly, cause-effect speeches are often satirical, one example being a speech recently presented in the speech-communication classroom on the topic "Why the Cubs Will Never Win the Pennant."

Most often, however, a cause-effect speech is phrased as an argument that something is related to something else in a causal way. An argument begins as an assertion that is phrased similarly to the following assertions:

Most teenagers start smoking because of increased peer pressure.

Welfare programs have created a new class of citizens: the institutionalized poor.

Installation of a wastewater treatment plant would reduce sewage flow into the bay, thus raising water quality and allowing fishing restrictions to be lifted that have crippled the area's largest industry and led to a severe unemployment problem.

Regardless of one's reason for using the cause-effect pattern, cause-effect discourse involves the giving of good reasons for the existence of a cause-effect relationship.[8]

The cause-effect pattern is concerned with such questions as why something occurred or what its effects will be. Be certain as you begin that your topic is best approached from the cause-effect point of view. For example, a student was interested in exploring the causes for dropping out of high school. As he probed the topic, he discovered that the process pattern would lead him to discussing "the dropout syndrome," a familiar pattern of steps that can be observed in students who drop out. The cause-effect probe led the student to that same dropout syndrome because it seemed to get at the "why" of dropping out as well as the process. But as the student thought about the matter, he discovered that he really wanted to know why this syndrome existed in some socioeconomic classes and not in others. Thus, for this student, cause-effect was the right choice. The point of this example is that the process and cause-effect patterns, because they are both based on time, have similar directions. Because of these similarities, when choosing a topic one must determine whether one's interest lies in the "why" or the "how" of the process pattern.

The typical cause-effect speech springs from a survey of the issues or controversies in which one is interested. Here are just a few cause-effect topics that have led to interesting speeches:

Looking for the root cause of unemployment

Three reasons that children fail

Anxiety: its basis in the human personality

The effects of television violence on children

Apathy and the American voter

Notice that the topics listed here fall within the realm of human affairs. Some of the topics will require an almost scientific objectivity, while some are more subject to opinion, both personal and expert. At the very minimum, however, each topic has ample room for critical analysis and debate. Topics that are absolutely demonstrable or purely speculative are not appropriate for a cause-effect speech. The following are some unsuitable topics:

Why the sky looks blue

The effects of nicotine injections on laboratory animals

Choosing a Topic for a Cause-Effect Speech

Why some politicians go astray

What would happen if everyone had a decent income

Choose a topic that will be of interest to the audience, one that will make them think and examine the issues of the day. Remember, the cause-effect pattern is a logical pattern, and one of its values in the speech-communication classroom is that it can initiate a reasoned discussion of the key events concerning us all.

Developing a Cause-Effect Speech

Begin to analyze your topic by drafting a critical-thinking statement. Remember that the critical-thinking statement should cue the audience to your role in the speech, your aim, and the pattern you intend to use. The statement shown here is taken from a speech asserting that products containing caffeine should require warning labels:

Caffeine, when used too frequently, has a number of potentially harmful effects on the individual. Caffeine can lead to loss of sleep, anxiety attacks, and physical changes in the body such as gum tissue decay. As a pharmacy major, I believe that products containing caffeine should be labelled so that people can monitor their intake. In this speech, I plan to document these negative effects and ask the audience to sign a letter that I will send to our senator asking him to propose legislation requiring warning labels on caffeinated products.

The above critical-thinking statement reveals the causal pattern to be used, and it helps the speaker understand her own role and her goal for the speech. The following statement comes from a speech using another causal pattern:

Illegal immigration may lead to lower prices for the products the immigrants pick, but these lower prices are artificial and simply lead to a false value for the goods in the marketplace, when in fact numerous costs, both economic and social, are felt indirectly throughout the society. As a citizen concerned about exploitation of migrant workers, I want to dispel the myth that enforcing immigration laws adds to inflation of prices.

In this critical-thinking statement, the speaker is proposing to refute a cause for an asserted effect: he contends that enforcement of immigration laws does not have an adverse effect on food prices. In this speech, the speaker was simply a "concerned citizen," which is a common role for those who speak on social issues.

When you have drafted the critical-thinking statement, you must begin to analyze the material. The goal of analysis in the cause-effect pattern is the establishment of proof beyond a reasonable doubt. You are attempting to establish your assertion as fact. Since every cause-effect speech begins with a speculation, an assertion of a causal relationship, you must follow standards for cause-effect reasoning in order to be successful. Let's begin our analysis of cause-effect reasoning by listing some guidelines and then looking at each one carefully.

1. Distinguish between correlation and cause.

2. Distinguish between conditions and causes.

3. Search for other causes for the same effect.

4. Ascertain the credentials of the person establishing the cause or the effect.

5. Distinguish between main effects and side effects.

We will examine each type of causal reasoning and the standards for verification. In so doing, we will also consider what are known as fallacies in reasoning from cause.

Distinguishing Between Correlations and Causes

A correlation is an assertion based on the observation that two phenomena are related. For instance, in a student speech, the speaker asserted that research had shown that physical attractiveness was positively correlated with sentencing by jurors; that is, the more attractive defendants are less likely to be judged guilty than are less attractive defendants. The conclusion drawn from this observation was that being physically attractive was positively correlated with sentencing.

But the fact that two phenomena are positively correlated does not mean that they are related as cause to effect. When the studies themselves are analyzed, it is clear that in real courtroom situations jurors rarely consider physical attractiveness without also considering other factors such as the evidence presented, repentance by the defendant, and instructions to the jury. The fact that two phenomena are positively correlated does not mean that one causes the other. A cause must be distinguished from a correlation by means of established procedures as well as common sense.

In the sciences and social sciences, when one asserts a cause-effect relationship, one must follow exacting standards for proving the claim before the results of the observations are accepted in the academic world. In everyday discussions, however, the same rigorous standards may not always have been applied before the person speaks. When standards determining cause and effect are not applied, claims based on correlation are often absurd and should be viewed with skepticism. One might argue, for instance, that the last five times the university changed presidents the football team had winning seasons. This would be a correlation, but certainly not a cause.

In numerous situations, determining whether something is a correlation or a cause is quite difficult. Following are some guidelines for judging whether two events are related as cause and effect or simply correlated.

First, use common sense. We can usually tell an absurdity from a reasonable claim. If it always seems to rain just after we wash the car, we might jokingly assume a positive correlation, but we would not assume a cause-effect relationship between the two activities because common sense tells us differently. To assume absurd correlations is to be guilty of a fallacy called the post hoc fallacy. The term comes from the Latin phrase *post hoc, ergo propter hoc*, which means "after this, therefore because of this."

When common sense does not help us analyze cause-effect relationships, we need to go beyond it to rules for verification. If someone, for instance, were to assert that every time oil-producing nations (OPEC) lowered the price of a barrel of oil it caused the stock market to go up, we would have to consider such a claim seriously. In such situations, we would need to ask the following questions:

1. Is there valid, objective support for the claim?

2. Do a variety of unbiased authorities agree on the claim?

3. Do facts, examples, or other sources of support verify the claim?

4. Are there other plausible causes for the same effect?

5. Is there an underlying cause for both events?

In addition, one special question that we might ask is "Does the correlation work both ways?" Theoretically, a correlation works both ways, while a causation works in only one direction.[9] For example, if the stock market goes up every time oil prices are raised, but oil prices do not go up every time the stock market rises, then the two events are not correlated, but one (oil prices) is a cause for the other (stock-market rises).

Distinguishing Between Conditions and Causes

A condition is a general state that can account for any number of events. For instance, capitalism is a general condition—an entire economic system—that is responsible for a wide range of events. In many arguments, capitalism is a condition within which almost anything could occur. Such arguments, then, would not be informative or convincing. Be certain that an argument based on the cause-effect pattern distinguishes between conditions and causes. Let's see how this can best be done.

A cause is directly related to an effect in that both are part of a small sphere of events. Therefore, a cause will usually result in a direct effect. To say that capitalism, for instance, is responsible for the high rates of suicide is to skip any number of intervening variables. An opponent to such an argument could claim that suicide rates were directly correlated to occupations such as dentistry and medicine, and argue that countries under other economic systems such as communism had lower suicide rates because they had few people in skilled professions such as medicine and dentistry. The latter argument accounts for the same effect in a more specific way, and thus it is more plausible than the first one.

When making a cause-effect argument, then, look for the difference between conditions and causes, or conditions and effects. Causes are specific, while conditions are usually general states, twice or three times removed from the effect.

Searching for Other Causes for the Same Effect

A cause-effect claim asserts a one-to-one relationship between cause and effect. When developing your topic, ask whether other causes might account for the same effect. For some time, for instance, it was assumed that lower IQ scores in the public school were the result of poor teaching, and this led politicians and school boards around the country to call for a "back to basics" curriculum. It was later discovered that a more plausible explanation for the lower IQ scores was the birth order of the children in the schools during the period studied. That is, IQ scores were rising in the 1950s because there were mostly first-born children in the schools, while scores were declining in the 1960s because many of the children taking the IQ tests were lower in the birth order: many were the third, fourth, fifth, and sixth children in their families.[10]

It is a good rule to assume that there are many causes for the same effect. When assessing the validity of an assertion, look with a skeptical eye at single cause-effect relationships.

Checking Source Credibility

In purely logical terms, of course, the accuracy of the supporting material or the reasonableness of the assertion establishes the validity of the argument. However, in many situations, the power of a cause-effect relationship rests on support by those considered authorities on the matter. One might assert that import quotas will improve the American economy. Support for such a claim and for counterclaims is rampant; that is, there are as many arguments to show that import quotas lead to a healthy economy as there are to show that import quotas cause artificial price increases for American goods, thus leading to an unhealthy economy. How is one to choose from competing assertions, given the global nature of the argument and the seeming reasonableness of both sides?

The first resort is to test the evidence (see Chapter 4) and to assess the reasoning supporting the assertion. In the final analysis, however, it may be necessary to assess the source of the argument. In such situations, ask the following questions:

1. Is the source really an expert on the matter?

2. Are the quotations taken from the source accurate, up-to-date, and in their proper contexts?

3. Are the experts on one side of the argument better than those on the other?

Distinguishing Between Main Effects and Side Effects

An effect is a direct result of a cause. A side effect is a result that was not intended. There is a familiar saying, "You can never do merely one thing."[11] You may, for instance, build a dam in order to bring hydroelectric power to a region, the power being the main effect intended. But in addition to power being brought to the people in the region, certain other side effects occur. Damming the river upstream changes the conditions of the water downstream, leading to a fish kill that causes the fishermen of the area to lose their livelihood or forces them into new occupations such as agriculture; this in turn changes their sociocultural patterns and ultimately affects the way the entire society behaves. When analyzing a topic, the speaker must decide which are main effects and which are side effects of the cause.

A common fallacy occurring in arguments from cause to effects is called the "slippery slope" fallacy, by which a sequence of effects from a single cause ultimately leads to a disaster in a sort of tumbling downhill chain of events. A clear and humorous example of this is the British Empire scenario presented at the beginning of this chapter.

Any disaster or negative effect can be traced backward to a series of causes and then presented as a "slippery slope" argument. One student recently argued that his best friend was causing him to flunk out of school. When asked to explain how this could be, the student said, "Well, I made an agreement with my best friend, John, to pay him for taking notes in our psychology class so I could sleep later. John went to the class, but on the mid-term exam review day he forgot his pen so he asked the woman next to him for her extra pen. They started talking and decided to head for the coffee shop so neither one of them took any notes. Not having any idea what was on the mid-term, I failed the exam, and since I am on academic probation, I need an A on the final to get a high enough average to stay in school. John really messed me up."

Of course, John is not the cause of the student's failure. The student is simply rationalizing: putting together a scenario that helps him explain his dilemma without blaming himself. Watch for such "slippery slope" arguments whenever cause-effect is the pattern operating.

When assessing a cause-effect argument, be certain to list the main and the side effects. Ask whether the effect was intended or whether it simply occurred as the result of the cause. A convincing cause-effect argument should include both main and side effects but should distinguish between them.

There is, then, much to be cautious of when analyzing a cause-effect topic. Cause-effect relationships are always hypothetical, and rest for their validity on the person making the connections. Follow the guidelines suggested here in order to insure a valid case and to anticipate opponents' objections to the argument.

Organizing and Outlining a Cause-Effect Speech

There are four kinds of cause-effect relationships.[12] Your choice of structure should depend upon the demands of your topic. Regardless of the type of cause-effect speech you intend to give, outline the speech by listing the cause(s) and the effect(s) as main headings, and continue to fill in the outline by subordinating lesser causes or effects and adding details to develop the argument as you discover them.

Single Cause to Single Effect

Many speeches using the cause-effect pattern assert a single cause as responsible for the effect. A speaker might assert that raising the drinking age to twenty-one is responsible for the decrease in highway deaths caused by teenage drinking. Similarly, someone might assert that the attack on Pearl Harbor in 1941 led to America's entry into World War II. When such an assertion is made, the body of the speech has a simple outline form:

A. Cause 1
B. Effect 1

The emphasis in such a speech is on the supporting details. Since it is difficult to show such simple causation, details will be essential to support the assertion.

Multiple Causes for a Single Effect

The second outline format involves showing multiple causes for a single effect. In this format, the causes themselves need not be linked to the effect through chronology. In a speech given recently, the speaker asserted four reasons that Americans did not express outrage over illegal immigration; for purposes of demonstration, let's see how the body of the speech was outlined.

A. Effect 1: Citizens are apathetic toward illegal immigration.
B. Cause 1: Public-opinion surveys show that Americans believe that allowing people to immigrate freely is a "liberal" thing to do.
C. Cause 2: Intellectuals often argue that an influx of new people keeps a fresh stock of ideas flowing into the culture.
D. Cause 3: Politicians and policymakers are faced with the long-standing notion that America is a land of immigrants and that one group has no right to "shut the gate" behind it.
E. Cause 4: Businesspersons and farmers argue that immigrants are good for the economy because they work for lower wages.

Notice that the reasons listed do not depend or build on one another sequentially. Even though some reasons are related and some may overlap, the reasons do not themselves form a causal sequence. The chronological order in this outline is simply that the causes all lead to the effect produced. Once again, proof must be given for each reason, and the validity of claims such as those advanced above is determined by the rules for cause-effect reasoning established in this chapter.

Single Cause to Multiple Effects

The third format is single cause to multiple effects. A speaker often asserts that one action will trigger numerous results. These results are not themselves based on chronology, (they can all occur together), but the cause must be linked to the effect chronologically. That is, no effect can occur before the cause occurs. One could not argue, for instance, that one effect of the 1969 law prohibiting cigarette advertising on television was a decrease in teenage smoking if statistics showed that teenage smoking had been declining steadily since 1965.

The basic outline format for the single-cause-to-multiple-effects speech is as follows:

A. Cause 1: The disappearance of hands from the faces of clocks and watches (the age of digital timekeeping)

B. Effect 1: The meaning of the terms *clockwise* and *counterclockwise*
C. Effect 2: The meaning of the term *o'clock*
D. Effect 3: An irregularity in the number system, with the loss of the base number sixty
E. Effect 4: An inability to locate things metaphorically by the time on the clock, such as in "Notice the object at two o'clock"[13]

Once again, each point must be filled in with details—examples, facts, and so on. The point is to begin the outline by listing the basics: cause and effects.

The Causal Sequence

The final pattern is the causal sequence, the classic cause-effect chain in which one event precedes and determines the next. Almost any cluster of events can be arranged in a causal sequence, since this pattern is based strictly on chronology. However, a speech structured as a causal sequence must list only those events that are essential to the cause-effect chain under discussion. Look at the following sample outline:

A. Event 1: A litter tax law is passed, which leads to
B. Event 2: New tax revenue for the state, which leads to
C. Event 3: Support for litter-education programs and trash barrels, which leads to
D. Event 4: Reduced litter, which leads to
E. A cleaner environment and a nicer place to live.

Of course, this argument could proceed to other points, such as the increased tourism brought about by a more pleasant environment. When making such an argument, be sure the event that begins the chain is essential to the final event in the sequence. Since all the events must be related to one thesis, the causal sequence appears as a unity in the speech.

Once you have rigorously analyzed the topic, you are ready to develop the other parts of the speech: introduction, conclusion, preview (if necessary), and the thesis statement. In so doing, remember to follow the guidelines presented in Chapter 5.

A cause-effect speech has a characteristic vocabulary. Commonly used terms include *as a result of, ends and means,* and *because of this.* This list could be much larger, but these examples make the point that when speaking with the cause-effect pattern it is important to cue the audience to the connections being made.

A cause-effect speech requires research. You will often be required to use quotations, statistics, and other forms of support such as those discussed in Chapter 4. There is an appropriate way to introduce such material.

When quoting authorities, it is best to present a complete source citation, particularly if the author is an expert but not well known to members of the audience. Here is an example of how to introduce quotations from little-known experts:

> *According to Walter Stone, statewide coordinator for the detoxification program, "One-third of the cost for alcohol rehabilitation counseling could be saved by using non-medical personnel."*

In the preceding example, the speaker provides the source of the quotation and the person's credentials. This is much better than simply saying,

> *It has been said that one-third of the cost of a detoxification program could be saved by using nonmedical personnel.*

When the quoted material comes from a printed source such as a magazine or a newspaper, note this as you introduce the material:

> *James Ruggles, vice-president of Apex Motors, is quoted in the July 13, 1985, issue of* Nation *as saying that, "unless workers grant more concessions at the bargaining table, this country is headed for a new, more serious recession than the one in 1980."*

Providing information about the source of a quotation adds credibility to the material. This is also true for statistical data and factual material. For an essay, the writer would list sources at the end of the piece; in a speech, however, the speaker must provide a sort of running bibliography as the speech proceeds. Look at this example:

> *I was able to locate the data on my chart in the United States Census for 1980. I found that these were the most accurate figures on birth rates available in our library.*

Wording and Delivery

By identifying the source of the material, the speaker allows the audience to judge its validity. If the source is well known, you can abbreviate the introduction accordingly. You would not, for instance, need to say, "Paul Newman, a well-known actor, says that . . ." or "*Time* magazine, a noted weekly, discovered that . . ." Use common sense, but do introduce your material in the speech.

Summary

The cause-effect pattern is based on the concept of time and on the natural, dependent relationships we see around us. It has to do with the reasons that something has occurred or with the implications of an action. Contrasted to narrative, a pattern based on the recounting of an experience, and process, which focuses on the steps involved in explaining the development of something, cause-effect is concerned with evaluation and judgment, with assessing why relationships exist as they do.

Cause-effect thinking is critical to our understanding of events. When we assert that we know why something has occurred, we assert knowledge of it. Because knowledge of the world around us determines how we behave toward the world, when someone claims to know why something has occurred, we demand proof.

Proof is a demonstration that one has discovered a true causal relationship. In order for a proof to stand, it must pass tests for causal reasoning. If a cause-effect relationship is demonstrated beyond a reasonable doubt, the relationship is said to be logical.

We all have to use the cause-effect pattern during our lives, regardless of our profession or our community interests. Public speeches are often organized according to the cause-effect pattern. Whether used in an explanation, as the basis for an argument, or in occasional lighthearted speeches, the cause-effect pattern is an essential tool for the educated person.

Cause-effect speech topics spring most often from the issues and controversies of the day. Some topics will require an almost scientific objectivity, while others will require reasoning that makes sense for the audience. Choose a topic that will make the audience think about the key issues of the day.

One develops a topic according to the cause-effect pattern by drafting a purpose statement that gives a clear understanding of the situation and then applying tests for reasonableness in cause-effect thinking. In this chapter we have examined the following guidelines: distinguishing between correlations and causes, distinguishing between conditions and causes, searching for other causes for the same effect, checking source credibility, and distinguishing between main and side effects.

There are four standard patterns for organizing a cause-effect speech: single cause to single effect, multiple causes for a single effect, single cause to multiple effects, and the causal sequence. Each pattern has a distinct outline form and method for proceeding. Finally, when wording a cause-effect speech, provide cue words for the audience and introduce quotations properly.

The model speech presented here is based on the single cause-multiple effects pattern. The topic is mandatory deposit legislation, sometimes called the bottle bill. Presented at a public hearing at the Rhode Island State House, the speech has been shortened and edited for purposes of this text.

Potential Impact of National Mandatory Deposit Legislation

Topic: Potential Impact of National Mandatory Deposit Legislation

Critical-Thinking Statement: As cofounder of the Rhode Island Bottle Bill Coalition, I hope to show our congressional delegation that a national mandatory deposit law would have a dramatic and beneficial impact on the state and the nation.

I. Introduction
   A. Present humorous anecdote to get audience involved.
   B. Present statistics showing the garbage crisis in America.

II. Preview
   A. Present background on the garbage crisis in America.
   B. Container trash is 35 percent of all garbage.
   C. Resource recovery is one way to reduce garbage, but it has not worked.
   D. Source reduction has been much more effective in reducing garbage.

III. Thesis: This speech will demonstrate the potential impact a national mandatory deposit law would have on both our state and our nation.

IV. Body
    A. Effect 1: Litter would be reduced dramatically.
        1. Drastic reductions occurred in Michigan after passage of the bottle bill.
            a. Michigan's container litter was reduced by 87 percent.
            b. Total litter was reduced by 21 percent.
        2. Connecticut experienced similar reductions in litter.
            a. Total litter was reduced by 50 percent in some Connecticut communities.
            b. Quotation by Gov. O'Neill shows success of bottle bill.
    B. Effect 2: Solid waste has decreased as a result of the bottle bill.
        1. In Maine, solid waste decreased by 6 percent after passage of the bottle bill.
        2. In Connecticut, solid waste was reduced anywhere from 4 to 15 percent.
    C. Effect 3: The bottle bill has brought significant gains in employment.
        1. Industry predicted huge layoffs from bottle bills, but this did not happen.
        2. In Michigan, 4,880 jobs were created by the bottle bill.
        3. Stroh's beer plant is a good example.
    D. Effect 4: The bottle bill has also had minor effects.
        1. Litter-related injuries are down.
        2. Costs associated with litter pick-up are down.
        3. The public is very much in favor of the bottle bill.

V. Conclusion: Given the success of the bottle bill in some states, it is reasonable to assume it would work nationwide. Please support the Hatfield Bill.

Introduction: The speaker used humor to gain attention and statistics to introduce the topic.

A comedian on "The Tonight Show" recently quipped that his garbage was beginning to feel heavier than his groceries. Humorously overstated, perhaps, but the remark does make a point. The comptroller general of the United States tells us that from 1958 to 1982, food consumption in the United States increased 2.3 percent, while the packaging used to contain food increased 33.3 percent. In 1982, the average American produced 1,000 pounds of garbage, compared to 250 pounds per person in the early 1950s. This "buy the sizzle and not the steak" attitude is responsible for what many experts have called the most pressing problem in America today: garbage.

In one year, 1973, Americans discarded over 2 million tons of major appliances, 22 million tons of food and food scraps, 10 million tons of newspaper, and 3 million tons of paper plates. In that same year, 195 million tires were discarded or left on abandoned vehicles. These figures, staggering as they are, do not even touch upon the largest contributor to solid waste: packaging.

Packages and containers account for approximately 35 percent of all solid waste. Using the example once again of 1973, Americans dumped close to 53 million tons of glass, steel, aluminum, paper, and plastic containers. Of this, only 7 million tons were recycled, the rest being either burned or buried in landfills.

The fastest-growing segment of packaging waste during the past generation has been the beer and soft-drink container. This champion of the throwaway society is now accounting for almost 10 percent of all solid waste produced in the country. In 1960, the average person discarded 75 beverage containers. Today, according to the Comptroller General's Office, this figure is 370. Americans purchase yearly over 65 billion beer and soft-drink containers, nearly 95 percent of which are disposable.

Efforts to cope with the container-waste dilemma have been focused in two areas: resource recovery and source reduction. Resource recovery is commonly known as recycling, and it occurs in both voluntary and involuntary forms. But recycling accounts for only about 8 percent of the container waste produced in the country, and advertisements featuring "teary-eyed Indians" have been virtually to no avail.

The other method, source reduction, has generally focused on deposit legislation, or the so-called bottle bill. Numerous studies have been published detailing a litany of effects of bottle bills in the nine states that have them. Today, I would like to demonstrate the potential impact a mandatory national deposit law would have on both our state and the nation.

The most dramatic effect of statewide bottle bills has been on litter. In Michigan, for example, according to Daniel B. Syrek of The Institute for Applied Research, beverage-container litter was reduced by 87 percent one year after the bottle bill passed into law, and total litter declined 21 percent. Such successes are reported in all bottle-bill states shortly after the law goes into effect. In Connecticut, litter was reduced by as much as 50 percent in some communities. In fact, the bill was so successful,

Governor Thomas O'Neill, in a press release issued on January 7, 1981, called for a repeal of the state's litter tax law because, as O'Neill said, "I am now convinced that with the continued strong support of our citizens, the bottle bill will fulfill its mission."

We can expect a related impact of a nationwide bottle bill; that is, on solid waste. About 10 percent of this is container waste for beer and soft drinks. One bottle-bill state, Maine, noted a 6 percent decrease in total solid waste shortly after the law's effective date in 1978. That adds up to approximately 40 tons less garbage in a state that is quickly running out of landfill space. In Connecticut, solid waste has decreased anywhere from 4 percent to 15 percent, depending upon whether the community was stocking refillable containers or simply deposit containers. The comptroller general estimates that a nationwide bottle bill would have the same effect nationally that it has had in bottle-bill states.

Perhaps the most controversial area of the bottle-bill debate has been the effect it would have on employment. Beverage container industry representatives have repeatedly warned that a bottle bill will cause massive layoffs, predicting in fact that as many as 61,400 jobs would be lost nationwide because of lowered demand for containers in a deposit system. But the dire predictions are not borne out by the experience in bottle-bill states.

There have been job losses in industries that produce containers. But in Michigan, while 240 jobs were lost in the container-production industry, 4,888 were gained in industries that distribute, retail, and recycle beverage containers. At the Stroh's beer plant in Michigan, 38 people were hired primarily in washing and refilling bottles. The new jobs in beverage container related industries are directly a result of the bottle bill.

There are other, indirect effects of the bottle bill. Litter-related injuries are down in bottle-bill states. Costs associated with litter pickup are also down, thus saving the taxpayer money. Maybe the greatest effect is the public's response to bottle bills, which is overwhelmingly positive in every instance.

Given the impact of bottle bills in the states that have adopted them, it seems clear that such legislation on the national level would have direct and dramatic effects on each and every one of us. I urge you to support the senate resolution submitted by Senator Mark Hatfield of Oregon.

The second model speech of the cause-effect pattern uses the multiple cause-single effect format to answer the question "Why do illegal aliens come to America from Mexico?" This speech was presented in a speech-communication classroom to a group of twenty-five university students. The speaker's intent was to show that illegal aliens do not necessarily want to leave their homeland, but that without work they find themselves with no alternative but to head north to America.

Topic: The Reasons for Illegal Immigration from Mexico

Critical-Thinking Statement: I have heard many people say that illegal aliens should be arrested and prosecuted, even shot. Illegals are blamed for taking jobs away from Americans, and they are thought of as sinister, dark-eyed criminals from south of the border. Actually, as I understand it, most illegals are decent, hard-working people who come to America for one reason: work. I'd like to show why illegals come to America, in the hope that the audience will understand this problem accurately.

I. Introduction
  A. Roper poll shows that Americans want illegal immigration stopped.
  B. Quotation from Burns Roper supports thesis.

II. Preview
  A. Background on illegal-alien problem helps us understand the situation.
  B. Present statistics on number of illegals from Mexico.

III. Thesis: If we understand the causes of illegal immigration, we can shape our opinions more accurately.

IV. Body
  A. Cause 1: Illegals come to America to work.
    1. 50 percent of Mexico's work force is unemployed.
    2. By the year 2,000, forty-five million Mexicans will be unemployed.
  B. Cause 2: Wage differentials are great between Mexico and the U.S.
    1. Quotation from Thomas Muller supports assertion.
    2. Present example from *Humanist* magazine showing worker sending money home.

C. Cause 3: America does have jobs.
  1. Quotation from Labor Secretary Marshall shows that illegals are getting work.
  2. Quotation from personnel manager in Chicago shows why companies hire illegals.

V. Conclusion
  A. Sum up the problem.
  B. Suggest possible solutions.

Introduction: Statistics and quotations are used to draw attention to the topic.	In 1977, the Roper polling organization took a public-opinion survey on the topic of illegal aliens. They discovered that 91 percent of the sample agreed that the U.S. should make an all-out effort to stop the illegal entry of 1.5 million foreigners each year. Commenting on this historic consensus, Burns Roper remarked, "It is rare on any poll to find such a lopsided opinion."
Background: The speaker tries to create a picture for the audience.	But while the overwhelming number of Americans want illegal immigration stopped, little consensus exists on how to stop it. The most popular approach at this point is to patrol the borders looking for "wetbacks." This lamentable name has been given to the most populous group of illegals, Mexicans, who swim across the Rio Grande River into America. But spending an estimated $300 million year year to stop illegal entry has done little to stop the exodus from Mexico into the United States. Corruption of officials and determination on the part of illegals are forces too powerful for good intentions.
The speaker makes a transition to the thesis of the speech.	I believe that we need to attack the cause of illegal immigration. Most Americans do not know the reasons that illegals are willing to risk imprisonment, bondage, and even their lives to reach our shores. I want to ask the question "Why do illegal aliens come to America?" If we understand the root causes of illegal immigration we can shape our opinions and our policies more accurately.
The thesis of the speech is stated in a single declarative sentence. Notice how the speaker cues the audience to the pattern of development with the word causes.	The illegal-immigration problem is reaching epidemic proportions. According to Robert Pear of *The New York Times*, more than three million illegal aliens were apprehended between 1978 and 1980. No one knows for sure how many illegals actually cross the border, but the Justice Department estimates that there are at least ten million illegal aliens in the United States today, most holding menial jobs and living lives of quiet desperation.

In the past few years, the illegal-immigration problem has become an increasingly Mexican problem. According to Edward Harwood of the Hoover Institution, Stanford University, Mexicans accounted for 60 percent of all arrests in the United States last year, and it is estimated that approximately 60 percent of all illegal aliens come from that country. Serious disagreement in governmental circles and among intellectuals exists for the crisis in illegal immigration. But on one point almost all analysts agree: illegal aliens come to America for one reason: jobs.

The speaker limits the topic to illegal immigration from Mexico.

The Hoover Institution is a conservative think tank. Does Harwood's association with Hoover affect his credibility?

The pull toward America is an irresistible force felt constantly by the majority of Mexico's people. The population of that country has doubled since 1945 and is expected to double again in the next twenty years. The Mexican labor force is now nineteen million people of whom 50 percent are unemployed. Estimates are that by the year 2,000 Mexico will have forty-five million unemployed workers. There is simply no work in this poorly developed, overpopulated nation.

Does the fact that 60 percent of all arrests involved Mexicans mean that all the Mexicans were illegal aliens? Think about statistics before accepting them.

Cause 1: Jobs are cited as the number-one cause for illegal immigration.

Added to the desire to work is the wage differential between Mexico and the United States. According to Thomas Muller, principal research associate for the Urban Institute, "Low-skilled, undocumented workers continue to enter regardless of economic conditions because wage differentials between the United States and nations south of the border are so large that even if immigrant workers can find jobs for only part of the year, their income will surpass earnings from year-round work in their native country, even assuming such stable work can be found."

The speaker supports the assertion with unemployment data. Is this data plausible proof of the relationship between illegal immigration and jobs?

Cause 2: Wage differentials are cited as the second reason for illegal immigration.

The cost of living in Mexico is so low that even the meager earnings of a migrant worker are worth the risk of passage. This is most clearly evidenced in the poignant anecdote of an illegal working on an Arizona farm, as recounted by Gina Allen, the illegal's employer, in a recent edition of *Humanist* magazine. "On Saturdays, paydays, I did his shopping for him and sent a money order to his wife in Mexico. The money he sent each week was enough to feed and clothe her and the children, he explained to me, and to pay two men to farm the few acres that were his in Mexico. The money order was always for fifty dollars."

Authority assertion is used to support the wage-differential argument. Is the quotation from Muller adequate to stand as proof of the asserted cause?

Notice the variety of supporting materials: statistics, authority assertions, and examples. Variety in detail adds to the plausibility of the argument.

So, for those out of work, America is the promised land. But even for those who can find work, the lure of Yankee dollars surpasses the desire to stay home.

And when they do arrive in America, most illegal aliens find work. Secretary of Labor Ray Marshall, commenting on the new wave of illegals into the big cities, noted that "there is a vigorous market for, and in

Cause 3: American companies want to hire illegal immigrants.

Once again, expert opinion is used to support the assertion. Does the fact that a person represents a federal agency give the person neutrality on a given topic?

Is the quotation from the personnel manager sufficient to establish the cause as valid? Why else might companies hire illegals?

Conclusion: The speaker sums up the cause-effect relationship as a "push-pull" force. This phrase helps to capture the essence of the problem for the audience.

Notice the way the speaker adapts the conclusion to the audience, showing them how they are involved. Notice also that the body of the speech focuses on causes. If this were a problem-solution speech, the solution might well be developed in the body in great detail. Since the speaker's purpose is to analyze causes, the solution can simply be suggested in the conclusion.

some instances active recruitment of, undocumented workers." Said one personnel agent for a Chicago manufacturing plant: "They like to work. They show up on time, they work overtime, and they don't get into fights. The citizen will gripe about working conditions. The citizen will demand workmen's compensation, will demand retirement. The alien is tickled to death to go in there and work 10 hours a day." Thus, whether it's picking grapes in California, or sorting microchips in an electronics firm in Detroit, illegals find that the host country may not want them in, but once they manage to cross safely, there is plenty to do to make money for those left behind.

This combination of unemployment in the sending country, work and wage differentials in the magnet country, and the general desire for a better life, have led to the steady stream of human beings who seek the simple basics of life: clothes, food, shelter, and a chance to dream.

If we are to develop attitudes and policies that confront the crisis of illegal immigration, we must recognize what political scientist Norman Zucker has called the "push-pull" factors of international migration. The natural movement of the have-nots toward the haves must be stopped at its source. The United States must be willing to help poorer countries improve their economic conditions so that natives of the country will desire to stay there. America must also address itself to the problems of worldwide population planning, food production, and general quality of life. If we are to retain our image as the world's open door, we must stop the clamor at the gates with a new sensitivity to our role as citizens of the world.

Exercises

1. In an in-class discussion, see whether your group can discover at least four plausible causes that might intervene between the causes and the effects listed below:

Effect	Cause
Anorexia nervosa	Models in magazines
Cheating on exams	Pressure to achieve
Price of gasoline	World supply
Love	Infatuation

2. Read the following passage from an article in *Time* for July 3, 1978. After you have read the story, answer the questions that follow.

Looking crisp and composed in a red shirtwaist dress, red-white-and-blue scarf and frosted hair, Phyllis Schlafly arrived last week at the Illinois capital with 500 followers. To symbolize their opposition to the Equal Rights Amendment, which was about to be voted on in the House, the women had brought loaves of home-baked bread—apricot, date nut, honey-bran, and pumpkin. But as she climbed onto a kitchen stool to address the cheering crowd, Schlafly the demure housewife turned into Schlafly the aggressive polemicist. The passage of ERA, she declared, would mean government-funded abortions, homosexual schoolteachers, women forced into military combat, and men refusing to support their wives.

For the past six years, Schlafly, 53, has been delivering similar exhortations to similar gatherings, helping to turn public opinion against ERA, which is still three states short of ratification. After passing 35 state legislatures in five years, ERA was defeated last year in Nevada, North Carolina, Florida and Illinois. Last week the amendment lost once again in Illinois when the House narrowly defeated it. With no other state legislature scheduled to vote on ERA, the amendment will expire on March 22, 1979, unless Congress agrees to extend the deadline.

ERA's decline has been largely the result of Schlafly's small (20,000 members) but highly disciplined organizations, Stop ERA and Eagle Forum. While the feminists have splintered over the issues of abortion and lesbian rights, Schlafly's troops have centered their efforts on ERA. They have evolved into a formidable lobbying force, allied with local and national right-wing groups, including HOW (Happiness of Women) and AWARE (American Women Are Richly Endowed).

Flying from state capital to state capital, the savvy, disarming Schlafly matches the feminists' rhetoric phrase for phrase. She bluntly proclaims that "All sensible people are against ERA," and dismisses the liberationists as "a bunch of bitter women seeking a constitutional cure for their personal problems." In many of her speeches, she continues to insist that "Women find their greatest fulfillment at home with their family." (Copyright 1978

HEADLINE: ANTI-ERA EVANGELIST WINS AGAIN

Time Inc. All rights reserved. Reprinted by permission from Time.)

a. The essay notes that "ERA's decline has been largely the result of Schlafly's small (20,000 members) but highly disciplined organizations, Stop ERA and Eagle Forum." Is that an accurate assertion? What evidence does the author offer for it? What other causes might there be?

b. The author says that Schlafly cited the following potential effects of ERA: government-funded abortions, homosexual school-teachers, women being forced into military combat, and men refusing to support their wives. Is Schlafly guilty of a "slippery slope" fallacy? Support your answer.

c. Does the author establish Schlafly as an expert on the issue? If you say "Yes," indicate the specific passages that establish her credentials. Are they objective?

3. Present a cause-effect speech to the class. Your instructor will provide guidelines and instructions.

References

1. *The New World Book of Knowledge* (NY: Grolier Incorporated, 1969), p. 40.

2. Garrett Hardin, *Exploring New Ethics for Survival: The Voyage of the Spaceship Beagle* (NY: Pelican Books, 1972), p. 39.

3. Chaim Perelman, *The New Rhetoric: A Treatise on Argumentation* (Notre Dame: University of Notre Dame Press, 1969), p. 263.

4. Charles W. Hendel, *An Inquiry Concerning Human Understanding: David Hume* (Indianapolis: Bobbs-Merrill, 1955), pp. 74–76.

5. Alan Monroe and Douglas Ehninger, *Principles and Types of Speech Communication*, 7th ed. (Glenview, IL: Scott, Foresman, and Co., 1974), p. 526.

6. William Broyles, Jr., "Why Men Love War," *Esquire,* November, 1984, pp. 55–65.

7. Isaac Asimov, "Dial Versus Digital," *American Way,* October 29, 1985, pp. 13–14.

8. Karl Wallace, "The Substance of Rhetoric: Good Reasons," *The Quarterly Journal of Speech* 49 (1963), pp. 239–249.

9. Trudy Govier, *A Practical Study of Argument* (Belmont, CA: Wadsworth Publishing Co., 1985), pp. 305–310.

10. Robert Zajonc, "Birth Order and Intelligence: Dumber by The Dozen," *Psychology Today*, January 1975, pp. 37–40.

11. Hardin, p. 38.

12. James William Johnson, *Logic and Rhetoric* (NY: MacMillan, 1962), p. 42.

13. Asimov, pp. 13–14.

Model Speech:
Erik Sayre, "The Reasons for Illegal Immigration from Mexico." Used by permission.

The cause-effect pattern probes a difficult domain: the search for why things happen as they do. It involves us in description and explanation, but more importantly in analysis, evaluation, and judgment. Cause-effect reasoning, because it conforms to logical rules, leads to much of what we consider knowledge in our society. Use the cause-effect pattern to both inform and convince others of your point of view.

One example of cause and effect on a grand scale is Egypt's Aswan High Dam, completed in 1967 (previous page). It was intended to have four major effects: to prevent severe flooding of the Nile River; to store water in a gigantic reservoir called Lake Nasser; to release the stored water as needed to irrigate the plains below the dam in order to increase Egypt's arable land (above); and to generate large amounts of electricity.

The dam has partially achieved these effects and has benefited Egypt's growing population. But there are other serious effects (side-effects) that weren't anticipated. Although the annual floods did hamper agricultural progress, they also washed away the harmful mineral salts from the soil and deposited rich silt in the plains. Now, the dam prevents the cleansing of the soil and holds back the silt—an important source of fertilizer. The lake above the dam has caused some flooding of ancient ruins (following page, top). The Egyptians also have lost their mackerel, lobster, sardine, and shrimp industries—important sources of protein that used to feed on the nutrient loaded silt that collected at the river's mouth.

In addition, the slow-moving irrigation water that has replaced the fast-flowing river has resulted in the spread of a parasitic disease called *schistosomiasis* (right). At one point, the infection rate rose from 6 to 90 percent for those living in the delta below the dam.

So far, the good effects seem to outweigh the bad; the Egyptians are developing methods for mitigating the harmful effects. But this example shows the immense power and range of cause and effect, and it points out the importance of the extensive analysis and evaluation that is needed before we embark on judgments and actions.

Chapter 12 - Static Analysis: Problems, Issues, Policies, and Objects

Early in the fourteenth century in England, there lived a man named William Ockham (1285?–1349). Ockham (also spelled "Occam") became a renowned Franciscan philosopher whose writings have influenced many of the great minds of Western civilization, including Copernicus, Descartes, and Martin Luther. During his lifetime, Ockham achieved a mastery of logic that he used to dissect the most profound questions of his day, such as the relationship of the mind to the body and the individual to the church, and the essential nature of time, space, and movement. Ockham was considered then—and still is today—to be a genius of logical analysis.

Ockham followed one essential rule in his analyses, which we know today as "the rule of parsimony." According to this rule, one should eliminate all unnecessary elements of a question. For Ockham, every issue was to be analyzed and dissected until only the essential elements remained. Because he was so adept at "shaving away" at a question until no aspect of it had escaped scrutiny, Ockham's rule of parsimony has become known as "Ockham's Razor," because it involves dissecting or dividing a question into minute parts.[1]

It is, indeed, a sign of critical thinking to dissect carefully a topic under discussion in order to understand it. This is what happens in static analysis: a topic is divided into its parts or components. In fact, the static-analysis pattern is sometimes called "division into parts," or simply "division."[2]

You may have already noted that the narrative, process, and cause-effect patterns involve dividing a topic into sequences of events. In narrative, for instance, a whole experience is divided into individual events, the recounting of which leads to a point or lesson about life. But static analysis offers the speaker an approach to a topic that is quite different from narrative, process, or cause-effect, and it is important to understand this difference in order to use static analysis properly when the situation so demands.

The narrative, process, and cause-effect patterns are based on the concept of time. The result of analysis in these three patterns is a sequence of events organized chronologically. We see how—within the time-bound, sequential framework—narrative, process, and cause-effect all arrange events to provide a unique perspective on them. Narrative helps us understand what happened, process helps us understand how something happened, and cause-effect helps us understand why something happened. Controlling each perspective, however, is time.

But there is another concept that can help us analyze ideas and experiences: the concept of space. Many topics are best understood

CHAPTER 12

by dividing them into units, like the pieces of a puzzle, rather than dividing them into sequences of events, as we would with a story or a recipe. Static analysis is one pattern we can use when division into parts is the best way to understand a topic.

The term *static* means "standing still or remaining stationary," and static analysis differs from analysis based on the time patterns.[3] In static analysis, the headings or divisions of the topic do not move us through a period of time but around a body of space, so that the analysis explains or otherwise covers the entire space. An example of this distinction will help clarify our thinking.

A professor of political science was asked recently to speak on the topic "Inherent Concerns in Safeguarding a Democracy." As he thought about the topic, it was obvious that the key term, *concerns*, required him to list the pitfalls or dangers to which democracies are prone. As he began to probe the topic, the professor listed the following items that he believed would cover the term *concerns:* apathy, ignorance, intolerance, and sanctions on freedom of expression. Each concern became a main idea in his outline, and the professor developed each in detail during the speech.

Notice that the four main ideas are not related in time—one main idea does not necessarily occur before the other. Furthermore, the four main ideas, as a group, do not make up a series of events, steps, or reasons. The relationship among the four headings is static in the sense that each concern covers a certain part of a territory. This division of the topic into headings related by space allowed the speaker to cover the key term in the topic, *concerns*, in a manner most appropriate to the topic and the situation.

Just as the concepts of time and space overlap in the physical world, there is some overlap between the time patterns and the space patterns. For instance, the cause-effect pattern and the static-analysis pattern are related in that sometimes the causes of something do not proceed through time (causes may occur simultaneously), and may thus bear a spatial relationship to one another. You may see other relationships as you study the patterns, but you will also see the difference in emphasis of the static-analysis pattern: the division rather than the sequencing of a body of material. In fact, incidental overlap among the patterns will become less important as you learn to use them to probe and structure a public speech in various situations.

There are many ways to express a static relationship. When you think about a controversial issue like divestiture in countries with apartheid, your mind automatically suggests a pro-and-con orientation. When you want to argue in favor of a proposed law or ordinance, you think quite naturally about a problem-solution format. When you are shopping for a new stereo system you list the key features of a stereo unit and look for them as you shop. Whether the division is mental, as in the arguments surrounding a controversy, or physical, as with the parts of a stereo system, static analysis is simply the natural division of some whole into its component parts.

The Intention of Static Analysis: Roles, Situations, and Purposes

Static analysis is intended to help a speaker discover the way a particular topic is most appropriately broken down for purposes of communication. The parts of an analysis are sometimes determined by the nature of the topic being analyzed and sometimes by the situation in which the analysis is to be presented. In this chapter we will discuss four of the most common types of topics analyzed: problems, issues, policies, and objects. If you know how to conduct and organize a basic static analysis, adjusting the format to fit your circumstances will not be difficult.

Public speakers frequently use static analysis to compose a speech. Most State of the Union addresses given recently by American presidents have been static analyses that divided the health of the nation into two key headings, domestic affairs and foreign affairs, with a discussion of problems and achievements under the two headings. Similarly, it is common for speakers at a town or city council meeting to use a problem-solution format to address an issue before the assemblage. Finally, in the speech-communication classroom, static analysis often forms the basis for a round of public speeches.

In some situations, the speaker will be expected to act as a consultant or a reporter on a particular topic. Consultants are often asked to explain an issue to a legislative body so that the committee can make an informed decision. In such situations, comprehension and objectivity are key qualities for the speaker to possess.

In other situations, the speaker will act as an advocate for a point of view. On such occasions, the speaker is required to state a position on an issue and then make a strong case supporting it. Most of us have found ourselves—or will find ourselves—trying to persuade others to join a group, sign a petition, support a motion made at a meeting, or believe in something. Static analysis and advocacy go together quite naturally because the static-analysis pattern often leads us to an examination of various positions on the important issues of the day.

Static analysis is especially helpful for speeches concerning social problems, controversial issues, proposals to adopt policies such as laws and ordinances, and objects of curiosity such as paintings, music, and buildings. In each instance the topic must be broken down into components, which serve as the main headings of the body of the speech. Let us look carefully, then, at problems, issues, policies, and objects as the focus of static analysis.

Developing a Topic Through Static Analysis

Problem Analysis

A problem is a condition, situation, or matter of some kind that is causing difficulty. As more and more students commute to your school, it may experience a parking problem; the local blood bank may be experiencing a shortage of donors; a city may have difficulty financing a new park or a social agency. Although problems come in all shapes, sizes, and degrees, the common element is that most of those who are involved with a problem agree that it is troubling and must be addressed.

Topics for problem analysis come from a variety of sources: one's personal affairs, social involvement, political interests, place of work, and so on. Here are just a few of the topics that have been the focus of problem analysis in recent speeches:

Conserving the nation's fresh water supply

Helping the children of drug addicts

Saving farmland and the family farm

Retraining workers replaced by new technologies

Funding the social security system

A problem-analysis speech may only detail a problem, but more likely it will include a recommended solution or alternative solutions. You will need to decide, based on the situation in which you find yourself, whether your analysis will focus on detailing the problem alone or on both problem and solution analysis.

Begin to develop the topic by drafting a critical-thinking statement. Remember that a problem or problem-solution analysis may require detachment or advocacy; be certain your critical-thinking statement indicates clearly the role you intend to play. The following statement provided the speaker with a precise understanding of her role in the speech situation.

> *Child abuse has reached epidemic proportions. I want the audience to know how serious the problem is and to convince them to volunteer for the CASA program (Court Appointed Special Advocates) to meet the needs of the abused child whose case is pending.*

Notice how clearly the speaker defines her role: she is interested in awareness and action, and she plans to get her audience to do something about the problem, not just learn about it (she had much success).

With a clear critical-thinking plan in mind, divide the topic into two main headings: "the problem" and "the solution." Analyze the problem first, following these guidelines:

1. CLARITY. State the problem in one clear sentence.

2. ACCURACY. Include key names, dates, places, and events that are essential to the audience's understanding of the situation.

3. TOPICALITY. Indicate why the problem has become critical, so that the audience feels the problem must be addressed now.

4. RELEVANCE. Adapt the problem to the audience so that audience members feel some personal stake in it.

5. VIVIDNESS. Provide vivid supporting material to help the audience comprehend the problem.

After you have analyzed the problem, turn your attention to the solution or to alternative solutions. Use the following guidelines when dividing the solution(s) into parts:

1. CLARITY. State the solution in one clear sentence.

2. PRECISION. Indicate who should solve the problem and how.

3. REASONING. Give your reasons for endorsing the solution and support each with evidence.

4. VIVIDNESS. Help the audience visualize the condition as it will be after your solution is adopted.

5. RELEVANCE. Personalize the solution for the audience so that they feel a sense of gratification in adopting it.

If the speech will present alternative solutions, follow the above guidelines for each alternative you present. After you have finished the body of the speech, which has now been divided into the problem section and the solution section, complete the development of the topic by drafting a thesis statement, a preview (if necessary), an introduction, and a conclusion. The following is the outline for a speech on Court Appointed Special Advocates, the critical-thinking statement for which appeared at the beginning of this discussion of problem analysis:

  I. Introduction: Tell the story of James Jones, a child who was badly abused.

 II. Thesis: Court Appointed Special Advocates can do much to insure fair treatment for abused children when their cases come to adjudication.

III. Preview
    A. Definition of the problem
       1. Present the law's definition of child abuse.
       2. Tell how the courts define child neglect.

IV. Body
    A. Analysis of the problem
       1. There is a long history of child abuse in America.
       2. The problem has recently become a center of attention.
       3. Statistics show that the problem is reaching epidemic proportions today.
          a. One and a half million cases were reported nationwide in 1982 (National Center on Child Abuse).
          b. In Rhode Island 9,187 children were targets of battering, according to Richard Gelles of the University of Rhode Island.
       4. Reasons for the problem
          a. Many biblical passages exhort parents not to "spare the rod and spoil the child."
          b. Ethnic traditions often prescribe corporal punishment.
    B. Solutions to the problem of child abuse
       1. Education is an essential element in the struggle against child abuse.

---

2. Prevention through mandatory sentencing has been proposed in the legislature.
3. Prosecution of violators is the most direct way to solve the problem of child abuse.
   a. CASAs protect the child's interests by investigating and submitting a report to the court.
   b. CASAs make recommendations about placement of the child.
   c. CASAs serve as a source of love and guidance for the children during the most stressful periods of the pre-trial and trial proceedings.
C. The benefits of CASAs are instantly realized.
   1. CASAs fill the role of professional family-court counsellors, many of whom have been cut because of recent budget cutbacks.
   2. My role as a CASA has been personally fulfilling, as in the case of the Jones child I mentioned in my introduction.
   3. There has been some criticism of CASAs because they are not necessarily certified guidance counsellors and work for no specific agency.

V. Conclusion: There are many children out there who need you right now. I wish you would volunteer your time for this worthy cause. See me for details.

Issue Analysis

An issue is a point, situation, or condition that is a matter of dispute. As opposed to a problem that most agree is harming an individual, a group, or a society, an issue is a matter about which one faction is arguing for change while another faction denies the need for change, or wants some other change. Issue analysis precedes or supersedes policy analysis, which we will cover in the next section of this chapter. That is, while a specific law or policy may be involved in the debate over the issue, the focus of the controversy is not the policy itself but the reasons for or against the point of view under discussion. Issues, then, are philosophical controversies pitting people and their ideas against one another.

It would be difficult to go through a normal day without being informed of, interested in, or even involved with an issue. Our very existence as individuals living in a free society and seeking an education means that we are the natural descendants of William

Ockham who would prefer to dissect and debate the great and complex issues of the day rather than allow others to determine the direction in which society should move.

Because they are matters of dispute and are yet to be resolved, issues are usually phrased as questions:

Is Harp seal hunting a way of life or a form of cruelty to animals?

Should student government recognize campus activities that are political in nature?

Should real estate developers be required to donate part of their land for recreation or open space?

Have intercollegiate athletics become too professional?

Should the federal government review children's TV programs for violent content?

Topics for issue analysis, as you can tell, range from local affairs to international crises. For each question there is a person or group saying "Yes" and a person or group saying "No." Thus, the natural essence of an issue analysis is "pro" and "con." Issue analysis begins with a critical-thinking statement that captures the essence of the controversy, the point about which people disagree. In the following critical-thinking statement you can see the issue divided clearly into its constituencies or parts:

Probably no topic has split the American people as much as the issue of legalized abortion. I have discovered in my research that both sides, the so-called "pro-choice" and the "pro-life" groups, cling tenaciously to their positions, so that little compromise seems possible. I have my own opinion on the matter, but in this speech it is my intent to review the grounds on which the two sides stand . . . and clash.

An issue analysis is developed by dividing the body of the speech into two sections: the "proponents" and the "opponents." Under each main heading list the arguments that each side offers in support of its position. Organize the list from most important to least important arguments, so that when you deliver the speech you can emphasize the most important arguments of each side. Follow the guidelines given in Chapter 4 for analyzing evidence, so that as you think about the arguments each side offers, you can judge their validity.

If you are acting as an advocate for one side or the other, think about how you will respond to the arguments of the opposition. Divide your note sheets down the middle and write each argument of the opposition on one side and your response to it on the other. It is not enough to say, "What nonsense!" when you encounter an argument you find weak or distasteful; you must be able to state in clear, well-supported terms why you disagree. The best time to develop your position is when you are reading and thinking about the position of those with whom you disagree.

When you have finished listing and thinking about the arguments of the various factions, proceed to organize the body of the speech according to one of two formats: the lines-of-argument format or the pro-con format. Since they are appropriate in different situations, let's discuss each in detail.

LINES-OF-ARGUMENT STRUCTURE. Sometimes an issue is disputed on common grounds. That is, both or all sides to a controversy have focused on the political argument or the medical argument, for example. Each argument is referred to as a "line of argument," meaning that each side to the dispute is offering a different interpretation of the same general argument. Let's trace the critical-thinking statement shown above for the speech on legalized abortion to show how the arguments might be organized in the body of a speech using the lines-of-argument format.

A. The controversy over legalized abortion can best be illustrated by dividing the questions into four arguments.
   1. The morality argument
      a. Pro-choice groups argue that having an abortion is a difficult but not immoral choice.
      b. Pro-life groups argue that having an abortion is the ultimate immoral act.
   2. The medical argument
      a. Pro-choice groups argue that life begins at birth.
      b. Pro-life groups argue that life begins at conception.
   3. The social-cost argument
      a. Pro-choice groups argue that unwanted pregnancies have enormous social costs.

b. Pro-life groups argue that society has provided many alternatives for caring for each child that is conceived.
4. The legal argument
   a. Pro-choice groups argue that women should have control over their own bodies.
   b. Pro-life groups believe that society has always, and should always, exercise some control over individual behavior.

Each statement, of course, was developed with evidence and reasoning. The lines-of-argument structure is especially useful in analyses designed to inform the audience. The presentation of the arguments is followed by an objective analysis of what, in the speaker's opinion, is likely to happen, or by a refutation of one side or the other if the speaker is acting as an advocate.

THE PRO-CON STRUCTURE.   Many issue-analysis speeches are given for the purpose of advocacy. Also, many issues do not proceed along parallel lines of argument. When either of these conditions exists, the pro-con structure may be the most appropriate format for the analysis. In the current debate over spending cuts for federal assistance programs begun in the 1960s, for instance, those favoring the cuts argue that the programs have failed and that circumstances have changed (argument by circumstance), while those opposed to cuts argue that there is a larger principle according to which no person should go without food, shelter, clothing, and basic medical care (argument by principle). The most appropriate way for this issue and others like it to be discussed is to present one side and then the other—the pro-con method.

The pro-con structure for the body of an issue-analysis speech shows the proponent's arguments first and then the opponent's arguments. The following outline shows the issue of legalized abortion approached from a pro-con perspective.

A. Supporters of legalized abortion take their stand on three fundamental principles.
   1. The woman has a right to control her own body.
   2. We have the right not to have unwanted children in society.
   3. People have the right to plan a family.
B. Opponents dispute these principles.
   1. Pro-lifers say society can prevent an individual from committing a crime.

2. Pro-life groups say there is no such thing as an unwanted child.
3. Pro-life groups believe that family planning is a form of fratricide.

The speech might then proceed to a refutation of the opponent's arguments and the giving of good reasons for one's own position, or to an objective analysis of the entire controversy.

Notice one important feature of the pro-con structure that makes it particularly adaptable to advocacy: the proponent's arguments dictate the opponent's arguments. That is, the advocate gets to name the grounds on which the argument will take place, enumerate the arguments that characterize the controversy from one side, present the opponent's argument in his or her own terms and as reactions to the proponent's arguments, and, finally, to refute the opponent's arguments. When your role is to be an advocate for a particular point of view, the pro-con format gives you the advantage you need, while remaining true to the standards for issue analysis.

Many students of public speaking find that the closer they get to an issue, the more they are able to agree with both sides of it. In fact, many who begin as advocates end up as objective analysts. You may decide, as the result of an issue analysis, to take a course in philosophy, psychology, or debate to learn more about how issues are resolved and why you lean one way or the other consistently on the issues of the day.

Policy Analysis

A policy is a principle, plan, or course of action pursued by a body or an individual. It can be a law, an ordinance, or a resolution that states how the person or group will actually behave.

Policy analysis, as we noted briefly earlier, is related to issue analysis. Once an issue has been decided on its merits, a policy is enacted to stand for the majority will on the matter. Dispute may also arise—and quite often does—at the point in the controversy when an issue has been settled but a specific policy cannot be agreed upon, or when an adopted policy needs changing. If a decision were made to curb excessive violence in children's television programming, for instance, would the best policy be government regulation, industry-controlled reviews, or self-censorship by the producers of the program? Policy analysis focuses on the appropriate means to the end sought.

Policies are often the focus of static analyses. In fact, many students notice that once they get into a problem or an issue analysis, they discover that their real interest shifts to the debate on policy. One student, for instance, was concerned with the problem of low voter turnout for student elections. As she looked carefully at the problem, she realized that the policies on voting, which required students to pick up a special ID number three days before the actual election, were the real problem. She quickly switched her focus to a speech requesting that the policy be changed.

Policy analysis, then, is future oriented—it deliberates on what should be done to resolve a controversy justly. Speeches based on policy analysis are a common variety. Here are a few topics for policy-analysis speeches that might work well in the speech-communication classroom:

Safety equipment in the sport of boxing

Import quotas

Regulations governing absentee voting

Labeling food preservatives used in restaurants

A national policy on nutrition

A policy statement is worded as a specific proposal for action. Quite often, the words *resolved that* or *I move that* will help in framing the proposal. These phrases do not necessarily need to appear in the thesis statement that ultimately appears in the speech, but they help while drafting the proposal. The following are two proposals for policy-analysis speeches:

The current policy governing reapportionment must be changed to provide for an independent reapportionment commission.

I move that a policy be established requiring an instructor to report incidents of cheating and plagiarism to the dean's office within fifteen days of the time the incident occurs.

Though one statement asks that a current policy be replaced and the other asks that one be established, both call for change from the way things are. It is improper to offer a proposal supporting a policy that already exists. It would not be appropriate to say, "I urge that we continue to hold our annual meeting in New York," since, until someone proposes that the meeting be moved, there is no point to the argument. A proposal is a request to consider a change for the future.

The critical-thinking statement of a policy-analysis speech must indicate the exact behavior desired, and the who, what, when, where, and how of the policy whenever possible. The earlier proposal requesting a change in reapportionment was originally suggested in the statement the speaker wrote for himself prior to composing the speech:

> *During the last reapportionment, the state spent over $1 million in attorney's fees and special election costs as a result of the gerrymandering that went on in the legislature. I believe an independent commission would take the politics out of reapportionment, giving the people a one person-one vote situation once again. I am going to propose that the members of the state constitutional convention which convenes next month establish an independent reapportionment commission through constitutional means to draw the state's district lines.*

Notice that the critical-thinking statement indicates what is to be done, who is to do it, when they are to do it, and even why. Not all critical-thinking statements can be written with such precision, but the more information you provide yourself as you begin to compose your speech, the better you will be able to guide your composing.

A policy analysis begins with careful attention to questions that must be answered when trying to anticipate the future. Look carefully at the following list of questions that are often used in policy analysis so that you can use them to develop your own policy-analysis speech.

TOPICALITY. What is the problem? The speaker must provide background on the entire problem to orient listeners to the topic.

SIGNIFICANCE. How has the present policy designed to solve the problem failed? Why is a policy needed to resolve the problem? The speaker must show the audience that a policy or a new policy is needed now before a crisis results, or to resolve a crisis that has already occurred.

INHERENCY. Is this the correct policy? The speaker must show that the policy being proposed is the right one for the situation. Indicate the specific clauses in the policy and discuss each one.

WORKABILITY. Is the policy practical? The speaker must indicate the costs of such a policy, both economic and social, and indicate whether a structure is in place that will allow the policy to work.

PLAN-MEET-NEED. Has the policy worked somewhere else? The speaker should show that the policy, or a similar policy, has been tried in another place and has worked. Help the audience visualize the situation once the policy has been established.

DISADVANTAGES. What problems might occur? The speaker must respond to opposing arguments, refuting them to the best of his or her ability. Indicate any problems the policy might cause and suggest ways to anticipate and resolve them.

In composing a speech analyzing a policy, begin with an introduction and a thesis statement framed as a proposal, and then proceed to the analysis using responses to the questions listed above as headings in the body of the outline. The policy-analysis speech on reapportionment (see the above critical-thinking statement) was outlined as follows:

I. Introduction: Tell the story of Eldredge Gerry, the man from whose name the term *gerrymandering* comes.

II. Thesis: It would be most prudent for the members of the constitutional convention to enact an independent reapportionment commission through constitutional means to draw district lines.

III. Body
  A. Topicality
    1. $1 million was spent last year fighting the legislative gerrymander.
    2. People are fed up with the intrusion of politics into the reapportionment process.
  B. Significance
    1. Reapportionment policy is not only corrupt but also illegal, as determined by Supreme Court decision Baker vs. Carr.
    2. The state now operates under a temporary statute.

3. We are about to convene a constitutional convention; it is now time to enact a legal, constitutionally established, independent reapportionment commission.

C. Inherency

1. It is better to have a policy written into the constitution than to operate under statute. This is the right place.

2. The legislature will not itself enact such a measure because of its self-interest. This is not the right group.

D. Workability

1. The new reapportionment process would begin with the screening of professional reapportionment commissions and selection of one.

2. The people would act in an oversight capacity by voting on any plan recommended by the commission.

3. Here are the steps in the reapportionment plan my policy recommends.

E. Plan-meet-need

1. Eight states now have independent commissions.

2. Arkansas, Missouri, and New Jersey have not had a court challenge to their reapportionment since adopting independent commissions.

3. We are very much a state like New Jersey.

F. Disadvantages

1. It is difficult to keep politics out of anything, and selection of the commision might become political.

2. According to the Council of State Governments, independent commissions have not had an overall better track record in the courts.

3. In our situation, the independent commission is worth a try as a way of recapturing public trust in government.

IV. Conclusion: We should give this policy our approval during the constitutional convention. Write to your elected representatives, asking them to approve it, and sign this petition I have brought with me this afternoon.

Policy analysis focuses on the details of a policy and is only peripherally concerned with the problem or issue it intends to address; the heart of the argument is the policy itself. Policy analysis can, of course, be objectively analytical; you do not have to conduct yourself as an advocate. If you do decide to take the role of informant on a matter of policy, however, it is probably better to use the issues-analysis format, since they provide the pro-and-con format that might serve your needs more appropriately.

Object Analysis

Object analysis seeks to identify and explain the essential nature of something. It involves dividing a person, place, or thing into its component parts, with the goal of appeasing the audience's curiosity about the topic or helping them understand it more thoroughly.

Topics for object analysis are as plentiful as are things themselves. A style of architecture is often analyzed by dividing it into such components as geometry, color, materials used, and aesthetic/functional appeal. A budget is analyzed by dividing it into income and expenses, and then refining those headings as much as is needed to understand the budget. Here is a list of subjects recently analyzed in the speech-communication classroom:

The military defense system in America

The movie rating system

The perfect dinner

Geodesic domes

Essentials of a healthy diet

The critical-thinking statement for an object analysis is quite important because of one problem inherent in object-analysis speeches: developing clear purpose. An object analysis can often appear to be irrelevant unless the audience is made to feel that the speech itself has some goal for them. When drafting the critical-thinking statement, the speaker must state the purpose clearly. In the following example, note how the speaker indicates a purpose for the speech other than simply to analyze:

It is easy to get ripped off when buying a used car. Most people think they know exactly what they are looking for, and that attitude plays right into the hands of the salesperson. Other people are afraid to ask the questions they should, or they don't know the right questions to ask. Having worked as a used-car salesman, I think I can help people get a good deal by reviewing the key variables they should cover as they shop around.

Object analysis begins by listing the main features of the topic under analysis. The goal is to indicate each distinctive component of the object and then to subordinate the parts of each main component as necessary. In the speech on used cars, the student discussed the major variables to ask about when shopping for a used car as follows:

1. The body
    a. Rocker panels
    b. Floorboards
    c. Paint
2. The engine
    a. The right sound
    b. Telltale signs of abuse
    c. The service record
3. Mileage and wear
    a. Tires
    b. Upholstery
    c. Muffler
4. Miscellaneous
    a. Previous owner
    b. Price

Having listed the variables one should ask about, the speaker discussed each one in detail. The point is that his analysis led him to dividing the object thoroughly.

There are five guidelines to use when probing an object-analysis speech. Be certain to consider each one when analyzing an object for a public speech:

SIGNIFICANCE. What is the topic and why is it worth learning about? Provide the audience with a sense of purpose for the speech. Look for an example of the object that the audience might be able to relate to.

BACKGROUND. What is the history of the topic? Tell what your involvement is with the object. Provide historical details if necessary. Names, dates, and places are important here.

FEATURES. What are the components of the object? The heart of the analysis is the division into parts and discussion of each part. Each feature becomes a main heading, with details of the feature subordinated to it. Comment on each feature as it is introduced.

PROBLEMS. What special problems does the object have? In some cases problems may occur, or disadvantages may be inherent in the object. Tell what is making the object problematic. If you are discussing an agency, indicate what special problems the agency is having right now. If you are discussing an inanimate object, discuss variables such as wear on the materials and grounds maintenance.

ADAPTATION. How can the audience benefit from the speech? Tailor the information to the audience, telling them how to see the object, when to use it, how to join it, and so on.[4]

These guidelines will provide you with the main headings for the outline of your object analysis. Follow the same procedures used in problem, issue, and policy analysis to develop your outline.

Businesses and agencies often use object analysis to help others understand the dimensions of something. You will find that object analysis is not difficult, but requires attention to detail and precise divisions. Most importantly, keep the purpose of your speech in the forefront of the audience members' minds.

Using Language and Supporting Material

Static analyses often involve complex topics, such as policies with long clauses or issues with a broad variety of opinions. When composing and delivering the analysis as a speech, avoid language that is slanted or suggestive. Slanting occurs when the speaker, perhaps inadvertently, uses a descriptive term that shows bias. For instance, instead of saying, "An aide to President Reagan was quoted as saying . . ." the speaker says, "A Reagan lieutenant . . . ." Notice the sudden smuggling in of a slanted expression. The same effect is achieved in other ways:

By emotional labeling, as in "John Smith, a narc for the feds, testified that . . . ."

By vocal emphasis, as in "Ms. Smith, as she demands to be called . . . ."

By comparison, as in "Brown is a man of great political ability, but he is also corrupt. Like a fish rotting in the moonlight, he both shines and stinks."

By suggestion, as in "Hoffmann, who never actually has served time, still believes that . . . ."

Avoid any suggestion of bias in your presentation of the opinion of others. It is better to allow the audience to judge your material on its own merits.

Summary

Static analysis involves dividing a topic into its component parts. It is based on the concept of space, and is distinguished from time-based patterns such as narrative, process, and cause-effect, which sequence events chronologically.

There are many ways to express a static relationship. Most static-analytical formats derive from the nature of the topic itself, or from the situation in which the analysis is to take place. A static analysis can divide a topic into its mental or physical characteristics, and is carried out by following guidelines that lead to a thorough and efficient division of the topic. Most static analyses occur for one of four types of topics: problems, issues, policies, and objects.

Speakers who conduct static analyses play many roles. In some situations they may serve as consultants, in others as advocates. In this chapter we have shown a variety of speaker roles and intentions in static-analysis situations.

Problems are often the topics of static analyses. A problem analysis may simply detail a problem, or it may propose a solution or alternative solutions to the problem. The guidelines for a problem analysis are clarity, accuracy, topicality, relevance, and vividness. When developing the solution to the problem, the speaker must consider clarity, precision, reasoning, vividness, and relevance.

Issues are matters of dispute. An issue is analyzed by responding to a question with the various arguments given for or against a view. In an issue analysis, one lists the arguments of the proponents and the arguments of the opponents, then analyzes and assesses each position. An issue analysis is organized according to one of two formats: the lines-of-argument format or the pro-con format.

A policy is a principle or plan of action, usually expressed as an ordinance or law. The focus of a policy analysis is the policy itself, rather than the problem or issue it addresses, although the latter are obviously involved. Policies are analyzed by following six guidelines: topicality, significance, inherency, workability, plan-meet-need, and disadvantages. These same guidelines are used to organize and outline the analysis.

Objects are single pieces of reality, and they are analyzed by looking for their distinctive features and arranging these features into main and subordinate headings. The key guidelines in developing an object analysis are significance, background, features, problems, and adaptation. Object analyses are intended to satisfy audience curiosity, but the speaker must indicate the intent of the object-analysis speech.

This model speech, a problem analysis with a problem-solution format, was presented to a speech-communication class of twenty students. The speaker's goal was to make the audience aware of the problem and to enlist their support in the war on animal neglect and abuse.

Controlling the American Pet Population

Topic: Controlling the American Pet Population

Critical-Thinking Statement: As a volunteer at our local animal impoundment, I am continually shocked at the neglect and abuse of pets. In this speech I am going to make the audience aware of the problem and ask them to make pet-owner responsibility a main priority.

I. Introduction: Present statistics on birth rates for cats and dogs.

II. Thesis: We must become aware of the pet population explosion in this country and find ways to remedy this painful and tragic problem.

III. Body
   A. Definition
      1. Most newborns are killed each year.
      2. Chances for adoption are slight.
         a. In New York, only 11,000 of 133,000 animals were placed in homes.
         b. Only 10 percent are placed nationally, the rest destroyed.

B. Background
    1. Cities and countrysides are home to millions of strays.
        a. Many are tortured, according to *Providence Journal.*
        b. Many are killed by cars.
    2. Strays pose a health problem.
        a. They eat garbage.
        b. They antagonize cattle.
C. Cause
    1. The "finding a good home" myth
    2. The "nature's way" myth
    3. The "humane society" myth
    4. The "spaying" myth
    5. The "children should see a birth" myth
    6. The "expense of neutering" myth
D. Solution
    1. Birth control should be made available to owners for their pets.
    2. Higher license fees should be set.
    3. Ordinances should be enforced.
    4. Neutering and spaying should be encouraged.
E. Benefits—an end to the suffering

IV. Conclusion: Quote from a popular song, "Born to Lose"

Introduction: Speaker startles audience with statistics showing magnitude of problem.

The American pet population increased by 25 percent in the last decade. It is estimated by the Humane Society of the United States that 80 to 100 million cats and dogs are born each year, at the rate of approximately 2,000 to 3,000 per hour. While this may seem like a bonanza to pet lovers, it is not. In fact, the pet population explosion has triggered a serious national emergency. Last year alone, approximately 14 million pets were destroyed at animal shelters across the country at a cost of more than 125 million dollars.

Thesis statement tells purpose of speech— awareness—and suggests mode of development: problem-solution analysis.

We must become aware of the pet population explosion in this country, and find ways to remedy this painful and tragic problem.

Body: The problem is analyzed with the stock issues.

Definition: The speaker explains shelter overcrowding.

Most newborn kittens and puppies were taken to shelters last year and automatically killed without any chance for adoption. Most female cats are disposed of as soon as they arrive at the shelter, since their chance for adoption is slight. In 1973, the New York Society for the Prevention of Cruelty to Animals (NYSPCA) found homes for 11,000 animals and destroyed another 122,000. Nationally, of the 15 to 17 million pets turned in to shelters, only 10 percent were adopted: the rest were put to death.

Our cities and countrysides have also become home to millions of free-roaming stray animals. These strays are the target of much abuse, being shot at and tortured by sick individuals. According to the *Providence Journal*, ten dogs that had been tortured and then shot were recently unearthed by a construction crew. According to the Humane Society, most abandoned strays die under the wheels of a car, freeze, or die of starvation. Very few ever get adopted.

Strays pose a threat to our health. Last year, 1.5 million dog bites were reported, most inflicted on children and joggers. Strays pose a sanitation problem also, as they tear open garbage bags and knock over garbage cans in search of food. In many rural areas, stray dogs run in packs and harass cattle and wildlife. Quite often, farmers have had to develop posses to rid the area of stray dogs.

What is the root of the problem? Animal overpopulation is caused by irresponsible pet owners who fail to exert control over their animals. Most animals reach puberty early, which causes frequent reproduction. A female dog is able to breed every six to nine months, and comes into heat at least twice a year. One dog can have as many as sixty puppies during a seven-year period. Cats can have three to four litters per year, making them even more prolific than dogs. Unfortunately, too many pet owners allow their pets to have litters.

There are six common myths behind allowing a pet to have a litter, all of which are faulty. The first is the myth of "finding a good home for the kittens and puppies." Unfortunately, even if homes are found, very few of the pets last more than a year in the home. Thus, the first belief of the irresponsible pet owner is false.

The second myth many pet owners believe is that nature intended for animals to have babies. This may be true, but humans intervened in a natural system, domesticating the animals and making them dependent on their owners. This changes the natural order of things.

The third myth many pet owners believe is that the humane society will take care of unwanted pets. The fact is, humane societies try, but they actually find homes for just a few pets: the rest are disposed of.

The fourth myth is that spaying a pet will hurt the animal permanently. This is simply not true. The procedure is simple, and the animal is more contented afterward.

The fifth myth is that children should have a chance to see puppies and kittens born. This is a selfish reason to have pet litters, and the suffering most pets will go through as a result is not worth the joy of seeing them born.

The sixth myth is that spaying or neutering is too expensive. The question is, can you afford not to have your dog or cat spayed or neutered? Can you risk the guilt you will feel knowing the suffering you are putting your pet's offspring through?

Solution:
1. Birth control
2. Higher license fees
3. Ordinances
4. Spaying or neutering

This problem can be solved. I would like to suggest four ways to cope with the problem, one or all of which will help to alleviate it.

First, there are currently three different birth-control devices for pets involving chemicals. Soon there will be a mechanical device capable of preventing pregnancy. Birth-control devices should be made available to pet owners.

Second, higher license fees should be set for unaltered animals where licenses are required. This is a specific law that would require a separate speech to explain, but it would help to solve the problem.

Third, practical and enforceable ordinances that protect animals from cruelty and that require animals to be leashed would do much to solve this problem.

Fourth, and most importantly, government agencies should encourage spaying and neutering of animals. Pet-food companies could set up a fund to assist those who cannot afford to have their animals fixed. Already there are shelters that provide spaying and neutering at the time the pet is adopted. There is every good reason for local and state government to make funds available to shelters to support spaying and neutering programs.

Benefits: Suffering would end.

The benefits of coping with our pet population explosion are many, but there is really one benefit that stands out: the end of the suffering we are now causing helpless creatures. Imagine what it must be like to huddle defenselessly against the cold winter night, slowly starving to death. A few simple actions on our part could end this suffering.

Conclusion: Speaker ends speech with a quotable quote and a handout.

As the words to a popular song go, "Some of us are born to lose." Nowhere is that more true than for unwanted pets, born to irresponsible pet owners. We should all resolve to alleviate this problem by our own behavior and by influencing our friends and neighbors to be responsible pet owners.

1. The class should divide into small groups of no more than five. Each group should agree to watch one of the television "news-magazine" programs such as "Sixty Minutes," "20-20," or "The MacNeil-Lehrer Report." Choose a segment that covers an issue of some kind, and, if possible request a transcript of the segment from the program's producers, or tape the segment. As you discuss the issue covered, decide whether the coverage was biased or balanced. Make a list of the evidence and supporting material used by those on both sides of the issue and decide which side wins the issue on the grounds of support. Make a group decision about the value of the report, asking whether it has helped the audience decide on the matter.

2. Divide the following objects into their key features. List all the headings you can think of that divide the topic into discrete features. After you have completed your division, compare your headings with another class member's headings to see how closely the two lists divide the same object. Discuss why you divided the object as you did, focusing on the criteria you used.

   The school's insignia

   The counselling center on campus

   A movie playing at the local cinema

   Rock music

   Friendship

3. Prepare an analysis speech to be delivered in class. Your instructor will provide details for the assignment.

1. *The American People's Encyclopedia* (NY: The Grolier Company, 1969), Vol. 19, pp. 325–326.

2. Frank D'Angelo, *A Conceptual Theory of Rhetoric* (Cambridge: Winthrop Publishers, 1975), p. 43.

3. D'Angelo, p. 44.

4. Adapted from Richard A. Katula, Celest Martin, and Robert Schwegler, *Communication: Writing and Speaking* (Boston: Little, Brown, 1982), pp. 232–236.

Speech Model:

Karen E. Levesque, "Controlling the American Pet Population." Used by permission.

Static analysis allows us to divide a topic into its parts or components so it can be examined and understood. Static analysis is helpful when examining complex problems, issues, policies, and objects that don't have simple right or wrong solutions and yes or no answers.

Our first amendment right—freedom of speech—involves the complex issue of censorship, which continually finds its way into our nation's courts (and which is an issue of importance to speech communication classes and book publishers). Static analysis can help us explore the intricacies of the censorship issue, clarify them, and present them succinctly to an audience.

In analyzing an issue such as censorship, it is particularly helpful to break it down and look at problems and solutions, pros and cons. You might want to examine those in favor and those opposed to some form of censorship and why. For example, many feminists favor censorship of pornography because they feel it depicts violence toward and the subjugation of women (right). Many fundamentalists, or so-called creationists, favor censorship of school textbooks because they believe some texts present young people with unacceptable religious or social beliefs. On the other hand, publishers and distributors of pornography oppose censorship because they feel it violates the right of freedom of the press (following page). Many well-respected authors and publishers oppose censorship, arguing for freedom of expression (previous page).

Censorship isn't an easy issue for most people. What do you do if you find pornography unacceptable but support the right of free speech? Or if you have strong religious beliefs, but you also believe in first amendment rights? There are no easy answers, but by employing the static-analysis pattern to examine the issues, you and your audience will come closer to understanding and solving a complex issue.

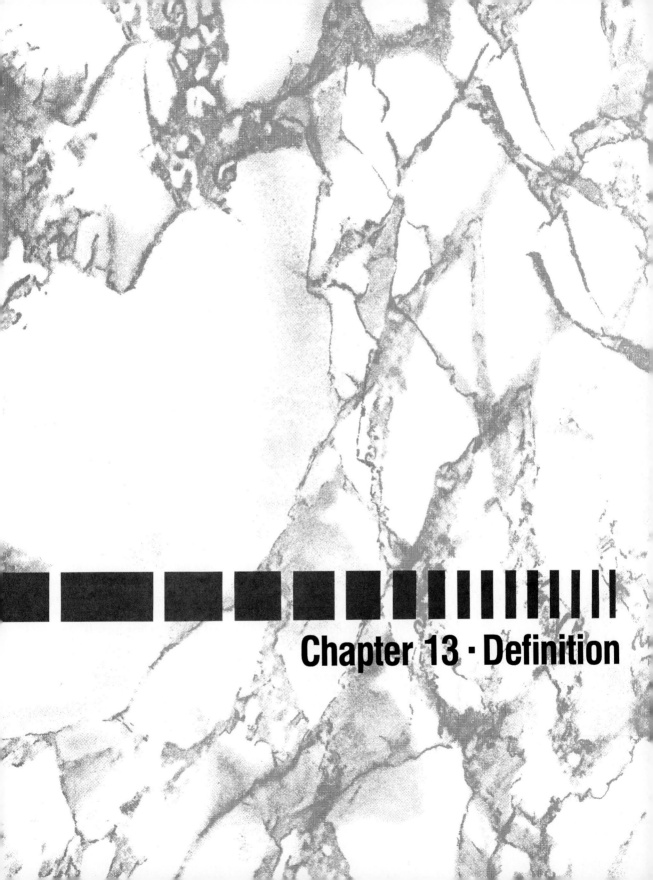

Chapter 13 · Definition

One of the twentieth century's great scientists, architects, and thinkers, R. Buckminster Fuller, was once asked to define *man*. He responded with the following:

> *Man is a self-balancing, 28 jointed adapter-based biped, an electro-chemical plant, integral with the segregated stowages of special energy extracts in storage batteries, for subsequent actuation of thousands of hydraulic and pneumatic pumps, with motors attached; 62,000 miles of capillaries, millions of warning signals, railroad and conveyor systems; crushers and cranes, and a universally distributed telephone system needing no service for 70 years if well managed. . . .*[1]

Interesting as Fuller's definition is, it is doubtful that most people would recognize this as an appropriate definition of *man*. Religious thinkers, for instance, might see in Fuller's definition a mechanized, godless creature, bereft of emotions and a soul. If you were asked to define *man*, you would most likely write something much different than either Fuller or a theologian would. And you might all be correct!

A definition is valid if it is based upon logically derived conclusions, stated in understandable terms, and consistent with common observations that you and anyone else might make. Aristotle noted that in order to explain anything we must first define it. An essential definition, according to Aristotle, is one that distinguishes a term or concept from all others and spells out a thing's nature.[2] The problem is that in order to define words we must use words themselves.

When we define words with other words, we begin to experience the tyranny of language, the oppressiveness of our own vocabulary as we try to capture agreeable meanings for our thoughts. We have all been in conversations that seemed to go nowhere because we couldn't agree on the meanings behind the words we were using: "Sara, exactly how are you using the term *euthanasia*?" "Tom, you called the Salvadoran Contras 'armed guerrilla insurgents,' but I would say they are liberation forces." And yet, we cannot escape the necessity of using words to define other words, because definitions allow us to set boundaries or limits on things, and, by doing so, to state their essential nature.[3] Defining, then, is an essential act in critical thinking. The definition pattern responds to those frequently asked questions, "What is it?" and "What does it mean?"

Definition is related to analysis, especially object analysis, because when we define we look for the essential nature of something, as we did in analysis.[4] The definition pattern is distinctive, however, because while the objective of analysis is to divide something into its parts in order to understand it, the objective of definition is to derive meaning through differentiating a term or concept from others; thus, when we define we look for the uniqueness of something in comparison to all other things. The distinctiveness of the definition pattern will become even clearer as you read this chapter.

Definitions also are commonly used as a form of supporting material in speeches organized around other patterns. Most frequently, a speaker will define key terms early in a speech so that the audience will understand them when they appear in the body. You will remember, for instance, that previewing terms, as discussed in Chapter 5, may be necessary for a speech regardless of its pattern. Similarly, in the analysis pattern covered in the preceding chapter, definitions often entered into the analysis as a main heading. When we use definition as part of another pattern it is called "limited definition."

But the definition pattern can also be used to think about terms and concepts in an extended manner. It is a method for reasoning through the subtle nuances of meaning that distinguish one thing from another. Whenever your goal is to know the complete meaning of something, whether for your own benefit or in communication with others, the definition pattern is an essential tool to have at your command.

The Intention of Definition: Roles, Situations, and Purposes

Public speakers frequently use the definition pattern to guide them through a topic. The pattern is particularly useful for inspirational speeches clarifying values or beliefs that the audience holds. In the nineteenth century, during the era of the public-lecture circuit, it was typical for one of the orators on the program to address a theme such as "The Meaning of Instinct" or "Safe and Sane Faith," using the definition pattern as the organizing principle.[5] Today, it is not uncommon to hear a religious sermon on a topic such as "What It Means to Be a Jew" (or Christian, Doubting Thomas, and so on) guided by the definition pattern.

Regardless of the topic, a definition speech is an excellent way to challenge yourself and your audience to think deeply about the meanings behind words as symbols. Whether the topic is a familiar but misunderstood term such as *average* or an unfamiliar but intriguing one such as *euthanasia*, the definition speech should make the audience think critically about symbols and their use in human communication. Because a speech structured with the definition pattern focuses intensely upon words, it is particularly useful for a course in communication.

Speeches based on the definition pattern serve a variety of purposes. In addition to the inspirational goal mentioned earlier, they can be used to satisfy audience curiosity, as with the model speech on the word *serendipity* at the end of this chapter. A similar speech was presented on the topic "The Hippies: A Romantic Retrospective." Speeches of this type are usually lighthearted in tone and presented for purposes of enjoyment and appreciation as much as for discovery.

A definition speech can be used to clarify a term. In a recent speech, an exchange student from India began his presentation on the concept of karma by noting that a popular song by John Lennon, "Instant Karma," had greatly distorted the actual meaning of the term; thus, his speech was intended to define the term correctly. Other speeches have been given for terms such as *radical, liberal,* and *conservative,* all of which, the speakers asserted, have precise meanings that have been distorted over time.

In addition, the definition pattern may be used to make an argument. When used for this purpose, the definition pattern can be used to distinguish a term from others, as in a speech on the nature of democracy. It can also associate a term with something the audience views favorably, as in a recent speech on the term *discrimination* in which the speaker proved that the term actually refers to refinement in choosing between and among objects rather than to prejudice. The definition pattern, as you will learn in this chapter, is a logical pattern when used correctly, and thus it has a built-in sense of validity. Rhetorician Chaim Perelman lists definition as a "quasi-logical" form of argument because it depends upon the logic the audience sees in the methods used to arrive at the definition.[6]

The goal of an argumentative-definition speech is to show that a term is appropriate as a label for something. This is Joseph Kraft's purpose in his argument, based on definition, against the Reagan administration shown in exercise 1 at the end of this chapter.[7] In addition, arguments based on the definition pattern can be aimed at redefining a term. One group may be calling a bank account "discretionary money," while another group may be calling the same account a "slush fund." A speech on the topic might center on the correct labeling of the account for purposes of accusation, or on defense of the practices associated with the account.

In the speech-communication classroom, students often find that a definition speech is an excellent exercise in critical thinking. Discovering the methods for constructing definitions and putting those methods to use often yields new insight into the meaning of terms commonly used but more commonly misused. In the area of values analysis especially, a definition often leads to discovery and discussion among audience members that is in itself a valuable learning experience. Thus, although it has practical application, a definition speech is quite frequently an intellectual experience in which the speaker takes on the role of critical examiner.

Choosing and Analyzing a Topic for a Definition Speech

Use the definition pattern when you feel the need to clarify a term or concept. Most of us have had the experience of having a new term catch our interest: *euthanasia*, *graffiti*, or *détente*, for example. The definition pattern can also be used when you want to clarify a term that you believe has been used improperly. Finally, you might have had the occasion to want to label something with a term to capture its uniqueness. In a recent talk at a town meeting, for example, a local activist referred to the transformation of a quaint New England downtown into a strip of fast-food restaurants as "pizza-fication," a term he defined as the stage of development of a community when it has ten pizza parlors or more in the local phone book. The point is to choose a topic that has some value for yourself and the audience.

Once you have chosen a topic for a definition speech, you must begin defining it. There are a number of ways to define a term, each illuminating a different aspect of the term and each adding to the reasonableness of the definition.

Term-Class Differentiation

The term-class-differentiation technique is the classical method of defining words or concepts, a method derived from the works of Aristotle. The objective of the term-class-differentiation method is to define a word (term) by placing it into a larger and more general class of words (class), and then to note how the word is different from other members of the class (differentiation). This method involves using the term to be defined as the subject of a sentence, then using the linking verb *is* to connect the term to a subject complement that states the class. The definition is completed by restricting the class with a qualifier, such as a relative-pronoun phrase. You can see how this is done by looking at the following examples:

Term	Class	Differentiation
Graffiti . . .	is a form of writing in public places . . .	that some call art and others call vandalism.
A Saturday Night Special . . .	is a type of handgun . . .	that is purchased from an illegal source.
Profanity . . .	is a form of obscene language . . .	that has as its subject a deity or sacred object.

The term-class-differentiation method of defining is a good place to begin thinking about a topic, since it will help you see the distinguishing characteristics of your term. Write as much as you can in the differentiation column so that you begin to "squeeze" various meanings out of the term. But term-class-differentiation is just a beginning, akin to looking up the term in the dictionary. Having started with this logical step, you should proceed to other methods for distinguishing your term from others.

Etymology

Etymology is the history of a word, particularly its origins. Defining a term etymologically involves tracing the term to its roots. By doing so, we can determine the original meaning of the term and discover how that meaning has changed over the years. A search through the history of a term often yields information we can use in a speech. Look, for instance, at the following excerpt from an argument by definition. It comes from an essay by Barbara Lawrence, "X Isn't a Dirty Word," on the origin of "dirty" words.

> *The argument that taboos exist only because of "sexual hang-ups" (middle class, middle age, feminist), or even that they are a result of class oppression—the contempt of Norman conquerors for the language of their Anglo-Saxon serfs—ignores*

*a much more likely explanation, it seems to me, and that is
the sources and functions of the words themselves.*

*The best known of the tabooed sexual verbs, for example,
comes from the German "ficken," meaning to "strike," combined, according to Partridge's etymological dictionary
Origins, with the Latin "fustis," a "staff" or "cudgel," the Celtic
"buc," a point, hence "to pierce"; the Irish "bot," the male
member; the Latin "battuere," which means "to beat"; the
Gaelic "batair," a "cudgeler"; the early Irish "bulaim," meaning
"I strike," and so forth. It is one of what etymologists call the
sadistic group of words for the man's part in copulation.*[8]

Based upon her search through the history of tabooed sexual
words, Lawrence concludes that the most notorious of the obscene
words is inherently bad because, by its very essence, it turns the
sexual act into an act of brutality and domination. Of course, you
may want to argue with Lawrence about her strict use of etymology
to support her argument, but the point she makes is well taken;
terms can be defined, and understood, by tracing their history.

Synonyms

Words are often defined through synonyms, words or phrases that
are close in meaning to the term being defined. Synonyms become
a way of suggesting equivalent words or phrases from the audience's
vocabulary to get at the meaning of the term being defined. The
following examples will give you a clear idea of synonymy as a form
of definition:

Vernacular = jargon, argot, lingo, slang

Intractable = unruly, stubborn, unmanageable

Ego = self, conceit, center

Synonyms can be found in any good dictionary. If no synonyms
are listed, you may want to look at a thesaurus, a book of synonyms
and antonyms (words that mean the opposite). Remember that every
word describes a different piece of the world; thus no two words
are exactly alike. Also, be careful to avoid euphemisms, terms that
may appear to be synonyms but are actually words that soften or

evade the true meaning of the term. The synonyms you choose should be words that state equivalent meanings, not exactly the same meaning as the word being defined.

Negation

A term or concept can be defined by negation, by stating what it is not. The term *darkness*, for instance, can be defined as "the absence of light," or *the normal person* might be defined as "someone who has no psychoses." Just as with the use of synonyms, defining by negation often requires the speaker to look up the antonyms of a word in the dictionary or a thesaurus.

It is not appropriate to base an entire definition speech upon negation, such as one might do with etymology. Use the negative as a technique to clarify a term, but do not extend it beyond that.

Examples

More than a specific technique for definition, examples are often used to clarify a definition, to make it concrete. Because they are colorful and concrete, examples are an excellent method for distinguishing unfamiliar or abstract terms. In the previously mentioned speech on karma, the speaker used the following example to clarify this somewhat abstract and often misused term:

> *A person's karma is the sum total of a person's behavior in this life up to the point that the life has been consciously lived. I am an engineering student and must make conscious decisions about the kind of engineering student I will be; a good one or a lazy one. My behavior as an engineering student is part of my karma, and it will be used to determine my fate. Karma is not something you have, it is something you accumulate as you act as a person in the world.*

Comparison and Analogy

A word or concept can often be made clearer by comparing it to something else; thus, while not a specific method for defining, comparisons and analogies can be used to illustrate a term or concept, and so aid in definition. A simple comparison will sometimes work:

"Software is to a computer as the brain is to the body." In other cases, a complete analogy may enliven and clarify the definition, as in the following example from a speech the Reverend Jesse Jackson gave at the Speech Communication Association Convention in 1974. Jackson is attempting to change the commonly held definition of America as the "melting pot" nation:

> A better example is that we're more like a bowl of vegetable soup than a melting pot. First of all, vegetable soup is more digestible than steel. The second point is that in the vegetable soup you may have a tomato base and that is the homogeneous dimension of American culture. There are many things that we have in common. We have common geographical soil, common air, common water, common tax system, common military system, common government. There is an American base, that's more American than it is European, African, or anything else. . . .

> But beyond that American base, corn and beans, peas and chunks of meat, are floating up on the top of that soup. And those things appeal to us. Our Irishness, our Italianness, our Catholicism, our Protestantism, our Jewishness, our Blackness, our Arabness, appeals to us, and it's up on the top of the soup. And when it gets hot, those elements do not lose their identity, but each one of them has extracted from it some of its vital juices. And that's what makes the soup tasty. Because there are some Blacks and Whites, some males, some females, some young and old, but no one loses his identity, just gives up some of his essence for the common wealth.

Once you have analyzed your topic using the various techniques for definition just discussed, you are ready to begin drafting the speech. Begin by composing a critical-thinking statement that gives you a sense of the situation, your role, and the purpose of your speech. In the following example, notice how the speaker captures the essence of the entire speech situation:

Composing a Definition Speech

> Beauty is an often used term, and, I think, one that is often misused. Although there are familiar clichés like "Beauty is only skin deep," I believe that most of the young people in this

room still judge beauty as a surface dimension of a person. As an older student, I have seen how this notion of beauty as the physical features a person is born with has caused relationships to break up and caused anguish to people who are not physically attractive. Although my speech may be on a term that is overdone, I want to talk about the beauty of a person that is inside the person. I want to talk about what beauty means to me, after thirty-five years of marriage to the same person. Maybe I can convince some of the younger people in the audience to look a little deeper than the skin when they search for a mate.

Notice that the speaker recognizes her role in the situation and her purpose—to convince others to see something differently.

With a clear critical-thought plan in mind to guide development of the topic, begin to flesh out the details of the speech. Look at all the definitions and aids to definition you have developed in your analysis, and start to decide how you will use them in the speech. You must decide how to use the various meanings you have uncovered to capture the essence of the term you are defining. At this point you might decide that etymology is the key to understanding the term, or that etymology is only a beginning and that the term can be made most clear through examples and comparisons. As you make these decisions, start to develop the speech outline.

There is no single structure for a definition speech; rather, the organization of the speech follows the techniques you have decided to use to define the term. You can, however, think of the skeleton structure of a definition speech in the following way:

I. Introduction

II. Thesis

III. Body
    A. Meaning 1
        1. Supporting detail
        2. Supporting detail
    B. Meaning 2
        1. Supporting detail
        2. Supporting detail
    C. Meaning 3 ...

IV. Conclusion

Your first meaning might be a definition by term-class differentiation, supported by the details you have uncovered in your research. The second meaning might be an etymological tracing of the term with the appropriate references and, perhaps, synonyms needed to clarify the term. The point is to use those techniques that are necessary to defining the term and achieving your purpose. In her speech on the concept of beauty, the speaker used the following outline to develop her idea:

I. Introduction: Cliché expressions about beauty, "Beauty is only skin deep" and "Beauty is in the eye of the beholder"

II. Thesis: A person's beauty is the sum total of his or her qualities, both physical and mental.

III. Body
    A. Beauty as distinguished from physical attractiveness
        1. Example of Barbra Streisand
        2. My own personal experience
    B. Beauty as defined in Keats's "Ode on a Grecian Urn"
        1. The meaning of Keats's phrase, "Beauty is truth, truth beauty"—universal qualities of beauty
        2. My own experience with lasting beauty
    C. What beauty is not
        1. Examples of things that are not beautiful
        2. Examples of things that are beautiful

IV. Conclusion: Quotation from Keats's poem

Summary

Defining terms is a fundamental skill. Through definitions we understand the essential nature of the world around us. But meanings change as conditions change, and using words to talk about words is an elusive art. Thus, we need to know how to define in order to communicate clearly.

Definition is a commonly used pattern of discourse. It is used to answer the frequently asked questions "What is it?" and "What does it mean?" The definition pattern is related to other patterns of discourse because it is based on the concept of space, but it is a distinctive pattern because of its emphasis on the essential meaning of something as discovered through differentiating it from other things.

Definitions are most commonly used as supporting material in a speech based upon another pattern; this is called "limited definition." But the definition pattern can be extended to govern a whole speech. Furthermore, the definition pattern can be used for a wide variety of purposes, from the most lighthearted and entertaining to the most serious arguments. Public speakers frequently use it as a guide in the definition of values such as loyalty and community.

A definition speech can clarify a term, reinforce a definition already accepted, or redefine a term to give it a purer or a different meaning. Use the definition pattern whenever the focus of your speech is on the meaning of something.

The definition pattern is considered to be based on logical reasoning because of the three techniques it uses to define a term: term-class differentiation, etymology, and synonymy. In addition, three aids to definition help the speaker fill in the details of a definition speech: comparison, negation, and example. Use all the tools for defining to reveal the full dimensions of a term.

A speech based on definition begins with a clear critical-thinking statement. Having drafted the critical-thinking statement, you should list the meanings and develop them with supporting material. To some degree, the methods you have chosen for defining the term will determine the structure of the speech.

The definition pattern allows the speaker and audience to practice critical thinking and language usage. It is also a good way to clarify for one's self and for the audience the meanings of values and concepts commonly used but often misused.

Serendipity

The model speech presented here takes as its subject the term *serendipity*. The speaker felt that the term was a source of curiosity and that it was confused with *dumb luck*. Presented in the speech-communication classroom, the speech was judged to be one of the five best for the semester in a group of classes numbering 120 students.

Topic: Serendipity

Critical-Thinking Statement: The term *serendipity* came to mind as soon as I began thinking about this speech. It is a word that has personal relevance for me, and, I have discovered, a word few others have ever heard or know much about. I think the audience will enjoy the speech and learn something about this fascinating term.

I. Introduction: A brief story about my personal interest in the term

II. Thesis: I have discovered that *serendipity* is a word deeply rooted in antiquity and one that has magical and alluring connotations.

III. Body
- A. Etymology of the term
  1. The term was coined by Horace Walpole in 1754.
  2. It comes from the fairy tale "The Three Princes of Serendip."
  3. Its original meaning is "the gift or faculty of discovering unexpected and valuable things not originally sought after."
  4. *Serendipity* is associated with the term *sagacity*.
  5. The background of the fairy tale shows that the word has historical meaning as the original name for Ceylon, the home of the three princes.
- B. Walpole's fascination with the term
  1. An example of serendipity in Walpole's life shows that he experienced it himself.
  2. A brief explanation shows how the term became associated with luck.
- C. Serendipity defined with term-class differentiation
  1. Present James Austin's definition.
  2. Tell my interpretation of the term.

IV. Conclusion: Two experiences I have had with the term *serendipity*

The word *serendipity* always sustained for me a certain, yet questionable meaning. At two distinct times in my life the word has suddenly appeared to me and left me with this insatiable curiosity. It was as if by some accident that this unusual word would finally reveal itself to me. I have discovered that *serendipity* is a word deeply rooted in antiquity and that it has magical and alluring connotations. In day-to-day life one might meet this word simply by chance.

Serendipity is a word coined by British author Horace Walpole around 1754. He was known for his wit and worldliness. Walpole wrote to Horace Mann, British Minister to the Court of Tuscany and lifelong friend, about, and I quote, "a silly fairy tale I read entitled, *The Three Princes of Serendip*, in which their highnesses travelled, always making discoveries by accident and sagacity, of things they were not in quest of." Hence comes the basis for Walpole's word *serendipity*—"the gift or faculty of discovering unexpected and valuable things not originally sought after." In this same correspondence with Mann, Walpole enlightened

Introduction: Speaker establishes her credibility by showing personal interest in the topic.

Thesis: The thesis is stated at the end of the introduction. Notice that the speaker suggests the definition pattern with the words deeply rooted.

Body: Speaker traces the etymology of the term, adding supporting material and especially interesting anecdotes to keep the audience's attention.

Body: Notice how the speaker subtly yet clearly shows how serendipity is at work even among those who coined the term. It was this clever touch that made this speech a winner with the audience.

him with the idea that "this discovery [of the word *serendipity*] indeed is almost of that kind which I call serendipity."

The word *sagacity* is often associated with *serendipity*. The archaic meaning of *sagacity* is "the acuteness of smell." In present-day dictionaries the definition of *sagacity* is the "the quality of being quick, keen, or acute in sense perceptions, to see what is seemingly relevant and significant." In Walpole's definition of *serendipity* he used sagacity to stress that there is a distinctive personal receptivity involved with the word, especially in interpersonal relationships.

Notice how the speaker does her own research to add to what Walpole discovered which she has already reported.

Walpole wrote to Mann that he derived the word *serendipity* from a Persian fairy tale. This tale of three princes is seven hundred years old, and parts of the story are more than 1500 years old. In 1557, Cristofaro Armeno, Christopher the Armenian, published this tale along with others that originated in Persia and India. Armeno's tale, *Peregrinaggio*, is a version of Khusrau's adaptation of the original, Nizami's *Khamse*, a story about three brothers and a camel driver. Armeno's tale told of three princes who lived on their island home of Ceylon. The medieval Arabian name for Ceylon is Serendippo, in later Persia, Sarandip or Serendip. In Ceylon or Serendippo the three princes travelled about exploring many things, encountering accidental good fortune every step of the way.

Notice the transition to other forms of defining that will be used in the speech.

Walpole came across this tale while reading Chevalier De Mailly's French adaptation of Armeno's *Peregrinaggio*. He discovered the word inadvertently when he accidentally found, in an old book, the coat of arms for a certain family that he had been searching for. In his letter to Mann of 28 January 1754, he used *serendipity* to describe how he came about this fortunate discovery much as the princes came across theirs. It is hard to understand the word *serendipity* from this letter, but there are certain key words that cue the meaning Walpole had in mind.

Notice the use of synonyms to suggest related meanings of the term.

In the letter to Mann, Walpole mentions his penchant for finding things as "Walpole's luck or Walpoliannae." He ascribes certain characteristics to his talent and relates it to the tale of the three princes of Serendip. His is a gift, a charm bringing apparent, magical, and miraculous effects. Within the letter are the terms *serene*, *luck*, *serendip*, and words with *-ity* endings, which all fall into the accidental discovery of *serendipity*. Thus, the continued use of this term.

Body: The speaker shifts to term-class-differentiation method for defining terms.

Serendipity is a unique word that exemplifies the way chance interacts with creativity. James Austin defines the word as "the weaving together of the threads of life and the times of its inventors." It is a happy word, a piece of art, which is regarded as a quality. *Serendipity* is the gift of discovering things by accident—chasing some other thing and finding that which you are not in pursuit of. One encounters good luck as a result of accident, sagacity, exploring, and chance.

I've accidentally discovered such good luck twice so far in my life. The very first time I stumbled upon the word *serendipity* was in a seventh-grade grammar workbook. The book was titled *Serendipity* and has since held a particular spot in my mind. I was struck by the unusual sound of the word, and struck even more so, after I learned what the term meant, by the way I had come upon it—almost by chance. The second time I found *serendipity* was in Alexandria, Virginia. While walking down a street I stopped in my tracks by a shop sign reading "serendipity." I entered the shop to find it filled with surprises and treasures.

Conclusion: The speaker shows that she too has experienced serendipity. The conclusion ties the speaker in with Walpole and shows the purpose for the speech.

Both experiences reinforced for me the essence of serendipity as the good luck one stumbles upon, either in a grammar lesson or upon entering a strange shop. Unfortunately, serendipity is understood as a result rather than an ability, as Walpole intended it to be. Today's meaning has been watered down to plain old good luck, quite different from the original definition. In other words, serendipity is something that must simply happen to you—you can't go out and get it.

Exercises

1. Read and critique the following essay by Joseph Kraft, using the principles discussed in this chapter. Evaluate the essay in your own terms, noting whether you like it or not.

   "I reject the use of the word 'sleaze,' and I don't think it fits any situation that we have here," President Reagan said at his news conference of April 4. As one of those who first advanced the term, I reject the rejection. Accordingly, there follows a brief foray into etymology.

   Sleazy, aka "sleezy," came into the language in the middle of the 17th century. The exact origin, the Oxford Dictionary says, is unknown. But there seems to be a clear association with cloth or thread of poor quality.

   The Unabridged Oxford Dictionary includes, under the date-line 1696, the following example: "It will not wear near so well by reason it is made of more sleazy thread than the former is." It also contains an entry, written in 1861, by Emerson: "You shall not conceal the sleazy, fraudulent, rotten hours you have slipped into the piece."

Thereafter, the term became a general synonym for inferior. Webster's Seventh New Collegiate Dictionary gives these definitions: "Carelessly made of inferior materials; shoddy," and "marked by cheapness of character or quality."

Partridge's Dictionary of slang offers as synonyms "slimy . . . greasy . . . garish . . . and disreputable." As an example it offers this sentence: "Half the wardroom was in some sleazy nightclub that was raided."

Note that sleaziness bears no necessary connection with criminality. The charges being made against the Reagan administration are not a matter of the old-fashioned corruption associated with the administrations of Warren Harding and U. S. Grant. Still less is it a question of the abuse of power. The tradition of being innocent until proved guilty, which President Reagan introduced as a standard in his news conference, does not come into play.

On the contrary, the emphasis is on reputation and seemliness, on high standards as distinct from low ones. The judgment that praised the Reagan administration at its inception for showing "a touch of class" is now up for review. What is essentially at issue, in other words, is what is done and what is not done. It is a matter of taste.

Examples clarify the distinction. Honoring Frank Sinatra at the White House, for instance, is certainly not criminal. The singer is not under indictment or anything of the kind. But he is well known for association with gangster elements. So holding him up for public admiration is the reverse of good taste: it is sleazy.

The Central Intelligence Agency performs sensitive missions relative to delicate questions of national security. The rules are largely unwritten, so there is a special premium on personal integrity, on austere renunciation of selfish interest.

Naming a director who buys and sells stock while in the post is surely not illegal. It is sleazy. Indeed, one of Bill Casey's colleagues once said, in defense of him, "He's not as sleazy as he seems."

Charles Wick, the Director of the United States Information Agency, regularly taped phone calls without telling his correspondents. That's not a crime. But it is not a highly respected practice either. It is, as Mr. Wick once acknowledged, sleazy. It does not become less so because Ronald Reagan gives his friend a clean bill of health.

The Deputy Secretary of Defense bears the chief responsibility for procurement involving billions of dollars. Paul Thayer, who held that post in the Reagan administration last year, now faces charges of insider trading. That is a crime of which he is innocent until proven guilty. But the indictment of Thayer sets forward highly detailed transactions for the benefit of cronies and girlfriends. That is sleazy.

Like the Wick case, moreover, the Thayer case puts into question a claim the President makes for himself. "I will be the first to remove anyone in the administration that does not have the highest integrity," Reagan said in his April 4 news conference. Thayer left office in January of this year. The papers reported in early October that he was under investigation. White House aides knew of his troubles before then. But Reagan apparently didn't.

Criminality and corruption, I repeat, are not at stake here. My impression is that the Reagan administration is not unusually bad on those counts. But bad taste does raise another issue. There is the President's claim that "I believe the halls of government are as sacred as our temples of worship."

That claim does not square with the record. Could it be that President Reagan is just an actor mouthing phrases to dupe the public? Elmer Gantry in the White House? Probably not. More likely is the proposition that he doesn't know the record, that he is an aging leader, out of touch with what is happening all around him. (© 1984, The Los Angeles Times Syndicate. Reprinted with permission.)

2. Look at the following words. In an in-class group exercise, define each term by differentiation, negation, example, and synonym. You might add etymology to the discussion if you have the information available to you. Each person in the group should take a turn at one technique. Upon completion of the exercise, discuss how each method for defining adds something to the meaning of the term.

football	euthanasia
soap opera	lasers
democracy	midterm exams

3. Present an 8–10 minute speech based upon definition. Your instructor will provide the necessary details.

References

1. R. Buckminster Fuller, quoted in Lewis Mumford, *The Pentagon of Power* (NY: Harcourt, Brace, Jovanovich, 1964), p. 56.

2. Edward P. J. Corbett, *Classical Rhetoric for the Modern Student* (NY: Oxford University Press, 1971), pp. 51–56.

3. C. K. Ogden and I. A. Richards, *The Meaning of Meaning* (NY: Harcourt, Brace, and World, 1923), Chaps. 1 and 2.

4. Frank D'Angelo, *A Conceptual Theory of Rhetoric* (Cambridge: Winthrop Publishers, 1975), p. 44.

5. Frederick Antczak, *Thought and Character: The Rhetoric of Democratic Education* (Ames, IA: Iowa State University Press, 1985), pp. 65, 78.

6. Chaim Perelman, *The New Rhetoric: A Treatise on Argumentation* (Notre Dame: University of Notre Dame Press, 1969), p. 210.

7. Joseph Kraft, "The Word 'Sleazy,' and Where It Fits," *The Providence Journal*, April 11, 1984, p. A-18.

8. Barbara Lawrence, "X Isn't a Dirty Word," *New York Times*, October 27, 1973, p. 29.

Speech Model:
Lisa Lepore, "Serendipity." Used by permission.

A View of the Definition Pattern: Sports

The definition pattern responds to the questions "What is it?" and "What does it mean?" Speakers use the definition pattern for a variety of purposes. A speech based on definition may appeal to the audience's curiosity such as when a term like "serendipity" is defined (see the model speech on page 350). Definition may also be used to persuade others to a point of view as in the case of the speech in exercise 1 (see pages 353-355). Finally, definition is often used to clarify a term that the speaker feels is being misused, a term like "euthanasia," or "moratorium," for instance.

When we define we look for the unique qualities of something as it is compared to all other things, and we use words to express those qualities. For example, in attempting to understand why so many people are drawn to sports, we may want to define the different meanings and purposes sports serve for different people.

When asked, "What do sports mean to you?" the variety of answers may include *skill development,* as in gymnastics (previous page) or ice skating; *thrill,* as in hang-gliding (above) or river rafting; *teamwork,* as in sailing (opposite, top) or soccer; or *competition,* as in bicycling (opposite, bottom) or boxing.

In fact, many people would use any combination of the above words to define one sport. But, as we can see, we need words to define and establish for ourselves and others. Through definition, then, we begin to examine and understand the many dimensions of one object or concept.

Chapter 14 - Classification

In 1940, a research group called Warner and Associates conducted an influential series of studies focusing on how Americans perceived themselves. The Warner group asked people in three communities, one in New England, one in the South, and one in the Midwest, to identify themselves according to one of the following social classes:

upper-upper class

lower-upper class

upper-middle class

lower-middle class

upper-lower class

lower-lower class

Each class was described for the respondents to give them criteria for identifying themselves. The lower-middle class, for example, was described this way:

> *The lower-middle class is composed of small business men, white collar workers, and a few skilled workers. Their small neat houses are on side streets. They are proper and conservative, careful with their money, concerned about respectability, and labeled as "good, common people."*[1]

The results of the Warner studies were controversial, as you might have suspected from the above description of just one class. But the results were also revealing. These studies demonstrated for the first time that Americans were able to identify themselves with a social class; in fact, the studies are said to be partly responsible for the emergence of class consciousness in the United States.

Furthermore, the Warner studies demonstrated that once one has identified with a class, the class itself begins to affect one's perceptions of others. For instance, the lower classes used money as the main criterion for class membership, the middle classes used money and morality, and the upper classes used life-style and ancestry. As soon as one classifies oneself, in other words, that very classification becomes an integral part of the way one sees everything else.

The Warner studies were the first to apply such familiar social-class labels as "middle class" to groups with discrete characteristics.

Many other studies followed. Most notably, a study conducted in 1945 by a social scientist, Richard Centers, inserted the term *working class* between *upper* and *middle*, giving people four classes with which to identify themselves. The term *working class* had such favorable connotations for post-World War II Americans that class identification surveys soon showed a significant shift away from self-identification as "middle class," which had been running about 80 to 90 percent in most surveys, into the "working class" group. One study, for instance, reported that 43 percent identified themselves as "middle class," while 51 percent identified with the "working class."[2]

These class-consciousness studies demonstrate a powerful motive in human behavior: the need to classify. Classification is a mental operation that adults perform on a regular basis. We observe classification all around us: politicians are classified as liberal, conservative, and moderate; music is classified as rock, funk, mellow, punk, and so on; movies are classified as "general audience," "parental guidance," "restricted," and "pornographic." Whenever we feel the need to take a diverse but related group of persons or things and organize them in some meaningful way, we turn to the classification pattern. Classifying enables us to answer the question "What are the common attributes of its members?"

The concept of classification is related to definition. In the definition pattern we determined the meaning of one thing by putting it into a class and then differentiating it from other members of that class. In classification, however, we engage in the actual development of those classes as well as the arrangement of a body of things (as opposed to one thing) into the classes we have established. To define, then, is to put a thing into a class, while classification involves dividing a body of things into categories.

The ability to classify is a sign of maturity in thinking, because when we classify we show our ability to distinguish among phenomena. Preschool children do not classify themselves very well within one social class, nor are they able to classify a group of objects, because they have not yet developed a set of categories into which things fit. Furthermore, young children do not yet have the ability to see likenesses and differences in things, so they cannot, on their own, devise sophisticated categories for classifying.

In a later stage of development the average child begins to classify objects according to such qualities as size, shape, and color. As we mature, we develop the capacity to classify in more and more sophisticated ways, often by mastering a scientific code or an abstract system such as the system of genus and species by which biologists classify living organisms. Classifying actually becomes a way of reasoning, of forming judgments and conclusions about things.

There are no universal categories for classifying. One culture might classify people by occupation, race, sex, and size; another may be concerned with marital status, economic class, and birth order. Each culture develops a classification system that makes sense for it based upon the culture's experience and its environment. Thus, while there are no universal classification systems, each culture does classify. Furthermore, one scholar, Michel Foucault, has noted that the classifications that exist within a given culture both reflect and direct its thinking.[3] The way we classify shapes the way we think about the world around us.

The Intention of Classification: Roles, Situations, and Purposes

Scientists often use classification as the organizing principle of their technical reports. Insurance agents classify people by age, driving record, and sex to determine insurance rates. Sociologists use classification to examine economic or political classes within a given society. Whenever a topic involves a large group of objects that share only a general set of characteristics, classification may be the most appropriate pattern.

Classification is often used as the analytical and organizational pattern in public speaking. In a recent speech delivered to the American Women in Radio and Television, psychologist Bonita Perry talked about the three "career traps" for women: "the perfectionism trap," "the burn-out blues," and "seduction by security."[4] By dividing her topic into these three categories, Perry was able to cover the multitude of problems women experience in the corporate world in an interesting and original manner; thus, her speech was both informative and entertaining.

In the speech-communication situation, classification is used when the speaker needs to organize the topic into classes or categories in order to talk about it. Recent speeches have discussed the following topics:

The four types of professors at the university

Categorizing the American holiday system

Fears we have known: phobias of every stripe

Collecting fans

Faces in the crowd at a rock concert

Use the classification pattern whenever your topic requires you to sort out or segregate a diverse body of persons, places, or objects that have some overall similarity but that are most easily understood when grouped into smaller units.

A classification speech can serve many purposes, but the most apparent is to introduce the audience to a new way to see a phenomenon. Awareness, then,is the most frequent goal of a classification speech. Classification is also used in humorous or entertaining speeches. The speech on fan collecting, which appears in this chapter, is a good example: it had the primary aim of informing the audience about the two types of fans, but was also quite entertaining as the speaker demonstrated the huge feather fans and the small hand fans that had funeral homes advertised on them.

Sometimes a clever or original classification system provides the audience with a new slant on an old topic. In a recent speech presented at a local Rotary Club luncheon, a successful professional football coach classified the various types of football fans around the country as "the animals," "the turncoats," "the sophisticates," and "the fanatics," building his commentary around the scheme he had invented. A classification speech can utilize an existing classification system or it can invent one—whichever facilitates analysis and organization of the topic.

Analyzing with the Classification Pattern

Once you have chosen to speak about a topic that lends itself to a classification pattern, go on to develop a critical-thinking statement that will serve as a guide throughout the composing process. In the following sample statement, note how the speaker carves out for herself the rhetorical situation in which she will be speaking:

I recently discovered that a friend of mine suffers from agoraphobia—she hates to come out of the house. I began to wonder about all the fears people have, and when I started to look into it, I discovered that there is an endless variety of fears or phobias. It seems to me that the audience would be surprised to find out how many known fears there are—I found some to be humorous and some to be serious, but I found that almost all of us have them, so the audience might learn something about themselves also. I plan to classify all the phobias into three categories: simple, social, and agoraphobias, and then to explain each category and give examples of each.

Once you have a clear plan in mind, you can begin to analyze and develop your topic. In order to conduct your analysis, you will need to be familiar with the rules for classification. Let's look carefully at five of these rules.

1. Begin with a body of unorganized material that you will organize for a specific purpose.

    As we have noted, many classification systems already exist, while others wait to be discovered. Whichever is the case for you, the material to be classified must have a common nature; that is, you would classify books within one system, but not books, restaurants, and blue jeans. Most importantly, know why you are doing the classification: What purpose do you have in mind for yourself and the audience? You need to know why your speech might be interesting, and how you can enhance that inherent interest with commentary of your own.

2. According to a determined plan, a plan based on your own reasoning or some logical set of categories that you know about, start to classify the material.

    You might begin by looking for physical distinctions such as size, shape, or color. Look at the people in a crowd and you will notice distinctions: some people are short, some tall; some of the people are black and some white; some people are male and some female. As you look closer, you will begin to see even finer distinctions among the people: some look hurried, some relaxed; some seem friendly, others standoffish. Each time you see physical distinctions you are on the verge of a category.

    You can go beyond physical distinctions such as size, shape, and color, into more abstract labels. If you want to talk about America's military buildup, you might classify weapons as offensive or defensive. If you are classifying television programs, you might use a familiar system such as sitcoms, mysteries, westerns, and talk shows; or, you might be creative and group the shows in another way, perhaps by the levels of violence or dullness. Let your thinking be guided by the qualities you observe in the events or the point that the events make. Any quality or any specific point may become the basis for a classification system. Once you have determined the distinctions you want to make, you are ready for rule 3.

3. Begin classifying by naming the categories.

If you wanted to examine religions, you might label your categories "Catholic," "Baptist," "Buddhist," "Islamic," and so on. Or, you might find the labels "evangelical," "mystical," "supernatural," and "metaphysical" to be more precise. If you were searching for a way to organize your books on your bookshelf, you might use an already-existing system such as fiction and nonfiction. You could further classify fiction as short stories, anthologies, plays, and novels. You must decide on the names or labels you will use to categorize your topic, adding color and originality whenever possible.

4. Be certain that your classes are discrete—that there is no excessive overlap, that each class has its distinctive qualities, and that the classes cover all possibilities.

Simple classification systems may not involve any overlap among the categories. If you were to categorize something like apples, you could use the terms *red, yellow,* and *green,* and account for all apples without overlap; that is, any apple you encountered would fit clearly into one category and one category only. The ideal situation, of course, is to develop categories that do not overlap.

But for complex topics, completely discrete categories are difficult to develop. You may have noticed, for example, that the classification of patterns used to label the various chapters in Part II of this text involves some admitted overlap. Overlap is sometimes unavoidable, since few things in the world exist in pure form. Some novels, such as *In Cold Blood,* are not clearly fictional or nonfictional; some weapons systems are not clearly offensive or defensive (the label usually depends on whether the weapons are ours or theirs). The speaker's task in coping with a complex system is to develop categories that are as discrete as the subject allows, while admitting and accounting for overlap in the speech itself.

Finally, the classification system should cover all possibilities. If you were classifying apples as red and green, you would soon find that not all the apples you encountered would fit into your system; you would need another category—yellow. Make certain that your system accounts for all possibilities.

5. There must be subclasses within each group.

You should obviously have at least two categories, each of which should have at least two members. In the speech on fans that appears at the end of the chapter, for example, the speaker noted that there were two basic classes of fans: the flag fan and the folding fan. The flag fan had a number of variations: large ceremonial fans and ostrich-feather fans no larger than a hand. Folding fans also came in varieties; Yale fans and lace, hand-painted, and wooden fans. Each fan fit into one of the two basic categories, but each added a new dimension to the class. Thus, the classification system worked.

Classifying your material according to the preceding rules will insure that your topic is both fully developed and instructive. In the following outline for the speech on phobias mentioned earlier, notice how the speaker indicated the classification system and then filled it in as the outline progressed:

I. Thesis: There are three major classes of phobias, each of which has interesting, sometimes surprising variations: simple phobias, social phobias, and agoraphobias.

II. Body
    A. A simple phobia is an isolated fear of a single object or situation.
        1. Animal phobias are the most common.
            a. Cynophobia: a fear of dogs
            b. Ophidiophobia: a fear of snakes
        2. Acrophobia is the second most common simple phobia: the fear of height.
        3. There are other simple phobias, some rather amusing.
            a. Ichnophobia: the fear of footprints
            b. Pogonophobia: the fear of beards
            c. Enterophobia: the fear of intestines
    B. A social phobia is any fear associated with being looked at.
        1. Fear of vomiting in public
        2. Fear of public speaking
        3. Fear of blushing
        4. Fear of being watched at work
    C. Agoraphobias, the final class, are clusters of complaints rather than just one.
        1. The fear of being in public
        2. Fear of open spaces

Once you have developed the basic classification scheme, start to fill in the commentary. Think of interesting definitions, observe unusual features that the audience might enjoy learning about, and search for stories and anecdotes that might add color to the speech. In general, the classification scheme is the outline of the speech; you need to fill in the details.

In the speech on phobias outlined earlier, the speaker added the following commentary as a preface to her lists of phobias:

> I want to distinguish between an anxiety and a fear. An anxiety is a response to a hidden and subjective danger, perhaps resulting from some repressed problem that developed early in the person's life. Fear is a reaction to an obvious and objective danger. Thus, a phobia usually contains both elements: anxiety about a situation that, when encountered in the real world, triggers a temporary surge of fear.

Details in a speech based on the classification pattern can be either objective, as in the example just shown, or subjective, as in the following anecdote from the speech on fan collecting:

> The Yale fan is a good example of a folding fan; this one is approximately sixty years old and was given to wives of alumni during reunion dinners. My grandmother attended the reunion in 1910, and this is the fan she was given. It may well be the only fan left from that occasion, and I treasure it.

Once you have developed the classification system by following the rules for classification discussed earlier, and have developed a critical-thinking statement and outlined the speech, all that remains is to develop an interesting introduction, a thesis statement, and a conclusion. Thus, the final structure of a classification speech looks like this:

Introduction: Gets audience attention for the topic.

Thesis: States the main point of the speech.

(Preview): Provides background, definitions, and so on, that the audience will need to follow the classification.

Body: Develops the classification system, using each group within the system as a main heading.
   A. Type 1

B. Type 2

C. Type 3 . . .

Conclusion: Reiterates main points and wraps up the discussion.

Language and the Classification Speech

A speech based on classification will use a characteristic vocabulary that may be new to many. Since one will encounter the terms used for classification during one's education and later in life, it is important to know and use them.

Classification is the term most commonly used to indicate an arrangement of material into groups or classes according to some system or principle.[5] Other terms are also used to indicate the act of classifying; some are synonymous with the term *classification*, while others have shadings of difference in meaning.

The term *genre*, pronounced "zhonru," is commonly used as a synonym for *classification*. A genre is a kind or type of something, and the term is usually reserved for discussions of kinds or types of literature or art. In literature, for instance, novels are often classified as "the Jewish novel," "the Southern novel," "the nonfiction novel," and so on. Once scholars have identified it as a distinct literary form, a type is awarded the status of a genre.

Another term commonly used with reference to classification is *taxonomy*. A taxonomy is a classification system, particularly one involving objects. The most familiar taxonomy is the system of genus and species that biologists use to classify animals and plants into groups based on common factors such as biochemistry, physical structure, and so on. In the social sciences, taxonomies are classes of phenomena such as communication anxieties, which are labeled, "shyness," "reticence," and "communication apprehension." Although the term *taxonomy* is somewhat synonymous with the term *classification*, use it to refer specifically to scientific or social-scientific classifications.

A less common term sometimes used interchangeably with *classification* is *nosology*. A nosology is a classification of diseases according to the symptoms exhibited by the person afflicted. One branch of medicine, in fact, is particularly concerned with the development of nosologies so that physicians can diagnose diseases more scientifically. Use the term *nosology* only in the context of medical classification.

In sum, the term *classification* refers to general classification schemes, while terms such as *genre*, *taxonomy*, and *nosology* are intended to refer to classification systems specific to certain fields of inquiry. It is important to know these distinctions so that you will use language more accurately in your speaking.

Summary

Classification is a fundamental pattern of thinking. Whenever we engage in sorting out a large body of related material into groups based upon common attributes we are classifying. The classification system a culture develops reflects the way that culture understands and organizes its objective world. It is important, therefore, to understand the concept of classification.

Classification is a commonly used pattern of communication, since many topics fall naturally into the classification pattern. Scientists, business persons, and teachers often find themselves discussing material according to a system of categories they have developed. When they do, the body of the speech will be structured according to the rules for classification.

The classification pattern can be defined as the act of segregating a diverse body of persons, places, or objects into classes according to some logical plan. Though a classification speech may fulfill a variety of purposes, it is usually devoted to helping the audience understand a diverse body of material in some systematic manner. Speeches based on the classification pattern range from serious discourse on scientific topics to lighthearted, humorous speeches on everyday phenomena classified with unusual, amusing terms.

Classifying must be done according to certain rules. Once the speaker has composed a clear critical-thinking statement, the analysis should proceed according to established procedures. In this chapter we discussed five rules for classifying: (1) the speaker must begin with a common body of material; (2) the classification scheme must have a reasonable basis; (3) the categories must be labeled; (4) the categories must be discrete; and (5) each group must contain subclasses.

When organizing the body of a speech according to the classification pattern, use each class as a main heading and discuss individual members of each class as subheadings. Develop the basic outline of main classes and subclasses with supporting material. Then complete the speech by composing an introduction, thesis, preview (if necessary), and a conclusion.

A classification speech is an experience in critical thinking. Since we must all know how to classify, and since we must come to understand the taxonomies that order our society, a classification speech is both revealing and instructive. If you experience a new awareness of the way categories have developed around you, the classification exercise has served a purpose.

Collecting Fans: A Beautiful Hobby

This model speech based on the classification pattern took as its topic one of the student's hobbies, collecting fans (her other hobby was gravestone rubbing). She had a large fan collection and wanted to talk to the class about it, so the assignment to present a speech based on classification presented the appropriate outlet for her. The speech was approximately twelve minutes long and included a number of visual aids. The speech was both enjoyable and instructive.

Topic: Collecting Fans: A Beautiful Hobby

Critical-Thinking Statement: I have been collecting fans for a long time. I find them fascinating not only for their designs and intricate artwork, but also for the memories they provoke of other times and places. I rarely get the opportunity to share my collection with others, so this is a perfect chance. I hope the speech will be informative as well as enjoyable.

   I. Introduction: The age of air conditioning compared to the age of fans

  II. Thesis statement: I thought it would be interesting to tell you about the two types of fans and show you some of the many varieties of these two types that have come from fan designers across the ages.

 III. Preview
     A. A definition of a fan
     B. A short history of fans
     C. How fans are constructed

 IV. Body
     A. The first type of fan is the flag or African fan.
        1. It was used for ceremonial and practical reasons since the time of the Egyptians.
        2. The first example is an Ethiopian fan woven from grasses.
        3. Other examples include fans made from ostrich feathers or papyrus used by the Egyptian and Minoan cultures (show and demonstrate).

B. The second type of fan is the folding or Yale fan.
1. The folding fan was invented by the Chinese, and today is also known as the accordion pleat fan.
2. The folding fan has six special components (show and demonstrate six parts).
3. The Yale fan is a good example of a folding fan.
4. Another variation is this lace and painted wood fan from the reign of French king Louis XIII.

V. Conclusion: How fans have been used throughout the ages. A word about fan collecting

The age of air conditioning has all but ended one of the most common human activities, an activity especially noticeable in the summertime. I am referring to waving a fan. But even more than the demise of fan waving, our age has all but brought to a close an art form, the art of designing fans.

Introduction: Speaker gains attention by comparing today to the age of fans.

My hobby is collecting fans. I have about fifty of them, many of which I have brought with me this evening. I thought it would be interesting to tell you about the two types of fans and show you some of the many varieties of these two types that have come from fan designers across the ages.

Thesis statement: Speaker states purpose of speech and indicates the pattern that will be used.

First, a definition. A fan is a folding device of paper, cloth, wood, or plastic, which, when opened, has the shape of a half sector of a circle and is used to set up a current of air for ventilating.

Preview: Speaker provides a definition of fans, a short background on the manufacture of fans, and a word about the material used in fans.

Fans have been manufactured for centuries; they are as old as civilization itself. The manufacture of fans is called "mounting," since the cloth or paper is mounted onto struts. Fan mounters would paint or sometimes print the fan leaf or skin with an etched plate of block print, then finish with freehand landscapes or other details. Foreground details were often omitted in favor of loose washes or nothing at all, in order to leave a margin which could be trimmed before the skin was put on the struts.

The struts were made of all kinds of material: ivory, tortoise shells, wood, bone, silver, and even cloth-covered metal. Metal fans were used in the Victorian era and were known as "Defenseless Maiden" fans, since they could be shut off—snapped shut—quickly to beat off the advances of an over-sexed suitor.

Transition: Speaker makes a transition from the preview to the body by indicating the two types of fans she will speak about.

Regardless of their appearance or their origin, all fans can be classified into two types: the flag or African fan, and the folding or Yale fan.

The flag or African fan is the first type. It is used for ceremonial and practical reasons, and has been around since the time of the Egyptians. Flag fans are the first in recorded history, and are also called palm fans because they are shaped like the palm of a hand.

The first fan of the flag-fan variety that I want to show you is this fan from Ethiopia. As you can see, it is made of handwoven grasses. The Egyptian and Minoan cultures used fans of this type, often manufacturing them out of feathers such as ostrich feathers or papyrus.

There are many other varieties of the flag fan, and I want to show you some of them. Here is a fan with a leaf for a skin, and here is one that uses a cloth skin. Here also are some fans with various types of struts.

The second type of fan is the folding or Yale fan. The Chinese are credited with the invention of this type of fan, which is also known as the accordion or pleat fan. The folding fan is distinguished by six special components, but most of all by the fact that it can be closed by snapping it shut. The six parts of the folding fan are the skin or leaf, the struts that allow the fan to be snapped shut, the main or "lady-face" strut, the breast knot, the washer-rivet component, and the wristlet or, in some cases, the waistlet.

The Yale fan I have here is a good example of the folding fan; this one is approximately sixty years old and was given to wives of alumni during reunion dinners at Yale University. My grandmother attended that reunion and this is the fan she was given. It may well be the only one left from that occasion.

The folding fan first came into vogue in the West during the reign of the French king Louis XIII (1610–1643). This lace and painted wood fan is typical of fans from that period. The fan was French in spirit, so much so that in the seventeenth century in Paris there were five hundred fanmakers or mounters.

In the Victorian and Edwardian periods, fans were a part of every woman's wardrobe. The language of the fan and fan management were arts taught to every young woman as part of her training in etiquette. There were fans for every occasion, such as this mourning fan, a Yale type, which was used with the black side facing out during the customary twelve- to eight-month period of mourning, and then it could be flipped to the other side.

CHAPTER 14

Fans were important as practical items also. Women, who were often corseted in extremely tight clothing, needed a fan to get fresh air. This Indian sandalwood fan, a flag-type fan, is about 125 years old and was brought from the Indian colony for ladies to moisten and then waft in to get the benefit of the sandalwood fragrance. Notice the intricate carving on this fan.

While fans went out of popular fashion as the twentieth century approached and progressed, their practicality never lessened, as advertisers began to print up their slogans on the backs of mass-produced flag or folding fans. People today still use advertising fans in churches and at carnivals, especially in hot weather.

Conclusion: The speaker sums up the discussion of fans by relating them to our times. She also tells the audience how they might get involved in such a hobby.

Fan collecting can be fun and inexpensive. With a little research and reading, and with an eye for color, shape, and beauty, and not just for the antiquity of the fan, you can have a collection like mine in a matter of two or three years.

Exercises

1. We have seen a proliferation of cola soft drinks recently, and passing through the cola section of a supermarket can be a confusing experience. How would you classify the various colas you encounter in a large supermarket? What are the bases for your classification scheme? Compare your classification with the systems developed by others in the class. Discuss the various criteria that led to the different taxonomies developed. Can you think of any bases not covered by the cola companies to meet the demands of consumers?

2. Classify the items in the following list according to the rules for classification presented in this chapter. When you have done so, answer the following questions:

movies	bad habits
taboo speech	children
junk food	leisure time activities

   a. What is the purpose of your classification system? What practical value does it serve for you or others who might have to deal with this item?

b. Is there any overlap in your system? If so, how can you justify it?

c. Which rule for classification was the most difficult for you to apply?

d. If you used existing terms for your classification system, can you think of other original and creative terms that might account for the items classified?

3. Present a speech based on the classification pattern. Your instructor will provide the details for the assignment.

References

1. Leonard Broom and Philip Selznick, *Sociology*, 3d ed. (NY: Harper and Row, 1963), p. 190.

2. Broom and Selznick, p. 194.

3. Carol Snyder, "Analyzing Classifications: Foucault for Advanced Writers," *College Composition and Communication* 35 (1984), pp. 209–216.

4. Bonita L. Perry, "The Three Career Traps for Women," *Vital Speeches*, November 15, 1981, p. 76.

5. All definitions taken from *Webster's New World Dictionary*, second college edition.

Speech Model:
Jody Finley, "Fan Collecting." Used by permission.

A View of the Classification Pattern: Jobs and Workers

Classification is a mental operation that we perform on a regular basis. When we attempt to understand various ideas, things, or people, we oftentimes try to find commonalities among them and group them together. In a sense, classification allows us to put something in its "place" so we can study and understand it.

For many years—and even today—we have classified jobs and occupations in terms of what we perceive as people's *roles:* men's work and women's work. We might tend to classify workers and their jobs according to *types* of work: skilled or unskilled, white collar or blue collar. Or we might try to understand jobs by classifying the kinds of *results* or output they produce: technical support, service, or manufactured goods. And sometimes we classify according to *skills:* physical, analytical, or technical. Not surprisingly, while all these classifications can help us examine the vast world of work, they also can reinforce stereotypes.

How would you classify the jobs and workers shown here? How might you use the classification pattern to structure a speech about jobs without falling back on stereotyped classifications? How could you use classification to examine one particular job?

INDEX

Emotion, displaying, 205
Encyclopedia of Associations, 92
Epideictic speeches, 65
Ethics of public speaking, 19–22
Etymology, 344–345
Examples
  definition by, 346
  hypothetical, 83–84
  illustration, 82–83
  of specific instances, 81–82
  of specific speeches
    See Model speeches
  use of women and men in, 187
Exhibits, 159–160
Experiences
  exploring, 46–48, 71
  recording, 50–53, 71
Expert opinion, 80–81
Experts, campus or local, 93–94
Expressions, colloquial, 185–186

Facial expression, 210
Facts, 84–86
Failure of speech, 107
Farb, Peter, 193
Feedback, 10
Filler speech, 206–207
Final format
  description of, 141–156, 168
  manuscript form, 141–147
  sentence-outline form, 153–156
  word-outline form, 147–153
Fluency, 213
Forensic speeches, 65
Form, 112
Freedom of speech, 26, 42
Fuller, R. Buckminster, 340

Gestures, 142, 204, 209
Gettysburg Address, 106–107
Glucksberg, Sam, 61
Goals, for composing speech, 107–108, 134
Good will, 62
Goss Model of Listening, 28
Government
  See United States government
Grammar, oral
  common errors, 207–208

correct, 207
Graphs, 157–158, 159, 160
Groups, as information sources, 92

Halberstam, David, 140
Handouts, 161
Hayakawa, S. I., 176
"He," generic, 186–187
Hearing, vs. listening, 27
Humor, in introduction, 126–127
Hypothetical comparisons, 87
Hypothetical examples, 83–84

Ideas
  exploring, 46–47, 48–50
  key, summarizing in conclusion, 131–132
  in main points of outline, 115–116
  recording, 50–53
Illustration, 82–83
Inaccuracy
  from loaded words, 182–183
  from using words incorrectly, 181–182
  See also Accuracy
Indexes, for magazines and periodicals, 97–99
Information, seeking through questions, 38
Information sources
  credibility, 293–294
    checking, 288
    for factual support of speech, 84–85
  governmental, 90–92, 99–100
  groups and organizations, 92–93
Interpreting, 30
Interruption of speech, 41
Interviews, conducting, 94
Introduction
  examples, 142
    from cause-effect speeches, 295, 296, 299, 300
    from classification speech, 372, 373
    from definition speech, 351
    from narrative, 249
    from narrative speech, 246
    from problem analysis speech, 329, 330
    from process speeches, 269, 272
  gaining attention in, 125–126
  humorous, 126–127
  purpose of, 135
  with questions, 128
  with references to the occasion, 128–129

Photo Credits

W9-ANG-264

Oracle® SQL™

INTERACTIVE WORKBOOK

Second Edition

D1

ISBN 0-13-100277-5

9 790131 002776

93999

THE PRENTICE HALL PTR ORACLE SERIES
The Independent Voice on Oracle

Oracle
SQL

INTERACTIVE WORKBOOK

Second Edition

ALICE RISCHERT

PRENTICE
HALL
PTR

PRENTICE HALL
Professional Technical Reference
Upper Saddle River, New Jersey 07458
www.phptr.com

Library of Congress Cataloging-in-Publication Data

A CIP record for this book can be obtained from the Library of Congress.

Editorial/production supervision: Jessica Balch (Pine Tree Composition, Inc.)
Cover design director: Jerry Votta
Cover design: Nina Scuderi
Art director: Gail Cocker-Bogusz
Interior design: Meg Van Arsdale
Manufacturing manager: Alexis Heydt-Long
Publisher: Jeffery Pepper
Marketing manager: Kate Hargett
Editorial assistant: Linda Ramagnano
Full-service production coordinator: Anne R. Garcia

 © 2003 Pearson Education, Inc.
Publishing as Prentice Hall Professional Technical Reference
Upper Saddle River, NJ 07458

Prentice Hall books are widely used by corporations and government agencies
for training, marketing, and resale.

For information regarding corporate and government bulk discounts, please contact:
Corporate and Government Sales (800)382-3419 or corpsales@pearsontechgroup.com

Other company and product names mentioned herein are the trademarks
or registered trademarks of their respective owners.

Printed in the United States of America
10 9 8 7 6 5 4 3

ISBN 0-13-100277-5

Pearson Education Ltd., *London*
Pearson Education Australia Pty, Limited, *Sydney*
Pearson Education Singapore, Pte. Ltd.
Pearson Education North Asia Ltd., *Hong Kong*
Pearson Education Canada, Ltd., *Toronto*
Pearson Educación de Mexico, S.A. de C.V.
Pearson Education—Japan, *Tokyo*
Pearson Education Malaysia, Pte. Ltd.

To my daughter, Kirsten, and my parents, Albert and Hilde

About Prentice Hall Professional Technical Reference

With origins reaching back to the industry's first computer science publishing program in the 1960s, Prentice Hall Professional Technical Reference (PH PTR) has developed into the leading provider of technical books in the world today. Formally launched as its own imprint in 1986, our editors now publish over 200 books annually, authored by leaders in the fields of computing, engineering, and business.

Our roots are firmly planted in the soil that gave rise to the technological revolution. Our bookshelf contains many of the industry's computing and engineering classics: Kernighan and Ritchie's *C Programming Language*, Nemeth's *UNIX System Administration Handbook*, Horstmann's *Core Java*, and Johnson's *High-Speed Digital Design*.

PH PTR acknowledges its auspicious beginnings while it looks to the future for inspiration. We continue to evolve and break new ground in publishing by providing today's professionals with tomorrow's solutions.

PRENTICE
HALL
PTR

CONTENTS

FOREWORD

THE ANCIENT PROBLEM

The year was AD 1680; the place was the Levant—a region on the eastern shores of the Mediterranean. The political climate was stable enough to allow peaceful trade among nations and the seaports were bustling with merchants who were making profits by expanding their markets outside of their country of origin. They met many challenges in the travel itself, as well as in adapting to other cultures and customs. A major obstacle was communication. How can you sell something if you cannot extol its virtues to your potential customer? Sign language and written symbols can be quite effective, but are not nearly as personal and understandable as the spoken word. The problem with spoken language in a situation like this is that there are many languages to master. As a seller of goods, your best chance for top sales is to target people whose language you know.

THE ANCIENT SOLUTION

The solution that emerged from this problem in the classical world was one that has been used by people of many lands throughout history: use a common language when gathered in a multicultural environment. In the Levant, the language that developed was a combination of Italian, Spanish, French, Greek, Arabic, and Turkish. This language, called *lingua franca*, became a standard in many ports as merchants used it to successfully communicate with their customers and fellow traders. Those who learned and mastered this language became the most effective and successful business people.

THE MODERN-DAY PROBLEM

In today's information technology (IT) industry, we face a similar situation. Companies are solving their data management requirements using relational and object-relational databases. Businesses have found these databases to offer the best features and most robust environments. The challenges that companies are facing when using databases are mainly in creating flexible and efficient human interfaces. Customized application development takes much in the way of effort and resources if it is to properly address the requirements of the business.

IT professionals who are tasked with creating modern database systems must rely on their training and expertise, both in designing the proper database storage objects and in programming the most efficient application programs. In the recent past, developers of relational and object-relational systems have used procedural programming languages such as COBOL, Fortran, and C to create application programs to access the data. Regardless of the procedural language used, there is an additional language embedded in these procedural programs. This language offers a standard way to define and manipulate the data structures in a relational or object-relational database. It is the lingua franca of database technology— Structured Query Language (SQL). Using SQL, all database developers can create commonly recognized programs for their applications. A standard language means that the written code is understood easily and can be supported fully and enhanced quickly. This is the promise of SQL, and this promise has been fulfilled successfully for decades in countless relational database application programs.

Therefore, the problem today is not the lack of a common language, as was the case in ancient times before lingua franca. The problem today is in the assimilation and proper use of the language. As the computer industry continues its logarithmic growth, the number of application developers increases similarly. Each new developer who comes into contact with a relational database must be trained in the lingua franca used to access it. In the recent past, with a smaller number of new developers, this was a manageable feat. When a new developer was in training, she or he would learn both a procedural programming language and the database language embedded in it—SQL.

Today, the trend is toward object orientation. Object-oriented analysis, design, and programming have come of age and, according to popular opinion, now make up the best way to create computer systems. This means that C++ and Java, which are object-oriented languages, are replacing the traditional procedural languages as the choice for building new systems. This is merely a shift in the main programming language that the developer uses to interface with the user. The core database language, SQL, is still required and of key importance.

However, something has gotten lost in this paradigm shift to object orientation. That something is a solid background in SQL. This problem persists for many reasons. Unfortunately, IT management professionals everywhere are employing Java programmers who do not have a solid grasp of the SQL language. This arrangement works up to a point, but there is, eventually, a collision with a brick wall. In many situations, this consultant has had to break into the SQL code used in a Java program only to find inefficient or incorrect use of the SQL language. Misunderstanding or misuse of the SQL language can have adverse effects on the program's efficiency and, without proper testing, can adversely affect production data systems, many of which are critical to the functioning of the business.

THE MODERN-DAY SOLUTION

The solution to the problem of misunderstanding the lingua franca of databases is simple—an increased focus on learning the foundations and abilities of SQL and the correct methods for coding SQL programs. Time and money spent in training on the basics of SQL are time and money well spent. There are many ways to learn a subject like SQL. In this writer's experience of over 18 years as a trainer in the IT and other industries, the best learning experience comes from a multifaceted approach. Human beings learn in different ways, and using different approaches to present the same subject ensures that the subject will be mastered. In addition, the repetition of concepts and material in different formats ensures a thorough understanding of the subject. Repetition and variety are proven learning techniques.

What Ms. Rischert has accomplished in this book is the epitome of the solution for the correct understanding of SQL. This book will be useful for seasoned IT professionals who need a refresher on the concepts and thought processes of using SQL, as well as for those who are new to the subject and want to learn it in the right way.

The multifaceted approach that the author uses allows the student of the subject to totally master the basics as well as the best ways to use the language. All core SQL subjects are treated with this approach, which includes a brief description of the concept followed by simple and easy-to-grasp examples. Examples make the concepts real and allow the reader to quickly master the subject.

The very best way to learn the concepts of any new technology is to be tasked with an application development project that uses that technology. However, a project in the real-world workplace is not the right place to learn—the stakes are too high and the pressure too great. This book gives you a taste of real-world application development needs and processes by assigning a series of labs in each chapter to apply the knowledge gained by the conceptual discussion and examples. The book then provides the solutions to these problems so that you can check your work. Proper use of these sections will lead you to a solid mastery of the language and give you the ability to use this lingua franca successfully to solve real-world business data problems. This type of mastery will serve you well in whatever type of database programming environment you find yourself.

Peter Koletzke
Quovera
Redwood Shores, CA
November 2002

ACKNOWLEDGMENTS

The work involved in writing a book is tremendous and anyone who has ever done this can attest to it. I am fortunate to acknowledge a number of people who contributed along the way in various ways by offering suggestions, corrections, guidance, ideas, comments, and advice.

In particular, I would like to thank Dan Diaz, Bernard Dadario, Gordon Green, Richard Kamm, and Tom Phipps for spending countless hours reviewing the material and putting it through the wringer. Many of their pointed comments and observations helped shape the book. Gnana Supramaniam probably read more chapters than anyone else, and his excellent comments made a significant impact on the overall quality of the book. Mitch Murov and Susan Hesse provided valuable feedback and comments from the student community and offered their perspective as SQL instructors. Thanks also to the students who test-drove the material. A number of readers of the first edition pointed out typos and suggested additional topics now covered in the new edition; all their ideas and perspectives were truly useful.

Ben Rosenzweig spearheaded the effort for the second edition of the Oracle Interactive Workbook series. His diligence and persistence helped tremendously in the coordination of the Prentice Hall template for writing the manuscript and pointing out some of the new Oracle 9*i* material to cover in the book. Thank you also to Victoria Jones at Prentice Hall for giving me the opportunity to make a great book even better. Jeffrey Pepper picked up where Victoria left off and guided this project to its end in spite of numerous obstacles. Anne Garcia at Prentice Hall and Jessica Balch at Pine Tree Composition saw to it that the book made it to the printer on time and in the quality you see in front of you.

This second edition was supposed to be "just an update," but it turned out to be a substantial rework of many topics and now includes hundreds of pages of additional material. Alex Morrison, my coauthor of the previous edition, knew how much work was involved and did not sign on. Some parts of her wonderful material have remained intact and unaffected by the version change. I would like to thank her for lending a sympathetic ear to the many topics covered on the e-mails trails coordinating this effort.

Thanks to the faculty and staff of Columbia University who are some of the most hard-working and knowledgeable individuals, in particular Dr. Art Langer and

xviii

Dennis Green. Mohammed Islam and Matthew Kirkpatrick kept the Oracle servers running smoothly and handled many technical details.

Thank you to Lonnie Blackwood at XWare for keeping my schedule light during the book-writing process and for understanding the many demands that were placed on me during this time. Thanks to my colleauges at XWare and friends at WMG who unwittingly provided some of the material. Their questions, problems, and challenges provided the framework for some of the book.

I want to thank Douglas Scherer not only initiating this book project but also for his support, friendship, and insights throughout. Peter Koletzke wrote the foreword to this edition and he has been a wonderful friend and supporter for so many years. While I was writing this book, Peter completed his new edition of the JDeveloper book and his enthusiasm and encouragements helped me see the light at the end of the tunnel.

Daniel Liao helped create some of the wonderful graphic illustrations for the book and was able to make sense out of my hand-drawn sketches. Thanks also to Embarcadero Software for providing a copy of ER/Studio to help with drawing some of the diagrams.

Espie Lising, Trisha Choi, Balo Garcia, Dr. Raymond Garcia, Marisue Rodriguez, and their families have given me invaluable support and inspiration over the last few years. My parents, sisters Irene and Christa, and my brother Guenter deserve a great deal of thanks for all their tremendous support, advice, and encouragement. Finally, I owe most of my thanks to my daughter, Kirsten, for her understanding, patience, and love. I feel very fortunate to have such a wonderful daughter.

Alice Rischert

ABOUT THE AUTHOR

Alice Rischert is the chair of Columbia University's Database Application Development and Design track in the Computer Technology and Application program, where she also teaches classes in Oracle SQL, PL/SQL, and database design. Ms. Rischert's wide-ranging technology experience encompasses systems integration, database architecture, and project management for a number of companies in the United States, Europe, and Asia. Ms. Rischert has worked with Oracle since Version 5, and she has presented on SQL and PL/SQL topics at Oracle conferences.

INTRODUCTION

The SQL language is the de facto standard language for relational databases, and Oracle's database server is the leading relational database on the market today. The *Oracle SQL Interactive Workbook, second edition,* presents an introduction to the Oracle SQL language in a unique and highly effective format. Rather than being a reference book, it guides you through the basic skills until you reach a mastery of the language. The book challenges you to work through hands-on guided tasks rather than read through descriptions. You will be able to retain the material more easily and the additional example questions reinforce and further enhance the learning experience.

WHO THIS BOOK IS FOR

This book is intended for anyone requiring a background in Oracle's implementation of the SQL language. In particular, application developers, system designers, and database administrators will find many practical and representative real-world examples. Students new to Oracle will gain the necessary experience and confidence to apply their knowledge in solving typical problems they face in the work situation. Individuals already familiar with Oracle SQL but wishing a firmer foundation or those interested in the new Oracle 9i features will discover many of the useful tips, tricks, and information.

The initial audience for the book was the students of the Oracle SQL class at Columbia University's Computer Technology and Applications program. The student body has a wide-ranging level of technology experience. Their questions, learning approaches, and feedback provided the framework for this book. Many students cited the hands-on exercises as critical to their understanding of database technology and the SQL language and continuously asked for more examples and additional challenging topics. This book shares much of the material presented in the classroom and looks at the various angles of many solutions to a particular issue.

WHAT MAKES THIS BOOK DIFFERENT

Unlike other SQL books, this book discusses Oracle's specific implementation of the language. Learning the language alone is not enough. The book also teaches you how to adopt good habits and educates you about many Oracle-specific technology features that are essential to successful systems development.

The book's exercises build knowledge step-by-step by introducing you to relational database concepts, the SQL*Plus environment, and the SQL language. Learning involves not just reading about a subject, but also doing it. The book's focus is to give the reader examples of how the SQL language is commonly used, with many exercises supporting the learning experience.

Unlike other SQL books, this book is *not* a reference book. The best way to learn the SQL language is to perform the exercises and compare your answers with the sample answers and accompanying explanations. After you have completed the exercises, the companion Web site contains additional questions to test your understanding. It also lists the solutions to the Test Your Thinking exercises at the end of each chapter. You can access the companion Web site at www.phptr.com/rischert.

This book does not cover the entire Oracle SQL syntax, but emphasizes the essentials of the most-frequently used features with many examples to reinforce the learning. We hope that you will enjoy this learning experience and come away with the knowledge you hoped to gain.

How This Book Is Organized

Each chapter of the book is divided into labs covering a particular topic. The objective of each lab is defined at its beginning, with brief examples that introduce the reader to the covered concepts.

Following the lab's introductory examples are exercises that are the heart of the lab which reinforce and expand the reader's knowledge of the subject. Each exercise consists of a series of steps to follow to perform specific tasks, or particular questions that are designed to help you discover the important aspects of the SQL language. The answers to these questions are given at the end of the exercises, along with more in-depth discussion of the concepts explored.

After you perform the exercises and compare the answers with the sample queries, answers, and explanations, the lab ends with multiple-choice Self-Review Questions. These are meant to test that you have understood the material covered in the lab. The answers to these questions appear in Appendix A. There are additional Self-Review questions at this book's companion Web site.

At the end of each chapter, the Test Your Thinking section reinforces the topics learned in labs, and solidifies your skills. The answers to these questions are found on the companion Web site for this book.

LAYOUT OF A CHAPTER

Chapter
     Lab
          Exercises
          Exercise Answers (with detailed discussion)
          Self-Review Questions
     Lab ...
     Test Your Thinking Questions

The chapters should be completed in sequence because concepts covered in earlier chapters are required for the completion of exercises in later chapters.

ABOUT THE COMPANION WEB SITE

The companion Web site is located at http://www.phptr.com/rischert. Here you will find three very important things:

1. Installation files you need before you begin reading the workbook.
2. Answers to the Test Your Thinking questions.
3. Additional Self-Review questions.

INSTALLATION FILES

All of the exercises and questions are based on a sample schema called STUDENT. The required files to install this STUDENT schema and the installation instructions can be downloaded from the Web site.

TEST YOUR THINKING

The answers to the Test Your Thinking sections are also found at the Web site.

ADDITIONAL SELF-REVIEW QUESTIONS

The Web site will have many other features, such as additional Self-Review questions, a message board, and periodically updated information about the book.

 Visit the companion Web site and download the required files before starting the labs and exercises.

WHAT YOU WILL NEED

To complete the exercises you need the following:

> The Oracle® database software
> Oracle's SQL*Plus software or a Web browser
> Access to the Internet

ORACLE 9*i*

Oracle 9*i* is Oracle's relational database software and its flagship product. You can use either the Personal Edition or Enterprise Edition. The Enterprise editions of Oracle 9.01 and 9.2 were used to create the exercises for this book, but subsequent versions should be compatible. If you have a previous version of the Oracle database you will be able to complete a large majority of the exercises, however some syntax options and features are only available in Oracle 9*i*.

ORACLE SQL*PLUS SOFTWARE OR WEB BROWSER

You can perform all the exercises in this book with Oracle's SQL*Plus software. Oracle introduced *i*SQL*Plus with Oracle version 8.1.7. This browser-based version does not require the installation of the Oracle SQL*Plus software on your individual machine. Only a browser is necessary and access to an HTTP *i*SQL*Plus server. The *i*SQL*Plus version simplifies the editing and offers a superior display of the result. However, *i*SQL*Plus does not allow certain functionality and this is pointed out where applicable. For a list of unsupported commands refer to Appendix C, "SQL*Plus Command Reference." Instead of SQL*Plus you can also use alternate SQL execution environments and a list is available in Appendix H, "Resources."

ACCESS TO THE INTERNET

You will need access to the Internet so that you can access the companion Web site: http://www.phptr.com/rischert. Here you will find files that are necessary to install the sample STUDENT schema.

ABOUT THE STUDENT SCHEMA

Throughout this workbook, you access data from a sample schema called STUDENT, which contains information about a computer education program. The schema was designed to record data about instructors, courses, students, and their respective enrollments and grades.

After you download the installation files to create the schema within your Oracle database, you will be able to follow the exercises in the workbook. In Chapter 1, "SQL and Data," you are introduced to the relational concepts necessary to read the schema diagram. Appendix D, "Student Database Schema," shows you a graphical representation of the schema and Appendix E, "Table and Column Descriptions" lists descriptive information about each table and column.

Conventions Used in This Book

There are several conventions used in this book to make your learning experience easier. These are explained here.

This icon denotes advice and useful information about a particular topic or concept from the author to you, the reader.

This icon flags tips that are especially helpful tricks that will save you time or trouble, for instance, a shortcut for performing a particular task or a method that the author has found useful.

Computers are delicate creatures and can be easily damaged. Likewise, they can be dangerous to work on if you're not careful. This icon flags information and precautions that not only save you headaches in the long run, but may even save you or your computer from harm.

Passages referring to the book's companion Web site are flagged with this icon. The companion Web site is located at http://www.phptr.com/ rischert.

Errata

I have made every effort to make sure there are no errors in the text and code. However, to err is human. As part of the companion Web site, you will find corrections as they're spotted. If you find an error that has not been reported, please let me know by contacting me at ar280@yahoo.com.

CHAPTER 1

SQL AND DATA

<table>
<tr><td colspan="2" align="center">CHAPTER OBJECTIVES</td></tr>
<tr><td colspan="2">In this chapter, you will learn about:</td></tr>
<tr><td>✔ Data, Databases, and the Definition of SQL</td><td align="right">Page 3</td></tr>
<tr><td>✔ Table Relationships</td><td align="right">Page 15</td></tr>
<tr><td>✔ The STUDENT Schema Diagram</td><td align="right">Page 37</td></tr>
</table>

W hat is SQL? SQL (pronounced *sequel*) is an acronym for *Structured Query Language,* a standardized language used to access and manipulate data. The history of SQL corresponds closely with the development of relational databases concepts published in a paper by Dr. E. F. Codd at IBM in 1970. He applied mathematical concepts to the specification of a method for data storage and access; this specification, which became the basis for relational databases, was intended to overcome the physical dependencies of the then-available database systems. The SQL language (originally called "System R" in the prototype and later called "SEQUEL") was developed by the IBM Research Laboratory as a standard language to use with relational databases. In 1979 Oracle, then called Relational Software, Inc., introduced the first commercially available implementation of a relational database incorporating the SQL language. The SQL language evolved with many additional syntax expansions incorporated into the American National Standards Institute (ANSI) SQL standards developed since. Individual database vendors continuously added extensions to the language, which eventually found their way into the latest ANSI standards used by relational databases today. Large-scale commercial implementations of relational database applications started to appear in the mid to late 1980s as early implementations were hampered by poor performance. Since then, relational databases and the SQL language have continuously evolved and improved.

Before you begin to use SQL, however, you must know about data, databases, and relational databases. What is a database? A *database* is an organized collection of data. A *database management system* (DBMS) is software that allows the creation, retrieval, and manipulation of data. You use such systems to maintain patient data in a hospital, bank accounts in a bank, or inventory in a warehouse. A *relational database management system* (RDBMS) provides this functionality within the context of the relational database theory and the rules defined for relational databases by Codd. These rules, called "Codd's Twelve Rules," later expanded to include additional rules, describe goals for database management systems to cope with ever-challenging and demanding database requirements. Compliance with Codd's Rules has been a major challenge for database vendors and early versions of relational databases and many desktop databases complied with only a handful of the rules.

Today, SQL is accepted as the universal standard database access language. Databases using the SQL language are entrusted with managing critical information affecting many aspects of our daily lives. Most applications developed today use a relational database and Oracle continues to be one of the largest and most popular database vendors. Although relational databases and the SQL language are already over 30 years old, there seems to be no slowing down of the popularity of the language. Learning SQL is probably one of the best long-term investments you can make for a number of reasons:

- SQL is used by most commercial database applications.
- Although the language has evolved over the years with a large array of syntax enhancements and additions, most of the basic functionality has remained essentially unchanged.
- SQL knowledge will continue to be a fundamental skill as there is currently no mature and viable alternative language that accomplishes the same functionality.
- Learning Oracle's specific SQL implementation provides you with great insight into the feature-rich functionality of one of the largest and most successful database vendors.

Understanding relational database concepts provides you with the foundation for understanding the SQL language. Those unfamiliar with relational concepts or interested in a refresher will receive an overview of basic relational theories in the next two labs. If you are already familiar with relational theory, you can skip the first two labs and jump directly to Lab 1.3, "The STUDENT Schema Diagram." The STUDENT database manages student enrollment data at a fictional university. Lab 1.3 teaches you about the organization and relationships of the STUDENT database, which is used throughout the exercises in this book.

L A B   1 . 1

DATA, DATABASES, AND THE DEFINITION OF SQL

LAB OBJECTIVES

After this lab, you will be able to:

✔ Identify and Group Data
✔ Define SQL
✔ Define the Structures of a RDBMS: Tables, Columns, Rows, and Keys

---

Data is all around you—you make use of it every day. Your hair may be brown, your flight leaves from gate K10, you try to get up in the morning at 6:30 A.M. Storing data in related groups and making the connections among them are what databases are all about.

You interact with a database when you withdraw cash from an ATM machine, order a book from a Web site, or check stock quotes on the Internet. The switch from the information processing society to the knowledge management society will be facilitated by databases. Databases provide a major asset to any organization by helping it run its business and databases represent the backbones of the many technological advances we enjoy today.

Before the availability of relational databases, data was stored in individual files that could not be accessed unless you knew a programming language. Data could not be combined easily and modifications to the underlying database structures were extremely difficult. The Relational Model conceived by E. F. Codd provided the framework to solve a myriad of these and many other database problems. Relational databases offer *data independence,* meaning a user does not need to know on which hard drive and file a particular piece of information is stored. The RDBMS provides users with *data consistency* and *data integrity.* For example, if an employee works in the Finance department and we know that he can only work for one department, there should not be duplicate department records or contradicting data in the database. As you work through this lab, you will discover many of these useful and essential features. Let's start with a discussion of the terminology used in relational databases.

TABLES

A relational database stores data in tables. Tables typically contain data about a single subject. Each table has a unique name that signifies the contents of the data. For example, you can store data about books you read in a table called BOOK.

COLUMNS

Columns in a table organize the data further and a table consists of at least one column. Each column represents a single, low-level detail about a particular set of data. The name of the column is unique within a table and identifies the data you find in the column. For example, the BOOK table may have a column for the title, publisher, date the book was published, and so on. The order of the columns is unimportant because SQL allows you to display data in any order you choose.

ROWS

Each row usually represents one unique set of data within this table. For example, the row in Figure 1.1 with the title "The Invisible Force" is unique within the BOOK table. All the columns of the row represent respective data for the row. Each intersection of a column and row in a table represents a value and some do not, as you see in the PUBLISH_DATE column. The value is said to be *NULL*. Null is an unknown value, so it's not even blank spaces. Nulls cannot be evaluated or compared because they are unknown.

BOOK Table

BOOK_ID	TITLE	PUBLISHER	PUBLISH_DATE	
1010	The Invisible Force	Literacy Circle		
1011	Into The Sky	Prentice Hall	10/02	◀— Row
1012	Making It Possible	Life Books	2/99	

Column

Figure 1.1 ■ Example of the BOOK table.

PRIMARY KEY

When working with tables, you must understand how to uniquely identify data within a table. This is the purpose of the *primary key*; it uniquely identifies a row within a table, which means that you find one, and only one row in the table by

CUSTOMER_ID	CUSTOMER_NAME	ADDRESS	PHONE	ZIP
2010	Movers, Inc.	123 Park Lane	212-555-1212	10095
2011	Acme Mfg. Ltd.	555 Broadway	212-566-1212	10004
2012	ALR Inc.	50 Fifth Avenue	212-999-1212	10010

PRIMARY KEY

Figure 1.2 ■ Primary key example.

looking for the primary key value. Figure 1.2 shows an example of the CUS-TOMER table with the CUSTOMER_ID as the primary key of the table.

At first glance you may think that the CUSTOMER_NAME column can serve as the primary key of the CUSTOMER table because it is unique. However, it is entirely possible to have customers with the same name. Therefore, the CUSTOMER_NAME column is not a good choice for the primary key. Sometimes the unique key is a system-generated sequence number; this type of key is called a *synthetic* or *surrogate key*. The advantage of such a surrogate key is that it is unique and does not have any inherent meaning or purpose; therefore, it is not subject to changes. In this example, the CUSTOMER_ID column is such a surrogate key.

It is best to avoid any primary keys that are subject to updates as they cause unnecessary complexity. For example, the phone number of a customer is a poor example of a primary key column choice. Though it may possibly be unique within a table, phone numbers can change and then cause a number of problems with updates of other columns that reference this column.

A table may have only one primary key, which consists of one or more columns. If the primary key contains multiple columns it is referred to as a *composite primary key* or *concatenated primary key*. (Choosing appropriate keys is discussed more in Chapter 11, "Create, Alter, and Drop Tables.") Oracle does not require that every table have a primary key and there may be cases where it is not appropriate to have one. However, it is strongly recommended that most tables have a primary key.

FOREIGN KEYS

If you store the customer and the customer's order information in one table, the customer's name and address is repeated for each order. Figure 1.3 depicts such a table. Any change to the address requires the update of all the rows in the table for that individual customer.

If, however, the data is split into two tables (CUSTOMER and ORDER as shown in Figure 1.4) and the customer's address needs to be updated, only one row in the CUSTOMER table needs to be updated. Furthermore, splitting data this way avoids data inconsistency whereby the data differs between the different rows.

ID	CUSTOMER_NAME	ADDRESS	PHONE	ZIP	ORDER_ID	ORDER_DATE	TOTAL_ORDER
2010	Movers, Inc.	123 Park Lane	212-555-1212	10095	100	12/23/01	$500
2010	Movers, Inc.	123 Park Lane	212-555-1212	10095	102	7/20/02	$100
2010	Movers, Inc.	123 Park Lane	212-555-1212	10095	103	8/25/02	$400
2010	Movers, Inc.	123 Park Lane	212-555-1212	10095	104	9/20/02	$200
2011	Acme Mfg. Ltd.	555 Broadway	212-566-1212	10004	105	8/20/02	$900
2012	ALR Inc.	50 Fifth Avenue	212-999-1212	10010	101	01/05/02	$600

Figure 1.3 ■ Example of CUSTOMER data mixed with ORDER data.

Eliminating redundancy is one of the key concepts in relational databases and this process, referred to as *normalization*, is discussed shortly.

Figure 1.4 illustrates how the data is split into two tables to provide data consistency. In this example, the CUSTOMER_ID becomes a *foreign key* column in the ORDER table. The foreign key is the column that links the CUSTOMER and ORDER table together. In this example, you can find all orders for a particular customer by looking for the particular CUSTOMER_ID in the ORDER table. The CUSTOMER_ID would correspond to a single row in the CUSTOMER table that provides the customer-specific information. The foreign key column CUSTOMER_ID happens to have the same column name in the ORDER table. This makes it easier to recognize the fact that the tables share common column values. Often the foreign key column and the primary key have identical column names, but it is not required. You will learn more about foreign key columns with the same and different names and how to create foreign key relationships in Chapter 11, "Create, Alter, and Drop

▼ **PRIMARY KEY**   **CUSTOMER**

CUSTOMER_ID	CUSTOMER_NAME	ADDRESS	PHONE	ZIP
2010	Movers, Inc.	123 Park Lane	212-555-1212	10095
2011	Acme Mfg. Ltd.	555 Broadway	212-566-1212	10004
2012	ALR Inc.	50 Fifth Avenue	212-999-1212	10010

▼**FOREIGN KEY**

ORDER_ID	CUSTOMER_ID	ORDER_DATE	TOTAL_ORDER
100	2010	12/23/01	$500
102	2010	7/20/02	$100
103	2010	8/25/02	$400
104	2010	9/20/02	$200
105	2011	8/20/02	$900
101	2012	01/05/02	$600

ORDER

Figure 1.4 ■ Primary and foreign key relationship between CUSTOMER and ORDER tables.

Tables." Chapter 6, "Equijoins," teaches you how to combine results from the two tables using SQL.

You connect and combine data between tables in a relational database via data common columns.

SQL LANGUAGE COMMANDS

You work with the tables, rows, and columns using the SQL language. SQL allows you to query data, create new data, modify existing data, and delete data. Within the SQL language you can differentiate between individual sublanguages, which are a collection of individual commands.

For example, the *Data Manipulation Language* (DML) commands allow you to query, insert, update, or delete data. SQL allows you to create new database structures such as tables or modify existing ones; this subcategory of SQL language commands is called the *Data Definition Language* (DDL). Using the SQL language you can control access to the data using *Data Control Language* (DCL) commands. Table 1.1 shows you an overview of different language categories with their respective SQL commands.

Table 1.1 ■ Overview of SQL Language Commands

Description	SQL Commands
Data Manipulation	SELECT, INSERT, UPDATE, DELETE, MERGE
Data Definition	CREATE, ALTER, DROP, TRUNCATE, RENAME
Data Control	GRANT, REVOKE
Transaction Control	COMMIT, ROLLBACK, SAVEPOINT

One of the first statements you will execute is the SELECT command, which allows you to retrieve data. For example, to retrieve the TITLE and PUBLISHER columns from the BOOK table you may issue a SELECT statement such as the following:

```
SELECT title, publisher
   FROM book
```

The INSERT command lets you add new rows to a table. The next command shows you an example of an INSERT statement that adds a row to the BOOK table. The row contains the values Oracle SQL as a book title, a BOOK_ID of 1013, and a publish date of 12/02 with Prentice Hall as the publisher.

```
INSERT INTO book
(book_id, title, publisher, publish_date)
VALUES
(1013, 'Oracle SQL', 'Prentice Hall', '12/02')
```

To create new tables you use the CREATE TABLE command. The following statement illustrates how to create a simple table called AUTHOR with three columns. The first column, called AUTHOR_ID, holds numeric data; the FIRST_NAME and LAST_NAME columns contain alphanumeric character data.

```
CREATE TABLE author
(author_id   NUMBER,
 first_name  VARCHAR2(30),
 last_name   VARCHAR2(30))
```

You can manipulate the column definitions of a table with the ALTER TABLE command. This allows you to add or drop columns. You can also create primary and foreign key constraints on a table. Constraints allow you to enforce business rules within the database. For example, a primary key constraint can enforce the uniqueness of the AUTHOR_ID column in the AUTHOR table.

To grant SELECT and INSERT access to the AUTHOR table, you issue a GRANT command. It allows the user Scott to retrieve and insert data in the AUTHOR table.

```
GRANT SELECT, INSERT ON author TO scott
```

Starting with Chapter 2, "SQL: The Basics," you will learn how to execute the SELECT command against the Oracle database; Chapter 10, "Insert, Update, and Delete," will teach you the details of data manipulation; and Chapter 11, "Create, Alter, and Drop Tables," introduces you to the creation of tables and the definition of constraints to enforce the required business rules. Chapter 14, "Security," discusses how to control the access to data and the various Oracle database features.

LAB 1.1 EXERCISES

1.1.1 IDENTIFY AND GROUP DATA

a) Give three examples of types of data.

b) What groupings of data do you use in your daily life?

c) Give an example of a database system you use outside of the workplace and explain how it helps you.

1.1.2 DEFINE SQL

a) What is SQL and why is it useful?

b) Try to match each of the SQL commands on the left with a verb from the list on the right.

1.	CREATE	a.	manipulate
2.	UPDATE	b.	define
3.	GRANT	c.	control

c) Why do you think it is important to control access to data in a database?

1.1.3 DEFINE THE STRUCTURES OF A RDBMS: TABLES, COLUMNS, ROWS, AND KEYS

a) How is data organized in a relational database?

b) Do you think it's possible to have a table with no rows at all?

c) Figure 1.5 displays a listing of an EMPLOYEE and a DEPART-MENT table. Identify the columns you consider to be primary keys and foreign keys for the tables.

EMPLOYEE_ID	FIRST_NAME	LAST_NAME	SALARY	DEPT_NO
230	Kyle	Hsu	80,000	40
231	Kirsten	Soehner	130,000	50
232	Madeline	Dimitri	70,000	40
234	Joshua	Hunter	90,000	20

DEPT_NO	DEPARTMENT_NAME
20	Finance
40	Human Resources
50	Sales
60	Information Systems

Figure 1.5 ■ EMPLOYEE and DEPARTMENT tables.

LAB 1.1 EXERCISE ANSWERS

1.1.1 ANSWERS

a) Give three examples of types of data.

Answer: The answer to this question will vary depending on your choices.

A circle, square, and triangle are all data about geometrical shapes. Your mother, father, and sister are data about your immediate family members. Fiction, comedy, cookbook, and computer are all data about types of books.

b) What groupings of data do you use in your daily life?

Answer: The answer to this question will vary depending on your situation.

I use my address book daily. It contains addresses and phone numbers of friends, relatives, and coworkers. I also keep a running to-do list of tasks at work, which groups together the tasks I have completed, as well as separately grouping those tasks I have yet to do.

When grouping data, each piece of data should be related to the others. A person's physical appearance is typically described by more than just brown hair; they may also have green eyes, be six feet tall, and be of the female sex. In my address book, I group together a person's name, address, and telephone number. I may keep a separate address book for my business contacts that would group together the person's name, company name, work telephone number, fax number, and email address.

c) Give an example of a database system you use outside of the workplace and explain how it helps you.

Answer: Again, the answer to this question will vary depending on your situation.

When I'm in a record store, I often use a computerized information kiosk to search for information about an album, such as where it is located in the store. Another example is an ATM machine, where I can inquire about my account balance.

1.1.2 ANSWERS

a) What is SQL and why is it useful?

Answer: SQL, the Structured Query Language, is a standardized relational database access language. It is useful because it allows a user to query, manipulate, define, and control data in a RDBMS.

The SQL language is sanctioned by ANSI, which determines standards on all aspects of the SQL language, including datatypes. However, most relational database products, including Oracle, have their own extensions to the ANSI standard, providing additional functionality within their respective products by further extending the use of SQL.

b) Try to match each of the SQL commands on the left with a verb from the list on the right:

Answer: The following shows how these commands match with the appropriate verb.

1. CREATE ⟶ a. manipulate
2. UPDATE ⟶ b. define
3. GRANT ⟶ c. control

DML is used to *manipulate* data, with the SELECT, INSERT, UPDATE, and DELETE commands. (Note that in some of Oracle's own documentation, the SELECT command is not part of the DML language, but is considered Data Retrieval Language.) DDL is used to *define* objects such as tables with the CREATE, ALTER, and DROP commands. DCL is used to *control* access privileges in a RDBMS, such as with the GRANT and REVOKE commands to give or remove privileges. These SQL commands are written and executed against the database using a software program. In this workbook, Oracle's SQL*Plus program or *i*SQL*Plus with your Web browser is used to communicate these commands to the RDBMS. The use of SQL*Plus and SQL commands will be covered in Chapter 2, "SQL: The Basics."

c) Why do you think it is important to control access to data in a database?

Answer: Data can contain sensitive information to which some users should have limited access privileges. Some users may be allowed to query certain data but not change it, while others are allowed to add data to a database, but not delete it. By controlling access to data, the security of the data is assured for all users. You learn about safeguarding your data in Chapter 14, "Security."

1.1.3 ANSWERS

a) How is data organized in a relational database?

Answer: Data is organized by placing like pieces of information together in a table that consists of columns and rows.

For example, the data found in a library is typically organized in several ways to facilitate finding a book. Figure 1.6 shows information specific to books. The data is organized into columns and rows; the columns represent a type of data (title vs. genre), and the rows contain data. A table in a database is organized in the same way. You might call this table BOOK as it contains information related to books only. Each intersection of a column and row in a table represents a value.

TITLE	AUTHOR	ISBN#	GENRE	LOCATION_ID
Magic Gum	Harry Smith	0-11-124456-2	Computer	D11
Desk Work	Robert Jones	0-11-223754-3	Fiction	H24
Beach Life	Mark Porter	0-11-922256-8	Juvenile	J3
From Here to There	Gary Mills	0-11-423356-5	Fiction	H24

Figure 1.6 ■ BOOK table.

Searching for a book by location might yield this excerpt of data shown in Figure 1.7. This set of columns and rows represents another database table called LOCATION, with information specific to locations in a library.

LOCATION_ID	FLOOR	SECTION	SHELF
D11	1	3	1
H24	2	2	3
J3	3	1	1

Figure 1.7 ■ LOCATION table.

The advantage to storing information about books and their locations separately is that information is not repeated unnecessarily, and maintenance of the data is much easier.

For instance, two books in the BOOK table have the same LOCATION_ID, H24. If the floor, section, and shelf information were also stored in the BOOK table, this information would be repeated for each of the two book rows. In that situation, if the floor of LOCATION_ID H24 changed, both of the rows in the BOOK table would have to change. Instead, by storing the location information separately, the floor information only has to change once in the LOCATION table.

The two tables (BOOK and LOCATION) have a common column between them, namely LOCATION_ID. In a relational database, SQL can be used to query information from more than one table at a time, making use of the common column they contain by performing a *join*. The join allows you to query both the BOOK and LOCATION tables to return a list of book titles together with floor, section, and shelve information to help you locate the books easily.

b) Do you think it's possible to have a table with no rows at all?

Answer: Yes, it is possible, though clearly it is not very useful to have a table with no data.

c) Figure 1.5 displays a listing of an EMPLOYEE and its respective DEPARTMENT table. Identify the columns you consider to be primary keys and foreign keys for the tables.

Answer: The primary key of the EMPLOYEE table is the EMPLOYEE_ID. The primary key of the DEPARTMENT table is DEPT_NO. The DEPT_NO is also the foreign key column of EMPLOYEE table and is common between the two tables.

In the DEPT_NO column of the EMPLOYEE table you can ONLY enter values that exist in the DEPARTMENT table. The DEPARTMENT table is the parent table from which the child table, the EMPLOYEE table, gets its DEPT_NO values. Establishing a foreign key relationship highlights the benefit of *referential integrity*. Only valid primary key values from the parent table are allowed in the child's foreign key column, therefore avoiding *orphan rows* (child rows without parent rows). For example, you cannot enter a DEPT_NO of 10 in the EMPLOYEE table if such a value does not exist in the DEPARTMENT table.

Note that the DEPARTMENT table contains one row with the department number of 60, which does not have any corresponding employees. The referential integrity rule allows a parent without child(ren), but does not allow a child without a parent because this would be considered an orphan row. You will learn how to establish primary key and foreign key relationships in Chapter 11, "Create, Alter, and Drop Tables."

LAB 1.1 SELF-REVIEW QUESTIONS

In order to test your progress, you should be able to answer the following questions.

1) A university's listing of students and the classes they are enrolled in is an example of a database system.

    a) _____ True
    b) _____ False

2) A table must always contain both columns and rows.

    a) _____ True
    b) _____ False

3) SQL is software that interacts with a relational database.

   a) _____ True
   b) _____ False

4) More than one user can be connected to a database at the same time.

   a) _____ True
   b) _____ False

5) Referential integrity ensures that each value in a foreign key column of the child table links back to a matching primary key value in the parent table.

   a) _____ True
   b) _____ False

Answers appear in Appendix A, Section 1.1.

LAB 1.2

TABLE RELATIONSHIPS

LAB OBJECTIVES

After this lab, you will be able to:

✔ Read a Schema Diagram
✔ Identify Data Normalization Rules and Table Relationships
✔ Understand the Database Development Context

Although this is a book about SQL, you must understand the basic concepts, terminology, and issues involving database design to be able to understand why tables are organized in specific ways. This lab will introduce you to the practical aspects of designing tables and determining their respective relationships to each other.

DATA NORMALIZATION

The objective of *normalization* is the elimination of redundancy in tables, therefore avoiding any future data manipulation problems. There are a number of different rules for minimizing duplication of data, which are formulated into the various *normal forms*.

The rules verify that the columns you placed in the tables do in fact belong there. You design your tables, the appropriate columns, and the matching primary and foreign keys to comply with these rules. This process is called normalization. The normalization rules will be quite intuitive after you have read through the examples in this lab. Although there are many normalization rules, the *five normal forms* and the *Boyce–Codd normal form* (BCNF) are the most widely accepted. This lab will discuss the first three normal forms as programmers and analysts typically don't bother normalizing beyond third normal form; with the exception of experienced database designers.

FIRST NORMAL FORM

For a table to be in *first normal form*, all repeating groups must be removed and placed in a new table. The example in Figure 1.8 illustrates the repeating groups

BOOK Table

BOOK_ID	TITLE	RETAIL_PRICE	LOCATION_1	LOCATION_2	LOCATION_3
1010	The Invisible Force	29.95	New York	San Francisco	
1011	Into The Sky	39.95	Chicago		
1012	Making It Possible	59.95	Miami	Austin	New York

Figure 1.8 ■ Repeating group.

in the BOOK table. The table has the location information of various warehouses across the country where the title is stocked. The location is listed in three columns as LOCATION_1 LOCATION_2, and LOCATION_3.

Imagine the scenario when you have more than three locations for a book. To avoid this and other problems, the database designer will move the location information to a separate table named BOOK_LOCATION, as illustrated in Figure 1.9. This design is more flexible and allows the storing of books at an unlimited number of locations.

BOOK Table

BOOK_ID	TITLE	RETAIL_PRICE
1010	The Invisible Force	29.95
1011	Into The Sky	39.95
1012	Making It Possible	59.95

BOOK_LOCATION Table

BOOK_ID	LOCATION
1010	New York
1010	San Francisco
1011	Chicago
1012	Miami
1012	Austin
1012	New York

Figure 1.9 ■ Tables in first normal form.

SECOND NORMAL FORM

Second normal form states that all nonkey columns must depend on the entire primary key, not just part of it. This form only applies to tables that have composite primary keys. Figure 1.10 shows the BOOK_AUTHOR table with both the BOOK_ID and AUTHOR_ID as the composite primary key. In this example, authors with the ID 900 and 901 coauthored the book with the ID of 10002. If you add the author's phone number to the table, the second normal form is violated because the phone

BOOK_ID	AUTHOR_ID	ROYALTY_SHARE	AUTHOR_PHONE_NO
10001	900	100	212-555-1212
10002	901	75	901-555-1212
10002	900	25	212-555-1212
10003	902	100	899-555-1212

Figure 1.10 ■ Violation of second normal form in the BOOK_AUTHOR table.

number is dependent only on the AUTHOR_ID, not on the BOOK_ID. Note ROYALTY_SHARE is dependent completely on the combination of both columns because the percentage of the royalty varies from book to book and is split among authors.

THIRD NORMAL FORM

The *third normal form* goes a step further than the second normal form: It states that every nonkey column must be a fact about the primary key column. The third normal form is quite intuitive. Figure 1.11 shows a table that violates third normal form. The PUBLISHER_PHONE_NO column is not dependent on the primary key column BOOK_ID but on the PUBLISHER_NAME column. Therefore, it should not be part of the BOOK table.

BOOK Table

BOOK_ID	TITLE	PUBLISHER_NAME	PUBLISH_DATE	PUBLISHER_PHONE_NO
1010	The Invisible Force	Literacy Circle	12/01	801-111-1111
1011	Into The Sky	Prentice Hall	10/02	999-888-1212
1012	Making It Possible	Life Books	2/99	777-555-1212
1013	Wonders of the World	Literacy Circle	5/99	801-111-1111

Figure 1.11 ■ Violation of third normal form.

Instead, the publisher's phone number should be stored in a separate table called PUBLISHER. This has the advantage that when a publisher's phone number is updated, it only needs to be updated in one place, rather than all occurrences of this publisher in the BOOK table. Removing the PUBLISHER_PHONE_NO column eliminates redundancy and avoids any possibilities of data inconsistencies (see Figure 1.12).

Also, the BOOK table can benefit by introducing a surrogate key, such as a PUBLISHER_ID. Such a key is not subject to changes and is easily referenced in any additional tables that may need to refer to data about the publisher.

**LAB
1.2**

BOOK Table

BOOK_ID	TITLE	PUBLISHER_ID	PUBLISH_DATE
1010	The Invisible Force	1	12/01
1011	Into The Sky	2	10/02
1012	Making It Possible	3	2/99
1013	Wonders of the World	1	5/99

PUBLISHER Table

PUBLISHER_ID	PUBLISHER_NAME	PUBLISHER_PHONE_NO
1	Literacy Circle	801-111-1111
2	Pen Books	999-888-1212
3	Life Books	777-555-1212

Figure 1.12 ■ Tables in third normal form.

BOYCE–CODD NORMAL FORM, FOURTH NORMAL FORM, AND FIFTH NORMAL FORM

The Boyce-Codd normal form is an even more elaborate version of the third normal form and deals with deletion anomalies. The *fourth normal form* tackles potential problems when three or more columns are part of the unique identifier and their dependencies to each other. The *fifth normal form* splits the tables even further apart to eliminate all redundancy. These different normal forms are beyond the scope of this book; for more details, please consult one of the many excellent books on database design.

TABLE RELATIONSHIPS

When two tables have a common column or columns, the tables are said to have a *relationship* between them. The *cardinality* of a relationship is the actual number of occurrences for each entity. We will explore one-to-one, one-to-many, and many-to-many relationships.

ONE-TO-MANY RELATIONSHIP (1:M)

Figure 1.13 shows the CUSTOMER table and the ORDER table. The common column is CUSTOMER_ID. The link between the two tables is a *one-to-many* relationship, the most common type of relationship. This means that "one" individual customer can have "many" order rows in the ORDER table. This relationship represents the business rule that "One customer can place one or many orders (or no orders)." Reading the relationship in the other direction, an order is associated with only one customer row (or no customer rows). In other words, "each order may be placed by one and only one customer."

CUSTOMER Table

PRIMARY KEY▼

CUSTOMER_ID	CUSTOMER_NAME	ADDRESS	PHONE	ZIP
2010	Movers, Inc.	123 Park Lane	212-555-1212	10095
2011	Acme Mfg Ltd.	555 Broadway	212-566-1212	10004
2012	ALR Inc.	50 Fifth Avenue	212-999-1212	10010

ORDER Table

PRIMARY KEY▼   ▼ FOREIGN KEY

ORDER_ID	CUSTOMER_ID	ORDER_DATE	TOTAL_ORDER_AMOUNT
100	2010	12/23/01	$500
101	2012	01/05/02	$600
102	2010	07/20/02	$100
103	2010	08/25/02	$400
104	2010	09/20/02	$200

Figure 1.13 ■ One-to-many relationship example between CUSTOMER and ORDER table.

ONE-TO-ONE RELATIONSHIP (1:1)

One-to-one relationships exist in the database world, but they are not typical because most often data from both tables are combined into one table for simplicity. Figure 1.14 shows an example of a *one-to-one* relationship between the PRODUCT table and the PRODUCT_PRICE table. For every row in the PRODUCT table you may find only "one" matching row in the PRODUCT_PRICE table. And for every row in the PRODUCT_PRICE table there is "one" matching row in the

PRODUCT

▼PRIMARY KEY

PRODUCT_ID	PRODUCT_NAME	MANUFACTURER
10001	Bolt	ACME, Inc.
10002	Screw	KR Mfg.
10003	Nail	ABC, Ltd.

PRODUCT_PRICE

▼FOREIGN KEY & PRIMARY KEY

PRODUCT_ID	RETAIL_PRICE	IN_STOCK_QTY
10001	$0.45	10,000
10002	$0.02	20,000
10003	$0.10	50,000

Figure 1.14 ■ One-to-one relationship example.

**LAB
1.2**

PRODUCT table. If the two tables are combined, the RETAIL_PRICE and IN_STOCK_QTY columns can be included in the PRODUCT table.

MANY-TO-MANY RELATIONSHIP (M:M)

The examination of Figure 1.15 reveals a *many-to-many* relationship between the BOOK and AUTHOR tables. One book can have one or more authors and one author can write one or more books. The relational database model requires the resolution of many-to-many relationships into one-to-many relationship tables. This is done by creating an *associative table* (also called an *intersection table*). The solution in this example is achieved via the BOOK_AUTHOR table. Figure 1.16 shows the columns of this table.

The BOOK_AUTHOR table lists the individual author(s) for each book and shows, for a particular author, the book(s) he or she wrote. The primary key of the BOOK_AUTHOR table is the combination of both columns: the BOOK_ID column and the AUTHOR_ID column. These two columns represent the concatenated primary key that uniquely identifies a row in the table. As you may recall from the previous lab, multicolumn primary keys are referred to as a composite or concatenated primary key. Additionally, the BOOK_AUTHOR table has the AUTHOR_ID and the BOOK_ID as two individual foreign keys linking back to the AUTHOR and the BOOK table, respectively.

The BOOK_AUTHOR table contains an additional column, the ROYALTY_SHARE column. It identifies the royalty percentage for each author for an individual book. When there are multiple authors, the percentage of the royalty is split; in the case of a sole author the share is 100 percent. This column is appropriately located in the BOOK_AUTHOR table as the values are relevant for the combination of the BOOK_ID and AUTHOR_ID. This combination of columns uniquely identifies both a book and an author and the respective percentage share of the royalty.

BOOK

BOOK_ID	TITLE	RETAIL_PRICE
10001	Call in the Dark	39.95
10002	The Spy	29.95
10003	Perspectives	59.95

Primary Key →

AUTHOR

AUTHOR_ID	FIRST_NAME	LAST_NAME
900	King	John
901	Oats	Heather
902	Turrow	Stephen

Primary Key →

Figure 1.15 ■ Many-to-many relationship example.

BOOK

BOOK_ID	TITLE	RETAIL_PRICE
10001	Call in the Dark	39.95
10002	The Spy	29.95
10003	Perspectives	59.95

AUTHOR

AUTHOR_ID	FIRST_NAME	LAST_NAME
900	King	John
901	Oats	Heather
902	Turrow	Stephen

Foreign Key   Foreign Key   **BOOK_AUTHOR**

BOOK_ID	AUTHOR_ID	ROYALTY_SHARE
10001	900	100
10002	901	75
10002	900	25
10003	902	100

Primary Key

Figure 1.16 ■ Associative BOOK_AUTHOR table that resolves the many-to-many relationship.

DRAWING RELATIONSHIPS

For clarity of meaning and conceptual consistency, it is useful to show table relationships using drawings (called *schema diagrams*) and there are a number of standard notations for this type of diagram. For example, Figure 1.17 illustrates one of the ways to graphically depict the relationship between tables. The convention used in this book for a one-to-many relationship is a line with a "crow's foot" (fork) on one end indicating the "many" side of the relationship; at the other end, a "single line" depicts the "one" side of the relationship. You will see

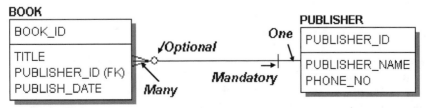

BOOK

BOOK_ID
TITLE
PUBLISHER_ID (FK)
PUBLISH_DATE

√Optional   *One*   **PUBLISHER**

PUBLISHER_ID
PUBLISHER_NAME
PHONE_NO

Mandatory

Many

Figure 1.17 ■ Crow's foot notation.

the use of the *crow's-foot notation* throughout this book. Software diagramming programs that support the graphical display of relational database models often allow you to choose your notation preference.

CARDINALITY AND OPTIONALITY

The cardinality expresses the ratio of a parent and child table from the perspective of the parent table. It describes how many rows you may find between the two tables for a given primary key value. For example, in Figure 1.13 you saw a one-to-many relationship between the CUSTOMER and ORDER tables and the relationship ratio is expressed in the form of a 1:M ratio.

Graphical relationship lines indicate the *optionality* of a relationship, whether a row is required or not (mandatory or optional). Specifically, optionality shows if one row in a table can exist without a row in the related table.

Figure 1.17 shows a one-to-many relationship between the PUBLISHER (parent) and the BOOK (child). Examining the relationship line on the "many" end, you notice a "circle" identifying the *optional relationship* and a crow's foot indicating "many." The symbols indicate that a publisher *may* publish zero, one, or many books. You use the word "may" to indicate that the relationship is *optional* and allows a publisher to exist without a corresponding value in the BOOK table.

The relationship line also reads the other way. The solid line on the PUBLISHER end of the line indicates the "one" side, a "vertical bar" intersects it and this bar identifies a *mandatory relationship*. You read this direction of the relationship as "One book *must* be published by one and only one publisher." This means a row in the BOOK table must always have the PUBLISHER_ID value filled in. It cannot be null because that means unknown and indicates there is no associated PUBLISHER row.

The "(FK)" symbol next to the PUBLISHER_ID column indicates that this is the foreign key column. In this diagram, the primary key is separated from the other columns with a line; you observe the BOOK_ID and the PUBLISHER_ID as the primary keys or unique identifiers.

Figure 1.18 shows an optional relationship on both sides; a book may be published by zero or one publisher. Effectively, this means the value in the

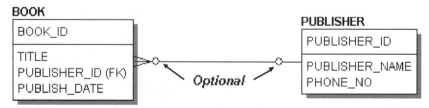

Figure 1.18 ■ Optional relationship on both sides.

PUBLISHER_ID column in BOOK is optional. Reading the relationship from the PUBLISHER, you can say that "one publisher may publish zero, one, or many books" (which is identical to Figure 1.17).

REAL WORLD BUSINESS PRACTICE

You will typically see only these two types of relationships: First, mandatory on the "one" side and optional on the "many" end as in Figure 1.17; and second, optional on both ends as in Figure 1.18. Only rarely will you find other types of relationships. For example, mandatory relationships on both sides are infrequently implemented; it means that rows must be inserted in both tables simultaneously. Occasionally you will find one-to-one relationships but most often the columns from both tables are combined into one table. Many-to-many relationships are not allowed in the relational database; they must be resolved via an associative or intersection table into one-to-many relationships.

LABELING RELATIONSHIPS

To clarify and explain the nature of the relationship on the diagram, it's useful to add a label or name with a verb on the relationship line. Figure 1.19 shows an example of a labeled relationship. For the utmost in clarity, a labeled relationship should be labeled on both sides. You then read it as: "One PUBLISHER may publish zero, one, or many BOOKs; and one BOOK must be published by one and only one PUBLISHER." This kind of labeling makes the relationship perfectly clear and states the relationship in terms that a business user can understand.

Figure 1.19 ■ Labeled relationship between BOOK and PUBLISHER.

IDENTIFYING AND NONIDENTIFYING RELATIONSHIPS

In an *identifying relationship,* the foreign key is propagated to the child entity as the primary key. This is in contrast to a *nonidentifying relationship,* in which the foreign key becomes one of the nonkey columns. Nonidentifying relationships may accept null value in the foreign key column.

Figure 1.20 depicts some of the tables used in the lab; the many-to-many relationship between the BOOK and AUTHOR tables is now resolved to the associative table called BOOK_AUTHOR. If a graphical representation of a table's box has *rounded edges* it means that the relationship is *identifying.* Effectively, one of the foreign keys became the primary key or part of the primary key. In the case of

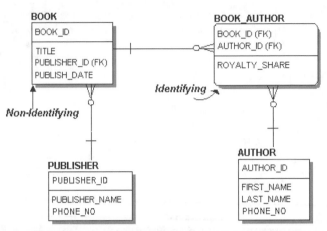

Figure 1.20 ■ Identifying and nonidentifying relationships.

the BOOK_AUTHOR table, both foreign key columns constitute the primary key and both columns may not be null because a primary key is never null.

The relationship between the PUBLISHER and BOOK tables is nonidentifying, as indicated by the sharp edges. The foreign key column PUBLISHER_ID is not part of the primary key. The foreign key columns of a nonidentifying relationship may be either NULL or NOT NULL. In this instance you can determine if a null is allowed by checking if the relationship is optional or mandatory. Although the foreign key column allows null values in non-identifying relationships, here the relationship depicts a single bar on the relationship line. Effectively, for every row in the BOOK table there must be a corresponding row in the PUBLISHER table and the PUBLISHER_ID column of the BOOK table cannot be null.

DATABASE DEVELOPMENT CONTEXT

Now that you are familiar with the some of the relational database terminology and its core concepts, you are ready to learn about how all this information fits into the context of database development. From the initial idea of an application until the final system implementation, the data model is continuously refined. Figure 1.21 indicates the essential phases of the development project with respect to the database.

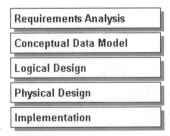

Figure 1.21 ■ Database development and design phases.

REQUIREMENTS ANALYSIS

Initially, the process starts off with gathering data requirements that identify the needs and wants of the users. One of the outputs of this phase is a list of individual data elements that need to be stored in the database.

CONCEPTUAL DATA MODEL

The *conceptual data model* logically groups the major data elements from the requirements analysis into individual *entities*. An entity is just something of significance for which you need to store data. For example, all data related to books such as the title, publish date, and retail price are placed in the book entity. Data elements such as the author's name and address are part of the author entity. The individual data elements are referred to as *attributes*.

You designate a *unique identifier* or *candidate key* that uniquely distinguishes a row in the entity. Notice that in this conceptual data model we use the terms entity, attribute, and candidate key or unique identifier instead of table, column, and primary key, respectively.

Noncritical attributes are not included in the model to emphasize the business meaning of those entities, attributes, and relationships. Many-to-many relationships are acceptable and not resolved. The diagram of the conceptual model is useful to communicate the initial understanding of the requirements to business users. The conceptual model gives no consideration to the implementation platform or database software. Many projects skip the conceptual model and go directly to the logical model.

LOGICAL DATA MODEL

The purpose of the *logical data model* is to show that all of the entities, their respective attributes, and the relationship between entities represent the business requirements without considering technical issues. The focus is entirely on business problems and considers a design that accommodates growth and change. The entities and attributes require descriptive names and documentation of their meaning. Labeling and documenting the relationships between entities clarify the business rules between them.

The diagram may show the datatype of an attribute in general terms such as text, number, and date. In many logical design models you will find foreign key columns identified, in others they are implied. (For example, Oracle's Designer software product doesn't show the foreign keys in the logical model diagram because they are an implementation detail that is implied by the relationships.)

The complete model is called the *logical data model* or *Entity Relationship Diagram* (ERD). At the end of the analysis phase the entities are fully normalized, the unique identifier for each entity is determined, and any many-to-many relationships are resolved into associative entities.

PHYSICAL DATA MODEL

The *physical data model*, also referred to as the *schema diagram,* is a graphical model of the physical design implementation of the database. This physical schema diagram is what the programmers and you will use to learn about the database and the relationship between the tables. In Lab 1.3 you will be introduced to the STUDENT schema diagram used throughout this workbook.

This physical data model is derived from the fully normalized logical model. Before the actual implementation (installation) of the physical data model in the database, multiple physical data models may exist. They represent a variety of alternative physical database designs that consider the performance implications and application constraints. One of the physical design models will be implemented in the database. The schema diagram graphically represents the chosen implemented physical data model; it is specific to a particular RDBMS product such as Oracle.

Figure 1.22 depicts the schema diagram of the book publishing database discussed in this chapter. It shows the structure of the tables with their respective columns, and it illustrates the relationships between the tables.

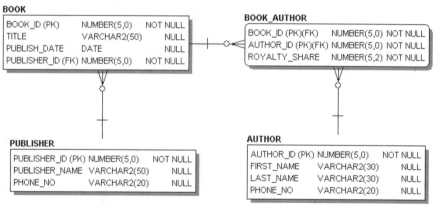

Figure 1.22 ■ Book publishing database diagram.

The physical data model has a different terminology than the conceptual or logical data model. The physical data model refers to tables instead of entities; the individual pieces of data are columns instead of attributes in the logical model.

TRANSFER FROM LOGICAL TO PHYSICAL MODEL

The transfer from the logical to the physical models, which ultimately means the actual implementation in a database as tables, columns, primary keys, foreign keys, indexes, and so on, requires a number of steps and considerations. The entities identified in the logical data model are resolved to physical tables; the entity name is often identical to the table name. Some designers use singular names for entities and plural names for tables; others abbreviate the entity names when implementing the physical model to follow certain business naming standards. Frequently, the physical data model includes additional tables for specific technical implementation requirements and programming purposes such as a report queue table or an error log table.

As mentioned, attributes become columns with names being either identical or following business naming conventions and abbreviations. The columns are associated with the database software vendor's specific datatypes, which considers valid column lengths and restrictions. Individual data entry formats are determined (e.g., phone numbers must be in numeric format with dashes between). Rules for maintaining data integrity and consistency are created and physical storage parameters for individual tables are determined. You will learn about these and many other aspects of creating these restrictions in Chapter 11, "Create, Alter, and Drop Tables." Sometimes additional columns are added that were never in the logical design with the purpose of storing precalculated values; this is referred to as *denormalization,* which we will discuss shortly.

Another activity that occurs in the physical data design phase is the design of indexes. *Indexes* are database objects that facilitate speedy access to data to a specific column or columns of a table. Placing indexes on tables is necessary to optimize efficient query performance, but indexes have the negative impact of requiring additional time for insert, update, or delete operations. Balancing the trade-offs with the advantages requires careful consideration of these factors, including knowledge in optimizing SQL statements and an understanding of the features of a particular database version. You will learn more about different types of indexes and the success factors of a well-placed index strategy in Chapter 12, "Views, Indexes, and Sequences."

 Poor physical database design is very costly and difficult to correct.

Database designers must be knowledgeable and experienced in many aspects of programming, design, and database administration to fully understand how design decisions impact cost, system interfaces, programming effort, and future maintenance.

You may wonder how the graphical models you see in this book are produced. Specific software packages allow you to visually design the various models and they allow you to display different aspects of it such as showing only table names or showing table names, columns, and their respective datatypes. Many of these tools even allow you to generate the DDL SQL statements to create the tables. For a list of software tools that allow you to visually produce the diagrams, see the book's Web site at http://www.phptr.com/rischert and Appendix H, "Resources."

DENORMALIZATION

Denormalization is the act of adding redundancy to the physical database design. Typically, logical models are fully normalized or at least in third normal form. When designing the physical model, database designers must weigh the benefit of eliminating all redundancy with data split into many tables against potentially poor performance when these many tables are joined.

Therefore database designers, also called database architects, sometimes purposely add redundancy to their physical design. Only experienced database designers should do denormalization. Increasing redundancy may greatly increase the overall programming effort because now many copies of the same data must be kept in sync; however, the time it takes to query data may be less.

In some applications, particularly data warehousing applications where massive amounts of detailed data are stored and summarized, denormalization is required. *Data warehouse applications* are database applications that benefit users that need to analyze large data sets from various angles and use this data for reporting and decision-making purposes. Typically, the source of the data warehouse is historical transaction data but can also include data from various other sources for the purpose of consolidating data. For example, the purchasing department of a supermarket chain could determine how many turkeys to order for a specific store on the week before Thanksgiving or use the data to determine what promotional offers have the largest sales impact on stores with certain customer demographics.

The primary purpose of a data warehouses is to query, report, and analyze data. Therefore redundancy is encouraged and necessary for queries to perform efficiently.

LAB 1.2 EXERCISES

1.2.1 READ A SCHEMA DIAGRAM

a) Describe the nature of the relationship between the ORDER_ HEADER table and the ORDER_DETAIL table (Figure 1.23).

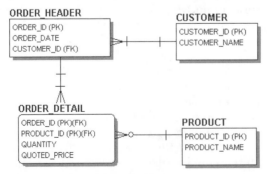

Figure 1.23 ■ Order tables.

1.2.2 IDENTIFY DATA NORMALIZATION RULES AND TABLE RELATIONSHIPS

a) One of the tables in Figure 1.24 is not fully normalized. Which normal form is violated? Draw a new diagram.

b) How would you change Figure 1.24 to add information about the sales representative that took the order?

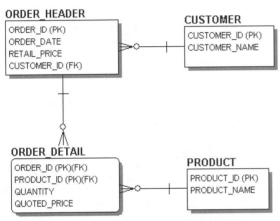

Figure 1.24 ■ Not fully normalized table.

c) How would you change Figure 1.25 if an employee does not need to belong to a department?

d) Based on Figure 1.25, why do you think the social security number (SSN) column should not be the primary key of the EMPLOYEE table?

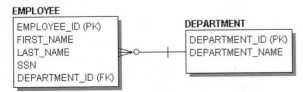

Figure 1.25 ■ EMPLOYEE to DEPARTMENT relationship.

**LAB
1.2**

a) Figures 1.26 and 1.27 depict the logical and physical model of a fictional movie rental database. What differences do you notice between the following entity relationship diagram and the physical schema diagram?

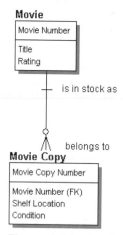

Figure 1.26 ■ Logical Data Model.

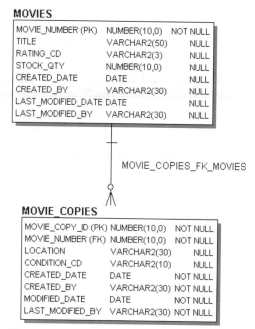

Figure 1.27 ■ Physical Data Model.

LAB 1.2 EXERCISE ANSWERS

a) Describe the nature of the relationship between the ORDER_HEADER table and the ORDER_DETAIL table (Figure 1.23).

Answer: The relationship depicts a mandatory one-to-many relationship between the ORDER_HEADER and the ORDER_DETAIL tables. The ORDER_HEADER table contains data found only once for each order, such as the ORDER_ID, the CUSTOMER_ID, and the ORDER_DATE. The ORDER_DETAIL table holds information about the individual order lines of an order. One row in the ORDER_HEADER table must have one or many order details. One ORDER_DETAIL row must have one and only one corresponding row in the ORDER_HEADER table.

MANDATORY RELATIONSHIP ON BOTH ENDS

The mandatory relationship indicates from the ORDER_HEADER to ORDER_
DETAIL that a row in the ORDER_HEADER table cannot exist unless a row in
ORDER_DETAIL is created simultaneously. This is a "chicken and egg" problem
whereby a row in the ORDER_HEADER table cannot be created without an
ORDER_DETAIL row and vice versa. In fact, it really doesn't matter as long as you
create the rows within one transaction. Furthermore, you must make sure that
every row in the ORDER_HEADER table has at least one row in the ORDER_
DETAIL table and rows in the ORDER_DETAIL table have exactly one corresponding row in the ORDER_HEADER table. There are various ways to physically implement this relationship.

Another example of a mandatory relationship on the figure is the relationship
between ORDER_HEADER and CUSTOMER. You can see the bar on the many side
of the relationship as an indication for the mandatory row. That means a customer must have placed an order before a row in the CUSTOMER table is saved,
and an order can only be placed by a customer.

However, for most practical purposes a mandatory relationship on both ends is
rarely implemented unless there is a very specific and important requirement.

NO DUPLICATES ALLOWED

On the previous diagrams, such as Figure 1.23, you noticed that some foreign
keys are part of the primary key. This is frequently the case in associative entities; in this particular example it requires the combination of ORDER_ID and
PRODUCT_ID to be unique. Ultimately the effect is that a single order containing the same product twice is not allowed. Figure 1.28 lists sample data in
the ORDER_DETAIL table for ORDER_ID 345 and PRODUCT_ID P90, which violates the primary key and is therefore not allowed. Instead, you must create
one order with a quantity of 10 or create a second order with a different
ORDER_ID so the primary key is not violated. You will learn about how Oracle
responds with error messages when you attempt to violate the primary key
constraint and other types of constraints in Chapter 10, "Insert, Update, and
Delete."

ORDER_DETAIL Table

ORDER_ID	PRODUCT_ID	QUANTITY	QUOTED_PRICE
123	P90	5	$50
234	S999	9	$12
345	P90	7	$50
345	X85	3	$10
345	P90	3	$50

Figure 1.28 ■ Sample data of the ORDER_DETAIL table.

**LAB
1.2**

a) One of the tables in Figure 1.24 is not fully normalized. Which normal form is violated? Draw a new diagram.

Answer: The third normal form is violated on the ORDER_HEADER table. The RETAIL_PRICE column belongs to the PRODUCT table instead (Figure 1.29).

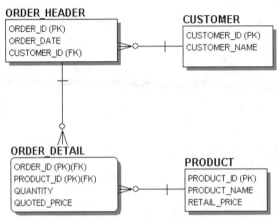

Figure 1.29 ■ Fully normalized tables.

Third normal form states that every nonkey column must be a fact about the primary key column, which is the ORDER_ID column in the ORDER_HEADER table. This is clearly not the case in the ORDER_HEADER table, as the RETAIL_PRICE column is not a fact about the ORDER_HEADER and does not depend upon the ORDER_ID; it is a fact about the PRODUCT. The QUOTED_PRICE column is included in the ORDER_DETAIL table because the price may vary over time, from order to order, and from customer to customer. (If you want to track any changes in the retail price, you may want to create a separate table called PRODUCT_PRICE_HISTORY that keeps track of the retail price per product and the effective date of each price change.) Table 1.2 provides a review of the normal forms.

Table 1.2 ■ The Three Normal Forms

Description	Rule
First Normal Form (1NF)	No repeating groups are permitted
Second Normal Form (2NF)	No partial key dependencies are permitted
Third Normal Form (3NF)	No nonkey dependencies are permitted.

b) How would you change Figure 1.24 to add information about the sales representative that took the order?

Answer: As you see in Figure 1.30, you need to add another table that contains the sales representative's name, SALES_REP_ID, and any other important information. The SALESREP_ID then becomes a foreign key in the ORDER_HEADER table.

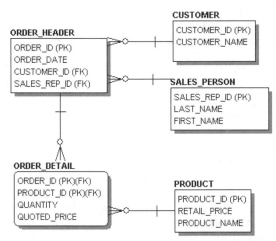

Figure 1.30 ■ ORDER_HEADER with SALES_REP_ID column.

c) How would you change Figure 1.25 if an employee does not need to belong to a department?

Answer: You change the relationship line on the DEPARTMENT table end to make it optional. This has the effect that the DEPARTMENT_ID column on the EMPLOYEE table can be null; that is, a value is not required (Figure 1.31).

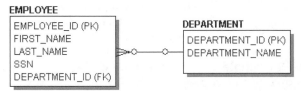

Figure 1.31 ■ EMPLOYEE to DEPARTMENT with optional relationship line.

d) Based on Figure 1.25, why do you think the social security number (SSN) column should not be the primary key of the EMPLOYEE table?

Answer: The requirement for a primary key is that it is unique, not subject to updates, and not null.

Although the SSN is unique, there have been incidents (though rare) of individuals with the same SSN or individuals who had to change their SSN. It is conceivable to have an employee without a SSN assigned yet (e.g., a legal alien with a work permit), hence the column is null. There is a myriad of reasons for not using a SSN, therefore it's best to create a surrogate or artificial key.

1.2.3 ANSWERS

a) Figures 1.26 and 1.27 depict the logical and physical model of a fictional movie rental database. What differences do you notice between the following entity relationship diagram and the physical schema diagram?

Answer: You can spot a number of differences between the logical model (entity relational diagram) and the physical model (schema diagram). While some logical and physical models are identical, these figures exhibit distinguishing differences you may find in the real world.

The entity name of the logical model is singular versus plural for the table name on the physical model. Some table names have special prefixes that denote the type of application the table belongs to. For example, if a table belongs to the purchase order system, it may be prefixed with PO_; if it belongs to the accounts payable system, the prefix is AP_; and so on. In the logical model, the spaces are allowed for table and column names. Typically, in Oracle implementations, table names are defined in uppercase and use the underscore (_) character to separate words.

Although the logical model may include the datatypes, here the datatype (such as DATE, VARCHAR2, NUMBER) shows on the physical model only. The physical model also indicates if a column allows NULL values.

The attribute and column names differ between the two models. For example, the RATING attribute changed to RATING_CD, which indicates the values are encoded such as for example "PG" rather than a descriptive "Parental Guidance" value. Designers create or follow established naming conventions and abbreviations for consistency. Naming conventions can help describe the type of values stored in the column.

The STOCK_QTY is another example of using the abbreviation QTY to express that the column holds a quantity of copies. Notice this column is absent from the logical model; it is a *derived column*. The quantity of movies for an individual movie title could be determined from the MOVIE_COPIES table. The database designer deliberately denormalized the table by adding this column. This simplifies any queries that determine how many copies of this particular title exist. Rather than issuing another query that counts the number of rows in the MOVIE_COPIES for the specific title, this column can be queried. Adding a derived column to a table requires that the value stay in sync with the data in the related table (MOVIE_COPIES in this case). The synchronization can be accomplished by writing a program that is executed from the end-user's screen. Alternatively, the developer could write a PL/SQL trigger on the table that automatically updates the STOCK_QTY value whenever a new row is added or deleted on the MOVIE_

COPIES table for each individual title. (For an example of a table trigger, refer to Chapter 12, "Create, Alter, and Drop Tables.")

The schema diagram prominently exhibits columns that did not exist in the logical data model, namely CREATED_DATE, MODIFIED_DATE, CREATED_BY, and MODIFIED_BY. Collectively these columns are sometimes referred to as "audit columns." They keep information about when a row was created and last changed together with the respective user that executed this action.

On the logical data model the relationship is labeled in both directions. On the physical model, the name of the foreign key constraint between the tables is listed instead. You may find that some physical models depict no label at all. There are no set standards for how a physical or logical model must graphically look and therefore the diagrams produced by various software vendors that offer diagramming tools not only look different, they also allow a number of different display options.

LAB 1.2 SELF-REVIEW QUESTIONS

In order to test your progress, you should be able to answer the following questions.

1) An entity relationship diagram depicts entities, attributes, and tables.
    a) _____ True
    b) _____ False

2) The crow's foot depicts the M of a 1:M relationship.
    a) _____ True
    b) _____ False

3) Repeating groups are a violation of the first normal form.
    a) _____ True
    b) _____ False

4) The logical model is derived from the schema diagram.
    a) _____ True
    b) _____ False

5) The concept of denormalization deals with eliminating redundancy.
    a) _____ True
    b) _____ False

6) When you issue a SQL statement, you are concerned with the logical design of the database.
    a) _____ True
    b) _____ False

7) In a mandatory relationship, null values are not allowed in the foreign key column.
    a) _____ True
    b) _____ False

8) A nonidentifying relationship means that the foreign key is propagated as a nonkey attribute in the child entity or child table.
    a) _____ True
    b) _____ False

Answers appear in Appendix A, Section 1.2.

LAB 1.3

THE STUDENT SCHEMA DIAGRAM

LAB OBJECTIVES

After this lab, you will be able to:

✔ Understand the STUDENT Schema Diagram and Identify Table Relationships

---

Throughout this series of Oracle Interactive Workbooks, the database for a school's computer education program is used as a case study upon which all exercises are based. If you have worked through the previous two labs, you know that the schema diagram is a model of data that reflects the relationships among data in a database. The name of the case study schema diagram is STUDENT. Before you begin to write SQL statements against the database, it is important to familiarize yourself with the diagram. You can find this graphical representation in Appendix D, "Student Database Schema."

In this book you will be frequently referring to the STUDENT schema diagram shown in Appendix D, "STUDENT Database Schema." Rather than flipping back and forth, you may find it more convenient to print out the schema diagram from the companion Web site of this book located at http://www.phptr.com/rischert.

THE STUDENT TABLE

Examine the STUDENT schema diagram and locate the STUDENT table. This table contains data about individual students, such as their name, address, employer, and date they registered in the program.

DATATYPES

Next to each column name in the diagram you find the datatype of the column. Each column contains a different kind of data, which can be classified by a datatype. You will notice that the FIRST_NAME column is of datatype VAR-CHAR2(25). This means that a variable length of (with a maximum of 25) alphanumeric characters (letters or numbers) may be stored in this column. Another datatype, the CHAR datatype, also stores alphanumeric data, but is a fixed-length datatype and pads any unused space in the column with blanks until it reaches the defined column length. The STUDENT_ID column is of datatype NUMBER with a maximum number of eight integer digits and no decimal place digits; the column is the primary key as denoted with the "(PK)" symbol. Oracle also provides a DATE datatype (as seen on the CREATED_DATE and MODIFIED_DATE columns) that stores both the date and time. You will learn more about the various datatypes in the next chapter.

Next to each column, the schema diagram indicates if a column allows NULL values. A NULL value is an unknown value. A space or value of zero is not the same as NULL. When a column in a row is defined as allowing NULL values, it means that a column does not need to contain a value. When a column is defined as NOT NULL it must always contain a value.

You will observe that the STUDENT table does not show the city and state. This information can be looked up via the foreign key column ZIP as indicated with the "(FK)" symbol after the column name. The ZIP column is a NOT NULL column and requires that every student row have a corresponding zip code entered.

THE COURSE TABLE

The COURSE table lists all the available courses that a student may take. The primary key of the table is the COURSE_NO column. The DESCRIPTION column shows the course description and the COST column lists the dollar amount charged for the enrollment in the course. The PREREQUISITE column displays the course number, which must be taken as a prerequisite to this course. This column is a foreign key column and its values refer back the COURSE_NO column. Only valid COURSE_NO values may be listed in this column. The relationship line of the COURSE table to itself represents a *recursive* or *self-referencing relationship*.

RECURSIVE RELATIONSHIP

As the term recursive or self-referencing relationship implies, a column in the COURSE table refers back to another column in the same table. The PREREQUISITE column refers back to the COURSE_NO column, which provides the list of acceptable values (also referred to as a *domain*) for the PREREQUISITE column. Because the relationship is optional, the foreign key column PREREQUISITE column allows null. Recursive relationships are always optional relationships; otherwise, there is no starting point in the hierarchy.

COURSE_NO	DESCRIPTION	PREREQUISITE	...
10	DP Overview		...
20	Intro to Computers		...
100	Hands-On Windows	20	...
140	Structured Analysis	20	...
25	Intro to Programming	140	...
...	...	...	...

Figure 1.32 ■ Data from the COURSE table.

Figure 1.32 lists an excerpt of data from the COURSE table. Notice that the courses with the COURSE_NO column values of 10 and 20 do not have a value in the PREREQUISITE column, those are the courses which a student must take to be able to take any subsequent courses (unless equivalent experience can be substituted). Course number 20 is a prerequisite course for course number 100, Hands-On-Windows, and course number 140, Structured Analysis. You will explore more about the intricacies of recursive relationships in Chapter 15, "Advanced SQL Queries."

THE SECTION TABLE

The SECTION TABLE includes all the individual sections a course may have. An individual course may have zero, one, or many sections, each of which can be taught at different rooms, times, and by different instructors. The primary key of the table is the SECTION_ID. The foreign key that links back to the COURSE table is the COURSE_NO column. The SECTION_NO column identifies the individual section number. For example, for the first section of a course, it contains the number 1; the second section lists the number 2, and so on. The two columns, COURSE_NO and SECTION_NO, also uniquely identify a row, but SECTION_ID has been created instead. This SECTION_ID column is called a surrogate key because it does not have any meaning to the user.

The column START_DATE_TIME shows the date and time the section meets for the first time. The LOCATION column lists the classroom. The CAPACITY column shows the maximum number of students that may enroll in this section. The INSTRUCTOR_ID column is another foreign key column within the SECTION table; it links back to the INSTRUCTOR table. The relationship between the SECTION and the INSTRUCTOR table indicates that an instructor must always be assigned to a section. The INSTRUCTOR_ID column of the SECTION table may never be null and when you read the relationship from the opposite end, you can say that an individual instructor may teach zero, one, or multiple sections.

The relationship line leading from the COURSE table to the SECTION table means that a course may have zero, one, or multiple sections. Conversely, every individual section *must* have a corresponding row in the COURSE table.

Relationships between tables are based on *business rules*. In this case, the business rule is that a course can exist without a section, but a section cannot exist unless it is assigned to a course. As mentioned, this is indicated with the bar (|) on the other end of the relationship line. Most of the child relationships on the schema diagram are considered mandatory relationships (with two exceptions); this dictates that the foreign key columns in the child table must contain a value (must be NOT NULL) and that value must correspond to a row in the parent table via its primary key value.

THE INSTRUCTOR TABLE

The INSTRUCTOR table lists information related to an individual instructor, such as name, address, phone, and zip code. The ZIP column is the foreign key column to the ZIPCODE table. The relationship between the INSTRUCTOR and the ZIPCODE is an optional relationship so a null value in the ZIP column is allowed. For a given ZIP column value there is one and only one value in the ZIPCODE table. For a given ZIP value in the ZIPCODE table you may find zero, one, or many of the same value in the INSTRUCTOR table. Another foreign key relationship exists to the SECTION table: an instructor may teach zero, one, or multiple sections and an individual section can be taught by one and only one instructor.

THE ZIPCODE TABLE

The primary key of ZIPCODE is the ZIP column. For an individual zip code it allows you to look up the corresponding CITY and STATE column values. The datatype of this column is VARCHAR2 and not a NUMBER, as it allows you to enter leading zeros. Both the STUDENT and the INSTRUCTOR table reference the ZIPCODE table. The relationship between the ZIPCODE and STUDENT tables is mandatory: For every ZIP value in the STUDENT table there must be a corresponding value in the ZIPCODE table, and for one given zip code, there may be zero, one, or multiple students with that zip code. In contrast, the relationship between the INSTRUCTOR and ZIPCODE table is optional; the ZIP column of the INSTRUCTOR table may be null.

WHAT ABOUT DELETE OPERATIONS?

Referential integrity does not allow deletion in a parent table of a primary key value that exists in a child table as a foreign key value. This would create orphan rows in the child table. There are many ways to handle deletes and you will learn about this topic and the effects of the deletes on other tables in Chapter 10, "Insert, Update, and Delete."

THE ENROLLMENT TABLE

The ENROLLMENT table is an intersection table between the STUDENT and the SECTION table. It lists the students enrolled in the various sections. The primary key of the table is a composite primary key consisting of the STUDENT_ID and

SECTION_ID columns. This unique combination does not allow a student to register for the same section twice. The ENROLL_DATE column contains the date the student registered for the section and the FINAL_GRADE column lists the student's final grade. The final grade is to be computed from individual grades such as quizzes, homework assignments, and so on.

The relationship line between the ENROLLMENT and STUDENT tables indicates that one student may be enrolled in zero, one, or many sections. For one row of the ENROLLMENT table you can find one and only one corresponding row in the STUDENT table. The relationship between the ENROLLMENT and SECTION table shows that a section may have zero, one, or multiple enrollments. A single row in the ENROLLMENT table always links back to one and only one row in the SECTION table.

THE GRADE_TYPE TABLE

The GRADE_TYPE table is a lookup table for other tables as it relates to grade information. The table's primary key is the GRADE_TYPE_CODE column that lists the unique category of grade, such as MT, HW, PA, and so on. The DESCRIPTION column describes the abbreviated code. For example, for the GRADE_TYPE_CODE of MT you will find the description Midterm, for HW you see Homework.

THE GRADE TABLE

This table lists the grades a student received for an individual section. The primary key columns are STUDENT_ID, SECTION_ID, GRADE_TYPE_CODE, and GRADE_CODE_OCCURRENCE. For an individual student you will find the all the grades related to the section the student is enrolled in. For example, the listed grades in the table may include the midterm grade, individual quizzes, final examination grade, and so on. For some grades (e.g., quizzes, homework assign-

STUDENT_ID	SECTION_ID	GRADE_ TYPE_ CODE	GRADE_ CODE_ OCCURRENCE	NUMERIC_ GRADE	...
221	104	FI	1	77	...
221	104	HM	1	76	...
221	104	HM	2	76	...
221	104	HM	3	86	...
221	104	HM	4	96	...
221	104	MT	1	90	...
221	104	PA	1	83	...
221	104	QZ	1	84	...
221	104	QZ	2	83	...
...	...	...	...	...	...

Figure 1.33 ■ Data from the GRADE table.

ments) there may be multiple grades and the sequence number is shown in the GRADE_CODE_OCCURRENCE column. Figure 1.33 displays an excerpt of data from the GRADE table. The NUMERIC_GRADE column lists the actual grade received. This grade may be converted to a letter grade with the help of the GRADE_CONVERSION table discussed later.

From the relationship between the ENROLLMENT and GRADE table, you can learn that rows only exist in the GRADE table if the student is actually enrolled in the section listed in the ENROLLMENT table. In other words, it is not possible for a student to have grades for a section in which he or she is not enrolled. The foreign key columns STUDENT_ID and SECTON_ID from the ENROLLMENT table enforce this relationship.

THE GRADE_TYPE_WEIGHT TABLE

The GRADE_TYPE_WEIGHT table aids in computation of the final grade a student receives for an individual section. This table lists how the final grade for an individual section is computed. For example, the midterm may constitute 50 percent of the final grade, all the quizzes 10 percent, and the final examination 40 percent. If there are multiple grades for a given GRADE_TYPE_CODE, the lowest grade may be dropped if the column DROP_LOWEST contains the value "Y". The final grade is determined by using the individual grades of the student and section in the GRADE table in conjunction with this table. This computed final grade value is stored in the FINAL_GRADE column of the ENROLLMENT table discussed previously. (The FINAL_GRADE column is a derived column. As mentioned, the values to compute this number are available in the GRADE and GRADE_TYPE_WEIGHT tables, but because the computation of this value is complex, it is stored to simplify queries.)

The primary key of this table consists of the SECTION_ID and GRADE_TYPE_CODE columns. A particular GRADE_TYPE_CODE value may exist zero, one, or multiple times in the GRADE_TYPE_WEIGHT table. For every row of the GRADE_TYPE_WEIGHT table you will find one and only one corresponding GRADE_TYPE_CODE value in the GRADE_TYPE table.

The relationship between the GRADE_TYPE_WEIGHT table and the SECTION table indicates that a section may have zero, one, or multiple rows in the GRADE_TYPE_WEIGHT table for a given SECTION_ID value. For one SECTION_ID value in the GRADE_TYPE_WEIGHT table there must always be one and only one corresponding value in the SECTION table.

THE GRADE_CONVERSION TABLE

The purpose of the GRADE_CONVERSION table is to convert a number grade to a letter grade. The table does not have any relationship with any other tables. The column LETTER_GRADE contains the unique grades, such as A+, A, A−, B, and so forth. For each of these letter grades, there is an equivalent number range. For example, for the letter B, the range is 83 through 86 and is listed in the MIN_GRADE and MAX_GRADE columns.

You can find the individual table and column descriptions of all the tables listed in the STUDENT schema diagram in Appendix E, "Table and Column Descriptions."

LAB 1.3 EXERCISES

1.3.1 UNDERSTAND THE SCHEMA DIAGRAM AND IDENTIFY TABLE RELATIONSHIPS

a) What does the STUDENT schema diagram represent?

b) Does the STUDENT schema diagram tell you where a student lives? Explain.

c) What four columns are common to all tables in the STUDENT schema diagram?

d) What is the primary key of the COURSE table?

e) How many primary keys does the ENROLLMENT table have? Name the column(s).

f) How many foreign keys does the SECTION table have?

g) Will a foreign key column in a table accept any data value? Explain using the STUDENT and ZIPCODE tables.

h) If the relationship between the ZIPCODE and STUDENT tables were optional, what would have to change in the STUDENT table?

i) From what domain of values (what column in what table) do you think the PREREQUISITE column of the COURSE table gets its values?

j) Explain the relationship(s) the ENROLLMENT table has to other table(s).

LAB 1.3 EXERCISE ANSWERS

1.3.1 ANSWERS

a) What does the STUDENT schema diagram represent?

Answer: The STUDENT schema diagram is a graphical representation of tables in a relational database.

A schema diagram is a useful tool during the software development lifecycle. English-like words should be used to name tables and columns so that anyone, whether developer or end-user, can look at a schema diagram and grasp the meaning of data, and the relationships among them, represented there. Developers study it to understand the design of a database, long before they put hands to keyboard to develop a system, and end-users can use it to understand how their data is stored.

b) Does the STUDENT schema diagram tell you where a student lives? Explain.

Answer: No. The STUDENT schema diagram tells you how data is organized in a relational database: the names of tables, the columns in those tables, and the relationship among them. It cannot tell you what actual data looks like. You use the SQL language to interact with a relational database to view, manipulate, and store the data in the tables.

c) What four columns are common to all tables in the STUDENT schema diagram?

Answer: The four columns are CREATED_BY, CREATED_DATE, MODIFIED_BY, and MODIFIED_DATE.

Database tables are often created with columns similar to these four to create an audit trail. These columns are designed to identify who first created or last modified a row of a table and when the action occurred. You will typically find these columns only on the physical schema diagram, not on the logical model. Some of these values in the columns can be filled in automatically by writing triggers. You will see an example of a table trigger in Chapter 12, "Create, Alter, and Drop

Tables." (Triggers are described in further detail in the *Oracle PL/SQL Interactive Workbook* by Benjamin Rosenzweig and Elena Silvestrova; Prentice Hall, 2003.)

d) What is the primary key of the COURSE table?

Answer: The primary key of the COURSE table is the column COURSE_NO.

You can identify the primary key with the "PK" symbol listed next to the column. In general a primary key uniquely identifies a row in a table, and the column or columns of the primary key are defined as NOT NULL.

e) How many primary keys does the ENROLLMENT table have? Name the column(s).

Answer: A table can have only one primary key. The primary key of the ENROLLMENT table consists of the two columns STUDENT_ID and SECTION_ID.

As mentioned earlier, a primary key uniquely identifies a single row in a table. In the case of the ENROLLMENT table, two columns uniquely identify a row and create a composite primary key.

Looking at the schema diagram you also notice that these two columns are also foreign keys. The STUDENT_ID column is the foreign key to the STUDENT table and the SECTION_ID is the foreign key to the SECTION table. Both foreign key relationships are identifying relationships.

f) How many foreign keys does the SECTION table have?

Answer: Two. The foreign keys of the SECTION table are COURSE_NO and INSTRUCTOR_ID.

g) Will a foreign key column in a table accept any data value? Explain using the STUDENT and ZIPCODE tables.

Answer: No. A foreign key must use the values of the primary key it references as its domain of values.

The ZIP column is the primary key in the ZIPCODE table. The STUDENT table references this column with the foreign key ZIP column. Only values that exist in the ZIP column of the ZIPCODE table can be valid values for the ZIP column of the STUDENT table. If you attempt to create a row or change an existing row in the STUDENT table with a zip code not found in the ZIPCODE table, the foreign key constraint on the STUDENT table will reject it.

In general, a foreign key is defined as being a column, or columns, in the child table. This column refers back to the primary key of another table, referred to as the parent table.

The primary key values are the domain of values for the foreign key column. A *domain* is a set of values that shows the possible values a column can have. The primary key values of the parent table are the only acceptable values that may appear in the foreign key column in the other table. (Domains are not only used in context with primary key and foreign key relationships, but can also be used for a list of values that may not be stored in a table. For example, common domains include Yes/No, Gender: Male/Female/Unknown, Weekday: Sun/Mon/Tue/Wed/Thu/Fri/Sat.)

h) If the relationship between the ZIPCODE and STUDENT tables were optional, what would have to change in the STUDENT table?

Answer: The foreign key column ZIP in the STUDENT table would have to be defined as allowing NULL values. It is currently defined as NOT NULL. The relationship should be indicated as optional instead of mandatory as shown in Figure 1.34.

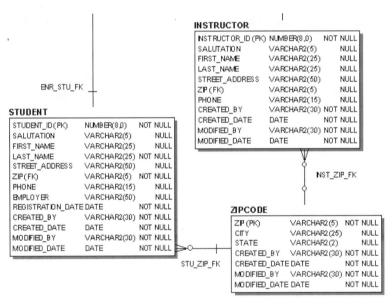

Figure 1.34 ■ The relationships of the ZIPCODE table.

There is such an optional relationship between the INSTRUCTOR and ZIPCODE tables. All the nonnull values of ZIP in the INSTRUCTOR table must be found in the ZIPCODE table.

i) From what domain of values (what column in what table) do you think the PRE-REQUISITE column of the COURSE table gets its values?

Answer: From the COURSE_NO column in the COURSE table.

In this case, the PREREQUISITE column refers back to the COURSE_NO column, which provides the domain of values for the PREREQUISITE column. A prerequisite is valid only if it is also a valid course number in the COURSE table. This relationship is shown in Figure 1.35.

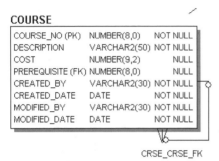

COURSE

COURSE_NO (PK)	NUMBER(8,0)	NOT NULL
DESCRIPTION	VARCHAR2(50)	NOT NULL
COST	NUMBER(9,2)	NULL
PREREQUISITE (FK)	NUMBER(8,0)	NULL
CREATED_BY	VARCHAR2(30)	NOT NULL
CREATED_DATE	DATE	NOT NULL
MODIFIED_BY	VARCHAR2(30)	NOT NULL
MODIFIED_DATE	DATE	NOT NULL

CRSE_CRSE_FK

Figure 1.35 ■ **The self-referencing relationship of the COURSE table.**

j) Explain the relationship(s) the ENROLLMENT table has to other table(s).

Answer: The STUDENT table and the SECTION table are the parent tables of the EN-ROLLMENT table. The ENROLLMENT table is one of the parent tables of the GRADE table.

As shown in Figure 1.36, the relationship between the STUDENT and SECTION tables signifies a student may be enrolled in zero, one, or many sections. One individual student can be enrolled in one specific section only once, otherwise the unique combination of the two columns in the ENROLLMENT table would be violated. The combination of these two foreign key columns represents the primary key of the ENROLLMENT table.

The relationship of the ENROLLMENT table as the parent of the GRADE table shows that for an individual student and her or his enrolled section there may be zero, one, or many grades. The primary key columns of the ENROLLMENT table (STUDENT_ID and SECTION_ID) are foreign keys in the GRADE table that become part of the GRADE table's composite primary key. Therefore, only enrolled students may have rows in the GRADE as indicated with the optional line. If a row in GRADE exists, it must be for one specific enrollment in a section for one specific student.

Note: In some cases, the foreign keys become part of a table's primary key, as in the ENROLLMENT or the GRADE table. If a composite primary key contains many columns (perhaps more than four or five), a surrogate key may be considered for simplicity. The decision to use a surrogate key is based on the database designer's understanding of how data is typically accessed by the application programs.

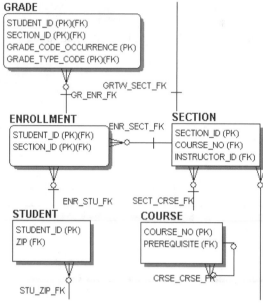

Figure 1.36 ■ The relationships of the ENROLLMENT table.

LAB 1.3 SELF-REVIEW QUESTIONS

In order to test your progress, you should be able to answer the following questions.

1) What role(s) does the STUDENT_ID column play in the GRADE table? Check all that apply.
   a) _____ Part of composite primary key
   b) _____ Primary key
   c) _____ Foreign key

2) The GRADE_TYPE table does not allow values to be NULL in any column.
   a) _____ True
   b) _____ False

3) The number of columns in a table matches the number of rows in that table.
   a) _____ True
   b) _____ False

4) The SECTION table has no foreign key columns.
   a) _____ True
   b) _____ False

5) A table can contain 10 million rows.
   a) _____ True
   b) _____ False

6) A primary key may contain NULL values.
   a) _____ True
   b) _____ False

7) A column name must be unique within a table.
   a) _____ True
   b) _____ False

LAB
1.3

8) If a table is a child table in three different one-to-many relationships, how many foreign key columns does it have?
   a) _____ One
   b) _____ Exactly three
   c) _____ Three or more

9) Referential integrity requires the relationship between foreign key and primary key to maintain values from the same domain.
   a) _____ True
   b) _____ False

10) A foreign key may be NULL.
    a) _____ True
    b) _____ False

11) Orphan rows are not allowed in the relational model.
    a) _____ True
    b) _____ False

Answers appear in Appendix A, Section 1.3.

CHAPTER 1

TEST YOUR THINKING

The projects in this section are meant to have you utilize all of the skills that you have acquired throughout this chapter. The answers to these projects can be found at the companion Web site to this book, located at *http://www.phptr.com/rischert*.

Visit the Web site periodically to share and discuss your answers.

In this chapter you learned about data, how data is organized in tables, and how the relationships among it is depicted in a schema diagram. Based on your newly acquired knowledge, design a schema diagram based on the fictional ACME Construction Company. Draw on your own work experience to design the following components.

1) Draw boxes for these three tables: EMPLOYEE, POSITION, and DEPARTMENT.
2) Create at least three columns for each of the tables and designate a primary key for each table.
3) Create relationships among the tables that make sense to you. At least one table should have a self-referencing relationship. Hint: Be sure to include the necessary foreign key columns.
4) Think about which columns should NOT allow NULL values.

CHAPTER 2
SQL: THE BASICS

Now that you are familiar with the concepts of databases and schema diagrams, you are ready to start with hands-on exercises. You will learn the basics of SQL*Plus, the software tool that allows you to execute statements against the Oracle database. After you familiarize yourself with SQL*Plus you will be ready to write SQL statements, or queries, to retrieve the data. SQL statements can range from very simple to highly complex; they can be a few words long, or a few hundred words long. In this chapter, you begin by writing simple SQL statements, but you will be able to build longer, more complex SQL queries very quickly.

LAB 2.1

THE SQL*PLUS ENVIRONMENT

> ## LAB OBJECTIVES
>
> After this lab, you will be able to:
>
> ✔ Identify Oracle's Client/Server Software
> ✔ Login and Logout of SQL*Plus

Oracle's software runs on many different operating systems and hardware environments. You can use the SQL*Plus software under three different architectural configurations: as a stand-alone machine, in a client–server setup, or as *i*SQL*Plus within a three-tier architecture. Another piece of Oracle software, called SQL*Net (Version 7), Net8 (Version 8), or Oracle Net (Version 9*i*), provides the required communication protocol to the server.

STAND-ALONE ENVIRONMENT

SQL*Plus may be run in a stand-alone environment where both the SQL*Plus client software and the Oracle database software reside on the same physical machine. This is the case when you install both the Oracle database server and the SQL*Plus software on your individual computer.

CLIENT–SERVER

A common setup is a client–server environment also referred to as two-tier architecture, where a client communicates with the server. In this type of environment, Oracle's SQL*Plus tool resides on a client computer such as a PC or Unix workstation; the Oracle RDBMS software resides on a server. Figure 2.1 shows such a client–server architecture.

The client sends SQL statements to the server and the server responds back with the result set. The job of the database server involves listening and managing many clients' requests, because in this configuration there are often multiple client machines involved.

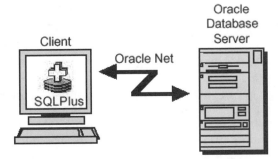

Figure 2.1 ■ Client–server architecture.

Instead of Oracle's SQL*Plus program, the client machine may run any other program with the ability to execute SQL statements against a database (e.g., Visual Basic™ or a custom-build Java program. For the client computer's programs to communicate with the Oracle database server, the individual client machine is typically configured with the Oracle Net software or the client may establish an Open Database Connectivity (ODBC) connection.

THREE-TIER ARCHITECTURE

Starting with Oracle 8.1.7 you can use the *i*SQL*Plus interface in a Web browser to access the Oracle database. It performs the same actions as SQL*Plus. The advantage of *i*SQL*Plus is that you don't need to install and configure the SQL*Plus program or Oracle Net software on your client machine. As long as you use a compatible browser on your machine and know the URL of the Oracle HTTP server, you can access the database. As with any connection, you obviously need a valid user account and password.

Figure 2.2 shows the three-tiered architecture of an *i*SQL*Plus configuration. The first tier is the client's Web browser and the middle tier is the Oracle HTTP server (Web server) that receives requests from the browser and forwards them via Oracle Net to the third tier, the Oracle database server. The Oracle HTTP server re-

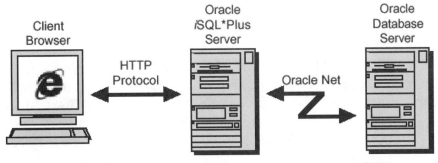

Figure 2.2 ■ Three-tier architecture.

turns results from the database server back to the Web browser for display. The three tiers may be on one machine but are typically on three different ones.

SQL AND THE ORACLE DATABASE SERVER

In the midst of all this software lies the SQL language. SQL commands are sent from the client software, also known as the *front end,* to the server, or *back end.* These commands send instructions to the server to tell it what services to provide. The server responds by sending back a result to the client, where it is displayed by the client software. Figure 2.3 shows a SQL statement that queries the DESCRIPTION column of the COURSE table. The SQL statement is sent to the Oracle server and the result is displayed by SQL*Plus.

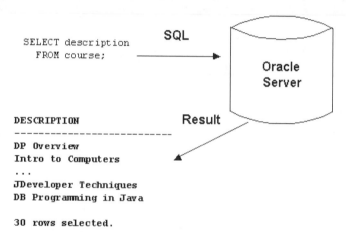

Figure 2.3 ■ SQL and the Oracle database server.

USER ID AND PASSWORD

To connect to the database and communicate via SQL*Plus, you must have a user ID that has been created for you. For the purposes of all examples in this workbook, you use the user name STUDENT and the password LEARN. Note that the user ID and password are not case sensitive.

If you have not yet created the STUDENT schema according to the instructions on the companion Web site located at http://www.phptr. com/rischert, you will not be able to log in with the STUDENT user ID and the LEARN password. You may want to continue to read through this lab first, and then create the STUDENT schema and lastly perform the exercises in this lab.

ACCESSING THE ORACLE DATABASE SERVER

You can access the Oracle server through various front-end tools. This workbook will discuss the use of Oracle's own SQL*Plus software (available as a graphical Windows environment and as a command line interface) and the browser-based *i*SQL*Plus.

This lab will teach you some of the basics of SQL*Plus as this tool is almost always found in any Oracle database environment. The log on screens for SQL*Plus and the browser-based *i*SQL*Plus are slightly different, but easily understood. You can use either SQL*Plus or *i*SQL*Plus to execute your SQL statements or perhaps you chose another front-end query tool that also allows you to enter SQL commands. (The companion Web site to this book lists other alternative query tools.) Differences between SQL*Plus or *i*SQL*Plus are pointed out to you as you work through the book. You can assume that with very few exceptions the functionality of *i*SQL*Plus and SQL*Plus are very similar if not identical.

When working through this workbook you have a choice to use either a browser and access iSQL*Plus or use the SQL*Plus software installed on your machine.

SQL*PLUS CLIENT FOR WINDOWS

If you have the SQL*Plus program installed on your Windows machine and you access the program, you will see the Log On dialog box displayed similar to Figure 2.4.

Enter as the User Name STUDENT and as the Password LEARN.

If your database is installed on the same machine as your SQL*Plus client, you don't need to enter a value in the Host String field. If you are connecting to a remote Oracle database, enter the Oracle Net connection string supplied to you by

```
Log On

User Name:      [                    ]

Password:       [                    ]

Host String:    [                    ]

        OK              Cancel
```

Figure 2.4 ■ **Windows graphical user interface log on dialog box.**

your Oracle database administrator and recorded in your TNSNAMES.ORA file. You will learn more about this special file later.

Figure 2.5 shows how your screen looks once you have successfully connected to the server. Effectively, you have established a connection with the Oracle database as the user STUDENT. The client and the server may now communicate with each other.

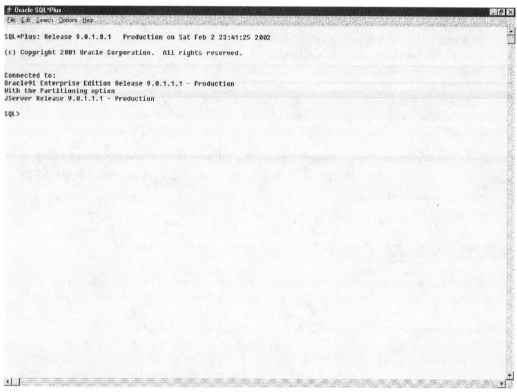

Figure 2.5 ■ **SQL*Plus prompt.**

When you see the SQL> command prompt, SQL*Plus is ready to accept your commands and you may begin to type. This is the default prompt for SQL*Plus.

To log out, either type EXIT or QUIT and press enter. Alternatively, you can choose Exit from the File menu or simply use your mouse to close the window.

LOG ON TO THE SQL*PLUS BROWSER VERSION: *i*SQL*PLUS

Instead of the SQL*Plus software program, you can also use the Web-based version called *i*SQL*Plus. To access the *i*SQL*Plus interface through your Web browser, enter the URL address of the server. A log on dialog similar to Figure 2.6 will appear. When you install the *i*SQL*Plus version in your environment you must know the URL for the server. In Figure 2.6, the URL is http://scooby:7778/isqlplus and will obviously be different for your individual installation.

For Oracle 9.2, a URL is in the form of http://machine_name.domain:port/isqlplus. For example, http://mymachine.acme.com:7778/isqlplus is a valid URL format. Previous Oracle versions did not require the port number. If you are unsure about your specific port number, refer to the port and listen directives in the httpd.config file on the Web server or try the default port 7778. In Figure 2.6, you notice that the domain is not shown because iSQL*Plus is located on a local machine.

Enter the user ID and password in the appropriate boxes. You don't need to supply the Connection Identifier (also called Host string) if your URL already points to the correct database instance.

Figure 2.7 displays the screen you see once you have successfully logged in. You notice the *i*SQL*Plus Work Screen and the message "Connected." below the boxes and buttons.

At the Enter statements text box, also referred to as the input area, you can enter commands. If you want to run a script (e.g., the script you need to execute to

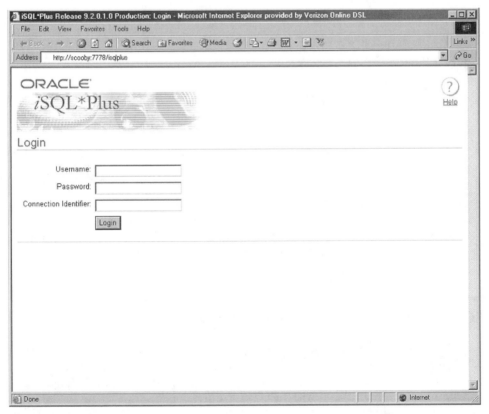

Figure 2.6 ■ *i*SQL*Plus log on screen.

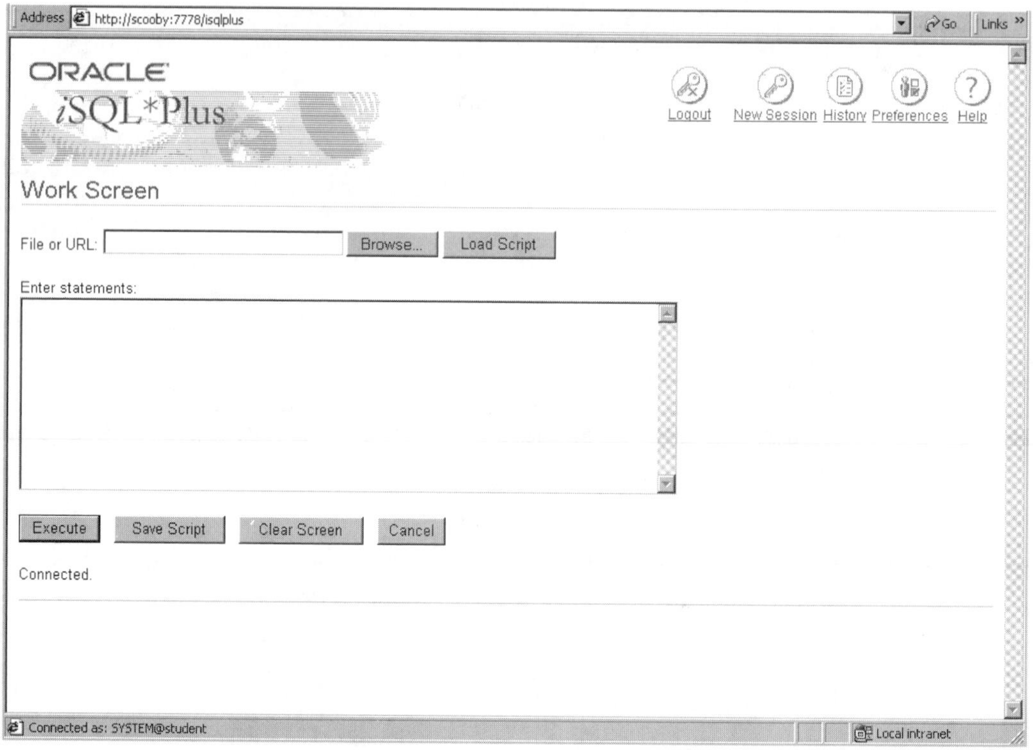

Figure 2.7 ■ *i*SQL*Plus work screen.

generate the STUDENT schema), you can enter the path and name of the script or click the Browse... button to locate the script. Once the script is loaded into the input area, you can edit the script or simply click the Execute button to execute the script.

*i*SQL*Plus has three options to show output. By default, the result displays in the Work Screen area below the input area. You can change this by clicking on the Preferences icon and choosing a different Interface Option. Alternatively, you can choose the New Window option, which shows the result in a new browser window, or you can choose the File option, which saves the output in an HTML format. When prompted for a file name, give it a .htm or .html extension.

To log out and return to the Log In screen, click on the Log Out icon.

SQL*PLUS IN THE UNIX/LINUX ENVIRONMENT

In place of a graphical user interface such as SQL*Plus for Windows or *i*SQL*Plus, you may use a command line interface. A command line interface is available with every Oracle version, no matter what operating system. In Figure 2.8 you see the command line interface for a Linux operating system installation. All SQL*Plus and SQL commands operate for this interface just the same. Note that your editor, as well as the cut and paste commands, may be different.

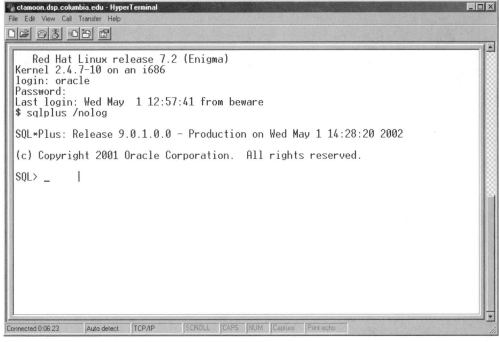

Figure 2.8 ■ **Command line-based SQL*Plus under the Linux operating system.**

THE REMOTE DATABASE AND COMMON
LOG-ON PROBLEMS

Often the database resides on a machine other than your client machine, or you have a choice of accessing different database servers. In these cases you need to supply the name of the database in the Host String box of the Log On dialog box (see Figure 2.9) or the Connection Identifier box in *i*SQL*Plus. For example, to connect to a database called ITCHY you have enter this name in the Host String box.

Figure 2.9 ■ **SQL*Plus Windows Graphical User Interface log on dialog box.**

The host string matches an entry in a file called TNSNAMES.ORA, which lists the database's IP address (or the machine name) and database instance name.

Essentially, the TNSNAMES.ORA file is a file containing a list of databases with their respective technical connection information. Your database administrator can help you with the configuration and setup of this file if you have a remote database setup.

Following is an excerpt of a TNSNAMES.ORA file. The entries in your file will obviously vary. If you supply the host string ITCHY at log in, SQL*Plus will look up the ITCHY entry in the TNSNAMES.ORA file. The HOST entry shows the IP address (if you use a TCP/IP network), which is listed as 169.254.147.245. Alternatively, you can enter the machine name. The SID entry identifies the name of the Oracle instance; here the instance is called ORCL. (When you install Oracle with the default options, you will be asked to supply such an instance name (SID). A common default name is ORCL.)

```
ITCHY =
  (DESCRIPTION =
    (ADDRESS_LIST =
        (ADDRESS =
           (PROTOCOL = TCP)
           (Host = 169.254.147.245)
           (Port = 1521)
        )
    )
    (CONNECT_DATA = (SID = ORCL)
    )
  )
```

Your TNSNAMES.ORA file may contain an entry called DEFAULT. If you do not supply a Host String in the log on dialog box, you will be connected to the database listed under the DEFAULT option. Note, depending on your individual setup, you may at times need to specify or omit the .WORLD suffix next to the host name (such as ITCHY.WORLD or simply ITCHY) in the TNSNAMES.ORA file.

Typical *i*SQL*Plus log-on problems involve specifying an invalid port number (Oracle 9.2) or an invalid machine name or domain. Refer to the companion Web site of this workbook for more suggestions.

COMMON LOG-ON PROBLEMS

Although we cannot possibly list all the errors and solutions to all log-on problems, here are two very common Oracle error messages.

A TNS error usually deals with the connectivity between the server and the client. The following message is typically displayed if the host string has an invalid entry in your TNSNAMES.ORA file. Check the values and retry.

```
ORA-12154: TNS: could not resolve service name
```

The next error occurs if you entered the wrong password or user name when the Oracle server attempted to authenticate you as a valid user. Double-check the spelling of your user name, which is STUDENT and password, which is LEARN. (If you cannot log on with this ID and password, check the readme.txt file regarding the installation of the STUDENT schema.)

```
ORA-01017: invalid username/password; logon denied
```

EXITING FROM SQL*PLUS OR *i*SQL*PLUS

When you type exit, or otherwise log out, your SQL*Plus or *i*SQL*Plus client session ends, and the user STUDENT is no longer connected to the database. However, there may be other clients connected to the Oracle database; the server software continues to run, regardless of whether a client is connected to it or not.

CREATING THE STUDENT SCHEMA

Now that you know how to log on to the Oracle database using SQL*Plus or *i*SQL*Plus, this is a good time to read the readme.txt file you downloaded from the Web site located at http://www.phptr.com/rischert and create the STUDENT schema if you have not already done so.

Unless specifically mentioned, we will not differentiate between SQL*Plus and *i*SQL*Plus commands because many are almost identical. For a list of differences see Appendix C, "SQL*Plus Command Reference."

All commands in SQL*Plus require the user to press the Enter key to execute them. In iSQL*Plus you always need to press the Execute button. The reminder to press the Enter key or the Execute button will not be included in the rest of the examples and exercises in this workbook.

LAB 2.1 EXERCISES

2.1.1 IDENTIFY ORACLE'S CLIENT/SERVER SOFTWARE

a) Identify which piece of Oracle software is the client, which is the server, and how they communicate with each other.

b) What is the role of SQL between client and server?

2.1.2 LOGIN AND LOGOUT OF SQL*PLUS

a) If you do not have access to SQL*Plus, please answer the question by referring to Figure 2.5. Once you have logged into SQL*Plus (not *i*SQL*Plus) with the user ID STUDENT and password LEARN, what information does the SQL*Plus screen show you?

b) What do you learn when you type `DESCRIBE student` and press `Enter`? If you use *i*SQL*Plus, click the Execute button instead of pressing ENTER.

c) Execute the following command and describe what you see: `SHOW ALL.`

LAB 2.1 EXERCISE ANSWERS

2.1.1 ANSWERS

a) Identify which piece of Oracle software is the client, which is the server, and how they communicate with each other.

Answer: SQL*Plus or the browser displaying iSQL*Plus is the client and the Oracle RDBMS is the server. In an Oracle 9i environment Oracle Net is the protocol that facilitates the communications.

b) What is the role of SQL between client and server?

Answer: SQL commands are issued from the client, telling the server to perform specific actions. The server sends back the results of those instructions to the client software, where they are displayed.

2.1.2 ANSWERS

a) If you do not have access to SQL*Plus, please answer the question by referring to Figure 2.5. Once you have logged into SQL*Plus (not *i*SQL*Plus) with the user ID STUDENT and password LEARN, what information does the SQL*Plus screen show you?

Answer: The screen shows which version of SQL*Plus you are using, the current date and time, Oracle copyright information, the version of the Oracle database you are con-

*nected to, and the version of PL/SQL you are using. After this information is displayed
you see the SQL> command prompt. At this prompt you are able to enter commands.*

PL/SQL is another Oracle language addressed in a separate Interactive Workbook
in this series—*Oracle PL/SQL Interactive Workbook* by Benjamin Rosenzweig and
Elena Silvestrova (Prentice Hall, 2003).

b) What do you learn when you type `DESCRIBE student` and press Enter? If
you use *i*SQL*Plus, click the Execute button instead of pressing ENTER.

*Answer: You find out about the structure of the STUDENT table, specifically its column
names, whether those columns allow nulls or not, and the datatype of each column.*

To write SQL statements, you need to know a table's column names and their
datatypes. The SQL*Plus DESCRIBE command displays this information and
shows if a column does not allow null values.

Many SQL*Plus commands may be abbreviated. For instance, DESCRIBE may be
shortened to DESC. Retype the command using this abbreviation and compare
the results. Figure 2.10 displays the result of the DESCRIBE command executed in
SQL*Plus.

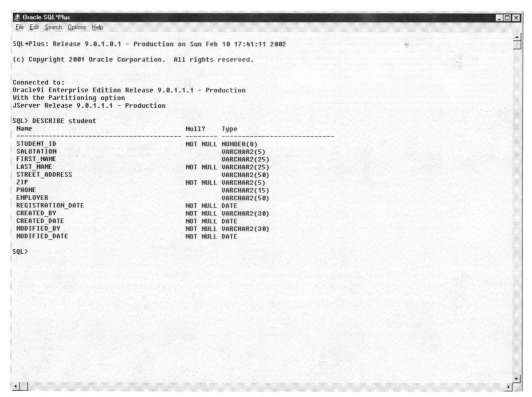

Figure 2.10 ■ Executing the SQL*Plus DESCRIBE command.

SQL*Plus is not case sensitive; the user ID, password, and SQL*Plus commands may all be entered in either upper or lowercase, or a combination of the two. Throughout this book, they are in uppercase for easy identification. In the next lab you will learn about formatting your SQL statements and when it is appropriate to capitalize words.

COMMON DATATYPES

Every column in Oracle must have a datatype, which determines what type of data can be stored. The DATE datatype is used to store date and time information. By default the display format for a date is DD-MON-YY. For example, July 4, 2003 displays as 04-JUL-03. There are a number of functions you can use to change the display format or to show the time, which you will learn about in Chapter 4, "Date and Conversion Functions."

Columns with the datatype NUMBER only allow numerical data; no text, hyphens, or dashes are allowed. A column defined as NUMBER(5,2) can have a maximum of three digits before the decimal point and two digits after the decimal point. The first digit (5) is called the *precision;* the second digit (2) is referred to as the *scale.* The smallest allowed number is –999.99 and the largest is 999.99. A column definition with a zero scale such as NUMBER(5) or NUMBER(5,0) allows integers in the range from –99,999 to 99,999.

The VARCHAR2 and CHAR datatypes store alphanumeric data (e.g., text, numbers, special characters, etc.). VARCHAR2 is the variable length datatype and the most commonly used alphanumeric datatype; its maximum size is 4,000 characters. The main difference between VARCHAR2 and CHAR is that the CHAR datatype is a fixed length datatype and any unused room is blank padded with spaces.

For example, a column defined as CHAR(10) and containing the four-character length value of JOHN in a row will have six blank characters padded at the end to make the total length 10 spaces. (If the column is stored in a VARCHAR2(10) column instead, it stores four characters only.) A CHAR column can store up to 2,000 characters. You will learn more about datatypes as you work through the exercises in this book. In Table 2.1 you find a list of Oracle's built-in datatypes.

For most SQL operations, you typically use the NUMBER, VARCHAR2, and DATE datatypes. These are the most commonly used datatypes where the vast majority of data is stored. Datatypes such as CLOB or BLOB require access through specific purpose functions in very highly specialized ways that go beyond the objectives of this workbook. In addition to the datatypes listed in Table 2.1, Oracle also has additional datatypes to support specific national character sets (e.g., NCLOB, NVARCHAR2), intermedia datatypes, and spatial (geographic) data. Oracle also gives you the ability to create your own customized object datatypes. For example, you can create a "customer order" datatype with specific properties; however, this remains a relatively infrequently used functionality with a number of restrictions.

Table 2.1 ■ Oracle's Most Commonly Used Built-In Datatypes

Datatype	Explanation
NUMBER [optional precision,[optional scale]]	Oracle stores zero, positive, and negative fixed- and floating-point numbers. The allowable values for precision are 1 to 38 and for the scale –84 to 127. If you don't specify the precision or scale, the magnitude of the number is between 1.0×10^{-130} and $9.9 \ldots 9 \times 10^{125}$ (38 nines followed by 88 zeroes) with 38 digits of precision.
VARCHAR2(size)	Variable length character string with a maximum size of 4,000 characters (or bytes). A length must always be specified.
CHAR[optional size]	Fixed character length data with maximum size of 2,000 characters; the default size is 1. Any space not used by the stored text is padded with blanks.
LONG	Character datatype with a maximum storage capacity of 2 gigabytes. LONGs are subject to a number of restrictions and Oracle recommends you convert data from this datatype to CLOBs, as the LONG datatype may be discontinued in the future.
CLOB	This stores large text objects with a maximum size of 4 gigabytes. Use this instead of the LONG datatype. Also useful for storing XML objects.
DATE	Stores date and time including seconds from January 1, 4712 BC to AD December 31, 9999.
TIMESTAMP [optional seconds precision]	Same as DATE but includes fractional seconds precision from 0 to 9 digits. The default is 6.
TIMESTAMP [optional seconds precision] WITH TIME ZONE	Same as TIMESTAMP including the time zone displacement value.
TIMESTAMP [optional seconds precision] WITH LOCAL TIME ZONE	Same as TIMESTAMP WITH TIME ZONE except time is displayed in session's time zone and stored in the database's time zone.
INTERVAL YEAR [optional year precision] TO MONTH	Period of years and months. The default precision is 2 years, with optional precision from 0 to 9 years.
INTERVAL DAY [optional day precision] TO SECOND [optional fractional seconds precision]	Period of time in days, hours, minutes, and seconds. The default day precision is 2 with acceptable values from 0 to 9. The default fractional seconds precision is 6 with acceptable values from 0 to 9.

(continued)

Table 2.1 ■ *continued*

Datatype	Explanation
ROWID	Represents the unique address of a row in a table, displayed in Hexadecimal format. Typically used in conjunction with the ROWID pseudocolumn. You will learn more about ROWIDs in Chapter 12, "Views, Indexes, and Sequences."
RAW (size)	Raw binary data with maximum length of 2,000 bytes. Useful for small binary data such as graphics.
LONG RAW	Same as RAW except holds up to 2 gigabytes. Used for binary data such as graphics, sounds, or documents. Oracle recommends that you convert LONG RAWS to binary BLOB columns as they have fewer restrictions than a LONG RAW.
BLOB	Stores unstructured binary large objects with a maximum size of 4 gigabytes. Often used for graphic images, video clips, and sounds.
BFILE	Points to large binary file stored outside of the database. Oracle can read the file only, not modify it. Oracle requires appropriate operating-system-level read permissions on the file.

Please note that the datatypes listed in Table 2.1 apply to data stored in database columns. PL/SQL has some of the same datatypes, but in some cases, PL/SQL places certain restrictions on manipulation and size. If you are working with datatypes within the PL/SQL language, please refer to the *PL/SQL Interactive Workbook* by Benjamin Rosenzweig and Elena Silvestrova for more details.

c) Execute the following command and describe what you see: SHOW ALL.

Answer: You will see a list of SQL*Plus environmental variables and their current settings. Using the SET command, many of them can be changed to suit your needs for a SQL*Plus session, which is defined as the time in between when you log in and log out of SQL*Plus. When you start your next SQL*Plus session, however, all commands will be set back to their defaults.

It is important to note here that SQL*Plus commands, such as SHOW and DE-SCRIBE, are *not* part of the SQL language. You will begin to type SQL commands using the SQL*Plus tool in the next lab.

If you use *i*SQl*Plus, you can change the environment variables by clicking the Preferences icon and Set system variables. Note that if you modify any of the settings, they take effect for subsequently executed statements, not for statements executed from the History screen that lets you recall previously issued statements.

LAB 2.1 SELF-REVIEW QUESTIONS

In order to test your progress, you should be able to answer the following questions.

1) The DESC command displays column names of a table.

   a) _____ True
   b) _____ False

2) Anyone can connect to an Oracle database as long as they have the SQL*Plus software.

   a) _____ True
   b) _____ False

3) The SQL*Plus command SHOW USER displays your login name.

   a) _____ True
   b) _____ False

4) Typing SHOW RELEASE at the prompt displays the version number of SQL*Plus you are using.

   a) _____ True
   b) _____ False

5) The COST column of the COURSE table is defined as NUMBER(9,2). The maximum cost of an individual course is 9,999,999.99.

   a) _____ True
   b) _____ False

Answers appear in Appendix A, Section 2.1.

LAB 2.2

THE ANATOMY
OF A SELECT STATEMENT

LAB OBJECTIVES

After this lab, you will be able to:

✔ Write a SQL SELECT Statement
✔ Use DISTINCT in a SQL Statement

THE SELECT STATEMENT

When you write a SQL query, it is usually to answer a question such as "How many students live in New York?" or "Where, and at what time, does the Unix class meet?" A SQL *SELECT statement,* or SQL *query,* is used to answer these questions. A SELECT statement can be broken down into a minimum of two parts: the *SELECT list* and the *FROM clause.* The SELECT list usually consists of the column or columns of a table(s) from which you want to display data. The FROM clause states on what table or tables this column or columns are found. Later in this chapter, you will learn some of the other clauses that can be used in a SELECT statement.

HOW DO YOU WRITE A SQL QUERY?

Before formulating the SELECT statement, you must first determine the table where the information is located. A study of the schema diagram reveals that the COURSE table provides descriptions of courses. (You can also refer to Appendix E, "Table and Column Descriptions.")

The following SELECT statement provides a list of course descriptions:

```
SELECT description
  FROM course
```

The SELECT list contains the single column called DESCRIPTION, which contains this information. The DESCRIPTION column is found on the COURSE table as specified in the FROM clause. When the statement is executed, the result set is a list of all the values found in the DESCRIPTION column of the COURSE table:

```
DESCRIPTION
---------------------------------------------------
DP Overview
Intro to Computers
...
JDeveloper Techniques
DB Programming in Java

30 rows selected.
```

Many of the result sets displayed throughout this workbook do not list all the rows. This is denoted with a line of ". . ." in the middle of the output. Typically, you will see the beginning and the ending rows of the result set and the number of rows returned. The resulting output of the SQL command is displayed in a bold font to easily distinguish the output from the commands you enter.

EXECUTING THE SQL STATEMENT

SQL*Plus does not require a new line for each clause, but it requires the use of a semicolon (";") at the end of each SQL statement to execute it. (Figure 2.11 shows the result of the execution of the previously mentioned SQL query in SQL*Plus.) Alternatively, the forward slash ("/") may be used on a separate line to accomplish the same. In *i*SQL*Plus a semicolon or forward slash is not required, you only need to press the Execute button:

```
SQL> SELECT description
  2    FROM course;
```

or:

```
SQL> SELECT description
  2    FROM course
  3  /
```

*The SQL*Plus commands such as DESC or SHOW USER discussed in the previous lab are not SQL commands and therefore do not require a semicolon or forward slash.*

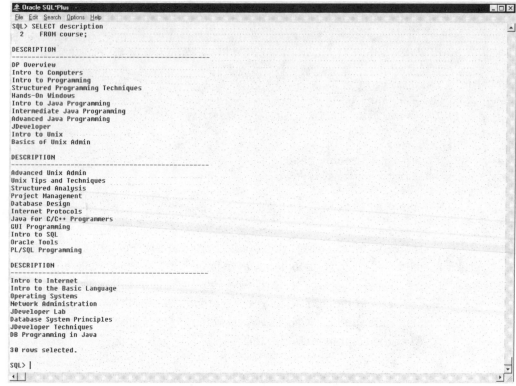

Figure 2.11 ■ Executing the SELECT statement in SQL*Plus.

RETRIEVING MULTIPLE COLUMNS

To retrieve a list of course descriptions and the cost of each course, include the COST column in the SELECT list:

```
SELECT description, cost
  FROM course
DESCRIPTION                   COST
-----------------------       ----
DP Overview                   1195
Intro to Computers            1195
...
JDeveloper Techniques         1195
DB Programming in Java

30 rows selected.
```

When you want to display more than one column in the SELECT list, separate the columns with commas. It is good practice to include a space after the comma for readability. The order of columns in a SELECT list will determine the order in which the columns are displayed in the output.

SELECTING ALL COLUMNS

You can also select all columns in a table with the asterisk (*) wildcard character. This is handy so you don't have to type all columns in the SELECT list. The columns are displayed in the order in which they are defined in the table. This is the same order you see when you use the SQL*Plus DESCRIBE command. If you execute this command you will notice that the columns wrap in SQL*Plus (not *i*SQL*Plus) as there is not sufficient room to display them in one line. You will learn how to format the output shortly.

```
SELECT *
  FROM course
```

ELIMINATING DUPLICATES WITH DISTINCT

The use of DISTINCT in the SELECT list eliminates duplicate data in the result set. The following SELECT statement retrieves the last name and the corresponding zip code for all rows of the INSTRUCTOR table.

```
SELECT last_name, zip
  FROM instructor
```

LAST_NAME	ZIP
Hanks	10015
Wojick	10025
Schorin	10025
Pertez	10035
Morris	10015
Smythe	10025
Chow	10015
Lowry	10025
Frantzen	10005
Willig	

10 rows selected.

Notice that there are 10 rows, yet only nine instructors have zip codes. Instructor Willig has a NULL value in the ZIP column. If you want to show only the distinct zip codes of the table, you write the following SELECT statement. The last row shows the NULL value.

```
SELECT DISTINCT zip
  FROM instructor
```

ZIP
10005

```
10015
10025
10035
```

```
5 rows selected.
```

By definition, a NULL is an unknown value, and a NULL does not equal another NULL. However, there are exceptions: If you write a SQL query using DISTINCT, SQL will consider a NULL value equal to another NULL value.

From Chapter 1, "SQL and Data," you already know that a primary key is always unique or distinct. Therefore, the use of DISTINCT in a SELECT list containing the primary key column(s) is unnecessary. The ZIP column in the INSTRUCTOR table is not the primary key and can therefore contain duplicate values.

DISPLAYING THE NUMBER OF ROWS RETURNED

You may notice that SQL*Plus sometimes does not show the number of rows returned by the query, but rather depends on the feedback settings for your SQL*Plus session. Typically, the feedback is set to 6 or more rows. In the previous example the feedback was set to 1, which displays the feedback line even when there is only one row returned. You will find this setting useful if your result set returns less than the default 6 rows and if any of the rows return nulls, which display as a blank. Otherwise, you may think it is not a row or value. To display the exact number of rows returned until you exit SQL*Plus, enter the SQL*Plus command:

```
SET FEEDBACK 1
```

To display your current settings use the SHOW ALL command or simply SHOW FEEDBACK. (If you want to retain certain SQL*Plus settings, you can create a login.sql file for your individual computer in a client–server setup. You can also create a glogin.sql file for all users if you want all to have the identical settings or if you use *i*SQL*Plus. See the companion Web site for more information.)

SQL STATEMENT FORMATTING CONVENTIONS

You will notice that the SQL statements presented in this and all other Oracle Interactive Workbooks in this series follow a common format. The use of uppercase for SELECT, FROM, and other Oracle keywords is for emphasis only, and distinguishes them from table and column names, which you see in the SQL statement as lowercase letters. A standard format enhances the clarity and readability of your SQL statements, and helps you detect errors more easily. Refer to Appendix B, "SQL Formatting Guide," for the formatting guidelines used throughout.

LAB 2.2 EXERCISES

2.2.1 WRITE A SQL SELECT STATEMENT

a) Write a SELECT statement to list the first and last names of all students.

b) Write a SELECT statement to list all cities, states, and zip codes.

c) Describe the result set of the following SQL statement:

```
SELECT *
   FROM grade_type
```

2.2.2 USE DISTINCT IN A SQL STATEMENT

a) Why are the result sets of each of the following SQL statements the same?

```
SELECT letter_grade
   FROM grade_conversion

SELECT DISTINCT letter_grade
   FROM grade_conversion
```

b) Explain the result set of the following SQL statement:

```
SELECT DISTINCT cost
   FROM course
```

c) Explain what happens, and why, when you execute the following SQL statement:

```
SELECT DISTINCT course_no
   FROM class
```

LAB 2.2 EXERCISE ANSWERS

2.2.1 ANSWERS

a) Write a SELECT statement to list the first and last names of all students.

Answer: The SELECT list contains the two columns that provide the first and last names of students; the FROM clause lists the STUDENT table where these columns are found.

```
SELECT first_name, last_name
  FROM student
FIRST_NAME                       LAST_NAME
------------------------------   ------------------------
George                           Eakheit
Leonard                          Millstein
...
Kathleen                         Mastandora
Angela                           Torres

268 rows selected.
```

You will also notice many rows are returned; you can examine each of the rows by scrolling up and down. There are many SET options in SQL*Plus that allow you to change the headings and the overall display of the data. As you work your way through this book you will examine and learn about the most important SQL*Plus settings.

b) Write a SELECT statement to list all cities, states, and zip codes.

Answer: The SELECT list contains the three columns that provide the city, state, and zip code; the FROM clause contains the ZIPCODE table where these columns are found.

```
SELECT city, state, zip
  FROM zipcode
CITY                       ST ZIP
------------------------   -- -----
Santurce                   PR 00914
North Adams                MA 01247
...
New York                   NY 10005
New York                   NY 10035

227 rows selected.
```

c) Describe the result set of the following SQL statement:

```
SELECT *
  FROM grade_type
```

Answer: *All columns and rows of the GRADE_TYPE table are returned in the result set. If you use iSQL*Plus your result will look similar to Figure 2.12. If you use SQL*Plus your result may resemble the first listing of SQL output in Figure 2.13.*

FORMATTING YOUR RESULT: THE SQL*PLUS COLUMN AND FORMAT COMMANDS

If you are using SQL*Plus, not *i*SQL*Plus, you will notice that the result set is difficult to read when data "wraps" itself onto the next line. The result may look similar to the screen you see in Figure 2.13. This will often occur when your SELECT statement contains multiple columns. To help you view the output more easily, SQL*Plus offers a number of formatting commands.

The SQL*Plus COLUMN command allows you to specify format attributes for specific columns. Because the SQL statement contains three alphanumeric columns, format each using these SQL*Plus commands:

```
COL description FORMAT A13
COL created_by FORMAT A8
COL modified_by FORMAT A8
```

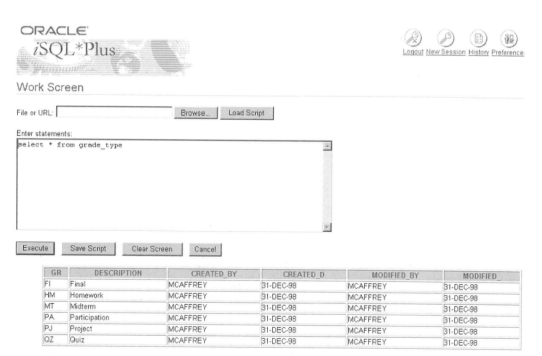

Figure 2.12 ■ **SELECT statement against the GRADE_TYPE table issued in *i*SQL*Plus.**

```
Oracle SQL*Plus                                                              _ 8 X
File  Edit  Search  Options  Help

SQL> SELECT *
  2     FROM grade_type
  3  /

GR DESCRIPTION                                         CREATED_BY                     CREATED_D
-- ----------------------------------------           --------------------------     ---------
MODIFIED_BY                       MODIFIED_
--------------------------------  ---------
FI Final                                              MCAFFREY                       31-DEC-98
MCAFFREY                          31-DEC-98

HM Homework                                           MCAFFREY                       31-DEC-98
MCAFFREY                          31-DEC-98

MT Midterm                                            MCAFFREY                       31-DEC-98
MCAFFREY                          31-DEC-98

PA Participation                                      MCAFFREY                       31-DEC-98
MCAFFREY                          31-DEC-98

PJ Project                                            MCAFFREY                       31-DEC-98
MCAFFREY                          31-DEC-98

QZ Quiz                                               MCAFFREY                       31-DEC-98
MCAFFREY                          31-DEC-98

6 rows selected.

SQL> COL description FORMAT A13
SQL> COL created_by FORMAT A8
SQL> COL modified_by FORMAT A8
SQL> /

GR DESCRIPTION   CREATED_ CREATED_D MODIFIED MODIFIED_
-- ------------- -------- --------- -------- ---------
FI Final         MCAFFREY 31-DEC-98 MCAFFREY 31-DEC-98
HM Homework      MCAFFREY 31-DEC-98 MCAFFREY 31-DEC-98
MT Midterm       MCAFFREY 31-DEC-98 MCAFFREY 31-DEC-98
PA Participation MCAFFREY 31-DEC-98 MCAFFREY 31-DEC-98
PJ Project       MCAFFREY 31-DEC-98 MCAFFREY 31-DEC-98
QZ Quiz          MCAFFREY 31-DEC-98 MCAFFREY 31-DEC-98

6 rows selected.

SQL>
```

Figure 2.13 ■ SELECT issued in SQL*Plus for Windows.

When you re-execute the SQL statement, the result is more readable as you see in the last result set shown in Figure 2.13.

The DESCRIPTION column is formatted to display a maximum of 13 characters; the CREATED_BY and MODIFIED_BY columns are formatted to display 8 characters. If the values in the columns do not fit into the space allotted, the data will wrap within the column. The column headings get truncated to the specified length.

The format for the column stays in place until you either respecify the format for the columns, specifically clear the format for the column, or exit SQL*Plus. To clear all the column formatting, execute the CLEAR COLUMNS command in SQL*Plus.

The two DATE datatype columns of this statement, CREATED_DATE and MODI-FIED_DATE, are not formatted by the COL command. By default, Oracle displays all DATE datatype columns with a nine-character width. You will learn about formatting columns with the DATE datatype in Chapter 4, "Date and Conversion Functions."

FORMATTING NUMBERS

If the column is of a NUMBER datatype column, you can change the format with a *format model* in the COLUMN command. For example, the 9 in the format model 999.99 represents the numeric digits, so the number 100 is displayed as 100.00. You can add dollar signs, leading zeros, angle brackets for negative numbers, and round values to format the display to your desire.

```
COL cost FORMAT $9,999.99
SELECT DISTINCT cost
  FROM course
        COST
----------
 $1,095.00
 $1,195.00
 $1,595.00


4 rows selected.
```

If you did not allot sufficient room for the number to fit in the column, SQL*Plus will show a # symbol instead.

```
COL cost FORMAT 999.99
    COST
-------
#######
#######
#######


4 rows selected.
```

For more SQL*Plus COLUMN FORMAT commands, see Appendix C, "SQL*Plus Command Reference."

Throughout this workbook you notice that the output is displayed in SQL*Plus rather than iSQL*Plus format. The reason for this is simply that it takes up less space in the book.

2.2.2 ANSWERS

a) Why are the result sets of each of the following SQL statements the same?

```
SELECT letter_grade
   FROM grade_conversion
```

```
SELECT DISTINCT letter_grade
   FROM grade_conversion
```

Answer: The result sets are the same because the data values in the LETTER_GRADE column in the GRADE_CONVERSION table are not repeated; the LETTER_GRADE column is the primary key of the table, so by definition its values are already distinct.

b) Explain the result set of the following SQL statement:

```
SELECT DISTINCT cost
   FROM course
```

Answer: The result set contains four rows of distinct costs in the COURSE table, including the NULL value.

```
SET FEEDBACK 1
```

```
SELECT DISTINCT cost
   FROM course
         COST
    -----------
         1095
         1195
         1595
```

4 rows selected.

Note that if you changed the feedback SQL*Plus environment variable to 1, using the SQL*Plus command SET FEEDBACK 1, the result will include the "4 rows selected." statement. There is one row in the COURSE table containing a null value in the COST column. Even though null is an unknown value, DISTINCT recognizes one or more null values in a column as one distinct value when returning a result set.

c) Explain what happens, and why, when you execute the following SQL statement:

```
SELECT DISTINCT course_no
   FROM class
```

Answer: Oracle returns an error because a table named CLASS does not exist.

```
FROM class
        *
ERROR at line 2:
ORA-00942: table or view does not exist
```

The asterisk in the error message indicates the error in the query. SQL is an exacting language. As you learn to write SQL, you will inevitably make mistakes. It is important to pay attention to the error messages returned to you from the database to learn from and correct your mistakes. This Oracle error message tells you that you referenced a table or a view does not exist in this database schema. (Views are discussed in Chapter 12, "Views, Indexes, and Sequences.") Correct your SQL statement and execute it again.

LAB 2.2 SELF-REVIEW QUESTIONS

In order to test your progress, you should be able to answer the following questions.

1) The column names listed in the SELECT list must be separated by commas.

   a) _____ True
   b) _____ False

2) A SELECT list may contain all the columns in a table.

   a) _____ True
   b) _____ False

3) The asterisk may be used as a wildcard in the FROM clause.

   a) _____ True
   b) _____ False

4) The following statement contains an error:
```
SELECT courseno
   FROM course
```

   a) _____ True
   b) _____ False

Answers appear in Appendix A, Section 2.2.

L A B   2 . 3

EDITING A SQL STATEMENT

LAB OBJECTIVES

After this lab, you will be able to:

✔ Edit a SQL Statement Using SQL*Plus Commands
✔ Edit a SQL Statement Using an Editor
✔ Save, Retrieve, and Run a SQL Statement in *i*SQL*Plus

THE LINE EDITOR

In *i*SQL*Plus you can easily edit your statement just like with any text. Sometimes you may not have access to *i*SQL*Plus, therefore you must learn how to write and edit a statement using the SQL*Plus line editor.

When using SQL*Plus you may have noticed that typing the same SQL statement over and over again to make a small change quickly becomes very tedious. You can use SQL*Plus's line editor to change your statement, indicating which line to change, then use a command to execute the change.

At the SQL prompt, type and execute the following statement to retrieve a list of course numbers:

```
SELECT course_no
   FROM course
```

SQL*Plus stores the last SQL command you typed in what is referred to as the *SQL buffer*. You can re-execute a statement by just pressing the "/", which reruns the command. The statement stays in the buffer until you enter another SQL command. Use the SQL*Plus LIST command, or simply the letter L, to list the contents of the buffer. The semicolon or the slash, both of which execute the statement, are not stored in the buffer. The asterisk next to the number 2 indicates this is the current line in the buffer.

```
SQL>LIST
  1 SELECT course_no
  2*   FROM course
```

For example, if you want to retrieve a list of descriptions instead, simply change the column course_no to description using the line editor. To make a change, indicate to the line editor which line to make current. To change it to the first line, type the number 1 at the SQL prompt:

```
SQL> 1
  1* SELECT course_no
```

Just the first line of the two-line statement is displayed, and the asterisk indicates this is now the current line in the buffer. You can make a change to that line with the CHANGE command:

```
SQL>CHANGE/course_no/description
```

The newly changed line is presented back to you:

```
  1* SELECT description
```

The CHANGE command is followed by a forward slash, followed by the text you want to change, and separated from the new text with another forward slash. The abbreviated command for the CHANGE command is the letter C. You are now ready to execute your statement to produce the new result set. Because you are not typing the statement for the first time, you cannot use the semicolon. Type a forward slash to execute the statement instead. The forward slash will always execute the current SQL statement in the buffer. Remember that certain commands you've learned so far, such as the LIST command, are not SQL, but SQL*Plus commands. Only SQL statements are saved in the buffer, never SQL*Plus commands.

USING AN EDITOR IN SQL*PLUS FOR WINDOWS

Although handy, using SQL*Plus's line editor capabilities can still be tedious, especially as your SQL statements grow in size and complexity. You may also want to save some statements for later use. This is where a *text editor* becomes useful. A text editor is a software program with no ability to format the text, such as with boldface or italics. Notepad, a text editor that comes with the Microsoft Windows operating systems, is one example of a text editor and is referenced in this workbook. Any other text editor will work just as well. For more about setting the default editor in SQL*Plus, see Appendix C, "SQL*Plus Command Reference."

To use a text editor in SQL*Plus for Windows or a SQL*Plus version with the command line interface, simply execute the EDIT or ED command. This command will *invoke*, or open, the default editor currently set in SQL*Plus. When you use the EDIT command at the SQL prompt, SQL*Plus will stay open in the back-

**LAB
2.3**

ground and your text editor will be in the foreground, automatically displaying the SQL statement in the buffer. The file already has a name, which can also be set as a default in SQL*Plus. For quick editing of statements, simply make your changes here, Save the file, and exit Notepad, which brings you back to SQL*Plus. If you wish to save the file for future reference, while still in Notepad select Save As to save the file with a different name and any extension you wish. It is common to save SQL files with a .sql extension.

If your editor puts a .txt after the file name (effectively creating a myfile.sql.txt file), change the Save As type to *All Files* instead of *Text documents (*.txt)*. Another way to ensure the file contains a .sql extension is to enclose the entire file name in quotes, (e.g., "myfile.sql" or if you want to include the path "c:\examples\myfile.sql"). Figure 2.14 displays the Save As dialog in SQL*Plus.

*Notice that when you invoke an editor, the SQL statement ends with a forward slash on a separate line at the end. SQL*Plus adds this character to the file so the file can be executed in SQL*Plus. When you invoke the editor from SQL*Plus, you can't go back to the SQL*Plus screen until you close the editor.*

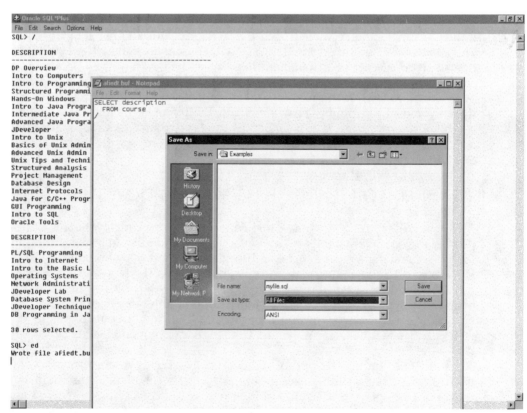

Figure 2.14 ■ Use of the Notepad text editor in SQL*Plus for Windows.

Type the following statement:

```
SELECT *
  FROM course
```

Now edit the file in Notepad and select Save As to save a second file with the name myfile2.sql. Exit Notepad and type and execute a new, different SQL statement:

```
SELECT state
  FROM zipcode
```

This statement is now in the buffer; however, you can execute a different SQL statement, such as the one you saved in myfile2.sql, with the START or @ command.

```
SQL>@myfile2
```

If the myfile2.sql file is stored in a directory other than the default directory, you need to specify the drive and directory name.

```
SQL>@c:\examples\myfile2
```

The statement in the file runs, producing a result set. Because the file already contains a forward slash, the SQL statement is executed automatically. If you save myfile2 with an extension other than .sql, you must type the file name and extension. If you want to change myfile2 again, simply type the following. Notepad will open with myfile2.sql containing your SQL statement.

```
ED c:\examples\myfile2
```

CHANGING THE DEFAULT DIRECTORY OF SQL*PLUS FOR WINDOWS

Whenever you execute a script or save a file in SQL*Plus without specifying a directory, it is assumed to be in the default directory. Typically this directory is named similar to C:\oracle\ora90\BIN. To change it to a different directory, such as the c:\guest directory, you need to create a shortcut. Modify the properties of the shortcut (see Figure 2.15) on the desktop to change the Start in field to the value c:\guest and then click OK. Whenever you evoke SQL*Plus through the shortcut, the c:\guest directory will be your default directory. If you are unsure how to create a shortcut in your Windows operating system, refer to the Windows documentation that came with your system. (Another way to change your default directory is by modifying your Windows registry. Only make these modifications if you are sufficiently knowledgeable about the Windows operating system. For more information, see Oracle's SQL*Plus manual.)

Figure 2.15 ■ Changing the default directory in SQL*Plus for Windows.

COPYING AND PASTING STATEMENTS
IN SQL*PLUS FOR WINDOWS

SQL*Plus for Windows allows you to copy and paste statements. You can open an editor such as Notepad in a separate window (without invoking it from SQL*Plus with the EDIT command) and enter your statements. Then copy the statement and paste it into SQL*Plus using the Paste menu option or the CTRL + V command key.

EDITING IN *i*SQL*PLUS

Editing a SQL statement in *i*SQL*Plus is rather intuitive. You can enter the statements in the input area, also called the Work Screen, and make changes using the delete and backspace keys or simply cut and paste. To save a statement to a text file you click on the Save Script button. You can reload the file later using the Load Script button. *i*SQL*Plus also has a SQL buffer; to see the latest statement type the LIST or L command, or simply press the browser's Back button. If you are using *i*SQL*Plus for Oracle 9*i* Release 2, your screen will have a History icon that allows you to see the previously issued statements.

DIFFERENCES BETWEEN SQL*PLUS AND *ISQL*PLUS

Throughout this workbook you will see both SQL*Plus and *i*SQL*Plus mentioned. For the most part the functionality between the two products is identical and does not impact on the result set, other than a different graphical output. If you are unclear if a certain SQL*Plus command performs identical in *i*SQL*Plus, refer to Appendix C, "SQL*Plus Command Reference."

Overall there are a small number of differences between the two products, particularly with respect to edits of SQL statements and the display of data. You will find these differences highlighted in Table 2.2.

*Unless specifically pointed out, all the mentioned SQL*Plus commands apply to both SQL*Plus and iSQL*Plus.*

Table 2.2 ■ Differences between SQL*Plus and *i*SQL*Plus

SQL*Plus	iSQL*Plus
Requires installation of SQL*Plus and Oracle Net software on individual machine.	No need to install special software, only browser is required.
Runs on individual workstation or on the server.	Run from a browser, which is typically a workstation with access to the Web server where iSQL*Plus is running.
Editing via line editor or with your own editor.	Editing in the Work Screen box.
Columns may not fit the whole width of your screen. You must use various SQL*Plus formatting commands to make them display on one line.	The browser automatically handles the formatting of columns to fit the width of the screen.
To recall any previously issued statements use the SAVE command, write the statement to file, or scroll back and cut and paste.	To recall any previous statement, use the browser's Back button, History icon, or save the statement to file.

LAB 2.3 EXERCISES

 If you have access to only SQL*Plus but not iSQL*Plus or vice versa, just perform the exercises that are applicable for the specific environment. Exercises 2.3.1 and 2.3.2 use SQL*Plus only, not iSQL*Plus.

2.3.1 EDIT A SQL STATEMENT USING SQL*PLUS COMMANDS

LAB 2.3

Type and execute the following SQL statement (use SQL*Plus, not iSQL*Plus):

```
SELECT employer
  FROM student
```

a) Using SQL*Plus commands, change the column `employer` to `registration_date` and execute the statement again.

b) Using SQL*Plus commands, add a second column, `phone`, to the statement you changed. Display the PHONE column first, then the REGISTRATION_DATE column, in the result set.

2.3.2 EDIT A SQL STATEMENT USING AN EDITOR

Perform these exercises using SQL*Plus, not iSQL*Plus.

a) Invoke the editor and change the statement in your buffer to the following. Then save the file and execute it in SQL*Plus.

```
SELECT salutation, first_name, last_name, phone
  FROM instructor
```

b) Edit the preceding statement, which is now in your buffer, save it as inst.sql, and use the `START` or @ command to execute it in SQL*Plus.

c) Edit inst.sql, save it as inst.x, and use the `RUN` or @ command to execute it in SQL*Plus.

2.3.3 SAVE, RETRIEVE, AND RUN A SQL STATEMENT IN iSQL*PLUS

a) Enter the following SELECT statement into the input area and execute the statement. Then save the statement in a file called state_zip.sql and press the Clear Screen button.

```
SELECT DISTINCT state
   FROM zipcode
```

b) Click the Browse... button and locate the state_zip.sql file you just saved. Then press the Load Script button to load it into input area. Execute the statement.

c) Explain the difference between the SQL language and SQL*Plus or *i*SQL*Plus.

LAB 2.3 EXERCISE ANSWERS

2.3.1 ANSWERS

Type and execute the following SQL statement (use SQL*Plus, not *i*SQL*Plus):

```
SELECT employer
   FROM student
```

a) Using SQL*Plus commands, change the column `employer` to `registration_date` and execute the statement again.

Answer: Select the first line in the buffer, then use the CHANGE command to change EMPLOYER to REGISTRATION_DATE.

Type `1` to select the first line in the buffer:

```
SQL> 1
  1* SELECT employer
```

Then use the CHANGE command:

```
SQL> c/employer/registration_date
  1* SELECT registration_date
```

Type L to list the changed statement:

```
SQL> L
  1 SELECT registration_date
  2*   FROM student
```

If you care to run the query, you can do so with the forward slash "/", which then executes the statement currently in the buffer.

b) Using SQL*Plus commands, add a second column, phone, to the statement you changed. Display the PHONE column first, then the REGISTRATION_DATE column, in the result set.

Answer: You must again select the first line in the buffer, then use the CHANGE command to add the PHONE column to the SELECT list.

Type 1 to select the first line in the buffer:

```
SQL> 1
  1* SELECT registration_date
```

Then use the CHANGE command:

```
C/SELECT/SELECT phone,
```

Here, the CHANGE command will replace SELECT with SELECT phone, (including the comma), changing your statement to the following:

```
  1 SELECT phone, registration_date
  2*   FROM student
```

The result set will display phone first, then the registration date:

```
PHONE              REGISTRAT
---------------    ---------
201-555-5555       18-FEB-93
201-555-5555       22-FEB-93
...
718-555-5555       22-FEB-93
718-555-5555       28-JAN-93

268 rows selected.
```

The CHANGE command looks for the first occurrence, from left to right, of the text you wish to change. When it locates it, it replaces this occurrence with the new text you wish to change it to.

OTHER USEFUL LINE EDITOR COMMANDS

Besides the CHANGE and LIST commands, the SQL*Plus line editor has a number of other commands. For example, to add another column to the SQL statement you use the APPEND command. The statement currently in the buffer lists as follows:

```
SQL> L
1 SELECT phone, registration_date
2*   FROM student
```

First choose the line to which you want to add at the end, then use the A command and add the text you want to append. In the following example the ", last_name" text was added to the statement.

```
SQL> 1
 1* SELECT phone, registration_date
SQL> A , last_name
 1* SELECT phone, registration_date, last_name
```

Another useful command is the INPUT command; it adds a new line after the current line. To insert the text ", first_name" on the next line, use the INPUT or I command. SQL*Plus prompts you for a new line and you enter the text and press Enter. SQL*Plus prompts you once more for another new line and if you are finished adding you press Enter again to indicate that you are done.

```
SQL> 1
 1* SELECT phone, registration_date, last_name
SQL> I
 2i       , first_name
 3i
SQL> L
 1  SELECT phone, registration_date, last_name
 2        , first_name
 3*   FROM student
```

If you need to insert the line before line 1, enter a 0 (zero). Use the DEL command to delete lines in the buffer. To delete line 2, you enter:

```
SQL> DEL 2
SQL> L
 1  SELECT phone, registration_date, last_name
 2*   FROM student
```

You can also save the statement using the SQL*Plus SAVE command. In the next example, the SQL query is saved in the c:\guest directory under the file name myexample.sql; if you don't specify the extension, by default it will be .sql.

```
SQL> SAVE c:\guest\myexample
Created file c:\guest\myexample
```

Note that you do not need to type a semicolon or forward slash, it will automatically be added. The statement can now be run either with the START or @ command. If you subsequently write other SQL statements and the statement is no longer in the SQL buffer, you can load it back into the buffer with the GET command. (The .sql extension is optional). You can then re-execute the statement with the forward slash.

```
SQL> GET c:\guest\myexample
  1    SELECT phone, registration_date, last_name
  2*   FROM student
```

2.3.2 ANSWERS

a) Invoke the editor and change the statement in your buffer to the following. Then save the file and execute it in SQL*Plus.

```
SELECT salutation, first_name, last_name, phone
  FROM instructor
```

Answer: Use the EDIT *command to edit the file and execute the changed statement in SQL*Plus with the forward slash.*

b) Edit the preceding statement, which is now in your buffer, save it as inst.sql, and use the START or @ command to execute it in SQL*Plus.

Answer: Use the EDIT *command to edit the file and save it as inst.sql. Execute the changed statement in SQL*Plus with the* START *or @ command.*

```
SQL>@inst.sql
```

c) Edit inst.sql, save it as inst.x, and use the START or @ command to execute it in SQL*Plus.

Answer: At the SQL prompt, type EDIT, *edit the file in your editor, save the file as inst.x, exit the editor, type at the SQL>prompt the command* @inst.x *to execute the changed statement.*

Because you saved the file with an extension other than .sql, you must explicitly reference both the file name and its extension. If you want to edit this file, you must type EDIT inst.x at the SQL prompt.

2.3.3 ANSWERS

a) Enter the following SELECT statement into the input area and execute the statement. Then save the statement in a file called state_zip.sql and press the Clear Screen button.

```
SELECT DISTINCT state
  FROM zipcode
```

Answer: When you execute this statement it returns a list of the state abbreviations from the ZIPCODE table. When you click on the Save Script button a message box informs you that the file is transferred from the Web browser to your individual computer. Click the Save button to save it on your computer (see Figure 2.16).

After you click the Save button you will receive a screen similar to Figure 2.17 and you are prompted to enter the file name. You see a suggested unique file name, but change it to state_zip.sql instead. The term *script* is just another word for command file containing one or multiple commands.

When you choose the Clear Screen button, the input area and output area are cleared, but note the SQL buffer is not cleared and it will still list the last statement if you enter the LIST command.

LAB 2.3

b) Click the Browse… button and locate the state_zip.sql file you just saved. Then press the Load Script button to load it into input area. Execute the statement.

Answer: When you click the Browse… button, you will see a dialog box that displays the directory and file name. Then you need to press the Load Script button to transfer the file into the input area for execution. Afterwards, you can execute the statement.

Figure 2.16 ■ **Save a file in *i*SQL*Plus.**

Figure 2.17 ■ **The Choose file dialog in *iSQL*Plus.**

RUNNING MULTIPLE STATEMENTS IN *iSQL*PLUS

You can run multiple SQL statements in *iSQL*Plus. For example, if you want to run the following two statements you either place them in a script file or simply type them into the input area. Just be sure to end every statement with either a semicolon or a forward slash at the beginning of a separate line. Note, you don't need a semicolon or forward slash for the last statement, but if you run the statements inside a script file you must end each statement with either one. Therefore, it is a good habit to place either the semicolon or forward slash after each statement.

On the following screen you see two query results. One shows the distinct zip codes for all instructors and the second result is a listing of first and last names for all students. The second statement does not quite fit on one screen, but you can scroll down to see the rest as you see in the screen displayed in Figure 2.18.

Be careful, do not add both a semicolon and a forward slash to the same statement, otherwise it will be executed twice. For example, the next SQL statement will be executed twice.

```
SELECT DISTINCT zip
  FROM zipcode;
/
```

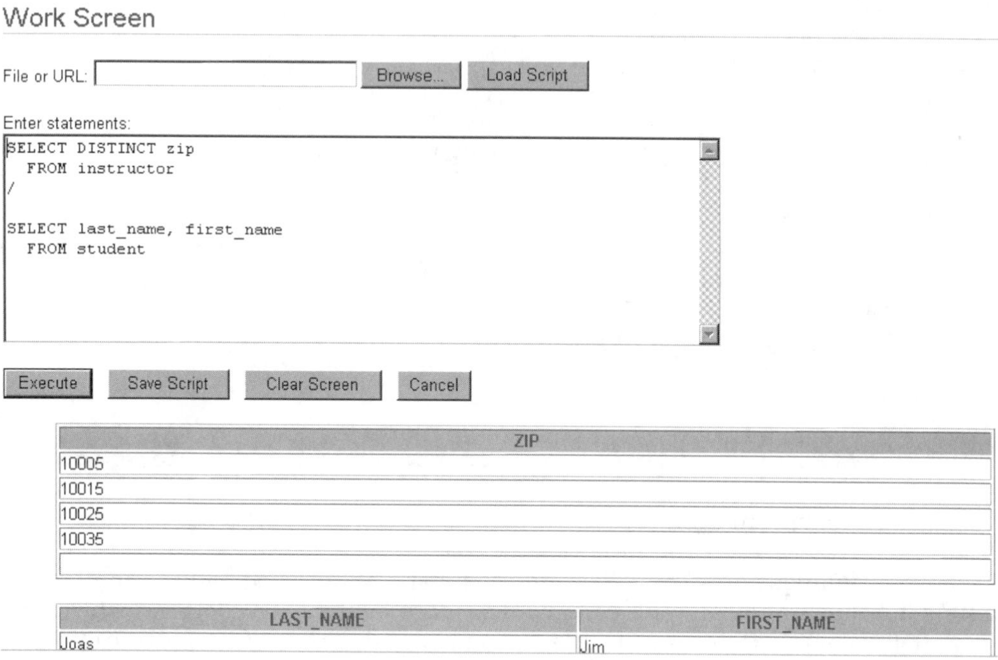

Work Screen

File or URL: [   ] [Browse...] [Load Script]

Enter statements:

```
SELECT DISTINCT zip
  FROM instructor
/

SELECT last_name, first_name
  FROM student
```

[Execute] [Save Script] [Clear Screen] [Cancel]

ZIP
10005
10015
10025
10035

LAST_NAME	FIRST_NAME
Joas	Jim

Figure 2.18 ■ Executing multiple SQL statements.

Make sure you add a return to the end of the file (most editors automatically do) and there are no stray characters; otherwise you may receive this harmless but annoying message when executing your script.

```
input truncated to 1 character
```

COMMENTS IN SQL SCRIPTS

Placing comments or remarks into a SQL script is very useful when you revisit the script later. It helps document the purpose, thoughts, and ideas or simply lists the author and creation date. You must identify the comment; otherwise you will receive an error when running the command. You can distinguish between two different types of comments: a single-line comment denoted with double dashes or a multi-line comment spawning multiple lines, which starts with an opening comment like this, /*, and ends with a closing comment, which looks like this, */.

Following is an example of a script file that includes comments, but comments can also be embedded within the SQL statement itself.

```
/* Multi-line comment
Homework #2
By: Kirsten Soehner
Date created: 4/30/2002
*/

-- Answer #1:  This is a single-line comment!
SELECT DISTINCT state
  FROM zipcode;

-- Answer #2:
COL cost FORMAT $9,999.99
SELECT DISTINCT cost
  FROM course

-- Answer #3:
SELECT instructor_id, -- Comment within a SQL statement!
       zip
  FROM instructor;
```

Note, SQL*Plus also has a REMARK command abbreviated as REM that allows single-line comments. This command is not recognized as a comment when your SQL statement is executed in an environment other than SQL*Plus or *i*SQL*Plus; it can also not be embedded in a SQL statement. Use the single-line and double-line comments mentioned previously instead!

c) Explain the difference between the SQL language and SQL*Plus or *i*SQL*Plus.

*Answer: SQL is a language that allows you to retrieve, manipulate, define, and control access to the database. SQL*Plus and iSQL*Plus are environments in which to execute the SQL statements and display the results.*

*i*SQL*Plus is the Web-based version of SQL*Plus and both programs are Oracle proprietary products. You can use other software programs to execute your SQL statements against an Oracle database. If you want to format your results in special ways use the SQL*Plus commands such as COLUMN FORMAT. If you don't execute the commands in *i*SQL*Plus or SQL*Plus these formatting commands are not available and you will need to use specific SQL functions to achieve somewhat similar results. Some of these SQL functions are discussed in the next chapter.

LAB 2.3 SELF-REVIEW QUESTIONS

In order to test your progress, you should be able to answer the following questions.

1) You can save a SQL statement to the SQL buffer for it to be referenced later.

    a) _____ True
    b) _____ False

2) After typing a SQL statement you can execute it with either the semicolon or the forward slash.

    a) _____ True
    b) _____ False

3) You cannot save a .sql file to the A: drive.

    a) _____ True
    b) _____ False

4) The SQL*Plus START command can execute what is in the SQL buffer.

    a) _____ True
    b) _____ False

Answers appear in Appendix A, Section 2.3.

L A B   2 . 4

THE WHERE CLAUSE: COMPARISON AND LOGICAL OPERATORS

> ## LAB OBJECTIVES
>
> After this lab, you will be able to:
>
> ✔ Use Comparison and Logical Operators in a WHERE Clause
> ✔ Use NULL in a WHERE Clause

The *WHERE clause,* also called the *predicate,* provides the power to narrow down the scope of data retrieved. In fact, most SQL statements you write will contain a WHERE clause.

COMPARISON OPERATORS

Comparison operators compare expressions. An *expression* can be a column of any datatype, a *string* or *text literal* (sometimes referred to as a *text constant* or *character literal*), a number, or any combination of these. An expression can also be a *function* or *mathematical computation,* which you will learn about in Chapter 3, "Character, Number, and Miscellaneous Functions." An expression always results in a value.

TESTING FOR EQUALITY AND INEQUALITY

Comparison operators compare one expression with another expression. One of the most commonly used comparison operators is the *equal* operator, denoted by the = symbol. For example, if you are asked to provide the first name, last name, and phone number of a teacher with the last name of Schorin, you write the following SQL statement:

```
SELECT first_name, last_name, phone
  FROM instructor
 WHERE last_name = 'Schorin'
FIRST_NAME LAST_NAME  PHONE
---------- ---------- ----------
Nina       Schorin    2125551212

1 row selected.
```

Here, the column LAST_NAME is the left side of the equation and the text literal 'Schorin' is the right side. Single quotes are used around the text literal 'Schorin'. This statement will only retrieve rows from the INSTRUCTOR table that satisfy this condition in the WHERE clause. In this case, only one row is retrieved.

When you describe the INSTRUCTOR table, you see the datatype of the LAST_NAME column is VARCHAR2. This means the data contained in this column is alphanumeric. When two values are compared to each other they must be of the same datatype; otherwise, Oracle returns an error. You will learn more about converting from one datatype to another in Chapter 4, "Date and Conversion Functions."

LAB 2.4

```
SQL> DESCR INSTRUCTOR
 Name                             Null?    Type
 -------------------------------- -------- -------------
 INSTRUCTOR_ID                    NOT NULL NUMBER(8)
 SALUTATION                                VARCHAR2(5)
 FIRST_NAME                                VARCHAR2(25)
 LAST_NAME                                 VARCHAR2(25)
 STREET_ADDRESS                            VARCHAR2(50)
 ZIP                                       VARCHAR2(5)
 PHONE                                     VARCHAR2(15)
 CREATED_BY                       NOT NULL VARCHAR2(30)
 CREATED_DATE                     NOT NULL DATE
 MODIFIED_BY                      NOT NULL VARCHAR2(30)
 MODIFIED_DATE                    NOT NULL DATE
```

SQL is case insensitive when it comes to column names, table names, and keywords such as SELECT. (There are some exceptions with regard to column names and table names. For more information see Chapter 11, "Create, Alter, and Drop Tables.") When you compare a text literal to a database column, the case of the data must match exactly. The syntax of the following statement is correct, but it does not yield any rows because the instructor's last name is obviously not in the correct case.

```
SELECT first_name, last_name, phone
  FROM instructor
 WHERE last_name = 'schorin'

no rows selected
```

Just as equality is useful, so is inequality.

```
SELECT first_name, last_name, phone
  FROM instructor
 WHERE last_name <> 'Schorin'
FIRST_NAME LAST_NAME  PHONE
---------- ---------- ----------
Fernand    Hanks      2125551212
Tom        Wojick     2125551212
...
Marilyn    Frantzen   2125551212
Irene      Willig     2125551212

9 rows selected.
```

All rows except the one with the last name of 'Schorin', are retrieved. Inequality can also be expressed with the != notation.

THE GREATER THAN AND LESS THAN OPERATORS

The comparison operators >, <, >=, and <= can all be used to compare values in columns. In the following example, the >=, or *greater than or equal to*, operator is used to retrieve a list of course descriptions whose cost is greater than or equal to 1195:

```
SELECT description, cost
  FROM course
 WHERE cost >= 1195
DESCRIPTION                    COST
------------------------------ ----
DP Overview                    1195
Intro to Computers             1195
...
Database System Principles     1195
PL/SQL Programming             1195

26 rows selected.
```

The value 1195 is not enclosed in single quotes because it is a number literal.

THE BETWEEN COMPARISON OPERATOR

The BETWEEN operator tests for a range of values:

```
SELECT description, cost
  FROM course
 WHERE cost BETWEEN 1000 AND 1100
```

```
DESCRIPTION                          COST
------------------------------   --------
Unix Tips and Techniques             1095
Intro to Internet                    1095
Intro to the Basic Language          1095

3 rows selected.
```

BETWEEN is inclusive of both values defining the range; the result set includes courses that cost 1000 and 1100 and everything in between. Note that the lower range of the values must be listed first.

If you use *i*SQL*Plus then your result may look similar to Figure 2.19. Note that the result is identical; the only difference is the formatting.

DESCRIPTION	COST
Unix Tips and Techniques	1095
Intro to Internet	1095
Intro to the Basic Language	1095

Figure 2.19 ■ *i*SQL*Plus result.

BETWEEN is most useful for number and date comparisons, but can also be used for comparing text strings in alphabetical order. Date comparisons are discussed in Chapter 4, "Date and Conversion Functions."

THE IN OPERATOR

The IN operator works with a *list of values,* separated by commas, contained within a set of parentheses. The following query looks for courses where the cost is either 1095 or 1595.

```
SELECT description, cost
  FROM course
 WHERE cost IN (1095, 1595)
DESCRIPTION                          COST
------------------------------   ---------
Structured Programming Techniques    1595
Unix Tips and Techniques             1095
Intro to Internet                    1095
Intro to the Basic Language          1095

4 rows selected.
```

THE LIKE OPERATOR

Another very useful comparison operator is LIKE, which performs pattern-matching using the percent (%) or underscore (_) characters as wildcards. The percent wildcard is used to denote multiple characters, while the underscore wildcard is used to denote a single character. The next query retrieves rows where the last name begins with the uppercase letter S and ends in anything else:

```
SELECT first_name, last_name, phone
  FROM instructor
 WHERE last_name LIKE 'S%'
```

FIRST_NAME	LAST_NAME	PHONE
Nina	Schorin	2125551212
Todd	Smythe	2125551212

```
2 rows selected.
```

The % character may be placed at the beginning, end, or anywhere within the literal text, but always within the single quotes. This is also true of the underscore wildcard character, as in this statement:

```
SELECT first_name, last_name
  FROM instructor
 WHERE last_name LIKE '_o%'
```

FIRST_NAME	LAST_NAME
Tom	Wojick
Anita	Morris
Charles	Lowry

```
3 rows selected.
```

The WHERE clause returns only rows where the last name begins with any character, but the second letter must be a lower case "o". The rest of the last name is irrelevant.

NEGATING USING NOT

All the previously mentioned operators can be negated with the NOT comparison operator; for example, NOT BETWEEN, NOT IN, NOT LIKE.

```
SELECT phone
  FROM instructor
 WHERE last_name NOT LIKE 'S%'
```

In the SQL statement the LAST_NAME column used in the WHERE clause doesn't appear in the SELECT list. There is no rule about columns in the WHERE clause having to exist in the SELECT list.

EVALUATING NULL VALUES

Recall that NULL means an unknown value. The IS NULL and IS NOT NULL operators evaluate whether a data value is NULL or not. The following SQL statement returns courses that do not have a prerequisite:

```
SELECT description, prerequisite
  FROM course
 WHERE prerequisite IS NULL
DESCRIPTION                      PREREQUISITE
------------------------------   ------------
DP Overview
Intro to Computers
Java for C/C++ Programmers
Operating Systems

4 rows selected.
```

Null values represent the unknown; a null cannot be equal or unequal to any value or to another null. Therefore, always use the IS NULL or IS NOT NULL operator when testing for nulls. There are a few exceptions when nulls are treated differently and a null can be equal to another null. One such example is the use of DISTINCT (see Lab 2.2). You will learn about the exceptions in the treatment of nulls throughout this workbook.

OVERVIEW OF COMPARISON OPERATORS

The comparison operators you have learned about so far are sometimes referred to as predicates or search conditions. A predicate is an expression that results in either a true, false, or unknown value. Table 2.3 provides you with a list of the most common comparison operators. You will learn about additional operators such as EXISTS, ANY, SOME, ALL in Chapter 7, "Subqueries," and the OVERLAPS operator in Chapter 4, "Date and Conversion Functions."

All these operators can be negated with the NOT logical operator.

LOGICAL OPERATORS

To harness the ultimate power of the WHERE clause, comparison operators can be combined with the help of the *logical operators* AND and OR. These logical operators are also referred to as *boolean operators*. They group expressions, all within the same WHERE clause of a single SQL statement.

Table 2.3 ■ SQL Comparison Operators

Comparison Operator	Definition
=	Equal
!=, <>	Not equal
>, >=	Greater than, greater than or equal to
<, <=	Less than, less than or equal to
BETWEEN ... AND ...	Inclusive of two values
LIKE	Pattern matching with wildcard characters % and _
IN (...)	List of values
IS NULL	Test for null values

**LAB
2.4**

For example, the following SQL query combines two comparison operators with the help of the AND boolean operator. The result shows rows where a course costs 1095 and the course description starts with the letter I:

```
SELECT description, cost
  FROM course
 WHERE cost = 1095
   AND description LIKE 'I%'
DESCRIPTION                              COST
-----------------------------------  ---------
Intro to Internet                        1095
Intro to the Basic Language              1095

2 rows selected.
```

With just the = operator in the WHERE clause, the result set contains three rows. With the addition of the AND description LIKE 'I%', the result is further reduced to two rows.

PRECEDENCE OF LOGICAL OPERATORS

When AND and OR are used together in a WHERE clause, the AND operator always takes precedence over the OR operator, meaning any AND conditions are evaluated first. If there are multiple operators of the same precedence, the left operator is executed before the right. You can manipulate the precedence in the WHERE clause with the use of parentheses. In the following SQL statement, the AND and OR logical operators are combined:

```
SELECT description, cost, prerequisite
  FROM course
```

```
WHERE cost = 1195
  AND prerequisite = 20
  OR prerequisite = 25
DESCRIPTION                           COST PREREQUISITE
------------------------------- --------- ------------
Hands-On Windows                      1195           20
Structured Analysis                   1195           20
Project Management                    1195           20
GUI Programming                       1195           20
Intro to SQL                          1195           20
Intro to the Basic Language           1095           25
Database System Principles            1195           25

7 rows selected.
```

The preceding SQL statement selects any record that has either a cost of 1195 and a prerequisite of 20, or just has a prerequisite of 25 no matter what the cost. The sixth row, `Intro to the Basic Language`, is selected because it satisfies the OR expression `prerequisite = 25`. The seventh row, `Database System Principles`, only satisfies one of the AND conditions, not both. However, the row is part of the result set because it satisfies the OR condition.

Here is the same SQL statement, but with parentheses to group the expressions in the WHERE clause:

```
SELECT description, cost, prerequisite
  FROM course
 WHERE cost = 1195
   AND (prerequisite = 20
        OR prerequisite = 25)
DESCRIPTION                           COST PREREQUISITE
------------------------------- ------ ------------
Database System Principles            1195           25
Hands-On Windows                      1195           20
Structured Analysis                   1195           20
Project Management                    1195           20
GUI Programming                       1195           20
Intro to SQL                          1195           20

6 rows selected.
```

The first expression selects only courses where the cost is equal to 1195. If the prerequisite is either 25 or 20, then the second condition is also true. Both expressions need to be true for the row to be displayed. These are the basic rules of logical operators. If two conditions are combined with the AND operator, both conditions must be true; if two conditions are connected by the OR operator, only one of the conditions needs to be true for the record to be selected.

**LAB
2.4**

The result set returns six rows instead of seven. The order in which items in the WHERE clause are evaluated is changed by the use of parentheses and results in a different output.

To ensure that your SQL statements are clearly understood, it is always best to use parentheses.

NULLS AND LOGICAL OPERATORS

SQL uses *tri-value logic*; this means a condition can evaluate to true, false, or unknown. (This is in contrast to boolean logic, where a condition must be either true or false.) A row gets returned when the condition evaluates to true. The following query returns rows from the COURSE table starting with the words Intro to as the description *and* a value equal or larger than 140 in the PREREQUISITE column.

```
SELECT description, prerequisite
  FROM course
 WHERE description LIKE 'Intro to%'
   AND prerequisite >= 140
DESCRIPTION                              PREREQUISITE
-------------------------------------    ------------
Intro to Programming                              140
Intro to Unix                                     310

2 rows selected.
```

Rows with a null value in the PREREQUISITE column are not included because null is an unknown value. This null value in the column is not equal or greater to 140. Therefore, the row Intro to Computers does not satisfy *both* conditions and is excluded from the result set. Following is the list of course descriptions with null values in the PREREQUISITE column. It shows the row Intro to Computers with a null value in the PREREQUISITE column.

```
SELECT description, prerequisite, cost
  FROM course
 WHERE prerequisite IS NULL
DESCRIPTION                     PREREQUISITE    COST
----------------------------    ------------    ---------
Operating Systems                               1195
Java for C/C++ Programmers                      1195
DP Overview                                     1195
Intro to Computers                              1195

4 rows selected.
```

Table 2.4 ■ AND Truth Table

AND	TRUE	FALSE	UNKNOWN
TRUE	TRUE	FALSE	UNKNOWN
FALSE	FALSE	FALSE	FALSE
UNKNOWN	UNKNOWN	FALSE	UNKNOWN

The AND truth table in Table 2.4 illustrates the combination of two conditions with the AND operator. Only if *both* conditions are true is a row returned for output. If one of the conditions evaluates to unknown, as is the case with the prerequisite being null, the condition is unknown and therefore the row not included in the result. The comparison against a null value yields unknown unless you specifically use the IS NULL operator.

For the OR condition, just *one* of the conditions needs to be true. Again, let's examine how nulls behave under this scenario using the same query, but this time with the OR operator. The Intro to Computers course is now listed because it satisfies the 'Intro to%' condition only. In addition, you will notice that rows such as DB Programming in Java do not start with the 'Intro to' as the description, but satisfy the second condition, which is a prerequisite of greater or equal to 140.

LAB
2.4

```
SELECT description, prerequisite
  FROM course
 WHERE description LIKE 'Intro to%'
    OR prerequisite >= 140
DESCRIPTION                              PREREQUISITE
------------------------------------    ------------
DB Programming in Java                        350
Database Design                               420
Internet Protocols                            310
Intro to Computers
Intro to Internet                              10
Intro to Java Programming                      80
Intro to Programming                          140
Intro to SQL                                   20
Intro to Unix                                 310
Intro to the Basic Language                    25
JDeveloper Techniques                         350
Oracle Tools                                  220
Structured Programming Techniques             204

13 rows selected.
```

Table 2.5 ■ OR Truth Table

OR	TRUE	FALSE	UNKNOWN
TRUE	TRUE	TRUE	TRUE
FALSE	TRUE	FALSE	UNKNOWN
UNKNOWN	TRUE	UNKNOWN	UNKNOWN

Table 2.5 shows the truth table for the OR operator; it highlights the fact that just one of the conditions need be true for the row to be returned in the result set. It is irrelevant if the second condition evaluates to false or unknown.

When you negate a condition with the NOT operator and the value you are comparing against is a null value, it also results in a null (see Table 2.6). The following query demonstrates that none of the null prerequisites are included in the result set.

```
SELECT description, prerequisite
   FROM course
  WHERE NOT prerequisite >= 140
DESCRIPTION                                 PREREQUISITE
------------------------------------------- ------------
Intro to Internet                                     10
GUI Programming                                       20
Intro to SQL                                          20
Hands-On Windows                                      20
Structured Analysis                                   20
Project Management                                    20
Intro to the Basic Language                           25
Database System Principles                            25
PL/SQL Programming                                    80
Intro to Java Programming                             80
Intermediate Java Programming                        120
Advanced Java Programming                            122
JDeveloper                                           122
JDeveloper Lab                                       125
Basics of Unix Admin                                 130
Network Administration                               130
Advanced Unix Admin                                  132
Unix Tips and Techniques                             134

18 rows selected.
```

Table 2.6 ■ NOT Truth Table

NOT	TRUE	FALSE	UNKNOWN
NOT	FALSE	TRUE	UNKNOWN

LAB 2.4 EXERCISES

2.4.1 USE COMPARISON AND LOGICAL OPERATORS IN A *WHERE* CLAUSE

a) Write a SELECT statement to list the last names of students living either in zip code 10048, 11102, or 11209.

b) Write a SELECT statement to list the first and last names of instructors with the letter "i" (either uppercase or lowercase) in their last name living in the zip code 10025.

c) Does the following statement contain an error? Explain.

```
SELECT last_name
  FROM instructor
 WHERE created_date = modified_by
```

d) What do you observe when you execute the following SQL statement?

```
SELECT course_no, cost
  FROM course
 WHERE cost BETWEEN 1500 AND 1000
```

2.4.2 USE *NULL* IN A *WHERE* CLAUSE

a) Write a SELECT statement to list descriptions of courses with prerequisites and cost less than 1100.

b) Write a SELECT statement to list the cost of courses without a prerequisite; do not repeat the cost.

LAB 2.4 EXERCISE ANSWERS

a) Write a SELECT statement to list the last names of students living either in zip code 10048, 11102, or 11209.

Answer: The SELECT statement selects a single column and uses the IN comparison operator in the WHERE clause.

```
SELECT last_name
  FROM student
 WHERE zip IN ('10048', '11102', '11209')
LAST_NAME
-------------------------
Masser
Allende
Winnicki
Wilson
Williams
McLean
Lefkowitz

7 rows selected.
```

The statement can also be written using the equal operator (=), in combination with the logical operator OR, and yields the same result set:

```
SELECT last_name
  FROM student
 WHERE zip = '10048'
    OR zip = '11102'
    OR zip = '11209'
```

There will be times when a SELECT statement can be written more than one way. The preceding statements are logically equivalent.

b) Write a SELECT statement to list the first and last names of instructors with the letter "i" (either uppercase or lowercase) in their last name living in the zip code 10025.

Answer: The SELECT statement selects two columns and uses the LIKE, =, and the AND and OR logical operators, combined with parentheses, in the WHERE clause.

```
SELECT first_name, last_name
  FROM instructor
 WHERE (last_name LIKE '%i%' OR last_name LIKE '%I%')
   AND zip = '10025'
FIRST_NAME                      LAST_NAME
------------------------------- --------------
Tom                             Wojick
Nina                            Schorin

2 rows selected.
```

The LIKE operator must be used twice in this example because there is no way of knowing whether there is an upper or lowercase 'i' anywhere in the last name. You must test for both conditions, which cannot be done using a single LIKE operator. If one of the OR conditions is true, the expression is true.

If you need to search for the actual % symbol within a column value, you can use a SQL function or an escape character. You learn more about this in Chapter 3, "Character, Number, and Miscellaneous Functions."

c) Does the following statement contain an error? Explain.

```
SELECT last_name
  FROM instructor
 WHERE created_date = modified_by
```

Answer: Yes. The two columns in the WHERE clause are not the same datatype and the Oracle database returns an error when this statement is executed.

You will get an error similar to the following when you execute the statement.

```
SQL> SELECT last_name
  2    FROM instructor
  3   WHERE created_date = modified_by
  4  /
 WHERE created_date = modified_by
                      *
ERROR at line 3:
ORA-01858: a non-numeric character was found where a numeric
was expected
```

There are times when the datatypes of columns do not agree and you need to convert from one datatype to another. You will learn about these circumstances in Chapter 4, "Date and Conversion Functions." (In this exercise example, data conversion is not fruitful because the data in these two columns is of a very different nature.)

d) What do you observe when you execute the following SQL statement?

```
SELECT course_no, cost
  FROM course
 WHERE cost BETWEEN 1500 AND 1000
no rows selected
```

Answer: The query returns no rows. Although there are courses that cost between 1000 and 1500, the BETWEEN clause requires the lower end of the range to be listed first. If the query is rewritten as follows, it returns rows.

```
SELECT course_no, cost
    FROM course
   WHERE cost BETWEEN 1000 AND 1500
```

BETWEEN AND TEXT LITERALS

As mentioned previously, BETWEEN is most often used for numbers and dates, which you will learn about in Chapter 4, "Date and Conversion Functions." You can apply the BETWEEN functions to text columns as you see in the next example, which utilizes the BETWEEN operator with text literals W and Z. The query lists the student's ID and the last name. Notice any students with a last name beginning with the letter "Z" are not included, because the STUDENT table has no student with a last name of the single letter "Z". If a student's last name was spelled "waldo", this student would not be included in the result, because the WHERE clause is only looking for last names that fall between the uppercase letters of W and Z.

```
SELECT student_id, last_name
  FROM student
 WHERE last_name BETWEEN 'W' AND 'Z'
STUDENT_ID LAST_NAME
---------- --------------------
       142 Waldman
...
       241 Yourish

11 rows selected.
```

If you are looking for "waldo", regardless of the case, use the OR operator to include both conditions.

```
SELECT student_id, last_name
  FROM student
 WHERE last_name BETWEEN 'W' AND 'Z'
    OR last_name BETWEEN 'w' AND 'z'
```

Here is another example of how you can use the BETWEEN and the >= and <= operators with text literals.

```
SELECT description
  FROM grade_type
 WHERE description BETWEEN 'Midterm' and 'Project'
```

This would be equivalent to:

```
SELECT description
  FROM grade_type
 WHERE description >= 'Midterm'
   AND description <= 'Project'
DESCRIPTION
-------------------------------- ---
Midterm
Participation
Project

3 rows selected.
```

2.4.2 ANSWERS

a) Write a SELECT statement to list descriptions of courses with prerequisites and cost less than 1100.

Answer: The SELECT statement selects a single column and uses the IS NOT NULL and less than (<) comparison operators in the WHERE clause.

```
SELECT description, cost, prerequisite
  FROM course
 WHERE prerequisite IS NOT NULL
   AND cost < 1100
DESCRIPTION                           COST PREREQUISITE
---------------- ---------------- --------- ------------
Intro to Internet                     1095           10
Intro to the Basic Language           1095           25
Unix Tips and Techniques              1095          134

3 rows selected.
```

Both conditions need to be true for the row to be returned. If the one of the conditions is not met, the row simply is not selected for output.

b) Write a SELECT statement to list the cost of courses without a prerequisite; do not repeat the cost.

Answer: The SELECT statement selects a single column in combination with DISTINCT, and uses the IS NULL comparison operator in the WHERE clause.

```
SELECT DISTINCT cost
  FROM course
 WHERE prerequisite IS NULL
COST
---------
     1195

1 row selected.
```

LAB 2.4 SELF-REVIEW QUESTIONS

In order to test your progress, you should be able to answer the following questions.

1) Comparison operators always compare two values only.

   a) _____ True
   b) _____ False

2) The BETWEEN operator uses a list of values.

   a) _____ True
   b) _____ False

3) The following statement is incorrect:
```
SELECT first_name, last_name
  FROM student
 WHERE employer = NULL
```

   a) _____ True
   b) _____ False

4) The following statement is incorrect:
```
SELECT description
  FROM course
 WHERE cost NOT LIKE (1095, 1195)
```

   a) _____ True
   b) _____ False

5) The following statement is incorrect:
```
SELECT city
  FROM zipcode
 WHERE state != 'NY'
```

   a) _____ True
   b) _____ False

6) The following statement returns rows in the STUDENT table where the last name begins with the letters SM.

```
SELECT last_name, first_name
  FROM student
 WHERE last_name = 'SM%'
```

a) _____ True

b) _____ False

Answers appear in Appendix A, Section 2.4.

L A B   2 . 5

THE ORDER BY CLAUSE

LAB OBJECTIVES

After this lab, you will be able to:

✔ Custom Sort Query Results

USING THE ORDER BY CLAUSE

Recall from Chapter 1, "SQL and Data," that data is not stored in a table in any particular order. In all of the examples used thus far, the result sets display data in the order in which they happen to be returned from the database. However, you may want to view data in a certain order and the ORDER BY clause accomplishes this by ordering the data any way you wish.

For example, the following statement retrieves a list of course numbers and descriptions for courses without a prerequisite, in alphabetical order by their descriptions:

```
SELECT course_no, description
  FROM course
 WHERE prerequisite IS NULL
 ORDER BY description
COURSE_NO DESCRIPTION
--------- --------------------------
       10 DP Overview
       20 Intro to Computers
      146 Java for C/C++ Programmers
      310 Operating Systems

4 rows selected.
```

By default, when the ORDER BY is used, the result set is sorted in *ascending* order; or you can be explicit by adding the abbreviation ASC after the column. If descending order is desired, the abbreviation DESC is used after the column in the ORDER BY clause:

```
SELECT course_no, description
  FROM course
 WHERE prerequisite IS NULL
 ORDER BY description DESC
```
COURSE_NO DESCRIPTION
--------- -------------------------
```
      310 Operating Systems
      146 Java for C/C++ Programmers
       20 Intro to Computers
       10 DP Overview
```

4 rows selected.

Instead of listing the name of the column to be ordered, you can list the sequence number of the column in the SELECT list. The next SQL statement returns the same result as the prior SQL statement, but uses a different ORDER BY clause. The number 2 indicates the second column of the SELECT list.

```
SELECT course_no, description
  FROM course
 WHERE prerequisite IS NULL
```
ORDER BY 2 DESC

A result set can be sorted by more than one column. The columns you wish to sort by need only be included in the ORDER BY clause, separated by commas. The ORDER BY clause is always the last clause in an SQL statement.

COLUMN ALIAS

A column alias can be used in the SELECT list to give a column or value an alias; it can also make the result much easier to read. In next example, different forms of a column alias are used to take the place of the column name in the result set. An alias may also contain one or more words or be spelled in exact case when enclosed in double quotes. The optional keyword AS can precede the alias name.

```
SELECT first_name first,
       first_name "First Name",
       first_name AS "First"
  FROM student
 WHERE zip = '10025'
```

FIRST	First Name	First
Jerry	Jerry	Jerry
Nicole	Nicole	Nicole
Frank	Frank	Frank

3 rows selected.

To format the column with the SQL*Plus COLUMN format, you must specify the alias in quotes as well. For example:

```
COL "First" FORMAT A13
```

You can also use the column alias to order by a specific column.

```
SELECT first_name first, first_name "First Name",
       first_name AS "First"
  FROM student
 WHERE zip = '10025'
 ORDER BY "First Name"
FIRST                           First Name               First
------------------------------  -----------------------  -----------
Frank                           Frank                    Frank
Jerry                           Jerry                    Jerry
Nicole                          Nicole                   Nicole

3 rows selected.
```

DISTINCT AND ORDER BY

The ORDER BY clause often contains columns listed in the SELECT clause, but it is also possible to ORDER BY columns that are not selected. One exception is columns qualified using the DISTINCT keyword—if the SELECT list contains DISTINCT, the column(s) the keyword pertains to must also be listed in the ORDER BY clause.

The next example shows that the STUDENT_ID column is not a column listed in the DISTINCT SELECT list and therefore results in an Oracle error message.

```
SQL> SELECT DISTINCT first_name, last_name
  2    FROM student
  3   WHERE zip = '10025'
  4   ORDER BY student_id
  5  /
 ORDER BY student_id
          *
ERROR at line 4:
ORA-01791: not a SELECTed expression
```

UNDERSTANDING ORACLE ERROR MESSAGES

As you begin to learn SQL you will inevitably make mistakes when writing statements. Oracle returns an error number and error message to inform you of your mistake. Some error messages are easy to understand, others are not. While we cannot anticipate every possible error you may encounter, you will see that throughout the book we point out common mistakes. Here are some general guidelines when dealing with Oracle errors.

1. READ THE ORACLE ERROR MESSAGE CAREFULLY

Oracle will tell you on which line the error occurred.

```
SQL> SELECT salutation, first_name, las_name
  2    FROM student
  3    WHERE first_name = 'John'
  4  /
SELECT salutation, first_name, las_name
                                *
ERROR at line 1:
ORA-00904: invalid column name
```

In this example the error is very easy to spot and the error message is self-explanatory. One of the column names is invalid and Oracle points out the error by indicating the line number. The error is on line one and the asterisk indicates in what position within the line the error is found; it is the misspelled LAST_NAME column name.

2. RESOLVE ONE ERROR AT A TIME

Sometimes you may have multiple errors in a single SQL statement. The Oracle *parser*, which checks the syntax of all statements, starts checking from the end of the entire statement.

```
SQL> SELECT salutation, first_name, las_name
  2    FROM studen
  3    WHER first_name = 'John'
  4  /
 WHER first_name = 'John'
      *
ERROR at line 3:
ORA-00933: SQL command not properly ended
```

This type of error message may leave you clueless as to what could be wrong with this query. In fact, the statement contains three errors, one in each line. Because the parser works its way backwards, it complains about the first error on line three. The position of the asterisk suggests that there is something wrong with the spelling of the FIRST_NAME column. But in fact, it is spelled correctly; otherwise you would see the ORA-00904 invalid column name error listed as in the previous example complaining about the incorrect column name. The WHERE key word is missing the letter E and therefore Oracle cannot interpret what you are attempting to do.

After you correct this error, you will see line two reported, exemplifying how the parser works its way backward.

```
SQL> SELECT salutation, first_name, las_name
  2     FROM studen
  3   WHERE first_name = 'John'
  4   /
  FROM studen
       *
  ERROR at line 2:
  ORA-00942: table or view does not exist
```

Here the table name is misspelled and Oracle indicates that such a table does not exist.

The last error in the statement is found on line one and is the misspelled LAST_NAME column name. The parser will report this error as the last error. If you are unsure about the spelling of a column or table name, you can always use the DESCRIBE SQL*Plus command to list the column names and their respective data types or you can refer to Appendix D, "Student Database Schema," for a list of table and column names.

LAB 2.5

3. DOUBLE-CHECK THE SYNTAX OF YOUR STATEMENT

Simple typos, such as a stray period or comma, a missing space, or single quote, can cause very strange and seemingly unrelated error message that may have nothing to do with the problem. Therefore, carefully reread the statement or simply retype it. After looking at a statement for a long time, the error may not be apparent. Perhaps put it aside, take a break, and look at it with a fresh mind later, or ask someone for help in spotting the error.

4. LOOK UP THE ORACLE ERROR NUMBER

You can look up the Oracle error number in the *Oracle Database Error Messages Manual*. If the error starts with an ORA message type, it is typically a database-related error whereas an error with an SP2 prefix indicates a SQL*Plus or *i*SQL*Plus specific error. Once you found the error in the manual, you will see the reason for the error and a recommended action on how to correct it. The recommended action may be general or very specific, once again depending on what type of error occurred.

Initially, the challenge may be finding the correct manual to look up the error message. Following are some suggestions on how to find this information. Besides looking at the online documentation that comes with your Oracle software and which is either found on your CDs or installed on your machine, you can also find the online manual on the Oracle Technology Network (Technet) Web site. Oracle offers a free subscription to the site, which includes a number of features such as access to the online manuals and discussion groups. The URL for the Oracle Technet Web site is http://technet.oracle.com; you must register first to become a member. Also refer to Appendix H, "Navigating through the Oracle

Documentation" and Appendix G, "Resources." These appendixes offer you tips on how to find the needed information.

In some operating systems such as Unix, Linux, and VMS, you can also use the Oracle program called oerr to look up the error message from the operating system prompt. This does not work in the Windows environment. For example, to look up the ORA-00939 error you type at the Unix operating system prompt (indicated with the $ sign):

```
$ oerr ora 00939
00939, 00000, " too many arguments for function"
// *Cause: The function was referenced with too many arguments.
// *Action: Check the function syntax and specify only the
//          required number of arguments.
$
```

LAB 2.5 EXERCISES

2.5.1 CUSTOM SORT QUERY RESULTS

**LAB
2.5**

a) Write a SELECT statement to list each city in New York or Connecticut, sorted in ascending order by zip code.

b) Write a SELECT statement to list course descriptions and their prerequisite course numbers, sorted in ascending order by description. Do not list courses without a prerequisite.

c) Show the salutation, first, and last name of students with the last name Grant. Order the result by salutation in descending order and the first name in ascending order.

d) Execute the following query. What do you observe about the last row returned by the query?

```
SELECT student_id, last_name
  FROM student
 ORDER BY last_name
```

LAB 2.5 EXERCISE ANSWERS

2.5.1 ANSWERS

a) Write a SELECT statement to list each city in New York or Connecticut, sorted in ascending order by zip code.

Answer: The SELECT statement selects two columns, uses the equal operator and OR logical operator to combine expressions in the WHERE clause, and uses ORDER BY with a single column to sort the results in ascending order.

```
SELECT city, zip
  FROM zipcode
 WHERE state = 'NY'
    OR state = 'CT'
 ORDER BY zip
CITY                                ZIP
--------------------------------    -----
Ansonia                             06401
Middlefield                         06455
...
Hicksville                          11802
Endicott                            13760

142 rows selected.
```

Alternatively, the WHERE clause can be written as:

```
WHERE state IN ('NY', 'CT')
```

b) Write a SELECT statement to list course descriptions and their prerequisite course numbers, sorted in ascending order by description. Do not list courses without a prerequisite.

Answer: The following query shows the use of the IS NOT NULL comparison operator in the WHERE clause. The result is sorted by the DESCRIPTION column in ascending order.

```
SELECT description, prerequisite
  FROM course
 WHERE prerequisite IS NOT NULL
 ORDER BY description
DESCRIPTION                              PREREQUISITE
------------------------------------    ------------
Advanced Java Programming                        122
Advanced Unix Admin                              132
...
```

```
Structured Programming Techniques          204
Unix Tips and Techniques                   134

26 rows selected.
```

Alternatively, the ORDER BY clause can be written as:

```
ORDER BY 1
```

You can even use the column alias.

```
SELECT description "Descr", prerequisite
  FROM course
 WHERE prerequisite IS NOT NULL
 ORDER BY "Descr"
```

In most of the previous examples you see the SELECT list is taking up one line only. By spreading it over several lines, it sometimes makes it easier to read and this is perfectly acceptable formatting. By putting elements in the SELECT list on separate lines, you control exactly when the next line begins and indent it for easy readability below the line above it. The following SELECT statement has multiple columns in the SELECT list.

```
SELECT description, prerequisite,
       cost, modified_date
  FROM course
 WHERE prerequisite IS NOT NULL
 ORDER BY description
```

DESCRIPTION	PREREQUISITE	COST	MODIFIED_
Advanced Java Programming	122	1195	05-APR-99
...			
Unix Tips and Techniques	134	1095	05-APR-99

```
26 rows selected.
```

c) Show the salutation, first, and last name of students with the last name Grant. Order the result by salutation in descending order and the first name in ascending order.

Answer: The ORDER BY clause contains two columns, the SALUTATION and the FIRST_NAME. The salutation is sorted first in descending order. Within each salutation, the first name is sorted in ascending order.

```
SELECT salutation, first_name, last_name
  FROM STUDENT
 WHERE LAST_NAME = 'Grant'
 ORDER BY salutation DESC, first_name ASC
```

```
SALUT FIRST_NAME          LAST_NAME
----- ----------------    ---------
Ms.   Eilene              Grant
Ms.   Verona              Grant
Mr.   Omaira              Grant
Mr.   Scott               Grant

4 rows selected.
```

Again, you can write the query also with this ORDER BY clause:

```
ORDER BY 1 DESC, 2 ASC
```

Or to use the default order for the second column, which is ASC and can be omitted:

```
ORDER BY 1 DESC, 2
```

If you give your column a column alias, you can also use the column alias in the ORDER BY clause.

```
SELECT salutation "Sal", first_name "First Name",
       last_name "Last Name"
  FROM STUDENT
 WHERE LAST_NAME = 'Grant'
 ORDER BY "Sal" DESC, "First Name" ASC
Sal   First Name          Last Name
----- ----------------    ----------------
Ms.   Eilene              Grant
Ms.   Verona              Grant
Mr.   Omaira              Grant
Mr.   Scott               Grant

4 rows selected.
```

d) Execute the following query. What do you observe about the last row returned by the query?

```
SELECT student_id, last_name
  FROM student
 ORDER BY last_name
```

Answer: The student with the STUDENT_ID of 206 has the last name entered in lower-case. When ordering the result set, the lowercase letters are listed after the uppercase letters.

```
STUDENT_ID LAST_NAME
---------- -------------------------
       119 Abdou
       399 Abdou
...
```

```
184 Zuckerberg
206 annunziato
```

268 rows selected.

LAB 2.5 SELF-REVIEW QUESTIONS

In order to test your progress, you should be able to answer the following questions.

1) The following is the correct order of all clauses in this SELECT statement:

```
SELECT ...
   FROM ...
 ORDER BY ...
 WHERE ...
```

a) _____ True
b) _____ False

2) You must explicitly indicate whether an ORDER BY is ascending.

a) _____ True
b) _____ False

**LAB
2.5**

3) The following statement is correct:
```
SELECT *
   FROM instructor
 ORDER BY phone
```

a) _____ True
b) _____ False

4) The following statement is incorrect:

```
SELECT description "Description",
          prerequisite AS prereqs,
          course_no "Course#"
   FROM course
 ORDER BY 3, 2
```

a) _____ True
b) _____ False

5) You can order by a column you have not selected.

a) _____ True
b) _____ False

Answers appear in Appendix A, Section 2.5.

CHAPTER 2

TEST YOUR THINKING

The projects in this section are meant to have you utilize all of the skills that you have acquired throughout this chapter. The answers to these projects can be found at the companion Web site to this book, located at http://www.phptr.com/rischert.

Visit the Web site periodically to share and discuss your answers.

1) Invoke an editor from SQL*Plus; create a file called first.sql containing an SQL statement that retrieves data from the COURSE table for courses that cost 1195, and whose descriptions start with 'Intro', sorted by their prerequisites.

2) Create another file called second.sql that retrieves data from the STUDENT table for students whose last names begin with 'A', 'B', or 'C', and who work for 'Competrol Real Estate', sorted by their last names.

3) Create yet another file called third.sql that retrieves all the descriptions from the GRADE_TYPE table, for rows that were modified by the user MCAFFREY.

4) Execute each of the files, in the order they were created.

C H A P T E R   3

CHARACTER, NUMBER, AND MISCELLANEOUS FUNCTIONS

CHAPTER OBJECTIVES

In this chapter, you will learn about:

Functions are a useful part of the SQL language. They can transform data in a way that is different from the way it is stored in a database. A function is a type of formula whose result is one of two things: either a *transformation,* such as changing the name of a student to upper-case letters, or *information,* such as the length of a word in a column. Most functions share similar characteristics, including a name, and typically at least one input parameter, also called *argument,* inside a pair of matching parentheses:

```
function_name(input_parameter)
```

All functions in this chapter and next chapter are performed on a single row. This chapter discusses the CHARACTER, NUMBER, and miscellaneous functions. Chapter 4, "Date and Conversion Functions," discusses the DATE-related functions together with datatype conversion functions. Single-row functions are in contrast to aggregate functions, which are performed against multiple rows. You will learn about aggregate functions in Chapter 5, "Aggregate Functions, GROUP BY, and HAVING."

DATATYPES

Each value in Oracle has a datatype associated with it. A datatype determines its respective attributes and acceptable values. For example, you cannot enter a text value into a NUMBER datatype column or enter an invalid date such as 32-DEC-2002 into the DATE column. In most SQL operations, you use the NUMBER, VARCHAR2, and DATE datatypes. These are the commonly used datatypes where the vast majority of data is stored. In this chapter you will concentrate on functions related to the character and numeric data.

HOW TO READ A SYNTAX DIAGRAM

In this lab and the following chapters you will learn about many essential SQL functions and commands. The syntax of the individual commands or functions is listed together with many examples of usage. Table 3.1 lists the symbols that describe the syntax usage.

Table 3.1 ■ Syntax Symbols

Symbol	Usage
[ ]	Square brackets enclose syntax options.
{ }	Braces enclose items of which only one is required.
|	The vertical bar denotes options.
...	The three dots indicate that the preceding expression can be repeated.
Delimiters	Delimiters other than brackets, braces, bars, or the three dots must be entered exactly as shown on the syntax. Examples of such delimiters are commas, parentheses, and so on.
CAPS	Words in capital letters indicate the Oracle keywords that identify the individual elements of the SQL command or the name of the SQL function. The case of the keyword or command does not matter, but for readability is in uppercase letter.
UNDERLINE	Default values are underlined.

L A B   3 . 1

CHARACTER FUNCTIONS

LAB OBJECTIVES

After this lab, you will be able to:

✔ Use a Character Function in a SQL Statement
✔ Concatenate Strings

All character functions require alphanumeric input parameters. The input can be a *text literal* or *character literal,* sometimes referred to as a *string* or *text constant,* or a column of datatype VARCHAR2 or CHAR. Text literals are always surrounded by single quotes. This lab discusses the most frequently used character functions.

THE LOWER FUNCTION

The LOWER function transforms data into lower case. The next query shows how both a column and a text constant serve as individual parameters for the LOWER function:

```
SELECT state, LOWER(state), LOWER('State')
  FROM zipcode
ST LO LOWER
-- -- -----
PR pr state
MA ma state
...
NY ny state
NY ny state

227 rows selected.
```

The first column in the SELECT list displays the STATE column without any transformation. The second column uses the LOWER function to transform the values of the STATE column in the ZIPCODE table into lowercase letters. The third column of the SELECT list transforms the text constant 'State' into lower-case letters. Text constants used in a SELECT statement are repeated for every row of resulting output.

THE UPPER AND INITCAP FUNCTIONS

The UPPER function is the exact opposite of the LOWER function and transforms data into uppercase. The INITCAP function capitalizes the first letter of a word.

```
SELECT UPPER(city), state, INITCAP(state)
  FROM zipcode
 WHERE zip = '10035'
UPPER(CITY)                 ST IN
------------------------- -- --
NEW YORK                    NY Ny

1 row selected.
```

The syntax of the UPPER, LOWER, and INITCAP function is listed here:

```
UPPER(char)
LOWER(char)
INITCAP(char)
```

THE LPAD AND RPAD FUNCTIONS

The LPAD and RPAD functions also transform data: they *left pad* and *right pad* strings, respectively. When you pad a string, you add to it. These functions can add characters, symbols, or even spaces to strings in your result set. Unlike the LOWER, UPPER, or INITCAP functions, these functions take more than one parameter as their input.

This SELECT statement displays cities right padded with asterisks, and states left padded with dashes:

```
SELECT RPAD(city, 20, '*') "City Name",
       LPAD(state, 10, '-') "State Name"
  FROM zipcode
City Name            State Name
-------------------- ----------
Santurce***********  --------PR
North Adams********* --------MA
...
New York***********  --------NY
New York***********  --------NY

227 rows selected.
```

The CITY column is right padded with the asterisk '*' character up to a length of 20 characters. The STATE column is left padded with '-' up to a total length of 10 characters. Both the LPAD and RPAD functions use three parameters, separated by commas. The first input parameter accepts either a text literal or a column of datatype VARCHAR2 or CHAR. The second argument specifies the total length the string should be padded. The third optional argument indicates the character the string should be padded with. If this parameter is not specified, the string is padded with spaces by default.

The syntax for the LPAD and RPAD functions is this:

```
LPAD(char1, n [, char2])
RPAD(char1, n [, char2])
```

Char1 is the string to perform the function on, n represents the length the string should be padded to, and char2 is the optional parameter (denoted by the brackets) used to specify which character(s) to pad the string with. The next SELECT statement shows an example of the LPAD function with the third optional argument missing, thus left padding the column with spaces.

```
SELECT LPAD(city, 20) AS "City Name"
   FROM zipcode
City Name
--------------------
            Santurce
         North Adams
...
            New York
            New York

227 rows selected.
```

THE DUAL TABLE

DUAL is a table unique to Oracle. It contains a single row and a single column called DUMMY and holds no significant data of its own. It can be used in conjunction with functions to select values that do not exist in tables, such as text literals or today's date.

```
SQL> DESCR dual
 Name                      Null?    Type
 ------------------------- -------- ----------------------
 DUMMY                              VARCHAR2(1)
```

A single row is always returned in the result set. In some of the subsequent SQL examples you are not concerned with specific rows, but instead use literals to demonstrate the purpose of the function.

```
SELECT *
  FROM dual
D
-
X
```

1 row selected.

THE LTRIM, RTRIM, AND TRIM FUNCTIONS

LTRIM and RTRIM are the opposite of LPAD and RPAD because they *trim,* or remove, unwanted characters, symbols, or spaces in strings. In this example you see the use of the DUAL table to trim the zero (0) from the left, the right, and both sides. If both the left and right side of the string is trimmed, you need to nest the function. The result of one function provides the input for the other function.

```
SELECT LTRIM('0001234500', '0') left,
       RTRIM('0001234500', '0') right,
       LTRIM(RTRIM('0001234500', '0'), '0') both
  FROM dual
LEFT      RIGHT      BOTH
-------   --------   -----
1234500   00012345   12345
```

1 row selected.

Here is the syntax for the LTRIM and RTRIM functions. The optional parameter char2 is used to specify which character to trim from the string. If char2 is not specified, then the string is trimmed of spaces.

```
LTRIM(char1 [, char2])
RTRIM(char1 [, char2])
```

The TRIM function removes either leading characters, trailing characters or both, effectively doing the job of LTRIM and RTRIM in one function. If you want the function to act like LTRIM, specify LEADING as the first parameter; for RTRIM, use the TRAILING option; for both, specify either the BOTH keyword or omit it altogether.

The syntax for TRIM is as follows. The char1 indicates the *single* character to be removed; char2 is the string to be trimmed. If you don't specify char1, blank spaces are assumed.

```
TRIM([LEADING|TRAILING|BOTH] char1 FROM char2)
```

The next example shows the use of LEADING, TRAILING, and BOTH (if neither LEADING nor TRAILING is specified); the result is identical to the previous query:

```
SELECT TRIM(LEADING '0' FROM '0001234500') leading,
       TRIM(TRAILING '0' FROM '0001234500') trailing,
       TRIM('0' FROM '0001234500') both
   FROM dual
LEADING TRAILING BOTH
------- -------- -----
1234500 00012345 12345
```

1 row selected.

To trim blank spaces only, you can use this syntax:

```
TRIM(char2)
```

Here is an example of a string with blank characters. Note only leading and trailing blanks are trimmed and blank spaces in the middle of the string are ignored.

```
SELECT TRIM('   00012345  00  ') AS "Blank Trim"
   FROM dual
Blank Trim
-----------
00012345  00
```

1 row selected.

THE SUBSTR FUNCTION

SUBSTR is another function that transforms a string, returning a *substring* or *subset* of a string, based on its input parameters. The following query displays student last names, the *first* five characters of those last names, and the *remaining* characters of those last names in the third column:

```
SELECT last_name,
       SUBSTR(last_name, 1, 5),
       SUBSTR(last_name, 6)
   FROM student
LAST_NAME                     SUBST SUBSTR(LAST_NAME,6)
------------------------- ----- --------------------
Eakheit                       Eakhe it
Millstein                     Mills tein
...
Mastandora                    Masta ndora
Torres                        Torre s
```

268 rows selected.

The SUBSTR function's first input parameter is a string; the second is the start position of the subset; the third is optional, indicating the length of the subset. If the third parameter is not used, the default is to display the remainder of the string. Here is the syntax for SUBSTR:

```
SUBSTR(char1, n [, n])
```

THE INSTR FUNCTION

INSTR, meaning *in string,* looks for the occurrence of a string inside another string, returning the starting position of the search string within the target string. Unlike the other string functions, INSTR does not return another string, but a number instead. This query displays course descriptions and the position in which the first occurrence of the string 'er', if any, in the DESCRIPTION column appears:

```
SELECT description, INSTR(description, 'er')
  FROM course
DESCRIPTION                     INSTR(DESCRIPTION,'ER')
------------------------------- -----------------------
DP Overview                                           6
Intro to Computers                                   16
...
JDeveloper Techniques                                 9
DB Programming in Java                                0

30 rows selected.
```

As you can see in the first row of the result set, the string 'er' starts in the sixth position of the DP Overview. The last row, DB Programming in Java, does not contain an 'er' string, therefore the result is 0. INSTR can take two other optional input parameters. The syntax for INSTR is:

```
INSTR(char1, char2 [,n1 [, n2]])
```

The third parameter allows you to specify the start position for the search. The fourth parameter specifies which occurrence of the string to look for. When these optional parameters are not used, the default value is 1.

THE LENGTH FUNCTION

The following SQL statement selects a text literal from the DUAL table in conjunction with the LENGTH function, which determines the length of a string expressed as a number.

```
SELECT LENGTH('Hello there')
  FROM dual
LENGTH('HELLOTHERE')
--------------------
                  11

1 row selected.
```

FUNCTIONS IN WHERE AND ORDER BY CLAUSES

The use of functions is not restricted to the SELECT list; they are also used in other SQL clauses. In a WHERE clause, a function restricts the output to rows that only evaluate to the result of the function. In an ORDER BY clause, rows are sorted based on the result of a function. The next query uses the SUBSTR function in the WHERE clause to search for student last names that begin with the string 'Mo'. The arguments are the LAST_NAME column of the STUDENT table, starting with the first character of the column for a length of two characters.

```
SELECT first_name, last_name
  FROM student
 WHERE SUBSTR(last_name, 1, 2) = 'Mo'
```

FIRST_NAME	LAST_NAME
Edgar	Moffat
Angel	Moskowitz
Vinnie	Moon
Bernadette	Montanez

4 rows selected.

Alternatively, you can achieve the same result by replacing the SUBSTR function with this WHERE clause:

```
WHERE last_name LIKE 'Mo%'
```

The following SQL statement selects student first and last names, where the value in the FIRST_NAME column contains a period, and also orders the result set based on the length of students' last names:

```
SELECT first_name, last_name
  FROM student
 WHERE INSTR(first_name, '.') > 0
 ORDER BY LENGTH(last_name)
```

FIRST_NAME	LAST_NAME
Suzanne M.	Abid
D.	Orent
...	
V.	Saliternan
Z.A.	Scrittorale

21 rows selected.

NESTED FUNCTIONS

As you have seen on the example of LPAD and RPAD, functions can be nested within each other. Nested functions are evaluated starting from the inner function and working outward. The following example shows you the CITY column formatted in uppercase, right padded with periods.

```
SELECT RPAD(UPPER(city), 20,'.')
   FROM zipcode
  WHERE state = 'CT'
RPAD(UPPER(CITY),20,
--------------------
ANSONIA.............
MIDDLEFIELD.........
...
STAMFORD............
STAMFORD............

19 rows selected.
```

Here is a more complicated but useful example. You may have noticed that middle initials in the STUDENT table are entered in the same column as the first name. To separate the middle initial from the first name, nest the SUBSTR and INSTR functions. First, determine the position of the middle initial's period in the FIRST_NAME column with the INSTR function. From this position, deduct the number one. This brings you to the position before the period, where the middle initial starts, which is where you want the SUBSTR function to start. The WHERE clause only selects rows where the third or any subsequent character of the first name contains a period.

```
SELECT first_name,
       SUBSTR(first_name, INSTR(first_name, '.')-1) mi,
       SUBSTR(first_name, 1, INSTR(first_name, '.')-2)
first
   FROM student
  WHERE INSTR(first_name, '.') >= 3
FIRST_NAME                 MI    FIRST
------------------------- ---   -------
Austin V.                  V.    Austin
John T.                    T.    John
...
Suzanne M.                 M.    Suzanne
Rafael A.                  A.    Rafael

7 rows selected.
```

For example, in the row for Austin V., the position of the period (.) is 9, but you need to start at 8 to include the middle initial letter. The last column of the result lists the first name without the middle initial. This is accomplished by starting with the first character of the string and ending the string before the position where the middle initial starts. The key is to determine the ending position of the string with the INSTR function, and count back two characters.

When using nested functions, a common pitfall is to misplace matching parentheses or forget the second half of the pair altogether. Start by writing a nested function from the inside out. Count the number of left parentheses, and make sure it matches the number of right parentheses.

CONCATENATION

Concatenation connects strings *together* to become one. Strings can be concatenated to produce a single column in the result set. There are two methods of concatenation in Oracle: one is with the CONCAT function, the other is with the || symbol, also known as two *vertical bars* or *pipes*. The syntax of the CONCAT function is this:

```
CONCAT(char1, char2)
```

When you want to concatenate cities and states together using the CONCAT function you can use the function as follows:

```
SELECT CONCAT(city, state)
   FROM zipcode
CONCAT(CITY,STATE)
---------------------------
SanturcePR
North AdamsMA
...
New YorkNY
New YorkNY

227 rows selected.
```

The result set is difficult to read without spaces between cities and states. The CONCAT function takes only two parameters, so to add spaces between the strings using CONCAT is complex. By using the || symbol, you can easily concatenate several strings:

```
SELECT city||state||zip
   FROM zipcode
CITY||STATE||ZIP
---------------------------------
SanturcePR00914
North AdamsMA01247
...
```

```
New YorkNY10005
New YorkNY10035
```

```
227 rows selected.
```

For a result set that is easier to read, concatenate the strings with spaces and separate the CITY and STATE columns with a comma:

```
SELECT city||', '||state||' '||zip
   FROM zipcode
CITY||','||STATE||''||ZIP
-------------------------
Santurce, PR   00914
North Adams, MA   01247
...
New York, NY   10005
New York, NY   10035

227 rows selected.
```

THE REPLACE FUNCTION

The REPLACE function literally *replaces* a string with another string. In the following example, when the string 'hand' is found within the string 'My hand is asleep', it is replaced by the string 'foot':

```
SELECT REPLACE('My hand is asleep', 'hand', 'foot')
   FROM dual
REPLACE('MYHANDISA
------------------
My foot is asleep

1 row selected.
```

The following is the syntax for the REPLACE function:

```
REPLACE(char, if, then)
```

The second parameter looks to see if a string exists within the first parameter. If so, then it displays the third parameter. If the second parameter is not found, then the original string is displayed:

```
SELECT REPLACE('My hand is asleep', 'x', 'foot')
   FROM dual
REPLACE('MYHANDISA
------------------
My hand is asleep

1 row selected.
```

THE TRANSLATE FUNCTION

Unlike REPLACE, which replaces an entire string, the TRANSLATE function provides a one-for-one character substitution. For instance, it allows you to determine if all the phone numbers in the STUDENT table follow the same format. In the next query, TRANSLATE substitutes the '#' character for every character from '0' to '9'. If the character in the PHONE column of the STUDENT table is a hyphen (-), then it is substituted with the same character. All numbers and hyphens in the PHONE column are translated to either '#' or '-'. To check if the hyphens are also placed at the correct positions, use TRANSLATE to convert the characters, and then the values are checked against the '###-###-####' format.

```
SELECT phone
  FROM student
 WHERE TRANSLATE(
       phone, '0123456789-',
              '##########-') <> '###-###-####'
```

no rows selected

If any phone number is entered in an invalid format, such as 'abc-ddd-efgh' or '555-1212', the query returns the row(s) with the incorrect phone format. The following is the syntax for the TRANSLATE function:

```
TRANSLATE(char, if, then)
```

WHICH CHARACTER FUNCTION SHOULD YOU USE?

It's easy to confuse character functions. When deciding which one to use, ask yourself exactly what is needed in your result set. Are you looking for the position of a string in a string? Do you need to produce a subset of a string? Do you need to know how long a string is? Or do you need to replace a string with something else? Table 3.2 lists the character functions discussed in this lab.

LAB 3.1 EXERCISES

3.1.1 USE A CHARACTER FUNCTION IN A SQL STATEMENT

a) Execute the following SQL statement. Based on the result, what is the purpose of the INITCAP function?

```
SELECT description "Description",
       INITCAP(description) "Initcap Description"
  FROM course
 WHERE description LIKE '%SQL%'
```

Table 3.2 ■ Character Functions

Function	Purpose
LOWER(char)	Converts to lowercase
UPPER(char)	Converts to uppercase
INITCAP(char)	Capitalizes the first letter
LPAD(char1, n [, char2])	Left pads
RPAD(char1, n [, char2])	Right pads
LTRIM(char1 [, char2])	Left trims
RTRIM(char1 [, char2])	Right trims
TRIM([LEADING|TRAILING|BOTH] char1 FROM char2)	Trims leading, trailing or both sides
SUBSTR(char1, n [, n])	Cuts out a piece of the string
INSTR(char1, char2 [,n1 [, n2]])	Determines starting location of a string
LENGTH(char)	Returns length of a string
CONCAT(char1, char2)	Concatenates two strings
REPLACE(char, if, then)	Replaces string with another string
TRANSLATE(char, if, then)	Substitutes individual character

b) Write the question answered by the following SQL statement.

```
SELECT last_name
  FROM instructor
 WHERE LENGTH(last_name) >= 6
```

c) Describe the result of the following SQL statement. Pay particular attention to the negative number parameter.

```
SELECT SUBSTR('12345', 3),
       SUBSTR('12345', 3, 2),
       SUBSTR('12345', -4, 3)
  FROM dual
```

d) Based on the result of the following SQL statement, describe the purpose of the LTRIM and RTRIM functions.

```
SELECT zip, LTRIM(zip, '0'), RTRIM(ZIP, '4')
  FROM zipcode
 ORDER BY zip
```

e) What do you observe when you execute the next statement? How would you change the statement to achieve the desired result?

```
SELECT TRIM('01' FROM '01230145601')
  FROM dual
```

f) What is the result of the following statement?

```
SELECT TRANSLATE('555-1212', '0123456789-',
                             '##########-')
  FROM dual
```

g) Write the SQL statement to retrieve those students that have a last name with the lowercase letter 'o' occurring three or more times.

3.1.2 CONCATENATE STRINGS

a) Write a SELECT statement that returns each instructor's last name, followed by a comma and a space, followed by the instructor's first name, all in a single column in the result set.

b) Using functions in the SELECT list, WHERE, and ORDER BY clauses, write the SELECT statement that returns course numbers and course descriptions from the COURSE table and looks like the following result set:

```
Description
-------------------------------------------------
204.......Intro to SQL
130.......Intro to Unix
```

```
230.......Intro to Internet
20........Intro to Computers
25........Intro to Programming
120.......Intro to Java Programming
240.......Intro to the Basic Language

7 rows selected.
```

LAB 3.1 EXERCISE ANSWERS

3.1.1 ANSWERS

a) Execute the following SQL statement. Based on the result, what is the purpose of the INITCAP function?

```
SELECT description "Description",
       INITCAP(description) "Initcap Description"
  FROM course
 WHERE description LIKE '%SQL%'
```

Answer: The INITCAP function capitalizes the first letter of a word and forces the remaining characters to be lowercase.

The result set contains two rows, one displaying a course description as it appears in the database, and one displaying each word with only the first letter capitalized. Notice that INITCAP forces any capitalized words, such as PL/SQL or SQL, to be lowercase.

```
Description                       Initcap Description
------------------------          ------------------------
Intro to SQL                      Intro To Sql
PL/SQL Programming                Pl/Sql Programming

2 rows selected.
```

b) Write the question answered by the following SQL statement.

```
SELECT last_name
  FROM instructor
 WHERE LENGTH(last_name) >= 6
```

Answer: The question answered by the query could be phrased like this: "Which instructors have last names longer than six characters?"

```
LAST_NAME
-------------------------
Wojick
Schorin
...
Frantzen
Willig


7 rows selected.
```

The LENGTH function returns the length of a string, expressed as a number. The LENGTH function takes only a single input parameter, as in the following syntax:

```
LENGTH(char)
```

c) Describe the result of the following SQL statement. Pay particular attention to the negative number parameter.

```
SELECT SUBSTR('12345', 3),
       SUBSTR('12345', 3, 2),
       SUBSTR('12345', -4, 3)
  FROM dual
```

Answer: The first column takes the characters starting from position three until the end, resulting in the string '345'. The second SUBSTR function also starts at position three but ends after two characters, and therefore returns '34'. The third column has a negative number as the first parameter. It counts from the end of the string to the left four characters; thus the substring starts at position 2 and for a length of three characters, resulting in '234'.

```
SUB SU SUB
--- -- ---
345 34 234


1 row selected.
```

d) Based on the result of the following SQL statement, describe the purpose of the LTRIM and RTRIM functions.

```
SELECT zip, LTRIM(zip, '0'), RTRIM(ZIP, '4')
  FROM zipcode
 ORDER BY zip
```

Answer: The LTRIM and RTRIM functions left trim and right trim strings based on the function's parameters. With the three columns in the result set side by side, you see the differences: the first column shows the ZIP column without modification, the second with ZIP left-trimmed of its 0s, and the third with ZIP right-trimmed of its 4s.

```
ZIP    LTRIM RTRIM
-----  ----- -----
00914  914   0091
01247  1247  01247
...
43224  43224 4322
48104  48104 4810

227 rows selected.
```

e) What do you observe when you execute the next statement? How would you change the statement to achieve the desired result?

```
SELECT TRIM('01' FROM '01230145601')
   FROM dual
```

Answer: The query results in an error indicating that only one character can be trimmed at a time. This query attempts to trim two characters, which are 0 and 1. Nest the LTRIM and RTRIM functions to achieve the desired result.

```
SQL> SELECT TRIM('01' FROM '01230145601')
  2     FROM dual
  3  /
SELECT TRIM('01' FROM '01230145601')
           *
ERROR at line 1:
ORA-30001: trim set should have only one character
```

To replace multiple characters, nest the LTRIM and RTRIM functions instead. If you tried the REPLACE function, you will notice that it will replace all occurrences of the '01' string, not just the first and last.

```
SELECT LTRIM('01230145601', '01') left,
       RTRIM('01230145601', '01') right,
       RTRIM(LTRIM('01230145601', '01'), '01') both,
       REPLACE('01230145601', '01') replace
   FROM dual
LEFT       RIGHT      BOTH     REPLA
---------- ---------- -------- -----
230145601  012301456  2301456  23456

1 row selected.
```

f) What is the result of the following statement?

```
SELECT TRANSLATE('555-1212', '0123456789-',
                             '##########-')
   FROM dual
```

Answer: It returns the result ####-#####. The TRANSLATE function is a character substitution function. The listed SQL statement uses each of the characters of the string '555-1212' to look up the corresponding character and then returns this character. One of the uses for this function is to determine if data is entered in the correct format.

```
TRANSLAT
--------
###-####


1 row selected.
```

USING TRANSLATE FOR PATTERN SEARCH

The TRANSLATE function also comes in handy when you need to perform a pattern search using the LIKE operator and you are looking for the actual wildcard characters % or _. Assume you need to query the STUDENT table and you want to find any students where the student's employer spells their name similar to the pattern 'B_B'. The underscore has to be taken as a literal underscore, not as a wildcard. Qualifying employer names are 'Bayer B_Biller' or 'ABCB_Bellman'. Unfortunately, no such employer names exist in the STUDENT database, but there are occasions when data entry errors occur and you need to figure out which are the offending rows. The following query will check if such an employer with the pattern 'B_B' exists in the table:

```
SELECT student_id, employer
  FROM student
 WHERE TRANSLATE(employer, '_', '+') LIKE '%B+B%'
```

As you can see, the TRANSLATE function performs this trick. Here the underscore is replaced with the plus sign and then the LIKE function is applied with the replaced plus sign in the character literal.

USING INSTR FOR PATTERN SEARCH

Another way to solve this query would be to use the INSTR function.

```
SELECT student_id, employer
  FROM student
 WHERE INSTR(employer, 'B_B') > 0
```

THE ESCAPE CHARACTER AND THE LIKE OPERATOR

Yet another way to determine any such employers in the STUDENT table is with the escape character functionality in conjunction with the LIKE operator. In the next example, the backslash (\) sign is selected as the escape character to indicate that the underscore character following the character is to be interpreted as a literal underscore and not as the wildcard underscore.

```
SELECT student_id, employer
  FROM student
 WHERE employer LIKE '%B\_B%' ESCAPE '\'
```

g) Write the SQL statement to retrieve those students that have a last name with the lowercase letter 'o' occurring three or more times.

Answer: The INSTR function determines the third or more occurrence of the lowercase letter o in the LAST_NAME column of the STUDENT table.

The INSTR function has two required parameters; the rest are optional and default to 1. The first parameter is the string or column where the function needs to be applied and where you are looking to find the desired values. The second parameter identifies the search string; here you are looking for the letter 'o'. The third parameter determines at which starting position the search must occur. The last parameter specifies which occurrence of the string is requested.

If the INSTR function finds the desired result it returns the starting position of the searched value. The WHERE clause condition looks for those rows where the result of the INSTR function is greater than 0.

```
SELECT student_id, last_name
  FROM student
 WHERE INSTR(last_name, 'o', 1, 3) > 0
STUDENT_ID LAST_NAME
---------- ------------------------
       280 Engongoro
       251 Frangopoulos
       254 Chamnonkool

3 rows selected.
```

3.1.2 ANSWERS

a) Write a SELECT statement that returns each instructor's last name, followed by a comma and a space, followed by the instructor's first name, all in a single column in the result set.

Answer: The instructor's last name, a comma and a space, and the instructor's first name are all concatenated using the || symbol.

```
SELECT last_name||', '||first_name
  FROM instructor
LAST_NAME||','||FIRST_NAME
--------------------------
Hanks, Fernand
Wojick, Tom
```

```
...
Frantzen, Marilyn
Willig, Irene

10 rows selected.
```

b) Using functions in the SELECT list, WHERE, and ORDER BY clauses, write the SELECT statement that returns course numbers and course descriptions from the COURSE table and looks like the following result set:

```
Description
-----------------------------------------------
204.......Intro to SQL
130.......Intro to Unix
230......Intro to Internet
20.......Intro to Computers
25........Intro to Programming
120.......Intro to Java Programming
240.......Intro to the Basic Language

7 rows selected.
```

Answer: The RPAD function right pads the COURSE_NO column with periods, up to 10 characters long; it is then concatenated with the DESCRIPTION column. The INSTR function is used in the WHERE clause to filter on descriptions starting with the string 'Intro'. The LENGTH function is used in the ORDER BY clause to sort the result set by ascending (shortest to longest) description length.

```
SELECT RPAD(course_no, 10, '.')||description
       AS "Description"
  FROM course
 WHERE INSTR(description, 'Intro') = 1
 ORDER BY LENGTH(description)
```

The same result can be obtained without the use of the INSTR function, as in the following WHERE clause:

```
WHERE description LIKE 'Intro%'
```

As you can see, concatenation combined with functions is a powerful way to quickly produce result sets that are useful and easy to read.

LAB 3.1 SELF-REVIEW QUESTIONS

In order to test your progress, you should be able to answer the following questions.

1) Functions that operate on single values can only have one input parameter.

    a) _____   True
    b) _____   False

2) The DUAL table can be used for testing functions.

    a) _____   True
    b) _____   False

3) The same function can be used twice in a SELECT statement.

    a) _____   True
    b) _____   False

4) The following SELECT statement contains an error:

```
SELECT UPPER(description)
   FROM LOWER(course)
```

    a) _____   True
    b) _____   False

5) The RTRIM function is useful for eliminating extra spaces in a string.

    a) _____   True
    b) _____   False

6) Which one of the following string functions tells you how many characters are in a string?

    a) _____   INSTR
    b) _____   SUBSTR
    c) _____   LENGTH
    d) _____   REPLACE

7) Which result will the following query return?

```
SELECT TRIM('   Mary Jones   ')
   FROM dual
```

    a) _____   Mary Jones
    b) _____   Mary Jones
    c) _____   MaryJones
    d) _____   The query returns an error.

8) The functions INSTR, SUBSTR, and TRIM are all single-row functions.

    a) _____ True
    b) _____ False

9) Which character function returns a specified portion of a character string?

    a) _____ INSTR
    b) _____ LENGTH
    c) _____ SUBSTR
    d) _____ INSTRING

Answers appear in Appendix A, Section 3.1.

L A B   3 . 2

NUMBER FUNCTIONS

LAB OBJECTIVES

After this lab, you will be able to:

✔ Use Number Functions and Perform Mathematical Computations

Number functions are valuable tools for operations such as rounding numbers or computing the absolute value of a number. There are several single-row number functions in Oracle; the most useful ones are discussed here.

THE ABS FUNCTION

The ABS function computes the *absolute value* of a number, measuring its magnitude:

```
SELECT 'The absolute value of -29 is '||ABS(-29)
  FROM dual
'THEABSOLUTEVALUEOF-29IS'||ABS(
-----------------------------
The absolute value of -29 is 29

1 row selected.
```

ABS takes only a single input parameter, and its syntax is this:

```
ABS(value)
```

THE SIGN FUNCTION

The SIGN function tells you the *sign* of a value, returning a number 1 for positive numbers, –1 for negative numbers, or 0 for a zero. The following example compares SIGN with the ABS function:

```
SELECT -14, SIGN(-14), SIGN(14), SIGN(0), ABS(-14)
  FROM dual
        -14 SIGN(-14) SIGN(14)    SIGN(0)  ABS(-14)
--------- --------- -------- ---------- ---------
        -14        -1        1          0        14
```

1 row selected.

SIGN also takes only a single input parameter, and its syntax is this:

```
SIGN(value)
```

*Most single-row functions return NULL when a NULL is the input
parameter.*

THE MOD FUNCTION

MOD is a function returning the *modulus,* or the remainder, of a value divided by
another value. It takes two input parameters, as in this SELECT statement:

```
SELECT MOD(20, 7)
  FROM dual
MOD(20,7)
----------
         6
```

1 row selected.

The MOD function divides 20 by 7 returning a remainder of 6. Here is the syntax
for MOD:

```
MOD(value, divisor)
```

The MOD function is particularly useful if you want to determine if a value is
odd or even. If you divide by 2 and the remainder is a zero, this indicates that the
value is even; if the remainder is one it means that the value is odd.

ROUND VS. TRUNC

ROUND and TRUNC are two useful functions that *round* and *truncate* (or cut off)
values, respectively, based on a given number of digits of precision. The next SE-
LECT statement illustrates the use of ROUND and TRUNC, which both take two
input parameters:

```
SELECT 222.34501,
       ROUND(222.34501, 2),
       TRUNC(222.34501, 2)
   FROM dual
222.34501 ROUND(222.34501,2) TRUNC(222.34501,2)
--------- ------------------ ------------------
222.34501            222.35             222.34

1 row selected.
```

Here, ROUND(2.34501,2) rounds the number 2.34501 to two digits to the right of the decimal, rounding the result up to 2.35, following the normal convention for rounding. In contrast, TRUNC has cut off all digits beyond two digits to the right of the decimal, resulting in 2.34. ROUND and TRUNC can be used to affect the *left* side of the decimal as well by passing a negative number as a parameter:

```
SELECT 222.34501,
       ROUND(222.34501, -2),
       TRUNC(222.34501, -2)
   FROM dual
222.34501 ROUND(222.34501,-2) TRUNC(222.34501,-2)
--------- ------------------- -------------------
222.34501                 200                 200

1 row selected.
```

Here is the syntax for both ROUND and TRUNC:

```
ROUND(value [, precision])
TRUNC(value [, precision])
```

Numbers with decimal places may be rounded to whole numbers by omitting the second parameter, or specifying a precision of 0:

```
SELECT 2.617, ROUND(2.617), TRUNC(2.617)
   FROM dual
2.617 ROUND(2.617) TRUNC(2.617)
----- ------------ ------------
2.617            3            2

1 row selected.
```

You can use the TRUNC and ROUND function not only on values of the NUMBER datatype but also on the DATE datatype, discussed in Chapter 4, "Date and Conversion Functions."

THE FLOOR AND CEIL FUNCTIONS

The CEIL function returns the smallest integer greater than or equal to a value; the FLOOR function returns the largest integer equal to or less than a value. These functions perform much like the ROUND and TRUNC functions without the optional precision parameter.

**LAB
3.2**

```
SELECT FLOOR(22.5), CEIL(22.5), TRUNC(22.5), ROUND(22.5)
  FROM dual
FLOOR(22.5) CEIL(22.5) TRUNC(22.5) ROUND(22.5)
----------- ---------- ----------- -----------
         22         23          22          23

1 row selected.
```

The syntax for the FLOOR and CEIL functions is:

```
FLOOR(value)
CEIL(value)
```

ARITHMETIC OPERATORS

The four mathematical operators (addition, subtraction, multiplication, and division) may be used in a SQL statement and can be combined.

Here, each of the four computations is used with course costs. Notice that one of the distinct course costs is null; here the computation with a null value yields another null.

```
SELECT DISTINCT cost, cost + 10,
       cost - 10, cost * 10, cost / 10
  FROM course
    COST    COST+10    COST-10    COST*10    COST/10
--------- ---------- ---------- ---------- ---------
     1095       1105       1085      10950     109.5
     1195       1205       1185      11950     119.5
     1595       1605       1585      15950     159.5


4 rows selected.
```

Parentheses are used to group computations, indicating precedence of the operators. The following SELECT statement returns distinct course costs increased by 10%. The computation within the parentheses is evaluated first, followed by the addition of the value in the COST column, resulting in a single number. NULL values can be replaced with a default value. You will learn about this topic in Lab 3.3.

```
SELECT DISTINCT cost + (cost * .10)
  FROM course
COST+(COST*.10)
---------------
        1204.5
        1314.5
        1754.5
```

4 rows selected.

WHICH NUMBER FUNCTION SHOULD YOU USE?

Table 3.3 lists the number functions discussed in this lab. Sometimes you may nest these functions within other functions. As you progress through the following chapters you will see specifically the usefulness of some of these function to write sophisticated SQL statements.

Table 3.3 ■ Number Functions

Function	Purpose
ABS(value)	Returns absolute value
SIGN(value)	Returns sign of a value such as 1, –1, and 0
MOD(value, divisor)	Returns remainder
ROUND(value [, precision])	Rounds value
TRUNC(value [, precision])	Truncates value
FLOOR(value)	Returns largest integer
CEIL(value)	Returns smallest integer

LAB 3.2 EXERCISES

3.2.1 USE NUMBER FUNCTIONS AND PERFORM MATHEMATICAL COMPUTATIONS

a) Describe the effect of the negative precision as a parameter of the ROUND function in the following SQL statement.

```
SELECT 10.245, ROUND(10.245, 1), ROUND(10.245, -1)
  FROM dual
```

b) Write a SELECT statement that displays distinct course costs. In a separate column, show the COST increased by 75% and round the decimals to the nearest dollar.

c) Write a SELECT statement that displays distinct numeric grades from the GRADE table, and half those values expressed as a whole number in a separate column.

LAB 3.2 EXERCISE ANSWERS

3.2.1 ANSWERS

a) Describe the effect of the negative precision as a parameter of the ROUND function in the following SQL statement.

```
SELECT 10.245, ROUND(10.245, 1), ROUND(10.245, -1)
  FROM dual
```

Answer: A negative precision rounds digits to the left of the decimal point.

```
  10.245 ROUND(10.245,1) ROUND(10.245,-1)
--------- --------------- ----------------
  10.245            10.2               10
```

```
1 row selected.
```

b) Write a SELECT statement that displays distinct course costs. In a separate column, show the COST increased by 75% and round the decimals to the nearest dollar.

Answer: The SELECT statement uses multiplication and the ROUND function.

```
SELECT DISTINCT cost, cost*1.75, ROUND(cost*1.75)
  FROM course
     COST COST*1.75 ROUND(COST*1.75)
--------- --------- ----------------
     1095   1916.25             1916
     1195   2091.25             2091
     1595   2791.25             2791
```

```
4 rows selected.
```

**LAB
3.2**

c) Write a SELECT statement that displays distinct numeric grades from the GRADE table, and half those values expressed as a whole number in a separate column.

Answer: The SELECT statement uses division to derive the value that is half the original value. That value becomes the input parameter for the ROUND function, without specifying a precision, to display the result as a whole number.

```
SELECT DISTINCT numeric_grade, ROUND(numeric_grade / 2)
  FROM grade
NUMERIC_GRADE ROUND(NUMERIC_GRADE/2)
------------- ----------------------
           70                     35
           71                     36
...
           98                     49
           99                     50

30 rows selected.
```

Here, a mathematical computation is combined with a function. Be sure to place computations correctly, either inside or outside the parentheses of a function, depending on the desired result. In this case, if the / 2 were on the outside of the ROUND function, a very different result occurs, not the correct answer to the task that was posed.

LAB 3.2 SELF-REVIEW QUESTIONS

In order to test your progress, you should be able to answer the following questions.

1) Number functions can be nested.

a) _____ True
b) _____ False

2) The ROUND function can take only the NUMBER datatype as a parameter.

a) _____ True
b) _____ False

3) The following SELECT statement is incorrect:

```
SELECT capacity - capacity
  FROM section
```

a) _____ True
b) _____ False

4) What does the following function return?

```
SELECT LENGTH(NULL)
  FROM dual
```

a) _____   4
b) _____   0
c) _____   Null

Answers appear in Appendix A, Section 3.2.

LAB 3.3

MISCELLANEOUS SINGLE-ROW FUNCTIONS

LAB OBJECTIVES

After this lab, you will be able to:

✔ Apply Substitution Functions and Other
  Miscellaneous Functions
✔ Utilize the Power of DECODE Function
  and the CASE Expression

In this lab you will learn about substitution functions to replace nulls with default values. You will also utilize the DECODE function and the CASE expression; these functions are destined to become your favorites, they allow you to perform powerful *if then else* comparisons.

THE NVL FUNCTION

The NVL function replaces a NULL value with a default value. NULLs represent a special challenge when used in calculations. A computation with an unknown value yields another unknown value, as you see in the following example.

```
SELECT 60+60+NULL
  FROM dual
60+60+NULL
----------


1 row selected.
```

To avoid this problem, you can use the NVL function to substitute the NULL for another value.

```
NVL(input_expression, substitution_expression)
```

The NVL function requires two parameters: an input expression (i.e., a column, literal, or a computation) and a substitution expression. If the input expression does *not* contain a NULL value, the input parameter is returned. If the input parameter does contain a NULL value, then the substitution parameter is returned.

In the following example, the substitution value is the number literal 1000. The NULL is substituted with 1000, resulting in the output 1120.

```
SELECT 60+60+NVL(NULL, 1000)
  FROM dual
60+60+NVL(NULL,1000)
--------------------
                1120

1 row selected.
```

When you substitute a value, the datatype of the substituted value must agree with the datatype of the input parameter. The next example uses the NVL function to substitute any NULL values with 'Not Applicable' in the PREREQUISITE column. An error is encountered when the statement is executed because the datatypes of the two parameters are different. The substitution parameter is a text literal, and the column PREREQUISITE is defined as a NUMBER datatype.

```
SELECT course_no, description,
       NVL(prerequisite, 'Not Applicable') prereq
  FROM course
 WHERE course_no IN (20, 100)
NVL(prerequisite, 'Not Applicable') prereq
                 *
ERROR at line 2:
ORA-01722: invalid number
```

The error indicates Oracle cannot convert the text literal 'Not Applicable' into a NUMBER. To overcome this problem, transform the output of the PREREQUISITE column into a VARCHAR2 datatype using the TO_CHAR datatype conversion function. This function takes a NUMBER or DATE datatype and converts it into a string.

```
SELECT course_no, description,
       NVL(TO_CHAR(prerequisite), 'Not Applicable') prereq
  FROM course
 WHERE course_no IN (20, 100)
COURSE_NO DESCRIPTION              PREREQ
--------- ------------------------ ----------------
      100 Hands-On Windows         20
       20 Intro to Computers       Not Applicable

2 rows selected.
```

THE COALESCE FUNCTION

The COALESCE function is similar to the NVL function, yet with an additional twist. Instead of specifying one substitution expression for a null value, you can optionally evaluate multiple substitution columns or substitution expressions. The syntax is:

```
COALESCE(input_expression, substitution_expression_1,
[, substitution_expression_n])
```

**LAB
3.3**

The next SQL query shows the case of multiple substitution expressions, two substitutions to be precise. A table called GRADE_SUMMARY, which is not part of the STUDENT schema, illustrates the idea.

The structure of the GRADE_SUMMARY TABLE is as follows:

```
SQL> DESCR grade_summary
 Name                              Null?      Type
 -------------------------------- --------   ----
 STUDENT_ID                                  NUMBER(8)
 MIDTERM_GRADE                               NUMBER(3)
 FINALEXAM_GRADE                             NUMBER(3)
 QUIZ_GRADE                                  NUMBER(3)
```

The resulting output of the "Coalesce" column shows that if the midterm grade is null, the final exam grade is substituted. If the final exam grade is also null then the grade for the quiz is substituted. You notice that this is the case with student 678 where both the MIDTERM_GRADE and the FINALEXAM_GRADE column values are null, therefore the value in the QUIZ_GRADE column is substituted. For student 999 all the column values are null, therefore the COALESCE function returns a null value.

```
SELECT student_id, midterm_grade, finalexam_grade, quiz_grade,
       COALESCE(midterm_grade, finalexam_grade, quiz_grade) "Coalesce"
  FROM grade_summary
```

STUDENT_ID	MIDTERM_GRADE	FINALEXAM_GRADE	QUIZ_GRADE	Coalesce
123	90	50	100	90
456	80	95		80
678			98	98
789		78	85	78
999				

5 rows selected.

(Note that the GRADE_SUMMARY table is a de-normalized table, not what we recommend you design unless you have a very good reason to de-normalize, but the purpose here is to illustrate the functionality of COALESCE. If you wish, you can create this table by downloading an additional script from the companion Web site.)

The following is an example using the COALESCE function with just a one substitution expression, which is equivalent to the NVL function discussed previously. The TO_CHAR function is necessary because the datatypes of the expressions do not agree. In this case, the PREREQUISITE column is of datatype NUMBER. The "Not Applicable" string is a character constant. You can use the TO_CHAR conversion function to make the two datatypes equivalent. The TO_CHAR function and conversion functions in general are covered in greater detail in Chapter 4, "Date and Conversion Functions."

```
SELECT course_no, description,
       COALESCE(TO_CHAR(prerequisite), 'Not Applicable') prereq
  FROM course
 WHERE course_no IN (20, 100)
COURSE_NO DESCRIPTION          PREREQ
--------- -------------------- ----------------
      100 Hands-On Windows     20
       20 Intro to Computers   Not Applicable

2 rows selected.
```

THE NVL2 FUNCTION

The NVL2 function is yet another extension of the NVL function. It checks for both not null and null values and has three parameters versus NVL's two parameters. The syntax for the function is as follows:

```
NVL2(input_expr, not_null_substitution_expr, null_substitution_expr)
```

If the input expression is not null, the second parameter of the function, the `not_null_substitution_expr`, is returned. If the input expression is null, then the last parameter, the `null_substitution_expr`, is returned instead. This query shows how the NVL2 function works. The distinct course costs are displayed; if the value in the COST column is not null, the literal `exists` is displayed; otherwise the result displays the word `none`.

```
SELECT DISTINCT cost,
       NVL2(cost, 'exists', 'none') "NVL2"
  FROM course
      COST NVL2
---------- ------
      1095 exists
      1195 exists
      1595 exists
           none

4 rows selected.
```

THE NULLIF FUNCTION

The NULLIF function is different because it generates null values. The function compares two expressions; if the values are equal, the function returns a null; otherwise, the function returns the first expression. The following SQL statement returns null for the NULLIF function if the values in the columns CREATED_DATE and MODIFIED_DATE are equal. This is the case for the row with the STUDENT_ID of 150. Both date columns are exactly the same, therefore the result of the NULLIF function is null. For the row with a STUDENT_ID of 340, the columns contain different values, therefore the first substitution expression is displayed. In this example, you see the use of the TO_CHAR function together with a DATE datatype as the input parameter. This allows the display of dates as formatted character strings. This functionality is explained in greater detail in Chapter 4, "Date and Conversion Functions."

```
SELECT student_id,
       TO_CHAR(created_date, 'DD-MON-YY HH24:MI:SS') "Created",
       TO_CHAR(modified_date, 'DD-MON-YY HH24:MI:SS') "Modified",
       NULLIF(created_date, modified_date) "Null if equal"
  FROM student
 WHERE student_id IN (150, 340)
STUDENT_ID Created             Modified            Null if e
---------- ------------------- ------------------- ---------
       150 30-JAN-99 00:00:00 30-JAN-99 00:00:00
       340 19-FEB-99 00:00:00 22-FEB-99 00:00:00 19-FEB-99

2 rows selected.
```

The syntax for the NULLIF function is as follows:

```
NULLIF(expression1, equal_expression2)
```

THE DECODE FUNCTION

The DECODE function substitutes values based on a condition using *if then else* logic. If a value is equal to another value, the substitution value is returned. If the value compared is not equal to any of the listed expressions, a default value can be returned. The syntax code for the DECODE function is:

```
DECODE (if_expr, equals_search,
        then_result [,else_default])
```

Note that the search and result values can be repeated.

In the following query, the text literals 'New York' and 'New Jersey' are returned when the state is equal to 'NY' or 'NJ', respectively. If the value in the STATE column is other than 'NY' or 'NJ', a null value is displayed. The second DECODE function shows the use of the *else* condition. In the case of 'CT', the function returns the value 'Other'.

```
SELECT DISTINCT state,
       DECODE(state, 'NY', 'New York',
                     'NJ', 'New Jersey') no_default,
       DECODE(state, 'NY', 'New York',
                     'NJ', 'New Jersey',
                           'OTHER') with_default
  FROM zipcode
 WHERE state IN ('NY','NJ','CT')
ST NO_DEFAULT WITH_DEFAU
-- ---------- ----------
CT            Other
NJ New Jersey New Jersey
NY New York   New York

3 rows selected.
```

**LAB
3.3**

THE DECODE FUNCTION AND NULLS

If you want to specifically test for the null value, you can use the keyword NULL. The following SQL statement shows for instructors with a null value in the ZIP column the text "NO zipcode!". Although one null does not equal another null, for the purpose of the DECODE function, null values are treated as equals.

```
SELECT instructor_id, zip,
       DECODE(zip, NULL, 'NO zipcode!', zip) "Decode Use"
  FROM instructor
 WHERE instructor_id IN (102, 110)
INSTRUCTOR_ID ZIP   Decode Use
------------- ----- -----------
          110       NO zipcode!
          102 10025 10025

2 rows selected.
```

The above result can be achieved with the NVL function.

```
SELECT instructor_id, zip,
       NVL(zip, 'NO zipcode!') "NVL Use"
  FROM instructor
 WHERE instructor_id IN (102, 110)
```

THE DECODE FUNCTION AND COMPARISONS

The DECODE function does not allow greater than or less than comparisons; however, combining the DECODE function with the SIGN function overcomes this shortcoming.

The following SELECT statement combines the DECODE and SIGN functions to display the course cost as 500 for courses that cost less than 1195. If the course cost is greater than or equal to 1195, the actual cost is displayed. The calculation of the value in the COST column minus 1195 results in a negative number, a positive number, a zero, or null. The SIGN function determines the sign of the calculation and returns respectively -1, +1, 0, or null. The DECODE function checks if the result equals -1. If so, this indicates that the cost is less than 1195 and the DECODE function returns 500; otherwise the regular cost is shown. See Chapter 15, "Advanced SQL Queries," for additional examples on the DECODE and SIGN functions.

```
SELECT course_no, cost,
       DECODE(SIGN(cost-1195),-1, 500, cost) newcost
  FROM course
 WHERE course_no IN (80, 20, 135, 450)
 ORDER BY 2
```

COURSE_NO	COST	NEWCOST
135	1095	500
20	1195	1195
80	1595	1595
450		

4 rows selected.

THE SEARCHED CASE EXPRESSION

A searched CASE expression is extremely powerful and can be utilized in many ways in SQL. It can be used in the SELECT list, the WHERE clause, the ORDER BY clause, as a parameter of a function, or anywhere an expression is allowed. Using a CASE expression is, in many cases, easier to understand, less restrictive, and more versatile than the DECODE function. For example, the following query accomplishes the same result as the previous query.

```
SELECT course_no, cost,
       CASE WHEN cost <1195 THEN 500
            ELSE cost
       END "Test CASE"
  FROM course
 WHERE course_no IN (80, 20, 135, 450)
 ORDER BY 2
```

COURSE_NO	COST	Test CASE
135	1095	500
20	1195	1195
80	1595	1595
450		

4 rows selected.

Each CASE expression starts with the keyword CASE and ends with the keyword END; the ELSE clause is optional. A condition is tested with the WHEN keyword; if the condition is true, the THEN clause is executed. The result of the query shows 500 in the column labeled "Test Case" when the value in the COST column is less than 1195, otherwise it just displays the value of the COST column. Following is the syntax of the searched CASE expression:

```
CASE {WHEN condition THEN return_expr
      [WHEN condition THEN return_expr]... }
      [ELSE else_expr]
END
```

LAB 3.3

The next example expands the WHEN condition of the CASE expression with multiple conditions being tested. The first condition checks whether the value in the COST column is less than 1100; when true, the result evaluates to 1000. If the value in the COST column is equal to or greater than 1100, but less than 1500, the value in the COST column is multiplied by 1.1, increasing the cost by 10%. If the value in the COST column is null then the value zero is the result. Lastly if none of the condition is true, the ELSE clause is returned.

```
SELECT course_no, cost,
       CASE WHEN cost <1100 THEN 1000
            WHEN cost >=1100 AND cost <1500 THEN cost*1.1
            WHEN cost IS NULL THEN 0
            ELSE cost
       END "Test CASE"
  FROM course
 WHERE course_no IN (80, 20, 135, 450)
 ORDER BY 2
```

COURSE_NO	COST	Test CASE
135	1095	1000
20	1195	1314.5
80	1595	1595
450		0

4 rows selected.

The CASE expression lets you evaluate if-then-else conditions more simply than the DECODE function.

NESTING CASE EXPRESSIONS

A CASE expression can be nested further with additional CASE expressions as shown in the next example. An additional row with the COURSE_NO of 230 is included in this query to demonstrate the result of the nested expression. This nested expression is evaluated only if the COST is less than 1100. If this expression is true, the value of the PREREQUISITE column is checked; if it is either 10 or 50, the cost is cut in half. If the PREREQUISITE column does not have the value of 10 or 50, just the value in the COST is displayed.

```
SELECT course_no, cost, prerequisite,
       CASE WHEN cost <1100 THEN
                  CASE WHEN prerequisite IN (10, 50) THEN cost/2
                       ELSE cost
                  END
            WHEN cost >=1100 AND cost <1500 THEN cost*1.1
            WHEN cost IS NULL THEN 0
            ELSE cost
       END "Test CASE"
  FROM course
 WHERE course_no IN (80, 20, 135, 450, 230)
 ORDER BY 2
```

COURSE_NO	COST	PREREQUISITE	Test CASE
230	1095	10	547.5
135	1095	134	1095
20	1195		1314.5
80	1595	204	1595
450		350	0

5 rows selected.

CASE EXPRESSION IN THE WHERE CLAUSE

CASE expressions are allowed anywhere expressions are allowed; the following example shows a CASE expression in the WHERE clause. It multiplies the CAPACITY column by the result of the CASE expression that returns either 2, 1.5, or null depending on the starting letter of the value in the LOCATION column. Only if the result of the CASE expression is greater than 30 the row is chosen for output.

```
SELECT DISTINCT capacity, location
  FROM section
 WHERE capacity*CASE
            WHEN SUBSTR(location, 1,1)='L' THEN 2
            WHEN SUBSTR(location, 1,1)='M' THEN 1.5
            ELSE NULL
       END  > 30
```

CAPACITY	LOCATION
25	L210
...	
25	M500

8 rows selected.

DATATYPE INCONSISTENCIES

You may come across the following error message when executing the CASE expression or the DECODE function. It indicates that the return datatype of the first condition does not agree with the datatype of the subsequent conditions. As you notice the first CASE condition returns a NUMBER datatype, the second condition returns the character literal "Room too small".

```
SQL> SELECT section_id, capacity,
  2         CASE WHEN capacity >=15 THEN capacity
  3              WHEN capacity < 15 THEN 'Room too small'
  4         END AS "Capacity"
  5    FROM section
  6   WHERE section_id IN (101, 146, 147)
  7  /
            WHEN capacity < 15 THEN 'Room too small'
                                *
ERROR at line 3:
ORA-00932: inconsistent datatypes
```

You match the two datatypes with a conversion function. The next example shows the use of the TO_CHAR conversion function to convert the values of the CAPACITY column to a character datatype.

```
SELECT section_id, capacity,
       CASE WHEN capacity >=15 THEN TO_CHAR(capacity)
            WHEN capacity < 15 THEN 'Room too small'
       END AS "Capacity"
  FROM section
 WHERE section_id IN (101, 146, 147)
SECTION_ID   CAPACITY Capacity
---------- ---------- -------------------
       147         15 15
       146         25 25
       101         10 Room too small

3 rows selected.
```

SIMPLE CASE EXPRESSION

If your conditions are testing for equality only, you can use the simple CASE expression. It has the following syntax.

```
CASE {expr WHEN comparison_expr THEN return_expr
          [WHEN comparison_expr THEN return_expr]...}
          [ELSE else_expr]
END
```

The next statement shows such an example. The query checks the value in the COST column to see if it equals the different amounts and if true, the appropriate THEN expression is executed.

```
SELECT course_no, cost,
       CASE cost WHEN 1095 THEN cost/2
                 WHEN 1195 THEN cost*1.1
                 WHEN 1595 THEN cost
                 ELSE cost*0.5
       END "Simple CASE"
  FROM course
 WHERE course_no IN (80, 20, 135, 450)
 ORDER BY 2
```

COURSE_NO	COST	Simple CASE
135	1095	547.5
20	1195	1314.5
80	1595	1595
450		

```
4 rows selected.
```

Rather than hard-coding literals in the CASE expressions, you can use subqueries to read dynamic values from tables instead. You will learn more about this in Chapter 7, "Subqueries."

OVERVIEW OF MISCELLANEOUS FUNCTIONS AND CASE EXPRESSIONS

Table 3.4 lists the miscellaneous functions and CASE expressions discussed in this lab.

LAB 3.3 EXERCISES

3.3.1 APPLY SUBSTITUTION FUNCTIONS AND OTHER MISCELLANEOUS FUNCTIONS

a) List the last name, first name, and phone number of students who do not have a phone number. Display '212-555-1212' for the phone number.

Table 3.4 ■ Miscellaneous Functions and the CASE Expressions

Function/Expression	Purpose
NVL(input_expression, substitution_expression)	Null value replacement
COALESCE(input_expression, substitution_expression_1, [, substitution_expression_*n*])	Null value replacement with multiple substitution expressions
NVL2(input_expr, not_null_substitution_expr, null_substitution_expr)	Null and not null substitution replacement
NULLIF(expression1, equal_expression2)	Returns null if the value of two expressions are identical, otherwise returns first expression
DECODE (if_expr, equals_search, then_result [,else_default])	Substitution function based on if then else logic
CASE {WHEN cond THEN return_expr {WHEN cond THEN return_ expr]...} [ELSE else_expr] END	Searched CASE expression. It allows for testing of null values, and greater than and less than comparisons.
CASE {expr WHEN expr THEN return_expr [WHEN expr THEN return_expr]...} [ELSE else_expr] END	The simple CASE expression tests for equality only. No greater than, less than, or IS NULL comparisons are allowed.

b) For course numbers 430 and greater, show the course cost. Add another column reflecting a discount of 10% off the cost and substitute any NULL values in the COST column with the number 1000. The result should look similar to the following output.

```
COURSE_NO     COST       NEW
---------  ---------  ---------
      430       1195     1075.5
      450                   900

2 rows selected.
```

c) Write the query to accomplish the following output using the NVL2 function in the column 'Get this result'.

```
ID NAME              PHONE          Get this result
--- --------------   ------------   ------------------
112 Thomas Thomas    201-555-5555   Phone# exists.
111 Peggy Noviello                  No phone# exists.

2 rows selected.
```

3.3.2 UTILIZE THE POWER OF THE DECODE FUNCTION AND THE CASE EXPRESSION

a) Rewrite the query from Exercise 3.3.1 c) using the DECODE function instead.

b) For course numbers 20, 120, 122, and 132, display the description, course number, and prerequisite course number. If the prerequisite is course number 120, display 200; if the prerequisite is 130, display 'N/A'. For courses with no prerequisites, display 'None'. Otherwise, list the current prerequisite. The result should look like the one listed below.

```
COURSE_NO DESCRIPTION                     ORIGINAL NEW
--------- ------------------------------  -------- ----
      132 Basics of Unix Admin                 130 N/A
      122 Intermediate Java Programming        120 200
      120 Intro to Java Programming             80 80
       20 Intro to Computers                       None

4 rows selected.
```

c) Display the student ID, zip code, and phone number for students with student IDs 145, 150, or 325. For those students living in the 212 area code and in zip code 10048, display 'North Campus'. List students living in the 212 area code but in a different zip code as 'West Campus'. Display students outside the 212 area code as 'Off Campus'. The result should look like the following result set. *Hint:* The solution to this query requires nested DECODE functions or nested CASE expressions.

```
STUDENT_ID ZIP   PHONE           LOC
---------- ----- --------------- -----------
       145 10048 212-555-5555    North Campus
       150 11787 718-555-5555    Off Campus
       325 10954 212-555-5555    West Campus

3 rows selected.
```

d) Display all the distinct salutations used in the INSTRUCTOR table. Order them alphabetically except for female salutations, which should be listed first. *Hint:* Use the DECODE function or CASE expression in the ORDER BY clause.

LAB 3.3 EXERCISE ANSWERS

3.3.1 ANSWERS

a) List the last name, first name, and phone number of students who do not have a phone number. Display '212-555-1212' for the phone number.

Answer: There are various solutions to obtain the desired result. The first determines the rows with a NULL phone number using the IS NULL operator. Then you apply the NVL function to the column with the substitution string '212-555-1212'. The second solution uses the NVL function in both the SELECT and WHERE clauses. Another way to achieve the result is to use the COALESCE function.

```
SELECT first_name||' '|| last_name name,
       phone oldphone,
       NVL(phone, '212-555-1212') newphone
  FROM student
 WHERE phone IS NULL
NAME                            OLDPHONE       NEWPHONE
------------------------------- -------------- ------------
Peggy Noviello                                 212-555-1212

1 row selected.
```

You can also retrieve the same rows by applying the NVL function in the WHERE clause.

```
SELECT first_name||' '|| last_name name,
       phone oldphone,
       NVL(phone, '212-555-1212') newphone
  FROM student
 WHERE NVL(phone, 'NONE') = 'NONE'
```

NAME	OLDPHONE	NEWPHONE
Peggy Noviello		212-555-1212

1 row selected.

The next query applies the COALESCE function to achieve the same result.

```
SELECT first_name||' '|| last_name name,
       phone oldphone,
       COALESCE(phone, '212-555-1212') newphone
  FROM student
 WHERE COALESCE(phone, 'NONE') ='NONE'
```

b) For course numbers 430 and greater, show the course cost. Add another column reflecting a discount of 10% off the cost and substitute any NULL values in the COST column with the number 1000. The result should look similar to the following output.

COURSE_NO	COST	NEW
430	1195	1075.5
450		900

2 rows selected.

Answer: Substitute 1000 for the null value, using the NVL function, before applying the discount calculation. Otherwise, the calculation yields a NULL..

```
SELECT course_no, cost,
       NVL(cost,1000)*0.9 new
  FROM course
 WHERE course_no >= 430
```

You can also use the COALESCE function instead.

```
SELECT course_no, cost,
       COALESCE(cost,1000)*0.9 new
  FROM course
 WHERE course_no >= 430
```

c) Write the query to accomplish the following output using the NVL2 function in the column 'Get this result'.

```
ID NAME            PHONE        Get this result
--- -------------- ------------ -----------------
112 Thomas Thomas  201-555-5555 Phone# exists.
111 Peggy Noviello              No phone# exists.

2 rows selected.
```

Answer: If the input parameter is not null, the NVL2 function's second parameter is returned. If the input parameter is null, then the third parameter is used.

```
SELECT student_id id, first_name||' '|| last_name name,
       phone,
       NVL2(phone, 'Phone# exists.', 'No phone# exists.')
        "Get this result"
  FROM student
 WHERE student_id IN (111, 112)
```

3.3.2 ANSWERS

a) Rewrite the query from Exercise 3.3.1 c) using the DECODE function instead.

Answer: The DECODE function can easily be substituted for the NVL2 function or the NVL function, because you can test for a NULL value. In this result, the DECODE function checks if the value is null. If this is true, the No phone# exists *literal is displayed; otherwise, it shows* Phone# exists.

```
SELECT student_id, first_name||' '|| last_name name,
       phone,
       DECODE(phone, NULL, 'No phone# exists.', 'Phone# exists.')
       "Get this result"
  FROM student
 WHERE student_id IN (111, 112)
```

b) For course numbers 20, 120, 122, and 132, display the description, course number, and prerequisite course number. If the prerequisite is course number 120, display 200; if the prerequisite is 130, display 'N/A'. For courses with no prerequisites, display 'None'. Otherwise, list the current prerequisite. The result should look like the one listed below.

```
COURSE_NO DESCRIPTION                     ORIGINAL NEW
--------- ------------------------------- -------- ----
      132 Basics of Unix Admin                 130 N/A
      122 Intermediate Java Programming        120 200
```

```
120 Intro to Java Programming                80 80
 20 Intro to Computers                       None
```

4 rows selected.

Answer: The solution can be achieved with either the CASE expression or the DECODE function.

SOLUTION USING THE CASE EXPRESSION

```
SELECT course_no, description, prerequisite "ORIGINAL",
       CASE WHEN prerequisite = 120 THEN '200'
            WHEN prerequisite = 130 THEN 'N/A'
            WHEN prerequisite IS NULL THEN 'None'
            ELSE TO_CHAR(prerequisite)
       END "NEW"
  FROM course
 WHERE course_no IN (20, 120, 122, 132)
 ORDER BY course_no DESC
```

The query checks for nulls with the IS NULL condition. The ELSE clause requires you to convert the NUMBER datatype into a VARCHAR2 using the TO_CHAR function, otherwise you receive an ORA-00932: inconsistent datatypes error, indicating that the output datatypes do not match. Oracle expects the datatype to be consistent with the same datatype as the first result expression, which is a string by placing the single quotes around the '200'.

If you attempt to use the simple CASE expression to solve the query, you will notice that the test for the null value cannot be accomplished because the simple CASE expression only allows testing for the equality (=). The IS NULL operator is not permitted and returns the error ORA-00936: missing expression.

```
SELECT course_no, description, prerequisite "ORIGINAL"
       CASE prerequisite WHEN 120 THEN '200'
                         WHEN 130 THEN 'N/A'
                         WHEN IS NULL THEN 'None'
                         ELSE TO_CHAR(prerequisite)
       END "NEW"
  FROM course
 WHERE course_no IN (20, 120, 122, 132)
 ORDER BY course_no DESC
                    WHEN IS NULL THEN 'None'
                    *
ERROR at line 4:
ORA-00936: missing expression
```

SOLUTION USING THE DECODE FUNCTION

```
SELECT course_no, description, prerequisite "ORIGINAL",
       DECODE(prerequisite, 120, '200',
                            130, 'N/A',
                            NULL, 'None',
                            TO_CHAR(prerequisite)) "NEW"
  FROM course
 WHERE course_no IN (20, 120, 122, 132)
 ORDER BY course_no DESC
```

The solution is best approached in several steps. The PREREQUISITE column is of datatype NUMBER. If you replace it in the DECODE function with another NUMBER for prerequisite 120, Oracle expects to continue to convert to the same datatype for all subsequent replacements. As the other replacements ('N/A' and 'None') are text literals, you need to enclose the number 200 with single quotes to predetermine the datatype for all subsequent substitutions as a VARCHAR2.

LAB
3.3

For any records that have a null prerequisite, "None" is displayed. Although one null does not equal another null, for the purpose of the DECODE function, null values are treated as equals.

The explicit datatype conversion with TO_CHAR function on the PREREQUISITE is good practice, though if you omit it Oracle will implicitly convert the value to a VARCHAR2 datatype. The automatic datatype conversion works in this example because the datatype is predetermined by the datatype of the first substitution value.

c) Display the student ID, zip code, and phone number for students with student IDs 145, 150, or 325. For those students living in the 212 area code and in zip code 10048, display 'North Campus'. List students living in the 212 area code but in a different zip code as 'West Campus'. Display students outside the 212 area code as 'Off Campus'. The result should look like the following result set. *Hint:* The solution requires nested DECODE functions or nested CASE expressions.

```
STUDENT_ID ZIP    PHONE            LOC
---------- -----  ---------------- ------------
       145 10048  212-555-5555     North Campus
       150 11787  718-555-5555     Off Campus
       325 10954  212-555-5555     West Campus

3 rows selected.
```

Answer:The CASE expressions can be nested within each other to allow for the required logic. A more complicated way to obtain the desired result is using nested DECODE statements; the output from one DECODE is an input parameter in a second DECODE function.

SOLUTION USING CASE EXPRESSION

```
SELECT student_id, zip, phone,
       CASE WHEN SUBSTR(phone, 1, 3) = '212' THEN
                 CASE WHEN zip = '10048' THEN 'North Campus'
                      ELSE 'West Campus'
                 END
            ELSE 'Off Campus'
       END loc
  FROM student
 WHERE student_id IN (150, 145, 325)
```

SOLUTION USING DECODE FUNCTION

```
SELECT student_id, zip, phone,
       DECODE(SUBSTR(phone, 1, 3), '212',
                    DECODE(zip, '10048', 'North Campus',
                                         'West Campus'),
              'Off Campus') loc
  FROM student
 WHERE student_id IN (150, 145, 325)
```

d) Display all the distinct salutations used in the INSTRUCTOR table. Order them alphabetically except for female salutations, which should be listed first. *Hint:* Use the DECODE function or CASE expression in the ORDER BY clause.

Answer:The DECODE function or the CASE expression is used in the ORDER BY clause to substitute a number for all female salutations, thereby listing them first when executing the ORDER BY clause.

```
SELECT DISTINCT salutation
  FROM instructor
 ORDER BY DECODE(salutation, 'Ms', 1,
                             'Mrs', 1,
                             'Miss', 1)
```

```
SALUT
-----
Ms
Dr
Hon
Rev
Mr

5 rows selected.
```

Or with the CASE expression:

```
SELECT DISTINCT salutation
   FROM instructor
   ORDER BY CASE salutation WHEN 'Ms' THEN '1'
                            WHEN 'Mrs' THEN '1'
                            WHEN 'Miss' THEN '1'
                            ELSE salutation
            END
```

The ASCII equivalent number of '1' is less than the ASCII equivalent of 'Dr', or any other salutation. Therefore Ms is listed first in the sort order. ASCII stands for American Standard Code for Information Interchange and deals with common formats.

To display the decimal representation of the first character of a string, use the ASCII function. Here is an example query of how you can determine the ASCII number of various values.

```
SELECT ASCII('1') "1", ASCII('0') "ZERO", ASCII('D') "D",
       ASCII('a') "a", ASCII('A') "A"
  FROM dual
```

1	ZERO	D	a	A
49	48	68	97	65

```
1 row selected.
```

LAB 3.3 SELF-REVIEW QUESTIONS

In order to test your progress, you should be able to answer the following questions.

1) A calculation with a null always yields another null.

a) _____ True
b) _____ False

2) The following query is valid.

```
SELECT NVL(cost, 'None')
  FROM course
```

a) _____ True
b) _____ False

3) The NVL2 function updates the data in the database.

a) _____ True
b) _____ False

4) The DECODE function lets you perform if then else functionality within the SQL language.

 a) _____ True
 b) _____ False

5) The DECODE function cannot be used in the WHERE clause of a SQL statement.

 a) _____ True
 b) _____ False

6) CASE expressions can be used in the ORDER BY clause of a SELECT statement.

 a) _____ True
 b) _____ False

7) The functions discussed in this lab can be used on the VARCHAR2 datatype only.

 a) _____ True
 b) _____ False

Answers appear in Appendix A, Section 3.3.

CHAPTER 3

TEST YOUR THINKING

The projects in this section are meant to have you utilize all of the skills that you have acquired throughout this chapter. The answers to these projects can be found at the companion Web site to this book, located at: http://www.phptr.com/rischert.

Visit the Web site periodically to share and discuss your answers.

1) Write the SELECT statement that returns the following output. Be sure to use spaces and punctuation exactly as you see them. (Use the SQL*Plus commands SET FEEDBACK OFF and SET HEADING OFF to turn off the number of rows displayed at the end of the statement and to turn off the column headings. Be sure to reset these options to their defaults when you are done. For more explanations on SQL*Plus commands, refer to Appendix C, "SQL*Plus Command Reference.")

```
Instructor: R. Chow...... Phone: 212-555-1212
Instructor: M. Frantzen.. Phone: 212-555-1212
Instructor: F. Hanks..... Phone: 212-555-1212
Instructor: C. Lowry..... Phone: 212-555-1212
Instructor: A. Morris.... Phone: 212-555-1212
Instructor: G. Pertez.... Phone: 212-555-1212
Instructor: N. Schorin... Phone: 212-555-1212
Instructor: T. Smythe.... Phone: 212-555-1212
Instructor: I. Willig.... Phone: 212-555-1212
Instructor: T. Wojick.... Phone: 212-555-1212
```

2) Rewrite the following query to replace all occurrences of the string 'Unix' with 'Linux'.

```
SELECT 'I develop software on the Unix platform'
   FROM dual
```

3) Determine which student does not have the first letter of her or his last name capitalized. Show the STUDENT_ID and LAST_NAME columns.

4) Check if any of the phone numbers in the INSTRUCTOR table have been entered in the *(###)###-####* format.

5) Explain the functionality of the following query:

```
SELECT section_id, capacity,
       CASE WHEN MOD(capacity, 2) <> 0 THEN capacity +1
       END "Even Number"
  FROM section
 WHERE section_id IN (101, 146, 147)
```

CHAPTER 4

DATE AND CONVERSION FUNCTIONS

In this chapter, you will gain an understanding of Oracle's unique date format, query date columns, and apply date functions in calculations. One of the most basic principles you will learn is datatype conversion, such as how to convert a literal or column from one datatype to another. Like character and number functions, date and conversion functions are single-row functions. The SQL novice often finds date and conversion functions challenging; the many examples in the labs will help you master these functions and avoid the common pitfalls.

L A B   4 . 1

APPLYING ORACLE'S
DATE FORMAT MODELS

LAB OBJECTIVES

After this lab, you will be able to:

✔ Compare a Text Literal to a DATE Column
✔ Apply Format Models

When working with an Oracle database, you will inevitably need to query columns containing dates. Oracle's DATE datatype consists of a *date and time stamp,* which is stored in an internal format that keeps track of the century, year, month, day, hour, minute, and second.

CHANGING THE DATE DISPLAY FORMAT

When you query a DATE datatype column, Oracle typically displays it in the default format such as 25-FEB-03. To change the display format of the column REGISTRATION_DATE in the following query, you use the TO_CHAR function together with a format model, also referred to as a *format mask.* The result shows the registration date in both the default date format and in the MM/DD/YYYY format.

```
SELECT last_name, registration_date,
       TO_CHAR(registration_date, 'MM/DD/YYYY')
       AS "Formatted"
  FROM student
 WHERE student_id IN (123, 161, 190)
```

```
LAST_NAME   REGISTRAT Formatted
----------  --------- ----------
Affinito    03-FEB-99 02/03/1999
Grant       02-FEB-99 02/02/1999
Radicola    27-JAN-99 01/27/1999

3 rows selected.
```

The TO_CHAR conversion function changes the DATE datatype into text and applies a format mask. The TO_DATE function converts a text literal into a DATE datatype. Table 4.1 shows the syntax of the two functions.

Table 4.1 ■ Date Related Conversion Functions

Function	Purpose	Return Datatype
TO_CHAR(date [,format_mask])	Converts DATE and DATETIME datatypes into VARCHAR2 to display it in a different format than the default date format. (The TO_CHAR function can be used with other datatypes besides the DATE, see Lab 4.5).	VARCHAR2
TO_DATE(char [,format_mask])	Converts a text literal to a DATE datatype. As with all other date-related conversion functions, the format_mask is optional if the literal is in the default format; otherwise, a format mask must be specified.	DATE

There are a number of display formats you can choose to format the dates to your liking. Table 4.2 provides an overview of the most frequently used DATE format masks.

The next SQL statement shows the same student record with the date and time formatted in various ways. You can see that the second and third columns have a different case because of the chosen format model; it is mixed case first, then uppercase. The next column has the month spelled out, but notice the extra spaces after the month. Oracle pads the month with nine spaces, which may be useful when you choose to align the month columns. If you want to eliminate the extra spaces, use the fill mask *fm*.

```
SELECT last_name,
       TO_CHAR(registration_date, 'Dy') AS "1.Day",
       TO_CHAR(registration_date, 'DY') AS "2.Day",
```

```
      TO_CHAR(registration_date, 'Month DD, YYYY')
      AS "Look at the Month",
      TO_CHAR(registration_date, 'HH:MI pm') AS "Time"
   FROM student
 WHERE student_id IN (123, 161, 190)
 LAST_NAME   1.D 2.D Look at the Month   Time
 ---------- --- --- ------------------ --------
 Affinito    Wed WED February   03, 1999 12:00 am
 Grant       Tue TUE February   02, 1999 12:00 am
 Radicola    Wed WED January    27, 1999 12:00 am

 3 rows selected.
```

Table 4.2 ■ Commonly Used Elements of the DATE Format Model

Format	Description
YYYY	Four-digit year.
YEAR	Year spelled out.
RR	Two-digit year based on century. If two-digit year is between 50 and 99, then it's the previous century; if the year is between 00 and 49, it's the current century.
MM	Two-digit month.
MON	Three-letter abbreviation of the month in capital letters.
MONTH	Month spelled out in capital letters and padded with blanks.
Month	Month spelled with first letter in caps and padded with blanks to a length of nine characters.
DD	Numeric day.
DAY	Day of the week in capital letters and padded with blanks to a length of nine characters.
DY	Three-letter abbreviation of the day of the week in caps.
D	Day of the week number (1–7). Sunday is day 1, Monday is day 2, and so forth.
HH or HH12	Hours (0–12).
HH24	Hours in military format (0–23).
MI	Minutes.
SS	Seconds.
AM or PM	Meridian indicator.
WW	Week of the year (1–53).
Q	Quarter of the year.

USING SPECIAL FORMAT MASKS

Here is a more elaborate example using the *fm* mask to eliminate the extra spaces between the month and the date in the second column of the following result set. In addition, this format mask uses the *th* suffix on the day (Dd) mask to include the "st", "nd", "rd," and "th" in lowercase after each number. The last column spells out the date using the *sp* format parameter with the first letter capitalized by using the Dd format. Also notice you can add a text literal, as in this case with the `"of"` text.

```
SELECT last_name,
       TO_CHAR(registration_date, 'fmMonth ddth, YYYY')
       "Eliminating Spaces",
       TO_CHAR(registration_date, 'Ddspth "of" fmMonth')
       "Spelled out"
  FROM student
 WHERE student_id IN (123, 161, 190)
LAST_NAME   Eliminating Spaces    Spelled out
----------  --------------------  -------------------------
Affinito    February 3rd, 1999    Third of February
Grant       February 2nd, 1999    Second of February
Radicola    January 27th, 1999    Twenty-Seventh of January

3 rows selected.
```

Table 4.3 shows you examples of how the format models can be used to format dates.

Table 4.3 ■ Date Format Model Examples

Format Mask	Example
DD-Mon-YYYY HH24:MI:SS	12-Apr-2003 17:00:00 (Note the case matters!)
MM/DD/YYYY HH:MI pm	04/12/2003 5:00 pm
Month	April
fmMonth DDth, YYYY	April 12th, 2003
Day	Sunday
DY	SUN
Qth YYYY	2nd 2003 (This shows the 2nd quarter of 2003)
Ddspth	Twelfth (Spells out the date)
DD-MON-RR	12-APR-03 (More on the RR format later in this lab)

USING DATES IN THE WHERE CLAUSE

Often you need to query data based on certain date criteria. For example, if you need to look for all those students that registered on January 22, 1999, you write a SQL statement similar to the following:

```
SELECT last_name, registration_date
  FROM student
 WHERE registration_date = TO_DATE('22-JAN-1999', 'DD-MON-YYYY')
```

LAST_NAME	REGISTRAT
Crocitto	22-JAN-99
Landry	22-JAN-99
...	
Sethi	22-JAN-99
Walter	22-JAN-99

8 rows selected.

In the WHERE clause, the text literal '22-JAN-1999' is converted to a DATE datatype using the TO_DATE function and the format model. This converted date is then compared to the REGISTRATION_DATE column, which is of datatype DATE. Now you are comparing identical datatypes: a datatype DATE column against a literal that is now converted into the equivalent Oracle DATE datatype.

You must inform Oracle about the format of your text literal, otherwise Oracle will not be able to interpret the text literal correctly and will return the following error message indicating that the text literal and the associated format mask do not agree.

```
SELECT last_name, registration_date
  FROM student
 WHERE registration_date = TO_DATE('22/01/1999', 'DD-MON-YYYY')
 WHERE registration_date = TO_DATE('22/01/1999', 'DD-MON-YYYY')
                           *
ERROR at line 3:
ORA-01843: not a valid month
```

IMPLICIT CONVERSION AND DEFAULT DATE FORMAT

In some cases Oracle will implicitly perform a conversion of the text literal to the DATE datatype because the text literal is in the default date format. The next SQL statement shows you such an example. The text literal is the default date format mask, which typically is DD-MON-YYYY and DD-MON-RR, so the implicit conversion is performed automatically by Oracle. The default date format can be changed with the initialization parameter NLS_DATE_FORMAT in your init.ora file (an Oracle initialization file on the database server) and your Windows Registry.

```
SELECT last_name, registration_date
  FROM student
 WHERE registration_date = '22-JAN-1999'
LAST_NAME                    REGISTRAT
------------------------     ---------
Crocitto                     22-JAN-99
Landry                       22-JAN-99
...
Sethi                        22-JAN-99
Walter                       22-JAN-99

8 rows selected.
```

The same result can also be achieved with this WHERE clause. Note that this will only work if your Oracle installation has the DD-MON-RR format model as the NLS_DATE_FORMAT default date format.

```
WHERE registration_date = '22-JAN-99'
```

It is best to explicitly use the TO_DATE function when converting a text literal! You will see the advantages of doing so as you go through some of the exercises.

THE RR DATE FORMAT MASK AND THE PREVIOUS CENTURY

Although the year 2000 is already behind us, you still have to deal with dates in the prior century. For example, the previous statement, repeated for your convenience, looks for students registered on January 22, 1999. But notice the century is missing.

```
SELECT last_name, registration_date
  FROM student
 WHERE registration_date = '22-JAN-99'
```

This statement will only return rows if your Oracle installation includes the DD-MON-RR format mask. This special RR format mask interprets the two-digit year from 50 until 99 as the prior century, which currently is for years from 1950 through 1999. Two-digit year numbers from 00 until 49 are interpreted as the current century, that is, as years 2000 through 2049.

You can also see what your session settings are by issuing this query, which returns session attributes.

```
SELECT SYS_CONTEXT ('USERENV', 'NLS_DATE_FORMAT')
  FROM dual
SYS_CONTEXT('USERENV','NLS_DATE_FORMAT')
----------------------------------------
DD-MON-RR

1 row selected.
```

If your default format mask is set to DD-MON-YY instead, Oracle interprets '22-JAN-99' as '22-JAN-2099', which is obviously not the desired result. Therefore, it's always best to be specific and to include the four-digit year in your WHERE clause.

The next query illustrates how a two-digit year gets interpreted with the RR format mask. The text literals '17-OCT-67' and '17-OCT-17' are converted to a DATE datatype with the format mask DD-MON-RR. Then the TO_CHAR function converts the DATE datatype back to text but this time with a four-digit year. This query shows you the result of the RR format. Effectively, the two-digit year 67 is interpreted as 1967 and the two-digit year literal 17 is interpreted as 2017.

```
SELECT TO_CHAR(TO_DATE('17-OCT-67','DD-MON-RR'),'YYYY') "1900",
       TO_CHAR(TO_DATE('17-OCT-17','DD-MON-RR'),'YYYY') "2000"
  FROM dual
1900 2000
---- ----
1967 2017

1 row selected.
```

The Whole Truth

The client-side program and database server changes regarding the format mask are automatically performed in any installation of Oracle Version 8.1.7 and higher. (For the server, the default mask entry NLS_DATE_FORMAT, found in the init.ora file—the database initialization file—ensures the correct century interpretation. For the Windows client software, you find the NLS_DATE_FORMAT parameter in the Windows registry.) If any of the aforementioned queries return a different century, see the companion Web site located at http://www.phptr.com/rischert for more details.

DON'T FORGET ABOUT THE TIME

As previously mentioned, the Oracle DATE datatype includes a time stamp. You can query records for a specific time or ignore the time altogether. The next SQL statement displays the time stamp in the result set. If no time was entered, Oracle assumes the time is midnight, which is 12:00:00 AM, or 00:00:00 military time (HH24 time format mask). The WHERE clause retrieves only those rows where the column has a value of January 22nd, 1999 midnight; other records with a different time are not returned, should any exist.

```
SELECT last_name,
       TO_CHAR(registration_date, 'DD-MON-YYYY HH24:MI:SS')
  FROM student
 WHERE registration_date = TO_DATE('22-JAN-1999', 'DD-MON-YYYY')
LAST_NAME                      TO_CHAR(REGISTRATION
------------------------       --------------------
Crocitto                       22-JAN-1999 00:00:00
Landry                         22-JAN-1999 00:00:00
...
Sethi                          22-JAN-1999 00:00:00
Walter                         22-JAN-1999 00:00:00

8 rows selected.
```

TIME AND THE TRUNC FUNCTION

You already learned about the TRUNC function in connection with the NUMBER datatype in Chapter 3, "Character and Number Functions." The TRUNC function can also take a DATE datatype as an input parameter, which interprets the time stamp as midnight (i.e. 12:00:00 AM). The next example shows the TRUNC function applied to the ENROLL_DATE column. This has the effect that the records are included no matter what the time, as long as the date is February 7th, 1999.

```
SELECT student_id, TO_CHAR(enroll_date, 'DD-MON-YYYY HH24:MI:SS')
  FROM enrollment
 WHERE TRUNC(enroll_date) = TO_DATE('07-FEB-1999', 'DD-MON-YYYY')
STUDENT_ID TO_CHAR(ENROLL_DATE,
---------- --------------------
       140 07-FEB-1999 10:19:00
       141 07-FEB-1999 10:19:00
...
       158 07-FEB-1999 10:19:00
       159 07-FEB-1999 10:19:00

20 rows selected.
```

THE ANSI DATE AND ANSI TIMESTAMP FORMATS

Instead of using Oracle's date literals, you can specify a date in the ANSI format listed in the next example. This format contains no time portion and must be listed exactly in the format YYYY-MM-DD with the DATE keyword prefix.

```
SELECT student_id, TO_CHAR(enroll_date, 'DD-MON-YYYY HH24:MI:SS')
  FROM enrollment
 WHERE enroll_date >= DATE '1999-02-07'
   AND enroll_date <  DATE '1999-02-08'
```

If you want to include the time portion, use the ANSI TIMESTAMP keyword. The literal must be in the ANSI TIMESTAMP format, which is defined as YYYY-MM-DD HH24:MI:SS.

```
SELECT student_id, TO_CHAR(enroll_date, 'DD-MON-YYYY HH24:MI:SS')
  FROM enrollment
 WHERE enroll_date >= TIMESTAMP '1999-02-07 00:00:00'
   AND enroll_date <  TIMESTAMP '1999-02-08 00:00:00'
```

LAB 4.1 EXERCISES

4.1.1 COMPARE A TEXT LITERAL TO A *DATE* COLUMN

a) Display the course number, section ID, and starting date and time for sections that were taught on May 4, 1999.

b) Show the student records that were modified on or before January 22, 1999. Display the date the record was modified and each student's first and last name concatenated in one column.

4.1.2 APPLY FORMAT MODELS

a) Display the course number, section ID, and starting date and time for sections that start on Tuesdays.

b) List the section ID and starting date and time for all sections that begin and end in July 1999.

c) Determine the day of the week for December 31, 1899.

d) Execute the following statement. Write the question to obtain the desired result. Pay particular attention to the ORDER BY clause.

```
SELECT 'Section '||section_id||' begins on '||
       TO_CHAR(start_date_time, 'fmDay')||'.' AS "Start"
  FROM section
 WHERE section_id IN (146, 127, 121, 155, 110, 85, 148)
 ORDER BY TO_CHAR(start_date_time, 'D')
```

LAB 4.1 EXERCISE ANSWERS

4.1.1 ANSWERS

a) Display the course number, section ID, and starting date and time for sections that were taught on May 4, 1999.

Answer: To display a DATE column in a nondefault format, use the TO_CHAR function. To compare a text literal with a DATE column, use the TO_DATE function. It is best to always use the four-digit year and the format mask when using the TO_DATE function. This is good practice and not subject to year interpretations or ambiguities if the default date format is different.

```
SELECT course_no, section_id,
       TO_CHAR(start_date_time, 'DD-MON-YYYY HH24:MI')
  FROM section
 WHERE start_date_time >= TO_DATE('04-MAY-1999', 'DD-MON-YYYY')
   AND start_date_time < TO_DATE('05-MAY-1999', 'DD-MON-YYYY')
COURSE_NO SECTION_ID TO_CHAR(START_DAT
--------- ---------- -----------------
       25         88 04-MAY-1999 09:30
      100        144 04-MAY-1999 09:30
      120        149 04-MAY-1999 09:30
      122        155 04-MAY-1999 09:30
```

4 rows selected.

The returned result set displays the starting date and time using the TO_CHAR function. In the WHERE clause the text literals '04-MAY-1999' and '05-MAY-1999' are transformed into the DATE datatype. If no format mask for the time is specified, Oracle assumes the time is midnight, which is 12:00:00 AM, or 00:00:00

military time (HH24 time format mask). The WHERE clause retrieves only those rows where the START_DATE_TIME column has values on or after '04-MAY-1999 12:00:00 AM' and before '05-MAY-1999 12:00:00 AM'.

You can also include the timestamp in your WHERE clause, such as in the following example. It is irrelevant if you choose AM or PM in the display 'DD-MON-YYYY HH:MI:SS AM' format mask for the display of the result, but obviously not in the WHERE clause with the actual date string listed as '04-MAY-1999 12:00:00 AM'.

```
SELECT course_no, section_id,
       TO_CHAR(start_date_time, 'DD-MON-YYYY HH24:MI')
  FROM section
 WHERE start_date_time >= TO_DATE('04-MAY-1999 12:00:00 AM',
                                  'DD-MON-YYYY HH:MI:SS AM')
   AND start_date_time <= TO_DATE('04-MAY-1999 11:59:59 PM',
                                  'DD-MON-YYYY HH:MI:SS AM')
```

The next SQL query returns the same result when the following WHERE clause is used instead. Here, note that Oracle has to perform the implicit conversion of the text literal into a DATE datatype.

```
WHERE start_date_time >= '04-MAY-1999'
  AND start_date_time <  '05-MAY-1999'
```

The next WHERE clause returns the same result again, but Oracle has to perform the implicit conversion and pick the correct century.

```
WHERE start_date_time >= '04-MAY-99'
  AND start_date_time < '05-MAY-99'
```

You can use the TRUNC function to ignore the timestamp.

```
SELECT course_no, section_id,
       TO_CHAR(start_date_time, 'DD-MON-YYYY HH24:MI')
  FROM section
 WHERE TRUNC(start_date_time) = TO_DATE('04-MAY-1999', 'DD-MON-YYYY')
```

The next WHERE clause is a valid alternative; however, the previous WHERE clause is preferable because it explicitly specifies the text literal to DATE datatype conversion together with the format mask and includes the four-digit year.

```
WHERE TRUNC(start_date_time) = '04-MAY-99'
```

When you modify a database column with a function in the WHERE clause, such as the TRUNC function on the database column START_DATE_TIME, you cannot take advantage of an index should one exist on the column, unless it is a function-based index. Indexes speed

up the retrieval of the data; you will learn more about the performance advantages of indexes in Chapter 12, "Views, Indexes, and Sequences."

The next statement does not return the desired rows. Only rows that have a START_DATE_TIME of midnight on May 4, 1999 qualify and because there are no such rows, no rows are selected for output.

```
SELECT course_no, section_id,
       TO_CHAR(start_date_time, 'DD-MON-YYYY HH24:MI')
  FROM section
 WHERE start_date_time = '04-MAY-99'
```

no rows selected

The ANSI format is listed in the next example. The ANSI DATE format does not have a time portion and it must be specified exactly in the format YYYY-MM-DD with the DATE keyword prefix.

```
SELECT course_no, section_id,
       TO_CHAR(start_date_time, 'DD-MON-YYYY HH24:MI')
  FROM section
 WHERE start_date_time >= DATE '1999-05-04'
   AND start_date_time <  DATE '1999-05-05'
```

Alternatively, you can apply the TRUNC function on the START_DATE_TIME column, but just be aware of the possible performance impact mentioned previously.

```
SELECT course_no, section_id,
       TO_CHAR(start_date_time, 'DD-MON-YYYY HH24:MI')
  FROM section
 WHERE TRUNC(start_date_time) = DATE '1999-05-04'
```

If you want to include the time portion, use the ANSI TIMESTAMP keyword. The literal must be exactly in the ANSI TIMESTAMP format defined as YYYY-MM-DD HH24:MI:SS.

```
SELECT course_no, section_id,
       TO_CHAR(start_date_time, 'DD-MON-YYYY HH24:MI')
  FROM section
 WHERE start_date_time >= TIMESTAMP '1999-05-04 00:00:00'
   AND start_date_time <  TIMESTAMP '1999-05-05 00:00:00'
```

ERROR WHEN ENTERING THE WRONG FORMAT

Any attempt to change the predetermined format or the use of the wrong keyword results in an error, as you see in the next example. For this query to work, the TIMESTAMP keyword must be used instead of the DATE keyword, because the literal is in the ANSI TIMESTAMP format.

```
SELECT course_no, section_id,
       TO_CHAR(start_date_time, 'DD-MON-YYYY HH24:MI')
  FROM section
 WHERE start_date_time >= DATE '1999-05-04 00:00:00'
   AND start_date_time <  DATE '1999-05-05 00:00:00'
 WHERE start_date_time >= DATE '1999-05-04 00:00:00'
                              *
ERROR at line 4:
ORA-01861: literal does not match format string
```

b) Show the student records that were modified on or before January 22, 1999. Display the date the record was modified and each student's first and last name concatenated in one column.

Answer: The query compares the MODIFIED_DATE column to the text literal. The text literal may be in either the Oracle default format or, better yet, formatted with the TO_DATE function, the appropriate format model, and the four-digit year.

```
SELECT first_name||' '||last_name fullname,
       TO_CHAR(modified_date, 'DD-MON-YYYY HH:MI P.M.')
       "Modified Date and Time"
  FROM student
 WHERE modified_date < TO_DATE('01/23/1999','MM/DD/YYYY')
```

FULLNAME	Modified Date and Time
Fred Crocitto	22-JAN-1999 12:00 A.M.
J. Landry	22-JAN-1999 12:00 A.M.
...	
Judy Sethi	22-JAN-1999 12:00 A.M.
Larry Walter	22-JAN-1999 12:00 A.M.

```
8 rows selected.
```

As previously mentioned, it is best practice to explicitly use the TO_DATE function to convert the text literal into a DATE datatype. It does not really matter which format mask you use (in this case MM/DD/YYYY was used in the WHERE clause) as long as you inform Oracle how to interpret it. Be sure to include the century to avoid ambiguities.

Another possible solution is the following WHERE clause utilizing the TRUNC function:

```
WHERE TRUNC(modified_date) <= TO_DATE('01/22/1999','MM/DD/YYYY')
```

a) Display the course number, section ID, and starting date and time for sections that start on Tuesdays.

Answer: The SQL statement shows all the sections that start on Tuesday by using the DY format mask, which displays the abbreviated day of the week in capitalized letters.

```
SELECT course_no, section_id,
       TO_CHAR(start_date_time, 'DY DD-MON-YYYY')
  FROM section
 WHERE TO_CHAR(start_date_time, 'DY') = 'TUE'
COURSE_NO SECTION_ID TO_CHAR(START_D
--------- ---------- ---------------
       25         88 TUE 04-MAY-1999
      100        144 TUE 04-MAY-1999
      120        149 TUE 04-MAY-1999
      122        155 TUE 04-MAY-1999

4 rows selected.
```

THE FILL MODE

Some of the format masks are tricky. For example, if you choose the 'Day' format mask, you must specify the correct case and add the extra blanks to fill it up to a total length of nine characters. The following query does not return any rows.

```
SELECT course_no, section_id,
       TO_CHAR(start_date_time, 'Day DD-Mon-YYYY')
  FROM section
 WHERE TO_CHAR(start_date_time, 'Day') = 'Tuesday'

no rows selected
```

Use the *fill mode (fm)* with the format mask to suppress the extra blanks:

```
SELECT course_no, section_id,
       TO_CHAR(start_date_time, 'Day DD-Mon-YYYY')
  FROM section
 WHERE TO_CHAR(start_date_time, 'fmDay') = 'Tuesday'
COURSE_NO SECTION_ID TO_CHAR(START_DATE_TI
--------- ---------- --------------------
       25         88 Tuesday   04-May-1999
      100        144 Tuesday   04-May-1999
      120        149 Tuesday   04-May-1999
      122        155 Tuesday   04-May-1999

4 rows selected.
```

b) List the section ID and starting date and time for all sections that begin and end in July 1999.

> *Answer: In the SQL language there are often several different solutions that may deliver the same result set. Examine the various correct solutions and avoid the pitfalls.*

SOLUTION ONE:

```
SELECT section_id,
       TO_CHAR(start_date_time, 'DD-MON-YYYY HH24:MI:SS')
  FROM section
 WHERE start_date_time >= TO_DATE('07/01/1999', 'MM/DD/YYYY')
   AND start_date_time <  TO_DATE('08/01/1999', 'MM/DD/YYYY')
SECTION_ID TO_CHAR(START_DATE_T
---------- --------------------
        81 24-JUL-1999 09:30:00
        85 14-JUL-1999 10:30:00
...
       147 24-JUL-1999 09:30:00
       153 24-JUL-1999 09:30:00

14 rows selected.
```

Based on the output, you see that the first solution takes the time stamp into consideration.

The following query will *not* yield the correct result if you have a section that starts on July 31, 1999 any time after midnight. The TO_DATE function converts the string to a DATE datatype and sets the time stamp to 12:00:00 AM. Therefore, a section starting on July 31, 1999 at 18:00 is not considered part of the range.

```
SELECT section_id,
       TO_CHAR(start_date_time, 'DD-MON-YYYY HH24:MI:SS')
  FROM section
 WHERE start_date_time BETWEEN
       TO_DATE('07/01/1999', 'MM/DD/YYYY')
   AND TO_DATE('07/31/1999', 'MM/DD/YYYY')
```

SOLUTION TWO:

This solution includes the 24-hour time format mask.

```
SELECT section_id,
       TO_CHAR(start_date_time, 'DD-MON-YYYY HH24:MI:SS')
  FROM section
 WHERE start_date_time BETWEEN
       TO_DATE('07/01/1999', 'MM/DD/YYYY')
   AND TO_DATE('07/31/1999 23:59:59', 'MM/DD/YYYY HH24:MI:SS')
```

This WHERE clause can also be used to obtain the desired output: The query ignores the date and time stamp on the column START_DATE_TIME completely.

```
WHERE TRUNC(start_date_time) BETWEEN
      TO_DATE('07/01/1999', 'MM/DD/YYYY')
  AND TO_DATE('07/31/1999', 'MM/DD/YYYY')
```

The following WHERE clause also returns the correct result because the literals are in the correct Oracle default format mask. However, it is best not to rely on Oracle's implicit conversion, and to specify the conversion function together with the four-digit year.

```
WHERE TRUNC(start_date_time) BETWEEN '1-JUL-99' AND '31-JUL-99'
```

Always think about the time when you compare dates.

AVOID THIS COMMON ERROR

Another common source of errors when using dates is applying the wrong datatype conversion function, as illustrated in this example:

```
SELECT section_id,
       TO_CHAR(start_date_time, 'DD-MON-YYYY HH24:MI:SS')
  FROM section
 WHERE TO_CHAR(start_date_time, 'DD-MON-YYYY HH24:MI:SS')
       >= '01-JUL-1999 00:00:00'
   AND TO_CHAR(start_date_time, 'DD-MON-YYYY HH24:MI:SS')
       <= '31-JUL-1999 23:59:59'
SECTION_ID TO_CHAR(START_DATE_T
---------- --------------------
        79 14-APR-1999 09:30:00
        80 24-APR-1999 09:30:00
...
       155 04-MAY-1999 09:30:00
       156 15-MAY-1999 09:30:00

78 rows selected.
```

The column START_DATE_TIME is converted to a character column in the WHERE clause and then compared to the text literal. The problem is that the dates are no longer compared. Instead, the character representation of the text literal and the character representation of the contents in column START_DATE_TIME in the format 'DD-MON-YYYY HH24:MI:SS' are compared.

A column value such as '14-APR-1999 09:30:00' is inclusive of the text literals '01-JUL-1999 00:00:00' and '31-JUL-1999 23:59:59' because the first digit of the column value 1 falls within the range of the characters 0 and 3. Therefore, the condition is true, but we know that April 14, 1999 is not in this date range.

This leads into a brief discussion about character comparison semantics. To illustrate the effect of character comparisons further, look at the next hypothetical examples. The query checks whether the text literal 9 is between the text literals 01 and 31, evaluated by the first digit, 0 and 3, and it returns no row, which indicates that it does not fall in this range.

```
SELECT *
  FROM dual
 WHERE '9' BETWEEN '01' AND '31'
```

no rows selected

With this knowledge, you can try the text literals. As you can see the comparison of text literals used in the query with the wrong datatype makes this condition true; however, not if you compared the DATE datatype values, because we know that April 14, 1999 does not fall in the month of July 1999. In conclusion, remember to make sure your datatype conversion does not cause incorrect results.

```
SELECT *
  FROM dual
 WHERE '14-APR-1999 09:30:00' BETWEEN '01-JUL-1999 00:00:00'
                                  AND '31-JUL-1999 23:59:59'
D
-
X
```

1 row selected.

Be sure to choose the correct datatype conversion function in your WHERE clause.

TO_CHAR FUNCTION VERSUS TO_DATE FUNCTION

The TO_DATE function converts text to the DATE datatype, typically used in the WHERE clause of a SELECT statement. The TO_CHAR function converts a DATE datatype to text, typically used in the SELECT clause to format the result. You can also use TO_CHAR to query for specifics in a format mask. For example, to find which sections meet on Tuesday, you use the TO_CHAR function in the WHERE clause as seen in the answer to exercise 4.1.2 (a) and listed here once again:

```
SELECT course_no, section_id,
       TO_CHAR(start_date_time, 'Day DD-Mon-YYYY')
  FROM section
 WHERE TO_CHAR(start_date_time, 'fmDay') = 'Tuesday'
```

c) Determine the day of the week for December 31, 1899.

Answer: The day of the week is Sunday.

You need to nest conversion functions by using the TO_DATE function to convert the text literal to a DATE datatype, then the TO_CHAR function to display the day of the week.

First, you translate the text literal '31-DEC-1899' using the format mask 'DD-MON-YYYY' into the Oracle DATE datatype. Then apply the TO_CHAR formatting function to convert the date into any format you wish, in this case to show the day of the week.

```
SELECT TO_CHAR(TO_DATE('31-DEC-1899', 'DD-MON-YYYY'),'Dy')
  FROM dual
TO_
--
Sun

1 row selected.
```

d) Execute the following statement. Write the question to obtain the desired result. Pay particular attention to the ORDER BY clause.

```
SELECT 'Section '||section_id||' begins on '|| TO_CHAR(start_date_time,
       'fmDay')||'.' AS "Start"
  FROM section
 WHERE section_id IN (146, 127, 121, 155, 110, 85, 148)
 ORDER BY TO_CHAR(start_date_time, 'D')
```

Answer: Your answer may be phrased similar to the following: "Display the day of the week when the sections 146, 127, 121, 155, 110, 85, and 148 start. Order the result by the day of the week starting with Sunday."

The result of the query will look similar to this result. Notice the statement uses the D format mask to order by the day of the week. This format assigns the number 1 for Sunday, 2 for Monday, and so on.

```
Starting Date
-----------------------------------
Section 146 begins on Sunday.
Section 148 begins on Monday.
Section 155 begins on Tuesday.
Section 85 begins on Wednesday.
Section 110 begins on Thursday.
Section 121 begins on Friday.
Section 127 begins on Saturday.

7 rows selected.
```

LAB 4.1 SELF-REVIEW QUESTIONS

In order to test your progress, you should be able to answer the following questions.

1) The TRUNC function on a date without a format model truncates the time stamp to 12:00:00 A.M.

   a) _____ True
   b) _____ False

2) Converting a text literal to a DATE format requires using the TO_CHAR function.

   a) _____ True
   b) _____ False

3) The format mask 'Dy' displays Monday as follows:

   a) _____ MON
   b) _____ Monday
   c) _____ MONDAY
   d) _____ Mon

4) Choose the format mask that displays "December 31st, 1999".

   a) _____ DD-MON-YYYY
   b) _____ MONTH DDth, YYYY
   c) _____ fmMONTH DD, YYYY
   d) _____ Month fmDD, YYYY
   e) _____ fmMonth ddth, yyyy

5) The SQL query displays the distinct hours and minutes from the SECTION table's START_DATE_TIME column.

```
SELECT DISTINCT TO_CHAR(start_date_time, 'HH24:MM')
  FROM section
```

a) _____ True
b) _____ False

Answers appear in Appendix A, Section 4.1.

LAB 4.2

PERFORMING DATE AND TIME MATH

LAB OBJECTIVES

After this lab, you will be able to:

✔ Understand the SYSDATE Function and Perform Date Arithmetic

---

THE SYSDATE FUNCTION

The SYSDATE function returns the computer operating system's current date and time and does not take any parameters. If you connect to the database server via a client machine, it returns date and time of the machine hosting the database, not the date and time of your client machine. For example, if your client workstation is located in New York, your local time zone is *Eastern Standard Time* (EST); if you connect to a server in California, you will receive the server's *Pacific Standard Time* (PST) date and time. To include the time in the result you use the TO_CHAR function.

```
SELECT SYSDATE, TO_CHAR(SYSDATE, 'DD-MON-YYYY HH24:MI')
  FROM dual
SYSDATE    TO_CHAR(SYSDATE,'
---------  -----------------
26-AUG-02 26-AUG-2002 10:38

1 row selected.
```

Using the SYSDATE function, you can determine the number of days until the year 2005. The following query subtracts today's date from January 1, 2005.

```
SELECT TO_DATE('01-JAN-2005','DD-MON-YYYY')-TRUNC(SYSDATE) int,
       TO_DATE('01-JAN-2005','DD-MON-YYYY')-SYSDATE dec
  FROM dual
         INT        DEC
---------- ----------
       859 858.560243
```

1 row selected.

To perform any date calculation, the column or text literal must be converted into the Oracle DATE datatype. For the first column, the text literal '01-JAN-2005' is converted into a DATE datatype using the TO_DATE function and the corresponding format mask. Because a time is not specified the time stamp of the text literal '01-JAN-2005' is set to 00:00:00 military time (the equivalent of 12:00:00 AM). From this date, the operating system's date (result of the SYSDATE function) is subtracted. SYSDATE is nested inside the TRUNC function, which truncates the timestamp to 00:00:00. As a result, the column shows 859 days.

The second column of the returned result performs the identical operation; however, this expression does not use the TRUNC function on SYSDATE function and therefore the time is factored into the calculation. The difference is now expressed in days with the time in decimal format. To display the decimal in hours or minutes, you can use the NUMTODSINTERVAL function discussed in the Lab 4.4.

THE ROUND FUNCTION

The ROUND function allows you to round days, months, or years. The following SQL statement lists the current date and time in the first column using the TO_CHAR function and a format mask. The next column shows the current date and time rounded to the next day. If the time stamp is at or past 12:00 noon, and no format mask is supplied, the ROUND function rounds to the next day. The last column displays the date rounded to the nearest month using the MM format mask.

```
SELECT TO_CHAR(SYSDATE,'DD-MON-YYYY HH24:MI') now,
       TO_CHAR(ROUND(SYSDATE),'DD-MON-YYYY HH24:MI') day,
       TO_CHAR(ROUND(SYSDATE,'MM'),'DD-MON-YYYY HH24:MI')
       mon
  FROM dual
NOW                DAY                MON
------------------ ------------------ ------------------
26-AUG-2002 10:33  26-AUG-2002 00:00  01-SEP-2002 00:00
```

1 row selected.

PERFORMING ARITHMETIC ON DATES

From the previous example on calculating the number of days until the year 2005, you know that you can perform arithmetic on a DATE datatype. In the following example, three hours are added to the current date and time. To determine tomorrow's date and time, simply add the number 1 to the SYSDATE function.

```
SELECT TO_CHAR(SYSDATE, 'MM/DD HH24:MI:SS') now,
       TO_CHAR(SYSDATE+3/24, 'MM/DD HH24:MI:SS')
       AS now_plus_3hrs,
       TO_CHAR(SYSDATE+1, 'MM/DD HH24:MI:SS') tomorrow,
       TO_CHAR(SYSDATE+1.5, 'MM/DD HH24:MI:SS') AS
       "36Hrs from now"
  FROM dual
```

NOW	NOW_PLUS_3HRS	TOMORROW	36Hrs from now
08/26 10:34:17	08/26 13:34:17	08/27 10:34:17	08/27 22:34:17

1 row selected.

The fraction 3/24 represents three hours; you can also express minutes as a fraction of 1440 (60 minutes × 24 hours = 1440, which is the total number of minutes in a day). For example, 15 minutes is 15/1440 or 1/96 or any equivalent fraction or decimal number.

Oracle has a number of functions to perform specific date calculations. To determine the date of the first Sunday of the year 2000, use the NEXT_DAY function as in the following SELECT statement.

```
SELECT TO_CHAR(TO_DATE('12/31/1999','MM/DD/YYYY'),
               'MM/DD/YYYY DY') "New Year's Eve",
       TO_CHAR(NEXT_DAY(TO_DATE('12/31/1999',
                                'MM/DD/YYYY'),
               'SUNDAY'),'MM/DD/YYYY DY')
       "First Sunday"
  FROM dual
```

New Year's Eve	First Sunday
12/31/1999 FRI	01/02/2000 SUN

1 row selected.

The text string '12/31/1999' is first converted to a date. To determine the date of the next Sunday, the NEXT_DAY function is applied. Lastly, format the output with a TO_CHAR format mask to display the result in the 'MM/DD/YYYY DY' format.

THE EXTRACT FUNCTION

The EXTRACT function extracts the year, month, or day from a column of the DATE datatype column. The next example shows rows with April values in the START_DATE_TIME column, and how the various elements of the DATE datatype can be extracted. Valid keyword choices are YEAR, MONTH, and DAY. You cannot extract hours, minutes, or seconds from the DATE datatype. These choices are only available on the other DATE-related datatypes you will learn about in Lab 4.3.

```
SELECT TO_CHAR(start_date_time, 'DD-MON-YYYY') "Start Date",
       EXTRACT(MONTH FROM start_date_time) "Month",
       EXTRACT(YEAR FROM start_date_time) "Year",
       EXTRACT(DAY FROM start_date_time) "Day"
  FROM section
 WHERE EXTRACT(MONTH FROM start_date_time) = 4
 ORDER BY start_date_time
Start Date      Month      Year       Day
----------- --------- --------- ---------
09-APR-1999         4       1999         9
09-APR-1999         4       1999         9
...
29-APR-1999         4       1999        29
08-APR-2000         4       2000         8

21 rows selected.
```

Here you see another example of the EXTRACT function. It passes a text literal as the parameter, which is in ANSI DATE format.

```
SELECT EXTRACT(YEAR FROM DATE '2002-03-11') year,
       EXTRACT(MONTH FROM DATE '2002-03-11') month,
       EXTRACT(DAY FROM DATE '2002-03-11') day
  FROM dual
    YEAR      MONTH        DAY
--------- --------- ---------
    2002          3         11

1 row selected.
```

Table 4.4 summarizes some of the most frequently used DATE calculation functions with their purpose and respective syntax.

Table 4.4 ■ Commonly Used Oracle DATE Calculation Functions

Function	Purpose	Return Datatype
ADD_MONTHS(date, integer)	Adds or subtracts number of months from a certain date.	DATE
MONTHS_BETWEEN (date2, date1)	Determines the number of months between two dates.	NUMBER
LAST_DAY(date)	Returns the last date of the month.	DATE
NEXT_DAY(date, day_of_the_week)	Returns the first day of the week that is later than the date parameter passed.	DATE
TRUNC(date)	Ignores the hours, minutes, and seconds on DATE datatype. Does not work on the new DATETIME datatypes discussed in Lab 4.3.	DATE
ROUND(date [,format_mask])	Rounds to various DATE components depending on the optional supplied format mask. Does not work on the new DATETIME datatypes.	DATE
NEW_TIME(date, current_time_zone, new_time_zone)	Returns the date and time in another time zone; for example, EST (Eastern Standard Time), PST (Pacific Standard Time), PDT (Pacific Daylight Time).	DATE

LAB 4.2

LAB 4.2 EXERCISES

4.2.1 UNDERSTAND THE SYSDATE FUNCTION AND PERFORM DATE ARITHMETIC

a) Determine the number of days between February 13, 1964 and the last day of the same month and year.

b) Compute the number of months between September 29, 1999 and August 17, 2003.

c) List the course number, section number, and starting date and time for courses meeting in location 'L500'. Display the date and time in EST and PST time zones using the NEW_TIME function.

d) Add three days to your current date and time.

LAB 4.2 EXERCISE ANSWERS

4.2.1 ANSWERS

a) Determine the number of days between February 13, 1964 and the last day of the same month and year.

Answer: First convert the text literal 13-FEB-1964 to a DATE datatype, then use the LAST_DAY function. The date returned is February 29, 1964, which was a leap year. The difference between the two dates is 16 days.

```
SELECT LAST_DAY(TO_DATE('13-FEB-1964','DD-MON-YYYY')) lastday,
       LAST_DAY(TO_DATE('13-FEB-1964','DD-MON-YYYY'))
       - TO_DATE('13-FEB-1964','DD-MON-YYYY') days
  FROM dual
```

LASTDAY	DAYS
29-FEB-64	16

1 row selected.

The LAST_DAY function takes a single parameter and accepts only parameters of the DATE datatype, either your column must be a DATE datatype column or you must convert it with the TO_DATE function.

b) Compute the number of months between September 29, 1999 and August 17, 2003.

Answer: The simplest solution is to use the MONTHS_BETWEEN function to determine the result.

```
SELECT MONTHS_BETWEEN(TO_DATE('17-AUG-2003','DD-MON-YYYY'),
       TO_DATE('29-SEP-1999','DD-MON-YYYY')) months
  FROM dual
```

```
MONTHS
--------------
46.6129032


1 row selected.
```

The MONTHS_BETWEEN function takes two dates as its parameters and returns a numeric value.

c) List the course number, section number, and starting date and time for courses meeting in location 'L500'. Display the date and time in EST and PST time zones using the NEW_TIME function.

Answer: The function NEW_TIME requires three parameters. The first parameter is the date you want to convert; the second parameter is the time zone on which the date is based; the third parameter is the time zone in which you want the result to be displayed.

```
SELECT course_no, section_no,
       TO_CHAR(start_date_time, 'DD-MON-YYYY HH:MI PM') est,
       TO_CHAR(NEW_TIME(start_date_time, 'EST','PST'),
       'DD-MON-YYYY HH:MI PM') pst
  FROM section
 WHERE location = 'L500'
```

COURSE_NO	SECTION_NO	EST	PST
230	1	07-MAY-1999 09:30 AM	07-MAY-1999 06:30 AM
100	2	24-JUL-1999 09:30 AM	24-JUL-1999 06:30 AM

```
2 rows selected.
```

Note that Oracle 9*i* has greatly expanded the capabilities to convert to and from various time zones. This is discussed in great detail in the next lab.

d) Add three days to your current date and time.

Answer: The answer will vary depending on when you execute this query. To add days to the current date and time, just add the number of days to the SYSDATE function.

```
SELECT TO_CHAR(SYSDATE, 'DD-MON-YYYY HH24:MI:SS') "Current",
       TO_CHAR(SYSDATE+3, 'DD-MON-YYYY HH24:MI:SS') "Answer"
  FROM dual
```

Current	Answer
06-MAR-2002 23:12:02	09-MAR-2002 23:12:02

```
1 row selected.
```

If you have to add hours you can express the hour as a fraction of the day. For example, five hours are SYSDATE+5/24. To find out yesterday's date, you can subtract days, thus the SELECT clause will read SYSDATE-1.

LAB 4.2 SELF-REVIEW QUESTIONS

In order to test your progress, you should be able to answer the following questions.

1) Using the ADD_MONTHS function, you can subtract months from a given date.

a) _____ True
b) _____ False

2) Which one of the following solutions adds 15 minutes to a given date?

a) _____ SELECT SYSDATE+1/96 FROM dual
b) _____ SELECT SYSDATE+1/128 FROM dual
c) _____ SELECT TO_DATE(SYSDATE+1/128) FROM dual
d) _____ SELECT TO_CHAR(SYSDATE+1/128, 'DD-MON-YYYY
   24HH:MI') FROM dual

3) Choose the date that is calculated by the following query:

```
SELECT TO_CHAR(NEXT_DAY(TO_DATE('02-JAN-2000 SUN',
             'DD-MON-YYYY DY'), 'SUN'),
             'fmDay Month DD, YYYY')
   FROM dual
```

a) _____ Sunday January 2, 2000
b) _____ Monday January 3, 2000
c) _____ Sunday January 9, 2000
d) _____ None of the above dates
e) _____ Invalid query

4) The following query gives you which of the following results?

```
SELECT ROUND(TO_DATE('2000/1/31 11:59', 'YYYY/MM/DD HH24:MI'))
   FROM dual
```

a) _____ Returns an Oracle error message
b) _____ 30-JAN-00
c) _____ 31-JAN-00
d) _____ 01-FEB-00

Answers appear in Appendix A, Section 4.2.

LAB 4.3

USING THE NEW ORACLE 9*i* DATETIME DATATYPES

LAB OBJECTIVES

After this lab, you will be able to:

✔ Learn about Oracle's new DATETIME Variants

Starting with Oracle 9*i*, the DATE datatype is extended to include several related datatypes referred to as DATETIME datatypes, which include fractional seconds and time zones. These new DATETIME datatypes are TIMESTAMP, TIMESTAMP WITH TIME ZONE, and TIMESTAMP WITH LOCAL TIME ZONE. In addition, you can store intervals between two dates in two datatypes called INTERVAL YEAR TO MONTH and INTERVAL DAY TO SECONDS. The INTERVAL datatype is discussed in Lab 4.4.

THE TIMESTAMP DATATYPE

The TIMESTAMP datatype allows you to store optional fractional seconds with a precision of up to 9; the default precision is 6. An example of a text literal in the default format looks like this: `'14-MAR-02 08.29.01.000123 AM'`. This represents the default format mask of 'DD-MON-RR HH:MI:SS.FF AM'. The fractional seconds are expressed with the FF format mask.

Instead of using the Oracle default format model, you can represent the format mask of a literal with the ANSI TIMESTAMP format as follows: TIMESTAMP `'2002-03-14  08:29:01.000123'`. Again, 000123 are the fractional seconds showing a six-digit precision.

THE TIMESTAMP WITH TIME ZONE DATATYPE

Besides the date, time, and fractional seconds, the TIMESTAMP WITH TIME ZONE datatype includes the *time zone displacement value*. The time zone displacement, also called *time zone offset value,* is expressed as the difference (in hours and minutes) between your local time and the *Greenwich Mean Time* (GMT) now called *Coordinated Universal Time* (UTC). The earth divides into 24 times zones. The time zone along the prime meridian in Greenwich, England is commonly known as GMT, against which all other time zones are compared. At noon Greenwich time, it is midnight at the international date line in the Pacific.

The time zone displacement value is shown as a positive or negative number (i.e., –5:00), indicating the hours and minutes before or after UTC. Alternatively, the time zone can be expressed as a time zone region name such as America/New_York instead of –5:00. The TIMESTAMP WITH TIME ZONE datatype is useful when storing date and time information across geographic regions. Oracle stores all values of this datatype in UTC.

The time zone region of the database is determined at the time of the database creation. If you don't specify any, the time zone defaults to your operating system's time zone. If all of these choices are invalid, the default becomes UTC. To find out the time zone value of your database, use the DBTIMEZONE function. The query returns the time zone displacement value indicating that the time zone is 5 hours before UTC.

```
SELECT DBTIMEZONE
  FROM dual
DBTIME
------
-05:00

1 row selected.
```

The Whole Truth

Instead of returning the offset number for the time zone displacement as you see indicated by the –5:00, the default can be changed for all displacement offsets to a region name instead. The time zone region equivalent for the EST (Eastern Standard Time) and EDT (Eastern Daylight Time) is 'America/New_York' and is listed in the V$TIMEZONE_NAMES data dictionary view, where you can find the list of valid time zone regions. (The data dictionary is a set of tables that provides information about the database. Data dictionary views are discussed in Chapter 13, "The Data Dictionary and Dynamic SQL Scripts." The server's time zone is determined at the creation of the database. It can be modified with an ALTER DATABASE statement. For more information on the CREATE and ALTER DATABASE statements, please see the *Oracle DBA Interactive Workbook* by Melanie Caffrey and Douglas Scherer.)

THE TIMESTAMP WITH LOCAL TIME ZONE DATATYPE

The TIMESTAMP WITH LOCAL TIME ZONE stores the date and time values of the database's own local time zone. When the user retrieves the data, the returned values are automatically converted to represent each individual user's time zone. In addition, the database does not store the time zone displacement value as part of the datatype and there is no text literal to represent this datatype. Although all other newly introduced datatypes are SQL:1999 standard compliant, this datatype is an Oracle proprietary datatype.

When performing arithmetic on this datatype, Oracle automatically converts all values to UTC before doing the calculation and then converts the value back to the local time. This is in contrast to the TIMESTAMP WITH TIME ZONE datatype, where the values are always stored in UTC and a conversion is unnecessary.

LAB 4.3

DAYLIGHT SAVINGS

Oracle provides automatic support for daylight savings time and for boundary cases when the time switches. Typically, daylight savings time starts on the first Sunday in April until the last Sunday in October; in Europe it starts a week earlier and ends at the same time.

DEFAULT FORMAT MASKS

Table 4.5 shows the DATE-related datatypes and their individual components together with default formats and example literals. Throughout this lab you will get to use these datatypes in different exercises.

Table 4.6 lists the valid range of values for the individual components of the DATE related datatypes.

NEW DATETIME FUNCTIONS

Oracle *9i* introduced a number of new functions related to these new datatypes. A listing of the DATE and DATETIME function to determine the current date and time is shown in Table 4.7.

THE LOCALTIMESTAMP FUNCTION

The next SQL statement shows the use of the LOCALTIMESTAMP function, which returns the current date and time including the fractional sections in Oracle's TIMESTAMP format. This function considers the local user's *session* time; that is, if the database server is in San Francisco and the user is in New York, the time displayed is the user's local New York time.

Table 4.5 ■ Overview of Oracle DATE-Related Datatypes

Datatype	Components	Default Formats

DATE	Century, Year, Month, Day, Hour, Minute, Second	Oracle Default Formats:
		`'DD-MON-RR'` and `'DD-MON-YYYY'`
		`'14-MAR-02'` and `'14-MAR-2002'`
		
		ANSI Formats:
		`DATE 'YYYY-MM-DD'`
		`DATE '2002-03-14'`
		`TIMESTAMP 'YYYY-MM-DD HH24:MI:SS'`
		`TIMESTAMP '2002-03-14 16:21:04'`

TIMESTAMP	Same as DATE with additional fractional seconds	Oracle Default Formats:
		`'DD-MON-RR HH.MI.SS.FF AM'`
		`'14-MAR-02 04.21.04.000001 PM'`
		`'DD-MON-YYYY HH.MI.SS.FF AM'`
		`'14-MAR-2002 04.21.04.000001 PM'`
		
		ANSI Format:
		`TIMESTAMP 'YYYY-MM-DD HH24:MI:SS.FF'`
		`TIMESTAMP '2002-03-14 16:21:04.000001'`

TIMESTAMP WITH TIME ZONE	Same as TIMESTAMP plus Time Zone Hour and Time Zone Minute (TZH:TZM) or Time Zone Region Name (TZR)	Oracle Default Formats with time offset values in hours and minutes:
		`'DD-MON-RR HH.MI.SS.FF AM TZH:TZM'`
		`'14-MAR-02 04.21.04.000001 PM -05:00'`
		`'DD-MON-YYYY HH.MI.SS.FF AM TZH:TZM'`
		`'14-MAR-2002 04.21.04.000001 PM -05:00'`
		
		Oracle Default Formats with time zone region:
		`'DD-MON-RR HH.MI.SS.FF AM TZR'`
		`'14-MAR-02 04.21.04.000001 PM America/`
		`New_York'`
		`'DD-MON-YYYY HH.MI.SS.FF AM TZR'`
		`'14-MAR-2002 04.21.04.000001 PM America/`
		`New_York'`
		
		ANSI Format with offset value:
		`TIMESTAMP 'YYYY-MM-DD HH24:MI:SS.FF TZH:TZM'`
		`TIMESTAMP '2002-03-14 16:21:04.000001 -5:00'`
		
		ANSI Format with time zone region:
		`TIMESTAMP 'YYYY-MM-DD HH:MI:SS.FF TZR'`
		`TIMESTAMP '2002-03-14 16:21:04.000001`
		`America/New_York'`

TIMESTAMP WITH LOCAL TIME ZONE	Same components as the TIMESTAMP datatype	See TIMESTAMP.

LAB 4.3

Table 4.6 ■ Valid Value Ranges for Date and Time Components

Date Component	Valid Values
YEAR	−4712 – 9999 (excluding year 0)
MONTH	01 – 12
DAY	01 – 31
HOUR	00 – 23
MINUTE	00 – 59
SECOND	00 – 59 (optional precision up to 9 digits for TIMESTAMP, TIMESTAMP WITH TIME ZONE, and TIMESTAMP WITH LOCAL TIME ZONE)
TIMEZONE_HOUR	−12 – +13
TIMEZONE_MINUTE	00 – 59

```
SELECT LOCALTIMESTAMP
  FROM dual
LOCALTIMESTAMP
----------------------------
14-MAR-02 04.21.04.000001 PM

1 row selected.
```

THE SYSTIMESTAMP FUNCTION

When compared to the SYSDATE function, the SYSTIMESTAMP function includes fractional seconds with a default six-digit precision. Like the SYSDATE function it shows the *database's* time zone, not that of the client machine executing the function. The time zone displacement or offset in the following SQL statement is −5.00, indicating the time is 5 hours before the UTC, which in this example represents EST. The format mask is expressed in the format mask [+|-] TZH:TZM, which means it is either a positive or negative number together with the time zone hours and time zone minutes offset numbers.

```
SELECT SYSTIMESTAMP
  FROM dual
SYSTIMESTAMP
-----------------------------------
10-MAR-02 03.23.34.000000 PM -05:00

1 row selected.
```

Table 4.7 ■ Session and Server DATE and DATETIME Functions

Function	Purpose	Return Datatype
CURRENT_DATE	Returns the date and time of the local *session* time zone in DATE datatype. (The local session time can be different than the server's date and time, if the client session is in a different time zone.)	DATE
CURRENT_TIMESTAMP [(optional_precison)]	Returns the individual's *session* date and time in the datatype TIMESTAMP WITH TIME ZONE value.	TIMESTAMP WITH TIME ZONE
DBTIMEZONE	Returns the time zone offset value of the database *server* time zone or time zone region name, depending on the setup of the database.	VARCHAR2
LOCALTIMESTAMP [(optional_precision)]	Returns in the TIMESTAMP format the current date and time in the local *session* time.	TIMESTAMP
SESSIONTIMEZONE	Returns the time zone offset value of the *session* time zone or the time zone region name, depending on the setup of the database.	VARCHAR2
SYSDATE	Returns the database *server* operating system current date and time.	DATE
SYSTIMESTAMP	Returns date, time, and six-digit fractional seconds and time zone of the *server*. This is similar to the SYSDATE function, but includes the fractional seconds and time zone.	TIMESTAMP WITH TIME ZONE

**LAB
4.3**

THE CURRENT_TIMESTAMP FUNCTION

The CURRENT_TIMESTAMP function returns the current *session's* time in the datatype TIMESTAMP WITH TIME ZONE value. It differs from the LOCALTIMESTAMP function in that the datatype is not TIMESTAMP, but TIMESTAMP WITH TIME ZONE and therefore includes the time zone displacement value.

```
SELECT CURRENT_TIMESTAMP, LOCALTIMESTAMP
   FROM dual
```

```
CURRENT_TIMESTAMP                    LOCALTIMESTAMP
-------------------------------- --------------------------
31-MAR-02 07.59.49.000000 PM -05:00 31-MAR-02 07.59.49.000000 PM
```

`1 row selected.`

THE CURRENT_DATE FUNCTION

The CURRENT_DATE function returns the date and time in the *session's* time zone. The returned values can be different than the values returned by the SYS-DATE function. For example, if you execute a query on your machine located on the east coast against a database server that is located on the west coast, the SYSDATE function returns the date and time of the server in PST and the CURRENT_DATE function returns your local east coast date and time. Note that the return datatype of the CURRENT_DATE function is a DATE datatype.

```
SELECT TO_CHAR(CURRENT_DATE, 'DD-MON-YYYY HH:MI:SS PM')
   FROM dual
TO_CHAR(CURRENT_DATE,'D
----------------------
01-APR-2002 02:37:11 AM
```

`1 row selected.`

You may wonder how the CURRENT_DATE function compares to the previously mentioned LOCALTIMESTAMP function. The difference is the return datatype of the function. CURRENT_DATE returns a DATE datatype and the LOCALTIMESTAMP function returns the TIMESTAMP datatype, which also includes the fractional seconds.

THE SESSIONTIMEZONE FUNCTION

Because an individual user may be in a different time zone than the server, you can execute different functions depending on what you want to accomplish. The SESSIONTIMEZONE returns the session's time zone displacement value; the DB-TIMEZONE function returns the server's time zone displacement value.

The next statement shows the execution of the SESSIONTIMEZONE function; you notice it includes the time zone displacement value indicating the difference in hours and minutes between the UTC and your local time. The user's local time zone is determined by either the most recent ALTER SESSION statement setting the local time zone or by your operating system's time zone. If none of them are valid, the default is UTC.

```
SELECT SESSIONTIMEZONE
   FROM dual
SESSIONTIMEZONE
----------------------
-05:00
```

`1 row selected.`

THE DBTIMEZONE FUNCTION

The DBTIMEZONE function is in contrast with the SESSIONTIMEZONE function. You can verify the database's local time zone with the DBTIMEZONE function. It displays the database's time zone; if none has been manually set, it displays UTC as the default value.

```
SELECT DBTIMEZONE
  FROM dual
DBTIME
------
-05:00

1 row selected.
```

CHANGING THE LOCAL TIME ZONE

You can experiment with changing the time zone of your local machine and the effect on the discussed functions. For example, on the Windows operating system, you can change the time zone in the Control Panel by choosing the Date/Time Properties (as shown in Figure 4.1). If you change your default time zone to another time zone with a different time zone displacement value, you will notice that the results of the SESSIONTIMEZONE function are different. Make sure to log out of the current SQL*Plus session first, so the effects of the time zone change are visible. If you use *i*SQL*Plus, you will not notice any difference, because your browser checks the *i*SQL*Plus HTTP server and not your local machine for the time zone.

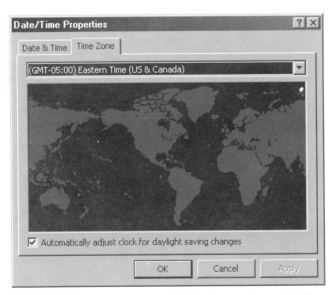

Figure 4.1 ■ Changing the time zone on the Windows operating system.

OVERRIDING THE INDIVIDUAL SESSION TIME ZONE

You can change the time zone for an individual session with the ALTER SESSION command. The setting remains until you exit the session. The following three example statements illustrate different ways you can change the time zone offset value. The first changes the value to a time zone region name, the second makes it equivalent to the database server's time zone, and the last resets it to the session's local time zone.

```
ALTER SESSION SET TIME_ZONE = 'America/New_York'
ALTER SESSION SET TIME_ZONE = dbtimezone
ALTER SESSION SET TIME_ZONE = local
```

EXTRACT FUNCTIONS

Extracting functions allow you to pull out various components of the DATE and DATETIME datatypes, such as the YEAR, MONTH, and so on (see Table 4.8). Similar results may also be accomplished with the TO_CHAR function and the respective format mask discussed in Lab 4.2.

Table 4.8 ■ Extracting Functions

Function	Purpose	Return Datatype
EXTRACT(YEAR FROM date)	Extracts year from a DATE datatype. Valid keyword choices are YEAR, MONTH, and DAY to extract the year, month, and day, respectively.	NUMBER
EXTRACT(YEAR FROM timestamp)	Extracts year from a TIMESTAMP datatype. Valid keyword choices are YEAR, MONTH, DAY, HOUR, MINUTE, SECOND to extract the year, month, day, hour, minute, and seconds including fractional seconds, respectively.	NUMBER
EXTRACT(YEAR FROM timestamp_with_time_zone)	Valid keywords are YEAR, MONTH, DAY, HOUR, MINUTE, SECOND, TIMEZONE_HOUR, TIMEZONE_MINUTE, TIMEZONE_REGION, TIMEZONE_ABBR. The values are returned in UTC.	NUMBER for TIME ZONE REGION (If TIME ZONE ABBREVIATION is passed the EXTRACT function returns VARCHAR2)
SYS_EXTRACT_UTC (timestamp with time zone)	Returns the date and time in UTC	TIMESTAMP WITH TIME ZONE
TZ_OFFSET(time_zone)	Returns the time difference between UTC and passed time zone value	VARCHAR2

THE SYS_EXTRACT_UTC FUNCTION

The purpose of the SYS_EXTRACT_UTC function is to extract the UTC from a passed date and time value. The next example shows two equivalent date and time values when translated to UTC. Both are ANSI literals of the datatype TIMESTAMP WITH TIME ZONE.

```
TIMESTAMP '2002-03-11 7:00:00 -8:00'
TIMESTAMP '2002-03-11 10:00:00 -5:00'
```

The first time stamp shows March 11, 2002 at 7:00 AM PST, which is eight hours before UTC. This value is identical to the next time stamp; it shows the same date with 10:00 AM EST local time, which is 5 hours before UTC. The 7:00 AM time on the west coast is identical to the 10:00 AM east coast as there is a three-hour time difference. When calculating the time in UTC, you will see that the two time stamps are identical in UTC. In fact, Oracle calculates the TIMESTAMP WITH TIME ZONE datatype always in UTC and then displays the local time with the time zone displacement.

```
SELECT SYS_EXTRACT_UTC(TIMESTAMP '2002-03-11 7:00:00 -8:00')
       "West coast to UTC",
       SYS_EXTRACT_UTC(TIMESTAMP '2002-03-11 10:00:00 -5:00')
       "East coast to UTC"
  FROM dual
West coast to UTC                  East coast to UTC
---------------------------------  ---------------------------------
11-MAR-02 03.00.00.000000000 PM  11-MAR-02 03.00.00.000000000 PM

1 row selected.
```

THE EXTRACT FUNCTION
AND THE TIMESTAMP DATATYPE

The following SQL statement extracts the various components of this datatype including the seconds. You cannot extract the fractional seconds only, they are included as part of the SECOND keyword specification. The passed TIMESTAMP literal is in the ANSI TIMESTAMP default format.

```
SELECT EXTRACT(HOUR FROM TIMESTAMP '2002-03-11 15:48:01.123') hour,
       EXTRACT(MINUTE FROM TIMESTAMP '2002-03-11 15:48:01.123')
       minute,
       EXTRACT(SECOND FROM TIMESTAMP '2002-03-11 15:48:01.123')
       second,
       EXTRACT(YEAR FROM TIMESTAMP '2002-03-11 15:48:01.123') year,
       EXTRACT(MONTH FROM TIMESTAMP '2002-03-11 15:48:01.123')
       month,
       EXTRACT(DAY FROM TIMESTAMP '2002-03-11 15:48:01.123') day
  FROM dual
```

HOUR	MINUTE	SECOND	YEAR	MONTH	DAY
15	48	1.123	2002	3	11

`1 row selected.`

EXTRACT AND THE TIMESTAMP WITH TIMEZONE DATATYPE

Following are examples of the EXTRACT function that illustrate how to pull out the various components of the TIMESTAMP WITH TIME ZONE datatype. Important to note here is that when using EXTRACT on this datatype only all date and time values are returned in UTC, not the time displayed by default in the column.

The next example shows just a few of the components. When examining the result you see that the column labeled HOUR displays the time as 21, which is 9 P.M., but the actual local time is stored as 4 P.M. in the column named COL_TIMESTAMP_W_TZ. This is a clear indication that the EXTRACT function uses UTC.

```
SELECT col_timestamp_w_tz,
       EXTRACT(YEAR FROM col_timestamp_w_tz) year,
       EXTRACT(MONTH FROM col_timestamp_w_tz) month,
       EXTRACT(DAY FROM col_timestamp_w_tz) day,
       EXTRACT(HOUR FROM col_timestamp_w_tz) hour,
       EXTRACT(MINUTE FROM col_timestamp_w_tz) min,
       EXTRACT(SECOND FROM col_timestamp_w_tz) sec
  FROM date_example
```

COL_TIMESTAMP_W_TZ	YEAR	MONTH	DAY	HOUR	MIN	SEC
24-MAR-02 04.25.32.000000 PM -05:00	2002	3	24	21	25	32

`1 row selected.`

The keywords TIMEZONE_HOUR and TIMEZONE_MINUTE allow you to display the time zone displacement value expressed in hours and minutes. The TIMEZONE_REGION and TIMEZONE_ABBR keywords indicate the time zone region information spelled out or in abbreviated format. If a region has not been setup for your database, you will see the value unknown, as in this example.

```
SELECT col_timestamp_w_tz,
       EXTRACT(TIMEZONE_HOUR FROM col_timestamp_w_tz) tz_hour,
       EXTRACT(TIMEZONE_MINUTE FROM col_timestamp_w_tz) tz_min,
       EXTRACT(TIMEZONE_REGION FROM col_timestamp_w_tz) tz_region,
       EXTRACT(TIMEZONE_ABBR FROM col_timestamp_w_tz) tz_abbr
  FROM date_example
```

```
COL_TIMESTAMP_W_TZ                      TZ_HOUR TZ_MIN TZ_REGION TZ_ABBR
-----------------------------------     ------- ------ --------- -------
24-MAR-02 04.25.32.000000 PM -05:00         -5      0 UNKNOWN   UNK
```

```
1 row selected.
```

THE DATE_EXAMPLE TABLE

In the two previous SQL statements you may have noticed the use of a table called DATE_EXAMPLE to illustrate the different variants of the DATETIME datatype. This table is not part of the STUDENT schema but can be created based on the additional script, available for download from the companion Web site. Listed here are the columns of the DATE_EXAMPLE table and their respective datatypes.

```
SQL> DESCR date_example
 Name                            Null?     Type
 ------------------------------- --------- ----------------------------
 COL_DATE                                  DATE
 COL_TIMESTAMP                             TIMESTAMP(6)
 COL_TIMESTAMP_W_TZ                        TIMESTAMP(6) WITH TIME ZONE
 COL_TIMESTAMP_W_LOCAL_TZ                  TIMESTAMP(6) WITH LOCAL TIME
```

The first column named COL_DATE is of the familiar DATE datatype. The second column called COL_TIMESTAMP includes fractional seconds with a six-digit precision. The third column called COL_TIMESTAMP_W_TZ additionally contains the time zone offset. Last, the fourth column is defined as the TIMESTAMP WITH LOCAL TIME ZONE datatype.

CONVERSION FUNCTIONS

To query against a column of the new datatype, you need to state any literal in the default format listed in Table 4.5 or use a function shown in Table 4.9 to convert the literal to the desired datatype. In the previous labs you became familiar with the TO_CHAR and the TO_DATE functions. The TO_TIMESTAMP and TO_TIMESTAMP_TZ work in a similar way. The TO_CHAR and TO_DATE functions are listed for completeness.

The next statement queries the DATE_EXAMPLE table and converts the text literal into a TIMESTAMP WITH TIME ZONE datatype to be able to compare the value against the column COL_TIMESTAMP_W_TZ of the same datatype.

```
        SELECT col_timestamp_w_tz
          FROM date_example
         WHERE col_timestamp_w_tz = TO_TIMESTAMP_TZ
                    ('24-MAR-02 04.25.32.000000 PM -05:00',
                     'DD-MON-RR HH.MI.SS.FF AM TZH:TZM')
```

Table 4.9 ■ Conversion Functions

Function	Purpose	Return Datatype
TO_TIMESTAMP(char [,format_mask])	Converts text to the TIMESTAMP datatype based on format mask (this works similar to the TO_DATE function).	TIMESTAMP
TO_TIMESTAMP_TZ(char [,format_mask])	Converts text or a database column of VARCHAR2 or CHAR datatype to TIMESTAMP WITH TIME ZONE datatype based on format mask.	TIMESTAMP WITH TIME ZONE
TO_DATE(char [,format_mask])	Converts a text literal to a DATE datatype. As with all other date-related conversion functions, the format_mask is optional if the literal is in the default format; otherwise, a format mask must be specified.	DATE
TO_CHAR(date [,format_mask])	Converts all DATE-related datatypes into VARCHAR2 to display it in a different format than the default date format. (The TO_CHAR function can be used with other datatypes; see Lab 4.5).	VARCHAR2
FROM_TZ(timestamp, hour_min_offset)	Converts a TIMESTAMP value into a TIMESTAMP WITH TIME ZONE datatype. An example of the hour_min_offset value (time zone displacement value) is '+5:00' or it can be a time zone region name such as 'America/New_York'.	TIMESTAMP WITH TIME ZONE

LAB 4.3

Note that Oracle does not provide a conversion function to convert to a TIMESTAMP WITH LOCAL TIME ZONE datatype. Use the CAST function discussed in Lab 4.5 instead.

```
COL_TIMESTAMP_W_TZ
---------------------------------------
24-MAR-02 04.25.32.000000 PM -05:00

1 row selected.
```

DATETIME EXPRESSION

A DATETIME expression can be a column of datatype TIMESTAMP WITH TIME ZONE, TIMESTAMP WITH LOCAL TIME ZONE, TIMESTAMP, or an expression that results in any of the three datatypes.

The expression can be shown in various time zones with the keywords AT TIME ZONE. The next example illustrates the value of 24-MAR-02 04.25.32.000000 P.M. -05:00 in the COL_TIMESTAMP_W_TZ column displayed in the Los Angeles local time instead. The expression uses the time zone region name 'America/Los_Angeles' after the keywords AT TIME ZONE.

```
SELECT col_timestamp_w_tz AT TIME ZONE 'America/Los_Angeles'
  FROM date_example
COL_TIMESTAMP_W_TZATTIMEZONE'AMERICA/LOS_ANGELES
--------------------------------------------------
24-MAR-02 01.25.32.000000 PM AMERICA/LOS_ANGELES

1 row selected.
```

The syntax of the DATETIME expression is as follows:

```
datetime_value_expr AT {
  LOCAL |
  TIME ZONE{'[+|-]hh:mm' |
            DBTIMEZONE |
            SESSIONTIMEZONE |
            'time_zone_name'}}
```

Besides showing the time in the local time zone, you can also choose a specific time zone displacement in the TZH:TZM format. Other syntax alternatives are DBTIMEZONE, which returns the value in the database server's time zone. The SESSIONTIMEZONE shows the session's time zone and the time zone name for a time zone region name.

The next example displays the same column expressed in the database server's time zone with the DBTIMEZONE keyword.

```
SELECT col_timestamp_w_tz AT TIME ZONE DBTIMEZONE
  FROM date_example
COL_TIMESTAMP_W_TZATTIMEZONEDBTIMEZONE
--------------------------------------
24-MAR-02 04.25.32.000000 PM -05:00

1 row selected.
```

In Lab 4.2 you learned about the NEW_TIME function. Compared to the NEW_TIME function, the DATETIME expression is more versatile because it allows a greater number of time zone values.

LAB 4.3 EXERCISES

4.3.1 LEARN ABOUT ORACLE'S NEW DATETIME VARIANTS

a) Describe the default display formats of the result returned by the following SQL query.

```
SELECT col_date, col_timestamp, col_timestamp_w_tz
  FROM date_example
COL_DATE   COL_TIMESTAMP                 COL_TIMESTAMP_W_TZ
---------  ----------------------------  -----------------------------------
24-MAR-02  24-MAR-02 04.25.32.000000 PM  24-MAR-02 04.25.32.000000 PM -05:00

1 row selected.
```

b) Explain the result of the following SELECT statement. Are there alternate ways to rewrite the query's WHERE clause?

```
SELECT col_timestamp
  FROM date_example
 WHERE col_timestamp = '24-MAR-02 04.25.32.000000 PM'
COL_TIMESTAMP
----------------------------
24-MAR-02 04.25.32.000000 PM

1 row selected.
```

c) What function can you utilize to display the seconds component of a TIMESTAMP datatype column?

d) What do you observe about the text literal of the following query's WHERE clause?

```
SELECT col_timestamp_w_tz
  FROM date_example
 WHERE col_timestamp_w_tz = '24-MAR-02 04.25.32.000000 PM -05:00'
COL_TIMESTAMP_W_TZ
-----------------------------------
24-MAR-02 04.25.32.000000 PM -05:00

1 row selected.
```

e) The following sets of SQL statements are issued against the database server. Explain the results.

```
SELECT SESSIONTIMEZONE
  FROM dual
SESSIONTIMEZONE
------------------
-05:00

1 row selected.

SELECT col_timestamp_w_tz, col_timestamp_w_local_tz
  FROM date_example
COL_TIMESTAMP_W_TZ                        COL_TIMESTAMP_W_LOCAL_TZ
---------------------------------- ----------------------------
24-MAR-02 04.25.32.000000 PM -05:00 24-MAR-02 04.25.32.000000 PM

1 row selected.

ALTER SESSION SET TIME_ZONE = '-8:00'
Session altered.

SELECT col_timestamp_w_tz, col_timestamp_w_local_tz
  FROM date_example
COL_TIMESTAMP_W_TZ                        COL_TIMESTAMP_W_LOCAL_TZ
---------------------------------- ----------------------------
24-MAR-02 04.25.32.000000 PM -05:00 24-MAR-02 01.25.32.000000 PM

1 row selected.

ALTER SESSION SET TIME_ZONE = '-5:00'
Session altered.
```

LAB 4.3 EXERCISE ANSWERS

4.3.1 ANSWERS

a) Describe the default display formats of the result returned by the following SQL query.

```
SELECT col_date, col_timestamp, col_timestamp_w_tz
  FROM date_example
COL_DATE   COL_TIMESTAMP                  COL_TIMESTAMP_W_TZ
--------- ---------------------------- ------------------------------------
24-MAR-02 24-MAR-02 04.25.32.000000 PM 24-MAR-02 04.25.32.000000 PM -05:00

1 row selected.
```

Answer: This query returns the default display format values of three columns: COL_DATE, COL_TIMESTAMP, and COL_TIMESTAMP_W_TZ.

You are already familiar with the DD-MON-RR DATE default format listed in the right column. The default display format for the Oracle TIMESTAMP datatype is DD-MON-RR HH.MI.SS.FF AM as shown in the second column. The third column named COL_TIMESTAMP_W_TZ also shows the time zone displacement value in the default format +/- TZH:TZM. (All the default display formats can be changed with the NLS_TIMESTAMP_FORMAT and NLS_TIMESTAMP_TZ_FORMAT parameters in the Oracle database initialization file, also referred to as the init.ora file, or they can also be changed with an ALTER SESSION statement. An ALTER SESSION statement changes certain values for the user's current session. These temporary settings remain until the user disconnects his session; i.e., exits from SQL*Plus or from any other program that created the session.)

b) Explain the result of the following SELECT statement. Are there alternate ways to rewrite the query's WHERE clause?

```
SELECT col_timestamp
  FROM date_example
 WHERE col_timestamp = '24-MAR-02 04.25.32.000000 PM'
COL_TIMESTAMP
----------------------------
24-MAR-02 04.25.32.000000 PM

1 row selected.
```

Answer: The query shows the use of the TIMESTAMP datatype. There are alternative ways available to achieve the same result. As you learned previously in context with the DATE datatype, it is always preferable to explicitly perform the datatype conversion instead of using the default text literal. The following query uses the TO_TIMESTAMP function to convert the text literal into an Oracle TIMESTAMP datatype and it uses the matching format masks. The FF format mask represents the fractional seconds; the AM format mask indicates the time listed in the AM/PM format, not the 24-hour military time format.

```
SELECT col_timestamp
  FROM date_example
 WHERE col_timestamp =
       TO_TIMESTAMP('24-MAR-2002 04:25:32.000000 PM',
                    'DD-MON-YYYY HH:MI:SS.FF AM')
```

If you exclude the fractional seconds together with the FF format mask, the fractional seconds are implied to be zero, as you can see in the next example.

```
SELECT col_timestamp
  FROM date_example
 WHERE col_timestamp =
       TO_TIMESTAMP('24-MAR-2002 04:25:32 PM',
                    'DD-MON-YYYY HH:MI:SS AM')
```

The following query using the ANSI TIMESTAMP format also returns the correct result.

```
SELECT col_timestamp
  FROM date_example
 WHERE col_timestamp = TIMESTAMP '2002-03-24 16:25:32.000000'
```

CONVERSION BETWEEN ORACLE DATE DATATYPES

You may wonder if you can apply any of the previously used TO_DATE format models to query the COL_TIMESTAMP column. The next SQL statement converts the text literal to a DATE datatype with the TO_DATE function. The DATE datatype is implicitly converted to the TIMESTAMP datatype. Because the fractional seconds in this example are equal to 000000, the result is considered equivalent and the row returned.

```
SELECT col_timestamp
  FROM date_example
 WHERE col_timestamp = TO_DATE('24-MAR-2002 04:25:32 PM',
                               'DD-MON-YYYY HH:MI:SS AM')
```

The following SQL statement shows what happens when you apply a TO_TIMESTAMP function to a DATE datatype column. Notice that the TO_TIMESTAMP function sets the time portion of the DATE column to zero.

```
SELECT TO_TIMESTAMP(col_date) "TO_TIMESTAMP",
       TO_CHAR(col_date, 'DD-MON-YYYY HH24:MI')
       AS "DISPLAY DATE"
  FROM date_example
TO_TIMESTAMP              DISPLAY DATE
----------------------   ----------------
24-MAR-02 12.00.00 AM    24-MAR-2002 16:25

1 row selected.
```

c) What function can you utilize to display the seconds component of a TIME-STAMP datatype column?

Answer: You can use either the TO_CHAR or the EXTRACT function to display components such as the year, month, date, hour, minute, and seconds from the TIMESTAMP datatype columns.

The next SQL statement shows how they are used and their respective differences.

```
SELECT col_timestamp,
       TO_CHAR(col_timestamp, 'SS') AS "CHAR Seconds",
       EXTRACT(SECOND FROM col_timestamp) AS "EXTRACT Seconds"
  FROM date_example
```

```
COL_TIMESTAMP                          CHAR Seconds EXTRACT Seconds
---------------------------------  ------------  ---------------
24-MAR-02 04.25.32.000000 PM 32                             32
```

1 row selected.

The first column displays the column's value in the default TIMESTAMP format; the second column utilizes the TO_CHAR function to display the seconds. If you want to include the fractional seconds, you need to add the FF format mask, which is omitted in this example. The third column shows the use of the EXTRACT function to return the seconds. You may notice the difference in the display of the result between the second and the third column. The TO_CHAR function returns the seconds as a string; the EXTRACT function returns the seconds as a NUMBER datatype. The fractional seconds are always included when using the SECOND keyword with this datatype, but because they are zero they are not shown in the result.

d) What do you observe about the text literal of the following query's WHERE clause?

```
SELECT col_timestamp_w_tz
  FROM date_example
 WHERE col_timestamp_w_tz = '24-MAR-02 04.25.32.000000 PM -05:00'
COL_TIMESTAMP_W_TZ
-----------------------------------
24-MAR-02 04.25.32.000000 PM -05:00
```

1 row selected.

Answer: This SQL statement queries the column called COL_TIMESTAMP_W_TZ using the default TIMESTAMP WITH TIMEZONE display format literal.

You may use other formats in the WHERE clause to accomplish the same. For example, you can use the TO_TIMESTAMP_TZ function to explicitly convert the text literal already in default format to a TIMESTAMP WITH TIME ZONE datatype.

```
SELECT col_timestamp_w_tz
  FROM date_example
 WHERE col_timestamp_w_tz =
       TO_TIMESTAMP_TZ('24-MAR-02 04.25.32.000000 PM -05:00')
```

If you choose a text literal not in default format, you must supply the format mask as illustrated in the next example. The TZH and TZM indicate the time zone displacement values in hours and minutes from UTC. In this example, the fractional seconds (FF) are not included because they are zero.

```
    SELECT col_timestamp_w_tz
      FROM date_example
```

```
WHERE col_timestamp_w_tz =
      TO_TIMESTAMP_TZ('24-MAR-2002 16:25:32 -05:00',
                      'DD-MON-YYYY HH24:MI:SS TZH:TZM')
```

The next WHERE clause uses the region name instead of the time zone offset number value. Region names are expressed in the TZR format mask.

```
SELECT col_timestamp_w_tz
  FROM date_example
 WHERE col_timestamp_w_tz =
       TO_TIMESTAMP_TZ('24-MAR-2002 16:25:32 America/New_York',
                       'DD-MON-YYYY HH24:MI:SS TZR')
```

You can retrieve valid time zone region names from the column TZNAME in the data dictionary view V$TIMEZONE_NAMES.

```
SELECT *
  FROM v$timezone_names
```

TZNAME	TZABBREV
Africa/Cairo	LMT
...	
America/Los_Angeles	PST
...	
America/Chicago	CST
...	
America/Denver	MST
...	
America/New_York	EST
...	

616 rows selected.

Alternatively, if you want to express the WHERE clause in PST, you can use the America/Los_Angeles region name and the actual hour literal needs to be changed from 16 to 13 to result in the same UTC:

```
WHERE col_timestamp_w_tz = TO_TIMESTAMP_TZ(
      '24-MAR-2002 13:25:32 America/Los_Angeles',
      'DD-MON-YYYY HH24:MI:SS TZR')
```

THE TZ_OFFSET FUNCTION

You can find out the time differences between the UTC and the individual time zones with the TZ_OFFSET function. Following is a query that illustrates the appropriate offset values. Note the query result is different when daylight savings time is in effect.

LAB 4.3

```
SELECT TZ_OFFSET('Europe/London') "London",
       TZ_OFFSET('America/New_York') "NY",
       TZ_OFFSET('America/Chicago') "Chicago",
       TZ_OFFSET('America/Denver') "Denver",
       TZ_OFFSET('America/Los_Angeles') "LA"
  FROM dual

London   NY      Chicago Denver  LA
-------  ------- ------- ------- -------
+01:00   -05:00  -06:00  -07:00  -08:00


1 row selected.
```

**LAB
4.3**

COMMON ERRORS

Here's one common mistake you can avoid in conjunction with the DATE-related datatypes. In the next query the HH24 mask is used simultaneously with the a.m./p.m. format mask. An Oracle error indicates that you must choose either HH24 or use the HH (or HH12) together with the a.m./p.m. mask to adjust the time to either 24-hour or 12-hour format.

```
SQL> SELECT col_timestamp_w_tz
  2    FROM date_example
  3   WHERE col_timestamp_w_tz =
  4         TO_TIMESTAMP_TZ('24-MAR-2002 16:25:32 PM -05:00',
  5                         'DD-MON-YYYY HH24:MI:SS PM TZH:TZM')
  6  /
                    'DD-MON-YYYY HH24:MI:SS PM TZH:TZM')
                     *
ERROR at line 5:
ORA-01818: 'HH24' precludes use of meridian indicator
```

The next example illustrates that not all DATE datatype functions work on the TIMESTAMP, TIMESTAMP WITH TIME ZONE, or TIMESTAMP WITH LOCAL TIME ZONE datatype. If you attempt to use the TRUNC function on any of these three datatypes, you will receive an error similar to the following.

```
SQL> SELECT col_timestamp_w_tz
  2    FROM date_example
  3   WHERE TRUNC(col_timestamp_w_tz) = '24-MAR-2002'
  4  /
  WHERE TRUNC(col_timestamp_w_tz) = '24-MAR-2002'
              *
ERROR at line 3:
ORA-00932: inconsistent datatypes
```

e) The following sets of SQL statements are issued against the database server. Explain the results.

```
SELECT SESSIONTIMEZONE
  FROM dual
SESSIONTIMEZONE
-------------------
-05:00

1 row selected.

SELECT col_timestamp_w_tz, col_timestamp_w_local_tz
  FROM date_example
COL_TIMESTAMP_W_TZ                          COL_TIMESTAMP_W_LOCAL_TZ
----------------------------------- ----------------------------
24-MAR-02 04.25.32.000000 PM -05:00 24-MAR-02 04.25.32.000000 PM

1 row selected.

ALTER SESSION SET TIME_ZONE = '-8:00'
Session altered.

SELECT col_timestamp_w_tz, col_timestamp_w_local_tz
  FROM date_example
COL_TIMESTAMP_W_TZ                          COL_TIMESTAMP_W_LOCAL_TZ
----------------------------------- ----------------------------
24-MAR-02 04.25.32.000000 PM -05:00 24-MAR-02 01.25.32.000000 PM

1 row selected.

ALTER SESSION SET TIME_ZONE = '-5:00'
Session altered.
```

**LAB
4.3**

Answer: The results are explained below each statement.

This query determines the session's current time zone offset value, which is –5 hours before UTC. When daylight savings time is in effect the time zone offset value changes.

```
SELECT SESSIONTIMEZONE
  FROM dual
SESSIONTIMEZONE
-------------------
-05:00

1 row selected.
```

The subsequent query of the exercise returns the currently stored values in the columns of the datatypes TIMESTAMP WITH TIME ZONE and TIMESTAMP WITH LOCAL TIME ZONE. Notice that the date and timestamps are identical in both columns. They represent the same date and time.

```
SELECT col_timestamp_w_tz, col_timestamp_w_local_tz
  FROM date_example;
COL_TIMESTAMP_W_TZ                       COL_TIMESTAMP_W_LOCAL_TZ
------------------------------------     ----------------------------
24-MAR-02 04.25.32.000000 PM -05:00 24-MAR-02 04.25.32.000000 PM
```

1 row selected.

Now the session's time zone is changed to be equivalent to the west coast time zone, which is 8 hours before UTC. This statement helps simulate a user's query result on the west coast.

```
ALTER SESSION SET TIME_ZONE = '-8:00'
```
Session altered.

The individual database user's local session time zone can be changed for the duration of the session with the ALTER SESSION command. When the user exits the session, the values are no longer effective. Alternatively, this could also be achieved by changing the user's operating system time zone value, but the ALTER SESSION commands will always override the operating system settings.

The query is reissued and when you compare the two column values, you notice that the second column with the datatype TIMESTAMP WITH LOCAL TIME ZONE shows a different value. The local time stamp is adjusted to the local west coast time.

```
SELECT col_timestamp_w_tz, col_timestamp_w_local_tz
  FROM date_example
COL_TIMESTAMP_W_TZ                       COL_TIMESTAMP_W_LOCAL_TZ
------------------------------------     ----------------------------
24-MAR-02 04.25.32.000000 PM -05:00 24-MAR-02 01.25.32.000000 PM
```

1 row selected.

The next statement resets the time zone to its initial time zone offset value to −5:00 as determined by the SESSIONTIMEZONE function issued previously.

```
ALTER SESSION SET TIME_ZONE = '-5:00'
```
Session altered.

When you reissue the query against the DATE_EXAMPLE table, you notice the local time is back to its original value.

```
SELECT col_timestamp_w_tz, col_timestamp_w_local_tz
  FROM date_example;
COL_TIMESTAMP_W_TZ                       COL_TIMESTAMP_W_LOCAL_TZ
------------------------------------     ----------------------------
24-MAR-02 04.25.32.000000 PM -05:00 24-MAR-02 04.25.32.000000 PM
```

1 row selected.

When the user exits the SQL*Plus session, these ALTER SESSION settings are no longer in effect. The ALTER SESSION settings only persist during the duration of the session.

LAB 4.3 SELF-REVIEW QUESTIONS

In order to test your progress, you should be able to answer the following questions.

1) What datatype will the following function return?

```
SELECT FROM_TZ(col_timestamp, '+5:00')
  FROM date_example
FROM_TZ(COL_TIMESTAMP,'+5:00')
-------------------------------------
24-MAR-02 04.25.32.000000 PM +05:00

1 row selected.
```

   a) _____ DATE
   b) _____ TIMESTAMP
   c) _____ TIMESTAMP WITH TIME ZONE
   d) _____ Returns an Oracle error message

2) The ALTER SESSION statement can change the session's time zone.

   a) _____ True
   b) _____ False

3) The TIMESTAMP WITH LOCAL TIME ZONE datatype always displays the local date and time.

   a) _____ True
   b) _____ False

4) The time zone displacement value indicates the time difference to UTC.

   a) _____ True
   b) _____ False

5) The TIMESTAMP WITH LOCAL TIME ZONE datatype allows fractional seconds.

   a) _____ True
   b) _____ False

Answers appear in Appendix A, Section 4.3.

**LAB
4.3**

LAB 4.4

PERFORMING CALCULATIONS WITH THE INTERVAL DATATYPE

LAB OBJECTIVES

After this lab, you will be able to:

✔ Understand the Functionality of the INTERVAL Datatype

THE INTERVAL DATATYPES

With the extension of the DATETIME datatypes in Oracle 9*i*, two new INTERVAL datatypes were introduced. They are INTERVAL YEAR TO MONTH and INTERVAL DAY TO SECOND. These datatypes store the difference between two date values. Table 4.10 provides you with an overview of the two datatypes and respective example literals.

USING INTERVALS

You can use intervals for calculations such as in the next example where an interval of one year and six months is added to a student's registration date. The interval is represented as the literal '01-06'. The TO_YMINTERVAL function converts this text literal to the INTERVAL YEAR TO MONTH datatype. The result of the query shows the graduation date as one year and six months after the REGISTRATION_DATE.

```
SELECT student_id, registration_date,
       registration_date+TO_YMINTERVAL('01-06') "Grad. Date"
  FROM student
 WHERE student_id = 123
STUDENT_ID REGISTRAT Grad. Dat
---------- --------- ---------
       123 27-JAN-99 27-JUL-00

1 row selected.
```

Table 4.10 ■ INTERVAL Datatypes

Datatype	Purpose and Example Literals
INTERVAL YEAR [year_precision] TO MONTH	Values are expressed in years and months. The default year precision is 2. Literal examples: INTERVAL '3-2' YEAR TO MONTH (3 years and 2 months) INTERVAL '2' YEAR (2 years) INTERVAL '4' MONTH (4 months) INTERVAL '36' MONTH (36 months or 3 years)
INTERVAL DAY [day_precision] TO SECOND (fractional_seconds_ precision)	Values are expressed in days, hours, minutes, and seconds. The default value for the day precision is 2, the fractional seconds precision has a six-digit default value. Literal examples: INTERVAL '30' DAY (30 days) INTERVAL '200' DAY (3) (300 days. Because the literal exceeds the default DAY precision of 2 you need to explicitly specify the precision.) INTERVAL '12:51' HOUR TO MINUTE (12 hours and 51 minutes) INTERVAL '15' MINUTE (15 minutes) INTERVAL '3 5:10:15.10' DAY TO SECONDS (3 days, 5 hours, 10 minutes, 15 seconds, and 10 fractional seconds) Note the components must be contiguous; for example, you cannot skip the MINUTE component between the HOUR and SECOND component.

LAB
4.4

The INTERVAL datatypes have individual components as listed in Table 4.11.

EXTRACT AND INTERVALS

Just like with the other DATE and DATETIME datatypes, you can use the EX-TRACT function to extract specific components. This query retrieves the minutes.

```
SELECT EXTRACT(MINUTE FROM INTERVAL '12:51' HOUR TO MINUTE)
   FROM dual
EXTRACT(MINUTEFROMINTERVAL'12:51'HOURTOMINUTE)
------------------------------------------------
                                              51

1 row selected.
```

Table 4.11 ■ Valid Value Ranges for INTERVAL Components

INTERVAL Component	Valid Values
YEAR	Positive or negative integer, default precision is 2
MONTH	00–11 Note that the 12th month will be converted to a year.
DAY	Positive or negative integer, default precision is 2.
HOUR	00–23
MINUTE	00–59
SECOND	00–59 (Plus optional precision up to 9-digit fractional seconds)

LAB 4.4

The INTERVAL datatype allows a number of useful functions that are listed in Table 4.12.

The next example expresses the time difference between the columns START_DATE_TIME and CREATED_DATE of the SECTION table. The first row of the output indicates that the difference between the two dates is the decimal result of 97.3958333 days; according to the fourth column where the NUMTODSINTERVAL function is applied, this translates into 97 days, 9 hours, 29 minutes, and 59.999999999 seconds.

Table 4.12 ■ Useful INTERVAL Functions

Function	Purpose	Return Datatype
TO_YMINTERVAL(char)	Convert a text literal to an INTERVAL YEAR TO MONTH datatype	INTERVAL YEAR TO MONTH
TO_DSINTERVAL(char)	Convert a text literal to an INTERVAL DAY TO SECOND datatype	INTERVAL DAY TO SECOND
NUMTOYMINTERVAL (number, 'YEAR') NUMTOYMINTERVAL (number, 'MONTH')	Convert a number to an INTERVAL YEAR TO MONTH literal	INTERVAL YEAR TO MONTH
NUMTODSINTERVAL (number, 'DAY')	Convert a number to an INTERVAL DAY TO SECOND literal. Instead of the DAY parameter you can pass the HOUR, MINUTE, or SECOND instead.	INTERVAL DAY TO SECOND
EXTRACT(MINUTE FROM interval_ datatype)	Extract specific components (i.e., YEAR, MONTH, DAY, HOUR, MINUTE, SECOND).	NUMBER

```
SELECT DISTINCT TO_CHAR(created_date, 'DD-MON-YY HH24:MI')
                "CREATED_DATE",
                TO_CHAR(start_date_time, 'DD-MON-YY HH24:MI')
                "START_DATE_TIME",
                start_date_time-created_date
                "Decimal",
                NUMTODSINTERVAL(start_date_time-created_date, 'DAY')
                "Interval"
  FROM section
 ORDER BY 3
```

CREATED_DATE	START_DATE_TIME	Decimal	Interval
02-JAN-99 00:00	09-APR-99 09:30	97.3958333	+000000097 09:29:59.999999999
02-JAN-99 00:00	14-APR-99 09:30	102.395833	+000000102 09:29:59.999999999
...			
02-JAN-99 00:00	24-JUL-99 09:30	203.395833	+000000203 09:29:59.999999999
02-JAN-99 00:00	08-APR-00 09:30	462.395833	+000000462 09:29:59.999999999

29 rows selected.

LAB 4.4

INTERVAL EXPRESSION

As an alternative to the NUMTODSINTERVAL or the NUMTOYMINTERVAL function you can use an *interval expression,* which can be either DAY TO SECOND or YEAR TO MONTH. The next example shows as the first column the value of datatype TIMESTAMP in the COL_TIMESTAMP column of the DATE_EXAMPLE table. The second column subtracts from the SYSTIMESTAMP function the COL_TIMESTAMP column and displays the difference as an interval of DAY TO SECOND, resulting in a difference of 108 days, 19 hours, 30 minutes, and 48 seconds. (The value of SYSTIMESTAMP at the time of the query was 11-JUL-02 11.56.20.000000 AM -04:00.)

```
SELECT col_timestamp, SYSTIMESTAMP,
       (SYSTIMESTAMP - col_timestamp) DAY TO SECOND
       "Interval Day to Second"
  FROM date_example
```

COL_TIMESTAMP	Interval Day to Second
24-MAR-02 04.25.32 PM	+000000108 19:30:48.000000

1 row selected.

If the same query is displayed as a YEAR TO MONTH interval instead, you will see this result displayed as zero years and 4 months.

```
SELECT col_timestamp,
       (SYSTIMESTAMP - col_timestamp) YEAR TO MONTH
       "Interval Year to Month"
  FROM date_example
```

```
COL_TIMESTAMP                Interval Year to Month
--------------------    --------------------------
24-MAR-02 04.25.32 PM   +000000000-04


1 row selected.
```

DETERMINING OVERLAPS

The OVERLAPS functionality was implemented in Oracle 9*i* but not documented. The OVERLAPS operator is useful to determine if two time periods overlap. For example, you can use this operator to determine if a planned meeting conflicts with other scheduled meetings.

The next example table is called MEETING and contains three columns: a MEETING _ID column and two columns that determine the start and end date and time of a meeting.

```
SQL> DESCR meeting
 Name                        Null?     Type
 --------------------    --------  ---------------
 MEETING_ID                        NUMBER(10)
 MEETING_START                     DATE
 MEETING_END                       DATE
```

The table has two rows, as you see from the following SELECT statement.

```
SELECT meeting_id,
       TO_CHAR(meeting_start, 'DD-MON-YYYY HH:MI PM') "Start",
       TO_CHAR(meeting_end, 'DD-MON-YYYY HH:MI PM') "End"
  FROM meeting
MEETING_ID Start                   End
---------- --------------------    --------------------
         1 01-JUL-2002 09:30 AM 01-JUL-2002 10:30 AM
         2 01-JUL-2002 03:00 PM 01-JUL-2002 04:30 PM


2 rows selected.
```

If you want to find out if a particular date and time conflicts with any of the already scheduled meetings, you can issue this SQL query with the OVERLAPS operator. This operator is used just like any of the other comparison operators in the WHERE clause of a SQL statement. Here it compares the column pair MEETING_START and MEETING_END with the date and time 01-JUL-2002 3:30 PM and a two-hour interval. The row that overlaps is returned in the output.

```
SELECT meeting_id,
       TO_CHAR(meeting_start, 'DD-MON-YYYY HH:MI PM') "Start",
       TO_CHAR(meeting_end, 'DD-MON-YYYY HH:MI PM') "End"
  FROM meeting
 WHERE (meeting_start, meeting_end)
```

```
      OVERLAPS
      (TO_DATE('01-JUL-2002 3:30PM', 'DD-MON-YYYY HH:MI PM'),
         INTERVAL '2' HOUR)
```
MEETING_ID Start   End
---------- -------------------- --------------------
         2 01-JUL-2002 03:00 PM 01-JUL-2002 04:30 PM

1 row selected.

Alternatively, if you want to find out which meetings do NOT conflict, you can negate the predicate with the NOT logical operator as shown in the next example.

```
SELECT meeting_id,
       TO_CHAR(meeting_start, 'DD-MON-YYYY HH:MI PM') "Start",
       TO_CHAR(meeting_end, 'DD-MON-YYYY HH:MI PM') "End"
  FROM meeting
 WHERE NOT (meeting_start, meeting_end)
       OVERLAPS
       (TO_DATE('01-JUL-2002 3:30PM', 'DD-MON-YYYY HH:MI PM'),
          INTERVAL '2' HOUR)
```
MEETING_ID Start   End
---------- -------------------- --------------------
         1 01-JUL-2002 09:30 AM 01-JUL-2002 10:30 AM

1 row selected.

LAB
4.4

The syntax for OVERLAPS is as follows:

```
event OVERLAPS event
```

Whereby event is either of the following:

```
(start_event_date_time, end_event_start_time)
```

Or:

```
(start_event_date_time, interval_duration)
```

LAB 4.4 EXERCISES

4.4.1 UNDERSTAND THE FUNCTIONALITY OF THE INTERVAL DATATYPE

a) Explain the result of this SQL statement.

```
SELECT section_id "ID",
       TO_CHAR(created_date, 'MM/DD/YY HH24:MI')
         "CREATED_DATE",
       TO_CHAR(start_date_time, 'MM/DD/YY HH24:MI')
```

```
     "START_DATE_TIME",
     NUMTODSINTERVAL(start_date_time-created_date, 'DAY')
       "Interval"
 FROM section
WHERE NUMTODSINTERVAL(start_date_time-created_date, 'DAY')
       BETWEEN INTERVAL '100' DAY(3) AND INTERVAL '120' DAY(3)
ORDER BY 3
 ID CREATED_DATE    START_DATE_TIM Interval
 --- -------------- -------------- -----------------------------
 79 01/02/99 00:00 04/14/99 09:30 +000000102 09:29:59.999999999
 87 01/02/99 00:00 04/14/99 09:30 +000000102 09:29:59.999999999
 ...
 152 01/02/99 00:00 04/29/99 09:30 +000000117 09:29:59.999999999
 125 01/02/99 00:00 04/29/99 09:30 +000000117 09:29:59.999999999

17 rows selected.
```

b) Explain the results of the two SQL statements. What differences do you notice?

```
SELECT meeting_id,
       TO_CHAR(meeting_start, 'DD-MON-YYYY HH:MI PM') "Start",
       TO_CHAR(meeting_end, 'DD-MON-YYYY HH:MI PM') "End"
  FROM meeting
 WHERE (meeting_start, meeting_end)
       BETWEEN
       TO_DATE('01-JUL-2002 4:30PM', 'DD-MON-YYYY HH:MI PM') AND
       TO_DATE('01-JUL-2002 6:00PM', 'DD-MON-YYYY HH:MI PM')
MEETING_ID Start                End
---------- -------------------- --------------------
         2 01-JUL-2002 03:00 PM 01-JUL-2002 04:30 PM

1 row selected.

SELECT meeting_id,
       TO_CHAR(meeting_start, 'DD-MON-YYYY HH:MI PM') "Start",
       TO_CHAR(meeting_end, 'DD-MON-YYYY HH:MI PM') "End"
  FROM meeting
 WHERE (meeting_start, meeting_end)
       OVERLAPS
       (TO_DATE('01-JUL-2002 4:30PM', 'DD-MON-YYYY HH:MI PM'),
          INTERVAL '1:30' HOUR TO MINUTE)

no rows selected
```

LAB 4.4 EXERCISE ANSWERS

4.4.1 ANSWERS

a) Explain the result of this SQL statement.

```
SELECT section_id,
       TO_CHAR(created_date, 'MM/DD/YY HH24:MI')
         "CREATED_DATE",
       TO_CHAR(start_date_time, 'MM/DD/YY HH24:MI')
         "START_DATE_TIME",
       NUMTODSINTERVAL(start_date_time-created_date, 'DAY')
         "Interval"
  FROM section
 WHERE NUMTODSINTERVAL(start_date_time-created_date, 'DAY')
       BETWEEN INTERVAL '100' DAY(3) AND INTERVAL '120' DAY(3)
 ORDER BY 3
SECTION_ID CREATED_DATE   START_DATE_TIM Interval
---------- -------------- -------------- ----------------------------
        79 01/02/99 00:00 04/14/99 09:30 +000000102 09:29:59.999999999
        87 01/02/99 00:00 04/14/99 09:30 +000000102 09:29:59.999999999
...
       152 01/02/99 00:00 04/29/99 09:30 +000000117 09:29:59.999999999
       125 01/02/99 00:00 04/29/99 09:30 +000000117 09:29:59.999999999

17 rows selected.
```

Answer: The query shows four columns: the SECTION_ID, the CREATED_DATE, the START_DATE_TIME (the date and time a section starts), and the "Interval" column. This last column subtracts the START_DATE_TIME column from the CREATED_DATE column. The time difference is expressed in days, hours, minutes, and seconds with the NUMTODSINTERVAL function. Without this function the calculation will return the time portion as a decimal. The WHERE clause of the query retrieves rows with a time difference value between 100 and 120 days.

The WHERE clause uses both the NUMTODSINTERVAL function and the INTERVAL expression and checks if the result falls BETWEEN the INTERVAL literals 100 and 120 days. Because the INTERVAL DAY has a default precision of 2, you must include the three-digit precision.

b) Explain the results of the two SQL statements. What differences do you notice?

Answer: The difference lies in the WHERE clause. The first statement uses the BETWEEN operator and the second uses the OVERLAPS operator and an interval.

In this example the meeting starts at 4:30 PM, and one of the rows in the database, MEETING_ID 2, ends exactly at that time. Instead of the OVERLAPS operator you can also use the BETWEEN operator when the INTERVAL datatypes as a duration is not involved. The one difference between the BETWEEN and the OVERLAPS operators is that if the two events start and end at the same time, the BETWEEN operator reports them as overlapping.

```
SELECT meeting_id,
       TO_CHAR(meeting_start, 'DD-MON-YYYY HH:MI PM') "Start",
       TO_CHAR(meeting_end, 'DD-MON-YYYY HH:MI PM') "End"
  FROM meeting
 WHERE (meeting_start, meeting_end)
       BETWEEN
       TO_DATE('01-JUL-2002 4:30PM', 'DD-MON-YYYY HH:MI PM') AND
       TO_DATE('01-JUL-2002 6:00PM', 'DD-MON-YYYY HH:MI PM')
MEETING_ID Start                End
---------- -------------------- --------------------
         2 01-JUL-2002 03:00 PM 01-JUL-2002 04:30 PM
```

LAB
4.4

`1 row selected.`

The next query returns no row because according to the OVERLAPS definition, the two events do not conflict if the meeting time ends at exactly the same time when another meeting starts.

```
SELECT meeting_id,
       TO_CHAR(meeting_start, 'DD-MON-YYYY HH:MI PM') "Start",
       TO_CHAR(meeting_end, 'DD-MON-YYYY HH:MI PM') "End"
  FROM meeting
 WHERE (meeting_start, meeting_end)
       OVERLAPS
       (TO_DATE('01-JUL-2002 4:30PM', 'DD-MON-YYYY HH:MI PM'),
          INTERVAL '1:30' HOUR TO MINUTE)
```

`no rows selected`

LAB 4.4 SELF-REVIEW QUESTIONS

In order to test your progress, you should be able to answer the following questions.

1) The TO_YMINTERVAL function converts a text literal to an INTERVAL DAY TO SECOND datatype.

   a) _____ True
   b) _____ False

2) The NUMTODSINTERVAL function converts a number to an INTERVAL YEAR TO MONTH datatype.

   a) _____ True
   b) _____ False

3) The OVERLAPS and BETWEEN operators always return identical results.

    a) _____ True
    b) _____ False

4) The EXTRACT function is not valid for the INTERVAL YEAR TO MONTH datatype.

    a) _____ True
    b) _____ False

5) The following interval literal is invalid.

```
INTERVAL '5 10:30:10.00' DAY TO SECOND
```

    a) _____ True
    b) _____ False

Answers appear in Appendix A, Section 4.4.

**LAB
4.4**

LAB 4.5

CONVERTING FROM ONE DATATYPE TO ANOTHER

LAB OBJECTIVES

After this lab, you will be able to:

✔ Convert between Different Datatypes
✔ Format Data

You know the good old phrase, "You can't compare apples to oranges." SQL works just the same way. When you compare two values or columns they must be of the same datatype or of a compatible datatype. Sometimes Oracle can implicitly convert from one datatype to the other. It is preferable to explicitly specify the conversion with a function to avoid any ambiguities or errors when your SQL statement is executed.

DATATYPE CONVERSION

You have already learned about implicit conversion in the context of DATE and DATETIME functions discussed in the previous labs. In the following SQL statement the WHERE clause compares a text literal against the numeric COURSE_NO column. When Oracle compares a character datatype, in this case the text literal '350', against the NUMBER datatype, which is the COURSE_NO column, Oracle implicitly converts the character data to a NUMBER. This works perfectly as you see from the query result.

```
SELECT course_no, description
  FROM course
 WHERE course_no = '350'
COURSE_NO DESCRIPTION
--------- ------------------------------------
      350 JDeveloper Lab

1 row selected.
```

Clearly, in this example, you have control over the literal and can simply change the text literal '350' to a NUMBER to avoid the implicit conversion. Such a change becomes more difficult or impossible when you are working within a programming language where you may not have influence over the datatype of a supplied value. Inevitably things can go wrong, as you see illustrated in this example table called CONVERSION_EXAMPLE. (This table is not part of the STUDENT schema, but can be downloaded from the companion Web site.)

```
SQL> DESCR conversion_example
 Name                           Null?    Type
 --------------------------     --------  -------------------
 COURSE_NO                               VARCHAR2(9)
```

The following SELECT statement retrieves all the rows from the table. Notice that the COURSE_NO column in this table is of datatype VARCHAR2 and therefore it accepts both numeric as well as alphanumeric entries. The table contains two rows, one with the value of 123 and another with the value xyz.

```
SELECT *
  FROM conversion_example
COURSE_NO
---------
123
xyz

2 rows selected.
```

To illustrate the effects of the implicit data conversion, first query the row with the value of 123 in the COURSE_NO column. As you can see, this statement executes flawlessly because the COURSE_NO column is a VARCHAR2 column and the text literal 123 is enclosed in single quotes.

```
SELECT *
  FROM conversion_example
 WHERE course_no = '123'
COURSE_NO
---------
123

1 row selected.
```

The next query does not enclose the literal in single quotes; in fact it now represents a number literal. Oracle implicitly converts the COURSE_NO column to a NUMBER datatype resulting in an ORA-01722 invalid number error. This error occurs because all the values in the COURSE_NO column are now implicitly converted into the NUMBER datatype. But this conversion cannot be completed because one of the rows, the row with the value xyz, obviously cannot be converted into a NUMBER. Therefore, the query does not return any rows.

```
SELECT *
  FROM conversion_example
 WHERE course_no = 123
ERROR:
ORA-01722: invalid number

no rows selected
```

To avoid this error, it is always best to explicitly specify the conversion function to make sure that the datatypes agree. You accomplish the conversion with the TO_CHAR function; it converts the passed parameter into a character datatype as you see in the next following SQL statement.

```
SELECT *
  FROM conversion_example
 WHERE course_no = TO_CHAR(123)
```

You may wonder why you would bother even adding the TO_CHAR function if you can just enclose the values with quotes. Clearly it is the easiest solution to simply enclose the value with single quotes, but as previously mentioned, you may encounter cases where you do not have control over the literal or when you are comparing one table's column against another table's column.

THE CAST FUNCTION

The CAST function also converts from one datatype to another. It can be applied to Oracle's most commonly used built-in datatypes (i.e., VARCHAR2, CHAR, NUMBER, DATE; including the DATETIME variants) or with a user-defined datatype or subquery. (The creation of user-defined datatypes is not a very commonly used feature and is beyond the scope of this workbook. You will learn about subqueries in Chapter 7, "Subqueries.")

The syntax for the CAST function is as follows:

```
CAST(expression AS datatype)
```

Following are examples on how CAST is used with Oracle's familiar datatypes. The SELECT statement contains CAST instead of the TO_CHAR function. When converting to a VARCHAR2 or CHAR datatype, also referred to as *casting,* you need to specify the length. Here it is three characters long.

```
SELECT *
  FROM conversion_example
 WHERE course_no = CAST(123 AS VARCHAR2(3))
```

The next query casts the text literal 29-MAR-02 into a DATE datatype in the first column and as a TIMESTAMP WITH LOCAL TIME ZONE datatype in the second column.

```
SELECT CAST('29-Mar-02' AS DATE),
       CAST('29-MAR-02' AS TIMESTAMP WITH LOCAL TIME ZONE)
  FROM dual
CAST('29-  CAST('29-MAR-02'ASTIMESTAMPWITHLOCALTIMEZONE)
---------  ------------------------------------------------
29-MAR-02  29-MAR-02 12.00.00.000000 AM

1 row selected.
```

You can use the CAST not only in the SELECT list, but also in the WHERE clause.

```
SELECT section_id,
       TO_CHAR(start_date_time, 'DD-MON-YYYY HH24:MI:SS')
  FROM section
 WHERE start_date_time >= CAST('01-JUL-1999' AS DATE)
   AND start_date_time <  CAST('01-AUG-1999' AS DATE)
```

The following statement casts the literal '04-JUL-2002 10:00:00 AM', shown in the default format, into the TIMESTAMP datatype, because the FROM_TZ function requires this datatype as the first parameter. The FROM_TZ function (discussed in Lab 4.3) converts the TIMESTAMP value into a TIMESTAMP WITH TIME ZONE datatype. The chosen time zone for date literal is the time zone region name 'America/New_York'. The AT TIME ZONE keywords of the resulting expression display the value in the local Los Angeles time.

```
SELECT FROM_TZ(CAST('04-JUL-2002 10:00:00 AM' AS TIMESTAMP),
       'America/New_York') AT TIME ZONE 'America/Los_Angeles'
       "FROM_TZ Example"
  FROM dual
FROM_TZ Example
------------------------------------------------------
04-JUL-02 07.00.00.000000 AM AMERICA/LOS_ANGELES

1 row selected.
```

The next example illustrates the use of CAST on intervals. The text literal '1-6' is converted into the INTERVAL YEAR TO MONTH datatype. As always, there are multiple ways to accomplish the same functionality in the SQL language; here the TO_YMINTERVAL function performs the identical function. This function requires a NUMBER datatype as input parameter. (See also Table 4.12 in Lab 4.4.)

```
SELECT CAST('1-6' AS INTERVAL YEAR TO MONTH) "CAST",
       TO_YMINTERVAL('1-6') "TO_YMINTERVAL",
       NUMTOYMINTERVAL(1.5, 'YEAR') "NUMTOYMINTERVAL"
  FROM dual
```

```
CAST    TO_YMINTERVAL NUMTOYMINTERVAL
------  ------------- ---------------
+01-06 +000000001-06 +000000001-06


1 row selected.
```

CAST VS. ORACLE'S CONVERSION FUNCTIONS

You may wonder why you should use the CAST instead of any of the other Oracle conversion functions. The CAST function is ANSI SQL:1999 compliant, so there is no need to learn multiple Oracle-specific functions. However, some of Oracle's built-in datatypes, such as the various LOB types, LONG RAWs, and LONGs, cannot be converted from one datatype to another using CAST. Instead, you must use Oracle's individual conversion functions. One disadvantage of the CAST function is casting into VARCHAR2 and CHAR datatypes as they need to be constrained to a determined length. The TO_DATE function and TO_CHAR functions are overall very versatile as they allow you a large variety of different format model choices. So you may choose whichever functions fit your specific requirements.

Table 4.13 provides you with an overview of Oracle conversion functions. In this lab you will concentrate on the TO_NUMBER, TO_CHAR, and CAST functions. In previous labs you already learned about the TO_DATE and the TO_CHAR conversion functions as well as conversion functions related to DATETIME datatypes and INTERVALS. (See Table 4.9 Conversion Functions, and Table 4.12, Useful INTERVAL Functions.)

Table 4.13 ■ Datatype Conversion Functions

Function	Purpose
TO_NUMBER(char [, format_mask])	Converts a VARCHAR2 or CHAR to a NUMBER.
TO_CHAR(date [, format_maks)	Converts a DATE or NUMBER to a VARCHAR2.
TO_CHAR(number [, format_mask])	Converts a NUMBER to a VARCHAR2
TO_DATE(char [, format_mask])	Converts a VARCHAR2, CHAR, or NUMBER to a DATE.
CAST(expression AS datatype)	Convert from one datatype to another. Can be used for Oracle's most commonly used datatypes and for user-defined datatypes.

FORMATTING DATA

The TO_CHAR conversion function is not only useful for data conversions between different datatypes, but also for formatting data. In the next SQL statement you see how a format mask can be applied with this function. To display a formatted result for the COST column, for instance, you can apply the format mask '999,999'. The values in the COST column are then formatted with a comma separating the thousands.

```
SELECT course_no, cost,
       TO_CHAR(cost, '999,999') formatted
  FROM course
 WHERE course_no < 25
COURSE_NO     COST FORMATTED
--------- --------- -----------
       10      1195       1,195
       20      1195       1,195

2 rows selected.
```

The conversion function used in the SELECT statement does not modify the values stored in the database, but rather performs a "temporary" conversion for the purpose of executing the statement. In Chapter 2, "SQL: The Basics," you learned about the SQL*Plus COLUMN FORMAT command, which achieves the same result. However, if you execute the SQL statement from a program other than SQL*Plus or *i*SQL*Plus, the COLUMN command is not available and you must use the TO_CHAR function to format the result.

The following statement shows both the effects of the SQL*Plus COLUMN FORMAT command and the TO_CHAR function. The column labeled "SQL*PLUS" is formatted with the `COL cost FORMAT 999,999` command, the last column labeled "CHAR" is formatted with the TO_CHAR function.

```
COL "SQL*PLUS" FORMAT 999,999

SELECT course_no, cost "SQL*PLUS",
       TO_CHAR(cost, '999,999') "CHAR"
  FROM course
 WHERE course_no < 25
COURSE_NO SQL*PLUS CHAR
--------- -------- --------
       10    1,195    1,195
       20    1,195    1,195

2 rows selected.
```

Table 4.14 gives an overview of the most popular NUMBER format models in conjunction with the TO_CHAR function.

Table 4.14 ■ Common NUMBER Format Models

Format Mask	Example Value	Applied TO_CHAR Function	Result
999,990.99	.45	TO_CHAR(.45, '999,990.99')	0.45 (Note the leading zero)
$99,999.99	1234	TO_CHAR(1234, '$99,999.99')	$1,234.00
999	123.59	TO_CHAR(123.59, '999')	124 (Note the rounding)

Notice that rounding can be accomplished not only with the ROUND function but also with a format model.

LAB 4.5 EXERCISES

4.5.1 CONVERT BETWEEN DIFFERENT DATATYPES

Type and execute the following query:

```
SELECT zip, city
  FROM zipcode
 WHERE zip = 10025
```

a) Rewrite the query using the TO_CHAR function in the WHERE clause.

b) Rewrite the query using the TO_NUMBER function in the WHERE clause.

c) Rewrite the query using CAST in the WHERE clause.

4.5.2 FORMAT DATA

a) Write the SQL statement that displays the following result. Note the last column in the result shows the formatted COST column with a leading dollar sign and a comma to separate the thousands. Include the cents in the result as well.

```
COURSE_NO      COST FORMATTED
---------- --------- ------------
       330      1195 $1,195.00

1 row selected.
```

b) List the COURSE_NO and COST columns for courses that cost more than 1500. In a third, fourth, and fifth column show the cost increased by 15%. Show the increased cost columns, one with a leading dollar sign and separate the thousands, and in another column show the same formatting but rounded to the nearest dollar. The result should look similar to the following output.

LAB 4.5

```
COURSE_NO    OLDCOST    NEWCOST FORMATTED     ROUNDED
---------- ---------- ---------- ------------ ------------
        80       1595    1834.25 $1,834.25    $1,834.00

1 row selected
```

c) Based on the previous question, write the query to achieve this result. Use the fm format mask to eliminate the extra spaces.

```
Increase
-----------------------------------------------------------
The price for course# 80 has been increased to $1,834.25.

1 row selected.
```

LAB 4.5 EXERCISE ANSWERS

4.5.1 ANSWERS

Type and execute the following query:

```
SELECT zip, city
  FROM zipcode
 WHERE zip = 10025
```

a) Rewrite the query using the TO_CHAR function in the WHERE clause.

Answer: The TO_CHAR function converts the number literal to a VARCHAR2 datatype, which makes it equal to the VARCHAR2 datatype of the ZIP column.

```
SELECT zip, city
  FROM zipcode
 WHERE zip = TO_CHAR(10025)
ZIP    CITY
----   ---------
10025  New York

1 row selected.
```

b) Rewrite the query using the TO_NUMBER function in the WHERE clause.

Answer: The VARCHAR2 datatype of the ZIP column is converted to a NUMBER datatype by applying the TO_NUMBER function. Oracle then compares it to the number literal 10025.

```
SELECT zip, city
  FROM zipcode
 WHERE TO_NUMBER(zip) = 10025
ZIP    CITY
-----  --------
10025  New York

1 row selected.
```

When you compare the results of the SQL statements from answers a and b, they are identical. Answer b is less desirable because a function is applied to a database column in the WHERE clause. This disables the use of any indexes that may exist on the ZIP column, and may require Oracle to read every row in the table instead of looking up the value in the index. Applying functions to database columns in the SELECT clause does not affect performance.

It is best to be explicit specifying the datatype conversion functions; your statements are easier to understand and the behavior predictable. Oracle's algorithms for implicit conversion may be subject to change across versions and products, and implicit conversion can have a negative impact on performance if the queried column is indexed. You will learn about indexes in Chapter 12, "Views, Indexes, and Sequences," and about performance considerations and function-based indexes in Chapter 16, "SQL Optimization."

c) Rewrite the query using CAST in the WHERE clause.

Answer: You can write the query in one of the following ways.

```
SELECT zip, city
  FROM zipcode
 WHERE CAST(zip AS NUMBER) = 10025
```

Or as:

```
SELECT zip, city
  FROM zipcode
 WHERE zip = CAST(10025 AS VARCHAR2(5))
```

If you specify a too short length of the VARCHAR2 datatype you will receive an error similar to this:

```
SELECT zip, city
  FROM zipcode
 WHERE zip = CAST(10025 AS VARCHAR2(3))
WHERE zip = CAST(10025 AS VARCHAR2(3))
                *
ERROR at line 3:
ORA-25137: Data value out of range
```

In the next SQL query result, observe the way SQL*Plus displays the result of a NUMBER column versus the result in a character type column. In the output you see as the first column the ZIP column in datatype VARCHAR2. It is left aligned, just like the VARCHAR2 column CITY. In general, values of the NUMBER datatype are always right aligned in SQL*Plus; character values are always left aligned.

```
SELECT zip, TO_NUMBER(zip) "TO_NUMBER",
       CAST(zip AS NUMBER) "CAST", city
  FROM zipcode
 WHERE zip = '10025'
ZIP      TO_NUMBER         CAST CITY
------ ---------- ---------- -----------
10025       10025        10025 New York

1 row selected.
```

a) Write the SQL statement that displays the following result. Note the last column in the result shows the formatted COST column with a leading dollar sign and a comma to separate the thousands. Include the cents in the result as well.

```
COURSE_NO     COST FORMATTED
---------  --------- ------------
      330     1195   $1,195.00
```

```
1 row selected.
```

Answer: The TO_CHAR function, together with the format mask in the SELECT clause of the statement, achieves the desired formatting.

```
SELECT course_no, cost,
       TO_CHAR(cost, '$999,999.99') Formatted
  FROM course
 WHERE course_no = 330
```

b) List the COURSE_NO and COST columns for courses that cost more than 1500. In a third, fourth, and fifth column show the cost increased by 15%. Show the increased cost columns, one with a leading dollar sign and separate the thousands, and in another column show the same formatting but rounded to the nearest dollar. The result should look similar to the following output.

```
COURSE_NO    OLDCOST    NEWCOST FORMATTED    ROUNDED
---------- ---------- ---------- ------------ ------------
        80       1595    1834.25  $1,834.25    $1,834.00
1 row selected
```

Answer: An increase of 15% means a multiplication of the column COST by 1.15. You can round to the nearest dollar with the ROUND function.

```
SELECT course_no, cost oldcost,
       cost*1.15 newcost,
       TO_CHAR(cost*1.15, '$999,999.99') formatted,
       TO_CHAR(ROUND(cost*1.15), '$999,999.99') rounded
  FROM course
 WHERE cost > 1500
```

Alternatively, the identical result is achieved with the format mask '$999,999', which omits the digits after the decimal point and rounds the cents as shown in the next statement:

```
SELECT course_no, TO_CHAR(ROUND(cost*1.15), '$999,999.99') rounded,
       TO_CHAR(cost*1.15, '$999,999') "No Cents"
  FROM course
 WHERE cost > 1500
```

```
COURSE_NO ROUNDED        No Cents
---------- ------------ ---------
       80    $1,834.00    $1,834
```

1 row selected.

c) Based on the previous question, write the query to achieve this result. Use the fm format mask to eliminate the extra spaces.

```
Increase
-----------------------------------------------------------
The price for course# 80 has been increased to $1,834.25.
```

1 row selected.

Answer: The following query achieves the desired result set. The fm format mask eliminates the blank padding.

```
SELECT 'The price for course# '||course_no||' has been increased to '||
       TO_CHAR(cost*1.15, 'fm$999,999.99')||'.'
       "Increase"
  FROM course
 WHERE cost > 1500
```

LAB 4.5 SELF-REVIEW QUESTIONS

In order to test your progress, you should be able to answer the following questions. There may be more than one correct answer, so choose all that apply.

1) Which SQL statement results in an error?

a) _____ SELECT TO_CHAR('123') FROM dual
b) _____ SELECT TO_CHAR(123) FROM dual
c) _____ SELECT TO_NUMBER('001.99999') FROM dual
d) _____ SELECT TO_NUMBER('A123') FROM dual
e) _____ SELECT TO_CHAR('A123') FROM dual
f) _____ SELECT TO_NUMBER(' 000123 ') FROM dual

2) Which of the following NUMBER format masks are valid?

a) _____ SELECT TO_CHAR(1.99,'9,9999.9X') FROM dual
b) _____ SELECT TO_CHAR(1.99,'A99.99) FROM dual
c) _____ SELECT TO_CHAR(1.99,'$000.99') FROM dual
d) _____ SELECT TO_CHAR(1.99,'999.99') FROM dual
e) _____ SELECT TO_CHAR(1.99,'.99') FROM dual

3) Explicit datatype conversion is preferable to Oracle's implicit conversion.

a) _____ True
b) _____ False

4) The TO_CHAR, TO_NUMBER, and TO_DATE conversion functions are single-row functions.

a) _____ True
b) _____ False

5) How can you correct the following SQL error message?

```
SQL> SELECT *
  2     FROM conversion_example
  3    WHERE course_no = CAST(123 AS VARCHAR2)
  4  /
  WHERE course_no = CAST(123 AS VARCHAR2)
                                          *
ERROR at line 3:
ORA-00906: missing left parenthesis
```

a) _____ Change the datatype to a CHAR
b) _____ Add a column length definition
c) _____ Choose a different aggregate function
d) _____ This query does not make sense

Answers appear in Appendix A, Section 4.5.

C H A P T E R   4

TEST YOUR THINKING

The projects in this section are meant to have you utilize all of the skills that you have acquired throughout this chapter. The answers to these projects can be found at the companion Web site to this book, located at http://www.phptr.com/rischert.

Visit the Web site periodically to share and discuss your answers.

1) Display all the sections where classes start at 10:30 AM.

2) Write the query to accomplish the following result. The output shows you all the days of the week where sections 82, 144, and 107 start. Note the order of the days.

```
DAY SECTION_ID
--- ----------
Mon         82
Tue        144
Wed        107

3 rows selected.
```

3) Select the distinct course costs of all the courses. If the course cost is unknown, substitute a zero. Format the output with a leading $ sign and separate the thousands with a comma. Display two digits after the decimal point. The query's output should look like the following result:

```
COST
-----------
      $0.00
  $1,095.00
  $1,195.00
  $1,595.00

4 rows selected.
```

4) What, if anything, is wrong with the following SQL statement?

```
SELECT zip + 100
  FROM zipcode
```

5) For the students enrolled on January 30, 1999, display the columns STUDENT_ID and ENROLL_DATE.

6) Execute the following SQL statements. Explain the individual statements.

```
SELECT SESSIONTIMEZONE, CURRENT_TIMESTAMP
  FROM dual;
ALTER SESSION SET TIME_ZONE = '-8:00';
SELECT SESSIONTIMEZONE, CURRENT_TIMESTAMP
  FROM dual;
ALTER SESSION SET TIME_ZONE = '-5:00';
```

CHAPTER 5

AGGREGATE FUNCTIONS, GROUP BY, AND HAVING

In the last two chapters, you learned about character functions, number functions, date functions, and miscellaneous functions, all *single-row* functions. In this chapter, you will learn about *aggregate functions,* which work on *groups of rows*. The most commonly used aggregate functions are discussed in this chapter. Aggregate functions allow you to generate summary data for a group of rows to obtain totals, averages, counts, minimum values, and maximum values. In Chapter 15, "Advanced SQL Queries," you will learn about advanced SQL aggregation topics involving the ROLLUP and CUBE operators.

L A B   5 . 1

AGGREGATE FUNCTIONS

> ## LAB OBJECTIVES
>
> After this lab, you will be able to:
>
> ✔ Use Aggregate Functions in a SQL Statement

Aggregate functions do just as you would expect: they *aggregate,* or group together, data to produce a single result. Questions such as "How many students are registered?" and "What is the average cost of a course?" can be answered by using aggregate functions. You count the individual students to answer the first question, and you calculate the average cost of all courses to answer the second. In each case, the result is a single answer based on several rows of data.

THE COUNT FUNCTION

One of the most common aggregate functions is the COUNT function which lets you count values in a table. The function takes a single parameter, which can be a column in a table of any datatype, and can even be the asterisk (*) wildcard. The following SELECT statement returns the number of rows in the ENROLLMENT table:

```
SELECT COUNT(*)
  FROM enrollment
COUNT(*)
---------
      226

1 row selected.
```

COUNT AND NULLS

This use of the COUNT function is useful for determining whether a table has data or not. If the result set returns the number 0 when using COUNT(*), it means there are no rows in the table, even though the table exists.

Following is an example of the COUNT function used with a database column as a parameter. The difference is that COUNT(*) counts rows that contain null values, whereas COUNT with a column excludes rows that contain nulls.

```
SELECT COUNT(final_grade), COUNT(section_id), COUNT(*)
  FROM enrollment
COUNT(FINAL_GRADE) COUNT(SECTION_ID)  COUNT(*)
------------------ ----------------- ---------
                 1               226       226
```

1 row selected.

The FINAL_GRADE column in the ENROLLMENT table allows null values, and there is only one row with a value in the FINAL_GRADE column. Therefore the result of the function is 1. The COUNT(section_id) returns the same number as the COUNT(*) because THE SECTION_ID column contains no nulls.

COUNT AND DISTINCT

DISTINCT is often used in conjunction with aggregate functions to determine the number of distinct values. There are 226 rows in the ENROLLMENT table, but 64 distinct section IDs. Several students are enrolled in the same section; some individual section IDs exist more than once in the ENROLLMENT table.

```
SELECT COUNT(DISTINCT section_id), COUNT(section_id)
  FROM enrollment
COUNT(DISTINCTSECTION_ID) COUNT(SECTION_ID)
------------------------- -----------------
                       64               226
```

1 row selected.

THE SUM FUNCTION

The SUM function adds values together for a group of rows. The following example adds up all the values in the CAPACITY column of the SECTION table. The result is the total capacity of all sections. If any values in the CAPACITY column contain a null, these values are ignored.

```
SELECT SUM(capacity)
  FROM section
SUM(CAPACITY)
-------------
         1652
```

1 row selected.

THE AVG FUNCTION

The AVG function returns the average within a group of rows. In the following example, the average capacity of each section is computed. Any nulls in the CAPACITY column are ignored. To substitute nulls with a zero, use the NVL or COALESCE function discussed in Chapter 3, "Character, Number, and Miscellaneous Functions."

```
SELECT AVG(capacity), AVG(NVL(capacity,0))
  FROM section
AVG(CAPACITY) AVG(NVL(CAPACITY,0))
------------- --------------------
   21.179487             21.179487

1 row selected.
```

In this example, there are no sections with null values in the CAPACITY column; therefore, the result of the two functions is identical.

THE MIN AND MAX FUNCTIONS

The MIN and MAX functions are opposites of each other, providing the minimum and maximum values, respectively, in a group of rows: The result shows the lowest value in the CAPACITY column of the SECTION; this value is 10 and the highest value is 25.

```
SELECT MIN(capacity), MAX(capacity)
  FROM section
MIN(CAPACITY) MAX(CAPACITY)
------------- -------------
           10            25

1 row selected.
```

MIN AND MAX WITH OTHER DATATYPES

The previous example operated on the CAPACITY column, which is of NUMBER datatype. The MIN and MAX functions can take other datatypes as a parameter. The next example shows the use with the DATE datatype and displays the first and last registration date in the STUDENT table.

```
SELECT MIN(registration_date) "First", MAX(registration_date) "Last"
  FROM student
First     Last
--------- ---------
22-JAN-99 23-FEB-99

1 row selected.
```

A less frequently used datatype for the MIN and MAX functions is the VAR-CHAR2 datatype. This query shows the minimum or maximum value of the DESCRIPTION column and returns the first and last values in an alphabetized list of values.

```
SELECT MIN (description) AS MIN, MAX (description) AS MAX
   FROM course
MIN                              MAX
--------------------------       -------------------------
Advanced Java Programming   Unix Tips and Techniques

1 row selected.
```

(The capital letter "A" is equal to the ASCII value 65, "B" is 66, and so on. Lowercase letters, numbers, and characters all have their own ASCII values. Therefore, MIN and MAX can be used to evaluate a character's respective first and last letters in alphabetical order.)

AGGREGATE FUNCTIONS AND NULLS

All aggregate functions ignore null values except for the COUNT(*) function. Use the NVL or COALESCE function to substitute for any null values. Aggregate functions always return a row. Even if the query returns no rows, the result is simply one row with a null value; the COUNT function always returns either a zero or a number.

AGGREGATE FUNCTIONS SYNTAX

Table 5.1 lists the most commonly used aggregate functions and their respective syntax. As you may notice, you can use the DISTINCT keyword with all these functions to only evaluate the distinct values. The ALL keyword is the default option and evaluates all rows. The DISTINCT keyword is really only useful for the AVG, SUM, and COUNT functions.

Table 5.1 ■ Aggregate Functions

Function	Purpose
COUNT({* | [DISTINCT|ALL] expression)	Counts number of rows. The wildcard (*) option includes duplicates and null values.
SUM([DISTINCT|ALL] value)	Computes total of a value, ignores nulls.
AVG([DISTINCT|ALL] value)	Average of a value, ignores nulls.
MIN([DISTINCT|ALL] expression)	Determines the minimum value of an expression, ignores nulls.
MAX([DISTINCT|ALL] expression)	Determines the maximum value of an expression, ignores nulls.

LAB 5.1 EXERCISES

5.1.1 USE AGGREGATE FUNCTIONS IN A SQL STATEMENT

a) Write a SELECT statement to determine how many courses do not have a prerequisite.

b) Write a SELECT statement to determine the total number of students enrolled in the program. Count students only once, no matter how many courses they are enrolled in.

c) Determine the average cost for all courses. If the course cost contains a null value, substitute the value 0.

d) Write a SELECT statement to determine the date of the most recent enrollment.

LAB 5.1 EXERCISE ANSWERS

5.1.1 ANSWERS

a) Write a SELECT statement to determine how many courses do not have a prerequisite.

Answer: The COUNT function is used to count the number of rows in the COURSE table where the values in the PREREQUISITE column are null.

```
SELECT COUNT(*)
  FROM course
 WHERE prerequisite IS NULL
 COUNT(*)
---------
        4

1 row selected.
```

b) Write a SELECT statement to determine the total number of students enrolled. Count students only once, no matter how many courses they are enrolled in.

Answer: DISTINCT is used in conjunction with the COUNT function to count distinct students, regardless of how many times they appear in the ENROLLMENT table.

```
SELECT COUNT(DISTINCT student_id)
  FROM enrollment
COUNT(DISTINCTSTUDENT_ID)
------------------------
                     165

1 row selected.
```

c) Determine the average cost for all courses. If the course cost contains a null value, substitute the value 0.

Answer: Both the NVL and the COALESCE function substitute any null value with a zero. The NVL or COALESCE function must be nested inside the AVG function.

```
SELECT AVG(NVL(cost, 0))
  FROM course
AVG(NVL(COST,0))
----------------
          1158.5

1 row selected.
```

or:

```
SELECT AVG(COALESCE(cost, 0))
  FROM course
```

If you do not substitute the nulls for the zero value, the average course cost returns a different, more accurate, result.

```
SELECT AVG(cost)
  FROM course
AVG(COST)
---------
1198.4483

1 row selected.
```

d) Write a SELECT statement to determine the date of the most recent enrollment.

Answer: The MAX function determines the most recent value in the ENROLL_DATE column of the ENROLLMENT table.

**LAB
5.1**

```
SELECT MAX(enroll_date)
  FROM enrollment
MAX(ENROL
---------
21-FEB-99

1 row selected.
```

LAB 5.1 SELF-REVIEW QUESTIONS

In order to test your progress, you should be able to answer the following questions.

1) How many of these functions are aggregate functions: AVG, COUNT, SUM, ROUND?

   a) _____ One
   b) _____ Two
   c) _____ Three
   d) _____ Four

2) Choose the correct question for the following SQL statement:

```
SELECT NVL(MAX(modified_date),
           TO_DATE('12-MAR-2005', 'DD-MON-YYYY'))
  FROM enrollment
```

   a) _____ Display the date when a STUDENT table was last modified.
   b) _____ Display the date a STUDENT record was last modified. Replace any null value with the date March 12, 2005.
   c) _____ Show the date a record in the ENROLLMENT table was last modified. If the result returns a null value, display March 12, 2005.
   d) _____ For all the ENROLLMENT records show the date 12-Mar-2005.

3) An aggregate function can be applied on a single row.

   a) _____ True
   b) _____ False

4) The following SQL statement contains an error:

```
SELECT AVG(*)
  FROM course
```

   a) _____ True
   b) _____ False

5) The following SQL statement determines the average of all capacities in a section:

```
SELECT AVG(DISTINCT capacity)
  FROM section
```

a) _____ True
b) _____ False

6) The following SQL statement contains an error:

```
SELECT SUM(capacity*1.5)
  FROM section
```

a) _____ True
b) _____ False

Answers appear in Appendix A, Section 5.1.

L A B   5 . 2

THE GROUP BY
AND HAVING CLAUSES

LAB OBJECTIVES

After this lab, you will be able to:

✔ Use the GROUP BY and HAVING Clauses

THE GROUP BY CLAUSE

Aggregate functions are often used with other columns in a SELECT list. This functionality lets you group data by other columns. When you do this, the GROUP BY clause must be used to present the information in the result. The result of the GROUP BY clause yields an output similar to that of the DISTINCT clause.

The following two queries will return the same result, which is a distinct listing of the values in the LOCATION column.

```
SELECT DISTINCT location
   FROM section
```

Or:

```
SELECT location
   FROM section
  GROUP BY location
LOCATION
------------
H310
L206
...
```

M311
M500

12 rows selected.

If you want to expand on this example and now include how many times each respective location value is listed in the SECTION table, you can include the COUNT(*) function in the query.

```
SELECT location, COUNT(*)
  FROM section
 GROUP BY location
```

LOCATION	COUNT(*)
H310	1
L206	1
L210	10
L211	3
L214	15
...	
M500	1

12 rows selected.

Essentially, the GROUP BY clause and the aggregate function work hand-in-hand. Based on the distinct values as listed in the GROUP BY clause, the aggregate function returns the result.

We can expand the SQL query to determine other values for the distinct LOCATION column. For example, the next statement adds the aggregate functions SUM, MIN, and MAX to the SELECT list. For each distinct location you see the total capacities with the SUM function, which adds up all the values in the CAPACITY column. The MIN and MAX functions return the minimum and maximum capacity for each respective location.

```
SELECT location, COUNT(*), SUM(capacity) AS sum,
       MIN(capacity) AS min, MAX(capacity) AS max
  FROM section
 GROUP BY location
```

LOCATION	COUNT(*)	SUM	MIN	MAX
H310	1	15	15	15
L206	1	15	15	15
L210	10	200	15	25
L211	3	55	15	25
L214	15	275	15	25
...				
M500	1	25	25	25

12 rows selected.

You can validate the result of the query by looking at one of the rows. For example, the row with the LOCATION value of L211 has three rows according to the COUNT function. The total of all the values in the CAPACITY column is 55 (25 + 15 + 15). The minimum value of the CAPACITY column is 15 and the maximum value is 25.

```
SELECT location, capacity, section_id
  FROM section
 WHERE location = 'L211'
LOCATION    CAPACITY SECTION_ID
--------  ---------- ----------
L211              25        119
L211              15        133
L211              15        153

3 rows selected.
```

GROUPING BY MULTIPLE COLUMNS

The next query applies the aggregate functions to the distinct values of the LOCATION and the INSTRUCTOR_ID columns; therefore, the statement returns more rows than the previous GROUP BY query.

```
SELECT location, instructor_id,
       COUNT(*), SUM(capacity) AS sum,
       MIN(capacity) AS min, MAX(capacity) AS max
  FROM section
 GROUP BY location, instructor_id
LOCATION INSTRUCTOR_ID COUNT(*)     SUM    MIN    MAX
-------- ------------- -------- ------ ------ ------
H310               103        1     15     15     15
L206               108        1     15     15     15
L210               101        1     15     15     15
L210               103        2     40     15     25
L210               104        1     25     25     25
L210               105        2     40     15     25
L210               106        1     25     25     25
L210               108        3     55     15     25
L214               102        4     70     15     25
...
M500               102        1     25     25     25

39 rows selected.
```

When you examine the result you notice there are six rows for the L210 location. For this location each row has a different INSTRUCTOR_ID value. On each of these six distinct LOCATION and INSTRUCTOR_ID combinations, the aggregate functions are applied. For example, the first row has only one row with this LO-

CATION and INSTRUCTOR_ID combination and the second row has two rows, as you see from the number in the COUNT(*) column. Once again, you can validate the result by issuing an individual query against the SECTION table.

```
SELECT location, instructor_id, capacity, section_id
  FROM section
 WHERE location = 'L210'
 ORDER BY 1, 2
LOCATION INSTRUCTOR_ID   CAPACITY SECTION_ID
-------- ------------- ---------- ----------
L210               101         15        117
L210               103         15         81
L210               103         25        150
L210               104         25         96
L210               105         25         91
L210               105         15        129
L210               106         25         84
L210               108         15         86
L210               108         15        155
L210               108         25        124

10 rows selected.
```

ORACLE ERROR ORA-00937

Every column you list in the SELECT list, except the aggregate function column itself, must be repeated in the GROUP BY clause. Following is the error Oracle returns when you violate this rule:

```
SQL> SELECT location, instructor_id,
  2          COUNT(*), SUM(capacity) AS sum,
  3          MIN(capacity) AS min, MAX(capacity) AS max
  4     FROM section
  5    GROUP BY location
  6  /
SELECT location, instructor_id,
                 *
ERROR at line 1:
ORA-00979: not a GROUP BY expression
```

The error message indicates that Oracle does not know how to process this query. The query lists the LOCATION and the INSTRUCTOR_ID column in the SELECT list, but only the LOCATION column in the GROUP BY clause. Essentially, Oracle is confused about the instruction. The GROUP BY clause lists only the LOCATION column, which determines the distinct values. But the statement fails to specify what to do with the INSTRUCTOR_ID column.

SORTING DATA

GROUP BY plays another role: It also orders data. The rows are always ordered by the columns listed in the GROUP BY clause. The ORDER BY clause is used when you want to change the sort order of the grouping. The ORDER BY must follow the GROUP BY clause in the SELECT statement. The columns used in the ORDER BY clause must appear in the SELECT list, which is unlike the normal use of ORDER BY. In the following example, the result is sorted in descending order by the total capacity. Note that you can also use the column alias in the ORDER BY clause.

```
SELECT location "Location", instructor_id,
       COUNT(location) "Total Locations",
       SUM(capacity) "Total Capacity"
  FROM section
 GROUP BY location, instructor_id
 ORDER BY "Total Capacity" DESC
```

THE HAVING CLAUSE

The purpose of the HAVING clause is to eliminate groups, just as the WHERE clause is used to eliminate rows. Using the previous example, apply the HAVING clause to restrict the result set to locations with a total capacity value of more than 50 students.

```
SELECT location "Location", instructor_id,
       COUNT(location) "Total Locations",
       SUM(capacity) "Total Capacity"
  FROM section
 GROUP BY location, instructor_id
 HAVING SUM(capacity) > 50
```

Location	INSTRUCTOR_ID	Total Locations	Total Capacity
L210	108	3	55
L214	102	4	70
L214	104	4	70
L214	106	3	55
L507	101	3	75
...			
L509	107	3	65

14 rows selected.

THE WHERE AND HAVING CLAUSES

As previously mentioned, the HAVING clause eliminates groups that do not satisfy its condition. This is in contrast to the WHERE clause, which eliminates rows before the aggregate functions and the GROUP BY and HAVING clauses are applied:

```
SELECT location "Location", instructor_id,
       COUNT(location) "Total Locations",
       SUM(capacity) "Total Capacity"
  FROM section
 WHERE section_no in (2, 3)
 GROUP BY location, instructor_id
HAVING SUM(capacity) > 50
```

Location INSTRUCTOR_ID Total Locations Total Capacity
-------- ------------- --------------- --------------
L214   104   3   55

1 row selected.

The WHERE clause is executed by the database first, narrowing the result set to rows in the SECTION table where the SECTION_NO equals either 2 or 3 (i.e., the second or third section of a course). The next step is to group the result by the columns listed in the GROUP BY clause and to apply the aggregate functions. Lastly, the HAVING condition is tested against the groups. Only those rows with a total capacity of greater than 50 are returned in the result.

MULTIPLE CONDITIONS IN THE HAVING CLAUSE

The HAVING clause can use multiple operators to further eliminate any groups, as in this example. The columns used in the HAVING clause must be found either in the GROUP BY clause or they must be aggregate functions.

```
SELECT location "Location",
       COUNT(location) "Total Locations",
       SUM(capacity) "Total Capacity"
  FROM section
 WHERE section_no = 3
 GROUP BY location
HAVING (SUM(capacity) > 75
        AND location LIKE 'L5%9')
```

FUNCTIONS WITHOUT PARAMETERS AND CONSTANTS

Any constant, such as a text or number literal or a function that does not take any parameters, such as the SYSDATE function, may be listed in the SELECT list without being repeated in the GROUP BY clause. This does not cause the ORA-00937 error message. The next query shows the text literal 'Hello', the number literal 1, and the SYSDATE function in the SELECT list of the query. You will notice that these expressions do not need to be repeated in the GROUP BY clause.

```
SELECT 'Hello', 1, SYSDATE, course_no "Course #",
       COUNT(*)
  FROM section
 GROUP BY course_no
HAVING COUNT(*) = 5
```

```
'HELL         1 SYSDATE    Course #  COUNT(*)
-----  ---------- ---------- --------- ---------
Hello         1 08-APR-02        100         5
Hello         1 08-APR-02        122         5
Hello         1 08-APR-02        125         5
```

3 rows selected.

NESTING AGGREGATE FUNCTIONS

Aggregate functions can also be nested, as in the following example. The query returns the largest number of students that enrolled in an individual section. The COUNT function determines a count for all the sections based on the GROUP BY clause, which lists the SECTION_ID. Against this result, the MAX function is applied and it returns 12 as the largest of the values. In other words, 12 students is the largest number of students enrolled in an individual section.

```
SELECT MAX(COUNT(*))
  FROM ENROLLMENT
 GROUP BY SECTION_ID
MAX(COUNT(*))
-------------
          12
```

1 row selected.

ORDER OF THE CLAUSES

The HAVING clause can also appear before the GROUP BY clause, but this is rarely seen in practice.

```
SELECT course_no "Course #",
       AVG(capacity) "Avg. Capacity",
       ROUND(AVG(capacity)) "Rounded Avg. Capacity"
  FROM section
HAVING COUNT(*) = 2
 GROUP BY course_no
```

All our examples so far have focused on a single table. You will learn about some of the potential pitfalls when joining multiple tables and applying aggregate functions in Chapter 7, "Subqueries."

LAB 5.2 EXERCISES

5.2.1 USE THE GROUP BY AND HAVING CLAUSES

a) Show a list of prerequisites and count how many times each appears in the COURSE table.

b) Write a SELECT statement showing student IDs and the number of courses they are enrolled in. Show only those enrolled in more than two classes.

c) Write a SELECT statement that displays the average room capacity for each course. Display the average expressed to the nearest whole number in another column. Use column aliases for each column selected.

d) Write the same SELECT statement as in the previous question except for classes with exactly two sections. Hint: Think about the relationship between the COURSE and SECTION tables, specifically how many times a course can be represented in the SECTION table.

LAB 5.2 EXERCISE ANSWERS

5.2.1 ANSWERS

a) Show a list of prerequisites and count how many times each appears in the COURSE table.

Answer: The COUNT function and GROUP BY clause are used to count distinct prerequisites. The last row of the result set shows the number of prerequisites with a null value.

```
SELECT prerequisite, COUNT(*)
  FROM course
 GROUP BY prerequisite
```

```
PREREQUISITE   COUNT(*)
------------   --------
          10          1
          20          5
...
         350          2
         420          1
                      4
```

`17 rows selected.`

NULLS AND AGGREGATE FUNCTIONS

If there are null values in a column and you group on the column, all the null values are considered equal. This is different from the typical handling of nulls, where one null is not equal to another. The aforementioned query and result shows that there are four null prerequisites. The nulls always appear last in the default ascending sort order.

You can change the default ordering of the nulls with the NULLS FIRST option in the ORDER BY clause as you see in the next statement. When you look at the result set you see that the nulls are now first, followed by the default ascending sort order.

```
SELECT prerequisite, COUNT(*)
  FROM course
 GROUP BY prerequisite
 ORDER BY prerequisite NULLS FIRST
PREREQUISITE   COUNT(*)
------------   --------
                      4
          10          1
...
         350          2
         420          1
```

`17 ROWS SELECTED.`

b) Write a SELECT statement showing student IDs and the number of courses they are enrolled in. Show only those enrolled in more than two classes.

Answer: To obtain the distinct students, use the STUDENT_ID column in the GROUP BY clause. For each of the groups, count records for each student with the COUNT function. Eliminate only those students enrolled in more than two sections from the groups with the HAVING clause.

```
SELECT student_id, COUNT(*)
  FROM enrollment
```

```
GROUP BY student_id
HAVING COUNT(*) > 2
STUDENT_ID  COUNT(*)
----------  ---------
       124          4
       184          3
...
       238          3
       250          3
```

7 rows selected.

c) Write a SELECT statement that displays the average room capacity for each course. Display the average expressed to the nearest whole number in another column. Use column aliases for each column selected.

Answer: The SELECT statement uses the AVG function and the ROUND function. The GROUP BY clause ensures that the average capacity is displayed for each course.

```
SELECT course_no "Course #",
       AVG(capacity) "Avg. Capacity",
       ROUND(AVG(capacity)) "Rounded Avg. Capacity"
  FROM section
 GROUP BY course_no
Course # Avg Capacity Rounded Avg Capacity
-------- ------------ --------------------
      10           15                   15
      20           20                   20
      25    22.777778                   23
...
     350    21.666667                   22
     420           25                   25
     450           25                   25
```

28 rows selected.

The previous SQL statement uses nested functions. Nested functions always work from the inside out, so the AVG(capacity) function is evaluated first and its result is the parameter for the ROUND function. ROUND's optional precision parameter is not used, so the result of AVG(capacity) rounds to a precision of 0, or no decimal places.

A COMMON ERROR YOU CAN AVOID

Sometimes you may copy the columns from the SELECT list—with the exception of the aggregate function, of course—down to the GROUP BY clause. After all, cut and paste saves a lot of typing. You then may end up with an error such as the next one. The error message on ORA-00933 "SQL command not properly ended" may leave you clueless as to how to solve the problem.

```
SQL> SELECT course_no "Course #",
  2         AVG(capacity) "Avg. Capacity",
  3         ROUND(AVG(capacity)) "Rounded Avg. Capacity"
  4    FROM section
  5   GROUP BY course_no "Course #"
  6  /
 GROUP BY course_no "Course #"
                    *
ERROR at line 5:
ORA-00933: SQL command not properly ended
```

Actually, to resolve the error, you must exclude table aliases in the GROUP BY clause. Notice how the "Course #" column alias remained in the GROUP BY clause.

Aliases are not allowed in the GROUP BY clause.

d) Write the same SELECT statement as in the previous question except for classes with exactly two sections. *Hint:* Think about the relationship between the COURSE and SECTION tables, specifically how many times a course can be represented in the SECTION table.

Answer: The HAVING clause is added to limit the result set to courses appearing exactly twice.

```
SELECT course_no "Course #",
       AVG(capacity) "Avg. Capacity",
       ROUND(AVG(capacity)) "Rounded Avg. Capacity"
  FROM section
 GROUP BY course_no
HAVING COUNT(*) = 2
```

Course #	Avg. Capacity	Rounded Avg. Capacity
132	25	25
145	25	25
146	20	20
230	13.5	14
240	12.5	13

5 rows selected.

Notice the COUNT(*) function in the HAVING clause does not appear as part of the SELECT list. You can eliminate any groups in the HAVING clause using aggregate functions that are not part of the SELECT list.

LAB 5.2 SELF-REVIEW QUESTIONS

In order to test your progress, you should be able to answer the following questions.

1) Which column(s) must be included in the GROUP BY clause of the following SELECT statement?

```
SELECT NVL(MAX(final_grade),0), section_id,
       MAX(created_date)
  FROM enrollment
 GROUP BY _____
```

a) _____ FINAL_GRADE
b) _____ SECTION_ID
c) _____ CREATED_DATE
d) _____ All three
e) _____ None of the above

2) You can combine DISTINCT and a GROUP BY clause in the same SELECT statement.

a) _____ True
b) _____ False

3) There is an error in the following SELECT statement.

```
SELECT COUNT(student_id)
  FROM enrollment
 WHERE COUNT(student_id) > 1
```

a) _____ True
b) _____ False

4) How many rows in the following SELECT statement will return a null prerequisite?

```
SELECT prerequisite, COUNT(*)
  FROM course
 WHERE prerequisite IS NULL
 GROUP BY prerequisite
```

a) _____ None
b) _____ One
c) _____ Multiple

5) Determine the error in the following SELECT statement.

```
SELECT COUNT(*)
  FROM section
 GROUP BY course_no
```

a) _____ No error
b) _____ Line 1
c) _____ Line 2
d) _____ Line 3

Answers appear in Appendix A, Section 5.2.

CHAPTER 5

TEST YOUR THINKING

The projects in this section are meant to have you utilize all of the skills that you have acquired throughout this chapter. The answers to these projects can be found at the companion Web site to this book, located at: *http://www.phptr.com/rischert.*

Visit the Web site periodically to share and discuss your answers.

1) List the order in which the WHERE, GROUP BY, and HAVING clauses are executed by the database in the following SQL statement.

```
SELECT section_id, COUNT(*), final_grade
  FROM enrollment
 WHERE TRUNC(enroll_date) >
       TO_DATE('2/16/1999', 'MM/DD/YYYY')
 GROUP BY section_id, final_grade
HAVING COUNT(*) > 5
```

2) Display a count of all the different course costs in the COURSE table.

3) Determine the number of students living in zip code 10025.

4) Show all the different companies for which students work. Display only companies where more than four students are employed.

5) List how many sections each instructor teaches.

6) Formulate the question for the following statement:

```
SELECT COUNT(*), start_date_time, location
  FROM section
 GROUP BY start_date_time, location
HAVING COUNT(*) > 1
```

7) Determine the highest grade achieved for the midterm within each section.

8) A table called CUSTOMER_ORDER contains 5,993 rows with a total order amount of $10,993,333.98. A total of 4,500 customers placed these orders. Given the following scenario, how many row(s) do you think the following query returns?

```
SELECT SUM(total_order_amount)
  FROM customer_order
```

CHAPTER 6

EQUIJOINS

So far, you have written SQL statements against a single table. In this chapter you will learn about joining tables, one of the most important aspects of the SQL language. The *equijoin* is by far the most common form of join and it allows you to connect two or more tables. Equijoins are based on equality of values in one or more columns. You will learn about other types of joins in Chapter 9, "Complex Joins."

LAB 6.1

THE TWO-TABLE JOIN

LAB OBJECTIVES

After this lab, you will be able to:

✔ Write Simple Join Constructs
✔ Narrow Down Your Result Set
✔ Understand the Cartesian Product

In this lab, you will join information from two tables into one meaningful result. Suppose you want to list the course number, course description, section number, location, and instructor ID for each section. This data is found in two separate tables: The course number and description are in the COURSE table; the SECTION table contains the course number, section number, location, and instructor ID. One approach is to query the individual tables and record the results on paper, then match every course number in the COURSE table with the corresponding course number in the SECTION table. The other approach is to formulate a SQL statement that accomplishes the join for you.

Figure 6.1 shows a partial listing of the COURSE table. Missing columns and rows are indicated with the three periods (…). The primary key of the COURSE table is the COURSE_NO.

COURSE_NO	DESCRIPTION	...	MODIFIED_DATE
10	DP Overview	...	05-APR-99
20	Intro to Computers	...	05-APR-99
25	Intro to Programming	...	05-APR-99
80	Structured Programming Techniques	...	05-APR-99
100	Hands-On Windows	...	05-APR-99
120	Intro to Java Programming	...	05-APR-99
...	...	...	...

Figure 6.1 ■ Excerpt of the COURSE table.

SECTION_ID	COURSE_NO	SECTION_NO	...	LOCATION
80	10	2	...	L214
81	20	2	...	L210
82	20	4	...	L214
83	20	7	...	L509
84	20	8	...	L210
85	25	1	...	M311
86	25	2	...	L210
87	25	3	...	L507
88	25	4	...	L214
89	25	5	...	L509
90	25	6	...	L509
91	25	7	...	L210
92	25	8	...	L509
93	25	9	...	L507
...	...	...	...	...
141	100	1	...	L214

Figure 6.2 ■ Excerpt of the SECTION table.

Figure 6.2 shows a partial listing of the SECTION table. The COURSE_NO column is the foreign key to the COURSE table.

Examine the result set listed in Figure 6.3. For example, for course number 10, one section exists in the SECTION table. The result of the match is one row. Looking at course number 20, Intro to Computers, you observe that this course has multiple rows in the SECTION table because there are multiple classes/sec-

COURSE_NO	SECTION_NO	DESCRIPTION	LOCATION	INSTRUCTOR_ID
10	2	DP Overview	L214	102
20	2	Intro to Computers	L210	103
20	4	Intro to Computers	L214	104
20	7	Intro to Computers	L509	105
20	8	Intro to Computers	L210	106
25	1	Intro to Programming	M311	107
25	2	Intro to Programming	L210	108
25	3	Intro to Programming	L507	101
25	4	Intro to Programming	L214	102
25	5	Intro to Programming	L509	103
25	6	Intro to Programming	L509	104
25	7	Intro to Programming	L210	105
25	8	Intro to Programming	L509	106
25	9	Intro to Programming	L507	107
100	1	Hands-On Windows	L214	102
...	...	...	...	...

Figure 6.3 ■ Result of join between COURSE and SECTION table.

tions for the same course. You may also notice that course number 80, Structured Programming Techniques, is missing from the result. This course number has no matching entry in the SECTION table and therefore this row is not in the result.

STEPS TO FORMULATE THE SQL STATEMENT

Before you write the SQL join statement, first choose the columns you want to include in the result. Next, determine the tables to which the columns belong. Then, identify the common columns between the tables.

Lastly, determine if there is a one-to-one, or a one-to-many relationship among the column values. Joins are typically used to join between the primary key and the foreign key. In the previous example, the COURSE_NO column in the COURSE table is the primary key, and the column COURSE_NO in the SECTION table is the foreign key. This represents a one-to-many relationship between the tables. (When you join tables related through a many-to-many relationship, it yields a *Cartesian product*. There is more on the Cartesian product later in this chapter.)

Following is the SQL statement that achieves the result shown in Figure 6.3. It looks much like the previous SELECT statements you have written so far, but two tables, separated by commas, are listed in the FROM clause.

```
SELECT course.course_no, section_no, description,
       location, instructor_id
  FROM course, section
 WHERE course.course_no = section.course_no
```

The WHERE clause formulates the join criteria between the two tables using the common COURSE_NO column. Since this is an equijoin, the values in the common columns must equal each other for a row to be displayed in the result set. Each COURSE_NO value from the COURSE table must match a COURSE_NO value from the SECTION table. To differentiate between columns of the same name, *qualify* the columns by prefixing the column with the table name and a period. Otherwise, Oracle returns an error—"ORA-00918: column ambiguously defined".

Instead of displaying the COURSE_NO column from the COURSE table in the SELECT list, you can use the COURSE_NO column from the SECTION table. Because it is an equijoin, it returns the same result.

> ### The Whole Truth
>
> The order in which the tables are listed in the FROM clause can have an effect on the efficiency of the SQL statement, but it has no effect on the query result. You will learn about this in Chapter 16, "SQL Optimization."

TABLE ALIAS

Instead of using the table name as a prefix to differentiate between the columns, you can use a *table alias,* which qualifies the table using a short abbreviation.

```
SELECT c.course_no, s.section_no, c.description,
       s.location, s.instructor_id
  FROM course c, section s
 WHERE c.course_no = s.course_no
```

The table alias names are arbitrary. However, you cannot use any Oracle *reserved words*. (Reserved words have a special meaning in the SQL language or in the Oracle database and are typically associated with a SQL command. For example, SELECT and WHERE are reserved words.) It is best to keep the name short and simple, as in this example. The COURSE table has the alias c, and the SECTION table has the alias s.

To easily identify the source table of a column and to improve the readability of a join statement, it is best to qualify all column names with the table alias. Furthermore, this avoids any future ambiguities that may arise if a new column with the same name is added to another table later. Without a qualified table alias, a subsequently issued SQL statement referencing both tables results in the Oracle error message "ORA-00918: column ambiguously defined".

NARROWING DOWN YOUR RESULT SET

The previous SQL statement lists all the rows in the SECTION and COURSE tables with matching COURSE_NO values. If you want to narrow down the criteria to specific rows, you can expand the WHERE clause to include additional conditions. The next statement chooses only those courses and their respective sections where the DESCRIPTION column starts with the text "Intro to".

```
SELECT c.course_no, s.section_no, c.description,
       s.location, s.instructor_id
  FROM course c, section s
 WHERE c.course_no = s.course_no
   AND c.description LIKE 'Intro to%'
```

NULLS AND JOINS

In an equijoin, a null value in the common column has the effect that the row is not included in the result. Look at the foreign key column ZIP on the INSTRUCTOR table, which allows nulls.

First, query the records with a null value.

**LAB
6.1**

```
SELECT instructor_id, zip, last_name, first_name
  FROM instructor
 WHERE zip IS NULL
INSTRUCTOR_ID ZIP    LAST_NAME   FIRST_NAME
------------- ----- ---------- ----------
          110        Willig      Irene

1 row selected.
```

Next, formulate the join to the ZIPCODE table via the ZIP column. Observe that instructor Irene Willig does not appear in the result.

```
SELECT i.instructor_id, i.zip, i.last_name, i.first_name
  FROM instructor i, zipcode z
 WHERE i.zip = z.zip
INSTRUCTOR_ID ZIP    LAST_NAME   FIRST_NAME
------------- ----- ---------- ----------
          101 10015 Hanks       Fernand
          105 10015 Morris      Anita
          109 10015 Chow        Rick
          102 10025 Wojick      Tom
          103 10025 Schorin     Nina
          106 10025 Smythe      Todd
          108 10025 Lowry       Charles
          107 10005 Frantzen    Marilyn
          104 10035 Pertez      Gary

9 rows selected.
```

A null value is not equal to any other value, including another null value. In this case, the zip code of Irene Willig's record is null; therefore, this row is not included in the result. In Chapter 9, "Complex Joins," you will learn how to include null values by formulating an *outer join* condition.

ANSI JOIN SYNTAX

Oracle 9*i* implements a number of additions to the SQL language to conform to many aspects of the SQL:1999 standard, one of which is the new ANSI join syntax. The advantage of the ANSI join syntax over the traditional, comma separated tables FROM clause is that SQL queries can run unmodified against other non-Oracle, ANSI SQL:1999 compliant databases.

THE INNER JOIN

The term *inner join* is used to express a join that satisfies the join condition; typically, the join condition is based on equality, thus creating an equijoin. (The inner join is in contrast to the outer join. Besides the matched rows, it also includes the unmatched rows from two tables.)

The ANSI syntax, compared to the previously discussed join syntax, has a number of differences. One is the JOIN keyword; it replaces the comma between the tables and identifies the to-be-joined tables.

The keyword INNER is optional and typically omitted. To express a join condition, you can specify either the USING condition or the ON condition.

THE **USING** CONDITION   The USING condition, also referred as the USING clause, identifies the common column between the tables. Here the common column is the COURSE_NO column, which has the same name and compatible datatype in both tables. An equijoin is always assumed with the USING clause.

```
SELECT course_no, s.section_no, c.description,
       s.location, s.instructor_id
  FROM course c JOIN section s
 USING (course_no)
```

Alternatively, you can include the optional INNER keyword, and as mentioned, this is usually omitted.

```
SELECT course_no, s.section_no, c.description,
       s.location, s.instructor_id
  FROM course c INNER JOIN section s
 USING (course_no)
```

The following query will not execute because you cannot use a table alias name with this syntax. The USING syntax implies that the column names are identical. The Oracle error identifies the C.COURSE_NO column as the column in the USING clause with the problem.

```
SQL> SELECT course_no, s.section_no, c.description,
  2          s.location, s.instructor_id
  3    FROM course c JOIN section s
  4    USING (c.course_no)
  5  /
 USING (c.course_no)
         *
ERROR at line 4:
ORA-01748: only simple column names allowed here
```

The next query shows the COURSE_NO column in the SELECT list prefixed with the alias name, thus resulting in an error as well. This alias must also be eliminated to successfully run the query.

```
  1  SELECT c.course_no, s.section_no, c.description,
  2          s.location, s.instructor_id
  3    FROM course c JOIN section s
  4* USING (course_no)
SQL> /
```

```
SELECT c.course_no, s.section_no, c.description,
       *
ERROR at line 1:
ORA-25154: column part of USING clause cannot have qualifier
```

The next example illustrates the error you receive when you omit the parentheses around the column COURSE_NO in the USING clause.

```
SQL> SELECT c.course_no, s.section_no, c.description,
  2            s.location, s.instructor_id
  3    FROM course c JOIN section s
  4    USING course_no
  5  /
  USING course_no
        *
ERROR at line 4:
ORA-00906: missing left parenthesis
```

THE ON CONDITION   In case the column names on the tables are different, you use the ON condition, also referred to as the ON clause. The next query is in functionality identical to the previous query, but is now expressed with the ON condition and the column name is qualified with the alias both in the SELECT list as well as in the ON condition. This syntax allows for conditions other than equality and different column names; you will see many such examples in Chapter 9, "Complex Joins."

```
SELECT c.course_no, s.section_no, c.description,
       s.location, s.instructor_id
  FROM course c JOIN section s
    ON (c.course_no = s.course_no)
```

The pair of parentheses around the ON condition is optional. When comparing this syntax to the traditional join syntax there are not many differences other than the ON clause and the JOIN keyword.

ADDITIONAL WHERE CLAUSE CONDITIONS   The ON or the USING conditions let you specify the join condition separate from any other WHERE condition. One of the advantages of the ANSI join syntax is that it separates the join condition from the filtering WHERE clause condition.

```
SELECT c.course_no, s.section_no, c.description,
       s.location, s.instructor_id
  FROM course c JOIN section s
    ON (c.course_no = s.course_no)
 WHERE description like 'B%'
```

THE NATURAL JOIN

The natural join joins the tables based on the columns with the same name and datatype. Here there is no need to prefix the column name with the table alias and the join is indicated with the keywords NATURAL JOIN. There is not even a mention of which column(s) to join. This syntax figures out the common columns between the tables. Any use of the ON or the USING clause is not allowed with the NATURAL JOIN keywords and the common columns may not list a column alias.

```
SELECT course_no, s.section_no, c.description,
       s.location, s.instructor_id
  FROM course c NATURAL JOIN section s
```

no rows selected

You may be surprised that the query does not return any result. However, when you examine the two tables you notice that the COURSE_NO column is not the only column with a common name. The columns CREATED_BY, CREATED_DATE, MODIFIED_BY, and MODIFIED_DATE are also common to both tables. These columns record the name of the last user updating a row and the original user creating the row, including the respective date and time. The SQL statement does not return any results because there are no rows that have identical values for all five common columns.

Using the natural join within a program is somewhat risky. There is always a chance for columns to be added to the table in the future that happen to have the same name as a column on another table, and you may not get the desired result. Therefore, the natural join works best for ad hoc queries, but not for repeated use within programs.

CARTESIAN PRODUCT

The Cartesian product is rarely useful in the real world. It usually indicates either the WHERE clause has no joining columns or that multiple rows from one table match multiple rows in another table; in other words, it indicates a many-to-many relationship.

To illustrate the multiplication effect of a Cartesian product, the following query joins the INSTRUCTOR table with the SECTION table. The INSTRUCTOR table contains 10 rows; the SECTION table has 78 rows. The multiplication of all the possible combinations results in 780 rows.

```
SELECT COUNT(*)
  FROM section, instructor
```

```
COUNT(*)
---------
      780
```

1 row selected.

Following is a partial listing of the rows showing all the different combinations of values between the two tables.

```
SELECT s.instructor_id s_instructor_id,
       i.instructor_id i_instructor_id
  FROM section s, instructor i
S_INSTRUCTOR_ID I_INSTRUCTOR_ID
--------------- ---------------
            101             101
            101             101
            101             101
            101             101
            101             101
            101             101
            101             101
            101             101
            101             101
            101             102
            101             102
            101             102
...
            108             110
            101             110
```

780 rows selected.

(If you wish to stop and examine the rows one screen at a time, you can use the SQL*Plus SET PAUSE ON command. This displays one screen at a time. To continue to the next screen, press the Enter key. If you want to stop scrolling through the screens and return to the SQL> prompt, press CTRL + C. Remember to issue the SET PAUSE OFF command to stop the feature when you are done! The SET PAUSE ON and SET PAUSE OFF commands are not available in *i*SQL*Plus.)

THE ANSI STANDARD CROSS-JOIN

To formulate a Cartesian product using the ANSI JOIN syntax you use the keyword CROSS JOIN. It replaces the comma between the two tables. Because of the nature of the cross-join as the combination of all possible values, the SQL statement does not have a join criteria. The result is obviously identical to that of the Cartesian product.

```
SELECT COUNT(*)
  FROM section CROSS JOIN instructor
```

LAB 6.1 EXERCISES

6.1.1 WRITE SIMPLE JOIN CONSTRUCTS

a) For all students, display last name, city, state, and zip code. Show the result ordered by zip code.

b) Select the first and last names of all enrolled students and order by the last name in ascending order.

6.1.2 NARROW DOWN YOUR RESULT SET

a) Execute the following SQL statement. Explain your observations about the WHERE clause and the resulting output.

```
SELECT c.course_no, c.description, s.section_no
  FROM course c, section s
 WHERE c.course_no = s.course_no
   AND c.prerequisite IS NULL
 ORDER BY c.course_no, s.section_no
```

b) Select the student ID, course number, enrollment date, and section ID for students who enrolled in course number 20 on January 30, 1999.

6.1.3 UNDERSTAND THE CARTESIAN PRODUCT

a) Select the students and instructors who live in the same zip code by joining on the common ZIP column. Order the result by the STUDENT_ID and INSTRUCTOR_ID columns. What do you observe?

LAB 6.1 EXERCISE ANSWERS

6.1.1 ANSWERS

a) For all students, display last name, city, state, and zip code. Show the result ordered by zip code.

Answer: The common column between the ZIPCODE table and the STUDENT table is the ZIP column. The ZIP column in both tables is defined as NOT NULL. For each row in the ZIPCODE table there may be zero, one, or multiple students living in one particular zip code. For each student's zip code there must be one matching row in the ZIPCODE table. Only those records that satisfy the equality condition of the join are returned.

```
SELECT s.last_name, s.zip, z.state, z.city
  FROM student s, zipcode z
 WHERE s.zip = z.zip
 ORDER BY s.zip
```

LAST_NAME	ZIP	ST	CITY
Norman	01247	MA	North Adams
Kocka	02124	MA	Dorchester
...			
Gilloon	43224	OH	Columbus
Snow	48104	MI	Ann Arbor

268 rows selected.

Because the ZIP column has the same name in both tables, you must qualify the column when you use the traditional join syntax. For simplicity, it is best to use an alias instead of the full table name because it saves you a lot of typing and improves readability. The ORDER BY clause lists the S.ZIP column, as does the SELECT clause. Choosing the Z.ZIP column instead of S.ZIP in the SELECT list or ORDER BY clause produces the same result because the values in the two columns have to be equal to be included in the result.

You can also write the query with the ANSI join syntax instead and use the ON or the USING condition. If you use the ON condition, you must alias the table names or prefix them with the full table name.

```
SELECT s.last_name, s.zip, z.state, z.city
  FROM student s JOIN zipcode z
    ON (s.zip = z.zip)
 ORDER BY s.zip
```

If you choose the USING condition instead, do not alias the common column as this will cause an error.

```
SELECT s.last_name, zip, z.state, z.city
  FROM student s JOIN zipcode z
 USING (zip)
 ORDER BY zip
```

b) Select the first and last names of all enrolled students and order by the last name in ascending order.

Answer: You need to join the ENROLLMENT and STUDENT tables. Only students who are enrolled have one or multiple rows in the ENROLLMENT table.

```
SELECT s.first_name, s.last_name, s.student_id
  FROM student s, enrollment e
 WHERE s.student_id = e.student_id
 ORDER BY s.last_name
```

FIRST_NAME	LAST_NAME	STUDENT_ID
Mardig	Abdou	119
Suzanne M.	Abid	257
...		
Salewa	Zuckerberg	184
Salewa	Zuckerberg	184
Salewa	Zuckerberg	184
Freedon	annunziato	206

```
226 rows selected.
```

Note that student Salewa Zuckerberg with STUDENT_ID 184 is returned three times. This is because Salewa Zuckerberg is enrolled in three sections. When the SECTION_ID column is included in the SELECT list, this fact becomes self-evident in the result set.

However, if you are not interested in the SECTION_ID and you want to only list the names without the duplication, use DISTINCT in the SELECT statement.

```
SELECT DISTINCT s.first_name, s.last_name, s.student_id
  FROM student s, enrollment e
 WHERE s.student_id = e.student_id
 ORDER BY s.last_name
```

The STUDENT_ID column is required in the SELECT clause because there may be students with the same first and last name but who are, in fact, different individuals. The STUDENT_ID column differentiates between these students; after all, it's the primary key that is unique to each individual row in the STUDENT table.

You may also notice that the student with the last name 'annunziato' is the last row. Because the last name is in lowercase, it has a higher sort order. (See Lab 3.3 regarding the sort order values and the ASCII function.)

If you use the ANSI syntax your SQL statement may look similar to this statement.

```
SELECT s.first_name, s.last_name, s.student_id
  FROM student s JOIN enrollment e
    ON (s.student_id = e.student_id)
 ORDER BY s.last_name
```

Or you may write the statement with the USING clause. In this query all aliases are omitted. Although this query looks quite simple and elegant, it has one drawback. You cannot easily recognize the source table for each column.

```
SELECT first_name, last_name, student_id
  FROM student JOIN enrollment
 USING (student_id)
 ORDER BY last_name
```

6.1.2 ANSWERS

a) Execute the following SQL statement. Explain your observations about the WHERE clause and the resulting output.

```
SELECT c.course_no, c.description, s.section_no
  FROM course c, section s
 WHERE c.course_no = s.course_no
   AND c.prerequisite IS NULL
 ORDER BY c.course_no, section_no
```

Answer: This query includes both a join condition and a condition that restricts the rows to classes that have no prerequisite. The result is ordered by the course number and the section number.

COURSE_NO	DESCRIPTION	SECTION_NO
10	DP Overview	2
20	Intro to Computers	2
...		
146	Java for C/C++ Programmers	2
310	Operating Systems	1

8 rows selected.

The COURSE and SECTION tables are joined to obtain the SECTION_NO column. The join requires the equality of values for the COURSE_NO columns in both tables. The courses without a prerequisite are determined with the IS NULL operator.

If the query is written with the ANSI join syntax and the ON clause, you see one advantage of the ANSI join syntax over the traditional join syntax. The ANSI join distinguishes the join condition from the filtering criteria.

```
SELECT c.course_no, c.description, s.section_no
  FROM course c JOIN section s
    ON (c.course_no = s.course_no)
 WHERE c.prerequisite IS NULL
 ORDER BY c.course_no, section_no
```

b) Select the student ID, course number, enrollment date, and section ID for students who enrolled in course number 20 on January 30, 1999.

Answer: The SECTION and ENROLLMENT tables are joined through their common column: SECTION_ID. This column is the primary key in the SECTION table and the foreign key column in the ENROLLMENT table. The rows are restricted to those records that have a course number of 20 and an enrollment date of January 30, 1999 by including this condition in the WHERE clause.

```
SELECT e.student_id, s.course_no,
       TO_CHAR(e.enroll_date,'MM/DD/YYYY HH:MI PM'),
       e.section_id
  FROM enrollment e JOIN section s
    ON (e.section_id = s.section_id)
 WHERE s.course_no = 20
   AND e.enroll_date >= TO_DATE('01/30/1999','MM/DD/YYYY')
   AND e.enroll_date < TO_DATE('01/31/1999','MM/DD/YYYY')
```

STUDENT_ID	COURSE_NO	TO_CHAR(ENROLL_DATE	SECTION_ID
103	20	01/30/1999 10:18 AM	81
104	20	01/30/1999 10:18 AM	81

2 rows selected.

Alternatively, you can use the USING clause or the more traditional join syntax, listed here.

```
SELECT e.student_id, s.course_no,
       TO_CHAR(e.enroll_date,'MM/DD/YYYY HH:MI PM'),
       e.section_id
  FROM enrollment e, section s
 WHERE e.section_id = s.section_id
   AND s.course_no = 20
   AND e.enroll_date >= TO_DATE('01/30/1999','MM/DD/YYYY')
   AND e.enroll_date < TO_DATE('01/31/1999','MM/DD/YYYY')
```

Note the WHERE clause considers the date and time values of the ENROLL_DATE column. There are alternative WHERE clause solutions, such as applying the TRUNC function on the ENROLL_DATE column. Refer to Chapter 4, "Date and Conversion Functions," for many examples on querying and displaying DATE datatype columns.

6.1.3 ANSWERS

a) Select the students and instructors who live in the same zip code by joining on the common ZIP column. Order the result by the STUDENT_ID and INSTRUCTOR_ID columns. What do you observe?

Answer: When you join the STUDENT and INSTRUCTOR tables, there is a many-to-many relationship, which causes a Cartesian product as a result.

```
SELECT s.student_id, i.instructor_id,
       s.zip, i.zip
  FROM student s, instructor i
 WHERE s.zip = i.zip
 ORDER BY s.student_id, i.instructor_id
STUDENT_ID INSTRUCTOR_ID ZIP   ZIP
---------- ------------- ----- -----
       163           102 10025 10025
       163           103 10025 10025
       163           106 10025 10025
       163           108 10025 10025
       223           102 10025 10025
       223           103 10025 10025
       223           106 10025 10025
       223           108 10025 10025
       399           102 10025 10025
       399           103 10025 10025
       399           106 10025 10025
       399           108 10025 10025
```

`12 rows selected.`

Initially this query and its corresponding result may not strike you as a Cartesian product because the WHERE clause contains a join criteria. However, the relationship between the STUDENT and the INSTRUCTOR table does not follow the primary key/foreign key path, and therefore a Cartesian product is possible. A look at the schema diagram reveals that no primary key/foreign key relationship exists between the two tables. To further illustrate the many-to-many relationship between the ZIP columns, select those students and instructors living in zip code 10025 in separate SQL statements.

```
SELECT student_id, zip
  FROM student
 WHERE zip = '10025'
STUDENT_ID ZIP
---------- -----
       223 10025
       163 10025
       399 10025
```

`3 rows selected.`

```
SELECT instructor_id, zip
  FROM instructor
 WHERE zip = '10025'
INSTRUCTOR_ID ZIP
------------- -----
          102 10025
          103 10025
          106 10025
          108 10025
```

4 rows selected.

These results validate the solution's output: the Cartesian product shows the three student rows multiplied by the four instructors, which results in 12 possible combinations. You can rewrite the query to include the DISTINCT keyword to select only the distinct student IDs. The query can also be written with a *subquery* construct, which avoids the Cartesian product. You will learn about this in Chapter 7, "Subqueries."

JOINING ALONG THE PRIMARY/FOREIGN KEY PATH

You can also join along the primary/foreign key path by joining the STUDENT table to the ENROLLMENT table, then to the SECTION table, and lastly to the INSTRUCTOR table. This involves a multitable join, discussed in Lab 6.2. However, the result is different from the Cartesian product result because it shows only instructors who teach a section in which the student is enrolled. In other words, an instructor living in zip code 10025 is included in the result only if the instructor teaches that student also living in the same zip code. This is in contrast to the Cartesian product example, which shows all of the instructors and students living in the same zip code, whether the instructor teaches this student or not. You will explore the differences between these two examples once more in the Test Your Thinking section at the end of the chapter.

LAB 6.1 SELF-REVIEW QUESTIONS

In order to test your progress, you should be able to answer the following questions.

1) Find the error(s) in the following SQL statement.

```
1 SELECT stud.last_name, stud.first_name,
2        stud.zip, zip.zip, zip.state, zip.city,
3        TO_CHAR(stud.student_id)
4   FROM student stud, zipcode zip
5  WHERE stud.student_id = 102
6    AND zip.zip = '11419'
7    AND zip.zip = s.zip
```

a) _____ No error
b) _____ This is not an equijoin
c) _____ Line 1, 2, 3
d) _____ Line 4
e) _____ Line 5, 6
f) _____ Line 7

2) Find the error(s) in the following SQL statement.

```
1 SELECT s.*, zipcode.zip,
2        DECODE(s.last_name, 'Smith', szip,
3               UPPER(s.last_name))
4   FROM student s, zipcode
5  WHERE stud.zip = zipcode.zip
6    AND s.last_name LIKE 'Smi%'
```

a) _____ Line 1 and 2
b) _____ Line 1 and 4
c) _____ Line 3
d) _____ Line 2 and 5
e) _____ Line 4

3) A table alias is the name of a duplicate table stored in memory.

a) _____ True
b) _____ False

4) To equijoin a table with another table involves matching the common column values.

a) _____ True
b) _____ False

5) Find the error(s) in the following SQL statement.

```
1 SELECT TO_CHAR(w.modified_date, 'dd-mon-yyyy'),
2        t.grade_type_code, description,
3        TO_NUMBER(TO_CHAR(number_per_section))
4   FROM grade_type t, grade_type_weight w
5  WHERE t.grade_type_code = w.grade_type_code_cd
6    AND ((t.grade_type_code = 'MT'
7        OR t.grade_type_code = 'HM'))
8    AND t.modified_date >=
9        TO_DATE('01-JAN-1999', 'DD-MON-YYYY')
```

a) _____ Line 1 and 8
b) _____ Line 4
c) _____ Line 5
d) _____ Line 6 and 7
e) _____ Line 5, 6, 7

6) Given two tables, T1 and T2, and their rows as shown, which result will be returned?

```
SELECT t1.val, t2.val, t1.name, t2.location
  FROM t1, t2
 WHERE t1.val = t2.val
```

Table T1		Table T2	
VAL	NAME	VAL	LOCATION
---	------------	---	---------
A	Jones	A	San Diego
B	Smith	B	New York
C	Zeta	B	New York
	Miller		Phoenix

a) _____

V	V	NAME	LOCATION
-	-	----------	---------
A	A	Jones	San Diego
B	B	Smith	New York
B	B	Smith	New York
		Miller	Phoenix

b) _____

V	V	NAME	LOCATION
-	-	----------	---------
A	A	Jones	San Diego
B	B	Smith	New York
B	B	Smith	New York

c) _____ None of the above

7) Find the error in the following SQL statement:

```
1 SELECT i.last_name, i.zip, section_id
2   FROM instructor INNER JOIN section
3   USING (instructor_id)
4   WHERE zip > '10025'
```

a) _____ Line 1
b) _____ Line 2
c) _____ Line 1 and 3
d) _____ Line 4
e) _____ Line 2 and 4

8) The USING clause of the ANSI join syntax always assumes an equijoin and identical column names.

a) _____ True
b) _____ False

9) The NATURAL JOIN keywords and the USING clause of the ANSI join syntax are mutually exclusive.

a) _____ True
b) _____ False

10) The common column used in the join condition must be listed in the SELECT list.

a) _____ True
b) _____ False

Answers appear in Appendix A, Section 6.1.

L A B   6 . 2

JOINING THREE
OR MORE TABLES

LAB OBJECTIVES

After this lab, you will be able to:

✔ Join Three or More Tables
✔ Join with Multicolumn Join Criteria

You often have to join more than two tables to determine the answer to a query. In this lab, you will practice these types of joins. Additionally, you will join tables with multicolumn keys.

THREE OR MORE TABLE JOINS

The join example at the beginning of the chapter involved two tables: the COURSE and SECTION tables. The following SQL statement repeats this query and the result of the join (see Figure 6.4). To include the instructor's first and last name, you will expand this statement to join to a third table, the INSTRUCTOR table.

```
SELECT c.course_no, s.section_no, c.description,
       s.location, s.instructor_id
  FROM course c, section s
 WHERE c.course_no = s.course_no
```

Figure 6.5 shows a partial listing of the INSTRUCTOR table. The INSTRUCTOR_ID column is the primary key of the table and is the common column with the SECTION table. Every row in the SECTION table with a value for the INSTRUCTOR_ID column must have one corresponding row in the INSTRUCTOR table. A particular INSTRUCTOR_ID in the INSTRUCTOR table may have zero, one, or multiple rows in the SECTION table.

COURSE_NO	SECTION_NO	DESCRIPTION	LOCATION	INSTRUCTOR_ID
10	2	DP Overview	L214	102
20	2	Intro to Computers	L210	103
20	4	Intro to Computers	L214	104
20	7	Intro to Computers	L509	105
20	8	Intro to Computers	L210	106
25	1	Intro to Programming	M311	107
25	2	Intro to Programming	L210	108
25	3	Intro to Programming	L507	101
25	4	Intro to Programming	L214	102
25	5	Intro to Programming	L509	103
25	6	Intro to Programming	L509	104
25	7	Intro to Programming	L210	105
25	8	Intro to Programming	L509	106
25	9	Intro to Programming	L507	107
100	1	Hands-On Windows	L214	102
...	...	...	...	...

Figure 6.4 ■ Result of join between COURSE and SECTION table.

To formulate the SQL statement, follow the same steps performed in Lab 6.1. First, determine the columns and tables needed for output. Then, confirm whether a one-to-one or a one-to-many relationship exists between the tables to accomplish the join. The changes to the previous SQL statement are indicated in bold.

```
SELECT c.course_no, s.section_no, c.description, s.location,
       s.instructor_id, i.last_name, i.first_name
  FROM course c, section s, instructor i
 WHERE c.course_no = s.course_no
   AND s.instructor_id = i.instructor_id
```

INSTRUCTOR_ID	LAST_NAME	FIRST_NAME	...
101	Hanks	Fernand	...
102	Wojick	Tom	...
103	Schorin	Nina	...
104	Pertez	Gary	...
105	Morris	Anita	...
106	Smythe	Todd	...
107	Frantzen	Marilyn	...
108	Lowry	Charles	...
109	Chow	Rick	...
110	Willig	Irene	...

Figure 6.5 ■ The INSTRUCTOR table.

COURSE _NO	SECT NO	DESCRIPTION	LOCA	INST _ID	LAST_NAME	FIRST_NAME
10	2	DP Overview	L214	102	Wojick	Tom
20	2	Intro to Computers	L210	103	Schorin	Nina
20	4	Intro to Computers	L214	104	Pertez	Gary
20	8	Intro to Computers	L210	106	Smythe	Todd
20	7	Intro to Computers	L509	105	Morris	Anita
25	2	Intro to Programming	L210	108	Lowry	Charles
25	8	Intro to Programming	L509	106	Smythe	Todd
25	9	Intro to Programming	L507	107	Frantzen	Marilyn
25	1	Intro to Programming	M311	107	Frantzen	Marilyn
25	7	Intro to Programming	L210	105	Morris	Anita
25	6	Intro to Programming	L509	104	Pertez	Gary
25	5	Intro to Programming	L509	103	Schorin	Nina
25	4	Intro to Programming	L214	102	Wojick	Tom
25	3	Intro to Programming	L507	101	Hanks	Fernand
100	1	Hands-On Windows	L214	102	Wojick	Tom
...	...	...	...	...	...	...

LAB 6.2

Figure 6.6 ■ Result of join between COURSE, SECTION, and INSTRUCTOR tables.

The join yields the result shown in Figure 6.6. The three-table join result now includes the instructor's first and last name. For example, notice the INSTRUCTOR_ ID with the 102 is listed multiple times in the SECTION table. This instructor teaches several sections; therefore, the INSTRUCTOR_ID's corresponding first and last names are repeated in the result.

ANSI JOIN SYNTAX FOR THREE AND MORE TABLE JOINS

The join across three tables can be expressed with the ANSI join syntax. Create the first join between the COURSE and SECTION tables via the JOIN keyword and the ON clause. To this result the next table and join condition are added. The set of parentheses around the ON clause is optional.

```
SELECT c.course_no, s.section_no, c.description, s.location,
       s.instructor_id, i.last_name, i.first_name
  FROM course c JOIN section s
    ON (c.course_no = s.course_no)
  JOIN instructor i
    ON (s.instructor_id = i.instructor_id)
```

Alternatively, the query can be expressed with the USING clause. The table and column aliases in the SELECT and FROM clauses are optional, but the parentheses in the USING clause are required.

```
SELECT course_no, s.section_no, c.description, s.location,
       instructor_id, i.last_name, i.first_name
  FROM course c JOIN section s
 USING (course_no)
  JOIN instructor i
 USING (instructor_id)
```

MULTICOLUMN JOINS

The basic steps of the multicolumn join do not differ from the previous examples. The only variation is to make multicolumn keys part of the join criteria.

One of the multikey column examples in the schema is the GRADE table. The primary key of the table consists of the four columns STUDENT_ID, SECTION_ID, GRADE_CODE_OCCURRENCE, and GRADE_TYPE_CODE. The GRADE table also has two foreign keys: the GRADE_TYPE_CODE column, referencing the GRADE_TYPE table, and the multicolumn foreign key STUDENT_ID and SECTION_ID, referencing the ENROLLMENT table.

To help you understand the data in the table, examine a set of sample records for a particular student. The student with ID 220 is enrolled in SECTION_ID 119 and has nine records in the GRADE table: four homework assignments (HM), two quizzes (QZ), one midterm (MT), one final examination (FI), and one participation (PA) grade.

```
SELECT student_id, section_id, grade_type_code type,
       grade_code_occurrence no,
       numeric_grade indiv_gr
  FROM grade
 WHERE student_id = 220
   AND section_id = 119
```

STUDENT_ID	SECTION_ID	TY	NO	INDIV_GR
220	119	FI	1	85
220	119	HM	1	84
220	119	HM	2	84
220	119	HM	3	74
220	119	HM	4	74
220	119	MT	1	88
220	119	PA	1	91
220	119	QZ	1	92
220	119	QZ	2	91

```
9 rows selected.
```

The next SQL query joins the GRADE table to the ENROLLMENT table to include the values of the ENROLL_DATE column in the result set. All the changes to the previous SQL query are indicated in bold.

```
SELECT g.student_id, g.section_id,
       g.grade_type_code type,
       g.grade_code_occurrence no,
       g.numeric_grade indiv_gr,
       TO_CHAR(e.enroll_date, 'MM/DD/YY') enrolldt
  FROM grade g, enrollment e
 WHERE g.student_id = 220
   AND g.section_id = 119
   AND g.student_id = e.student_id
   AND g.section_id = e.section_id
```

STUDENT_ID	SECTION_ID	TY	NO	INDIV_GR	ENROLLDT
220	119	FI	1	85	02/16/99
220	119	HM	1	84	02/16/99
220	119	HM	2	84	02/16/99
220	119	HM	3	74	02/16/99
220	119	HM	4	74	02/16/99
220	119	MT	1	88	02/16/99
220	119	PA	1	91	02/16/99
220	119	QZ	1	92	02/16/99
220	119	QZ	2	91	02/16/99

```
9 rows selected.
```

To join between the tables ENROLLMENT and GRADE, use both the SECTION_ID and STUDENT_ID columns. These two columns represent the primary key of the ENROLLMENT table and foreign key of the GRADE table, a one-to-many relationship between the tables exists.

The values for the ENROLL_DATE column are repeated, because for each individual grade you have one row showing the ENROLL_DATE in the ENROLLMENT table.

EXPRESSING MULTICOLUMN JOINS USING THE ANSI JOIN SYNTAX

A join involving multiple columns on a table requires the columns to be listed in the ON or the USING clause as a join criteria. The next SQL statement shows the ON clause.

```
SELECT g.student_id, g.section_id,
       g.grade_type_code type,
       g.grade_code_occurrence no,
       g.numeric_grade indiv_gr,
       TO_CHAR(e.enroll_date, 'MM/DD/YY') enrolldt
  FROM grade g JOIN enrollment e
```

LAB 6.2

```
        ON (g.student_id = e.student_id
       AND g.section_id = e.section_id)
     WHERE g.student_id = 220
       AND g.section_id = 119
```

When you write the query with the USING clause, you list the join columns separated by commas.

```
SELECT student_id, section_id,
       grade_type_code type,
       grade_code_occurrence no,
       numeric_grade indiv_gr,
       TO_CHAR(enroll_date, 'MM/DD/YY') enrolldt
  FROM grade JOIN enrollment
 USING (student_id, section_id)
 WHERE student_id = 220
   AND section_id = 119
```

JOINING ACROSS MANY TABLES

Joining across multiple tables is repeating the same steps of a two-join or three-join table over again. The first two tables are joined and then the result is joined to each subsequent table using the common column(s). This is then repeated until all the tables are joined.

To join *n* tables together, you need at least *n*–1 join conditions. For example, to join five tables, at least four join conditions are required unless your join deals with tables containing multicolumn keys. You will obviously need to include these multicolumns as part of the join condition.

The Oracle optimizer determines the order in which the tables are joined based on the join condition, the indexes on the table, and the various statistics about the tables (such as number of rows or the number of distinct values in each column). The join order has a tremendous impact on the performance of multitable joins. You can learn more about this topic and how to influence the optimizer in Chapter 16, "SQL Optimization."

THE ANSI JOIN VERSUS THE TRADITIONAL JOIN SYNTAX

You may wonder which one of the join syntax options is better. The ANSI join syntax has a number of advantages.

1. Easy to identify the join criteria and the filtering condition
2. Accidental Cartesian product is avoided because you must explicitly specify the join criteria and any missing join conditions become evident because an error is generated

3. Easy to read and understand

4. The USING clause requires less typing, but the datatypes of the colums must match

5. SQL is understood by other ANSI-compliant non-Oracle databases

Although the traditional join syntax with the columns separated by commas in the FROM clause and the join condition listed in the WHERE clause may become the old way of writing SQL, you must nevertheless familiarize yourself with this syntax as millions of SQL statements already use it and it clearly performs its intended purpose. As of this writing (November 2002), the traditional join syntax for equijoins sometimes outperforms the ANSI join syntax. It is expected that this performance difference will disappear shortly. The ANSI join syntax has some distinct functional advantages over the traditional join syntax when it comes to outer joins, which you can learn about in Chapter 9, "Complex Joins."

Table 6.1 ■ Types of Joins

Join Type	Base of Join Condition	Learn About It	Syntax
Equijoin or Inner Join	Equality	This chapter	Traditional comma-separated join or ANSI JOIN syntax (including optional INNER keyword).
Natural Join	Equality	This chapter	NATURAL JOIN keyword.
Cross-Join or Cartesian Product	No join condition	This chapter	Traditional comma-separated with the missing join condition in the WHERE clause or CROSS JOIN keyword.
Self-Join	Equality	Chapter 9, "Complex Joins"	(See Equijoin or Inner Join).
Outer Join (left, right, full)	Equality and extending the result set	Chapter 9, "Complex Joins"	OUTER JOIN keywords or outer join operator(+).
Non-Equijoin	Nonequality of values	Chapter 9, "Complex Joins"	Traditional comma-separated join or ANSI join syntax with the ON clause. The join criteria is not based on equality.

DIFFERENT TYPES OF JOINS

Most of the joins you will come across are based on equality, with the equijoin being the most dominant. In this chapter you learned about equijoins; there are other types of joins you must become familiar with, most notably the self-join, the non-equijoin, and the outer join. (See Table 6.1 for a listing of the various types of joins.)

LAB 6.2

LAB 6.2 EXERCISES

6.2.1 JOIN THREE OR MORE TABLES

a) Display the student ID, course number, and section number of enrolled students where the instructor of the section lives in zip code 10025. Additionally, the course should not have any prerequisites.

b) Produce the mailing addresses for instructors who taught sections starting in June of 1999.

c) List the student IDs of enrolled students living in Connecticut.

6.2.2 JOIN WITH MULTICOLUMN JOIN CRITERIA

a) Show all the grades student Fred Crocitto received for SECTION_ID 86.

b) List the final examination grades for all enrolled Connecticut students of course number 420. Note final examination does not mean final grade.

c) Display the LAST_NAME, STUDENT_ID, PERCENT_OF_FINAL, GRADE_TYPE_CODE, and NUMERIC_GRADE columns for students who received 80 or less for their class project (GRADE_TYPE_CODE = 'PJ'). Order the result by student last name.

LAB 6.2 EXERCISE ANSWERS

6.2.1 ANSWERS

**LAB
6.2**

a) Display the student ID, course number, and section number of enrolled students where the instructor of the section lives in zip code 10025. Additionally, the course should not have any prerequisites.

Answer: This query involves joining four tables. The course number is found in the SEC-TION and COURSE tables, the PREREQUISITE column in the COURSE table. To deter-mine the zip code of an instructor, use the INSTRUCTOR table. To choose only enrolled students, join to the ENROLLMENT table.

```
SELECT c.course_no, s.section_no, e.student_id
  FROM course c, section s, instructor i, enrollment e
 WHERE c.prerequisite IS NULL
   AND c.course_no = s.course_no
   AND s.instructor_id = i.instructor_id
   AND i.zip = '10025'
   AND s.section_id = e.section_id
```

COURSE_NO	SECTION_NO	STUDENT_ID
10	2	128
146	2	117
146	2	140
...		
20	8	158
20	8	199

12 rows selected.

To obtain this result, build the four-table join just like any other join, step by step. First start with one of the tables, such as the COURSE table.

```
SELECT course_no
  FROM course
 WHERE prerequisite IS NULL
```

For each of these courses you find the corresponding sections when you join the COURSE table with the SECTION table. Notice the bolded additions to the SQL statement.

```
SELECT c.course_no, s.section_no
  FROM course c, section s
 WHERE c.prerequisite IS NULL
   AND c.course_no = s.course_no
```

Then include instructors who live in zip code 10025. The common column between SECTION and INSTRUCTOR is INSTRUCTOR_ID.

```
SELECT c.course_no, s.section_no
  FROM course c, section s, instructor i
 WHERE c.prerequisite IS NULL
   AND c.course_no = s.course_no
   AND s.instructor_id = i.instructor_id
   AND i.zip = '10025'
```

Finally, join the results of the ENROLLMENT table via the SECTION_ID column, which leads you to the solution shown previously.

Instead of using the traditional join syntax to obtain the result, you can opt for the ANSI join syntax instead. The query may look similar to the following statement.

```
SELECT course_no, section_no, student_id
  FROM course JOIN section
 USING (course_no)
  JOIN instructor
 USING (instructor_id)
  JOIN enrollment
 USING (section_id)
 WHERE prerequisite IS NULL
   AND zip = '10025'
```

Another possible alternative using the ANSI join syntax is listed next: It uses the ON condition instead.

```
SELECT c.course_no, s.section_no, e.student_id
  FROM course c JOIN section s
    ON (c.course_no = s.course_no)
  JOIN instructor i
    ON (s.instructor_id = i.instructor_id)
  JOIN enrollment e
    ON (s.section_id = e.section_id)
 WHERE c.prerequisite IS NULL
   AND i.zip = '10025'
```

b) Produce the mailing addresses for instructors who taught sections starting in June of 1999.

Answer: This solution requires the join of three tables: you join the INSTRUCTOR, SECTION, and ZIPCODE tables to produce the mailing list.

```
SELECT i.first_name || ' ' ||i.last_name name,
       i.street_address, z.city || ', ' || z.state
       || ' ' || i.zip "City State Zip",
       TO_CHAR(s.start_date_time, 'MM/DD/YY') start_dt,
       section_id sect
  FROM instructor i, section s, zipcode z
 WHERE i.instructor_id = s.instructor_id
   AND i.zip = z.zip
   AND s.start_date_time >=
       TO_DATE('01-JUN-1999','DD-MON-YYYY')
   AND s.start_date_time <
       TO_DATE('01-JUL-1999','DD-MON-YYYY')
```

```
NAME            STREET_ADDRESS City State Zip     START_DT SECT
--------------- -------------- ------------------ -------- ----
Fernand Hanks   100 East 87th  New York, NY 10015 06/02/99 117
Anita Morris    34 Maiden Lane New York, NY 10015 06/11/99  83
Anita Morris    34 Maiden Lane New York, NY 10015 06/12/99  91
Anita Morris    34 Maiden Lane New York, NY 10015 06/02/99 113
...
Gary Pertez     34 Sixth Ave   New York, NY 10035 06/12/99  90
Gary Pertez     34 Sixth Ave   New York, NY 10035 06/10/99 120
Gary Pertez     34 Sixth Ave   New York, NY 10035 06/03/99 143
Gary Pertez     34 Sixth Ave   New York, NY 10035 06/12/99 151

17 rows selected.
```

LAB 6.2

One of the first steps in solving this query is to determine the columns and tables involved. Look at the schema diagram in Appendix D, "Student Database Schema," or refer to the table and column comments listed in Appendix E, "Table and Column Descriptions."

In this example, the instructor's last name, first name, street address, and zip code are found in the INSTRUCTOR table. The CITY, STATE, and ZIP are columns in the ZIPCODE table. The join also needs to include the SECTION table because the column START_DATE_TIME lists the date and time on which the individual sections started. The next step is to determine the common columns. The ZIP column is the common column between the INSTRUCTOR and ZIPCODE tables. For every value in the ZIP column of the INSTRUCTOR table you have one corresponding ZIP value in the ZIPCODE table. For every value in the ZIPCODE table there may be zero, one, or multiple records in the INSTRUCTOR table. The join returns only the matching records.

The other common column is the INSTRUCTOR_ID in the SECTION and INSTRUCTOR tables. Only instructors who teach have one or more rows in the SECTION table. Any section that does not have an instructor assigned is not taught.

As always, the query can be expressed with one of the ANSI join syntax variations.

```
SELECT first_name || ' ' ||last_name name,
       street_address, city || ', ' || state
       || ' ' || zip "City State Zip",
       TO_CHAR(start_date_time, 'MM/DD/YY') start_dt,
       section_id sect
  FROM instructor JOIN section s
 USING (instructor_id)
  JOIN zipcode
 USING (zip)
 WHERE start_date_time >=TO_DATE('01-JUN-1999','DD-MON-YYYY')
   AND start_date_time < TO_DATE('01-JUL-1999','DD-MON-YYYY')
```

Looking at the result, notice there are instructors teaching multiple sections. To see only the distinct addresses, use the DISTINCT keyword and drop the START_DATE_TIME and SECTION_ID columns from the SELECT list.

c) List the student IDs of enrolled students living in Connecticut.

Answer: Only students enrolled in classes are in the result; any student who does not have a row in the ENROLLMENT table is not considered enrolled. The STUDENT_ID is the common column between the STUDENT and ENROLLMENT tables. The STATE column is in the ZIPCODE table. The common column between the STUDENT and the ZIPCODE tables is the ZIP column.

```
SELECT student_id
  FROM student JOIN enrollment
 USING (student_id)
  JOIN zipcode
 USING (zip)
 WHERE state = 'CT'
STUDENT_ID
-----------
       220
       270
       270
...
       210
       154

13 rows selected.
```

Because students can be enrolled in more than one class, add the DISTINCT keyword if you want to display each STUDENT_ID once.

Following is the SQL statement expressed using the traditional join syntax.

```
SELECT s.student_id
  FROM student s, enrollment e, zipcode z
 WHERE s.student_id = e.student_id
   AND s.zip = z.zip
   AND z.state = 'CT'
```

a) Show all the grades student Fred Crocitto received for SECTION_ID 86.

Answer: The grades for each section and student are stored in the GRADE table. The primary key of the GRADE table consists of the STUDENT_ID, SECTION_ID, GRADE_TYPE_CODE, and GRADE_CODE_OCCURRENCE columns. This means a student, such as Fred Crocitto, has multiple grades for each grade type.

LAB 6.2

```
SELECT s.first_name|| ' '|| s.last_name name,
       e.section_id, g.grade_type_code,
       g.numeric_grade grade
  FROM student s JOIN enrollment e
    ON (s.student_id = e.student_id)
  JOIN grade g
    ON (e.student_id = g.student_id
   AND e.section_id = g.section_id)
 WHERE s.last_name = 'Crocitto'
   AND s.first_name ='Fred'
   AND e.section_id = 86
```

The SQL statement using the traditional join syntax may look similar to this query.

```
SELECT s.first_name|| ' '|| s.last_name name,
       e.section_id, g.grade_type_code,
       g.numeric_grade grade
  FROM student s, enrollment e, grade g
 WHERE s.last_name = 'Crocitto'
   AND s.first_name ='Fred'
   AND e.section_id = 86
   AND s.student_id = e.student_id
   AND e.student_id = g.student_id
   AND e.section_id = g.section_id
```

NAME	SECTION_ID	GR	GRADE
Fred Crocitto	86	FI	85
...			
Fred Crocitto	86	QZ	90
Fred Crocitto	86	QZ	84
Fred Crocitto	86	QZ	97
Fred Crocitto	86	QZ	97

```
11 rows selected.
```

To build up the SQL statement step by step, you may want to start with the STUDENT table and select the record for Fred Crocitto.

```
SELECT last_name, first_name
  FROM student
 WHERE last_name = 'Crocitto'
   AND first_name = 'Fred'
```

Next, choose the section with the ID of 86 in which Fred is enrolled. The common column between the two tables is STUDENT_ID.

```
SELECT s.first_name||' '|| s.last_name name,
       e.section_id
  FROM student s, enrollment e
 WHERE s.last_name = 'Crocitto'
   AND s.first_name = 'Fred'
   AND e.section_id = 86
   AND s.student_id = e.student_id
```

Lastly, retrieve the individual grades from the GRADE table. The common columns between the GRADE table and the ENROLLMENT table are SECTION_ID and STUDENT_ID. They represent the primary key in the ENROLLMENT table, and are foreign keys in the GRADE table. Both columns need to be in the WHERE clause.

Expanding on the query, add the DESCRIPTION column of the GRADE_TYPE table for each GRADE_TYPE_CODE. The common column between the tables GRADE and GRADE_TYPE is GRADE_TYPE_CODE. Add the DESCRIPTION column to the SELECT list and prefix the GRADE_TYPE_CODE column to indicate from which table the column is selected.

```
SELECT s.first_name||' '|| s.last_name name,
       e.section_id, g.grade_type_code grade,
       g.numeric_grade, gt.description
  FROM student s, enrollment e, grade g, grade_type gt
 WHERE s.last_name = 'Crocitto'
   AND s.first_name = 'Fred'
   AND e.section_id = 86
   AND s.student_id = e.student_id
   AND e.student_id = g.student_id
   AND e.section_id = g.section_id
   AND g.grade_type_code = gt.grade_type_code
```

If you also show the COURSE_NO column, join to the SECTION table via the ENROLLMENT table column SECTION_ID.

```
SELECT s.first_name||' '|| s.last_name name,
       e.section_id, g.grade_type_code,
       g.numeric_grade grade, gt.description,
       sec.course_no
  FROM student s, enrollment e, grade g, grade_type gt,
       section sec
```

```
WHERE s.last_name = 'Crocitto'
  AND s.first_name = 'Fred'
  AND e.section_id = 86
  AND s.student_id = e.student_id
  AND e.student_id = g.student_id
  AND e.section_id = g.section_id
  AND g.grade_type_code = gt.grade_type_code
  AND e.section_id = sec.section_id
```

```
NAME            SECTION_ID GR GRADE DESCRIPTION COURSE_NO
-------------   ---------- -- ----- ----------- ---------
Fred Crocitto        86 FI    85 Final             25
...
Fred Crocitto        86 QZ    90 Quiz              25
Fred Crocitto        86 QZ    84 Quiz              25
Fred Crocitto        86 QZ    97 Quiz              25
Fred Crocitto        86 QZ    97 Quiz              25

11 rows selected.
```

b) List the final examination grades for all enrolled Connecticut students of course number 420. Note final examination does not mean final grade.

Answer: This answer requires joining five tables. The required joins are: the ZIPCODE table with the STUDENT table to determine the Connecticut students and the STUDENT and ENROLLMENT tables to determine the SECTION_IDs in which the students are enrolled. From these SECTION_IDs you only include sections where the course number equals 420. This requires a join of the ENROLLMENT table to the SECTION table. Lastly, the ENROLLMENT table needs to be joined to the GRADE table to display the grades.

```
SELECT e.student_id, sec.course_no, g.numeric_grade
  FROM student stud, zipcode z,
       enrollment e, section sec, grade g
 WHERE stud.zip = z.zip
   AND z.state = 'CT'
   AND stud.student_id = e.student_id
   AND e.section_id = sec.section_id
   AND e.section_id = g.section_id
   AND e.student_id = g.student_id
   AND sec.course_no = 420
   AND g.grade_type_code = 'FI'
STUDENT_ID COURSE_NO NUMERIC_GRADE
---------- --------- -------------
       196       420            84
       198       420            85

2 rows selected.
```

You may list any of the columns you find relevant to solving the query. For this solution, the columns STUDENT_ID, COURSE_NO, and NUMERIC_GRADE were chosen.

Obviously, the query can be expressed with the ANSI join syntax here showing the USING clause.

```
SELECT student_id, course_no, numeric_grade
  FROM student JOIN zipcode
USING (zip)
   JOIN enrollment
USING (student_id)
  JOIN section
USING (section_id)
  JOIN grade g
USING (section_id, student_id)
 WHERE course_no = 420
   AND grade_type_code = 'FI'
   AND state = 'CT'
```

c) Display the columns LAST_NAME, STUDENT_ID, PERCENT_OF_FINAL, GRADE_TYPE_CODE, and NUMERIC_GRADE for students who received 80 or less for their class project (GRADE_TYPE_CODE = 'PJ'). Order the result by student last name.

Answer: Join the tables GRADE_TYPE_WEIGHT, GRADE, ENROLLMENT, and STUDENT.

The column PERCENT_OF_FINAL_GRADE of the GRADE_TYPE_WEIGHT table stores the weighted percentage a particular grade has on the final grade. One of the foreign keys of the GRADE table is the combination of the GRADE_TYPE_ CODE and SECTION_ID; these columns represent the primary key of the GRADE_TYPE_WEIGHT table.

To include the student's last name, you have two choices. Either follow the primary and foreign key relationships by joining the tables GRADE and ENROLL-MENT via the STUDENT_ID and SECTION_ID columns, and then join the ENROLLMENT table to the STUDENT table via the STUDENT_ID column, or skip the ENROLLMENT table and join GRADE directly to the STUDENT table via the STUDENT_ID. Examine the first option of joining to the ENROLLMENT table and then joining it to the STUDENT table.

```
SELECT g.student_id, g.section_id,
       gw.percent_of_final_grade pct, g.grade_type_code,
       g.numeric_grade grade, s.last_name
  FROM grade_type_weight gw, grade g,
       enrollment e, student s
 WHERE g.grade_type_code = 'PJ'
   AND gw.grade_type_code = g.grade_type_code
```

```
   AND gw.section_id = g.section_id
   AND g.numeric_grade <= 80
   AND g.section_id = e.section_id
   AND g.student_id = e.student_id
   AND e.student_id = s.student_id
 ORDER BY s.last_name
STUDENT_ID SECTION_ID          PCT GR      GRADE LAST_NAME
---------- ----------   --------- --   --------- -----------
       245         82          75 PJ         77 Dalvi
       176        115          75 PJ         76 Satterfield
       244         82          75 PJ         76 Wilson
       248        155          75 PJ         76 Zapulla
```

**LAB
6.2**

4 rows selected.

SKIPPING THE PRIMARY/FOREIGN KEY PATH

The second choice is to join the STUDENT_ID from the GRADE table directly to the STUDENT_ID of the STUDENT table, thus skipping the ENROLLMENT table entirely. The following query returns the same result.

```
SELECT g.student_id, g.section_id,
       gw.percent_of_final_grade pct, g.grade_type_code,
       g.numeric_grade grade, s.last_name
  FROM grade_type_weight gw, grade g,
       student s
 WHERE g.grade_type_code = 'PJ'
   AND gw.grade_type_code = g.grade_type_code
   AND gw.section_id = g.section_id
   AND g.numeric_grade <= 80
   AND g.student_id = s.student_id
 ORDER BY s.last_name
STUDENT_ID SECTION_ID          PCT GR      GRADE LAST_NAME
---------- ----------   --------- --   --------- -----------
       245         82          75 PJ         77 Dalvi
       176        115          75 PJ         76 Satterfield
       244         82          75 PJ         76 Wilson
       248        155          75 PJ         76 Zapulla
```

4 rows selected.

This shortcut is perfectly acceptable, even if it does not follow the primary/foreign key relationship path. In this case, you can be sure not to build a Cartesian product as you can guarantee only one STUDENT_ID in the STUDENT table for every STUDENT_ID in the GRADE table. In addition, it also saves another join; thus, the query executes a little faster and takes up less resources, which is probably negligible with this small result set.

LAB 6.2 SELF-REVIEW QUESTIONS

In order to test your progress, you should be able to answer the following questions.

1) Which SQL statement shows the sections that have instructors assigned to them?

a) _____

```
SELECT c.course_no, s.section_id, i.instructor_id
  FROM course c, section s, instructor i
 WHERE c.course_no = s.course_no
   AND i.instructor_id = s.section_id
```

b) _____

```
SELECT c.course_no, s.section_id, i.instructor_id
  FROM course c, section s, instructor i
 WHERE c.course_no = s.course_no
   AND i.instructor_id = s.instructor_id
```

c) _____

```
SELECT course_no, section_id, instructor.instructor_id
  FROM section, instructor
 WHERE instructor.instructor_id = section.section_id
```

d) _____

```
SELECT c.section_id, i.instructor_id
  FROM course c, instructor i
 WHERE i.instructor_id = c.section_id
```

e) _____

```
SELECT c.course_no, i.instructor_id
  FROM course c JOIN innstructor
 USING (instructor_id)
```

2) How do you resolve the Oracle error `ORA-00918: column ambiguously defined`?

a) _____ Correct the join criteria and WHERE clause condition
b) _____ Choose another column
c) _____ Add the correct table alias
d) _____ Correct the spelling of the column name

3) Joins involving multiple columns must always follow the primary/foreign key relationship path.

a) _____ True
b) _____ False

4) Find the error(s) in the following SQL statement.

```
1 SELECT g.student_id, s.section_id,
2        g.numeric_grade, s.last_name
3   FROM grade g,
4        enrollment e, student s
5  WHERE g.section_id = e.section_id
6    AND g.student_id = e.student_id
7    AND s.student_id = e.student_id
8    AND s.student_id = 248
9    AND e.section_id = 155
```

a) _____ Line 1
b) _____ Line 5
c) _____ Line 6
d) _____ Line 5, 6
e) _____ Line 1, 5, 6
f) _____ No error

5) Equijoins are the most common type of joins and are always based on equality of values.

a) _____ True
b) _____ False

6) To join four tables you must have at least three join conditions.

a) _____ True
b) _____ False

Answers appear in Appendix A, Section 6.2.

CHAPTER 6

TEST YOUR THINKING

The projects in this section are meant to have you utilize all of the skills that you have acquired throughout this chapter. The answers to these projects can be found at the companion Web site to this book, located at: *http://www.phptr.com/rischert.*

Visit the Web site periodically to share and discuss your answers.

1) Select the course description, section number, and location for sections meeting in location L211.

2) Show the course description, section number, and starting date and time of the courses Joseph German is taking.

3) List the instructor ID, last name of the instructor, and section ID of sections where class participation contributes to 25% of the total grade. Order the result by the instructor's last name.

4) Display the first and last names of students who received 99 or more points on their class project.

5) Select the grades for quizzes of students living in zip code 10956.

6) List the course number, section number, and instructor first and last names of classes with course number 350 as a prerequisite.

7) Write the questions for the following two SELECT statements. Explain the difference between the two results.

```
SELECT stud.student_id, i.instructor_id,
       stud.zip, i.zip
  FROM student stud, instructor i
 WHERE stud.zip = i.zip

SELECT stud.student_id, i.instructor_id,
       stud.zip, i.zip
  FROM student stud, enrollment e, section sec,
       instructor i
 WHERE stud.student_id = e.student_id
   AND e.section_id = sec.section_id
   AND sec.instructor_id = i.instructor_id
   AND stud.zip = i.zip
```

CHAPTER 7

SUBQUERIES

A subquery is a SELECT statement nested in various clauses of a SQL statement. It allows you to use the output from one query as the input of another SQL statement. Subqueries make it easy to break down problems into logical and manageable pieces.

L A B   7 . 1

SIMPLE SUBQUERIES

LAB OBJECTIVES

After this lab, you will be able to:

✔ Write Subqueries in the WHERE and HAVING Clauses
✔ Write Subqueries Returning Multiple Rows
✔ Write Subqueries Returning Multiple Columns

Subqueries are not used just in SELECT statements, but in other SQL statements that allow subqueries as well (e.g., the WHERE clause of DELETE statements, the SET and WHERE clause of UPDATE statements, or part of the SELECT clause of INSERT statements). You use these SQL statements in Chapter 10, "INSERT, UP-DATE, and DELETE."

In this workbook, the subquery is referred to as the inner query and the surrounding statement is known as the outer query. In the simple subquery, the inner query is executed once, before the execution of the outer query. (This is in contrast to the correlated subquery, where the inner query executes repeatedly. You will learn to write correlated subqueries in Lab 7.2.)

A subquery allows you to break down a problem into individual pieces and solve it by nesting the queries. Although subqueries can be nested several levels deep, it is impractical beyond four or five levels. Subqueries are sometimes also referred to as *sub-SELECTs* or *nested SELECTs*.

SCALAR SUBQUERIES

The *scalar subquery* is also called the *single row subquery*; it returns a single column with one row. When you want to show the courses with the lowest course cost, you can write two separate queries. First, determine the lowest cost by applying the aggregate function MIN to the COST column of the COURSE table.

```
SELECT MIN(cost)
  FROM course
MIN(COST)
---------
     1095
```

1 row selected.

Then, write another SELECT statement that retrieves courses equaling the cost.

```
SELECT course_no, description, cost
  FROM course
 WHERE cost = 1095
```

COURSE_NO	DESCRIPTION	COST
135	Unix Tips and Techniques	1095
230	Intro to Internet	1095
240	Intro to the Basic Language	1095

3 rows selected.

The subquery construct simplifies the writing of two separate queries and the recording of the intermediate result. The following SQL statement nests the subquery determining the lowest course cost in the WHERE clause of the outer query. The inner query, which is the query determining the lowest cost from the COURSE table, is executed first. The result is fed to the outer query, which retrieves all the values that qualify.

```
SELECT course_no, description, cost
  FROM course
 WHERE cost =
       (SELECT MIN(cost)
          FROM course)
```

COURSE_NO	DESCRIPTION	COST
135	Unix Tips and Techniques	1095
230	Intro to Internet	1095
240	Intro to the Basic Language	1095

3 rows selected.

Instead of performing equality conditions, you may need to construct >, <, >=, <=, or <> comparisons against a set of rows. These comparisons will only work, just like the aforementioned statement, if the subquery returns a single row.

SUBQUERIES RETURNING MULTIPLE ROWS

Subqueries can return one or multiple rows. If a subquery returns a single row, the =, <, >, <=, >=, or <> operator may be used for comparison with the subquery. If multiple records are returned, the IN, ANY, ALL, or SOME operator must be used; otherwise, Oracle returns an error message.

The following query displays the course number, description, and cost of courses with a cost equal to the highest cost of all the courses. The highest cost requires the use of the aggregate function MAX. As you recall from Chapter 5, "Aggregate Functions, GROUP BY, and HAVING," aggregate functions when used alone without the presence of any nonaggregate expressions in the SELECT list always return one row. The subquery returns the single value 1595. All the rows of the COURSE table are compared to this value to see if any rows have the same course cost. Only one record in the COURSE table equals this cost.

```
SELECT course_no, description, cost
  FROM course
 WHERE cost =
       (SELECT MAX(cost)
          FROM course)
COURSE_NO DESCRIPTION                               COST
--------- -------------------------------- ------
       80 Structured Programming Techniques   1595

1 row selected.
```

The next SQL statement is an example of a subquery that returns several rows.

```
SELECT course_no, description, cost
  FROM course
 WHERE cost =
       (SELECT cost
          FROM course
         WHERE prerequisite = 20)
ERROR at line 4:
ORA-01427: single-row subquery returns more than one row
```

Multiple rows of the subquery satisfy the criteria of a prerequisite course number equal to 20. Therefore, Oracle returns an error message. To eliminate the error, change the = operator of the outer query to the IN operator. The IN operator compares a list of values for equivalency. If any of the values in the list satisfy the condition, the record is included in the result set.

```
SELECT course_no, description, cost
  FROM course
 WHERE cost IN
       (SELECT cost
          FROM course
         WHERE prerequisite = 20)
```

```
COURSE_NO DESCRIPTION                                        COST
-------------------------------------------------------- ---
       10 DP Overview                                        1195
       20 Intro to Computers                                 1195
...
      122 Intermediate Java Programming                      1195
      100 Hands-On Windows                                   1195

    25 rows selected.
```

You can also negate the criteria of the subquery and include only records with values that are not in the subquery's result. You accomplish this by applying the NOT IN operator.

```
SELECT course_no, description, cost
  FROM course
 WHERE cost NOT IN
       (SELECT cost
          FROM course
         WHERE prerequisite = 20)
COURSE_NO DESCRIPTION                                 COST
--------- -------------------------------- ---------
       80 Structured Programming Techniques    1595
      135 Unix Tips and Techniques             1095
      230 Intro to Internet                    1095
      240 Intro to the Basic Language          1095

4 rows selected.
```

If the subquery returns multiple rows and you want to perform a comparison other than equality or inequality, use the ALL, ANY, and SOME operators discussed in Lab 7.4 to perform such comparisons.

Table 7.1 provides an overview of the various comparison operators available for subqueries. If your subquery returns more than one row you have to choose a different operator than if your subquery retrieves at most one row only.

NESTING MULTIPLE SUBQUERIES

You can nest one subquery within another subquery. The innermost query is always evaluated first, then the next higher one, and so on. The result of each subquery is fed into the enclosing statement.

Determine the last and first names of students enrolled in section number 8 of course number 20.

Table 7.1 ■ Comparison Operators for Subqueries

Comparison Operator	Subquery Returns One Row	Subquery Returns Multiple Rows
Equality	=	IN
Inequality	<>	NOT IN
Greater than	>	Use the ANY, ALL, SOME
Less than	<	operators (see Lab 7.4).
Greater than and equal	>=	
Less than and equal	<=	

```
SELECT last_name, first_name
  FROM student
 WHERE student_id IN
       (SELECT student_id
          FROM enrollment
         WHERE section_id IN
               (SELECT section_id
                  FROM section
                 WHERE section_no = 8
                 AND course_no = 20))
LAST_NAME                       FIRST_NAME
------------------------------- ----------
Limate                          Roy
Segall                          J.

2 rows selected.
```

The innermost nested subquery, the last subquery in the example, is executed first; it determines the SECTION_ID for section number 8 and course number 20. The surrounding query uses this resulting SECTION_ID in the WHERE clause to select student IDs from the ENROLLMENT table. These STUDENT_ID rows are fed to the outermost SELECT statement, which then displays the first and last names from the STUDENT table.

SUBQUERIES AND JOINS

Sometimes subqueries using the IN or = operator can be expressed as joins if the subquery does not contain an aggregate function. The following query can be transformed into an equijoin. Oracle sometimes performs this conversion implicitly as part of its optimization strategy if the primary and foreign keys exist on the tables and the join does not cause a Cartesian product.

```
SELECT course_no, description
  FROM course
```

```
WHERE course_no IN
        (SELECT course_no
            FROM section
          WHERE location = 'L211')
```

COURSE_NO DESCRIPTION
--------- -----------------------------
    142 Project Management
    125 JDeveloper
    122 Intermediate Java Programming

3 rows selected.

Here is the same query now expressed as an equijoin:

```
SELECT c.course_no, c.description
  FROM course c, section s
 WHERE c.course_no = s.course_no
   AND s.location = 'L211'
```

SUBQUERIES RETURNING MULTIPLE COLUMNS

SQL allows you to compare multiple columns in the WHERE clause to multiple columns of a subquery. The values in the columns must match both sides of the equation in the WHERE clause for the condition to be true. This means the datatype must be compatible and the number and order of columns must match.

For example, for each section, determine the students with the highest grade for their project (PJ). The following query does not accomplish this goal. It returns the highest project grade for each section, but does not list the individual student(s).

```
SELECT section_id, MAX(numeric_grade)
  FROM grade
 WHERE grade_type_code = 'PJ'
 GROUP BY section_id
```

SECTION_ID MAX(NUMERIC_GRADE)
---------- ------------------
      82   **77**
      88   **99**
...
    149   **83**
    155   **92**

8 rows selected.

The following query obtains the desired result by transforming the query into a subquery. The outer query displays the desired STUDENT_ID column and the

WHERE clause compares the column pairs against the column pairs in the sub-query.

```
SELECT student_id, section_id, numeric_grade
  FROM grade
 WHERE grade_type_code = 'PJ'
   AND (section_id, numeric_grade) IN
       (SELECT section_id, MAX(numeric_grade)
          FROM grade
         WHERE grade_type_code = 'PJ'
         GROUP BY section_id)
```

STUDENT_ID	SECTION_ID	NUMERIC_GRADE
245	82	77
166	88	99
...		
232	149	83
105	155	92

8 rows selected.

The execution steps are just like the previous simple subqueries. First, the inner-most query is executed, determining the highest grade for each section. Then the pairs of columns are compared. If the column pair matches, Oracle displays the record.

SUBQUERIES AND NULLS

One easily overlooked behavior of subqueries is the occurrence of null values. The next example illustrates this subject on the COURSE table and the PREREQ-UISITE column. The first query shows a subquery that returns all the COURSE_NO and PREREQUISITE column values for courses with the COURSE_NO of 120, 220, and 310 of the COURSE table. Note that the course number 310 has a null value for in the PREREQUISITE column, meaning that the individual course does not have any prerequisites.

```
SELECT course_no, prerequisite
  FROM course
 WHERE course_no IN (120, 220, 310)
```

COURSE_NO	PREREQUISITE
120	80
220	80
310	

3 rows selected.

If you use this result and now formulate a subquery for these rows specifically and negate it with NOT, you will notice an interesting result. The outer query does not return any rows despite the fact that there are rows with PREREQUISITE column values other than 80 and null.

```
SELECT course_no, prerequisite
   FROM course
  WHERE prerequisite NOT IN
          (SELECT prerequisite
              FROM course
             WHERE course_no IN (310, 220))
```

no rows selected

If you translate the result of the subquery into a list of values, you will see the same identical result. No rows are returned from the query because the condition evaluates to unknown when any member of the values in the list has a null.

```
SELECT course_no, prerequisite
   FROM course
  WHERE prerequisite NOT IN (80, NULL)
```

no rows selected

You typically only come across this type of scenario in subqueries; therefore, you must be aware of any NOT IN operator subqueries that can potentially return null values. The way to solve this null dilemma is to use the NOT EXISTS operator discussed in Lab 7.2. The next query will return the desired result.

```
SELECT course_no, prerequisite
   FROM course c
  WHERE NOT EXISTS
          (SELECT '*'
              FROM course
             WHERE course_no IN (310, 220)
               AND c.prerequisite = prerequisite)
```

The NVL or COALESCE functions are useful to deal with null values. You can substitute a default value and apply the function to both the subquery and the WHERE clause condition.

ORDER BY CLAUSE IN SUBQUERIES

The ORDER BY clause is not allowed inside a subquery with the exception of the inline view discussed in Lab 7.3. If you attempt to include an ORDER BY clause you will get an error message. It is not immediately apparent where the problem lies unless you already know about this rule. The message essentially indicates that an ORDER BY clause is not allowed in a subquery and that Oracle is expecting to see the right parenthesis signifying the closing of the subquery. An ORDER BY clause is certainly valid for the outer query, just not for the nested subquery.

```
SELECT course_no, description, cost
  FROM course
 WHERE cost IN
         (SELECT cost
            FROM course
           WHERE prerequisite = 420
           ORDER BY cost)
         ORDER BY cost)
         *
ERROR at line 7:
ORA-00907: missing right parenthesis
```

You cannot use the ORDER BY clause inside a nested subquery. Another type of subquery, the inline view discussed in Lab 7.3, allows such a construct.

LAB 7.1 EXERCISES

7.1.1 WRITE SUBQUERIES IN THE *WHERE* AND *HAVING* CLAUSES

a) Write a SQL statement that displays the first and last names of students who registered first.

b) Show the sections with the lowest course cost and a capacity equal to or lower than the average capacity. Also display the course description, section number, capacity, and cost.

c) Select the course number and total capacity for each course. Show only the courses with a total capacity less than the average capacity of all the sections.

d) Choose the most ambitious students: display the STUDENT_ID for students enrolled in the most sections.

7.1.2 WRITE SUBQUERIES RETURNING MULTIPLE ROWS

a) Select the STUDENT_ID and SECTION_ID of enrolled students living in zip code 06820.

b) Display the course number and course description of the courses taught by instructor Fernand Hanks.

c) Select the last name and first name of students not enrolled in any class.

7.1.3 WRITE SUBQUERIES RETURNING MULTIPLE COLUMNS

a) Determine the STUDENT_ID and last name of students with the highest FINAL_GRADE for each section. Also include the SECTION_ID and the FINAL_GRADE columns in the result.

b) Select the sections and their capacity where the capacity equals the number of students enrolled.

LAB 7.1 EXERCISE ANSWERS

7.1.1 ANSWERS

a) Write a SQL statement that displays the first and last names of students who registered first.

Answer: The query is broken down into logical pieces by first determining the earliest registration date of all students. The aggregate function MIN obtains the result in the subquery. The earliest date is compared to the REGISTRATION_DATE column for each student, and only records that are equal to the same date and time are returned.

```
SELECT first_name, last_name
  FROM student
 WHERE registration_date =
       (SELECT MIN(registration_date)
          FROM student)
```

```
FIRST_NAME                               LAST_NAME
------------------------------           ----------
J.                                       Landry
Judith                                   Olvsade
...
Larry                                    Walter
Catherine                                Mierzwa

8 rows selected.
```

b) Show the sections with the lowest course cost and a capacity equal to or lower than the average capacity. Also display the course description, section number, capacity, and cost.

Answer: First, break down the problem into individual queries. Start by determining the average capacity of all sections and the lowest course cost of all courses. To compare both cost and capacity against the subqueries, the SECTION and COURSE tables require a join.

```
SELECT c.description, s.section_no, c.cost, s.capacity
  FROM course c, section s
 WHERE c.course_no = s.course_no
   AND s.capacity <=
       (SELECT AVG(capacity)
          FROM section)
   AND c.cost =
       (SELECT MIN(cost)
          FROM course)
```

```
DESCRIPTION                      SECTION_NO   COST   CAPACITY
------------------------------   ----------   ------ ---------
Intro to Internet                        1    1095         12
Intro to Internet                        2    1095         15
...
Unix Tips and Techniques                 2    1095         15
Unix Tips and Techniques                 4    1095         15

6 rows selected.
```

c) Select the course number and total capacity for each course. Show only the courses with a total capacity less than the average capacity of all the sections.

Answer: To determine the total capacity per course, use the SUM function to add the values in the SECTION table's CAPACITY column. Compare the total capacity for each course to the average capacity for all sections and return those courses that have a total capacity less than the average capacity.

```
SELECT course_no, SUM(capacity)
  FROM section
```

```
GROUP BY course_no
HAVING SUM(capacity) <
       (SELECT AVG(capacity)
          FROM section)
```

COURSE_NO	SUM(CAPACITY)
10	15
144	15

2 rows selected.

The solution shows only those courses and their respective capacities that satisfy the condition in the HAVING clause.

To determine the solution, first write the individual queries and then combine them. The following query first determines the total capacity for each course.

```
SELECT course_no, SUM(capacity)
  FROM section
 GROUP BY course_no
```

COURSE_NO	SUM(CAPACITY)
10	15
20	80
...	
420	25
450	25

28 rows selected.

The average capacity for all sections is easily obtained using the AVG function.

```
SELECT AVG(capacity)
  FROM section
```

AVG(CAPACITY)
21.179487

1 row selected.

d) Choose the most ambitious students: display the STUDENT_ID for students enrolled in the most sections.

Answer: A count of records for each student in the ENROLLMENT table shows how many sections each student is enrolled in. Determine the most number of enrollments per student by nesting the aggregate functions MAX and COUNT.

```
SELECT student_id, COUNT(*)
  FROM enrollment
```

```
GROUP BY student_id
HAVING COUNT(*) =
        (SELECT MAX(COUNT(*))
           FROM enrollment
          GROUP BY student_id)
STUDENT_ID  COUNT(*)
----------  --------
       124         4
       214         4
```

2 rows selected.

To reach the subquery solution, determine the number of enrollments for each student. Notice that the STUDENT_ID column is not listed in the SELECT list. Therefore, only the result of the COUNT function is shown.

```
SELECT COUNT(*)
  FROM enrollment
 GROUP BY student_id
COUNT(*)
---------
        2
        1
...
        2
        2
```

165 rows selected.

The second query combines two aggregate functions to determine the highest number of sections any student is enrolled in. This subquery is then applied in the HAVING clause of the solution.

```
SELECT MAX(COUNT(*))
  FROM enrollment
 GROUP BY student_id
MAX(COUNT(*))
-------------
            4
```

1 row selected.

7.1.2 ANSWERS

a) Select the STUDENT_ID and SECTION_ID of enrolled students living in zip code 06820.

Answer: The IN operator is necessary because the subquery returns multiple rows.

```
SELECT student_id, section_id
  FROM enrollment
 WHERE student_id IN
        (SELECT student_id
           FROM student
          WHERE zip = '06820')
STUDENT_ID SECTION_ID
---------- ----------
       240         81
```

1 row selected.

Alternatively, you can achieve the same result using an equijoin.

```
SELECT e.student_id, e.section_id
  FROM enrollment e, student s
 WHERE e.student_id = s.student_id
   AND s.zip = '06820'
```

b) Display the course number and course description of the courses taught by instructor Fernand Hanks.

Answer: To determine the courses taught by this instructor, nest multiple subqueries. This question can also be solved using an equijoin.

```
SELECT course_no, description
  FROM course
 WHERE course_no IN
        (SELECT course_no
           FROM section
          WHERE instructor_id IN
                (SELECT instructor_id
                   FROM instructor
                  WHERE last_name = 'Hanks'
                    AND first_name = 'Fernand'))
COURSE_NO DESCRIPTION
--------- ----------------------------
       25 Intro to Programming
      240 Intro to the Basic Language
...
      120 Intro to Java Programming
      122 Intermediate Java Programming
```

9 rows selected.

The alternative solution is an equijoin:

```
SELECT c.course_no, c.description
  FROM course c, section s, instructor i
```

```
WHERE c.course_no = s.course_no
  AND s.instructor_id = i.instructor_id
  AND i.last_name = 'Hanks'
  AND i.first_name = 'Fernand'
```

c) Select the last name and first name of students not enrolled in any class.

Answer: Use the NOT IN operator to eliminate those student IDs not found in the EN-ROLLMENT table. The result is a listing of students with no rows in the ENROLLMENT table. They may be newly registered students that have not yet enrolled in any courses.

```
SELECT last_name, first_name
  FROM student
 WHERE student_id NOT IN
       (SELECT student_id
          FROM enrollment)
```

LAST_NAME	FIRST_NAME
Eakheit	George
Millstein	Leonard
...	
Larcia	Preston
Mastandora	Kathleen

103 rows selected.

You may wonder why the solution does not include the DISTINCT keyword in the subquery. It is not required and does not alter the result, nor change the efficiency of the execution. Oracle automatically eliminates duplicates in a list of values as a result of the subquery.

7.1.3 ANSWERS

a) Determine the STUDENT_ID and last name of students with the highest FINAL_GRADE for each section. Also include the SECTION_ID and the FINAL_GRADE columns in the result.

Answer: The solution requires pairs of columns to be compared. First, determine the subquery to show the highest grade for each section. Then match the result to the columns in the outer query.

```
SELECT s.student_id, s.last_name, e.final_grade,
       e.section_id
  FROM enrollment e, student s
 WHERE e.student_id = s.student_id
   AND (e.final_grade, e.section_id) IN
       (SELECT MAX(final_grade), section_id
          FROM enrollment
         GROUP BY section_id)
```

```
STUDENT_ID LAST_NAME   FINAL_GRADE SECTION_ID
---------- ----------  ----------- ----------
       102 Crocitto            92          89
```

1 row selected.

Note, there is no need to add a table alias to the subquery. Table aliases in subqueries are typically only used in correlated subqueries or in subqueries that contain joins. Correlated subqueries are discussed in Lab 7.2.

b) Select the sections and their capacity where the capacity equals the number of students enrolled.

Answer: The subquery determines the number of enrolled students per section. The resulting set is then compared to the column pair of SECTION_ID and CAPACITY.

```
SELECT section_id, capacity
  FROM section
 WHERE (section_id, capacity) IN
       (SELECT section_id, COUNT(*)
          FROM enrollment
         GROUP BY section_id)
SECTION_ID  CAPACITY
----------  --------
        99        12
```

1 row selected.

LAB 7.1 SELF-REVIEW QUESTIONS

In order to test your progress, you should be able to answer the following questions.

1) The ORDER BY clause is not allowed in subqueries.

a) _____ True
b) _____ False

2) Subqueries are used only in SELECT statements.

a) _____ True
b) _____ False

3) The most deeply nested, noncorrelated subquery always executes first.

a) _____ True
b) _____ False

4) What operator would you choose to prevent this Oracle error message?
ORA-01427: single-row subquery returns more than one row

    a) _____ Use the >= operator
    b) _____ Use the = operator
    c) _____ Use the IN operator
    d) _____ Use the <= operator

5) Subqueries can return multiple rows and columns.

    a) _____ True
    b) _____ False

Answers appear in Appendix A, Section 7.1.

LAB 7.2

CORRELATED SUBQUERIES

LAB OBJECTIVES

After this lab, you will be able to:

✔ Write Correlated Subqueries
✔ Write Correlated Subqueries Using the EXISTS
  and NOT EXISTS Operators

CORRELATED SUBQUERIES

Correlated subqueries are probably one of the most powerful, yet initially very difficult, concepts of the SQL language. Correlated subqueries are different from the simple subqueries discussed so far because they allow you to reference columns used in the outer query. The correlation is achieved by executing the inner query once for each row in the outer query. This is in contrast to previous subquery examples, where the inner query is executed only once.

In the previous lab, one example illustrates how to determine the students with the highest grade for their project (PJ), within their respective sections. The solution is accomplished with the IN operator which compares the column pairs. The following SELECT statement repeats the solution.

```
SELECT student_id, section_id, numeric_grade
  FROM grade
 WHERE grade_type_code = 'PJ'
   AND (section_id, numeric_grade) IN
       (SELECT section_id, MAX(numeric_grade)
          FROM grade
         WHERE grade_type_code = 'PJ'
         GROUP BY section_id)
```

Here is the query rewritten as a correlated subquery.

```
SELECT student_id, section_id, numeric_grade
  FROM grade outer
 WHERE grade_type_code = 'PJ'
   AND numeric_grade =
       (SELECT MAX(numeric_grade)
          FROM grade
         WHERE grade_type_code = outer.grade_type_code
           AND section_id = outer.section_id)
```

STUDENT_ID	SECTION_ID	NUMERIC_GRADE
245	82	77
166	88	99
...		
232	149	83
105	155	92

8 rows selected.

This query is a correlated subquery because the inner query refers to columns from the outer query. The GRADE table is the parent query, or the outer query. For simplicity, a table alias of outer is used.

Now you can refer to columns of the outer query using the alias. In this example, the values of the column SECTION_ID of the outer query are compared to the values of the inner query. The inner query determines the highest project grade for the SECTION_ID and GRADE_TYPE_CODE values of the current outer row.

STEPS PERFORMED BY THE CORRELATED SUBQUERY

To select the correct records, the following steps are performed by Oracle.

1. Select a row from the outer query.
2. Determine the value of the correlated column(s).
3. Execute the inner query for each record of the outer query.
4. The result of the inner query is then fed to the outer query and evaluated. If it satisfies the criteria, the row is returned for output.
5. The next record of the outer query is selected and steps 2 through 4 are repeated until all the records of the outer query are evaluated.

Here are the steps in more detail.

STEP 1: SELECT A ROW FROM THE OUTER QUERY   Choose a record in the outer query where the GRADE_TYPE_CODE, equals 'PJ'. The row returned in this step will be further evaluated in the steps that follow.

```
SELECT student_id, section_id, numeric_grade
  FROM grade outer
 WHERE grade_type_code = 'PJ'
```

```
STUDENT_ID SECTION_ID NUMERIC_GRADE
---------- ---------- -------------
       105        155            92
       111        133            90
...
       245         82            77
       248        155            76
```

21 rows selected.

STEP 2: DETERMINE THE VALUE OF THE CORRELATED COLUMN(S)   Starting with the first returned row with a STUDENT_ID 105, the value of the correlated column OUTER.SECTION_ID equals 155. For the column OUTER.GRADE_TYPE_CODE, the value is 'PJ'.

STEP 3: EXECUTE THE INNER QUERY   Based on the correlated column values, the inner query is executed. It shows the highest grade for the respective section and grade type code.

```
SELECT MAX(numeric_grade)
  FROM grade
 WHERE grade_type_code = 'PJ'
   AND section_id = 155
MAX(NUMERIC_GRADE)
------------------
                92
```

1 row selected.

STEP 4: EVALUATE THE CONDITION   Because the NUMERIC_GRADE equals 92, the row for STUDENT_ID 105 evaluates to true and is included in the result.

STEP 5: REPEAT STEPS 2 THROUGH 4 FOR EACH SUBSEQUENT ROW OF THE OUTER QUERY   Evaluate the next row containing values STUDENT_ID 111 and SECTION_ID 133. The highest grade for the section and grade type code happens to be 92, but student 111 does not have a NUMERIC_GRADE equal to this value. Therefore, the row is not returned. Each row of the outer query repeats these steps until all the rows are evaluated.

```
SELECT MAX(numeric_grade)
  FROM grade
 WHERE grade_type_code = 'PJ'
   AND section_id = 133
MAX(NUMERIC_GRADE)
------------------
                92
```

1 row selected.

Unlike the subqueries discussed in Lab 7.1 where the inner query is evaluated once, the correlated subquery executes the inner query repeatedly, once for each row in the outer table.

LAB 7.2

THE EXISTS OPERATOR

The EXISTS operator is used for correlated subqueries. It tests if the subquery returns at least one row. The EXISTS operator returns either true or false, never unknown. Because EXISTS tests only if a row exists, the columns shown in the SELECT list are irrelevant. Typically, you use a single character text literal such as '1' or 'X' or the keyword NULL.

Display the INSTRUCTOR_ID, FIRST_NAME, LAST_NAME, and ZIP column values of instructors assigned to at least one section. The following correlated subquery displays instructors where the INSTRUCTOR_ID has a matching row in the SECTION table.

```
SELECT instructor_id, last_name, first_name, zip
  FROM instructor i
 WHERE EXISTS
       (SELECT 'X'
          FROM section
         WHERE i.instructor_id = instructor_id)
```

INSTRUCTOR_ID	LAST_NAME	FIRST_NAME	ZIP
101	Hanks	Fernand	10015
102	Wojick	Tom	10025
103	Schorin	Nina	10025
104	Pertez	Gary	10035
105	Morris	Anita	10015
106	Smythe	Todd	10025
108	Lowry	Charles	10025
107	Frantzen	Marilyn	10005

```
8 rows selected.
```

The query can also be written using the IN operator.

```
SELECT instructor_id, last_name, first_name, zip
  FROM instructor
 WHERE instructor_id IN
       (SELECT instructor_id
          FROM section)
```

Alternatively, you can write this query with an equijoin.

```
SELECT DISTINCT i.instructor_id, i.last_name,
       i.first_name, i.zip
```

```
FROM instructor i JOIN section s
   ON i.instructor_id = s.instructor_id
```

THE NOT EXISTS OPERATOR

The NOT EXISTS operator is the opposite of the EXISTS operator; it tests if a matching row cannot be found. The next query displays the instructors not assigned to any section.

```
SELECT instructor_id, last_name, first_name, zip
  FROM instructor i
 WHERE NOT EXISTS
       (SELECT 'X'
          FROM section
         WHERE i.instructor_id = instructor_id)
```

INSTRUCTOR_ID	LAST_NAME	FIRST_NAME	ZIP
109	Chow	Rick	10015
110	Willig	Irene	

2 rows selected.

You cannot rewrite this particular query using an equijoin, but you can rewrite it with the NOT IN operator. However, the NOT IN operator does not always yield the same result if null values are involved, as you see in the following example.

NOT EXISTS VERSUS NOT IN

Display the INSTRUCTOR_ID, FIRST_NAME, LAST_NAME, and ZIP columns from the INSTRUCTOR table where there is no corresponding zip code in the ZIP-CODE table. Note the ZIP column in the INSTRUCTOR table allows NULL values.

USING NOT EXISTS

```
SELECT instructor_id, last_name, first_name, zip
  FROM instructor i
 WHERE NOT EXISTS
       (SELECT 'X'
          FROM zipcode
         WHERE i.zip = zip)
```

INSTRUCTOR_ID	LAST_NAME	FIRST_NAME	ZIP
110	Willig	Irene	

1 row selected.

USING NOT IN

```
SELECT instructor_id, last_name, first_name, zip
   FROM instructor
  WHERE zip NOT IN
           (SELECT zip
               FROM zipcode)
```

no rows selected

As you can see, the difference between NOT EXISTS and NOT IN lies in the way NULL values are treated. Instructor Irene Willig's ZIP column contains a NULL value. The NOT EXISTS operator tests for NULL values, the NOT IN operator does not.

AVOIDING INCORRECT RESULTS
THROUGH THE USE OF SUBQUERIES

Many SQL statements perform joins, together with aggregate functions. When you join tables together, some values may be repeated as a result of a one-to-many relationship between the joined tables. If you apply an aggregate function to the resulting repeating values, the result of the calculation may be incorrect. The following example shows a listing of the total capacity for courses with enrolled students.

```
SELECT s.course_no, SUM(s.capacity)
   FROM enrollment e, section s
  WHERE e.section_id = s.section_id
  GROUP BY s.course_no
```

COURSE_NO	SUM(S.CAPACITY)
10	15
20	175
...	
420	50
450	25

25 rows selected.

To illustrate that the result is incorrect, look at the value for the capacity column of COURSE_NO 20. The following query shows the capacity for each section, resulting in a total capacity of 80 students, rather than 175 students as seen on the previous result.

```
SELECT section_id, capacity
   FROM section
  WHERE course_no = 20
```

```
SECTION_ID  CAPACITY
----------  --------
    81         15
    82         15
    83         25
    84         25
```

4 rows selected.

A closer look at the effect of the join without the aggregate function reveals the problem.

```
SELECT s.section_id, s.capacity, e.student_id,
       s.course_no
  FROM enrollment e, section s
 WHERE e.section_id = s.section_id
   AND s.course_no = 20
 ORDER BY section_id
```

SECTION_ID	CAPACITY	STUDENT_ID	COURSE_NO
81	15	103	20
81	15	104	20
81	15	240	20
82	15	244	20
82	15	245	20
83	25	124	20
83	25	235	20
84	25	158	20
84	25	199	20

9 rows selected.

For each enrolled student, the capacity record is repeated as the result of the join. This is correct, because for every row in the ENROLLMENT table, the corresponding SECTION_ID is looked up in the SECTION table. But when the SUM aggregate function is applied to the capacity, the capacity value of every returned record is added to the total capacity for each course. To achieve the correct result the query needs to be written as follows.

```
SELECT course_no, SUM(capacity)
  FROM section s
 WHERE EXISTS
       (SELECT NULL
          FROM enrollment e, section sect
         WHERE e.section_id = sect.section_id
           AND sect.course_no = s.course_no)
 GROUP BY course_no
```

```
COURSE_NO SUM(CAPACITY)
--------- -------------
       10    15
       20    80
...
      420    25
      450    25

25 rows selected.
```

The EXISTS operator checks to see if the COURSE_NO exists in the subquery. If it exists, the course has enrollment records for the particular course. The outer query sums up the values for every row of the SECTION table. The EXISTS operator solves this particular problem, but not all queries can be solved this way; some may need to be written using inline views (see Lab 7.3).

LAB 7.2 EXERCISES

7.2.1 WRITE CORRELATED SUBQUERIES

a) Write a correlated subquery to display the SECTION_ID and course number of sections with less than two students enrolled. Remember to include sections that have no students enrolled!

b) Show the sections and their number of enrollments where the enrollment exceeds the capacity of the section, using a correlated subquery.

7.2.2 WRITE CORRELATED SUBQUERIES USING THE *EXISTS* AND *NOT EXISTS* OPERATORS

a) Write a SQL statement to determine the total number of students enrolled using the EXISTS operator. Count students enrolled in more than one course as one.

b) Show the STUDENT_ID, last name, and first name of students enrolled in three or more classes.

c) Which courses do not have sections assigned? Use a correlated subquery in the solution.

d) Which sections have no students enrolled? Use a correlated subquery in the solution and order the result by the course number in ascending order.

LAB 7.2 EXERCISE ANSWERS

7.2.1 ANSWERS

a) Write a correlated subquery to display the SECTION_ID and course number of sections with less than two students enrolled. Remember to include sections that have no students enrolled!

Answer:You query the SECTION table and correlate it with the ENROLLMENT table.

```
SELECT section_id, course_no
  FROM section s
 WHERE 2 >
       (SELECT COUNT(*)
          FROM enrollment
         WHERE section_id = s.section_id)
SECTION_ID COURSE_NO
---------- ---------
        79       350
        80        10

       145       100
       149       120
```

27 rows selected.

For each row of the SECTION table the number literal 2 is compared to the result of the COUNT(*) function of the correlated subquery. The inner query is executed for each row of the outer SECTION table with the S.SECTION_ID column being the correlated column. If no enrollment is found for the particular section, the COUNT function returns a zero; the row satisfies the criteria that 2 is greater than zero and is included in the result set.

For example, for SECTION_ID 80, the subquery returns a count of 1.

```
SELECT COUNT(*)
  FROM enrollment
 WHERE section_id = 80
COUNT(*)
----------
         1
```

1 row selected.

When the number 1 is compared in the WHERE clause of the outer query, you see that 2 > 1 is true; therefore, this section is returned in the result.

You can write two queries to verify that the result is correct. First, write a query that shows sections where the enrollment is less than 2 students. This query returns 13 rows.

```
SELECT section_id, COUNT(*)
  FROM enrollment
 GROUP BY section_id
HAVING COUNT(*) < 2
SECTION_ID   COUNT(*)
----------  ---------
        80          1
        96          1
...
       145          1
       149          1
```

13 rows selected.

Then write a second query to show the sections without any enrollments (i.e., the SECTION_ID does not exist in the ENROLLMENT table). To determine these sections, you can use the NOT IN operator because the SECTION_ID in the EN-ROLLMENT table is defined as NOT NULL.

```
SELECT section_id
  FROM section
 WHERE section_id NOT IN
        (SELECT section_id
           FROM enrollment)
SECTION_ID
----------
        79
        93
...
       136
       139
```

14 rows selected.

The combination of the 13 and 14 rows from the last two queries returns a combined total of 27, as in the exercise solution.

Alternatively, you can combine the results of the two queries with the UNION operator discussed in Chapter 8, "Set Operators."

b) Show the sections and their number of enrollments where the enrollment exceeds the capacity of the section, using a correlated subquery.

Answer: The correlated query solution executes the outer query's GROUP BY clause first; then for every group, the subquery is executed to determine if it satisfies the condition in the HAVING clause. Only sections where the number of enrolled students exceeds the capacity for the respective section are returned for output.

```
SELECT section_id, COUNT(*)
  FROM enrollment e
 GROUP BY section_id
HAVING COUNT(*) >
        (SELECT capacity
           FROM section
          WHERE e.section_id = section_id)
SECTION_ID   COUNT(*)
---------- ---------
       101        12
```

1 row selected.

Alternatively, this can be solved using an equijoin and an aggregate function. The enrollment count is evaluated in the HAVING clause and compared with the capacity. The additional CAPACITY column in the output validates the correct result.

```
SELECT e.section_id, COUNT(*), s.capacity
  FROM enrollment e, section s
 WHERE e.section_id = s.section_id
 GROUP BY e.section_id, s.capacity
HAVING COUNT(*) > s.capacity
SECTION_ID   COUNT(*)   CAPACITY
---------- ---------- --------
       101        12         10
```

1 row selected.

When you join tables and apply aggregate functions, be sure the resulting rows provide the correct result of the aggregate function.

**LAB
7.2**

a) Write a SQL statement to determine the total number of students enrolled using the EXISTS operator. Count students enrolled in more than one course as one.

Answer: For every student, the query checks to see if a row exists in the ENROLLMENT table. If this is true, the record is part of the result set. After Oracle determines all the rows that satisfy the EXISTS condition, the aggregate function COUNT is applied to determine the total number of students.

```
SELECT COUNT(*)
  FROM student s
 WHERE EXISTS
       (SELECT NULL
          FROM enrollment
         WHERE student_id = s.student_id)
COUNT(*)
---------
     165

1 row selected.
```

The same result can be obtained with the next query. Because the ENROLLMENT table may contain multiple STUDENT_IDS if the student is enrolled in several sections, you need to count the distinct occurrences of the STUDENT_ID to obtain the correct result.

```
SELECT COUNT(DISTINCT student_id)
  FROM enrollment
COUNT(DISTINCT STUDENT_ID)
--------------------------
                       165

1 row selected.
```

b) Show the STUDENT_ID, last name, and first name of students enrolled in three or more classes.

Answer: There are four possible solutions: two of them use a correlated subquery, one uses an equijoin, and another uses the IN operator with a subquery.

SOLUTION 1: CORRELATED SUBQUERY

```
SELECT first_name, last_name, student_id
  FROM student s
 WHERE EXISTS
       (SELECT NULL
          FROM enrollment
```

```
        WHERE s.student_id = student_id
        GROUP BY student_id
        HAVING COUNT(*) >= 3)
FIRST_NAME                      LAST_NAME       student_id
----------------------          -------------   ----------
Daniel                          Wicelinski             124
Roger                           Snow                   238
...
Salewa                          Zuckerberg             184
Yvonne                          Williams               214
```

7 rows selected.

For each record in the STUDENT table, the inner query is executed to determine if the STUDENT_ID occurs three or more times in the ENROLLMENT table. The inner query's SELECT clause lists the NULL keyword whereas in the previous examples, a text literal was selected. It is completely irrelevant what columns are selected in the subquery with the EXISTS and NOT EXISTS operators as these operators only check for the existence or nonexistence of rows.

SOLUTION 2: EQUIJOIN

```
SELECT first_name, last_name, student_id
  FROM enrollment e, student s
 WHERE e.student_id = s.student_id
 GROUP BY first_name, last_name, s.student_id
HAVING COUNT(*) >= 3
```

This solution joins the STUDENT and ENROLLMENT tables. Students enrolled multiple times are grouped into one row and the COUNT function counts the occurrences of each student's enrollment record. Only those having three or more records in the ENROLLMENT table are included.

Although Solution 2 achieves the correct result, you need to be aware of the dangers of aggregate functions in joins.

SOLUTION 3: IN SUBQUERY

This subquery returns only STUDENT_IDs with three or more enrollments. The result is then fed to the outer query.

```
SELECT first_name, last_name, student_id
  FROM student
 WHERE student_id IN
       (SELECT student_id
          FROM enrollment
        GROUP BY student_id
       HAVING COUNT(*) >= 3)
```

SOLUTION 4: ANOTHER CORRELATED SUBQUERY

The number literal 3 is compared to the result of the correlated subquery. It counts the enrollment records for each individual student. This solution is similar to the solution in Exercise 7.2.1a.

```
SELECT last_name, first_name, student_id
  FROM student s
 WHERE 3 <= (SELECT COUNT(*)
               FROM enrollment
              WHERE s.student_id = student_id)
```

c) Which courses do not have sections assigned? Use a correlated subquery in the solution.

Answer: For every course in the COURSE table, the NOT EXISTS condition probes the SECTION table to determine if a row with the same course number exists. If the course number is not found, the WHERE clause evaluates to true and the record is included in the result set.

```
SELECT course_no, description
  FROM course c
 WHERE NOT EXISTS
       (SELECT 'X'
          FROM section
         WHERE c.course_no = course_no)
```

COURSE_NO DESCRIPTION
```
--------- ----------------------------------
       80 Structured Programming Techniques
      430 JDeveloper Techniques
```

2 rows selected.

Note you can also write the query as follows:

```
SELECT course_no, description
  FROM course c
 WHERE NOT EXISTS
       (SELECT 'X'
          FROM section s
         WHERE c.course_no = s.course_no)
```

The SECTION table uses the table alias s which the S.COURSE_NO column refers to. This alias is not required; it simply clarifies the column's source table. When you use column(s) without an alias, it is understood that the column(s) refers to the table in the current subquery. However, you must use a table alias for the C.COURSE_NO column, referencing the COURSE_NO in the outer query; otherwise, the query is not correlated.

As an alternative, the same result can be obtained using the NOT IN operator. Because the COURSE_NO column in the SECTION table is defined as NOT NULL, the query returns the same result.

```
SELECT course_no, description
  FROM course
 WHERE course_no NOT IN
         (SELECT course_no
            FROM section)
```

d) Which sections have no students enrolled? Use a correlated subquery in the solution and order the result by the course number in ascending order.

Answer: The result contains only rows where the SECTION_ID does not exist in the EN-ROLLMENT table. The inner query executes for each row of the outer query.

```
SELECT course_no, section_id
  FROM section s
 WHERE NOT EXISTS
         (SELECT NULL
            FROM enrollment
           WHERE s.section_id = section_id)
 ORDER BY course_no
```

COURSE_NO	SECTION_ID
25	93
124	129
...	
350	79

14 rows selected.

You can achieve the same result using the NOT IN operator because the SECTION_ID column in the ENROLLMENT table is defined as NOT NULL.

```
SELECT course_no, section_id
  FROM section
 WHERE section_id NOT IN
         (SELECT section_id
            FROM enrollment)
 ORDER BY course_no
```

LAB 7.2 SELF-REVIEW QUESTIONS

In order to test your progress, you should be able to answer the following questions.

1) The NOT EXISTS operator tests for occurrences of nulls.

   a) _____ True
   b) _____ False

2) In a correlated subquery the inner query is executed repeatedly.

   a) _____ True
   b) _____ False

3) The operators IN and EXISTS are equivalent.

   a) _____ True
   b) _____ False

4) Determine the correct question for the following SQL statement.

```
SELECT student_id, section_id
  FROM enrollment e
 WHERE NOT EXISTS
         (SELECT '1'
            FROM grade g
           WHERE e.section_id = section_id)
             AND e.student_id = student_id)
```

   a) _____ Show the enrolled students and their respective sections that have grades assigned.
   b) _____ Determine the students and their sections where no grades have been assigned.
   c) _____ Determine which students are not enrolled.
   d) _____ Determine the students that are not enrolled and do not have grades.
   e) _____ This is an invalid query.

5) Always evaluate the result of a join first, before applying an aggregate function.

   a) _____ True
   b) _____ False

6) The following SQL statement is valid.

```
1  SELECT *
2    FROM student
3   WHERE (SELECT student_id
4            FROM enrollment
5           WHERE section_id) = student_id
```

a) _____ True
b) _____ False

Answers appear in Appendix A, Section 7.2.

L A B   7 . 3

INLINE VIEWS, SCALAR SUBQUERY EXPRESSIONS, AND THE SUBQUERY WITH CLAUSE

LAB OBJECTIVES

After this lab, you will be able to:

✔ Write Inline Views, Write Scalar Subquery Expressions, and Utilize the WITH Clause

---

INLINE VIEWS

Inline views, also referred to as queries in the FROM clause, allow you to treat a query as a virtual table or view. The following example illustrates the concept of the inline view.

```
SELECT e.student_id, e.section_id, s.last_name
  FROM (SELECT student_id, section_id, enroll_date
          FROM enrollment
         WHERE student_id = 123) e,
        student s
 WHERE e.student_id = s.student_id
STUDENT_ID SECTION_ID LAST_NAME
---------- ---------- ----------
       123         87 Radicola

1 row selected.
```

The inline view is written in the FROM clause of the query and receives an alias called e. The result of this query is evaluated and executed first, and then the result is joined to the STUDENT table.

The inline view acts just like a virtual table, or, for that matter, like a view. A view is a query definition stored in the database that looks just like a table. It does not have any physical rows, because a view is actually a stored query that is only executed when the view is accessed. You learn more about views in Chapter 12, "Views, Indexes, and Sequences."

The difference between a view and an inline view is that the inline view does not need to be created and stored in the data dictionary. You can create this inline view or virtual table by placing your query into the FROM clause of a SQL statement.

Inline view queries may look very complicated, but are very easy to understand. They allow you to break down complex problems into simple queries. The following query uses two inline views to return the actual number of enrollments for course number 20 and joins this result to the capacity of the course. The actual and potential revenue is then computed by multiplying the course cost with the number of enrollments and the respective capacity of the course.

```
SELECT enr.num_enrolled "Enrollments",
       enr.num_enrolled * c.cost "Actual Revenue",
       cap.capacity "Total Capacity",
       cap.capacity * c.cost "Potential Revenue"
  FROM (SELECT COUNT(*) num_enrolled
          FROM enrollment e, section s
         WHERE s.course_no = 20
           AND s.section_id = e.section_id) enr,
       (SELECT SUM(capacity) capacity
          FROM section
         WHERE course_no = 20) cap,
       course c
 WHERE c.course_no = 20
```

Enrollments	Actual Revenue	Total Capacity	Potential Revenue
9	10755	80	95600

1 row selected.

The easiest way to understand the query is to look at the result set for each inline view. The first query, referenced with the alias ENR, returns the number of students enrolled in course number 20. It requires a join between the ENROLLMENT and the SECTION table, because the number of students enrolled per section is in the ENROLLMENT table and the COURSE_NO column is found in the SECTION table. The column joining the two tables is the SECTION_ID. The query returns one row and indicates that 9 students are enrolled in course number 20.

```
SELECT COUNT(*) num_enrolled
  FROM enrollment e, section s
 WHERE s.course_no = 20
   AND s.section_id = e.section_id
NUM_ENROLLED
------------
           9
```

1 row selected.

The second query, with the alias CAP, uses the aggregate function SUM to add all the values in the CAPACITY column for course number 20. Since the SUM function is an aggregate function, it returns one row with the total capacity of 80 for all the sections for course number of 20.

```
SELECT SUM(capacity) capacity
  FROM section
 WHERE course_no = 20
CAPACITY
---------
       80
```

1 row selected.

The last table in the FROM clause of the query is the COURSE table. This table holds the course cost to compute the actual revenue and the potential revenue. The query also retrieves one row.

Note the results of the inline views, which are identified with the aliases ENR and CAP, are not joined together with the COURSE table, thus creating a Cartesian product. Because a multiplication of the number of rows from each inline view, 1*1*1, results in one row, this query returns the one row for course number 20. A join condition is not required in this case, but can be added for clarification if so desired.

TOP-N QUERY

An example of a top-n query is a query allowing you to determine the top three students for a particular section. The ROWNUM pseudocolumn, together with an inline view, helps achieve this result. A pseudocolumn is not a real column in a table; you can select from this column, but you cannot manipulate its values. You will learn more about other pseudocolumns (e.g., LEVEL, NEXTVAL, CURRVAL, and ROWID) throughout this workbook.

The ROWNUM pseudocolumn returns a number indicating the order in which Oracle returns the rows from a table or set of tables. You can use ROWNUM to limit the number of rows returned, as in the following example. It returns the first five rows.

```
SELECT last_name, first_name
  FROM student
 WHERE ROWNUM <=5
LAST_NAME                            FIRST_NAME
-------------------------            -----------
Eakheit                              George
Millstein                            Leonard
Cadet                                Austin V.
Zapulla                              Tamara
Goldsmith                            Jenny
```

5 rows selected.

To determine the three highest final examination grades of section 101, combine the ROWNUM pseudocolumn together with an inline view as follows.

```
SELECT ROWNUM, numeric_grade
  FROM (SELECT DISTINCT numeric_grade
          FROM grade
         WHERE section_id = 101
           AND grade_type_code = 'FI'
         ORDER BY numeric_grade DESC)
 WHERE ROWNUM <= 3
    ROWNUM NUMERIC_GRADE
--------- -------------
        1            99
        2            92
        3            91
```

3 rows selected.

The inline view selects the distinct values in the NUMERIC_GRADE column for all final examination grades where the SECTION_ID equals 101. This result is ordered by the NUMERIC_GRADE in descending order, with the highest NUMERIC_GRADE listed first. The outer query uses the ordered result of the inline view and the ROWNUM column to return only the first three. By ordering the results within the inline view this construct provides a method to both limit and order the number of rows returned. For even more sophisticated ranking functionality and more on analytical and statistical functions refer to Chapter 15, "Advanced SQL Queries."

SCALAR SUBQUERY EXPRESSIONS

You already learned about the scalar subquery, which is a query returning a single-column, single-row value. You can use a scalar subquery expression in most syntax that calls for an expression. The next examples show you how to use this functionality in the SELECT list, the WHERE clause, the ORDER BY clause of a query, a CASE expression, or as part of a function call.

SCALAR SUBQUERY EXPRESSION IN THE SELECT CLAUSE

This query returns all the Connecticut zip codes and a count of how many students live in each zip code. The query is correlated as the scalar subquery and it is executed for each individual zip code. For some zip codes, no students are in the STUDENT table; therefore, the subquery's COUNT function returns a zero. The query can also be written as an outer join discussed in Chapter 9, "Complex Joins."

**LAB
7.3**

```
SELECT city, state, zip,
       (SELECT COUNT(*)
          FROM student s
         WHERE s.zip = z.zip) AS student_count
  FROM zipcode z
 WHERE state = 'CT'
```

CITY	ST	ZIP	STUDENT_COUNT
Ansonia	CT	06401	0
...			
Stamford	CT	06907	1

19 rows selected.

Note that scalar subquery expressions can become notoriously inefficient because Oracle can often execute table joins in a more efficient manner, particularly when scans of the entire result set are involved. Following is one example where the results of an equijoin is achieved using a scalar subquery.

```
SELECT student_id, last_name,
       (SELECT state
          FROM zipcode z
         WHERE z.zip = s.zip) AS state
  FROM student s
 WHERE student_id BETWEEN 100 AND 120
```

STUDENT_ID	LAST_NAME	ST
102	Crocitto	NY
...		
120	Alexander	NY

17 rows selected.

SCALAR SUBQUERY EXPRESSION IN THE WHERE CLAUSE

The next query is an example of a scalar subquery expression in the WHERE clause of a SELECT statement. The result shows the students that enrolled in more courses than the average student. The equivalent equijoin is probably more efficient.

```
SELECT student_id, last_name
  FROM student s
 WHERE (SELECT COUNT(*)
          FROM enrollment e
         WHERE s.student_id = e.student_id) >
              (SELECT AVG(COUNT(*))
                 FROM enrollment
                GROUP BY student_id)
 ORDER BY 1
STUDENT_ID LAST_NAME
---------- ---------------
       102 Crocitto
...
       283 Perkins

52 rows selected.
```

SCALAR SUBQUERY EXPRESSION IN THE ORDER BY CLAUSE

You may wonder why you need to ever execute a scalar subquery expression in the ORDER BY clause. The next example illustrates that you can ORDER BY a column that does not even exist in the STUDENT table or is not displayed in the query. The query lists the STUDENT_ID and LAST_NAME columns of those students with an ID between 150 and 160. The result is ordered by the number of courses a respective student is enrolled in. If you execute a separate query to verify the result, you will notice that student Brendler is enrolled in one section and the student called Jung in three sections.

```
SELECT student_id, last_name
  FROM student s
 WHERE student_id BETWEEN 230 AND 235
 ORDER BY (SELECT COUNT(*)
             FROM enrollment e
            WHERE s.student_id = e.student_id) DESC
STUDENT_ID LAST_NAME
---------- ------------
       232 Jung
...
       234 Brendler

5 rows selected.
```

SCALAR SUBQUERY EXPRESSION AND THE CASE EXPRESSION

Scalar subquery expressions are particularly handy in CASE expressions or within the DECODE function. The following example demonstrates their extraordinarily powerful functionality. The SELECT statement lists the costs of courses with the

COURSE_NO of 20 and 80. The column labeled "Test CASE" illustrates the result of the CASE expression.

Depending on the value of the COST column, a comparison against a scalar subquery expression is executed. For example, the COST column is compared to the average COST of all courses and if the value in the COST column is less than or equal to that average, the value in the COST column is multiplied by 1.5.

The next WHEN comparison checks to see if the cost is equal to the highest course cost and if so it displays the value of the COST column for COURSE_NO 20. Note that if the scalar subquery expression determines that the row with the COURSE_NO 20 does not exist, the scalar subquery expression will evaluate to a null.

```
SELECT course_no, cost,
       CASE WHEN cost <= (SELECT AVG(cost) FROM course) THEN
                  cost *1.5
            WHEN cost =  (SELECT MAX(cost) FROM course) THEN
                         (SELECT cost FROM course WHERE
                          course_no = 20)
            ELSE cost
       END "Test CASE"
  FROM course
 WHERE course_no IN (20, 80)
 ORDER BY 2
COURSE_NO      COST Test CASE
--------- --------- ---------
       20      1195    1792.5
       80      1595      1195
```

2 rows selected.

The next example shows the use of the scalar subquery expression in the condition part of the CASE expression. The cost of course number 134, which happens to be 1195, is multiplied by 2, effectively doubling the cost. This result is then compared to see if it's less than or equal to the average cost of all courses.

```
SELECT course_no, cost,
       CASE WHEN (SELECT cost*2
                    FROM course
                   WHERE course_no = 134)
                <= (SELECT AVG(cost) FROM course) THEN
                      cost *1.5
            WHEN cost =  (SELECT MAX(cost) FROM course) THEN
                         (SELECT cost FROM course WHERE
                          course_no = 20)
            ELSE cost
       END "Test CASE"
  FROM course
```

```
WHERE course_no IN (20, 80)
ORDER BY 2
COURSE_NO     COST  Test CASE
----------  --------- ----------
       20      1195       1195
       80      1595       1195
```

2 rows selected.

SCALAR SUBQUERY EXPRESSIONS AND FUNCTIONS

The next example shows the use of the scalar subquery expression within a function. For every retrieved row, the UPPER function is executed, which in turn retrieves the respective student's last name from the STUDENT table. A join between the STUDENT and ENROLLMENT table to retrieve the same information is typically more efficient, but the example illustrates another of the many versatile uses of scalar subquery expressions.

```
SELECT student_id, section_id,
       UPPER((SELECT last_name
               FROM student s
              WHERE student_id = e.student_id))
       "Last Name in Caps"
  FROM enrollment e
 WHERE student_id BETWEEN 100 AND 110
STUDENT_ID SECTION_ID Last Name in Caps
---------- ---------- -------------------------
       102         86 CROCITTO
       102         89 CROCITTO
...
       110         95 MARTIN
       110        154 MARTIN
```

13 rows selected.

ERRORS IN SCALAR SUBQUERY EXPRESSIONS

Just like you learned in Lab 7.1, the scalar subquery expression must always return one row, otherwise the error message `ORA-01427: single-row subquery returns more than one row` is returned by Oracle. If your subquery does not return any rows, a null value is returned.

SUBQUERIES AND THE WITH CLAUSE

The WITH clause, also referred to as the *subquery factoring clause*, offers the benefit of re-using a query when it occurs more than once within the same statement. Instead of storing the query results in a temporary table and performing queries against this temporary table, you can use the WITH clause; it gives the query a name and allows you to reference it multiple times. This avoids a re-read and re-execution of the query, which improves overall query execution time and resources utilization, particularly when very large tables and/or joins are involved. The WITH clause also simplifies the writing of SQL statements.

The WITH keyword identifies that multiple SQL statements are involved. The following example determines the revenue generated by each instructor. The query result returns only those instructors and their respective revenue that have a greater than average revenue generated by all instructors combined.

The WITH clause creates a name for the "temporary" result called REVENUE_PER_INSTRUCTOR. This result is then referred to in the subsequent SELECT statements within the context of the original query.

```
WITH
revenue_per_instructor AS
(SELECT instructor_id, SUM(cost) AS revenue
   FROM section s, course c, enrollment e
  WHERE s.section_id = e.section_id
    AND c.course_no = s.course_no
  GROUP BY instructor_id)
SELECT *
  FROM revenue_per_instructor
 WHERE revenue > (SELECT AVG(revenue)
                    FROM revenue_per_instructor)
```

INSTRUCTOR_ID	REVENUE
101	51380
103	44215
107	35745
108	39235

4 rows selected.

Because the REVENUE_PER_INSTRUCTOR query involves a join and an aggregate function, it is useful to examine the result of the join to ensure the accuracy of the aggregate function.

```
SELECT instructor_id, cost, s.section_id, student_id
  FROM section s, course c, enrollment e
 WHERE s.section_id = e.section_id
   AND c.course_no = s.course_no
 ORDER BY instructor_id
```

INSTRUCTOR_ID	COST	SECTION_ID	STUDENT_ID
101	1195	87	256
...			
105	1195	152	138
105	1195	152	144

105	1195	152	206
105	1195	152	207
105	1195	144	153
105	1195	144	200
105	1095	113	129
105	1195	105	202
105	1195	91	232
105	1195	105	263
105	1195	105	261
105	1195	105	259
105	1195	105	260
105	1195	83	124
105	1195	91	271
...			
108	1195	86	102

226 rows selected.

For example, review INSTRUCTOR_ID 105. Effectively, the SUM function adds up all the individual values of the COST column resulting in a total of 19020. Adding the GROUP BY and the SUM function to the joined tables produces this output, which is identical to the result achieved by the REVENUE_PER_INSTRUCTOR query:

```
SELECT instructor_id, SUM(cost)
  FROM section s, course c, enrollment
 WHERE s.section_id = e.section_id
   AND c.course_no = s.course_no
 GROUP BY instructor_id
INSTRUCTOR_ID  SUM(COST)
-------------  ----------
          101      51380
          102      24995
          103      44215
          104      29675
          105      19020
          106      21510
          107      35745
          108      39235
```

8 rows selected.

To determine the average revenue for all instructors, you nest the two aggregate functions AVG and SUM. The REVENUE_PER_INSTRUCTOR, however, reuses the previous result instead of executing the following query.

```
SELECT AVG(SUM(cost))
  FROM section s, course c, enrollment e
 WHERE s.section_id = e.section_id
```

```
   AND c.course_no = s.course_no
GROUP BY INSTRUCTOR_ID
AVG(SUM(COST))
--------------
     33221.875
```

1 row selected.

Without the subquery factoring clause you will need to write the following statement, which effectively performs the reading of the tables and the join twice—once for the subquery and once for the outer query. This requires more resources and consumes more time than writing the query with the subquery factoring clause, particularly when large tables, many joins, and complex aggregations are involved.

```
SELECT instructor_id, SUM(cost) AS revenue
  FROM section s, course c, enrollment e
 WHERE s.section_id = e.section_id
   AND c.course_no = s.course_no
 GROUP BY instructor_id
HAVING SUM(cost) > (SELECT AVG(SUM(cost))
              FROM section s, course c, enrollment e
             WHERE s.section_id = e.section_id
               AND c.course_no = s.course_no
             GROUP BY instructor_id)
```

INSTRUCTOR_ID	REVENUE
101	51380
103	44215
107	35745
108	39235

4 rows selected.

Do not confuse the WITH clause in subqueries with the START WITH clause used in hierarchical queries, discussed in Chapter 15, "Advanced SQL Queries."

LAB 7.3 EXERCISES

7.3.1 WRITE INLINE VIEWS, WRITE SCALAR SUBQUERY EXPRESSIONS, AND UTILIZE THE WITH CLAUSE

a) Write the query that displays the SECTION_ID and COURSE_NO columns along with the number of students enrolled for sections with the ID of 93, 101, and 103. Utilize a scalar subquery to write the query. The result should look similar to the following output.

```
SECTION_ID COURSE_NO NUM_ENROLLED
---------- --------- ------------
        93        25            0
       103       310            4
       101       240           12

3 rows selected.
```

b) Write the exercise question that is answered by the following query.

```
SELECT g.student_id, section_id, g.numeric_grade,
       gr.average
  FROM grade g JOIN
       (SELECT section_id, AVG(numeric_grade) average
          FROM grade
         WHERE section_id IN (94, 106)
           AND grade_type_code = 'FI'
         GROUP BY section_id) gr
 USING (section_id)
 WHERE g.grade_type_code = 'FI'
   AND g.numeric_grade > gr.average
```

```
STUDENT_ID SECTION_ID NUMERIC_GRADE   AVERAGE
---------- ---------- ------------- ---------
       140         94            85      84.5
       200        106            92        89
       145        106            91        89
       130        106            90        89

4 rows selected.
```

c) For each course number, display the total capacity of the individual sections. Include the number of students enrolled and the percentage of the course that is filled. The result should look similar to the following output.

COURSE_NO	TOTAL_CAPACITY	TOTAL_STUDENTS	Filled Percentage
240	25	13	52
230	27	14	51.85
...			
450	25	1	4
134	65	2	3.08

25 rows selected.

d) Determine the top five courses with the largest number of enrollments.

e) Explain the result of this query.

```
WITH
num_enroll AS
(SELECT COUNT(*) num_students, course_no
  FROM enrollment e JOIN section s
 USING (section_id)
 GROUP BY course_no),
avg_stud_enroll AS
(SELECT AVG(num_students) avg#_of_stud
  FROM num_enroll
 WHERE num_students <> (SELECT MAX(num_students)
                         FROM num_enroll))
SELECT course_no, num_students
  FROM num_enroll
 WHERE num_students > (SELECT avg#_of_stud
                        FROM avg_stud_enroll)
   AND num_students < (SELECT MAX(num_students)
                        FROM num_enroll)
```

LAB 7.3 EXERCISE ANSWERS

7.3.1 ANSWERS

a) Write the query that displays the SECTION_ID and COURSE_NO columns along with the number of students enrolled for sections with the ID of 93, 101, and 103. Utilize a scalar subquery to write the query. The result should look similar to the following output.

```
SECTION_ID COURSE_NO NUM_ENROLLED
---------- --------- ------------
        93        25            0
       103       310            4
       101       240           12
```

3 rows selected.

Answer: This query uses a scalar subquery in the SELECT clause of the SQL statement. The scalar subquery is correlated and determines for each of the three SECTION_ID values the number of rows in the ENROLLMENT table.

```
SELECT section_id, course_no,
       (SELECT COUNT(*)
          FROM enrollment e
         WHERE s.section_id = e.section_id)
       AS num_enrolled
  FROM section s
 WHERE section_id IN (101, 103, 93)
```

b) Write the question that is answered by the following query.

```
SELECT g.student_id, section_id, g.numeric_grade,
       gr.average
  FROM grade g JOIN
       (SELECT section_id, AVG(numeric_grade) average
          FROM grade
         WHERE section_id IN (94, 106)
           AND grade_type_code = 'FI'
         GROUP BY section_id) gr
 USING (section_id)
 WHERE g.grade_type_code = 'FI'
   AND g.numeric_grade > gr.average
```

STUDENT_ID	SECTION_ID	NUMERIC_GRADE	AVERAGE
140	94	85	84.5
200	106	92	89
145	106	91	89
130	106	90	89

4 rows selected.

Answer: Show for sections 94 and 106 those students that have a final examination grade higher than the average for each respective section.

The inline view determines the average final examination grade for each of the sections 94 and 106. This query is executed first. The result is then joined with the GRADE table where the SECTION_ID column agrees. The filtering criteria is that the GRADE_TYPE_CODE column equals to 'FI', which stands for final examination grade, and the last condition chooses only those rows that have a grade higher than the average for each respective section.

c) For each course number, display the total capacity of the individual sections. Include the number of students enrolled and the percentage of the course that is filled. The result should look similar to the following output.

COURSE_NO	TOTAL_CAPACITY	TOTAL_STUDENTS	Filled Percentage
240	25	13	52
230	27	14	51.85
...			
450	25	1	4
134	65	2	3.08

25 rows selected.

Answer: The query uses inline views to retrieve the total capacity and number of students enrolled. The percentage filled column is calculated using the resulting values from the inline views and is used to order the result.

```
SELECT a.course_no, total_capacity, total_students,
       ROUND(100/total_capacity*total_students, 2)
       "Filled Percentage"
  FROM (SELECT COUNT(*) total_students, s.course_no
          FROM enrollment e, section s
         WHERE e.section_id = s.section_id
         GROUP BY s.course_no) a,
       (SELECT SUM(capacity) total_capacity, course_no
          FROM section
         GROUP BY course_no) b
 WHERE b.course_no = a.course_no
 ORDER BY "Filled Percentage" DESC
```

It helps to build the query step by step by looking at the individual queries. The first query, with the alias a, returns the total number of students enrolled for each course.

```
SELECT COUNT(*) total_students, s.course_no
  FROM enrollment e, section s
 WHERE e.section_id = s.section_id
 GROUP BY s.course_no
TOTAL_STUDENTS COURSE_NO
-------------- ---------
             1        10
             9        20
...
             2       420
             1       450

25 rows selected.
```

The second query, with the alias b, returns the total capacity for each course.

```
SELECT SUM(capacity) total_capacity, course_no
  FROM section
 GROUP BY course_no
TOTAL_CAPACITY COURSE_NO
-------------- ---------
            15        10
            80        20
...
            25       420
            25       450

28 rows selected.
```

Then, the two queries are joined by the common column, the COURSE_NO, using the aliases a and b assigned in the inline view queries. The outer query references the columns TOTAL_STUDENTS and TOTAL_CAPACITY. The ROUND function computes the percentage with a two-digit precision after the comma. The result is sorted by this percentage in descending order.

d) Determine the top five courses with the largest number of enrollments.

Answer: This question is solved with an inline view and the ROWNUM pseudocolumn.

```
SELECT ROWNUM Ranking, course_no, num_enrolled
  FROM (SELECT COUNT(*) num_enrolled, s.course_no
          FROM enrollment e, section s
         WHERE e.section_id = s.section_id
         GROUP BY s.course_no
         ORDER BY 1 DESC)
 WHERE ROWNUM <= 5
```

RANKING	COURSE_NO	NUM_ENROLLED
1	25	45
2	122	24
3	120	23
4	140	15
5	230	14

`5 rows selected.`

e) Explain the result of this query.

```
WITH
num_enroll AS
(SELECT COUNT(*) num_students, course_no
  FROM enrollment e JOIN section s
 USING (section_id)
 GROUP BY course_no),
avg_stud_enroll AS
(SELECT AVG(num_students) avg#_of_stud
  FROM num_enroll
 WHERE num_students <> (SELECT MAX(num_students)
                        FROM num_enroll))
SELECT course_no, num_students
  FROM num_enroll
 WHERE num_students > (SELECT avg#_of_stud
                        FROM avg_stud_enroll)
   AND num_students < (SELECT MAX(num_students)
                        FROM num_enroll)
```

Answer:The query will return those courses and the respective enrollment above the average enrollment per course, excluding any courses with the highest enrollment.

COURSE_NO	NUM_STUDENTS
20	9
100	13
120	23
122	24
124	8
125	8
130	8
140	15
230	14
240	13
350	9

`11 rows selected.`

This query uses two inline queries NUM_ENROLL and AVG_STUD_ENROLL. The first query, called NUM_ENROLL, computes the number of enrolled students per course. The second query, labeled AVG_STUD_ENROLL, uses the previous query to determine the average number of students enrolled excluding the course with the highest enrollment. The last query shows the COURSE_NO column together with the number of enrolled students where the course has an enrollment that is higher than the average enrollment. Remember this average excludes the course with the highest enrollment. The last condition specifically excludes the course with the highest enrollment in the result as it would otherwise be included as it obviously has a higher than average enrollment.

As you discovered already, the SQL language allows many different ways of expressing a query and still achieving the same result. The differences often lie in the efficiency of the statement. The result can also be obtained using this query; notice that several joins are required with each execution of the condition, thus requiring more resources and time than simply re-using the temporarily stored query result. Furthermore, the WITH clause breaks down the problem into individual pieces, therefore simplifying the writing of complex queries.

```
SELECT course_no, COUNT(*) num_students
  FROM enrollment e JOIN section s
 USING (section_id)
 GROUP BY course_no
HAVING COUNT(*) > (SELECT AVG(COUNT(*))
                     FROM enrollment e JOIN section s
                    USING (section_id)
                    GROUP BY course_no
                   HAVING COUNT(*) <> (SELECT MAX(COUNT(*))
                                         FROM enrollment e JOIN
                                         section s
                                        USING (section_id)
                                        GROUP BY course_no))
   AND COUNT(*) <>(SELECT MAX(COUNT(*))
                     FROM enrollment e JOIN section s
                    USING (section_id)
                    GROUP BY course_no)
```

LAB 7.3 SELF-REVIEW QUESTIONS

In order to test your progress, you should be able to answer the following questions.

1) Scalar subquery expressions are not allowed in the GROUP BY clause.

a) _____ True
b) _____ False

2) Scalar subqueries return one or more rows.

   a) _____ True
   b) _____ False

3) Inline views are stored in the data dictionary.

   a) _____ True
   b) _____ False

4) The ROWNUM is an actual column in a table.

   a) _____ True
   b) _____ False

5) The ORDER BY clause is allowed in an inline view.

   a) _____ True
   b) _____ False

Answers appear in Appendix A, Section 7.3.

LAB 7.4

ANY, SOME, AND ALL OPERATORS IN SUBQUERIES

> ### LAB OBJECTIVES
>
> After this lab, you will be able to:
>
> ✔ Use the ANY, SOME, and ALL Operators in Subqueries

You are already familiar with the IN operator, which compares a list of values for equality. The ANY, SOME, and ALL operators are related to the IN operator as they also compare against a list of values. Additionally, these operators allow >, <, >=, and <= comparisons.

The ANY operator checks whether any value in the list makes the condition true. The ALL operator returns rows if the condition is true for all the values in the list. The SOME operator is identical to ANY and the two can be used interchangeably. Before applying these operators to subqueries, examine their effect on a simple list of values.

This query retrieves all the grades for SECTION_ID 84.

```
SELECT section_id, numeric_grade
  FROM grade
 WHERE section_id = 84
```

SECTION_ID	NUMERIC_GRADE
84	88
84	99
84	77
84	88

4 rows selected.

The familiar IN operator in the next SQL statement chooses all the grades that are either equal to 77 or equal to 99.

```
SELECT section_id, numeric_grade
  FROM grade
 WHERE section_id = 84
   AND numeric_grade IN (77, 99)
SECTION_ID NUMERIC_GRADE
---------- -------------
        84            99
        84            77
```

2 rows selected.

If you want to perform a comparison such as less than (<) against a list of values, use either the ANY, SOME, or ALL operator.

ANY AND SOME

This SQL query looks for any rows where the value in the NUMERIC_GRADE column is less than either value in the list.

```
SELECT section_id, numeric_grade
  FROM grade
 WHERE section_id = 84
   AND numeric_grade < ANY (80, 90)
SECTION_ID NUMERIC_GRADE
---------- -------------
        84            88
        84            88
        84            77
```

3 rows selected.

The query returns the NUMERIC_GRADE values 77 and 88. For the rows with the NUMERIC_GRADE of 88, the condition is true as 88 is less than 90, but the condition is not true for the value 80. However, because the condition needs to be true for any of the records compared in the list, the row is included in the result.

The following query performs a greater-than comparison with the ANY operator.

```
SELECT section_id, numeric_grade
  FROM grade
 WHERE section_id = 84
   AND numeric_grade > ANY (80, 90)
```

```
SECTION_ID NUMERIC_GRADE
---------- -------------
        84            88
        84            99
        84            88
```

3 rows selected.

Because the records with the NUMERIC_GRADE 88 are greater than 80, they are included. The NUMERIC_GRADE of 99 is greater than both 80 and 90, and, therefore, is also included in the result set, although just one of the conditions is sufficient to be included in the result set.

The ANY operator with the = operator is the equivalent of the IN operator. There are no rows that have a NUMERIC_GRADE of either 80 or 90.

```
SELECT section_id, numeric_grade
  FROM grade
 WHERE section_id = 84
   AND numeric_grade = ANY (80, 90)
```

no rows selected

The following query is the logical equivalent to the IN operator.

```
SELECT section_id, numeric_grade
  FROM grade
 WHERE section_id = 84
   AND numeric_grade IN (80, 90)
```

no rows selected

ALL

The ALL operator returns true if every value in the list satisfies the condition. In the following example, all the records in the GRADE table must be less than 80 and 90. This condition is true only for the row with the NUMERIC_GRADE value of 77, which is less than both 80 and 90.

```
SELECT section_id, numeric_grade
  FROM grade
 WHERE section_id = 84
   AND numeric_grade < ALL (80, 90)
SECTION_ID NUMERIC_GRADE
---------- -------------
        84            77
```

1 row selected.

LAB
7.4

A SQL statement using <> ALL is equivalent to NOT IN.

```
SELECT section_id, numeric_grade
  FROM grade
 WHERE section_id = 84
   AND numeric_grade <> ALL (80, 90)
SECTION_ID NUMERIC_GRADE
---------- -------------
        84            88
        84            99
        84            77
        84            88

4 rows selected.
```

LAB 7.4

Whenever a subquery with the ALL operator fails to return a row, the query is automatically true. This is different from the ANY operator, which returns false.

LAB 7.4 EXERCISES

7.4.1 USE THE ANY, SOME, AND ALL OPERATORS IN SUBQUERIES

a) Write a SELECT statement to display the STUDENT_ID, SECTION_ID, and grade for students who received a final examination grade better than *all* of their individual homework grades.

b) Based on the result of question a, what do you observe about the row with the STUDENT_ID 102 and the SECTION_ID 89?

c) Select the STUDENT_ID, SECTION_ID, and grade of students who received a final examination grade better than *any* of their individual homework grades.

d) Based on question c, explain the result of the row with the STUDENT_ID 102 and the SECTION_ID 89.

LAB 7.4 EXERCISE ANSWERS

7.4.1 ANSWERS

a) Write a SELECT statement to display the STUDENT_ID, SECTION_ID, and grade for students who received a final examination grade better than *all* of their individual homework grades.

Answer: A correlated subquery is used to compare each individual student's final examination grade with his or her respective homework grades for a particular section. The output includes only those records where the final examination grade is higher than all of the homework grades.

```
SELECT student_id, section_id, numeric_grade
  FROM grade g
 WHERE grade_type_code = 'FI'
   AND numeric_grade > ALL
        (SELECT numeric_grade
           FROM grade
          WHERE grade_type_code = 'HM'
            AND g.section_id = section_id
            AND g.student_id = student_id)
```

STUDENT_ID	SECTION_ID	NUMERIC_GRADE
102	89	92
124	83	99
143	85	92
...		
215	156	90
283	99	85

96 rows selected.

To verify the result, use the STUDENT_ID 143 and SECTION_ID 85 as an example. The highest grade for all of the homework is 91 and the lowest is 81. The grade achieved in the final examination is 92.

```
    SELECT student_id, section_id, grade_type_code,
           MAX(numeric_grade) max, MIN(numeric_grade) min
      FROM grade
     WHERE student_id = 143
       AND section_id = 85
       AND grade_type_code IN ('HM', 'FI')
     GROUP BY student_id, section_id, grade_type_code
```

```
STUDENT_ID SECTION_ID GR        MAX       MIN
---------- ---------- --  --------- ---------
       143         85 FI         92        92
       143         85 HM         91        81
```

```
2 rows selected.
```

The student with the ID of 143 enrolled in section 85 is correctly selected for output as it satisfies the condition that the final examination grade be greater than all of the homework grades.

The following query verifies that the student with the ID of 179 enrolled in section 116 has a lower grade in the final exam than in all the homework grades. Therefore, the row is not included in the set.

```
SELECT student_id, section_id, grade_type_code,
       MAX(numeric_grade) max, MIN(numeric_grade) min
  FROM grade
 WHERE student_id = 179
   AND section_id = 116
   AND grade_type_code IN ('HM', 'FI')
 GROUP BY student_id, section_id, grade_type_code
STUDENT_ID SECTION_ID GR        MAX        MIN
---------- ---------- --  --------- ----------
       179        116 FI         90         90
       179        116 HM         99         99
```

```
2 rows selected.
```

b) Based on the result of question a, what do you observe about the row with the STUDENT_ID 102 and the SECTION_ID 89?

Answer: Whenever the subquery with the ALL operator fails to return a row, the query is automatically true. Therefore, this student is also included in the result set.

The interesting aspect of the relationship between ALL and NULL is that here the student for this section has no homework grades, yet the row is returned for output.

```
SELECT student_id, section_id, grade_type_code,
       MAX(numeric_grade) max, MIN(numeric_grade) min
  FROM grade
 WHERE student_id = 102
   AND section_id = 89
   AND grade_type_code IN ('HM', 'FI')
 GROUP BY student_id, section_id, grade_type_code
STUDENT_ID SECTION_ID GR        MAX        MIN
---------- ---------- --  --------- ---------
       102         89 FI         92         92
```

```
1 row selected.
```

c) Select the STUDENT_ID, SECTION_ID, and grade of students who received a final examination grade better than *any* of their individual homework grades.

Answer: The ANY operator together with the correlated subquery achieves the desired result.

```
SELECT student_id, section_id, numeric_grade
  FROM grade g
 WHERE grade_type_code = 'FI'
   AND numeric_grade > ANY
       (SELECT numeric_grade
          FROM grade
         WHERE grade_type_code = 'HM'
           AND g.section_id = section_id
           AND g.student_id = student_id)
STUDENT_ID SECTION_ID NUMERIC_GRADE
---------- ---------- -------------
       102         86            85
       103         81            91
       143         85            92
...
       283         99            85
       283        101            88

157 rows selected.
```

Examine the grades for the homework and the final for STUDENT_ID 102 and SECTION_ID 86. This student's final grade of 85 is better than the homework grade of 82. The ANY operator tests for an OR condition, so the student and section are returned because only one of the homework grades has to satisfy the condition.

```
SELECT student_id, section_id, grade_type_code,
       numeric_grade
  FROM grade
 WHERE student_id = 102
   AND section_id = 86
   AND grade_type_code IN ('HM', 'FI')
 GROUP BY student_id, section_id, grade_type_code,
       numeric_grade
STUDENT_ID SECTION_ID GR NUMERIC_GRADE
---------- ---------- -- -------------
       102         86 FI            85
       102         86 HM            82
       102         86 HM            90
       102         86 HM            99

4 rows selected.
```

LAB
7.4

d) Based on question c, explain the result of the row with the STUDENT_ID 102 and the SECTION_ID 89.

Answer: This record is not returned because unlike the ALL operator, the ANY operator returns false.

The following example illustrates the effect of no records in the subquery on the ANY operator. The student 102 enrolled in SECTION_ID 89 has no homework grades, and, therefore, does not appear in question c's result set.

```
SELECT student_id, section_id, grade_type_code,
       numeric_grade
  FROM grade
 WHERE student_id = 102
   AND section_id = 89
   AND grade_type_code IN ('HM', 'FI')
STUDENT_ID SECTION_ID GR NUMERIC_GRADE
---------- ---------- -- -------------
       102         89 FI            92

1 row selected.
```

LAB 7.4 SELF-REVIEW QUESTIONS

In order to test your progress, you should be able to answer the following questions.

1) Are the operators NOT IN and <> ANY equivalent as illustrated in the following example?

```
SELECT 'TRUE'
  FROM dual
 WHERE 6 <> ANY (6, 9)

SELECT 'TRUE'
  FROM dual
 WHERE 6 NOT IN (6, 9)
```

a) _____ Yes
b) _____ No

2) The following queries are logically equivalent.

```
SELECT 'TRUE'
  FROM dual
 WHERE 6 IN (6, 9)

SELECT 'TRUE'
  FROM dual
 WHERE 6 = ANY (6,9)
```

a) _____ True
b) _____ False

3) The operators ANY and SOME are equivalent.

a) _____ True
b) _____ False

LAB
7.4

4) To perform any >=, <=, >, or < comparison with a subquery returning multiple rows, you need to use either the ANY, SOME, or ALL operator.

a) _____ True
b) _____ False

5) The ANY, SOME, and ALL operators do not work with multiple columns.

a) _____ True
b) _____ False

Answers appear in Appendix A, Section 7.4.

C H A P T E R   7

TEST YOUR THINKING

The projects in this section are meant to have you utilize all of the skills that you have acquired throughout this chapter. The answers to these projects can be found at the companion Web site to this book, located at: *http://www.phptr.com/rischert.*

Visit the Web site periodically to share and discuss your answers.

1) Using a subquery construct, determine which sections the student Henry Masser is enrolled in.
2) Write the question for the following SELECT statement.

```
SELECT zip
  FROM zipcode z
 WHERE NOT EXISTS
        (SELECT '*'
           FROM student
          WHERE z.zip = zip)
   AND NOT EXISTS
        (SELECT '*'
           FROM instructor
          WHERE z.zip = zip)
```

3) Display the course number and description of courses with no enrollment. Also include courses that have no section assigned.
4) Can the ANY and ALL operators be used on the DATE datatype? Write a simple query to prove your answer.
5) If you have a choice to write either a correlated subquery or a simple non-correlated subquery, which one would you choose and why?
6) Determine the top three zip codes where most of the students live.

CHAPTER 8

SET OPERATORS

Set operators combine two or more sets of data to produce a single result set. Oracle has four set operators: UNION, UNION ALL, MINUS, and INTERSECT. The UNION and UNION ALL operators combine results. The INTERSECT operator determines common rows. The MINUS operator shows differences between sets of rows. In this chapter you will use set operators to combine data from many tables throughout the STUDENT schema.

L A B   8 . 1

THE POWER OF UNION
AND UNION ALL

The UNION operator is probably the most commonly used set operator. It combines two or more sets of data to produce a single set of data. Think of the UNION operator as two overlapping circles, as illustrated in Figure 8.1. The union of the two circles is everything from both circles. There are duplicates where they overlap, and there may even be duplicates within each set, but the final result shows these values only once. The UNION ALL operator includes these duplicates.

The sets of data in a set operation are SELECT statements, as simple or as complex as SELECT statements can be written. When writing any set operation, there are two rules to remember:

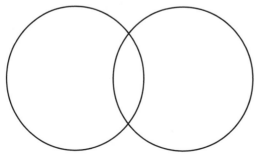

Figure 8.1 ■ UNION and UNION ALL set operators.

- Each of the SELECT lists must contain the same number of columns
- The matching columns in each of the SELECT lists must be the same datatype (Oracle considers CHAR and VARCHAR2 to be datatype compatible)

Imagine you need to create a phone list of all instructors and students. The following set operation uses the UNION operator to combine instructor and student names and phone numbers from the INSTRUCTOR and STUDENT tables into a single result set.

```
SELECT first_name, last_name, phone
  FROM instructor
UNION
SELECT first_name, last_name, phone
  FROM student
```

FIRST_NAME	LAST_NAME	PHONE
A.	Tucker	203-555-5555
Adele	Rothstein	718-555-5555
...		
Z.A.	Scrittorale	203-555-5555
Zalman	Draquez	718-555-5555

```
276 rows selected.
```

The same three columns are selected from each table, effectively stacking the columns one on top of the other in the result set. The results are automatically sorted by the order in which the columns appear in the SELECT list.

Notice the result returns 276 rows, even though there are 268 student rows and 10 instructor rows. What happened to the other two rows? The following query shows duplicate rows in the STUDENT table.

```
SELECT first_name, last_name, phone, COUNT(*)
  FROM student
 GROUP BY first_name, last_name, phone
HAVING COUNT(*) > 1
```

FIRST_NAME	LAST_NAME	PHONE	COUNT(*)
Kevin	Porch	201-555-5555	2
Thomas	Edwards	201-555-5555	2

```
2 rows selected.
```

Because the UNION operator eliminates duplicates, both of the duplicate student rows appear just once in the result of the UNION set operation. To list all the instructors and students, including duplicates, there are two approaches. One ap-

proach is to add the ID of the INSTRUCTOR and STUDENT tables to the set operation, plus a text literal such as 'instructor' and 'student'. The other approach is
to use the UNION ALL operator. UNION ALL includes any duplicates when sets
of data are added. Think again of the two overlapping circles shown in Figure 8.1.
UNION ALL not only adds the two sets of data, but includes the overlapping duplicates as well. Duplicates that may exist within each set are also included.

```
SELECT first_name, last_name, phone
  FROM instructor
UNION ALL
SELECT first_name, last_name, phone
  FROM student
FIRST_NAME LAST_NAME        PHONE
---------- ----------------  ----------
Fernand    Hanks             2125551212
Tom        Wojick            2125551212
...
Kathleen   Mastandora        718-555-5555
Angela     Torres            718-555-5555

278 rows selected.
```

UNION ALL results in 278 rows, which includes the duplicates in the STUDENT
table. Also, the result set is no longer sorted; UNION ALL does not perform a sort.

ORDER BY AND SET OPERATIONS

Just like the result of any SELECT statement, the result of a set operation can be
sorted using the ORDER BY clause. Instead of naming the column you want to
sort the result by, refer to its position in the SELECT list instead. Consider what
happens if you add the instructor and student IDs to the previous example using
UNION and order the results by the LAST_NAME column:

```
SELECT instructor_id id, first_name, last_name, phone
  FROM instructor
UNION
SELECT student_id, first_name, last_name, phone
  FROM student
ORDER BY 3
        ID FIRST_NAME LAST_NAME        PHONE
---------- ---------- ----------------  ------------
       119 Mardig     Abdou             718-555-5555
       399 Jerry      Abdou             718-555-5555
...
       184 Salewa     Zuckerberg        718-555-5555
       206 Freedon    annunziato        718-555-5555

278 rows selected.
```

The ORDER BY clause can also refer to a column alias, such as id used for the first column. However, referring to the column position in the ORDER BY clause is ANSI-standard, and is also independent of the column names in either SELECT statement.

With the addition of the instructor and student IDs, the unique combination of those IDs with first name, last name, and phone number now produces all 278 rows between the INSTRUCTOR and STUDENT tables.

The first columns in each of the individual SELECT statements, INSTRUCTOR_ID and STUDENT_ID, have different names but are the same datatype. Oracle uses the alias to name the column in the result set to a meaningful name for both instructor and student IDs.

SQL will always take its cue from the topmost SELECT statement when naming columns in the result set. When you want the result set to display a specific column name that is not dependent on the names of columns listed in the topmost statement, you must use a column alias.

LAB 8.1 EXERCISES

8.1.1 USE THE UNION AND UNION ALL SET OPERATORS

a) Explain the result of the following set operation, and why it works.

```
SELECT first_name, last_name,
       'Instructor' "Type"
  FROM instructor
 UNION
SELECT first_name, last_name,
       'Student'
  FROM student
```

b) Write a set operation, using the UNION set operator, to list all the zip codes in the INSTRUCTOR and STUDENT tables.

**LAB
8.1**

c) Write the question for the following set operation.

```
SELECT created_by
  FROM enrollment
UNION
SELECT created_by
  FROM grade
UNION
SELECT created_by
  FROM grade_type
UNION
SELECT created_by
  FROM grade_conversion
CREATED_BY
-----------------------
ARISCHER
BMOTIVAL
BROSENZW
CBRENNAN
DSCHERER
JAYCAF
MCAFFREY

7 rows selected.
```

d) Explain the result of the following set operation:

```
SELECT course_no, description
  FROM course
 WHERE prerequisite IS NOT NULL
 ORDER BY 1
UNION
SELECT course_no, description
  FROM course
 WHERE prerequisite IS NULL
```

e) What is wrong with the following set operation, and what do you have to change to make it work correctly?

```
SELECT instructor_id, last_name
  FROM instructor
UNION
SELECT last_name, student_id
  FROM student
```

LAB 8.1 EXERCISE ANSWERS

8.1.1 ANSWERS

a) Explain the result of the following set operation, and why it works.

```
SELECT first_name, last_name,
       'Instructor' "Type"
  FROM instructor
 UNION
SELECT first_name, last_name,
       'Student'
  FROM student
```

Answer: The result set displays the first and last names of instructors and students. The third column identifies what type of person it is, which also identifies the tables where the record originates. 'Instructor' and 'Student' are both text literals and are in the same position in each SELECT list. Therefore, the two SELECT statements are row-compatible.

```
FIRST_NAME LAST_NAME                    Type
---------- ------------------------     -------

A.         Tucker                       Student
Adele      Rothstein                    Student
...
Z.A.       Scrittorale                  Student
Zalman     Draquez                      Student

276 rows selected.
```

As your SELECT statements and set operations become more complex, it can be difficult to identify the data in your result sets accurately. This technique of identifying each row in the result set coming from one or the other set of data may be very useful.

b) Write a set operation, using UNION, to list all the zip codes in the INSTRUCTOR and STUDENT tables.

Answer: Two SELECT statements are combined using the UNION set operator for a result set displaying zip codes from both tables, eliminating any duplicates.

```
SELECT zip
  FROM instructor
 UNION
SELECT zip
  FROM student
ZIP
-----
01247
```

```
02124
...
43224
48104


149 rows selected.
```

c) Write the question for the following set operation.

```
SELECT created_by
   FROM enrollment
 UNION
SELECT created_by
   FROM grade
 UNION
SELECT created_by
   FROM grade_type
 UNION
SELECT created_by
   FROM grade_conversion
CREATED_BY
----------------
ARISCHER
BMOTIVAL
BROSENZW
CBRENNAN
DSCHERER
JAYCAF
MCAFFREY


7 rows selected.
```

Answer: Create a list of users who created rows in the ENROLLMENT, GRADE, GRADE_TYPE, and GRADE_CONVERSION tables. Show each user name only once.

As mentioned in the beginning of this lab, set operators can be used with two or more sets of data. This exercise combines the data from four separate tables into a single result set, eliminating duplicates where they occur.

CONTROLLING THE SORT ORDER

Sometimes you want to choose a specific sort order. This can be accomplished with a literal by which you can order the result.

```
SELECT created_by, 'GRADE' AS SOURCE, 1 AS SORT_ORDER
   FROM grade
 UNION
SELECT created_by, 'GRADE_TYPE', 2
   FROM grade_type
```

```
   UNION
   SELECT created_by, 'GRADE_CONVERSION', 3
     FROM grade_conversion
   UNION
   SELECT created_by, 'ENROLLMENT', 4
     FROM enrollment
   ORDER BY 3
```

CREATED_BY	SOURCE	SORT_ORDER
ARISCHER	GRADE	1
BROSENZW	GRADE	1
CBRENNAN	GRADE	1
MCAFFREY	GRADE_TYPE	2
BMOTIVAL	GRADE_CONVERSION	3
DSCHERER	ENROLLMENT	4
JAYCAF	ENROLLMENT	4

7 rows selected.

d) Explain the result of the following set operation:

```
SELECT course_no, description
  FROM course
 WHERE prerequisite IS NOT NULL
 ORDER BY 1
 UNION
SELECT course_no, description
  FROM course
 WHERE prerequisite IS NULL
```

Answer: Oracle returns the following error message because the ORDER BY clause must be used at the end of a set operation.

```
ORA-00933: SQL command not properly ended
```

SQL always expects the ORDER BY clause to be the very last command in a SQL statement, including set operations. An ORDER BY clause logically has no purpose in the top most statement; it is applied only to the single set of data in the result set, which is a combination of all data from all SELECT statements in a set operation.

e) What is wrong with the following set operation, and what do you have to change to make it work correctly?

```
SELECT instructor_id, last_name
  FROM instructor
 UNION
SELECT last_name, student_id
  FROM student
```

Answer: Oracle returns an error: `ORA-01790: expression` must have same datatype as corresponding expression. *The datatypes of columns must be the same for columns in the same position in each SELECT list of a set operation. Either the order of the columns in the first or the second statement must be switched for the statement to work correctly.*

Sometimes the datatype of columns do not match because of the way the columns were created, in which case you can use the data conversion functions to change from one datatype to another. Sometimes you want to combine distinct result sets together with the UNION ALL operator and place a null value for those columns where you want to omit the value. The next example query uses the CAST function and the TO_DATE function to make sure the null columns agree with the same datatype.

```
SELECT DISTINCT salutation, CAST(NULL AS NUMBER),
       state, z.created_date
  FROM instructor i, zipcode z
 WHERE i.zip = z.zip
UNION ALL
SELECT salutation, COUNT(*),
       state, TO_DATE(NULL)
  FROM student s, zipcode z
 WHERE s.zip = z.zip
 GROUP BY salutation, state
SALUT CAST(NULLASNUMBER) ST CREATED_D
----- ------------------ -- ---------
DR                          NY 03-AUG-99
HON                         NY 03-AUG-99
...
MS.                      69 NY
MS.                       1 WV
REV                       1 NJ

19 rows selected.
```

LAB 8.1 SELF-REVIEW QUESTIONS

In order to test your progress, you should be able to answer the following questions.

1) It is redundant to use DISTINCT in a UNION set operation.

  a) _____ True
  b) _____ False

2) Each of the SELECT statements in a set operation must have an ORDER BY clause when you want the results to be ordered.

   a) _____ True
   b) _____ False

3) A UNION set operation always returns the same result set as an equijoin.

   a) _____ True
   b) _____ False

4) You cannot use UNION to join two tables that do not have a primary key/foreign key relationship.

   a) _____ True
   b) _____ False

5) There must be the same number of columns in each SELECT statement of a set operation.

   a) _____ True
   b) _____ False

Answers appear in Appendix A, Section 8.1.

LAB 8.2

**LAB
8.2**

THE MINUS AND INTERSECT
SET OPERATORS

LAB OBJECTIVES

After this lab, you will be able to:

✔ Use the MINUS Set Operator
✔ Use the INTERSECT Set Operator

The MINUS set operator subtracts one set of data from another, identifying what data exists in one table but not the other. The INTERSECT set operator is the intersection of sets of data, identifying data common to all of them.

THE MINUS OPERATOR

The MINUS operation returns the difference between two sets. Effectively, you are subtracting one set from another set. The gray area of the circle in Figure 8.2 depicts the difference between the sets and indicates the data that is in one circle, but not in another.

The following set operation lists instructors not currently teaching any classes (sections).

```
SELECT instructor_id
  FROM instructor
 MINUS
SELECT instructor_id
  FROM section
INSTRUCTOR_ID
-------------
          109
          110

2 rows selected.
```

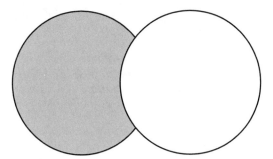

Figure 8.2 ■ **The MINUS set operator.**

Looking at the statements separately, the first SELECT statement returns the complete list of instructors.

```
SELECT instructor_id
  FROM instructor
INSTRUCTOR_ID
-------------
          101
          102
          103
          104
          105
          106
          109
          108
          107
          110

10 rows selected.
```

The second SELECT statement returns a distinct list of instructors currently teaching.

```
SELECT DISTINCT instructor_id
  FROM section
INSTRUCTOR_ID
-------------
          101
          102
          103
          104
          105
          106
          107
          108

8 rows selected.
```

Subtracting the second statement from the first statement leaves a list of instructors not currently teaching, which are the INSTRUCTOR_ID values of 109 and 110.

Just like the UNION set operator, MINUS eliminates duplicates when evaluating sets of data. Note DISTINCT is used in the preceding second SELECT statement when it is written separately. The following set operation implies distinct values in both SELECT statements.

**LAB
8.2**

```
SELECT created_by
  FROM enrollment
 MINUS
SELECT created_by
  FROM course
CREATED_BY
------------------------------
JAYCAF


1 row selected.
```

Written separately, the two SELECT statements use DISTINCT:

```
SELECT DISTINCT created_by
  FROM enrollment
CREATED_BY
--------------------------
DSCHERER
JAYCAF


2 rows selected.

SELECT DISTINCT created_by
  FROM course
CREATED_BY
------------------------------
DSCHERER


1 row selected.
```

The second SELECT statement results in the distinct value 'DSCHERER'. This is subtracted from the result of the first statement, which consists of the distinct values 'JAYCAF' and 'DSCHERER'. This results in the value 'JAYCAF' because 'JAYCAF' does not exist in the COURSE table, only in the ENROLLMENT table. A result set that exists in one table, but not in another, is sometimes referred to as an *antijoin*.

Be careful when positioning the SELECT statements in a MINUS set operation because their order makes a big difference. Be sure to place the set you want to subtract from first.

THE INTERSECT OPERATOR

The INTERSECT operator determines the common values between two sets. Figure 8.3 illustrates the two overlapping circles. The gray color indicates the area where the two circles intersect.

When you use INTERSECT instead of MINUS in the previous statement, the result is quite different:

```
SELECT created_by
  FROM enrollment
INTERSECT
SELECT created_by
  FROM course
CREATED_BY
------------------------------
DSCHERER

1 row selected.
```

The result set contains 'DSCHERER', which is the distinct value where the two sets overlap or intersect. Unlike MINUS, the order of the SELECT statements in an INTERSECT set operation does not matter.

INTERSECT INSTEAD OF EQUIJOINS

The INTERSECT set operator can replace the equijoin, which you learned about in Chapter 6, "Equijoins." The equijoin produces a result set that is the intersection of two or more tables, the same result as with INTERSECT.

Here is an equijoin that returns a list of course numbers for courses with corresponding sections:

```
SELECT DISTINCT c.course_no
  FROM course c, section s
 WHERE c.course_no = s.course_no
```

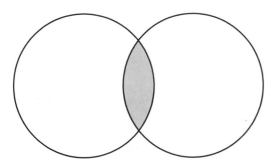

Figure 8.3 ■ The **INTERSECT** set operator.

```
COURSE_NO
---------
       10
       20
...
      420
      450
```

28 rows selected.

This INTERSECT set operation returns the same result:

```
SELECT course_no
  FROM course
INTERSECT
SELECT course_no
  FROM section
COURSE_NO
---------
       10
       20
...
      420
      450
```

28 rows selected.

The drawback to using INTERSECT instead of an equijoin is that INTERSECT operates on all columns in each SELECT list of the set operation. Therefore, you cannot include columns that exist in one table and not the other.

LAB 8.2 EXERCISES

8.2.1 USE THE *MINUS* SET OPERATOR

a) Explain the result of the following set operation.

```
SELECT course_no, description
  FROM course
 MINUS
SELECT s.course_no, c.description
  FROM section s, course c
 WHERE s.course_no = c.course_no
```

b) Use the MINUS set operator to create a list of courses and sections with no students enrolled. Add a column to the result set with the title `Status` and display the text `No Enroll-ments` in each row. Order the results by the COURSE_NO and SECTION_NO columns.

8.2.2 USE THE INTERSECT SET OPERATOR

a) Use the INTERSECT set operator to list all zip codes that are in both the STUDENT and INSTRUCTOR tables.

b) Use the INTERSECT set operator to list student IDs for students who are enrolled.

LAB 8.2 EXERCISE ANSWERS

8.2.1 ANSWERS

a) Explain the result of the following set operation.

```
SELECT course_no, description
  FROM course
 MINUS
SELECT s.course_no, c.description
  FROM section s, course c
 WHERE s.course_no = c.course_no
```

Answer: The set operation subtracts all courses having sections from all courses, result-ing in the two courses without matching sections.

```
COURSE_NO DESCRIPTION
--------- --------------------------------
       80 Structured Programming Techniques
      430 JDeveloper Techniques

2 rows selected.
```

Another way to formulate the query is to write a subquery using the NOT IN or the NOT EXISTS operator:

```
SELECT course_no, description
  FROM course c
 WHERE NOT EXISTS
        (SELECT '*'
           FROM section
          WHERE c.course_no = course_no)
```

b) Use the MINUS set operator to create a list of courses and sections with no students enrolled. Add a column to the result set with the title `Status` and display the text `No Enrollments` in each row. Order the results by the COURSE_NO and SECTION_NO columns.

Answer: The first SELECT statement is the set of all courses with sections. The second SELECT statement subtracts the set of courses and sections having enrollments, leaving the difference of courses and sections without enrollments.

```
SELECT course_no, section_no, 'No Enrollments' "Status"
  FROM section
 MINUS
SELECT course_no, section_no, 'No Enrollments'
  FROM section s
 WHERE EXISTS (SELECT section_id
                 FROM enrollment e
                WHERE e.section_id = s.section_id)
 ORDER BY 1, 2
COURSE_NO SECTION_NO Status
--------- ---------- --------------
       25          9 No Enrollments
      124          4 No Enrollments
...
      220          1 No Enrollments
      350          3 No Enrollments

14 rows selected.
```

This statement uses a trick to display `'No Enrollments'` in the result set. Even though it is not a column in either table, as long as it is in the first statement there is a column for it in the result set. And, as long as it is in the second statement, it matches the first and, therefore, allows the MINUS to work correctly, subtracting one set from a similar set.

8.2.2 ANSWERS

a) Use the INTERSECT set operator to list all zip codes that are in both the STUDENT and INSTRUCTOR tables.

Answer: INTERSECT is used to find the intersection of distinct zip codes in the INSTRUCTOR and STUDENT tables.

```
SELECT zip
  FROM instructor
INTERSECT
SELECT zip
  FROM student
ZIP
-----
10025
```

1 row selected.

Be careful when deciding to use INTERSECT versus UNION. The key phrase in the question asked is ". . . zip codes that are in both. . . ." INTERSECT achieves the intersection of both tables alone, whereas UNION returns all zip codes combined from both tables.

b) Use the INTERSECT set operator to list student IDs for students who are enrolled.

Answer: The intersection of student IDs in the STUDENT and ENROLLMENT tables yields all students who are enrolled.

```
SELECT student_id
  FROM student
INTERSECT
SELECT student_id
  FROM enrollment
STUDENT_ID
----------
       102
       103
...
       282
       283
```

165 rows selected.

LAB 8.2 SELF-REVIEW QUESTIONS

In order to test your progress, you should be able to answer the following questions.

1) The following two SELECT statements are equivalent and return the same rows.

```
SELECT student_id                SELECT student_id
  FROM enrollment                  FROM student
MINUS                            MINUS
SELECT student_id                SELECT student_id
  FROM student                     FROM enrollment
```

a) _____ True
b) _____ False

2) The SELECT statements in an INTERSECT set operation can contain a correlated subquery.

    a) _____ True
    b) _____ False

**LAB
8.2**

3) The following SQL statement executes without an error.

```
SELECT TO_CHAR(1)
  FROM dual
MINUS
SELECT TO_NUMBER('1')
  FROM dual
```

    a) _____ True
    b) _____ False

4) It is redundant to use DISTINCT in either a MINUS or INTERSECT set operation.

    a) _____ True
    b) _____ False

Answers appear in Appendix A, Section 8.2.

CHAPTER 8

TEST YOUR THINKING

The projects in this section are meant to have you utilize all of the skills that you have acquired throughout this chapter. The answers to these projects can be found at the companion Web site to this book, located at: *http://www.phptr.com/rischert.*

Visit the Web site periodically to share and discuss your answers.

1) List all the zip codes in the ZIPCODE table that are not used in the STUDENT or INSTRUCTOR tables. Write two different solutions, using set operators for both.
2) Write a SQL statement, using a set operator, to show which students enrolled in a section on the same day they registered.
3) Find the students that are not enrolled in any classes. Write three solutions: a set operation, a subquery, and a correlated subquery.
4) Show the students who have received grades for their class. Write four solutions: a set operation, a subquery, a correlated subquery, and a join.

C H A P T E R 9

COMPLEX JOINS

Outer joins and self-joins are extensions of the equijoin you learned about in Chapter 6, "Equijoins." The outer join includes the result rows returned by the equijoin, plus extra rows where no matches are found. The self-join, as implied by the name, joins a table to itself. This type of join is useful for tables with a self-referencing relationship or when you want to determine data inconsistencies.

You will see the usefulness of these types of joins for analyzing and exploring the relationships within your data.

L A B   9 . 1

OUTER JOINS

LAB OBJECTIVES

After this lab, you will be able to:

✔ Write Outer Joins with Two Tables
✔ Write Outer Joins with Three Tables

MISSING ROWS?

The outer join is similar to the equijoin because it returns all the records the equijoin returns. But it also returns records that are in one of the tables with no matching records in another table. The following is an equijoin and its result. The SQL statement returns all the rows where a match for the COURSE_NO column is found in both the COURSE and the SECTION tables.

```
SELECT course_no, description,
       section_id, course_no
  FROM course JOIN section
 USING (course_no)
 ORDER BY course_no
```

COURSE_NO	DESCRIPTION	SECTION_ID	COURSE_NO
10	DP Overview	80	10
20	Intro to Computers	81	20
...			
420	Database System Principles	108	420
450	DB Programming in Java	109	450

78 rows selected.

Some courses are not included in the result because there are no matching course numbers in the SECTION table. To determine those courses not assigned to any sections, write a NOT EXISTS subquery, a NOT IN subquery, or use the MINUS operator.

```
SELECT course_no, description
  FROM course c
 WHERE NOT EXISTS
       (SELECT 'X'
          FROM section
         WHERE c.course_no = course_no)
COURSE_NO DESCRIPTION
--------- ---------------------------------
       80 Structured Programming Techniques
      430 JDeveloper Techniques

2 rows selected.
```

The previous equijoin did not return the two courses because there are no matches for course numbers 80 and 430 in the SECTION table. To include these courses in the result, you need to perform an outer join.

THE ANSI OUTER JOIN

The outer join is typically formed with one of three different syntax options. Either you can use the ANSI join syntax, Oracle's outer join operator denoted with the (+), or you can express the query as a UNION. This lab will teach you how to write the queries using various ways. Typically it is best to use the ANSI outer join syntax as it greatly increases the SQL functionality and flexibility. It can also be easily understood by any non-Oracle databases and it is not subject to the many limitations the Oracle-specific outer-join operator imposes. If your SQL needs to run against Oracle versions prior to *9i*, you have no choice but to use Oracle's outer-join operator or a UNION ALL set operator.

The following query shows the use of the ANSI outer join syntax. The keywords LEFT OUTER are added to the JOIN keyword. It indicates that the rows in the table to the left side of the JOIN keyword are to be listed, including any rows where a match to the SECTION table cannot be found.

```
SELECT c.course_no, c.description,
       s.section_id, s.course_no
  FROM course c LEFT OUTER JOIN section s
    ON c.course_no = s.course_no
 ORDER BY c.course_no
COURSE_NO DESCRIPTION            SECTION_ID COURSE_NO
--------- ---------------------- ---------- ---------
       10 DP Overview                    80        10
       20 Intro to Computers             81        20
...
       80 Structured Programming
          Techniques
...
      430 JDeveloper Techniques
```

```
      450 DB Programming in Java          109          450
```

```
80 rows selected.
```

Look closely at the result for course numbers 80 and 430. These courses have no sections assigned. For example, COURSE_NO 430 of the COURSE table (c.course_no) contains the COURSE_NO value, but the COURSE_NO from the SECTION table s.course_no contains a null. The outer join includes null values for the columns s.course_no and s.section_id where a match is not found.

If you wanted to include all the rows in the SECTION table you can also use the RIGHT OUTER JOIN syntax. This doesn't really make any sense because when you look at the schema diagram, you notice that every row in the SECTION table must have a corresponding row in the COURSE table. Orphan rows, which are rows that exist in the SECTION table but not the COURSE table, are not allowed.

However, notice that if we switch the order of the tables to list the SECTION table first, you can write a RIGHT OUTER JOIN. This is essentially the same as the LEFT OUTER JOIN listed previously. The only difference is the order of the tables in the FROM clause and the RIGHT keyword. Based on the order of the tables in the FROM clause, you must choose either the RIGHT or the LEFT keyword to include all the rows of the outer joined table.

```
SELECT c.course_no, c.description,
       s.section_id, s.course_no
  FROM section s RIGHT OUTER JOIN course c
    ON c.course_no = s.course_no
 ORDER BY c.course_no
```

You can also write the outer join with another ANSI join syntax, such as the USING clause.

```
SELECT course_no, description,
       section_id
  FROM section RIGHT OUTER JOIN course
 USING (course_no)
 ORDER BY course_no
COURSE_NO DESCRIPTION                    SECTION_ID
--------- ---------------------------- ----------
       10 DP Overview                           80
       20 Intro to Computers                    81
...
       80 Structured Programming
          Techniques
...
      430 JDeveloper Techniques
      450 DB Programming in Java               109
```

```
80 rows selected.
```

Notice that the query and the returned result do not include both COURSE_NO columns because you are not allowed to alias the joined column when writing the query with the USING clause. The column now also contains a non-null value, unlike the previous result where the corresponding COURSE_NO column from the SECTION table showed a null. For the SECTION_ID column, you continue to see a null value as there obviously is no matching valve in the SECTION table.

THE ORACLE OUTER JOIN OPERATOR (+)

The next query looks very much like the equijoin you are already familiar with, except for the (+) symbol next to the SECTION table's COURSE_NO column in the WHERE clause. Oracle uses the outer join operator '(+)' to indicate that nulls are generated for nonmatching rows. All the nonmatching columns from the SECTION table have a NULL value in the result set, exactly like the previous result.

You place the outer join operator on the table for which you want to generate nulls. In this case, all the rows from the COURSE table are required and for every row in the COURSE table for which a match cannot be found in the SECTION table, a null is generated. Therefore, the (+) operator needs to be on the COURSE_NO column of the SECTION table.

```
SELECT c.course_no, c.description,
       s.section_id, s.course_no
  FROM course c, section s
 WHERE c.course_no = s.course_no(+)
 ORDER BY c.course_no
```

If the order of the tables in the FROM clause changes, the (+) operator still needs to remain on the S.COURSE_NO column. This syntax and the UNION ALL syntax are the only way to express outer joins in Oracle versions prior to Oracle 9*i*. If you have a choice, use the ANSI join syntax instead; it is easy and overall more flexible and functional.

THE OUTER JOIN AND THE UNION ALL OPERATOR

Alternatively, you can achieve the same result with two SQL statements—an equijoin and a correlated subquery—with the results combined using the UNION ALL operator.

```
SELECT c1.course_no, c1.description,
       s.section_id, s.course_no
  FROM course c1, section s
 WHERE c1.course_no = s.course_no
UNION ALL
SELECT c2.course_no, c2.description,
       TO_NUMBER(NULL), TO_NUMBER(NULL)
  FROM course c2
 WHERE NOT EXISTS
```

```
(SELECT 'X'
    FROM section
   WHERE c2.course_no = course_no)
```

In this example, the UNION ALL operator is used to combine the result of the equijoin (all courses with sections) with the result of the correlated subquery (courses with no match in the SECTION table). Duplicate rows are not returned between the two SELECT statements; each SELECT statement returns a different set. Therefore, it is more efficient to use UNION ALL rather than the UNION operator because the UNION ALL avoids the sort required by the UNION operator to eliminate the duplicates.

The TO_NUMBER datatype conversion is performed to match the datatypes of the columns in each of the SELECT statements in the set operation. Alternatively, you can substitute CAST(NULL AS NUMBER) for the TO_NUMBER(NULL) function.

FULL OUTER JOIN

A full outer join includes rows from both tables. Oracle does not support a full outer join with the (+) outer join operator. To accomplish a full outer join, you need to use either the ANSI FULL OUTER JOIN syntax or the UNION operator.

ANSI FULL OUTER JOIN

To fully illustrate the effects of an outer join, here are tables named T1 and T2 (not found in the STUDENT schema unless you installed the additional tables from the companion Web site) and the data in them. Table T1 has one numeric column named COL1 and table T2 also consists of a numeric column called COL2.

```
SELECT col1
  FROM t1
     COL1
---------
        1
        2
        3

3 rows selected.

SELECT col2
  FROM t2
     COL2
---------
        2
        3
        4

3 rows selected.
```

To understand the effect of a full outer join on the tables T1 and T2, first write an outer join on table T1 with the following SELECT statement. This SELECT statement is referred to as a left outer join. The result includes all the rows from table T1.

```
SELECT col1, col2
  FROM t1 LEFT OUTER JOIN t2
    ON t1.col1 = t2.col2
    COL1        COL2
--------- ---------
       1
       2           2
       3           3
```

3 rows selected.

The next SELECT statement returns all the rows from T2, whether a match is found or not. This outer join is a right outer join. All the rows on the right table are returned, including nonmatching rows.

```
SELECT col1, col2
  FROM t1 RIGHT OUTER JOIN t2
    ON t1.col1 = t2.col2
    COL1        COL2
--------- ---------
       2           2
       3           3
                   4
```

3 rows selected.

The full outer join includes all the rows from both tables, whether a match is found or not.

```
SELECT col1, col2
  FROM t1 FULL OUTER JOIN t2
    ON t1.col1 = t2.col2
    COL1        COL2
--------- ---------
       1
       2           2
       3           3
                   4
```

4 rows selected.

FULL OUTER JOIN USING THE UNION OPERATOR

You can also express the same full outer join using the Oracle outer join operator and combining the two SELECT statements with the UNION operator. The UNION operator eliminates the duplicate rows from the two statements.

```
SELECT col1, col2
  FROM t1, t2
 WHERE t1.col1 = t2.col2(+)
UNION
SELECT col1, col2
  FROM t1, t2
 WHERE t1.col1(+) = t2.col2
```

The first SELECT statement performs an outer join on the T1 table; the second SELECT statement performs an outer join on the T2 table. The result of each query is combined and duplicates are eliminated with the UNION operator.

LAB 9.1 EXERCISES

9.1.1 WRITE OUTER JOINS WITH TWO TABLES

a) Explain why Oracle returns an error message when you execute the following SELECT statement.

```
SELECT c.course_no, s.course_no, s.section_id,
       c.description, s.start_date_time
  FROM course c, section s
 WHERE c.course_no(+) = s.course_no(+)
```

b) Show the description of all courses with the prerequisite course number 350. Include the location where the sections meet in the result. Return course rows even if no corresponding row in the SECTION table is found.

c) Rewrite the following SQL statement using an outer join.

```
SELECT course_no, description
  FROM course c
 WHERE NOT EXISTS
       (SELECT 'X'
          FROM section
         WHERE c.course_no = course_no)
COURSE_NO DESCRIPTION
--------- --------------------------------
       80 Structured Programming Techniques
      430 JDeveloper Techniques

2 rows selected.
```

d) Show all the cities, state, and zip codes for Connecticut. Display a count of how many students live in each zip code. Order the result alphabetically by city. The result should look similar to the following output. Note, the result returns a zero when no student lives in a particular zip code.

```
CITY                        ST ZIP   STUDENT_COUNT
------------------------    -- -----  ------------
Ansonia                     CT 06401            0
Bridgeport                  CT 06605            1
...
Wilton                      CT 06897            0
Woodbury                    CT 06798            1

19 rows selected.
```

9.1.2 WRITE OUTER JOINS WITH THREE TABLES

a) Display the course number, description, cost, class location, and instructor's last name for all the courses. Also include courses where no sections or instructors have been assigned.

b) For students with the student ID of 102 and 301, determine the sections they are enrolled in. Also show the numeric grades and grade types they received, no matter if they are enrolled or received any grades.

LAB 9.1 EXERCISE ANSWERS

9.1.1 ANSWERS

a) Explain why Oracle returns an error message when you execute the following SELECT statement.

```
SELECT c.course_no, s.course_no, s.section_id,
       c.description, s.start_date_time
  FROM course c, section s
 WHERE c.course_no(+) = s.course_no(+)
```

Answer: The outer join symbol can be used only on one side of the equation, not both.

```
ERROR at line 4:
ORA-01468: a predicate may reference only one outer-joined table
```

This SQL statement attempts to include rows from the COURSE table for which no match exists in the SECTION table and include rows from the SECTION table where no match is found in the COURSE table. This is referred to as a full outer join; you want to include the rows from both tables, including those rows for which a match cannot be found in either table.

You can write the full outer join with the ANSI join syntax.

```
SELECT c.course_no, s.course_no, s.section_id,
       c.description, s.start_date_time
  FROM course c FULL OUTER JOIN section s
    ON c.course_no = s.course_no
```

When you look at the relationship between the SECTION and COURSE tables, you notice a section cannot exist unless a corresponding course exists. Therefore, finding any sections for which no course exists is impossible unless the foreign key constraint is disabled or dropped. (For information on how to create and drop foreign keys, see Chapter 11, "Create, Alter, and Drop Tables." To learn how to determine if the foreign keys are disabled or enabled, see Chapter 13, "The Data Dictionary and Dynamic SQL Scripts.")

b) Show the description of all courses with the prerequisite course number 350. Include the location where the sections meet in the result. Return course rows even if no corresponding row in the SECTION table is found.

Answer: To show all the courses with this prerequisite, include rows without any corresponding course number in the SECTION table. This involves writing an outer join and applying a left outer join to the COURSE table. For any records where no match in the SECTION table is found, null values are generated for the SECTION table columns.

```
SELECT c.course_no cno, s.course_no sno,
       c.description,
       c.prerequisite prereq,
       s.location loc, s.section_id
  FROM course c LEFT OUTER JOIN section s
    ON c.course_no = s.course_no
 WHERE c.prerequisite = 350
```

CNO	SNO	DESCRIPTION	PREREQ	LOC	SECTION_ID
430		JDeveloper Techniques	350		
450	450	DB Programming in Java	350	L507	109

```
2 rows selected.
```

Or:

```
SELECT c.course_no cno, s.course_no sno,
       c.description,
       c.prerequisite prereq,
       s.location loc, s.section_id
  FROM course c, section s
 WHERE c.course_no = s.course_no(+)
   AND c.prerequisite = 350
```

Course number 430, JDeveloper Techniques, does not have a matching section. Therefore, you cannot determine the column values of the SECTION table, such as LOCATION, S.COURSE_NO (SNO as the column alias), and SECTION_ID; null values are generated for these columns.

This query can be expressed with the USING clause. The COURSE_NO column does not have an alias and the result will show the value from the COURSE table, which is not null.

```
SELECT course_no cno,
       description,
       prerequisite prereq,
       location loc, section_id
  FROM course LEFT OUTER JOIN section
 USING (course_no)
 WHERE prerequisite = 350
```

ORACLE OUTER JOIN OPERATOR RESTRICTIONS

Oracle imposes a number of other restrictions and caveats when using the (+) outer join operator. For example, if you don't correctly place the (+) on WHERE clause conditions and join criteria you may get the result of the equijoin rather than the outer join without any warning or error message. The outer join operator also restricts the use of an outer joined column involving a subquery and prohibits the use of the OR logical operator and the IN comparison. All these conditions issue an error message indicating that the query is invalid.

WHERE CONDITIONS AND THE ORACLE OUTER JOIN OPERATOR

There are some things you need to watch out for when you use Oracle's proprietary outer join operator, particularly when it comes to using conditions in WHERE clauses. The previously listed outer join is repeated for your reference. Note that the condition in the WHERE clause is applied to the PREREQUISITE column. This column is in the COURSE table—the outer joined table—which includes all rows including nonmatching rows.

```
SELECT c.course_no cno, s.course_no sno,
       c.description,
       c.prerequisite prereq,
```

```
            s.location loc, s.section_id
    FROM course c, section s
   WHERE c.course_no = s.course_no(+)
     AND c.prerequisite = 350
```

The next SQL statement modifies the WHERE condition and adds a condition specific to the SECTION table. The query retrieves classes that only meet in LO-CATION L507. Observe the output of the query and compare it to the previous result.

```
SELECT c.course_no cno, s.course_no sno,
       c.description,
       c.prerequisite prereq,
       s.location loc, s.section_id
  FROM course c, section s
 WHERE c.course_no = s.course_no(+)
   AND c.prerequisite = 350
   AND s.location = 'L507'
```

CNO	SNO	DESCRIPTION	PREREQ	LOC	SECTION_ID
450	450	DB Programming in Java	350	L507	109

```
1 row selected.
```

You may wonder what happened to course number 430? The course is no longer included in the result, even though the outer join operator is applied to return all the rows whether a match is found in the SECTION table or not.

When a WHERE clause contains a condition that compares a column from the outer joined table to a literal, such as the text literal 'L507', you also need to include the outer join operator on the column. Otherwise, Oracle returns only the results of the equijoin, rather than generating nulls for the columns. The following query adds the outer join symbol to the LOCATION column.

```
SELECT c.course_no cno, s.course_no sno,
       c.description,
       c.prerequisite prereq,
       s.location loc, s.section_id
  FROM course c, section s
 WHERE c.course_no = s.course_no(+)
   AND c.prerequisite = 350
   AND s.location(+) = 'L507'
```

CNO	SNO	DESCRIPTION	PREREQ	LOC	SECTION_ID
430		JDeveloper Techniques	350		
450	450	DB Programming in Java	350	L507	109

```
2 rows selected.
```

These two records satisfy the condition of the prerequisite. The outer join operator applied to the LOCATION column includes records where either (a) the location equals L507, (b) the location is null, or (c) the location is different from 'L507'. You will see an example shortly of why the location can be different.

Once you apply the outer join operator to a column on the outer joined table, you need to understand the order in which the conditions are processed. First, the records on the table where you want to include all the rows are processed. This is the condition `prerequisite = 350`. Next, the matching records in the SECTION table are identified. If a match is not found, the records with the prerequisite 350 are still returned. The next condition, `location(+) = 'L507'`, shows rows in the SECTION table that satisfy this condition; otherwise, a null is returned.

What happens when you choose a different location, such as L210? Neither course meets in this location.

```
SELECT c.course_no cno, s.course_no sno,
       SUBSTR(c.description, 1,20),
       c.prerequisite prereq,
       s.location loc, s.section_id
  FROM course c, section s
 WHERE c.course_no = s.course_no(+)
   AND c.prerequisite = 350
   AND s.location(+) = 'L210'
```

CNO	SNO	DESCRIPTION	PREREQ	LOC	SECTION_ID
430		JDeveloper Techniques	350		
450		DB Programming in Java	350		

```
2 rows selected.
```

Here you see both courses with this prerequisite. This contrasts with the earlier output because now both the LOCATION and SECTION_ID columns contain nulls. When the WHERE clause is evaluated, the PREREQUISITE condition is evaluated first, then matches are found in the SECTION table with the condition `location(+) = 'L210'`. Since none of the sections match this LOCATION condition for this course number, nulls are generated for the SECTION_ID and the LOCATION.

WHERE CONDITIONS AND THE ANSI OUTER JOINS

When you compare the Oracle syntax to the ANSI outer join syntax, you see that there are some differences. Following is the query of the first outer join with the LOCATION = 'L507'. The ANSI join returns the result of the equijoin, which is one row. This is not the desired result.

```
SELECT c.course_no cno, s.course_no sno,
       c.description,
       c.prerequisite prereq,
```

```
                  s.location loc, s.section_id
          FROM course c LEFT OUTER JOIN section s
            ON c.course_no = s.course_no
         WHERE c.prerequisite = 350
           AND location = 'L507'
```

```
CNO SNO DESCRIPTION                   PREREQ LOC   SECTION_ID
--- --- --------------------- --------- ---- ----------
450 450 DB Programming in Java           350 L507          109
```

```
1 row selected.
```

Instead the query needs to be changed with the use of parentheses to obtain the correct result. The order of execution matters indeed, and the order is determined by the parentheses! The join on the COURSE_NO column together with the condition location = 'L507' is enclosed by parentheses; they determine that the join and LOCATION condition are executed first. This intermediate result includes all matching rows between the COURSE and SECTION tables based on the COURSE_NO column and those rows from the SECTION table where the LOCATION column has a value of L507.

```
SELECT c.course_no cno, s.course_no sno,
       c.description,
       c.prerequisite prereq,
       s.location loc, s.section_id
  FROM course c LEFT OUTER JOIN section s
    ON (c.course_no = s.course_no
   AND location = 'L507')
 WHERE c.prerequisite = 350
```

Here is an intermediate result listing of the join condition without the WHERE clause condition applied.

```
          ON (c.course_no = s.course_no
         AND location = 'L507')
```

```
CNO SNO DESCRIPTION                   PREREQ LOC   SECTION_ID
--- --- --------------------- --------- ---- ----------
100 100 Hands-On Windows                  20 L507          144
450 450 DB Programming in Java           350 L507          109
...
350     JDeveloper Lab                   125
430     JDeveloper Techniques            350
220     PL/SQL Programming                80
230     Intro to Internet                 10
```

```
33 rows selected.
```

Based on this intermediate result set the WHERE clause is applied, only rows with a prerequisite value of 350 are chosen for output and just two rows qualify for the final result. This works because the LOCATION column condition is part of the outer join criteria on the table for which nulls are to be generated.

USING INLINE VIEWS AND OUTER JOINS   You can also use inline views to gain control over the execution order. The same result can also be obtained with the following query, which chooses all the rows from the COURSE table with a value of 350 in the PREREQUISITE column. This result set is then left outer joined with the inline view of the SECTION table, which retrieves only sections with a LOCATION column value of 'L507'.

```
SELECT c.course_no cno, s.course_no sno,
       c.description,
       c.prerequisite prereq,
       s.location loc, s.section_id
  FROM (select *
          FROM course
         WHERE prerequisite = 350) c LEFT OUTER JOIN
       (SELECT * FROM section
         WHERE location = 'L507') s
    ON (c.course_no = s.course_no)
```

WHERE clauses and outer joins may give you unexpected results unless you carefully craft your conditions. Inline views and ANSI joins are best for complicated conditions as they allow you control over the execution order of the conditions and joins. ANSI joins are preferable over Oracle's proprietary outer join operator as ANSI joins are less restrictive, easier to read, and allow your SQL statements to be portable to non-Oracle databases.

c) Rewrite the following SQL statement using an outer join.

```
SELECT course_no, description
  FROM course c
 WHERE NOT EXISTS
       (SELECT 'X'
          FROM section
         WHERE c.course_no = course_no)
COURSE_NO DESCRIPTION
--------- --------------------------------
       80 Structured Programming Techniques
      430 JDeveloper Techniques

2 rows selected.
```

Answer: A NOT EXISTS condition can be rewritten as an outer join condition by querying the SECTION table for nulls.

Your query can be written in many different ways. The following example shows the use of the (+) outer join operator:

```
SELECT c.course_no, c.description
  FROM course c, section s
 WHERE c.course_no = s.course_no(+)
   AND s.course_no IS NULL
```

Or you can write it with the ANSI outer join syntax and the USING clause.

```
SELECT course_no, description
  FROM course LEFT OUTER JOIN section
 USING (course_no)
 WHERE section_id IS NULL
```

d) Show all the cities, state, and zip codes for Connecticut. Display a count of how many students live in each zip code. Order the result alphabetically by city. The result should look similar to the following output. Note, the result returns a zero when no student lives in a particular zip code.

```
CITY                        ST ZIP   STUDENT_COUNT
-------------------------   -- ----- -------------
Ansonia                     CT 06401             0
Bridgeport                  CT 06605             1
...
Wilton                      CT 06897             0
Woodbury                    CT 06798             1

19 rows selected.
```

Answer: The query that achieves the correct solution requires the use of an outer join on the ZIPCODE table and the use of the aggregate function COUNT. When using an aggregate function together with outer joins, you must be careful to apply the aggregate function to the correct column.

```
SELECT city, state, z.zip,
       COUNT(s.zip) AS student_count
  FROM zipcode z LEFT OUTER JOIN student s
    ON (z.zip = s.zip)
 WHERE state = 'CT'
 GROUP by city, state, z.zip
```

Notice the parameter in the COUNT function is the S.ZIP column instead of Z.ZIP. The COUNT function requires the STUDENT table's ZIP column as a parameter to assure that if the zip code is not found in the STUDENT table, the COUNT function will return a zero.

Just for illustration of this important issue, the next query shows the result of both the Z.ZIP and the S.ZIP column in the SELECT list and as a parameter in the

COUNT function. Notice that the SZIP column in the result is null and the column WRONG_VALUE has a count of one even though this zip code does not exist in the STUDENT table. The COUNT function for this column is counting the occurrence of the zip code in the ZIPCODE table, not the desired STUDENT table's zip code.

```
SELECT city, state, z.zip AS zzip, s.zip AS szip,
       COUNT(s.zip) AS student_count,
       COUNT(z.zip) AS wrong_value
  FROM zipcode z LEFT OUTER JOIN student s
    ON (z.zip = s.zip)
 WHERE state = 'CT'
 GROUP by city, state, z.zip, s.zip
```

CITY	ST	ZZIP	SZIP	STUDENT_COUNT	WRONG_VALUE
Ansonia	CT	06401		0	1
...					
Woodbury	CT	06798	06798	1	1

19 rows selected.

ALTERNATIVE SOLUTION WITH A SCALAR SUBQUERY

The scalar subquery, discussed in Chapter 7, "Subqueries," can provide some simplicity and less chance for errors. The query is correlated as the scalar subquery is executed for each individual zip code. However, scalar subqueries can be notoriously inefficient because Oracle can often execute table joins more quickly, particularly when scans of the entire result set are involved.

```
SELECT city, state, zip,
       (SELECT COUNT(*)
          FROM student s
         WHERE s.zip = z.zip) AS student_count
  FROM zipcode z
 WHERE state = 'CT'
```

CITY	ST	ZIP	STUDENT_COUNT
Ansonia	CT	06401	0
...			
Stamford	CT	06907	1

19 rows selected.

9.1.2 ANSWERS

a) Display the course number, description, cost, class location, and instructor's last name for all courses. Also include courses where no sections or instructors have been assigned.

Answer: This outer join involves three tables: the COURSE, SECTION, and INSTRUCTOR tables. You want to include all the courses from the COURSE table, whether a section exists for it or not. Also, if no instructor is assigned to a section or no match is found, the rows of the SECTION table should still be included.

The SELECT statement requires the outer join operator to be placed on the COURSE_NO column of the SECTION table. This indicates you want to see all the courses, whether there are corresponding sections or not. The outer join operator is also applied to the INSTRUCTOR_ID column of the INSTRUCTOR table. This directs Oracle to include rows from the SECTION table even if it doesn't find a matching record in the INSTRUCTOR table.

```
SELECT course_no cou, description, cost,
       location, last_name
  FROM course LEFT OUTER JOIN section
USING (course_no)
  LEFT OUTER JOIN instructor
USING (instructor_id)
ORDER BY course_no
COU DESCRIPTION                     COST LOCA LAST_NAME
---- ---------------------- --------- ---- ---------
  10 DP Overview                    1195 L214 Wojick
  20 Intro to Computers             1195 L210 Schorin
  20 Intro to Computers             1195 L214 Pertez
  20 Intro to Computers             1195 L509 Morris
  20 Intro to Computers             1195 L210 Smythe
...
 430 JDeveloper Techniques          1195
 450 DB Programming in Java              L507 Hanks

80 rows selected.
```

When you review the result, recall from the previous examples that course number 430 does not have a section assigned. Therefore, the column LOCATION is NULL. Also, the instructor's last name is NULL because there cannot be an instructor assigned if the row does not exist.

You can also use the Oracle outer join operator and the SQL statement will look similar to the following:

```
SELECT c.course_no cou, c.description, c.cost,
       s.location, i.last_name
```

```
   FROM course c, section s, instructor i
  WHERE c.course_no = s.course_no(+)
    AND s.instructor_id = i.instructor_id(+)
  ORDER BY c.course_no
```

The join between the SECTION and INSTRUCTOR tables is defined with the following criteria: If you leave out the outer join operator (+) on the INSTRUCTOR_ID column, you get the result of an equijoin.

```
    AND s.instructor_id = i.instructor_id(+)
```

b) For students with the student ID of 102 and 301, determine the sections they are enrolled in. Also show the numeric grades and grade types they received, no matter if they are enrolled or received any grades.

Answer: You can write outer joins that include rows from all three tables: STUDENT, EN-ROLLEMNT, and GRADE.

```
SELECT student_id, section_id, grade_type_code,
       numeric_grade
  FROM student LEFT OUTER JOIN enrollment
 USING (student_id)
  LEFT OUTER JOIN grade
 USING (student_id, section_id)
 WHERE student_id IN (102, 301)
```

Or:

```
SELECT s.student_id, en.section_id, grade_type_code,
       numeric_grade
  FROM student s LEFT OUTER JOIN enrollment en
    ON (s.student_id = en.student_id)
  LEFT OUTER JOIN grade g
    ON (s.student_id = g.student_id
   AND en.section_id = g.section_id)
 WHERE s.student_id IN (102, 301)
```

STUDENT_ID	SECTION_ID	GR	NUMERIC_GRADE
102	86	FI	85
102	86	HM	90
102	86	HM	99
102	86	HM	82
102	86	HM	82
102	86	MT	90
102	86	PA	85
102	86	QZ	90
102	86	QZ	84
102	86	QZ	97
102	86	QZ	97

```
102        89 FI        92
102        89 MT        91
301
```

14 rows selected.

The student with ID 102 is enrolled and received grades. His rows are returned as part of an equijoin. However, student 301 is not enrolled in any section, and does not have any grades.

You can also write the query using the traditional join syntax and the Oracle (+) outer join operator.

```
SELECT s.student_id, e.section_id, g.grade_type_code,
       g.numeric_grade
  FROM student s, enrollment e, grade g
 WHERE s.student_id IN (102, 301)
   AND s.student_id = e.student_id(+)
   AND e.student_id = g.student_id(+)
   AND e.section_id = g.section_id(+)
```

Because the outer join operator is applied to both the SECTION and the GRADE tables, STUDENT_ID 301 is included in the result. The condition s.student_id IN (102, 301) does not require an outer join operator because it is based on the STUDENT table and it is the table from which you want all the rows that satisfy this condition.

LAB 9.1 SELF-REVIEW QUESTIONS

In order to test your progress, you should be able to answer the following questions.

1) A WHERE clause containing an outer join (+) operator cannot contain another condition with the OR operator, as in this example:

```
SELECT *
  FROM course c, section s
 WHERE c.course_no = s.course_no(+)
    OR c.course_no = 100
```

a) _____ True
b) _____ False

2) A column with the outer join (+) operator may not use the IN operator, as in this example:

```
SELECT *
  FROM course c, section s
 WHERE c.course_no = s.course_no(+)
   AND c.course_no(+) IN (100, 200)
```

a) _____ True
b) _____ False

3) An outer join between two tables returns all rows that satisfy the equijoin condition plus those records from the outer joined tables for which no matches are found.

a) _____ True
b) _____ False

4) Which of the WHERE clauses results in this error message?

```
SELECT c.course_no, s.course_no,
       SUBSTR(c.description, 1,20), s.start_date_time
  FROM course c, section s
```

ORA-01468: a predicate may reference only one outer joined table

a) _____ WHERE course_no = course_no
b) _____ WHERE c.course_no(+) = s.course_no
c) _____ WHERE c.course_no = s.course_no(+)
d) _____ WHERE c.course_no(+) = s.course_no(+)

Answers appear in Appendix A, Section 9.1.

LAB 9.2

SELF-JOINS

LAB OBJECTIVES

After this lab, you will be able to:

✔ Write Self-Joins and Detect Data Inconsistencies

Equijoins always join one or multiple tables. A self-join joins a table to itself by pretending there are different tables involved. This is accomplished by using table aliases. One table has one alias and the same table another alias. For the purpose of executing the query, Oracle treats them as two different tables.

Self-joins are quite useful to perform comparisons and to check for inconsistencies in data. Sometimes a self-join is needed to report on recursive relationships. Chapter 15, "Advanced SQL Queries," covers detailed examples on hierarchical reporting of recursive relationships using the CONNECT BY operator.

One example that lends itself very well to showing the functionality of the self-join is the COURSE table. The PREREQUISITE column is a foreign key to the primary key column COURSE_NO of the COURSE table, reflecting a recursive relationship between the two columns. A PREREQUISITE is valid only if it is also a valid COURSE_NO; otherwise, the data manipulation operation on the table is rejected.

Many queries executed on the course table so far in this workbook typically only show the prerequisite number:

```
SELECT course_no, description, prerequisite
   FROM course
```

If you also want to show the description of the prerequisite, you will need to write a self-join. This is accomplished by pretending to have two separate tables via table aliases, such as C1 and C2. Join the PREREQUISITE column of table C1 with the COURSE_NO column of table C2. If matching records are found, the description of the prerequisite is displayed.

```
SELECT c1.course_no,
       c1.description course_descr,
       c1.prerequisite,
       c2.description pre_req_descr
  FROM course c1 JOIN course c2
    ON (c1.prerequisite = c2.course_no)
 ORDER BY 3
```

COURSE_NO	COURSE_DESCR	PREREQUISITE	PRE_REQ_DESCR
230	Intro to Internet	10	DP Overview
100	Hands-On Windows	20	Intro to Computers
...			
450	DB Programming	350	JDeveloper Lab
144	Database Design	420	Database Systems

26 rows selected.

Examine the first row, COURSE_NO 230, with the prerequisite course number of 10. The course description for course number 10 is DP Overview. This join works just like the equijoins you learned about in Chapter 6, "Equijoin." If a prerequisite is NULL or a match is not found, the self-join, just like the equijoin, does not return the record.

The self-join acts like other joins with primary key and foreign key columns. However, here the relationship is to the table itself. The PREREQUISITE column is a foreign key to the primary key COURSE_NO. The PREREQUISITE comes from the child table and the COURSE_NO comes from the parent table. Every COURSE_NO may have zero or one PREREQUISITE. Note: To qualify as a prerequisite, the PREREQUISITE course number must be listed in the PREREQUISITE column for at least one or multiple courses.

The USING clause cannot be used with the self-join because the USING clause requires identical column names on both tables. This is obviously a problem, because the join needs to be executed on the columns PREREQUISITE and COURSE_NO.

The query can also be expressed in the traditional join format with the following SQL statement.

```
SELECT c1.course_no,
       c1.description course_descr,
       c1.prerequisite,
       c2.description pre_req_descr
  FROM course c1, course c2
 WHERE c1.prerequisite = c2.course_no
 ORDER BY 3
```

THE NON-EQUIJOIN

Occasionally you need to construct joins that are not based on equality of values. The next query illustrates such an example using BETWEEN where you have values that fall into a range. The result shows a listing of grades for student ID 107 including the respective letter. The BETWEEN operator checks for each value in the NUMERIC_GRADE column to see if the individual grade is between the values found in the columns MIN_GRADE and MAX_GRADE of the GRADE_CONVERSION table. If a match is found the appropriate letter grade is returned. For example, the first row of the result shows the value of 76 in the NUMERIC_GRADE column for a final examination. The appropriate letter grade for the value of 76 is a C.

```
SELECT grade_type_code, numeric_grade, letter_grade
  FROM grade g JOIN grade_conversion c
    ON (g.numeric_grade BETWEEN c.min_grade AND c.max_grade)
 WHERE g.student_id = 107
 ORDER BY 1, 2 DESC
GR NUMERIC_GRADE LE
-- ------------- --
FI            76 C
HM            96 A
HM            96 A
...
HM            73 C
MT            91 A-

12 rows selected.
```

You can express the query with the traditional join syntax instead.

```
SELECT grade_type_code, numeric_grade, letter_grade, min_grade,
max_grade
  FROM grade g, grade_conversion c
 WHERE g.numeric_grade BETWEEN c.min_grade AND c.max_grade
   AND g.student_id = 107
 ORDER BY 1, 2 DESC
```

LAB 9.2 EXERCISES

9.2.1 WRITE SELF-JOINS AND DETECT DATA INCONSISTENCIES

a) For SECTION_ID 86, determine which students received a lower grade on their final than on their midterm. In your result, list the columns STUDENT_ID and the grade for the midterm and final.

b) Formulate the question for the following query.

```
SELECT DISTINCT a.student_id, a.first_name, a.salutation
  FROM student a, student b
 WHERE a.salutation <> b.salutation
   AND b.first_name = a.first_name
   AND a.student_id <> b.student_id
 ORDER BY a.first_name
```

c) Display the student ID, last name, and street address of students living at the same address and zip code.

d) Write a query showing the course number, course description, prerequisite, and description of the prerequisite. Include courses without any prerequisites. Note this requires a self-join and an outer join.

LAB 9.2 EXERCISE ANSWERS

9.2.1 ANSWERS

a) For SECTION_ID 86, determine which students received a lower grade on their final than on their midterm. In your result, list the columns STUDENT_ID and the grade for the midterm and final.

Answer: Using a self-join, you can compare the grade for the midterm with the grade for the final and determine if the final is lower than the midterm grade.

```
SELECT fi.student_id, mt.numeric_grade "Midterm Grade",
       fi.numeric_grade "Final Grade"
  FROM grade fi JOIN grade mt
    ON (fi.section_id = mt.section_id
   AND fi.student_id = mt.student_id)
 WHERE fi.grade_type_code = 'FI'
   AND fi.section_id = 86
   AND mt.grade_type_code = 'MT'
   AND fi.numeric_grade < mt.numeric_grade
```

STUDENT_ID	Midterm Grade	Final Grade
102	90	85
108	91	76
211	92	77

3 rows selected.

**LAB
9.2**

Notice three students have a lower grade in the final than the grade they achieved in the midterm. Using a self-join allows you to easily determine the correct result. Imagine you are actually joining to a different table, even though it is really the same table. Visualize one table as the midterm table and the other as the final table, and the formulation of your SQL statement falls into place.

Start with the table representing the final grade for SECTION_ID 86. Then compare the result with the table representing the midterm grade (grade_type_code = 'MT'). Also join the columns STUDENT_ID and SECTION_ID to make sure you match the same individuals and section. Finally, compare the numeric grades between the midterm and final.

Using the traditional join syntax, you can also write the query as follows:

```
SELECT fi.student_id, mt.numeric_grade "Midterm Grade",
       fi.numeric_grade "Final Grade"
  FROM grade fi, grade mt
 WHERE fi.grade_type_code = 'FI'
   AND fi.section_id = 86
   AND mt.grade_type_code = 'MT'
   AND fi.section_id = mt.section_id
   AND fi.student_id = mt.student_id
   AND fi.numeric_grade < mt.numeric_grade
```

Alternatively, a somewhat similar solution can be obtained using the ANY operator and a correlated subquery (see Chapter 7, "Subqueries").

```
SELECT student_id, section_id, numeric_grade
  FROM grade g
 WHERE grade_type_code = 'FI'
   AND section_id = 86
   AND numeric_grade < ANY
       (SELECT numeric_grade
          FROM grade
         WHERE grade_type_code = 'MT'
           AND g.section_id = section_id
           AND g.student_id = student_id)
```

b) Formulate the question for the following query.

```
SELECT DISTINCT a.student_id, a.first_name, a.salutation
  FROM student a, student b
 WHERE a.salutation <> b.salutation
   AND a.first_name = b.first_name
   AND a.student_id <> b.student_id
 ORDER BY a.first_name
```

Answer:Determine the students who might have inconsistent salutations for their respective first names.

Answer:Determine the students who might have inconsistent salutations for their respective first names.

This self-join is used to check for errors and inconsistency of data. A number of students have different salutations for the same first name. For example, Kevin is both a female and male name. The same holds true for Daniel, Roger, and some other students as well.

STUDENT_ID	FIRST_NAME	SALUT
124	Daniel	Mr.
242	Daniel	Mr.
315	Daniel	Ms.
...		
272	Kevin	Ms.
341	Kevin	Mr.
368	Kevin	Mr.
238	Roger	Mr.
383	Roger	Ms.

17 rows selected.

The query self-joins by the first name and shows only those having a different salutation for the same name. Because there are multiple names for each table alias, this results in a Cartesian product. Eliminate any records where the STUDENT_IDs are identical with the condition a.student_id <> b.student_id. Duplicate rows are also eliminated using DISTINCT.

c) Display the student ID, last name, and street address of students living at the same address and zip code.

Answer:The self-join compares the street address and the zip code.

```
SELECT DISTINCT a.student_id, a.last_name,
       a.street_address
  FROM student a, student b
 WHERE a.street_address = b.street_address
   AND a.zip = b.zip
   AND a.student_id <> b.student_id
 ORDER BY a.street_address
```

```
STUDENT_ID LAST_NAME              STREET_ADDRESS
---------- -------------------    --------------------
       390 Greenberg              105-34 65th Ave.   #6B
       392 Saliternan             105-34 65th Ave.   #6B
       234 Brendler               111 Village Hill Dr.
       380 Krot                   111 Village Hill Dr.
...
       217 Citron                 PO Box 1091
       182 Delbrun                PO Box 1091

22 rows selected.
```

The condition `a.student_id <> b.student_id` eliminates the student itself from the result.

Alternatively, the ANSI join solution may look similar to the following SELECT statement.

```
SELECT DISTINCT a.student_id, a.last_name,
       a.street_address
  FROM student a JOIN student b
    ON (a.street_address = b.street_address
   AND a.zip = b.zip
   AND a.student_id <> b.student_id)
 ORDER BY a.street_address
```

Or, your join and WHERE clause may look like this. It actually does not change the result. The ON clause and the WHERE condition all need to be true and are connected by the logical AND.

```
    ON (a.street_address = b.street_address
   AND a.zip = b.zip)
 WHERE a.student_id <> b.student_id
 ORDER BY a.street_address
```

You can also expand the query to include the city and state information for the particular zip code by joining to a third table, the ZIPCODE table.

```
SELECT DISTINCT b.student_id id, b.last_name,
       b.street_address ||' '|| city || ', '
       || state address
  FROM student a, student b, zipcode z
 WHERE a.street_address = b.street_address
   AND a.zip = b.zip
   AND a.student_id <> b.student_id
   AND z.zip = b.zip
 ORDER BY address
```

```
   ID LAST_NAME     ADDRESS
 ---- ------------  ------------------------------------------
  390 Greenberg     105-34 65th Ave.  #6B Forest Hills, NY
  392 Saliternan    105-34 65th Ave.  #6B Forest Hills, NY

  ...
  217 Citron        PO Box 1091 Ft. Lee, NJ
  182 Delbrun       PO Box 1091 Ft. Lee, NJ

22 rows selected.
```

As always, there are many alternatives to achieve the same result; for example, you can also write a subquery.

```
SELECT DISTINCT student_id id, last_name,
       street_address ||' '|| city || ', '
       || state address
  FROM student s, zipcode z
 WHERE s.zip = z.zip
   AND (street_address, s.zip) IN
       (SELECT street_address, zip
          FROM student
         GROUP BY street_address, zip
        HAVING COUNT(*) > 1)
 ORDER BY address
```

d) Write a query showing the course number, course description, prerequisite, and description of the prerequisite. Include courses without any prerequisites. Note this requires a self-join and an outer join.

Answer: The SELECT statement joins the courses and their corresponding prerequisites. It also includes those courses that do not have any prerequisites using an outer join, and generates a NULL for the prerequisite description column labeled PRE_REQ_DESCR.

```
SELECT c1.course_no,
       SUBSTR(c1.description, 1,15) course_descr,
       C1.prerequisite,
       SUBSTR(c2.description,1,15) pre_req_descr
  FROM course c1 LEFT OUTER JOIN course c2
    ON c1.prerequisite = c2.course_no
 ORDER BY 1
COURSE_NO COURSE_DESCR      PREREQUISITE PRE_REQ_DESCR
--------- ----------------  ------------ ---------------
       10 DP Overview
       20 Intro to Comput
       25 Intro to Progra            140 Structured Anal
...
      145 Internet Protoc            310 Operating Syste
      146 Java for C/C++
```

```
          147 GUI Programming              20 Intro to Comput
    . . .
          430 JDeveloper Tech            350 JDeveloper Lab
          450 DB Programming             350 JDeveloper Lab
```

30 rows selected.

Using the traditional syntax you can write the query as follows.

```
SELECT c1.course_no,
       SUBSTR(c1.description, 1,15) course_descr,
       C1.prerequisite,
       SUBSTR(c2.description,1,15) pre_req_descr
  FROM course c1, course c2
 WHERE c1.prerequisite = c2.course_no(+)
 ORDER BY 1
```

Or, you can even write the query with a UNION ALL.

```
SELECT c1.course_no, c1.description course_descr,
       c1.prerequisite, c2.description pre_req_descr
  FROM course c1 JOIN course c2
    ON (c1.prerequisite = c2.course_no)
 UNION ALL
SELECT course_no, description, prerequisite, NULL
  FROM course
 WHERE prerequisite is null
```

LAB 9.2 SELF-REVIEW QUESTIONS

In order to test your progress, you should be able to answer the following questions.

1) A self-join requires you to always join the foreign key with the primary key in the same table.

   a) _____ True
   b) _____ False

2) Self-joins work only when you have a recursive relationship in your table.

   a) _____ True
   b) _____ False

3) You cannot use subqueries or ORDER BY clauses with self-joins.

   a) _____ True
   b) _____ False

4) A self-join joins a table to itself.

    a) _____ True
    b) _____ False

5) You need to use a table alias to be able to write a self-join.

    a) _____ True
    b) _____ False

Answers appear in Appendix A, Section 9.2.

**LAB
9.2**

CHAPTER 9

TEST YOUR THINKING

The projects in this section are meant to have you utilize all of the skills that you have acquired throughout this chapter. The answers to these projects can be found at the companion Web site to this book, located at: *http://www.phptr.com/rischert.*

Visit the Web site periodically to share and discuss your answers.

1) Write a query that shows all the instructors that live in the same zip code.
2) Are any of the rooms overbooked? Determine if any sections meet at the same date, time, and location.
3) Determine if there is any scheduling conflict for instructors: Are any instructors scheduled to teach one or more sections at the same date and time? Order the result by the INSTRUCTOR_ID and the starting date and time of the sections.
4) Show the course number, description, course cost, and section ID for courses that cost 1195 or more. Include courses that have no corresponding section.
5) Write a query that lists the section numbers and students IDs of students enrolled in classes held in location 'L210'. Include sections for which no students are enrolled.

CHAPTER 10

INSERT, UPDATE, AND DELETE

<hr>

CHAPTER OBJECTIVES

In this chapter, you will learn about:

✔ Creating Data and Transaction Control	Page 440
✔ Updating and Deleting Data	Page 463

<hr>

In Chapters 1 through 9 you learned what data is, and how to query and present data. In this chapter, you will learn how to modify the data in tables with the INSERT, UPDATE, DELETE, and MERGE statements, also known as Data Manipulation Language (DML). These statements give you the ability to create, change, or delete data from tables. In the first lab you will learn about creating data in tables with the different INSERT command options and how to make this change permanent. The second lab illustrates various ways to change existing data in the tables and discusses Oracle's locking and read-consistency features. Finally you will learn how to remove or delete data from the table.

LAB 10.1

CREATING DATA AND TRANSACTION CONTROL

> ## LAB OBJECTIVES
>
> After this lab, you will be able to:
>
> ✔ Insert Data

INSERTING DATA

The INSERT statement creates new data in a table. It can insert a single row or multiple rows (based on a subquery) into a single table at one time.

INSERTING AN INDIVIDUAL ROW

The following INSERT statement inserts a row into the ZIPCODE table.

```
INSERT INTO zipcode
VALUES
   ('11111', 'Westerly', 'MA',
    USER, TO_DATE('18-JAN-2000', 'DD-MON-YYYY'),
    USER, SYSDATE)
```

When the statement is executed, Oracle responds with this message:

1 row created.

The INSERT INTO keywords always precede the name of the table into which you want to insert data. The VALUES keyword precedes a set of parentheses that enclose the values you want to insert. For each of the seven columns of the ZIPCODE table there are seven corresponding values with matching datatypes in the INSERT statement separated by commas. The values in the list are in the same order as the columns when you DESCRIBE the ZIPCODE table. It is good practice to include a column list nevertheless in case of future database changes. Following is the INSERT statement with the column list.

```
INSERT INTO zipcode
   (zip, city, state,
    created_by, created_date,
    modified_by, modified_date)
VALUES
   ('11111', 'Westerly', 'MA',
    USER, TO_DATE('18-JAN-2000', 'DD-MON-YYYY'),
    USER, SYSDATE)
```

The syntax of the single-row, single-table INSERT statement is:

```
INSERT INTO tablename [(column [, column]...)]
VALUES (expression|DEFAULT [,expression|DEFAULT]...)
```

As a reminder, the syntax convention for optional parts is enclosed in brackets denoted as [ ]. Keywords are in uppercase. The three dots(. . .) mean that the expression can be repeated. The braces, { }, enclose items of which only one is required.

You notice from the INSERT statement into the ZIPCODE table that a text literal such as 'Westerly' is enclosed with single quotes and to insert a date requires the TO_DATE function with the format mask unless the date is in the default format (typically DD-MON-YYYY or DD-MON-RR).

The INSERT statement uses the SYSDATE function to insert the current date and time into the MODIFIED_DATE column. Similar to the SYSDATE function, the USER function is another function that does not take a parameter. It returns the schema name of the user logged in; in this case, the value STUDENT. This value is inserted in the CREATED_BY and MODIFIED_BY columns. You see the result of the USER function in the following example.

```
SELECT USER
   FROM dual
USER
--------------------
STUDENT

1 row selected.
```

(Note, the SQL*Plus SHOW USER command also returns the schema name of the user logged in, but you cannot use this in an INSERT statement.)

Not all columns of the ZIPCODE table require values, only columns defined as NOT NULL. When you are not inserting data into all columns of a table, you must explicitly name the columns to insert data into. The following statement inserts values into just five of the seven columns in the ZIPCODE table; no data is inserted into the CITY and STATE columns.

```
INSERT INTO zipcode
   (zip, created_by, created_date,
    modified_by, modified_date)
VALUES
   ('11111', USER, SYSDATE, USER, SYSDATE)
```

Alternatively, the statement can be written to not explicitly list the columns, and to insert NULL values in the columns instead.

```
INSERT INTO zipcode
VALUES
   ('11111', NULL, NULL, USER, SYSDATE, USER, SYSDATE)
```

Some columns may have default values defined as part of their column definition. Not listing the column in the INSERT statement automatically places the default value in the column, or you can also explicitly use the keyword DEFAULT.

INSERTING DATES AND TIMES

Inserting a value of the DATE or the DATETIME datatypes is very similar to using these literals in the WHERE clause of a SELECT statement. Following is the structure of the DATE_EXAMPLE table used in Chapter 4, "Date and Conversion Functions."

```
SQL> DESCR date_example
```

Name	Null?	Type
COL_DATE		DATE
COL_TIMESTAMP		TIMESTAMP(6)
COL_TIMESTAMP_W_TZ		TIMESTAMP(6) WITH TIME ZONE
COL_TIMESTAMP_W_LOCAL_TZ		TIMESTAMP(6) WITH LOCAL TIME ZONE

This INSERT statement populates in the table; it explicitly converts the literals with the conversion functions into the respective datatype. The first column value is a DATE and you use the TO_DATE function; the second value is a TIMESTAMP and the literal is converted to this datatype with the TO_TIMESTAMP function. The third column value is of datatype TIMESTAMP WITH TIME ZONE and uses the corresponding TO_TIMESTAMP_TZ function to convert it into the correct datatype. Finally, the fourth column is the date and time in the local time zone. There is no specific conversion function for this datatype; it always displays the value in the local time.

```
INSERT INTO date_example
   (col_date,
    col_timestamp,
```

```
            col_timestamp_w_tz,
            col_timestamp_w_local_tz)
       VALUES
          (TO_DATE('24-MAR-2002 16:25:32',
                    'DD-MON-YYYY HH24:MI:SS'),
           TO_TIMESTAMP('24-MAR-2002 16:25:32.0000000',
                         'DD-MON-YYYY  HH24:MI:SS.FF'),
           TO_TIMESTAMP_TZ('24-MAR-2002 16:25:32.0000000 -5:00',
                            'DD-MON-YYYY HH24:MI:SS.FF TZH:TZM'),
           TO_TIMESTAMP('24-MAR-2002 16:25:32.0000000',
                         'DD-MON-YYYY HH24:MI:SS.FF'))
```

ROUNDING

The next statement attempts to insert a value that exceeds in scale of the COST
column of the COURSE table. The COST column is defined as NUMBER(9,2) and
the inserted value is 50.57499.

```
       INSERT INTO course
          (course_no, description, cost, prerequisite,
           created_by, created_date, modified_by, modified_date)
       VALUES
          (900, 'Test Course', 50.57499, NULL,
           'Your name', SYSDATE, 'Your name', SYSDATE)
       1 row created.
```

The INSERT statement proceeds successfully without any error, and the SELECT
statement against the table reveals that Oracle rounds the number to 50.57.

```
       SELECT cost, course_no
         FROM course
        WHERE course_no = 900
              COST COURSE_NO
       --------- ---------
             50.57       900

       1 row selected.
```

If the value exceeded the precision of the COST column, then you get an error
like the next message. The precision is exceeded by one digit; the COST column
is defined as NUMBER(9,2) with a two-digits scale, thus allowing a maximum
number of seven digits before the comma.

```
INSERT INTO course
   (course_no, description, cost, prerequisite,
    created_by, created_date, modified_by, modified_date)
VALUES
   (901, 'Test Course',12345678, NULL,
    'Your name', SYSDATE, 'Your name', SYSDATE)
```

```
(901, 'Test Course',12345678, NULL,
                    *
ERROR at line 5:
ORA-01438: value larger than specified precision allows for this
column
```

INSERTS AND SCALAR SUBQUERIES

Scalar subqueries, which are defined as subqueries returning a single row and column, are allowed within the VALUE clause of an INSERT statement. The following example shows two scalar subqueries: one inserts the description of COURSE_NO 10 and concatenates it with the word " – Test"; the second scalar subquery inserts the highest cost of any rows in the COURSE table into the COST column.

```
INSERT INTO course
   (course_no, description, cost,
    prerequisite, created_by, created_date,
    modified_by, modified_date)
VALUES
   (1000, (SELECT description||' - Test'
             FROM course
            WHERE course_no = 10),
    (SELECT MAX(cost)
       FROM course),
    20, 'MyName', SYSDATE,
    'MyName', SYSDATE)
```

Verify the result of the INSERT statement by querying the COURSE table for the COURSE_NO equal to 1000.

```
SELECT description, cost, course_no
  FROM course
 WHERE course_no = 1000
```

DESCRIPTION	COST	COURSE_NO
DP Overview - Test	1595	1000

```
1 row selected.
```

INSERTING MULTIPLE ROWS

Another method for inserting data is to select data from another table via a subquery. The subquery may return one or multiple rows; thus, the INSERT statement inserts one or multiple rows at a time. Suppose there is a table called INTRO_COURSE in the STUDENT schema with columns similar to the COURSE table; that is, the corresponding columns have a compatible datatype and column length. They do not have to have the same column names or column order. The following INSERT statement inserts data into the INTRO_COURSE table based on a query against the rows of the COURSE table. According to the subquery's WHERE clause only those rows are chosen where the course has no prerequisite.

```
INSERT INTO intro_course
    (course_no, description_tx, cost, prereq_no,
     created_by, created_date, modified_by,
     modified_date)
SELECT course_no, description, cost, prerequisite,
       created_by, created_date, 'Melanie',
       TO_DATE('01-JAN-2001', 'DD-MON-YYYY')
  FROM course
 WHERE prerequisite IS NULL
```

The syntax for a multiple row INSERT based on a subquery is:

```
INSERT INTO tablename [(column [, column]...)]
SUBQUERY
```

INSERTING INTO MULTIPLE TABLES

While most often you use the single-table, single-row INSERT command, you may occasionally have a need to insert rows into multiple tables simultaneously. This new Oracle *9i* feature is useful when data is transferred from other system sources and the destination is a data warehouse system where the data is consolidated and denormalized for the purpose of providing end-users simple query access to this data. Another use for the multitable INSERT command is when you need to archive old data into separate tables.

Rather than executing multiple individual INSERT statements, the multitable INSERT is not only faster but allows additional syntax options providing further flexibility by allowing the conditional insert of data and perhaps eliminating the need to write specific programs. There are two different types of multitable inserts: the INSERT ALL and the INSERT FIRST. The INSERT ALL can be divided into the unconditional INSERT and the conditional INSERT.

The next examples demonstrate multirow INSERT statements with the SECTION_HISTORY and the CAPACITY_HISTORY tables. You can add them to the STUDENT schema with the supplemental table scripts available from the companion Web site at *http://www.phptr.com/rischert.*

THE UNCONDITIONAL INSERT ALL

The INSERT statement chooses the sections that started more than one year ago and inserts these rows into both tables—the SECTION_HISTORY and the CAPACITY_HISTORY tables. There is no condition on the INSERT statement, other than the WHERE clause condition that determines the rows to be selected from the SECTION table.

```
INSERT ALL
  INTO section_history
    VALUES (section_id, start_date_time, course_no, section_no)
  INTO capacity_history
    VALUES (section_id, location, capacity)
SELECT section_id, start_date_time, course_no, section_no,
      location, capacity
  FROM section
 WHERE TRUNC(start_date_time) < TRUNC(SYSDATE)-365
156 rows created.
```

THE CONDITIONAL INSERT ALL

The next statement chooses the same sections and inserts these rows into the tables depending on whether the individual INSERT condition is satisfied. For example, for a SECTION_ID value of 130 and a CAPACITY of 25, the statement will enter the row in both tables. If only one of the conditions is true, it inserts the row only into the table with the true condition. If both conditions are false, the selected row is not inserted into either of the tables.

```
INSERT ALL
  WHEN section_id BETWEEN 100 and 400 THEN
   INTO section_history
     VALUES (section_id, start_date_time, course_no, section_no)
  WHEN capacity >= 25 THEN
   INTO capacity_history
     VALUES (section_id, location, capacity)
SELECT section_id, start_date_time, course_no, section_no,
      location, capacity
  FROM section
 WHERE TRUNC(start_date_time) < TRUNC(SYSDATE)-365
106 rows created.
```

The syntax for the conditional INSERT ALL is as follows:

```
INSERT ALL
WHEN condition THEN
insert_clause [insert_clause...]
[WHEN condition THEN
insert_clause [insert_clause...]...]
[ELSE
insert_clause [insert_clause...]]
(query)
```

insert_clause:

```
INTO tablename [(column [, column]...)]
[VALUES (expression|DEFAULT[,expression|DEFAULT]...)]
```

THE CONDITIONAL INSERT FIRST

The INSERT FIRST statement evaluates the WHEN clauses in order; if the first condition is true, the row is inserted and subsequent conditions are no longer tested. For example, with a SECTION_ID value of 130 and a CAPACITY of 25, the statement will insert the row in the SECTION_HISTORY tables only because the first condition of the WHEN clause is satisfied. You can have an optional ELSE condition in case none of the conditions are true.

```
INSERT FIRST
 WHEN section_id BETWEEN 100 and 400 THEN
  INTO section_history
    VALUES (section_id, start_date_time, course_no, section_no)
 WHEN capacity >= 25 THEN
  INTO capacity_history
    VALUES (section_id, location, capacity)
SELECT section_id, start_date_time, course_no, section_no,
       location, capacity
  FROM section
 WHERE TRUNC(start_date_time) < TRUNC(SYSDATE)-365
71 rows created.
```

The syntax for the INSERT FIRST command is identical to that of the conditional INSERT ALL command except for the FIRST keyword instead of the ALL keyword.

THE PIVOTING INSERT ALL

The pivoting INSERT ALL statement is just like the unconditional INSERT ALL statement—it inserts the rows into multiple tables and is also does not have a WHEN condition. Here is the example of pivoting a table; that is, flipping it on its side. The following example table called GRADE_DISTRIBUTION has a count of the different grades per each section. The first row with SECTION_ID of 400 shows 5 students with the letter grade A, 10 students with the letter grade B, 3 students with the letter grade C, and no D or F grade for any students of the section.

```
select *
  FROM grade_distribution
```

SECTION_ID	GRADE_A	GRADE_B	GRADE_C	GRADE_D	GRADE_F
400	5	10	3	0	0
401	1	3	5	1	0
402	5	10	3	0	1

```
3 rows selected.
```

Suppose you want to move the data into a more normalized table format. Then you can use a pivoting INSERT ALL statement. This example illustrates the inserting of the data into the table GRADE_DISTRIBUTION_NORMALIZED, which just lists the letter grade and the number of students. Here is the structure of the table. To insert the same data about SECTION_ID 400, five individual rows are needed.

```
SQL> DESCR grade_distribution_normalized
Name                        Null?    Type
--------------------------  -------- -------------
SECTION_ID                           NUMBER(8)
LETTER_GRADE                         VARCHAR2(2)
NUM_OF_STUDENTS                      NUMBER(4)
```

The following INSERT ALL statement transfers each individual selected row into the same table, but in a normalized format whereby each grade is its own row.

```
INSERT ALL
  INTO grade_distribution_normalized
    VALUES (section_id, 'A', grade_a)
  INTO grade_distribution_normalized
    VALUES (section_id, 'B', grade_b)
  INTO grade_distribution_normalized
    VALUES (section_id, 'C', grade_c)
  INTO grade_distribution_normalized
    VALUES (section_id, 'D', grade_d)
  INTO grade_distribution_normalized
    VALUES (section_id, 'F', grade_f)
SELECT section_id, grade_a, grade_b,
       grade_c, grade_d, grade_f
  FROM grade_distribution
15 rows created.
```

When selecting from the GRADE_DISTRIBUTION_NORMALIZED table you see the rows in a normalized format.

```
select *
  FROM grade_distribution_normalized
SECTION_ID LE NUM_OF_STUDENTS
---------- -- ---------------
       400 A                5
       401 A                1
       402 A                5
       400 B               10
...
       400 F                0
       401 F                0
       402 F                1

15 rows selected.
```

TRANSACTION CONTROL

Just as important as manipulating data is controlling when the manipulation becomes permanent. DML statements are controlled within the context of a *transaction*. A transaction is a DML statement or group of DML statements that logically belong together, also referred to as a *logical unit of work*. The group of statements is defined by the commands COMMIT and ROLLBACK, in conjunction with the SAVEPOINT command.

COMMIT

The COMMIT command makes the change to the data permanent. Any previously uncommitted changes are now committed and cannot be undone. The effect of the COMMIT command is that it allows other sessions to see the data. The session issuing the DML command can always see the changes, but other sessions can only see the changes after you COMMIT. Another effect of a COMMIT is that locks for the changed rows are released and other users may perform changes on the rows. You will learn more about locking in Lab 10.2.

DDL statements such as the CREATE TABLE command or DCL statements such as GRANT implicitly issue a COMMIT to the database; there is no need to issue a COMMIT command. You learn about DDL commands in Chapter 11, "Create, Alter, and Drop Tables," and DCL commands in Chapter 14, "Security."

WHAT IS A SESSION?

A session is an individual connection to the Oracle database server. It starts as soon as the user is logged in and authenticated by the server with a valid login ID and password. The session ends when the user logs out with either a DISCONNECT command, an EXIT command to exit SQL*Plus, a click on the log off icon in *i*SQL*Plus, or when there is an abnormal termination, such as the system crashes or the user shuts off his or her or machine without properly exiting. An individual database user may be connected to multiple concurrent sessions simultaneously. For example, you can log into SQL*Plus multiple times, each time establishing an individual session. In *i*SQL*Plus you can startup multiple Browser windows or use the New Session icon in Oracle 9*i* Release 2.

ROLLBACK

The ROLLBACK command undoes any DML statements back to the last COMMIT command issued. Any pending changes are discarded and any locks on the affected rows are released.

EXAMPLE OF A TRANSACTION

The following SQL statements all constitute a single transaction. The first INSERT statement starts the transaction and the ROLLBACK command ends it.

```
INSERT INTO zipcode
   (zip, city, state,
    created_by, created_date, modified_by, modified_date)
VALUES
   ('22222', NULL, NULL,
    USER, SYSDATE, USER, SYSDATE)
```
1 row created.

```
INSERT INTO zipcode
   (zip, city, state,
    created_by, created_date, modified_by, modified_date)
VALUES
   ('33333', NULL, NULL,
    USER, SYSDATE, USER, SYSDATE)
```
1 row created.

```
INSERT INTO zipcode
   (zip, city, state,
    created_by, created_date, modified_by, modified_date)
VALUES
   ('44444', NULL, NULL,
    USER, SYSDATE, USER, SYSDATE)
```
1 row created.

Now query the ZIPCODE table for the values inserted.

```
SELECT zip, city, state
  FROM zipcode
 WHERE zip IN ('22222', '33333', '44444')
```
ZIP   CITY   ST
----- -------------------------- --
22222
33333
44444

3 rows selected.

Then, issue the ROLLBACK command and perform the same query.

```
ROLLBACK
```
Rollback complete.

```
SELECT zip, city, state
  FROM zipcode
 WHERE zip IN ('22222', '33333', '44444')
```

no rows selected

The values inserted are no longer in the ZIPCODE table; the ROLLBACK command prevents the values inserted by all three statements from being committed to the database. If a COMMIT command is issued between the first and second statements, the value '22222' would be found in the ZIPCODE table, but not the values '33333' and '44444'.

SAVEPOINT

The SAVEPOINT command allows you to save the result of DML transactions temporarily. The ROLLBACK command can then refer back to a particular SAVEPOINT and roll back the transaction up to that point; any statements issued after the SAVEPOINT are rolled back.

EXAMPLE OF A SAVEPOINT

Here are the same three DML statements used previously, but with SAVEPOINT commands issued in between.

```
INSERT INTO zipcode
   (zip, city, state,
    created_by, created_date, modified_by, modified_date)
VALUES
   ('22222', NULL, NULL,
    USER, SYSDATE, USER, SYSDATE)
1 row created.

SAVEPOINT zip22222
Savepoint created.

INSERT INTO zipcode
   (zip, city, state,
    created_by, created_date, modified_by, modified_date)
VALUES
   ('33333', NULL, NULL,
    USER, SYSDATE, USER, SYSDATE)
1 row created.

SAVEPOINT zip33333
Savepoint created.

INSERT INTO zipcode
   (zip, city, state,
    created_by, created_date, modified_by, modified_date)
VALUES
   ('44444', NULL, NULL,
    USER, SYSDATE, USER, SYSDATE)
1 row created.
```

Now query the ZIPCODE table for the values inserted.

```
SELECT zip, city, state
  FROM zipcode
 WHERE zip IN ('22222', '33333', '44444')
ZIP   CITY                        ST
----- ------------------------- --
22222
33333
44444

3 rows selected.
```

Then, issue the command ROLLBACK TO SAVEPOINT zip33333 and perform the same query.

```
ROLLBACK TO SAVEPOINT zip33333
Rollback complete.

SELECT zip, city, state
  FROM zipcode
 WHERE zip IN ('22222', '33333', '44444')
ZIP   CITY                        ST
----- ------------------------- --
22222
33333

2 rows selected.
```

All statements issued after the zip33333 savepoint are rolled back. When you rollback to the previous savepoint, the same result occurs, and so on.

```
ROLLBACK TO SAVEPOINT zip22222
Rollback complete.

SELECT zip, city, state
  FROM zipcode
 WHERE zip IN ('22222', '33333', '44444')
ZIP   CITY                        ST
----- ------------------------- --
22222

1 row selected.
```

The three statements still constitute a single transaction; however, it is possible to mark parts of the transaction with a SAVEPOINT in order to control when a statement is rolled back with the ROLLBACK TO SAVEPOINT command.

CONTROLLING TRANSACTIONS

It is important to control DML statements using COMMIT, ROLLBACK, and SAVEPOINT. If the three previous statements logically belong together—in other words, one does not make sense without the others occurring—then another session should not see the results until all three are committed at once. Until the user performing the inserts issues a COMMIT command, no other database users or sessions are able to see the changes. A typical example of such a transaction is the transfer from a savings account to a checking account. You obviously want to avoid the scenario where transactions from one account are missing and the balances are out of sync. Unless both data manipulations are successful, the change does not become permanent and visible to other users.

Oracle places a lock on a row whenever the row is manipulated through a DML statement. This prevents other users from manipulating the row until it is either committed or rolled back. Users can continue to query the row and see the old values until the row is committed.

STATEMENT-LEVEL ROLLBACK

If one individual statement fails in a series of DML statements, only this statement is rolled back and Oracle issues an implicit SAVEPOINT. The other changes remain until a COMMIT or ROLLBACK occurs to end the transactions.

The next example shows two SQL statements: the first INSERT statement executes successfully and the second fails.

```
INSERT INTO zipcode
   (zip, city, state,
    created_by, created_date, modified_by, modified_date)
VALUES
   ('99999', NULL, NULL,
    USER, SYSDATE, USER, SYSDATE)
1 row created.

INSERT INTO zipcode
   (zip, city, state,
    created_by, created_date, modified_by, modified_date)
VALUES
   (NULL, NULL, NULL,
    USER, SYSDATE, USER, SYSDATE)
INSERT INTO zipcode
*
ERROR at line 1:
ORA-01400: cannot insert NULL into ("STUDENT"."ZIPCODE"."ZIP")
```

The error message indicates the problem with the statement; it shows that a null value cannot be inserted into the ZIP column of the ZIPCODE table located in the STUDENT schema.

Only the second statement is rolled back. The first statement remains intact and uncommitted as you see when executing the next query. The entire transaction ends when a ROLLBACK or COMMIT occurs.

```
SELECT zip
  FROM zipcode
 WHERE zip = '99999'
ZIP
-----
99999

1 row selected.
```

LAB 10.1 EXERCISES

10.1.1 INSERT DATA

a) Write and execute an INSERT statement to insert a row into the GRADE_TYPE table for a grade type of 'Extra Credit', identified by a code of 'EC'. Issue a COMMIT command afterward.

b) Explain what is wrong with the following INSERT statement. Hint: It is not the value COURSE_NO_SEQ.NEXTVAL, which inserts a value from a sequence, thus generating a unique number.

```
INSERT INTO course
   (course_no, description, cost)
VALUES
   (course_no_seq.NEXTVAL, 'Intro to Linux', 1295)
```

c) Make students with the first name of Yvonne into instructors by inserting their records into the INSTRUCTOR table. Hint: Use INSTRUCTOR_ID_SEQ.NEXTVAL to generate the instructor IDs. Once the INSERT statement is successful, issue a ROLLBACK command.

d) Issue the following INSERT statements. Are the statements successful? If not, what do you observe?

```
INSERT INTO section
   (section_id, course_no, section_no,
   start_date_time,
   location, instructor_id, capacity, created_by,
   created_date, modified_by, modified_date)
VALUES
   (500, 90, 1,
   TO_DATE('03-APR-2002 15:00', 'DD-MON-YYYY HH24:MI'),
   'L500', 103, 50, 'Your name here',
   SYSDATE, 'Your name here', SYSDATE)


INSERT INTO instructor
   (last_name, salutation, instructor_id,
   created_by, created_date, modified_by, modified_date)
VALUES
   ('Spencer', 'Mister', 200,
   'Your name', SYSDATE, 'Your name', SYSDATE)
```

e) Insert the following row into the GRADE table and exit/logoff SQL*Plus or *i*SQL*Plus without issuing a COMMIT statement. Log back into the server and query the GRADE table for the inserted row. What do you observe?

```
INSERT INTO grade
   (student_id, section_id, grade_type_code,
   grade_code_occurrence, numeric_grade, created_by,
   created_date, modified_by, modified_date)
VALUES
   (124, 83, 'MT',
   1, 90, 'MyName',
   SYSDATE, 'MyName', SYSDATE)
```

LAB 10.1 EXERCISE ANSWERS

10.1.1 ANSWERS

a) Write and execute an INSERT statement to insert a row into the GRADE_TYPE table for a grade type of 'Extra Credit', identified by a code of 'EC'. Issue a COMMIT command afterward.

Answer: All columns of the GRADE_TYPE table are identified as NOT NULL, so the INSERT statement needs to list all the columns and corresponding values.

```
INSERT INTO grade_type
   (grade_type_code, description,
    created_by, created_date, modified_by, modified_date)
VALUES
   ('EC', 'Extra Credit',
    USER, SYSDATE, USER, SYSDATE)
1 row created.


COMMIT
Commit complete.
```

It is not necessary to explicitly list the columns of the GRADE_TYPE table because values are supplied for all columns. However, it is good practice to name all the columns in the column list, because if additional columns are added in the future or the order of columns in the table changes, the INSERT statement will fail. This is particularly important when the INSERT statement is used in a program for repeated use.

b) Explain what is wrong with the following INSERT statement. Hint: It is not the value COURSE_NO_SEQ.NEXTVAL, which inserts a value from a sequence, thus generating a unique number.

```
INSERT INTO course
   (course_no, description, cost)
VALUES
   (course_no_seq.NEXTVAL, 'Intro to Linux', 1295)
```

Answer: The INSERT statement fails because it does not insert values into the NOT NULL columns CREATED_BY, CREATED_DATE, MODIFIED_BY, and MODIFIED_DATE in the COURSE table.

```
INSERT INTO course
             *
ERROR at line 1:
ORA-01400: cannot insert NULL into
("STUDENT"."COURSE"."CREATED_BY")
```

The Oracle error message informs you that the column CREATED_BY requires a value. The correct command includes the NOT NULL columns and is successfully executed when issued as follows:

```
INSERT INTO course
   (course_no, description, cost, created_date,
    modified_date, created_by, modified_by)
VALUES
   (course_no_seq.NEXTVAL, 'Intro to Linux', 1295, SYSDATE,
    SYSDATE, 'AliceRischert', 'AliceRischert')
1 row created.
```

If you don't want to make this change permanent in the database, issue the ROLLBACK command.

```
ROLLBACK
Rollback complete.
```

The value supplied for the COURSE_NO column, COURSE_NO_SEQ.NEXTVAL, is not a text literal, number, or date. It is a value generated from a sequence called COURSE_NO_SEQ. A sequence is an Oracle database object that generates sequential numbers to ensure uniqueness whenever it is used, most commonly for generating primary keys. The keyword NEXTVAL indicates to Oracle to select the next value from the sequence. You learn more about sequences in Chapter 12, "Views, Indexes, and Sequences."

c) Make students with the first name of Yvonne into instructors by inserting their records into the INSTRUCTOR table. Hint: Use INSTRUCTOR_ID_SEQ .NEXTVAL to generate the instructor IDs. Once the INSERT statement is successful, issue a ROLLBACK command.

Answer: An INSERT statement selects values from all columns of the STUDENT table for students with a first name of Yvonne and inserts them into the INSTRUCTOR table.

```
INSERT INTO instructor
  (instructor_id,
   salutation, first_name, last_name,
   street_address, zip, phone,
   created_by, created_date, modified_by, modified_date)
SELECT instructor_id_seq.NEXTVAL,
       salutation, first_name, last_name,
       street_address, zip, phone,
       USER, SYSDATE, USER, SYSDATE
  FROM student
 WHERE first_name = 'Yvonne'
3 rows created.

ROLLBACK
Rollback complete.
```

d) Issue the following INSERT statements. Are the statements successful? If not, what do you observe?

```
INSERT INTO section
   (section_id, course_no, section_no,
    start_date_time,
    location, instructor_id, capacity, created_by,
    created_date, modified_by, modified_date)
VALUES
   (500, 90, 1,
    TO_DATE('03-APR-2002 15:00', 'DD-MON-YYYY HH24:MI'),
    'L500', 103, 50, 'Your name here',
    SYSDATE, 'Your name here', SYSDATE)

INSERT INTO instructor
   (last_name, salutation, instructor_id,
    created_by, created_date, modified_by, modified_date)
VALUES
   ('Spencer', 'Mister', 200,
    'Your name', SYSDATE, 'Your name', SYSDATE)
```

Answer: Both of the INSERT statements fail. You see the reason why after each individual statement is issued.

```
INSERT INTO section
   (section_id, course_no, section_no,
    start_date_time,
    location, instructor_id, capacity, created_by,
    created_date, modified_by, modified_date)
VALUES
   (500, 90, 1,
    TO_DATE('03-APR-2002 15:00', 'DD-MON-YYYY HH24:MI'),
    'L500', 103, 50, 'Your name here',
    SYSDATE, 'Your name here', SYSDATE)
```
INSERT INTO section
*
ERROR at line 1:
ORA-02291: integrity constraint (STUDENT.SECT_CRSE_FK)
violated - parent key not found

This statement fails because a parent row cannot be found. The foreign key constraint SECT_CRSE_FK is violated; that means a course number with the value of 500 does not exist in the COURSE table, thus the creation of an orphan row is prevented by the foreign key constraint. The constraint name is determined when you create a foreign key constraint, discussed in Chapter 12, "Create, Alter, and Drop Tables." Ideally, you want to name the constraint so that it is apparent which columns and tables are involved. If you are unsure which column and table the constraint references, you can query the data dictionary views USER_CONSTRAINTS or ALL_CONSTRAINTS discussed in Chapter 13, "The Data Dictionary and Dynamic SQL Scripts." Note also that the constraint name is prefixed with the STUDENT schema name; this is unrelated to the STUDENT table name.

The next INSERT statement also fails because it attempts to insert a value that is larger than the defined five-character width of the SALUTATION column of the INSTRUCTOR table. The value of 'Mister' is six characters long and therefore causes the following error message.

```
INSERT INTO instructor
   (last_name, salutation, instructor_id,
    created_by, created_date, modified_by, modified_date)
VALUES
   ('Spencer', 'Mister', 200,
    'Your name', SYSDATE, 'Your name', SYSDATE)
INSERT INTO instructor
             *
ERROR at line 1:
ORA-01401: inserted value too large for column
```

INSERTING SPECIAL CHARACTERS

If you attempt to insert the following record, notice the error you will receive. Any attempt to insert or update a column with an ampersand (&) is interpreted by Oracle as a substitution parameter for a SQL*Plus script and prompts you to enter a value. You will learn about this parameter in Chapter 13, "The Data Dictionary and Dynamic SQL Scripts." The & substitution parameter is specific to SQL*Plus or *i*SQL*Plus; you will not encounter such a prompt in other SQL execution environments.

```
INSERT INTO instructor
   (salutation, last_name, instructor_id,
    created_by, created_date, modified_by, modified_date)
VALUES
   ('Mr&Ms', 'Spencer', 300,
    'Your name', SYSDATE, 'Your name', SYSDATE)
Enter value for ms:
old   5:   ('Mr&Ms', 'Spencer', 300,
new   5:   ('Mr', 'Spencer', 300,

1 row created.


ROLLBACK
Rollback complete.
```

To temporarily turn off the substitution parameter functionality you issue the SET DEFINE OFF command. Don't forget to reset it back to its default value with the SET DEFINE ON command.

```
SQL> set define off
SQL> INSERT INTO instructor
  2     (salutation, last_name, instructor_id,
  3       created_by, created_date, modified_by, modified_date)
  4  VALUES
  5     ('Mr&Ms', 'Spencer', 300,
  6       'Your name', SYSDATE, 'Your name', SYSDATE)
  7  /
1 row created.

SQL> SET define on
```

If you have another instructor named O'Neil, you need to use a double set of single quotes to make Oracle understand that this single quote is to be taken as a literal quote.

```
INSERT INTO instructor
   (salutation, last_name, instructor_id,
    created_by, created_date, modified_by, modified_date)
VALUES
   ('Mr.', 'O''Neil', 305,
    'Your name', SYSDATE, 'Your name', SYSDATE)
1 row created.

SELECT last_name
  FROM instructor
 WHERE instructor_id = 305
LAST_NAME
-------------------------
O'Neil

1 row selected.
```

e) Insert the following row into the GRADE table and exit/logoff SQL*Plus or iSQL*Plus without issuing a COMMIT statement. Log back into the server and query the GRADE table for the inserted row. What do you observe?

```
INSERT INTO grade
   (student_id, section_id, grade_type_code,
    grade_code_occurrence, numeric_grade, created_by,
    created_date, modified_by, modified_date)
VALUES
   (124, 83, 'MT',
    1, 90, 'MyName',
    SYSDATE, 'MyName', SYSDATE)
1 row created.
```

*Answer: SQL*Plus and iSQL*Plus implicitly issue a COMMIT when you properly exit the program.*

After you log back into the server and you query the GRADE table, you notice that the row exists, despite the missing COMMIT command. SQL*Plus and *i*SQL*Plus implicitly issue the COMMIT when you correctly exit the program by typing the EXIT or DISCONNECT command or by clicking the Lout Out icon in *i*SQL*Plus.

```
SELECT student_id, section_id, created_by, created_date,
       grade_type_code
  FROM grade
 WHERE section_id = 83
   AND student_id = 124
   AND grade_type_code = 'MT'
   AND TRUNC(created_date) = TRUNC(SYSDATE)
STUDENT_ID SECTION_ID CREATED_BY CREATED_D
---------- ---------- ---------- ---------
       124         83 MyName     08-MAY-02

1 row selected.
```

The implicit commit behavior is part of Oracle's SQL*Plus programs; do not expect identical functionality in any other programs. Typically, you must explicitly commit or rollback your transactions. However, if you exit from either program by clicking the CLOSE button in the window, the INSERT statement will not COMMIT to the database. This is considered an abnormal exit and modified rows will be locked.

LOCKING OF ROWS THROUGH ABNORMAL TERMINATION

Rows may also become locked when a session abnormally terminates such as when the user reboots the machine without properly exiting or the application program connected to the database raises an unhandled exception. If you do not exit properly from your session, an uncommitted transaction may be pending and the row will be locked until Oracle eventually detects the dead session and rolls back the transaction. You can verify if in fact a lock is held on a particular row and table by querying the Oracle data dictionary views. Sometimes the Database Administrator (DBA) must intervene and manually release the lock if Oracle does not resolve the problem automatically. You will find more information on locking in the *Oracle DBA Interactive Workbook* by Melanie Caffrey and Douglas Scherer.

Clean exits and frequent commits are part of good habits that you should adopt; otherwise, locks will not be released and other users cannot make modifications to the same rows you changed.

(Note the SQL*Plus command AUTOCOMMIT can be set to automatically commit every statement issued during a SQL*Plus session by typing `SET AUTOCOMMIT`

ON or SET AUTOCOMMIT IMMEDIATE. This SQL*Plus command is dangerous because it means a ROLLBACK command issued during that session has no effect because every transaction is automatically committed. If you use *i*SQL*Plus, you may notice that after a period of inactivity you get a SP2-0864: Session has expired. Please log in again message. This is due to a time out interval parameter set on *i*SQL*Plus. Typically, this interval is 30 minutes and can be changed. If you exceed the inactivity of the *i*SQL*Plus session, your uncommitted changes are automatically committed and the locks released.)

LAB 10.1 SELF-REVIEW QUESTIONS

In order to test your progress, you should be able to answer the following questions.

1) A DML command automatically issues a COMMIT.

    a) _____ True
    b) _____ False

2) A statement-level rollback ends a transaction.

    a) _____ True
    b) _____ False

3) An INSERT statement can only insert one row at a time into a table.

    a) _____ True
    b) _____ False

4) A COMMIT or ROLLBACK command ends a transaction.

    a) _____ True
    b) _____ False

5) Uncommitted changes can be seen by all users.

    a) _____ True
    b) _____ False

6) A transaction is a logical unit of work.

    a) _____ True
    b) _____ False

Answers appear in Appendix A, Section 10.1.

L A B   1 0 . 2

UPDATING AND DELETING DATA

LAB OBJECTIVES

After this lab, you will be able to:

✔ Update Data
✔ Delete Data

UPDATING DATA

Updating data manipulates existing data in a table. An UPDATE statement always refers to a single table. For example, the following UPDATE statement updates the FINAL_GRADE column in the ENROLLMENT table to 90 for all students who enrolled in January 1999.

```
UPDATE enrollment
   SET final_grade = 90
 WHERE enroll_date >= TO_DATE('01/01/1999', 'MM/DD/YYYY')
   AND enroll_date < TO_DATE('02/01/1999', 'MM/DD/YYYY')
11 rows updated.
```

The keyword UPDATE always precedes the name of the table to be updated, and the SET keyword precedes the column or columns to be changed. An UPDATE statement can update all rows in a table at once, or just certain rows when restricted with a WHERE clause as in the previous example. The general syntax for the UPDATE command is as follows:

```
UPDATE tablename
SET {{(column[,column]...)=(subquery)|
       column={expression|(subquery)|DEFAULT}
     }[,{(column[,column]...)=(subquery)|
```

```
        column={expression|(subquery)|DEFAULT}
    }]...}
[WHERE condition]
```

UPDATING COLUMNS TO NULL VALUES

An UPDATE statement can also update columns with a NULL value. The following UPDATE statement sets the FINAL_GRADE column to NULL for all rows in the ENROLLMENT table.

```
UPDATE enrollment
    SET final_grade = NULL
```

Note the IS NULL operator is used only in a WHERE clause, not in the SET clause of an UPDATE statement.

COLUMN DEFAULT VALUE

A column may have a default value defined; this value is entered if an INSERT statement did not specify an explicit value for a column. Alternatively, you can use the DEFAULT keyword in the UPDATE or INSERT command to explicitly set the default value defined for the column. The NUMERIC_GRADE column of the GRADE table has such a default value of 0 defined. Examine the row before the change to the DEFAULT value.

```
SELECT numeric_grade
  FROM grade
WHERE student_id = 211
  AND section_id = 141
  AND grade_type_code = 'HM'
  AND grade_code_occurrence = 1
NUMERIC_GRADE
-------------
           99
```

1 row selected.

To update the column to the default value of 0 for the first homework grade of student ID 211 in SECTION_ID 141, you issue the following UPDATE command.

```
UPDATE grade
   SET numeric_grade = DEFAULT
 WHERE student_id = 211
   AND section_id = 141
   AND grade_type_code = 'HM'
   AND grade_code_occurrence = 1
1 row updated.
```

Examine the result of the change by re-querying the record. Notice that the column default value of 0 is now entered.

```
SELECT numeric_grade
  FROM grade
WHERE student_id = 211
   AND section_id = 141
   AND grade_type_code = 'HM'
   AND grade_code_occurrence = 1
NUMERIC_GRADE
-------------
            0

1 row selected.
```

Now restore the value to the original value of 99 with the ROLLBACK command.

```
ROLLBACK
Rollback complete.
```

If you want to find out which columns have column default values, you query the data dictionary views USER_TAB_COLUMNS or ALL_TAB_COLUMNS discussed in greater detail in Chapter 13, "The Data Dictionary and Dynamic SQL Scripts." You will learn about the syntax to create column defaults in Chapter 12, "Create, Alter, and Drop Tables."

UPDATES AND THE CASE EXPRESSION

CASE expressions can be used anywhere expressions are allowed. The next example shows the CASE expression in the SET clause of the UPDATE statement. The FINAL_GRADE column of the ENROLLMENT table is updated whereby students enrolled in SECTION_ID 100 receive extra points for their FINAL_GRADE score.

```
UPDATE enrollment
   SET final_grade = CASE WHEN final_grade <=80 THEN
                               final_grade+5
                          WHEN final_grade > 80 THEN
                               final_grade+10
                     END
WHERE section_id = 100
```

The CASE expression evaluates the current value of the FINAL_GRADE column. If the value is less than or equal to 80, the value of the FINAL_GRADE is increased by 5 points, if the value is greater than 80, the increase is 10 points. No provision is made for null values; they remain unchanged because they do not satisfy any of the WHEN conditions. A null value is not greater, less than, or equal to any value and there is no ELSE clause in this statement.

SUBQUERIES AND THE UPDATE COMMAND

An update can occur based on data from other tables using a subquery. The next example uses a subquery in the SET clause of the UPDATE command and it updates the ZIP column of INSTRUCTOR_ID 108 to be equal to the ZIP value of the state of Florida.

```
UPDATE instructor
   SET zip = (SELECT zip
                FROM zipcode
                WHERE state = 'FL')
 WHERE instructor_id = 108
```

In our ZIPCODE table the state of Florida has a single value in the ZIPCODE table.

```
select zip
  FROM zipcode
 WHERE state = 'FL'
ZIP
-----
33431

1 row selected.
```

The result of the update effectively changes the zip code to 33431 for INSTRUCTOR_ID 108.

```
SELECT instructor_id, zip
  FROM instructor
 WHERE instructor_id = 108
INSTRUCTOR_ID ZIP
------------- -----
          108 33431

1 row selected.
```

SUBQUERIES RETURNING NULL VALUES

The following UPDATE query statement attempts to update the same instructor's zip code with a value for which you will not find any zip code in the ZIPCODE table.

```
UPDATE instructor
   SET zip = (SELECT zip
                FROM zipcode
                WHERE state = 'CA')
 WHERE instructor_id = 108
1 row updated.
```

When you issue the query to see the effect of the update. You notice that the sub-query returned a null value and therefore updated the ZIP column to a null.

```
SELECT instructor_id, zip
  FROM instructor
WHERE instructor_id = 108
INSTRUCTOR_ID ZIP
------------- -----
          108
```

1 row selected.

SUBQUERIES RETURNING MULTIPLE VALUES

The next subquery returns multiple zip codes for the state of Connecticut. The error message indicates that the subquery returns multiple rows, which is not allowed for an equal sign (=) and therefore the UPDATE statement fails.

```
UPDATE instructor
   SET zip = (SELECT zip
                 FROM zipcode
                WHERE state = 'CT')
 WHERE instructor_id = 108
   SET zip = (SELECT zip
              *
ERROR at line 2:
ORA-01427: single-row subquery returns more than one row
```

If you want just any one of the zip codes, no matter which one, you can utilize the MAX or MIN function. An aggregate function guarantees the return of a single row.

```
UPDATE instructor
   SET zip = (SELECT MAX(zip)
                 FROM zipcode
                WHERE state = 'CT')
 WHERE instructor_id = 108
1 row updated.
```

UPDATES AND CORRELATED SUBQUERIES

The following statement updates the FINAL_GRADE column to 90 and the MODIFIED_DATE column to March 13, 2000 for those sections taught by the instructor Hanks.

```
UPDATE enrollment e
   SET final_grade = 90,
       modified_date = TO_DATE('13-MAR-2000', 'DD-MON-YYYY')
 WHERE EXISTS
```

```
(SELECT '*'
   FROM section s, instructor i
  WHERE e.section_id = s.section_id
    AND s.instructor_id = i.instructor_id
    AND i.last_name = 'Hanks')
```

**LAB
10.2**

As you see, you can use any of the SELECT statements you learned about to re-strict the result set. In this example, a correlated subquery identifies the rows to be updated. A column from the outer table, in this case ENROLLMENT, is refer-enced in the subquery through the column E.SECTION_ID. Every row of the EN-ROLLMENT table is updated where a corresponding SECTION_ID is returned by the subquery. Just like other correlated subqueries, every row in the outer table, here the ENROLLMENT table, is examined and evaluated against the inner query. The update occurs for those rows where the condition of the correlated subquery evaluates to true.

AVOID THIS COMMON SCENARIO
WITH CORRELATED SUBQUERIES

The following correlated update changes one column with a value from another table. Here are two example tables: TA and TB. The values from TA need to be up-dated to reflect changes made in TB. The query shows a listing of all the rows the example table called TA.

```
SELECT *
  FROM ta
          ID COL1
--------- ----
         1 a
         2 b
         3 c
         4 d
```

4 rows selected.

This is a listing of all the rows in table TB. The idea of the correlated update is to up-date the rows of TA based on table TB by joining the common column called ID.

```
SELECT *
  FROM tb
          ID COL2
--------- ----
         1 w
         2 x
         5 y
         6 z
```

4 rows selected.

When you execute the UPDATE statement and subsequently query table TA, you will notice that the rows with the ID 3 and 4 were updated with null values. The intention was to retain the original values.

```
UPDATE ta
   SET col1 = (SELECT col2
                      FROM tb
                 WHERE ta.id = tb.id)
```
4 rows updated.

```
SELECT *
  FROM ta
        ID COL1
--------- ----
        1 w
        2 x
        3
        4
```

4 rows selected.

The correlated update query does not have a WHERE clause; therefore, all the rows of table TA are evaluated. The correlated subquery returns a null value for any row that was not found in table TB. You can avoid this behavior and retain the values in COL1 by including only the rows found in table TB with an appropriate WHERE clause in the UPDATE statement.

```
ROLLBACK
```
Rollback complete.

```
UPDATE ta
   SET col1 = (SELECT col2
                      FROM tb
                 WHERE ta.id = tb.id)
  WHERE id IN (SELECT id
                      FROM tb)
```
2 rows updated.

A query against the TB table verifies that the desired updates are done correctly.

```
SELECT *
  FROM ta
        ID COL1
--------- ----
        1 w
        2 x
        3 c
        4 d
```

4 rows selected.

Be sure to check your results before committing, especially when you perform complicated updates to a table.

UPDATES AND SUBQUERIES RETURNING MULTIPLE COLUMNS

Following are two example tables called EMPLOYEE and EMPLOYEE_CHANGE. The EMPLOYEE table holds a list of employees with their ID, name, salary, and title. The purpose of the EMPLOYEE_CHANGE table is to hold all the changes that need to be made to the EMPLOYEE table. Perhaps the names, title, and salary information comes from various other systems and is then recorded in the EMPLOYEE_CHANGE table that is to be used for updates to the master EMPLOYEE table.

```
SELECT *
  FROM employee
EMPLOYEE_ID NAME          SALARY TITLE
----------- ----------   ------- ----------
          1 John            1000 Analyst
          2 Mary            2000 Manager
          3 Stella          5000 President
          4 Fred             500 Janitor

4 rows selected.

SELECT *
  FROM employee_change
EMPLOYEE_ID NAME          SALARY TITLE
----------- ----------   ------- ----------
          1 John            1500 Programmer
          3 Stella          6000 CEO
          4 Fred             600 Clerk
          5 Jean             800 Secretary
          6 Betsy           2000 SalesRep

5 rows selected.
```

The next statement updates both the SALARY and TITLE columns of the EMPLOYEE table with the corresponding values from the EMPLOYEE_CHANGE table for the employee with the ID of 4, which is Fred the Janitor. When you review the subquery of this UPDATE statement, you will notice the equal sign indicates that the subquery must return a single row.

```
UPDATE employee
   SET (salary, title) = (SELECT salary, title
                            FROM employee_change
```

```
                                        WHERE employee_id = 4)
        WHERE employee_id = 4
1 row updated.
```

You now see the change and Fred now earns a different salary and has the title of
Clerk.

```
SELECT *
  FROM employee
EMPLOYEE_ID NAME        SALARY TITLE
----------- ---------- --------- ----------
          1 John          1000 Analyst
          2 Mary          2000 Manager
          3 Stella        5000 President
          4 Fred           600 Clerk

4 rows selected.


ROLLBACK
Rollback complete.
```

Undo the change with the ROLLBACK command. The next example shows how
to update all the rows in the EMPLOYEE table instead of just one individual employee.

```
UPDATE employee e
   SET (salary, title) =
       (SELECT salary, title
          FROM employee_change c
         WHERE e.employee_id = c.employee_id)
   WHERE employee_id IN (SELECT employee_id
                           FROM employee_change)
3 rows updated.
```

Notice three rows are updated and they are for the employees John, Stella, and
Fred. The records for employees Jean and Betsy are not inserted into the EM-
PLOYEE table because the UPDATE statement just updates existing records, not
insert any new rows.

```
SELECT *
  FROM employee
EMPLOYEE_ID NAME        SALARY TITLE
----------- ---------- --------- ----------
          1 John          1500 Programmer
          2 Mary          2000 Manager
          3 Stella        6000 CEO
          4 Fred           600 Clerk

4 rows selected.
```

ROLLBACK
Rollback complete.

MERGE: INSERTS AND UPDATES

You can perform combined INSERT and UPDATE operations with the MERGE command using the following syntax:

```
MERGE INTO tablename
USING query|tablename ON (condition)
WHEN MATCHED THEN UPDATE set_clause
WHEN NOT MATCHED THEN INSERT values_clause
```

The table EMPLOYEE_CHANGE contains two additional rows, Jean and Betsy, not found in the EMPLOYEE table. The MERGE statement allows you to update the matching rows and lets you insert those rows found in the EMPLOYEE_CHANGE table but that are missing from the EMPLOYEE table.

```
MERGE INTO employee e
USING (SELECT employee_id, salary, title, name
         FROM employee_change) c
  ON (e.employee_id = c.employee_id)
WHEN MATCHED THEN
  UPDATE SET e.salary = c.salary,
             e.title = c.title
WHEN NOT MATCHED THEN
  INSERT (e.employee_id, e.salary, e.title, e.name)
  VALUES (c.employee_id, c.salary, c.title, c.name)
5 rows merged.
```

When you query the EMPLOYEE table you observe the changed values and the addition of the employees Jean and Betsy. Note that Mary did not have a record in the EMPLOYEE_CHANGE table; therefore, no modification to her record is performed.

```
SELECT *
  FROM employee
```

EMPLOYEE_ID	NAME	SALARY	TITLE
1	John	1500	Programmer
2	Mary	2000	Manager
3	Stella	6000	CEO
4	Fred	600	Clerk
5	Jean	800	Secretary
6	Betsy	2000	SalesRep

6 rows selected.

DELETING DATA

Data is removed from a table with the DELETE statement. It can delete all rows or just specific rows. The syntax is:

```
DELETE FROM tablename
[WHERE condition]
```

The following statement deletes all rows in the GRADE_CONVERSION table.

```
DELETE FROM grade_conversion
```
15 rows deleted.

When a ROLLBACK command is issued, the DELETE command is undone and the rows are back in the GRADE_CONVERSION table.

```
ROLLBACK
```
Rollback complete.

```
SELECT COUNT(*)
  FROM grade_conversion
```
  COUNT(*)

       15

1 row selected.

REFERENTIAL INTEGRITY AND THE DELETE COMMAND

A DELETE operation on a row that has children rows has a different effect depending on how deletes on the foreign key are defined. There are three different ways you can specify a foreign key constraint with respect to deletes: restrict, cascade, or set null.

If you issue a DELETE on a parent table with associated children records and the foreign key constraint is set to ON DELETE CASCADE, the children are automatically deleted. If the foreign key constraint is set to ON DELETE SET NULL, the children rows are updated to a null value, providing the foreign key column of the child table allows nulls. The default option for a foreign key constraint with respect to deletes is restrict. It disallows the delete of a parent if children rows exist. In this case you must delete the children rows first, before you delete the parent row.

In the STUDENT schema all foreign key constraints are set to the default option, which restricts insert, update, and delete operations.

DELETES AND REFERENTIAL INTEGRITY IN ACTION

If a foreign key constraint is DELETE RESTRICT, you will not be able to delete any parent row, if any child records exist. In the following example, an attempt is made to delete the zip code 10025. Because the ZIP column of the ZIPCODE table is referenced as a foreign key column in the STUDENT table and the table contains student rows with this zip code, you cannot delete the row. Oracle prevents you from creating orphan rows and responds with an error message.

```
DELETE FROM zipcode
  WHERE zip = '10025'
DELETE FROM zipcode
*
ERROR at line 1:
ORA-02292: integrity constraint (STUDENT.INST_ZIP_FK)
violated - child record found
```

The constraint name error message consists of not only the constraint name but also the name of the schema, which in this case is the STUDENT schema. If you installed the tables into another user account, your schema name will be different. You will learn how to create constraints and specify constraint names in the next chapter.

A DELETE statement may delete rows in other tables. If the foreign key constraint specifies the ON DELETE CASCADE option, a delete of a parent row automatically deletes the associated child rows. Imagine that the referential integrity constraint between the STUDENT and ENROLLMENT tables is DELETE CASCADE. A DELETE statement would delete not only the individual STUDENT row, but also any associated ENROLLMENT rows.

To take the scenario a step further, suppose that the student also has records in the GRADE table. The delete will only be successful if the constraint between the ENROLLMENT table and the GRADE table is also DELETE CASCADE. Then the corresponding rows in the GRADE tables are deleted as well. If the delete is RE-STRICT, the ORA-02292 error will appear, informing you to delete all the children records first.

As you know, the ZIPCODE table is not only referenced by the STUDENT table, but also by the INSTRUCTOR table. Suppose you have the ON DELETE SET NULL constraint as the foreign key. A delete of the zip code 10025 would cause an update of the ZIP column on the INSTRUCTOR table to a null value providing the STUDENT table does not have this zipcode.

To find out which foreign keys have either the DELETE RESTRICT, the DELETE CAS-CADE, or SET NULL constraint, you can query the data dictionary views USER_CONSTRAINTS or ALL_CONSTRAINTS discussed in Chapter 13, "The Data Dictionary and Dynamic SQL Scripts."

THE SCHEMA DIAGRAM

Sometimes schema diagrams depicting the physical relationships between tables show the referential integrity rules in place. Three types of data manipulation operations are possible in SQL: INSERT, UPDATE, and DELETE. On some schema diagrams you may also find the letters I, U, and D, which are abbreviations for Insert, Update, and Delete, respectively. These abbreviated letters indicate the valid rules that these data manipulation operations must follow.

Figure 10.1 shows a schema diagram of the PUBLISHER and the BOOK table. The foreign key column PUBLISHER_ID is found in the BOOK table. A one-to-many, mandatory relationship exists between the PUBLISHER and BOOK tables. The I:R indicates that any INSERT operation filling in values in PUBLISHER_ID of the BOOK table is RESTRICTED to values found in the PUBLISHER table. By default most database systems require this condition when a foreign key is defined on a column.

The U:R notation indicates that any UPDATE to the PUBLISHER_ID column of the BOOK table is RESTRICTED to values found in the PUBLISHER table. Attempting to UPDATE an invalid value violates the U:R data integrity constraint and generates an error. Both the U:R and the I:R referential integrity rules are the default behaviors and often are not listed on schema diagrams.

The notation for the DELETE operation is listed as D:R, indicating that DELETE operations are restricted. Specifically, this means that you cannot delete a publisher row that is referenced in the BOOK table. If you were allowed to delete the row, you would not be able to tell the publisher of the book and you would create an orphan row. The relationship between the two tables is mandatory, indicating that a null value for the PUBLISHER_ID is not acceptable.

If instead you see a D:C notation, it depicts a DELETE CASCADE meaning a delete of a PUBLISHER row deletes any associated children rows in the BOOK table.

The D:N identifies the DELETE SET NULL. This means that upon the deletion of a PUBLISHER row any corresponding children rows are automatically set to null in the PUBLISHER_ID column of the BOOK table, providing nulls are allowed. This referential functionality is new in Oracle 9*i* and could previously only be implemented with customized PL/SQL trigger code.

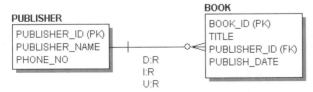

Figure 10.1 ■ Relationship between PUBLISHER and BOOK tables.

THE TRUNCATE COMMAND

The TRUNCATE command deletes all rows from a table, just like the DELETE command. However, the TRUNCATE command does not allow a WHERE clause and automatically issues a COMMIT. All rows are deleted without the ability to roll back the change.

```
TRUNCATE TABLE class
Table truncated.
```

The TRUNCATE statement works more quickly than a DELETE statement to remove all rows from a table because the database does not have to store the undo information in case a ROLLBACK command is issued.

If you attempt to TRUNCATE a table that is referenced by another table as a foreign key, Oracle will issue an error message indicating that this action is not allowed; otherwise, you may create orphan rows. You must disable the foreign key constraint first before you can succeed. Enabling and disabling constraints is discussed in Chapter 12, "Create, Alter, and Drop Tables."

```
TRUNCATE TABLE student;
TRUNCATE TABLE student
                 *
ERROR at line 1:
ORA-02266: unique/primary keys in table referenced by
enabled foreign keys
```

The Whole Truth

Oracle has the capability to attach triggers to tables that fire on DELETE, INSERT, and UPDATE commands. A table's triggers will not execute when the table is truncated. Triggers are written in the PL/SQL language and may perform sophisticated actions (i.e., recording changes to another table for auditing purpose or updating summary values on derived columns).

LOCKING

The real world scenario of a database system is one where many users are accessing data concurrently. Occasionally, users collide and want to manipulate the same piece of information. Locking ensures data consistency.

When you issue an INSERT, UPDATE, DELETE, or MERGE statement, Oracle automatically locks the modified rows. The lock prevents other sessions from making changes to these rows. The lock is released when the session initiating the change commits or rolls back. Other users or sessions may now modify the rows.

Queries do not place locks on rows. Data can always be queried despite being locked; however, other sessions can see the uncommitted data only. After the successful commit of the transaction, the new change is visible to all sessions and the lock is released.

If a row is locked by a session, another session cannot acquire the lock and modify the row. The session attempting to acquire the locked row waits until the lock is released. The session might appear frozen while it waits. Users often think that perhaps their connection to the server dropped or that the DML operation is extremely slow. Users might terminate their session or reboot the machine, only to find out that if they retry the same action the session continues to behave identically. Oracle waits until the lock is released by the other session to proceed with the new change.

Especially when you anticipate multiple users contending for the same row simultaneously, you should commit frequently.

THE LOST UPDATE PROBLEM

The WHERE clause of the next UPDATE statement lists not only the primary key column (the COURSE_NO column) but also includes the old COST column value.

```
UPDATE course
   SET cost = 800
 WHERE course_no = 25
   AND cost = 1195
```

Although this is may seem unnecessary, it can be helpful in case another user made changes to the values in the meantime. Then the UPDATE statement will not be successful and will return 0 rows updated. This indicates that the row containing the old value is no longer found. Many end-user application programs append the values displayed on a user's screen to the WHERE clause of an UPDATE statement. If the UPDATE returns with the 0 rows updated message, the program can alert the user that changes have been made and request the user to re-query the data. This prevents the user from unknowingly overwriting data that changed since he or she last retrieved the data.

You may wonder why Oracle doesn't automatically lock the data to prevent such a situation or place locks on queries. Oracle releases the lock after the user issues a COMMIT or ROLLBACK. A SELECT does not cause any locks; the other user may have queried the data, updated the data, and issued a COMMIT immediately after the UPDATE. Therefore, any subsequent updates do not interfere with another user's UPDATE statement as the lock is already released.

While Oracle automatically takes care of locking, you can explicitly acquire a lock with the SELECT FOR UPDATE or the LOCK TABLE statement. This will override the default locking mechanism; however, this functionality is infrequently used in the real world. Oracle's implicit and automatic locking mechanism works very well for the vast majority of scenarios and adding the retrieved "old" values to the WHERE clause avoids overwriting any unwanted changes.

LOCKING OF ROWS BY DDL OPERATIONS

Locks are not just acquired on individual rows, but also on the entire table when a DDL operation such as ALTER TABLE or CREATE INDEX command is issued. A DML operation cannot update the table while the DDL operation is in progress (e.g., you cannot update rows while a table is being altered) and the same holds true for the reverse: A DDL command on a table cannot be executed if users are holding locks on the table (with some exceptions such as the creation of online indexes discussed in Chapter 12, "Views, Indexes, and Sequences").

READ-CONSISTENCY OF DATA

Whenever a user changes data with a DML operation, Oracle keeps track of the old values on a rollback segment. If the user rolls back the transaction with the ROLLBACK command, Oracle reads the old values from the rollback segment and returns the data to the previous state.

WHAT IS A ROLLBACK SEGMENT OR THE UNDO TABLESPACE?

The purpose of a rollback segment, or UNDO tablespace as it is called in Oracle 9*i*, is to keep track of changes not yet committed. It allows users to issue the ROLLBACK command to restore the data to its original state. Uncommitted data is not permanent and therefore not ready for other users to see yet. Before any data is changed on the actual table, the change is written to the undo/rollback segments first.

Figure 10.2 illustrates the visibility and timing of any changes made to the COST column of the COURSE table for two individual sessions. For example, session #2 updates the COST column value for COURSE_NO 20 to 2000 but does not COMMIT the change. Session #1 will still see the old values, which are retrieved from the rollback segments. Session #1, or any other session for that matter, will not see the data until the user performing the change makes it permanent by issuing a COMMIT.

THE SYSTEM CHANGE NUMBERS (SCN) AND MULTI-VERSIONING

When long-running queries and DML operations occur simultaneously, Oracle automatically handles this with the use of the System Change Number (SCN) that tracks the order in which events occur. This feature enables queries to return a read-consistent result. For example, a query starts at 10:00 A.M. and ends at

TIME	SESSION #1	SESSION #2

T1	`SELECT cost`
	`   FROM course`
	`   WHERE course_no=20`
	`COST`
	`---------`
	`1195`
	
	`1 row selected.`	

T2		`UPDATE course`
		`   SET cost = 2000`
		`   WHERE course_no=20`
		`1 row updated.`

T3	`SELECT cost`
	`   FROM course`
	`   WHERE course_no=20`
	`COST`
	`---------`
	`1195`
	
	`1 row selected.`	

T4		`SELECT cost`
		`   FROM course`
		`   WHERE course_no=20`
		`COST`
		`---------`
		`2000`
		
		`1 row selected.`

T5		`COMMIT` **`Commit complete.`**

T6	`SELECT cost`
	`   FROM course`
	`   WHERE course_no=20`
	`COST`
	`---------`
	`2000`
	
	`1 row selected.`	

Figure 10.2 ■ **The effect of the COMMIT command.**

10:05 A.M. and computes the sum of all salaries for all employees. At 10:03 A.M. the salary of one employee is updated and a COMMIT is issued. What result does the query return? Because the query began before the UPDATE was issued, the result will return a read-consistent result based on the point in time when the query started, which is 10:00 A.M. When a query reads the newly changed salary row, it will recognize that the SCN of the UPDATE is issued after the start of the query and look for the old salary value on the rollback segment.

If you have very long-running queries, you may get an ORA-1555 snapshot too old error message; this indicates that Oracle had to overwrite the rollback information you are attempting to access and therefore cannot return a read-consistent result. Rollback data can be overwritten by other transactions when the previous transaction is committed or rolled back. When this rollback data is no longer available, the long-running query is looking for undo information that no longer exists and returns the error message. To eliminate this error, you can attempt to reissue the query; or if there is a lot of activity on the system, you may need to increase the size of the rollback segments.

For more information on read-consistency, database recovery, and the management of the rollback/UNDO tablespace, refer to the *DBA Interactive Workbook* by Melanie Caffrey and Douglas Scherer.

FLASHBACK QUERIES

Oracle 9i introduced a new feature called *flashback query* that allows you to look at values before specific DML statements occurred. This can be useful in case of a user accidentally performing an unintended but committed DML change. The feature can also be used to compare the current data against the previous day's data to see the changes. When using the flashback query you may specify either an explicit time interval, such as data one day ago, or indicate an individual SCN. Data for flashback queries is kept only for a certain time period that is dependent on the undo management implemented by the DBA. You must familiarize yourself with the limitations of this feature. For example, issuing certain DDL commands, such as altering a table by dropping or modifying columns, invalidates the undo data for the individual table.

LAB 10.2 EXERCISES

10.2.1 UPDATE DATA

    a) Using an UPDATE statement, change the location to B111 for all sections where the location is currently L210.

    b) Update the MODIFIED_BY column with the user login name and update the MODIFIED_DATE column with a date of March 31, 2001 using the TO_DATE function for all the rows updated in Exercise a.

c) Update instructor Irene Willig's zip code to 90210. What do you observe?

d) What does this query accomplish?

```
UPDATE enrollment e
   SET final_grade = (SELECT AVG(numeric_grade)
                        FROM grade g
                       WHERE e.student_id = g.student_id
                         AND e.section_id = g.section_id),
       modified_date = SYSDATE,
       modified_by = 'Your name here'
 WHERE student_id IN (SELECT student_id
                        FROM student
                       WHERE last_name like 'S%')
```

e) Update the first name from Rick to Nick for the instructor with the ID of 104.

f) Write and execute an UPDATE statement to update the phone numbers of instructors from 2125551212 to 212-555-1212 and the MODIFIED_BY and MODIFIED_DATE columns with the user logged in and today's date, respectively. Write a SELECT statement to prove the update worked correctly. Do not issue a COMMIT command.

g) Start another SQL*Plus session on your computer and login as STUDENT with the password LEARN while your current session is still open. Execute the same SELECT statement you executed in Exercise f to prove your update worked correctly. Explain what data you see and why.

h) What do you think will be the result of the following statement?

```
MERGE INTO enrollment e
USING (SELECT AVG(numeric_grade) final_grade,
              section_id, student_id
        FROM grade
       GROUP BY section_id, student_id) g
```

```
ON (g.section_ID = e.section_id
AND g.student_id = e.student_id)
WHEN MATCHED THEN
  UPDATE SET e.final_grade = g.final_grade
WHEN NOT MATCHED THEN
  INSERT (e.student_id, e.section_id, e.enroll_date,
          e.final_grade, e.created_by, e.created_date,
          e.modified_date, e.modified_by)
  VALUES (g.section_id, g.student_id, SYSDATE,
          g.final_grade, 'MERGE', SYSDATE,
          SYSDATE, 'MERGE')
```

10.2.2 DELETE DATA

a) Delete all rows from the GRADE_CONVERSION table. Then SELECT all the data from the table, issue a ROLLBACK command, and explain your observations.

b) If TRUNCATE is used in Exercise a instead of DELETE, how would this change your observations? Caution: Do not actually execute the TRUNCATE statement unless you are prepared to reload the data.

c) Delete the row inserted in Exercise 10.1.1a in the GRADE_TYPE table.

d) Formulate the question for the following query.

```
DELETE FROM enrollment
 WHERE student_id NOT IN
        (SELECT student_id
           FROM student s, zipcode z
          WHERE s.zip = z.zip
            AND z.city = 'Brooklyn'
            AND z.state = 'NY')
```

LAB 10.2 EXERCISE ANSWERS

10.2.1 ANSWERS

a) Using an UPDATE statement, change the location to B111 for all sections where the location is currently L210.

Answer: The UPDATE statement updates the LOCATION column in 10 rows of the SEC-TION table.

```
UPDATE section
   SET location = 'B111'
 WHERE location = 'L210'
10 rows updated.
```

Without the WHERE clause, all rows in the SECTION table are updated, not just 10 rows. For example, if you want to make sure all students have their last names begin with a capital letter, issue the following UPDATE statement.

```
UPDATE student
   SET last_name = INITCAP(last_name)
```

UPDATES TO MULTIPLE TABLES

Typically your UPDATE statement affects a single table. However, if the table has a trigger associated with it, it may fire if the certain conditions specified in the trigger are true. The code in the trigger may cause insert, updates, or deletes to other tables. Triggers can also add or modify values to rows you are changing. You can query the data dictionary view USER_TRIGGERS to see if any triggers are associated with your tables.

b) Update the MODIFIED_BY column with the user login name and update the MODIFIED_DATE column with a date of March 31, 2001 using the TO_DATE function for all the rows updated in Exercise a.

Answer: The MODIFIED_BY column is updated with the USER function to reflect an update by the user logged in, namely STUDENT, and the MODIFIED_DATE column is updated using the TO_DATE function. The update is based on the previously updated location.

```
UPDATE section
   SET modified_by = USER,
       modified_date = TO_DATE('31-MAR-2001', 'DD-MON-YYYY')
 WHERE location = 'B111'
10 rows updated.
```

Instead of writing them as individual UPDATE statements, Exercises a and b can be combined in a single UPDATE statement with the columns separated by commas.

```
UPDATE section
   SET location = 'B111',
       modified_by = USER,
       modified_date = TO_DATE('31-MAR-2001', 'DD-MON-YYYY')
 WHERE location = 'L210'
```

c) Update instructor Irene Willig's zip code to 90210. What do you observe?

Answer: The attempt to change the zip code to a value that does not exist in the ZIP-CODE table results in a referential integrity constraint error.

```
UPDATE instructor
   SET zip = '90210'
 WHERE last_name = 'Willig'
   AND first_name = 'Irene'
UPDATE instructor
*
ERROR at line 1:
ORA-02291: integrity constraint (STUDENT.INST_ZIP_FK)
violated - parent key not found
```

Oracle does not allow any invalid values in a column if the foreign key constraint exists and is enabled.

A query checking for this zip code in the ZIPCODE table retrieves no rows.

```
SELECT zip
  FROM zipcode
 WHERE zip = '90210'
```

```
no rows selected
```

UNIQUELY IDENTIFYING RECORDS

The WHERE clause in this statement lists the first and last name of the instructor and it happens to be unique and sufficient to identify the individual. Imagine a scenario where you may have instructors with the identical name, but who are in fact different individuals. When you perform manipulation of data, it is best to include the primary key value, such as the INSTRUCTOR_ID, to ensure that the correct row is changed.

d) What does this query accomplish?

```
UPDATE enrollment e
   SET final_grade = (SELECT AVG(numeric_grade)
                        FROM grade g
                       WHERE e.student_id = g.student_id
                         AND e.section_id = g.section_id),
       modified_date = SYSDATE,
```

```
                modified_by = 'Your name here'
WHERE student_id IN (SELECT student_id
                        FROM student
                        WHERE last_name like 'S%')
```

Answer:This query updates the FINAL_GRADE, MODIFIED_DATE, and MODIFIED_BY columns of the ENROLLMENT table for students with the last name starting with the letter S.The computed average grade is based on the individual grades received by the student for the respective section.

The example illustrates a correlated UPDATE statement. The outer query identifies the students with the last name of S. For each individual outer row the inner correlated subquery executes and computes the average of the individual grades from the GRADE table. The result is then updated in the FINAL_GRADE column of the ENROLLMENT table.

e) Update the first name from Rick to Nick for the instructor with the ID of 104.

Answer:The primary key column INSTRUCTOR_ID identifies the instructor uniquely and is therefore used in the WHERE clause.Additionally, it helps to add the old value of the FIRST_NAME column to the WHERE clause, in case any previous changes to the column have been made.

```
UPDATE instructor
   SET first_name = 'Nick'
 WHERE instructor_id = 109
   AND first_name = 'Rick'
1 row updated.
```

f) Write and execute an UPDATE statement to update the phone numbers of instructors from 2125551212 to 212-555-1212 and the MODIFIED_BY and MODIFIED_DATE columns with the user logged in and today's date, respectively. Write a SELECT statement to prove the update worked correctly. Do not issue a COMMIT command.

Answer:A single UPDATE statement updates three columns in 10 rows simultaneously in the INSTRUCTOR table.The MODIFIED_BY column is updated with the USER function and the MODIFIED_DATE column is updated with the SYSDATE function entering today's date and time into the column.

```
UPDATE instructor
   SET phone = '212-555-1212',
       modified_by = USER,
       modified_date = SYSDATE
 WHERE phone = '2125551212'
10 rows updated.

SELECT instructor_id, phone, modified_by, modified_date
  FROM instructor
```

```
INSTRUCTOR_ID PHONE            MODIFIED_BY MODIFIED_
------------- -------------    ----------- ---------
          101 212-555-1212 STUDENT          09-MAY-02
          102 212-555-1212 STUDENT          09-MAY-02
...
          109 212-555-5555 STUDENT          09-MAY-02
          110 212-555-5555 STUDENT          09-MAY-02
```

10 rows selected.

g) Start another SQL*Plus session on your computer and login as STUDENT with the password LEARN while your current session is still open. Execute the same SELECT statement you executed in Exercise f to prove your update worked correctly. Explain what data you see and why.

Answer: The session does not reflect the changes made. Any other database user or session cannot see the updated values in the INSTRUCTOR table until a COMMIT command is issued in the original session.

```
SELECT instructor_id, phone, modified_by, modified_date
   FROM instructor
INSTRUCTOR_ID PHONE               MODIFIED_BY  MODIFIED_
------------- ---------------     -----------  ---------
          101 2125551212          ESILVEST     02-JAN-99
          102 2125551212          ESILVEST     02-JAN-99
...
          109 2125555555          ESILVEST     02-JAN-99
          110 2125555555          ARISCHER     11-MAR-99
```

10 rows selected.

When you are ready to move on to the next exercise, please issue the ROLLBACK command in the first session to undo your changes.

h) What do you think will be the result of the following statement?

```
MERGE INTO enrollment e
USING (SELECT AVG(numeric_grade) final_grade, section_id, student_id
         FROM grade
        GROUP BY section_id, student_id) g
   ON (g.section_ID = e.section_id
   AND g.student_id = e.student_id)
WHEN MATCHED THEN
   UPDATE SET e.final_grade = g.final_grade
WHEN NOT MATCHED THEN
   INSERT (e.student_id, e.section_id, e.enroll_date,
           e.final_grade, e.created_by, e.created_date,
           e.modified_date, e.modified_by)
   VALUES (g.section_id, g.student_id, SYSDATE,
```

```
          g.final_grade, 'MERGE', SYSDATE,
          SYSDATE, 'MERGE')
```

Answer:The MERGE statement will update the column FINAL_GRADE to the average grade per student and section based on the GRADE table. If the section and student is not found in the ENROLLMENT table the MERGE command will insert the row.

Actually, the INSERT part of the MERGE statement will probably never be executed because a row in the GRADE table cannot exist unless an ENROLLMENT row exists. The foreign key relationship between the two tables enforces this. In this instance, the following correlated subquery UPDATE will achieve the same result as the MERGE statement.

```
UPDATE enrollment e
    SET final_grade = (SELECT AVG(numeric_grade)
                          FROM grade g
                         WHERE g.section_id = e.section_id
                           AND g.student_id = e.student_id)
```

10.2.2 ANSWERS

a) Delete all rows from the GRADE_CONVERSION table. Then SELECT all the data from the table, issue a ROLLBACK command, and explain your observations.

Answer:A DELETE statement deletes all rows in the GRADE_CONVERSION table. A subsequently issued SELECT statement shows no rows in the table. Issuing a ROLLBACK undoes the delete. You can verify this by issuing another SELECT statement against the table.

```
DELETE FROM grade_conversion
```
15 rows deleted.

```
SELECT *
  FROM grade_conversion
```

no rows selected

```
ROLLBACK
```
Rollback complete.

b) If TRUNCATE is used in Exercise a instead of DELETE, how would this change your observations? Caution: Do not execute the TRUNCATE statement unless you are prepared to reload the data.

Answer:When TRUNCATE is used the data cannot be rolled back; the ROLLBACK statement has no effect. A subsequent SELECT statement reflects no rows in the GRADE_CONVERSION table.

```
TRUNCATE TABLE grade_conversion
```
Table truncated.

```
ROLLBACK
```
Rollback complete.

```
SELECT COUNT(*)
  FROM grade_conversion
  COUNT(*)
---------
        0
```

1 row selected.

> *Notice, when the ROLLBACK command is issued, Oracle returns the* `Rollback complete` *message. This is misleading, because in this case a rollback did not occur; the data is permanently deleted. Be sure to use caution when using the TRUNCATE TABLE command.*

c) Delete the row inserted in Exercise 10.1.1a in the GRADE_TYPE table.

Answer: A DELETE statement is written for the row where the grade type code is 'EC'.

```
DELETE FROM grade_type
 WHERE grade_type_code = 'EC'
```
1 row deleted.

d) Formulate the question for the following query.

```
DELETE FROM enrollment
 WHERE student_id NOT IN
        (SELECT student_id
           FROM student s, zipcode z
          WHERE s.zip = z.zip
            AND z.city = 'Brooklyn'
            AND z.state = 'NY')
```

Answer: Delete enrollment rows for all students except those who live in Brooklyn, NY.

The DELETE statement narrows down the records in the WHERE clause using a NOT IN subquery to find students who do not live in Brooklyn, NY. Alternatively, the DELETE statement can be rewritten as a correlated subquery using the NOT EXISTS operator, which under certain circumstances can execute faster.

```
DELETE FROM enrollment e
 WHERE NOT EXISTS
        (SELECT 'x'
           FROM student s, zipcode z
          WHERE s.zip = z.zip
```

```
AND s.student_id = e.student_id
AND z.city = 'Brooklyn'
AND z.state = 'NY')
```

Because the STUDENT_ID in the STUDENT table is defined as NOT NULL, the NOT IN and NOT EXISTS statements are equivalent. For more information on the differences between NOT IN and NOT EXISTS see Chapter 7, "Subqueries," and Chapter 16, "SQL Optimization."

LAB 10.2 SELF-REVIEW QUESTIONS

In order to test your progress, you should be able to answer the following questions.

1) It is possible to restore rows deleted with a DELETE statement.

    a) _____ True
    b) _____ False

2) There is no syntax error in the following UPDATE statement.

```
UPDATE grade_type
   SET description = 'Exams'
 WHERE grade_type_code IN ('FI', 'MT')
```

    a) _____ True
    b) _____ False

3) The SELECT command always places locks on the retrieved rows.

    a) _____ True
    b) _____ False

4) Oracle achieves read-consistency by reading uncommitted data.

    a) _____ True
    b) _____ False

5) Oracle releases the lock of a row after the session issues a COMMIT or ROLL-BACK command.

    a) _____ True
    b) _____ False

Answers appear in Appendix A, Section 10.2.

CHAPTER 10

TEST YOUR THINKING

The projects in this section are meant to have you utilize all of the skills that you have acquired throughout this chapter. The answers to these projects can be found at the companion Web site to this book, located at: *http://www.phptr.com/rischert*.

Visit the Web site periodically to share and discuss your answers.

1) Write and execute two INSERT statements to insert rows into the ZIP-CODE table for the following two cities: Newton, MA 02199; Cleveland, OH 43011. After your INSERT statements are successful, make the changes permanent.

2) Make yourself a student by writing and executing an INSERT statement to insert a row into the STUDENT table with data about you. Use one of the zip codes you inserted in Exercise 1. Only insert values into the columns STUDENT_ID (use a value of '900'), FIRST_NAME, LAST_NAME, ZIP, REGISTRATION_DATE (use a date that is five days after today), CREATED_BY, CREATED_DATE, MODIFIED_BY, and MODIFIED_DATE. Issue a COMMIT command afterwards.

3) Write an UPDATE statement to update the data about you in the STUDENT table. Update the columns SALUTATION, STREET_ADDRESS, PHONE, and EMPLOYER. Be sure to also update the MODIFIED_DATE column and make the changes permanent.

4) Delete the row in the STUDENT table and the two rows in the ZIPCODE table you created. Be sure to issue a COMMIT command afterward.

If you performed the exercises in this chapter, you will have changed data in most of the tables of the STUDENT schema. If you go back to the previous chapters and re-execute the queries, you may find that the results are different. Therefore, if you want to re-load the tables and data, you can run the rebuildStudent.sql script. In SQL*Plus you execute: SQL>@c:\guest\schemasetup\rebuildStudent.sql. If you use iSQL*Plus, enter the script location, load, and execute the script.

C H A P T E R   1 1

CREATE, ALTER, AND DROP TABLES

This chapter introduces you to the Data Definition Language (DDL) commands associated with tables, the type of database object most frequently used. Table 11.1 provides you with an overview of other commonly used object types discussed in later chapters.

The DDL commands allow you to create, modify, and remove database objects. This chapter discusses the options available with respect to tables, which allow the manipulating of column definitions and constraints. Because database constraints enforce business rules and data integrity, understanding constraints such the as primary key, foreign key, check or unique constraints are essential to learning about a relational database.

Keep in mind that all DDL statements automatically issue an implicit COMMIT.

Table 11.1 ■ Commonly Used Database Object Types

Database Object	Purpose	Find More Information
Table	Stores data	This chapter
View	Used for security and to hide complexity	Chapter 12
Index	Improves data access speed	Chapter 12
Sequence	Generates unique key values	Chapter 12
Synonym	Provides an alternative name for a database object	Chapter 14
Directory	Points to a directory location outside the Oracle database	This chapter
Stored Database Objects Created Using the PL/SQL Language		
Trigger	Individual PL/SQL programs that executes on DML operations	
Function	Program that returns a single value	
Procedure	Accomplishes a specific task; the program may return zero, one, or many values	
Package	Collection of procedures, functions, or other PL/SQL constructs bundled together	

L A B   1 1 . 1

CREATING AND
DROPPING TABLES

LAB OBJECTIVES

After this lab, you will be able to:

✔ Create and Drop Tables
✔ Create Constraints

CREATING TABLES

Tables are created with the CREATE TABLE command and can be created in one of two ways. The first method is to specify the columns and their datatypes explicitly; the second method is to create a table based on an existing table.

The following statement creates a table called TOY, consisting of four columns. A NOT NULL constraint is specified for the DESCRIPTION column. The newly created table contains no data.

```
CREATE TABLE toy
   (toy_id              NUMBER(10),
    description         VARCHAR2(15) NOT NULL,
    last_purchase_date  DATE,
    remaining_quantity  NUMBER(6))
```

TABLE NAMES

A table name must be unique within a database schema; no other database object, such as another table or an index, can have the same name. All database object names must be no longer than 30 characters; cannot include spaces or hyphens, but can have underscores; and must begin with a letter. The table name should describe the nature of the data contained in it; for consistency, choose either singular or plural names.

COLUMN NAMES

A column name must be unique within a table, should not exceed 30 characters, and should be descriptive of the values stored in the column. A column is defined by a name, datatype, and length, where appropriate. A comma separates each column definition.

By default, table and column names are stored in the Oracle database in uppercase format. You can create table names and column names with mixed cases, special characters, and spaces if you use double quotes around the table and column names. This is rarely used and defies the conventions used by most Oracle database installations.

Many corporations have standard column and naming conventions. Compliance with naming standards simplifies the task of identifying database objects for developers. Furthermore, it shortens the learning curve for individuals involved in the maintenance and support of the system.

Be consistent with your table and column names in terms of abbreviations and the use of either the single or plural form.

Following is the simplified syntax of a CREATE TABLE statement.

```
CREATE [GLOBAL TEMPORARY] TABLE tablename
   (columnname datatype [DEFAULT expr]
     [column_constraint_clause]
      [, columname datatype [DEFAULT expr]
          [column_constraint_clause]...]
    [table_constraint_clause]
   )
[physical_storage_clause]
[temporary_table_clause]
[AS query]
```

The CREATE TABLE syntax shows that you must list the individual column name and the respective datatype; the default expression and a column constraint clause are optional. The column constraint clause has a number of individual syntax options that allow you to restrict the values in an individual column. Because a table actually doesn't consist of just one column, the syntax shows that the various syntax portions, consisting of column name, datatype, default expression, and column constraint clause, may be repeated for each subsequent column. Besides an individual column constraint, a table may have table constraints that restrict one or

·multiple columns. Tables require physical storage with individual storage parameters defined in the storage clause. As previously mentioned, you can create a table based on another table; this is accomplished with the AS QUERY clause. Using the CREATE TABLE statement you can create a temporary table with the GLOBAL TEMPORARY keywords and the use of a temporary_table_clause.

As you work your way through this lab, you will learn about all the different clauses and you will gain a good understanding about the fundamental functionality of the CREATE TABLE command.

COMMONLY USED ORACLE DATATYPES

Character data is stored in columns of datatype VARCHAR2, CHAR, LONG, or CLOB. When creating or altering a table, the VARCHAR2 and CHAR datatypes require a column length. The maximum length of a VARCHAR2 column is 4,000 characters. A fixed length CHAR column stores 2,000 characters at most. A name such as Smith stored in the LAST_NAME column defined as VARCHAR2(25) stores only 6 characters versus a 25 characters in fixed-length CHAR(25) defined column because the CHAR adds trailing spaces to pad the remaining spaces. The LONG datatype stores up to 2 gigabytes of data in a single column; one LONG column per table is allowed, and you cannot use character functions on a LONG column. Oracle recommends the use of the CLOB datatype instead of LONG. CLOBs store up to 4 gigabytes of data and a table may have multiple CLOB columns. LONG and CLOB datatypes come with a number of restrictions related to the use of character functions you learned about in Chapter 3, "Character, Number and Miscellaneous Functions," most of which are overcome with Oracle 9i Text, formerly known as ConText and *inter*Media Text. Using various operators and PL/SQL packages it allows full-text search capabilities against these datatypes.

The NUMBER datatype does not require a precision and scale and it can store up to 38 decimal digits of precision. The definition of NUMBER(5,2) on a column allows you to store values between –999.99 and 999.99. A number such as 1,000 is rejected, and a value such as 80.999 is rounded up to 81.00. Use the NUMBER datatype for data on which you need to calculate, not for phone numbers or zip codes. For example, in the STUDENT schema the ZIP column of the ZIPCODE table is stored as a VARCHAR2 rather than a NUMBER datatype because it requires leading zeros.

The DATE datatype stores the century, year, month, day, hour, minute, and second. It has its own internal format, which can be displayed using different format masks. You can store dates from January 1, 4712 BC to December 31, 4712 AD. Oracle 9i adds new datatypes: The TIMESTAMP datatype includes additional fractional seconds and TIMESTAMP WITH TIME ZONE enables you to keep track of time across geographic regions. The TIMESTAMP WITH LOCAL TIME ZONE is concerned with the date and time in the local region only. The INTERVAL YEAR TO MONTH and INTERVAL DAY TO SECOND handle differences between dates. Prior to Oracle 9i you had to use the NUMBER datatype to represent intervals.

Oracle allows you to save binary data such as images, audio, and video in datatypes called BLOB, RAW, LONG RAW, or BFILE. A BFILE datatype points to a binary operating system file.

For more details about each datatype, refer to Chapter 2, "SQL: The Basics," and Table 2.1 for Oracle's most commonly used build-in datatypes.

INTEGRITY CONSTRAINTS

When creating tables, you typically create them with integrity constraints. These constraints enforce the business rules of a system. For instance, "The salary of an employee may not be a negative number," may be enforced with a check constraint on the salary column, or "An employee must have a unique social security number" is enforced with a NOT NULL constraint and a unique constraint. Constraints ensure the data integrity and data consistency among all applications, no matter which program. They ease the burden of programming the business rules in individual applications because the database enforces the constraint.

The following CREATE TABLE statement creates a table called TAB1 with several types of constraints.

```
CREATE TABLE tab1
   (col1  NUMBER(10)    PRIMARY KEY,
    col2  NUMBER(4)     NOT NULL,
    col3  VARCHAR2(5)   REFERENCES zipcode(zip)
             ON DELETE CASCADE,
    col4  DATE          DEFAULT SYSDATE,
    col5  VARCHAR2(20)  UNIQUE,
    col6  NUMBER        CHECK(col6 < 100))
```

THE PRIMARY KEY CONSTRAINT

The first column of the table, COL1, has a PRIMARY KEY constraint, also referred to as an *entity integrity constraint*. The primary key ensures all values in this column are NOT NULL and are unique. This is enforced through a unique index automatically created by Oracle, unless such a unique index already exists. (Indexes are discussed in Chapter 12, "Views, Indexes, and Sequences.") When the table TAB1 is created, Oracle automatically creates a name for this constraint, which looks something like this: SYS_C0030291. This constraint name is not terribly meaningful because it does not identify the table the constraint was created for or the constraint type. You learn how to name constraints shortly.

Every table usually has one primary key, consisting of one or more columns. The combination of all values in a multicolumn primary key, also called a concatenated primary key, must be unique. Tables without a primary key should have at least a unique key. Primary keys should be static, which means no updates are usually performed. The primary key values are typically created by a number-generating sequence. This type of key is also referred to as an *artificial* or *surrogate* key and has the advantage that these values are completely meaningless and therefore not subject to updates. As a primary key datatype, the NUMBER datatype is a better choice than the VARCHAR2 datatype because it is not prone to punctuation, case-sensitivity, and spelling mistakes, which make it more difficult to distinguish if two records are identical.

THE UNIQUE CONSTRAINT

To enforce unique values on an individual or a group of columns, you create a unique constraint for a table. In this example, column COL5 has a UNIQUE constraint. Before determining the primary key, there are often alternate keys that are candidates for the primary key. Phone numbers or social security numbers are examples of alternate keys with unique constraints. However, these keys are often not chosen as the primary key because they may allow null values or the values are subject to updates. Often these keys are extremely useful for end-users querying the data and perhaps uniqueness may still need to be enforced through the unique constraint. Just like with a primary key constraint, Oracle automatically creates a unique index when a UNIQUE constraint is specified. The most distinguishing characteristic between the primary key constraint and the unique constraint is that a unique constraint allows null values.

THE FOREIGN KEY CONSTRAINT

The foreign key constraint, also referred to as *referential integrity constraint,* ensures that the values in the foreign key correspond to values of a primary key. The column COL3 contains a FOREIGN KEY constraint. The keyword REFERENCES, followed by the ZIPCODE table and the ZIP column in the ZIPCODE table in parentheses, indicates COL3 is a foreign key to the ZIP column of the ZIPCODE table. The FOREIGN KEY constraint indicates the domain of values for COL3; in other words, the only valid values for the COL3 column are zip codes found in the ZIP column of the ZIPCODE table and null values. Following is the excerpt from the previous CREATE TABLE statement, which shows the relevant foreign key constraint syntax.

```
CREATE TABLE tab1
...
    col3  VARCHAR2(5) REFERENCES zipcode(zip)
          ON DELETE CASCADE,
...
```

Alternatively, the foreign key can be created with this syntax; it does not mention the ZIP column. It is simply assumed that it is the primary key of the referenced table.

```
    col3  VARCHAR2(5) REFERENCES zipcode
          ON DELETE CASCADE,
```

When defining a FOREIGN KEY constraint on a table, the column name does not have to be identical to the column name it references. For example, COL3 is the foreign key name and ZIP is the referencing column name, but note that the datatype and length must agree. Foreign keys almost always reference primary keys, but occasionally may reference unique constraints.

DELETES AND THE FOREIGN KEY

By default the foreign key constraint is of type DELETE RESTRICT; in effect, parent rows cannot be deleted if children rows exist. An ON DELETE CASCADE clause indicates that when a parent row is deleted, the corresponding row or rows in this child table will be deleted as well. In the previous SQL statement DELETE CASCADE is explicitly specified, so if a row in the ZIPCODE table is deleted, any rows with the same zip code are deleted from the TAB1 table.

Another possible clause for defining the delete behavior of the foreign key is the clause ON DELETE SET NULL. A delete of a zip code will update the corresponding children rows in TAB1 to null providing the COL3 allows null values.

RECURSIVE RELATIONSHIP

A *recursive relationship* is also known as a self-referencing relationship; the PRE-REQUISITE and the COURSE_NO columns of the COURSE table are an example where a foreign key references the primary key constraint of the same table. A recursive relationship enforced just like any other foreign key; you will see an example how you create such a relationship later in the chapter.

THE CHECK CONSTRAINT

Check constraints enforce logical expressions on column(s), which must evaluate to true for every row in the table. The COL6 column has a CHECK constraint, constraining the column to values less than 100. Note that a null value is allowed, as the column does not have a not null constraint.

```
CREATE TABLE tab1
...
   col6  NUMBER CHECK(col6 < 100))
...
```

Here is another example of a check constraint. The following constraint on a column called STATE restricts the values to the states listed in the IN clause.

```
state VARCHAR2(20) CHECK(state IN
      ('NY','NJ','CT','FL','CA'))
```

THE NOT NULL CHECK CONSTRAINT

The column COL2 contains a check constraint you are already familiar with, namely NOT NULL. Any inserts or changes to data changing the values in this column to NULL are rejected.

```
CREATE TABLE tab1
...
    col2  NUMBER(4) NOT NULL,
...
```

Alternatively, the check constraint can also be written like this, but the previous form is simpler.

```
    col2  NUMBER(4) CHECK (col2 IS NOT NULL),
```

You define the NOT NULL constraints for columns that must always contain a value. For example, the LAST_NAME column of the INSTRUCTOR table is defined as a NOT NULL column and therefore you cannot create or update a row in the INSTRUCTOR table unless a value exists in the column.

THE DEFAULT COLUMN OPTION

The column COL4 specifies a DEFAULT option, which is not a constraint. When a row is inserted into TAB1 and no value is supplied for COL4, SYSDATE is inserted by default.

```
CREATE TABLE tab1
...
    col4  DATE DEFAULT SYSDATE,
...
```

In INSERT statements the keyword DEFAULT explicitly specifies the default value, or if the column is omitted in the statement. In an UPDATE statement the DEFAULT keyword resets a column value to the default value. Refer to Lab 11.2 for more examples.

A default value can be created for any column except for the column or columns of the primary key. Often you choose a default value that represents a typical value. You may combine a default value with a NOT NULL constraint to avoid null values in columns. For example, if the typical COST of a course is 1095, you may want to create a default value for this column. The effect is that if you want to retrieve costs that are less than 1595 or null, you write this query:

```
SELECT *
  FROM course
WHERE NVL(cost,0) < 1595
```

With a default value and a NOT NULL constraint, you simplify the query to the following statement:

```
WHERE cost < 1595
```

NAMING CONSTRAINTS

Applying names to all constraints is a good habit you must adopt; it simplifies identifying constraint errors and avoids confusion and further research. Following is an example of how to name constraints in a CREATE TABLE statement.

```
CREATE TABLE tab1
  (col1   NUMBER(10),
   col2   NUMBER(4) CONSTRAINT tab1_col2_nn NOT NULL,
   col3   VARCHAR2(5),
   col4   DATE DEFAULT SYSDATE,
   col5   VARCHAR2(20),
   col6   NUMBER,
   CONSTRAINT tab1_pk PRIMARY KEY(col1),
   CONSTRAINT tab1_zipcode_fk FOREIGN KEY(col3)
     REFERENCES zipcode(zip),
   CONSTRAINT tab1_col5_col6_uk UNIQUE(col5, col6),
   CONSTRAINT tab1_col6_ck CHECK(col6 < 100),
   CONSTRAINT tab1_col2_col6_ck CHECK(col2 > 100 OR COL6 >20))
```

Table created.

Some of the constraint names are next to each column; these are column-level constraints. The constraint names at the end of the statement are table-level constraints each of which are separated by commas. Constraint names cannot exceed 30 characters and must be unique within the user's schema. In this example the constraint names consist of the name of the table and column (or an abbreviated version) and a two-letter abbreviation identifying the type of constraint.

Ideally, you follow a standard naming convention determined by your organization. In this book, the convention for naming primary key constraints is the name of the table plus the _PK suffix. The foreign key constraint contains the abbreviated name of the child table, then the parent table and the _FK suffix. The unique constraint lists the table name and the columns plus the _UK suffix. Often you must abbreviate table and column names; otherwise, you exceed the 30-character constraint name limit. The last constraint, a CHECK constraint called TAB1_COL6_CK, contains the name table and column name plus the _CK suffix. When compared to the previous example with the unnamed constraints, the unique constraint is now enforced for the values of the combined columns COL5 and COL6 instead. Another difference to the previous CREATE TABLE statement is that the last constraint combines the two columns COL2 and COL6 to ensure that both columns meet the condition specified in the constraint.

All the examples listed here show the constraints added at the time of the table creation. In Lab 11.2 you will see how to add constraints after the table exists.

It is best to name constraints explicitly, for clarity and to manipulate them more easily, as you see in Lab 11.2. Also, when a SQL statement, such as an INSERT, UPDATE, or DELETE statement violates a constraint, Oracle returns an error message with the name of the constraint, making it easy to identify the source of the error.

TABLE-LEVEL AND COLUMN-LEVEL CONSTRAINTS

Constraints are defined on two possible levels—either on the column level or on the table level. A column-level constraint refers to a single column and is defined together with the column. A table-level constraint references one or multiple columns and is defined separately after the definition of all the columns.

All constraints can be defined at the table level except for the NOT NULL constraint. You must use a table-level constraint if you are constraining more than one column.

The general syntax for the column constraint clause is listed as follows: It shows the not null, primary, foreign, unique, and check constraint options.

```
[CONSTRAINT constraintname]
 [NULL|NOT NULL] |
 [REFERENCES tablename [(columname)]
   [ON DELETE {CASCADE|ON DELETE SET NULL}] |
 [[UNIQUE|PRIMARY KEY]
   [USING INDEX
    [(CREATE INDEX indexname
       ON tablename (columnname[,columname...])]
         [storage_clause])]] |
 [CHECK (check_condition)]
 [ENABLE|DISABLE]
 [VALIDATE|NOVALIDATE]
```

The constraint name is optional and must be preceded with the keyword CONSTRAINT. Unless you specify otherwise, your column allows nulls; the underline indicates that this is the default. The foreign key constraint is defined with the REFERENCES keyword; it has two choices with regard to deletes as indicated with the vertical bar or pipe symbol (|). One is the ON DELETE CASCADE keyword, the other is the ON DELETE SET NULL. If you don't list either of these two choices the deletion of rows is restricted; that is, your delete is only successful if no children rows exist. Because the unique and primary key constraint automatically create a unique index, you can use an optional index clause to explicitly create an index with predefined storage parameters. This allows you to define the index on a different tablespace (which is often on a different physical device) for better performance.

The next constraint option is the check constraint syntax. You see that the check condition is within a set of parentheses. All constraints can be either disabled or enabled (the default). The validate and novalidate options indicate if the constraint is enforced for existing and new data or only for subsequently created data.

The table-level constraint is listed after the column definitions. The syntax is listed here:

```
[CONSTRAINT constraintname]
  [UNIQUE (columnname[,columnname...])|
   PRIMARY KEY (columnname[,columnname...])]
    [USING INDEX
    [CREATE INDEX indexname ON tablename
         (columnname[,columnname...])]
      [storage_clause]] |
  [FOREIGN KEY (columnname[,columnname...])]
    REFERENCES tablename [(columnname[,columnname...])]
      [ON DELETE {CASCADE|ON DELETE SET NULL}] |
  [CHECK (check_condition)]
  [ENABLE|DISABLE]
  [VALIDATE|NOVALIDATE]
```

WHAT ARE BUSINESS RULES?

Constraints enforce rules and procedures in organizations. For example, a rule that a student must have a last name is enforced through a NOT NULL constraint. Another rule may state that students must live in a valid zip code and this rule can be imposed with a referential integrity constraint to the ZIPCODE table and a NOT NULL constraint on the ZIP column of the STUDENT table. You can apply a check constraint to make sure course costs fall within a certain range. The datatype of a column determines what kind of data is allowed for entry and perhaps the maximum length. A unique constraint prevents duplicate entry of social security numbers into an EMPLOYEE table. A data consistency rule may state that for any delete of a student record, all corresponding enrollment and grade records are deleted; this is done with a referential integrity foreign key constraint and the ON DELETE CASCADE keyword.

Other business rules may not be as easily enforceable with any of Oracle's declarative constraints. For instance, your rule states that a student cannot enroll after a class has already started. To enforce this rule you have to check that the value in the ENROLL_DATE column of the ENROLLMENT table contains a value less than or equal to the value in the START_DATE_TIME column of the SECTION table for the student's enrolled section. Database triggers enforce such rules and fire on the INSERT, UPDATE, or DELETE operation of a specific table and check other tables to see if the values satisfy the business rule criteria. If not, the operation will fail and the statement will be rejected.

WHAT IS A DATABASE TRIGGER?

Database triggers are PL/SQL programs associated with a table, view, or system event. The following trigger is used to audit data modification. The trigger fires before the UPDATE of each row on the STUDENT table and it automatically updates the MODIFIED_DATE column with the SYSDATE function, filling in the current date and time whenever any update in the table takes place. This database trigger is written in Oracle's PL/SQL language and you will learn more about the language and triggers in general in the *Oracle PL/SQL Interactive Workbook* by Benjamin Rosenzweig and Elena Silvestrova.

```
CREATE OR REPLACE TRIGGER student_trg_ai BEFORE UPDATE ON STUDENT
FOR EACH ROW
BEGIN
 :new.modified_date:=SYSDATE;
END;
/
```

Triggers can also enforce referential integrity constraints instead of applying a foreign key constraint. However, it is preferable to use Oracle's built-in declarative constraints, such as the foreign key constraint, to enforce these rules. Constraints are easier to maintain, simpler, and faster than duplicating identical functionality in a trigger.

WHERE TO ENFORCE BUSINESS RULES?

Business rules can be enforced either on the client side through the front-end program or on the database server. Alternatively, the business logic can also reside on a third tier, perhaps an application server. At times you may see that some rules are enforced in multiple places. The decision often depends on a number of factors: Rules imposed across all applications are often done on the database server, so the need to program and enforce this rule consistently in various programs may be unnecessary.

On the other hand, certain data validation needs to be performed in the front-end program. For example, if your business rule states that a salary must be larger than zero and not null, you may perform this validation within the data entry screen. Some validation is very easy to perform on the front-end screen and the user receives a friendly error message to correct the data entry. Otherwise it is annoying to the user to enter the data only to find out the server rejected the entry. If the salary can be updated by programs other than the front-end screen, you may consider enforcing the rules on both the client front-end program and the server. Be sure to keep the rules consistent throughout.

There are many options to keep in mind regarding the placement of business rules when you are designing applications and database systems, including considerations about user-friendliness, data integrity, consistency, future maintenance, and elimination of duplicate efforts on both the front-end and the back-end.

CREATING TABLES BASED ON OTHER TABLES

Another method of creating a table is to base it on another table or tables using a query construct. You can choose to include the data or not. The following example creates a table called JAN_99_ENROLLMENT based on the January 1999 enrollment rows in the ENROLLMENT table.

```
CREATE TABLE jan_99_enrollment AS
SELECT *
  FROM enrollment
 WHERE enroll_date >= TO_DATE('01/01/1999',
       'MM/DD/YYYY')
   AND enroll_date <  TO_DATE('02/01/1999',
       'MM/DD/YYYY')
Table created.
```

The database feedback `Table created` confirms the JAN_99_ENROLLMENT table is successfully created. Notice the columns and their datatypes when you DESCRIBE the new table.

```
SQL> DESC jan_99_enrollment
 Name                        Null?     Type
 ----------------------      --------  ---------------
 STUDENT_ID                  NOT NULL  NUMBER(8)
 SECTION_ID                  NOT NULL  NUMBER(8)
 ENROLL_DATE                 NOT NULL  DATE
 FINAL_GRADE                           NUMBER(3)
 CREATED_BY                  NOT NULL  VARCHAR2(30)
 CREATED_DATE                NOT NULL  DATE
 MODIFIED_BY                 NOT NULL  VARCHAR2(30)
 MODIFIED_DATE               NOT NULL  DATE
```

The new table has the same columns, datatypes, and lengths as the ENROLLMENT table on which it is based. A SELECT statement on the new table confirms that the inserted data is equal to the condition listed in the WHERE clause.

```
SELECT student_id, section_id, enroll_date
  FROM jan_99_enrollment
STUDENT_ID SECTION_ID ENROLL_DA
---------- ---------- ---------
       102         89 30-JAN-99
       102         86 30-JAN-99
...
```

```
  109        101 30-JAN-99
  109         99 30-JAN-99
```

11 rows selected.

You can use the same syntax to create a table without data. Instead of the WHERE clause restricting specific rows from the ENROLLMENT table, here no rows are returned. The ROWNUM pseudocolumn indicates the order in which Oracle selects a row from a table or set of tables. The first selected row has a ROWNUM of 1, the second has a 2, and so on. Because the query asks for less than 1 row, the statement subsequently creates an empty table.

```
CREATE TABLE jan_99_enrollment AS
SELECT *
  FROM enrollment
 WHERE rownum < 1
```

Alternatively, you can also write the statement with a query that never evaluates to true, such as in the next example. However, this takes more time than the previously issued statement with the ROWNUM.

```
CREATE TABLE jan_99_enrollment AS
SELECT *
  FROM enrollment
 WHERE 1 = 2
```

Tables created with this construct do not inherit referential integrity, indexes, or any other objects associated with the base table except the not null constraints, which receive a system-generated name starting with the letters SYS_.

If a SELECT statement in a CREATE TABLE statement joins two tables or more, it is best not to use the asterisk wildcard in the SELECT list. The tables being joined may contain columns with the same name, resulting in an error message when Oracle attempts to create two columns with the same name in one table.

RENAMING TABLES

Tables can be renamed with the RENAME command. The syntax of the command is as follows:

```
RENAME oldname TO newname
```

You can use the RENAME command not only to rename tables but also views and synonyms; these object types are discussed in the following chapters.

The next statement renames the JAN_99_ENROLLMENT table to JAN_99.

```
RENAME jan_99_enrollment TO jan_99
```
Table renamed.

Alternatively, you can use the ALTER TABLE command, which will be discussed in Lab 11.2.

```
ALTER TABLE jan_99_enrollment RENAME TO jan_99
```

Constraint names and dependent database objects, such as indexes and triggers, are not renamed when the table name is changed. Any granted privileges on the table to other users remain intact. Dependent objects such as views become invalid and need to be recompiled.

DROPPING TABLES

Tables can be dropped when they are no longer needed, using the DROP TABLE command. The syntax is:

```
DROP TABLE tablename [CASCADE CONSTRAINTS]
```

When you drop a table, the table as well as its data is removed from the database. Any indexes or triggers associated with the table are automatically dropped.

```
DROP TABLE jan_99
```
Table dropped.

Other tables may be dependent on the dropped table as a domain for a foreign key reference. For example, if you drop the ZIPCODE table, an Oracle error message occurs because there are other tables with a foreign key referencing the ZIP column of the ZIPCODE table. One solution is to disable or drop the individual foreign key constraints with individual ALTER TABLE commands on these dependent tables, which you will learn in Lab 11.2. Another is to let Oracle drop the foreign key constraints with the CASCADE CONSTRAINTS option. Caution: Do not actually execute the following statement unless you are prepared to reload the data from the ZIPCODE table and add the foreign key constraints on the STUDENT and INSTRUCTOR tables.

```
DROP TABLE zipcode CASCADE CONSTRAINTS
```

Database objects that depend on the table, such as a view referencing the table, synonyms, or PL/SQL packages, procedures, and functions, become invalid. To find out which objects reference a table, query the data dictionary view ALL_DEPENDENCIES or USER_DEPENDENCIES.

STORAGE CLAUSE

A CREATE TABLE statement may have an optional storage clause specifying space definition attributes. Each table allocates an initial extent that specifies how much diskspace is reserved for the table at the time of creation. After the table runs out of the initial extent, Oracle automatically allocates additional space based on the storage parameters of the NEXT extent parameter.

The following statement creates a table called CTX_BOOKMARK with a storage clause specifying an initial size of 5 megabytes on the tablespace called USERS. Once the table is out of the allocated space, each subsequent extent allotted is one additional megabyte in size.

```
CREATE TABLE ctx_bookmark
   (bookmark_id    NUMBER,
    container_id   NUMBER,
    bookmark_tx    VARCHAR2(300) NULL,
    modified_date  DATE)
     TABLESPACE users
       STORAGE (INITIAL 5M NEXT 1M)
       PCTFREE 20
```

A tablespace consists of one or more physical data files. For performance reasons, tables and indexes are usually stored in separate tablespaces located on different physical disk drives. To find out which tablespaces are available to you query the data dictionary view USER_TABLESPACES and to determine your default tablespace look at the USER_USERS data dictionary view.

If no specific storage parameters are defined, the default storage parameters of the tablespace apply. Statements with a missing tablespace name create the data on the default tablespace assigned when the user was created. If a user account does not have any rights to create any table objects, or no rights on certain tablespaces, these rights must be granted to the user first. You will learn more about granting access to tablespaces in Chapter 14, "Security."

ESTIMATING THE TABLE SIZE

How do you determine how much initial space to allocate? You estimate a rough size by entering sample data in the table and then computing statistics with the ANALYZE TABLE command (discussed in Chapter 16, "SQL Optimization"). This will update the data dictionary information with statistics about the table including the average row length in bytes (AVG_ROW_LEN column in the USER_TABLES data dictionary view). Multiply this figure by the number of rows you expect in the table plus about 10 to 15 percent for overhead. Increase the number by how much free space you want to leave in each data block for updates that increase the size of the rows; this figure is determined as a percentage with the PCTFREE ("percent free") parameter in the storage clause.

```
avg_row_len in bytes * number of rows * (1 + PCTFREE/100) * 1.15
```

Next you see the most frequently used options of the storage clause. The PCTUSED parameter determines when a block becomes available again for inserts after its used space falls below the PCTUSED integer. The storage parameters for indexes discussed in the next chapter are identical; however, the PCTUSED parameter is not applicable for indexes.

```
[TABLESPACE tablespacename]
[PCTFREE integer]
[PCTUSED integer]
[STORAGE
  ([INITIAL integer [K|M]]
   [NEXT integer [K|M]])]
```

To determine the total allocated space of an existing table, you query the BYTES column in the data dictionary views USER_SEGMENTS or DBA_SEGMENTS.

Please note that the SQL command syntax in this book highlights the most relevant syntax options. Oracle's SQL commands often include a myriad of different options, some of which are rarely used and therefore not included here. If you need to look up the complete syntax in the Oracle documentation, please refer to Appendix G, "Navigating through the Oracle Documentation."

ORACLE'S OTHER TABLE TYPES

The vast majority of data is stored in an "ordinary" Oracle table. The following paragraphs list other table types for completeness only; a detailed discussion of these table types goes beyond the scope of this book. The other Oracle table types available are: temporary tables, index-organized tables, and external tables. You will obtain a brief overview of their capabilities. Additionally, Oracle allows object-oriented capabilities with tables; in practice, object-oriented database table features are still not very commonly used.

TEMPORARY TABLES

When a query becomes too complicated you can resolve it by writing part of the data to a temporary table before continuing with the main query. Oracle allows two types of temporary tables: session-specific or transaction-specific temporary tables. The data in the temporary table is visible to multiple sessions or transactions, but only with respect to the data created by each session or transaction. Once the session or transaction is complete, the data is deleted.

CREATING TEMPORARY TABLES. The table is session-specific when created with the ON COMMIT PRESERVE ROWS keywords and transaction-specific when created with the ON COMMIT DELETE ROWS keywords.

The following statement creates a session-specific temporary table that will retain its value until the session ends, not when a transaction ends because of an issued COMMIT or ROLLBACK command.

```
CREATE GLOBAL TEMPORARY TABLE s_num_rows
  (student_id              NUMBER,
   last_name               VARCHAR2(25),
   num_classes_enrolled NUMBER)
ON COMMIT PRESERVE ROWS
```

You enter values into the table with an INSERT statement.

```
INSERT INTO s_num_rows
VALUES (123, 'Hesse', 5)
```

The next temporary table is transaction-specific as you see from the ON COM-
MIT DELETE ROWS keywords and uses the SELECT command to populate rows
to the table.

```
CREATE GLOBAL TEMPORARY TABLE t_grade
  ON COMMIT DELETE ROWS as
  SELECT student_id, AVG(numeric_grade) AS avg_grade
    FROM grade
  WHERE student_id IN (SELECT student_id
                         FROM enrollment
                        WHERE final_grade IS NOT NULL)
  GROUP BY student_id
```

Temporary tables behave much like regular tables whereby you can add indexes,
triggers, and some types of constraints, but certain restrictions apply; for example, no referential integrity constraints are allowed.

```
SQL> DESCR t_grade
 Name                          Null?      Type
 ------------------------------ --------- ---------
 STUDENT_ID                    NOT NULL  NUMBER(8)
 AVG_GRADE                                NUMBER
```

When are temporary tables useful? Use temporary tables in cases where it simplifies the query logic and the query is infrequently executed. Be sure to keep in
mind that this may not be the most efficient way to execute the query, but as
with all queries, only testing against a representative data set will determine if
this temporary table solves your complicated query dilemma.

*Data in temporary tables is not stored permanently and only persists
during a session or transaction; however, the structure of the temporary
table exists until explicitly dropped with a DROP TABLE command.*

INDEX-ORGANIZED TABLES

When the primary key of a table comprises most or all of the columns in a table, you may want to consider storing the data in an index-organized table. An index-organized table is useful for frequently used lookup tables that hold currencies, state abbreviations, or stock prices with their respective dates. This type of table executes queries quickly that are looking for the primary key value and as this does not require the lookup of a value in the index first, and then the corresponding retrieval of the row in the table. You cannot disable or drop the primary key of an index-organized table.

```
CREATE TABLE states
   (state_code      VARCHAR2(2),
    state_tx        VARChAR2(200),
    CONSTRAINT state_pk PRIMARY KEY (state_code))
   ORGANIZATION INDEX
```

EXTERNAL TABLES

With the help of external tables, Oracle 9*i* allows read access to data stored outside the database, such as legacy systems. SELECT statements are issued against external tables much like any other table. You cannot insert into or update and delete from an external table, nor can you build an index on an external table.

To define an external table, you describe the individual columns with Oracle datatypes and how to map to these columns. A data access driver and external table layer perform the necessary transformation. Because external data remains stored outside the database, no backup or recovery capabilities within Oracle are performed. External tables are useful to load data into the database, but their setup requires the help of a DBA and some knowledge of Oracle's SQL*Loader bulk-load utility is useful.

Here is a simple example of a flat ASCII example file that is located on the one of the directories of the Oracle database server. Such a file may have data such as the following where the values are separated by commas.

```
102,Crocitto,Fred
103,Landry,J.
104,Enison,Laetia
105,Moskowitz,Angel
106,Olvsade,Judith
107,Mierzwa,Catherine
108,Sethi,Judy
109,Walter,Larry
```

Then you create a ORACLE DIRECTORY entry so the database knows where to find the file on an accessible directory and drive. If you use the Windows operating system, you may choose to specify a directory such as the C:\GUEST as the directory, or wherever your file is located.

```
CREATE DIRECTORY dir_guest AS 'C:\GUEST'
Directory created.
```

You must make sure the Oracle database has operating system read and write access to the operating system directory; otherwise, Oracle cannot load the data! To create an ORACLE DIRECTORY entry within the Oracle database, you must have the DBA privilege or the CREATE ANY DIRECTORY system privilege. Logon as a user with DBA rights or the SYSTEM account then issue the following command: GRANT CREATE ANY DIRECTORY TO student.

You create the external table based on the contents of the flat file with the CREATE TABLE command. The name of the table is STUDENT_EXTERNAL with three columns: STUDENT_ID, LAST_NAME, and FIRST_NAME. The keywords ORGANIZATION EXTERNAL identify that this table is located outside the Oracle database. The TYPE indicates the driver used to read the data. The DEFAULT DIRECTORY identifies the directory where the file is located. The structure of the flat file is defined by the individual field names that are to be read as well as how these individual fields are separated from each other. In this example a comma separates the fields. Additionally, you see the LOCATION keyword indicating the name of the file. This temp.lst file must be located in the directory defined as DIR_GUEST, which maps to the server's C:\GUEST directory.

```
CREATE TABLE student_external
  (student_id NUMBER(3),
   last_name VARCHAR2(25),
   first_name VARCHAR2(25))
  ORGANIZATION EXTERNAL
  (TYPE oracle_loader
   DEFAULT DIRECTORY dir_guest
   ACCESS PARAMETERS
  (FIELDS TERMINATED BY ','
   (student_id, last_name, first_name))
  LOCATION ('temp.lst'))
```

Table created.

There are different types of files; this example shows a comma-separated value file (CSV). Some files enclose the text fields in double quotes, others have fixed lengths where the starting and ending position of each column is predetermined.

Although you have learned about the different Oracle table types, you must know that most of the time you will deal with ordinary Oracle tables and the aforementioned table types currently represent the exception to the norm.

LAB 11.1 EXERCISES

11.1.1 CREATE AND DROP TABLES

a) Explain the error(s) in the following CREATE TABLE statement, if any. If there are errors, rewrite the statement correctly.

```
CREATE TABLE student candidate
   (name     VARCHAR2(25)
    address  VARCHAR2(20)
    city     VARCHAR2
    zip      NUMBER)
```

b) Write and execute a CREATE TABLE statement to create an empty table called NEW_STUDENT containing the following columns: first name, last name, the description of the first course the student takes, and the date the student registered in the program. Determine the datatype and length necessary for each column based on the tables in the STUDENT schema. DESCRIBE the table when you have finished.

c) Execute the following CREATE TABLE statement and explain the result.

```
CREATE TABLE school_program AS
SELECT last_name||', '||first_name name
  FROM student
UNION
SELECT last_name||', '||first_name
  FROM instructor
```

d) Rename the SCHOOL_PROGRAM table you created in Exercise c to a table called SCHOOL_PROGRAM2. Then, drop both the SCHOOL_PROGRAM and SCHOOL_PROGRAM2 tables and explain your observations.

11.1.2 CREATE CONSTRAINTS

a) Execute the following SQL statements to create an empty table called COURSE2 and insert two rows into COURSE2, respectively. What do you observe about the values of the COURSE_NO column in the COURSE2 table?

```
CREATE TABLE course2 AS
SELECT *
  FROM course
 WHERE 1 = 2
Table created.

INSERT INTO course2
   (course_no, description, cost, prerequisite,
    created_by, created_date, modified_by, modified_date)
VALUES
   (999, 'Teaching SQL - Part 1', 1495, NULL,
    'AMORRISON', SYSDATE, 'AMORRISON', SYSDATE)
1 row created.

INSERT INTO course2
   (course_no, description, cost, prerequisite,
    created_by, created_date, modified_by, modified_date)
VALUES
   (999, 'Teaching SQL - Part 2', 1495, NULL,
    'AMORRISON', SYSDATE, 'AMORRISON', SYSDATE)
1 row created.
```

b) Identify the constraints in the following CREATE TABLE statement and explain their purpose.

```
CREATE TABLE extinct_animal
   (animal_id       NUMBER,
    species_id      NUMBER,
    name            VARCHAR2(30) NOT NULL,
    native_country  VARCHAR2(20)
      CONSTRAINT extinct_animal_country_fk
      REFERENCES country(country_name),
    remaining       NUMBER(2,0),
    CONSTRAINT extinct_animal_pk PRIMARY KEY(animal_id, species_id),
    CONSTRAINT extinct_animal_remaining_ck
      CHECK (remaining BETWEEN 0 and 10))
```

c) Rewrite and execute the following CREATE TABLE statement to give the primary key and the foreign key constraints a name.

```
CREATE TABLE former_student
   (studid      NUMBER(8) PRIMARY KEY,
    first_nm    VARCHAR2(25),
    last_nm     VARCHAR2(25),
    enrolled    VARCHAR2(1) DEFAULT 'N',
    zip         VARCHAR2(5) REFERENCES zipcode(zip))
```

d) Rewrite the solution to Exercise c to add a UNIQUE constraint on the FIRST_NM and LAST_NM columns.

LAB 11.1 EXERCISE ANSWERS

11.1.1 ANSWERS

a) Explain the error(s) in the following CREATE TABLE statement, if any. If there are errors, rewrite the statement correctly.

```
CREATE TABLE student candidate
   (name       VARCHAR2(25)
    address    VARCHAR2(20)
    city       VARCHAR2
    zip        NUMBER)
```

Answer: The statement will not execute, as there are three errors: One is that the table name contains spaces. Another is that the length of the CITY column is not specified and lastly, commas are required to separate the column definitions.

```
CREATE TABLE student_candidate
   (name       VARCHAR2(25),
    address    VARCHAR2(20),
    city       VARCHAR2(15),
    zip        NUMBER)
```

b) Write and execute a CREATE TABLE statement to create an empty table called NEW_STUDENT containing the following columns: first name, last name, the description of the first course the student takes, and the date the student registered in the program. Determine the datatype and length necessary for each column based on the tables in the STUDENT schema. DESCRIBE the table when you have finished.

Answer: The table contains the four columns FIRST_NAME, LAST_NAME, DESCRIP-TION, and REGISTRATION_DATE. The first three are of datatype VARCHAR2 and REGISTRATION_DATE is of datatype DATE.

```
CREATE TABLE new_student
   (first_name                      VARCHAR2(25),
    last_name                       VARCHAR2(25),
    description                     VARCHAR2(50),
    registration_date               DATE)
```

```
SQL> DESC new_student
Name                               Null?      Type
---------------------------        --------   -------------
FIRST_NAME                                    VARCHAR2(25)
LAST_NAME                                     VARCHAR2(25)
DESCRIPTION                                   VARCHAR2(50)
REGISTRATION_DATE                             DATE
```

DOCUMENTING THE TABLES AND COLUMNS

When you create tables and columns, you can add comments to them thereby documenting their purposes. This is accomplished with the COMMENT statement. These comments are stored in the data dictionary for reporting and self-documentation purposes. If you want to view the comments, you can query the involved data dictionary views ALL_COL_COMMENTS and ALL_TAB_COMMENTS.

Here is an example of how to create a *table comment* on the NEW_STUDENT table. The comment is enclosed in a single quote.

```
COMMENT ON TABLE new_student IS 'Table holding student
information used for exercises'
Comment created.
```

Next is an example of a *column comment* for the FIRST_NAME column on the NEW_STUDENT table. Notice two individual quotes are necessary to represent a single quote.

```
COMMENT ON COLUMN new_student.first_name is 'The student''s
first name.'
Comment created.
```

c) Execute the following CREATE TABLE statement and explain the result.

```
CREATE TABLE school_program AS
SELECT last_name||', '||first_name name
  FROM student
UNION
SELECT last_name||', '||first_name
  FROM instructor
```

Answer: The statement creates a table called SCHOOL_PROGRAM based on a query of two other tables combining student and instructor names. The first and last names are concatenated into one column.

```
SQL> DESC school_program
 Name                             Null?    Type
 ------------------------------   -------- ------------
 NAME                                      VARCHAR2(52)
```

Notice the length of the name column in the new table: It is long enough to accommodate the combined length of first and last names, plus a comma and a space.

d) Rename the SCHOOL_PROGRAM table you created in Exercise c to a table called SCHOOL_PROGRAM2. Then drop both the SCHOOL_PROGRAM and SCHOOL_PROGRAM2 tables and explain your observations.

Answer: The RENAME and DROP TABLE commands are used. The SCHOOL_PROGRAM table no longer exists because it is renamed to SCHOOL_PROGRAM2, so it cannot be dropped.

```
RENAME school_program TO school_program2
Table renamed.

DROP TABLE school_program
DROP TABLE school_program
           *
ERROR at line 1:
ORA-00942: table or view does not exist

DROP TABLE school_program2
Table dropped.
```

11.1.2 ANSWERS

a) Execute the following SQL statements to create an empty table called COURSE2 and insert two rows into COURSE2, respectively. What do you observe about the values of the COURSE_NO column in the COURSE2 table?

```
CREATE TABLE course2 AS
SELECT *
  FROM course
 WHERE 1 = 2
Table created.

INSERT INTO course2
  (course_no, description, cost, prerequisite,
   created_by, created_date, modified_by, modified_date)
```

```
VALUES
  (999, 'Teaching SQL - Part 1', 1495, NULL,
   'AMORRISON', SYSDATE, 'AMORRISON', SYSDATE)
```
1 row created.

```
INSERT INTO course2
  (course_no, description, cost, prerequisite,
   created_by, created_date, modified_by, modified_date)
VALUES
  (999, 'Teaching SQL - Part 2', 1495, NULL,
   'AMORRISON', SYSDATE, 'AMORRISON', SYSDATE)
```
1 row created.

Answer: The primary key constraint is not preserved.

When a table is created from another table, constraints are not automatically pre-served in the new table, except for the NOT NULL constraint. The COURSE_NO column is the primary key in the COURSE table, and, therefore, prevents dupli-cate values. But, when the COURSE2 table is created from the COURSE table, a primary key constraint is not created so the COURSE_NO column in the COURSE2 table allows duplicate values to be inserted.

After creating a table based on another, you can add constraints with the ALTER TABLE command discussed in Lab 11.2.

b) Identify the constraints in the following CREATE TABLE statement and explain their purpose.

```
CREATE TABLE extinct_animal
  (animal_id       NUMBER,
   species_id      NUMBER,
   name            VARCHAR2(30) NOT NULL,
   native_country  VARCHAR2(20)
     CONSTRAINT extinct_animal_country_fk
     REFERENCES country(country_name),
   remaining       NUMBER(2,0),
   CONSTRAINT extinct_animal_pk PRIMARY KEY(animal_id, species_id),
   CONSTRAINT extinct_animal_remaining_ck
     CHECK (remaining BETWEEN 0 and 10))
```

Answer: The first constraint in the EXTINCT_ANIMAL table is a NOT NULL constraint on the NAME column and because it is not named, it receives a system-generated name. The NATIVE_COUNTRY column is a constraint with a foreign key to values from the COUNTRY_NAME column in a table called COUNTRY, which must exist before the command is successful.

The concatenated PRIMARY KEY constraint called EXTINCT_ANIMAL_PK consists of the ANIMAL_ID and SPECIES_ID columns. When a primary key on a table consists of more than one column, the constraint must be written as a table-level constraint on a separate line of the CREATE TABLE statement. The CHECK constraint on the column called EXTINCT_ANIMAL_REMAINING_CK checks whether a number inserted or updated is between the values 0 and 10 inclusively.

A NOT NULL constraint on the ANIMAL_ID and SPECIES_ID columns is not required because the columns are defined as the primary key.

c) Rewrite and execute the following CREATE TABLE statement to give the primary key and the foreign key constraints a name.

```
CREATE TABLE former_student
  (studid    NUMBER(8) PRIMARY KEY,
   first_nm    VARCHAR2(25),
   last_nm     VARCHAR2(25),
   enrolled  VARCHAR2(1) DEFAULT 'N',
   zip         VARCHAR2(5) REFERENCES zipcode(zip))
```

Answer: The constraint definitions are moved to the end of the CREATE TABLE statement where they are created with specific names.

```
CREATE TABLE former_student
  (studid    NUMBER(8),
   first_nm  VARCHAR2(25),
   last_nm   VARCHAR2(25),
   enrolled  VARCHAR2(1) DEFAULT 'N',
   zip       VARCHAR2(5),
   CONSTRAINT former_student_pk PRIMARY KEY(studid),
   CONSTRAINT former_student_zipcode_fk FOREIGN KEY(zip)
     REFERENCES zipcode(zip))
```

Alternatively, you can also use the column-level constraints. Your solution may look similar to this statement:

```
CREATE TABLE former_student
  (studid    NUMBER(8) CONSTRAINT former_student_pk PRIMARY KEY,
   first_nm  VARCHAR2(25),
   last_nm   VARCHAR2(25),
   enrolled  VARCHAR2(1) DEFAULT 'N',
   zip        VARCHAR2(5) CONSTRAINT former_student_zipcode_fk
              REFERENCES zipcode(zip))
```

When a constraint is not named and an error occurs you will receive a system-generated constraint error name. Here is such an example.

```
INSERT INTO former_student
  (studid, first_nm, last_nm, enrolled, zip)
VALUES
  (101, 'Alex', 'Morrison', NULL, '10005')
1 row created.
```

```
INSERT INTO former_student
  (studid, first_nm, last_nm, enrolled, zip)
VALUES
  (101, 'Alex', 'Morrison', NULL, '11717')
INSERT INTO former_student
          *
ERROR at line 1:
ORA-00001: unique constraint (STUDENT.SYS_C001293) violated
```

From the error message, it is impossible to figure out which column(s) caused the error; you can only determine that the constraint is in the STUDENT schema. You need to look up the name of the constraint in the Oracle data dictionary views USER_CONSTRAINTS or ALL_CONSTRAINTS to determine the reason for the error. The system-generated name is not informative; therefore, always name your constraints.

d) Rewrite the solution to Exercise c to add a UNIQUE constraint on the FIRST_NM and LAST_NM columns.

Answer: The constraint is added to the end of the CREATE TABLE statement with a specific name.

```
CREATE TABLE former_student
  (studid    NUMBER(8),
   first_nm  VARCHAR2(25),
   last_nm   VARCHAR2(25),
   enrolled  VARCHAR2(1) DEFAULT 'N',
   zip       VARCHAR2(5),
   CONSTRAINT former_student_pk PRIMARY KEY(studid),
   CONSTRAINT former_student_zipcode_fk FOREIGN KEY(zip)
     REFERENCES zipcode(zip),
   CONSTRAINT former_student_uk UNIQUE(first_nm, last_nm))
```

 A UNIQUE constraint prevents duplicate values from being inserted into a column. It is different from a PRIMARY KEY constraint because a UNIQUE constraint allows NULL values.

LAB 11.1 SELF-REVIEW QUESTIONS

In order to test your progress, you should be able to answer the following questions.

1) The primary key of the following CREATE TABLE statement is a concatenated primary key.

```
CREATE TABLE class_roster
  (class_id         NUMBER(3),
   class_name       VARCHAR2(20) UNIQUE,
   first_class      DATE NOT NULL,
   num_of_students  NUMBER(3),
   CONSTRAINT class_roster_pk
    PRIMARY KEY(class_id, class_name))
```

a) _____ True
b) _____ False

2) It is possible to create one table from three different tables in a single CREATE TABLE statement.

a) _____ True
b) _____ False

3) The CASCADE CONSTRAINTS keywords in a DROP TABLE statement drop all referencing child tables.

a) _____ True
b) _____ False

4) Every column of a table can have one or more constraints.

a) _____ True
b) _____ False

5) You cannot create a table from another table if it has no rows.

a) _____ True
b) _____ False

6) A CREATE TABLE statement automatically commits all previously issued DML statements.

a) _____ True
b) _____ False

7) A foreign key must match a primary key or unique key.

    a) _____ True
    b) _____ False

8) Primary key values should always be subject to frequent change.

    a) _____ True
    b) _____ False

9) The STORAGE clause on a CREATE TABLE statement can specify how much space to allocate.

    a) _____ True
    b) _____ False

Answers appear in Appendix A, Section 11.1.

L A B   1 1 . 2

ALTERING TABLES AND MANIPULATING CONSTRAINTS

LAB OBJECTIVES

After this lab, you will be able to:

✔ Alter Tables and Manipulate Constraints

Once a table is created, you sometimes find you must change its characteristics. The ALTER TABLE command, in conjunction with the ADD, DROP, and MODIFY clauses, allows you to do this. You can add or delete a column; change the length, datatype, or default value of a column; or add, drop, enable, or disable a table's integrity constraints.

Following is the general syntax for the ALTER TABLE command: You will see examples of these many options throughout this lab and in the following exercises.

```
ALTER TABLE tablename
    [ADD [(columnname datatype[DEFAULT expr]
        [column_constraint]
        [, columname datatype[DEFAULT expr]
        [column_constraint]]...)]
        [, table_constraint [, table_constraint...]]]
    [MODIFY [(columname datatype [DEFAULT expr]
        [column_constraint]
    [MODIFY CONSTRAINT constraint_name
        [ENABLE|DISABLE] [NOVALIDATE|VALIDATE]]
    [DROP CONSTRAINT constraint_name|
        PRIMARY KEY|
        UNIQUE (columnname[,columnname...])
        [CASCADE]
    [DISABLE|ENABLE [VALIDATE|NOVALIDATE]
        CONSTRAINT constraint_name|
```

```
    PRIMARY KEY|
    UNIQUE (columnname[,columnname]...)
    [USING INDEX indexname [storage_clause]
 [RENAME CONSTRAINT constraint_name TO new_constraint_name
 [DROP (columnname)|DROP COLUMN (columnname[,columnname...])]
 [SET UNUSED COLUMN columnname|SET UNUSED (columnname[,colum-
name...])]
    [DROP UNUSED COLUMNS]
    [RENAME COLUMN columnname TO newcolumnname]
    [RENAME TO newtablename]
    [storage_clause]
```

ADDING COLUMNS

This is a list of the columns of the TOY TABLE created in Lab 11.1.

```
SQL> DESC toy
Name                              Null?      Type
------------------------------    --------   -----------
TOY_ID                                       NUMBER(10)
DESCRIPTION                       NOT NULL   VARCHAR2(15)
LAST_PURCHASE_DATE                           DATE
REMAINING_QUANTITY                           NUMBER(6)
```

The following statement alters the TOY table to add a new column called MANU-FACTURER.

```
ALTER TABLE toy
  ADD (manufacturer VARCHAR2(30) NOT NULL)
Table altered.
```

The `Table altered` command indicates the successful completion of the operation. When the column is added, it is defined as VARCHAR2(30). The column also has a NOT NULL constraint. When you issue another DESCRIBE command, you see the new column.

```
SQL> DESC toy
Name                              Null?      Type
------------------------------    --------   -----------
TOY_ID                                       NUMBER(10)
DESCRIPTION                       NOT NULL   VARCHAR2(15)
LAST_PURCHASE_DATE                           DATE
REMAINING_QUANTITY                           NUMBER(6)
MANUFACTURER                      NOT NULL   VARCHAR2(30)
```

Alternatively, you can add the column and name the constraint as in the following example.

```
ALTER TABLE TOY
   ADD (manufacturer VARCHAR2(30)
      CONSTRAINT toy_manufacturer_nn NOT NULL)
```

You can only add a column together with a NOT NULL constraint if the table contains no data. Otherwise, add the column first without the NOT NULL constraint, then update the column with data and change the column definition to a NOT NULL constraint with the MODIFY clause of the ALTER TABLE statement.

DROPPING COLUMNS

Columns can also be dropped from a table with the ALTER TABLE command using the DROP clause. The following statement drops the LAST_PURCHASE_DATE column from the TOY table.

```
ALTER TABLE toy
   DROP (last_purchase_date)
```
Table altered.

If you want to drop multiple columns, separate the columns with commas.

```
ALTER TABLE toy
   DROP (manufacturer, remaining_quantity)
```
Table altered.

Instead of dropping a column, you can mark it as unused with the SET UNUSED clause of the ALTER TABLE statement.

```
ALTER TABLE toy
   SET UNUSED (last_purchase_date)
```
Table altered.

Setting the column as unused is useful if you want to make the column no longer visible but do not want to physically remove it yet. When you issue a subsequent ALTER TABLE with the DROP COLUMN clause, or the ALTER TABLE command with the DROP UNUSED COLUMNS clause, Oracle physically removes the column from the database.

```
ALTER TABLE toy
   DROP UNUSED COLUMNS
```
Table altered.

Changing a column to unused instead of dropping it is quicker, because it does not demand a lot of system resources. When the database system resources are less in demand, you can then physically remove the column.

RENAMING COLUMNS

With Oracle 9*i* Release 2 (Version 9.2), you may rename an individual column with the following command:

```
ALTER TABLE toy RENAME COLUMN description TO description_tx
```

MODIFYING COLUMNS

You modify the datatype, length, and column default of existing columns with the ALTER TABLE statement. There are a number of restrictions, as you see in the lab exercises.

The following statement changes the length of the DESCRIPTION column from 15 to 25 characters.

```
ALTER TABLE toy
  MODIFY (description VARCHAR2(25))
Table altered.
```

The following statement modifies the datatype of the REMAINING_QUANTITY column from NUMBER to VARCHAR2, and makes the column NOT NULL simultaneously. This statement executes successfully because the table contains no data.

```
ALTER TABLE toy
  MODIFY (remaining_quantity VARCHAR2(6) NOT NULL)
Table altered.
```

You can also execute the statements individually.

```
ALTER TABLE toy
  MODIFY (remaining_quantity VARCHAR2(6))
Table altered.
```

```
ALTER TABLE toy
  MODIFY (remaining_quantity NOT NULL)
Table altered.
```

If you want to give the NOT NULL constraint a name, you use this command. Instead of the system-generated SYS_ name, the constraint's name will be REMAIN_ QT_NN.

```
ALTER TABLE toy
  MODIFY (remaining_quantity
  CONSTRAINT remain_qt_nn NOT NULL)
Table altered.
```

Other database objects, such as views and stored PL/SQL objects, may be dependent on the table, making them invalid when the table is altered. These objects need to be recompiled and you find the list of invalid objects in the ALL_OBJECTS or ALL_OBJECTS data dictionary view. Before invalidating any objects you can find out which objects are dependent on the table by querying the USER_DEPENDENCIES or ALL_DEPENDENCIES data dictionary news.

**LAB
11.2**

ADDING, DROPPING, DISABLING, AND ENABLING CONSTRAINTS

ADDING CONSTRAINTS

When the TOY table was created, no primary key was specified. The following statement alters the TOY table to add a primary key constraint based on the TOY_ID column.

```
ALTER TABLE toy
   ADD PRIMARY KEY(toy_id)
Table altered.
```

The same statement can be rewritten with a constraint name and a storage clause for the index as well as the tablespace on which the index is to be stored on.

```
ALTER TABLE toy
   ADD CONSTRAINT toy_pk PRIMARY KEY(toy_id)
   USING INDEX TABLESPACE store_idx
   STORAGE (INITIAL 1M NEXT 500 K)
Table altered.
```

For performance reasons, you typically separate indexes and data by storing them on separate tablespaces on different physical devices. The index is created in a tablespace called STORE_IDX. Other characteristics of a table, such as its storage parameters and size, can also be specified with the ALTER TABLE command. In the previous example, one megabyte of space is allocated, regardless of whether any rows exist or not. After this space is used, each subsequent amount of space allocated is 500 kilobytes in size.

The following statement is an example of a SQL statement that creates the concatenated primary key constraint for the GRADE table consisting of four columns. Additionally, the space allocation and tablespace for the automatically associated unique index is located on the INDX tablespace and 100 kilobytes are used for the initial extent.

```
ALTER TABLE grade
  ADD CONSTRAINT gr_pk PRIMARY KEY
  (student_id, section_id, grade_type_code, grade_code_occurrence)
```

```
USING INDEX TABLESPACE indx
STORAGE (INITIAL 100K NEXT 100K)
```

FOREIGN KEY   The following statement illustrates the creation of the two-column foreign key constraint on the GRADE table referencing the concatenated primary key columns of the ENROLLMENT table.

```
ALTER TABLE grade
   ADD CONSTRAINT gr_enr_fk FOREIGN KEY (student_id, section_id)
   REFERENCES enrollment (student_id, section_id)
```

SELF-REFERENCING FOREIGN KEY   The COURSE table has a recursive relationship; the PREREQUISITE column refers back to the COURSE_NO column. It checks to see if the values in the PREREQUISITE column are in fact valid COURSE_NO values. The following SQL statement shows the foreign key constraint command used to create the self-referencing constraint on the COURSE table.

```
ALTER TABLE course
   ADD CONSTRAINT crse_crse_fk FOREIGN KEY (PREREQUISITE)
   REFERENCES course (course_no)
```

If you are loading large amounts of data you may want to consider temporarily disabling this constraint unless you can be sure that the sequence in which the data is inserted into the table is correct. The correct order requires any courses that are prerequisites for other courses to be entered first.

UNIQUE INDEX   The next example shows how the ALTER TABLE command on the SECTION table creates the unique index on the SECTION_NO and COURSE_NO columns. Because unique constraints automatically create an associated index, you want to place the index on a separate tablespace. Following is the syntax to place the index on the INDX tablespace, and the command also defines the initial and each subsequent extent.

```
ALTER TABLE section
   ADD CONSTRAINT sect_sect2_uk
      UNIQUE (section_no, course_no)
   USING INDEX TABLESPACE indx
   STORAGE
   (INITIAL 120K NEXT 120K)
```

CHECK CONSTRAINTS   The following statement adds a check constraint to the ZIP-CODE table. It verifies that the entries in the ZIP primary key column are exactly five characters long and only numbers, not letters or special characters. The TRANSLATE function converts each entered digit into a 9 and then checks to see if the format equals to 99999. Any nonnumeric digits are not translated; therefore, the result of the TRANSLATE is unequal to 99999 and the value is rejected.

```
ALTER TABLE zipcode
   ADD CONSTRAINT zipcode_zip_ck
```

```
CHECK (TRANSLATE(zip, '1234567890',
                      '9999999999') = '99999')
```

Alternatively, you could come up with the following check constraint, but it has one drawback. A value such as '123.4' does not raise an error when the TO_NUMBER conversion function is applied. The LENGTH function is also fine because this is a string with a five-character length. There are many ways to handle checking of data validity; check constraints are just one option.

```
ALTER TABLE zipcode
    ADD CONSTRAINT zipcode_zip_ck
    CHECK (TO_NUMBER(zip)>0 AND LENGTH(zip)= 5)
```

This check constraint is applied to the SALUTATION column of the INSTRUCTOR table.

```
ALTER TABLE instructor
    ADD CONSTRAINT instructor_salutation_ck
    CHECK (salutation IN ('Dr', 'Hon', 'Mr', 'Ms', 'Rev')
         OR salutation IS NULL)
```

Any of the constraints you learned in Lab 11.1 can be added to a table with the ALTER TABLE . . . ADD command.

DROPPING CONSTRAINTS

When a constraint is no longer needed, you drop it with the ALTER TABLE command and the DROP clause. The next statement drops a constraint by explicitly specifying the constraint name.

```
ALTER TABLE toy
    DROP CONSTRAINT toy_pk
Table altered.
```

Alternatively, you can drop a primary key constraint with the following statement.

```
ALTER TABLE toy
    DROP PRIMARY KEY
```

If there is a unique constraint you either issue the command with the constraint name or use a statement similar to this:

```
ALTER TABLE toy
    DROP UNIQUE (description)
```

RENAMING CONSTRAINTS

Starting with Oracle Version 9.2, you may rename a constraint name with the following command:

```
ALTER TABLE section RENAME CONSTRAINT sect_crse_fk TO sect_fk_crse
```

DISABLING AND ENABLING CONSTRAINTS

Constraints are enabled or disabled as necessary with the ALTER TABLE command. By default, when a constraint is created it is enabled, unless you explicitly disable it. You may want to disable constraints when updating massive volumes of data or inserting large amounts of data at once to decrease overall time for these operations. Once the data manipulation is performed, you re-enable the constraint.

The following statement disables an existing primary key constraint named TOY_PK on the TOY table.

```
ALTER TABLE toy
   DISABLE CONSTRAINT toy_pk
Table altered.
```

Note, when primary key or unique constraint is disabled, any associated index is dropped. When the constraint is re-enabled a unique index is recreated.

Naming constraints helps when you want to disable or enable them. Once data changes are completed, you can enable the primary key again with either of the following two statements.

```
ALTER TABLE toy
   ENABLE PRIMARY KEY
   USING INDEX TABLESPACE store_idx
   STORAGE (INITIAL 1 M
            NEXT 500 K)
Table altered.
```

This statement explicitly specifies the constraint name.

```
ALTER TABLE toy
   ENABLE CONSTRAINT toy_pk
   USING INDEX TABLESPACE store_idx
   STORAGE (INITIAL 1 M
            NEXT 500 K)
Table altered.
```

To find out the name of a constraint and its status (enabled or disabled), query the data dictionary views USER_CONSTRAINTS and USER_CONS_COLUMNS.

If you don't specify the tablespace name when you enable the index, the index will be stored on your default tablespace with the default storage size parameters of the tablespace. Storage parameters on constraints are only relevant with primary and unique constraints because they create indexes.

The following statement disables the foreign key constraint between the COURSE and the SECTION tables.

```
ALTER TABLE section
   DISABLE CONSTRAINT sect_crse_fk
Table altered.
```

If you want to disable multiple constraints, you can issue multiple statements or issue them in one ALTER TABLE statement. Note that the individual DISABLE clauses are not separated by commas.

```
ALTER TABLE section
   DISABLE CONSTRAINT sect_crse_fk
   DISABLE CONSTRAINT sect_inst_fk
```

NOVALIDATE OPTION   As part of the ENABLE clause of the ALTER TABLE statement, Oracle also provides a NOVALIDATE option, allowing only subsequent DML operations on the table to comply with the constraint; existing data can violate the constraint.

DETERMINE WHICH ROWS VIOLATE CONSTRAINTS

Unless the NOVALIDATE option is used, when a constraint is re-enabled, Oracle checks to see if all the rows satisfy the condition of the constraint. If some rows violate the constraint, the statement fails and Oracle issues an error message. The constraint cannot be enabled unless all exceptions are fixed or the offending rows are deleted.

FOREIGN KEY CONSTRAINT VIOLATIONS

In the following example, a course number was added to the SECTION table but the COURSE table has no such COURSE_NO. Therefore, the foreign key constraint cannot be enabled.

```
ALTER TABLE section
   ENABLE CONSTRAINT sect_crse_fk
ALTER TABLE section
*
ERROR at line 1:
ORA-02298: cannot validate (STUDENT.SECT_CRSE_FK) - parent
keys not found
```

There are a variety of ways to determine the offending rows. For example, you can issue the following statement to display the rows:

```
SELECT course_no
  FROM section
 MINUS
SELECT course_no
  FROM course
```

PRIMARY KEY CONSTRAINT VIOLATIONS

To determine which rows violate the primary key constraint, you can issue the following SQL command:

```
SELECT section_id, COUNT(*)
  FROM section
 GROUP BY section_id
HAVING COUNT(*) > 1
```

A subsequent DELETE operation of the duplicate rows may look like this:

```
DELETE
  FROM section
 WHERE ROWID IN (SELECT MAX(ROWID)
                   FROM section
                  GROUP BY section_id
                 HAVING COUNT(*) > 1)
```

The subquery identifies the duplicates as it groups the subquery by the SECTION_ID column. The SELECT of the subquery shows the largest ROWID pseudocolumn. Each Oracle table has a pseudocolumn called ROWID, which is not visible when describing the table or with a SELECT * statement. The ROWID is unique for every row and this subquery statement picks the largest ROWID value using the MAX function. The rows with these duplicate SECTION_ID values will be deleted. (Make sure that the non-primary key column values are identical, so you don't inadvertantly delete rows that you want to keep.

The Whole Truth

Another way to identify constraint violations: Oracle also allows you to record all the rows violating a constraint in a table called EXCEPTIONS with the Oracle script utlexcpt.sql found in the %ORACLE_HOME%\rdbms\admin directory. You can then use the ALTER TABLE tablename ENABLE CONSTRAINT constraint_name EXCEPTIONS INTO exceptions syntax to place the violating rows into the EXCEPTIONS table.

MODIFYING THE STORAGE CHARACTERISTICS OF A TABLE

After a table is created you can change some of its storage characteristics, such as the size of the next extent or the PCTFREE parameter determining how much free space to leave in each block for updates that increase the size of the row.

The next statement alters the table's storage characteristics. Any subsequently allocated extent will be 200 kilobytes in size.

```
ALTER TABLE section
  STORAGE (NEXT 200 K)
```

ONLINE TABLE DEFINITION

Oracle will only execute your DDL command if there are no sessions holding any locks; otherwise, it will wait for the release of the locks to process the statement. This is just one of the many reasons why data maintenance tasks such as the modification of table structures must take place during off-hours when users are not using the system. As the demand for 24/7 database availability has significantly increased, Oracle has put functionality into place that allows you to perform DDL tasks that restructure the table while users are performing data manipulation on the tables. This is accomplished with a set of PL/SQL procedures within the DBMS_REDEFINITION package that copies the data to an interim table and keeps track of the changes until the new table with the desired characteristics is ready to be used.

LAB 11.2 EXERCISES

11.2.1 ALTER TABLES AND MANIPULATE CONSTRAINTS

a) Alter the table called NEW_STUDENT you created in Exercise 11.1.1 b to add four columns called PHONE, NUM_COURSES with datatype and length NUMBER(3), CREATED_BY, and CREATED_DATE. Determine the other column datatypes and lengths based on the STUDENT table. The PHONE, NUM_ COURSES, and CREATED_BY columns should allow null values with the CREATED_BY column defaulting to the schema user logged in. The CREATED_DATE column should not allow null values and default to today's date. DESCRIBE the table when you have finished.

b) Execute the following INSERT statement to insert a row into the NEW_STUDENT table. Then alter the table to change the PHONE column from NULL to NOT NULL. What do you observe?

```
INSERT INTO new_student
   (first_name, last_name, description, registration_date)
VALUES
   ('Joe', 'Fisher', 'Intro to Linux', SYSDATE)
```

c) Alter the NEW_STUDENT table to change the REGISTRATION_DATE column from DATE datatype to VARCHAR2 datatype. What do you observe?

d) Alter the NEW_STUDENT table to create a primary key consisting of the FIRST_NAME and LAST_NAME columns.

e) Alter the NEW_STUDENT table to change the length of the LAST_NAME column from 25 to 2. What do you observe?

f) Disable the primary key constraint on the NEW_STUDENT table and write an INSERT statement with the values "Joe Fisher" for the first and last name to prove it is successful. Then enable the constraint again and describe the result.

g) Add the column STUDY_DURATION of datatype INTERVAL YEAR TO MONTH and the column ALUMNI_JOIN_DATE with a datatype of TIMESTAMP WITH TIME ZONE and a six-digit precision to the NEW_STUDENT table.

h) Drop the foreign key constraint FORMER_STUDENT_ZIPCODE_FK on the FORMER_STUDENT table and change it to an **ON DELETE SET NULL** foreign key constraint. Test the behavior by inserting a new zip code in the ZIPCODE table and creating a new student row with this new zip code, and then deleting the same zip code from the ZIPCODE table. Query the FORMER_STUDENT table to see the effect.

i) Drop all the tables created throughout the labs. The table names are: STUDENT_CANDIDATE, NEW_STUDENT, COURSE2, EXTINCT_ANIMAL, and FORMER_STUDENT.

LAB 11.2 EXERCISE ANSWERS

11.2.1 ANSWERS

a) Alter the table called NEW_STUDENT you created in Exercise 11.1.1 b to add four columns called PHONE, NUM_COURSES with datatype and length NUMBER(3), CREATED_BY, and CREATED_DATE. Determine the other column datatypes and lengths based on the STUDENT table. The PHONE, NUM_COURSES, and CREATED_BY columns should allow null values with the CREATED_BY column defaulting to the schema user logged in. The CREATED_DATE column should not allow null values and default to today's date. DESCRIBE the table when you have finished.

Answer: The four columns are added with a single ALTER TABLE...ADD command, separated by commas. The CREATED_BY column has a DEFAULT clause to default the column to the value of the current user; the CREATED_DATE column contains a NOT NULL constraint and defaults the column to the value SYSDATE.

```
ALTER TABLE new_student
  ADD (phone VARCHAR2(15),
       num_courses NUMBER(3),
       created_by VARCHAR2(30) DEFAULT USER,
       created_date DATE DEFAULT SYSDATE NOT NULL)
Table altered.

SQL> DESC new_student
 Name                                   Null?    Type
 -------------------------------------- -------- ------------
 FIRST_NAME                                      VARCHAR2(25)
 LAST_NAME                                       VARCHAR2(25)
```

DESCRIPTION	VARCHAR2(50)
REGISTRATION_DATE	DATE
PHONE	VARCHAR2(15)
NUM_COURSES	NUMBER(3)
CREATED_BY	VARCHAR2(30)
CREATED_DATE	NOT NULL DATE

A column or columns can be added to a table regardless of whether the table contains data or not. However, you cannot add columns with a NOT NULL constraint if the column contains NULL values. Therefore, you must first add the column with the NULL constraint, update the column with values, then alter the table to modify the column to add the NOT NULL constraint.

SETTING COLUMNS TO THE DEFAULT VALUES

How do default values behave when you insert data into the column? The CREATED_DATE column has a default value of SYSDATE. If you want this default value to appear in an INSERT statement, you can either not list the column on the INSERT statement or explicitly state the DEFAULT keyword. The CREATED_BY default returns the value of the USER function, which is the name of the user currently logged in. Because it's not listed in the following INSERT statement, this default value is used. The CREATED_DATE column is explicitly specified and the DEFAULT keyword is used. It places the current date and time into the column.

```
INSERT INTO new_student
    (first_name, last_name, description, created_date)
VALUES
    ('Julian', 'Soehner', 'Test#1', DEFAULT)

SELECT description, created_by, created_date
    FROM new_student
```

DESCRIPTION	CREATED_BY	CREATED_D
Test#1	STUDENT	18-MAY-02

```
1 row selected.

ROLLBACK
Rollback complete.
```

MODIFYING OR REMOVING COLUMN DEFAULT VALUES

A column with a DEFAULT option can also be changed to another default value or the default value can be removed. The next example removes the default value for the CREATED_BY column and changes the value for CREATED_DATE column to '01-JAN-2003'.

```
ALTER TABLE new_student
  MODIFY (created_by VARCHAR2(30) DEFAULT NULL,
          created_date DATE DEFAULT TO_DATE('01-Jan-2003'))
Table altered.
```

**LAB
11.2**

Note that DDL commands such as this ALTER TABLE command cannot be rolled back, and they COMMIT any previously issued DML statements.

An update of a column to reset its present value to the default value using the DEFAULT keyword would look like this:

```
UPDATE new_student
   SET created_date = DEFAULT
 WHERE description = 'Test#1'
```

The result now shows the CREATED_DATE column with the 01-Jan-2003 value.

```
SELECT description, created_date
   FROM new_student
DESCRIPTION      CREATED_D
---------------  ---------
Test#1           01-JAN-03

1 row selected.
```

b) Execute the following INSERT statement to insert a row into the NEW_STUDENT table. Then alter the table to change the PHONE column from NULL to NOT NULL. What do you observe?

```
INSERT INTO new_student
   (first_name, last_name, description, registration_date)
VALUES
   ('Joe', 'Fisher', 'Intro to Linux', SYSDATE)
```

Answer: The column cannot be modified to have a NOT NULL constraint because there is already a row in the table containing a NULL value in the column.

```
ALTER TABLE new_student
   MODIFY (phone NOT NULL)
MODIFY (phone NOT NULL)
        *
ERROR at line 2:
ORA-02296: cannot enable (STDENT.) - null values found
```

Just as you are unable to add a column with a NOT NULL constraint to a table, you cannot modify an existing column to NOT NULL if it contains NULL values.

You must first add data to the column and then modify the column to add the constraint.

```
UPDATE new_student
    SET phone = '917-555-1212'
```

```
ALTER TABLE new_student
    MODIFY (phone NOT NULL)
```
Table altered.

```
SQL> DESC new_student
```

Name	Null?	Type
FIRST_NAME		VARCHAR2(25)
LAST_NAME		VARCHAR2(25)
DESCRIPTION		VARCHAR2(50)
REGISTRATION_DATE		DATE
PHONE	NOT NULL	VARCHAR2(15)
NUM_COURSES		NUMBER(3)
CREATED_BY	NOT NULL	VARCHAR2(30)
CREATED_DATE	NOT NULL	DATE

The column can also be changed back to NULL with the following statement.

```
ALTER TABLE new_student
    MODIFY (phone NULL)
```
Table altered.

```
SQL> DESC new_student
```

Name	Null?	Type
FIRST_NAME		VARCHAR2(25)
LAST_NAME		VARCHAR2(25)
DESCRIPTION		VARCHAR2(50)
REGISTRATION_DATE		DATE
PHONE		VARCHAR2(15)
NUM_COURSES		NUMBER(3)
CREATED_BY	NOT NULL	VARCHAR2(30)
CREATED_DATE	NOT NULL	DATE

DEFINING A COLUMN AS NULL VERSUS NOT NULL

Deciding if a column should be NOT NULL or NULL leads into a discussion of nulls in general. A column allowing null values is subject to different interpretations. If you find a null value in a column it may mean many things: Perhaps the value is simply unknown, unspecified (user didn't pick any of the available choices), or perhaps not applicable. An encoded value can help distinguish between these differences.

Suppose you have a table holding client data containing a GENDER column. There simply aren't just two genders—male and female. What if your client is not an individual, but a corporation? Do you enter a null value and does a null value mean not applicable? What if the gender is unknown? You can come up with a lot of different other scenarios for a seemingly simple GENDER column. Therefore, database designers use consistent values throughout to ensure that null values are interpreted correctly. For example, you can enter a value of "?" for unknown, a "N/A" for not applicable, "OTH" for other, or create a default value for unspecified.

Writing queries against data that contains null values poses another challenge. Unless you specifically use the IS NULL operator (or the NVL or COALESCE function) on a column, null values are ignored. You must always keep the possibility of null values in mind when dealing with data. Nulls can also have positive effects. An example of this is if you have an order status flag column on your order table indicating if the order needs processing. If you enter a "YES" it indicates the order is incomplete if you enter a "NO" it indicates that the order is processed. If instead you only allow "YES" or a null value, you can actually improve the performances of queries looking for orders to be processed. You can build an index on this status flag column and only nonnull entries are stored in the index, which is rather small because there are few entries and the values are retrieved quickly.

c) Alter the NEW_STUDENT table to change the REGISTRATION_DATE column from DATE datatype to VARCHAR2 datatype. What do you observe?

Answer: A column's datatype cannot be changed when there is data in the column.

```
ALTER TABLE new_student
  MODIFY (registration_date VARCHAR2(12))
MODIFY (registration_date VARCHAR2(12))
       *
ERROR at line 2:
ORA-01439: column to be modified must be empty to change datatype
```

CHANGING A COLUMN'S DATATYPE

It is possible to change a column's datatype under two sets of circumstances. The first is when changing from one datatype to a compatible datatype, such as VARCHAR2 to CHAR. The next statement changes the REGISTRATION_DATE column from the DATE datatype to the compatible TIMESTAMP datatype. You can't change from a TIMESTAMP back to a DATE dataype unless the column is null.

```
    ALTER TABLE new_student
      MODIFY (registration_date TIMESTAMP(3))
    Table altered.
```

The second circumstance is when the column is empty, as in the following example. This statement sets the column to null to facilitate the change to a completely different datatype.

```
UPDATE new_student
   SET registration_date = NULL
1 row updated.


ALTER TABLE new_student
  MODIFY (registration_date VARCHAR2(12))
Table altered.
```

d) Alter the NEW_STUDENT table to create a primary key consisting of the FIRST_NAME and LAST_NAME columns.

Answer: The NEW_STUDENT table is altered to add a PRIMARY KEY constraint consisting of the two columns, separated by commas inside the parentheses.

```
ALTER TABLE new_student
  ADD CONSTRAINT new_student_pk
    PRIMARY KEY(first_name, last_name)
Table altered.
```

The ADD PRIMARY KEY keywords are used to add the primary key constraint. (Actually, the choice of this column as a primary key is not a very good one, because a name entered in all uppercase is considered different than a name entered in mixed case.)

e) Alter the NEW_STUDENT table to change the length of the LAST_NAME column from 25 to 2. What do you observe?

Answer: The length of a column cannot be decreased when the values in the column are larger than the new column width.

```
ALTER TABLE new_student
  MODIFY (last_name VARCHAR2(2))
MODIFY (last_name VARCHAR2(2))
        *
ERROR at line 2:
ORA-01441: cannot decrease column length because some value
is too big
```

INCREASING AND DECREASING THE COLUMN WIDTH

For columns containing data, the length of the column can always be increased, as in the following example, but not decreased if existing data is larger than the new column width. In versions before Oracle 9*i*, a decrease was not possible at all if the table contained any data.

```
ALTER TABLE new_student
  MODIFY (last_name VARCHAR2(30))
Table altered.
```

f) Disable the primary key constraint on the NEW_STUDENT table and write an INSERT statement with the value "Joe Fisher" for the first and last name to prove it is successful. Then enable the constraint again and describe the result.

Answer: The value "Joe Fisher" exists twice in the FIRST_NAME and LAST_NAME columns, respectively, so a primary key constraint cannot be enabled on the table.

```
ALTER TABLE new_student
  DISABLE PRIMARY KEY
Table altered.

INSERT INTO new_student
  (first_name, last_name, phone, created_by, created_date)
VALUES
  ('Joe', 'Fisher', '718-555-1212', USER, SYSDATE)
1 row created.

ALTER TABLE new_student
  ENABLE PRIMARY KEY
ALTER TABLE new_student
*
ERROR at line 1:
ORA-02437: cannot enable (STUDENT.SYS_C001265) - primary key
violated
```

It is dangerous to disable a table's primary key because the integrity of the data may be violated. The only time you may want to disable constraints is when you are performing large data loads. Otherwise, if the constraints are enabled, each row must be evaluated to ensure it does not violate any of the constraints, thus slowing down the data loading process. Therefore, for large data loads or updates, it's best to disable constraints temporarily, load the data, and re-enable the constraints.

In Chapter 13, "The Data Dictionary and Dynamic SQL Scripts," you will learn how to do this easily for many constraints at once by generating a SQL statement to generate other SQL statements. The chapter also teaches you how to query the Oracle Data Dictionary for existing constraints and their respective status, such as enabled or disabled.

g) Add the column STUDY_DURATION of datatype INTERVAL YEAR TO MONTH and the column ALUMNI_JOIN_DATE with a datatype of TIMESTAMP WITH TIME ZONE and a six-digit precision to the NEW_STUDENT table.

Answer: The ALTER TABLE statement adds both columns simultaneously. The six-digit fractional seconds are the default for the TIMESTAMP WITH TIME ZONE datatype and do not need to be specified explicitly.

```
ALTER TABLE new_student
   ADD (study_months INTERVAL YEAR TO MONTH,
        alumni_join_date TIMESTAMP (6) WITH TIME ZONE)
Table altered.
```

LAB 11.2

h) Drop the foreign key constraint FORMER_STUDENT_ZIPCODE_FK on the FORMER_STUDENT table and change it to an ON DELETE SET NULL foreign key constraint. Test the behavior by inserting a new zip code in the ZIPCODE table and creating a new student row with this new zip code, and then deleting the same zip code from the ZIPCODE table. Query the FORMER_STUDENT table to see the effect.

Answer: The DROP CONSTRAINT clause removes the constraint and you can then add the foreign key with the ON DELETE SET NULL constraint instead.

```
ALTER TABLE former_student DROP CONSTRAINT
former_student_zipcode_fk
Table altered.

ALTER TABLE former_student
   ADD CONSTRAINT former_student_zipcode_fk FOREIGN KEY(zip)
      REFERENCES zipcode (ZIP) ON DELETE SET NULL
Table altered.
```

Insert a new zip code into the ZIPCODE table with the value of 90210.

```
INSERT INTO zipcode
   (zip, city, state, created_by,
   created_date, modified_by, modified_date)
VALUES
   ('90210','Hollywood', 'CA', 'Alice',
   sysdate, 'Alice', sysdate);
1 row created.
```

To demonstrate the functionality, insert a zip code into the FORMER_STUDENT table.

```
INSERT INTO former_student
   (studid, first_nm, last_nm, enrolled, zip)
VALUES
   (109, 'Alice', 'Rischert', 3, '90210')
1 row created.
```

Now delete the zip code 90210 from the ZIPCODE table.

```
DELETE FROM zipcode
 WHERE zip = '90210'
1 row deleted.
```

A check of the effect on the FORMER_STUDENT table reveals that the column ZIP is updated to a null value.

```
SELECT studid, zip
  FROM former_student
 WHERE studid = 109
    STUDID ZIP
---------- -----
       109

1 row selected.
```

If you attempt to delete a row that exists not just in the NEW_STUDENT table, but perhaps also in the STUDENT or INSTRUCTOR table, such as the value 10025, you will be prevented from the DELETE operation because these other tables are referencing the ZIPCODE with a DELETE restrict. In this case, it indicates that the INSTRUCTOR table is referencing this value as well and that orphan rows are not allowed.

```
DELETE FROM zipcode
 WHERE zip = '10025'
DELETE FROM zipcode
*
ERROR at line 1:
ORA-02292: integrity constraint (STUDENT.INST_ZIP_FK)
violated - child record found
```

Note, if your schema name is not STUDENT, but a different account name, the constraint name error will be prefixed with the respective name.

The other foreign key alternatives to the ON DELETE SET NULL options are the two statements listed next. The first would add the DELETE RESTRICT default instead, and the second shows the ON DELETE CASCADE constraint alternative.

```
ALTER TABLE former_student
  ADD CONSTRAINT former_student_zipcode_fk FOREIGN
KEY(zip)
     REFERENCES zipcode (ZIP)

ALTER TABLE former_student
  ADD CONSTRAINT former_student_zipcode_fk FOREIGN
KEY(zip)
     REFERENCES zipcode (ZIP) ON DELETE CASCADE
```

i) Drop all the tables created throughout the labs. The table names are: STUDENT_CANDIDATE, NEW_STUDENT, COURSE2, EXTINCT_ANIMAL, and FORMER_STUDENT.

Answer: Use the DROP TABLE command to remove the tables from the schema.

```
DROP TABLE student_candidate
```
Table dropped.

```
DROP TABLE new_student
```
Table dropped.

```
DROP TABLE course2
```
Table dropped.

```
DROP TABLE extinct_animal
```
Table dropped.

```
DROP TABLE former_student
```
Table dropped.

TRUNCATE TABLE VERSUS DROP TABLE

The TRUNCATE TABLE command, discussed in Chapter 10, "Insert, Update, and Delete," removes all data from the table; however, the structure of table remains intact. Like the DROP TABLE command, it does not generate any rollback information and does not fire any triggers should they exist on the table. The TRUNCATE statement is a DDL command and implicitly issues a COMMIT. By default the TRUNCATE TABLE command deallocates all of the table's storage except for the initial extent(s); you can retain all the existing storage extents with the REUSE STORAGE clause.

```
TRUNCATE TABLE grade REUSE STORAGE
```

LAB 11.2 SELF-REVIEW QUESTIONS

In order to test your progress, you should be able to answer the following questions.

1) The following ALTER TABLE statement contains an error.

```
ALTER TABLE new_student
  DROP CONSTRAINT PRIMARY_KEY
```

a) _____ True
b) _____ False

2) The ADD and MODIFY keywords can be used interchangeably in an ALTER TABLE statement.

a) _____ True
b) _____ False

3) You can add a NOT NULL constraint to a column providing all the rows of the column contain data.

a) _____ True
b) _____ False

4) A constraint must have a name in order for it to be disabled.

a) _____ True
b) _____ False

5) A column's datatype can be changed only when the column contains no data.

a) _____ True
b) _____ False

6) The following statement constrains values in the PHONE column of the STU-DENT table to a particular format.

```
ALTER TABLE student
   ADD CONSTRAINT student_phone_ck CHECK
      (TRANSLATE (phone,'1234567890-', '9999999999-') =
      '999-999-9999')
```

a) _____ True
b) _____ False

Answers appear in Appendix A, Section 11.2.

CHAPTER 11

TEST YOUR THINKING

The projects in this section are meant to have you utilize all of the skills that you have acquired throughout this chapter. The answers to these projects can be found at the companion Web site to this book, located at: *http://www.phptr.com/rischert.*

Visit the Web site periodically to share and discuss your answers.

1) Create a table called TEMP_STUDENT with the following columns and constraints: a column STUDID for student ID that is NOT NULL and is the primary key, a column FIRST_NAME for student first name, a column LAST_NAME for student last name, a column ZIP that is a foreign key to the ZIP column in the ZIPCODE table, and a column REGISTRATION_ DATE that is NOT NULL and has a CHECK constraint to restrict the registration date to dates after January 1, 2000.

2) Write an INSERT statement violating one of the constraints for the TEMP_STUDENT table you just created. Write another INSERT statement that succeeds when executed and commit your work.

3) Alter the TEMP_STUDENT table to add two more columns called EMPLOYER and EMPLOYER_ZIP. The EMPLOYER_ZIP column should have a foreign key constraint referencing the ZIP column of the ZIPCODE table. Update the EMPLOYER column and alter the table once again to make the employer column NOT NULL. Drop the TEMP_STUDENT table once you're done with the exercise.

CHAPTER 12

VIEWS, INDEXES, AND SEQUENCES

This chapter covers three different yet very important database objects: views, indexes, and sequences.

Views are significant in a database as they provide row-level and column-level security to the data. They allow you to look at the data differently and/or display only specific information to the user. Views are also useful to simplify the writing of queries for end-users as they can hide the complexities of joins and conditional statements.

Indexes are required for good performance of any database. A well-thought-out indexing strategy entails the careful placement of indexes on relevant columns. You will gain an understanding about the advantages and trade-offs when using indexes on tables.

Sequences generate unique values and are used mainly for creating primary key values. You will learn how to create and use sequences.

L A B   1 2 . 1

CREATING AND
MODIFYING VIEWS

LAB OBJECTIVES

After this lab, you will be able to:

✔ Create, Alter, and Drop Views
✔ Understand the Data Manipulation Rules for Views

The view is a virtual table consisting of columns and rows, but it is only the SE-LECT statement that is stored, not a physical table with data. A view's SELECT query may reference one or multiple tables. These tables are called *base tables*. The base tables are typically actual tables or other views.

PURPOSE OF VIEWS

The data retrieved from the view can show only certain columns by listing those columns in the SELECT list of the query. You can also restrict the view to display specific rows with the WHERE clause of the query.

In a view, you can give a column a different name from the one in the base table. A view looks just like any other table, you may describe and query the view and also issue INSERT, UPDATE, and DELETE statements to a certain extent.

Views are useful for security reasons because they can hide data. They also simplify the writing of queries. You can query a single view instead of writing a complicated SQL statement joining many tables. The complexity of the underlying SQL statement is hidden from the user and contained only in the view. Views may be used to isolate an application from a change in the definition of the base tables. Suppose a view contains five columns of a 10-column base table and another column is added to the table. The view is not affected and neither is any program accessing the view.

CREATING A VIEW

The simplified syntax for creating a view is as follows:

```
CREATE [OR REPLACE] [FORCE|NOFORCE] VIEW viewname
[(column_alias[, column_alias]...)]
AS query
[WITH CHECK OPTION|WITH READ ONLY [CONSTRAINT constraintname]]
```

The next statements create a view called COURSE_NO_COST and describe the new view.

```
CREATE OR REPLACE VIEW course_no_cost AS
SELECT course_no, description, prerequisite
  FROM course
View created.


SQL> DESC course_no_cost
 Name                         Null?     Type
 --------------------------- --------- ----------------
 COURSE_NO                   NOT NULL  NUMBER(8)
 DESCRIPTION                 NOT NULL  VARCHAR2(50)
 PREREQUISITE                          NUMBER(8)
```

The COURSE_NO_COST view hides a number of columns that exist in the COURSE table. You do not see the COST column or the CREATED_DATE, CRE-ATED_BY, MODIFIED_DATE, and MODIFIED_BY columns. The main purpose of this view is security. You can grant access just to the view COURSE_NO_COST instead of to the COURSE table itself. For more information on granting access privileges to database objects, see Chapter 14, "Security."

USING COLUMN ALIASES

The following statement demonstrates a view with column names different from the column names in the base tables. Here the view named STUD_ENROLL shows a listing of the STUDENT_ID, the last name of the student in capital letters, and the number of classes the student is enrolled in. The column STUDENT_ID from the STUDENT table is renamed in the view to STUD_ID using a column alias. When a column contains an expression such as a function, a column alias is required. The two expressions in the STUD_ENROLL view, namely the student last name in caps and the count of classes enrolled, are therefore aliased.

```
CREATE OR REPLACE VIEW stud_enroll AS
SELECT s.student_id stud_id,
       UPPER(s.last_name) last_name,
       COUNT(*) num_enrolled
  FROM student s, enrollment e
 WHERE s.student_id = e.student_id
 GROUP BY s.student_id, UPPER(s.last_name)
```

The OR REPLACE keywords are useful in case the view already exists. It allows you to replace the view with a different SELECT statement without having to drop the view first. This also means you do not have to regrant privileges to the view; the rights to the view are retained by those who have already been granted privileges.

The next example shows an alternate SQL statement for naming columns in a view, whereby the view's columns are listed in parentheses after the view name.

```
CREATE OR REPLACE VIEW stud_enroll
       (stud_id, last_name, num_enrolled) AS
SELECT s.student_id,
       UPPER(s.last_name),
       COUNT(*)
  FROM student s, enrollment e
 WHERE s.student_id = e.student_id
 GROUP BY s.student_id, UPPER(s.last_name)
```

ALTERING A VIEW

You use the ALTER VIEW command to recompile an invalid view after altering one of the base tables to ensure that the view continues to be valid. The syntax of the ALTER VIEW statement is:

```
ALTER VIEW viewname COMPILE
```

(The ALTER VIEW command in Oracle 9*i* allows for additional syntax options not mentioned. These options let you create primary or unique constraints on views. However, these constraints are not enforced, do not maintain data integrity, and an index is never built, because they can only be created in DISABLE NOVALIDATE mode. These new constraint types are primarily useful with *materialized views,* a popular data warehousing feature that allows you to physically store pre-aggregated results and/or joins for speedy access. Unlike the views discussed in this chapter, materialized views result in physical data stored in tables.)

RENAMING A VIEW

The RENAME command allows you to change the name of a view.

```
RENAME stud_enroll to stud_enroll2
```

All underlying constraints and granted privileges remain intact. However, any objects that use this view (perhaps another view or a PL/SQL procedure, package, or function) become invalid and need to be compiled.

DROPPING A VIEW

To drop a view you use the DROP VIEW command. The next statement drops the STUD_ENROLL2 view.

```
DROP VIEW stud_enroll2
View dropped.
```

LAB 12.1 EXERCISES

12.1.1 CREATE, ALTER, AND DROP VIEWS

a) Create a view called LONG_DISTANCE_STUDENT with all the columns in the STUDENT table plus the CITY and STATE columns from the ZIPCODE table. Exclude students from New York, New Jersey, and Connecticut.

b) Create a view named CHEAP_COURSE showing all columns of the COURSE table where the course cost is 1095 or less.

c) Issue the following INSERT statement. What do you observe when you query the CHEAP_COURSE view?

```
INSERT INTO cheap_course
   (course_no, description, cost,
   created_by, created_date, modified_by,
   modified_date)
VALUES
   (900, 'Expensive', 2000,
   'ME', SYSDATE, 'ME', SYSDATE)
```

d) Drop the views named LONG_DISTANCE_STUDENT and CHEAP_COURSE.

e) Using the following statement, create a table called TEST_TAB and build a view over it. Then, add a column to the table and attempt to DESCRIBE the view. What do you observe? Drop the table and view after you complete the exercise.

```
CREATE TABLE test_tab
   (col1 NUMBER)
```

**LAB
12.1**

12.1.2 UNDERSTAND THE DATA MANIPULATION RULES FOR VIEWS

a) Create a view called BUSY_STUDENT based on the following query. Update the number of enrollments for STUDENT_ID 124 to five through the BUSY_STUDENT view. Record your observation.

```
SELECT student_id, COUNT(*)
  FROM enrollment
 GROUP BY student_id
HAVING COUNT(*) > 2
```

b) Create a view listing the addresses of students. Include the columns STUDENT_ID, FIRST_NAME, LAST_NAME, STREET_ADDRESS, CITY, STATE, and ZIP. Using the view, update the last name of STUDENT_ID 237 from Frost to O'Brien. Then, update the state for the student from NJ to CT. What do you notice for the statements you issue?

LAB 12.1 EXERCISE ANSWERS

12.1.1 ANSWERS

a) Create a view called LONG_DISTANCE_STUDENT with all the columns in the STUDENT table plus the CITY and STATE columns from the ZIPCODE table. Exclude students from New York, New Jersey, and Connecticut.

Answer: To select all columns from the STUDENT table, use the wildcard symbol. For the columns CITY and STATE in the view, join to the ZIPCODE table. With this view definition you see only records where the state is not equal to New York, Connecticut, or New Jersey.

```
CREATE OR REPLACE VIEW long_distance_student AS
SELECT s.*, z.city, z.state
  FROM student s, zipcode z
 WHERE s.zip = z.zip
   AND state NOT IN ('NJ','NY','CT')
View created.
```

You can issue a query against the view or DESCRIBE the view. As you observe, you can restrict the columns and/or the rows of the view.

```
SELECT state, first_name, last_name
  FROM long_distance_student
ST FIRST_NAME            LAST_NAME
-- ------------------    -----------
MA James E.              Norman
MA George                Kocka
...
OH Phil                  Gilloon
MI Roger                 Snow

10 rows selected.
```

You might want to validate the view by querying for students living in New Jersey.

```
SELECT *
  FROM long_distance_student
 WHERE state = 'NJ'

no rows selected
```

As you see, there are none because the view's defining query excludes these records.

b) Create a view named CHEAP_COURSE showing all columns of the COURSE table where the course cost is 1095 or less.

Answer: The view restricts the rows to courses with a cost of 1095 or less.

```
CREATE OR REPLACE VIEW cheap_course AS
SELECT *
  FROM course
 WHERE cost <= 1095
```

c) Issue the following INSERT statement. What do you observe when you query the CHEAP_COURSE view?

```
INSERT INTO cheap_course
  (course_no, description, cost,
   created_by, created_date, modified_by,
   modified_date)
VALUES
  (900, 'Expensive', 2000,
   'ME', SYSDATE, 'ME', SYSDATE)
```

Answer: You can insert records through the view, violating the view's defining query condition.

A cost of 2000 is successfully inserted into the COURSE table through the view, even though this is higher than 1095, which is the defining condition of the view.

You can query the CHEAP_VIEW to see if the record is there. The course was successfully inserted in the underlying COURSE base table, but it does not satisfy the view's definition and is not displayed.

```
SELECT course_no, cost
  FROM cheap_course
COURSE_NO      COST
---------  ---------
      135       1095
      230       1095
      240       1095

3 rows selected.
```

A view's WHERE clause works for any query, but not for DML statements. The course number 900 is not visible through the CHEAP_COURSE view, but insert, update, or delete operations are permitted despite the conflicting WHERE condition. To change this security-defying behavior, create the view with the WITH CHECK OPTION constraint. But first undo the INSERT statement with the ROLL-BACK command, because any subsequent DDL command, such as the creation of a view, automatically commits the record.

```
ROLLBACK
Rollback complete.

CREATE OR REPLACE VIEW cheap_course AS
SELECT *
  FROM course
 WHERE cost <= 1095
WITH CHECK OPTION CONSTRAINT check_cost
View created.
```

It is a good habit to name constraints. You understand the benefit of well-named constraints when you query the Oracle data dictionary or when you violate constraints with data manipulation statements.

The following error message appears when inserts, updates, and deletes issued against a view violate the view's defining query. The previous INSERT statement would now be rejected with the following error message.

```
ORA-01402: view WITH CHECK OPTION where-clause violation
```

What happens if you attempt to insert a record with a value of NULL for the course cost? Again, Oracle rejects the row because the condition is not satisfied. The NULL value is not less than or equal to 1095.

VIEW CONSTRAINTS

You can enforce constraints in a variety of ways: The underlying base tables automatically ensure data integrity or you can use the WITH CHECK OPTION. You can also avoid any data manipulation on the view through the READ ONLY option. The following statement creates a read-only view named COURSE_V.

```
CREATE OR REPLACE VIEW course_v AS
SELECT course_no, description,
       created_by, created_date,
       modified_by, modified_date
  FROM course
  WITH READ ONLY CONSTRAINT course_v_read_check
View created.
```

d) Drop the views named LONG_DISTANCE_STUDENT and CHEAP_COURSE.

Answer: Just like other operations on data objects, the DROP keyword removes a database object from the database.

```
DROP VIEW long_distance_student
View dropped.
```

```
DROP VIEW cheap_course
View dropped.
```

Remember, any DDL operation, such as the creation of a view, cannot be rolled back, and any prior DML operations, such as inserts, updates, and deletes, are automatically committed.

e) Using the following statement, create a table called TEST_TAB and build a view over it. Then, add a column to the table and attempt to DESCRIBE the view. What do you observe? Drop the table and view after you complete the exercise.

```
CREATE TABLE test_tab
  (col1 NUMBER)
```

Answer: The view becomes invalid after the underlying table is altered.

```
CREATE OR REPLACE VIEW test_tab_view AS
SELECT *
  FROM test_tab
View created.
```

After the table creation, the view is created. Here, the name TEST_TAB_VIEW is used. Then add an additional column to the table; here it is named col2.

```
ALTER TABLE test_tab
   ADD (col2 NUMBER)
Table altered.
```

You would expect the SQL*Plus DESCRIBE command on the view to show the additional column, but it shows an error. Whenever there is any database change to the underlying base table, the view becomes invalid.

```
SQL> DESC test_tab_view
ERROR:
ORA-24372: invalid object for describe
```

The next time you attempt to access the view through a SQL statement, not a SQL*Plus statement such as DESCRIBE, Oracle automatically attempts to revalidate the view by compiling it. Access the view by issuing a SELECT statement against it to see if it causes any errors.

```
SELECT *
   FROM test_tab_view
```

```
no rows selected
```

COMPILE A VIEW

You can explicitly issue the COMPILE command to make sure the view is valid. The command to compile is:

```
ALTER VIEW test_tab_view COMPILE
View altered.
```

A subsequently issued DESCRIBE of the view reveals another interesting fact.

```
SQL> DESC test_tab_view
 Name                                 Null?    Type
 ------------------------------------ -------- ------
 COL1                                          NUMBER
```

Where is the new column that was added? Whenever a view is created with the wildcard (*) character, Oracle stores the individual column names in the definition of the view. A query against the data dictionary table USER_VIEWS shows how Oracle stores the view's definition. Note, the column is listed with enclosed quotation marks, just in case of mixed case column names.

```
SELECT text
   FROM user_views
  WHERE view_name = 'TEST_TAB_VIEW'
```

```
TEXT
-----------------------------------------
SELECT "COL1"
   FROM test_tab
```

1 row selected.

Altering the table by adding or dropping columns invalidates the view. In this case, the view is automatically recompiled and working, but the new column is missing. You need to re-issue the creation of the view statement for the view to include the new column.

```
CREATE OR REPLACE VIEW test_tab_view AS
SELECT *
  FROM test_tab
```
View created.

Now, when DESCRIBE is issued on the view, the new column is included.

```
SQL> DESC test_tab_view
```
Name	Null?	Type
COL1		NUMBER
COL2		NUMBER

Drop the no-longer-needed table and notice the effect on the view.

```
DROP TABLE test_tab
```
Table dropped.

```
ALTER VIEW test_tab_view COMPILE
```
Warning: View altered with compilation errors.

REFERENCING AN INVALID VIEW

When you access an invalid view, Oracle returns an error message to the user indicating that the view exists. However, it is currently invalid because the underlying objects were altered or dropped. Any subsequent attempt to access the view or to compile it returns an error.

```
SELECT *
   FROM test_tab_view
```
ERROR at line 2:
ORA-04063: view "STUDENT.TEST_TAB_VIEW" has errors

Drop the view to restore the STUDENT schema to its previous state.

```
DROP VIEW test_tab_view
```
View dropped.

**LAB
12.1**

FORCING THE CREATION OF A VIEW

If the view's base tables do not exist or the creator of the view doesn't have privileges to access the view, the creation of the view will fail. The next example shows the creation of the view named TEST based on a nonexistent SALES table.

```
CREATE VIEW test AS
SELECT *
  FROM sales
ERROR at line 3:
ORA-00942: table or view does not exist
```

If you want to create the view despite it being invalid you can create it with the FORCE option; the default on the CREATE VIEW syntax is NOFORCE. This FORCE option is useful if you need to create the view and you add the referenced table later or you expect to obtain the necessary privileges to the referenced object shortly.

```
CREATE FORCE VIEW test AS
SELECT *
  FROM sales
Warning: View created with compilation errors.
```

The view, though invalid, now exists in the database.

12.1.2 ANSWERS

a) Create a view called BUSY_STUDENT based on the following query. Update the number of enrollments for STUDENT_ID 124 to five through the BUSY_STUDENT view. Record your observation.

```
SELECT student_id, COUNT(*)
  FROM enrollment
 GROUP BY student_id
HAVING COUNT(*) > 2
```

Answer: The UPDATE operation fails. Data manipulation operations on a view impose a number of restrictions.

To create the view, you need to give the COUNT(*) expression a column alias; otherwise, this error occurs:

```
ERROR at line 2:
ORA-00998: must name this expression with a column alias
```

```
CREATE OR REPLACE VIEW busy_student AS
SELECT student_id, COUNT(*) enroll_num
  FROM enrollment
```

```
    GROUP BY student_id
    HAVING COUNT(*) > 2
View created.
```

You can now attempt to update the ENROLLMENT table using the view with the following UPDATE statement.

```
UPDATE busy_student
    SET enroll_num = 5
 WHERE student_id = 124
ORA-01732: data manipulation operation not legal on this view
```

For a view to be updateable, it needs to conform to a number of rules: The view may not contain an expression, aggregate function, set operator, DISTINCT keyword, GROUP BY clause, or ORDER BY clause. Special rules apply to views containing join conditions, as you see in the next exercise.

b) Create a view listing the addresses of students. Include the columns STUDENT_ID, FIRST_NAME, LAST_NAME, STREET_ADDRESS, CITY, STATE, and ZIP. Using the view, update the last name of STUDENT_ID 237 from Frost to O'Brien. Then, update the state for the student from NJ to CT. What do you notice for the statements you issue?

Answer: Not all updates to views containing joins are allowed. The update of the last name is successful, but not the update of the STATE column.

```
CREATE OR REPLACE VIEW student_address AS
SELECT student_id, first_name, last_name,
       street_address, city, state, s.zip szip,
       z.zip zzip
  FROM student s, zipcode z
 WHERE s.zip=z.zip
View created.
```

Now update the last name to O'Brien with the following statement. To indicate a single quote, prefix the single quote with another single quote.

```
UPDATE student_address
    SET last_name = 'O''Brien'
 WHERE student_id = 237
1 row updated.
```

Because the test was successful, rollback the UPDATE to retain the current data in the table.

```
ROLLBACK
Rollback complete.
```

As you can see, you are able to update the data in the underlying base table STU-DENT. Now update the column STATE in the base table ZIPCODE through the STUDENT_ADDRESS view.

```
UPDATE student_address
   SET state = 'CT'
 WHERE student_id = 237
ORA-01779: cannot modify a column which maps to a nonkey-
preserved table
```

The understanding of a key-preserved table is essential to understanding the restrictions on join views. A table is considered key-preserved if every key of the table can also be a key of the result of the join. In this case, the STUDENT table is the key-preserved or child table.

For a join view to be updateable, the DML operation may affect only the key-preserved table (also known as the child base table) and the child's primary key must be included in the view's definition. In this case, the child table is the STU-DENT table and the primary key is the STUDENT_ID.

If you are in doubt regarding which table is the key-preserved table, query the Oracle data dictionary table USER_UPDATABLE_COLUMNS. The result shows you which columns are updateable. Also, note the STUDENT table's ZIP column is updateable, but not the ZIP column from the ZIPCODE table. Only the STUDENT table's ZIP column (aliased as SZIP) is considered key-preserved.

```
SELECT column_name, updatable
  FROM user_updatable_columns
 WHERE table_name = 'STUDENT_ADDRESS'
```

COLUMN_NAME	UPD
STUDENT_ID	YES
FIRST_NAME	YES
LAST_NAME	YES
STREET_ADDRESS	YES
CITY	NO
STATE	NO
SZIP	YES
ZZIP	NO

```
8 rows selected.
```

The data dictionary is covered in greater detail in Chapter 13, "The Data Dictionary and Dynamic SQL Scripts."

LAB 12.1 SELF-REVIEW QUESTIONS

In order to test your progress, you should be able to answer the following questions.

1) Views are useful for security, for simplifying the writing of queries, and for hiding data complexity.

    a) _____ True
    b) _____ False

2) Under what circumstances can views become invalid? Check all that apply.

    a) _____ The datatype of a column changes.
    b) _____ The underlying table(s) are dropped.
    c) _____ Views never become invalid, they automatically recompile.

3) Identify the error in the following view definition.

```
CREATE OR REPLACE VIEW my_student
      (studid, slname, szip) AS
SELECT student_id, last_name, zip
  FROM student
 WHERE student_id BETWEEN 100 AND 200
```

    a) _____ Line 1
    b) _____ Line 2
    c) _____ Line 4
    d) _____ Line 1, 2, 4
    e) _____ No error

4) An UPDATE to the STATE column in the ZIPCODE table is permitted using the following view.

```
CREATE OR REPLACE VIEW my_zipcode AS
SELECT zip, city, state, created_by,
       created_date, modified_by,
       TO_CHAR(modified_date, 'DD-MON-YYYY') modified_date
  FROM zipcode
```

    a) _____ True
    b) _____ False

5) Views provide security by restricting access to specific rows and/or columns of a table.

    a) _____ True
    b) _____ False

6) A column in a view may have a different name than in the base table.

    a) _____ True
    b) _____ False

Answers appear in Appendix A, Section 12.1.

L A B   1 2 . 2

INDEXES

> ## LAB OBJECTIVES
>
> After this lab, you will be able to:
>
> ✔ Create B-Tree Indexes
> ✔ Understand When Indexes Are Useful

To achieve good performance for data retrieval and data manipulation statements, you need to understand Oracle's use of indexes. Just like the index in the back of a book, Oracle uses indexes to look up data quickly. If the appropriate index does not exist on a table, Oracle needs to examine every row. This is called a *full table scan*.

If the index speeds up query time, you may wonder why not just index every column in the table? When you retrieve a large number of rows in a table, it may be more efficient to read the entire table rather than look up the values from the index. It also takes a significant amount of time and storage space to build and maintain an index. For each DML statement that changes a value in an indexed column, the index needs to be maintained.

THE B-TREE INDEX

In this workbook, you will perform exercises centered on Oracle's most popular index storage structure—the B-tree index. The merits and uses of another type of index, the bitmapped index, will be discussed briefly at the end of the lab; this type of index can only be created in Oracle's Enterprise Server Edition.

The B-tree (balanced tree) index is by far the most common type of index. It provides excellent performance in circumstances where there are many distinct values on a column or columns. If you have several low-selectivity columns, you can also consider combining them into one *composite index*, also called a *concatenated index*. B-tree indexes are best for exact match and range searches against both small and very large tables.

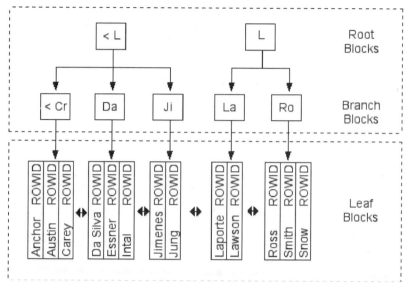

Figure 12.1 ■ **B-tree Index.**

Figure 12.1 illustrates the structure of a B-tree index. It looks like an inverted tree and consists of two types of blocks: *Root/branch blocks* and *leaf blocks*. Root or branch blocks are used for storing the key together with a pointer to the child block containing the key; leaf blocks store the key values along with the ROWID, which is the physical storage location for the data in the table.

STEPS PERFORMED TO SEARCH FOR VALUES IN AN B-TREE INDEX

The first step is to start with the root block of the index. The searched value is compared with the root block keys. For example, if you are looking for the student with the last name of Essner, you must go down the root block of <L. This block points to the next leaf blocks, which are greater than Da and less than Ji; going down on this leaf block, you find the value Essner and the associated ROWID, the physical address of the row. A leaf block also contains links to the next and previous leaf block, which allow scanning the index for ranges.

THE ROWID PSEUDOCOLUMN

Every row in the database has a unique address called the ROWID. The address determines exactly where the row is located. Indexes store the ROWID to retrieve rows quickly. The ROWID consists of several components: the data object number, the number of the data block of the file, the number of rows within the data block, and the data file number. The data block and the data file define the physical storage characteristics of data within the individual Oracle database.

```
SELECT ROWID, student_id, last_name
  FROM student
 WHERE student_id = 123
ROWID                  STUDENT_ID LAST_NAME
------------------     ---------- ---------
AAADA1AABAAARAIAAD            123 Radicola

1 row selected.
```

A ROWID is always unique. It is the fastest way to access a row.

You can use the ROWID in UPDATE statements to directly access the row, rather than searching the index. For example, because the ROWID of the student named Radicola is already selected as part of the query, a subsequent update to the name of the student can find the row in the table immediately without having to scan the entire table or use an index.

```
UPDATE student
   SET last_name = 'Radicolament'
 WHERE student_id = 123
   AND ROWID = 'AAADA1AABAAARAIAAD'
   AND last_name = 'Radicola'
```

You cannot update the ROWID, but the ROWID may change if you first delete the row and then re-insert the row as it may now be placed in another physical location. Never use the ROWID as a table's primary key because it is subject to change.

As you learned in Chapter 10, "Insert, Update, and Delete," it is always good practice to include the old values in the WHERE clause of the UPDATE to ensure that another session or user has not changed the name in the meantime.

A pseudocolumn is not an actual column, but it acts like one. One of the pseudocolumns you have already used is the ROWNUM, which restricts the number of rows a query returns. You will learn about other Oracle pseudocolumns, namely NEXTVAL and CURRVAL, shortly.

CREATE AN INDEX

You create an index using the following general syntax:

```
CREATE [UNIQUE|BITMAPPED] INDEX indexname
  ON tablename
   (column|col_expression [,column|col_expression]...)
```

```
[PCTFREE integer]
[TABLESPACE tablespacename|DEFAULT]
[STORAGE ([INITIAL integer [K|M]]
          [NEXT integer [K|M)]])]
[ONLINE]
```

The following statement creates an index named SECT_LOCATION_I on the LO-CATION column of the SECTION table.

```
CREATE INDEX sect_location_i
  ON section(location)
Index created.
```

A subsequent query to find all the classes held in LOCATION L206 can take advantage of this index. Oracle looks up the value in the index. This retrieves the row faster than reading every row, particularly if the table has many records.

```
SELECT course_no, section_no, start_date_time, location
  FROM section
 WHERE location = 'L206'
COURSE_NO SECTION_NO START_DAT LOCATION
--------- ---------- --------- --------
      120          2 24-JUL-99 L206

1 row selected.
```

COMPOSITE INDEXES

Sometimes it is useful to build indexes based on multiple columns; this type of index is called a *composite index* or *concatenated index*. For example, you can create a composite index on two columns with a low selectivity (i.e., not many distinct values). The combination of these low selectivity values makes the composite index highly selective. If you compare the query access time of a composite index to that of two individual single-column indexes, the composite index offers better performance.

The next statement creates a composite index on the columns DESCRIPTION and COST. The first column of the index, also called the leading edge of the index, is the DESCRIPTION column; the second column of the index is the COST column.

```
CREATE INDEX course_description_cost_i
  ON course (description, cost)
```

Columns that are used together frequently in a WHERE clause and combined with the AND logical operator are often good candidates for a composite index, particularly if their combined selectivity is high. The order of the individual columns in the index can affect query performance. Choose the column you use most frequently in the WHERE clause first. If both columns are accessed with equal frequency, then choose the column with the highest selectivity. In this example, the COST column has very few distinct values and is therefore considered a low-selectivity column; access against an index with a low-selectivity column as the leading edge requires more index blocks reads and is therefore less desirable.

There are some caveats about composite indexes you must know about when writing queries. When executed in Oracle versions prior to 9*i* a query such as the following using the COST column in the WHERE clause cannot use the COURSE_DESCRIPTION_COST_I index, because it's not the leading edge of the index.

```
SELECT course_no, description, cost
  FROM course
 WHERE cost = 1095
```

Starting with version 9i, Oracle can use a technique called skip scan, which may use the index nonetheless. As you work your way through this lab, you will learn more about this feature.

To find out what columns of a table are indexed and the order of the columns in an index, you can query the data dictionary views USER_INDEXES and USER_IND_COLUMNS.

NULLS AND INDEXES

NULL values are not stored in a B-tree index unless it is a composite index where at least the first column of the index contains a value. The following query does not make use of the single-column index on the FIRST_NAME column.

```
SELECT student_id, first_name
  FROM student
 WHERE first_name IS NULL
```

FUNCTIONS AND INDEXES

Even when you create an index on one or multiple columns of a table, Oracle may not be able to use it. In the next scenario assume that the LAST_NAME column of the STUDENT table is indexed. The following SQL query applies the UPPER function on the LAST_NAME column. You may use this WHERE clause expression if you don't know how the last name is stored in the column—it may be stored with the first initial in uppercase, all uppercase, or perhaps in mixed case. This query will not take advantage of the index because the column is modified by a function.

```
SELECT student_id, last_name, first_name
  FROM student
 WHERE UPPER(last_name) = 'SMITH'
```

Starting with Oracle version 8.1 you can avoid this behavior by creating a function-based index instead, as in the following example. This allows for case-insensitive searches on the LAST_NAME column.

```
CREATE INDEX stud_last_name_i
   ON student(UPPER(last_name))
```

For function-based indexes to work, you must also set two Oracle initialization parameters in the Oracle initialization file (init.ora). Alternatively, you can issue two ALTER SESSION commands in SQL*Plus: ALTER SESSION SET query_rewrite_enabled = TRUE and ALTER SESSION SET query_rewrite_integrity = TRUSTED.

INDEXES AND TABLESPACES

To optimize performance, it is important that you separate indexes from data by placing them in separate tablespaces residing on different physical devices. This significantly improves the performance of your queries. Use the following statement to create an index named SECT_LOCATION_I on a tablespace called INDEX_TX with an initial size of 500 kilobytes and 100 kilobytes in size for each subsequent extent.

```
CREATE INDEX sect_location_i
  ON section(location)
  TABLESPACE index_tx
  STORAGE (INITIAL 500K NEXT 100K)
```

The storage clause of indexes is similar to the storage clause discussed in Chapter 11, "Create, Alter, and Drop Tables." If you want to see a list of tablespaces accessible to you, query the data dictionary view USER_TABLESPACES.

UNIQUE INDEX VERSUS UNIQUE CONSTRAINT

At times you may want to enforce a unique combination of the values in a table, (e.g., the COURSE_NO and SECTION_NO columns of the SECTION table). You can create a unique constraint on the table that automatically creates a unique index:

```
alter table section
  ADD CONSTRAINT sect_sect2_uk UNIQUE (section_no, course_no)
  USING INDEX
  TABLESPACE index_tx
  STORAGE (INITIAL 12K NEXT 12K)
```

Or you can use the CREATE UNIQUE INDEX command:

```
CREATE UNIQUE INDEX section_sect_course_no_i
  ON section (section_no, course_no)
  TABLESPACE index_tx
  STORAGE (INITIAL 12K NEXT 12K)
```

Oracle prefers if you use the unique constraint syntax for future compatibility.

CREATING AN INDEX ASSOCIATED WITH A CONSTRAINT

When creating a primary key constraint or a unique constraint, Oracle creates the index automatically. In Chapter 11, "Create, Alter, and Drop Tables," you learned about various syntax options you can use. If you want control over the storage characteristics of an index, you can use this syntax, already listed in Chapter 11.

The index NEW_TERM_PK is created as part of the CREATE TABLE statement and is associated with the primary key constraint.

```
CREATE TABLE new_term
   (term_no NUMBER(8) NOT NULL PRIMARY KEY USING INDEX
      (CREATE INDEX new_term_pk ON new_term(term_no)
         STORAGE (INITIAL 100 K NEXT 100K)),
    season_tx VARCHAR2(20),
    sequence_no NUMBER(3))
```

The advantage of using this syntax is that you can create an index in the same statement of the CREATE TABLE command whereby you have control over the storage characteristics of the index. It doesn't require two separate statements: a CREATE TABLE statement and an ALTER TABLE statement that adds the constraint and the index plus storage clause.

If you already have an existing index and you want to associate a constraint with it you can use a statement similar to the following. It assumes an existing index called SEMESTER_SEMESTER_ID_I based on the SEMESTER_ID column.

```
ALTER TABLE semester
   ADD CONSTRAINT semester_pk PRIMARY KEY (semester_id)
   USING INDEX semester_semester_id_i
```

The next statement shows an example of a unique constraint that is associated with a unique index.

```
CREATE TABLE semester
   (semester_id NUMBER(8),
    semester_name VARCHAR2(8) NOT NULL,
    year_no  NUMBER(4) NOT NULL,
    CONSTRAINT semester_uk UNIQUE (semester_name, year_no)
    USING INDEX
    (CREATE UNIQUE INDEX semester_sem_yr_uk
       ON semester(semester_name, year_no)))
```

These syntax alternatives are advantageous when you drop or disable the primary key or unique constraint, as the index will continue to exist. This saves time, particularly on large tables where it may take many hours to recreate the index.

**LAB
12.2**

INDEXES AND FOREIGN KEYS

You should almost always index foreign keys as they are frequently used in joins. Additionally, if you intend to delete or update unique or primary keys on the parent table and you use versions prior to Oracle 9*i*, you should index the foreign keys to improve the locking of child records. Foreign keys that are not indexed require locks to be placed on the entire child table when a parent row is deleted or the primary or unique keys of the parent table are updated. This prevented any inserts, updates, and deletes on the child table. The advantage of an index on the foreign key column is that the locks are placed on the affected indexed child rows instead, thus not locking up the entire child table. This is more efficient and allows data manipulation of child rows *not* affected by the updates and deletes of the parent table.

In Oracle 9i, a lock is still acquired in case of updates or deletes on the primary key, but it is released immediately.

DROP AN INDEX

To drop an index, use the DROP INDEX command. You might drop an index if queries in your applications do not utilize the index.

```
DROP INDEX sect_location_i
Index dropped.
```

You can monitor the use of an index with the ALTER INDEX indexname MONITORING USAGE command. If you notice that within a sufficiently wide time period the index is not used by any of the SQL statements, you may consider dropping it. There is no point in keeping the associated space tied up and to occur the additional time required for maintaining index entries through insert, update, and delete statements. If the index is used just once a month for a large batch job that may take 15 hours if no index exists, you may consider keeping the index, or perhaps creating the index before the start of the job. You must carefully test your scenarios. Issue the NOMONITORING USAGE clause when you want to stop monitoring the index; the V$OBJECT_USAGE data dictionary view records the usage information.

When you drop a table, all associated indexes are dropped automatically.

BITMAPPED INDEX

The bitmapped index is another type of index supported by Oracle. This index is typically used in a data warehouse where the primary goal is the querying and analyzing of data with bulk data loads occurring at certain intervals. Bitmapped indexes are not suitable for tables with heavy data manipulation activity by many users as any such changes on this type of index may significantly slow down the transactions. A bitmapped index is typically used on columns with a very low selectivity; that is, columns with very few distinct values. For example, a column like GENDER, with four distinct values of female, male, unknown, and not applicable (in case of a legal entity such as a corporation), has a very low selectivity.

A low selectivity is expressed as the number of distinct values as a total against all the rows in the database. For example, if you had 9,000 distinct values in a table with one million rows, it would be considered a low-selectivity column. In this scenario, the number of distinct values represents less than 1% of the entire rows in the table and this column may be a good candidate for a bitmapped index.

Figure 12.2 illustrates the concept of a bitmapped index. The example is a hypothetical CUSTOMER table with a bitmapped index on the GENDER column. The bitmapped index translates the distinct values for the GENDER column of indi-

CUSTOMER Table

ID	FIRST_NAME	LAST_NAME	GENDER
1	Mary	Jones	F
2	Carol	Smith	F
3	Fred	Olson	M
4		ABC, Inc.	N/A
...	...	...	...

Bitmapped index on GENDER column

CUSTOMER ID	1	2	3	4	...
GENDER = F	1	1	0	0	...
GENDER = M	0	0	1	0	...
GENDER = N/A	0	0	0	1	...
GENDER = Unknown	0	0	0	0	...

Figure 12.2 ■ A bitmapped index.

vidual customers. In this simplified example, the customer with the IDs of 1 and 2 has the GENDER = F, which makes the bit turned on to 1. The other values such as GENDER = M, GENDER = N/A, and GENDER = UNKNOWN have a 0, indicating that these values are not true for the row. The next customer with the ID of 3 has the 1 bit turned on GENDER = M, the other values are zero.

The next statement creates a bitmapped index on the GENDER column of a CUSTOMER table.

```
CREATE BITMAP INDEX customer_bm_gender_i
    ON customer(gender)
```

If you have multiple bitmapped indexes, such as one for GENDER, MARTIAL STATUS, and ZIP, and you need to retrieve rows based on certain AND and OR conditions, then bitmapped indexes perform very fast. They quickly compare and merge the bit settings of these conditions and are therefore highly effective for large tables. Bitmapped indexes require less storage space than traditional B-tree indexes, but they do not perform as well for less than or greater than comparisons. Note that bitmapped indexes are only available with Oracle's Enterprise Edition.

GUIDELINES WHEN TO INDEX

You want to consider indexing columns frequently used in the WHERE clause of SQL statements and foreign key columns. Oracle automatically creates a unique index to enforce the primary key constraint and the unique constraint. Here are some general guidelines for when an index is typically useful:

1. Columns used in the WHERE clause or join condition.
2. Frequent queries against large tables retrieving less than 5 to 15 percent of the rows. The percentage may vary depending on a number of factors, including the size of the table.
3. Frequently accessed columns containing highly slective data for B-tree indexes.
4. Columns frequently accessed with a small range of values for bitmapped indexes.
5. Columns frequently accessed with many null values, but the query is looking for the NOT NULL values

Building an index is often useless if:

1. The table is small, but you should nevertheless create unique and primary constraints to enforce business rules.
2. The query retrieves more than 5 to 15 percent of the rows.
3. The indexed column part of an expression. Then consider creating a function-based index.

In Chapter 16, "SQL Optimization," you learn to verify that SQL statements issued actually use an index.

Although adding indexes may improve performance of certain queries, you must realize that Oracle may use this new index for other queries that previously used a different index. This rarely has an adverse effect, but you must nevertheless make certain that your overall application performance does not suffer because of this change. Keep in mind that adding indexes may increase the time required for data manipulation operations, such as INSERT, UPDATE, and DELETE.

REBUILDING OF INDEXES

Periodically, you need to rebuild indexes to compact the data and balance the index tree. This is particularly important after data is subject to a large number of DML changes and the rebuild operation will improve the performance of the queries. Oracle provides the index rebuild option. It is faster to rebuild the index than dropping and recreating the index; furthermore, the index continues to be available for queries while the rebuild operation is in progress.

```
ALTER INDEX stu_zip_fk_i REBUILD
Index altered.
```

The ALTER INDEX command allows you to change the storage characteristics of an index or rename an index. Here are some of the general syntax options:

```
ALTER INDEX indexname
   [STORAGE (([INITIAL integer [K|M]]
             [NEXT integer [K|M)]])]
   [REBUILD [ONLINE]]
   [RENAME TO newindexname]
```

DML AND DDL OPERATIONS

When a DML operation, such as an insert, update, or delete command, is not yet committed, a lock is placed on the affected rows. Because a DDL command requires exclusive access to the table or index, another session cannot issue such a command unless the DML command is committed or rolled back. This is just one of the many reasons why data structure changes are performed during times when users are not accessing the system.

You can create or rebuild indexes while users are performing DML commands manipulating a small percentage of the rows in the table with the ONLINE option.

```
CREATE INDEX student_ix_employer
   ON student(employer)
   STORAGE (INITIAL 10K)
   ONLINE
```

or:

```
ALTER INDEX stu_zip_fk_i REBUILD ONLINE
```

LOADING LARGE AMOUNTS OF DATA

When you insert or update large amounts of data, you may want to consider dropping certain indexes to improve performance. After the operation is complete, recreate the indexes.

LAB 12.2 EXERCISES

12.2.1 CREATE B-TREE INDEXES

a) Create an index on the PHONE column of the STUDENT table. Drop the index after you successfully create it to return the STUDENT schema to its original state.

b) Create a composite index on the first and last name columns of the STUDENT table. Drop the index when you have finished.

c) Create an index on the DESCRIPTION column of the COURSE table. Note that queries against the table often use the UPPER function. Drop the index after you successfully create it.

d) Execute the following SQL statements. Explain the reason for the error.

```
CREATE TABLE test (col1 NUMBER)
CREATE INDEX test_col1_i ON test(col1)
DROP TABLE test
DROP INDEX test_col1_i
```

12.2.2 UNDERSTAND WHEN INDEXES ARE USEFUL

a) Would you create a B-tree index on a frequently accessed column with few distinct values? Explain.

b) List the advantages and disadvantages of indexes on performance.

c) Assume an index exists on the column ENROLL_DATE in the ENROLLMENT table. Change the following query so it uses the index.

```
SELECT student_id, section_id,
       TO_CHAR(enroll_date,'DD-MON-YYYY')
  FROM enrollment
 WHERE TO_CHAR(enroll_date,'DD-MON-YYYY') = '12-MAR-1999'
```

LAB 12.2 EXERCISE ANSWERS

12.2.1 ANSWERS

a) Create an index on the PHONE column of the STUDENT table. Drop the index after you successfully create it to return the STUDENT schema to its original state.

Answer: To create the index on the table, issue a CREATE INDEX statement.

```
CREATE INDEX stu_phone_i
  ON student(phone)
Index created.
```

Include the name of the table and the indexed column(s) in the index name; this allows you to identify the indexed columns in a particular table without querying the data dictionary views USER_INDEXES and USER_IND_COLUMNS. But remember, no database object's name, such as an index, may be longer than 30 characters.

To drop the index, simply issue the DROP INDEX command.

```
DROP INDEX stu_phone_i
Index dropped.
```

LAB
12.2

b) Create a composite index on the first and last name columns of the STUDENT table. Drop the index when you have finished.

Answer: There are two possible solutions for creating a composite index using the first and last name columns.

A composite or concatenated index is an index that consists of more than one column. Depending on how you access the table, you need to order the columns in the index accordingly.

To determine the best column order in the index, determine the selectivity of each column. That means determining how many distinct values each column has. You also need to determine what types of queries to write against the table. All this information helps you choose the best column order for the index.

SOLUTION 1:

The index is created in the order first_name, last_name.

```
CREATE INDEX stu_first_last_name_i
   ON student(first_name, last_name)
```

This index is used in a SQL statement only if you refer in the WHERE clause to either both columns or the FIRST_NAME column. Oracle can access the index only if the WHERE clause lists the leading column of the index. The leading column, also called the leading edge, of the aforementioned index is the FIRST_NAME column. If the WHERE clause of a SQL statement lists only the LAST_NAME column, the SQL statement cannot access the index. For example, the next two WHERE clauses do not use the index.

```
WHERE last_name = 'Smith'
WHERE last_name LIKE 'Sm%'
```

SOLUTION 2:

The index is created in the order LAST_NAME, FIRST_NAME. The LAST_NAME column is the leading column of the index.

```
CREATE INDEX stu_last_first_name_i
   ON student(last_name, first_name)
```

This index is used in a SQL statement if you query both columns or only the LAST_NAME column. If a WHERE clause in a SQL statement lists only the FIRST_NAME column, Oracle does not use the index because it is not the leading column of the index.

COMPOSITE INDEXES VERSUS INDIVIDUAL INDEXES

An alternative to the composite index is to create two separate indexes: one for the FIRST_NAME and one for the LAST_NAME column.

```
CREATE INDEX stu_first_name_i
   ON student(first_name)
Index created.

CREATE INDEX stu_last_name_i
   ON student(last_name)
Index created.
```

A SQL statement with one of the columns in the WHERE clause uses the appropriate index. In the case where both columns are used in the WHERE clause, Oracle typically merges the two indexes together to retrieve the rows. You may wonder, why, then, have concatenated indexes at all? A composite index outperforms individual column indexes, provided all the columns are referenced in the WHERE clause.

Oracle 9i has a new feature called skip scan that allows the skipping of the leading edge of an index. During a skip scan, the B-tree index is probed for the distinct values of the leading edge column; ideally this column has few distinct values. The skip scan feature allows queries that previously had to read the entire table to use the composite index instead. A second benefit of the skip scan feature is the reduced need for indexes; fewer indexes require less storage space and therefore result in better performance of DML statements. Note that skip scan is not supported for bitmapped and function-based indexes.

The database designer, together with the application developer, decides how to structure the indexes to make them most useful, based on the SQL statements issued. Make sure to verify that Oracle actually uses the index; you can do this with the help of an explain plan, which is covered in Chapter 16, "SQL Optimization."

■ *FOR EXAMPLE*

Assume that on a given table you create a composite index on columns A, B, and C in this order. To make use of the index, specify in the WHERE clause either column A; columns A and B; columns A, B, and C; or columns A and C. Queries listing column C only, or B only, or B and C only do not use the index because they are not leading edge columns.

To determine the best order, again think about the types of queries issued and the selectivity of each column. The following three indexes cover all the query possibilities. This solution requires with the least amount of storage and offers the best overall performance.

```
CREATE INDEX test_table_a_b_c ON test_table(a, b, c)
CREATE INDEX test_table_b_c ON test_table(b, c)
CREATE INDEX test_table_c ON test_table(c)
```

If you use Oracle 9i, your queries may take advantage of the skip scan, and you may not need to build as many indexes. You must test your statements carefully to ensure adequate performance.

c) Create an index on the DESCRIPTION column of the COURSE table. Note that queries against the table often use the UPPER function. Drop the index after you successfully create it.

Answer: A function-based index is created on the DESCRIPTION column.

```
CREATE INDEX crse_description_i
  ON course(UPPER(description))
```

A function-based index stores the indexed values and uses the index based on the following SELECT statement, which retrieves the course number for the course called Hands-On Windows. If you don't know in what case the description was entered into the COURSE table, you may want to apply the UPPER function to the column.

```
SELECT course_no, description
  FROM course
WHERE UPPER(description) = 'HANDS-ON WINDOWS'
```

Any query that modifies a column with a function in the WHERE clause does not make use of an index unless you create a function-based index.

An index like the following cannot be used for the previously issued SQL statement.

```
CREATE INDEX crse_description_i
  ON course(description)
```

To restore the schema to its previous state, drop the index.

```
DROP INDEX crse_description_i
Index dropped.
```

d) Execute the following SQL statements. Explain the reason for the error.

```
CREATE TABLE test (col1 NUMBER)
CREATE INDEX test_col1_i ON test(col1)
DROP TABLE test
DROP INDEX test_col1_i
```

Answer: Dropping a table automatically drops any associated index. There is no need to drop the index separately.

```
DROP INDEX test_col1_i
            *
ERROR at line 1:
ORA-01418: specified index does not exist
```

12.2.2 ANSWERS

a) Would you create a B-tree index on a frequently accessed column with few distinct values? Explain.

Answer: It may be advantageous to create a B-tree index even on a low-selectivity column.

Assume you have an EMPLOYEE table with a column named GENDER that you consider indexing. Also assume that 90 percent of your employees are male and 10 percent are female. You frequently query for female employees. In this case, the index is helpful and improves the performance of your query. A query for male employees might also access the index, even though a full table scan of the table is more efficient than looking up all the values in the index.

b) List the advantages and disadvantages of indexes on performance.

Answer: Advantages: Adding an index on a table increases the performance of SQL statements using the indexed column(s) in the WHERE clause. This assumes that only a small percentage of the rows are accessed. Should you access many rows in the table, accessing the entire table via a full table scan probably yields better performance. Indexes on the foreign key columns also improve locking. Disadvantages: Adding indexes may increase the time required for insert, update, and delete operations. Indexes also require additional disk space.

c) Assume an index exists on the column ENROLL_DATE in the ENROLLMENT table. Change the following query so it uses the index.

```
SELECT student_id, section_id,
       TO_CHAR(enroll_date,'DD-MON-YYYY')
  FROM enrollment
 WHERE TO_CHAR(enroll_date,'DD-MON-YYYY') = '12-MAR-1999'
```

Answer: When you modify an indexed column with a function, such as the function TO_CHAR in the WHERE clause, the SQL statement is not able to access the index. The exception is when you create a function-based index on the column.

In this case you do not need a function-based index. The SQL statement is changed so it does not modify the indexed column with a function. Refer to Chapter 4, "Date and Conversion Functions," about the dangers of using TO_CHAR with a DATE column in the WHERE clause.

```
SELECT student_id, section_id,
       TO_CHAR(enroll_date,'DD-MON-YYYY')
  FROM enrollment
 WHERE enroll_date = TO_DATE('12-MAR-1999','DD-MON-YYYY')
```

LAB 12.2 SELF-REVIEW QUESTIONS

In order to test your progress, you should be able to answer the following questions.

1) For the following query, choose which index(es), if any, probably yield the best performance.

```
SELECT student_id, last_name, employer, phone
  FROM student
 WHERE employer = 'FGIC'
   AND phone = '201-555-5555'
```

a) _____ Index on employer
b) _____ Index on phone
c) _____ Index in the order employer, phone
d) _____ Index in the order phone, employer
e) _____ No index

2) You should always index as many columns as possible.

a) _____ True
b) _____ False

3) Frequently queried columns and foreign keys should almost always be indexed.

a) _____ True
b) _____ False

4) The ROWID is the fastest way to access a row.

a) _____ True
b) _____ False

5) The following query uses the single-column index on the ZIP column of the INSTRUCTOR table.

```
SELECT instructor_id, last_name, first_name, zip
  FROM instructor
 WHERE zip IS NULL
```

a) _____ True
b) _____ False

6) The following SQL statement benefits from an index on the column INSTRUCTOR_ID.

```
UPDATE instructor
   SET phone = '212-555-1212'
 WHERE instructor_id = 123
```

a) _____ True

b) _____ False

Answers appear in Appendix A, Section 12.2.

LAB 12.3

SEQUENCES

> ## LAB OBJECTIVES
>
> After this lab, you will be able to:
>
> ✔ Create and Use Sequences

Sequences are Oracle database objects allowing you to generate unique integers. Recall the STUDENT table with the primary key column STUDENT_ID. The value of STUDENT_ID is a *surrogate key* or *artificial key* generated from a sequence. This key is useful to the system but usually has no meaning for the user, is not subject to changes, and is never NULL.

Assume a student is uniquely identified by the first name, last name, and address. These columns are called the alternate key. If you choose these columns as the primary key, imagine a scenario where a student's name or address changes. This requires a large amount of updates in many tables because all the foreign key columns need to be changed, involving a lot of customized programming. Instead, a surrogate key column is created and populated by a sequence. This surrogate key is not subject to change and the users rarely see this column.

Sequences assure that no user gets the same value from the sequence, thus guaranteeing unique values for primary keys. Sequences are typically incremented by 1, but other increments can be specified. You can also start sequences at a specific number.

Because you still need to enforce your users' business rule and prevent duplicate student entries, consider creating a unique constraint on the alternate key.

CREATE A SEQUENCE

The simplified syntax for creating sequences is as follows:

```
CREATE SEQUENCE sequencename
[INCREMENT BY integer]
[START WITH integer]
```

```
[CACHE integer|NOCACHE]
[MAXVALUE integer|NOMAXVALUE]
[MINVALUE integer|NOMINVALUE]
```

To create a sequence named STUDENT_ID_SEQ_NEW, issue the CREATE SE-QUENCE command.

```
CREATE SEQUENCE student_id_seq_new START WITH 1 NOCACHE
Sequence created.
```

Basing the name of the sequence on the name of the column for which you want to use it is helpful for identification, but it does not associate the sequence with a particular column or table. The START WITH clause starts the sequence with the number 1. The NOCACHE keyword indicates the sequence numbers should not be kept in memory, so that when the system shuts down you will not lose any cached numbers. However, losing numbers is not a reason for concern because there are many more available from the sequence. It is useful to leave the sequence numbers in the cache only if you access the sequence frequently. If you don't specify a CACHE choice, the first 20 numbers are cached. The MAXVALUE and MINVALUE parameters determine the minimum and maximum range values of the sequence; the defaults are NOMAXVALUE and NOMINVALUE.

LAB 12.3

USING SEQUENCE NUMBERS

To increment the sequence and display the unique number, use the NEXTVAL pseudocolumn. The following SQL statement takes the next value from the sequence. Because the sequence was just created and starts with the number 1, it takes the number 1 as the first available value.

```
SELECT student_id_seq_new.NEXTVAL
  FROM dual
  NEXTVAL
---------
        1

1 row selected.
```

Typically, you use NEXTVAL in INSERT and UPDATE statements. To display the current value of the sequence after it is incremented, use the CURRVAL pseudocolumn.

ALTERING SEQUENCES

The ALTER SEQUENCE command allows you to change the properties of a sequence, such as the increment value, min and max values, and cache option. The general syntax of the ALTER SEQUENCE command is listed as follows:

```
ALTER SEQUENCE sequencename
  [INCREMENT BY integer]
```

```
[MAXVALUE integer|NOMAXVALUE]
[MINVALUE integer|NOMINVALUE]
[CACHE integer|NOCACHE]
```

To restart sequence numbers at a lower number, you must drop and recreate the sequence. Any GRANTs to other users of the sequence must be reissued. For more on the GRANT command see Chapter 14, "Security."

LAB 12.3 EXERCISES

12.3.1 CREATE AND USE SEQUENCES

a) Describe the effects of the following SQL statement on the sequence SECTION_ID_SEQ.

```
INSERT INTO section
   (section_id, course_no, section_no,
   start_date_time, location,
   instructor_id, capacity, created_by,
   created_date, modified_by, modified_date)
VALUES
   (section_id_seq.NEXTVAL, 122, 5,
   TO_DATE('15-MAY-1999', 'DD-MON-YYYY'), 'R305',
   106, 10, 'ARISCHERT',
   SYSDATE, 'ARISCHERT', SYSDATE)
```

b) Write a SQL statement to increment the sequence STUDENT_ ID_ SEQ_NEW with NEXTVAL and then issue a ROLLBACK command. Determine the effect on the sequence number.

c) Drop the sequence STUDENT_ID_SEQ_NEW.

LAB 12.3 EXERCISE ANSWERS

12.3.1 ANSWERS

a) Describe the effects of the following SQL statement on the sequence SECTION_ID_SEQ.

```
INSERT INTO section
   (section_id, course_no, section_no,
   start_date_time, location,
   instructor_id, capacity, created_by,
   created_date, modified_by, modified_date)
VALUES
   (section_id_seq.NEXTVAL, 122, 5,
   TO_DATE('15-MAY-1999', 'DD-MON-YYYY'), 'R305',
   106, 10, 'ARISCHERT',
   SYSDATE, 'ARISCHERT', SYSDATE)
```

Answer: The sequence is accessible from within an INSERT statement. The sequence is incremented with the next value and this value is inserted in the table.

b) Write a SQL statement to increment the sequence STUDENT_ID_SEQ_NEW with NEXTVAL and then issue a ROLLBACK command. Determine the effect on the sequence number.

Answer: Once a sequence is incremented, the ROLLBACK command does not restore the number.

```
SELECT student_id_seq_new.NEXTVAL
   FROM dual
   NEXTVAL
---------
       2

1 row selected.


ROLLBACK
Rollback complete.

SELECT student_id_seq_new.NEXTVAL
   FROM dual
   NEXTVAL
---------
       3

1 row selected.
```

If there are any gaps in the primary key sequence numbers it really doesn't matter because the numbers have no meaning to the user and there are many more numbers available from the sequence. One of the unique properties of sequences is that no two users receive the same number.

You can see information about the sequence in the USER_SEQUENCES data dictionary view. Here the LAST_NUMBER column indicates the last used number of the sequence.

```
SELECT sequence_name, last_number, cache_size
  FROM user_sequences
 WHERE sequence_name = 'STUDENT_ID_SEQ_NEW'
SEQUENCE_NAME                           LAST_NUMBER CACHE_SIZE
-------------------------------------   ----------- ----------
STUDENT_ID_SEQ_NEW                                3          0

1 row selected.
```

The current number of the sequence may be obtained using CURRVAL providing the sequence was incremented by the user's session.

```
SELECT student_id_seq_new.CURRVAL
  FROM dual
    CURRVAL
----------
         3

1 row selected.
```

c) Drop the sequence STUDENT_ID_SEQ_NEW.

Answer: Just as with other database objects, you use the DROP command to drop a sequence.

```
DROP SEQUENCE student_id_seq_new
Sequence dropped.
```

LAB 12.3 SELF-REVIEW QUESTIONS

In order to test your progress, you should be able to answer the following questions.

1) Sequences are useful for generating unique values.

    a) _____ True
    b) _____ False

2) A student's social security number is a good choice for a primary key value instead of a sequence.

a) _____ True
b) _____ False

3) The default increment of a sequence is 1.

a) _____ True
b) _____ False

4) When you drop a table the associated sequence is also dropped.

a) _____ True
b) _____ False

5) The following statement creates a sequence named EMPLOYEE_ID_SEQ, which starts at the number 1000.

```
CREATE SEQUENCE employee_id_seq START WITH 1000
```

a) _____ True
b) _____ False

Answers appear in Appendix A, Section 12.3.

C H A P T E R   1 2

TEST YOUR THINKING

The projects in this section are meant to have you utilize all of the skills that you have acquired throughout this chapter. The answers to these projects can be found at the companion Web site to this book, located at: *http://www.phptr.com/rischert.*

Visit the Web site periodically to share and discuss your answers.

1) Who can update the SALARY column through the MY_EMPLOYEE view? Hint: The USER function returns the name of the currently logged in user.

```
CREATE OR REPLACE VIEW my_employee AS
SELECT employee_id, employee_name, salary, manager
  FROM employee
 WHERE manager = USER
   WITH CHECK OPTION CONSTRAINT my_employee_ck_manager
```

2) Which columns in a table should you consider indexing?
3) Explain the purpose of the following Oracle SQL command.

```
ALTER INDEX crse_crse_fk_i REBUILD
```

4) Are null values stored in an index? Explain.

C H A P T E R 1 3

THE DATA DICTIONARY AND DYNAMIC SQL SCRIPTS

The Oracle data dictionary is a set of tables and views that contains data about the database; it is also sometimes referred to as the *catalog*. The data dictionary is used internally by Oracle for many purposes; for instance, to determine if a SQL statement contains valid column and table names or to determine the privileges of an individual user. You will find it useful to query the data dictionary because it contains a wealth of information about the database.

Dynamic SQL scripts expand your knowledge of SQL*Plus and its capabilities as a SQL execution environment. In many situations you can simplify the writing of SQL statements and the administration of the database by writing SQL scripts that execute other SQL statements.

L A B   1 3 . 1

THE ORACLE DATA DICTIONARY VIEWS

LAB OBJECTIVES

After this lab, you will be able to:

✔ Query the Data Dictionary

The data dictionary has two distinct sets of views: the *static* data dictionary views and the *dynamic* data dictionary views, also referred to as *dynamic performance views* or as *V$TABLES* (V-Dollar tables).

THE STATIC DATA DICTIONARY VIEWS

The static data dictionary stores details about database objects, such as tables, indexes, and views. It also lists information about referential integrity constraints and indexed columns. Whenever a new object is added or an object is changed, data about the object is recorded in the data dictionary.

Most of the static dictionary views begin with the prefix USER_, ALL_, or DBA_. The USER_ views show information belonging to the user querying the data dictionary. For example, when you login as STUDENT, the views beginning with the USER_ prefix show all the objects belonging to the STUDENT schema.

The ALL_ views show the same information, plus any information granted to the STUDENT user by another user, and public objects. You learn how to grant and receive access rights in Chapter 14, "Security." The DBA_ views show all objects, but you need DBA privileges to be able to query these views.

Table 13.1 ▪ Overview of Oracle Data Dictionary Views

Prefix	Purpose
USER_	Objects belonging to the user querying
ALL_	Objects belonging to the user and objects accessible to the user
DBA_	All objects, accessible only to users with DBA privileges
V$	Dynamic performance views, accessible only to users with DBA privileges

THE DYNAMIC DATA DICTIONARY VIEWS

The dynamic views begin with V$ and are typically used by the DBA to monitor the system. They are called dynamic because they are continuously updated by the database but never by the user. Table 13.1 shows the different types of data dictionary views.

THE DICTIONARY

The collection of static and dynamic data dictionary tables and views, along with a description of each, is listed in the view called DICTIONARY, also known by the synonym DICT. A synonym is another name for a database object; instead of using DICTIONARY, you can refer to its shorter synonym DICT. You learn about synonyms and their use in Chapter 14, "Security." Take a look at the columns of the DICT view by issuing the SQL*Plus DESCRIBE command.

```
SQL> DESC dict
 Name                      Null?      Type
 -------------------       --------   --------------
 TABLE_NAME                           VARCHAR2(30)
 COMMENTS                             VARCHAR2(4000)
```

The column TABLE_NAME contains a list of all the individual data dictionary tables and views accessible to you, together with a brief description in the COMMENTS column.

For example, to find information about sequences in the database, you can query the DICT view. The column TABLE_NAME stores the names of the data dictionary tables and views in uppercase. The following query results in all data dictionary views with the letters SEQ in their name.

```
SELECT table_name, comments
  FROM dict
 WHERE table_name LIKE '%SEQ%'
```

```
TABLE_NAME           COMMENTS
---------------      --------------------------------------------------
ALL_SEQUENCES        Description of SEQUENCEs accessible to the user
DBA_SEQUENCES        Description of all SEQUENCEs in the database
USER_SEQUENCES       Description of the user's own SEQUENCEs
SEQ                  Synonym for USER_SEQUENCES
```

4 rows selected.

Four different data dictionary views contain information about sequences. Note that if you do not have DBA access privileges, you may not see the DBA_SEQUENCES view. To display the columns of the SEQ view, issue the DESCRIBE command at the SQL*Plus prompt.

```
SQL> DESC SEQ
 Name                                 Null?      Type
 -------------------------------      --------   ---------
 SEQUENCE_NAME                        NOT NULL   VARCHAR2(30)
 MIN_VALUE                                       NUMBER
 MAX_VALUE                                       NUMBER
 INCREMENT_BY                         NOT NULL   NUMBER
 CYCLE_FLAG                                      VARCHAR2(1)
 ORDER_FLAG                                      VARCHAR2(1)
 CACHE_SIZE                           NOT NULL   NUMBER
 LAST_NUMBER                          NOT NULL   NUMBER
```

To find out which individual sequences are in the STUDENT schema, query the view.

```
SELECT sequence_name
  FROM seq
SEQUENCE_NAME
-------------------------------
COURSE_NO_SEQ
INSTRUCTOR_ID_SEQ
SECTION_ID_SEQ
STUDENT_ID_SEQ
```

4 rows selected.

If you are unclear about the meaning of the different columns in the SEQ view, query yet another view named DICT_COLUMNS for a description of each column.

```
SELECT column_name, comments
  FROM dict_columns
 WHERE table_name = 'USER_SEQUENCES'
COLUMN_NAME        COMMENTS
---------------    ------------------------------------
SEQUENCE_NAME      SEQUENCE name
MIN_VALUE          Minimum value of the sequence
```

```
. . .
CACHE_SIZE          Number of sequence numbers to cache
LAST_NUMBER         Last sequence number written to disk
```

8 rows selected.

If you have performed most of the exercises in the previous chapters of this workbook your results will differ from the results shown in the outputs of this chapter as you have added new objects and altered existing objects in the STUDENT schema. To bring back the STUDENT schema to its original state, run the rebuildStudent.sql script at the SQL*Plus prompt. For example: SQL>@c:\guest\schemasetup\ rebuildStudent.sql. *This script drops the STUDENT database-related tables, recreates the tables, and reloads the data. If you added the supplemental tables mentioned in the previous chapters, you can drop them with the sql_book_drop_extra_tables.sql script. This script will not recreate them. To run the script execute this command at the SQL*Plus prompt:* SQL>@:c:\guest\schemasetup\sql_book_drop_ extra_tables.sql. *Both SQL*Plus commands assume that you are running the Windows environment and your scripts are stored in the c:\guest\schemasetup directory. If you are using iSQL*Plus, refer to Chapter 2, "SQL: The Basics," about loading the file and executing the script.*

LAB 13.1 EXERCISES

13.1.1 QUERY THE DATA DICTIONARY

a) Execute the following SQL statement. Describe the result of the query and name the different object types.

```
SELECT object_name, object_type
  FROM user_objects
```

b) Based on the USER_OBJECTS view, what information is stored in the columns CREATED, LAST_DDL_TIME, and STATUS?

c) Name the data dictionary view listing tables only in the STUDENT schema.

d) Query the data dictionary view USER_TAB_COLUMNS for the GRADE table and describe the information found in the columns DATA_TYPE, DATA_LENGTH, NULLABLE, and DATA_DEFAULT.

e) Show a list of all indexes and their columns for the ENROLL-MENT table.

f) Display a list of all the sequences in the STUDENT schema and the current value of each.

g) Execute the following two SQL statements. The first statement creates a view and the second queries the data dictionary view called USER_VIEWS. What information is stored in the TEXT column of USER_VIEWS? Drop the view afterward.

```
CREATE OR REPLACE VIEW my_test AS
SELECT first_name, instructor_id
  FROM instructor

SELECT view_name, text
  FROM user_views
 WHERE view_name = 'MY_TEST'
```

h) Execute the following query. What do you observe?

```
SELECT constraint_name, table_name, constraint_type
  FROM user_constraints
```

i) What columns are listed in the data dictionary view USER_CONS_COLUMNS?

j) Execute the following SQL statement. Describe the result.

```
SELECT username
  FROM all_users
```

k) Execute the following query. What do you observe about the result?

```
SELECT segment_name, segment_type, bytes/1024
  FROM user_segments
 WHERE segment_name = 'ZIPCODE'
   AND segment_type = 'TABLE'
```

LAB 13.1 EXERCISE ANSWERS

13.1.1 ANSWERS

a) Execute the following SQL statement. Describe the result of the query and name the different object types.

```
SELECT object_name, object_type
  FROM user_objects
```

Answer: The query returns a list of all the objects owned by the current user. The object types listed are table, sequence, and index.

OBJECT_NAME	OBJECT_TYPE
COURSE	TABLE
...	
COURSE_NO_SEQ	SEQUENCE
...	
ZIP_PK	INDEX

36 rows selected.

Depending on the objects created in your individual schema, you see different results. Most likely, you see a list of tables, indexes, and sequences, but the list can also include views, procedures, packages, functions, synonyms, triggers, and other object types.

The ALL_OBJECTS view is different from the USER_OBJECTS view because it includes an additional column called OWNER and lists all the objects accessible to the user. It identifies the name of the schema in which the object is stored. The USER_OBJECTS view shows only those objects in the user's own schema.

The columns OWNER and OBJECT_NAME represent the unique identifier of the ALL_OBJECTS data dictionary view. There can be objects with the same name in other schemas, but within a schema, the object name has to be unique.

b) Based on the USER_OBJECTS view, what information is stored in the columns CREATED, LAST_DDL_TIME, and STATUS?

Answer: The CREATED column shows when an object was created in the schema. The LAST_DDL_TIME column indicates when an object was last modified via a DDL command, such as when a column was added to a table or a view was recompiled. The STATUS column indicates whether an object is valid or invalid.

The resulting output may vary depending on the objects in your schema.

```
SELECT object_name, created, last_ddl_time, status
  FROM user_objects
OBJECT_NAME            CREATED    LAST_DDL_ STATU
--------------------   ---------  --------- -----
COURSE                 14-AUG-99  23-OCT-99 VALID
...
ZIP_PK                 14-AUG-99  14-AUG-99 VALID

36 rows selected.
```

A view may become invalid if the underlying table is modified or dropped. Other objects, such as PL/SQL procedures, packages, or functions, may become invalid if dependent objects are modified, and they subsequently need to be recompiled.

If you are unclear about the meaning of a particular column, refer to the DICT_COLUMNS view for information.

```
SELECT column_name, comments
  FROM dict_columns
 WHERE table_name = 'USER_OBJECTS'
   AND column_name IN ('STATUS', 'LAST_DDL_TIME',
                       'CREATED')
COLUMN_NAME          COMMENTS
------------------   --------------------------------------------
CREATED              Timestamp for the creation of the object
LAST_DDL_TIME        Timestamp for the last DDL change (including
                     GRANT and REVOKE) to the object
STATUS               Status of the object

3 rows selected.
```

c) Name the data dictionary view listing tables only in the STUDENT schema.

Answer: The view is USER_TABLES. You can find out which data dictionary table contains this information by querying the DICT view.

```
SELECT table_name
  FROM user_tables
```

```
TABLE_NAME
-------------------
COURSE
...
ZIPCODE
```

10 rows selected.

d) Query the data dictionary view USER_TAB_COLUMNS for the GRADE table and describe the information found in the columns DATA_TYPE, DATA_LENGTH, NULLABLE, and DATA_DEFAULT.

Answer: The column DATA_TYPE shows the datatype of the column, DATA_LENGTH displays the length of the column in bytes, and there is either a 'Y' or 'N' in the column NULLABLE indicating whether or not NULL values are allowed in the column. The column DATA_DEFAULT represents the default value for the column, if any.

```
SELECT table_name, column_name, data_type, data_length,
       nullable, data_default
  FROM user_tab_columns
 WHERE table_name = 'GRADE'
```

TABLE_NA	COLUMN_NAME	DATA_TYP	DATA_LENGTH	N	DATA_
GRADE	STUDENT_ID	NUMBER	22	N	
...					
GRADE	NUMERIC_GRADE	NUMBER	22	N	0
...					
GRADE	MODIFIED_BY	VARCHAR2	30	N	
GRADE	MODIFIED_DATE	DATE	7	N	

10 rows selected.

Note the zero value in the last column named DATA_DEFAULT. This means the column called NUMERIC_GRADE has a column default value of zero. This value is inserted into a table's row if the NUMERIC_GRADE column is not specified during an INSERT operation. For example, the following INSERT statement does not list the NUMERIC_GRADE column and, therefore, the NUMERIC_GRADE column is zero; alternatively, you can use the DEFAULT keyword discussed in Chapter 10, "Insert, Update, and Delete."

```
INSERT INTO GRADE
   (student_id, section_id, grade_type_code,
    grade_code_occurrence,
    created_by, created_date,
    modified_by, modified_date)
VALUES
   (102,89, 'FI',
    2,
```

```
'ARISCHERT', SYSDATE,
'ARISCHERT', SYSDATE)
1 row created.
```

e) Show a list of all indexes and their columns for the ENROLLMENT table.

Answer: The data dictionary view USER_IND_COLUMNS lists the desired result.

```
SELECT index_name, table_name, column_name,
       column_position
  FROM user_ind_columns
 WHERE table_name = 'ENROLLMENT'
 ORDER BY 1, 4
INDEX_NAME       TABLE_NAME COLUMN_NAM COLUMN_POSITION
---------------- ---------- ---------- ---------------
ENR_PK           ENROLLMENT STUDENT_ID               1
ENR_PK           ENROLLMENT SECTION_ID               2
ENR_SECT_FK_I    ENROLLMENT SECTION_ID               1

3 rows selected.
```

The ENROLLMENT table has two indexes: ENR_SECT_FK_I and ENR_PK. The first index consists of the column SECTION_ID. The second index, a unique index created by the primary key constraint, has the columns STUDENT_ID and SEC-TION_ID in that order. The COLUMN_POSITION shows the order of the columns within the index.

If you want to show just the indexes you can query USER_INDEXES. This view also indicates if an index is unique or not. Details about function-based indexes are listed in the USER_IND_EXPRESSIONS view.

f) Display a list of all the sequences in the STUDENT schema and the current value of each.

Answer: The USER_SEQUENCES data dictionary view shows the sequence name and the current value of the sequence.

The resulting output may vary depending on the sequences in your schema.

```
SELECT sequence_name, last_number
  FROM user_sequences
SEQUENCE_NAME                       LAST_NUMBER
------------------------------      -----------
COURSE_NO_SEQ                               451
INSTRUCTOR_ID_SEQ                           111
SECTION_ID_SEQ                              157
STUDENT_ID_SEQ                              400

4 rows selected.
```

g) Execute the following two SQL statements. The first statement creates a view and the second queries the data dictionary view called USER_VIEWS. What information is stored in the TEXT column of USER_VIEWS? Drop the view afterward.

```
CREATE OR REPLACE VIEW my_test AS
SELECT first_name, instructor_id
  FROM instructor

SELECT view_name, text
  FROM user_views
 WHERE view_name = 'MY_TEST'
```

Answer: The TEXT column of the USER_VIEWS data dictionary view stores the view's defining SQL statement.

```
VIEW_NAME   TEXT
----------  --------------------------------
MY_TEST     SELECT first_name, instructor_id
              FROM instructor

1 row selected.
```

From Chapter 12, "Views, Indexes, and Sequences," recall the definition of a view as a stored query. The query is stored in the column named TEXT of USER_VIEWS.

The TEXT column in the USER_VIEWS data dictionary is of the LONG datatype. By default SQL*Plus does not display more than 80 characters of a LONG. You can increase this length with the SQL*Plus SET LONG command and wrap whole words using the SQL*Plus FORMAT COLUMN command with the WORD_WRAPPED option.

OBJECT DEPENDENCIES

Some objects, such as a view, synonym, procedure, function, or package, depend on other objects. For example, the view MY_TEST depends on the INSTRUCTOR table. You can find out about these dependencies in the USER_DEPENDENCIES view. The query shows that this object is a view and that it references the INSTRUCTOR table. While this is easy to determine with a simple view, some objects are more complicated and querying this view helps identify the effect of any potential change.

```
SELECT name, type, referenced_name
  FROM user_dependencies
 WHERE name = 'MY_TEST'
NAME        TYPE          REFERENCED_NAME
----------  ------------  --------------------
MY_TEST     VIEW          INSTRUCTOR

1 row selected.
```

**LAB
13.1**

The MY_TEST view is dropped with the DROP VIEW command.

```
DROP VIEW my_test
View dropped.
```

h) Execute the following query. What do you observe?

```
SELECT constraint_name, table_name, constraint_type
  FROM user_constraints
```

Answer: The output shows the constraints on the various tables. The foreign key constraint is listed as constraint type R (Referential Integrity constraint), the NOT NULL and check constraints are shown as constraint type C, and the primary key constraints are displayed as constraint type P. The SECTION table has a unique constraint listed as constraint type U.

```
CONSTRAINT_NAME                     TABLE_NAME C
----------------------------------- ---------- -
CRSE_CRSE_FK                        COURSE     R
...
SYS_C001441                         GRADE      C
ENR_STU_FK                          ENROLLMENT R
...
SECT_SECT2_UK                       SECTION    U
...
ZIP_PK                              ZIPCODE    P
...
ZIP_MODIFIED_BY_NNULL               ZIPCODE    C

94 rows selected.
```

Note any constraint not explicitly named receives a system-assigned name, such as the constraint called SYS_C001441.

The USER_CONSTRAINTS view contains more useful columns in addition to the ones shown in the previous query, particularly for referential integrity constraints.

For example, query the view for the foreign key constraint called ENR_STU_FK. The result shows the name of the primary key constraint. This constraint is referenced by the foreign key.

```
SELECT r_owner, r_constraint_name, delete_rule
  FROM user_constraints
 WHERE constraint_name = 'ENR_STU_FK'
R_OWNER    R_CONSTRAINT_NAME                     DELETE_RU
---------- ------------------------------------- ---------
STUDENT    STU_PK                                NO ACTION

1 row selected.
```

You'll notice from the result that the delete rule on the ENR_STU_FK constraint specifies NO ACTION, which means any delete of a student row (parent record) is restricted if dependent enrollment rows (child records with the same STUDENT_ ID) exist. This is in contrast to a CASCADE, which means if a parent record is deleted the children are automatically deleted. If the referential integrity constraint is on delete set null, you would see the value SET NULL in the DELETE_ RULE column.

The referential integrity constraints avoid the creation of orphan rows, meaning enrollment records without corresponding students. Also, the parent table may not be dropped unless the foreign key constraint is dropped. To disable constraints use the ALTER TABLE command. Alternatively, the parent table may be dropped using the DROP TABLE command with the CASCADE CONSTRAINTS clause, automatically dropping the foreign key constraints.

OTHER CONSTRAINT TYPES

In addition to the constraint types mentioned, Table 13.2 shows additional constraint types, they are the view constraint with check option (V) and the view constraint with the read-only option (O).

Table 13.2 ■ Constraint Types

Constraint Type	Description
R	Referential Integrity Constraint
C	Check Constraint including Not Null Constraint
P	Primary Key Constraint
U	Unique Constraint
V	View Constraint with Check Option
R	View Constraint with Read-Only Option

DISTINGUISH NOT NULL CONSTRAINTS FROM CHECK CONSTRAINTS

The NOT NULL constraint is listed as a check constraint and you can distinguish this type from other user-defined check constraints by looking at the SEARCH_ CONDITION column. The next query shows the constraints of the GRADE_TYPE table. For example, the NOT NULL constraint called GRTYP_DESCRIPTION_ NNULL on the DESCRIPTION column lists the NOT NULL column with the column name in quotes (in case of case-sensitive column names) together with the words IS NOT NULL. By comparison the GRTYP_GRADE_TYPE_CODE_LENGTH constraint checks for the length of the GRADE_TYPE_CODE column to be exactly 2.

```
SELECT constraint_name, search_condition
  FROM user_constraints
 WHERE constraint_type = 'C'
   AND table_name = 'GRADE_TYPE'
```

CONSTRAINT_NAME	SEARCH_CONDITION
GRTYP_DESCRIPTION_NNULL	"DESCRIPTION" IS NOT NULL
...	
GRTYP_GRADE_TYPE_CODE_LENGTH	LENGTH(grade_type_code)=2

7 rows selected.

i) What columns are listed in the data dictionary view USER_CONS_COLUMNS?

Answer: The columns are OWNER, CONSTRAINT_NAME, TABLE_NAME, COLUMN_NAME, and POSITION.

This data dictionary view shows which columns are referenced in a constraint. A query against the view illustrates this on the example of the primary key constraint ENR_PK which consists of the two columns STUDENT_ID and SECTION_ID.

```
SELECT constraint_name, column_name, position
  FROM user_cons_columns
 WHERE constraint_name = 'ENR_PK'
```

CONSTRAINT_NAME	COLUMN_NAME	POSITION
ENR_PK	STUDENT_ID	1
ENR_PK	SECTION_ID	2

2 rows selected.

j) Execute the following SQL statement. Describe the result.

```
SELECT username
  FROM all_users
```

Answer: It shows a list of all the users in the database.

The resulting output may vary, depending on your database.

USERNAME
SYS
SYSTEM
...
SCOTT
...
STUDENT

15 rows selected.

Note that there are two users named SYS and SYSTEM. The SYS user is the owner of the Oracle data dictionary. The default password for this user is typically CHANGE_ON_INSTALL. This password should be changed as soon as the database installation is complete. Never log in as this "super user" unless you are an experienced Oracle DBA or are instructed by Oracle to do so. Otherwise, you may inadvertently perform actions that could adversely affect the database.

The SYSTEM user has DBA privileges, but does not own the data dictionary. Always change the default password, MANAGER, to another password. Be sure to keep track of all these passwords.

Another useful view is the USER_USERS view. Following is a query displaying information about the current user or schema. It shows your login name and the name of the default tablespace on which any tables or indexes you create are stored, unless you explicitly specify another tablespace. It also shows when your account was created.

```
SELECT username, default_tablespace, created
  FROM user_users
```

USERNAME	DEFAULT_TABLESPACE	CREATED
STUDENT	USERS	04-MAY-02

1 row selected.

k) Execute the following query. What do you observe about the result?

```
SELECT segment_name, segment_type, bytes/1024
  FROM user_segments
 WHERE segment_name = 'ZIPCODE'
   AND segment_type = 'TABLE'
```

Answer: The query displays the size of the ZIPCODE table.

SEGMENT_NA	SEGMENT_TYPE	BYTES/1024
ZIPCODE	TABLE	64

1 row selected.

The most common segment types are tables and indexes. The USER_SEGMENT view shows the storage in bytes for a particular segment. Dividing the bytes by 1024 displays the size in kilobytes (KB). Note, your actual number of bytes may vary from the figure listed here depending on the storage parameter chosen for the default tablespace in your individual user account.

To see a listing of the different available tablespaces, you query the USER_TABLESPACES or DBA_TABLESPACES view. It may yield a result similar to the following.

```
SELECT tablespace_name
  FROM user_tablespaces
  ORDER BY tablespace_name
```
TABLESPACE_NAME

**INDX
SYSTEM
TEMP
USERS**

4 rows selected.

To find out how much space is available in total on each of the tablespaces you write a SQL statement against the view USER_FREE_SPACE. The result shows you the available megabytes (MB) for each tablespace. You learn more about table-space and space management topics in the *Oracle DBA Interactive Workbook* by Melanie Caffrey and Douglas Scherer.

```
SELECT tablespace_name, SUM(bytes)/1024/1024
  FROM user_free_space
  GROUP BY tablespace_name
```

TABLESPACE_NAME	**SUM(BYTES)/1024/1024**
INDX	24.8125
SYSTEM	14.6796875
USERS	82.8125

3 rows selected.

LAB 13.1 SELF-REVIEW QUESTIONS

In order to test your progress, you should be able to answer the following questions.

1) The data dictionary contains data about the database.

a) _____ True
b) _____ False

2) The data dictionary view USER_OBJECTS stores information about tables, indexes, and sequences.

a) _____ True
b) _____ False

3) The dynamic data dictionary is updated only by the Oracle database.

a) _____ True
b) _____ False

4) The ALL_TABLES data dictionary view shows all the tables in the entire database.

    a) _____ True
    b) _____ False

5) The OBJ view is a public synonym for the USER_OBJECTS view.

    a) _____ True
    b) _____ False

Answers appear in Appendix A, Section 13.1.

L A B   1 3 . 2

DYNAMIC SQL SCRIPTS

LAB OBJECTIVES

After this lab, you will be able to:

✔ Write Dynamic SQL Statements
✔ Write Dynamic SQL Scripts

So far, you have executed many SQL statements in the SQL*Plus environment. In this lab, you learn how to write SQL statements that create and execute other SQL statements.

SQL*PLUS SUBSTITUTION VARIABLES

You probably find yourself executing the same command over and over again, sometimes just with slight modifications. Instead of editing the SQL statement each time, you can substitute part of the SQL statement with a variable. When the statement is executed, you supply the appropriate value for the variable.

For example, the variable in the following statement is named v_course_no. You identify a variable by prefixing an arbitrary variable name with an ampersand (&) symbol. When you execute the statement, SQL*Plus prompts you for a value and the supplied value is assigned to the variable.

```
SELECT course_no, description
  FROM course
 WHERE course_no = &v_course_no
```

The prompt you see in *i*SQL*Plus looks similar to Figure 13.1.

If you use SQL*Plus your prompt looks like this:

```
Enter value for v_course_no:
```

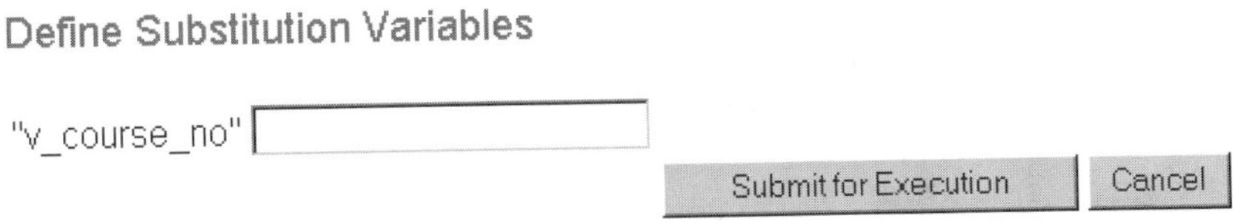

Define Substitution Variables

"v_course_no" [   ]

[Submit for Execution]   [Cancel]

Figure 13.1 ■ Substitution variables prompt in *iSQL*Plus*.

Once you enter the value of 240 and press Enter or the Submit for Execution button, SQL*Plus will assign the variable v_course_no the value of 240, which then subsequently executes the statement and displays the result similar to the result you see in Figure 13.2 if you use *iSQL*Plus*.

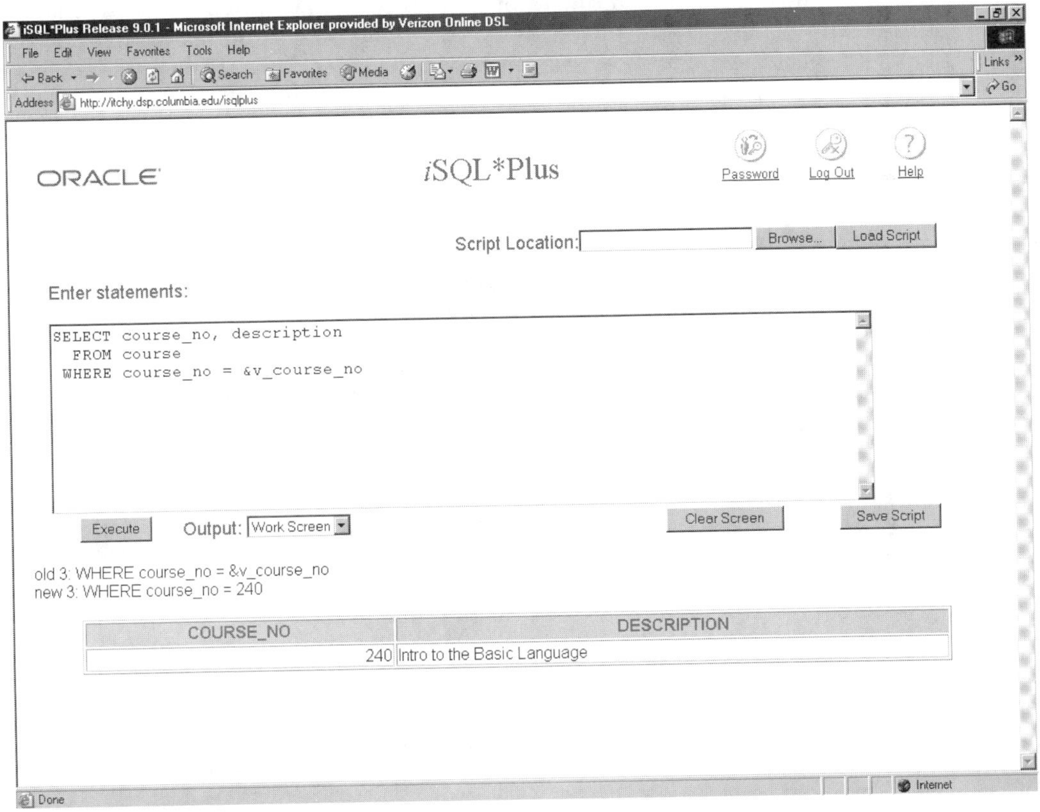

Figure 13.2 ■ Result in *iSQL*Plus*.

If you use SQL*Plus you will see a result much like the following:

```
SQL> SELECT course_no, description
  2    FROM course
  3   WHERE course_no = &v_course_no
  4  /
```

```
Enter value for v_course_no: 240
old    3:   WHERE course_no = &v_course_no
new    3:   WHERE course_no = 240


COURSE_NO DESCRIPTION
--------- ------------------------------------
      240 Intro to the Basic Language

1 row selected.
```

The text displayed after the substitution variable prompt shows the value before (old) and after the substitution of the value (new). The number 3 indicates that the substitution variable is found on line 3 of the SQL statement. You can change this default behavior with the SET VERIFY OFF SQL*Plus command that will no longer display the old and new values.

If you want to re-execute the statement in the buffer, use the forward slash (/) and you are prompted for a value for the v_course_no substitution variable each time.

You can use a substitution variable in any SQL statement executed within the SQL*Plus environment. The next statement shows you an example of a query against the USER_OBJECTS data dictionary view. This SQL statement determines if the name of a particular database object is valid and its object type. Instead of repeatedly editing the same statement, use a variable to substitute the value of the object name. Because the datatype of the OBJECT_NAME column and the variable name must agree, the variable name is enclosed in single quotation marks.

```
SELECT object_name, object_type, status
   FROM obj
 WHERE object_name LIKE UPPER('&v_object_name')
Enter value for v_object_name: student
old    3:   WHERE object_name LIKE UPPER('&v_object_name')
new    3:   WHERE object_name LIKE UPPER('student')


OBJECT_NAME                      OBJECT_TYPE         STATUS
------------------------------   -----------------   ------
STUDENT                          TABLE               VALID

1 row selected.
```

You can save the file so you may re-execute it at a later time. Substitution variables are not limited to the WHERE clause of a statement. For example, you can also use them in the ORDER BY clause, the FROM clause to substitute a table name, as an individual column expression, or even substitute an entire WHERE clause.

GENERATE DYNAMIC SQL

Dynamic SQL allows you to execute SQL commands built at runtime. Dynamic SQL is often executed in Oracle's PL/SQL language, but can also be generated and executed in SQL*Plus using SQL*Plus scripts. These scripts are often referred to as *SQL to generate SQL scripts* or *master/slave scripts*.

Please note that there are a number of SQL*Plus commands not supported in the iSQL*Plus release. They include the SPOOL, SET TERMOUT, HOST, and ACCEPT commands, among others. For a complete list see Appendix C, "SQL*Plus Command Reference." Attempting to use any of the unsupported commands or command options raises an SP2-0850 error message. To complete this portion of the lab and the accompanying exercises please use the client–server SQL*Plus software instead of the Web-based iSQL*Plus version.

Using SQL*Plus you can automatically generate SQL statements and spool them to a file for use. The SPOOL command captures all the output from the SQL*Plus prompt in a file.

For example, you made some database changes to tables, causing other database objects, such as views, to become invalid. To compile the views, you can repeatedly type the ALTER VIEW command for each invalid view or you can wait for the user to access the views and let Oracle compile them. However, it is best to compile them after the table changes to make sure there are no errors. This is achieved by writing a script to generate the ALTER VIEW statement for each invalid view. The following SQL statement generates the dynamic SQL.

```
SELECT 'ALTER VIEW '|| object_name || ' COMPILE;'
  FROM user_objects
 WHERE object_type = 'VIEW'
   AND status <> 'VALID'
```

If you have any invalid views, your result may look like this:

```
'ALTERVIEW'||OBJECT_NAME||'COMPILE;'
-------------------------------------
ALTER VIEW CAPACITY_V COMPILE;
ALTER VIEW CT_STUDENT_V COMPILE;
ALTER VIEW NJ_STUDENT_V COMPILE;
ALTER VIEW NY_STUDENT_V COMPILE;

4 rows selected.
```

The text literal 'ALTER VIEW' is concatenated with the view name and then with the text literal `'COMPILE;'`. You can spool the result into a file using the SPOOL command.

LAB 13.2 EXERCISES

13.2.1 WRITE DYNAMIC SQL STATEMENTS

a) Execute the following statements. What result do you see when you substitute the variable with the value `enr_pk`?

```
COL column_name FORMAT A20
COL owner FORMAT A10
COL constraint_name HEADING 'Constraint|Name' FORMAT A20
UNDEFINE vname
SELECT t.constraint_type, c.column_name,
       t.constraint_name, t.owner
  FROM all_constraints t, all_cons_columns c
 WHERE t.owner = c.owner
   AND t.constraint_name = c.constraint_name
   AND t.constraint_name LIKE UPPER('%&vname%')
 ORDER BY position
```

b) Execute the SQL*Plus command `SET VERIFY OFF`. Re-execute the SQL statement from Exercise a by entering the forward slash. What do you observe?

c) Enter the following SQL statement into a text file named s_query.sql. Don't forget to end the statement with a semi-colon or a forward slash on a separate line. Save the file and execute it at the SQL*Plus prompt with the command `@s_query 252`. What result do you see?

```
SELECT last_name, student_id
  FROM student
 WHERE student_id = &1
```

d) Execute the following SQL*Plus commands and the SQL statement that determines the maximum and minimum value of a column in a table. When prompted for the value of the vcol

variable, enter the value `cost`; for the vtable variable, enter
`course`. Describe your observation about the SQL*Plus
prompts.

```
UNDEFINE vcol
UNDEFINE vtable
SET VERIFY OFF
SELECT MIN(&vcol), MAX(&vcol)
   FROM &vtable
```

e) Enter all the following commands in a file named maxval.sql,
then execute the script. For the column name supply the value
`capacity` and for the table name enter the value `section`.
What do you observe?

```
PROMPT Determine the maximum and minimum value of a column
ACCEPT vcol CHAR PROMPT 'Enter the column name: '
ACCEPT vtable CHAR PROMPT 'Enter the corresponding table name:
SET VERIFY OFF
SELECT MIN(&vcol), MAX(&vcol)
   FROM &vtable
```

13.2.2 WRITE DYNAMIC SQL SCRIPTS

The following SQL statement disables the foreign key constraint on the ZIP column of the STUDENT table.

```
ALTER TABLE student DISABLE CONSTRAINT stu_zip_fk
```

Disabling the constraint allows child values to be entered where no corresponding parent exists. This means you can insert or update a zip code in the STUDENT
table that does not have a corresponding value in the ZIPCODE table. There are
times when you want to disable constraints temporarily, such as when you must
bulk load data or update large quantities of data quickly. Afterward you enable
the constraints again. The following exercises show you how to disable and enable constraints using a dynamic SQL script.

a) Execute the following SQL statement to generate other SQL
statements. What do you observe?

```
SELECT 'ALTER TABLE ' || table_name
   FROM user_constraints
  WHERE constraint_type = 'R'
```

b) Expand the SQL statement in Exercise a by adding the constraint name dynamically. The resulting output should look like this:

```
ALTER TABLE COURSE DISABLE CONSTRAINT CRSE_CRSE_FK;
...
ALTER TABLE SECTION DISABLE CONSTRAINT SECT_CRSE_FK;
ALTER TABLE SECTION DISABLE CONSTRAINT SECT_INST_FK;
ALTER TABLE STUDENT DISABLE CONSTRAINT STU_ZIP_FK;

11 rows selected.
```

c) Save the SQL statement in Exercise b to a file named disable_fk.sql. Add the following SQL*Plus statements at the beginning of the file. Note that the double dashes represent single-line comments.

```
-- File Name: disable_fk.sql
-- Purpose: Disable Foreign Key constraints.
-- Created Date: Place current date here
-- Author: Put your name here
SET PAGESIZE 0
SET LINESIZE 80
SET FEEDBACK OFF
SET TERM OFF
SPOOL disable_fk.out
```

Add a semicolon at the end of the SQL statement and the following SQL*Plus commands afterward.

```
SPOOL OFF
SET PAGESIZE 20
SET LINESIZE 100
SET FEEDBACK ON
SET TERM ON
```

Save the file and run the disable_fk.sql file at the SQL*Plus prompt with the @ command. Describe the output from the spooled file named disable_fk.out.

d) Write a dynamic SQL script performing the opposite operation, which is enabling the foreign key constraints.

e) Explain each line in the following SQL script and then describe the purpose of the script in one sentence.

```
01 /*
02 -----------------------------------------------------
03 File name:   rows.sql
04 Purpose:
05 Created by:  H. Ashley on January 7, 2000
06 Modified by: A. Christa on September 29, 2001
07 -----------------------------------------------------
08 */
09 SET TERM OFF
10 SET PAGESIZE 0
11 SET FEEDBACK OFF
12 SPOOL temp
13 SELECT 'SELECT ' || '''' || table_name || '''' ||
14         ', COUNT(*) '||CHR(10) ||
15         ' FROM '|| LOWER(table_name) || ';'
16   FROM user_tables;
17 SPOOL OFF
18 SET FEEDBACK 1
19 SET PAGESIZE 20
20 SET TERM ON
21 @temp.lst
22 HOST DEL temp.lst
```

**LAB
13.2**

f) Enter the following commands in a file called ascii_test.sql. Describe the result of the ascii_test.out file.

```
-- File Name: ascii_test.sql
SET PAGESIZE 0
SET LINESIZE 100
SET FEEDBACK OFF
PROMPT Enter the starting and ending course numbers
ACCEPT v_start_course_no CHAR PROMPT 'Enter starting course number: '
ACCEPT v_end_course_no CHAR PROMPT 'Enter ending course number: '
SET TERM OFF
SPOOL ascii_test.out
SELECT course_no||','''||description||''','||
       Cost||','''||modified_date||''''
  FROM course
 WHERE course_no BETWEEN &v_start_course_no
       AND &v_end_course_no;
SPOOL OFF
SET PAGESIZE 20
SET LINESIZE 80
SET FEEDBACK ON
SET TERM ON
```

g) Explain the result of the following script.

```
--File: dump_file.sql
SET PAGESIZE 0
SET LINESIZE 100
SET FEEDBACK OFF
SPOOL dump_file.out
SELECT 'INSERT INTO STUDENT_TEST VALUES
('|| student_id||','''||last_name||
   ''','''||first_name||''');'
 FROM student
SPOOL OFF
SET PAGESIZE 20
SET LINESIZE 80
SET FEEDBACK ON
SET TERM ON
```

h) Imagine a scenario in which you would execute a script like the following.

```
--File: re_create_seq.sql
SET PAGESIZE 0
SET LINESIZE 100
SET FEEDBACK OFF
SPOOL re_create_seq.out
SELECT 'CREATE SEQUENCE '||sequence_name||
       ' START WITH '||last_number||chr(10)||
       ' INCREMENT BY '||increment_by ||
       DECODE(cache_size, 0, ' nocache', 'cache '||cache_size)||';'
  FROM SEQ;
SPOOL OFF
SET PAGESIZE 20
SET LINESIZE 80
SET FEEDBACK ON
SET TERM ON
```

LAB 13.2 EXERCISE ANSWERS

13.2.1 ANSWERS

a) Execute the following statements. What result do you see when you substitute the variable with the value `enr_pk`?

```
COL column_name FORMAT A20
COL owner FORMAT A10
COL constraint_name HEADING 'Constraint|Name' FORMAT A20
UNDEFINE vname
SELECT t.constraint_type, c.column_name,
       t.constraint_name, t.owner
  FROM all_constraints t, all_cons_columns c
 WHERE t.owner = c.owner
   AND t.constraint_name = c.constraint_name
   AND t.constraint_name LIKE UPPER('%&vname%')
 ORDER BY position
```

Answer: The old and new substitution values for the vname variable are displayed. After the value is entered, the SQL statement displays constraints with a similar name.

The number 6, after the old and new values, represents the line number of the substitution variable within the SQL statement.

```
Enter value for vname: enr_pk
old  6:     AND t.constraint_name LIKE UPPER('%&vname%')
new  6:     AND t.constraint_name LIKE UPPER('%enr_pk%')


                        Constraint
C COLUMN_NAME           Name                 OWNER
- -------------------- -------------------- --------
P STUDENT_ID           ENR_PK               STUDENT
P SECTION_ID           ENR_PK               STUDENT

2 rows selected.
```

The result includes the constraint type; in this example it is the primary key constraint. Additionally, you see the individual primary key columns STUDENT_ID and SECTION_ID. Also, note the substitution value can be entered in either lowercase or uppercase; the UPPER function in the SQL statement converts it into uppercase.

The query that provides this result joins the table constraints (ALL_CONSTRAINTS) and column constraints (ALL_CONS_COLUMNS) via the OWNER and CONSTRAINT_NAME columns. These two columns represent the unique identifier of the ALL_CONSTRAINTS view. Although a view cannot have a primary key or unique constraint, the view's underlying data dictionary tables have these columns as a unique identifier.

The UNDEFINE command deletes any previous reference to the vname SQL*Plus variable. A variable is typically defined when you explicitly use the DEFINE command, the ampersand (&), the double ampersand (&&), or the ACCEPT command. You learn about the double ampersand and the ACCEPT command shortly. The value of the variable is retained until you UNDEFINE the variable, use the variable with a single ampersand, use the variable with the ACCEPT command, or exit SQL*Plus.

The SQL*Plus FORMAT command shows the use of the COL HEADING command. The vertical pipe permits splitting of a column name across multiple lines.

SUPPRESSING THE USE OF SUBSTITUTION VARIABLES

There are times in SQL*Plus when you don't want the ampersand to be an indicator that a substitution variable follows, but a literal ampersand instead.

```
UPDATE student
   SET employer = 'Soehner & Peter'
 WHERE student_id = 135
Enter value for peter:
```

SQL*Plus thinks you want to use a substitution parameter rather than the literal ampersand. To remedy this, use the SET DEFINE command to turn the use of substitution parameters on or off.

```
SET DEFINE OFF
UPDATE student
   SET employer = 'Soehner & Peter'
 WHERE student_id = 135
1 row updated.
SET DEFINE ON
```

Lastly, issue a ROLLBACK command to undo the change of employer and set it back to the original value.

```
ROLLBACK
Rollback complete.
```

b) Execute the SQL*Plus command SET VERIFY OFF. Re-execute the SQL statement from Exercise a by entering the forward slash. What do you observe?

Answer: The VERIFY command suppresses the listing of the OLD and NEW substitution values.

Reset it back to its SQL*Plus default with the SET VERIFY ON command.

c) Enter the following SQL statement into a text file named s_query.sql. Don't forget to end the statement with a semicolon or a forward slash on a separate line. Save the file and execute it at the SQL*Plus prompt with the command @s_query 252. What result do you see?

```
SELECT last_name, student_id
  FROM student
 WHERE student_id = &1
```

Answer: The result displays the last name of the student with the STUDENT_ID of 252.

```
old    3:   WHERE student_id = &1
new    3:   WHERE student_id = 252


LAST_NAME                      STUDENT_ID
------------------------    ----------
Barogh                              252

1 row selected.
```

You can pass parameters (arguments) when running a script file in SQL*Plus. This works only if your substitution variable is a numeral. The &1 parameter is substituted with the first parameter passed (in this example with the value 252). If you include another parameter, such as &2, you can pass a second argument, and so on.

d) Execute the following SQL*Plus commands and the SQL statement that determines the maximum and minimum value of a column in a table. When prompted for the value of the vcol variable, enter the value `cost`; for the vtable variable, enter `course`. Describe your observation about the SQL*Plus prompts.

```
UNDEFINE vcol
UNDEFINE vtable
SET VERIFY OFF
SELECT MIN(&vcol), MAX(&vcol)
  FROM &vtable
```

*Answer: When a variable with the same name is preceded multiple times using an ampersand (&), SQL*Plus prompts you for each one.*

```
Enter value for vcol: cost
Enter value for vcol: cost
Enter value for vtable: course


MIN(COST) MAX(COST)
--------- ---------
     1095      1595

1 row selected.
```

To avoid being reprompted, define the variable with a double ampersand (&&).

```
UNDEFINE vcol
UNDEFINE vtable
SET VERIFY OFF
SELECT MIN(&&vcol), MAX(&&vcol)
  FROM &vtable
Enter value for vcol: cost
```

```
Enter value for vtable: course

MIN(COST) MAX(COST)
--------- ---------
     1095      1595
```

```
1 row selected.
```

Note that, until you exit SQL*Plus, the && variable is defined with the entered value, so any subsequent execution of the statement has the value for the variable vcol already defined without reprompting. Observe the effect of yet another execution. Only the prompt for the table name will appear because the vtable variable has only one & symbol. When the value section is now entered for a table name, this leads to an error because the value cost was retained for the v_col variables. The COST column is not a valid column name for the SECTION table.

```
Enter value for vtable: section
SELECT MIN(cost), MAX(cost)
                      *
ERROR at line 1:
ORA-00904: invalid column name
```

It can also be confusing to use the && if you forget you defined the variable because you are not prompted again. Undefine the vcol variable and rerun the statement.

```
UNDEFINE vcol
/
Enter value for vcol: capacity
Enter value for vtable: section

MIN(CAPACITY) MAX(CAPACITY)
------------- -------------
           10            25
```

```
1 row selected.
```

To display the values defined and their associated values, use the DE-FINE command.

e) Enter all the following commands in a file named maxval.sql, then execute the script. For the column name supply the value capacity and for the table name enter the value section. What do you observe?

```
PROMPT Determine the maximum and minimum value of a column
ACCEPT vcol CHAR PROMPT 'Enter the column name: '
ACCEPT vtable CHAR PROMPT 'Enter the corresponding table
name: '
SET VERIFY OFF
SELECT MIN(&vcol), MAX(&vcol)
   FROM &vtable
```

Answer: The PROMPT command prompts the user for input.

```
@maxval
Determine the maximum and minimum value of a column
Enter the column name: capacity
Enter the corresponding table name: section

MIN(CAPACITY) MAX(CAPACITY)
------------- -------------
          10            25

1 row selected.
```

Notice the ACCEPT SQL*Plus command defines a variable that can then be referenced with the ampersand symbol. The SQL*Plus ACCEPT command allows for datatype checking of the entered value. Other valid datatypes used with the ACCEPT command are NUMBER and DATE.

13.2.2 ANSWERS

a) Execute the following SQL statement to generate other SQL statements. What do you observe?

```
SELECT 'ALTER TABLE ' || table_name
   FROM user_constraints
 WHERE constraint_type = 'R'
```

Answer: The statement generates a list of all the tables with foreign key constraints together with a literal "ALTER TABLE".

```
'ALTERTABLE'||TABLE_NAME
-----------------------------------
ALTER TABLE COURSE
...
ALTER TABLE SECTION
ALTER TABLE SECTION
ALTER TABLE STUDENT

11 rows selected.
```

Note there are multiple rows with the same table name because a table may have multiple foreign keys.

b) Expand the SQL statement in Exercise a by adding the constraint name dynamically. The resulting output should look like this:

```
ALTER TABLE COURSE DISABLE CONSTRAINT CRSE_CRSE_FK;
...
ALTER TABLE SECTION DISABLE CONSTRAINT SECT_CRSE_FK;
ALTER TABLE SECTION DISABLE CONSTRAINT SECT_INST_FK;
ALTER TABLE STUDENT DISABLE CONSTRAINT STU_ZIP_FK;

11 rows selected.
```

Answer: The disable clause is added to the statement by concatenating the text literal 'DISABLE CONSTRAINT' with the constraint name and then with another text literal containing the semicolon.

```
SELECT 'ALTER TABLE ' || table_name ||
       ' DISABLE CONSTRAINT '|| constraint_name||';'
  FROM user_constraints
 WHERE constraint_type = 'R'
'ALTERTABLE'||TABLE_NAME||'DISABLECONSTRAINT'||CONSTRAIN
--------------------------------------------------------
ALTER TABLE COURSE DISABLE CONSTRAINT CRSE_CRSE_FK;
...
ALTER TABLE SECTION DISABLE CONSTRAINT SECT_CRSE_FK;
ALTER TABLE SECTION DISABLE CONSTRAINT SECT_INST_FK;
ALTER TABLE STUDENT DISABLE CONSTRAINT STU_ZIP_FK;

11 rows selected.
```

c) Save the SQL statement in Exercise b to a file named disable_fk.sql. Add the following SQL*Plus statements at the beginning of the file. Note that the double dashes represent single-line comments.

```
-- File Name: disable_fk.sql
-- Purpose: Disable Foreign Key constraints.
-- Created Date: Place current date here
-- Author: Put your name here
SET PAGESIZE 0
SET LINESIZE 80
SET FEEDBACK OFF
SET TERM OFF
SPOOL disable_fk.out
```

Add a semicolon at the end of the SQL statement and the following SQL*Plus commands afterward.

```
SPOOL OFF
SET PAGESIZE 20
SET LINESIZE 100
SET FEEDBACK ON
SET TERM ON
```

Save the file and run the disable_fk.sql file at the SQL*Plus prompt with the @ command. Describe the output from the spooled file named disable_fk.out.

Answer: The spooled file contains a list of all SQL statements necessary to disable the foreign constraints.

After editing the file, the disable_fk.sql script should look similar to the following:

```
-- File Name: disable_fk.sql
-- Purpose: Disable Foreign Key constraints.
-- Created Date: Place current date here
-- Author: Put your name here
SET PAGESIZE 0
SET LINESIZE 80
SET FEEDBACK OFF
SET TERM OFF
SPOOL disable_fk.out
SELECT 'ALTER TABLE ' || table_name || CHR(10)||
       '        DISABLE CONSTRAINT '|| constraint_name||';'
  FROM user_constraints
 WHERE constraint_type = 'R';
SPOOL OFF
SET PAGESIZE 20
SET LINESIZE 100
SET FEEDBACK ON
SET TERM ON
```

Executing the script disable_fk.sql with the @ command results in the disable_fk.out file, which looks like the following:

```
ALTER TABLE COURSE
  DISABLE CONSTRAINT CRSE_CRSE_FK;
...
ALTER TABLE STUDENT
       DISABLE CONSTRAINT STU_ZIP_FK;
```

You can now execute the commands in the file by typing @disable_fk.out at the SQL*Plus prompt. You need to specify the extension here because the file does not have the default .SQL extension.

Note the SQL statement contains the function CHR(10). This column function automatically returns a new line in the result.

COMMON SQL*PLUS COMMANDS IN SQL*PLUS SCRIPTS

The SQL*Plus commands before and after the SQL statement in the script change the settings of the SQL*Plus environment.

The SPOOL command, together with a filename, spools any subsequently issued SQL*Plus or SQL command to a file named disable_fk.out. If you don't add an extension, the default extension is .LST. The following command creates a file named temp.lst. If a file with the same name already exists, it is overwritten without warning.

```
SPOOL temp
```

To show the file name you're currently spooling to, use the SPOOL command.

```
SPOOL
currently spooling to temp.lst
```

To end the spooling and close the file, enter this command:

```
SPOOL OFF
```

Just as with other file names, you can add a path to store the file in a directory other than your default directory. To learn how to change your default directory, see Chapter 2, "SQL: The Basics."

The PAGESIZE 0 command suppresses the column headings.

The FEEDBACK command returns the number of records returned by a query. Because you don't want to see this in the resulting file you subsequently execute, issue either the command SET FEEDBACK 0 or the command SET FEEDBACK OFF.

The SET TERMOUT OFF or SET TERM OFF command controls the display of output generated by the commands. The OFF setting suppresses the output from the screen only when the command is executed from a script file.

The SET LINESIZE command determines the total number of characters SQL*Plus displays in one line before beginning a new line. Setting it to 80 makes it easy to read the spooled output in a text editor.

You want to reset all the SQL*Plus environmental variables to their previous settings. To see the current settings of all environmental variables, use the SHOW ALL command at the SQL*Plus prompt.

DOCUMENTING YOUR SCRIPT

You can document your scripts by using comments. You begin a single-line comment with two hyphens (--). A multiline comment begins with a slash and an asterisk (/*) and ends with an asterisk and a slash (*/). In SQL*Plus scripts, you can also use the REMARK (REM) command.

```
/* This is a multi-line
comment */
-- A single-line comment, it ends with a line break.
REM Another single-line comment, only used in SQL*Plus.
```

d) Write a dynamic SQL script performing the opposite operation, which is enabling the foreign key constraints.

Answer: The spooled file contains a list of all SQL statements necessary to enable the foreign key constraints.

```
-- File Name: enable_fk.sql
-- Purpose: Enable Foreign Key constraints.
-- Created Date: Place current date here
-- Author: Put your name here
SET PAGESIZE 0
SET LINESIZE 80
SET FEEDBACK OFF
SET TERM OFF
SPOOL enable_fk.out
SELECT 'ALTER TABLE ' || table_name || CHR(10)||
       '        ENABLE CONSTRAINT '|| constraint_name||';'
  FROM user_constraints
 WHERE constraint_type = 'R';
SPOOL OFF
SET PAGESIZE 20
SET LINESIZE 80
SET FEEDBACK ON
SET TERM ON
```

e) Explain each line in the following SQL script and then describe the purpose of the script in one sentence.

```
01 /*
02 -----------------------------------------------------
03 File name:   rows.sql
04 Purpose:
05 Created by:  H. Ashley on January 7, 2000
06 Modified by: A. Christa on September 29, 2001
07 -----------------------------------------------------
08 */
09 SET TERM OFF
10 SET PAGESIZE 0
11 SET FEEDBACK OFF
12 SPOOL temp
13 SELECT 'SELECT ' || '''' || table_name || '''' ||
14        ', COUNT(*) '||CHR(10) ||
15        ' FROM '|| LOWER(table_name) || ';'
16   FROM user_tables;
17 SPOOL OFF
18 SET FEEDBACK 1
19 SET PAGESIZE 20
20 SET TERM ON
21 @temp.lst
22 HOST DEL temp.lst
```

Answer:The purpose of the script is to display a list of all user-accessible tables, together with a row count for each.

The script dynamically generates these statements and spools them to the resulting temp.lst file as follows.

```
SELECT 'course', COUNT(*)
  FROM course;
...
SELECT 'zipcode', COUNT(*)
  FROM zipcode;
```

The temp.lst file is then executed with the @temp.lst command and a count of all rows for each table is displayed.

```
'STUDEN  COUNT(*)
-------  ---------
student       268

1 row selected.
...
'ZIPCOD  COUNT(*)
-------  ---------
zipcode       227

1 row selected.
```

Lines 1 through 8 show a multiline comment; the comment starts with a /* and ends with */. Line 9 listing the command SET TERM OFF turns the output to the screen off. Line 10 sets the PAGESIZE to zero, line 11 avoids any FEEDBACK, and line 12 spools the result of all subsequent statements to the temp.lst file in the current directory. Line 13 shows an example of the literal SELECT concatenated with four single quotes. The four single quotes result in a single quote in the spooled file and the table name is concatenated between the single quotes.

USING QUOTES IN SQL

As you see in many SQL statements, a single quote is used to enclose a text literal.

```
SELECT last_name
  FROM student
 WHERE last_name = 'Smith'
```

If you want to query, insert, update, or delete a value containing a single quote, prefix the quote with another quote.

```
SELECT last_name
  FROM student
 WHERE last_name = 'O''Neil'
```

To replicate a single quote in a dynamic SQL script, you need four quotes: two individual quotes to represent a single quote and two quotes to surround this text literal.

Line 14 displays the COUNT function to count rows. The CHR(10) function results in a new line in the spooled file. The resulting concatenation is then further combined with the literal FROM in line 15 together with the table name in lowercase and a semicolon.

Line 16 shows the query is issued against the USER_TABLES data dictionary view. Line 17 ends the spooling to the file. Lines 18, 19, and 20 reset the SQL*Plus settings to their defaults. Line 21 runs the spooled temp.lst file. Line 22 uses the HOST command to execute the operating system DEL (Delete) command to delete the temp.lst file. Instead of the HOST command, you can also use a $ (Windows and VMS operating systems) or a ! (Unix operating system). Note the delete command is really not necessary because the file is overwritten the next time you run the script. But it demonstrates the use of a Windows operating system command within SQL*Plus.

*Frequently used SQL*Plus commands are listed in Appendix C, "SQL*Plus Command Reference."*

f) Enter the following commands in a file called ascii_test.sql. Describe the result of the ascii_test.out file.

```
-- File Name: ascii_test.sql
SET PAGESIZE 0
SET LINESIZE 100
SET FEEDBACK OFF
SET VERIFY OFF
PROMPT Enter the starting and ending course numbers
ACCEPT v_start_course_no CHAR PROMPT 'Enter starting course number: '
ACCEPT v_end_course_no CHAR PROMPT 'Enter ending course number: '
SET TERM OFF
SPOOL ascii_test.out
SELECT course_no||','''||description||''','||
       cost||','''||modified_date||''''
  FROM course
 WHERE course_no BETWEEN &v_start_course_no
       AND &v_end_course_no;
SPOOL OFF
SET PAGESIZE 20
SET LINESIZE 80
SET FEEDBACK ON
SET TERM ON
SET VERIFY ON
```

Answer: The script prompts the user to enter starting and ending course number values, which in turn select only certain course numbers and their respective description, cost, and last modification date. Commas separate the column value and single quotes surround text and DATE information.

This type of file is called a *comma-separated ASCII file*. You can use files of this nature to load data into other systems that accept comma-separated ASCII files. If you need to create *fixed-width ASCII files,* use the LPAD commands to pad values.

The output result of the file looks like this when the user enters a starting course number of 120 and an ending course number of 150.

```
120,'Intro to Java Programming',1195,'05-APR-99'
122,'Intermediate Java Programming',1195,'05-APR-99'
124,'Advanced Java Programming',1195,'05-APR-99'
125,'JDeveloper',1195,'05-APR-99'
130,'Intro to Unix',1195,'05-APR-99'
132,'Basics of Unix Admin',1195,'05-APR-99'
134,'Advanced Unix Admin',1195,'05-APR-99'
135,'Unix Tips and Techniques',1095,'05-APR-99'
140,'Structured Analysis',1195,'05-APR-99'
142,'Project Management',1195,'05-APR-99'
144,'Database Design',1195,'05-APR-99'
145,'Internet Protocols',1195,'05-APR-99'
146,'Java for C/C++ Programmers',1195,'05-APR-99'
147,'GUI Programming',1195,'05-APR-99'
```

g) Explain the result of the following script.

```
--File: dump_file.sql
SET PAGESIZE 0
SET LINESIZE 100
SET FEEDBACK OFF
SPOOL dump_file.out
SELECT 'INSERT INTO student_test VALUES
('|| student_id||','''||last_name||
''',''||first_name||''');'
 FROM student;
SPOOL OFF
SET PAGESIZE 20
SET LINESIZE 80
SET FEEDBACK ON
SET TERM ON
```

Answer: This script produces INSERT statements for a table called STUDENT_TEST with values from the STUDENT_ID, LAST_NAME, and FIRST_NAME columns of the STUDENT table.

The result in the created file named dump_file.out will look similar to this result. You can then use the dump_file.out and run it to insert the values into the STU-DENT_TEST table.

```
INSERT INTO student_test VALUES
(102,'Crocitto','Fred');
INSERT INTO student_test VALUES
(103,'Landry','J.');
...
INSERT INTO student_test VALUES
(397,'Lloyd','Margaret');
INSERT INTO student_test VALUES
(399,'Abdou','Jerry');
```

h) Imagine a scenario in which you would execute a script like the following.

```
--File: re_create_seq.sql
SET PAGESIZE 0
SET LINESIZE 100
SET FEEDBACK OFF
SPOOL re_create_seq.out
SELECT 'CREATE SEQUENCE '||sequence_name||
       ' START WITH '||last_number||CHR(10)||
       ' INCREMENT BY '||increment_by ||
       DECODE(cache_size, 0, ' nocache', ' cache '||cache_size)||';'
  FROM seq;
SPOOL OFF
SET PAGESIZE 20
SET LINESIZE 80
SET FEEDBACK ON
SET TERM ON
```

Answer:There are times when you need to recreate certain database objects; perhaps you need to replicate the same setup in another database or to make changes to database objects without creating the scripts from scratch.

```
CREATE SEQUENCE COURSE_NO_SEQ START WITH 454
  INCREMENT BY 1 nocache;
...
CREATE SEQUENCE STUDENT_ID_SEQ START WITH 401
  INCREMENT BY 1 nocache;
```

The example of recreating a sequence based on the data dictionary is rather simple. If have to perform these more involved activities, you should know that you don't have to reinvent the wheel. Utility scripts that perform these tasks are often found on many of the Oracle-related Web sites. Alternatively, SQL tool vendors offer such capabilities as one of their product's features. Refer to Appendix H, "Resources," for more information on this topic.

LAB 13.2 SELF-REVIEW QUESTIONS

In order to test your progress, you should be able to answer the following questions.

1) The following statements are SQL*Plus commands, not SQL commands.

```
SET FEEDBACK ON
SET HEADING ON
COL student FORMAT A20
START
DEFINE v_stud_id
```

   a) _____ True
   b) _____ False

2) What is the result of the following SELECT statement?

```
SELECT 'HELLO ' || CHR(10) || 'THERE'
  FROM dual
```

   a) _____ HELLO THERE
   b) _____ HELLO
             THERE
   c) _____ Invalid query

3) Dynamic SQL scripts are useful for generating SQL statements.

   a) _____ True
   b) _____ False

4) The $ command and the HOST command are equivalent in SQL*Plus.

   a) _____ True
   b) _____ False

5) The following SELECT statement returns a single quote.

```
SELECT ''''
  FROM dual
```

   a) _____ True
   b) _____ False

6) Dynamic SQL scripts avoid repetitive coding.

   a) _____ True
   b) _____ False

Answers appear in Appendix A, Section 13.2.

C H A P T E R   1 3

TEST YOUR THINKING

The projects in this section are meant to have you utilize all of the skills that you have acquired throughout this chapter. The answers to these projects can be found at the companion Web site to this book, located at: *http://www.phptr.com/rischert.*

Visit the Web site periodically to share and discuss your answers.

1) Formulate the question that is answered by the following query.

```
SELECT table_name, column_name, comments
  FROM user_col_comments
```

2) Describe the differences between the views USER_USERS, ALL_USERS, and DBA_USERS.
3) Name the underlying data dictionary views for the public synonyms TABS and COLS.
4) Write a dynamic SQL script to drop all views in the STUDENT schema. If there are no views, create some to test your script.

C H A P T E R   1 4

SECURITY

Protecting the data in a database is done by implementing security via users, roles, and privileges. The SQL language commands used to accomplish these security tasks are known as DCL commands.

Oracle provides several different ways to enforce access control to ensure that only authorized users can login to the database. Every database user has certain *system privileges* that determine the type of actions a user can perform, such as create tables, drop views, or create other users. You want to avoid situations whereby a user can accidentally drop an important table or sidestep security rules.

Once a user is successfully authenticated, various privileges avoid any wrongful data modifications to individual tables or columns. The owner of the database objects, can control exactly who can access what objects and to what extent; these privileges are referred to as *object privileges*.

System and object privileges can be grouped together into a *role*. Setting up the correct security for database users is a task performed by a DBA. It is vital that the database is properly protected against any wrongful actions and unauthorized access.

L A B   1 4 . 1

USERS, PRIVILEGES, ROLES, AND SYNONYMS

LAB OBJECTIVES

After this lab, you will be able to:

✔ Create Users and Grant and Revoke Privileges
✔ Create and Use Synonyms
✔ Create User-Defined Roles

WHAT IS A SCHEMA?

A *schema* is a collection of objects (e.g., tables, views, indexes, sequences, triggers, synonyms). Each schema is owned by a single user account with the same name; in fact, the two terms are often used interchangeably.

You can list the types of objects in the STUDENT schema by querying the USER_OBJECTS data dictionary view.

```
SELECT DISTINCT object_type
  FROM user_objects
OBJECT_TYPE
-----------------
INDEX
SEQUENCE
...
VIEW

5 rows selected.
```

To see all the different types of objects available for the user accessing the database, query the ALL_OBJECTS view. The result set on your database may vary from this result, as various users may have different object types and different privileges.

```
select distinct object_type
  FROM all_objects
OBJECT_TYPE
------------------
...
INDEX
...
PACKAGE
PACKAGE BODY
PROCEDURE
SEQUENCE
SYNONYM
TABLE
TABLE PARTITION
TRIGGER
...

25 rows selected.
```

SPECIAL USERS: SYSTEM AND SYS

When an Oracle database is created it comes with a number of default accounts. Two extremely important accounts are SYS and SYSTEM.

The SYS account is the most privileged user. It owns the data dictionary. Do not drop any of the objects of the SYS schema as you will endanger the critical operation of the Oracle database. The default password is change_on_install.

The SYSTEM account is automatically granted the DBA role. This role includes all the database administration privileges, except for the startup and shutdown privilege of the database. The SYSTEM account is typically used to create regular user accounts or accounts with the DBA role. The default password is manager.

To prevent any inappropriate access, the default passwords are changed immediately after creating the Oracle database.

Oracle suggests that you create an administrative type of account after the creation of the database with the DBA role. This account is used to perform daily administrative tasks and avoids the use of the SYS and SYSTEM accounts.

CREATING USERS

To log into the Oracle database, a user must have a user name, a password, and certain system privileges. A user name is created with the CREATE USER command. Following is the syntax for the CREATE USER command:

```
CREATE USER user IDENTIFIED {BY password|EXTERNALLY}
[{DEFAULT TABLESPACE tablespace |
```

```
TEMPORARY TABLESPACE tablespace |
QUOTA {integer[K|M] | UNLIMITED} ON tablespace
   [[QUOTA {integer[K|M] | UNLIMITED} ON tablespace]...]|
PROFILE profile |
PASSWORD EXPIRE |
ACCOUNT {LOCK|UNLOCK}
   }]
```

To create a new user, first login as a user that has DBA privileges or as the user SYS-TEM. The creation of user accounts is a task a database administrator performs. The following statement creates a new user called MUSIC with a password of LISTEN.

```
CREATE USER music IDENTIFIED BY listen
   DEFAULT TABLESPACE users
   TEMPORARY TABLESPACE temp
   QUOTA 15 M ON users
User created.
```

The User created message indicates the successful creation of the user. The key-words DEFAULT TABLESPACE indicate where any of the user's objects are stored. Here the tablespace is called USERS. The TEMPORARY TABLESPACE keywords de-termine where any sorting of data that cannot be performed in memory is tem-porarily stored.

In preparation for creating users in your database, you must find out what table-spaces exist in your Oracle database. Query the USER_TABLESPACES or DBA_TABLESPACES data dictionary views with the following query:

```
SELECT tablespace_name
   FROM dba_tablespaces
   ORDER BY tablespace_name
```

You can also refer to the readme.txt file on the companion Web site located at: *http://www.phptr.com/rischert* for an example of how the STUDENT user was created.

After you assign a default tablespace to the user, this does not mean that the user can actually store objects in this tablespace. The QUOTA 15 M ON users clause al-lows the MUSIC user to use up to 15 megabytes on the USERS tablespace.

If you do not specify a default tablespace or temporary tablespace clause, the de-fault tablespace and temporary tablespace will default to the SYSTEM tablespace. It is never good practice to use the SYSTEM tablespace as the default or temporary tablespace because the SYSTEM tablespace should only contain the data diction-ary and other internal Oracle system-related objects. If you run out of space on this SYSTEM tablespace it will bring the system to a complete halt.

In Oracle *9i* you can specify a default temporary tablespace at the time of data-base creation or later on through an ALTER DATABASE command. This avoids the use of the SYSTEM tablespace in case the default and/or temporary tablespace for a user was not setup.

CHANGING THE PASSWORD
AND ALTERING THE USER SETTINGS

When a individual user's account settings need to change, such as the password or the default tablespace, the user can be altered. The syntax of the ALTER USER command is as follows:

```
ALTER USER {user {IDENTIFIED {BY password|EXTERNALLY}
   DEFAULT TABLESPACE tablespace |
   TEMPORARY TABLESPACE tablespace |
   QUOTA {integer [K|M] | UNLIMITED} ON tablespace
    [[QUOTA {integer [K|M] | UNLIMITED} ON tablespace]...]|
   PROFILE profile |
   DEFAULT ROLE
    {role [,role]...|ALL[EXCEPT role [,role]...]|NONE}|
   PASSWORD EXPIRE |
   ACCOUNT {LOCK|UNLOCK}
   }}
```

The following statement changes MUSIC's password from LISTEN to TONE and changes the default tablespace from USERS to USER_DATA.

```
ALTER USER music IDENTIFIED BY tone
   DEFAULT TABLESPACE USER_DATA
```
User altered.

Note, a user can instead be authenticated by the operating system account; this is done via the IDENTIFIED BY EXTERNALLY password option.

Oracle creates a number of default user accounts as part of the database installation process that may need to be locked. You can use the ALTER USER command with the ACCOUNT LOCK option to lock those accounts that are not being used by your user community.

As you have noticed, Oracle has a large number of syntax options as part of the ALTER USER command. You will explore these different options throughout this lab.

DROPPING USERS

A user is dropped with the following command.

```
DROP USER music
```
User dropped.

The DROP USER command drops the user if the user does not own any objects This is the syntax for the DROP USER command:

```
DROP USER user [CASCADE]
```

If you want to also drop the objects owned by the user, execute the DROP USER command with the CASCADE keyword:

```
DROP USER music CASCADE
```

If the objects and their data need to be preserved, be sure to first back up the data using the Oracle EXPORT utility program or any other reliable method.

LOGIN AND LOGOUT OF SQL*PLUS

Instead of exiting *i*SQL*Plus or SQL*Plus and starting another session, you can login with the CONNECT command at the SQL*Plus prompt. The CONNECT command can be abbreviated to CONN, followed by the user ID, a forward slash, and the password:

```
SQL> CONN system/manager
Connected.
```

This example shows how you include the host string identifying the name of the database you want to connect if you are connecting to a remote database. In this case the remote database link name is called ITCHY and is referenced with the @ symbol.

```
CONN system/manager@itchy
```

When you connect as another user while you are running a SQL*Plus session, you are no longer logged in as the previous user. If you prefer, you can just start a new SQL*Plus session to keep both sessions connected.

WHAT ARE PRIVILEGES?

A privilege is a right to execute a particular type of SQL statement. There are two types of privileges: System Privileges and Object Privileges. An example of a system privilege is the right to create a table or an index. A particular object privilege allows you to access an individual object, such as the privilege to SELECT from the INSTRUCTOR table, to DELETE from the ZIPCODE table, or to SELECT a number from an specific sequence.

SYSTEM PRIVILEGES

To establish a connection to the database, the user must be granted certain system privileges. These privileges are granted either individually or in the form of roles. A role is a collection of privileges.

Although the user MUSIC is created, the user cannot start a SQL*Plus session, as you see from the following error message. The user lacks the CREATE SESSION system privilege to login to the database.

```
CONN music/tone
ERROR: ORA-01045: user MUSIC lacks CREATE SESSION
privilege; logon denied
```

Table 14.1 lists a few examples of individual system privileges that can be granted to a user.

For example, if you have the CREATE TABLE privilege you may create tables in your schema; if you have the CREATE ANY TABLE privilege you may create tables in another user's schema. The CREATE TABLE privilege includes the CREATE INDEX privilege, but before you are allowed to create these objects you must

Table 14.1 ■ Examples of System Privileges

Privilege	Example
Session	CREATE SESSION ALTER SESSION
Table	CREATE TABLE CREATE ANY TABLE ALTER ANY TABLE DROP ANY TABLE SELECT ANY TABLE UPDATE ANY TABLE DELETE ANY TABLE
Index	CREATE ANY INDEX ALTER ANY INDEX DROP ANY INDEX
Sequence	CREATE SEQUENCE CREATE ANY SEQUENCE ALTER ANY SEQUENCE DROP ANY SEQUENCE
View	CREATE VIEW CREATE ANY VIEW DROP ANY VIEW

make sure you have been granted a quota on the individual tablespace on which you would like to place the object.

OBJECT PRIVILEGES

Object privileges are granted for a particular object (i.e., table, view, sequence). Examples of object privileges are listed in Table 14.2.

Table 14.2 ■ Examples of Commonly Used Object Privileges

Object Type	Privilege	Purpose
TABLE	SELECT	The right to query from an individual table.
	INSERT	The right to add new rows into an individual table
	UPDATE	The right to change rows in an individual table. You can optionally specify to allow UPDATE rights only on individual columns.
	DELETE	The right to remove rows from an individual table.
	REFERENCES	The right to reference a table in a foreign key constraint.
	ALTER	The right to change table definitions.
	INDEX	The right to create indexes on the individual table.
	ALL	All possible object privileges on a table.
SEQUENCE	SELECT	Increment values from a sequence and retrieve current values.
	ALTER	Change the sequence definition.
PL/SQL Stored Objects	EXECUTE	Execute any stored procedure, function, or package.

THE GRANT COMMAND

A system privilege or an object privilege is given to a user with the GRANT command. Privileges can be granted individually or through a role.

The syntax to grant system privileges is as follows:

```
GRANT {system_privilege|role|ALL PRIVILEGES}
  [,{system_privilege|role|ALL PRIVILEGES}]...
TO {user|role|PUBLIC}[,{user|role|PUBLIC}]...
[WITH ADMIN OPTION]
```

The following statement grants the CREATE SESSION system privilege to the MUSIC user. This allows the MUSIC user to establish a session to the database.

```
GRANT CREATE SESSION TO music
```

Object privileges grant certain privileges on specific objects such as tables, views, or sequences. You grant object privileges to other users when you want them to have access to objects you created. You can also grant users access to objects you do not own if the object's owner gave you permission to extend rights to others.

The following lists the general syntax for granting object privileges:

```
GRANT {object_privilege|ALL [PRIVILEGES]}
        [(column[,column]... )]
    [,{object_privilege|ALL [PRIVILEGES]}
        [(column[,column]... )]]...
ON objectname
TO {user|role|PUBLIC}[,{user|role|PUBLIC}]...
[WITH GRANT OPTION]
```

For example, the following statement connects as the STUDENT user account and grants the SELECT privilege on the COURSE table to the new user MUSIC.

```
CONN student/learn
Connected.

GRANT SELECT ON course TO music
Grant succeeded.
```

In this case, the STUDENT user is the grantor and MUSIC is the grantee, the recipient of the privileges. Now the MUSIC user can query the COURSE table.

In addition to SELECT, other object privileges can be granted on a table, such as INSERT, UPDATE, DELETE, ALTER, INDEX, and REFERENCES. The ALTER privilege allows another user to change table definitions with the ALTER table command, the INDEX privilege allows the creation of indexes on the table, and the REFERENCES privilege allows the table to be referenced with a foreign key constraint. You can also grant all object privileges at once with the GRANT ALL command.

Object privileges can be assigned to other database objects such as sequences, packages, procedures, and functions. SELECT and ALTER privileges can be granted on sequences. Packages, procedures, and functions require the EXECUTE privilege if other users want to run these stored programs.

If an object, such as a table, is dropped and then recreated, the grants need to be reissued. This is not the case if the object is replaced with the CREATE OR REPLACE keywords available for views and stored programs.

GRANTING PRIVILEGES ON COLUMNS

You can grant UPDATE and REFERENCE privileges on individual columns on a table. For example, to grant UPDATE on the columns COST and DESCRIPTION of the COURSE table, execute the following command.

```
GRANT UPDATE (cost, description) ON course TO music
Grant succeeded.
```

ROLES

Roles are several privileges collected under one role name. Oracle includes predefined roles; three popular ones are CONNECT, RESOURCE, and DBA.

The CONNECT role includes the CREATE SESSION privilege that allows a user to start a SQL*Plus session, as well as create views, tables, and sequences among other operations. The RESOURCE role allows the user to create tables and indexes on any tablespace and to create PL/SQL stored objects (packages, procedures, functions). The DBA role includes all system privileges. This role is usually granted only to a user who performs database administration tasks. Table 14.3 lists the system privileges associated with each role. You also can query the DBA_SYS_PRIVS data dictionary view to list the individual system privileges for each role as this may change in future versions.

Table 14.3 ■ The **CONNECT, RESOURCE, and DBA** Roles

Role	Purpose
CONNECT	This role encompasses the following system privileges: CREATE SESSION, CREATE TABLE, CREATE VIEW, CREATE SYNONYM, CREATE SEQUENCE, ALTER SESSION, CREATE CLUSTER, CREATE DATABASE LINK
RESOURCE	This role includes these system privileges: CREATE TABLE, CREATE SEQUENCE, CREATE TRIGGER, CREATE PROCEDURE, CREATE CLUSTER, CREATE INDEXTYPE, CREATE OPERATOR, CREATE TYPE
DBA	This role includes all system privileges and allows them to be granted WITH ADMIN OPTION.

When a user is granted a role, the user acquires all the privileges defined within the role. The following statement uses the two predefined Oracle roles, CONNECT and RESOURCE, to grant a number of system privileges to the new user.

```
GRANT CONNECT, RESOURCE TO music
Grant succeeded.
```

ABILITY TO EXTEND THE PRIVILEGES TO OTHERS

You can grant users the privilege to pass system privileges to other users with the WITH ADMIN OPTION. For example, after execution of the following statement the user MUSIC will be able to grant the CONNECT role to other users:

```
GRANT CONNECT TO music WITH ADMIN OPTION
Grant succeeded.
```

Object privilege grants can be extended to other users as well with the WITH GRANT OPTION. The following SQL statement grants all object privileges on the COURSE table to the MUSIC user. It also passes on to the MUSIC user the ability to grant these privileges to yet other users using the WITH GRANT OPTION. Here, MUSIC is the grantee, but can become a grantor if the privilege is passed on to another user.

```
GRANT ALL ON course TO music WITH GRANT OPTION
Grant succeeded.
```

You can see which system privileges you received through a role by querying the Oracle data dictionary view ROLE_SYS_PRIVS. For granted system privileges, query the data dictionary views USER_SYS_PRIVS or DBA_SYS_PRIVS. Table 14.4 lists a number of data dictionary views you may find useful when trying to determine individual object privileges, system privileges, and roles.

Table 14.4 ■ Useful Data Dictionary Views

Data Dictionary View	Purpose
SESSION_PRIVS	All current system privileges available to an individual user
USER_SYS_PRIVS	System privileges granted to the user
ROLE_SYS_PRIVS	System privileges received through a role
ROLE_TAB_PRIVS	Object privileges received through a role
USER_TAB_PRIVS	Object grants
USER_COL_PRIVS	Individual column grants
USER_TAB_PRIVS_RECD	Object privileges received by the user
USER_TAB_PRIVS_MADE	Object privileges made by the user

THE REVOKE COMMAND

Privileges can be taken away with the REVOKE command. Use this syntax to revoke system privileges.

```
REVOKE {system_privilege|role|ALL PRIVILEGES}
   [,{system_privilege|role|ALL PRIVILEGES}]...
FROM {user|role|PUBLIC}[,{user|role|PUBLIC}]...
```

The next example shows how the RESOURCE role is revoked from the user named MUSIC.

```
REVOKE RESOURCE FROM music
Revoke succeeded.
```

Object privileges can also be revoked, as in the following statement.

```
REVOKE UPDATE ON course FROM music
Revoke succeeded.
```

The syntax for revoking object privileges is listed here:

```
REVOKE {object_privilege|ALL [PRIVILEGES]}
  [( column[,column]... )]
  [,{object_privilege|ALL [PRIVILEGES]}
  [(column[,column]...)]]...
ON objectname
FROM {user|role|PUBLIC}[,{user|role|PUBLIC}]...
[CASCADE CONSTRAINTS]
```

The CASCADE CONSTRAINTS clause is only needed if you revoke the REFER-
ENCES or ALL privileges. The REFERENCES privilege allows you to create a referential integrity constraint based on another user's object. The CASCADE
CONSTRAINT options will drop any defined referential constraints when you revoke the REFERENCES privilege.

Object privileges granted using the WITH GRANT OPTION are revoked if the
grantor's object privilege is revoked. For example, assume USER1 is granted SE-
LECT privilege on the COURSE table using the WITH GRANT OPTION and grants
the same privilege to USER2. If the SELECT privilege is revoked from USER1, then
the revoke cascades to USER2.

*Revoking object privileges cascades the REVOKE to other users. How-
ever, revoking system privileges does not have a cascading effect.*

REFERRING TO OBJECTS IN OTHER SCHEMAS

The MUSIC user still has the SELECT privilege on the COURSE table issued earlier. Observe what occurs when you connect as the MUSIC user and attempt to
query the table.

```
CONN music/tone
Connected.

SELECT description
  FROM course
  FROM course
        *
ERROR at line 2:
ORA-00942: table or view does not exist
```

Even though the user MUSIC is allowed to query the COURSE table, MUSIC does not own the COURSE table and must qualify the name of the schema where the object exists. Because the COURSE table exists in the STUDENT schema, you prefix the table name with the schema name.

```
SELECT description
  FROM student.course
DESCRIPTION
---------------------------
DP Overview
Intro to Computers
...
JDeveloper Techniques
DB Programming in Java

30 rows selected.
```

The COURSE table is now qualified with the name of the user who owns the COURSE table, namely STUDENT. When any query, DML, or DDL statement is issued in Oracle, the database assumes the object being referenced is in the user's own schema unless it is otherwise qualified.

PRIVATE SYNONYMS

Instead of qualifying the name of an object with the object owner's name, a synonym can be used. A synonym is a way to alias an object with another name. You can create private and public synonyms. A private synonym is a synonym in a user's schema; public synonyms are visible to everyone.

The syntax for creating synonyms is as follows:

```
CREATE [PUBLIC] SYNONYM [schema.]synonymname
  FOR [schema.]objectname[@dblink]
```

The next CREATE SYNONYM command creates a private synonym called COURSE in the MUSIC schema for the COURSE table located in the STUDENT schema.

```
CREATE SYNONYM course FOR student.course
Synonym created.
```

If you are not logged in as the MUSIC user, but as a user who has rights to create synonyms in another user's schema, such as a DBA, you must prefix the synonym's name with the schema name in which the synonym should be created.

```
CREATE SYNONYM music.course FOR student.course
```

After the synonym is successfully created in the MUSIC schema, you can select from the COURSE table without prefixing the table with the schema name.

```
SELECT description
  FROM course
DESCRIPTION
---------------------------
DP Overview
Intro to Computers
...
JDeveloper Techniques
DB Programming in Java

30 rows selected.
```

The SELECT statement is resolved by looking at the synonym COURSE, which points to the COURSE table located in the STUDENT schema.

Whenever any statement is executed, Oracle looks in the current schema for the object. If there is no object of that name in the current schema, Oracle checks for a public synonym of that name.

When you create a synonym, the validity of the underlying object is not checked; that is, you can create a synonym without the object existing. The synonym will be created without error, but will get an error message if you attempt to access the synonym. The next synonym called SYN_TEST is based on a nonexisting TEST_ME object, which could be a view, table, another synonym, or another type of Oracle object.

```
CREATE SYNONYM syn_test FOR test_me
Synonym created.
```

The access of the synonym results in this message:

```
SQL>SELECT *
  2    FROM test_me;
  FROM test_me
        *
ERROR at line 2:
ORA-00942: table or view does not exist
```

PUBLIC SYNONYMS

All synonyms are private unless the keyword PUBLIC is specified. Public synonyms are visible to all users of the database. However, this does not automatically grant any object privileges to the underlying objects. Grants still need to be issued to either individual users or to PUBLIC by referring to either the public synonym or the underlying object. For the user MUSIC, the following statements create a table, create a public synonym for the table, and grant the SELECT privilege on the table to the user STUDENT.

```
CREATE TABLE instrument
   (instrument_id  NUMBER(10),
    description     VARCHAR2(25))
Table created.


CREATE PUBLIC SYNONYM instrument FOR instrument
Synonym created.


GRANT SELECT ON instrument TO student
Grant succeeded.
```

Now the user STUDENT can perform queries against the public synonym or table INSTRUMENT located in the MUSIC schema. The user STUDENT, or for that matter any other user, does not need to prefix the INSTRUMENT table with the owner. However, users other than the user STUDENT do not have access to the table. If you want every user in the database system to have SELECT privileges, you can grant the SELECT privilege to PUBLIC:

```
GRANT SELECT ON instrument TO PUBLIC
```

 The ability to create public synonyms is typically granted to users with DBA privileges. To complete the exercises in this chapter for public synonyms, have your database administrator grant the user STUDENT this privilege or login as SYSTEM and grant the system privilege CREATE PUBLIC SYNONYM with the following statement: GRANT CREATE PUBLIC SYNONYM TO student.

Synonyms are dropped with the DROP SYNONYM command. The next commands drop the COURSE synonym and the public INSTRUMENT synonym.

```
DROP SYNONYM course
Synonym dropped.

DROP PUBLIC SYNONYM instrument
Synonym dropped.
```

Should a synonym already exist and you want to change the definition, you can use the CREATE OR REPLACE SYNONYM command, instead of dropping and recreating a synonym.

```
CREATE OR REPLACE PUBLIC SYNONYM instrument FOR guitar
```

RESOLVING SCHEMA REFERENCES

Suppose your schema contains a public synonym INSTRUMENT referring to a table in another user's schema and a table named INSTRUMENT in your own schema. When you issue a query against INSTRUMENT, Oracle resolves the schema reference by referring to the object in your own schema first. If such an object does not exist, it refers to the public synonym.

USER-DEFINED ROLES

In addition to Oracle's predefined roles, user-defined roles can be created to customize a grouping of system and/or object privileges. There may be different types of users for a given system. Sometimes, there are users who only view data, so those users only need SELECT privileges. There are other users who maintain the data, so they typically need a combination of SELECT, INSERT, UPDATE, and DELETE privileges on certain tables and columns.

The syntax to create a role is as follows:

```
CREATE ROLE rolename
```

The following statement creates a role named READ_DATA_ONLY for users who only need to query the data in the STUDENT schema.

```
CREATE ROLE read_data_only
Role created.
```

The role still does not have any privileges associated with it. The following SELECT statement generates other statements, granting SELECT privileges on all of the STUDENT schema's tables to the new role READ_DATA_ONLY.

```
SELECT 'GRANT SELECT ON '||table_name||
       ' TO read_data_only;'
  FROM user_tables
```

When the statement is executed from a script that in turn executes each resulting statement, the individual commands issued look similar to the following. If you are unsure how dynamic SQL scripts work, refer to Chapter 13, "The Data Dictionary and Dynamic SQL Scripts."

```
GRANT SELECT ON COURSE TO read_data_only;
...
GRANT SELECT ON STUDENT TO read_data_only;
GRANT SELECT ON ZIPCODE TO read_data_only;
```

With these individually executed statements, the role READ_DATA_ONLY obtains a collection of privileges. The next step is to grant the READ_DATA_ONLY role to users so these users have the privileges defined by the role. The following statement grants every user in the database this role by granting the READ_DATA_ONLY role to PUBLIC.

```
GRANT read_data_only TO PUBLIC
Grant succeeded.
```

Now all users of the database have SELECT privileges on all of the STUDENT schema's tables. All privileges defined by the role can be revoked in a single statement, as in the following.

```
REVOKE read_data_only FROM PUBLIC
Revoke succeeded.
```

If you want none of the users to have the SELECT privilege to the COURSE table anymore, you can revoke this privilege from the individual role only and all users that have been granted this role will no longer have access to the table. You see that this makes the management of privileges fairly easy. If you want to grant the READ_DATA_ONLY role only to individual users, such as the MUSIC user instead of PUBLIC, you can issue a statement such as this:

```
GRANT read_data_only TO MUSIC
```

Roles can be granted with the WITH ADMIN option. It allows the user to pass these privileges on to others.

The data dictionary views shown in Table 14.5 list information about roles.

Table 14.5 ■ Data Dictionary Views Related to Roles

Data Dictionary View	Purpose
DBA_ROLES	All roles in the database
user_ROLE_PRIVS	Roles granted to current user
Dba_role_privs	Shows roles granted to users and other roles
Role_role_privs	Roles granted to roles
Role_sys_privs	System privileges granted to roles
Dba_sys_privs	System privileges granted to roles and users
ROLE_TAB_PRIVS	Object privileges granted to roles
SESSION_ROLES	Roles a user has currently enabled

The ability to create roles may be performed only by users with DBA privileges, or by individual users granted the CREATE ROLE privilege. To complete the exercises in this chapter for user-defined roles, have your DBA grant this privilege to the STUDENT user or login as SYSTEM and

grant this system privilege by executing the following statement: GRANT CREATE ROLE TO student.

Roles are dropped with the DROP ROLE command.

```
DROP ROLE read_data_only
Role dropped.
```

PROFILE

A profile is a name for identifying specific resource limits or password features. A user account is always associated with a profile. If at the creation of an account a profile is not specified, the default profile is used. With a profile you can enforce features such as password expiration settings, maximum idle times (maximum time without any activity for a session), or the maximum number of concurrent sessions.

The most commonly used syntax options are listed here:

```
CREATE PROFILE profilename LIMIT
{{SESSIONS_PER_USER|
  CPU_PER_SESSION|
  CPU_PER_CALL|
  CONNECT_TIME|
  IDLE_TIME}
   {integer|UNLIMITED|DEFAULT}}|
{{FAILED_LOGIN_ATTEMPTS|
  PASSWORD_LIFE_TIME|
  PASSWORD_REUSE_TIME|
  PASSWORD_REUSE_MAX|
  PASSWORD_LOCK_TIME|
  PASSWORD_GRACE_TIME}
   {expression|UNLIMITED|DEFAULT}}
```

The next statement creates a profile named MEDIUM_SECURITY. The effect of this profile is that the password expires after 30 days and if the user logs in with the wrong password, the account is locked after three failed attempts. The password will be locked for one hour (1/24th of a day). The maximum number of concurrent sessions a user may have is three and the inactivity time, excluding long-running queries, is 15 minutes.

```
CREATE PROFILE medium_security
 LIMIT
  PASSWORD_LIFE_TIME 30
  FAILED_LOGIN_ATTEMPTS 3
  PASSWORD_LOCK_TIME 1/24
  SESSIONS_PER_USER 3
  IDLE_TIME 15
Profile created.
```

You can assign a user a profile with the ALTER USER command.

```
ALTER USER music
   PROFILE medium_security
User altered.
```

Profiles can be changed with the ALTER PROFILE command and removed with the DROP PROFILE statement. If you drop a profile any assigned users associated with this profile will automatically be assigned the DEFAULT profile. You can see information about profiles in the data dictionary views DBA_PROFILES and DBA_USERS. These views are only available if you have the right to see DBA_ views.

The ability to create profiles may be performed only by users with DBA privileges or by individual users granted the CREATE PROFILE system privilege.

SECURITY IMPLEMENTATION

In live production environments users typically never log on as the owner of the tables they access. Imagine the scenario whereby an application user knows the password of the STUDENT account. If the user logs in as the owner of the objects, he or she has the ability to drop tables, update any of the data, or drop any of the indexes in the schema. Needless to say this situation is a disaster waiting to happen. Therefore a responsible and cautious DBA creates one user account that receives grants for the objects. For example, the DBA may create a STUDENT_USER account to which the application users have access instead. This account is granted SELECT, INSERT, UPDATE, and DELETE privileges on the various tables. The DBA creates synonyms (private or public) so the STUDENT_USER's queries do not need the owner prefix. This STUDENT_USER account cannot drop individual

---

The Whole Truth

You can implement stored PL/SQL procedures to encapsulate the security access and business rules to certain transactions. For example, you can create a PL/SQL procedure to update individual employee salaries only during certain hours and within a certain percentage increase range. This avoids granting UPDATE rights on the SALARY column of the EMPLOYEE table; instead, you grant the users the right to execute the procedure through which all salary updates must be performed. All the security and logic is enforced and encapsulated within the procedure. For even finer grained access control, Oracle provides a feature called the *virtual private database* (VPD); it allows very sophisticated control over many aspects of data manipulation and data access.

tables or alter them because the account is not the owner of the table, and the DBA does not grant the system privileges such as the DROP ANY TABLE or ALTER ANY TABLE privilege. There are many ways to implement security and fine-grained security will probably be accomplished through the individual application screens that determine which users have access to specific screens. Each individual security implementation will depend on the unique requirements of an application. Oracle provides a variety of ways to control user access including administration through granting of various privileges and administration through roles or different user accounts.

CONNECTING WITH SPECIAL PRIVILEGES: SYSOPER AND SYSDBA

Oracle allows special privileged modes of connection to the database. They are called SYSOPER and SYSDBA. In previous Oracle versions the CONNECT INTERNAL command accomplished similar functionality. The SYSOPER privilege allows startup and shutdown operations and other basic operational tasks such as backups, but does not allow the user to look at the user data. The SYSDBA privilege allows you to perform startup and shutdown of the database and to effectively connect as the most privileged user, which is the SYS user account.

You connect with your user schema name and append AS SYSOPER or AS SYSDBA. For example, to connect in SQL*Plus (not *i*SQL*Plus), you can issue the following CONNECT command if the MUSIC user has been granted the SYSDBA privilege.

```
CONNECT music AS SYSDBA
```

In *i*SQL*Plus version 9.0.1, you select the either AS SYSDBA or AS SYSOPER from the box labeled Privilege on the logon screen. If you use Oracle 9*i* Release2, you will see the Priviledge box only if you connect to *i*SQL*Plus DBA. The URL is in the format http:// machine_name.domain:port/isqlplusdba.

After you connect as SYSDBA or SYSOPER, you don't connect with the schema associated with your username. But rather if you connect as SYSOPER you connect as PUBLIC and for SYSDBA as the owner SYS. Starting with Oracle 9*i*, you can no longer connect with the SYS account unless you connect with the SYSDBA or SYSOPER privileges.

LAB 14.1 EXERCISES

14.1.1 CREATE USERS AND GRANT AND REVOKE PRIVILEGES

The text `<default_tablespace>` and `<temporary_tablespace>` in the following exercise solutions is where the name of the appropriate tablespaces in your database should appear in your answers.

a) Login to SQL*Plus as SYSTEM/MANAGER (or any other account that allows you to create a new user) and create a user called TEACHER with a password of SUBJECT, with the appropriate default and temporary tablespaces for your database. Using Oracle's predefined roles, grant enough privileges to the new user to start a SQL*Plus session, create a table, and create a view. Login to SQL*Plus as the new user and create a table called ACCOUNT with these three columns: ACCOUNT_NUM as the primary key column and the columns ACCOUNT_TYPE and ACCOUNT_STATUS. Determine appropriate datatypes for the columns. Insert a row with the values 1001, Checking, and Active, respectively. Create a view based on the ACCOUNT table called ACCOUNT_STATUS with the ACCOUNT_NUM and STATUS columns.

b) While logged in as the new user TEACHER created in Exercise a, execute the following SELECT statements against the data dictionary views. What do these views tell you about the new user?

```
SELECT username, granted_role, admin_option
  FROM user_role_privs

SELECT *
  FROM session_privs
```

c) While logged in as the user TEACHER, grant SELECT privileges for the ACCOUNT table to the STUDENT user and allow the STUDENT user to grant the same privilege to another user. Then, login as the STUDENT user and execute the following three statements. What do you observe?

```
SELECT *
  FROM teacher.account

INSERT INTO teacher.account
  (account_num, type, status)
VALUES
  (1002, 'Savings', 'Active')

SELECT *
  FROM teacher.account_status
```

d) Connect as SYSTEM/MANAGER and change the password for the user TEACHER from SUBJECT to CLASS. Login as TEACHER and revoke the SELECT privileges from STUDENT on the ACCOUNT table.

e) Execute the following query as the TEACHER user. What purpose do you think this data dictionary view serves?

```
SELECT username, default_tablespace, temporary_tablespace
    FROM user_users
```

14.1.2 CREATE AND USE SYNONYMS

a) While logged in as the STUDENT user, create a private synonym called COURSE for the COURSE table. Describe your observations.

b) Explain the result of the following SELECT statement.

```
SELECT 'CREATE PUBLIC SYNONYM '||table_name||
       ' FOR '||table_name||';'
    FROM user_tables
```

14.1.3 CREATE USER-DEFINED ROLES

a) While logged in as the STUDENT user, create a role called STUDENT_ADMIN. Grant INSERT and UPDATE privileges on the COURSE table to the role. Then, grant the role to TEACHER.

b) Execute the following SELECT statement and describe the result.

```
SELECT *
    FROM user_tab_privs_made
```

LAB 14.1 EXERCISE ANSWERS

14.1.1 ANSWERS

a) Login to SQL*Plus as SYSTEM/MANAGER (or any other account that allows you to create a new user) and create a user called TEACHER with a password of SUBJECT, with the appropriate default and temporary tablespaces for your database. Using Oracle's predefined roles, grant enough privileges to the new user to start a SQL*Plus session, create a table, and create a view. Login to SQL*Plus as the new user and create a table called ACCOUNT with these three columns: ACCOUNT_NUM as the primary key column and the columns ACCOUNT_TYPE and ACCOUNT_STATUS. Determine appropriate datatypes for the columns. Insert a row with the values 1001, Checking, and Active, respectively. Create a view based on the account table called ACCOUNT_STATUS with the ACCOUNT_NUM and STATUS columns.

Answer: The CONNECT command is used to connect as the SYSTEM user. The CREATE USER command and the GRANT commands are used to create the new user and grant system privileges to the user. The CONNECT command is used again to connect as the new user and the CREATE TABLE and CREATE OR REPLACE VIEW commands are used to create two new objects for the new user.

```
CONN system/manager
Connected.

CREATE USER teacher IDENTIFIED BY subject
  DEFAULT TABLESPACE <default_tablespace>
  TEMPORARY TABLESPACE <temporary_tablespace>
User created.

GRANT CONNECT, RESOURCE to TEACHER
Grant succeeded.

CONN teacher/subject
Connected.

CREATE TABLE account
  (account_num  NUMBER(15),
   type      .  VARCHAR(10),
   status       VARCHAR(6),
   CONSTRAINT account_pk PRIMARY KEY(account_num))
Table created.

INSERT INTO account
  (account_num, type, status)
VALUES
  (1001, 'Checking', 'Active')
1 row created.
```

```
CREATE OR REPLACE VIEW account_status AS
SELECT account_num, status
  FROM account
View created.
```

Note that a COMMIT command does not need to be issued after the INSERT statement, because the DDL command CREATE OR REPLACE VIEW implicitly issues a COMMIT.

b) While logged in as the new user TEACHER created in Exercise a, execute the following SELECT statements against the data dictionary views. What do these views tell you about the new user?

```
SELECT username, granted_role, admin_option
  FROM user_role_privs
```

```
SELECT *
  FROM session_privs
```

Answer: The query against the USER_ROLE_PRIVS view lists what Oracle roles the user TEACHER has been granted and whether the user has been granted the administration option on those roles. The query against the SESSION_PRIVS view shows the privileges currently available to the user TEACHER.

```
SELECT username, granted_role, admin_option
  FROM user_role_privs
```

USERNAME	GRANTED_ROLE	ADM
TEACHER	CONNECT	NO
TEACHER	RESOURCE	NO

```
2 rows selected.
```

```
SELECT *
  FROM session_privs
```

PRIVILEGE
CREATE SESSION
ALTER SESSION
UNLIMITED TABLESPACE
...
CREATE SEQUENCE

```
14 rows selected.
```

The user TEACHER, or grantee, can grant the same system privileges to another user, becoming the grantor and enabling the TEACHER account to grant these same privileges to another user if the following statement is issued by the SYSTEM account instead.

```
GRANT CONNECT, RESOURCE TO teacher WITH ADMIN OPTION
```
Grant succeeded.

If you were to subsequently re-execute the query against the USER_ROLE_PRIVS view, you would see 'YES' in the ADMIN_OPTION column.

```
SELECT username, granted_role, admin_option
  FROM user_role_privs
```

USERNAME	GRANTED_ROLE	ADM
TEACHER	CONNECT	YES
TEACHER	RESOURCE	YES

2 rows selected.

These privileges are sufficient to create tables, views, and other objects, but not user accounts. The ability to create users must be granted individually or via the DBA role to the TEACHER user if you choose to do so. The following grant would need to be issued by the SYSTEM user:

```
GRANT CREATE USER TO teacher
```
Grant succeeded.

c) While logged in as the user TEACHER, grant SELECT privileges for the AC-COUNT table to the STUDENT user and allow the STUDENT user to grant the same privilege to another user. Then, login as the STUDENT user and execute the following three statements. What do you observe?

```
SELECT *
  FROM teacher.account

INSERT INTO teacher.account
  (account_num, type, status)
VALUES
  (1002, 'Savings', 'Active')

SELECT *
  FROM teacher.account_status
```

Answer: Some of the statements result in errors due to insufficient privileges.

While logged on as the TEACHER user, issue the GRANT SELECT command on the ACCOUNT table. The WITH GRANT option allows the STUDENT user to pass this privilege on to others.

```
CONN teacher/subject
```
Connected.

```
GRANT SELECT ON account TO student WITH GRANT OPTION
```
Grant succeeded.

The first statement queries the ACCOUNT table in the TEACHER schema without any problems. The SELECT privilege on the ACCOUNT table was granted. The table name must be prefixed with the schema name.

```
CONN student/learn
Connected.

SELECT *
  FROM teacher.account
ACCOUNT_NUM TYPE        STATUS
----------- ----------  ------
       1001 Checking    Active

1 row selected.
```

The second statement attempts to insert a row into the ACCOUNT table. However, the STUDENT user does not have the privilege to perform this action. No INSERT grant on the table was issued to the STUDENT user; therefore, this leads to the insufficient privileges error.

```
INSERT INTO teacher.account
   (account_num, type, status)
VALUES
   (1002, 'Savings', 'Active')
INSERT INTO teacher.account
              *
ERROR at line 1:
ORA-01031: insufficient privileges
```

The last statement queries the ACCOUNT_STATUS view of the TEACHER schema, but the STUDENT user has not been granted SELECT privileges on the view.

```
SELECT *
  FROM teacher.account_status
  FROM teacher.account_status
          *
ERROR at line 2:
ORA-00942: table or view does not exist
```

d) Connect as SYSTEM/MANAGER and change the password for the user TEACHER from SUBJECT to CLASS. Login as TEACHER and revoke the SELECT privileges from STUDENT on the ACCOUNT table.

Answer: The ALTER USER command is used to change the password from SUBJECT to CLASS. The REVOKE command is used to revoke SELECT privileges on the ACCOUNT table from the STUDENT user.

```
CONN system/manager
Connected.
```

```
ALTER USER teacher identified by class
User altered.

CONN teacher/class
Connected.

REVOKE SELECT ON account FROM student
Revoke succeeded.
```

**LAB
14.1**

e) Execute the following query as the TEACHER user. What purpose do you think this data dictionary view serves?

```
SELECT username, default_tablespace, temporary_tablespace
  FROM user_users
```

Answer: It shows the current user's default and temporary tablespace.

USERNAME	DEFAULT_TABLESPACE	TEMPORARY_TABLESPACE
TEACHER	USERS	TEMP

```
1 row selected.
```

If the user has any tablespace quotas assigned you can issue this query to determine the quota for each tablespace. Your result may obviously differ from the output listed here.

```
SELECT tablespace_name, bytes/1024/1024 "MB"
  FROM user_ts_quotas
```

TABLESPACE_NAME	MB
SYSTEM	.95703125
USERS	13.8125
INDX	.125

```
3 rows selected.
```

Quotas are assigned with the ALTER USER command such as one of the following statements. The first assigns 100 megabytes of space on the USERS tablespace to the TEACHER user. Alternatively, the second statement assigns unlimited use of the tablespace USERS to the TEACHER account.

```
ALTER USER teacher QUOTA 100 M ON users
ALTER USER teacher QUOTA UNLIMITED ON users
```

A user must have a quota for the tablespace or have been granted the UNLIMITED TABLESPACE system privilege (e.g., through the RESOURCE role) to be able to create indexes and tables.

14.1.2 ANSWERS

a) While logged in as the STUDENT user, create a private synonym called COURSE for the COURSE table. Describe your observations.

Answer: Two objects with the same name cannot exist in the same schema.

```
CREATE SYNONYM course FOR course
CREATE SYNONYM course FOR course
*
ERROR at line 1:
ORA-01471: cannot create a synonym with same name as object
```

It is not necessary to create private synonyms for objects you already own. However, it is possible to do so but the synonym must have a different name from the underlying object. Within one schema, all object names must be unique, regardless of the type of object. You may create a public synonym called COURSE, which is then available to all schemas.

Public synonyms are not owned by the user who creates them, so there is no conflict between the public synonym name and the name of the object on which it is based.

b) Explain the result of the following SELECT statement.

```
SELECT 'CREATE PUBLIC SYNONYM '||table_name||
       ' FOR '||table_name||';'
  FROM user_tables
```

Answer: The SELECT statement generates other SELECT statements dynamically. Each statement generated creates a public synonym for each table owned by the current user.

When you create public synonyms for other users to see your objects, you typically do it for many objects in your schema. Using a SELECT statement to generate other statements is the fastest way to do this.

14.1.3 ANSWERS

a) While logged in as the STUDENT user, create a role called STUDENT_ADMIN. Grant INSERT and UPDATE privileges on the COURSE table to the role. Then, grant the role to TEACHER.

Answer: First, the CREATE ROLE command is used to create the role. Then a GRANT command is used to grant INSERT and UPDATE privileges, separated by commas, to the role. Then another GRANT statement grants the role to the user TEACHER.

```
CREATE ROLE student_admin
```
Role created.

```
GRANT INSERT, UPDATE ON course TO student_admin
```
Grant succeeded.

```
GRANT student_admin TO TEACHER
```
Grant succeeded.

The WITH ADMIN OPTION can be used to pass on the ability to grant the privileges being granted. The following statement is the same as the previous GRANT statement, but also gives the ability to the TEACHER user to pass on the privileges being granted.

```
GRANT student_admin TO teacher WITH ADMIN OPTION
```
Grant succeeded.

Now the user TEACHER can pass the same set of privileges on to other users.

b) Execute the following SELECT statement and describe the result.

```
SELECT *
  FROM user_tab_privs_made
```

Answer: The result shows the details of all grants made on tables by the STUDENT user: the recipient of the grant (the grantee); the table on which the grant was based; the grantor, or the user who granted the privilege; the privilege granted on the table; and whether the privilege is grantable to other users.

The results vary depending on the privileges you have granted, and have been granted by other users.

GRANTEE	TABLE_NAME	GRANTOR	PRIVILEGE	GRA
STUDENT_ADMIN	COURSE	STUDENT	INSERT	NO
STUDENT_ADMIN	COURSE	STUDENT	UPDATE	NO

2 rows selected.

You can see that the STUDENT_ADMIN role is the grantee of INSERT and UPDATE privileges on the COURSE table, and the STUDENT user is the grantor.

The DICT data dictionary view can be queried to list several other data dictionary views containing information about the roles created and privileges granted in a system.

LAB 14.1 SELF-REVIEW QUESTIONS

In order to test your progress, you should be able to answer the following questions.

1) A user's objects must be dropped in a separate statement before the user can be dropped.

   a) _____ True
   b) _____ False

2) The SQL*Plus CONNECT command is not the same as the CONNECT role.

   a) _____ True
   b) _____ False

3) The following statement contains an error.

   ```
   REVOKE resource, SELECT ON course FROM music
   ```

   a) _____ True
   b) _____ False

4) System privileges cannot be granted through a role.

   a) _____ True
   b) _____ False

5) Dropping a role drops the underlying object the role's privileges are based on.

   a) _____ True
   b) _____ False

6) Grants can be given to users, roles, or public.

   a) _____ True
   b) _____ False

Answers appear in Appendix A, Section 14.1.

CHAPTER 14

TEST YOUR THINKING

The projects in this section are meant to have you utilize all of the skills that you have acquired throughout this chapter. The answers to these projects can be found at the companion Web site to this book, located at: *http://www.phptr.com/rischert.*

Visit the Web site periodically to share and discuss your answers.

To complete the following exercises, create a new user called SCHOOL with the password PROGRAM and grant CONNECT and RESOURCE privileges to it. Then logon as the STUDENT user.

1) Create two roles: one called REGISTRAR the other called INSTRUCTOR.
2) Create a view called CURRENT_REGS reflecting all students that registered today. Grant the SELECT privilege on the new view to the REGISTRAR role.
3) Create a view called ROSTER, reflecting all students taught by the instructor Marilyn Frantzen. Grant the SELECT privilege on the new view to the INSTRUCTOR role.
4) Grant the REGISTRAR and INSTRUCTOR roles to the new user called SCHOOL.
5) Start a SQL*Plus session as the user SCHOOL and select from the two previously created views.

C H A P T E R   1 5

ADVANCED
SQL QUERIES

This chapter revisits some of the concepts and functionality discussed in previous chapters, namely the DECODE function, the CASE expression, and aggregate functions. You will expand on your existing knowledge and solve more complex queries.

Oracle 9*i* implemented new analytical functions that allow you to explore the data in ways never imagined before. The new functions let you analyze data to determine rankings, perform complex aggregate calculations, and reveal period-to-period changes.

The CUBE and ROLLUP operators perform multiple aggregation levels at once. All this functionality offers you a glimpse into some of the incredibly powerful capabilities of Oracle's data warehousing features, which allows users to query large volumes of summarized data.

In Lab 15.3 you use the CONNECT BY clause and the PRIOR operators for hierarchical queries. These operators let you graphically display a hierarchy and reveal the relationship of records within a table.

LAB 15.1

ADVANCED SQL CONCEPTS AND ANALYTICAL FUNCTIONS

LAB OBJECTIVES

After this lab, you will be able to:

✔ Transpose a Result Set
✔ Utilize Analytical Functions

TRANSPOSE RESULTS

USING THE DECODE FUNCTION

The DECODE function permits you to perform not only powerful *if then else* comparisons but also allows you to transpose or pivot the results of queries. For example, the following query returns a listing of the number of courses held for each day of the week. The day of the week is formatted using the DY format mask.

```
SELECT TO_CHAR(start_date_time, 'DY') Day, COUNT(*)
  FROM section
 GROUP BY TO_CHAR(start_date_time, 'DY')
DAY  COUNT(*)
---  ---------
FRI        15
MON         5
...
TUE         4
WED        17

7 rows selected.
```

If you want to transpose the result and show it horizontally, with the days of the week as columns and a count below, you nest the DECODE function within the COUNT function.

```
SELECT COUNT(DECODE(
        TO_CHAR(start_date_time, 'DY'), 'MON', 1)) MON,
       COUNT(DECODE(
        TO_CHAR(start_date_time, 'DY'), 'TUE', 1)) TUE,
       COUNT(DECODE(
        TO_CHAR(start_date_time, 'DY'), 'WED', 1)) WED,
       COUNT(DECODE(
        TO_CHAR(start_date_time, 'DY'), 'THU', 1)) THU,
       COUNT(DECODE(
        TO_CHAR(start_date_time, 'DY'), 'FRI', 1)) FRI,
       COUNT(DECODE(
        TO_CHAR(start_date_time, 'DY'), 'SAT', 1)) SAT,
       COUNT(DECODE(
        TO_CHAR(start_date_time, 'DY'), 'SUN', 1)) SUN
  FROM section
```

MON	TUE	WED	THU	FRI	SAT	SUN
5	4	17	12	15	18	7

1 row selected.

Recall the syntax of the DECODE function:

```
DECODE (if_expr, equals_search,
        then_result [,else_default])
```

Note: Search and result values can be repeated.

When each row of the expression TO_CHAR(start_date_time, 'DY') is evaluated, it returns the day of the week in the format DY, which is MON for Monday, TUE for Tuesday, and so on. If the DECODE expression is equal to the search value, the result value of 1 is returned. Because no ELSE condition is specified, a NULL value is returned.

The COUNT function without an argument does not count NULL values; NULLs are counted only with the wildcard COUNT(*). Therefore, when the COUNT function is applied to the result of either NULL or 1, it only counts those records with NOT NULL values.

USING CASE

Instead of the DECODE function, you can also write the statement with the equivalent CASE expression for an identical result.

```
SELECT COUNT(CASE WHEN TO_CHAR(start_date_time, 'DY')
             = 'MON' THEN 1 END) MON,
       COUNT(CASE WHEN TO_CHAR(start_date_time, 'DY')
             = 'TUE' THEN 1 END) TUE,
       COUNT(CASE WHEN TO_CHAR(start_date_time, 'DY')
             = 'WED' THEN 1 END) WED,
       COUNT(CASE WHEN TO_CHAR(start_date_time, 'DY')
             = 'THU' THEN 1 END) THU,
       COUNT(CASE WHEN TO_CHAR(start_date_time, 'DY')
             = 'FRI' THEN 1 END) FRI,
       COUNT(CASE WHEN TO_CHAR(start_date_time, 'DY')
             = 'SAT' THEN 1 END) SAT,
       COUNT(CASE WHEN TO_CHAR(start_date_time, 'DY')
             = 'SUN' THEN 1 END) SUN
  FROM section
```

USING A SCALAR SUBQUERY

The next query shows yet another way you can accomplish the identical result. The drawback of this solution is that you execute seven individual queries; this is not as efficient as the DECODE or CASE, which executes only once against the table.

```
SELECT (SELECT COUNT(*)
          FROM section
         WHERE TO_CHAR(start_date_time, 'DY') = 'MON') MON,
       (SELECT COUNT(*)
          FROM section
         WHERE TO_CHAR(start_date_time, 'DY') = 'TUE') TUE,
       (SELECT COUNT(*)
          FROM section
         WHERE TO_CHAR(start_date_time, 'DY') = 'WED') WED,
       (SELECT COUNT(*)
          FROM section
         WHERE TO_CHAR(start_date_time, 'DY') = 'THU') THU,
       (SELECT COUNT(*)
          FROM section
         WHERE TO_CHAR(start_date_time, 'DY') = 'FRI') FRI,
       (SELECT COUNT(*)
          FROM section
         WHERE TO_CHAR(start_date_time, 'DY') = 'SAT') SAT,
       (SELECT COUNT(*)
          FROM section
         WHERE TO_CHAR(start_date_time, 'DY') = 'SUN') SUN
  FROM DUAL
```

Note: For very difficult queries where the result cannot be performed using any of the previously mentioned solutions, you may want to consider the creation of a temporary table to hold intermediate results. Creating temporary tables is discussed in Chapter 11, "Create, Alter, and Drop Tables."

ANALYTICAL FUNCTIONS

Why should you use analytic functions? Starting with Oracle 8*i* and continuing with each subsequent release, Oracle implemented a number of very useful functions that allow you to analyze, aggregate, and rank vast amounts of stored data. You can use these analytical functions to find out the top-n revenue-generating courses, compare revenues of one course with another, or compute various statistics about student's grades.

Although this lab does not discuss all of the available analytical functions, it does provide you with an overview of the most commonly used functions. You will gain an appreciation of their core functionality and usefulness, particularly with regard to the calculation of rankings or generation of moving averages, moving sums, and so on.

Analytical functions execute queries fairly quickly as they allow you to make one pass through the data, rather than writing multiple queries or complicated SQL to achieve the same result. This significantly speeds up query performance.

The general syntax of analytic functions is listed here:

```
analytic_function([arguments]) OVER (analytic_clause)
```

Note the use of the OVER keyword. It indicates that the function operates after the results of the FROM, WHERE, GROUP BY, and HAVING clauses have been formed.

The ANALYTIC_CLAUSE may contain three other clauses: A QUERY_PARTITIONING, ORDER_BY, or WINDOWING clause:

```
[query_partition_clause] [order_by_clause [windowing_clause]]
```

There are slight variations in the general syntax with certain functions whereby some require specific clauses and others do not. The QUERY_PARTIONING clause allows you to split the result into smaller subsets on which you can apply the analytical functions. The ORDER_BY_CLAUSE is much like the familiar ordering clause; however, it is applied to the result of the analytic function. The WINDOWING_CLAUSE lets you compute moving and accumulative aggregates such as moving averages, moving sums, or cumulative sums by choosing only certain data within a specified window.

QUERY PROCESSING WITH ANALYTICAL FUNCTIONS

Query processing with analytical functions is performed in several steps (see Figure 15.1). First, joins, WHERE, GROUP BY, and HAVING clauses are carried out. This result is then utilized by the analytic functions. If any partitions are involved, they are formed after the GROUP BY clause. If a windowing clause is involved the functions are based against the specified window. Analytical functions may have an ORDER BY clause as part of the function specification that allows

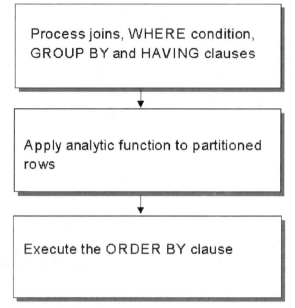

Figure 15.1 ■ Query processing steps with analytical functions.

you to order the result before the analytical function is applied. Last, if an ORDER BY clause is present at the end of the statement, the result set is sorted accordingly.

ANALYTICAL FUNCTION TYPES

Analytical functions can be categorized into various types: An overview of the different types is listed in Table 15.1. Ranking functions determine the ranking of a value (e.g., to determine the top three students based on their grade averages or to determine the first and last values of an ordered group). The reporting functions take the familiar aggregate function capabilities a step further by allowing you to aggregate values without the need for a GROUP BY clause. The windowing capability allows you to generate moving averages, cumulative sums, and the like. The LAG/LEAD functions allow you to easily see how much values changed from one period to another.

RANKING FUNCTIONS

In Chapter 7, "Subqueries," you explored the subject of top-*n* queries using an inline view and the ROWNUM pseudocolumn. Ranking functions allow for even more advanced functionality. As you read through this lab you will learn about the differences between the ranking functions.

The first example of a ranking function is DENSE_RANK and the next query shows the ranking of the grades for student ID 254 in section 87. The grades are

Table 15.1 ■ Type and Purpose of Analytical Functions

Type	Purpose
Ranking	Compute ranking. Function examples are RANK, DENSE_RANK, NTILE, ROW_NUMBER.
Hypothetical Ranking	Determine the rank of hypothetical data values within a result set.
FIRST/LAST	Finds the FIRST and LAST value within an ordered group.
Reporting	Use aggregate functions such as SUM, AVG, MIN, MAX, COUNT, VARIANCE, or STDDEV. Also calculate ratios using functions as RATIO_TO_REPORT.
Windowing	Calculate moving averages and cumulative values using AVG, SUM, MIN, MAX, COUNT, FIRST_VALUE, LAST_VALUE. Note, FIRST_VALUE and LAST_VALUE are only available within a WINDOWING_CLAUSE, unlike the FIRST/LAST function.
LAG/LEAD	These two functions allow you to specify an individual row relative to before or after the current row. The functionality is somewhat similar to windowing and these functions are very useful to compare period-to-period changes.
Inverse Percentile	The value in a data set that is equal to a specific percentile. This functionality is beyond the scope of this book.
Linear Regression	Compute linear regression and other related statistics. These functions are beyond the scope of this book.

ranked by the lowest grade first. Notice the use of the ORDER BY clause within the analytical function.

```
SELECT numeric_grade,
       DENSE_RANK() OVER (ORDER BY numeric_grade) AS rank
  FROM grade
 WHERE student_id = 254
   AND section_id = 87
NUMERIC_GRADE        RANK
------------- ----------
           71           1
           71           1
           75           2
  ...
           91           5
           98           6
           98           6

12 rows selected.
```

The NUMERIC_GRADE value of 71 is the lowest grade of the student; it holds rank number 1. The next higher grade, which is 75, holds rank number 2, and so on. The ORDER BY clause controls the ordering of the ranking. If you want the highest grade to have rank number 1, use DESCENDING in the ORDER BY clause. The default is ASCENDING. You may already have noticed one difference to the inline view; the DENSE_RANK function allows identical values to share the same rank.

To find out the three lowest grades of the student, rather than all the grades, you can modify the query by using the ranking function and an inline view as follows:

```
SELECT *
  FROM (SELECT numeric_grade,
               DENSE_RANK() OVER (ORDER BY numeric_grade)
               AS rank
          FROM grade
         WHERE student_id = 254
           AND section_id = 87)
 WHERE rank <= 3
```

NUMERIC_GRADE	RANK
71	1
71	1
75	2
76	3

4 rows selected.

To contrast this with the inline view solution discussed in Chapter 7, "Subqueries," you will only receive three rows. The lowest grade is listed twice and unlike the DENSE_RANK function, the ROWNUM pseudocolumn does not distinguish between grades that share the same values.

```
SELECT *
  FROM (SELECT numeric_grade
          FROM grade
         WHERE student_id = 254
           AND section_id = 87
         ORDER BY numeric_grade)
 WHERE rownum <=3
```

NUMERIC_GRADE
71
71
75

3 rows selected.

The next query shows you the revenue generated per course. It is based on a table named COURSE_REVENUE and its columns are defined as follows:

```
SQL> DESCR course_revenue
 Name                          Null?     Type
 ---------------------------   --------  ------------
 COURSE_NO                     NOT NULL  NUMBER(8)
 REVENUE                                 NUMBER
 COURSE_FEE                              NUMBER(9,2)
 NUM_ENROLLED                            NUMBER
 NUM_OF_SECTIONS                         NUMBER
```

The REVENUE column holds the revenue generated by the respective COURSE_NO. The COURSE_FEE column shows the amount charged for enrollment in one individual course, the NUM_ENROLLED column stores the number of students enrolled in a specific course. The NUM_OF_SECTIONS column holds the number of sections per course.

This table is not part of the STUDENT schema, but can be created from the additional script called sql_book_add_tables.sql available for download from the companion Web site.

RANK, DENSE_RANK, AND ROW_NUMBER

The next query shows three different ranking functions: RANK, DENSE_RANK, and ROW_NUMBER. The simplest function of the three is the ROW_NUMBER and it is listed as the last column in the result; it has similar functionality to the ROWNUM pseudocolumn. It sequentially assigns a unique number to each row starting with the number 1 based on the ORDER BY clause ranking of the revenue. Notice that when rows share duplicate revenue values, such as the course numbers 20 and 350, one of them arbitrarily gets the next number assigned.

```
SELECT course_no, revenue,
       RANK() OVER (ORDER BY revenue DESC)
         rev_rank,
       DENSE_RANK() OVER (ORDER BY revenue DESC)
         rev_dense_rank,
       ROW_NUMBER() OVER (ORDER BY revenue DESC)
         row_number
  FROM course_revenue
```

COURSE_NO	REVENUE	REV_RANK	REV_DENSE_RANK	ROW_NUMBER
25	53775	1	1	1
122	28680	2	2	2
120	27485	3	3	3
...				
240	14235	7	7	7

20	10755	8	8	8
350	10755	8	8	9
124	9560	10	9	10
125	**9560**	**10**	**9**	**11**
130	**9560**	**10**	**9**	**12**
142	**8365**	**13**	**10**	**13**
147	**5975**	**14**	**11**	**14**
310	**4780**	**15**	**12**	**15**
...				
204	**1195**	**23**	**16**	**24**

24 rows selected.

The RANK function assigns each row a unique number except for duplicate rows, which receive the identical ranking and a gap appears in the sequence to the next rank. In the column labeled REV_RANK, course numbers 20 and 350 share the identical revenue and therefore obtain the same rank. You can observe a gap to the next rank.

The ranking function DENSE_RANK assigns duplicate values the same rank. The result of this function is displayed in the column labeled as REV_DENSE_RANK.

The syntax of the three functions is as follows:

```
ROW_NUMBER()OVER ([query_partition_clause] order_by_clause)
RANK() OVER ([query_partition_clause] order_by_clause)
DENSE_RANK() OVER ([query_partition_clause] order_by_clause)
```

The ORDER_BY_CLAUSE is required as it determines the ordering of the rows and therefore ranking. Although in the previous example no null values were present, you should understand that nulls are assumed to be equal to another null value. Just like the ORDER BY clause at the end of a SQL statement, you can include the NULLS FIRST or NULLS LAST clause to indicate the position of any nulls in the ordered sequence. If you need a refresher on NULLS FIRST or NULLS LAST, refer to Lab 5.2 in Chapter 5, "Aggregate Functions, GROUP BY, and HAVING."

The syntax includes the optional QUERY_PARTITION_CLAUSE. This option allows you to rank across portions of the result set as you see in the following examples.

PARTITIONING THE RESULT

The previous query generated the ranking over the entire result. The optional partitioning clause lets you create independent rankings and resets the rank whenever the partitioned values change. In the next query the COURSE_FEE column is added to show the respective fee per course number. The ranking is now partitioned by a course's fee instead of the entire result. You will observe that the ranking changes after each value change in the COURSE_FEE column.

```
SELECT course_no, course_fee fee, revenue,
       RANK() OVER (PARTITION BY course_fee
          ORDER BY revenue DESC) rev_rank,
       DENSE_RANK() OVER (PARTITION BY course_fee
          ORDER BY revenue DESC) rev_dense_rank,
       ROW_NUMBER() OVER (PARTITION BY course_fee
          ORDER BY revenue DESC) row_number
  FROM course_revenue
```

COURSE_NO	FEE	REVENUE	REV_RANK	REV_DENSE_RANK	ROW_NUMBER
230	1095	15330	1	1	1
240	1095	14235	2	2	2
135	1095	4380	3	3	3
25	1195	53775	1	1	1
122	1195	28680	2	2	2
120	1195	27485	3	3	3
140	1195	17925	4	4	4
100	1195	15535	5	5	5
20	1195	10755	6	6	6
350	1195	10755	6	6	7
124	1195	9560	8	7	8
125	1195	9560	8	7	9
130	1195	9560	8	7	10
...					
204	1195	1195	20	13	21

24 rows selected.

The first step in the query execution is the forming of the partition, then for each distinct partition value the ORDER BY clause is executed. This example demonstrates the use of a single partitioned value, the COURE_FEE column. You can partition over multiple values/columns by listing each individual expression and separating them with a comma in the partitioning clause.

Note: Do not confuse the partitioning clause in analytical functions with the concept of physically splitting very large tables or indexes into smaller partitioned tables and indexes. Table and index partitioning functionality is beyond the scope of this book and independent of analytical functions discussed in this lab.

NTILE

The NTILE function is another ranking function. You can use the NTILE function to divide data into buckets of fourth, thirds, or any other groupings. The next SELECT statement shows the result split into four buckets (4 quartiles or 4 × 25% buckets). Those in the first quartile of the revenue receive the number 1 in the NTILE column. The next quartile displays the number 2, and so on.

```
SELECT course_no, revenue,
       NTILE(4) OVER (ORDER BY revenue DESC) ntile
  FROM course_revenue
```

COURSE_NO	REVENUE	NTILE
25	53775	1
122	28680	1
120	27485	1
140	17925	1
100	15535	1
230	15330	1
240	14235	2
20	10755	2
...		
204	1195	4

24 rows selected.

The syntax of the NTILE function is as follows:

```
NTILE(expr) OVER ([query_partition_clause] order_by_clause)
```

Other less frequently used ranking functions are CUME_DIST and PERCENT_RANK. CUME_DIST determines the position of a specific value relative to a set of values and PERCENT_RANK calculates the percent rank relative to the number of rows.

HYPOTHETICAL RANKING

Sometimes you may want to find out how a specific data value ranks if it was part of the result set. You can perform this type of what-if analysis with the HYPO-THETICAL RANKING syntax, which uses the WITHIN GROUP keywords. The next query determines the rank of the value 20,000 if it was present in REVENUE column of the COURSE_REVENUE table. As you see from the result of the query it would have a rank of 4.

```
SELECT RANK(20000) WITHIN GROUP (ORDER BY revenue DESC)
       "Hypothetical Rank"
  FROM course_revenue
```

Hypothetical Rank

                4

1 row selected.

The syntax for hypothetical ranking is as follows:

```
[RANK|DENSE_RANK|PERCENT_RANK|CUME_DIST](constant[, ...])
WITHIN GROUP (order_by_clause)
```

FIRST/LAST FUNCTIONS

The FIRST and LAST functions operate on a set of values to show the lowest or highest value within a result. The syntax of this function is:

```
aggregate_function KEEP (DENSE_RANK {LAST|FIRST} order_by_clause)
[OVER query_partitioning_clause]
```

The next query displays for the GRADE table and SECTION_ID 99 a count of the number of rows with the highest and the lowest grade.

```
SELECT COUNT(*),
       MIN(numeric_grade) min, MAX(numeric_grade) max,
       COUNT(*) KEEP (DENSE_RANK FIRST ORDER BY numeric_grade)
       lowest,
       COUNT(*) KEEP (DENSE_RANK LAST ORDER BY numeric_grade)
       highest
  FROM grade g
 WHERE section_id = 99
```

COUNT(*)	MIN	MAX	LOWEST	HIGHEST
108	73	99	2	9

1 row selected.

This result indicates a total of 108 rows or individual grades. Of these rows, the lowest grade is 73 and the highest is 99, as computed with the familiar MIN and MAX functions. The query's last two columns apply the FIRST and LAST functions; two grade rows exist for the lowest grade of 73 and nine rows have 99 as the highest grade.

The purpose of the FIRST and LAST functions is that they allow you to ORDER BY one column but apply the aggregate to another column. This effectively eliminates the writing of a subquery that reads the same table yet again.

The equivalent statement to determine the result of the FIRST and LAST ranking functions would be this query, which makes multiple passes through the SECTION table.

```
SELECT numeric_grade, COUNT(*)
  FROM grade
 WHERE section_id = 99
   AND (numeric_grade IN (SELECT MAX(numeric_grade)
                            FROM grade
                           WHERE section_id = 99)
        OR
        numeric_grade IN (SELECT MIN(numeric_grade)
                            FROM grade
                           WHERE section_id = 99))
 GROUP BY numeric_grade
```

```
NUMERIC_GRADE     COUNT(*)
-------------    ----------
           73             2
           99             9
```

2 rows selected.

REPORTING FUNCTIONALITY

The reporting functionality allows you to compute aggregates for a row in a partition. The syntax is as follows:

```
{SUM|AVG|MAX|MIN|COUNT|STDDEV|VARIANCE}
    ([ALL|DISTINCT] {expression|*})
        OVER ([PARTITION BY expression2[,...]])
```

The next example lists the individual grades for each grade type for STUDENT_ID 254 enrolled in SECTION_ID 87. The last column labeled AVG displays the grade average for each grade type.

```
SELECT numeric_grade, grade_type_code,
       AVG(numeric_grade)
         OVER(PARTITION BY grade_type_code) AS avg
  FROM grade
 WHERE student_id = 254
   AND section_id = 87
```

```
NUMERIC_GRADE GR        AVG
------------- --  ----------
           91 FI          91
           91 HM        84.8
           75 HM        84.8
           98 HM        84.8
...
           91 HM        84.8
           76 MT          76
```

12 rows selected.

Notice that there is no GROUP BY clause, even though an aggregate function is used in the SELECT statement. The aggregate function is processed last and works over the GRADE_TYPE_CODE column partition. Effectively, the partitioning clause works similarly to the GROUP BY clause, as it groups those rows together and builds the aggregate for the distinct value of the partition.

If you don't specify a partition as indicated with the empty set of parentheses, the aggregate is computed for all the rows of the result set as you see in the next query.

```
SELECT numeric_grade, grade_type_code,
       AVG(numeric_grade) OVER() AS avg
  FROM grade
```

```
WHERE student_id = 254
  AND section_id = 87
NUMERIC_GRADE GR        AVG
------------- -- ----------
          91 FI 84.5833333
          91 HM 84.5833333
          75 HM 84.5833333
          98 HM 84.5833333
...

          76 MT 84.5833333

12 rows selected.
```

RATIO_TO_REPORT

The RATIO_TO_REPORT function is another reporting function; it computes the ratio of a value to the sum of a set of values. The syntax is as follows:

```
RATIO_TO_REPORT(expression) OVER ([query_partition_clause])
```

The next SQL statement illustrates the use of the function. The result of the RATIO column represents the ratio of the entire revenue because the partitioning clause is absent. The first row shows the total revenue of COURSE_NO 10 for 1195; the RATIO column indicates that the computed value represents 4.496284% of the entire revenue.

```
SELECT course_no, revenue,
       RATIO_TO_REPORT(revenue) OVER () AS ratio
  FROM course_revenue
COURSE_NO     REVENUE       RATIO
---------- ---------- ----------
       10        1195 .004496284
       20       10755 .04046656
       25       53775  .2023328
      100       15535 .058451698
      120       27485 .103414542
...
      350       10755 .04046656
      420        2390 .008992569

24 rows selected.
```

WINDOWING

The WINDOWING clause allows you to compute cumulative, moving, and centered aggregates. A window has a defining starting and ending point. All the parameters in the windowing clause are always relative to the current row. A sliding window changes the starting or ending points depending on the definition of window.

A window that defines a cumulative sum starts with the first row and then slides forward with each subsequent row. A moving average has sliding starting and ending rows for a constant logical or physical range.

The next SELECT statement illustrates the computation of a cumulative average and a cumulative sum that is based on the values from the first row until and including the current row. The result shows the individual course numbers and their respective revenues. The CumAvg column shows the cumulative average and the CumSum column the cumulative sum.

```
SELECT course_no, revenue,
       AVG(revenue) OVER (ORDER BY course_no
         ROWS BETWEEN UNBOUNDED PRECEDING AND CURRENT ROW)
         "CumAvg",
       SUM(revenue) OVER (ORDER BY course_no
         ROWS BETWEEN UNBOUNDED PRECEDING AND CURRENT ROW)
         "CumSum"
  FROM course_revenue
```

COURSE_NO	REVENUE	CumAvg	CumSum
10	1195	1195	1195
20	10755	5975	11950
25	53775	21908.3333	65725
100	15535	20315	81260
120	27485	21749	108745
...			
350	10755	11451.5217	263385
420	2390	11073.9583	265775

24 rows selected.

Examine the third row with COURSE_NO equal to 25. The average was built based on the revenue values of COURSE_NO 10, 20, and 25, which have REVENUE column values of 1195, 10755, and 53775, respectively. The average of these three values is 21908.3333. The next row builds the average from the previously mentioned values plus the current value, which is 15535; divided by four this yields 20315. The value in the CumAvg column changes for each subsequent row.

The CumSum column is the cumulative sum and for each subsequent row it adds the revenue value to the previously computed sum.

The next example shows a centered average; it is computed with the row preceding the current row and the row following the current row. The column is labeled CentAvg. A moving average takes the current row and the previous row and the result is shown in the MovAvg column.

```
SELECT course_no, revenue,
       AVG(revenue) OVER (ORDER BY course_no
         ROWS BETWEEN 1 PRECEDING AND 1 FOLLOWING)
```

```
    "CentAvg",
    AVG(revenue) OVER (ORDER BY course_no
      ROWS 1 PRECEDING)
    "MovAvg"
  FROM course_revenue
  COURSE_NO    REVENUE    CentAvg      MovAvg
  ---------- ---------- ---------- ----------
         10       1195       5975        1195
         20      10755 21908.3333        5975
         25      53775 26688.3333       32265
        100      15535      32265       34655
        120      27485      23900       21510
  ...
        420       2390     6572.5      6572.5

24 rows selected.
```

You can expand this functionality for any of the aggregate functions, not just averages. This allows you to compute moving sums, centered sums, moving min and max values, and so on.

The syntax of the windowing clause is as follows:

```
order_by_clause {ROWS|RANGE}
  {BETWEEN
    {UNBOUNDED PRECEDING|CURRENT ROW|
     expression {PRECEDING|FOLLOWING}}
  AND
    {UNBOUNDED FOLLOWING|CURRENT ROW|
     expression {PRECEDING|FOLLOWING}}|
    {UNBOUNDED PRECEDING|CURRENT ROW|expression PRECEDING}}
```

The ROWS and RANGE keywords allow you to define a window, either *physically* through the number of ROWS or *logically* such as a time interval or a positive numeric value in the RANGE keyword. The BETWEEN...AND clause defines the starting and ending point of the window and if none are specified, defaults to RANGE BETWEEN UNBOUNDED PRECEDING AND CURRENT ROW.

UNBOUNDED PRECEDING indicates the window starts at the first row of the partition and UNBOUNDED FOLLOWING indicates the window ends at the last row of the partition.

Besides the aggregate functions such as AVG, COUNT, MIN, MAX, SUM, STDDEV, and VARIANCE, you can use the FIRST_VALUE and LAST_VALUE functions, which return the first value and last value in the window, respectively.

LOGICAL AND PHYSICAL WINDOWS

As mentioned previously, a window can be defined as either a logical or a physical window. A physical window is defined with the ROWS keyword. A logical

Table 15.2 ■ Differences between Physical and Logical Windows

Physical Window	Logical Window
Specify window with the ROWS keyword.	Specify the window with the RANGE keyword.
Ability to specify the exact number of rows.	Logical offset that determines the starting and ending point of the window; this can be a constant (i.e., RANGE 5 PRECEDING), an expression that evaluates to a constant, or an interval (i.e., RANGE INTERVAL 10 DAYS PRECEDING).
Duplicate values in the ORDER BY clause do not affect the definition of the *current row.*	Duplicate values are considered the same for the purpose of defining the *current row;* therefore, the aggregate function includes all duplicate values, even if they follow after the current physical row.
Allows multiple ORDER BY expressions.	Only one ORDER BY expression is allowed.

window uses the RANGE keyword. Table 15.2 highlights the main differences between logical and physical windows. You will explore these differences in the following exercises.

THE ORDER BY CLAUSE

The ORDER BY clause in a windowing clause is mandatory and determines the order in which the rows are sorted. Based on this order, the starting and ending points of the window are defined.

```
SELECT numeric_grade, grade_type_code,
       AVG(numeric_grade) OVER(ORDER BY grade_type_code)
       AS cumavg
  FROM grade
 WHERE student_id = 254
   AND section_id = 87
NUMERIC_GRADE GR     CUMAVG
------------- -- ----------
           91 FI         91
           91 HM 85.3636364
           75 HM 85.3636364
           98 HM 85.3636364
  . . .
           76 MT 84.5833333

12 rows selected.
```

The SELECT statement computes the average of grades based on the GRADE_TYPE_CODE column. Notice the moving average changes upon each change in the GRADE_TYPE_CODE value. Because no windowing clause is specified, the window defaults to RANGE BETWEEN UNBOUNDED PRECEDING AND CURRENT ROW. Effectively this is a logical window. Therefore the cumulative average value changes upon the change of the value in the GRADE_TYPE_CODE column.

One of the keys to understanding LOGICAL windows is that the current row equals all the rows with the same ORDER BY values.

Again, in the next statement the windowing clause is missing but now there are four columns in the ORDER BY clause. These columns represent the primary key and make the values in the ORDER BY clause unique. In the CUMAVG_OVER_PK column you notice that the average changes with each row. The PARTITION column is formed with a combination of the PARTIONING clause and the WINDOWING clause. The rows are partitioned by GRADE_TYPE_CODE, and the cumulative average change is reset with each change in the partition.

```
SELECT numeric_grade, grade_type_code,
       grade_code_occurrence AS occur,
       AVG(numeric_grade) OVER(ORDER BY student_id,
        section_id, grade_type_code,
        grade_code_occurrence) AS cumavg_over_pk,
       AVG(numeric_grade) OVER(PARTITION BY
        grade_type_code
        ORDER BY student_id, section_id,
        grade_type_code, grade_code_occurrence)
        AS partition
   FROM grade
  WHERE student_id = 254
    AND section_id = 87
```

NUMERIC_GRADE	GR	OCCUR	CUMAVG_OVER_PK	PARTITION
91	FI	1	91	91
91	HM	1	91	91
75	HM	2	85.6666667	83
98	HM	3	88.75	88
98	HM	4	90.6	90.5
81	HM	5	89	88.6
71	HM	6	86.4285714	85.6666667
71	HM	7	84.5	83.5714286
81	HM	8	84.1111111	83.25
91	HM	9	84.8	84.1111111
91	HM	10	85.3636364	84.8
76	MT	1	84.5833333	76

12 rows selected.

INTERVALS AND LOGICAL WINDOW

The next SQL statement shows another example of the functionality of a logical window and the RANGE keyword. The resulting output of the statement lists the number of students that enrolled on specific dates. The sliding windowing functionality with the moving AVG function is applied to the last three columns named PREV 10 DAYS, NEXT 10 DAYS, and 20-DAY WINDOW.

The column PREV 10 DAYS indicates the average number of students that enrolled 10 days prior to the listed ENROLL_DATE. The starting point of the window is 10 days prior to the ENROLL_DATE of the current row and the ending point of the window is the current row. The next column labeled NEXT 10 DAYS is a window that defines itself from the current row until 10 days after the ENROLL_DATE. The column 20-DAY WINDOW shows a 20-day sliding window, starting with 10 days prior to the current row and 10 days after the current row.

```
SELECT TRUNC(enroll_date) ENROLL_DATE, COUNT(*) "# ENROLLED",
       AVG(COUNT(*))OVER(ORDER BY TRUNC(enroll_date)
        RANGE INTERVAL '10' DAY PRECEDING) "PREV 10 DAYS",
       AVG(COUNT(*))OVER(ORDER BY TRUNC(enroll_date)
        RANGE BETWEEN CURRENT ROW
        AND INTERVAL '10' DAY FOLLOWING) "NEXT 10 DAYS",
       AVG(COUNT(*))OVER(ORDER BY TRUNC(enroll_date)
        RANGE BETWEEN INTERVAL '10' DAY PRECEDING
        AND INTERVAL '10' DAY FOLLOWING) "20-DAY WINDOW"
   FROM enrollment
  GROUP BY TRUNC(enroll_date)
```

ENROLL_DA	# ENROLLED	PREV 10 DAYS	NEXT 10 DAYS	20-DAY WINDOW
30-JAN-99	11	11	17	17
02-FEB-99	14	12.5	20.6	19
04-FEB-99	23	16	22.8	19.8571429
07-FEB-99	20	17	23.4	20.625
10-FEB-99	22	19.75	24.4	22.375
11-FEB-99	24	20.6	27.2	23.8888889
13-FEB-99	25	22.8	28	25.125
16-FEB-99	26	23.4	29	25.4285714
19-FEB-99	25	24.4	30.5	26.3333333
21-FEB-99	36	27.2	36	27.2

10 rows selected.

Examine the first row; it displays 30-JAN-99 in the ENROLL_DATE column. You will notice that 11 students enrolled on the respective date. The average number of enrollments for the previous 10 days is computed by the nested AVG(COUNT(*)) function, which computes the average of the number of enrolled students per ENROLL_DATE within the last 10 days. Because this is the first row and there are no prior values, the average is equal to the number of enrolled students. Note that all the values in the ENROLL_DATE column are truncated to ensure only date not time values are considered.

All the cumulative window values change as you move forward within each subsequent enrollment date. For example, the row with the ENROLL_DATE value of 10-FEB-99 shows the average number of enrollments for the previous 10 days (including the current date) as 19.75. This value is computed by averaging the number of enrollments up to and including the 2-FEB-99 value. The value in the NEXT 10 DAYS column is computed once again through the sliding window of 10 days after the current date and inclusive of the current row. This includes all the enrollments up to and including 19-FEB-99. The value in the 20-DAY WINDOW column includes the prior 10 days and the 10 days following the current date of the row.

Notice that the query shows the use of interval literals; remember that interval literals are expressed in the format:

```
INTERVAL n DAY|MONTH|YEAR
```

If you need to compute the time interval between two dates use the NUMTOYMINTERVAL or NUMTODSINTERVAL functions discussed in Chapter 4, "Date and Conversion Functions."

LAG/LEAD FUNCTIONS

The LAG/LEAD functionality allows you to get values from other rows relative to the position of the current row. The syntax is:

```
{LAG|LEAD}(expression[,offset][,default])
   OVER ([query_partition_clause] order_by_clause)
```

The LAG function will return one of the values of the previous rows, the LEAD function will return one of the values of the next rows. The optional OFFSET parameter identifies the relative position of the row and if no parameter is specified it defaults to 1. The default optional parameter returns the value if the offset falls outside of the boundaries of the table or the partition, such as the last and first rows. The LAG and LEAD functions do not have a windowing clause because the offset indicates the exact row.

The next SQL statement shows a useful example of the LAG function. The column labeled "This Month's Revenue" displays the revenue generated for the month in which an individual section begins. The column "Previous Month" is computed using the LAG function. The offset number is specified as 1, which indicates to always use the previous row's value. The "Monthly Change" column computes the change to the previous month by subtracting the value of the "This Month's Revenue" column from the value in the "Previous Month" column.

```
SELECT TO_CHAR(start_date_time, 'MM') "Month",
       SUM(cost) "This Month's Revenue",
       LAG(SUM(cost),1) OVER
         (ORDER BY TO_CHAR(start_date_time, 'MM'))
         "Previous Month",
       SUM(cost)-LAG(SUM(cost),1) OVER
         (ORDER BY TO_CHAR(start_date_time, 'MM'))
         "Monthly Change"
  FROM enrollment e, section s, course c
 WHERE e.section_id = s.section_id
   AND s.course_no = c.course_no
   AND c.cost IS NOT NULL
 GROUP BY TO_CHAR(start_date_time, 'MM')
```

Mo	This Month's Revenue	Previous Month	Monthly Change
04	59745		
05	98780	59745	39035
06	48695	98780	-50085
07	58555	48695	9860

4 rows selected.

ADVANTAGES OF ANALYTICAL FUNCTIONS

Analytical functions have a number of advantages. Unlike SELECT statements containing aggregate functions and the GROUP BY clause, they allow you to display summary and detail data together rather than writing separate queries. The next SELECT statements illustrate this advantage.

This query shows the average revenue per number of sections in a course.

```
SELECT num_of_sections, AVG(revenue)
  FROM course_revenue
 GROUP BY num_of_sections
```

NUM_OF_SECTIONS	AVG(REVENUE)
1	2987.5
2	10369.2857
3	7833.33333
4	10157.5
5	22107.5
6	27485
8	53775

7 rows selected.

The next statement allows you to show any of the table's columns; you are not limited to only the columns listed in the GROUP BY clause and you avoid the "ORA-00937" error. The result demonstrates a listing of both summary and detail data.

```
SELECT course_no, revenue, num_of_sections,
       AVG(revenue) OVER (PARTITION BY
          num_of_sections) AS avg_rev_per_cour
  FROM course_revenue
```

COURSE_NO	REVENUE	NUM_OF_SECTIONS	AVG_REV_PER_COUR
10	1195	1	2987.5
132	2390	1	2987.5
145	2390	1	2987.5
...			
147	5975	1	2987.5
134	2390	2	10369.2857
350	10755	2	10369.2857
...			
146	3585	2	10369.2857
...			
135	4380	3	7833.33333
...			
25	53775	8	53775

24 rows selected.

Analytical functions perform postprocessing on the result, which makes them very efficient and simple to use. Some analytical functions cannot be duplicated using any other SQL syntax. For example, the DENSE_RANK or moving and cumulative values cannot be computed without the use of the analytical clause in a statement.

As you have discovered throughout this book, there are often times when there are many ways to write a SQL statement. Recall from Chapter 7, "Subqueries," the subquery WITH clause, which allows you to build temporary results against which you can write further queries. One of the example queries from Chapter 7 is listed here and displays the total revenue per instructor. The result only shows those instructors and the respective revenues they generate that are above the average revenue per instructor.

```
WITH
revenue_per_instructor AS
(SELECT instructor_id, SUM(cost) AS revenue
   FROM section s, course c, enrollment e
  WHERE s.section_id = e.section_id
    AND c.course_no = s.course_no
  GROUP BY instructor_id)
SELECT *
  FROM revenue_per_instructor
 WHERE revenue > (SELECT AVG(revenue)
                    FROM revenue_per_instructor)
```

The query can also be written with an analytical function and partitioning clause, resulting in the following SELECT statement.

```
select *
  FROM (SELECT instructor_id, SUM(cost) AS revenue,
               AVG(SUM(cost)) OVER() AS avg
          FROM section s, course c, enrollment e
         WHERE s.section_id = e.section_id
           AND c.course_no = s.course_no
         GROUP BY instructor_id) t
 WHERE revenue > avg
```

INSTRUCTOR_ID	REVENUE	AVG
101	51380	33221.875
103	44215	33221.875
107	35745	33221.875
108	39235	33221.875

4 rows selected.

Again, there are often many solutions to determine a result. Knowing your options is useful and allows you to choose the most efficient statement.

CREATING YOUR OWN CUSTOM FUNCTION

So far you have used a variety of the rich offerings of Oracle's built-in functions. Using the PL/SQL language, you can write your own functions. Although this book will not discuss the PL/SQL language in detail, this brief section will offer you a glimpse into what a customized PL/SQL function can accomplish when used within a SQL statement.

Why would you write your own PL/SQL function? This functionality is quite useful in the case of complicated query logic as it allows you to easily call the function that hides the complexity of the logic. The next example shows a custom function that chooses the next business day if the passed date falls on a weekend day. The function queries the HOLIDAY table to make sure the next business day does not fall on a company holiday. You can use this function much like any of the single-row functions you have learned about.

The next example shows how the function called NEXT_BUSINESS_DAY works. As you can see it hides all the complexity of figuring out the date for you and simply returns the next business day.

```
SELECT next_business_day('10-AUG-2002')
  FROM dual
```

NEXT_BUSI

```
---------
```

12-AUG-02

1 row selected.

Because August 10, 2002 falls on a Saturday, the next business day is a Monday. So if you're trying to write a report to list the due dates of invoices and you must always display a business day as the due date, it is easier to use this function. Furthermore, it is simpler than writing a long CASE expression, and you may be unable to do this at all if you are working with an old Oracle version that does not support the CASE expression. Other statements can use the stored function and take advantage of the functionality. Furthermore, a stored function ensures subsequent changes to the logic are automatically applied to any statement that calls the function.

There is the PL/SQL code that implements and stores the NEXT_BUSINESS_DAY function in the database.

```
CREATE OR REPLACE FUNCTION next_business_day(i_date DATE)
   RETURN DATE IS
   v_date DATE;
BEGIN
  v_date:=i_date;
  SELECT NVL(MAX(holiday_end_date)+1, v_date)
    INTO v_date
    FROM holiday
   WHERE v_date BETWEEN holiday_start_date AND holiday_end_date;
  IF TO_CHAR(v_date, 'DY') = 'SAT' THEN
     v_date:=v_date+2;
  ELSIF TO_CHAR(v_date, 'DY') = 'SUN' THEN
     v_date:=v_date+1;
  END IF;
  RETURN v_date;
EXCEPTION
  WHEN OTHERS THEN
    RETURN NULL;
END next_business_day;
/
```

Note that in previous Oracle versions, functions executed from a SQL statement required that they be wrapped inside a package—a type of PL/SQL object.

Clearly writing your own custom functions simplifies the logic of complicated business rules and can overcome SQL limitations. However, you must keep in mind that the function will be executed for every row of the result set; the key is to eliminate as many rows as possible first before applying the function.

To learn more about the PL/SQL language refer to the companion book in the Oracle Interactive Workbook series called *Oracle PL/SQL Interactive Workbook* by Benjamin Rosenzweig and Elena Silvestrova (Prentice Hall).

LAB 15.1 EXERCISES

15.1.1 TRANSPOSE A RESULT SET

a) The following query result is a listing of all the distinct course costs and a count of each. Write the query to achieve the result.

```
    1095       1195       1595       NULL
--------- --------- --------- ---------
        3         25          1          1
```

1 row selected.

b) Build upon Exercise a to include a range so the output looks like the following. Hint: You can write the query with the CASE expression or use the DECODE and SIGN function.

```
1500 OR LESS MORE THAN 1500
------------ --------------
          29              1
```

1 row selected.

15.1.2 UTILIZE ANALYTICAL FUNCTIONS

a) Modify the following query to display the top-3 revenue-generating courses. If there is a tie in the revenue, include the duplicates. Hint: Use an inline view to achieve the desired result.

```
SELECT course_no, revenue,
       RANK() OVER (ORDER BY revenue DESC)
         rev_rank,
       DENSE_RANK() OVER (ORDER BY revenue DESC)
         rev_dense_rank,
       ROW_NUMBER() OVER (ORDER BY revenue DESC)
         row_number
  FROM course_revenue
```

b) Based on the following statement explain how the result of the AVG column is achieved.

```
SELECT numeric_grade AS grade, grade_type_code,
       grade_code_occurrence AS occurrence,
       AVG(numeric_grade) OVER(PARTITION BY grade_type_code
       ORDER BY grade_code_occurrence) AS avg
  FROM grade
 WHERE student_id = 254
   AND section_id = 87
```

GRADE	GR	OCCURRENCE	AVG
91	FI	1	91
91	HM	1	91
75	HM	2	83
98	HM	3	88
98	HM	4	90.5
81	HM	5	88.6
71	HM	6	85.6666667
71	HM	7	83.5714286
81	HM	8	83.25
91	HM	9	84.1111111
91	HM	10	84.8
76	MT	1	76

12 rows selected.

c) How would you formulate the question this query is attempting to solve?

```
SELECT e.*, SUM(diff) OVER (ORDER BY 1 ROWS BETWEEN
       UNBOUNDED PRECEDING AND CURRENT ROW) AS cum_sum
  FROM (SELECT TRUNC(enroll_date),
              TRUNC(enroll_date)-LAG(TRUNC(enroll_date),1)
               OVER (ORDER BY TRUNC(ENROLL_DATE)) DIFF
         FROM enrollment
        GROUP BY TRUNC(enroll_date)) e
```

TRUNC(ENR	DIFF	CUM_SUM
30-JAN-99		
02-FEB-99	3	3
04-FEB-99	2	5
07-FEB-99	3	8
10-FEB-99	3	11
11-FEB-99	1	12
13-FEB-99	2	14
16-FEB-99	3	17
19-FEB-99	3	20
21-FEB-99	2	22

10 rows selected.

LAB 15.1 EXERCISE ANSWERS

15.1.1 ANSWERS

a) The following query result is a listing of all the distinct course costs and a count of each. Write the query to achieve the result.

```
    1095        1195        1595        NULL
--------- --------- --------- ---------
        3          25           1           1
```

`1 row selected.`

Answer: The answer requires the use of the DECODE function nested inside the aggregate function COUNT or you can write the query using the CASE expression.

```
SELECT COUNT(DECODE(cost, 1095, 1)) "1095",
       COUNT(DECODE(cost, 1195, 1)) "1195",
       COUNT(DECODE(cost, 1595, 1)) "1595",
       COUNT(DECODE(cost, NULL, 1)) "NULL"
  FROM course
```

Or:

```
SELECT COUNT(CASE WHEN cost = 1095 THEN 1 END) "1095",
       COUNT(CASE WHEN cost = 1195 THEN 1 END) "1195",
       COUNT(CASE WHEN cost = 1595 THEN 1 END) "1595",
       COUNT(CASE WHEN cost IS NULL THEN 1 END) "NULL"
  FROM course
```

The transposed result uses the COUNT function to count the row only if it meets the search criteria of the DECODE function or CASE expression. The first column of the SELECT statement tests for courses with a cost of 1095. If this expression is equal to 1095, then the DECODE function or CASE expression returns the value 1; otherwise, it returns a NULL value. The COUNT function counts NOT NULL values; the NULL values are not included. Note that this is different from the way the COUNT(*) function works, which includes NULL values in the count.

The last column in the SELECT statement tests for courses with a NULL cost. If this condition of a NULL course cost is true, the DECODE function or the CASE expression returns a 1 and the row is included in the count.

You can also expand on the previous example to show all the course costs by prerequisite. Here, two courses with prerequisite 25 have a course cost of 1095 and 1195, respectively.

```
SELECT prerequisite,
       COUNT(DECODE(cost, 1095, 1)) "1095",
       COUNT(DECODE(cost, 1195, 1)) "1195",
```

```
        COUNT(DECODE(cost, 1595, 1)) "1595",
        COUNT(DECODE(cost, NULL, 1)) "NULL"
   FROM course
   GROUP BY prerequisite
```

PREREQUISITE	1095	1195	1595	NULL
10	1	0	0	0
20	0	5	0	0
25	1	1	0	0
...				
350	0	1	0	1
420	0	1	0	0
	0	4	0	0

17 rows selected.

The CASE expression can be used instead of the DECODE function. The query would then look similar to the following statement:

```
SELECT prerequisite,
       COUNT(CASE WHEN cost = 1095 THEN 1 END) "1095",
       COUNT(CASE WHEN cost = 1195 THEN 1 END) "1195",
       COUNT(CASE WHEN cost = 1595 THEN 1 END) "1595",
       COUNT(CASE WHEN cost IS NULL THEN 1 END) "NULL"
  FROM course
  GROUP BY prerequisite
```

It is best to use the CASE expression as it is always easier to understand than DECODE functionality. It also has the added benefit of being ANSI compatible. You should know about DECODE nonetheless because sometimes your SQL queries may need to run against an Oracle version prior to the implementation of the CASE functionality.

b) Build upon Exercise a to include a range so the output looks like the following. Hint: You can write the query with the CASE expression or use the DECODE and the SIGN function.

1500 OR LESS	MORE THAN 1500
29	1

1 row selected.

Answer: The simplest query statement is achieved with the CASE expression. Otherwise use the SIGN function nested within the DECODE function to compare the values.

```
SELECT COUNT(CASE WHEN NVL(cost,0) <=1500 THEN 1 END)
       "1500 OR LESS",
       COUNT(CASE WHEN cost >1500 THEN 1 END)
       "MORE THAN 1500"
  FROM course
```

You can only express the same logic with the DECODE and SIGN functions.

```
SELECT COUNT(DECODE(SIGN(NVL(cost, 0) -1500), 1, NULL, 'A'))
       "1500 OR LESS",
       COUNT(DECODE(SIGN(NVL(cost,0) -1500), 1, 'A', NULL))
       "MORE THAN 1500"
  FROM course
```

To evaluate the function, read it from the inside out. Look at the first column of the SELECT statement. First, the NVL function is evaluated; if the cost equals NULL, a zero is substituted. The result of the expression NVL(cost, 0) – 1500 returns either a zero, a negative number, or a positive number. The SIGN function is applied to this expression and the SIGN function returns a 1 if the result of the expression NVL(COST, 0) – 1500 is positive. If the result is negative, the SIGN function returns a –1; if the result is zero, the SIGN function returns a zero. Based on the return value of the SIGN function, the DECODE function compares it to the search criteria.

For example, look at the first column, which counts the courses with a cost of 1500 or less. If the course cost of the row equals 1095, then the result of the expression 1095 – 1500 equals –405, a negative number. The SIGN function returns a –1. Therefore, the else condition of the DECODE function is executed, which returns the value 'A'. The COUNT function counts this record, because it is a NOT NULL value.

If the cost is greater than 1500, the expression SIGN(NVL(cost, 0) – 1500) returns a positive number, for which you find the search value of 1; then the resulting return value of the DECODE function is a NULL value. This row is not included in the count.

For the second column, which lists the costs greater than 1500, the same logic is repeated, but the search and resulting condition of the DECODE change accordingly.

Alternatively, you can write this with a SUM function to achieve the same result. Note that with the SUM function, the substitution value of the DECODE matters because it is added up. This is in contrast to the COUNT function, where only the NOT NULL values are counted, but the actual value does not matter.

```
SELECT SUM(DECODE(SIGN(NVL(cost, 0) -1500), 1, NULL, 1))
       "1500 OR LESS",
       SUM(DECODE(SIGN(NVL(cost, 0) -1500), 1, 1, NULL))
       "MORE THAN 1500"
  FROM course
```

15.1.2 ANSWERS

a) Modify the following query to display the top-3 revenue-generating courses. If there is a tie in the revenue, include the duplicates. Hint: Use an inline view to achieve the desired result.

```
SELECT course_no, revenue,
       RANK() OVER (ORDER BY revenue DESC)
         rev_rank,
       DENSE_RANK() OVER (ORDER BY revenue DESC)
         rev_dense_rank,
       ROW_NUMBER() OVER (ORDER BY revenue DESC)
         row_number
  FROM course_revenue
```

Answer: Using an inline view you restrict the rows to only those where the values in the REV_DENSE_RANK column are 3 or less. The DENSE_RANK function is the better choice just in case some courses share the same revenue.

```
SELECT course_no, revenue, rev_dense_rank
  FROM (SELECT course_no, revenue,
               DENSE_RANK() OVER (ORDER BY revenue DESC)
                 rev_dense_rank
          FROM course_revenue) t
 WHERE rev_dense_rank <= 3
```

COURSE_NO	REVENUE	REV_DENSE_RANK
25	53775	1
122	28680	2
120	27485	3

3 rows selected.

BOTTOM-*N* RANKING

The bottom-*n* ranking is similar to top-*n* except now you change the order of the ranking. Instead of ordering the revenue by descending order, the ORDER BY clause is now in ascending order. The query to determine the bottom three revenue ranking courses is listed here.

```
SELECT course_no, revenue, rev_dense_rank
  FROM (SELECT course_no, revenue,
               DENSE_RANK() OVER (ORDER BY revenue ASC)
                 rev_dense_rank
          FROM course_revenue) t
 WHERE rev_dense_rank <= 3
```

COURSE_NO	REVENUE	REV_DENSE_RANK
10	1195	1
204	1195	1
132	2390	2
145	2390	2
420	2390	2
134	2390	2
146	3585	3
330	3585	3

8 rows selected.

b) Based on the following statement explain how the result of the AVG column is achieved.

```
SELECT numeric_grade AS grade, grade_type_code,
       grade_code_occurrence AS occurrence,
       AVG(numeric_grade) OVER(PARTITION BY grade_type_code
       ORDER BY grade_code_occurrence) AS avg
  FROM grade
 WHERE student_id = 254
   AND section_id = 87
```

GRADE	GR	OCCURRENCE	AVG
91	FI	1	91
91	HM	1	91
75	HM	2	83
98	HM	3	88
98	HM	4	90.5
81	HM	5	88.6
71	HM	6	85.6666667
71	HM	7	83.5714286
81	HM	8	83.25
91	HM	9	84.1111111
91	HM	10	84.8
76	MT	1	76

12 rows selected.

Answer: The statement computes a cumulative average for each partition. The average is reset after the values listed in the partition clause change. The ORDER BY clause determines the definition of the window.

After the WHERE clause is executed, postprocessing with the analytical function takes over. The partitions are built first. The result shows three distinct values: FI, HM, and MT for final, homework, and midterm, respectively. After a change in partition the average is reset.

It's easiest to follow the logic by examining the individual computations for each respective row. They are listed next to the result.

```
  GRADE GR OCCURRENCE          AVG
----------  --  ----------  ----------
     91 FI           1           91  /* (91)/1 */
     91 HM           1           91  /* (91)/1 partition change*/
     75 HM           2           83  /* (91+83)/2 */
     98 HM           3           88  /* (91+83+98)/3 */
     98 HM           4         90.5  /* (91+83+98+98)/4 */
...
     76 MT           1           76  /* (76)/1 partition change*/
```

12 rows selected.

You will notice that for the HM partition there are duplicates for the NU-MERIC_GRADE column values (row 4 and 5 show 98). Because the column GRADE_CODE_OCCURRENCE is part of the ORDER BY clause and has different and ever-changing values, the cumulative average is computed for each row.

c) How would you formulate the question this query is attempting to solve?

```
SELECT e.*, SUM(diff) OVER (ORDER BY 1 ROWS BETWEEN
        UNBOUNDED PRECEDING AND CURRENT ROW) AS cum_sum
  FROM (SELECT TRUNC(enroll_date),
               TRUNC(enroll_date)-LAG(TRUNC(enroll_date),1)
               OVER (ORDER BY TRUNC(ENROLL_DATE)) DIFF
         FROM enrollment
        GROUP BY TRUNC(enroll_date)) e
```

```
TRUNC(ENR      DIFF    CUM_SUM
---------  ----------  ----------
30-JAN-99
02-FEB-99       3          3
04-FEB-99       2          5
07-FEB-99       3          8
10-FEB-99       3         11
11-FEB-99       1         12
13-FEB-99       2         14
16-FEB-99       3         17
19-FEB-99       3         20
21-FEB-99       2         22
```

10 rows selected.

Answer: Determine the difference in days between the distinct ENROLL_DATE values; only consider the date not the time values. In the result list the distinct ENROLL_DATE values, the difference in days between each value, and the cumulative sum of days in the last column.

LAB 15.1 SELF-REVIEW QUESTIONS

In order to test your progress, you should be able to answer the following questions.

1) What value does the following expression return?

```
DECODE(SIGN(100-500), 1, 50, -1, 400, NULL)
```

a) _____ −400
b) _____ 50
c) _____ 400
d) _____ −1
e) _____ NULL

2) The difference between the RANK and DENSE_RANK functions is that DENSE_RANK leaves no gaps in ranking sequence when there are ties in the values.

a) _____ True
b) _____ False

3) If you use the RANK function without a partitioning clause, the ranking works over the entire result set.

a) _____ True
b) _____ False

4) The ROWS keyword in a windowing clause defines a logical window.

a) _____ True
b) _____ False

5) The presence of duplicate rows in an ORDER BY clause of a logical window will cause the analytical function such as an average to be computed for the rows with identical value.

a) _____ True
b) _____ False

6) The LAG and LEAD functions may have a windowing clause.

a) _____ True
b) _____ False

7) The FIRST_VALUE or LAST_VALUE functions only work with a windowing clause.

   a) _____ True
   b) _____ False

   Answers appear in Appendix A, Section 15.1.

LAB 15.2

ROLLUP AND CUBE OPERATORS

> ## LAB OBJECTIVES
>
> After this lab, you will be able to:
>
> ✔ Use the ROLLUP, CUBE, GROUPING, and GROUPING SET Capabilities

---

In versions 8*i* and 9*i* Oracle introduced many enhancements to the GROUP BY clause that make aggregating data from many different perspectives simpler and more efficient. These enhancements come in the form of the ROLLUP and CUBE operators, the GROUPING function, and GROUPING SETS capabilities. The ROLLUP and CUBE operators allow you to create subtotals and grand totals; it simply eliminates the need to run multiple queries against the data.

You will see how useful these capabilities are for analyzing data and discovering relationships between data elements. This functionality is primarily used in data warehousing environments with the goal of providing users with reporting and decision support functionality against summarized data.

End-user access is often accomplished with various querying tools that read this summarized data and allow users to "slice and dice" the information in any way they desire. As many companies are increasingly using their databases to gain competitive market advantage and to better support their customers as well as reduce costs, this capability allows you to uncover much information about the data.

Many software vendors offer various types of tools that present the summarized data in an easily understandable format to users; Oracle itself also supplies its own version of an end-user decision support software tool called Oracle Discoverer. While we will not discuss the capabilities and merits of such tools, we will illustrate the summarization capabilities of Oracle to discover relationships and information about the data. You will see that this functionality is quite powerful, extremely valuable, and yet very easy to use.

THE ROLLUP OPERATOR

The ROLLUP operator allows you to create subtotals and grand totals, also referred to as *super aggregate rows*, for various groupings and for all rows.

The table used for the exercises in this lab is called INSTRUCTOR_SUMMARY and is included in the supplemental tables you can download from the companion Web site. It contains summary data generated from the various tables in the STUDENT schema.

The DESCRIBE command lists the following columns. The primary key of the table consists of the INSTRUCTOR_ID, SEMESTER_YEAR, and SEMESTER_MONTH columns.

```
SQL> DESCR instructor_summary
 Name                      Null?     Type
 ------------------------- --------  ---------------
 INSTRUCTOR_ID             NOT NULL  NUMBER(8)
 GENDER                              CHAR(1)
 CAMPUS                              VARCHAR2(11)
 SEMESTER_YEAR             NOT NULL  VARCHAR2(4)
 SEMESTER_MONTH            NOT NULL  VARCHAR2(2)
 NUM_OF_CLASSES                      NUMBER
 NUM_OF_STUDENTS                     NUMBER
 REVENUE                             NUMBER
```

The INSTRUCTOR_ID is identical to the familiar column in the INSTRUCTOR table. The GENDER column identifies the gender as either male (M), female (F), or unknown (U) if the title of an instructor is different than Mr., Mrs., or Ms. The CAMPUS column indicates the name of the campus where the instructor's office is located. The SEMESTER_YEAR and SEMESTER_MONTH columns display the year and month the instructor worked. The column NUM_OF_CLASSES holds the number of sections the instructor taught, the NUM_OF_STUDENTS shows the column number of students for all the sections, and the REVENUE column contains the revenue generated by the individual instructor for these classes.

Using the familiar GROUP BY clause, the following query produces a listing of instructors grouped by the GENDER, SEMESTER_YEAR, and SEMESTER_MONTH columns, including the total number of students taught.

```
SELECT gender, semester_year AS year,
       semester_month AS month,
       SUM(num_of_students) AS total
  FROM instructor_summary
 GROUP BY gender, semester_year, semester_month
```

```
G YEAR MO       TOTAL
- ---- -- -----------
F 1999 05           0
F 1999 06          16
F 2000 07          37
M 1999 06          45
M 1999 07          79
U 1999 05           0
U 1999 07          49


7 rows selected.
```

Based on the result you notice that all the distinct occurrences of these three columns are summarized.

Instead of using the GROUP BY clause, the next query uses the ROLLUP operator. You will discover the formation of subtotals for each of the groups. Your individual result will not show the actual shading shown here; they are shown here to clearly illustrate the location of the formed super aggregate rows.

```
SELECT gender, semester_year AS year,
       semester_month AS month,
       SUM(num_of_students) AS total
  FROM instructor_summary
 GROUP BY ROLLUP(gender, semester_year, semester_month)
```

G	YEAR	MO	TOTAL	
F	1999	05	0	
F	1999	06	16	
F	1999		16	Subtotal for female in year 1999
F	2000	07	37	
F	2000		37	Subtotal for female in year 2000
F			53	Subtotal for entire female gender
M	1999	06	45	
M	1999	07	79	
M	1999		124	Subtotal for male in year 1999
M			124	Subtotal for entire male gender
U	1999	05	0	
U	1999	07	49	
U	1999		49	Subtotal for unknown gender 1999
U			49	Subtotal for entire unknown gender
			226	Grand Total

```
15 rows selected.
```

Examining the result, you will observe the same rows as those shown in the issued GROUP BY query. What is different are additional rows. These additional rows indicate subtotals for the GENDER and YEAR columns, a subtotal for the GENDER column only, and a grand total column. The subtotals are formed for each change in value.

The first shaded set of summary rows indicates 16 female students for the year 1999 and 53 female students in total.

Notice that you only needed one query to generate different groupings of data. The individual groupings are: group #1: gender, year, and month; group #2: gender and year; group #3: gender; and group #4: grand total.

The number of columns or expressions appearing in the ROLLUP clause determines the number of groupings. The formula is $n + 1$ whereby n is the number of columns listed in the ROLLUP clause. Without the ROLLUP clause you would need to write four individual queries.

The first query is already listed at the beginning of this lab, but repeated together with partial output. This query represents the different individual rows grouped by the columns GENDER, SEMESTER_YEAR, and SEMESTER_MONTH.

```
SELECT gender, semester_year AS year,
       semester_month AS month,
       SUM(num_of_students) AS total
  FROM instructor_summary
 GROUP BY gender, semester_year, semester_month
 G YEAR MO      TOTAL
 - ---- -- ----------
 F 1999 05          0
 F 1999 06         16
 ...
 U 1999 07         49

 7 rows selected.
```

The second query lists the GENDER and SEMESTER_YEAR columns and computes the respective summary data.

```
SELECT gender, semester_year AS year,
       SUM(num_of_students) AS total
  FROM instructor_summary
 GROUP BY gender, semester_year
 G YEAR       TOTAL
 - ----  ----------
 F 1999          16
 F 2000          37
 M 1999         124
 U 1999          49

 4 rows selected.
```

The third query is a listing grouped to give you a subtotal for the gender.

```
SELECT gender, SUM(num_of_students) AS total
  FROM instructor_summary
 GROUP BY gender
G       TOTAL
-  ----------
F          53
M         124
U          49

3 rows selected.
```

And the last query is the grand total for all the rows.

```
SELECT SUM(num_of_students) AS total
  FROM instructor_summary
    TOTAL
----------
      226

1 row selected.
```

The idea of the ROLLUP operator is that you don't need to write multiple queries and Oracle doesn't need to process the table multiple times, but rather does all the necessary work in one pass through the table. This is a very efficient and quick way to accomplish the desired result. (If you wanted to perform this functionality and the same result in versions prior to Oracle 8*i*, you had to write these individual queries and combine the result using the UNION ALL set operator discussed in Chapter 8, "Set Operators.")

THE CUBE OPERATOR

The CUBE operator takes the formation of super aggregates yet another step further; it allows you to generate all the possible combinations of groups. If you have n columns or expressions in the GROUP BY clause, the CUBE operator generates 2^n groupings. The CUBE operator received its name from the different combinations that can be achieved from an n-dimensional cube. The next example illustrates the combinations based on the previously used query. The CUBE operator is now substituted for the ROLLUP operator.

```
SELECT gender, semester_year AS year,
       semester_month AS month,
       SUM(num_of_students) AS total
  FROM instructor_summary
 GROUP BY CUBE(gender, semester_year, semester_month)
```

G	YEAR	MO	TOTAL
F	1999	05	0
F	1999	06	16
F	1999		16
F	2000	07	37
F	2000		37
F		05	0
F		06	16
F		07	37
F			53
M	1999	06	45
M	1999	07	79
M	1999		124
M		06	45
M		07	79
M			124
U	1999	05	0
U	1999	07	49
U	1999		49
U		05	0
U		07	49
U			49
	1999	05	0
	1999	06	61
	1999	07	128
	1999		189
	2000	07	37
	2000		37
		05	0
		06	61
		07	165
			226

31 rows selected.

The shading around the rows indicate the new additionally formed subtotals. Observe a subtotal for GENDER and SEMESTER_MONTH, another for SEMESTER_YEAR and SEMESTER_MONTH, a subtotal for SEMESTER_YEAR only, and lastly a total by SEMESTER_MONTH.

The cube determined the 2^3 different combinations for the three columns, which results in a total of eight different subtotals. The ROLLUP already determined four and the CUBE added four more combinations.

DETERMINING THE ROLLUP AND CUBE COMBINATIONS

Assume you have three rollup groups in your GROUP BY ROLLUP clause listed like the following hypothetical columns named YEAR, MONTH, and WEEK.

```
GROUP BY ROLLUP (year, month, week)
```

You will get the following four rollup groups according to the $n + 1$ formula: group #1, which consists of year, month, and week; group #2 shows year and month; group #3 shows year; and group #4 shows the grand total. Hierarchies such as time periods or sales territories (continent, country, state, county) lend themselves naturally to the ROLLUP operator, though you can obviously create your own or use your own combination of columns to rollup.

If you use the CUBE operator instead, you generate eight different combinations, all of which are listed in Table 15.3. Note the empty set of parentheses, (), indicates the grand total.

Table 15.3 ■ Grouping Combinations

Operator	Formula	Grouping Combinations
ROLLUP (year, month, week)	$n + 1$ $3 + 1 = 4$	(year, month, week), (year, month), (year), ()
CUBE (year, month, week)	2^n $2^3 = 8$	(year, month, week), (year, month), (year), (month, week), (year, week), (week), (month), ()

PARTIAL CUBE AND ROLLUP RESULTS

To exclude certain subtotals from the CUBE or the ROLLUP result, you can selectively remove columns from the CUBE or ROLLUP clause and place them into the GROUP BY clause or generate summaries based on composite columns. Although it is useful to know about these options, you may simplify this with the GROUPING SETS clause discussed shortly.

Table 15.4 lists the partial ROLLUP and CUBE results when a column moves into the GROUP BY clause. The example uses three columns called YEAR, MONTH, and WEEK. Most notably the summary grand total is missing from all the partial rollups.

In Oracle 9*i* you can further group on composite columns. A composite column defined within this context is a collection of columns and is listed within a set of parentheses. As such, a composite column is treated as a single unit; this avoids

Table 15.4 ■ Partial ROLLUP and CUBE Operations

GROUP BY Clause	Grouping Combinations
year, ROLLUP (month, week)	(year, month, week), (year, month), (year)
year, month ROLLUP (week)	(year, month, week), (year, month)
year, CUBE(month, week)	(year, month, week), (year, month), (year, week), (year)
year, month, CUBE (week)	(year, month, week), (year, month)

any unnecessary aggregations for specific levels. The results of operations on composite columns are listed in Table 15.5.

Table 15.5 ■ Composite Column ROLLUP and CUBE Operations

Composite Columns	Grouping Combinations
ROLLUP ((year, month), week)	(year, month, week), (year, month), ()
ROLLUP (year), (month, week)	(year, month, week), (month, week)
CUBE ((year, month), week)	(year, month, week), (year, month), (week), ()
CUBE (year), (month, week)	(year, month, week), (month, week)

GROUPING SETS

Computing and displaying only selective results can actually be simplified with the Oracle 9*i* GROUPING SETS extension of the GROUP BY clause. You explicitly state which summaries you want to generate. The following query applies the GROUPING SETS functionality to the example query drawn on previously.

```
SELECT gender, semester_year AS YEAR,
       semester_month AS month,
       SUM(num_of_students) AS total
  FROM instructor_summary
 GROUP BY GROUPING SETS
       ((gender, semester_year),   -- 1st Group
        (semester_month),          -- 2nd Group
        ())                        -- 3rd Group

G YEAR MO       TOTAL
- ---- -- ----------
F 1999             16
F 2000             37
M 1999            124
U 1999             49
        05          0
        06         61
```

```
07              165
                226
```

8 rows selected.

The query produces three sets: one for the GENDER and SEMESTER_YEAR columns, a second for the SEMESTER_MONTH, and the last group is the grand total. Each individual set must be enclosed in parentheses; the empty set of parentheses indicates the grand total. The GROUPING SETS clause provides the advantage of reading the table once and generating the results at once and only for those summaries in which you are interested. GROUPING SETS functionality is very efficient and yet selective about the results you choose to report.

COMBINE GROUPING SETS

If you have many hierarchy groupings, you may not want to specify all the different groupings individually. You can combine multiple GROUPING SETS to generate yet more combinations.

The next example lists two GROUPING SETS clauses in the GROUP BY clause.

```
GROUP BY GROUPING SETS (year, month),
         GROUPING SETS (week, day)
```

The cross product results in the following equivalent groupings.

```
GROUP BY GROUPING SETS (
           (year, week),
           (year, day),
           (month, week),
           (month, day))
```

THE GROUPING FUNCTION

One of the purposes of the GROUPING function is that it helps you distinguish the summary rows from any rows that are a result of null values. The next query shows a CUBE operation on the columns SEMESTER_YEAR and CAMPUS. As it turns out, the CAMPUS column contains null values and it is difficult to distinguish between the summary row and an individual row holding a null value.

```
SELECT semester_year AS year, campus,
       SUM(num_of_classes) AS num_of_classes
  FROM instructor_summary
 GROUP BY CUBE (semester_year, campus)
```

YEAR	CAMPUS	NUM_OF_CLASSES
1999	DOWNTOWN	10
1999	LIBERTY	19

```
1999 MORNINGSIDE                29
1999                            10 Summary row or null?
1999                            68
2000 MORNINGSIDE                10
2000                            10
     DOWNTOWN                   10
     LIBERTY                    19
     MORNINGSIDE                39
                                10 Summary row or null?
                                78
```

12 rows selected.

The GROUPING function eliminates any ambiguities. Whenever you see a value of 1 in a column where the GROUPING function is applied, it indicates a super aggregate row, such as a subtotal or grand total row created by the ROLLUP or CUBE operator.

```
SELECT semester_year AS year, campus,
       SUM(num_of_classes) AS num_of_classes,
       GROUPING (semester_year) GP_YEAR,
       GROUPING (campus) GP_CAMPUS
  FROM instructor_summary
 GROUP BY CUBE (semester_year, campus)
```

YEAR	CAMPUS	NUM_OF_CLA	GP_YEAR	GP_CAMPUS	
1999	DOWNTOWN	10	0	0	
1999	LIBERTY	19	0	0	
1999	MORNINGSIDE	29	0	0	
1999		10	0	0	NULL value GP_CAMPUS
1999		68	0	1	
2000	MORNINGSIDE	10	0	0	
2000		10	0	1	
	DOWNTOWN	10	1	0	
	LIBERTY	19	1	0	
	MORNINGSIDE	39	1	0	
		10	1	0	NULL value GP_CAMPUS
		78	1	1	

12 rows selected.

When examining the result, you observe the columns where the GROUPING function is applied and has a value of zero or one. The number one indicates that this column is a super aggregate row.

The first shaded area on the resulting output shows a zero in the GP_CAMPUS column; this indicates that the null value in the CAMPUS column is indeed a null. The following row lists the number one in the GP_CAMPUS column; this designates the row as a summary row. The value for the CAMPUS column is aggregated and lists as a result 10 classes for all campus locations in 1999.

The second shaded row shows the number 1 in the GP_YEAR column, this indicates that the SEMESTER_YEAR column is an aggregate just like the previous three rows. That means the rows display the aggregate values for each individual campus for all years.

The last row contains the number one for both the GP_YEAR and the GP_CAMPUS columns. This indicates the grand total.

You can use the GROUPING function not only to determine if it's a generated row or null value, but to return certain rows from the result set with the HAVING clause. This is yet another way to selectively choose certain summary rows only.

```
HAVING GROUPING(campus) = 1
```

The GROUPING function can be utilized to add labels to the super aggregate rows. Instead of a blank column, a label such as 'GRAND TOTAL:' is displayed.

```
SELECT CASE WHEN GROUPING(semester_year) = 1
              AND GROUPING(campus) = 1 THEN 'GRAND TOTAL:'
          ELSE semester_year
       END AS year,
       CASE WHEN GROUPING(semester_year) = 1
              AND GROUPING(campus) = 1 THEN NULL
          ELSE campus
       END AS campus,
       SUM(num_of_classes) AS num_of_classes,
       GROUPING (semester_year) GP_YEAR,
       GROUPING (campus) GP_CAMPUS
  FROM instructor_summary
 GROUP BY CUBE (semester_year, campus)
```

YEAR	CAMPUS	NUM_OF_CLAS	GP_YEAR	GP_CAMPUS
1999	DOWNTOWN	10	0	0
1999	LIBERTY	19	0	0
1999	MORNINGSIDE	29	0	0
1999		10	0	0
1999		68	0	1
2000	MORNINGSIDE	10	0	0
2000		10	0	1
	DOWNTOWN	10	1	0
	LIBERTY	19	1	0
	MORNINGSIDE	39	1	0
		10	1	0
GRAND TOTAL:		78	1	1

```
12 rows selected.
```

> *Remember you can also use the NVL or COALESCE function to test for null values and return a substitute value.*

THE GROUPING_ID FUNCTION

If your query includes many GROUPING functions, you may want to consider consolidating the columns with the GROUPING_ID function. This function is not only similar in name and functionality but allows multiple columns as a parameter; it returns a number indicating the level of aggregation in the rollup or cube.

The GROUPING_ID returns a single number that identifies the exact aggregation level of every row.

```
SELECT semester_year AS year,
       campus,
       SUM(num_of_classes) AS num_of_classes,
       GROUPING (semester_year) GP_YEAR,
       GROUPING (campus) GP_CAMPUS,
       GROUPING_ID(semester_year, campus)
       AS GROUPING_ID
  FROM instructor_summary
 GROUP BY CUBE (semester_year, campus)
```

YEAR	CAMPUS	NUM_OF_C	GP_YEAR	GP_CAMPUS	GROUPING_ID
1999	DOWNTOWN	10	0	0	0
1999	LIBERTY	19	0	0	0
1999	MORNINGSIDE	29	0	0	0
1999		10	0	0	0
1999		68	0	1	1
2000	MORNINGSIDE	10	0	0	0
2000		10	0	1	1
	DOWNTOWN	10	1	0	2
	LIBERTY	19	1	0	2
	MORNINGSIDE	39	1	0	2
		10	1	0	2
		78	1	1	3

12 rows selected.

The GROUPING_ID function works just like the GROUPING function that generates zeros and ones. However, the GROUPING_ID function concatenates the zeros and ones and forms a bit vector, which is treated as a binary number. The GROUPING_ID returns the binary number's base-10 value. A value of 1 for each GROUPING column indicates that this is the grand total. This 11 binary number for the two-level column aggregation represents the number 3, which is returned by GROUPING_ID function. Zeros in all the columns of the GROUPING functions indicate that this is the lowest aggregation level.

Table 15.6 lists binary numbers and their numeric equivalent on the example of a four-column cube, representative of a GROUP BY clause such as CUBE(year, month, week, day). The column labeled GROUPING_ID displays the result of the GROUPING_ID function for each individual column; the bit-vector column indicates which bits are turned on and off.

You can use the GROUPING_ID function for labeling columns as discussed previously. However, its primary use is the application of *materialized views*, an Oracle object that allows you to create and maintain aggregate summary tables. Storing pre-aggregate summary information is an important technique for maximizing query performance in large decision support applications. The effect of the creation of this materialized view is that data is physically stored in a table. Any

Table 15.6 ■ Bit to Numeric Representation on the Example of a 4-Column CUBE

GROUPING_ID Numeric Equivalent	Bit-Vector	Aggregation Level
0	0 0 0 0	(year, month, week, day)
1	0 0 0 1	(year, month, week)
2	0 0 1 0	(year, month, day)
3	0 0 1 1	(year, month)
4	0 1 0 0	(year, week, day)
5	0 1 0 1	(year, week)
6	0 1 1 0	(year, day)
7	0 1 1 1	(year)
8	1 0 0 0	(month, week, day)
9	1 0 0 1	(month, week)
10	1 0 1 0	(month, day)
11	1 0 1 1	(month)
12	1 1 0 0	(week, day)
13	1 1 0 1	(week)
14	1 1 1 0	(day)
15	1 1 1 1	()

changes to the underlying tables are reflected in the materialized view through various refresh methods. (Unlike views, discussed in Chapter 12, "Views, Indexes, and Sequences," materialized views require physical storage.)

```
CREATE MATERIALIZED VIEW instructor_sum_mv
STORAGE(INITIAL 5 M PCTINCREASE 0)
AS
SELECT semester_year AS year,
       campus,
       SUM(num_of_classes) AS num_of_classes,
       GROUPING_ID(semester_year, campus)
       AS GROUPING_ID
  FROM instructor_summary
 GROUP BY CUBE (semester_year, campus)
Materialized view created.
```

You must have the CREATE MATERIALIZED VIEW privilege to be able to perform this operation.

GROUP_ID FUNCTION

The GROUP_ID function lets you distinguish among duplicate groupings; they may be generated as a result of combinations of columns listed in the GROUP BY clause. The GROUP_ID returns the number zero to the first row in the set that is not yet duplicated; any subsequent duplicate grouping row receives a higher number, starting with the number 1.

```
SELECT semester_year AS year, campus,
       SUM(num_of_classes) AS num_of_classes,
       GROUPING_ID(semester_year, campus) GROUPING_ID,
       GROUP_ID()
  FROM instructor_summary
 GROUP BY GROUPING SETS
       (semester_year, ROLLUP(semester_year, campus))
```

YEAR	CAMPUS	NUM_OF_CLASSES	GROUPING_ID	GROUP_ID()
1999	DOWNTOWN	10	0	0
1999	LIBERTY	19	0	0
1999	MORNINGSIDE	29	0	0
1999		10	0	0
2000	MORNINGSIDE	10	0	0
		78	3	0
1999		68	1	0
2000		10	1	0
1999		68	1	1
2000		10	1	1

```
10 rows selected.
```

This query illustrates the result of the GROUP_ID function, which returns a zero for the first row; the subsequent identical group returns the number 1.

If you have complicated queries that may generate duplicate values, you can eliminate those rows by including the condition HAVING GROUP_ID() = 0.

LAB 15.2 EXERCISES

15.2.1 USE THE ROLLUP, CUBE, GROUPING, AND GROUPING SET CAPABILITIES

a) Describe the effect of the following SQL statement and its resulting output.

```
COL SALUTATION FORMAT A5
COL "Area Code" FORMAT A9
COL "Reg.Month" FORMAT A10
SET pagesize 1000

SELECT salutation AS SALUTATION, SUBSTR(phone, 1,3)
       AS "Area Code",
       TO_CHAR(registration_date, 'MON') AS "Reg.Month",
       COUNT(*)
  FROM student
 WHERE SUBSTR(phone, 1,3) IN ('201','212','718')
   AND salutation IN ('Mr.', 'Ms.')
 GROUP BY ROLLUP (salutation, SUBSTR(phone, 1,3),
          TO_CHAR(registration_date, 'MON'))
```

SALUT	Area Code	Reg.Month	COUNT(*)
Mr.	201	FEB	34
Mr.	201	JAN	9
Mr.	201		43
Mr.	212	FEB	1
Mr.	212	JAN	1
Mr.	212		2
Mr.	718	FEB	72
Mr.	718	JAN	17
Mr.	718		89
Mr.			134
Ms.	201	FEB	27
Ms.	201	JAN	5
Ms.	201		32
Ms.	212	FEB	2
Ms.	212	JAN	1
Ms.	212		3
Ms.	718	FEB	52
Ms.	718	JAN	13

```
Ms.    718                        65
Ms.                               100
                                  234
```

```
21 rows selected.
```

b) Answer the following questions about the result set:

How many female students are there in total?
How many male students live in area code 212?
What is the total number of students?
How many female students live in the area code 718 and registered in January?

c) If the CUBE operator is used on the query in Question a instead, how many different combinations of groups do you get? List the groups.

d) Describe the result of the following query using the GROUPING SET extension to the GROUP BY clause.

```
COL "Area Code" FORMAT A9
COL "Reg.Month" FORMAT A9

SELECT SALUTATION, SUBSTR(phone, 1,3) "Area Code",
       TO_CHAR(registration_date, 'MON') "Reg.Month",
       COUNT(*)
  FROM student
 WHERE SUBSTR(phone, 1,3) IN ('201','212','718')
   AND salutation IN ('Mr.', 'Ms.')
   GROUP BY
        GROUPING SETS
        ((SALUTATION, SUBSTR(phone, 1,3)),
         (SALUTATION, TO_CHAR(registration_date, 'MON')),
         ()
        )
SALUT Are Reg   COUNT(*)
----- --- ---   ---------
Mr.   201            43
Mr.   212             2
Mr.   718            89
Ms.   201            32
Ms.   212             3
```

```
Ms.    718                65
Mr.            FEB       107
Mr.            JAN        27
Ms.            FEB        81
Ms.            JAN        19
                         234
```

```
11 rows selected.
```

e) Write the necessary individual queries to create the results similar to Question d. There is no need to include the null values in the columns.

LAB 15.2 EXERCISE ANSWERS

15.2.1 ANSWERS

a) Describe the effect of the following SQL statement and its resulting output. (For space reasons, the code is not repeated here.)

Answer: The query generates summary totals for three different groupings of students by using the ROLLUP operator. This effectively creates groupings which are counting rows in the STUDENT table. Four rollup groups are generated based on the columns: salutation, area code, and registration month (labeled "Reg.Month").

The first ROLLUP group is salutation, area code, and registration date; the second group is salutation and area code; the third is salutation; and the last is a grand total of all the rows. The shaded rows indicate the first occurrence of a group.

SALUT	Area Code	Reg.Month	COUNT(*)	
Mr.	201	FEB	34	Group #1
Mr.	201	JAN	9	
Mr.	201		43	Group #2
Mr.	212	FEB	1	
Mr.	212	JAN	1	
Mr.	212		2	
Mr.	718	FEB	72	
Mr.	718	JAN	17	
Mr.	718		89	
Mr.			134	Group #3
Ms.	201	FEB	27	

```
Ms.    201       JAN           5
Ms.    201                    32
Ms.    212       FEB           2
Ms.    212       JAN           1
Ms.    212                     3
Ms.    718       FEB          52
Ms.    718       JAN          13
Ms.    718                    65
Ms.                          100
                             234   Group #4
```

21 rows selected.

b) Answer the following questions about the result set:

How many female students are there in total?
How many male students live in area code 212?
What is the total number of students?
How many female students live in the area code 718 and registered in January?

Answer:You can obtain all these answers by examining the result set.

The first question, "How many female students are part of the result set?", can be easily answered by looking at the result set. The correct answer is that there are 100 female students. Following is an excerpt of the output.

```
SALUT Area Code Reg.Month   COUNT(*)
----- --------- ----------  ---------
...
Ms.                             100
```

The next question about the male students living in area code 212 can be obtained from this row. As you can see the number of students is 2.

```
SALUT Area Code Reg.Month   COUNT(*)
----- --------- ----------  ---------
...
Mr.    212                        2
```

The total number of students satisfying the WHERE clause of the query can be obtained with the last row, the grand total row. There are 234 in total.

```
SALUT Area Code Reg.Month   COUNT(*)
----- --------- ----------  ---------
...
                                234
```

Lastly, there are 13 female students that live in area code 718 and registered in January.

```
SALUT Area Code Reg.Month    COUNT(*)
----- --------- ----------   ---------
...
Ms.   718       JAN                 13
```

c) If the CUBE operator is used on the query in Question a instead, how many different combinations of groups do you get? List the groups.

Answer: There are three columns involved; therefore, there are 2^3 possible combinations, which translates to 8 different groupings.

Group #1: Salutation, area code, registration date
Group #2: Salutation, area code
Group #3: Salutation
Group #4: Area code, registration date
Group #5: Registration date
Group #6: Salutation, registration date
Group #7: Area code
Group #8: Grand total

d) Describe the result of the following query using the GROUPING SET extension to the GROUP BY clause.

```
COL "Area Code" FORMAT A9
COL "Reg.Month" FORMAT A9

SELECT SALUTATION, SUBSTR(phone, 1,3) "Area Code",
       TO_CHAR(registration_date, 'MON') "Reg.Month",
       COUNT(*)
  FROM student
 WHERE SUBSTR(phone, 1,3) IN ('201','212','718')
   AND salutation IN ('Mr.', 'Ms.')
 GROUP BY
       GROUPING SETS
       ((SALUTATION, SUBSTR(phone, 1,3)),
        (SALUTATION, TO_CHAR(registration_date, 'MON')),
        ()
       )
```

```
SALUT Are Reg   COUNT(*)
----- --- ---   ---------
Mr.   201              43
Mr.   212               2
Mr.   718              89
Ms.   201              32
Ms.   212               3
Ms.   718              65
Mr.       FEB         107
Mr.       JAN          27
Ms.       FEB          81
```

```
Ms.        JAN        19
                      234
```

11 rows selected.

Answer:The query result shows students with the salutations Mr. and Ms. that live in the area codes 201, 212, and 718. The GROUPING SETS extension to the GROUP BY clause allows you to selectively group specific information. There are three individual groups. The first set is salutation and area code and is indicated as a set with the enclosed parentheses. The next set is the registration month and the salutation is again enclosed in the parentheses. The third and last set is an empty set of parentheses; this indicates the grand total. The GROUPING SETS clause is very efficient as it queries the table once to generate the result.

e) Write the necessary individual queries to create the results similar to Question d. There is no need to include the null values in the columns.

Answer: From the previous question, we already identified the three groupings, which then translate into three individual queries.

Query #1:

```
SELECT salutation, SUBSTR(phone, 1, 3), COUNT(*)
  FROM student
 WHERE SUBSTR(phone, 1,3) IN ('201','212','718')
   AND salutation IN ('Mr.', 'Ms.')
 GROUP BY salutation, SUBSTR(phone, 1, 3)
SALUT SUB  COUNT(*)
----- ---  ---------
Mr.   201        43
Mr.   212         2
Mr.   718        89
Ms.   201        32
Ms.   212         3
Ms.   718        65
```

6 rows selected.

Query #2:

```
SELECT salutation, TO_CHAR(registration_date, 'MON'),
       COUNT(*)
  FROM student
 WHERE SUBSTR(phone, 1,3) IN ('201','212','718')
   AND salutation IN ('Mr.', 'Ms.')
 GROUP BY salutation, TO_CHAR(registration_date, 'MON')
SALUT TO_  COUNT(*)
----- ---  ---------
Mr.   FEB       107
Mr.   JAN        27
```

```
Ms.    FEB        81
Ms.    JAN        19
```

`4 rows selected.`

Query #3:

```
SELECT COUNT(*)
  FROM student
 WHERE SUBSTR(phone, 1,3) IN ('201','212','718')
   AND salutation IN ('Mr.', 'Ms.')
 COUNT(*)
---------
      234
```

`1 row selected.`

LAB 15.2 SELF-REVIEW QUESTIONS

In order to test your progress, you should be able to answer the following questions.

1) A query has the following GROUP BY clause. How many different groupings are visible on the result?

   `GROUP BY CUBE (color, price, material, store_location)`

   a) _____ 4
   b) _____ 5
   c) _____ 16
   d) _____ 24
   e) _____ Unknown

2) A query has the following GROUP BY clause. How many different groupings are visible on the result?

   `GROUP BY ROLLUP (color, price, material, store_location)`

   a) _____ 4
   b) _____ 5
   c) _____ 16
   d) _____ 24
   e) _____ Unknown

3) A return value of 1 from the GROUPING function indicates an aggregate row.

   a) _____ True
   b) _____ False

4) How many groups are generated by the following query.

```
GROUP BY GROUPING SETS((color, price), material, store_location)
```

     a) _____ 3
     b) _____ 4
     c) _____ 5
     d) _____ 16
     e) _____ Unknown

Answers appear in Appendix A, Section 15.2.

**LAB
15.2**

LAB 15.3

HIERARCHICAL QUERIES

> ### LAB OBJECTIVES
>
> After this Lab, you will be able to:
>
> ✔ Restrict the Result Set in Hierarchical Queries
> ✔ Move Up and Down the Hierarchy Tree

A recursive relationship, also called a self-referencing relationship, exists on the COURSE table in the STUDENT schema (see Figure 15.2). This recursive relationship is between the columns COURSE_NO and PREREQUISITE. It is just like any other parent–child table relationship, except the relationship is with itself.

The PREREQUISITE column is a foreign key referencing its own table's primary key. Only valid course numbers can be entered as prerequisites. Any attempt to insert or update the PREREQUISITE column to a value for which no COURSE_NO exists is rejected. A course can have zero or one prerequisite. For a course to be considered a prerequisite, it must appear at least once in the PREREQUISITE column.

This relationship between the parent and child can be depicted in a query result as a hierarchy or tree, using Oracle's CONNECT BY clause and the PRIOR opera-

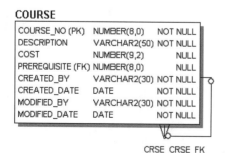

COURSE

COURSE_NO (PK)	NUMBER(8,0)	NOT NULL
DESCRIPTION	VARCHAR2(50)	NOT NULL
COST	NUMBER(9,2)	NULL
PREREQUISITE (FK)	NUMBER(8,0)	NULL
CREATED_BY	VARCHAR2(30)	NOT NULL
CREATED_DATE	DATE	NOT NULL
MODIFIED_BY	VARCHAR2(30)	NOT NULL
MODIFIED_DATE	DATE	NOT NULL

CRSE CRSE FK

Figure 15.2 ■ The self-referencing relationship of the COURSE table.

tor. The following result visually displays the relationship of the courses that have the course number 310, Operating Systems, as their prerequisite.

```
310  Operating Systems
   130  Intro to Unix
      132  Basics of Unix Admin
         134  Advanced Unix Admin
            135  Unix Tips and Techniques
      330  Network Administration
   145  Internet Protocols
```

Reading from the outside in, the student first needs to take Operating Systems and then decide on either Intro to Unix or Internet Protocols. If the student completes the Intro to Unix course, he or she may choose between the Basics of Unix Admin class and the Network Administration class. If the student completes the Basics of Unix Admin, he or she may enroll in Advanced Unix Admin. After completion of this course, the student may enroll in Unix Tips and Techniques.

You can also travel the hierarchy in the reverse direction. If a student wants to take course number 134, Advanced Unix Administration, you can determine the required prerequisite courses until you reach the first course required.

In the business world, you may often encounter hierarchical relationships, such as the relationship between a manager and employees. Every employee may have at most one manager (parent) and to be a manager (parent) one must manage one or multiple employees (children). The root of the tree is the company's president; the president does not have a parent and, therefore, shows a NULL value in the parent column.

THE CONNECT BY CLAUSE AND THE PRIOR OPERATOR

To accomplish the hierarchical display, you need to construct a query with the CONNECT BY clause and the PRIOR operator. You identify the relationship between the parent and the child by placing the PRIOR operator before the parent column. To find the children of a parent, Oracle evaluates the PRIOR expression for the parent row. Rows for which the condition is true are the children of the parent. With the following CONNECT BY clause, you can see the order of courses and the sequence in which they need to be taken.

```
CONNECT BY PRIOR course_no = prerequisite
```

The COURSE_NO column is the parent and the PREREQUISITE column is the child. The PRIOR operator is placed in front of the parent column COURSE_NO. Depending on which column you prefix with the PRIOR operator, you can change the direction of the hierarchy.

The CONNECT BY condition can contain additional conditions to filter the rows and eliminate branches from the hierarchy tree, but cannot contain a subquery.

THE START WITH CLAUSE

The START WITH clause determines the root rows of the hierarchy. The records for which the START WITH clause is true are first selected. All children are retrieved from these records going forward. Without this clause, Oracle uses all rows in the table as root rows.

The syntax of the CONNECT BY clause in the SELECT statement is listed here:

```
[START WITH condition] CONNECT BY condition
```

The following query selects the parent course number 310, its child rows, and for each child its respective descendents. The LPAD function, together with the LEVEL pseudocolumn, accomplishes the indentation.

```
SELECT LPAD(' ', 3*(LEVEL-1)) ||course_no
       || ' ' ||description
  FROM course
 START WITH course_no = 310
CONNECT BY PRIOR course_no = prerequisite
LPAD('',3*(LEVEL-1))||COURSE_NO||''||DESCRIPTION
-------------------------------------------------
310  Operating Systems
   130  Intro to Unix
      132  Basics of Unix Admin
         134  Advanced Unix Admin
            135  Unix Tips and Techniques
      330  Network Administration
   145  Internet Protocols

7 rows selected.
```

UNDERSTANDING LEVEL AND LPAD

The pseudocolumn LEVEL returns the number 1 for the root of the hierarchy, 2 for the child, 3 for the grandchild, and so on. The LPAD function allows you to visualize the hierarchy by indenting it with spaces. The length of the padded characters is calculated with the LEVEL function.

In Chapter 9, "Complex Joins," you learned about self-joins. You may wonder how they compare to the hierarchical query. There are some fundamental differences: Only the hierarchical query with the CONNECT BY clause allows you to visually display the hierarchy; the self-join shows you the prerequisite in a vertical fashion only.

HIERARCHY PATH

You can show the path of a value from the root to the last node of the branch for any of the rows using the SYS_CONNECT_BY_PATH function. The following query example displays the hierarchy path and each course number is separated by a forward slash.

```
SELECT LPAD(' ', 1*(LEVEL-1))
       ||SYS_CONNECT_BY_PATH(course_no, '/') AS "Path" ,
       description
  FROM course
 START WITH course_no = 310
CONNECT BY PRIOR course_no = prerequisite
```

Path	DESCRIPTION
/310	Operating Systems
/310/130	Intro to Unix
/310/130/132	Basics of Unix Admin
/310/130/132/134	Advanced Unix Admin
/310/130/132/134/135	Unix Tips and Techniques
/310/130/330	Network Administration
/310/145	Internet Protocols

7 rows selected.

The SYS_CONNECT_BY_PATH function is only valid for a hierarchical query and its syntax is as follows:

```
SYS_CONNECT_BY_PATH (column, char)
```

PRUNING THE HIERARCHY TREE

A hierarchy can be described as a tree; if you want to remove specific rows from the result, you can use either the WHERE clause to eliminate individual rows or the CONNECT BY clause to eliminate branches.

The effect of the WHERE clause on the rest of the hierarchy is graphically depicted in Figure 15.3. It effectively eliminates individual rows from the hierarchy.

Only those rows that satisfy the CONDITION of the WHERE clause are included in the result. The following SQL statement shows the WHERE clause that eliminates the specific row. Notice that the child rows of the eliminated course are listed.

```
SELECT LPAD(' ', 3*(LEVEL-1)) ||course_no
       || ' ' ||description AS hierarchy
  FROM course
 WHERE course_no <> 132
```

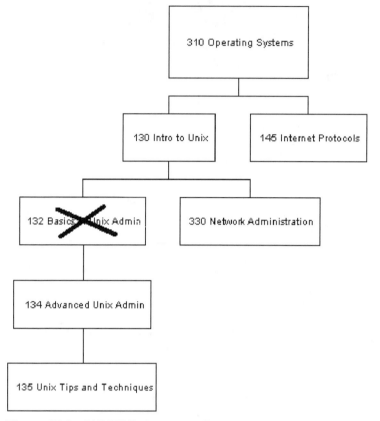

Figure 15.3 ■ WHERE clause to eliminate rows.

```
  START WITH course_no = 310
  CONNECT BY PRIOR course_no = prerequisite
  HIERARCHY
  --------------------------------------------
  310  Operating Systems
     130  Intro to Unix
           134  Advanced Unix Admin
                135  Unix Tips and Techniques
         330  Network Administration
     145  Internet Protocols

  6 rows selected.
```

Figure 15.4 displays the scenario when the condition is moved to the CONNECT BY clause causing the removal of a branch of the tree.

The condition is part of the CONNECT BY clause and when you examine the result you find that COURSE_NO 132 and its respective descendants are eliminated.

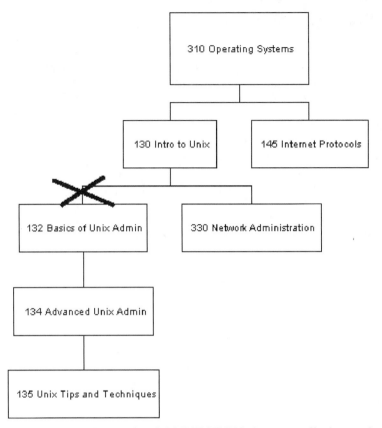

Figure 15.4 ▪ Use of the **CONNECT BY** clause to eliminate the entire branch.

```
SELECT LPAD(' ', 3*(LEVEL-1)) ||course_no
       || '   ' ||description AS hierarchy
  FROM course
 START WITH course_no = 310
CONNECT BY PRIOR course_no = prerequisite
   AND course_no <> '132'
HIERARCHY
----------------------------------
310  Operating Systems
   130  Intro to Unix
      330  Network Administration
   145  Internet Protocols

4 rows selected.
```

JOINING TABLES

Prior to Oracle *9i*, joins in hierarchical queries were not allowed. To achieve somewhat similar results, you had to write inline views or use custom-written PL/SQL functions to display any columns from related tables. The effect of a join in a hierarchical query is shown following; the query joins to the SECTION table to include the SECTION_ID column in the result.

The join uses the common COURSE_NO column. The root rows are determined via the START WITH clause. Here only those root rows with a COURSE_NO of 310 are selected as the root rows on which the hierarchy will be based. From the root row, the children, grandchildren, and any further descendants are determined.

As a result, you will notice a large number of rows because some courses have multiple sections. For example, COURSE_NO 132, Basics of Unix Admin, has two sections: they are SECTION_ID 139 and 138. For each section the hierarchy is listed with the respective sections. The individual child sections then show their child rows and so on.

```
SELECT LPAD(' ', 3*(LEVEL-1)) || c.course_no||' '||
       description AS hierarchy, s.section_id
  FROM course c, section s
 WHERE c.course_no = s.course_no
START WITH c.course_no = 310
CONNECT BY PRIOR c.course_no = prerequisite
HIERARCHY                                   SECTION_ID
------------------------------------------- ----------
310 Operating Systems                              103
   130 Intro to Unix                               107
      330 Network Administration                   104
      132 Basics of Unix Admin                     139
         134 Advanced Unix Admin                   110
            135 Unix Tips and Techniques           112
            135 Unix Tips and Techniques           115
            135 Unix Tips and Techniques           114
            135 Unix Tips and Techniques           113
         134 Advanced Unix Admin                   111
            135 Unix Tips and Techniques           112
            135 Unix Tips and Techniques           115
            135 Unix Tips and Techniques           114
            135 Unix Tips and Techniques           113
         134 Advanced Unix Admin                   140
            135 Unix Tips and Techniques           112
            135 Unix Tips and Techniques           115
            135 Unix Tips and Techniques           114
            135 Unix Tips and Techniques           113
      132 Basics of Unix Admin                     138
```

LAB 15.3

```
      134 Advanced Unix Admin              110
        135 Unix Tips and Techniques       112
        135 Unix Tips and Techniques       115
    ...
    139 rows selected.
```

SORTING

The following query lists all the courses that require COURSE_NO 20 as a prerequisite. Examine the order of the rows with COURSE_NO 100, 140, 142, 147, and 204 in the next result. These five rows share the same hierarchy level (and the same parent PREREQUISITE value). The order within a hierarchy level is rather arbitrary.

```
SELECT LEVEL, LPAD(' ', 2*(LEVEL-1)) || c.course_no
       AS course_no,
       description, prerequisite AS pre
  FROM course c
 START WITH c.course_no = 20
CONNECT BY PRIOR c.course_no = prerequisite
```

LEVEL	COURSE_NO	DESCRIPTION	PRE
1	20	Intro to Computers	
2	100	Hands-On Windows	20
2	140	Structured Analysis	20
3	25	Intro to Programming	140
4	240	Intro to the Basic Language	25
4	420	Database System Principles	25
5	144	Database Design	420
2	142	Project Management	20
2	147	GUI Programming	20
2	204	Intro to SQL	20
3	80	Structured Programming Techniq	204
4	120	Intro to Java Programming	80
...			
5	210	Oracle Tools	220

20 rows selected.

If you want to order the result by the DESCRIPTION column in alphabetical order, without destroying the hierarchical default order of the CONNECT BY clause, you use the ORDER SIBLINGS BY clause. It preserves the hierarchy and orders the siblings as specified in the ORDER BY clause.

```
SELECT LEVEL, LPAD(' ', 2*(LEVEL-1)) || c.course_no
       AS course_no,
       description, prerequisite AS pre
  FROM course c
```

```
START WITH c.course_no = 20
CONNECT BY PRIOR c.course_no = prerequisite
ORDER SIBLINGS BY description
```

LEVEL	COURSE_NO	DESCRIPTION	PRE
1	20	Intro to Computers	
2	147	GUI Programming	20
2	100	Hands-On Windows	20
2	204	Intro to SQL	20
3	80	Structured Programming Techniq	204
4	120	Intro to Java Programming	80
5	122	Intermediate Java Programming	120
6	124	Advanced Java Programming	122
6	125	JDeveloper	122

...

20 rows selected.

Any other ORDER BY clause has the effect of the DESCRIPTION column now taking precedence over the default ordering. For example, the result of ordering by the DESCRIPTION column without the SIBLINGS keyword results in this listing. As you notice, the hierarchy order is no longer intact.

```
SELECT LEVEL, LPAD(' ', 2*(LEVEL-1)) || c.course_no
       AS course_no,
       description, prerequisite AS pre
  FROM course c
 START WITH c.course_no = 20
CONNECT BY PRIOR c.course_no = prerequisite
 ORDER BY description
```

LEVEL	COURSE_NO	DESCRIPTION	PRE
6	124	Advanced Java Programming	122
8	450	DB Programming in Java	350
5	144	Database Design	420
...			
2	140	Structured Analysis	20
3	80	Structured Programming Techniq	204

20 rows selected.

Ordering by the LEVEL pseudocolumn results in all the parents being grouped together, then all children, all the grandchildren, and so on.

```
SELECT LEVEL, LPAD(' ', 2*(LEVEL-1)) || c.course_no
       AS course_no,
       description, prerequisite AS pre
  FROM course c
 START WITH c.course_no = 20
```

```
CONNECT BY PRIOR c.course_no = prerequisite
  ORDER BY LEVEL
```

LEVEL	COURSE_NO		DESCRIPTION	PRE
1	20		Intro to Computers	
2	100		Hands-On Windows	20
2	142		Project Management	20
2	147		GUI Programming	20
...				
8		450	DB Programming in Java	350

20 rows selected.

LAB 15.3 EXERCISES

15.3.1 RESTRICT THE RESULT SET IN HIERARCHICAL QUERIES

a) Show the course number and course description of courses with course number 310 as a prerequisite. Make these records the root of your hierarchical query. Display all the courses that can be taken after these root courses have been completed as child records. Include the LEVEL pseudocolumn as an additional column.

b) Execute the following query. What do you observe about the result?

```
SELECT LEVEL, LPAD(' ', 6*(LEVEL-1)) ||course_no
       || ' ' ||description hier
  FROM course
 START WITH course_no = 310
CONNECT BY PRIOR course_no = prerequisite
    AND LEVEL <= 3
```

c) What does the following START WITH clause accomplish?

```
SELECT LEVEL, LPAD(' ', 3*(LEVEL-1)) ||course_no
       || ' ' ||description hier
  FROM course
 START WITH prerequisite IS NULL
CONNECT BY PRIOR course_no = prerequisite
```

15.3.2 MOVE UP AND DOWN THE HIERARCHY TREE

a) Execute the following query, placing the PRIOR operator on the PREREQUISITE column. How does the result compare to the previously issued queries?

```
SELECT LEVEL, LPAD(' ', 6*(LEVEL-1)) ||course_no
        || ' ' ||description hierarchy
  FROM course
 START WITH course_no = 132
CONNECT BY course_no = PRIOR prerequisite
```

LAB
15.3

b) Write the SQL statement to display the following result.

```
LEVEL HIERARCHY
----- ------------------------------------
    5 310   Operating Systems
    4    130   Intro to Unix
    3       132   Basics of Unix Admin
    2          134   Advanced Unix Admin
    1             135   Unix Tips and Techniques

5 rows selected.
```

c) Insert the following record into the COURSE table and execute the query. What error message do you get and why? ROLLBACK the INSERT statement after you issue the SELECT statement.

```
INSERT INTO course
   (course_no, description, prerequisite,
    created_by, created_date, modified_by, modified_date)
VALUES
   (1000, 'Test', 1000,
    'TEST', SYSDATE, 'TEST', SYSDATE)

SELECT course_no, prerequisite
  FROM course
 START WITH course_no = 1000
CONNECT BY PRIOR course_no = prerequisite

ROLLBACK
```

LAB 15.3 EXERCISE ANSWERS

15.3.1 ANSWERS

a) Show the course number and course description of courses with course number 310 as a prerequisite. Make these records the root of your hierarchical query. Display all the courses that can be taken after these root courses have been completed as child records. Include the LEVEL pseudocolumn as an additional column.

Answer: The START WITH clause starts the hierarchy at the prerequisite course number 310. The PRIOR operator identifies the COURSE_NO as the parent record for which all the children are retrieved.

```
SELECT LEVEL, LPAD(' ', 6*(LEVEL-1)) ||course_no
          || ' ' ||description hierarchy
   FROM course
 START WITH prerequisite = 310
CONNECT BY PRIOR course_no = prerequisite
    LEVEL HIERARCHY
--------- -------------------------------------------------
        1 130    Intro to Unix
        2      132    Basics of Unix Admin
        3          134    Advanced Unix Admin
        4              135    Unix Tips and Techniques
        2      330    Network Administration
        1 145    Internet Protocols

6 rows selected.
```

The START WITH condition returns two records, one for the Intro to Unix class and the second for Internet Protocols. These are the root records from the hierarchy.

```
START WITH prerequisite = 310
```

The PRIOR operator in the CONNECT BY clause identifies the COURSE_NO as the parent. Child records are those records with the same course number in the PREREQUISITE column. The following two CONNECT BY clauses are equivalent.

```
CONNECT BY PRIOR course_no = prerequisite
```

and

```
CONNECT BY prerequisite = PRIOR course_no
```

If you use the PRIOR operator on the PREREQUISITE column, you will reverse the hierarchy and travel in the opposite direction. You will see examples of this shortly.

Lastly, you need to add the LEVEL function as a single column to display the hierarchy level of each record. If you also want to show the hierarchy visually with indents, the combination of LEVEL and LPAD does the trick. Recall the syntax of LPAD:

```
LPAD(char1, n [, char2])
```

The LPAD function uses the first argument as a literal. If char2 is not specified, by default it will be filled from the left with blanks up to the length shown as parameter n. The following SELECT clause indents each level with six additional spaces. Obviously, you may choose any number of spaces you like.

```
SELECT LEVEL, LPAD(' ', 6*(LEVEL-1)) ||course_no
             || ' ' ||description hierarchy
```

The length for the first level is 0 (Level 1 − 1 = 0); therefore, this level is not indented. The second level is indented by six spaces (6 * (2 − 1) = 6), the next by twelve (6 * (3 − 1) = 12), and so on. The resulting padded spaces are then concatenated with the course number and course description.

b) Execute the following query. What do you observe about the result?

```
SELECT LEVEL, LPAD(' ', 6*(LEVEL-1)) ||course_no
             || ' ' ||description hier
   FROM course
 START WITH course_no = 310
CONNECT BY PRIOR course_no = prerequisite
    AND LEVEL <= 3
```

Answer: The LEVEL pseudocolumn restricts the rows in the CONNECT BY clause to show only the first three levels of the hierarchy.

```
LEVEL HIER
--------- ------------------------------------------
    1 310   Operating Systems
    2       130   Intro to Unix
    3             132   Basics of Unix Admin
    3             330   Network Administration
    2       145   Internet Protocols

5 rows selected.
```

From the previous exercise you learned that the WHERE clause eliminates the particular row but not its children. You restrict child rows with conditions in the CONNECT BY clause. Here the PRIOR operator applies to the parent row and the other side of the equation applies to the child record. A qualifying child needs to have the correct parent and it must have a LEVEL number of 3 or less.

c) What does the following START WITH clause accomplish?

```
SELECT LEVEL, LPAD(' ', 3*(LEVEL-1)) ||course_no
       || ' ' ||description hier
  FROM course
 START WITH prerequisite IS NULL
CONNECT BY PRIOR course_no = prerequisite
```

Answer: This query's START WITH clause identifies all the root rows of the COURSE table. Those are the courses without any prerequisites.

While the START WITH is optional with hierarchical queries, you typically identify the root rows of the hierarchy. That's the starting point for all rows.

The next statement displays the result of a query without a START WITH clause.

```
SELECT LEVEL, LPAD(' ', 3*(LEVEL-1)) ||course_no
       || ' ' ||description hier
  FROM course
CONNECT BY PRIOR course_no = prerequisite
    LEVEL HIER
--------- --------------------------------------------
        1 10   DP Overview
        2    230   Intro to Internet
        ...
        1 310   Operating Systems
        2    130   Intro to Unix
        3       132   Basics of Unix Admin
        4          134   Advanced Unix Admin
        5          135  Unix Tips and Techniques
        3       330   Network Administration
        2    145   Internet Protocols
        1 330   Network Administration
        ...
        1 130   Intro to Unix
        2    132   Basics of Unix Admin
        3       134   Advanced Unix Admin
        4       135  Unix Tips and Techniques
        2    330   Network Administration
        1 132   Basics of Unix Admin
        2    134   Advanced Unix Admin
        3          135  Unix Tips and Techniques
        1 134   Advanced Unix Admin
        2    135  Unix Tips and Techniques
        1 135  Unix Tips and Techniques
        1 350   JDeveloper Lab
        ...
        1 430   JDeveloper Techniques
        1 450   DB Programming in Java

107 rows selected.
```

**LAB
15.3**

Though such a query is not very useful, it helps to understand why the records appear multiple times. When the START WITH clause is not specified, every record in the table is considered the root of the hierarchy. Therefore, for every record in the table, the hierarchy is displayed and the courses are repeated multiple times.

For example, the course number 135, Unix Tips and Techniques, is returned five times. From the root 310, Operating Systems, it is five levels deep in the hierarchy. It is repeated for the root course number 130, Intro to Unix, then for 132, Basics of Unix Admin, then for 134, Advanced Unix Admin, and lastly for itself.

LAB 15.3

15.3.2 ANSWERS

a) Execute the following query, placing the PRIOR operator on the PREREQUISITE column. How does the result compare to the previously issued queries?

```
SELECT LEVEL, LPAD(' ', 6*(LEVEL-1)) ||course_no
       || ' ' ||description hierarchy
  FROM course
 START WITH course_no = 132
CONNECT BY course_no = PRIOR prerequisite
```

Answer: The PREREQUISITE column becomes the parent and the COURSE_NO column becomes the child. This effectively reverses the direction of the hierarchy compared to the previously issued queries.

The result of the query shows all the prerequisites a student needs to take before enrolling in course number 132, Basics of Unix Administration.

```
LEVEL HIERARCHY
--------- -----------------------------------
        1 132  Basics of Unix Admin
        2      130  Intro to Unix
        3           310  Operating Systems

3 rows selected.
```

The student needs to take course number 310, Operating Systems, then course number 130, Intro to Unix, before taking the COURSE_NO 132, Basics of Unix Admin.

b) Write the SQL statement to display the following result.

```
LEVEL HIERARCHY
----- -----------------------------------
    5 310  Operating Systems
    4      130  Intro to Unix
    3           132  Basics of Unix Admin
```

2	134	Advanced Unix Admin
1	135	Unix Tips and Techniques

5 rows selected.

Answer: The rows show you the prerequisite courses for 135 as a root, thus resulting in the use of the START WITH clause. The ORDER BY clause orders the result by the hierarchy level.

```
SELECT LEVEL, LPAD(' ', 2*(5-LEVEL)) ||course_no
              || ' ' ||description hierarchy
  FROM course
  START WITH course_no = 135
CONNECT BY course_no = PRIOR prerequisite
  ORDER BY LEVEL DESC
```

Because the result shows you the prerequisites, the PRIOR operator needs to be applied on the PREREQUISITE column. PREREQUISITE becomes the parent column.

```
CONNECT BY course_no = PRIOR prerequisite
```

The ORDER BY clause orders the records by the hierarchy LEVEL in descending order. The indentation with the LPAD function is different from previous examples. You now subtract the number five from each level and multiply the result by two, resulting in the largest indentation for the root.

c) Insert the following record into the COURSE table and execute the query. What error message do you get and why? ROLLBACK the INSERT statement after you issue the SELECT statement.

```
INSERT INTO course
   (course_no, description, prerequisite,
    created_by, created_date, modified_by, modified_date)
VALUES
   (1000, 'Test', 1000,
    'TEST', SYSDATE, 'TEST', SYSDATE)

SELECT course_no, prerequisite
  FROM course
 START WITH course_no = 1000
CONNECT BY PRIOR course_no = prerequisite

ROLLBACK
```

Answer: The INSERT statement causes the course number 1000 to be its own parent and child. This results in a loop in the hierarchy and is reported by the hierarchical query.

```
SELECT course_no, prerequisite
  FROM course
```

```
START WITH course_no = 1000
CONNECT BY PRIOR course_no = prerequisite
```

ERROR:
ORA-01436: CONNECT BY loop in user data

no rows selected

This is quite an obvious loop; because it is in the same record, the row is both the parent and the child. Here is another example that can cause a loop:

```
COURSE_NO PREREQUISITE
--------- ------------
     2000         3000
     3000         2000
```

Loops can be buried deep within the hierarchy and are then more difficult to find.

LAB 15.3 SELF-REVIEW QUESTIONS

In order to test your progress, you should be able to answer the following questions.

1) The ORDER BY clause does not order the columns within a hierarchy, but does order the columns in the order stated in the ORDER BY clause unless the SIBLINGS keyword is used.

a) _____ True
b) _____ False

2) Which column is the parent in the SQL statement below?

```
CONNECT BY PRIOR emp = manager
```

a) _____ The EMP column
b) _____ The MANAGER column
c) _____ None of the above

3) The CONNECT BY condition cannot contain a subquery.

a) _____ True
b) _____ False

4) Joins were not allowed in hierarchical queries in Oracle versions prior to 9i.

a) _____ True
b) _____ False

Answers appear in Appendix A, Section 15.3.

C H A P T E R   1 5

TEST YOUR THINKING

The projects in this section are meant to have you utilize all of the skills that you have acquired throughout this chapter. The answers to these projects can be found at the companion Web site to this book, located at: *http://www.phptr.com/rischert*.

Visit the Web site periodically to share and discuss your answers.

1) Write the question for the following query and answer.

```
SELECT COUNT(DECODE(SIGN(total_capacity-20),
            -1, 1, 0, 1)) "<=20",
       COUNT(DECODE(SIGN(total_capacity-21),
            0, 1, -1, NULL,
            DECODE(SIGN(total_capacity-30), -1, 1)))
            "21-30",
       COUNT(DECODE(SIGN(total_capacity-30), 1, 1)) "31+"
  FROM (SELECT SUM(capacity) total_capacity, course_no
          FROM SECTION
         GROUP BY COURSE_NO)

     <=20      21-30        31+
 --------- --------- ---------
        2        10         16

1 row selected.
```

2) Determine the top three zip codes where most of the students live. Use an analytical function.

3) Explain the result of the following query.

```
SELECT 'Q'||TO_CHAR(start_date_time, 'Q') qtr,
       TO_CHAR(start_date_time, 'DY') day, COUNT(*),
       DENSE_RANK() OVER (
          PARTITION BY 'Q'||TO_CHAR(start_date_time, 'Q')
          ORDER BY COUNT(*) DESC) rank_qtr,
       DENSE_RANK() OVER (ORDER BY COUNT(*) DESC) rank_all
  FROM enrollment e, section s
 WHERE s.section_id = e.section_id
 GROUP BY 'Q'||TO_CHAR(start_date_time, 'Q'),
```

```
              TO_CHAR(start_date_time, 'DY')
     ORDER BY 1
     QT DAY     COUNT(*)     RANK_QTR     RANK_ALL
     -- ---    ----------   ----------   ----------
     Q2 FRI          42            1            1
     Q2 SAT          36            2            2
     Q2 WED          30            3            3
     Q2 THU          28            4            5
     Q2 SUN          15            5            7
     Q2 MON          13            6            8
     Q2 TUE          13            6            8
     Q3 WED          29            1            4
     Q3 SAT          20            2            6

     9 rows selected.
```

4) Name other hierarchical relationships you are familiar with.

CHAPTER 16

SQL OPTIMIZATION

Throughout this book you find alternate SQL statements for many solutions. This chapter focuses on determining the most effective SQL statement to efficiently and quickly return results. You gain an overview of the workings of the Oracle Optimizer and an understanding of SQL performance tuning techniques. The list of tuning suggestions in this chapter is by no means comprehensive, but merely a starting point. After you understand how to read the execution steps of SQL statements, you learn to focus on tuning problem areas with alternate SQL statements.

L A B   1 6 . 1

THE ORACLE OPTIMIZER AND WRITING EFFECTIVE SQL STATEMENTS

LAB OBJECTIVES

After this lab, you will be able to:

✔ Gather Statistics for Tables and Indexes
✔ Read the Execution plan
✔ Understand Join Operations and Alternate SQL Statements

Poor performance of a system is often caused by one or a combination of problems: poor database design, improper tuning of the Oracle server, and poorly written SQL statements. A well-thought-out database design has the greatest positive impact on database performance, followed by effectively written SQL statements, and then by tuning the Oracle server itself. This chapter focuses on writing effective SQL statements only.

The Oracle database server provides you with a number of tools that help you improve the efficiency of SQL statements. This chapter focuses on the use of the SQL*Plus AUTOTRACE command. This utility provides you with the *execution plan*, which is a sequence of the steps that Oracle carries out to perform a specific SQL command. You can change the execution plan by choosing an alternate SQL statement or by adding a *hint*, which is a directive to execute the statement differently. Using hints, you can force the use of a specific index, change the join order, or change join method. Before learning more about the execution plan and the query tuning tools, you must understand the basics of how a SQL statement is evaluated by the Oracle database server.

SQL STATEMENT PROCESSING

Before a SQL statement returns a result set, the server performs a number of operations that are completely transparent to the user. The first step is the creation of a cursor, an area in memory where Oracle stores the SQL statement and all associated information.

Next, Oracle parses the SQL statement. This entails checking the syntax for validity, checking if all the column and table names exist, and determining if the user has permission to access these tables and columns. Part of the parsing operation is also the determination of the execution plan.

Because parsing requires time and resources, there are ways to eliminate parsing when repeatedly executing similar statements. Oracle maintains a cache of recently executed SQL statements and their respective execution plan so if an identical statement has been used previously it does not need to be re-parsed. This is accomplished by using bind variables, which are placeholders for values. If bind variables are used in a statement the variable names must be associated with an actual value at execution time. More on bind variables is discussed shortly.

If bind variables are used they are associated with the appropriate values. Next the SQL statement is executed. If the SQL statement is a query, the result needs to be fetched. Once all the rows are fetched, the cursor is closed. Figure 16.1 graphically shows an overview of these various steps.

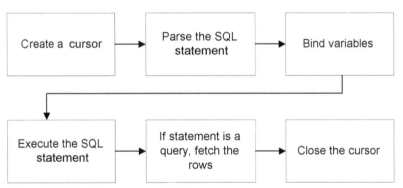

Figure 16.1 ■ Overview of SQL statement processing steps.

THE OPTIMIZER

The Oracle optimizer is part of the Oracle software; it examines each SQL statement and chooses the best execution plan for it. The execution plan consists of a sequence of steps that are necessary to execute your SQL statement. Oracle has two optimizers: the rule-based optimizer and the cost-based optimizer.

The rule-based optimizer is the optimizer employed by Oracle since its beginnings. It determines the execution plan through a number of rigid rules. The cost-based optimizer takes statistics into consideration and it takes into account the number of rows in the table and the selectivity of columns, among other factors, to determine the best execution path.

THE RULE-BASED OPTIMIZER

Each rule has a ranking and the condition with the highest rank is the first executed because the optimizer considers it more efficient. Table 16.1 lists the 15-step ranking employed by the rule-based optimizer. For example, if a WHERE clause condition contains a column with a unique index as well as a nonindexed column, the optimizer creates a plan to process the condition with the unique index first because it has a higher ranking than accessing the row by a full table scan. The rule-based optimizer does not take into consideration that perhaps the query may potentially retrieve all the rows of the table and that a full table scan may be more efficient than access through the index. (If you retrieve all the rows through the use of an index, it takes longer, because both the index and the table needs to be read.)

THE COST-BASED OPTIMIZER

The cost-based optimizer takes statistics into consideration to choose the execution plan. These statistics are gathered through the ANALYZE command or the

Table 16.1 ■ Rule-Based Optimizer Ranking

Rank	Access Path
1	Single row by ROWID
2	Single row by cluster join
3	Single row by hash cluster key with unique or primary key
4	Single row by unique or primary key
5	Cluster join
6	Hash cluster key
7	Indexed cluster key
8	Composite index (consists of more than one column)
9	Single column index
10	Bounded range search on an indexed column (i.e. >= AND <=)
11	Unbounded range search on indexed column (i.e. >=)
12	Sort-merge join
13	MIN or MAX function on an indexed column
14	ORDER BY clause on indexed column
15	Full-table scan

DBMS_STATS procedure. Gathering the statistics lets the optimizer know how many rows are in each table or how many distinct values there are in each column (also known as the selectivity of a column). You can even find out about the distribution of the individual values by generating a *histogram,* which is discussed shortly. These statistics are stored in the data dictionary and must be updated frequently if the distribution or volume of data changes significantly.

Oracle advises that all SQL statements be written using the cost-based optimizer because the rule-based optimizer may not be supported in future releases.

 Oracle continually enhances the optimizer with each subsequent version. Nevertheless you always want to test your SQL statement carefully to ensure that there is no adverse impact on the performance when you upgrade the Oracle software.

CHOOSING THE OPTIMIZER

The choice of optimizer is determined in one of three ways: on the database instance level in the database initialization file (init.ora), on the session level with an ALTER SESSION SET OPTIMIZER_GOAL command, or with a hint that overrides the default optimizer.

You can set the optimizer to CHOOSE mode, causing Oracle to select the cost-based optimizer if statistics are collected for any of the tables involved in the SQL statement; otherwise, the rule-based optimizer is used. If you want to use only the cost-based optimizer, you can decide whether you want to optimize for best overall throughput (ALL_ROWS goal), which is most useful for reporting and batch processing, or for quickly retrieving the first n rows (FIRST_ROWS goal) (see Table 16.2).

Table 16.2 ■ Optimizer Goal

Optimizer Goal	Explanation
RULE	This setting uses the rule-based optimizer.
CHOOSE	If any tables have statistics, the cost-based optimizer is chosen; otherwise, it's the rule-based optimizer.
ALL_ROWS	This always uses the cost-based optimizer with the goal of best performance for retrieving all the rows. This is the default behavior of the cost-based optimizer.
FIRST_ROWS(n)	This setting uses the cost-based optimizer and has the goal of retrieving the first n row(s) first. This is best for interactive programs that need to display a few initial rows of data on a screen.

GATHERING STATISTICS FOR THE COST-BASED OPTIMIZER

You can gather statistics with either the ANALYZE command or with the DBMS_STATS package. These statistics are then stored in a number of data dictionary tables, ALL_TABLES, ALL_TAB_COL_STATISTICS, ALL_TAB_COLUMNS, and ALL_INDEXES to name a few.

Statistics must be gathered periodically, particularly if the number of records in the table and/or the distribution of the values in the columns changes significantly. Query the data dictionary news USER_TABLES and USER_INDEXES and check the LAST_ANALYZED column for the last date statistics were collected.

EXACT STATISTICS OR SAMPLE SIZE

When you gather statistics you can either compute them exactly or choose to estimate them by choosing a specific sample size. Oracle picks a random data sample or you can pick your own sampling percentage (i.e., 20 percent of all the data, 5,000 rows). Because calculating exact statistics may take a long time on very large tables, it is sometimes more practical to estimate sufficiently accurate statistics. For large tables, a sampling percentage size of 10 to 25 percent is often fine.

THE ANALYZE COMMAND

The ANALYZE command gathers statistics for either a table or an index. If you choose the TABLE option of the syntax, it automatically gathers both table and index statistics. You use the INDEX option if you create a new index and you need to determine statistics for the index only. The simplified syntax of the command is as follows:

```
ANALYZE {TABLE tablename|INDEX indexname}
  {COMPUTE STATISTICS|
   ESTIMATE STATISTICS [SAMPLE integer {ROWS|PERCENT}]|
   DELETE STATISTICS}
```

The next statement shows the use of the ANALYZE TABLE command; it computes the exact statistics for the COURSE table together with any associated indexes.

```
ANALYZE TABLE course COMPUTE STATISTICS
Table analyzed.
```

(The DELETE option of the ANALYZE table command deletes the statistics if your optimizer mode is set to CHOOSE and you want to switch back to the rule-based optimizer. The ANALYZE command has additional syntax options to validate table structures and to identify rows that migrated from one data block to another due to insufficient space in a data block. A database administrator typically uses these options.)

THE DBMS_STATS PACKAGE

The DBMS_STATS package is an Oracle-supplied PL/SQL package that generates and manages statistics for use by the cost-based optimizer; a few of the many procedures in the package to gather statistics are listed in Table 16.3.

Table 16.3 ■ DBMS_STATS Procedures That Gather Statistics

Procedure	Purpose
GATHER_TABLE_STATS	Gather table, column, and index statistics
GATHER_INDEX_STATS	Gather index statistics
GATHER_SCHEMA_STATS	Gather statistics for all objects in a schema
GATHER_DATABASE_STATS	Gather statistics for all objects in a database instance
GATHER_SYSTEM_STATS	Gathers system statistics about the CPU and I/O

Following are some examples on how you execute the procedures to collect statistics. The next statement gathers exact statistics for the COURSE table located in the STUDENT schema.

```
EXEC DBMS_STATS.GATHER_TABLE_STATS(ownname=>'STUDENT',
                                   tabname=>'COURSE');
PL/SQL procedure successfully completed.
```

The two parameters OWNNAME for the schema name and the TABNAME for the table name are required. The example uses the named notation syntax (ownname=>) to identify each parameter with the appropriate value. You do not need to list the parameter names OWNNAME and TABLENAME if you supply the PL/SQL procedure the parameter values in the order in which the parameters are defined in the package.

```
EXEC DBMS_STATS.GATHER_TABLE_STATS('STUDENT', 'COURSE');
```

The procedure has additional parameters (e.g., ESTIMATE_PERCENT) that let you specify the sample percentage. If you don't specify the additional parameters, default values are assigned. In the previous examples the ESTIMATE_PERCENT is not specified so the default is to compute the exact statistics.

If the different parameters do not fit on one line or if you want to separate each parameter, write the procedure call as follows:

```
BEGIN
   DBMS_STATS.GATHER_TABLE_STATS(
      ownname=>'STUDENT',
```

```
           tabname=>'COURSE');
END;
/
```

To find out the different parameter names of a procedure, you issue the DESC-RIBE command in SQL*Plus. It lists all the individual procedures available and their respective parameters. The In/Out column indicates if the procedure requires an input parameter or returns an output value. You can find out more information about each parameter and the respective default values in the *Oracle 9i Supplied PL/SQL Packages and Types References* manual.

```
SQL> DESCR DBMS_STATS
PROCEDURE ALTER_DATABASE_TAB_MONITORING
 Argument Name                 Type           In/Out Default?
 ---------------------------  ------------   ------  --------
 MONITORING                   BOOLEAN         IN      DEFAULT
 SYSOBJS                      BOOLEAN         IN      DEFAULT
 ...
PROCEDURE GATHER_TABLE_STATS
 Argument Name                 Type           In/Out Default?
 ---------------------------  ------------   ------  --------
 OWNNAME                      VARCHAR2        IN
 TABNAME                      VARCHAR2        IN
 PARTNAME                     VARCHAR2        IN      DEFAULT
 ESTIMATE_PERCENT             NUMBER          IN      DEFAULT
 BLOCK_SAMPLE                 BOOLEAN         IN      DEFAULT
 METHOD_OPT                   VARCHAR2        IN      DEFAULT
 DEGREE                       NUMBER          IN      DEFAULT
 GRANULARITY                  VARCHAR2        IN      DEFAULT
 CASCADE                      BOOLEAN         IN      DEFAULT
 ...
```

You must also collect statistics not only for tables but also for the indexes, otherwise the optimizer makes poor choices. The ANALYZE TABLE command by default gathers the index statistics. The DBMS_STATS package does perform this by default. You must explicitly specify that you also want to gather index statistics by setting the CASCADE option to True. The default if FALSE.

```
BEGIN
  DBMS_STATS.GATHER_TABLE_STATS(
    ownname=>'STUDENT',
    tabname=>'COURSE',
    cascade=>TRUE);
END;
/
```

The next procedure gathers statistics for the entire STUDENT schema including the indexes and uses AUTO_SAMPLE_SIZE as a parameter value to let Oracle automatically determine the best sample size.

```
BEGIN
  DBMS_STATS.GATHER_SCHEMA_STATS(
    ownname=>'STUDENT',
    cascade=>TRUE);
    estimate_percent=>DBMS_STATS.AUTO_SAMPLE_SIZE);
END;
/
```

MANAGING STATISTICS

Besides gathering statistics, the DBMS_STATS package includes procedures to modify, view, export, import, and delete statistics. For example, you can save the current statistics before gathering new statistics so you can restore them should the performance of the system be adversely affected. The statistics can also be copied from one database instance to another. This is useful if you want to test how your SQL statements behave in a different environment (e.g., test vs. production). Table 16.4 shows a few of the DBMS_STATS procedures that manage statistics for an individual table.

Gathering statistics is necessary to ensure the statistics accurately reflect the distribution of data over time. Periodic gathering of statistics can be accomplished by executing SQL scripts that are scheduled using the cron job facility in Unix or "at" service in Windows. Alternatively, you can schedule the execution of the package with Oracle's built-in DBMS_JOB package.

Instead of gathering statistics for all the objects, you can gather statistics only when the statistics become stale. This is the case when more then 10 percent of the rows change due to INSERT, UPDATE, or DELETE operations. You identify stale statistics by monitoring the data modifications in a table. This is accomplished with the ALTER TABLE statement. For example, this statement monitors the COURSE table.

```
ALTER TABLE course MONITORING
```

The modifications are recorded on the data dictionary view USER_TAB_ MODIFICATIONS. Alternatively, you can use the DBMS_STATS procedures ALTER_

Table 16.4 ■ Selected DBMS_STATS Procedures

Procedure	Purpose
DELETE_TABLE_STATS	Deletes statistics for an individual table
CREATE_STAT_TABLE	Creates a table to hold statistics for import/export
EXPORT_TABLE_STATS	Exports statistics about an individual table so it may be used for a later import
IMPORT_TABLE_STATS	Imports table statistics into the data dictionary

SCHEMA_TAB_MONITORING or ALTER_DATABASE_TAB_MONITORING to accomplish the same.

```
BEGIN
  DBMS_STATS.ALTER_SCHEMA_TAB_MONITORING(
    ownname=>'STUDENT', monitoring=>TRUE);
END;
/
```

Instead of gathering the statistics for all tables, you can only gather statistics for stale tables. For example, you can use the GATHER STALE option of the GATHER_SCHEMA_STATS procedure.

```
BEGIN
  DBMS_STATS.GATHER_SCHEMA_STATS(
    ownname=>'STUDENT', cascade=>TRUE,
    options=>'GATHER STALE');
END;
/
```

TIMING THE EXECUTION OF A STATEMENT

If a SQL statement does not perform well, you need a baseline to compare the execution time of other alternative SQL statements. This is accomplished simply in SQL*Plus by executing the SQL*Plus command SET TIMING ON. This command returns the execution time.

Note that repeated executions of the same or similar statements take less time than the initial execution because the data no longer needs to be retrieved from disk since it is cached in memory. Just because you made a minor change to the statement doesn't mean the statement is actually running faster.

```
SQL> SET TIMING ON
SQL> SELECT COUNT(*)
       FROM student
  COUNT(*)
---------
       268

1 row selected.
Elapsed: 00:00:00.30
```

Tuning a SQL statement is effective only if your SQL statement executes against realistic data volumes and column distributions similar to what is expected in a production environment. For instance, the execution plan for a join involving two tables varies if the data in the test environment is 100 rows, but in production it is 50,000 rows. The Oracle optimizer also evolves with each subsequent version of the Oracle database so having a test environment that closely resembles your production environment greatly aids in this process.

THE EXECUTION PLAN

The optimizer creates the execution plan also referred to as the *explain plan*. It shows the individual steps the Oracle database executes to process a statement. You read the execution plan from the inside out, meaning the most indented step is performed first. If two steps have the same level of indentation, the step listed first is the first executed. Following is a SQL statement and its execution plan. You learn how to obtain such an output shortly.

```
SELECT student_id, last_name
  FROM student
 WHERE student_id = 123
Execution Plan
----------------------------------------------------------
0 SELECT STATEMENT Optimizer=CHOOSE
   (Cost=2 Card=1 Bytes=12)
1    0   TABLE ACCESS (BY INDEX ROWID) OF 'STUDENT'
           (Cost=2 Card=1 Bytes=12)
2    1      INDEX (UNIQUE SCAN) OF 'STU_PK' (UNIQUE)
              (Cost=1 Card=1)
```

The first step performed is a lookup of the value 123 in the index STU_PK. Using the index entry, the row is retrieved from the STUDENT table via the ROWID.

Notice the optimizer is in CHOOSE mode—that is, the Optimizer chooses between the rule-based or cost-based optimizer based on whether any of the tables involved are analyzed. In this example, the cost-based optimizer is used because you see in parentheses the cost for each step of the statement. This cost helps you determine how involved each step is so you can focus on tuning the steps with the highest cost. The cost is determined using estimated amounts of memory, input/output, and CPU time required to execute the statement. The card parameter shows the cardinality of the step (i.e., how many rows the optimizer expects to process at this step). Lastly, the bytes parameter shows the size in bytes expected for the step. The numbers on the far left side indicate the parent step number and the number of each individual step.

USING AUTOTRACE

There are various ways to obtain an execution plan. The simplest way is to use the AUTOTRACE command in SQL*Plus. Other popular ways to obtain an execution plan include the EXPLAIN PLAN FOR command and the Oracle TKPROF utility. A plan is also easily obtained by using one of the popular third-party tools listed in Appendix H, "Resources." The use of the TKPROF utility is discussed in the *Oracle DBA Interactive Workbook* by Melanie Caffrey and Douglas Scherer and allows for a very accurate assessment of the resources involved in processing the statement.

To enable the AUTOTRACE facility you need to have access to the PLUSTRACE role. If the role is not already enabled, run the following script in SQL*Plus when logged in as a DBA (such as SYSTEM) with the SYSDBA privilege. The script is usually found in the sqlplus\admin directory; the location varies depending on the operating system, Oracle version, and individual installation. In the following example, the script is located on a Windows machine in the directory e:\oracle\ora92\sqlplus\admin.

```
SQL> CONN / AS SYSDBA
Connected.
SQL> @e:\oracle\ora92\sqlplus\admin\plustrce.sql
```

After the script executes successfully, grant the PLUSTRACE role to PUBLIC. This makes the role accessible to everyone in the database, no matter who logs in.

```
GRANT plustrace TO PUBLIC
Grant succeeded.
```

Then, log back into the STUDENT schema.

```
CONN student/learn
Connected.
```

You also need a table called the PLAN_TABLE in your schema. The script to create the table is named utlxplan.sql and is usually found in the %ORACLE_HOME%\rdbms\admin directory. In this example, the file is located on a Windows machine in the directory e:\oracle\ora92\rdbms\admin. Again, run the file. In SQL*Plus you execute it as follows:

```
@e:\oracle\ora92\rdbms\admin\utlxplan.sql
```

Now you can enable the AUTOTRACE at the SQL*Plus prompt with the following command. This command does not show the result set of the SQL statement, only the execution plan.

```
SET AUTOTRACE TRACE EXPLAIN
```

Alternatively, to include the result set, execute the following command:

```
SET AUTOT ON
```

Each subsequently issued SQL statement shows the result plus additional summary statistics.

```
SELECT student_id, last_name
  FROM student
 WHERE student_id = 123
STUDENT_ID LAST_NAME
---------- --------------------------
       123 Radicola


1 row selected.


Execution Plan
-----------------------------------------------------------
0 SELECT STATEMENT Optimizer=CHOOSE
  (Cost=2 Card=1 Bytes=12)
1     0   TABLE ACCESS (BY INDEX ROWID) OF 'STUDENT'
          (Cost=2 Card=1 Bytes=12)
2     1     INDEX (UNIQUE SCAN) OF 'STU_PK' (UNIQUE)
            (Cost=1 Card=1)


Statistics
-----------------------------------------------------------
        272  recursive calls
          1  db block gets
         90  consistent gets
          7  physical reads
          0  redo size
        440  bytes sent via SQL*Net to client
        430  bytes received via SQL*Net from client
          4  SQL*Net roundtrips to/from client
          4  sorts (memory)
          0  sorts (disk)
          1  rows processed
```

To turn autotrace off, issue this command:

```
SET AUTOT OFF
```

HINTS

If you are not satisfied with the optimizer's plan, you can change it by using hints. Hints are directives to the optimizer. For example, you can ask to use a particular index or to choose a specific join order. Because you know the distribution of the data best, sometimes you can come up with a better execution plan by overriding the default plan with specific hints. In certain instances this may result in a better plan. For example, if you know that a particular index is more selective for certain queries, you can ask the optimizer to use this index instead.

Following are examples of useful hints. The hint is always enclosed by either a multiline comment with a plus sign (/*+ */) or a single line comment with a plus sign (--+).

The following statement uses an index hint to scan the STU_ZIP_FK_I index on the STUDENT table. This index is actually a poorer choice than the STU_PK index, but the example demonstrates how you can override the optimizer's default plan.

```
SELECT /*+ INDEX (student stu_zip_fk_i) */ student_id,
       last_name
  FROM student
 WHERE student_id = 123
Execution Plan
----------------------------------------------------------
0   SELECT STATEMENT Optimizer=CHOOSE
    (Cost=826 Card=6 Bytes=162)
1     0   TABLE ACCESS (BY INDEX ROWID) OF 'STUDENT'
          (Cost=826 Card=6 Bytes=162)
2     1     INDEX (FULL SCAN) OF 'STU_ZIP_FK_I'
            (NON-UNIQUE) (Cost=26 Card=6)
```

In Table 16.5 you see some of the frequently used hints. You will use some of them in the exercises throughout this lab.

Table 16.5 ■ Popular Hints

Hint	Purpose
FIRST_ROWS	Return the first row as quickly as possible.
ALL_ROWS	Return all rows as quickly as possible.
RULE	Unlike any of the other hints, this hint uses the rule-based optimizer.
CHOOSE	If one of the tables has statistics, the cost-based optimizer with the ALL_ROWS approach is used; otherwise, it's the rule-based optimizer.
INDEX(tablename indexname)	Use the specified index. If an alias is used in the FROM clause of the query, be sure to list the alias instead of the tablename.
ORDERED	Joins the tables as listed in the FROM clause of the query.
LEADING(tablename)	The specified table is the first table in the join order.
USE_MERGE(tablename)	Use the sort-merge join method to join tables.
USE_HASH(tablename)	Use the hash join method to join tables.
USE_NL(tablename)	Use the nested loop join method; the specified table name is the inner table.

INCORRECTLY SPECIFYING HINTS

If you incorrectly specify the hint, the optimizer ignores it and you are left to wonder why the hint does not work. Here is an example of the index hint specified incorrectly.

```
SELECT /*+ INDEX (student stu_zip_fk_i) */ student_id,
       last_name
  FROM student s
 WHERE student_id = 123
Execution Plan
-------------------------------------------------------
0   SELECT STATEMENT Optimizer=CHOOSE
    (Cost=2 Card=1 Bytes=12)
1      0   TABLE ACCESS (BY INDEX ROWID) OF 'STUDENT'
           (Cost=2 Card=1 Bytes=12)
2      1      INDEX (UNIQUE SCAN) OF 'STU_PK' (UNIQUE)
              (Cost=1 Card=1)
```

Instead of the table name STUDENT, the table alias s should be used because an alias is used in the FROM clause of the statement. This incorrect hint causes the optimizer to use a different index.

Your hint may also be ignored if you use the FIRST_ROWS hint in a query that contains a GROUP BY clause, aggregate function, set operator, the DISTINCT key word, or an ORDER BY clause (if not supported by an index). All these Oracle keywords require that the result or sort is first determined based on all the rows before returning the first row.

Only the cost-based optimizer understands hints. If you want the cost-based optimizer to act like the rule-based optimizer, you can add the RULE hint.

JOIN TYPES

Determining the type of join and the join order of tables has a significant impact on how efficiently your SQL statement executes. Oracle chooses one of four types of join operations: Nested Loop Join, Sort-Merge Join, Hash Join, or Cluster Join. This lab discusses only the first three, which are the most popular ones.

NESTED LOOP JOIN

With the nested loop join, the optimizer picks a driving table that is the first table in the join chain. In this example, the driving table is the STUDENT table. A full table scan is executed on the driving table and for each row in the STUDENT table, the primary key index of the ENROLLMENT table is probed to see if the WHERE clause condition is satisfied. If so, the row is returned in the result set. This probing is repeated until all the rows of the driving table, in this case the STUDENT table, are tested.

The execution plan of a nested loop join looks like the following.

```
SELECT /*+ RULE */ *
  FROM enrollment e, student s
 WHERE s.student_id = e.student_id
Execution Plan
----------------------------------------------------------
0        SELECT STATEMENT Optimizer=HINT: RULE
1    0     NESTED LOOPS
2    1       TABLE ACCESS (FULL) OF 'STUDENT'
3    1       TABLE ACCESS (BY INDEX ROWID) OF 'ENROLLMENT'
4    3         INDEX (RANGE SCAN) OF 'ENR_PK' (UNIQUE)
```

Note that the execution plan for a nested loop is read differently from the other execution plans because it contains a loop. The access to the ENR_PK index, the most indented row, is not read first, but rather is probed for every row of the driving STUDENT table.

The nested loop join is typically the fastest join when the goal is to retrieve the first row as quickly as possible. It is also the best join when you access approximately 1 to 10 percent of the total rows from the tables involved. This percentage varies depending on the total number of rows returned, various parameters in your Oracle initialization file (init.ora), and the Oracle version. But it gives you a general idea of when this join is useful.

The selection of the driving table is essential to good performance of the nested loop join. Making the driving table return the least number of rows is critical for probing fewer records in subsequent joins to other tables. Therefore, eliminate as many rows as possible from the driving table.

You will also notice on the execution plan that no cardinality and cost values are returned. This is because in this statement a rule hint was used that caused a rule-based optimizer to be used and therefore such values are missing from the execution plan.

SORT-MERGE JOIN

To perform this join, a full table scan is executed on the ENROLLMENT table, the result is sorted by the joining column, and then the STUDENT table is scanned and sorted. The two results are then merged and the matching rows are returned for output. The first row is returned only after all the records from both tables are processed. This join is typically used when the majority of the rows are retrieved, when no indexes exist on the table to support the join condition, or when a USE_MERGE hint is specified.

```
SELECT /*+ USE_MERGE (e, s)*/ *
  FROM enrollment e, student s
```

```
 WHERE s.student_id = e.student_id
Execution Plan
---------------------------------------------------------
0   SELECT STATEMENT Optimizer=CHOOSE
    (Cost=24 Card=226 Bytes=38420)
1    0   MERGE JOIN (Cost=24 Card=226 Bytes=37968)
2    1     SORT (JOIN) (Cost=9 Card=226 Bytes=11074)
3    2       TABLE ACCESS (FULL) OF 'ENROLLMENT'
                (Cost=2 Card=226 Bytes=11074)
4    1     SORT (JOIN) (Cost=16 Card=268 Bytes=31892)
5    4       TABLE ACCESS (FULL) OF 'STUDENT'
                (Cost=3 Card=268 Bytes=31892)
```

HASH JOIN

The hash join is available only in the cost-based optimizer. Oracle performs a full table scan on each of the tables and splits each into many partitions in memory. Oracle then builds a hash table from one of these partitions and probes it against the partition of the other table. The hash join typically out-performs the sort-merge join.

```
SELECT /*+ ALL_ROWS */ *
   FROM enrollment e, student s
  WHERE s.student_id = e.student_id
Execution Plan
---------------------------------------------------------
0   SELECT STATEMENT Optimizer=HINT: ALL_ROWS
    (Cost=8 Card=226 Bytes=37968)
1    0   HASH JOIN (Cost=8 Card=226 Bytes=37968)
2    1     TABLE ACCESS (FULL) OF 'ENROLLMENT'
                (Cost=2 Card=226 Bytes=11074)
3    1     TABLE ACCESS (FULL) OF 'STUDENT'
                (Cost=3 Card=268 Bytes=31892)
```

BIND VARIABLES AND THE OPTIMIZER

If you repeatedly execute the same statement with only slightly different values in the WHERE clause you can eliminate the parsing with the use of bind variables also referred to as *host variables*. For example, if the users of your program repeatedly issue this query, but substitute a different phone number each time, you should consider substituting the literal value with a bind variable.

```
SELECT last_name, first_name
   FROM student
  WHERE phone = '614-555-5555'
```

The use of the bind variable eliminates the parsing of the SQL statement. This overhead is significant when you have many users on a system. Bind variables are prefixed with a colon. The new statement with a bind variable looks like this:

```
SELECT last_name, first_name
  FROM student
 WHERE phone = :phone_no
```

The :PHONE_NO bind variable gets a new value assigned whenever the user issues the statement. The statement with the bind variable is already parsed and the execution plan is determined and therefore ready for execution (see Figure 16.1).

You typically use bind variables in application programs where you expect to issue the same statement over and over again. The next example illustrates the use of a bind variable in SQL*Plus. The VARIABLE command creates a bind variable. The next PL/SQL block assigns the variable a value, which is 914-555-5555.

```
SQL> VARIABLE phone_no VARCHAR2(20)
SQL> BEGIN
  2     :phone_no :='914-555-5555';
  3  END;
  4  .
SQL> /
```

PL/SQL procedure successfully completed.

The subsequent execution of the SQL statement using the bind variable associates the assigned value with the variable and returns the correct row.

```
SQL> SELECT last_name, first_name
  2    FROM student
  3   WHERE phone = :phone_no
  4  /
```

LAST_NAME	FIRST_NAME
Mwangi	Paula

1 row selected.

Bind variables are advantageous in applications where the same statement is executed repeatedly. At the first invocation of the statement with the bind variables, the optimizer looks at the selectivity of the value and determines the best possible execution plan. In repeated executions of the statement, no peeking at the value takes place. This assumes that every value associated with the bind variable has the same selectivity.

In a scenario where the statement is executed with a literal value instead, the next statement's literal values may be more selective and result in a more favorable execution plan.

In general, you should use bind variable if the same statements are executed frequently and the difference in the selectivity between the different values is minimal. This is typically the case in transaction processing oriented environments and the use of bind variable results in time and resource savings due to the elimination of the parsing step.

This is in contrast to data warehousing environments where the queries are long running or of an ad-hoc nature and therefore executed infrequently. Therefore the use of literals is preferred because the optimizer can make a better determination about the most efficient execution plan. Also, the parsing time is negligible in comparison to the execution time.

HISTOGRAMS

For table columns where the data is not uniformly distributed, (i.e., the value in the column have a large variation in the number of duplicates), you may want to consider creating histograms. For example, Oracle may determine that the values of a particular column are distributed as 10 percent with values of >=500 and 90 percent with values of <500. Creating a histogram for skewed data allows the cost-based optimizer to better understand the distribution of data. Note the optimizer cannot utilize the histograms if you use bind variables.

The following procedure creates a histogram for the COURSE table on the indexed columns.

```
BEGIN
  DBMS_STATS.GATHER_TABLE_STATS(
    ownname => 'STUDENT',
    tabname => 'COURSE',
    cascade => TRUE,
    method_opt =>'FOR ALL INDEXED COLUMNS');
END;
/
```

STORED OUTLINES

The rule-based optimizer never changes the execution plan if the distribution of the data changes. The cost-based optimizer always takes the latest statistics and the selectivity of individual values in the WHERE clause into consideration to determine the best execution plan. Perhaps you have already decided that you want a specific plan executed, no matter what the statistics are or if the distribution of the data changes. Oracle implemented a feature called stored outline, which stores the execution plan for a SQL statement. Outlines ensure execution plan stability; any changes in the distribution of the data or statistics do not affect the subsequently issued statements.

To create an outline, use the CREATE OUTLINE command. The next SQL statement creates an outline called COURSE_OUTLINE.

```
CREATE OR REPLACE OUTLINE course_outline
   FOR CATEGORY active_ol ON
SELECT *
  FROM course c, section s
 WHERE cost > :cost_val
   AND c.course_no = s.course_no
Outline created.
```

The category name is used to simplify the management of multiple outlines. You can find the stored outlines in the data dictionary view USER_OUTLINES. The data dictionary view USER_OUTLINE_HINTS shows the hints Oracle uses to re-create the same execution plan that was used when an outline was created. For Oracle to use the stored outline, you have to activate the outline with the ALTER SESSION, ALTER SYSTEM command or you must activate the outlines in the init.ora file of the server that's read when the database instance starts up.

```
ALTER SESSION SET USE_STORED_OUTLINES = active_ol
Session altered.
```

If you execute the statement, you may notice that you see the execution plan is actually different. You can check to see if an outline is used by querying the V$SQL data dictionary view. It contains a column called OUTLINE_CATEGORY and shows the category name. In fact, this is one of the characteristics of stored outline where the actual execution plan is only shown when you use the SQL trace command and the TKPROF utility. To make sure the SQL in the outline is exactly like the SQL being executed, you use bind variables.

SQL PERFORMANCE IMPROVEMENT TIPS

There are a few good habits to adopt when you write SQL statements. Keep the following list of suggestions in mind when writing or rewriting SQL statements.

- Functions applied to indexed columns in the WHERE clause do not take advantage of the index. Instead create a function-based index. (The exceptions are the MIN and MAX functions.)
- Use analytical functions where possible instead of multiple SQL statements as it simplifies the query writing and requires only a single pass through the table.
- Build indexes on columns you frequently use in the WHERE clause but keep the performance trade-offs of DML statements in mind. Adding

an index can also adversely affect the performance of other SQL statements accessing the table. Be sure to test your scenarios carefully.

- Consider restructuring existing indexes. You can improve the selectivity by adding additional columns to an index. Alternatively you can change the order of columns in a composite index.

- Full-table scans may at times be more efficient than the use of indexes if the table is relatively small in size.

- If you are retrieving more than 5 to 20 percent of the rows, a full table scan may also be more efficient than retrieving the rows from an index.

- When joining tables make sure to choose the table that returns the fewest number of rows as the driving table.

- Consider replacing the NOT IN operator with the NOT EXISTS operator when writing correlated subqueries and eliminate as many rows as possible in the outer query of a correlated subquery.

- If you have very large tables, consider partitioning the tables. This is a feature found only in the Oracle Enterprise edition.

- If your queries involve aggregates and joins against large tables you can use materialized views to pre-store results and periodically refresh them. Oracle has a set of advisor procedures that help you design and evaluate the benefits of materialized views.

- Make sure you did not forget the joining criteria so as to avoid the building of a Cartesian product.

- Update the statistics for the cost-based optimizer periodically, particularly after heavy DML activity.

- Rebuild indexes periodically to improve the performance of the index. This is accomplished with the ALTER INDEX indexname REBUILD command. Make sure to analyze the index afterwards. Use this particularly after many DELETE statements have been issued.

- Use the CASE expression to avoid visiting tables multiple times. For example, if you need to aggregate rows that have different WHERE conditions within the same table, you can use the CASE expression to aggregate only those rows that satisfy the necessary condition.

While the cost-based optimizer makes fairly good choices about the best optimization path and therefore makes the tuning process easier, the optimizer cannot rewrite badly constructed SQL statements or automatically create indexes. Make sure you test your SQL statements carefully in a representative test environment where the data distribution, data volume, and hardware setup is similar to a production environment. Be sure to make a copy of your statistics with the DBMS_STATS. EXPORT_SCHEMA_STATS procedure. In case the performance degrades after analyzing, you can restore the old statistics with the DBMS_STATS> IMPORT_SCHEMA_STATS procedure.

LAB 16.1 EXERCISES

16.1.1 GATHER STATISTICS FOR TABLES AND INDEXES

a) Gather statistics for the STUDENT table together with the associated indexes.

b) Create an index on the REGISTRATION_DATE column of the STUDENT table. Check the data dictionary for the statistics for this index. Record your result. Drop the index afterward.

16.1.2 READ THE EXECUTION PLAN

The following exercises assume the cost-based optimizer as your default optimizer and that your tables are analyzed. If they are not, execute the following PL/SQL procedure at the SQL*Plus prompt to generate statistics for your entire schema.

```
BEGIN
  DBMS_STATS.GATHER_SCHEMA_STATS(
    ownname=>'student', cascade=>TRUE);
END;
/
PL/SQL procedure successfully completed.
```

a) Describe the result of the following query.

```
SELECT index_name, column_name, column_position
  FROM user_ind_columns
 WHERE table_name = 'STUDENT'
 ORDER BY 1, 3
```

b) Execute the SQL*Plus command SET AUTOT TRACE EXPLAIN at the SQL*Plus prompt. Then execute the following SQL statement. What do you observe about the use of the index?

```
SELECT *
  FROM student
 WHERE student_id <> 101
```

c) Create an index called STU_FIRST_I on the FIRST_NAME column of the STUDENT table. Gather statistics for the index, then execute the following SQL statement and describe the result of the execution plan.

```
SELECT student_id, first_name
  FROM student
 WHERE first_name IS NULL
```

d) Execute the following SQL query and describe the result of the execution plan.

```
SELECT student_id, first_name
  FROM student
 WHERE UPPER(first_name) = 'MARY'
```

e) Examine the following SQL queries and their respective execution plan. What do you notice about the use of the index? Drop the index STU_FIRST_I afterward.

```
SELECT student_id, first_name
  FROM student
 WHERE first_name LIKE '%oh%'
Execution Plan
-------------------------------------------------------
0       SELECT STATEMENT Optimizer=CHOOSE
        (Cost=4 Card=14 Bytes=574)
1    0    TABLE ACCESS (FULL) OF 'STUDENT'
          (Cost=4 Card=14 Bytes=574)


SELECT student_id, first_name
  FROM student
 WHERE first_name LIKE 'Joh%'
Execution Plan
-------------------------------------------------------
0       SELECT STATEMENT Optimizer=CHOOSE
        (Cost=4 Card=2 Bytes=82)
1    0    TABLE ACCESS (BY INDEX ROWID) OF 'STUDENT'
          (Cost=4 Card=2 Bytes=82)
2    1      INDEX (RANGE SCAN) OF 'STU_FIRST_I'
            (NON-UNIQUE) (Cost=2 Card=2)
```

f) Execute the following SQL query and describe the result of the execution plan.

```
SELECT *
  FROM zipcode
 WHERE zip = 10025
```

g) Explain why the following query does not use an index. Note, to reset the AUTOTRACE facility, issue the SET AUTOTRACE OFF command.

```
SELECT *
  FROM grade
 WHERE grade_type_code = 'HW'
```

16.1.3 UNDERSTAND JOIN OPERATIONS AND ALTERNATE SQL STATEMENTS

a) Given the following SELECT statement and the resulting execution plan, determine the driving table and the type of join performed.

```
SELECT --+ first_rows
       i.last_name, c.description, c.course_no
  FROM course c, section s, instructor i
 WHERE c.course_no = s.course_no
   AND s.instructor_id = i.instructor_id
   AND s.section_id = 133
```

Execution Plan

```
----------------------------------------------------------
0        SELECT STATEMENT Optimizer=HINT: FIRST_ROWS
         (Cost=4 Card=1 Bytes=119)
1    0     NESTED LOOPS (Cost=4 Card=1 Bytes=119)
2    1       NESTED LOOPS (Cost=3 Card=1 Bytes=92)
3    2         TABLE ACCESS (BY INDEX ROWID) OF 'SECTION'
                (Cost=2 Card=1 Bytes=39)
4    3           INDEX (UNIQUE SCAN) OF 'SECT_PK' (UNIQUE)
                  (Cost=1 Card=1)
5    2         TABLE ACCESS (BY INDEX ROWID) OF 'COURSE'
                (Cost=1 Card=30 Bytes=1590)
6    5           INDEX (UNIQUE SCAN) OF 'CRSE_PK' (UNIQUE)
7    1       TABLE ACCESS (BY INDEX ROWID) OF 'INSTRUCTOR'
              (Cost=1 Card=10 Bytes=270)
8    7         INDEX (UNIQUE SCAN) OF 'INST_PK' (UNIQUE)
```

b) Execute the following SELECT statement. Determine the driving table and the type of join performed.

```
SELECT /*+ RULE */ *
  FROM student s, enrollment e
 WHERE s.student_id = e.student_id
```

c) Reverse the order of the tables in the SELECT statement in Exercise b. Determine the driving table.

d) Execute an execution plan for these alternate SQL statements. Describe your results.

```
SELECT /*+ RULE */ *
  FROM student
 WHERE student_id NOT IN
       (SELECT student_id
          FROM enrollment)
```

```
SELECT /*+ RULE */ *
  FROM student s
 WHERE NOT EXISTS
       (SELECT 'X'
          FROM enrollment
         WHERE s.student_id = student_id)
```

```
SELECT /*+ RULE */ student_id
  FROM student
 MINUS
SELECT student_id
  FROM enrollment
```

e) Show the execution plan for the following SELECT statements and describe the difference.

```
SELECT student_id, last_name, 'student'
  FROM student
UNION
SELECT instructor_id, last_name, 'instructor'
  FROM instructor
```

```
SELECT student_id, last_name, 'student'
  FROM student
UNION ALL
SELECT instructor_id, last_name, 'instructor'
  FROM instructor
```

LAB 16.1 EXERCISE ANSWERS

16.1.1 ANSWERS

a) Gather statistics for the STUDENT table together with the associated indexes.

Answer: Issue the DBMS_STATS.GATHER_TABLE_STATS procedure or the ANALYZE TABLE command against the STUDENT table. Indexes associated with the table will automatically also get their statistics updated.

```
BEGIN
  DBMS_STATS.GATHER_TABLE_STATS(
    ownname=>'STUDENT',
    tabname=>'STUDENT',
    cascade=>TRUE,
END;
/
```
PL/SQL procedure successfully completed.

If instead of computing the exact statistics, you prefer to estimate them you can issue this command. The result of the estimate is probably identical with that of the compute because the STUDENT table is a relatively small table.

```
BEGIN
  DBMS_STATS.GATHER_TABLE_STATS(
    ownname=>'STUDENT',
    tabname=>'STUDENT',
    cascade=>TRUE,
    estimate_percent=>DBMS_STATS.AUTO_SAMPLE_SIZE);
END;
/
```

Alternatively, you can issue the ANALYZE command, which looks like this:

```
ANALYZE TABLE student COMPUTE STATISTICS
```
Table analyzed.

Alternatively, you can specify a certain percentage of rows or a specific number of rows.

```
ANALYZE TABLE student ESTIMATE STATISTICS
```

b) Create an index on the REGISTRATION_DATE column of the STUDENT table. Check the data dictionary for the statistics for this index. Record your result. Drop the index afterward.

Answer: After the index is created, you also need to compute the statistics.

```
CREATE INDEX stu_reg_date_i
  ON student (registration_date)
Index created.
```

Now, check the statistics of the index:

```
SELECT distinct_keys, num_rows, sample_size,
       last_analyzed
  FROM user_indexes
 WHERE index_name = 'STU_REG_DATE_I'
DISTINCT_KEYS  NUM_ROWS SAMPLE_SIZE LAST_ANAL
-------------- --------- ----------- ---------


1 row selected.
```

After you create an index, you also need to gather the statistics with the DBMS_STATS.GATHER_INDEX_STATS procedure or the ANALYZE INDEX command, for the previous statement to reflect them. If you are unsure what the parameters of the GATHER_INDEX_STATS procedure are, you can issue the DESCRIBE command against DBMS_STATS to see the parameters.

```
SQL> DESCR dbms_stats
...
PROCEDURE GATHER_INDEX_STATS
  Argument Name           Type          In/Out Default?
  ----------------------  ------------  ------ --------
  OWNNAME                 VARCHAR2      IN
  INDNAME                 VARCHAR2      IN
  PARTNAME                VARCHAR2      IN     DEFAULT
  ESTIMATE_PERCENT        NUMBER        IN     DEFAULT
  STATTAB                 VARCHAR2      IN     DEFAULT
  STATID                  VARCHAR2      IN     DEFAULT
  STATOWN                 VARCHAR2      IN     DEFAULT
...
```

The first two parameters are required and identify the schema name and the name of the index.

```
BEGIN
  DBMS_STATS.GATHER_INDEX_STATS(
      ownname=>'STUDENT',
      indname=>'STU_REG_DATE_I');
END;
/
```

Make sure you do not misspell the index name, otherwise you will get an error indicating that you misspelled the name or that you don't have sufficient privileges to perform this operation. The name of the index is misspelled here:

```
SQL> BEGIN
  2      DBMS_STATS.GATHER_INDEX_STATS(
  3          ownname=>'STUDENT',
  4          indname=>'STUDENT_REG_DATE_I');
  5  END;
  6  /
BEGIN
*
ERROR at line 1:
ORA-20000: Unable to analyze INDEX
"STUDENT"."STUDENT_REG_DATE_I", insufficient
privileges or does not exist
ORA-06512: at "SYS.DBMS_STATS", line 6984
ORA-06512: at line 2
```

You could also get a similar error if you misspelled the schema name.

As always, you can use the ANALYZE command.

```
ANALYZE INDEX stu_reg_date_i COMPUTE STATISTICS
Index analyzed.
```

Remember, if you add an index, you must also collect the statistics for it, otherwise the optimizer cannot come up with a good execution plan. The next SELECT statement shows that the statistics for the index are now available.

```
SELECT distinct_keys, num_rows, sample_size,
       last_analyzed
  FROM user_indexes
 WHERE index_name = 'STU_REG_DATE_I'
```

DISTINCT_KEYS	NUM_ROWS	SAMPLE_SIZE	LAST_ANAL
14	268	268	09-OCT-02

```
1 row selected.
```

DELETING STATISTICS

You can delete statistics for a table or index. If the optimizer is set to CHOOSE this will force the use of the rule-based optimizer. If you have the cost-based optimizer as your default, Oracle will assume certain values as your default if the statistics are not present. To delete the index statistics, execute this statement:

```
BEGIN
   DBMS_STATS.DELETE_INDEX_STATS(
```

```
        ownname=>'STUDENT',
        indname=>'STU_REG_DATE_I');
END;
/
```

Alternatively, you can use the ANALYZE INDEX command:

```
ANALYZE INDEX stu_reg_date_i DELETE STATISTICS
Index analyzed.
```

The statistics then disappear as you see from the subsequent query against the data dictionary.

```
SELECT distinct_keys, num_rows, sample_size,
       last_analyzed
  FROM user_indexes
 WHERE index_name = 'STU_REG_DATE_I'
DISTINCT_KEYS  NUM_ROWS SAMPLE_SIZE LAST_ANAL
------------- --------- ----------- ---------


1 row selected.
```

Don't forget to drop the index to restore the schema to its original state.

```
DROP INDEX stu_reg_date_i
Index dropped.
```

16.1.2 ANSWERS

The following exercises assume the cost-based optimizer as your default optimizer and that your tables are analyzed. If they are not, execute the following PL/SQL procedure at the SQL*Plus prompt to generate statistics for your entire schema.

```
BEGIN
  DBMS_STATS.GATHER_SCHEMA_STATS(
      ownname=>'STUDENT', cascade=>TRUE);
END;
/
PL/SQL procedure successfully completed.
```

a) Describe the result of the following query.

```
SELECT index_name, column_name, column_position
  FROM user_ind_columns
 WHERE table_name = 'STUDENT'
 ORDER BY 1, 3
```

Answer: The result of the query shows a listing of all indexes on the STUDENT table and the order in which the columns are indexed.

INDEX_NAME	COLUMN_NAME	COLUMN_POSITION
STU_ZIP_FK_I	ZIP	1
STU_PK	STUDENT_ID	1

```
2 rows selected.
```

b) Execute the SQL*Plus command SET AUTOT TRACE EXPLAIN at the SQL*Plus prompt. Then execute the following SQL statement. What do you observe about the use of the index?

```
SELECT *
  FROM student
 WHERE student_id <> 101
```

Answer: The index is not used in this query; every record is examined with the full table scan instead.

```
Execution Plan
--------------------------------------------------------
0       SELECT STATEMENT Optimizer=CHOOSE
        (Cost=4 Card=267 Bytes=29370)
1   0     TABLE ACCESS (FULL) OF 'STUDENT'
          (Cost=4 Card=267 Bytes=29370)
```

Inequality conditions, such as <>, !=, or any negation using NOT typically never make use of an index.

c) Create an index called STU_FIRST_I on the FIRST_NAME column of the STU-DENT table. Gather statistics for the index, then execute the following SQL statement and describe the result of the execution plan.

```
SELECT student_id, first_name
  FROM student
 WHERE first_name IS NULL
```

Answer: The query does not make use of the index on the FIRST_NAME column because NULL values are not stored in the index. Therefore, a full table scan is executed.

```
CREATE INDEX stu_first_i ON student(first_name)
Index created.

BEGIN
  DBMS_STATS.GATHER_INDEX_STATS(
    'STUDENT','STU_FIRST_I');
END;
/
PL/SQL procedure successfully completed.
```

The subsequently issued query results in this execution plan:

```
Execution Plan
----------------------------------------------------
0        SELECT STATEMENT Optimizer=CHOOSE
         (Cost=4 Card=1 Bytes=41)
1    0   TABLE ACCESS (FULL) OF 'STUDENT'
         (Cost=4 Card=1 Bytes=41)
```

If you expect to execute this query frequently and want to avoid a full table scan, you may want to consider adding a row with a default value for FIRST_NAME such as 'Unknown'. When this value is inserted in the index, a subsequently issued query, such as the following, uses the index.

```
SELECT student_id, first_name
  FROM student
 WHERE first_name = 'Unknown'
```

The index is not efficient, however, if you expect a significant number of the values to be 'Unknown'. In this case, retrieving values through the index rather than the full table scan takes longer.

d) Execute the following SQL query and describe the result of the execution plan.

```
SELECT student_id, first_name
  FROM student
 WHERE UPPER(first_name) = 'MARY'
```

Answer: The query does not make use of the index on the FIRST_NAME column.

```
Execution Plan
----------------------------------------------------
0        SELECT STATEMENT Optimizer=CHOOSE
         (Cost=4 Card=3 Bytes=123)
1    0   TABLE ACCESS (FULL) OF 'STUDENT'
         (Cost=4 Card=3 Bytes=123)
```

The UPPER function can be used in the SQL statement if you are unsure which case the first name was entered. The query returns records with the values of MARY, Mary, or combinations thereof. Each time you modify an indexed column, the use of the index is disabled. The solution is to create a function-based index. For more information on this topic, refer to Chapter 12, "Views, Indexes, and Sequences."

e) Examine the following SQL queries and their respective execution plan. What do you notice about the use of the index? Drop the index STU_FIRST_I afterward.

**LAB
16.1**

```
SELECT student_id, first_name
  FROM student
 WHERE first_name LIKE '%oh%'
Execution Plan
----------------------------------------------------------
0        SELECT STATEMENT Optimizer=CHOOSE
         (Cost=4 Card=14 Bytes=574)
1    0     TABLE ACCESS (FULL) OF 'STUDENT'
           (Cost=4 Card=14 Bytes=574)


SELECT student_id, first_name
  FROM student
 WHERE first_name LIKE 'Joh%'
Execution Plan
----------------------------------------------------------
0        SELECT STATEMENT Optimizer=CHOOSE
         (Cost=4 Card=2 Bytes=82)
1    0     TABLE ACCESS (BY INDEX ROWID) OF 'STUDENT'
           (Cost=4 Card=2 Bytes=82)
2    1       INDEX (RANGE SCAN) OF 'STU_FIRST_I'
             (NON-UNIQUE) (Cost=2 Card=2)
```

Answer: The first query does not make use of the index on the FIRST_NAME column because the index cannot determine the index entries. The second query allows the use of the index.

If you execute the queries in your individual database environment and you use the cost-based optimizer you may experience that the second query does not use an index. The optimizer may determine that the table is so small it is more efficient to simply read the entire table.

Drop the index from the schema afterward to restore the schema to its original state.

```
DROP INDEX stu_first_i
Index dropped.
```

f) Execute the following SQL query and describe the result of the execution plan.

```
SELECT *
  FROM zipcode
 WHERE zip = 10025
```

Answer: The query does not make use of the primary key index on the ZIP column.

```
Execution Plan
----------------------------------------------------------
0        SELECT STATEMENT Optimizer=CHOOSE
         (Cost=2 Card=3 Bytes=24)
1    0     TABLE ACCESS (FULL) OF 'ZIPCODE'
           (Cost=2 Card=3 Bytes=24)
```

The full table access is used because the datatypes between the ZIP column and the number literal do not agree. The ZIP column is of VARCHAR2 datatype to store leading zeros for zip codes such as '00706' and the literal is a NUMBER. This query is an example of when Oracle performs an implicit conversion. In this case, Oracle converts the ZIP column to a NUMBER and, therefore, disables the use of the index. If the WHERE clause is written as follows, it uses the index.

```
WHERE zip = '10025'
Execution Plan
-------------------------------------------------------
0        SELECT STATEMENT Optimizer=CHOOSE
         (Cost=2 Card=1 Bytes=48)
1    0     TABLE ACCESS (BY INDEX ROWID) OF 'ZIPCODE'
            (Cost=2 Card=1 Bytes=48)
2    1       INDEX (UNIQUE SCAN) OF 'ZIP_PK' (UNIQUE)
               (Cost=1 Card=2)
```

g) Explain why the following query does not use an index. Note, to reset the AUTOTRACE facility, issue the SET AUTOTRACE OFF command.

```
SELECT *
  FROM grade
 WHERE grade_type_code = 'HW'
```

Answer: The GRADE_TYPE_CODE column is not the leading column on any index of the GRADE table.

```
Execution Plan
-------------------------------------------------------
0        SELECT STATEMENT Optimizer=CHOOSE
         (Cost=2 Card=144 Bytes=144)
1    0     TABLE ACCESS (FULL) OF 'GRADE'
            (Cost=2 Card=144 Bytes=144)
```

The following query shows the indexes on the GRADE table. As you see, the GRADE_TYPE_CODE is a column in two different indexes but is never the leading column, nor are any of the leading columns in the WHERE clause of the query.

```
SELECT index_name, column_name, column_position
  FROM user_ind_columns
 WHERE table_name = 'GRADE'
 ORDER BY 1, 3
```

INDEX_NAME	COLUMN_NAME	COLUMN_POSITION
GR_GRTW_FK_I	SECTION_ID	1
GR_GRTW_FK_I	GRADE_TYPE_CODE	2
GR_PK	STUDENT_ID	1
GR_PK	SECTION_ID	2

| GR_PK | GRADE_TYPE_CODE | 3 |
| GR_PK | GRADE_CODE_OCCURRENCE | 4 |

6 rows selected.

The following query makes use of the index GR_GRTW_FK_I because the leading edge of the index is in the WHERE clause.

```
SELECT *
  FROM grade
 WHERE grade_type_code = 'HW'
   AND section_id = 123
```

And this query uses the primary key index GR_PK.

```
SELECT *
  FROM grade
 WHERE grade_type_code = 'HW'
   AND section_id = 123
   AND student_id = 567
```

Oracle 9i introduced a new feature called skip scan, which improves index scans when the leading portion of the index is not specified. This only works with the cost-based optimizer. Essentially, scanning an index is faster than scanning the table and skip scanning splits the index into smaller subindexes. These different subindexes show the number of distinct values in the leading index. Skip indexes are most useful when there are few distinct values in the leading column of the index.

16.1.3 ANSWERS

a) Given the following SELECT statement and the resulting execution plan, determine the driving table and the type of join performed.

```
SELECT --+ first_rows
       i.last_name, c.description, c.course_no
  FROM course c, section s, instructor i
 WHERE c.course_no = s.course_no
   AND s.instructor_id = i.instructor_id
   AND s.section_id = 133
```

Execution Plan
```
----------------------------------------------------------
0        SELECT STATEMENT Optimizer=HINT: FIRST_ROWS
         (Cost=4 Card=1 Bytes=119)
1     0    NESTED LOOPS (Cost=4 Card=1 Bytes=119)
2     1      NESTED LOOPS (Cost=3 Card=1 Bytes=92)
```

```
3      2        TABLE ACCESS (BY INDEX ROWID) OF 'SECTION'
                (Cost=2 Card=1 Bytes=39)
4      3          INDEX (UNIQUE SCAN) OF 'SECT_PK' (UNIQUE)
                  (Cost=1 Card=1)
5      2        TABLE ACCESS (BY INDEX ROWID) OF 'COURSE'
                (Cost=1 Card=30 Bytes=1590)
6      5          INDEX (UNIQUE SCAN) OF 'CRSE_PK' (UNIQUE)
7      1      TABLE ACCESS (BY INDEX ROWID) OF 'INSTRUCTOR'
              (Cost=1 Card=10 Bytes=270)
8      7          INDEX (UNIQUE SCAN) OF 'INST_PK' (UNIQUE)
```

Answer:The driving table of this nested loop join is the SECTION table.

The following steps are performed by this query: The index SECT_PK is probed for the SECTION_ID of 133 and one record in the SECTION table is accessed. Then, the index CRSE_PK on the COURSE table is checked for the COURSE_NO matching the row. The row is retrieved for the DESCRIPTION and COURSE_NO. Finally, the instructor index INST_PK is used to find a match for the INSTRUCTOR_ ID from the initial row in the SECTION table, and then the corresponding record in the INSTRUCTOR table is retrieved.

b) Execute the following SELECT statement. Determine the driving table and the type of join performed.

```
SELECT /*+ RULE */ *
  FROM student s, enrollment e
 WHERE s.student_id = e.student_id
```

Answer: Oracle performs a nested loop join because indexes exist on the tables.The driving table is the ENROLLMENT table.

Execution Plan
```
------------------------------------------------------
0        SELECT STATEMENT Optimizer=HINT: RULE
1    0     NESTED LOOPS
2    1       TABLE ACCESS (FULL) OF 'ENROLLMENT'
3    1       TABLE ACCESS (BY INDEX ROWID) OF 'STUDENT'
4    3          INDEX (UNIQUE SCAN) OF 'STU_PK' (UNIQUE)
```

The nested loop join performs a full table scan on the ENROLLMENT table; for every row retrieved, the nested loop checks if a corresponding student exists in the STUD_PK index. If the row exists, the row is then retrieved from the STUDENT table. The rule-based optimizer does not recognize that a full table scan with a hash or sort-merge join is more efficient than looking at the rows through the index.

Comparing the execution time of the nested loop to the sort-merge join or the hash join does not show a great variance, but if you are joining larger tables, the differences may be significant.

c) Reverse the order of the tables in the SELECT statement in Exercise b. Determine the driving table.

Answer: The driving table is the STUDENT table.

```
SELECT /*+ RULE */ *
  FROM enrollment e, student s
 WHERE s.student_id = e.student_id
Execution Plan
----------------------------------------------------
0     SELECT STATEMENT Optimizer=HINT: RULE
1  0     NESTED LOOPS
2  1        TABLE ACCESS (FULL) OF 'STUDENT'
3  1        TABLE ACCESS (BY INDEX ROWID) OF 'ENROLLMENT'
4  3           INDEX (RANGE SCAN) OF 'ENR_PK' (UNIQUE)
```

The optimizer chooses the join order based on the order of the tables listed in the FROM clause, provided the WHERE clause conditions of the tables are equivalent. For the rule-based optimizer, the last table listed in the FROM clause is the driving table, as long as the indexes in the WHERE clause have the same ranking.

For the cost-based optimizer, given that the conditions in the WHERE clause are equivalent, it chooses the first table listed in the FROM clause. With the cost-based optimizer you can influence the join order with the ORDERED or the LEADING hint.

d) Execute an execution plan for these alternate SQL statements. Describe your results.

```
SELECT /*+ RULE */ *
  FROM student
 WHERE student_id NOT IN
       (SELECT student_id
          FROM enrollment)

SELECT /*+ RULE */ *
  FROM student s
 WHERE NOT EXISTS
       (SELECT 'X'
          FROM enrollment
         WHERE s.student_id = student_id)

SELECT /*+ RULE */ student_id
  FROM student
MINUS
SELECT student_id
  FROM enrollment
```

Answer: The NOT IN subquery does not take advantage of the index on the ENROLLMENT table, but the NOT EXISTS query does. The MINUS operator has a different execution plan.

```
SELECT /*+ RULE */ *
  FROM student
 WHERE student_id NOT IN
          (SELECT student_id
             FROM enrollment)
Execution Plan
-------------------------------------------------------
0       SELECT STATEMENT Optimizer=HINT: RULE
1    0    FILTER
2    1      TABLE ACCESS (FULL) OF 'STUDENT'
3    1      TABLE ACCESS (FULL) OF 'ENROLLMENT'
```

The NOT IN operator under the rule-based optimizer is very inefficient and is best replaced with a NOT EXISTS. Note that the cost-based optimizer for subqueries has greatly improved the notorious slowness of the NOT IN operator and optimizes the results.

```
SELECT /*+ RULE */ *
  FROM student s
 WHERE NOT EXISTS
          (SELECT 'X'
             FROM enrollment
            WHERE s.student_id = student_id)
Execution Plan
-------------------------------------------------------
0       SELECT STATEMENT Optimizer=HINT: RULE
1    0    FILTER
2    1      TABLE ACCESS (FULL) OF 'STUDENT'
3    1      INDEX (RANGE SCAN) OF 'ENR_PK' (UNIQUE)
```

The NOT EXISTS operator takes advantage of the index on the ENROLLMENT table.

```
SELECT /*+ RULE */ student_id
  FROM student
MINUS
SELECT student_id
  FROM enrollment
Execution Plan
-------------------------------------------------------
0       SELECT STATEMENT Optimizer=HINT: RULE
1    0    MINUS
2    1      SORT (UNIQUE)
3    2        TABLE ACCESS (FULL) OF 'STUDENT'
4    1      SORT (UNIQUE)
5    4        TABLE ACCESS (FULL) OF 'ENROLLMENT'
```

The execution plan of the MINUS operator does not look very impressive, but can actually be one of the fastest ways to retrieve the result, especially when a large number of records is involved.

Always consider alternative SQL syntax when writing queries and tune your SQL statements with a representative data set. If the distribution of the data changes, so will the statistics, and the optimizer may favor a different execution plan.

e) Show the execution plan for the following SELECT statements and describe the difference.

```
SELECT student_id, last_name, 'student'
  FROM student
UNION
SELECT instructor_id, last_name, 'instructor'
  FROM instructor

SELECT student_id, last_name, 'student'
  FROM student
UNION ALL
SELECT instructor_id, last_name, 'instructor'
  FROM instructor
```

Answer: The UNION statement involves an additional sort, which is not performed on the UNION ALL statement.

```
SELECT student_id, last_name, 'student'
  FROM student
UNION
SELECT instructor_id, last_name, 'instructor'
  FROM instructor
Execution Plan
-------------------------------------------------------
0       SELECT STATEMENT Optimizer=CHOOSE
        (Cost=14 Card=278 Bytes=7506)
1   0     SORT (UNIQUE) (Cost=14 Card=278 Bytes=7506)
2   1       UNION-ALL
3   2         TABLE ACCESS (FULL) OF 'STUDENT'
              (Cost=4 Card=268 Bytes=7236)
4   2         TABLE ACCESS (FULL) OF 'INSTRUCTOR'
              (Cost=1 Card=10 Bytes=270)

SELECT student_id, last_name, 'student'
  FROM student
UNION ALL
SELECT instructor_id, last_name, 'instructor'
  FROM instructor
Execution Plan
-------------------------------------------------------
0       SELECT STATEMENT Optimizer=CHOOSE
        (Cost=5 Card=278 Bytes=7506)
1   0     UNION-ALL
```

2	1	TABLE ACCESS (FULL) OF 'STUDENT'
		(Cost=4 Card=268 Bytes=7236)
3	1	TABLE ACCESS (FULL) OF 'INSTRUCTOR'
		(Cost=1 Card=10 Bytes=270)

Whenever possible, avoid any unnecessary sorts required by the use of UNION or DISTINCT.

LAB 16.1 SELF-REVIEW QUESTIONS

In order to test your progress, you should be able to answer the following questions.

1) The rule-based optimizer requires tables to be analyzed.

   a) _____ True
   b) _____ False

2) An ORDERED hint can influence the join order of SQL statements using the cost-based optimizer.

   a) _____ True
   b) _____ False

3) The join order of tables is important for good performance of the nested loop join.

   a) _____ True
   b) _____ False

4) An execution plan is read from the bottom to the top and then from the inside to the outside.

   a) _____ True
   b) _____ False

5) Incorrectly written hints are treated as comments and ignored.

   a) _____ True
   b) _____ False

Answers appear in Appendix A, Section 16.1.

C H A P T E R   1 6

TEST YOUR THINKING

The projects in this section are meant to have you utilize all of the skills that you have acquired throughout this chapter. The answers to these projects can be found at the companion Web site to this book, located at: *http://www.phptr.com/rischert.*

Visit the Web site periodically to share and discuss your answers.

1) Given the following execution plan, describe the steps and their order of execution.

```
SELECT /*+ RULE */ c.course_no, c.description,
       i.instructor_id
  FROM course c, section s, instructor i
 WHERE prerequisite = 30
   AND c.course_no = s.course_no
   AND s.instructor_id = i.instructor_id
Execution Plan
--------------------------------------------------------
0       SELECT STATEMENT Optimizer=HINT: RULE
1    0    NESTED LOOPS
2    1      NESTED LOOPS
3    2        TABLE ACCESS (BY INDEX ROWID) OF 'COURSE'
4    3          INDEX (RANGE SCAN) OF 'CRSE_CRSE_FK_I' (NON-UNIQUE)
5    2        TABLE ACCESS (BY INDEX ROWID) OF 'SECTION'
6    5          INDEX (RANGE SCAN) OF 'SECT_CRSE_FK_I' (NON-UNIQUE)
7    1      INDEX (UNIQUE SCAN) OF 'INST_PK' (UNIQUE)
```

2) Describe the steps of the following execution plan.

```
UPDATE enrollment e
   SET final_grade =
       (SELECT NVL(AVG(numeric_grade),0)
          FROM grade
         WHERE e.student_id = student_id
           AND e.section_id = section_id)
 WHERE student_id = 1000
   AND section_id = 2000
 0 rows updated.
```

```
Execution Plan
-----------------------------------------------------
0     UPDATE STATEMENT Optimizer=CHOOSE
         (Cost=2 Card=1 Bytes=47)
1  0     UPDATE OF 'ENROLLMENT'
2  1        INDEX (UNIQUE SCAN) OF 'ENR_PK' (UNIQUE)
              (Cost=1 Card=1 Bytes=47)
3  0     SORT (AGGREGATE)
4  3        TABLE ACCESS (BY INDEX ROWID) OF 'GRADE'
              (Cost=3 Card=1 Bytes=39)
5  4           INDEX (RANGE SCAN) OF 'GR_PK' (UNIQUE)
                 (Cost=2 Card=1)
```

3) The following SQL statement has an error in the hint. Correct the statement so Oracle can use the hint.

```
SELECT /*+ INDEX (student stu_pk) */ *
  FROM student s
 WHERE last_name = 'Smith'
```

ANSWERS
TO SELF-REVIEW
QUESTIONS

CHAPTER 1

Lab 1.1 ■ Self-Review Answers

Question	Answer	Comments
1)	a	
2)	b	A table must always have at least one column. Rows are not required.
3)	b	SQL is a language. For example, SQL*Plus is a software program (which you will learn about in Chapter 2, "SQL: The Basics") that allows you to use SQL language to interact with the database.
4)	a	Most database systems are multiuser systems.
5)	a	

Lab 1.2 ■ Self-Review Answers

Question	Answer	Comments
1)	b	The entity relationship diagram is a logical model that doesn't deal with physical tables yet, but instead with entities and attributes.
2)	a	Another cardinality notation used to depict a one-to-many relationship is 1:M or 1:N.
3)	a	
4)	b	The schema diagram or physical model is derived from the logical data model.
5)	b	Actually, when you denormalize you reintroduce redundancy.

6)	b	The logical database design is one of the steps in the database development life cycle that ends with the actual physical database implementation. SQL works with the physical database implementation.
7)	a	
8)	a	

Lab 1.3 ■ Self-Review Answers

Question	Answer	Comments
1)	a, c	
2)	a	
3)	b	The number of rows is completely independent of the number of columns in a table.
4)	b	The SECTION table has COURSE_NO and INSTRUCTOR_ID columns as foreign keys.
5)	a	Each individual database system software may have limits constrained by the hardware and software. It is not uncommon to have tables exceeding 10 million rows.
6)	b	A primary key may never contain NULL values.
7)	a	
8)	c	The table has at least three foreign key columns. Some foreign keys may consist of multiple columns.
9)	a	
10)	a	An example of a foreign key that allows null values is the ZIP column on the INSTRUCTOR table.
11)	a	The prevention of orphan rows, thereby preserving the parent–child relationship between tables, is key to the success of a relational database design.

CHAPTER 2

Lab 2.1 ■ Self-Review Answers

Question	Answer	Comments
1)	a	The DESC command is an easy way to find out about the structure of a table; that is, column names, datatypes, and if a column allows NULL values or not.
2)	b	SQL*Plus is not necessary to connect to Oracle. You may use other types of software that allows database connectivity. You can also use *i*SQL*Plus, which only requires a Web browser. As with any database connection you will obviously need a valid user ID and password.
3)	a	
4)	a	
5)	a	

Lab 2.2 ■ Self-Review Answers

Question	Answer	Comments
1)	a	
2)	a	To show all the columns, it is easiest to use the asterisk wildcard character (*).
3)	b	The asterisk is used for the column list only.
4)	a	A column with the COURSENO does not exist on the COURSE table.

Lab 2.3 ■ Self-Review Answers

Question	Answer	Comments
1)	b	Only the most recent statement is saved in the buffer.
2)	a	Note that the forward slash must be in a separate line and start at the first position.
3)	b	You can save a file anywhere you have permission to access the drive.
4)	b	The SQL*Plus START command executes a file; the RUN command or the forward slash executes the contents of the buffer.

Lab 2.4 ■ Self-Review Answers

Question	Answer	Comments
1)	b	Comparison operators can compare multiple values, such as the IN operator, which compares against a list of values.
2)	b	The BETWEEN operator is inclusive of the two values specified.
3)	a	Testing for nulls must be done using the IS NULL operator. This query will not return any rows!
4)	a	The LIKE operator cannot compare against a list of values.
5)	b	This query is valid. Alternatively, the <> operator or the WHERE clause NOT state = 'NY' can be used.
6)	b	Because the comparison operator is the equal sign (=), not the LIKE operator, it looks for a last name exactly equal to 'SM%', including the % sign. If you use the LIKE operator instead then last names beginning with the uppercase letters SM are returned.

Lab 2.5 ■ Self-Review Answers

Question	Answer	Comments
1)	b	The order should be SELECT, FROM, WHERE, ORDER BY.
2)	b	The default ORDER BY sort order is ascending.
3)	a	There is no error in this statement.
4)	b	The query does not contain an error.
5)	a	Typically yes, the exception is the use of the DISTINCT keyword in the SELECT clause.

Chapter 3

Lab 3.1 ■ Self-Review Answers

Question	Answer	Comments
1)	b	For example, the INSTR function, which converts single values, requires two parameters and may have optional parameters.
2)	a	You will see other uses of the DUAL table throughout this workbook.
3)	a	
4)	a	You may not apply a function to the table name in the FROM clause of a SQL statement.
5)	a	The RTRIM right trims characters. If a parameter is not specified, it trims spaces.
6)	c	The LENGTH function returns the length of a string.
7)	a	
8)	a	This is in contrast to the aggregate functions where one or more rows are involved. Aggregate functions are discussed in Chapter 5, "Aggregate Functions, GROUP BY and HAVING."
9)	c	The SUBSTR function returns a specified portion of a character string.

Lab 3.2 ■ Self-Review Answers

Question	Answer	Comments
1)	a	
2)	b	The ROUND function works on the DATE and the NUMBER datatypes. It can also take a string consisting of numbers as a parameter, providing it can be implicitly converted into a NUMBER datatype.
3)	b	This SELECT statement subtracts the CAPACITY columns from each other. It is perfectly valid to use another column rather than a literal, as we used in most other examples. The result of the query will not make much sense in this case, resulting in zero values. If any of the CAPACITY column values contains a null value, the result is another null.
4)	c	Most functions return a null with a null argument. There are a few exceptions such as the REPLACE, NVL, and CONCAT functions.

Lab 3.3 ■ Self-Review Answers

Question	Answer	Comments
1)	a	Any calculation with a null always yields null. If you want to avoid this behavior, you can use the NVL function to substitute another value.
2)	b	If the datatypes are different, Oracle attempts to convert the substitution expression's datatype to the input expres-

sion's datatype. If this is not possible, the function returns an error as in this example. The text literal 'None', which is the substitution expression, cannot be converted into the input expression's NUMBER datatype. The corrected statement looks like this: `SELECT NVL(TO_CHAR(cost), 'None') FROM course.`

3)   b   The UPDATE command (discussed in Chapter 10, "Insert, Update, and Delete," updates data in the database. Any of the functions you have learned about so far will not modify the value in the database.

4)   a

5)   b   The DECODE function is allowed in any SQL statement where functions are allowed.

6)   a   The CASE expression is allowed anywhere expressions are allowed including ORDER BY clauses or inside functions.

7)   b   The functions in this lab can be used on most datatypes. For example, the NVL function is most frequently used on DATE, NUMBER, and VARCHAR2 datatypes.

CHAPTER 4

Lab 4.1 ■ Self-Review Answers

Question	Answer	Comments
1)	a	The TRUNC function, without a format model, sets the timestamp to midnight. TRUNC can also take a NUMBER datatype as a parameter.
2)	b	The TO_DATE function is required instead. For example, `SELECT TO_DATE('01/12/2000','MM/DD/YYYY') FROM dual.`
3)	d	The case is identical to the case of the format mask. The format mask DY returns MON, Day returns Monday, DAY returns MONDAY.
4)	e	The fill mode (fm) prevents any blank padding between December and 31. The date format element suffix th adds the ordinal number.
5)	b	Note the minutes (MI) are displayed as months (MM) instead. This is a mistake beginners often make by confusing the month (MM) format with the minutes (MI) format.

Lab 4.2 ■ Self-Review Answers

Question	Answer	Comments
1)	a	You need to supply a negative value as a parameter. For example, the following statement subtracts one month from the current date: `SELECT ADD_MONTHS(SYSDATE,-1), SYSDATE FROM dual.`

2)	a	You compute this by multiplying 24 hours by the 4 quarters of every hour. You can verify this with the following query: SELECT TO_CHAR(SYSDATE, 'HH24:MI'), TO_CHAR (SYSDATE+1/96, 'HH24:MI') FROM dual.
3)	c	The NEXT_DAY function takes two parameters: a date and a day of the week. Sunday, January 9 is the next Sunday after January 2, 2000.
4)	c	The ROUND function rounds not just numbers, but also dates. If a format model is not specified, as in this example, it rounds to the nearest date. Because the time is before noon, it rounds to the current date. If the time is after noon, the next day is returned.

Lab 4.3 ■ Self-Review Answers

Question	Answer	Comments
1)	c	The FROM_TZ function returns a TIMESTAMP WITH TIME ZONE datatype.
2)	a	The ALTER SESSION command can, among other things, change the individual's session time zone.
3)	a	The date and time are stored in the database server's own time zone, but the result is displayed in the individual user's respective time zone.
4)	a	The time zone displacement value, also called the time zone offset value, is the difference in hours and minutes between the local time and UTC (Coordinated Universal Time).
5)	a	

Lab 4.4 ■ Self-Review Answers

Question	Answer	Comments
1)	b	The TO_YMINTERVAL function converts the text literal to an INTERVAL YEAR TO MONTH datatype instead.
2)	b	The NUMTODSINTERVAL function returns a INTERVAL DAY TO SECOND datatype.
3)	b	The operators will return different results if two events start and end at the same time.
4)	b	You can use the EXTRACT function on INTERVAL datatypes.
5)	b	The interval literal is valid.

Lab 4.5 ■ Self-Review Answers

Question	Answer	Comments
1)	d	The solution d results in an error because 'A123' cannot be converted to a NUMBER. (Note, Oracle versions prior to 9i may return an error message on statement e) because the

TO_CHAR function expects a NUMBER or DATE datatype, not a character datatype. The passed literal 'A123' is assumed to be a NUMBER and Oracle attempts to implicitly convert the literal to a NUMBER; therefore an error is returned.)

2)   c, d, e   These are all valid, including e, but the solution e does not show all the digits because the passed parameter exceeds the specified precision. The solutions a and b are invalid NUMBER masks; solution b also misses a single quote at the end of the format mask.

3)   a   It is always best to explicitly specify the datatype and not to rely on Oracle's implicit conversion.

4)   a   Conversion functions operate on a single row at a time.

5)   b   Changing the query as follows will correct the error.

```
SELECT *
  FROM conversion_example
 WHERE course_no = CAST(123 AS VARCHAR2(3))
```

CHAPTER 5

Lab 5.1 ■ Self-Review Answers

Question	Answer	Comments
1)	c	Only AVG, COUNT, and SUM are aggregate functions. ROUND is a single-row function.
2)	c	The aggregate function MAX determines the most recently modified record for the ENROLLMENT table. If a null value is returned, the value March 12, 2005 is substituted.
3)	a	Typically, aggregate functions work on groups of rows, but can also be applied to a single row. For example, the following two statements return the same result. SELECT MAX(modified_date) FROM zipcode WHERE zip = '10025'; SELECT modified_date FROM zipcode WHERE zip = '10025'.
4)	a	The asterisk is not a permissible argument for the AVG function.
5)	b	It computes the average capacity of only the DISTINCT capacities of the SECTION table.
6)	b	The statement is correct and shows an example of an expression as an argument of an aggregate function. The values in the CAPACITY columns are multiplied by 1.5, then the aggregate function SUM is applied.

Lab 5.2 ■ Self-Review Answers

Question	Answer	Comments
1)	b	Only the SECTION_ID column. The other columns contain aggregate functions, which are computed based on the grouping by SECTION_ID.

2)   a   It is syntactically correct to do this, but it is redundant because GROUP BY implies distinct values.

3)   a   Aggregate functions are not allowed in the WHERE clause unless they are part of a subquery. (See Chapter 7 for more on subqueries.)

4)   b   One row, because all the NULL values are grouped together. Although one NULL does not equal another, in a GROUP BY clause they are grouped together.

5)   a   The SQL statement is correct. You do not need to list the columns of the GROUP BY clause in the SELECT list as well. This type of query is typically not very useful as this individual example displays only the value of the COUNT function and not the column by which the group is formed. The result of the query looks like the following output.

```
COUNT(*)
----------
         1
...
         1

28 rows selected.
```

CHAPTER 6

Lab 6.1 ■ Self-Review Answers

Question	Answer	Comments
1)	f	The alias is incorrect on the STUDENT table's ZIP column.
2)	d	Lines 2 and 5 are incorrect. In line 5 the STUD.ZIP column does not exist; it needs to be changed to S.ZIP to correspond to the STUDENT table's alias s listed in the FROM clause. Line 2 lists a nonexistent SZIP column. Change it to S.ZIP for the query to work.
3)	b	The table alias is just another name to reference the table.
4)	a	The equijoin tests for equality of values in one or multiple columns.
5)	c	The column W.GRADE_TYPE_CODE_CD is misspelled and needs to be changed to W.GRADE_TYPE_CODE for the query to work.
6)	b	The NULL value from one table does not match the NULL value from another table; therefore, the records are not included in the result.
7)	a or b	The aliases used for the columns are not listed as table alias. The keyword INNER is acceptable but typically omitted with the ANSI JOIN syntax.
8)	a	The USING clause assumes the equality of the values and identical column names. If you want to specify inequality or the join columns do not share the same name, use the

		traditional WHERE clause or use the ON clause. For more on inequality in joins refer to Chapter 9, "Complex Joins."
9)	a	The natural join does not allow any USING or ON clause. The common column names are assumed to be the joining criteria.
10)	b	This is not required, but is often included to understand the result set.

Lab 6.2 ■ Self-Review Answers

Question	Answer	Comments
1)	b	This statement has the correct join criteria between the tables SECTION, COURSE, and INSTRUCTOR. Note, the COURSE table is not necessary to show the instructors assigned to sections.
2)	c	You get this error if you list two columns with the same name. Resolve it by prefixing the column with a table name or a table alias.
3)	b	Multicolumn joins need to have all the common columns listed. Some joins do not follow the primary/foreign key path because either a foreign key relationship does not exist or a shortcut is used to obtain the information.
4)	a	The SECTION_ID column has the wrong table alias; change it to E.SECTION_ID or G.SECTION_ID instead.
5)	a	The most common type of join is the equijoin, which is based on the equality of values. This is typically expressed with the equal (=) sign, or in ANSI syntax with the NATURAL JOIN or INNER JOIN together with the USING clause or the ON condition. You will explore nonequijoin conditions, self-joins, and outer joins in Chapter 9, "Complex Joins."
6)	a	Remember the n − 1 formula? In the case of multicolumn keys, you may have additional conditions in your WHERE clause or multiple columns in your ANSI join ON or USING clause.

CHAPTER 7

Lab 7.1 ■ Self-Review Answers

Question	Answer	Comments
1)	a	A subquery with the ORDER BY clause results in an error, except for inline views discussed in Lab 7.3.
2)	b	Subqueries can also be used in other types of SQL statements. Most frequently they are used in SELECT statements or in INSERT, DELETE, or UPDATE statements.
3)	a	The most deeply nested subquery is executed first. This is in contrast to the correlated subquery, which executes the

outer query first, then repeatedly executes the inner sub-query for every row of the outer query.

4)	c	The IN operator allows multiple rows.
5)	a	You can compare column pairs by enclosing them in parentheses and comparing them to the subquery using the IN operator. Make sure the datatype and column pairs match on both sides of the IN operator.

Lab 7.2 ■ Self-Review Answers

Question	Answer	Comments
1)	a	The NOT EXISTS operator tests for NULL values, in contrast to the NOT IN operator which does not.
2)	a	For every row of the outer query, the inner query is executed.
3)	a	They result in the same output, although one may execute more efficiently than the other.
4)	b	The query looks only for enrolled students that have no corresponding record in the GRADE table for the particular section.
5)	a	The join may repeat some of the values from the child table and applying the aggregate function to these rows may not yield the correct result. Therefore, check the result of the join first!
6)	b	The syntax of the SQL statement is incorrect because the subquery's WHERE clause is incomplete. It does not compare the column SECTION_ID to any value.

Lab 7.3 ■ Self-Review Answers

Question	Answer	Comments
1)	a	
2)	b	A scalar subquery returns a single column and single row.
3)	b	Inline views, unlike regular views, are not stored in the data dictionary.
4)	b	It is a pseudocolumn, appearing as though it was an actual column in the table, but it is not.
5)	a	Just like other types of views, this is allowed.

Lab 7.4 ■ Self-Review Answers

Question	Answer	Comments
1)	b	The first query tests if the number 6 is unequal to any of the values in the list. It is unequal to the number 9 and therefore the query returns the value `True`. The second query checks if the number 6 is not in the list of values. The value is included, and the query returns `no rows selected`.

2)	a	The two queries return the identical result.
3)	a	These operators can be used interchangeably.
4)	a	ANY, SOME, and ALL operators allow you to compare a list of values with the comparison operators. The IN operator tests for equivalency of values only.
5)	a	Only one column can be compared, not pairs of columns.

CHAPTER 8

Lab 8.1 ■ Self-Review Answers

Question	Answer	Comments
1)	a	The UNION set operator already performs a sort and only lists distinct values.
2)	b	The ORDER BY clause is always the last clause in a set operation.
3)	b	A UNION set operation does not eliminate rows; rather, it combines rows from each SELECT statement, eliminating duplicates only. An equijoin returns only rows where values from each table are equal.
4)	b	You can UNION any tables as long as you conform to the rules of the UNION operation; that is, the same number of columns and the same datatype.
5)	a	One of the rules of set operations is that the number of columns must be the same, as well as the datatypes of those columns.

Lab 8.2 ■ Self-Review Answers

Question	Answer	Comments
1)	b	The two SELECT statements are two different sets of data. Only one can be subtracted from the other for the desired, correct result.
2)	a	The SELECT statements in a set operation can be any SELECT statements.
3)	b	The datatype of the columns must agree.
4)	a	All set operators, except UNION ALL, eliminate duplicate values, so DISTINCT is not needed.

CHAPTER 9

Lab 9.1 ■ Self-Review Answers

Question	Answer	Comments
1)	a	The OR operator is not allowed in the outer join. The result is an error message such as this one: ORA-01719: outer join operator (+) not allowed in operand of OR or IN.

2)	a	The IN operator may not be used. The error message is identical to the one in Question 1. Note that the new ANSI join syntax overcomes some of these limitations.
3)	a	The Oracle outer join operator indicates from which table you want to generate NULLs for nonmatching values. Alternatively, this can be expressed with the ANSI outer join syntax or a UNION.
4)	d	You cannot write a full outer join with two (+) outer join operators. You need to write two outer join statements and combine the result with the UNION set operator or use the ANSI full outer join syntax.

Lab 9.2 ■ Self-Review Answers

Question	Answer	Comments
1)	b	Any kinds of joins do not have to follow the foreign/primary key path. But you have to carefully examine the result to make sure it is correct. Otherwise, it could result in a Cartesian product.
2)	b	You can join a table to itself without a recursive relationship, (e.g., to determine data inconsistencies).
3)	b	Such restrictions do not exist.
4)	a	
5)	a	Yes, an alias is required.

CHAPTER 10

Lab 10.1 ■ Self-Review Answers

Question	Answer	Comments
1)	b	Only DDL or DCL commands issue implicit commits.
2)	b	
3)	b	You can insert multiple rows by selecting from another table.
4)	a	
5)	b	Only committed changes can be seen by all users. The session issuing the change can always see the change.
6)	a	

Lab 10.2 ■ Self-Review Answers

1)	a	If the rows have not been committed to the database, they can be restored.
2)	a	
3)	b	Queries never place locks on rows. The exception is the SELECT FOR UPDATE command; it retrieves the rows and explicitly places a lock on them.

4)	b	Reading uncommitted data is called "dirty reads." Oracle only shows data that has been committed and achieves read-consistency be reading old data from the rollback (or undo) segments to present the user a picture of how the data looked at the time the query started.
5)	a	If the same session issues a DCL or DDL command, it will force an implicit commit and therefore release the lock on the row.

CHAPTER 11

Lab 11.1 ■ Self-Review Answers

Question	Answer	Comments
1)	a	The primary key consists of multiple columns.
2)	a	When the CREATE TABLE statement uses the AS SELECT keywords to select from another table or tables, the SELECT statement can contain a join of multiple tables.
3)	b	The foreign key constraints of the child tables are dropped, but not the child tables themselves.
4)	a	
5)	b	You can create a table from another regardless if the table has rows or not.
6)	a	Any DDL commands, such as CREATE TABLE, ALTER TABLE, TRUNCATE TABLE, issue an implicit commit.
7)	a	If the foreign key column is defined as nulls allowed, a null value is also acceptable.
8)	b	Ideally, primary key values should be generic and never subject to changes; otherwise, this requires updates to the corresponding foreign key columns.
9)	a	The INITIAL extent specifies the storage allocation when the table is initially created. Once the data is entered and the space filled, Oracle will automatically allocate another extent in a size indicated with the NEXT parameter.

Lab 11.2 ■ Self-Review Answers

Question	Answer	Comments
1)	a	The syntax should not include both keywords CONSTRAINT and PRIMARY KEY. The correct syntax is either ALTER TABLE tablename DROP CONSTRAINT followed by the constraint name, or ALTER TABLE tablename DROP PRIMARY KEY.
2)	b	The ADD keyword is used to add columns or constraints to a table, whereas the MODIFY keyword is used to change characteristics of a column.
3)	a	You can only add a NOT NULL constraint if the referenced column contains values or the table is empty.

4)	b	The ALTER TABLE...DISABLE Primary KEY command is an example of the command used without the name of the constraint.
5)	b	A column's datatype can also be changed to a compatible datatype, such as from a VARCHAR2 to CHAR.
6)	a	The TRANSLATE functionnn in the CHECK constraint checks if the format of a telephone number is correct when inserted or changed in the table. It also checks that the value contains only numbers and hyphens, and not letters.

CHAPTER 12

Lab 12.1 ■ Self-Review Answers

Question	Answer	Comments
1)	a	
2)	a, b	
3)	e	
4)	a	Views must follow a number of rules to be updateable. This view allows inserts and updates and deletes referencing the STATE column, but not to the MODIFIED_DATE column. If you are in doubt, query the data dictionary view called USER_UPDATABLE_COLUMNS.
5)	a	You can list only certain columns in a view, and/or you can restrict the view with the WHERE clause for specific rows.
6)	a	You can choose to keep the name or create a different name; however, expressions require a column alias.

Lab 12.2 ■ Self-Review Answers

Question	Answer	Comments
1)	c, d	A concatenated index typically outperforms individual column indexes. However, as with any query, you need to know how many rows you expect to retrieve with the criteria. If you retrieve a large number of records, the full table scan may outperform the retrieval from the index. Oracle's optimizer will automatically make this determination. If you create a concatenated index, choose the column order carefully. If you have a choice, choose the most selective column first; that is, the column with the most distinct values. In Oracle 9*i*, a new feature called skip scan can overturn these "old" rules. Be sure to test your options carefully to determine the best performance.
2)	b	Indexes slow down INSERT, UPDATE, and DELETE operations. Retrieving data from an index may take more time if the retrieved data set is relatively large because both table and index need to be accessed.

3)	a	These columns are often listed in the WHERE clause and therefore accessed frequently. Indexing these columns improves the performance of joins and locking.
4)	a	
5)	b	Nulls are not stored in a B-tree index; therefore, a search for null values will not use the index. However, a concatenated index will store nulls as long as the leading column of the concatenated index is not null.
6)	a	Indexes are not only useful for SELECT statements, but also for UPDATE and DELETE statements to quickly locate the record. Note that INSERT, UPDATE, and DELETE operations on columns containing indexes are much slower because the index needs to be updated with the changed or newly inserted values.

Lab 12.3 ■ Self-Review Answers

Question	Answer	Comments
1)	a	
2)	b	It is best to use a generated value for a primary key, such as from a sequence, because it is generic, not subject to any change, and prevents duplicates or null values.
3)	a	
4)	b	These two objects are independent of each other. For example, you can use the same sequence for multiple tables.
5)	a	

CHAPTER 13

Lab 13.1 ■ Self-Review Answers

Question	Answer	Comments
1)	a	
2)	a	Other object types are also listed in this view.
3)	a	
4)	b	The ALL_TABLES view shows only the tables accessible to a user.
5)	a	

Lab 13.2 ■ Self-Review Answers

Question	Answer	Comments
1)	a	
2)	b	The CHR(10) function issues a line feed.
3)	a	
4)	a	Note that the $ command is not available on all operating systems.

5)   a

6)   a   Rather than retyping the same commands over again, dynamic SQL scripts, also referred to as master/slave scripts or SQL to generate SQL, simplify this task.

CHAPTER 14

Lab 14.1 ■ Self-Review Answers

Question	Answer	Comments
1)	b	A user's objects can be dropped with the CASCADE keyword at the end of the DROP USER statement.
2)	a	
3)	a	System and object privileges cannot be granted or revoked in the same statement. However, system and object privileges, in separate statements, can be granted to or revoked from a single role.
4)	b	Both system and object privileges can be granted to a user through a role.
5)	b	Dropping a role has no effect on the underlying objects.
6)	a	

CHAPTER 15

Lab 15.1 ■ Self-Review Answers

Question	Answer	Comments
1)	c	
2)	a	
3)	a	
4)	b	The ROWS keyword defines a physical window.
5)	a	
6)	b	LAG and LEAD do not need a windowing clause, the position is defined with the offset value.
7)	a	

Lab 15.2 ■ Self-Review Answers

Question	Answer	Comments
1)	c	The formula to determine the number of different combinations for the CUBE operator is 2^n. With four columns the answer is 2^4, which equals 16.
2)	b	The formula for ROLLUP is $n + 1$. With four columns there will be a total of five groupings.

3)	a	A super aggregate row generated by the CUBE or ROLLUP operator will return the number 1 with the GROUPING function.
4)	a	These are three sets. The first set is a combination of the columns COLOR and PRICE as indicated with the parentheses around the columns. The second group is MATERIAL and the last group STORE_LOCATION.

Lab 15.3 ■ Self-Review Answers

Question	Answer	Comments
1)	a	
2)	a	The PRIOR operator determines the parent.
3)	a	
4)	a	

CHAPTER 16

Lab 16.1 ■ Self-Review Answers

Question	Answer	Comments
1)	b	
2)	a	
3)	a	The join order has a significant impact on performance.
4)	b	It is read from the inside to the outside. If two statements have the same level of indentation, the topmost statement is read first. The exception to this rule is the nested loop join.
5)	a	

A P P E N D I X   B

SQL FORMATTING GUIDE

SQL formatting guidelines are a set of written instructions, similar to a style sheet in publishing, that help programmers determine what the program code should look like. The main rule is *consistency;* once you have decided on the style, use it rigorously.

Why have guidelines? The major benefit of standardized formatting is ease of reading. This is particularly important if someone else has to maintain, upgrade, or fix your programs. The easier a program is to read, the easier it is to understand, and the faster changes can be made. This ultimately saves time and money.

CASE

SQL is case insensitive. However, there are guidelines to follow when writing SQL, for the sake of readability:

- Use UPPER case for SQL commands and keywords (SELECT, INSERT, UPDATE, DELETE, ALTER, etc.), datatypes (VARCHAR2, DATE, NUMBER), functions (COUNT, TO_DATE, SUBSTR, etc.), and SQL*Plus commands (CONNECT, SET, etc.).
- Use lowercase for column and tables names, as well as variable names.

FORMATTING SQL CODE

White space is important for readability. Put spaces on both sides of an equality sign or comparison operator. All examples in this workbook use a monospaced font (Courier) that makes the formatting easier to read. Proportionally spaced fonts can hide spaces and make it difficult to line up clauses. Most text and programming editors use monospace fonts by default.

IN QUERIES

For SELECT statements, right-align keywords (SELECT, FROM, WHERE, the ORDER of ORDER BY), as in this example:

```
SELECT *
  FROM course
 WHERE prerequisite IS NULL
 ORDER BY course_no
```

IN DML STATEMENTS

For DML statements, right-align keywords (the INSERT of INSERT INTO, VALUES, SELECT). List columns on a separate line, indenting the open parenthesis two spaces. Align columns underneath each other, putting only a few columns on each line, as in this example:

```
INSERT INTO zipcode
  (zip, created_by, created_date,
   modified_by, modified_date)
VALUES
  ('11111', USER, SYSDATE,
   USER, SYSDATE)
```

IN DDL STATEMENTS

When using CREATE TABLE and defining columns, or using ALTER to alter a table, indent the second line and all other lines thereafter by two spaces, as in this example:

```
CREATE TABLE toy
  (description          VARCHAR2(15) NOT NULL,
   last_purchase_date   DATE,
   remaining_quantity   NUMBER(6))
```

When creating a table from another, right-align keywords (CREATE, SELECT, FROM, WHERE), as in this example:

```
CREATE TABLE jan_99_enrollment AS
SELECT *
  FROM enrollment
 WHERE 1 = 2
```

COMMENTS

Comments are very important when writing SQL code. Comments should explain the main sections of the program or SQL statement and any major logic or business rules that are involved or nontrivial.

Suggestion: Use the '--' comments instead of the '/*' comments. It is easier to comment out a set of code for debugging using the '/*' comments if the code has only '--' comments. This is because you cannot embed '/*' comments within '/*' comments.

A P P E N D I X   C

SQL*PLUS COMMAND REFERENCE

UNSUPPORTED SQL*PLUS COMMANDS IN ISQL*PLUS

*i*SQL*Plus does not support some of the SQL*Plus commands; they are simply not applicable and if you issue the command it will raise an SP2–0850 error message. Table C.1 lists these unsupported commands.

Table C.1 ■ Unsupported SQL*Plus Commands

Command	Purpose
ACCEPT	Reads input and stores it in a variable.
CLEAR SCREEN	Clears screen of commands.
COLSEP	Set a column separation character.
EDITFILE	Sets the default file name for the EDIT file. The default file name in the Windows environment is afiedt.buf.
EXIT	Exits SQL*Plus and returns to the operating system.
FLUSH	Setting FLUSH OFF allows the operating system to buffer the output.
GET	Loads a file into the SQL buffer.
HOST	Executes an operating system command from within SQL*Plus.
NEWPAGE	The SET NEWPAGE command sets the number of blank lines printed on the top of a page. This is used to create and format reports in SQL*Plus.
PASSWORD	Changes the password without displaying the password on the screen.
PAUSE	Allows pausing of the output for each screen. To continue scrolling, you press the Enter key.

(continued)

Table C.1 ▪ continued

Command	Purpose
SAVE	Saves the contents of the SQL buffer to a file.
SHIFTINOUT	Used only for terminals that display shift characters.
SPOOL	Allows recording of commands in a file.
SQLBLANKLINES	Controls if blank lines are allowed within a SQL command or script.
SQLCONTINUE	Controls the line continuation prompt when a command doesn't fit in a line and needs to be continued. The default continuation character is a hyphen (-).
SQLNUMBER	Sets numeric sequence for subsequent prompt lines.
SQLPREFIX	Changes the SQLPREFIX character from the default value of # to another non-alphanumeric character.
SQLPROMPT	Changes the default SQL> prompt.
STORE	Saves all the settings of the SQL*Plus environment in a file.
TAB	Sets how SQL*Plus formats using either white spaces or tab characters.
TERMOUT	Controls the terminal output.
TIME	Shows the current time.
TRIMOUT	Allows trailing blanks at the end of each displayed line.
WHENEVER OSERROR EXIT	Exits SQL*Plus in case of an operating system error during the execution of a script.
WHENEVER SQLERROR EXIT	Exits SQL*Plus in case of a SQL command error during the execution of a script.

FORMATTING OUTPUT IN SQL*PLUS

The SQL*Plus COLUMN command allows you to change the column heading and format the query result. These formatting options are useful within SQL*Plus and allow for better readability.

FORMATTING THE QUERY RESULT

To allow a better viewing of the query result, you can use the COLUMN command with the FORMAT clause to change the formatting of the column. The syntax of the COLUMN command is as follows:

```
COLUMN columnname FORMAT formatmodel
```

The COLUMN keyword can be abbreviated as COL. The columnname indicates the name of the column or the column alias. If you choose a mixed case column alias or one that contains spaces, you must enclose it with double quotes.

The formatmodel allows for formatting of numeric and alphanumeric columns. For alphanumeric columns, it consists of the letter A and a column width. Numeric columns allow formatting for $ signs and commas.

To format the alphanumeric LAST_NAME column of the STUDENT table to a width of 20 characters, you would issue the following command:

```
COLUMN last_name FORMAT A20
```

The A20 format model indicates that you want the column formatted in alphanumeric format with a maximum width of 20 characters. If any value does not fit within the column, it will wrap. If you prefer that the values get truncated, use the SET WRAP OFF command or the TRUNCATED option of the FORMAT command.

```
COLUMN last_name FORMAT A5 TRUNCATED
```

Optionally, you can also wrap whole words with the COLUMN command.

```
COLUMN description FORMAT A20 WORD_WRAPPED
```

The effect on text such as "Intro to the Basic Language" is as follows:

```
Intro to the Basic
Language
```

Following is an example of a numeric format model that formats the COST column with a leading dollar sign and separates the thousands with a comma.

```
COL cost FORMAT $9,999.99
```

The result of this format model on different values is shown as follows:

```
 945.99     $945.99
1945.99   $1,945.99
10945.99  ##########
```

Notice that the last value cannot fit within the specified column width of the format model and SQL*Plus indicates this overflow with a pound (#) symbol for each allowed digit.

Alphanumeric values are displayed left-justified and numeric values are shown as right-justified.

To display the current attributes of a column, you use the COLUMN command with the column name.

```
COLUMN cost
COLUMN    cost ON
FORMAT    $9,999.99
```

To show the attributes of all columns, enter the COLUMN command without a column name or alias. To reset the display attributes to their default, use this syntax:

```
COL cost CLEAR
```

To reset the display attributes for all columns, issue the CLEAR COLUMNS command.

You can temporarily suppress the display attributes and return them to the default values with this syntax:

```
COL cost OFF
```

To restore the attributes use the COL cost ON command.

To give another column the same attributes as an existing column's attributes, you can copy the attributes with the LIKE clause of the COLUMN command. The FIRST_NAME column obtains the identical display attributes.

```
COL last_name FORMAT A10
COL first_name LIKE last_name
```

CHANGING THE COLUMN HEADING

You can change the column heading with the HEADING clause of the COLUMN command. The syntax is as follows:

```
COLUMN columnname HEADING columnheading
```

To display a heading over more than one line, you use the vertical bar (|) where a new line begins.

```
COL last_name HEADING STUDENT|LAST|NAME
STUDENT
LAST
NAME
--------
Crocitto
Landry
```

SQL*PLUS LINE EDITOR EDITING COMMANDS

This section is not applicable for *i*SQL*Plus. SQL*Plus stores SQL and PL/SQL commands (not SQL*Plus commands) in the SQL*Plus buffer.

To edit SQL*Plus commands that have been entered at the SQL*Plus command prompt, simply backspace over the command. SQL and PL/SQL commands that have been stored in the SQL*Plus buffer may be edited from within SQL*Plus using the SQL*Plus editing commands listed in Table C.2.

Table C.2 ■ SQL*Plus Editing Commands

Command	Abbreviation	Purpose
Append text	A text	Add text at the end of a line
Change /old/new	C /old/new	Change old to new in a line
Change /text	C /text	Delete text from a line
Clear Buffer	CL Buff	Delete all lines
Del	(none)	Delete a line
Input	I	Add one or more lines
Input text	I text	Add a line consisting of text
List	L	List all lines in the SQL buffer
List n	L n or n	List 1 line
List *	L *	List the current line
List Last	L Last	List the last line
List m n	L m n	List a range of lines (m to n)

USING THE SQL*PLUS LINE EDITOR TO SAVE AND RETRIEVE FILES

To save the current contents of the SQL*Plus buffer to a command script, use the SAVE command. An .sql extension is attached to the filename by default.

```
SQL> SAVE create_table_cat
```

To save the contents of the SQL*Plus buffer to a filename that already exists, use the SAVE command with the REPLACE option.

```
SQL> SAVE create_table_cat REPLACE
```

USING AN EDITOR TO CREATE A COMMAND SCRIPT

If you want to retrieve a file and place the contents of a command script into the SQL*Plus buffer, use the SQL*Plus GET command.

```
SQL> GET create_table_cat
```

If you have a set of commands (SQL*Plus, SQL, or a combination of the two) that may be used more than once, it is strongly recommended that you store them in a command script. A command script is a text file that can be run from the SQL*Plus command prompt:

```
SQL> @create_table_cat.sql
```

or you can run it from the operating system command prompt. The next command runs SQL*Plus from the Windows operating system command line and connects via the STUDENT account and the LEARN password. It automatically also runs the file CREATE_TABLE_CAT.SQL file located in the c:\guest directory. The .sql extension is optional.

```
C:\>sqlplus student/learn @c:\guest\create_table_cat.sql
```

USING AN EDITOR THAT IS EXTERNAL TO SQL*PLUS

To use your default operating system editor, type EDIT at the SQL*Plus prompt. EDIT loads the contents of the SQL*Plus buffer into the default editor.

You can start and create a new file with the EDIT command, which will invoke the editor.

```
SQL> EDIT
```

To load an already existing file with the user-supplied filename, that file will be opened for editing. SQL*Plus will supply the extension .sql by default.

```
SQL> EDIT create_table_cat
```

CHANGING THE DEFAULT EDITOR

To load the SQL*Plus buffer contents into a text editor other than the default, use the SQL*Plus DEFINE command to change the value of the variable, _EDITOR, to contain the name of the new editor.

```
SQL> DEFINE _EDITOR = ED
```

SQL*PLUS COMMANDS

The following are just some of the most commonly used commands available for use with SQL*Plus. Some of them are discussed in Chapter 2, "SQL: The Basics." This listing is not intended to be a thorough guide to SQL*Plus commands and some of the listed commands take additional parameters. Note that certain SQL*Plus commands can be toggled on or off (e.g., ECHO and FEEDBACK commands) or changed from one value to another with the SET command. (e.g., the LINESIZE command). All of the current values of the commands can be viewed when you type SHOW ALL at the SQL*Plus prompt. Note the letters appearing in square brackets are optional.

```
@ ("at") and @@ (double "at" sign)
```

The "at" symbol (@) precedes a file name to run a SQL script. It is equivalent to the START command. For example: @@filename[.ext] An @@ command runs a nested command file and runs in the same directory path as the calling script.

```
&variablename
```

The ampersand (&) symbol is used as a substitution variable. Use the SET DEFINE OFF command to turn off the use of the ampersand as the substitution variable.

```
&&variablename
```

The double ampersand symbol (&&) is also a substitution variable, but it avoids reprompting. The variable is declared for the duration of the SQL*Plus session. Use UNDEFINE to undefine the variable and allow for reprompting.

The forward slash is entered at the SQL*Plus prompt to execute the current SQL statement or PL/SQL block in the buffer.

```
ACC[EPT] variablename
```

The ACCEPT command reads a line of input and stores it in a user variable. This command is not available in *i*SQL*Plus.

```
A[PPEND]
```

The APPEND command appends text at the end of a line.

```
C[HANGE]
```

The CHANGE command changes text on the line indicated by following the CHANGE command with a forward slash, the old text, another forward slash, and the new text.

```
CL[EAR] BUF[FER]
```

The CLEAR BUFFER command clears all lines of a SQL statement from the buffer.

```
CL[EAR] COL[UMNS]
```

The CLEAR COLUMNS command clears all formatting of columns issued previously during the current session.

```
CL[EAR] SCR[EEN]
```

The CLEAR SCREEN command clears the entire screen of all commands. This command is not available in *i*SQL*Plus.

```
COL[UMN]
```

The COLUMN command shows the display attributes for all columns. To show a specific column, use COLUMN columnname. To reset the attributes, use the COLUMN columnname CLEAR command. Also refer to the FORMAT command.

```
CONN[ECT]
```

When the CONNECT command is followed by a user ID and password and the connect identifier (if any), it allows you to connect to the Oracle database as another user, and it closes the active session for the current user. You can also use the DISCONNECT command to close an active session.

```
COPY
```

Allows you to copy results between tables or databases. It allows you to create or append rows to existing tables or create new tables.

```
DEF[INE] [variablename]
```

The DEFINE command defines a SQL*Plus variable and stores it in a CHAR datatype variable. Without a variable name, it shows all the defined variables. SET DEFINE defines the substitution character—by default the ampersand symbol (&). SET DEFINE OFF turns the use of the substitution character off.

```
DEL
```

The DEL command deletes the current line in the buffer.

```
DESC[RIBE]
```

The DESCRIBE command describes the structure of a table or view, detailing its columns and their datatypes and lengths.

```
ED[IT] [filename.ext]
```

The EDIT command invokes the editor specified in SQL*Plus, opening a file with the current SQL statement. You can edit a specific file by executing the EDIT command followed by a filename. This command is not available in *i*SQL*Plus.

```
EXIT
```

The EXIT command disconnects the current user from the database and closes the SQL*Plus software. This command is not available in *i*SQL*Plus.

```
EXE[CUTE] statement
```

The EXECUTE command executes a single PL/SQL statement.

```
FOR[MAT] formatmodel
```

The FORMAT command, together with the COLUMN command, specifies the display format of a column. For example, COL "Last Name" FORMAT A30, or COL cost FORMAT $999.99, or COL description FORMAT A20.

```
GET filename[.ext]
```

Loads a file into the SQL buffer. This command is not available in *i*SQL*Plus.

```
HELP [topic]
```

The HELP command accesses the SQL*Plus help system.

```
HO[ST]
```

The HOST command executes an operating system command without exiting SQL*Plus. Depending on the operating system, ! or $ can be specified instead of the HOST command. This command is not available in *i*SQL*Plus.

```
I[NPUT]
```

The INPUT command adds one or more lines to the current SQL statement.

```
L[IST]
```

The LIST command lists the contents of the buffer.

```
PROMPT [text]
```

The PROMPT command sends the specified message or a blank line to the user's screen.

```
REM[ARK]
```

The REMARK command begins a comment in a command file.

REP[LACE]

The REPLACE command is used in conjunction with the SAVE command to save a SQL statement to an existing file and overwrite it. The syntax is: SAVE filename[.sql] REPLACE.

RUN

The RUN command lists and executes a SQL command in the SQL buffer.

SAV[E] filename[.ext]

When followed by a file name, the SAVE command saves the file to the operating system. A directory can be specified. This command is not available in *i*SQL*Plus.

SET AUTO[COMMIT]

The AUTOCOMMIT command can be set for a session to automatically commit all DML statements, rather than having to issue an explicit COMMIT command.

SET DEFINE [ON|OFF]

The DEFINE command turns the use of the substitution character on and off. See also DEFINE command.

SET ECHO [OFF|ON]

The ECHO command controls whether or not the commands in a SQL*Plus script are shown when the script is executed.

SET FEED[BACK] [6|n|OFF|ON]

The FEEDBACK command displays the number of records returned by a query when a query selects at least n records.

SET LIN[ESIZE] [80|n]

The LINESIZE command sets the number of characters that SQL*Plus displays on a line before beginning a new line.

SET PAGES[IZE] [14|n]

The PAGESIZE command sets the number of lines from the top title to the end of the page. A value 0 suppresses SQL*Plus formatting information such as headings.

```
SET PAU[SE] [OFF|ON|text]
```

The PAUSE command allows control of scrolling and text displayed during pause. This command is not available in *i*SQL*Plus.

```
SET SQLPROMPT
```

The SET SQLPROMPT command changes the SQL*Plus prompt. This command is not available in *i*SQL*Plus.

```
SET TIME [ON|OFF]
```

The TIME command shows the current time. This command is not available in *i*SQL*Plus.

```
SET TIMING [ON|OFF]
```

The TIMING command turns on/off the display of timing statistics.

```
SET TERM[OUT] [OFF|ON]
```

The TERMOUT command controls the display of output. This command is not available in *i*SQL*Plus.

```
SET VER[IFY] [OFF|ON]
```

The VERIFY command controls whether SQL*Plus lists text of a command before and after SQL*Plus replaces substitution variables with values.

```
SHO[W] ALL
```

The SHOWALL command lists the value of all SQL*Plus system variables. The SHOW USER command is also useful to display the current login name.

```
SHUTDOWN
```

The SHUTDOWN command shuts down an Oracle database instance.

```
SPO[OL] [filename[.ext]|OFF|OUT]
```

When you issue the SPOOL command followed by a file name, all commands subsequently issued in SQL*Plus are written to the file. The SPOOL OFF command stops writing to the file. If you do not specify an extension, the default extension is LIS or LST. This command is not available in *i*SQL*Plus.

```
START filename[.ext]
```

When followed by a file name, the START command executes the file. This is the same as the @ symbol.

```
STARTUP
```

The STARTUP command starts up an Oracle instance and optionally mounts and opens the database.

```
UNDEFINE variablename
```

The UNDEFINE command deletes a user variable that was explicitly defined with the DEFINE command or implicitly with the & or && substitution variables.

```
WHENEVER OSERROR
```

The OSERROR command exits SQL*Plus if an operating system command generates an error. Not available in *i*SQL*Plus.

```
WHENEVER SQLERROR
```

The SQLERROR command exits SQL*Plus if an SQL command generates an error. Not available in *i*SQL*Plus.

A P P E N D I X   D

STUDENT DATABASE SCHEMA

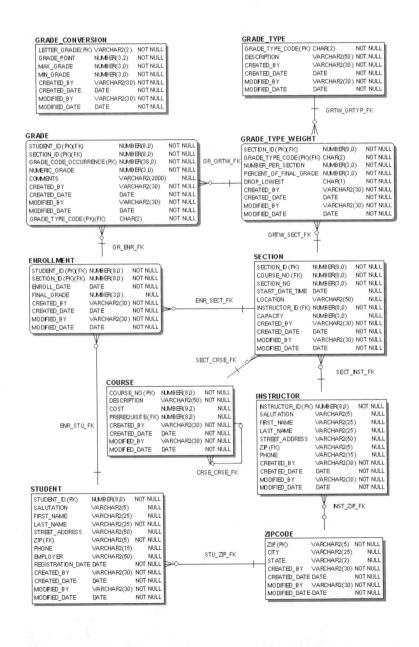

APPENDIX E

TABLE AND COLUMN DESCRIPTIONS

COURSE: Information for a course

Column Name	Null	Type	Comments
COURSE_NO	NOT NULL	NUMBER(8, 0)	The unique ID for a course.
DESCRIPTION	NULL	VARCHAR2(50)	The full name for this course.
COST	NULL	NUMBER(9,2)	The dollar amount charged for enrollment in this course.
PREREQUISITE	NULL	NUMBER(8, 0)	The ID number of the course which must be taken as a prerequisite to this course.
CREATED_BY	NOT NULL	VARCHAR2(30)	Audit column—indicates user who inserted data.
CREATED_DATE	NOT NULL	DATE	Audit column—indicates date of insert.
MODIFIED_BY	NOT NULL	VARCHAR2(30)	Audit column—indicates who made last update.
MODIFIED_DATE	NOT NULL	DATE	Audit column—date of last update.

SECTION: Information for an individual section (class) of a particular course

Column Name	Null	Type	Comments
SECTION_ID	NOT NULL	NUMBER(8,0)	The unique ID for a section.
COURSE_NO	NOT NULL	NUMBER(8,0)	The course number for which this is a section.
SECTION_NO	NOT NULL	NUMBER(3)	The individual section number within this course.
START_DATE_TIME	NULL	DATE	The date and time on which this section meets.
LOCATION	NULL	VARCHAR2(50)	The meeting room for the section.
INSTRUCTOR_ID	NOT NULL	NUMBER(8,0)	The ID number of the instructor who teaches this section.
CAPACITY	NULL	NUMBER(3,0)	The maximum number of students allowed in this section.
CREATED_BY	NOT NULL	VARCHAR2(30)	Audit column—indicates user who inserted data.
CREATED_DATE	NOT NULL	DATE	Audit column—indicates date of insert.
MODIFIED_BY	NOT NULL	VARCHAR2(30)	Audit column—indicates who made last update.
MODIFIED_DATE	NOT NULL	DATE	Audit column—date of last update.

STUDENT: Profile information for a student

Column Name	Null	Type	Comments
STUDENT_ID	NOT NULL	NUMBER(8,0)	The unique ID for a student.
SALUTATION	NULL	VARCHAR2(5)	This student's title (Ms., Mr., Dr., etc.).
FIRST_NAME	NULL	VARCHAR2(25)	This student's first name.
LAST_NAME	NOT NULL	VARCHAR2(25)	This student's last name.
STREET_ADDRESS	NULL	VARCHAR2(50)	This student's street address.
ZIP	NOT NULL	VARCHAR2(5)	The postal zip code for this student.

PHONE	NULL	VARCHAR2(15)	The phone number for this student, including area code.
EMPLOYER	NULL	VARCHAR2(50)	The name of the company where this student is employed.
REGISTRATION_DATE	NOT NULL	DATE	The date this student registered in the program.
CREATED_BY	NOT NULL	VARCHAR2(30)	Audit column—indicates user who inserted data.
CREATED_DATE	NOT NULL	DATE	Audit column—indicates date of insert.
MODIFIED_BY	NOT NULL	VARCHAR2(30)	Audit column—indicates who made last update.
MODIFIED_DATE	NOT NULL	DATE	Audit column—date of last update.

ENROLLMENT: Information for a student registered for a particular section (class)

Column Name	Null	Type	Comments
STUDENT_ID	NOT NULL	NUMBER(8,0)	The unique ID for a student.
SECTION_ID	NOT NULL	NUMBER(8,0)	The unique ID for a section.
ENROLL_DATE	NOT NULL	DATE	The date this student registered for this section.
FINAL_GRADE	NULL	NUMBER(3,0)	The final grade given to this student for all work in this section (class).
CREATED_BY	NOT NULL	VARCHAR2(30)	Audit column—indicates user who inserted data.
CREATED_DATE	NOT NULL	DATE	Audit column—indicates date of insert.
MODIFIED_BY	NOT NULL	VARCHAR2(30)	Audit column—indicates who made last update.
MODIFIED_DATE	NOT NULL	DATE	Audit column—date of last update.

INSTRUCTOR: Profile information for an instructor

Column Name	Null	Type	Comments
INSTRUCTOR_ID	NOT NULL	NUMBER(8)	The unique ID for an instructor.
SALUTATION	NULL	VARCHAR2(5)	This instructor's title (Mr., Ms., Dr., Rev., etc.).
FIRST_NAME	NULL	VARCHAR2(25)	This instructor's first name.
LAST_NAME	NULL	VARCHAR2(25)	This instructor's last name.
STREET_ADDRESS	NULL	VARCHAR2(50)	This instructor's street address.
ZIP	NULL	VARCHAR2(5)	The postal zip code for this instructor.
PHONE	NULL	VARCHAR2(15)	The phone number for this instructor, including area code.
CREATED_BY	NOT NULL	VARCHAR2(30)	Audit column—indicates user who inserted data.
CREATED_DATE	NOT NULL	DATE	Audit column—indicates date of insert.
MODIFIED_BY	NOT NULL	VARCHAR2(30)	Audit column—indicates who made last update.
MODIFIED_DATE	NOT NULL	DATE	Audit column—date of last update.

ZIPCODE: City, state, and zipcode information

Column Name	Null	Type	Comments
ZIP	NOT NULL	VARCHAR2(5)	The zip code number, unique for a city and state.
CITY	NULL	VARCHAR2(25)	The city name for this zip code.
STATE	NULL	VARCHAR2(2)	The postal abbreviation for the U.S. state.
CREATED_BY	NOT NULL	VARCHAR2(30)	Audit column—indicates user who inserted data.
CREATED_DATE	NOT NULL	DATE	Audit column—indicates date of insert.
MODIFIED_BY	NOT NULL	VARCHAR2(30)	Audit column—indicates who made last update.
MODIFIED_DATE	NOT NULL	DATE	Audit column—date of last update.

GRADE_TYPE: Lookup table of a grade type (code) and its description

Column Name	Null	Type	Comments
GRADE_TYPE_CODE	NOT NULL	CHAR(2)	The unique code that identifies a category of grade (e.g., MT, HW).
DESCRIPTION	NOT NULL	VARCHAR2(50)	The description for this code (e.g., Midterm, Homework).
CREATED_BY	NOT NULL	VARCHAR2(30)	Audit column—indicates user who inserted data.
CREATED_DATE	NOT NULL	DATE	Audit column—indicates date of insert.
MODIFIED_BY	NOT NULL	VARCHAR2(30)	Audit column—indicates who made last update.
MODIFIED_DATE	NOT NULL	DATE	Audit column—date of last update.

GRADE_TYPE_WEIGHT: Information on how the final grade for a particular section is computed. For example, the midterm constitutes 50 percent, the quiz 10 percent, and the final examination 40 percent of the final grade

Column Name	Null	Type	Comments
SECTION_ID	NOT NULL	NUMBER(8)	The unique ID for a section.
GRADE_TYPE_CODE	NOT NULL	CHAR(2)	The code which identifies a category of grade.
NUMBER_PER_SECTION	NOT NULL	NUMBER(3)	How many of these grade types can be used in this section (i.e., there may be three quizzes).
PERCENT_OF_FINAL_GRADE	NOT NULL	NUMBER(3)	The percentage this category of grade contributes to the final grade.
DROP_LOWEST	NOT NULL	CHAR(1)	Is the lowest grade in this type removed when determining the final grade? (Y/N).
CREATED_BY	NOT NULL	VARCHAR2(30)	Audit column—indicates user who inserted data.
CREATED_DATE	NOT NULL	DATE	Audit column—indicates date of insert.
MODIFIED_BY	NOT NULL	VARCHAR2(30)	Audit column—indicates who made last update.
MODIFIED_DATE	NOT NULL	DATE	Audit column—date of last update.

GRADE: The individual grades a student received for a particular section (class)

Column Name	Null	Type	Comments
STUDENT_ID	NOT NULL	NUMBER(8)	The unique ID for a student.
SECTION_ID	NOT NULL	NUMBER(8)	The unique ID for a section.
GRADE_TYPE_CODE	NOT NULL	CHAR(2)	The code which identifies a category of grade.
GRADE_CODE_OCCURRENCE	NOT NULL	NUMBER(38)	The sequence number of one grade type for one section. For example, there could be multiple assignments numbered 1, 2, 3, etc.
NUMERIC_GRADE	NOT NULL	NUMBER(3)	Numeric grade value (e.g., 70, 75).
COMMENTS	NULL	VARCHAR2(2000)	Instructor's comments on this grade.
CREATED_BY	NOT NULL	VARCHAR2(30)	Audit column—indicates user who inserted data.
CREATED_DATE	NOT NULL	DATE	Audit column—indicates date of insert.
MODIFIED_BY	NOT NULL	VARCHAR2(30)	Audit column—indicates who made last update.
MODIFIED_DATE	NOT NULL	DATE	Audit column—date of last update.

GRADE_CONVERSION: Converts a number grade to a letter grade

Column Name	Null	Type	Comments
LETTER_GRADE	NOT NULL	VARCHAR(2)	The unique grade as a letter (A, A–, B, B+, etc.).
GRADE_POINT	NOT NULL	NUMBER(3,2)	The number grade on a scale from 0 (F) to 4 (A).
MAX_GRADE	NOT NULL	NUMBER(3)	The highest grade number that makes this letter grade.
MIN_GRADE	NOT NULL	NUMBER(3)	The lowest grade number that makes this letter grade.
CREATED_BY	NOT NULL	VARCHAR2(30)	Audit column—indicates user who inserted data.
CREATED_DATE	NOT NULL	DATE	Audit column—indicates date of insert.
MODIFIED_BY	NOT NULL	VARCHAR2(30)	Audit column—indicates who last made update.
MODIFIED_DATE	NOT NULL	DATE	Audit column—date of last update.

A P P E N D I X   F

ADDITIONAL EXAMPLE TABLES

Throughout this workbook some exercises made use of tables not part of the STU-DENT schema diagram listed in Appendix D, "STUDENT Schema Diagram." These additional tables can be created in your STUDENT schema by downloading the script sql_book_add_tables.sql from the companion Web site located at: http://www.phptr.com/rischert. The purpose of these additional tables is to illustrate SQL concepts that could otherwise not be shown within the available data and datatypes in the STUDENT schema.

Chapter 4: Date and Conversion Functions

DATE_EXAMPLE

```
COL_DATE
COL_TIMESTAMP
COL_TIMESTAMP_W_TZ
COL_TIMESTAMP_W_LOCAL_TZ
```

CONVERSION_EXAMPLE

```
COURSE_NO
```

GRADE_SUMMARY

```
STUDENT_ID
MIDTERM_GRADE
FINALEXAM_GRADE
QUIZ_GRADE
```

MEETING

```
MEETING_ID
MEETING_START
MEETING_END
```

Chapter 9: Complex Joins

T1

```
COL1
```

T2

```
COL2
```

Chapter 10: Insert, Update, and Delete

INTRO_COURSE

```
COURSE_NO
DESCRIPTION_TX
COST
PREREQ_NO
CREATED_BY
CREATED_DATE
MODIFIED_BY
MODIFIED_DATE
```

GRADE_DISTRIBUTION

```
SECTION_ID
GRADE_A
GRADE_B
GRADE_C
GRADE_D
GRADE_F
```

GRADE_DISTRIBUTION_NORMALIZED

```
SECTION_ID
LETTER_GRADE
NUM_OF_STUDENTS
```

EMPLOYEE

```
EMPLOYEE_ID
NAME
SALARY
TITLE
```

EMPLOYEE_CHANGE

```
EMPLOYEE_ID
NAME
TITLE
SALARY
```

SECTION_HISTORY

```
SECTION_ID
START_DATE_TIME
COURSE_NO
SECTION_NO
```

CAPACITY_HISTORY

```
SECTION_ID
LOCATION
CAPACITY
```

TA

```
ID
COL1
```

TB

```
ID
COL2
```

Chapter 15: Advanced SQL Queries

COURSE_REVENUE

```
COURSE_NO
REVENUE
COURSE_FEE
NUM_ENROLLED
NUM_OF_SECTIONS
```

INSTRUCTOR_SUMMARY

```
INSTRUCTOR_ID (PK)
SEMESTER_YEAR (PK)
SEMESTER_MONTH (PK)
GENDER
CAMPUS
NUM_OF_CLASSES
NUM_OF_STUDENTS
REVENUE
```

TABLE AND COLUMN DESCRIPTIONS

CHAPTER 4: DATE AND CONVERSION FUNCTIONS

DATE_EXAMPLE: This table holds data to illustrate the use of **DATE** and **DATETIME** related datatypes

Column Name	Null	Type	Comments
COL_DATE	NULL	DATE	Holds data in the DATE datatype.
COL_TIMESTAMP	NULL	TIMESTAMP(6)	Holds data in TIMESTAMP datatype with a 6-digit precision for fractional seconds.
COL_TIMESTAMP_W_TZ	NULL	TIMESTAMP(6) WITH TIME ZONE	Holds data in TIMESTAMP WITH TIME ZONE datatype.
COL_TIMESTAMP_W_LOCAL_TZ	NULL	TIMESTAMP(6) WITH LOCAL TIMES ZONE	Holds data in TIMESTAMP WITH LOCAL TIME ZONE datatype.

CONVERSION_EXAMPLE: This table helps demonstrate the effect of Oracle's implicit datatype conversion

Column Name	Null	Type	Comments
COURSE_NO	NULL	VARCHAR2(9)	Course number.

GRADE_SUMMARY: This table shows the use of the **COALESCE** function

Column Name	Null	Type	Comments
STUDENT_ID	NULL	NUMBER(8,0)	The unique ID for a student.
MIDTERM_GRADE	NULL	NUMBER(3)	Midterm grade of a student.
FINALEXAM_GRADE	NULL	NUMBER(3)	Final grade of a student.
QUIZ_GRADE	NULL	NUMBER(3)	Quiz grade of a student.

MEETING:This table shows the use of the OVERLAP and BETWEEN operators

Column Name	Null	Type	Comments
MEETING_ID	NULL	NUMBER(10)	The unique ID for a meeting.
MEETING_START_DATE	NULL	DATE	The meeting's starting date and time.
MEETING_END_DATE	NULL	DATE	The meeting's ending date and time.

CHAPTER 9: COMPLEX JOINS

T1:This table combined with table T2 illustrates outer joins and full outer joins

Column Name	Null	Type	Comments
COL1	NULL	NUMBER	Column holds numeric data.

T2:This table combined with table T1 illustrates outer joins and full outer joins

Column Name	Null	Type	Comments
COL2	NULL	NUMBER	Column holds numeric data.

CHAPTER 10: INSERT, UPDATE, AND DELETE

INTRO_COURSE:This table is similar in structure to the COURSE table and is used to show examples of insert statements

Column Name	Null	Type	Comments
COURSE_NO	NULL	NUMBER(8, 0)	The unique ID for a course.
DESCRIPTION	NULL	VARCHAR2(50)	The full name for this course.
COST	NULL	NUMBER(9,2)	The dollar amount charged for enrollment in this course.
PREREQ_NO	NULL	NUMBER(8, 0)	The ID number of the course which must be taken as a prerequisite to this course.
CREATED_BY	NULL	VARCHAR2(30)	Audit column—indicates user who inserted data.
CREATED_DATE	NULL	DATE	Audit column—indicates date of insert.
MODIFIED_BY	NULL	VARCHAR2(30)	Audit column—indicates who made last update.
MODIFIED_DATE	NULL	DATE	Audit column—date of last update.

GRADE_DISTRIBUTION: This table is used to demonstrate multi-table INSERT statements

Column Name	Null	Type	Comments
SECTION_ID	NULL	NUMBER(8)	The unique ID for a section.
GRADE_A	NULL	NUMBER(4)	Number of students with grade of A.
GRADE_B	NULL	NUMBER(4)	Number of students with a grade of B.
GRADE_C	NULL	NUMBER(4)	Number of students with a grade of C.
GRADE_D	NULL	NUMBER(4)	Number of students with a grade of D.
GRADE_F	NULL	NUMBER(4)	Number of students with a grade of F.

GRADE_DISTRIBUTION_NORMALIZED: This table helps illustrate the use of the multi-table INSERT statements

Column Name	Null	Type	Comments
SECTION_ID	NULL	NUMBER(8)	The unique ID for a section.
LETTER_GRADE	NULL	VARCHAR(2)	The unique grade as a letter (A, A-, B, B+, etc.).
NUM_OF_STUDENTS	NULL	NUMBER(4)	Number of students.

EMPLOYEE: The table holds employee information

Column Name	Null	Type	Comments
EMPLOYEE_ID	NULL	NUMBER	The unique ID for an employee.
NAME	NULL	VARCHAR2(10)	Employee's name.
SALARY	NULL	NUMBER	Employee's salary.
TITLE	NULL	VARCHAR2(10)	Employee's job title.

EMPLOYEE_CHANGE: This table contains changes to the EMPLOYEE table for the purpose of showing INSERT/MERGE functionality

Column Name	Null	Type	Comments
EMPLOYEE_ID	NULL	NUMBER	The unique ID for an employee.
NAME	NULL	VARCHAR2(10)	Employee's name.
SALARY	NULL	NUMBER	Employee's salary.
TITLE	NULL	VARCHAR2(10)	Employee's job title.

SECTION_HISTORY: This table lists historical data from the SECTION table to help illustrate the use of the multi-table INSERT command

Column Name	Null	Type	Comments
SECTION_ID	NOT NULL	NUMBER(8,0)	The unique ID for a section.
START_DATE_TIME	NULL	DATE	The date and time on which this section meets.
COURSE_NO	NOT NULL	NUMBER(8,0)	The course number for which this is a section.
SECTION_NO	NOT NULL	NUMBER(3)	The individual section number within this course.

CAPACITY_HISTORY: This table holds historical data from the SECTION table related to the CAPACITY column and is used to show the use of the multi-table INSERT command

Column Name	Null	Type	Comments
SECTION_ID	NOT NULL	NUMBER(8,0)	The unique ID for a section.
LOCATION	NULL	VARCHAR2(50)	The meeting room for the section.
CAPACITY	NULL	NUMBER(3,0)	The maximum number of students that can be enrolled in this section.

TA: This table helps illustrate a correlated update problem

Column Name	Null	Type	Comments
ID	NULL	NUMBER	The unique ID the table.
COL1	NULL	VARCHAR2(4)	The column holds alphanumeric data.

TB: This table helps illustrate a correlated update problem

Column Name	Null	Type	Comments
ID	NULL	NUMBER	The unique ID the table.
COL2	NULL	VARCHAR2(4)	The column holds alphanumeric data.

CHAPTER 15: ADVANCED SQL QUERIES

COURSE_REVENUE: This table contains data about the total revenue per course, the total number of students enrolled, and the number of sections for this course

Column Name	Null	Type	Comments
COURSE_NO	NULL	NUMBER(8, 0)	The unique ID for a course.
REVENUE	NULL	NUMBER	The revenue for this course.
COURSE_FEE	NULL	NUMBER(9,2)	The course fee (course cost) of this course.
NUM_ENROLLED	NULL	NUMBER	The number of students enrolled in this course.
NUM_OF_SECTIONS	NULL	NUMBER	The number of sections for this course.

INSTRUCTOR_SUMMARY: This table holds revenue and enrollment information by instructor, year, and month

Column Name	Null	Type	Comments
INSTRUCTOR_ID	NOT NULL	NUMBER(8,0)	The ID number of the instructor who teaches this section.
SEMESTER_YEAR	NOT NULL	VARCHAR2(4)	Semester year in which this instructor teaches.
SEMESTER_MONTH	NOT NULL	VARCHAR2(2)	Month in which the instructor teaches.
GENDER	NULL	CHAR(1)	Gender.
CAMPUS	NULL	VARCHAR2(11)	Campus location.
NUM_OF_CLASSES	NULL	NUMBER	Number of sections.
NUM_OF_STUDENTS	NULL	NUMBER	The number of enrolled students.
REVENUE	NULL	NUMBER	This column holds the generated revenue amount, which is computed by multiplying the course cost by the number of enrolled students.

APPENDIX G

NAVIGATING THROUGH THE ORACLE DOCUMENTATION

WHY DO YOU NEED TO READ THIS APPENDIX?

After reading this book and performing the exercises, you will have gained significant experience and knowledge with the Oracle database. Congratulations! Not every topic and syntax option can be discussed in this book; otherwise it would have several thousands of pages. The emphasis is on highlighting the most commonly used features. What do you do to learn more about a particular topic or what if you have further questions? One of the ways to research the answer is to consult the Oracle supplied documentation.

Another reason you may need to consult the Oracle documentation is when versions change (an inevitable fact of software development). Additional features are often added and existing functionality enhanced. Perhaps you are working with a previous Oracle version (prior to Oracle 9*i*) and want to check if certain features are available. As you can see, there are many reasons why consulting the documentation is unavoidable.

WHERE DO YOU FIND THE ORACLE DOCUMENTATION?

The Oracle documentation can be installed using Oracle's installer program or you can look up the documentation on the OTN (Oracle Technology Network) Web site. The OTN site is Oracle's own site that contains a wealth of information including the documentation and is geared towards developers and DBAs. Before you can access the site, you must register (registration is free). The URL for OTN is http://otn. oracle.com. After you register, you can find all Oracle documentation (including previous Oracle versions) at this URL: http://otn.oracle.com/docs/content.html. If you do not want to join OTN, you can use this direct link: http://tahiti.oracle.com.

After you navigated through the different options, you will receive a screen similar to Figure G.1, which shows the Oracle 9*i* Search screen.

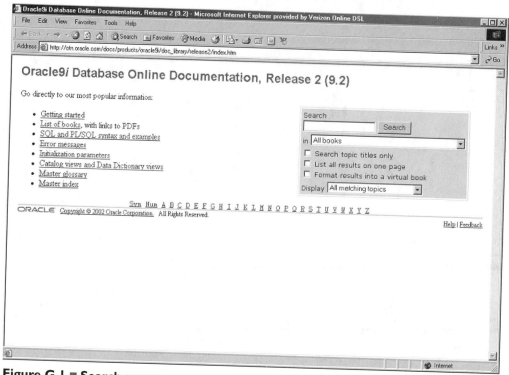

Figure G.1 ■ Search screen.

JUMPSTART YOUR SEARCH

On the left side of the Search screen is a menu that lets you jumpstart your search for specific subjects. You can look for Oracle error messages by clicking on the Oracle Error messages link, which allows you to search for an individual error message and determine the cause and recommended action along with it.

If you already know in which book you will find the needed information, you can click directly on the List of Books link. Most manuals can be viewed in PDF format, if you care to print the information.

Clicking on to the Catalog Views and Data Dictionary Views link displays all the views and lets you click on the respective view to read the column definitions. It also provides a link that shows you where the individual view is mentioned in the documentation.

The Master Glossary is a great way to start a search for definitions, especially when you are new to Oracle database technology.

The Master Index link contains the index entries for all books. This is just another way to search and find relevant information in the documentation.

The Initialization Parameters link allows you to list all the different init.ora settings, their definitions, and possible values.

The right side of the screen presents a Search box that allows you to enter a word or phrase you want to search for in either upper or lowercase. If you already know the specific Oracle documentation you are looking for, you can choose from a selected list of books. The last box lets you choose the level of detail you want that is you can search all matching topics, only introductory information, only tasks, only examples, or only troubleshooting.

You can enter a phrase or an individual word. Multiple words or phrases can be connected with AND to query for items that contains both words—this is useful if your initial search result yielded too many matches. You can also use the OR and the NOT Boolean operators to improve your search results.

The search result presents a listing of books and the number of matching topics in each. You can then read the books and matches you consider most relevant. The most widely used books are listed first, and when you have chosen a book the search result is listed in alphabetical order.

VIRTUAL BOOK FEATURE

If you are unsure which book is the best choice, you can click on the Virtual Book checkbox to format the search results into a virtual book. This may make it easier to read through the search results. It also presents introductory material first. The Virtual Book does not support the AND and OR operators in the search, and the checkboxes and drop-down menu have no effect on the search result. All the books and all topics are examined; however, the search only looks at the titles rather than the entire text for an individual topic.

ORACLE DOCUMENTATION TITLES

It is useful to know what topics are covered in the various Oracle manuals. Table G.1 lists of the most commonly used manuals and the major topics covered in each.

ERROR MESSAGES

The Oracle Error Messages manual, together with the SQL*Plus User's Guide and Reference manual, lists the most common error messages. Error messages are usually prefixed with a three-letter code that indicates the program that issued the error. It also gives you an indication in which manual to look for the error or which of Oracle's products causes the error. Most error messages are found in the Oracle Error Messages manual; however, some product-specific errors are found in that product's individual manual (i.e., SP2 errors are found in the SQL*Plus User's Guide and Reference manual). Table G.2 lists the most common error message codes.

Table G.1 ■ Selected Oracle Documentation Titles

Book	Contents
Administrator's Guide	Basic database administration tasks, such as creating new databases, starting up and shutting down a database, managing the files, backup and recovery, storage management, creating, altering, and dropping database objects, managing users and permissions.
Application Developer's Guide—Fundamentals	This guide is one of the most useful Oracle documentation books. It contains a wealth of information from a developer's perspective. Information such as the management of database objects, the selection of datatypes, and the enforcement of data integrity via constraints is discussed. You will find information about choosing an indexing strategy for good performance as well as an introduction into application security and a discussion of PL/SQL triggers.
Backup and Recovery Concepts	This book details backup and recovery strategies to ensure adequate protection of your database.
Concepts	This manual discusses the Oracle architecture and its core concepts and is intended for database administrators and database application developers. It explains the details of data blocks, tablespaces, the data dictionary, the database instance with startup and shutdown, the different types of database objects, data types, triggers, and dependency amongst objects, data integrity and security.
Data Warehousing Guide	This book covers the issues evolving around designing, building and maintaining a data warehouse. It explains the analytical functions and discusses data transformation and loading.
Error Messages	You will find most error messages in this manual, except for SQL*Plus SP2 errors. You will find those in the SQL*Plus User's Guide and Reference. Other product-specific errors are also found in the respective Oracle product manual.
Getting Started with Windows	This is an introductory text to the features of SQL*Plus.
Installation Guide for Windows or Installation Guide for Unix Systems	An installation guide to installing the Oracle software for the individual operating system environment (e.g., Windows, Unix).
Performance Tuning Guide and Reference	This manual is concerned with tuning SQL statements and the Oracle database for optimal performance. The various methods illustrate how you can collect performance statistics on your database and how to tune SQL statements.

Table G.1 ■ Continued

Book	Contents
Reference	The dynamic and static data dictionary views are listed in this book along with the Oracle initialization parameters for the initialization file (init.ora).
SQL Reference	This is an alphabetical reference to all SQL commands. Furthermore, it contains a list of all functions, operators, and expressions. Diagrams show and explain the different syntax options. If you are unsure of a command's syntax options, this is the manual to consult.
Supplied PL/SQL Packages and Types Reference	Information about the procedures and functions of Oracle supplied packages appear in this manual. For example, you find examples and parameter listings about collecting statistics with the DBMS_STATS package in this book.
SQL*Plus Getting Started for Windows	An introduction to using SQL*Plus.
SQL*Plus User's Guide and Reference	Guide to SQL*Plus including all SP2 error messages. Contains a listing of all SQL*Plus commands and formatting options.

Table G.2 ■ Common Oracle Error Message Codes

Message Prefix	Oracle Software
ORA	Oracle server message
TNS	Oracle Net messages
SP2	SQL*Plus message
EXP	Export utility message
IMP	Import utility message
SQL*Loader	SQL*Loader message
KUP	External table message
RMAN	Recovery Manager message
PLS	PL/SQL message

READING ORACLE SYNTAX DIAGRAMS

In Chapter 3, "Character, Number, and Miscellaneous Functions," you were introduced to a variant of the BNF (Backus-Naur Form) style syntax (see Table 3.1). A very similar style is also listed in the Oracle manuals if you click on the text description link below the syntax.

You will notice that most of Oracle's manuals now show the graphic syntax diagrams. To read such a diagram, you should follow the path of the line, starting from the left to the right. Keywords such as commands are in uppercase and inside rectangular boxes. Required syntax always appears on the main path; an optional choice is listed above the main path. Multiple choices are indicated through multiple paths either on or above the main path.

Figure G.2 lists the partial syntax diagram of the CREATE INDEX command. As you see, the CREATE INDEX command allows for a number of choices. You can choose between the syntax options CREATE INDEX, CREATE UNIQUE INDEX, and CREATE BITMAP INDEX. The UNIQUE and BITMAP keywords are optional and let you create different types of indexes.

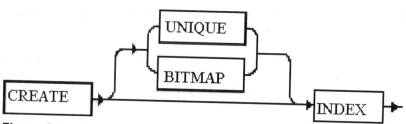

Figure G.2 ■ Excerpt of CREATE INDEX syntax.

Figure G.3 shows you additional syntax conventions on the example of the VALUES clause of the INSERT command. Inside circles you will find punctuation, operators, and delimiters such as commas or parentheses. Object names, expressions, parameters, and variables appear in lowercase and inside ovals. If you are allowed to choose more than one option, the diagram has a loopback path that lets you repeat the choices. In this example, expression or the DEFAULT keyword within the set of parentheses may be repeated but are separated from each other by a comma.

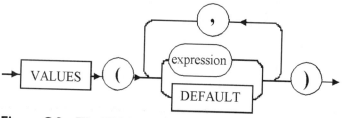

Figure G.3 ■ The VALUES clause of an INSERT command.

APPENDIX H

RESOURCES

This appendix lists Oracle-related Web sites where you will be able to explore topics in greater detail and find information beyond the scope of the book. Because Web links always change, also refer to the companion Web site located at http://www.phptr.com/rischert for up-to-date listings and additions. The companion Web site also features a bulletin board to exchange messages.

ORACLE PORTAL

This is a well-organized Oracle portal called *Oracle FAQ* features extensive links to many useful Oracle related sites. This is a great site for further research on Oracle topics. You can find it at http://www.orafaq.com.

ORACLE NEWSGROUPS

You can search through the following newsgroups with the Google search engine: http://groups.google.com. Often the answer to your question may already be out there. Be sure to check it out.

comp.databases.oracle.tools

comp.databases.oracle.misc

comp.databases.oracle.server

comp.databases.oracle.marketplace

ORACLE'S OWN WEB SITES

Oracle's home page is located at http://www.oracle.com.

The Oracle Technology Network (OTN) offers free product downloads, discussion forums, white papers, sample code, documentation, and technical articles on a variety of Oracle related issues. You can find the site at http://otn.oracle.com. The site requires registration, but is free.

839

Sometimes Oracle offers free online tutorials and presentations that are accessible via this link: http://www.oracle.com/education/oln/index.html.

Oracle support via Metalink is available only if you purchase an Oracle support contract.

http://www.oracle.com/support

http://metalink.oracle.com/index.html

ALTERNATIVE SQL*PLUS SOFTWARE TOOLS

This book uses SQL*Plus and *i*SQL*Plus as execution environments because one of these tools is always available with every Oracle installation. There are many excellent tools on the market that make you wonder how you could have ever lived without them. These tools often feature an easy-to-use editor and a graphical execution environment with a browser showing all the database objects. You can easily execute queries, generate execution plans for SQL statements, export and import tables, and reverse-engineer the DDL for existing objects. We recommend that you download one of the trial versions to help you determine the suitability for you individual needs. Following is a list of popular vendors. The ORAFAQ Web site which is located at http://www.orafaq.com/tools/index.htm, lists many more including a comparison chart.

PL/SQL Developer by Allaround Automations: http://www.allroundautomations.nl/plsqldevaddons.html

RapidSQL by Embarcadero Technologies: http://www.embarcadero.com

SQL Navigator and Toad by Quest Software: http://www.quest.com

DATABASE DESIGN SOFTWARE

Besides Oracle's own Designer tool, there are a many vendors that offer tools that allow you to create logical and physical data models for Oracle databases. Following are a few of the popular vendors.

DeZign by Datanamic: http://www.datanamic.com

ER/Studio: http://www.embarcadero.com

ERwin Data Modeler by Computer Associates: http://www.cai.com

USER GROUPS

Joining a user group is one of the best ways to gain knowledge and experience using Oracle. Be sure to check out the group in your geographical area.

International Oracle User Group: http://www.ioug.org

Search Oracle's Web site for a listing of all user groups: http://www.oracle.com/corporate/overview/index.html?usergroups.html

Oracle Development Tools User Group: http://odtug.com

ORACLE-RELATED PUBLICATIONS

SELECT Magazine, a publication of the IOUG user group: http://www.selectonline.org

Oracle Magazine, a free Oracle publication that contains technology articles as well as tips and techniques: http://www.oramag.com/publications

ACADEMIC RESOURCES

Mailing list and repository related to using Oracle in an academic teaching environment: http://mail.uindy.edu/mailman/listinfo/oracle_in_academia

Oracle Academic Initiative (OAI): http://oai.oracle.com

Oracle Workforce: http://workforce.oracle.com

BOOKS

Following is a list of titles that allow you to explore advanced subjects in further detail.

SQL for Smarties: Advanced SQL Programming by Joe Celko; Morgan Kaufman Publishers, Inc., 1995. Excellent coverage of many advanced SQL topics.

SQL Puzzles & Answers by Joe Celko; Morgan Kaufman Publishers, Inc., 1997. This book contains many clever and humorous real-life examples and solutions.

Oracle SQL High-Performance Tuning, 2nd edition, by Guy Harrison; Prentice Hall, 2001. An excellent resource if you want to know more about writing efficient SQL statements and getting the most out of your database. This book is a must-read for developers and DBAs alike.

Oracle PL/SQL Interactive Workbook, 2nd edition, by Benjamin Rosenzweig and Elena Silvestrova; Prentice Hall, 2003. This book is the logical choice to take you to the next level of Oracle knowledge. It is based on the same workbook pedagogy as this book, with exercises and labs. It is a perfect introduction into the PL/SQL language.

Oracle DBA Interactive Workbook by Melanie Caffrey and Douglas Scherer; Prentice Hall, 2003. If you are interested in learning how to administer a database, this book teaches you the essentials of database maintenance, security, optimization, backup, and recovery. The hands-on approach of the workbook will provide you with the practical expert knowledge to successfully administer a database.

Oracle 8i *Tips & Techniques* by Douglas Scherer, William Gaynor, Arlene Valentinsen, and Xerxes Cursetjee; Oracle Press, 2000. While the book covers the 8*i* version, many of the topics, such as security and interMedia, are still relevant in Oracle 9*i*.

Oracle Design by Dave Ensor and Ian Stevenson; O'Reilly, 1997. The book is primarily centered around Oracle 7 (a newer companion book called Oracle 8 Design Tips is also available). However, a number of the excellent design tips contained within still hold true.

Building Intelligent Databases with Oracle PL/SQL Triggers and Stored Procedures, 2nd edition, by Kevin T. Owens; Prentice Hall, 1998. Contains extensive coverage of integrity constraints and explains in detail how triggers can facilitate the storing of business logic within the Oracle database.

INDEX

844

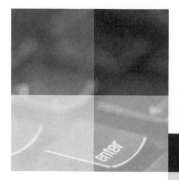

informIT

YOUR GUIDE TO IT REFERENCE

Articles

Keep your edge with thousands of free articles, in-depth features, interviews, and IT reference recommendations – all written by experts you know and trust.

Online Books

Answers in an instant from **InformIT Online Book's** 600+ fully searchable on line books. Sign up now and get your first 14 days **free**.

POWERED BY

Safari

Catalog

Review online sample chapters, author biographies and customer rankings and choose exactly the right book from a selection of over 5,000 titles.